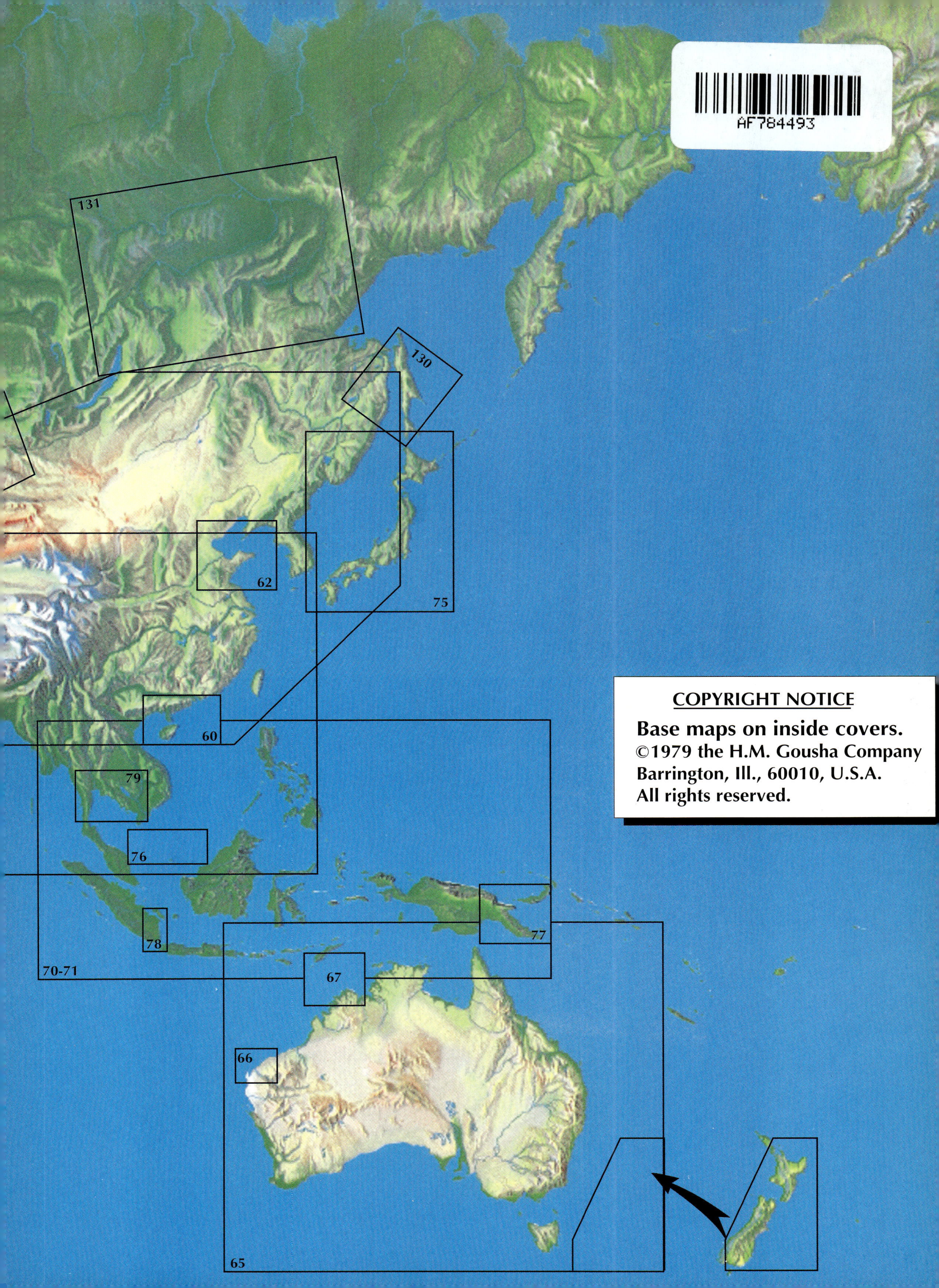
131
130
75
62
60
79
76
78
77
70-71
67
66
65

International Petroleum Encyclopedia

PennWell Publishing Co.
Box 1260, Tulsa, OK 74101

Library of Congress
CIP 77-76966
ISBN 0878146601
Printed in U.S.A.

West Texas pumping unit. Photo courtesy of Kent Abernathie, Amerada Hess Corp.

INTERNATIONAL PETROLEUM ENCYCLOPEDIA

TABLE OF CONTENTS

SPECIAL FEATURES

Argentina's YPF SA became a major international oil company in what was among the first and most thorough of Latin America's oil-industry privatization campaigns. Shown here is a reforming section at YPF's 176,000 b/cd La Plata refinery near Buenos Aires.

International Petroleum Encyclopedia

International Petroleum Encyclopedia is published annually by PennWell Publishing Co., 1421 S. Sheridan Rd., Box 1260, Tulsa, Okla. 74101. Phone: (918) 835-3161. Fax: (918) 831-9555.
Editorial offices: 3050 Post Oak Blvd., Suite 200, Houston, Tex. 77056. Phone: (713) 621-9720. Fax: (713) 963-6285. Editor's e-mail: bobt@ogjonline.com.

Gas pipeline in Argentina is operated by YPF SA, former state petroleum company that was successfully privatized. Since privatization, oil and gas production in Argentina has risen dramatically. Photo courtesy YPF.

Privatization sweeps oil industry in Latin America

Venezuelans call it *"la apertura"* (the "opening"). In Bolivia, it's "capitalization;" in Brazil, "flexibilization."

Whatever it's called, the juggernaut of privatization continued to roll across Latin America's petroleum industry in 1996.

While not always privatization in a strict sense of the word, this trend at least involved a greater willingness by governments to let private investment participate in the region's petroleum operations. That participation includes efforts to strip state companies of their monopolies even while those firms remain in state hands.

Signs are that this trend will accelerate in 1997 and beyond, expanding business opportunities for petroleum companies and for petroleum service and supply sectors.

Latin America thus will play an increasingly important role in global oil and gas markets. Economic expansion is helping to bolster demand for oil and gas and in many Latin American countries. At the same time, a growing emphasis on free-market principles is brightening the outlook for profitability of the companies—private and state-owned—that provide those commodities.

In addition, increased investment in Latin America's petroleum sector is increasing the region's importance as a source of supply. Colombia, within scarcely a decade, has become a significant oil exporter. Trinidad and Tobago, long thought of as a marginal player in the petroleum industry, suddenly is on track to start up the Western Hemisphere's first grassroots liquefied natural gas complex in more than 25 years and is emerging as one of the world's top methanol producers.

There remain obstacles to privatization—such as the dogged resistance by Mexican state petroleum company Petroleos Mexicanos to private ownership of the country's oil and gas—and other problems—some countries' onerous petroleum fiscal regimes and environmental and security issues throughout the region.

But the trend toward the once-taboo concept of foreign/private ownership of the "people's resources" (*la patrimonia*, in some countries) appears to be irreversible and fundamental.

As Alirio Parra, former Venezuelan oil minister and currently with London's Centre for Global Energy Studies, puts it: "Latin America is undergoing a fundamental economic change that is more profound and perhaps less subject to reversal than any shift we have witnessed in the past.

"Throughout the region, there is a strong commitment to representative democracy and a common concern regarding corruption, governance, poverty, and the environment. If structural reform is to be successful, it must take into account these political concerns and the existing social inequalities."

Parra notes that Latin America's recovery has been led by liberal macroeconomic reforms.

"However, the consensus means much more than achieving economic stabilization; it is aimed at promoting development, establishing competitiveness, and bringing about fiscal discipline in a market-driven economy."

Parra contends that the recent wave of privatization in Latin America is what distinguishes the current economic-reform process from any in the past.

"The role of the state as an entrepreneur is set to diminish progressively. It is indeed a break with the past."

Parra thinks Latin America is entering the most positive period in the history of its economic development. He cites a healthy economic record during 1990-95 that, while not spectacular, shows a solid 3.7%/year growth.

"Moreover, the economies of the region seem to have settled down to a path of steady expansion in the order of 5%/year for the rest of the decade and perhaps beyond."

BP Exploration Colombia drilled the 1 Cusiana discovery well, which opened Colombia's biggest oil play. BP in 1996 was embroiled in a controversy with Bogota over contract terms, which the government began to try sweetening for foreign investors. Photo courtesy BP.

Petroleum privatization

It is within this context of macroeconomic reform that Parra traces the path of privatization in Latin America's oil and gas industry.

He notes that a mere 10 years ago, the petroleum industry in Latin America was largely in the hands of the private sector and largely shielded from internal competition.

Today, many state oil companies with a long history in the public sector are either set on the road to privatization or turning to strategic alliances with private investors.

"Such changes are hedged with all sorts of difficulties, but the prize is increased growth, greater efficiency, and an open competitive setting.

"The reinvigoration of the oil and gas industries in the region is taking place within a context inspired by the prospects for sustainable growth, accelerating regional integration, and the interplay of advanced technology on exploration prospectivity and costs."

"But the driving force behind these value-adding changes has undoubtedly been the opening up of the sector to private investment. Privatization in its broadest sense is firmly embedded in the new 'vision' of macroeconomic development."

Parra contends that privatization goes beyond the simple act of selling public sector assets with or without yielding control. It can also denote the removal of the legal or statutory barriers to entry or even the outsourcing of certain peripheral activities to private entrepreneurs on a concessionary basis or for a fixed-term basis.

There are three basic kinds of privatization under way in Latin America's petroleum industry today:

- Privatization in the classic sense, typified by the outright sale of state assets and yielding of most control to private entrepreneurs, as in the Argentine government's floating the shares of state petroleum company Yacimientos Petroliferos Fiscales SA (now simply YPF SA).
- Venezuela's *la apertura*, which fits the category of removal of barriers to entry or private investment.
- Demonopolization, involving the partial opening of the hydrocarbon sector, such as the flexibilization program under way in Brazil.

Parra points that a chief obstacle to the mechanics of privatization in Latin America is the relatively small size of capital markets throughout the region.

"Wherever possible, however, a portion of the shares (of a company to be privatized) should be placed on the local stock exchange offering an incentive of 5% or even 10% for smaller investors. Instead of the state, a vast number of local citizens would have the opportunity to become part owners of their own industries."

Latin American hydrocarbons

The promising potential of Latin America's hydrocarbon resource underlies oil and gas companies' generally enthusiastic response to the privatization push in the region.

These potential resources are large enough to affect global oil and gas balances, especially supply and demand in the Western Hemisphere.

Proved oil reserves in Latin America total more than 130 billion bbl, about 13% of the world total. More importantly, these reserves represent more than 40 years of production at current levels, greater than in any other area of the world outside the Middle East.

And that's just proved reserves, not taking into consideration such enormous deposits as Venezuela's Orinoco heavy oil belt, deemed the world's largest oil accumulation at about 1.7 trillion bbl.

Natural gas reserves in the region are pegged at 300 tcf, undervalued because of underdeveloped gas infrastructure. But a heightened emphasis on gas exploration and development is accompanying expansion and regional integration of the gas grids in Latin American countries.

Centre for Global Energy Studies' Alirio Parra
"Politics, economics, and technology are combining admirably with local and foreign capital both private and public to set the scene for a major energy push in Latin America."

Latin America's importance as a net exporter of oil is likely to grow. Almost 35% of the region's oil production is exported.

Parra estimates that by 2000, Latin American oil production will reach 11.7 million b/d, representing an exportable surplus and a net flow of foreign exchange into the region equivalent to 40% of total output.

Country breakout

Parra offers these snapshots of the status of privatization in some of the key petroleum-producing countries in Latin America, followed by detailed sketches of the two biggest oil producers, Mexico and Venezuela:

- In Argentina, the oil and gas sector has been successfully privatized. All that remains in the hands of the state is a 20% share of YPF. "As a result of these measures, together with changes in the investment laws, we have seen oil and natural gas production rise to record levels.
- In Bolivia, the "capitalization" program entails selling 50% of the upstream business of state petroleum concern Yacimientos Petroliferos Fiscales Bolivianos SA (YPFB) and setting aside the balance to create a pension fund for all Bolivians. The sale was successfully concluded at the end of 1996.
- In Brazil, the focus is on "flexibilization," which will allow the private sector to enter into partnerships with the state oil monopoly Petroleo Brasileiro SA (Petrobras). There are, however, efforts to go beyond this simple demonopolization toward a more straightforward privatization.
- Colombia already allows for private investment in exploration and development of oil and gas. However, to attract further interest in its shared-risk contracts, the terms for entry are being made more competitive.
- In Peru, privatization of the petroleum sector is only a few steps from completion, involving the breakup and disposal of all of Petroperu's assets. "Peru is the most under-explored country on the continent and, with the exception of natural gas in the Camisea fields, little has been discovered in recent years."
- In Ecuador, progress toward attracting private capital has been halted while contracts signed by previous administrations are renegotiated. In some quarters of the country, however, there was talk as 1996 came to a close of privatizing state-owned Petroleos del Ecuador, perhaps selling 50% of the firm to private investors.

Mexico

Since 1985, oil policy in Mexico has focused on efforts to maintain production at steady levels.

That strategy has been tied to the availability of capital rather than the state of Mexico's reserves or the country's goals.

"We are now witnessing a shift in this situation," Parra said. "Pemex is moving cautiously into an expansion program of modest proportions. In 1996, crude oil output is estimated to reach 2.82 million b/d from 2.6 million b/d in 1995 and is projected to move up to 3.1 million b/d or more by the end of the century."

In addition to the production push, there is under way a fundamental restructuring of the organization and focus of Pemex as well as shifts in public policy that will have profound effects on oil and gas operations in the country and upon the country itself.

Parra notes that Pemex has undergone a series of organizational changes involving the restructuring of operations, but its main focus now is on enhancing value, cutting costs, and decentralizing control.

At the same time, the Mexican government "has taken decisions on divestiture without precedent since nationalization in 1938.

"It is liberalizing the transportation, distribution, storage, and sale of natural gas and opening the state secondary petrochemical industry to private investment—although without yielding control."

There have been setbacks with secondary petrochemicals. The government shied away from sale of these assets in their entirety, opting instead to offer, in increments, as much as 49% of the businesses to local and foreign private capital.

"In the Mexican case," Parra pointed out, "public opinion was not yet ready to accept the sell-off of what are still considered strategic assets."

On the other hand, gas privatization is accelerating, with Pemex itself promoting competition in the downstream gas sector ahead of forthcoming clean-air legislation. Pemex hopes to demonopolize the downstream gas sector by 1998.

Opening the downstream gas sector in Mexico will give it an infusion of fresh capital, estimated at $5 billion, that will encourage development of more domestic production capacity by permitting more efficient access to markets.

Venezuela

Unlike Mexico, the focus of upstream investment in Venezuela has always been on adding reserves and production capacity—albeit not always successfully, Parra noted.

In the first 10 years since nationalization in 1975, while production capacity remained essentially flat, the foundations for growth were laid.

Exploration successes by state-owned Petroleos de Venezuela SA (Pdvsa) in that decade included a major new oil trend in the eastern part of the country and a significant offshore gas province. During this period, it also delineated the Orinoco oil belt.

Cadereyta complex operated by Mexico's state oil company Petroleos Mexicanos includes secondary petrochemical operations slated to be partly privatized in 1997. Photo courtesy Pemex.

In the subsequent 10 years, production capacity shot up by 650,000 b/d, and oil reserves rose sharply. And by yearend 1995, the effects of private sector investment in Venezuela's petroleum industry also were becoming apparent.

"The happy coincidence of the discovery of new oil provinces together with the inflow of private capital is strengthening immeasurably the upstream sector of the Venezuelan oil industry," Parra said. "It also marks the beginning of structural changes for the state oil company that will play themselves out over the next decade."

Venezuela's privatization strategy is three-pronged and focuses on inviting in private local and foreign capital and technology.

The first piece of the strategy, launched in 1992, was the program to reactivate marginal oil fields. A second round followed in 1993 and a third in 1996. As of early 1997, more than 15 operating contracts had been awarded under the marginal-fields reactivation program.

"The biggest surprise of this program has been the impact of technology in reducing costs and the discovery of important new but deeper trends, with at least one well testing at over 14,000 b/d," Parra said.

Total investments under this program are projected at $3.5 billion, with resulting incremental production expected to peak at almost 500,000 b/d.

The second part of the strategy concentrates on exploiting the vast Orinoco heavy oil resource. The approach here is an integrated one, involving not just producing heavy and extra-heavy crude but also upgrading, transporting, and marketing the resulting synthetic crude. There are no exploration risks and minimal production costs, but "success depends on the economics of conversion of Orinoco bitumen to a fungible synthetic crude."

Under this program, five strategic associations are planned involving $8-10 billion and a minimum production level of 500,000 b/d of syncrude.

The latest strategy push involves the profit-sharing program, which focuses on exploration in virgin areas. The award of eight exploration licenses in 1996 represents Venezuela's "most ambitious step to date embracing the private sector," Parra said.

Postulated reserves in the eight licenses are 5-6 billion bbl, and wildcat success ratios in Venezuela average 40%.

In addition to this three-part strategy, Venezuela is accelerating the outsourcing of operations, a type of privatization that Parra expects will total $3.3 billion in the next few years.

And privatization is by no means confined to the upstream sector in Venezuela. Private companies have been active for some time in the petrochemical industry there. The most dramatic evidence that this trend will accelerate was the disclosure late in 1996 of plans by Mobil Corp. and Pdvsa affiliate Pequiven SA to form a 50-50 joint venture to develop a $1.5 billion grassroots olefins complex at Jose, Venezuela.

Brazil's new regime

A seminar held in 1996 in Rio de Janeiro by the Brazilian Petroleum Institute and the economic research group Getulio Vargas Foundation looked at the likely outcome of efforts to establish a new regulatory regime for Brazil's petroleum sector as Petrobras' 42-year monopoly comes to an end.

Brazil's Congress in 1995 passed a constitutional amendment that effectively ended the Petrobras monopoly but retains the concern as a state-owned petroleum company. Congress then wrestled with draft legislation designed to establish a federal regulatory body, National Petroleum Agency (ANP), to regulate Brazil's petroleum sector in the vacuum created by demonopolization. This new approach is referred to as "flexibilization."

Energy Minister Raimundo Brito said the agency will have financial and administrative autonomy and on behalf of the government will regulate and monitor the industry's activities. ANP would be responsible for the creation of a national oil supply program as well as the formulation of a national refining plan. It also would promote tenders to grant concessions for petroleum exploration and development as well as authorize contracts for all other activities linked to the industry.

> **Centre for Global Energy Studies' Alirio Parra**
> *"The portfolio of investment opportunities for local and foreign private capital in Latin America's petroleum industry is greater now than at any other time in the last 50 years."*

The bill also proposes the creation of a National Council of Petroleum Policies to directly assist the Minister of Mines and Energy in questions related to the petroleum industry.

The draft bill further assigns to the government all rights covering basins and prospective hydrocarbon provinces where Petrobras has no activity. In this way, within 10 months after the bill is passed, the government will be able to publish tenders granting exploration rights to private companies, domestic and international.

If a bill was hammered out early in 1997, concessions could have been made available in second half 1997.

Petrobras will retain the rights to fields it already has delineated or developed for 3 years after the bill is passed, as well as rights to any commercial discovery or oil or gas production that starts up during the same period. Although Petrobras will retain the rights to fields it now operates, the draft bill requires that 6 months after the bill is passed, Petrobras will have to submit to ANP proposals concerning accurate reservoir delineation.

Bill debate

Regarding the draft bill's clauses for investors, Louis E. Smith, planning adviser for Exxon Exploration Co., said, "The most important consideration for both the authorities and the company is that sufficient time be allowed for full evaluation of the acreage. I fear that 5 years, as indicated in the synopsis of Brazil's enabling legislation, will be sufficient time to fail but not to be successful. I believe that the exploration period needs to be in the range of 6-12 years, depending upon the maturity of the area."

Brito pointed out that of the 29 sedimentary basins covering an area of 5.7 million sq km in the country, only eight basins get about 80% of Petrobras's investments in exploration. This shows that most of Brazil's basins are underdeveloped or underexplored.

Antonio Carlos Agostini, Petrobras E&P director, said that his company's E&P program calls for production capacity of 1.5 million b/d by 2000. By forming joint ventures, he believes, Petrobras will manage an added increment of 200,000 b/d during the same period.

Willem Goebel, president of Shell do Brasil, said he is skeptical about Petrobras reaching the 1.5 million b/d target because of its cash constraints. The state oil company had been investing $2-3 billion/year. Goebel estimated that at least $5 billion/year would be needed for Petrobras to reach that figure.

Investors' consensus

From the point of view of potential investors in E&P in Brazil, panelists agreed that:

- There is commercial interest in E&P in Brazil in gas as well as oil.
- The type of contract is not as important as is the way it is structured; the contract should include parameters that permit a rate of return in accordance with the project and its real risks.
- A level playing field is a must.
- Legal and tax rules should be stable and competitive at an international level, avoiding double taxation.
- Provided that the minimum work commitment has been met, companies should be granted flexibility to determine their work programs.
- E&P contract periods should be compatible with the type of areas under contract and reflect consideration of risk, infrastructure, and market conditions.
- Excessive licensing fees or bonuses, high income tax on production or gross revenues, high royalties, and "special" taxes are investment disincentives.
- Accounts should be in a stable currency.
- Investor companies should have the freedom to market their production as long as prices are based upon the international market and there are no risks of domestic shortfall.
- There must be a provision for international arbitration to resolve technical disputes. This serves as a stimulus for parties involved to reach consensus solutions and avoid conflicts.

Supply, refining

A seminar panel on oil supply and refining concluded, from those perspectives, that the goals of Brazil's new petroleum regime should include productivity and efficiency, an open market with adequate regulations due to the nature of the sector, supply guarantees, respect for consumers' needs, and refined product prices compatible with the international market.

All participants agreed upon the need for a transition period to a climate of free competition because of lingering market distortions left by policies under the former monopoly, notably cross-subsidization of product prices, the fuel ethanol mandate, and the fact that consumers near producing centers subsidize consumers in remote regions of the country.

Marcelo Castilho, commercial superintendent of Petrobras, estimates the government owes the company about $5.5 billion in subsidies Petrobras has paid since 1990. This amount represents subsidies for refined products, with the biggest share, $3 billion, for subsidies paid to ethanol producers.

The panelists agreed that Petrobras must no longer be responsible for such subsidies, and they instead should be the responsibility of the National Treasury.

The panel also recommended the transition period be sufficient for establishing well-defined regulations, guarantee equal economic access to existing transportation and storage facilities, urge investments in transportation infrastructure with an emphasis on pipelines, and examine carefully oil import programs so as not to incur unnecessary risks to the refining sector.

Self-sufficiency in refining is not necessarily a target to be pursued, the panel concluded, because there is surplus refining capacity in the world. However, the largely low gravities of crude oil produced in Brazil may make necessary new investments to upgrade Brazil's refineries.

There is also the need to revise the present tax structure related to products distribution so as to avoid fraud and unfair competition.

To guarantee implementation of these objectives, said panelists, it is necessary to create a regulatory agency with these responsibilities:

- Guarantee domestic supply at the lowest feasible cost to consumers.
- Promote investments in the sector.
- Respect consumer rights and needs.
- Promote competition and preservation of the environment.

Most panelists felt such an agency should be autonomous and independent, with the heads retaining a predetermined mandate not subject to dismissal but submitted for approval by the Senate.

Panelists also agreed this agency should work with stable rules, administrative flexibility, equal treatment of participants, continuous dialogue with all sectors of the industry, transparent regulatory processes, employees with strong technical backgrounds, appropriate legislation, operational and financial autonomy, and administrative continuity.

Bolivia's "capitalization" program included upstream activities of partly state-owned oil company Yacimientos Petroliferos Fiscales Bolivianos (YPFB). Two of the state company's upstream units were sold to private investors at the end of 1996. Photo courtesy YPFB.

Brazilian privatization?

Even with debate over the concept of partial—out of political necessity—privatization that "flexibilization" entails, there are efforts to embrace true privatization.

Congressman Eliseu Resende, head of a special commission studying the draft bill setting up the new regulatory framework for the petroleum industry, planned to introduce into that bill language for privatizing Petrobras.

Brazilian President Cardoso promised in his 1994 election campaign and to the senate that he would not privatize Petrobras. Resende nevertheless favors that and is trying to persuade others on the commission to amend the draft bill to include privatization of Petrobras.

Resende also differs with Cardoso on the president's proposal that the members of ANP be named by the mines and energy minister and approved by the president. He wants to see independent people from all sectors, including the private sector, represented in the agency and appointed for fixed terms to ensure their freedom from political pressure.

Bolivia: mission accomplished

It came a year late and was accompanied by ugly protests, but the privatization of half of Bolivian state company YPFB was wrapped up at the end of 1996.

Under the capitalization program, three winning bidders paid a total of $835 million for YPFB's two E&P units and its pipeline operations.

Winners were Amoco Corp.; a group of three Argentine companies led by YPF SA; and a combine of Enron Corp. and Shell International Overseas Holdings.

Argentine companies YPF SA, Perez Companc, and Pluspetrol combined to buy their 50% interest in upstream unit Empresa Petrolera Andina for $264.8 million. Amoco topped bids for the second upstream unit Empresa Petrolera Chaco with $306.7 million.

YFB's pipeline unit Transportadora de Hidrocarburos went to Enron and Shell in a joint bid for $263.5 million.

YPFB retains its refining and domestic marketing operations along with some technical and maintenance units.

Potential trouble still lay ahead for winning bidders.

All three major opposition parties signed an agreement vowing to overturn the partial sale of YPFB and start impeachment proceedings against the president once he completed his term of office in 1997.

Some analysts saw this as a populist electioneering stunt to make the most of the government's unpopularity over the sale. But indications were that this opposition alliance had a good chance of forming the next government, after general elections in June 1997.

YPFB capitalization

What makes YPFB capitalization different from other state asset sales is that the companies' bids represent direct investments in YPFB and will not be soaked up by the Bolivian treasury.

Companies had 5 years to budget the funds but were required to lodge the amounts bid in the respective company accounts immediately prior to closing. This provides a strong incentive for bidders to spend early in order to get an early return on their investments.

Such early capital spending had occurred in the other state industries Bolivia sold, so the pattern was likely to be repeated in Bolivia's privatized oil industry.

Centre for Global Energy Studies' Alirio Parra

Total oil and gas investment requirements in Latin America are estimated at $25 billion/year during 10 years. "By no means can all of this value be financed internally or locally, but will require substantial inflows of foreign private capital of perhaps 50% or more of this amount."

The much-needed capital injection combined with the winning companies' strong regional interests looked set to ensure the rapid development of Bolivia's oil and gas reserves.

Ecuador's turnabout

Advocates of increasing openness and privatization efforts in Latin America's petroleum industry likely were disappointed by a surprising turn of events in Ecuador in 1996.

Ecuador had been making steady if unspectacular progress in opening its petroleum sector to foreign investment (making more acreage available to foreign operators while amicably taking over Texaco Inc.'s operations).

However, the new government of President Abdala Bucaram undertook a widespread review of service contracts in 1996 that followed a dispute over one such contract with YPF unit Maxus Energy Corp.

Service contracts put under review are held by Oryx Ecuador Energy Co., Occidental Exploration & Production, ARCO Oriente Inc., Elf Aquitaine, and Tripetrol SA. But the review was not confined to just those.

What was especially puzzling was that Bucaram pledged to make Ecuadorian economic development a priority—notably with foreign investment.

By some observations, the fiery populist's theatrics belied a more market-oriented approach to foreign investment. That approach was seen in a politically unpopular, market-oriented effort to end some state subsidies for refined product prices.

New measures

Bucaram in 1996 also disclosed new measures aimed at boosting foreign investment in all economic sectors, with a special focus on oil policy.

Energy proposals under review and discussion in Ecuador included:

- Flashing a green light to laying private pipelines to carry heavy oil from southern Oriente fields, as well as expanding the trans-Ecuadorian Lago Agrio-Balao pipeline.
- Allowing private investors to build refineries.
- Implementing new types of contracts to promote E&P, namely concession and association contracts previously used.
- Restructuring Petroecuador as a centralized entity by combining operations of affiliates Petroproduccion, Petrocomercial, and Petroindustrial.

Peru's success

Another Latin American country that marked significant progress in privatizing its petroleum sector in 1996 was Peru.

A privatization committee overseeing the process sold the last oil field operated by Petroleos del Peru (Petroperu) as 1996 wound down.

In the fourth asset auction during second half 1996, Perez Companc bought the Talara basin's Block X on the northern coast for a surprisingly high $202 million.

In the other three auctions, the government sold a 50% interest in the 102,000 b/d La Pampilla refinery at Lima, Petroperu's lubricants business, and northern jungle Blocks 8 and 8X.

Pluspetrol SA, Buenos Aires, and partners took over operation of Petroperu's former northern jungle Blocks 8 and 8X and signed an exploration license with Perupetro for the first stage of development in the central jungle's Block 79, near the Aguaytia gas fields.

Mobil Oil del Peru won the auction held for Petrolube SA, Petroperu's lubricants business. Mobil won the lube operation with an offer of $18.85 million, two and a half times the $7.5 million base price. The purchase includes a 300,000 bbl/year lubes blending plant, a grease plant, and the brand name. Mobil intends to continue marketing Petrolube products and will produce Mobil and Petrolube lubricants at the same plant. The company said both brands combined cover almost half the country's market. Mobil already has a lube blending plant at Callao with capacity of 160,000 bbl/year. Mobil also has a 9% share in the group led by Repsol that bought a 60% stake in the La Pampilla refinery.

Refinadores del Peru SA, a new company formed by a group led by Spain's Repsol SA, formally took over operations of the La Pampilla refinery and disclosed investment plans late in 1996. It changed the company's name to Refineria La Pampilla SA (Relapasa). Repsol Peruvian unit Empresa Repsol SA is the plant operator. Relapasa will continue to supply all domestic and foreign clients. The new owners of La Pampilla must invest at least $50 million in upgrading the refinery in 5 years. Petroperu's privatization committee will contribute $37 million to environmental remediation programs at La Pampilla in 5 years. After that, it will be the responsibility of the new owners.

Sale delayed

A fifth Petroperu unit, encompassing the 62,000 b/d Talara refinery, was slated for auction in December 1996, but that was delayed.

EIA: Energy privatization trend historic opportunity

THE U.S. ENERGY INFORMATION ADMINISTRATION said privatizations of formerly state-owned energy enterprises during the 1990s presented energy investment opportunities of historic dimensions.

"Around the globe, energy privatizations have led to several billions of dollars in cross-border capital flows thus far, and the level of future foreign investment activity looks larger still. In former socialist countries, privatization represents an important part of the transition from centrally planned economies to free markets."

In its report Privatization and the Globalization of Energy Markets, EIA said the privatization of electric resources may be the most important development.

"Electric power is expected to be the fastest-growing source of end-use energy supply over the next 2 decades. Several developing countries have removed restrictions on private and foreign investment in new electric power generation facilities. Several formerly state-owned electric utilities have also been fully privatized, and often sold to foreign investors."

EIA said that among nations within the Organisation for Economic Cooperation and Development, Australia and the U.K. have led global electricity privatization efforts, and U.S. electric utilities have been the most prominent of all foreign investors in those two countries.

FSU privatization

"Privatization in the countries of the former Soviet Union (FSU) and in other formerly socialist nations has clearly widened the scope of investment opportunities of the major petroleum companies to include previously off-limit exploration and development areas," EIA said.

"However, although several major U.S. petroleum companies (and other multinational energy companies) are committing billions of dollars to future exploration and development in the FSU, persisting political and economic uncertainties continue to cast substantial doubt as to whether these investments will come into fruition."

EIA said privatization has encouraged greater integration of traditional oil companies into electric power and in several regions has fostered a greater convergence of the electric power and natural gas industries.

"This latter development has been particularly prominent in the U.K., where several recently privatized electricity companies and recently privatized natural gas companies have merged or formed cooperative ventures."

Regional differences

The report said giant firms such as British Petroleum Co. plc, British Gas plc, Elf Aquitaine, ENI, Petro-Canada, Repsol SA, and Total have all undergone transitions from state-ownership to some significant degree of private ownership.

"However, traditionally, OECD governments have exerted a much more limited degree of control over their nationalized petroleum companies than governments in most regions. Thus far, the most pronounced impact of privatization...may be the increased level of ownership of several formerly state-run petroleum companies by foreign investors, particularly those from the U.S."

EIA said oil privatizations in Latin America have occurred against a backdrop of sweeping free market economic reform, but various nations have taken different routes to privatization.

"At one extreme lies Argentina, which completely privatized its formerly state-owned petroleum company, YPF. At the other end of the spectrum lies Mexico, which has largely maintained its state-owned petroleum monopoly, Pemex. The privatization of electricity generation in Latin America has also been widespread."

Petroperu postponed the sale because high oil prices and stiff competition, especially in middle distillates, squeezed its earnings.

The privatization committee early in 1997 planned an industry tour in the U.S. and Venezuela to promote the refinery sale.

Petroperu will sell the Talara refinery under the same terms as those for the La Pampilla refinery, offering a 60% share, with the state keeping 40%, and refinery employees able to buy as much as 10%.

The state may keep a "golden share" in the refinery to maintain control over sensitive issues, such as a possible resale of the plant.

Despite the delay in the Talara sale, officials predicted that Petroperu would complete privatization of its basic assets by yearend 1997.

Other units slated for privatization include the concession on the 200,000 b/d North Peruvian pipeline, the Iquitos and Conchan refineries, and marine terminals.

Sale of these other units will not necessarily have to wait on the Talara refinery offering, although the privatization committee would prefer to sell the refinery first.

The outlook

Alirio Parra contends that with the opening of the oil and gas industries in Latin America, the scope for private sector investment both upstream and downstream is growing.

"In fact, the portfolio of investment opportunities for local and foreign private capital is greater now than at any other time in the last 50 years," he said.

He estimated total oil and gas investment requirements in Latin America at $25 billion/year for 10 years.

"By no means can all of this value be financed internally or locally but will require substantial inflows of foreign private capital of perhaps 50% or more of this amount."

In short, said Parra, "Politics, economics, and technology are combining admirably with local and foreign capital both private and public to set the scene for a major energy push in Latin America." IPE

UNITED STATES

CAPITAL: Washington, D.C.
MONETARY UNIT: Dollar
REFINING CAPACITY: 15.433 million b/d
PRODUCTION: 6.478 million b/d
RESERVES: 22.351 billion bbl

The long-awaited recovery of the U.S. upstream oil and gas industry came clearly into view in 1996. Early in the year, it was apparent that companies had learned not only how to make money with oil and gas prices stuck in ranges once considered disastrously low but also how to add significantly to reserves and production. By the end of the year, prices had further lifted industry fortunes by piercing the ceiling of the former range.

Rising prices notwithstanding, the turnaround was largely self-made. The oil market's collapse of 1986 forced the industry in the following decade to seek profits in a price environment much different from earlier expectations: $15-20/bbl for crude oil indefinitely instead of steady increases forever. The 1995 performance data reported in 1996 reflected the consequent gains in efficiency, with costs down dramatically in most crucial operating categories.

The organizational changes and technological advances that made these improvements possible had other important effects that were especially important in the mature U.S. For one thing, they added to the industry's prospect list portions of the resource once considered uneconomic or physically impossible to explore and develop. The deepwater and subsalt plays reviving activity in the Gulf of Mexico were the best examples of this phenomenon in 1996 (see section on Gulf of Mexico). New work patterns and technology also yielded economic opportunities in old areas. Interdisciplinary teams within companies and alliances among companies sought ways to add reserves and make money not only through new plays but also through new applications of technology in old producing regions. In many cases, the new focus on old reservoirs yielded improvements in recovery rates if not whole new, previously undetectable, drilling targets.

With opportunities thus multiplying and costs falling because of rapidly advancing technology, U.S. upstream prospects became once again competitive on a global scale. As a result, another important trend reversal that became evident in 1996 was a leveling of U.S. vs. non-U.S. upstream capital outlays. Since the late 1980s, exploration and production spending had increased much more rapidly outside the U.S. than within it.

Period of growth

In its 1996 survey of reserves data published by publicly traded U.S. oil and gas companies, Arthur Andersen LLP in August heralded a period of strong U.S. and international growth for exploration and production companies based in the U.S. The company said key measures of performance, based on 1995 data, showed the U.S. petroleum industry to be in its best health in 15 years.

Capital spending by companies in the Arthur Andersen survey increased by 12% in 1995 to $57.8 billion from a 5-year low in 1994. U.S. spending grew by 11% during the year to $22.3 billion, an 8 year high. Non-U.S. capital spending increased 12% to $35.5 billion. The survey covered information filed with the U.S. Securities and Exchange Commission by 231 companies, including 23 with headquarters outside the U.S.

For exploration and development spending alone, the U.S. total increased 8% to $17.3 billion in 1995, the highest level since 1991. All of the increase came from major companies, which as a group in the previous few years had been moving capital away from the U.S. Spending in the U.S. by majors increased 14% in 1995 to $9.8 billion. The low point in U.S. exploration and development spending came in 1992. The 1995 figures were up 21% for majors and 47% for independents.

The Arthur Andersen survey reflected large decreases in the costs of replacing produced reserves though exploration, development, and acquisition. Worldwide, the costs decreased 6% in 1995 for the surveyed companies to $4.22/bbl of oil equivalent (BOE), the lowest level since 1987. Replacement costs for independents declined 13% to $4.43/BOE in 1995, while majors' costs increased 2% to $4.03/BOE.

During 1992-95, the entire group replaced U.S. reserves at an average cost of $4.44/BOE—$4.05/BOE for majors and $4.85/BOE for independents.

Surveyed companies replaced 99% of their U.S. oil production from all sources in 1995. The majors' replacement rate was 79%, independents' 185%, both 5 year highs. The U.S. gas production replacement rate from all sources for all companies was 132% in 1995—102% for the majors and 172% for independents.

According to the survey, production costs in the U.S. fell by 5% in 1995 to $4/BOE. That compared with a 5 year high of $4.96/BOE in 1991. Production costs of independents in the survey averaged $3.71/BOE, compared with $4.13/BOE for the majors. The difference reflects the greater percentage of gas in the independents' production total: 70% vs. 42%.

Production costs outside the U.S. were higher for the surveyed group: $4.75/BOE, up slightly from 1994.

Oil reserves held by the group in the U.S. fell slightly to 19.2 billion bbl, 83% of the total held by majors. Oil production by the group declined to 1.8 billion bbl. Sales of oil reserves increased by 50% in 1995.

Gas reserves held by surveyed companies in the U.S. increased by 3% in 1995 to 109.6 tcf. Gas production increased slightly to 11.3 tcf. Sales of U.S. gas reserves totaled 2.2 tcf, up for the first time since 1992.

U.S. regaining ground

A 1996 study by John S. Herold Inc. highlighted the economics behind the slowdown, if not end, of migration of capital away from North America.

Focusing on reserve replacement costs (RCCs), the firm declared the U.S. once again competitive with the rest of the world for upstream investments. In 1995, 102 companies tracked by Herold invested $51.5 billion in exploration and production, 49% of it in North America. In 1992, 42% of the companies' E&P spending was in North America.

E&P spending in the U.S. totaled $19.9 billion in 1995, up 6% from the 1994 total and the third consecutive yearly increase. The U.S. share of worldwide E&P budgets increased to 39% in 1995 from 37% in 1992. Canadian E&P spending fell 21% in 1995 to $5.1 billion but was still nearly twice the 1992 level.

In Herold's analysis, RRCs covered reserves added in all categories. The firm also estimated finding and development costs (FDCs), which exclude effects of proved property purchases and essentially measure costs of adding reserves through drilling.

RRCs in the U.S. fell to $4.13/BOE in 1995 from $4.72/BOE in 1994. Worldwide RRCs were higher at $4.35/BOE in 1995 and, for a larger group of companies, $4.77/BOE in 1994.

FDCs in the U.S. fell to $4.16/BOE in 1995 from $4.77/BOE in 1994. They compared with worldwide FDCs of $4.53/BOE in 1995 and $4.98/BOE in 1994.

Herold's survey report, published in advance of its annual RRC survey analysis, predicted that the North American gains in share of worldwide E&P capital spending—paced by the U.S.—would endure. Although large discoveries were more probable elsewhere, the firm noted, reserves size wasn't the attraction that it once was. Companies were increasingly focused on rapid investment turnover and quick payoffs and less interested than before on projects with slow depletion rates and high reserves-to-production ratios.

Outside the U.S., large prospects tended to be remote, requiring large expenditures of time and money on infrastructure. Such requirements helped North American prospects, though usually smaller, to compete economically.

Reserve patterns

The improving upstream economics in the U.S. cited in the Arthur Andersen and J.S. Herold surveys slowed a long-standing decline in oil reserves and enabled natural gas reserves to increase for the second year in a row in 1995.

According to a September 1996 report by the U.S. Energy Information Administration, reserves of crude oil at the end of 1995 were down only 0.5% at 22.351 billion bbl, of natural gas up 0.8% at 165.146 tcf, and of natural gas liquids up 3.2% at 7.399 billion bbl.

For crude oil, the 1995 estimate was the eighth consecutive annual decline. But it reflected the smallest percentage change since the increase of 1987. Additions in federal waters of the Gulf of Mexico offset combined decreases in Alaska, California, and Texas. Reserves in the Lower 48 increased for the first time in a decade, by 81 million bbl. Additions to crude oil reserves in 1995 represented 95% of the year's total production.

Total discoveries of crude oil in 1995, at 957 million bbl, were at their highest level in a decade and exceeded the 1994 figure by 67%. The federal Gulf of Mexico accounted for 60% of total discoveries, Texas for 16%, and Alaska for 8%. Within the discoveries category, new reservoir discoveries in old fields totaled 343 million bbl, new field discoveries 114 million bbl, and field extensions 500 million bbl.

The figure for new reservoir discoveries in old fields was more than three times its 1994 level and prior 10 year average for the U.S. The federal Gulf of Mexico accounted for 91% of the 1995 total. Federal gulf waters accounted for a large share of new field discoveries as well—79%. New field discoveries were up 78% from their 1994 total. Field extensions were up 26% from a year earlier.

Revisions and adjustments, totaling 1.15 billion bbl in 1995, were down 4% from their 1994 total but still accounted for more than half of all reserves additions. Texas, Alaska, and California accounted for 59% of the total.

The oil reserves pattern showed the effects of the industry's new operating strategies. Most additions to reserves occurred in categories other than new field discoveries, and that category was dominated by large discoveries in the Gulf of Mexico. The large finds there, of course, depended on technological advances in seismic and deepwater drilling, completion, and transportation technology.

Elsewhere, reserves additions came from drilling near existing production or from revisions and adjustments, which result largely from enhanced recovery. These additions, too, depended heavily on technology as companies used increasingly sophisticated geophysical, modeling, and engineering techniques to learn more and more about producing reservoirs. The increased knowledge enabled them to increase recoveries through a variety of means and to identify previously overlooked pay zones.

Gas, NGL reserves

Gas reserves increased by 2.731 bcf in 1995, a volume that represented 107% of the year's total production.

U.S. gas reserves have changed only insignificantly since 1988, when reserves on Alaska's North Slope were written down to reflect the absence of a transportation system that will have to be installed before development can proceed.

Total discoveries of dry gas declined by 11% from their 1994 level to 10.961 tcf. Texas and the Gulf of Mexico accounted for more than two thirds of the total.

New field discoveries made up 1.666 bcf of the discoveries total, down 12% from 1994 but one-third higher than the prior 10 year average. Field extensions declined 1% to 6.843 bcf. New reservoir discoveries in old fields totaled 2.452 bcf, down 30% from 1994 but 14% higher than the prior 10 year average.

Net revisions and adjustments added 8.314 tcf to reserves in 1995, up 12% from the year earlier.

Reserves of coalbed methane represented 6% of 1995 dry gas reserves and contributed 5% to total gas production in 1995.

Reserves of natural gas liquids increased by 5 million bbl in Alaska and by 224 million bbl in the Lower 48. Additions to reserves represented 129% of production. Total discoveries of NGL accounted for 54% of additions to reserves, revisions and adjustments the rest.

UNITED STATES

State	No. Refineries
Alabama	3
Alaska	6
Arkansas	3
California	23
Colorado	2
Delaware	1
Georgia	2
Hawaii	2
Illinois	6
Indiana	3
Kansas	3
Kentucky	2
Louisiana	19
Michigan	3
Minnesota	2
Mississippi	4
Montana	4
Nevada	1
New Jersey	6
New Mexico	3
North Dakota	1
Ohio	4
Oklahoma	5
Oregon	1
Pennsylvania	6
Tennessee	1
Texas	28
Utah	5
Virginia	1
Washington	7
West Virginia	1
Wisconsin	1
Wyoming	4
Total	**163**

CANADA

Province	No. Refineries
Alberta	5
British Columbia	2
New Brunswick	1
Newfoundland	1
Nova Scotia	1
Ontario	7
Quebec	3
Saskatchewan	2
Total	**22**

For individual locations and capacities, see detailed maps on following pages.

Drilling patterns

The industry spent $10.5 billion in 1995 to drill and equip oil and gas wells in the U.S., according to the annual Joint Association Survey on Drilling Costs (JAS) by the American Petroleum Institute, Independent Petroleum Association of America, and Mid-Continent Oil and Gas Association. The figure was up 8.9% from the 1994 total.

Spending on development wells increased 15% to $8.9 billion, while spending on exploratory wells fell 15% to $1.6 billion.

The JAS, released in November 1996, reported that the industry drilled 20,528 wells in 1995, 2.5% more than in 1994, and a total of 120,834,000 ft of hole.

The drilling included 7,745 oil wells, up 18.8%, 7,863 gas wells, down 7.1%, and 4,920 dry holes, down 2.3%. The pattern followed trends in field-level revenues in 1995, when average wellhead prices reported by EIA were up for oil ($14.62/bbl in 1995 dollars vs. $13.53/bbl in 1994) and down for gas ($1.55/Mcf vs. $1.93/Mcf in 1994).

The average cost per well was $513,415 and average cost per foot, $87.22. Both figures were up from their

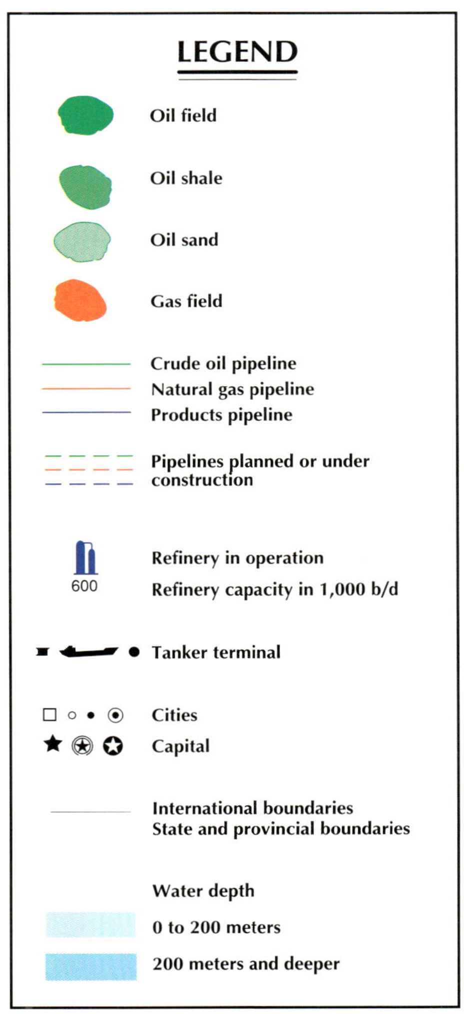

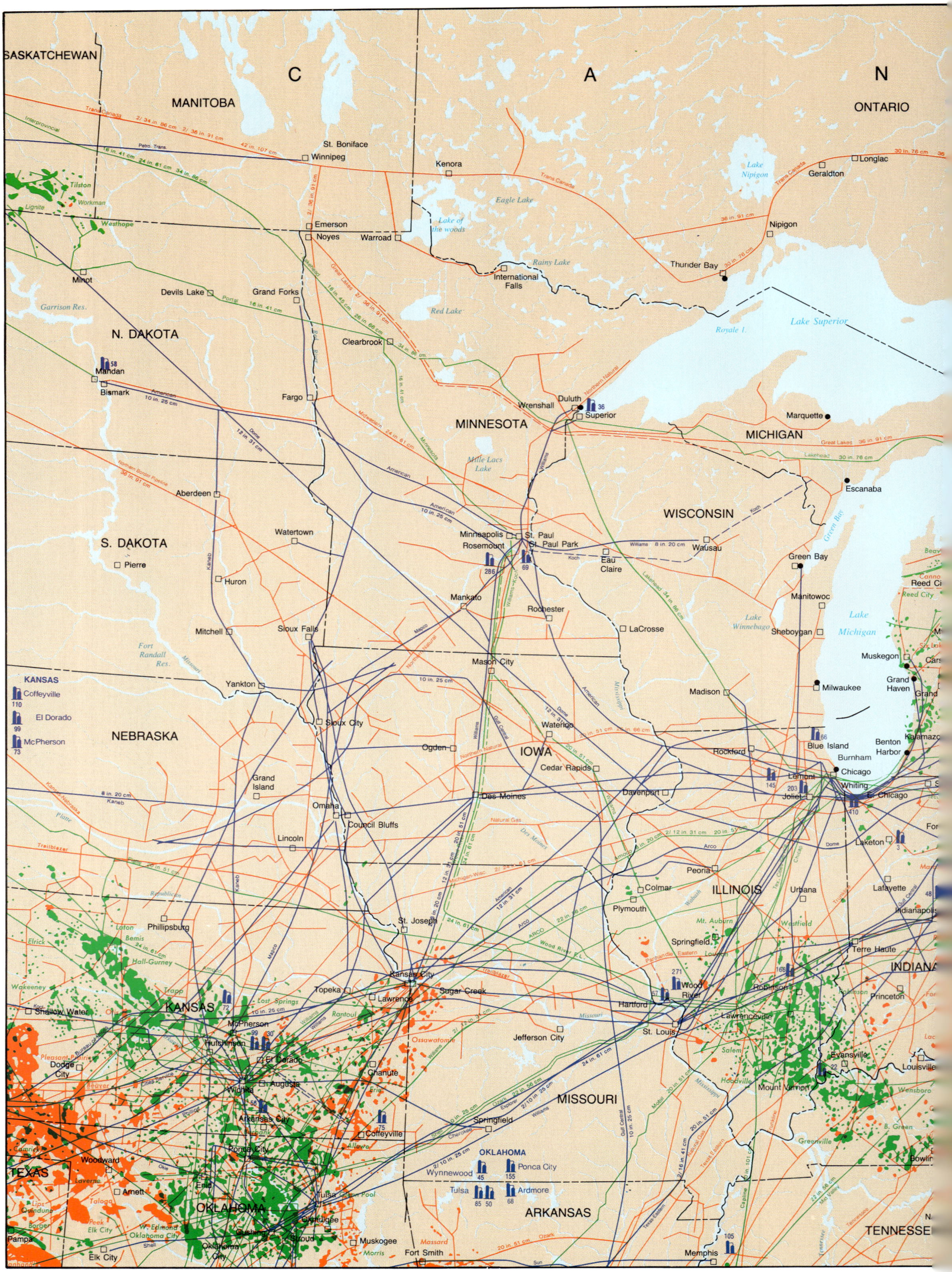
C A N
SASKATCHEWAN
MANITOBA
ONTARIO
N. DAKOTA
S. DAKOTA
NEBRASKA
KANSAS
OKLAHOMA
TEXAS
MINNESOTA
IOWA
MISSOURI
ARKANSAS
WISCONSIN
MICHIGAN
ILLINOIS
INDIANA
TENNESSEE
Lake Superior
Lake Michigan
Lake Nipigon
Lake of the woods
Red Lake
Rainy Lake
Eagle Lake
Mille Lacs Lake
Lake Winnebago
Green Bay
Garrison Res.
Fort Randall Res.
St. Boniface
Winnipeg
Kenora
Emerson
Noyes
Warroad
International Falls
Thunder Bay
Nipigon
Geraldton
Longlac
Minot
Devils Lake
Grand Forks
Clearbrook
Mandan
Bismark
Fargo
Duluth
Wrenshall
Superior
Marquette
Escanaba
Aberdeen
Watertown
Pierre
Huron
Mitchell
Sioux Falls
Yankton
Minneapolis
Rosemount
St. Paul
St. Paul Park
Eau Claire
Wausau
Mankato
Rochester
LaCrosse
Green Bay
Manitowoc
Sheboygan
Milwaukee
Madison
Muskegon
Grand Haven
Benton Harbor
Mason City
Waterloo
Sioux City
Ogden
Cedar Rapids
Rockford
Blue Island
Burnham
Chicago
Lemont
Joliet
Whiting
E. Chicago
Grand Island
Omaha
Council Bluffs
Lincoln
Des Moines
Davenport
Peoria
Laketon
Colmar
Plymouth
Urbana
Lafayette
Indianapolis
Springfield
Terre Haute
Phillipsburg
St. Joseph
Kansas City
Topeka
Lawrence
Sugar Creek
Wood River
Hartford
St. Louis
Robinson
Lawrenceville
Princeton
Jefferson City
Shallow Water
McPherson
Hutchinson
El Dorado
Dodge City
Augusta
Wichita
Chanute
Arkansas City
Coffeyville
Springfield
Evansville
Mount Vernon
Louisville
Ponca City
Woodward
Enid
Tulsa
Amett
Okmulgee
Cushing
Stroud
Oklahoma City
Muskogee
Fort Smith
Memphis
Elk City
Pampa
KANSAS
Coffeyville
El Dorado
McPherson
OKLAHOMA
Wynnewood
Ponca City
Tulsa
Ardmore
Trans Canada
Interprovincial
Lakehead
Great Lakes
Williams
American
Northern Natural
Northern Border Pipeline
Kaneb
Dome
Koch
Mapco
Amoco
Arco
Explorer
Texas Eastern
Mid Valley
Capline
Sun

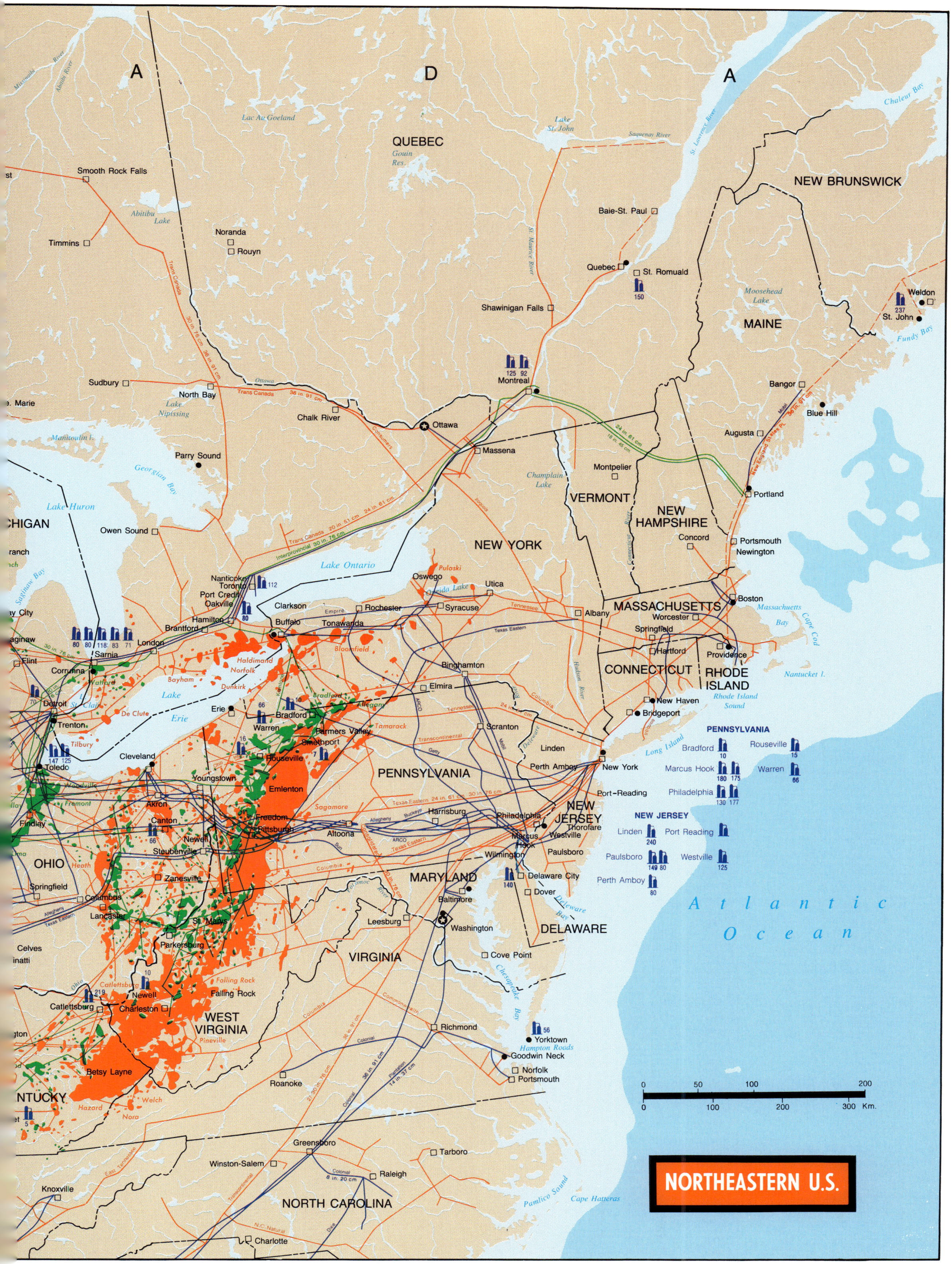
NORTHEASTERN U.S.
QUEBEC
NEW BRUNSWICK
MAINE
VERMONT
NEW HAMPSHIRE
NEW YORK
MASSACHUSETTS
CONNECTICUT
RHODE ISLAND
PENNSYLVANIA
NEW JERSEY
MARYLAND
DELAWARE
VIRGINIA
WEST VIRGINIA
NORTH CAROLINA
OHIO
Atlantic Ocean
Lake Ontario
Lake Erie
Lake Huron
Georgian Bay
Smooth Rock Falls
Timmins
Noranda
Rouyn
Sudbury
North Bay
Chalk River
Parry Sound
Owen Sound
Ottawa
Montreal
Massena
Shawinigan Falls
Quebec
St. Romuald
Baie-St. Paul
Weldon
St. John
Bangor
Blue Hill
Augusta
Portland
Montpelier
Concord
Portsmouth
Newington
Boston
Worcester
Springfield
Hartford
Providence
New Haven
Bridgeport
Albany
Syracuse
Utica
Oswego
Rochester
Buffalo
Tonawanda
Clarkson
Nanticoke
Toronto
Port Credit
Oakville
Hamilton
Brantford
London
Sarnia
Corrunna
Detroit
Trenton
Toledo
Erie
Bradford
Warren
Farmers Valley
Smethport
Rouseville
Emlenton
Freedom
Pittsburgh
Youngstown
Cleveland
Akron
Canton
Newell
Steubenville
Zanesville
Columbus
Lancaster
St. Marys
Parkersburg
Catlettsburg
Charleston
Falling Rock
Betsy Layne
Binghamton
Elmira
Scranton
Linden
Perth Amboy
New York
Port Reading
Harrisburg
Altoona
Philadelphia
Marcus Hook
Westville
Thorofare
Paulsboro
Wilmington
Delaware City
Dover
Baltimore
Washington
Leesburg
Cove Point
Richmond
Yorktown
Goodwin Neck
Norfolk
Portsmouth
Roanoke
Greensboro
Winston-Salem
Raleigh
Tarboro
Knoxville
Charlotte
PENNSYLVANIA
Bradford 10
Rouseville 15
Marcus Hook 180 175
Warren 66
Philadelphia 130 177
NEW JERSEY
Linden 240
Port Reading
Paulsboro 149 80
Westville 125
Perth Amboy 80
0 50 100 200
0 100 200 300 Km.

levels of 1994. In its report on the JAS, API attributed the gains to increased outlays for seismic surveys, material, and equipment and a shift to drilling of development gas wells deeper than 15,000 ft. Adjusted for inflation and drilling activity, the cost to drill a well was 3% lower than in 1994 and 31% lower than in 1984, API said.

Drilling of onshore development wells less than 10,000 ft deep rebounded in 1995. Activity was concentrated in Kern County, Calif., Central and West Texas, and Utah. Development gas drilling nearly doubled in Michigan's shallow Devonian Antrim shale gas play, where well depths tended to be less than 2,500 ft, and in the deeper Gulf Coast basin province of East Texas, with wells commonly deeper than 15,000 ft. In the Gulf of Mexico, by far the busiest U.S. offshore drilling theater, the number of deep wells drilled in 1995 rose 50%, and their costs rose 40%, according to the JAS.

The most expensive onshore wells in the survey, at more than $1 million each, were drilled in south Louisiana and the Gulf Coast basin in Texas. The least expensive wells on a per-unit basis, at less than $100,000 apiece, were drilled in the Illinois basin of Illinois, Indiana, and Western Kentucky.

The Gulf Coast basin was first in expenditures, followed by Louisiana, the Permian basin, and the Anadarko and Chautauqua basin of Oklahoma.

A total of 1,175 horizontal wells were completed in 1995, up 32% from 1994, and costing a total of $1.4 billion.

The number of coalbed methane wells drilled fell 15% in 1995 to 180.

Rig utilization rises

The market for rigs in the U.S. reapproached balance in 1996 after a long period of oversupply.

Drilling in general was up. The Baker Hughes rotary rig count for the first week in December was 856, up 84 from the same week a year earlier.

The number of available rigs declined by 80 units to 1,649 in 1996, according to the annual rig census by Reed Tool Co. The figure represented an all-time low, breaking the record set just a year earlier.

The low point of the previous rig fleet cycle came in 1973 at 1,767. With crude prices leaping in the years following, the rig fleet zoomed to a peak of 5,644 units in 1982.

By Reed's count, there were 1,263 active rigs in 1996. The firm defines "active rigs" as units drilling in a specific 45 day period, which was May 25-July 8 for the 1996 census. The 1996 census of active rigs was up almost 3% from the year earlier.

The utilization rate of the rig fleet was 77% in 1996, compared with 72% in 1995. It was the highest utilization rate in 15 years. Average utilization over the history of the Reed census is 73%.

"We believe a sustained utilization rate above 80% is necessary for business conditions to be healthy for drilling contractors," said Reed President Alex Newton when he presented the census at the October 1996 annual meeting of the International Association of Drilling Contractors. "The five percentage point increase in rig utilization this year has given hope that further rig rate increases will follow."

Only 6% of the available rigs were not being marketed, the lowest percentage since 1989, when the census began counting rigs being bid for jobs.

Deletions from the rig fleet totaled 141 in 1996 vs. 195 in 1995. Of that total, 42 rigs fell from the fleet because they required capital expenditures exceeding $50,000. The comparable figure in 1995 was 62.

Thirty-six rigs were deleted because they were stacked more than 3 years (vs. 29 in 1995). Another 36 rigs were cannibalized or auctioned for parts, a practice characteristic of periods of low rig rates. In 1995, 71 rigs were deleted for this reason. Twenty-four rigs were moved out of the U.S., and three were destroyed. In 1995, 30 rigs moved out of the U.S., and three were destroyed.

Additions to the U.S. rig fleet totaled 61 in 1996, compared with 83 in 1995. Thirty-three rigs were reactivated (vs. 38 in 1995), 24 were assembled from components (vs. 35 in 1995), 3 were newly manufactured (vs. 0 in 1995), and 1 moved into the U.S. (vs. 10 in 1995). The three newly built rigs were the first land rigs built for the U.S. market since 1992.

At the time of the census, 35% of the active rigs were drilling for gas (down from 39% in 1995), 24% were drilling for oil (down from 30%), and 41% were reported to be drilling for both oil and gas (up from 30%).

In another sign of improving conditions in the drilling industry, the percentage of active rigs working under day work contracts increased for the fourth consecutive year to 54% in 1996 from 50% in 1995 and 36% in 1992.

The offshore rig fleet totaled 244 units available and was 85.7% utilized at the time of the census. Utilization rates by rig type were 78.3% for inland barges, 95.5% for floating units, 64.5% for platforms, and 94.9% for jack-ups.

For land rigs, the utilization rate jumped to 75% in 1996 from 70% in 1995.

Offshore fleet tight

By the end of 1996, operators and analysts were feeling a squeeze in rig availability for the active Gulf of Mexico, especially deepwater units.

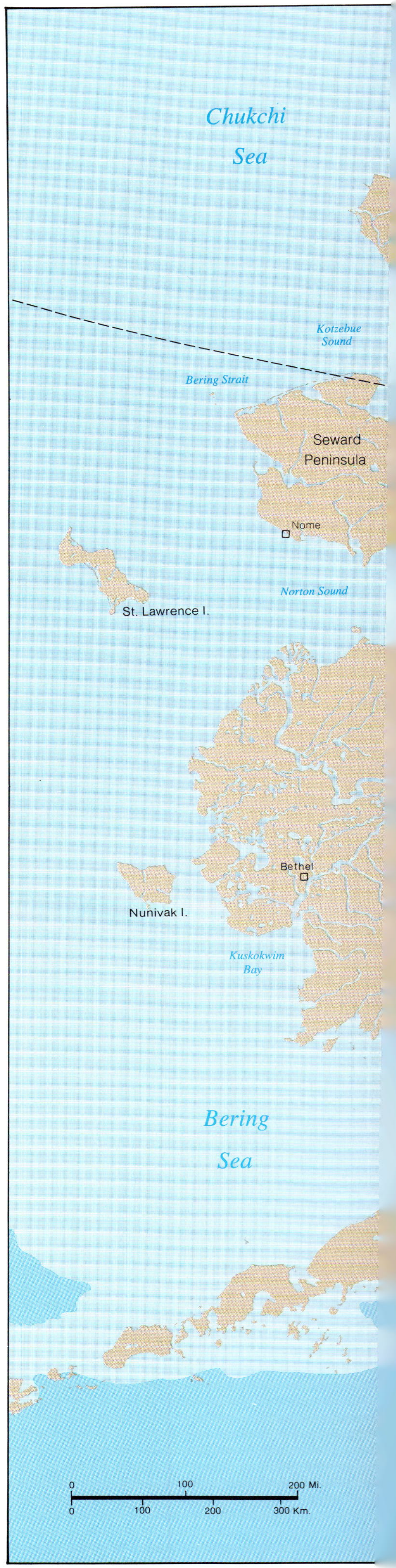

Beaufort Sea
Point Barrow
Barrow
Smith Bay
Simpson
Arctic Plains
Harrison Bay
Prudhoe Bay Field unit
Prudhoe Bay
Kuparuk
Endicott
Flaxman Is.
Point Thomson
Camden Bay
Naval Petroleum Reserve No. 4
Umiat
Gubik
E. Umiat
Kavik
Brooks Range
Arctic Wildlife Reserve
Tuktoyaktuk Pen.
Koakoak
Kopanoar
Issungnak
Amauligak
Atkinson
Pitsiulak
Tarsiut
Itiyok
Richards I.
Ivik
Mayogiak
Adgo
Mallik
Taglu
Tuk
Niglintgak
Ya Ya
Kumak
Parsons Lake
Mackenzie Bay
Titalik
Reindeer
Inuvik
Fort Good Hope
Norman Wells
Arctic Circle
Fort Yukon
Circle
YUKON
NORTHWEST TERRITORIES
Tanana
Yukon River
Fairbanks
North Pole
ALASKA
Delta Jct.
Dawson
Alaska Range
CANADA
Willow
Palmer
Anchorage
Chugach Mountains
Valdez
Gravina Point
Cordova
Beluga River
Ivan River
Granite Point
North Cook Inlet
Trading Bay
Birch Hills
McArthur River
Swanson River
Drift River
Nikiski
Kenai
Kenai Pen.
Cook Inlet
Montague I.
Haines Jct.
Whitehorse
Watson Lake
Yakataga
Yakutat
Skagway
Haines
Juneau
Sitka
Wrangell
Ketchikan
Kodiak
Kodiak I.
Alaska Peninsula
Gulf of Alaska
ALASKA

LOS ANGELES BASIN
CALIFORNIA
Pacific
Ocean
Point Arguello
Point Conception
Gaviota
Capitan
Goleta
Santa Barbara
Alegria
Molino
Naples
Elwood
Sacate
Pescado
Hondo
Santa Ynez Unit Area
South Elwood
Coal Oil Point
Mesa
Sanctuary
Carpinteria
Summerland
Dos Cuadras
Rincon
San Miguelito
Santa Barbara Channel
Pitas Point Ridge
Santa Rosa
Santa Clara
Sockeye
Hueneme
West Montalvo
Ventura
Oxnard
Ojai
Temescal
Timber Creek
Oak Canyon
Ramona
Castaic Hills
Canton Creek
Tapia
Wayside Canyon
Honor Rancho
Saugas
Castaic Junction
Newhall Potrero
Newhall
Placerita
Fillmore
Del Valle
South Mountain
Cascade
San Fernando
Simi
Aliso Canyon
Mission
Conejo
Canoga Park
Los Angeles
Sherman
San Vicente
Beverly Hills
Los Angeles City
Union Station
Boyle Heights
Los Angeles Downtown
Montebello
Santa Fe Springs
Walnut
Whittier
Sansinena
Brea-Olinda
Chino-Soquel
Yorba Linda
Mahala
Prado-Corona
Esperanza
Kraemer
Richfield
Olive
Venice Beach
Playa Del Rey
Hyperion
El Segundo
Rosecrans
Dominguez
Torrance
Carson
Wilmington
Long Beach
Long Beach Airport
Signal Hill
Seal Beach
Sunset Beach
Huntington Beach
Belmont Offshore
Newport Beach
Newport
W. Newport
San Clemente
San Bernardino
San Miguel I.
Santa Rosa I.
Santa Cruz I.
Anacapa I.
Santa Catalina I.
3 mile boundary
0 5 10 15 Mi.
0 5 10 15 Km.

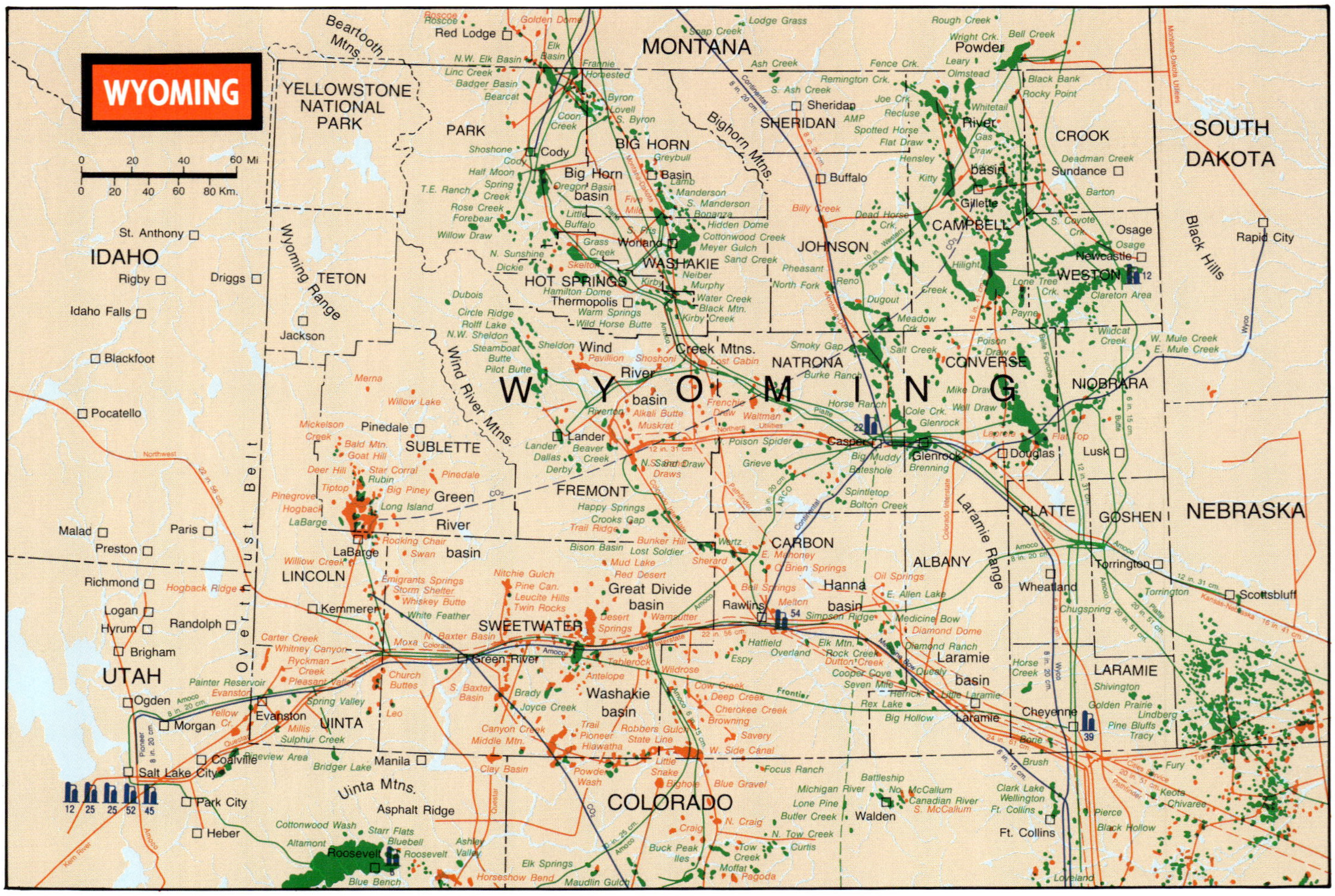
WYOMING
W Y O M I N G
MONTANA
IDAHO
UTAH
COLORADO
SOUTH DAKOTA
NEBRASKA
YELLOWSTONE NATIONAL PARK
Beartooth Mtns.
Bighorn Mtns.
Wind River Mtns.
Wyoming Range
Laramie Range
Uinta Mtns.
Overthrust Belt
Black Hills
PARK
BIG HORN
SHERIDAN
JOHNSON
CAMPBELL
CROOK
WESTON
WASHAKIE
HOT SPRINGS
TETON
FREMONT
NATRONA
CONVERSE
NIOBRARA
SUBLETTE
LINCOLN
SWEETWATER
CARBON
ALBANY
PLATTE
GOSHEN
LARAMIE
UINTA
Big Horn basin
Wind River basin
Powder River basin
Green River basin
Great Divide basin
Washakie basin
Hanna basin
Laramie basin
Red Lodge
Cody
Basin
Sheridan
Buffalo
Gillette
Sundance
Osage
Newcastle
Rapid City
Thermopolis
Casper
Glenrock
Douglas
Lusk
Torrington
Scottsbluff
Wheatland
Cheyenne
Laramie
Rawlins
Green River
Kemmerer
LaBarge
Pinedale
Jackson
Lander
Riverton
Evanston
Salt Lake City
Ogden
Morgan
Coalville
Park City
Heber
Roosevelt
Manila
Walden
Ft. Collins
St. Anthony
Rigby
Driggs
Idaho Falls
Blackfoot
Pocatello
Malad
Preston
Paris
Richmond
Logan
Hyrum
Randolph
Brigham
0 20 40 60 Mi
0 20 40 60 80 Km.

CALIFORNIA
OREGON
IDAHO
NEVADA
ARIZONA
MEXICO
Pacific Ocean
State CALIFORNIA
No. Refineries
Bakersfield 4
Benicia 2
Carson 2
El Segundo 1
Martinez 2
McKittrick 1
Oildale 1
Oxnard 1
Paramount 1
Richmond 1
Santa Maria/ San Francisco 1
South Gate 1
Torrance 1
Wilmington 4
Total 23
Carson 255 118
El Segundo 258
Oxnard 4
Paramount 42
South Gate 7
Torrance 130
Wilmington 118 5 91 68
Benicia 128 8
Martinez 156 155
Hercules 50
Richmond 255
San Francisco 103
Oildale 10
Bakersfield 18 58 21 15
Eureka
Santa Rosa
Sacramento
Oakland
San Jose
Santa Cruz
Salinas
Modesto
Fresno
Hanford
San Luis Obispo
Santa Maria
Santa Barbara
Ventura
Oxnard
Newhall
Los Angeles
Torrance
Long Beach
Santa Fe Springs
San Bernardino
Carlsbad
San Diego
Tijuana
El Centro
Mexicali
Yuma
Barstow
Needles
Kingman
Las Vegas
Henderson
Boulder City
Hoover Dam
Davis Dam
Reno
Sparks
Carson City
Virginia City
Tonopah
Warm Springs
Bishop
Susanville
Alturas
Klamath Falls
Medford
Grants Pass
Ashland
Talent
Fields
Rome
Triangle
Humboldt
Elko
Indian Springs
Overton
Nelson
Yucca
0 50 100 Mi.
0 50 100 Km.

WESTERN U.S.
For detail on California refineries, see California maps
BRITISH COLUMBIA
WASHINGTON
OREGON
IDAHO
MONTANA
ALBERTA
WYOMING
NEVADA
UTAH
CALIFORNIA
ARIZONA
Pacific Ocean
Vancouver
Cherry Point
Ferndale
Anacortes
Port Angeles
Seattle
Tacoma
Olympia
Aberdeen
Longview
Portland
Salem
Corvallis
Eugene
Coos Bay
Roseburg
Medford
Klamath Falls
Bend
Yakima
Richland
Pasco
Walla Walla
The Dalles
Pendleton
Spokane
Coeur d'Alene
Moses Lake
Moscow
Lewiston
Missoula
Helena
Great Falls
Anaconda
Butte
Billings
Laurel
Dillon
Boise
Caldwell
Ontario
Baker
Mountain Home
Twin Falls
Pocatello
Logan
Brigham City
Ogden
Woods Cross
Salt Lake City
Provo
Grand Junction
Montrose
Durango
Farmington
Bloomfield
Gallup
Albuquerque
Eureka
Santa Rosa
Sacramento
Richmond
San Francisco
Oakland
Stockton
Hayward
Redwood City
San Jose
Santa Clara
Santa Cruz
Salinas
Modesto
Fresno
Hanford
Oildale
Bakersfield
Estero Bay
San Luis Obispo
Santa Maria
Santa Barbara
Ventura
Oxnard
Newhall
Los Angeles
Long Beach
Santa Fe Springs
San Bernardino
Carlsbad
San Diego
Tijuana
Rosarito
Mexicali
El Centro
Yuma
Ajo
Phoenix
Tucson
Nogales
Douglas
Las Vegas
Boulder City
Hoover Dam
Kingman
Flagstaff
Winslow
Prescott
Reno
Fallon
Carson City
Yerington
Tonopah
Ely
Elko
Cedar City
Fredonia
Nelson
Trail
Babb
Medicine Hat
Rock Springs
Sinclair
Casper
Thermopolis
Cody
Greybull
Cowley
Frannie
Elk Basin
Mosby
Bascom
Hardin
Sheridan
La Barge
Fort Washakie
Roosevelt
Rangely
0 100 200 Mi.
0 100 200 Km.

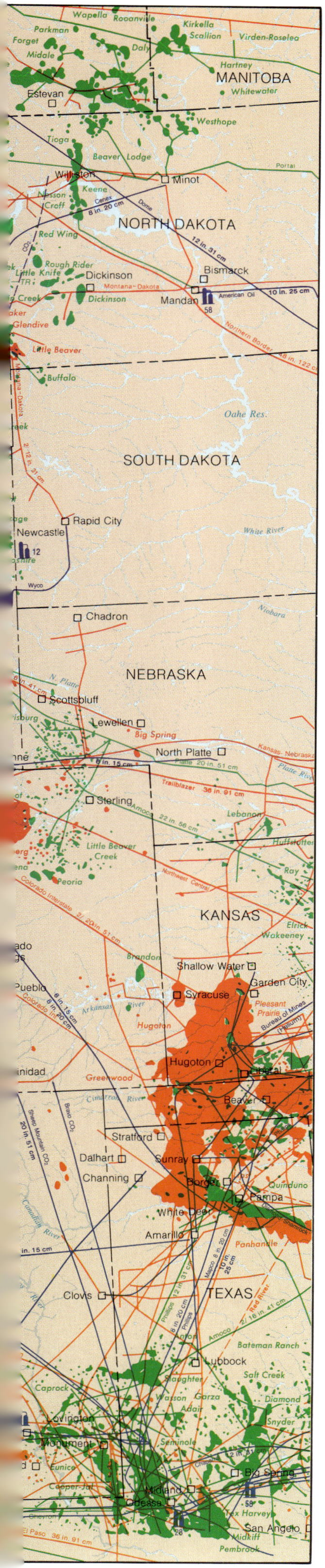

In a presentation to the British American Business Association at the end of October 1996, Matthew R. Simmons, president of Simmons & Co. International, estimated that 91% of rigs available in the gulf were under contract, 5% were cold-stacked, and 4% were in shipyards. And there was little surplus worldwide to supplement supply in the gulf or anywhere else. The spare but ready-to-use supply of offshore rigs had shrunk to only 1% of the worldwide fleet, Simmons said.

He further estimated that the number of deepwater rigs in the gulf needed to triple. Outer Continental Shelf lease sales in 1996 increased the number of leases in waters 800 m and deeper by 70%, he explained. Eight such rigs were available at the time.

Simmons said efficiency gains can't eliminate the need for new rigs.

"Well efficiency is essentially flat," he said. And technology hasn't eliminated the drilling of dry holes.

The need to add oil and gas supplies through drilling rather than increasing production from spare capacity would significantly raise industry costs, Simmons predicted, pointing out that not just rig but also oil and gas markets had ended a long period of surplus.

"We have finally entered 'the golden era' where everything works once more, and tightness is not so severe," Simmons said. "Are we about to exit this golden age and propel into the era of chronic tightness?"

Louisiana chalk play

One of the hottest onshore drilling plays in the U.S. during 1996 showed how steady gains in technology were creating opportunities. Horizontal drilling extended exploration and development of the Cretaceous Austin chalk from Texas, where they had been active since the late 1980s, into technically more challenging but potentially more profitable locations in western Louisiana.

Advances in measurement-while-drilling (MWD) techniques, improved mud and bit programs, and sophisticated use of 2D and 3D seismic data were credited with making the Louisiana chalk economic to explore and develop. In general, the type of technological advances that greatly lowered costs in the more-mature Texas side of the chalk play brought the deeper, hotter, geologically more complex chalk prospects of Louisiana into the realm of the economically worthwhile.

The modern era of the Texas Austin chalk began in the mid-1980s, when Oryx Energy Co. in Pearsall field of Southwest Texas and Union Pacific Resources in Giddings field of South Central Texas scored major production gains with horizontal wells. Their successes revived interest in the chalk and touched off a horizontal drilling binge that continued, at least in the Giddings area, into 1996.

The play skipped to the Louisiana border when Union Pacific drilled its first horizontal well in Brookeland field in 1992. Discovered in 1983, the field was thought to be in decline. Horizontal drilling, among other things, opened development of downdip parts of the field in chalk at depths exceeding 10,000 ft.

The Louisiana chalk, drilled vertically since the 1920s, began to receive new industry interest after Cliffs Oil & Gas Co. in 1991 reentered a well drilled in 1978 by Gulf Oil Co. in North Bayou Jack field and recompleted it with a 2,135 ft horizontal lateral that tested 2,600 b/d of oil and 1.5 MMcfd of gas.

After that, a number of major and independent oil and gas companies became active in the Louisiana chalk. In 1996, most drilling and development activity was in and around Brookeland field, which straddles the Louisiana-Texas border, and in and near North Bayou Jack, North Hadden, Masters Creek, Burr Ferry, and South Burr Ferry fields in Louisiana. The play extended from the state line to the Livingston area just east of Baton Rouge.

In November 1996, 20 rigs were reported to be active in the Louisiana chalk, most of them in the western part of the trend.

Union Pacific Resources, which had drilled 1,300 horizontal wells in the Texas chalk, said a Louisiana chalk well required 90-120 days to drill, compared with 30 days or less in Giddings field. Although deeper and thus more costly to drill, Louisiana chalk wells were more oil-prone than their Texas counterparts and benefited from a Louisiana tax holiday. Gas from the Louisiana chalk also has a high BTU content and thus receives a premium price.

UBS Securities LLC, in a November 1996 analysis, traced the economic improvement that had occurred in chalk drilling. Early in the Texas chalk play, it said, typical horizontal wells reached an average vertical depth of 9,000 ft and had a single lateral reach of 2,000 ft. Average finding cost in this period was $1.25/Mcf of gas equivalent (McfE). Reserves lives were short, so economics depended on quick payouts.

The advent of MWD and improvements in the steering of wells lowered finding costs in the Texas chalk to 75¢/McfE in 1993-94, while operators drilled into deeper, more heavily pressured, and more-fractured parts of the chalk—which also held potential for

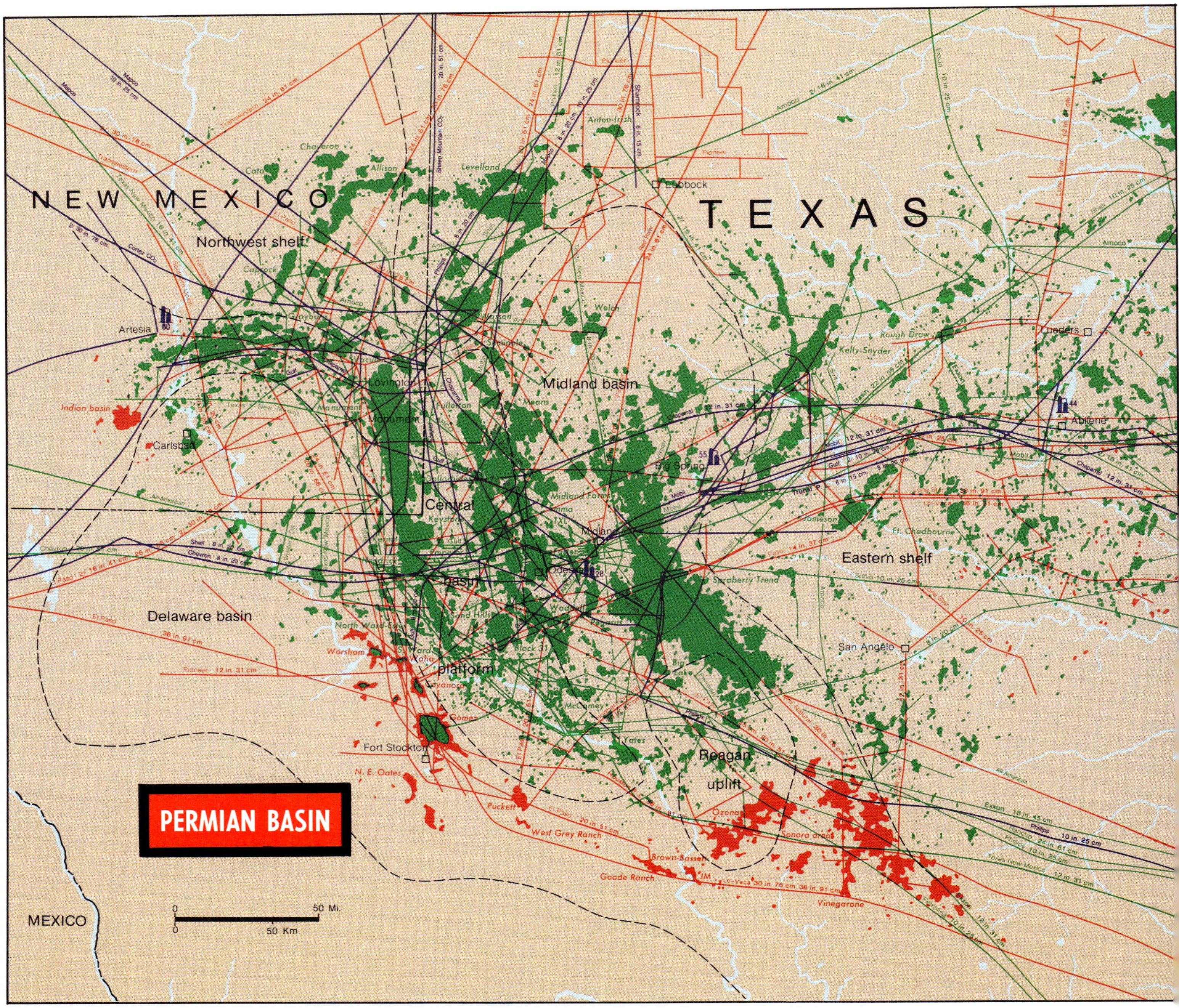

higher reserves.

Dual-opposing laterals, in which two horizontal sections were drilled in opposite directions from a single vertical well bore, entered the scene in 1993 and lowered finding costs to 50¢/McfE in 1994-95. Typical dual-opposing lateral horizontal wells reached depths of 12,000-15,000 ft and had horizontal reaches of about 4,000 ft on each side.

In 1995, companies increasingly drilled quadrilateral horizontal wells, involving four horizontal legs extending from a single vertical well bore.

UBS estimated that finding costs in the Texas chalk in 1996 had fallen to as low as 35¢/McfE.

Louisiana wells weren't comparable. UBS estimated that dual lateral wells in the Texas chalk cost $2-3 million, while like wells in the Louisiana chalk cost $4-5 million. A single-lateral completion in the Louisiana chalk cost $2.5-3.5 million.

Lessons learned in Texas chalk were certainly contributing to success in Louisiana, however, and UBS predicted that Louisiana costs would decline as operators learned more about geology and reservoirs there.

"Much like the deepwater plays in the Gulf of Mexico," it said, "the Austin Chalk is truly a technology play."

Price movements

Price increases in 1996 added a bonus to the profitability gains the upstream industry had earned from a decade of cost-cutting and technological progress.

The average wellhead price of crude oil in the U.S. increased 25.4% in 1996 to an estimated $18.33/bbl. It was the second straight year of increase following 4 years of decline. The wellhead crude oil price averaged $20.03/bbl in 1990 and fell steadily to $13.19/bbl in 1994.

The average landed cost of crude oil imports by the U.S. increased 20.5% in 1996 to $20.20/bbl.

Crude prices rose in part because supplies tightened somewhat worldwide and in part because produce prices rose on the strength of continued increases in demand.

The average pump price for unleaded gasoline rose 7.2% in

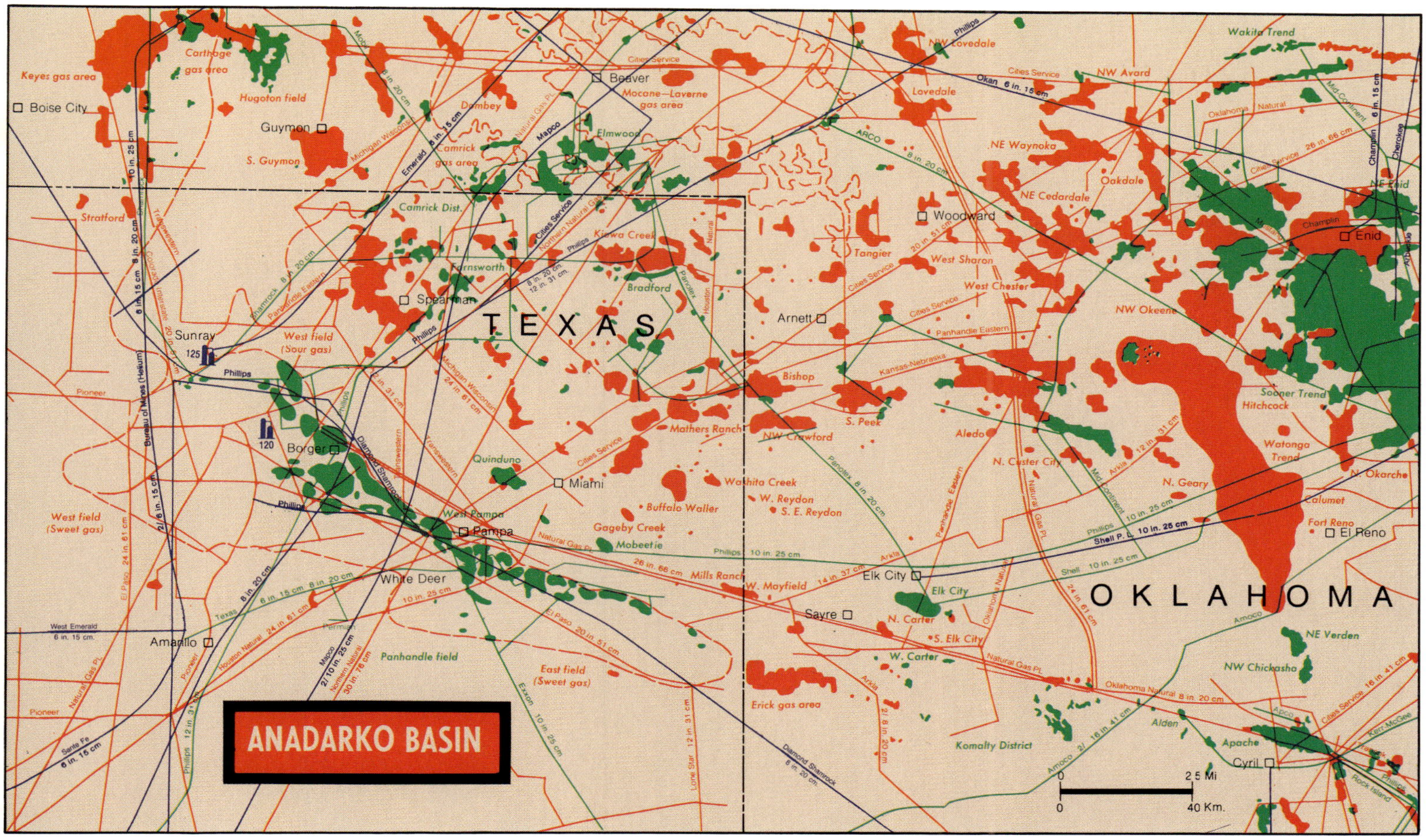

1996 to an estimated average of \$1.23/gal. This followed a 3.1% increase in 1995 to \$1.147/gal, highest since 1983. The refiners' wholesale price of finished motor gasoline increased 16.6% to an estimated average of 73¢/gal in 1996. Although gasoline demand ran ahead of year-earlier levels for most of the year, that increment of increase appeared to be diminishing at yearend.

Total gasoline taxes at the pump averaged 39.5¢/gal in 1996, up from 39.3¢/gal in 1995 and 37.5¢/gal in 1994.

The strongest price gain came in distillate heating oil. Extreme cold early in 1996 raised demand, and inventories were low at the beginning of the 1996-97 heating season. The average wholesale price of No. 2 fuel oil increased 23% to an estimated 62.9¢/gal in 1996 following a 1% increase in 1995 to 51.1¢/gal. Fuel oil prices had fallen for 4 consecutive years through 1994.

Refining trends

With crude oil prices up more than prices of the principal petroleum products, refining margins were narrow most of 1996.

Except for a few weeks in the first quarter of the year, when gasoline prices rose along with heating oil, and in the fourth quarter, when heating oil values jumped because of high demand and low inventories, gross operating margins were thin to negative most of the year.

A heating oil price surge late in the year didn't help margins much. Refiners, straining to build inventories of a product that accounts for less than one-fourth of their average yield, produced more gasoline than the market needed and thus suppressed prices for the product that makes up about half their average yield.

For the first 9 months of 1996, the Gulf Coast cash operating margin as calculated by Wright Killen & Co. and published in Oil & Gas Journal averaged 53¢/bbl, up from 25¢/bbl for the same period of 1995. Much of that strength came early in the year, however, when prices were high across the product barrel.

By August, the average refining margin had fallen to −6¢/bbl, a sharp contrast to the 58¢/bbl of the same month a year earlier. It was considered unlikely that average Gulf Coast refining margins for the year would appreciably exceed the 33¢/bbl of 1995. Earlier margin averages were 88¢/bbl in 1994 and \$1.39/bbl in 1993.

Weak margins persisted even though refineries operated at close to full capacity throughout the year.

Crude oil runs to stills increased 1.3% in 1996 to average an estimated 14.16 million b/d. Total input to stills rose 1.2% to average 14.29 million b/d.

Average refining capacity over the course of the year slipped to 15.335 million b/d from 15.346 million b/d in 1995. The increase in input to stills coupled with the reduction in capacity boosted the refinery utilization rate to an average of 93.2% from 92% in 1995. This is essentially full capacity utilization since some idle capacity is needed for maintenance and contingencies.

Total industry imports of crude oil and petroleum products increased by 6.8% to 9.44 million b/d in 1996. The total included 7.54 million b/d of crude (up 4.3%), and 1.9 million b/d of products (up 18.4%).

Capacity changes

A major reason for margin weakness in a period of high capacity utilization was an excess of conversion capacity.

In response to requirements for reformulated and oxygenated gasoline and low-sulfur diesel fuel under the Clean Air Act Amendments of 1990 (CAAA), refiners had to invest heavily in processing equipment that would produce no return. The general expectation was that old refineries would have to be shut down in a process that would eliminate large amounts of dis-

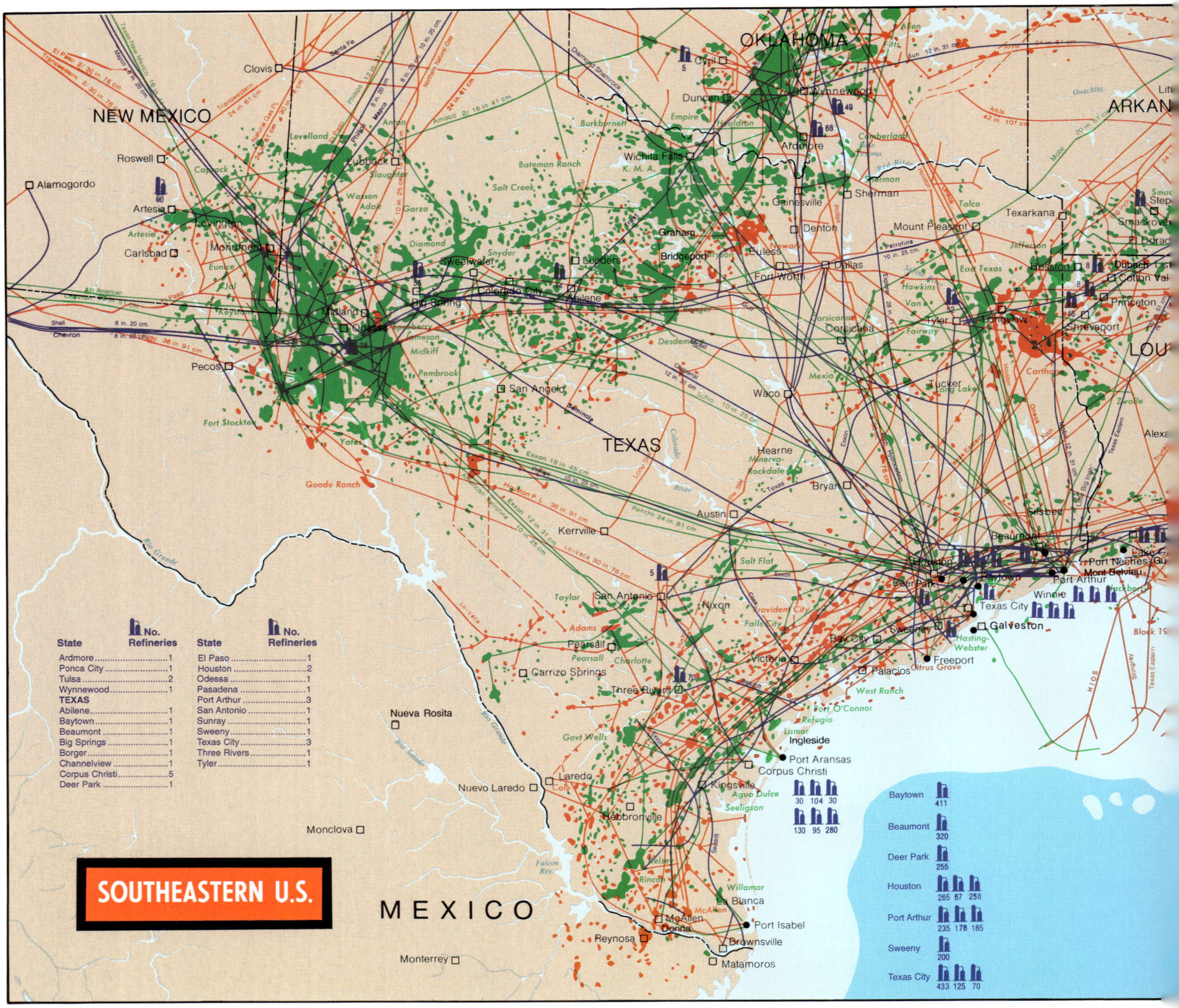

tillation capacity and enlarge refining margins.

At the same time, refiners planning to stay in business increased conversion capacity, partly to help meet the new requirements but also to improve plant efficiency and recoup investments in hydrotreating and alkylation capacity for CAAA compliance. The increased ability to upgrade the heavy products of distillation, they believed, would both help them meet expected increases in demand for light products and enable them to profit from the spreads between values of heavy and light products.

At least through 1996, those expectations had not come true. While a few refineries did close, cuts in U.S. distillation capacity were relatively modest, about 600,000 b/d during 1992-96. High clean-up costs and potentially endless environmental liabilities discouraged many companies from shutting down plants. A larger trend was toward mergers or sales by major oil companies of unwanted facilities to independent companies able to operate them cheaply—and keep distillation capacity on stream.

Meanwhile, refiners needed to keep new conversion capacity occupied, which meant running a lot of crude and making a lot of light products. The results: failure of heavy-light spreads to remain at levels on which conversion investments had been based and pressure on refining margins overall.

Refineries shut down in 1996 included Barrett Refining Corp., 10,500 b/cd, Thomas, Okla.; Crystal Refining Co. Inc., 4,000 b/cd, Carson City, Mich.; Intermountain Refining Co. Inc., 5,710 b/cd, Fredonia, Ariz.; and Total Petroleum Inc., 56,000 b/cd, Arkansas City, Kan.

In addition, BP Oil Co. idled its 180,500 b/cd refinery at Marcus Hook, Pa., during a labor dispute then sold it in February 1996 to Tosco Corp., which kept it idle for economic reasons but planned to restart it, possibly in mid-1997. Tosco, a Stamford, Conn., independent refiner and marketer, was building a strong refining and marketing presence in the U.S. with purchases from major companies. Before the BP purchase, it had acquired the 165,000 b/d Avon refinery on San Francisco Bay, the 90,000 b/d Ferndale plant on Puget Sound in Washington, and the 285,000 b/d Bayway refinery on New York Harbor. In May 1996 it greatly expanded its marketing operations with the $900 million purchase of Circle K Corp. And in November,

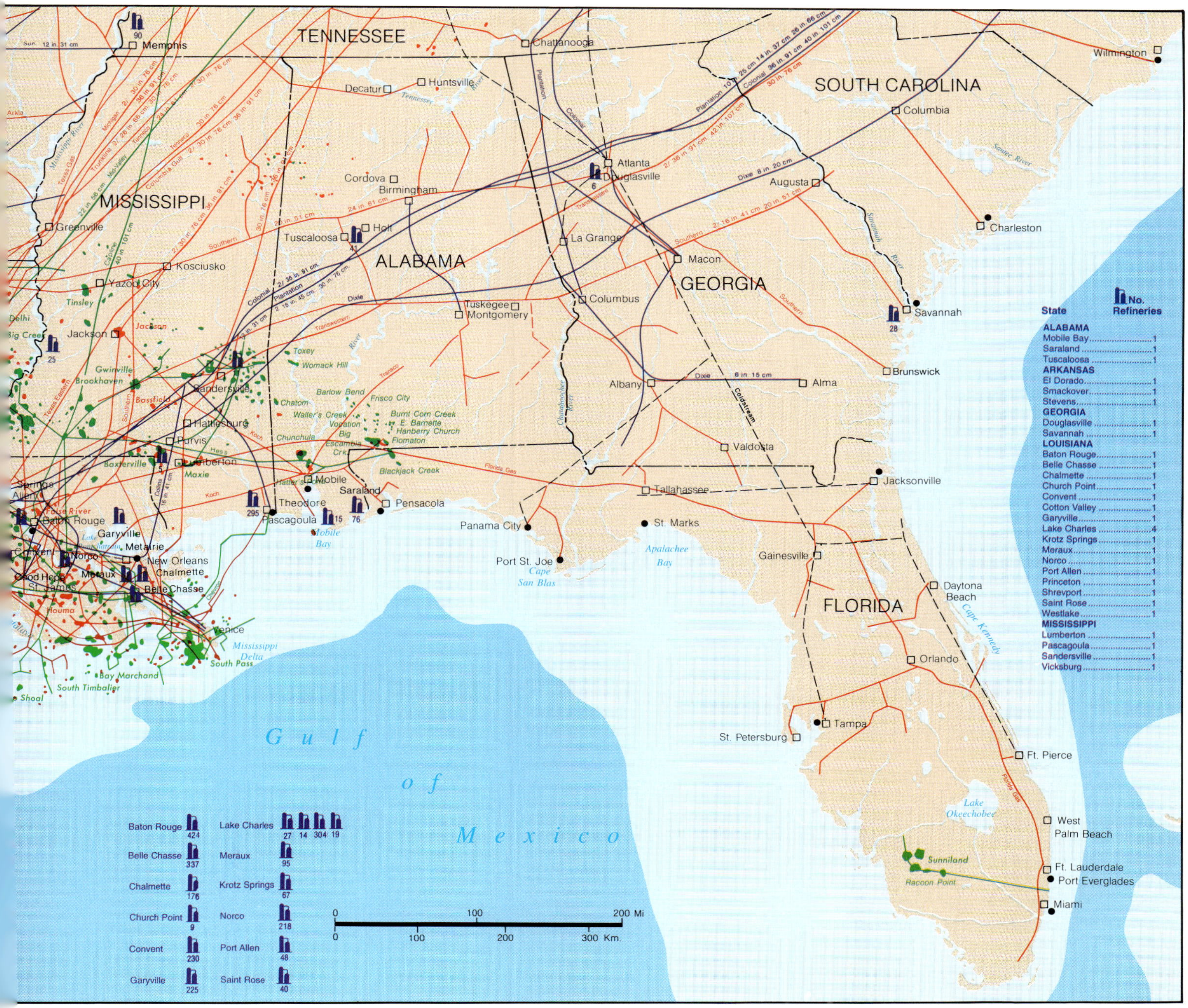

Tosco announced plans to buy Unocal Corp.'s 76 Products division.

At the end of 1996, Oil & Gas Journal estimated U.S. crude distillation capacity in place and operable as of Jan. 1, 1997, at 15.433 million b/cd, compared with 15.354 million b/cd at the start of 1996. The only processing category that changed significantly during the year was catalytic cracking, total capacity for which decreased by 103,400 b/d to 1.351 million b/d. Most of the decline came from Sun Refining & Marketing, which eliminated the 30,000 b/d fluid catalytic cracking unit at its Tulsa refinery and the 80,000 b/d unit at its Marcus Hook facility. The latter unit was being revamped and expanded.

Refinery mergers, acquisitions

U.S. refiners could not deal with chronically low margins in what would seem to be the rational way: by closing refineries. They faced huge clean-up and environmental compliance costs for refinery sites, and environmental liabilities could be endless.

The pressures in 1996 sustained a wave of merger and partnership activity involving refining and marketing properties. The impulses behind this activity were clear. In straight refinery sales, sellers shed themselves of underperforming assets without incurring the exorbitant exit costs of closing refineries, and buyers acquired properties able to generate cash flow at prices significantly below replacement costs. In mergers and alliances, parties sought ways to reduce costs and strengthen marketing efforts.

In addition to Tosco's acquisitions, 1996 merger, acquisition, and alliance activity included a merger of Ultramar Corp. and Diamond Shamrock Inc. and a proposed, then scuttled, merger of the downstream assets of Conoco Inc. and Phillips Petroleum Co.

The year's most sweeping proposal, although not consummated by yearend, was a three-way blending of the downstream assets of Texaco Inc., Shell Oil Co., and Star Enterprise, Texaco's refining partnership with Saudi Arabian Oil Co. (Saudi Aramco). The companies were discussing what they described as "joint operational arrangements," which may or may not have led to outright merger.

A full combination of the companies would involve refining

TEXAS
BEAUREGARD
ALLEN
ST. LANDRY
LOUISIANA
CALCASIEU
JEFFERSON DAVIS
ACADIA
LAFAYETTE
ST. MARTIN
IBERVILLE
CAMERON
VERMILION
IBERIA
ASSUMPTIC
ST. MARY
Lake Charles
Jennings
Port Neches
Port Arthur
Sabine Lake
Calcasieu Lake
Grand Lake
White Lake
Vermilion Bay
New Iberia
Abbeville
Lafayette
Baton Rouge
Port Allen
Morgan City
Atchafalaya Bay
WEST CAMERON
SABINE PASS
EAST CAMERON
HIGH ISLAND
WEST CAMERON WEST ADDITION
HIGH ISLAND EAST ADDITION
WEST CAMERON SOUTH ADDITION
HIGH ISLAND EAST ADDITION SOUTH EXTENSION
EAST CAMERON SOUTH ADDITION
VERMILION
VERMILION SOUTH ADDITION
SOUTH MARSH ISLAND NORTH ADDITION
SOUTH MARSH ISLAND
SOUTH MARSH ISLAND SOUTH ADDITION
EUGENE ISLAND
EUGENE ISLAND SOUTH ADDITION
SHIP SHOAL
GARDEN BANKS NG 15-2
THREE LINE

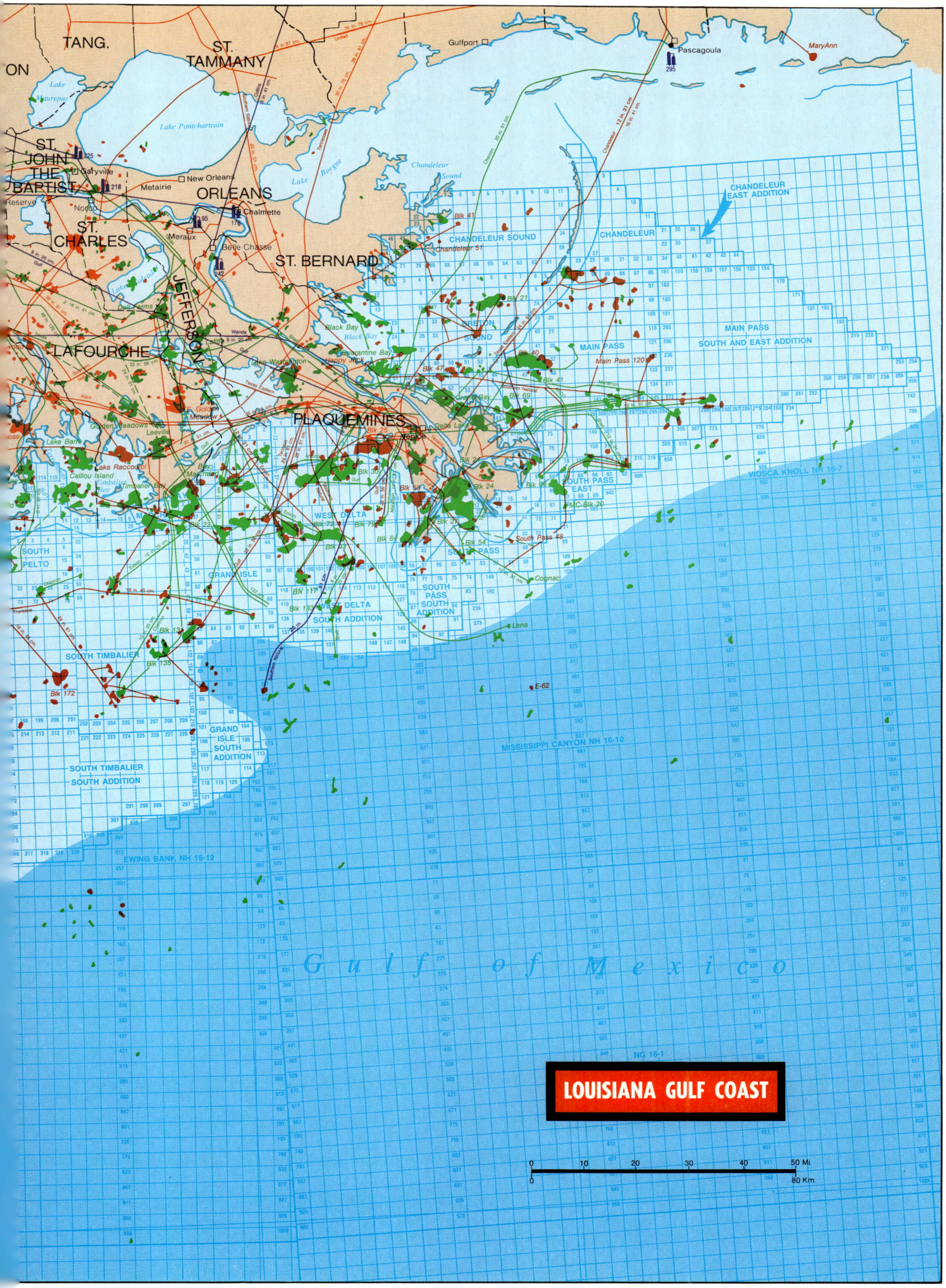
TANG.
ST. TAMMANY
ST. JOHN THE BAPTIST
ORLEANS
ST. CHARLES
ST. BERNARD
JEFFERSON
LAFOURCHE
PLAQUEMINES
Lake Maurepas
Lake Pontchartrain
Lake Borgne
Chandeleur Sound
Gulfport
Pascagoula
MaryAnn
Garyville
Reserve
Norco
Metairie
New Orleans
Chalmette
Meraux
Belle Chasse
Black Bay
Venice
Lake Barre
Leeville
Caillou Island
Timbalier Bay
CHANDELEUR SOUND
CHANDELEUR
CHANDELEUR EAST ADDITION
BRETON SOUND
MAIN PASS
MAIN PASS SOUTH AND EAST ADDITION
SOUTH PASS EAST
SOUTH PASS
SOUTH PASS SOUTH ADDITION
WEST DELTA
WEST DELTA SOUTH ADDITION
GRAND ISLE
GRAND ISLE SOUTH ADDITION
SOUTH PELTO
SOUTH TIMBALIER
SOUTH TIMBALIER SOUTH ADDITION
EWING BANK NH 15-12
VIOSCA KNOLL NH 16-7
MISSISSIPPI CANYON NH 16-10
NG 16-1
Cognac
Lena
E-62
Gulf of Mexico
LOUISIANA GULF COAST
0 10 20 30 40 50 Mi.
0 80 Km.

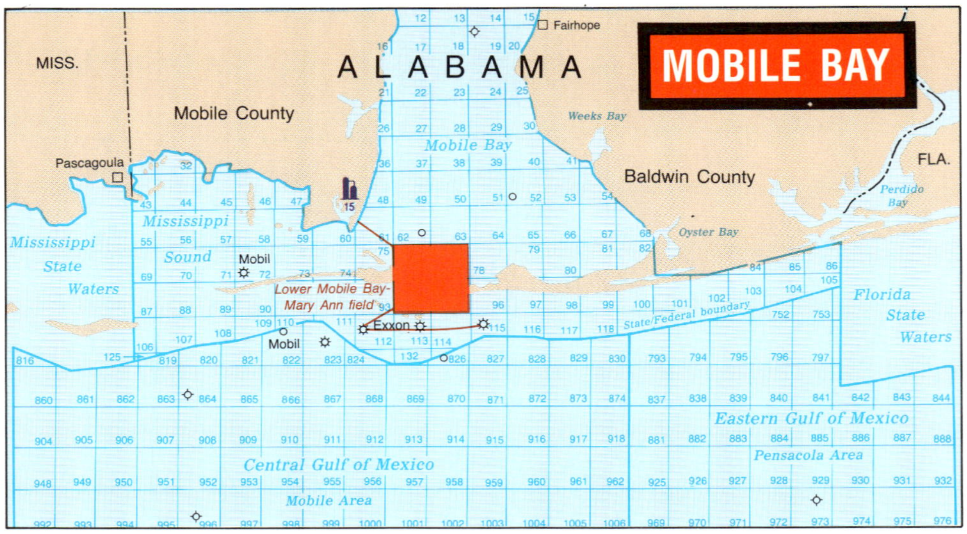

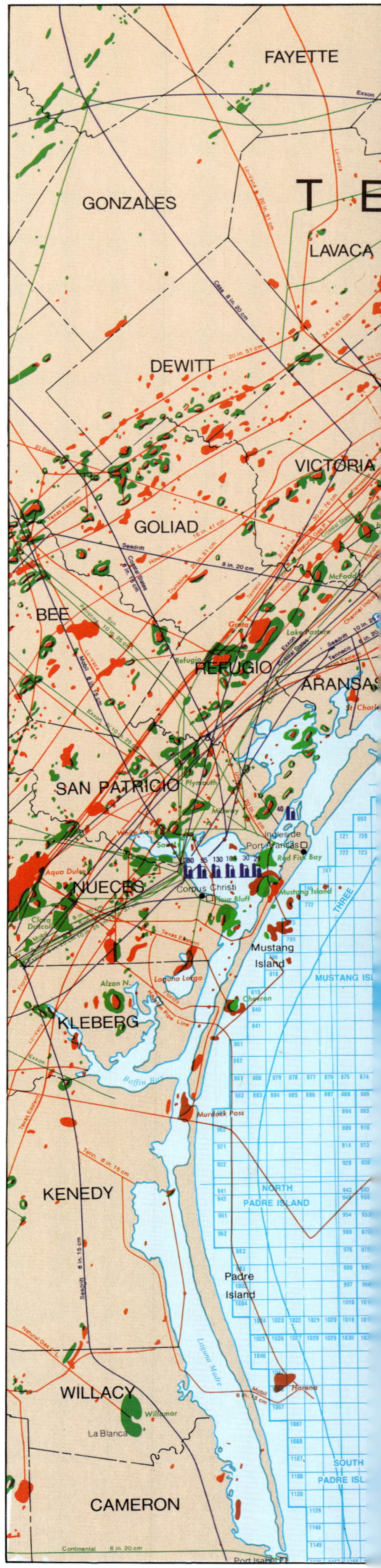

capacity of 1.8 million b/d. Texaco had 14,000 branded service stations in the U.S. in 1996, Shell 8,800.

The gas industry

As it was in refining and marketing, merger and acquisition activity was a highlight of the natural gas industry in 1996.

A large example was El Paso Energy Corp.'s midyear acquisition of Tenneco Energy in a deal worth an estimated $4 billion. The companies had combined assets of $8 billion. The merger created the third largest interstate gas pipeline system in the U.S. and the only one capable of shipping gas to both the East and West coasts.

Most 1996 company mergers in the gas industry, however, were part of a larger blending of the gas and electricity businesses. In 1996, the Federal Energy Regulatory Commission, with its Orders 888 and 889, deregulated much of the wholesale electricity business in a move partly parallel to its earlier deregulation of interstate natural gas. The order accommodated the already well-established convergence of the gas and electricity markets. It left retail deregulation largely up to states.

Faced with diminishing regulation and intense competition from independent power generators, electric utilities needed to look at new activities for growth potential. And a number of them saw natural gas as a natural route to expansion. In many of the larger mergers announced in 1996, electric utilities expanded to varying degrees into natural gas production, transportation, and marketing.

In an important exception with the gas company as buyer, Enron Corp. in 1996 acquired Portland General Corp., gaining an important electricity transmission system in California and access to federally subsidized electric power from the Bonneville Power Administration. The deal was seen as giving Enron a price advantage against California utilities forced to buy power from independent generators.

In late 1996, one of California's biggest utilities, San Diego Gas & Electric announced plans to merge with an important California gas holding company, Pacific Enterprises, in a deal more characteristic of the trend. Acquisitions announced earlier in the year included one by Texas Utilities Corp. of Enserch Corp. and another by Houston Industries Inc. of NorAm Energy Corp. Late in 1996, Duke Power Co., Charlotte, N.C., and PanEnergy Corp., Houston, agreed to merge in a deal worth an estimated $23 billion. Early in 1997, Valero Energy Corp. was trying to sell its natural gas business.

Most analysts expected the merger and acquisition activity to continue, most often with electric utilities absorbing gas assets and operations. The electric utility industry, with three to four times the market capitalization of the gas industry, had the greater takeover muscle of the two. And, with growth prospects in its core functions limited and competition growing, electric utilities needed acquisitions in order both to grow and to add the services they needed to be competitive.

Like its oil counterpart, the gas market tightened in 1996, with prices of near-month futures contracts on the New York Mercantile Exchange at times exceeding $4/MMBTU. In mid-November, working inventories of natural gas were 6% below their levels a year earlier. This made prices very sensitive to weather changes for the rest of the year.

The average wellhead price of natural gas in 1996 jumped to $2.25/Mcf from $1.59/Mcf in 1995 and $1.88/Mcf in 1994. Annual averages had stayed in the range of $1.64-1.74/Mcf during 1987-92 before jumping to $2.03/Mcf in 1993.

Gas consumption in 1996 rose 1.2% to 21.9 tcf. Production was up 0.4% to 19.81 tcf, highest since 1981. Gas imports increased 1.3% in 1996 to 2.878 tcf; imports from Canada rose 0.5% to 2.83 tcf.

Import pipelines from Canada operated at near their practical capacities in 1996. Major capacity expansions were not expected to be complete before 1998. IPE

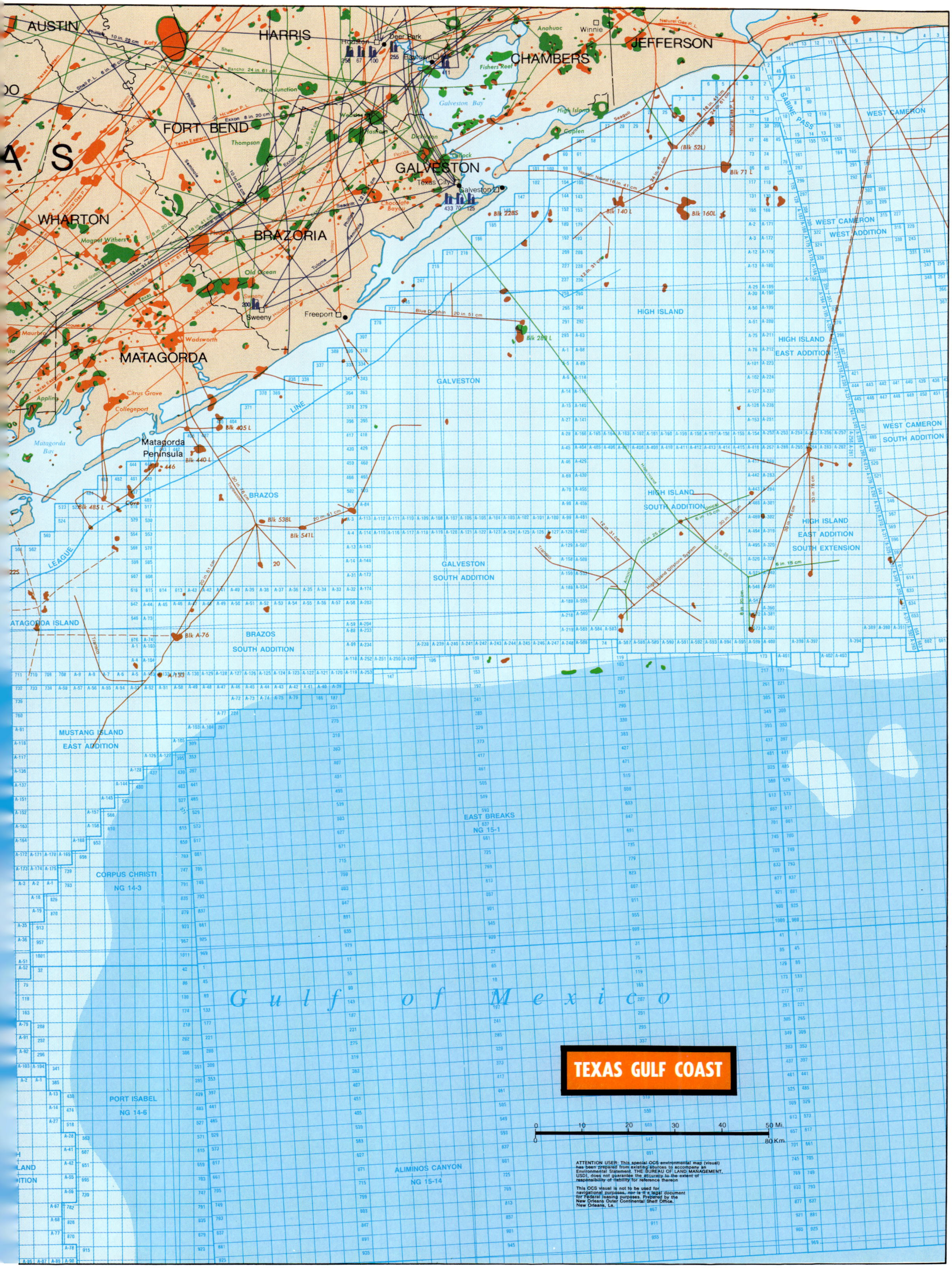
AUSTIN
HARRIS
CHAMBERS
JEFFERSON
FORT BEND
GALVESTON
WHARTON
BRAZORIA
MATAGORDA
Galveston Bay
Freeport
Sweeny
Matagorda Peninsula
WEST CAMERON
WEST CAMERON WEST ADDITION
HIGH ISLAND
HIGH ISLAND EAST ADDITION
WEST CAMERON SOUTH ADDITION
GALVESTON
BRAZOS
HIGH ISLAND SOUTH ADDITION
HIGH ISLAND EAST ADDITION SOUTH EXTENSION
GALVESTON SOUTH ADDITION
BRAZOS SOUTH ADDITION
MATAGORDA ISLAND
MUSTANG ISLAND EAST ADDITION
CORPUS CHRISTI NG 14-3
EAST BREAKS NG 15-1
PORT ISABEL NG 14-6
ALIMINOS CANYON NG 15-14
Gulf of Mexico
TEXAS GULF COAST
0 10 20 30 40 50 Mi.
0 80 Km
ATTENTION USER: This special OCS environmental map (visual) has been prepared from existing sources to accompany an Environmental Statement. THE BUREAU OF LAND MANAGEMENT, USDI, does not guarantee the accuracy to the extent of responsibility of liability for reference thereon.
This OCS visual is not to be used for navigational purposes, nor is it a legal document for Federal leasing purposes. Prepared by the New Orleans Outer Continental Shelf Office, New Orleans, La.

CANADA

CAPITAL: Ottawa
MONETARY UNIT: Dollar
REFINING CAPACITY: 1.852 million b/d
PRODUCTION: 1.82 million b/d
RESERVES: 4.894 billion bbl (conventional crude)

Oil and gas drilling activity improved in Canada during 1996 as the long period of development for Hibernia oil field off the East Coast entered its final stages. New capacity to export natural gas to the U.S. was expected to begin coming on stream in 1998, easing a production restraint that kept wellhead gas prices below U.S. levels for producers in Alberta and British Colombia.

The average active-rig count, as reported by Baker Hughes Inc., broke its 10 year high of 259 in 1994, reaching 270 for 1996. Because of the suppressed gas prices, about 60% of the year's completions were oil wells. That drilling could finish strong despite the drag on gas activity showed potential for strong Canadian exploration and production once new pipeline capacity enters service.

Oil & Gas Journal estimated total wells drilled in 1996 at 11,738. The National Energy Board reported 11,062 completions of all types in 1995.

In addition, development was strong in 1996 in Canada's huge deposits of oilsands. The activity resulted from a combination of rising oil prices, cost-cutting technological advances, and tax measures by the federal government designed to stimulate the oilsands industry (see section on Canadian oilsands).

Newfoundland's offshore

The approach of first production from Hibernia late in 1997 gave activity off Newfoundland a huge lift. In August 1996, Petro-Canada and partners filed an application for the $2 billion (Canadian) development of Terra Nova oil field, 22 miles southeast of Hibernia and 285 miles southeast of St. John's, Newf. The activity, plus royalty incentives enacted by Newfoundland, raised prospects for development of other discoveries in the area.

Hibernia, discovered in 1979 and delineated in 1980-84, lies in 250 ft of water and will have cost $5 billion to develop by the time production starts. Including operating outlays over the 19 year production life of the field, total costs will reach $6.258 billion. The breakeven crude price is estimated at $12.95/bbl in 1995 U.S. dollars.

The field holds 615 million bbl of reserves in Cretaceous Hibernia sandstone encountered at 3,700 m and Cretaceous Avalon sand at 2,400 m. Production will climb to a sustained level of 135,000 b/d of 32º gravity crude in mid-2000. Mobil Oil Canada holds a 33.125% interest in the field, Chevron Canada Resources 26.875%, Petro-Canada 25%, Canada Hibernia Holding Corp. 8.5%, and Murphy Atlantic Offshore Oil Co. 6.5%.

Workers in 1996 were completing a gravity base structure able to store 1.3 million bbl of oil and designed to withstand 10 ft waves and the impact of a 6 million ton iceberg. Average iceberg size around Hibernia is 300,000 tons. Platform topsides, also nearly complete in 1996, will accommodate drilling of 64 wells drilled to an average depth of 9,000 m with lateral displacements of as much as 7,500 m. More wells will be drilled from floating rigs and completed subsea for tie-back to the platform.

Mating of the gravity base structure and topsides was to have occurred in March 1997, with tow-out to the field scheduled for June. Drilling was to begin in August, production in December.

First offloading of crude was scheduled for February 1998. Two ice-reinforced tankers with capacities of 850,000 bbl each will shuttle crude to refineries in the U.S. and Canada. The single-point mooring near the Hibernia platform will be able to offload 900,000 bbl in 24 hr.

Three of the Hibernia partners—Mobil, Chevron, and Petro-Canada—announced in 1996 that they planned to build a $100 million oil transshipment terminal at Whiffin Head, Newf., to handle oil from Hibernia and other fields on the Grand Banks. The terminal was seen as an economic alternative to construction of two additional tankers at $150 million each.

The terminal, on the Avalon Peninsula in Placentia Bay, will be able to hold 1.5 million bbl of crude. It will have one tanker berth and three tanks. Another tanker berth and three more tanks might eventually be built.

Construction of the terminal was to begin in spring 1997 and be completed late in 1998. Mobil will own a 41% interest in the terminal, Chevron 34%, and Petro-Canada 25%.

Action around Hibernia

The development application filed for Terra Nova field in 1996 initiated public and regulatory review procedures expected to take about 1 year. A decision by the Terra Nova partners to proceed with development depended on approval of the application by the Canada-Newfoundland Offshore Petroleum Board.

Terra Nova, in 90-100 m of water, holds an estimated 406 million bbl of 33º gravity, low-sulfur crude oil and would produce at peak rates of about 100,000 b/d of oil and 75 MMcfd of gas, beginning in 2001. Production life would be 15-18 years.

Petro-Canada and its partners had spent about $400 million by mid-1996 on exploration, delineation, and preliminary engineering on Terra Nova. Capital cost to start-up would be about $1.6 billion. Total capital and operating cost for development but not transportation would be about $4.2 billion.

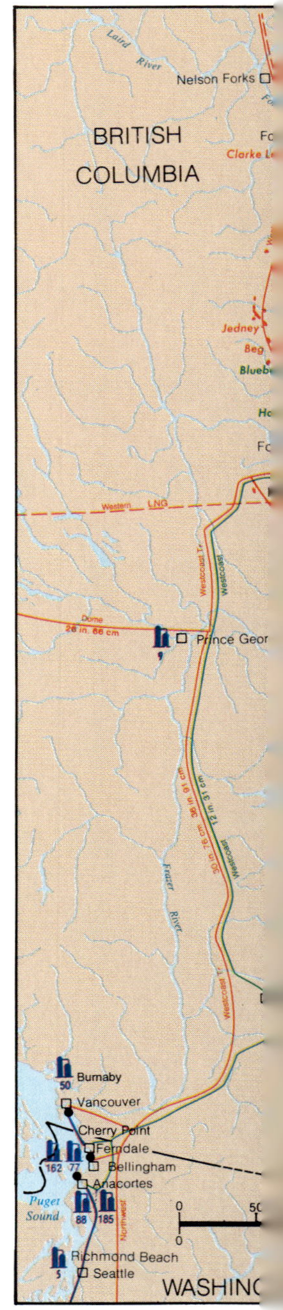

Interests in the field at the time the application was filed were Petro-Canada 49.2%, Mobil Oil Canada Ltd. 20.7%, Husky Oil Operations Ltd. 15.8%, Murphy Oil Co. Ltd. 10.7%, and Mosbacher Operating Co. Ltd. 3.6%. They were subject to change following unitization of the field and an exchange of Canadian and Norwegian interests.

Petro-Canada discovered the field in 1984. It expected to develop the field through a semisubmersible or ship, drilling 19 production and 13 pressure-maintenance wells in the upper Jurassic Jeanne d'Arc sand at 3,200-3,700 m and completing them in seabed holes to protect them from ice gouging.

On a 44,500-acre block adjacent to Terra Nova, Amoco Canada in 1995 bid $90 million for exploration rights and planned to drill one or two wells in 1997.

Separately, Husky Oil Operations Ltd. planned to develop Whiterose oil and gas field, a 1984 discovery 50 km east of Hibernia and 320 km east of St. John's. The company estimated reserves of the field, which lies in 125 m of water, at 250 million bbl of oil and 1.5 tcf of natural gas in Ben Nevis/Avalon sands.

Husky planned to drill as many as four delineation wells beginning in 1998. Production might start by 2004 through a floating vessel and rise to an average of 75,000 b/d, with a peak rate of 100,000 b/d. Husky planned a seismic survey in 1997.

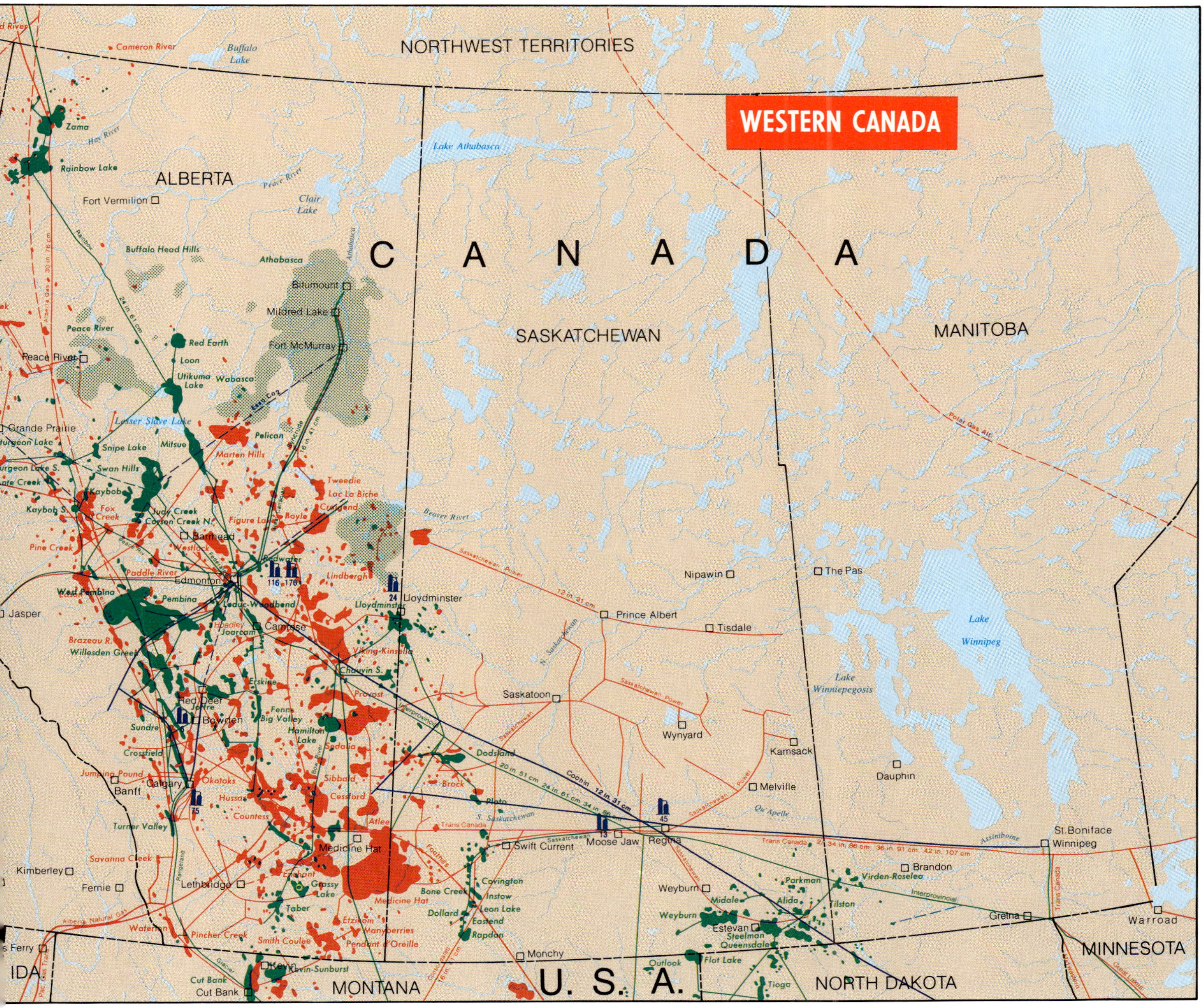

After filing development plans about 2000, it expected to drill 13 horizontal or highly deviated production wells and 10 injection wells. Husky holds 42%, Petro-Canada 25%, Talisman Energy Inc. 17%, and Gulf Canada Resources Ltd. and Parex 8% each.

New royalty regime

In what it described as an effort to sustain offshore oil and gas work, the government of Newfoundland in 1996 established a generic royalty regime based on oil recovery rates. The scheme applies to fields other than Hibernia and Terra Nova.

A basic royalty applies at rates of 1% of gross revenues until production of 20% of initially established reserves or 50 million bbl, whichever comes first. The rate rises to 2.5% of gross revenues until production totals 100 million bbl, 5% through 200 million bbl of production, and 7.5% thereafter.

A two-tier net royalty also applies to production. Tier 1 is 20% of net revenue after achievement of a 5% rate of return plus the long-term government bond rate. Tier 2 is 10% of net revenues after a 15% rate of return plus the long-term government bond rate.

According to Newfoundland Premier Brian Tobin, the industry through mid-1996 had discovered 1.6 billion bbl of recoverable oil, 4.6 tcf of natural gas, and 237 million bbl of natural gas liquids off Newfoundland. The Geological Survey of Canada estimated that a further 5-6 billion bbl of oil might be discovered on the northern Grand Banks alone, Tobin said.

In addition to the Grand Banks area, leasing and drilling were active on and off Newfoundland's western coast. Hunt Oil Co. and PanCanadian Petroleum Ltd. were thought to have discovered hydrocarbons in a tight hole, 1 Port au Port, southwest of Cape St. George. They were drilling other wells in the area in 1996.

Gas pipelines

The key to Canadian upstream activity overall in 1996 remained expansion of pipeline capacity for natural gas bound for the U.S. New capacity was planned from both the western producing provinces and gas fields off Sable Island, Nova Scotia.

Exports of natural gas rose 11% to a total of 79.3 billion cu m in 1995, according to the National Energy Board, which noted that further increases would require greater export capacity. Total Canadian production in 1995 rose 5.2% to 150 billion cu m.

Because of the export bottleneck, Canadian producers essentially didn't benefit from the gas price increases in the U.S. during 1996. Gas unable to move south had to compete with other gas in Canada, which suppressed wellhead realizations. A number of pipeline projects were proposed in 1996, not all of which will reach the construction stage. Little additional capacity was expected to enter service before 1998.

TransCanada PipeLines in 1996 had plans to add 287 MMcfd of capacity to its 8,600 mile mainline network, of which 169 MMcfd would be shared among the Chippewa, Iroquois, and Niagara export outlets to the U.S. and the rest delivered within Canada. Nova Corp., Alberta's gas network, announced plans to expand its capacity to accommodate the TransCanada increase. Its Nova Gas Transmission Ltd. unit delivered a record 4.3 tcf of gas in 1995, its ninth consecutive annual record. The total was up 4.9% from 1994 and amounted to average deliveries of 11.5 bcfd.

In response to a rate dispute involving producers in southern Alberta, PanCanadian and Westcoast Energy Inc. proposed to build the 1,900 mile Palliser Pipeline to move 1.2 bcfd of gas from near Calgary into southern Saskatchewan. It would take advantage of the expansion planned by TransCanada as well as one in the U.S. by Norther Border Pipeline, which runs 967 miles from the Saskatchewan-Montana border to Harper, Iowa. Northern Border planned to add 700 MMcfd to its existing capacity of 1.7 bcfd and to extend the system by 243 miles to Manhattan, Ill., near Chicago. Foothills Pipeline, which feeds Northern Border from Canada, also would be expanded.

The rate dispute related to Nova's "postage stamp" tolls, in which producers in all parts of the province pay identical tariffs. Some producers considered the practice an unfair subsidy of northern fields. Late in 1996, Nova and PanCanadian were discussing a way to use a negotiation provision to Alberta's toll policy that would preclude the Palliser proposal. Another pipeline proposal surfaced, however: Alberta Pipeline Project by Amoco, Shell, and CU Gas to carry 1-1.4 bcfd to two export points as well as Alberta utilities.

Another producer-backed pipeline proposal was the 1,900 mile Alliance gas line from western Canada to the U.S. Midwest. The 36 in. line would extend from near Fort St. John, B.C., to Chicago and be designed to carry 1 bcfd of gas in dense phase. The proposal, by a group of 19 producers and marketers led by general partner Alliance Pipeline Ltd., grew out of a feasibility study known as the Northern Area Transportation Study (NATS).

Sable Island projects

In the Sable Island area, two gas pipeline proposals were advancing in 1996.

One was called the Maritimes & Northeast Pipeline, the transportation unit for the Sable Offshore Energy Project. It would ultimately carry as much as 400 MMcfd of gas 630 miles across

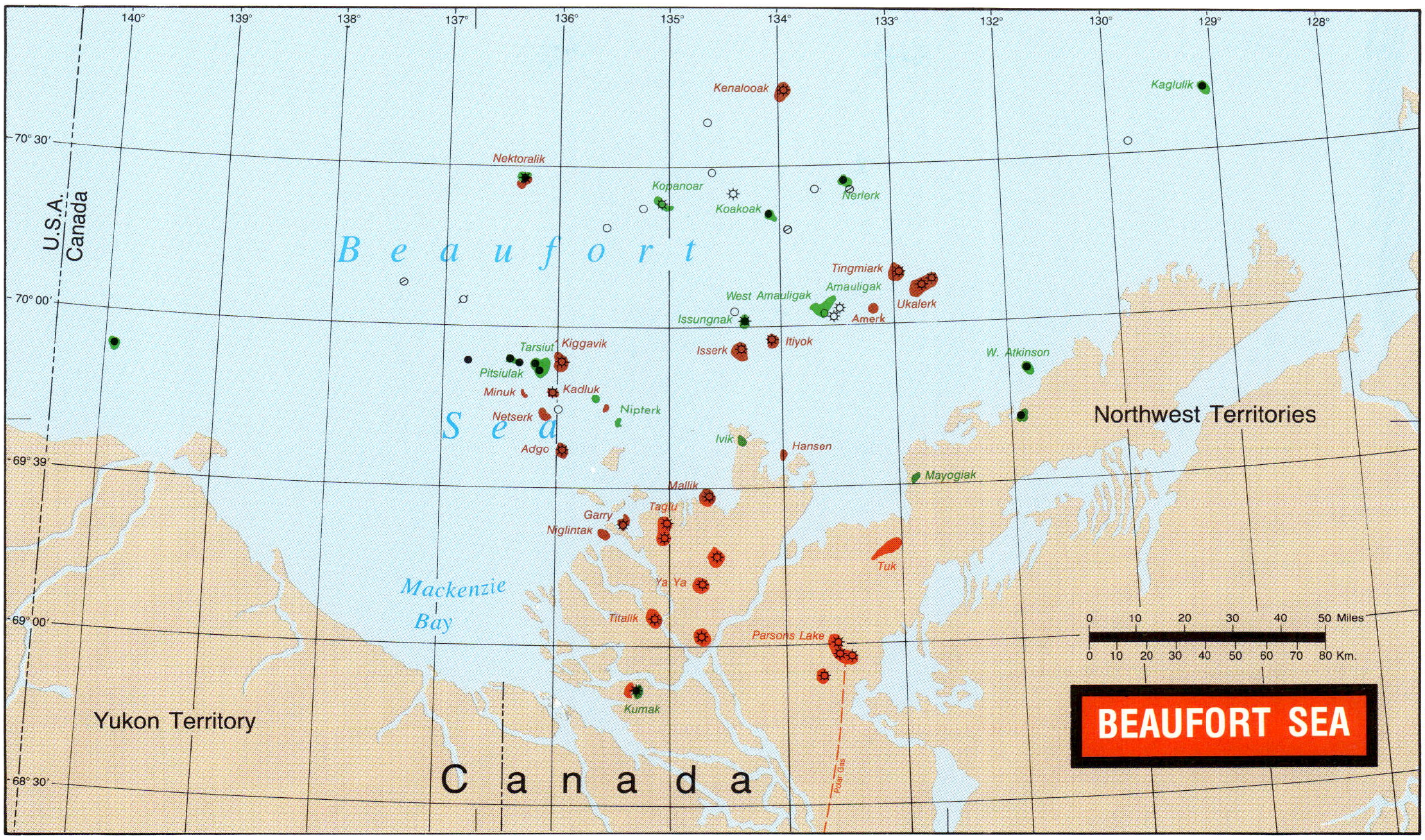

Nova Scotia, New Brunswick, Maine, and New Hampshire and link up with the North American pipeline grid in Massachusetts.

About 3 tcf of gas reserves were undergoing predevelopment work in 1996 by Mobil Oil Canada Properties, Shell Canada Ltd., Petro-Canada, Imperial Oil Resources Ltd., and Nova Scotia Resources Ltd. Westcoast Energy was handling the Canadian portion of the pipeline, PanEnergy Corp. the U.S. portion.

Services under the first phase of the system were fully subscribed in 1996. Maritimes & Northeast Pipelines LLC planned to begin construction by 1997. For the second phase the partnership held an open season in which prospective customers could select from among a number of transportation and supply options.

The first phase involves a 64 mile, 24 in. line between Dracut, Mass., and Wells, Me., with a capacity of 60 MMcfd.

In the second phase, the partnership would lay about 340 miles of 24 in. pipeline between Country Harbour, N.S., and St. Stephens, N.B., and 225 miles of 24 in. line and related facilities between Woodland and Wells, Me. The second phase would raise system capacity to 400 MMcfd.

A competing proposal to transport Sable Island gas emerged in 1996 from TransCanada PipeLines and Montreal utility Gaz Metropolitain Co. The companies proposed to lay a $1 billion pipeline through New Brunswick to link at Quebec City with the TransQuebec & Maritimes pipeline, in which each owns a 50% interest.

TransCanada also hoped to ship some Sable Island gas through the proposed Portland Natural Gas System in the U.S., a 250 mile, 175 MMcfd pipeline that would connect with the TransCanada mainline in Vermont or the TransQuebec & Maritimes line at the Quebec border and extending to Portland, Me. TransCanada holds a 20% interest in the Portland project.

Outlook improves

Spending on exploration and production in Canada looked set to increase in 1997 as operators reported an improved outlook for Canadian exploration and production.

A Salomon Bros. survey of 97 companies operating in Canada projected an E&P spending increase to $8.4 billion from an estimated $7.5 billion in 1996. That's an 11.6% increase following a 17.8% jump estimated for 1996, a year for which spending initially was projected to be down. Oil price strength overcame the problems of gas export capacity and resultant gas price weakness, Salomon Bros. said.

Canadian operators were the most sensitive of all survey respondents to oil price levels, the firm said. Outside Canada, access to attractive prospects and operating cash flow levels were the key issues of concern to survey respondents. For surveyed Canadian operators, prospect access was secondary to oil and gas prices.

In response to survey questions, 44% of the Canadian operators said they planned to shift spending emphasis to natural gas in 1997, while 22% said they expected a shift to oil, and 34% said they expected no shift. In 1996, 40% shifted to oil, 20% to natural gas, and 40% made no shift in spending emphasis.

For 1997, 39% of the companies expected to spend a larger share of their E&P budgets on exploration than in 1996, while 44% planned no change and 17% planned to spend a larger share on development. The percentages changed little from actual patterns of 1996.

Among the Canadian operators, 53% expected outlays for leases to consume a larger share of their E&P budgets in 1997 than in 1996, while 30% expected the leasing share to remain the same, and 17% expected the share to decline.

For budget allocations to seismic activities, 53% of the Canadian operators in the survey expected the share to increase in 1997, 38% expected it to stay the same, and 9% expected declines. Of the respondents, 51% reported growth in the seismic share of 1996 spending, 33% reported no change, and 16% reported declines.

Asked to evaluate oil exploration economics, 21% rated Canada excellent in 1996, 51% good, 25% fair, and 3% poor. The 1995 ratings were much different: 6% excellent, 40% good, 41% fair, and 12% poor.

Natural gas exploration ratings were 20% excellent in 1996 vs. 5% in 1995, 44% good vs. 35%, 27% fair vs. 34%, and 10% poor vs. 26%. IPE

Noble Drilling Corp.'s Eddie Paul jack up, working for Texaco on Eugene Island Block 354 in the Gulf of Mexico, was formerly a slot-type unit. It was upgraded and converted with a 70-ft, extended-reach cantilever, and additional legs were installed to enable the rig to work in up to 390 ft of water.

Development projects lead Gulf of Mexico march into deep water

Development was the operational byword during 1996 in the Gulf of Mexico, and projects slated for 1997 start-up were shaping up to surpass existing water depth and production records set just in 1996. There was plenty of non-record-breaking action as well in the U.S.'s most prolific offshore operating theater.

As 1996 drew to a close, drilling activity levels were at or near record-setting levels, new alliances had been formed to lower the costs and risks of exploration and development, and numerous pipeline transportation schemes were announced to move to market new volumes of oil and gas.

Driven by strong oil and gas prices, new government incentives under the U.S. Deep Water Royalty Relief Act, anticipated expiration of primary term leases, and constantly improving technological efficiencies, operators were pressing exploration and development projects in virtually all water depths during 1996. Industry experts said the pace had not been seen since the onset of areawide leasing early in the 1980s.

The spotlight shone most intensely on deepwater and ultra-deepwater E&D action, in depths generally 1,200 ft and greater, with major oil reserves the most highly sought prize.

A shortage of premium available deepwater-service mobile offshore drilling units (MODUs) was becoming particularly acute late in the year. Drilling contractors said the tightness was attributable, in part, to major oil companies placing available MODUs, especially semisubmersibles and drillships, under long-term contracts for existing and planned programs in 1997 and beyond.

The year also saw high levels of deepwater mobile rig upgrades and conversions commissioned by major oil companies to increase contracted drilling units' water depth capabilities.

The level of interest shown by industry in the two Minerals Management Service Gulf of Mexico lease sales during 1996 indicated the health of the offshore region, portending robust exploratory activity for years to come. Western Gulf Sale 161, which drew $352.5 million in high bids in September 1996, was the most successful western gulf sale ever in terms of the number of bids received and the number of blocks receiving bids.

Industry also showed heavy interest in Central Gulf of Mexico Sale 157. The April 1996 sale drew almost $521 million in high bids on 924 blocks.

Impetus of technology

Industry experts maintain that technology and application of it have caught up with industry's continual move into deeper waters. New and enhanced technology, involving 3D seismic, extended-reach drilling, and subsea and floating production systems to name only a few, together with increased innovation and efficiencies on the part of operators and service companies, were yielding big rewards and lowering costs of the search for hydrocarbons in the Gulf of Mexico in 1996.

In a Sept. 9, 1996, article in Oil & Gas Journal, Don Henery, Shell Offshore Inc.'s (SOI) manager of offshore engineering and pipelines, noted the number of deepwater exploration successes that had occurred and development projects foreseen in the

Where Shell Group will develop Ursa deepwater field

Fig. 1

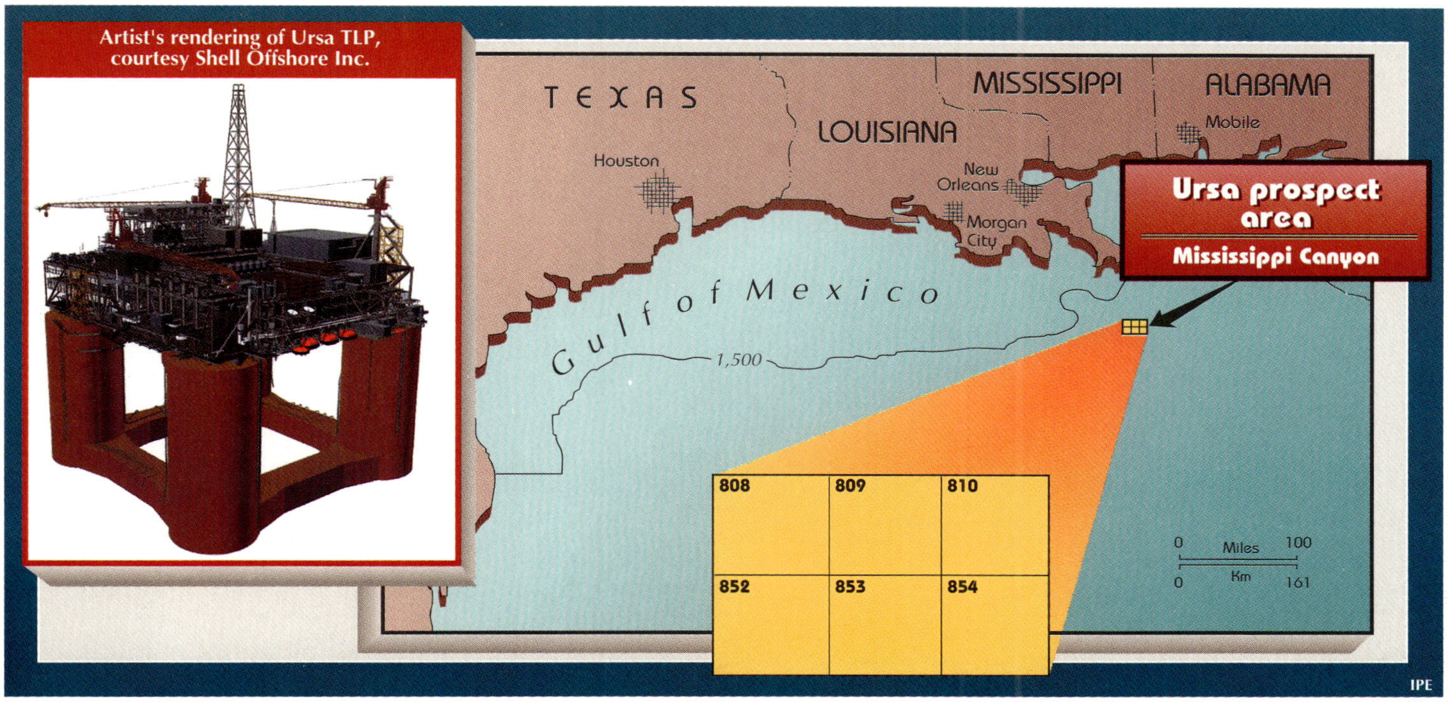

Gulf of Mexico. Henery said that as of yearend 1995, there had been almost 300 exploratory wells and more than 50 development wells drilled in the gulf in water deeper than 1,475 ft (450 m).

"At least 36 confirmed discoveries have been made to date in water depths greater than 450 m," he said. "Of these, 18 have been found by Shell. It appears that at least 2.4 billion bbl of oil equivalent (BOE) reserves have been discovered to date, with two thirds of this from Shell projects."

Henery added, "Further potential for the Gulf of Mexico deepwater development is estimated at 8-15 billion BOE," he said. "By the year 2000…it is likely that 25-35% of production from the Gulf of Mexico will come from deep water."

The effects of technological advances are nowhere more evident than in cost reductions Shell has made and expects to make since installing the 100% SOI-owned Auger platform in February 1994 in 2,860 ft of water on Garden Banks Block 426, about 255 miles southeast of Houston.

Auger project cost totals $1.1 billion, excluding about $11.3 million in lease costs for Garden Banks Blocks 426, 427, 470, and 471 acquired during Sale 84 in July 1984 and Sale 102 in August 1985. Production began in April 1994 and was averaging about 155 MMcfd of gas and 71,000 b/d of oil as of second quarter 1996.

As of early December 1996, oil production averaged about 76,000 b/d, and SOI reported that Auger's A-17 well had established a record gulf production rate of 21,700 b/d.

Total gross ultimate recovery from Auger is estimated at 220 million BOE with an oil:gas ratio of 2:1.

According to industry figures, the capital portion of daily production costs totaled $13.25/1,000 BOE for Auger vs. anticipated costs of $6.80/1,000 BOE when Ursa comes on stream.

Ursa

SOI Group's Ursa tension leg platform (TLP) will be installed in 1997 in 3,950 ft of water on Mississippi Canyon Block 810, about 130 miles southeast of New Orleans. Production from the $1.5 billion project is anticipated to begin in early or mid-1999.

Construction began in July 1996.

Ursa will develop Mississippi Canyon Blocks 808, 809, 810, 852, 853, and 854 (Fig. 1). The leases were acquired in Sale 72 in May 1983, Sale 81 in April 1984, and Sale 113 in March 1988.

"Ursa is another important advancement in the evolution of deepwater development," said Rich Pattarozzi, Deepwater Division general manager for SOI. "The platform will be the largest structure in the Gulf of Mexico, and its individual wells are expected to produce at rates not thought possible just a few years ago."

Ursa is expected to achieve record rates of production—150,000 b/d of oil and 400 MMcfd of gas. Ultimate recovery is estimated at 400 million BOE.

Operator SOI holds a 45% interest in the project. Other interest owners are BP Exploration Inc. 23% and Conoco Inc. and Exxon Co. U.S.A. 16% each.

Ursa's current development plans involve only 14 wells, but some are expected to produce initial rates of as much as 30,000 b/d of oil and 80 MMcfd of gas. Eleven wells are planned from the TLP, and three will be subsea wells. Shell said the highest individual well rate achieved as of third quarter 1996 in the Gulf of Mexico was about 13,000 b/d from its Auger TLP.

Production will be moved about 47 miles via an 18-in. oil pipeline and a 20-in. gas pipeline to a gathering platform in West Delta Block 143. Pipeline construction was scheduled to begin in 1997. Contractor selection had not been made late in 1996.

Ursa design will be similar to that of Shell's Mars TLP, which was installed in May 1996 and Ram-Powell TLP, scheduled for installation during 1997. But it will be significantly larger to accommodate the high anticipated production rates. Ursa will weigh about 63,300 tons vs. 36,500 tons for Mars. Ursa's total displacement will be about 97,500 tons.

Ursa will have complete separation, dehydration, and treatment facilities designed to process 150,000 b/d of oil and condensate, 400 MMcfd of gas, and 50,000 b/d of produced water.

Ram-Powell

SOI's Ram-Powell TLP, which was scheduled for installation late in May 1997 in 3,218 ft of water on Viosca Knoll Block 956, about 125 miles east-southeast of New Orleans, will hold the world water depth record for a permanent drilling and production platform—but only until Ursa is installed. First production was scheduled during August 1997.

Ram-Powell will surpass the depth record for the Gulf of Mexico set when SOI installed the Mars TLP in 2,960 ft of water on Mississippi Canyon Block 807.

Total cost of the project is about $1 billion, excluding lease costs. MMS in June 1989 approved the Ram-Powell Unit, which consists of Viosca Knoll Blocks 867, 868, 911, 912, 913, 955, 956, and 957. The leases were acquired during 1984, 1986, 1987, and 1988 for a total bonus of almost $16.2 million.

Operator SOI has a 38% interest in the project. Other interest owners are Amoco Corp. and Exxon Co. U.S.A., 31% each.

Estimated gross recovery from Ram-Powell Unit is about 250 million BOE, with a 50:50 oil:gas ratio.

Complete separation, dehydration, and treatment facilities were being designed for peak gross production of about 60,000 b/d of oil, 200 MMcfd of gas, and 30,000 b/d of produced water.

Production will be transported about 25 miles via a 12-in. oil pipeline and a 14-in. gas pipeline to platforms on the Outer Continental Shelf. Both lines will be installed by Allseas as part of the Ram-Powell development. Gas will be moved to a platform on Viosca Knoll Block 817, and oil will be moved to facilities on Main Pass Block 289-C.

Fig. 2

Conoco/Reading & Bates ultradeepwater drilling capability

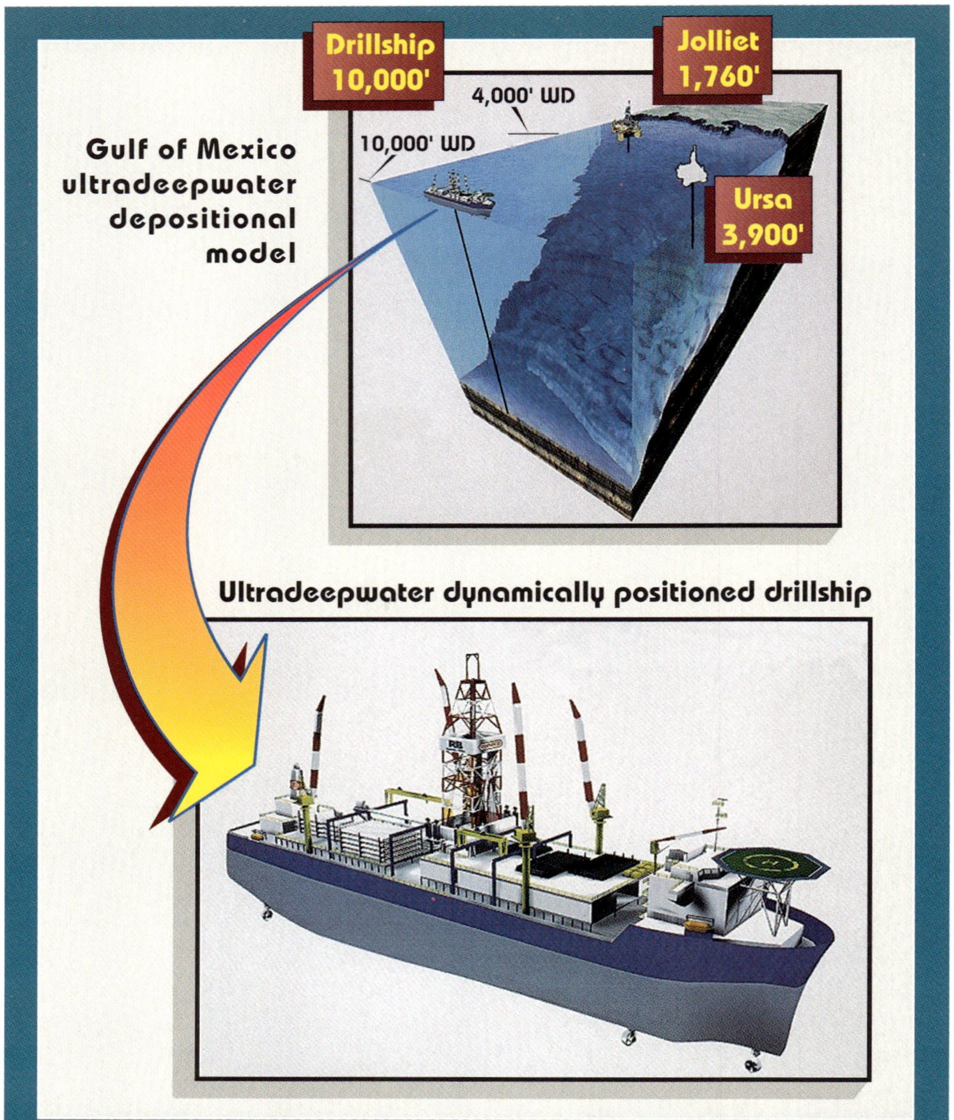

Source: Conoco Inc.

IPE

Mensa

When on stream in mid-1997 in 5,300 ft in the Mississippi Canyon area, SOI's 100%-owned Mensa subsea development project was to be a world record-breaker.

Shell said Mensa, with a total system cost of about $280 million, would capture the record for the world's deepest production, surpassing the existing 3,370 ft subsea production record set in 1994 by Petroleo Brasileiro SA in Marlim field in the Campos basin off Brazil.

Also, Shell said, Mensa's subsea wells would grab the record for the longest tie-back in the world—68 miles.

First production was scheduled for mid-1997. Ultimate recovery is estimated at 720 bcf of gas.

Development plans call for a subsea system of three wells connected to a subsea manifold 5 miles away, which will then be tied back via a 63-mile, 12-in. flowline to the West Delta Block 143 platform utilized by Mars, which will also be utilized by Ursa.

The Discoverer Seven Seas drillship drilled the Mensa discovery in 1987, about 140 miles southeast of New Orleans. Mensa encompasses Mississippi Canyon Blocks 686, 687, 730, and 731.

Mars

The Mars TLP was installed in May 1996 in 2,940 ft of water on Mississippi Canyon Block 807, about 130 miles southeast of New Orleans. Operator SOI holds a 71.5% interest in the project, and BP Exploration owns the remainder.

Cost of the initial phase of development totals $1.2 billion.

Production, which began July 8, 1996, is expected to peak at rates of 100,000 b/d of oil and 110 MMcfd of gas. At yearend 1996, rates were averaging 52,000 b/d of oil and 57 MMcfd of gas, SOI reported.

Oil is transported 116 miles via an 18-in. and 24-in. pipeline to the Clovelly, La., area, and the gas is moved 55 miles via a 14-in. pipeline to the West Delta Block 143 gathering platform. Both pipelines were installed as part of Mars development.

Shell designed the 36,500-ton, 24-slot Mars TLP.

Belleli SpA fabricated the 15,650-ton hull, which consists of four circular steel columns, 66.5 ft in diameter and 162 ft high and four 27 ft by 24 ft pontoons connecting to the bottom of the four columns.

McDermott fabricated the deck modules, including wellbay, quarters, process, power, and drilling. Aker Gulf Marine, Ingleside, Tex., handled the integration portion of the project, including setting of the modules and interconnecting steel, piping, electrical, and instrumentation systems. Integration was completed during second quarter 1996.

Aker fabricated the piles and tendons. There are 12 tendons, three per corner, each with a diameter of 28 in. and a wall thickness of 1.2 in. Each tendon is about 2,852 ft long, and the total weight of the tendons is 6,150 tons. Tendons are connected directly to seafloor piles. There are 12 piles about 84 in. in diameter and 375 ft long, weighing 260 tons each.

Heeremac, Leiden, Netherlands, handled installation.

Development involves Mississippi Canyon Blocks 762, 763,

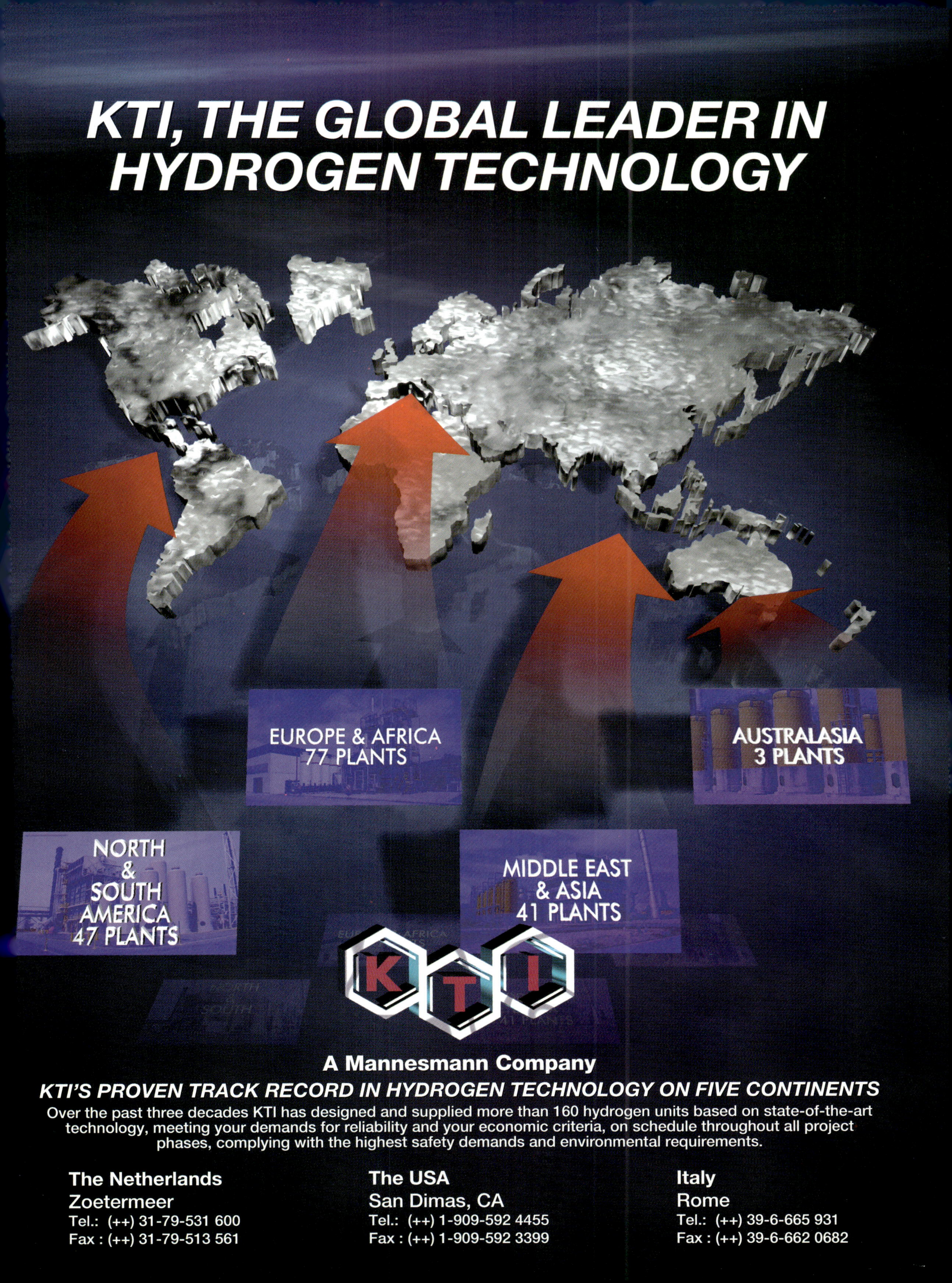
KTI, THE GLOBAL LEADER IN HYDROGEN TECHNOLOGY
EUROPE & AFRICA 77 PLANTS
AUSTRALASIA 3 PLANTS
NORTH & SOUTH AMERICA 47 PLANTS
MIDDLE EAST & ASIA 41 PLANTS
KTI
A Mannesmann Company
KTI'S PROVEN TRACK RECORD IN HYDROGEN TECHNOLOGY ON FIVE CONTINENTS
Over the past three decades KTI has designed and supplied more than 160 hydrogen units based on state-of-the-art technology, meeting your demands for reliability and your economic criteria, on schedule throughout all project phases, complying with the highest safety demands and environmental requirements.
The Netherlands
Zoetermeer
Tel.: (++) 31-79-531 600
Fax : (++) 31-79-513 561
The USA
San Dimas, CA
Tel.: (++) 1-909-592 4455
Fax : (++) 1-909-592 3399
Italy
Rome
Tel.: (++) 39-6-665 931
Fax : (++) 39-6-662 0682

Neptune spar, shown after 1996 installation by Oryx and CNG on Viosca Knoll Block 826, is the world's first spar-based offshore oil and gas production system.

806, 807, 850, and 851. MMS approved the Mars Unit in December 1992.

Popeye

Subsea production from the Popeye Unit, located in about 2,000 ft of water in the Green Canyon Area about 140 miles south of New Orleans, began in January 1996. The unit is being developed in phases and consists of Green Canyon Blocks 72, 73, 116, and 117.

Peak production rates from two wells in 1996 were 160 MMcfd of gas and 9,000 b/d of condensate, according to SOI. Average production was 145 MMcfd of gas and 7,200 b/d of oil at yearend 1996. Single well rates of 105 MMcfd had been achieved.

First phase, at a cost of about $110 million, is designed to recover about 200 bcf of gas and 7 million bbl of condensate. Phase one includes two subsea wells drilled in 1994-95 on Block 116, directionally drilled to bottomhole locations on Blocks 73 and 116 and connected via 4-in. ID jumpers to an adjacent subsea gathering manifold.

Additional subsea wells could be drilled in subsequent development phases, with locations and wells required to be based on production performance in phase one.

Operator SOI has a 37.5% interest in the field. Other interest owners are CNG Producing Co. 37.5%; and Mobil Exploration & Producing Co. and BP, 12.5% each.

The subsea system is designed to produce as much as 120 MMcfd of gas and condensate. Production is moved 24 miles by two nominal 6-in. flowlines to SOI's Cougar platform on South Timbalier Block 300.

Tahoe, Southeast Tahoe

The Tahoe Unit is in its second phase of development at a cost of about $150 million, while adjacent Southeast Tahoe field was a March 1996 discovery.

The Tahoe Unit, owned by SOI and partners, encompasses Viosca Knoll Area Blocks 783 and 827 in about 1,500 ft of water, about 140 miles east of New Orleans and about 105 miles south of Mobile, Ala. Operator SOI has a 70% interest in the wells and subsea systems and a 100% interest in the platforms and surface facilities. Remaining interest is owned by Murphy Exploration & Production Co.

The discovery well was drilled in 1984 on Viosca Knoll Area Block 783, and four wells and three sidetracks were drilled to evaluate the discovery.

Phase one development cost about $27 million and was designed to produce about 30 MMcfd of gas and 1,000 b/d of condensate. Production began in January 1994.

Phase one was developed initially with one subsea well tied back to SOI's Bud platform on Main Pass Block 252, 12 miles away.

Phase two consists of three gas wells and one oil well. The cost of second-phase work includes wells, facilities, and a platform. Drilling began in September 1995, and all of the wells will be horizontal.

Phase two wells are tied back to SOI's Bud Lite platform on Main Pass Block 252. Bud Lite facilities are located on a jacket bridge connected to the Bud platform.

Platform installation was completed in May 1996, and phase two production began in August 1996. Production design capacity for Bud Lite is 300 MMcfd of gas, 8,000 b/d of oil, and 7,000 b/d of condensate. Peak production for phase two is estimated at 235 MMcfd of gas.

Total ultimate recovery from both phases of development is estimated at 120 million BOE.

Diamond Offshore Drilling Inc. semis Ocean Quest in drydock, background, and Ocean Star, foreground, underwent deepwater upgrading during 1996 by Texas Drydock Inc. at its Port Arthur, Tex., complex. Also upgraded was Diamond Offshore's Ocean Victory. All units had blisters and sponsons added, increasing their variable deck loads to 5,000 tons, as well as increasing their water depth capability. Photo courtesy of Texas Drydock Inc.

Growing spar fleet

The world's first spar-based offshore oil and gas production system, Neptune, was installed late in 1996 in 1,930 ft of water on Viosca Knoll Block 826 by Oryx Energy Co., Dallas, and CNG Producing Co., New Orleans.

Meanwhile, during 1996, Chevron U.S.A. Production Co. and partners were advancing plans for a $750 million development using Genesis, the world's second production spar, scheduled to begin producing late in 1998 from 2,600 ft of water on Green Canyon Block 205. It will develop blocks 160 and 161, also.

Oryx and CNG are 50-50 partners in the $300 million Neptune project. Production from Neptune field was scheduled to begin in January 1997. Equipment on Neptune spar's topsides are designed to produce 25,000 b/d of oil and 30 MMcfd of gas.

The spar consists of a 705 ft tall by 72 ft wide, 12,640-ton cylindrical hull and three-deck topsides that weigh about 3,600 tons. Because the unit has a buoyancy center above the center of gravity, a key advantage is its stability in the Gulf of Mexico during hurricane conditions.

The Genesis spar, which will measure 705 ft tall by 122 ft across, will be industry's largest production spar and be the first such unit to be equipped for drilling. The unit will draw 650 ft of water. The hull will be moored to the seabed with 14 anchor lines.

Genesis will be the first Chevron-operated deepwater development. Chevron has a 56.67% interest in the project. Other interest owners are Exxon Co. U.S.A., 38.38%, and a unit of Fina Inc., 4.95%.

Production from Genesis field, about 150 miles south of New Orleans, is expected to peak in 2000 at 72 MMcfd of gas and 55,000 b/d of oil. Reserves have been placed at more than 160 million BOE with a life of 15-20 years.

Petronius

Texaco Inc. and Marathon Oil Co. were advancing plans during 1996 to develop Petronius, a $400 million deepwater field that will utilize a compliant tower to be installed in 1,754 ft of water on Viosca Knoll Block 786, about 130 miles southeast of New Orleans.

Industry's first compliant tower ever installed was Lena, in a little more than 1,000 ft of water in Mississippi Canyon Block 281 by Exxon Co. U.S.A. early in the 1980s.

Petronius, a 1995 discovery, is scheduled to come on stream early in 1999. It is being designed to handle 100 MMcfd of gas and 60,000 b/d of oil.

Petronius will be developed with a 21-slot, 1,870-ft compliant tower. Its total weight, including tower sections, foundation template, piles, and conductors is estimated at 43,000 tons. The tower will be built in two sections: a base and a top.

A total of 12 piles, three at each corner leg, will extend from the tower legs 450 ft through the mudline and into the seabed.

Topsides, weighing more than 7,500 tons and including a full drilling package, will measure 210 ft by 140 ft by 60 ft tall. They will contain all processing equipment, water injection facilities, export pipeline pumps, and utilities.

The unit will be designed for 10 producing wells and seven water injection wells. Estimated peak injection rate will be about 72,000 b/d of water.

Subsalt action

Mahogany, the Gulf of Mexico's first subsalt discovery in 370 ft of water on Ship Shoal South Addition Block 349, came on stream Dec. 30,1996, about 80 miles off Louisiana.

The field was expected to average 30 MMcfd of gas and 20,000 b/d of oil initially from four salt wells predrilled to develop blocks 349 and 359. Additional drilling was scheduled after production start.

Operator Phillips Petroleum Co. and partners installed an eight-pile, 20-slot platform in August 1996 to develop the 1993 strike as part of a $200 million project expected to produce at peak 100 MMcfd of gas and 45,000 b/d of oil.

Phillips and Anadarko Petroleum Corp., Houston, each own 37.5% interest in the project. Amoco holds 25%.

The four predrilled wells were connected to the platform after installation. Production will flow via subsea pipelines to gulf gathering systems. Oil will come ashore via the Poseidon

Pipeline System, operated by a unit of Texaco Inc. through Poseidon Oil Pipeline Co., a 50-50 joint venture of Texaco and Leviathan Gas Pipeline Partners LP, Houston.

Gas comes ashore through the Louisiana Offshore Gathering System (LOGS). A 9-mile, 16-in. Leviathan-operated pipeline transports Mahogany gas to LOGS.

Meanwhile, another subsalt discovery was advancing toward development during 1996. SOI was making plans to start work early in 1997 to develop Enchilada, a subsalt discovery in Garden Banks Block 172.

Also during 1996, Texaco disclosed that its Gemini subsalt condensate strike, drilled in 3,393 ft of water on Mississippi Canyon Block 292 about 90 miles southeast of New Orleans, was commercial.

Other work

In mid-1995, Marathon, BP, and Shell reported their Green Canyon Block 200 appraisal well extended their Green Canyon Block 244 field 1½ miles north into Green Canyon Block 200, confirming a development potential of more than 100 million bbl of oil. The appraisal was drilled to 18,758 ft in 2,672 ft of water, and additional drilling was planned.

Known initially as Wasatch, the find is now referred to by the partners as Troika. The partners own one-third interests each in the unit, which consists of Green Canyon Blocks 200, 201, 244, and 245.

In 1996, BP said Troika deserves special attention because it sets some new benchmarks for subsea development.

BP said in May 1996 Troika is a 200-plus million barrel field that will be developed with five subsea wells in about 3,000 ft of water. Wells will be tied back to Shell's Bullwinkle platform in about 1,350 ft of water. The 15-mile long flow line will set a Gulf of Mexico distance record, and (Troika will) produce at a rate of 80,000 b/d, according to BP.

Meanwhile, Chevron, Murphy, and Conoco late in 1996 took the initial steps to gain government approvals for a gas development off Florida on the Destin Dome Block 56 Unit, an 11-block area on the Destin Dome structure, about 25 miles south of Pensacola. MMS was reviewing the application, which included a 16-volume development plan, at yearend.

Leasing in federal waters off Florida has been under a 10-year moratorium since 1990, but companies holding leases prior to that time have been able to drill their leases. Stiff environmental opposition to the Chevron group's plan was building at yearend.

Ultradeep exploration drilling

Conoco and Amoco Corp. unit Amoco Exploration & Production took strategic steps in 1996 to position themselves to be able to expeditiously drill their leases in ultradeep water using the latest designs in new dynamically positioned drillships.

In a move aimed at lowering the costs and risks of exploration—as well as giving the operator the ability to get its wells drilled in a timely fashion in an extremely tight 1996 rig market—a $600 million ultradeepwater exploration and drilling joint-venture (JV) alliance by Conoco and Reading & Bates Corp. was disclosed late in the year.

The 50-50 JV, via a limited liability company known as Deepwater Drilling LLC, will employ a first-of-its kind dynamically positioned drillship under construction in Korea to initially drill on 60 ultradeepwater Conoco-interest gulf blocks in 2,000-9,000 ft of water that Conoco acquired during 1996 (Fig. 2).

The vessel will be capable of drilling in as much as 10,000 ft of water and will carry the most stringent American Bureau of Shipping requirements for dynamic positioning systems, DP-3. It will be initially outfitted to drill in as much as 7,500 ft of water.

The vessel, which will be 721 ft long and equipped with a double hull, was scheduled to be delivered in 1998 by Samsung Heavy Industries Co. Ltd., Seoul.

In the other significant move, earlier in 1996, Amoco agreed to a long-term commitment with Transocean Offshore enabling Transocean to proceed with construction of a leading-edge DP drillship, representing the next generation of DP drillships over the successful Discoverer-class series. The new vessel, named Discoverer Enterprise, will be initially equipped to drill in 7,000 ft of water but will be capable of exploration and development drilling in as much as 10,000 ft of water.

The new dual-activity drilling function, double-hulled vessel was expected to be operational in mid-1998. Transocean said the vessel's dual-drilling function uses a new trademarked methodology called Expedrill, which will allow for drilling tasks associated with a single well to be accomplished in a concurrent rather than sequential manner, decreasing critical path activities and allowing for improved efficiencies in both exploration and development drilling. This will be accomplished with Discoverer Enterprise's greater deck space and variable deck load, the company said.

The unit will measure about 840 ft in length and 125 ft in width, or about 60% greater than the current Discoverer-class units. The Discoverer Seven Seas drillship, for comparison, is 534 ft long and 80 ft wide.

Discoverer Enterprise will displace 98,000 metric tons, and Discoverer Seven Seas displaces 21,562 metric tons.

Transportation

Numerous transportation schemes were announced during 1996, most designed to accommodate increasing production from deepwater and ultradeepwater gulf areas.

Units of Shell Oil Co. and Amerada Hess Corp. proposed a 1 bcfd natural gas system in the Garden Banks area. The Garden Banks Gas Gathering Pipeline LLC plans a 50-mile, 30-in. pipeline to gather deepwater and shelf edge gas and redeliver it offshore to existing interstate transmission systems. The system will extend from the Enchilada platform on Garden Banks Block 128 to a new platform on South Marsh Island Block 76.

Tenneco Energy, acquired by El Paso Energy Corp. late in 1996, and National Fuel Gas Supply Corp. formed a partnership to develop a $200 million Green Canyon Gathering System. The 24-in., 153-mile offshore pipeline system will move production from Green Canyon, Ewing Bank, Mississippi Canyon, Ship Shoal, Grand Isle, and South Timbalier areas and have a capacity of 515 MMcfd, accessing 3.4 tcf of estimated reserves.

Transcontinental Gas Pipeline Corp. planned an expansion of the Southeast Louisiana Gathering System in a two-phase, $129 million project that will add 660 MMcfd of capacity to the system.

Texaco Natural Gas announed a $300 million project to build the Discovery gas gathering, processing, and transmission system to provide 600-750 MMcfd of new capacity for fields in the Central Gulf of Mexico, primarily.

Marathon, Shell, and DeepTech International will build the Nautilus offshore pipeline and expand the Manta Ray gathering system in a project pegged at about $220 million to add as much as 600 MMcfd of new capacity in the Eugene Island, Ship Shoal, South Timbalier, Ewing Bank, and Green Canyon areas.

Destin Pipeline Co., a unit of Southern Natural Gas Co., Birmingham, Ala., was planning a $294 million program to add about 1 bcfd of capacity off Mississippi in the Mobile, Viosca Knoll, and Main Pass East Addition areas.

Dauphin Island Gathering Partners, Houston, planned to increase capacity of the Dauphin Island Gathering System by 450-550 MMcfd off Alabama in the Mobile, Viosca Knoll, and Main Pass East Addition areas.

The Poseidon pipeline system, a project that consists of about 200 miles of 16-in., 20-in., and 24-in. crude oil pipeline from Garden Banks Block 72, came on stream in 1996. As much as 400,000 b/d of sour crude moves from Block 72 to a Leviathan Gas Pipeline Partners LP platform on Ship Shoal South Addition Block 332. IPE

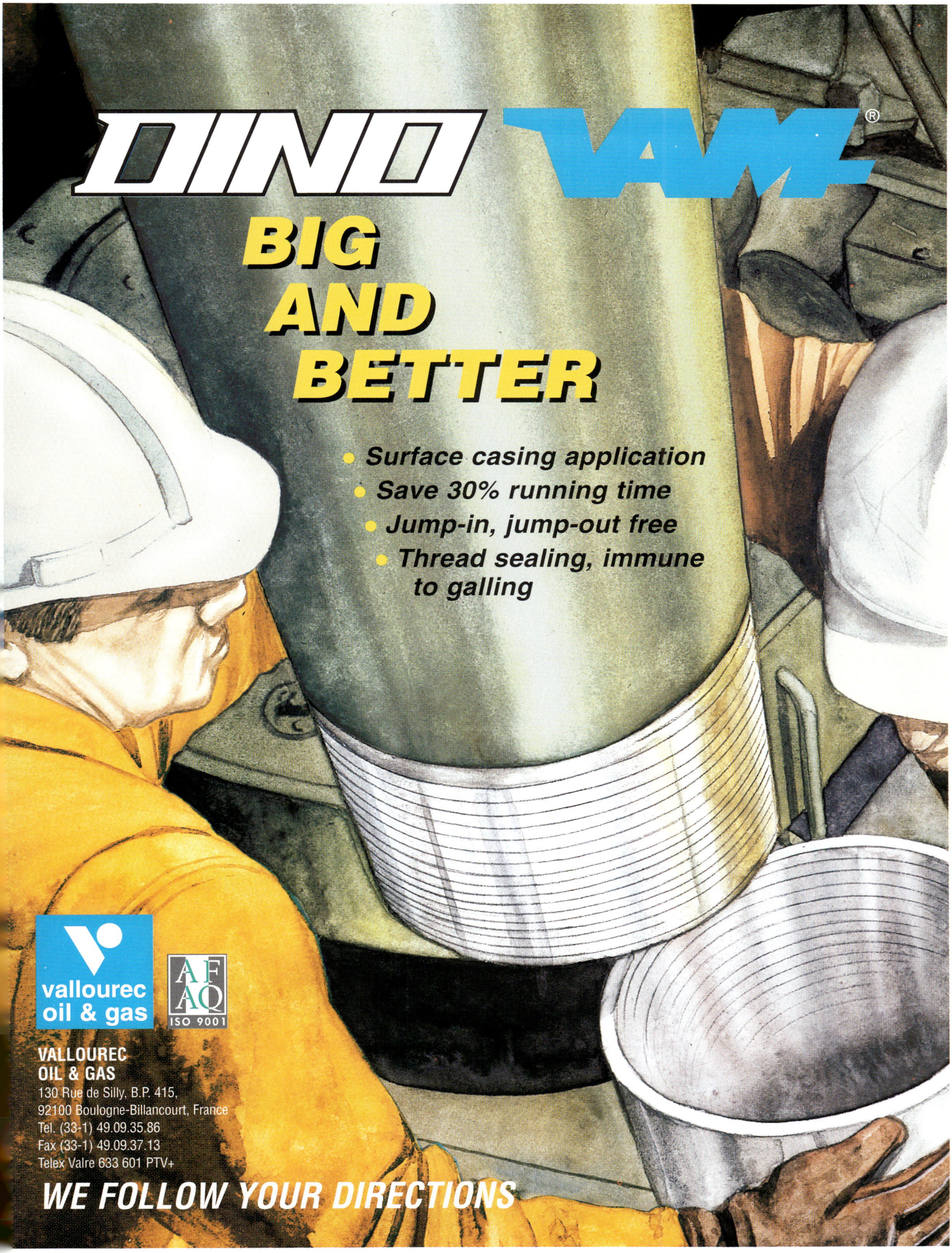
DINO VAM®
BIG AND BETTER
• Surface casing application
• Save 30% running time
• Jump-in, jump-out free
• Thread sealing, immune to galling
vallourec oil & gas
AFAQ ISO 9001
VALLOUREC OIL & GAS
130 Rue de Silly, B.P. 415,
92100 Boulogne-Billancourt, France
Tel. (33-1) 49.09.35.86
Fax (33-1) 49.09.37.13
Telex Valre 633 601 PTV+
WE FOLLOW YOUR DIRECTIONS

Alaska poised for new E&D surge

Alaska is poised for a fresh burst of exploration and development activity on and off the North Slope and in the Cook Inlet area.

Driving this surge in part are new fiscal incentives from the state designed to bolster economics of marginal field development.

Just as strong a contribution, however, comes from technological advances that have bolstered E&D elsewhere in the world. And the higher oil and gas prices that prevailed in 1996 and seemed likely to continue at least early in 1997 certainly helped the economics of exploring, drilling, and producing in one of the world's costliest oil and gas arenas.

Still another positive influence on future Alaskan E&D is the lifting of the ban on Alaskan North Slope (ANS) oil exports in 1996: By diversifying its prospective markets beyond the traditional one of the U.S. West Coast, ANS crude may now be able to command a greater wellhead price.

A negative factor is also a contributor to the state's E&D momentum: concern over declining oil production. That carries with it not only the specter of budget deficits as oil revenues fall but also the prospect of the Trans-Alaska Pipeline System (TAPS) being shut down as declining capacity utilization renders that venerable megaproject uneconomic—in turn shutting in potential billions of barrels of untapped oil resources on the North Slope.

That's an imperative not just for the state but also for the North Slope producers. They not only must replace ANS production but in the biggest instances are also equity owners of TAPS.

Capital spending

All of these trends underpin an imminent surge in upstream capital spending by the two companies that account for most E&D outlays in Alaska every year: BP Exploration (Alaska) Inc. and ARCO Alaska Inc.

More than half the Alaskan production level projected in 2000 depends on investments still to be made, say state officials.

In late December 1996, BP disclosed plans to hike its capital spending in Alaska by $1 billion in the next 5 years and help reverse the decline in ANS production.

BP outlays in the period will jump to an average $700 million/year from $500 million/year. Total capital spending will rise to $3.5 billion the next 5 years from $2.5 billion under earlier plans.

The accelerated investment is key to parent British Petroleum Co. plc's strategy to increase its worldwide oil production to 1.8 million b/d by 2000 from the current 1.5 million b/d.

BP expects to hike its North Slope production to almost 600,000 b/d by 2002 from the current 525,000 b/d.

This is a dramatic turnaround from a perspective held only 3 years earlier, said BP Alaska Pres. John Morgan, that a perpetual slow decline was inevitable for North Slope production.

"I think it's a story now of a very healthy future for the industry in Alaska," he said.

BP's 5-year capital spending program will include $1.2 billion for enhanced oil recovery projects and development drilling and $1.5 billion for development of Northstar, Badami, and other new fields.

During the next 10 years, BP hopes to increase its Alaska reserves by 4-5 billion bbl, excluding any prospective resource underlying the Coastal Plain of the Arctic National Wildlife Refuge—currently locked up by opposition on environmental grounds by the Congress and White House.

Prudhoe's role

Along with the expanded BP investment will be some production job cuts because of an impending restructuring at Prudhoe Bay.

Prudhoe output had fallen to a little more than 800,000 b/d early in 1997 from its peak of 1.5 million b/d in the late 1980s. Even with the aggressive development of satellite pools and

3-D Geophysical Inc. conducts an ocean-bottom cable, shallow-water, 3D seismic survey in August 1996 in the Beaufort Sea off Prudhoe Bay field. Operators are increasing E&D spending in Alaska as technology and efficiency improvements continue to drive down costs. Photo courtesy 3-D Geophysical Inc.

EOR programs, Prudhoe production is expected to drop further to 500,000-600,000 b/d by 2000.

Prudhoe accounted for most of the drop in Alaska's overall oil production in recent years. The state's total oil output early in 1997 was 1.4 million b/d, compared with its peak of more than 2 million b/d during the late 1980s.

The decline notwithstanding, Prudhoe remains the hub of a North Slope infrastructure that will accommodate other, more-marginally economic development of oil reserves in the vicinity.

Such new sources of oil will be less manpower-intensive than Prudhoe and other, older fields.

ARCO's capital program

Also in December 1996, ARCO disclosed plans to boost its capital spending in Alaska during the next 5 years by $500 million beyond the $1.2 billion in outlays previously projected for 1997-2001.

Driving the capital spending increase is the state's improved business climate and the company's success in driving down costs through technology and efficiency improvements, said ARCO Alaska Pres. Ken Thompson.

ARCO's Alaska 5-year capital spending plans call for:

- About $475 million for exploration and delineation drilling.
- About $400 million to develop the Alpine oil discovery east of Kuparuk River oil field in the Colville River delta area.
- $300 million for EOR and infill drilling programs in Prudhoe Bay field.
- $275 million for Kuparuk River EOR.
- $120 million for a pilot project to determine feasibility of producing heavy oil from West Sak, a massive, thin, shallow reservoir that overlies main producing zones in the Prudhoe-Kuparuk area.
- About $100 million for miscellaneous projects.

Ending ban

Ending the 23-year ban on ANS exports in mid-1996 was a boost to North Slope producers psychologically, even if little effect had been seen by early 1997.

President Bill Clinton in May 1996 determined that allowing ANS exports is in the national interest.

Taiwan's Chinese Petroleum Corp. was the first non-U.S. buyer of ANS crude, signing a contract for 10,000 b/d with BP.

However, only four shipments of ANS crude were exported to the Far East by yearend 1996 since the ban was lifted in May. Foreign shippers at first apparently objected to U.S. requirements in lifting the ban that the exported crude must be carried in U.S. vessels.

North Slope producers expect that most of the ANS volumes that had been going to the Gulf Coast, about 25% of the total, eventually will be redirected to markets outside the U.S.

When Congress approved enabling legislation in the 1970s allowing construction of TAPS to proceed, a rider was attached reserving ANS production solely for domestic use.

A law enacted in 1995 repealed the export ban, but it required more study and a finding by the President that exports were in the national interest.

The law allows the President to impose new export restrictions in the event of severe oil supply shortages.

Clinton also required that tankers carrying the oil must remain outside the 200-mile Exclusive Economic Zone, for environmental reasons.

Further, ANS export tankers must: have a satellite communications system to allow the Coast Guard to monitor their positions; be inspected yearly by the Coast Guard; and flush their ballast water in deep ocean before entering Alaska's Prince William Sound.

An interagency review found that lifting the export ban would generate as many as 25,000 added jobs, increase oil production by 100,000 b/d, and bring in as much as $2 billion in added royalty and tax payments.

Fig. 1

Alaska North Slope oil production forecast

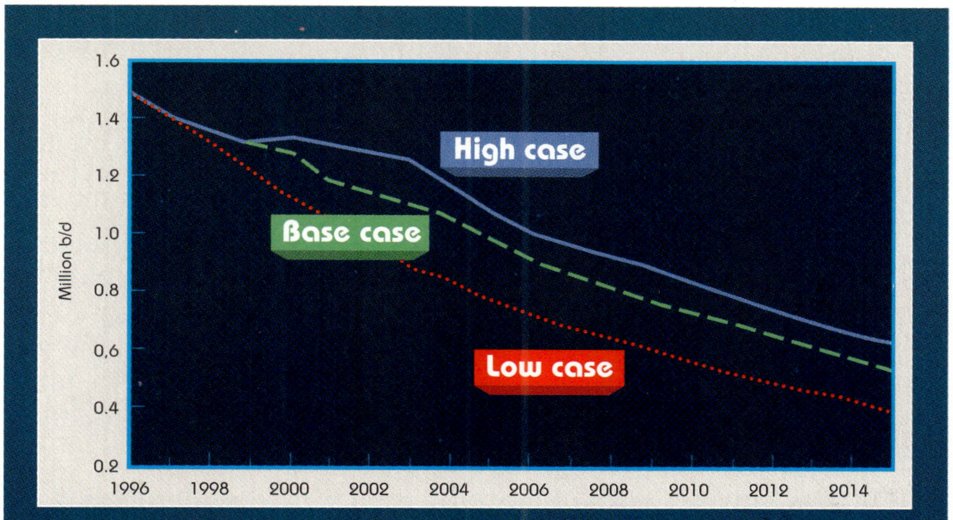

Source: Alyeska Pipeline Service Co. from Alaska Department of Revenue data

IPE

Improved fiscal regime

A new spirit of cooperation between government and the petroleum industry paved the way for an improved climate for investment in the state.

Thompson cited the relationship between government and industry in the Large Scale Enhanced Oil Recovery (Lseor) project—involving injection of miscible gas—nearing completion in ARCO-operated Kuparuk River field. The $175 million Lseor project involves expanding the Kuparuk miscible gas EOR project to 20 drillsites from three.

"The state worked for us there to prevent double taxation of the natural gas liquids that are being injected," Thompson said. "Under the old regulations, we were taxed at Prudhoe Bay when a barrel of NGL was produced, and once it's injected at Kuparuk and later produced again, we'd be taxed a second time."

A proposal to change regulations had been made by Gov. Wally Hickel's administration in 1994. The successor administration of Tony Knowles then supported the proposal, and the change took effect in 1995. The change will apply not only to Kuparuk but also to future enhanced oil recovery projects in Alaska.

Lseor is expected to bolster Kuparuk reserves by 200 million bbl and production by 35,000 b/d and enable ARCO to maintain Kuparuk output near its current level of 280,000 b/d through 2000. The project is limited to the best part of the field, and if it performs as expected, the EOR program is likely to be expanded to the rest of the Kuparuk River Unit.

Alaska also improved its tax regime for oil and gas producers, adding a tax appeals process and clarifying some tax regulations.

The producers long had complained that the tax laws were so complex that disputes were common and often resulted in lawsuits. In addition to the simpler tax language, producers now can take their tax appeals to an independent panel for a hearing.

Another boon to Alaskan operators was a push for areawide leasing that resulted in new legislation that would implement this concept in place of the existing, often sporadic lease schedule.

Perhaps the biggest benefit targeting oil and gas producers was 1995 legislation that encouraged development of marginal fields by cutting royalty rates.

That mission was put to the test with an agreement in 1996 between the Knowles administration and BP designed to encourage development of Northstar field in the Beaufort Sea off the Kuparuk River delta.

The field is on state and federal leases awarded in 1979. The state leases, sold to Amerada Hess Corp., hold the largest share of reserves. They carried a 20% royalty and an 89% net profits provision.

Federal leases, originally leased to Shell Western E&P Inc. with 16.67% royalty, would not be affected by the Knowles administration/BP agreement. Northstar field was a 1982 discovery by Shell from manmade Seal Island. Amerada Hess followed Shell's discovery with an extension find drilled from Northstar Island. Both companies considered development schemes but shelved them because of the high cost of laying a buried pipeline to transport oil to existing onshore facilities and the high net profits percentage to be paid on state leases.

BP entered the picture in January 1995 by acquiring Amerada Hess' 81% interest in the Northstar Unit and followed up with acquisition of Shell's 17% interest. Murphy Oil retained the remaining 2% interest.

In the agreement reached between the Knowles administration and BP, the state agreed to drop the 89% of net profits provision and substitute for it a supplemental royalty that would rise whenever North Slope oil prices exceeded a $17.35/bbl West Coast benchmark to a maximum additional 7.5% above the 20% the state already would receive.

Northstar development

BP plans to develop the 30,788-acre Northstar Unit by first expanding the size of Northstar Island from which Amerada Hess drilled in the 1980s for use as a base from which to drill new wells.

The drilling program calls for 23 wells, including 13 producers, six water injectors, three gas injectors, and one waste disposal well. Oil will be transported from the drilling island through a subsea pipeline buried 10 ft below the seabed.

Reserves are estimated at 130 million bbl of oil, potentially as much as 145-150 million bbl of an estimated 260 million bbl in place.

Production is expected to peak at 50,000 b/d of 40° gravity oil.

Alpine development

A group led by ARCO will develop an oil field in the western Colville area, marking the North Slope's first major new field development in some years.

The Alpine field development project, 8 miles north of the village of Nuiqsut, is the first North Slope oil discovery on Native-owned mineral estate since passage of the Alaska Native Claims Settlement Act in 1971.

The project's cost is estimated at $700-800 million, with initial production of 30,000 b/d expected early in 2000, rising to 60,000 b/d a year later.

The 10-mile long, 40,000 acre oil field has proven and potential reserves of 250-300 million bbl of oil and 800 million-1 billion bbl of oil in place.

Partners are operator ARCO 56%; Anadarko Petroleum Corp. 22%; and Union Texas Petroleum Alaska Corp. 22%.

The partners plan two drill sites and 100-150 wells covering 85 surface acres with a stand-alone processing complex.

Four delineation wells were tested and flowed high-quality, 40° gravity oil. An unstimulated rate of 2,380 b/d of oil was achieved from the Alpine formation, a sandstone discovered at a depth of about 6,850 ft.

Engineering design for field development and pipeline construction got under way in mid-1996.

Plans call for a 3-mile gravel road connecting the two drill sites and ice roads to move equipment and supplies. Alpine oil would move to market through an elevated, 34-mile, 16-20 in. pipeline linking Alpine to TAPS via the Kuparuk River pipeline.

Pending permitting, field construction and development would begin in winter 1997-98.

Fig. 2

Selective 40 acre infill drilling

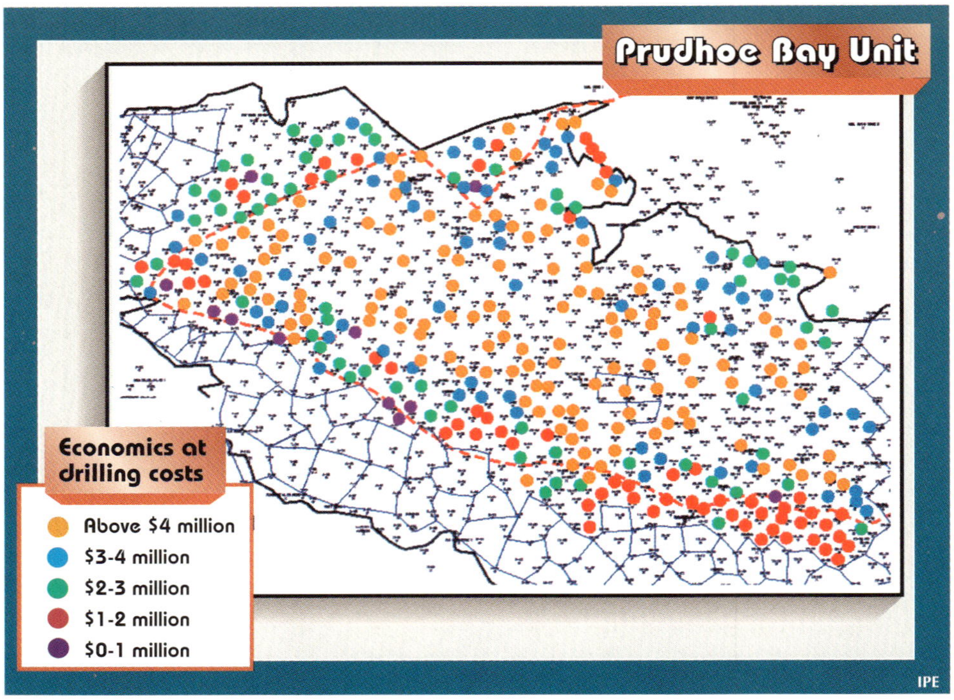

Prudhoe work

Even with the decline at Prudhoe, there remains much work to be done in North America's biggest oil field.

On tap is selective 40-acre infill drilling. Prudhoe development started with 160-acre spacing, but most of the field's development has been on 80-acre spacing.

Field operators ARCO and BP plan almost 500 reservoir penetrations the next 4 years, more than in any year since Prudhoe was discovered, and including coiled tubing drilling, horizontal drilling, sidetracking, and slim holes. Eighty percent of these penetrations will be horizontal wells.

Also figuring in the Prudhoe scenario is ARCO's proposed miscible injectant expansion (MIX) project, still pending approval by partners at the start of 1997.

The idea is to boost natural gas liquid and field gas production while also expanding manufacture of miscible injectant for added EOR. If approved, this would involve a sealift of equipment to the slope by fall 1998.

"MIX would increase black oil rate by boosting field gas offtake to over 8 bcfd," Thompson added. "It would boost natural gas liquids production by increasing CGF (Central Gas Facility) throughput, raising miscible injectant production, and accelerating recovery of enhanced oil recovery oil. MIX will cost approximately $200 million and add significant new reserves."

Prudhoe operators also are eying a host of satellite developments in the greater Prudhoe Bay area, including the ARCO-operated Lisburne Production Center/Greater Point McIntyre field area.

In 1993, production through the Lisburne processing center was 40,000 b/d from a single reservoir—the Lisburne part of Prudhoe Bay Unit. Today the Lisburne center processes more than 200,000 b/d from five reservoirs: Lisburne, Point McIntyre, West Beach, North Prudhoe Bay, and BP/ARCO/Exxon's Niakuk.

Satellite exploration

North Slope operators will increase their focus on exploring for and developing more such satellites.

ARCO alone has identified another 40 prospective satellite accumulations across the slope that it thinks range in size from a few million bbl to a few hundred million bbl. It thinks the satellites just in the immediate Prudhoe Bay vicinity may contain as much as 1.3 billion bbl of oil, with 300 million bbl recoverable.

"Over the next 3 years, our exploration program will be focused on testing a large number of these prospects as well as prospects surrounding other fields," ARCO's Thompson said. "We expect to drill six to eight exploratory wells a year."

Such efforts have enabled ARCO to rein its decline to only 6%/year vs. the 12%/year for Prudhoe Bay field overall.

In all, ARCO expects the continuing work in Prudhoe and Kuparuk, in tandem with phased West Sak development and development of satellite accumulations, could level ARCO's production by 2000.

West Sak's potential is enormous. An estimated 16 billion bbl of oil is in place at West Sak, or about 6 billion bbl less than Prudhoe's OOIP. West Sak crude has a gravity of 15-22°, but its closeness to permafrost gives it a high viscosity.

ARCO plans to use existing technology and lower operating costs by more than 30% to make West Sak viable. If successful, a phased development of West Sak could begin in 1997.

"We'll do an area, learn from it, next year do some more, and just keep going if the economics are there," Thompson said. "It could be significant because we see ARCO's share of recoverable barrels at 300-500 million bbl."

Milne Point revival

Meantime, a surprising revival is in store for a North Slope marginal field that only a few years ago remained in the limbo of a "warm shut-in" awaiting higher oil prices.

BP and Oxy U.S.A. Inc. were projecting that output of Milne Point field would more than double to 65,000 b/d by yearend 1996, a level that would place the field among the 10 most productive in the U.S.

Maintaining steady E&D programs, including expansion into new areas, has been the key to growth in production and reserves. BP doubled the number of Milne Point wells during 1995-96 and maintains a two-rig drilling program in the field.

The two partners also recently completed a $180 million project to expand capacity of Milne Point's oil processing facilities to 60,000 b/d from 30,000 b/d. When BP took over the Milne Point operation at the start of 1994, the field was producing 20,000 b/d.

If they can overcome some persistent commercial and technical challenges, BP and Oxy by 2000 could drill as many as 300 more wells in the field, boost production to as much as 100,000 b/d, and add 200-800 million bbl of reserves.

The increased E&D efforts led the partners to increase estimates of Milne Point reserves to 330 million bbl from 100 million bbl under the original development plan.

Schrader Bluff, the largest of Milne Point's three productive oil-bearing formations, is the eastern extension of West Sak formation, which overlies Kuparuk River intervals in Kuparuk River unit. Shallow, unconsolidated Schrader Bluff oil sands hold about 2 billion bbl of 14-20° gravity crude.

BP and Oxy in 1995 drilled five Schrader Bluff wells from existing gravel pads to test new well designs and drilling techniques. They aimed to reduce costs and improve productivity of the formation's heavy, viscous crude. They were encouraged by results of a gravel-packing program in Schrader Bluff wells that prevents granules from the formation's crumbly sands from entering the well bore, thereby lowering the risk of damaging production equipment.

A Milne Point field well was drilling ahead in 1996 for BP Exploration (Alaska) Inc., which set the stage for a tripling of production in the field, part of industry's efforts to arrest the decline in Alaskan North Slope production. Photo courtesy of BP.

Badami

Elsewhere on the slope, BP is experimenting with new approaches with contractors and regulators to come up with a commercial development scheme for Badami field, 35 miles east of Prudhoe Bay.

BP drilled two appraisal wells in 1995 that indicated reserves of 100 million bbl. This fell short of the targeted 150 million bbl, making development extremely challenging despite significant cost-cutting efforts ahead of the two-well program.

Capital outlays had been pegged at $780 million, and BP had wanted to cut costs to $320 million for a project based on 150 million bbl of reserves.

BP exploration

BP's drilling plans for the 1996-97 winter drilling season included the 3 Sourdough, in 29-9n-24e, in the Staines River area 1 mile west of the ANWR Coastal Plain.

The permitted drill site is about 1 mile north and slightly east of BP's 2 Sourdough, in 31-9n-24e, drilled to TD 12,600 ft in 1994. The state classified the No. 2 well as "capable of producing in paying quantities."

BP also let contract to the Northern Geophysical unit of 3-D Geophysical Inc., Englewood, Colo., for $7.5-9.5 million in North Slope seismic surveys during the 1996-97 winter. The contract adds to shallow-water work the contractor performed for BP in summer 1996 near Prudhoe Bay field.

Late in 1996, U.S. Minerals Management Service approved BP's exploration plan for the Liberty prospect in the Beaufort Sea.

The plan was submitted for two leases BP received in OCS Lease Sale 144, held Sept. 18, 1996.

BP plans to build a spray ice island and drill a wildcat to test the Liberty prospect, about 6 miles east of Endicott oil field. Plans called for a February 1997 spud date from the ice island, which is to be built from the remnants of a gravel island that Shell Oil Co. used to explore the Tern prospect in the early 1980s.

Cook Inlet

Alaska's other producing province, Cook Inlet, continues to hold its own, albeit on a much smaller scale.

While some major oil companies are increasingly reticent to commit E&D funds to Cook Inlet, an independent has jumped into the region with a big splash.

Cook Inlet production declined only 0.6% in 1995, compared with an overall drop of 4% in Alaskan oil production.

While disappointed that the first phase of its Chakachatna project did not increase production as hoped, Unocal believes there is more oil to be found in Cook Inlet basin.

Of the $45 million in Unocal's 1996 budget for capital investment in Alaska, $30 million was earmarked for Cook Inlet projects, with the remaining $15 million to pay for Unocal's share of investment in Kuparuk River and Endicott fields.

Swanson River field, which supplies gas to fuel the company's fertilizer plant, will claim almost one third of Unocal's Cook Inlet funds for new wells and upgrading facilities to sustain gas deliveries. Remaining funds will pay for new wells, reworks, and facility upgrades on platforms in Granite Point, Middle Ground Shoal, and McArthur River fields and improvements to onshore processing facilities.

ARCO Alaska Inc. reassessed its Cook Inlet holdings after its Bufflehead wildcat, drilled in 1995, proved dry.

The Bufflehead well was the first for ARCO in the Cook Inlet area since the abandonment in 1993 of two follow-up wildcats south of the Sunfish discovery well drilled in 1991. In the wake of unsuccessful follow-up wells, ARCO described Sunfish as noncommercial by itself.

Shell, whose involvement with Cook Inlet production goes back to the 1960s, put its statewide producing properties up for sale, including Platforms A and C in Middle Ground Shoal field, an onshore processing facility near Nikiski, interest in Beluga River gas field on the west side of Cook Inlet, and a 0.1377% interest in Prudhoe Bay field.

Marathon Oil Co. opened an exploratory campaign targeting gas on the Kenai Peninsula in late February 1996, spudding the 1 Corea Creek Federal, in 12-1n-13w, about 3 miles southwest of Clam Gulch. The directional well was targeted to 3,000 ft northwest of the surface location. The well went to 9,000 ft TD, and testing began with no release of results.

Stewart Petroleum Co., Anchorage, had planned by yearend 1996 to spud a deep exploratory well in the Cape Starich area of the Kenai Peninsula, 25 miles southwest of Falls Creek gas field and about 10 miles northwest of North Fork gas field. The high angle, long reach well was to be drilled from an onshore pad to bottom under Cook Inlet waters at about 22,000 ft.

New independent player

Miami independent Forcenergy Inc. quickly took a leading role in Cook Inlet E&D.

Forcenergy and Unocal agreed to jointly pursue lease sale activities and further develop Unocal's existing properties in the Cook Inlet basin.

The producing properties in the Cook Inlet area and the Cook Inlet Pipeline Co. are operated by Unocal.

"We believe that the Cook Inlet basin is underexplored and offers the potential for significant new discoveries," said Stig Wennerstrom, Forcenergy president and chief executive officer.

The disclosure came on the heels of a separate yet parallel deal, in which Forcenergy will acquire for $128.2 million Marathon Oil Co.'s interest in crude oil properties in Alaska's Cook Inlet and Prudhoe Bay unit. That deal includes purchase of Marathon's 30% working interest in Cook Inlet Pipeline Co. IPE

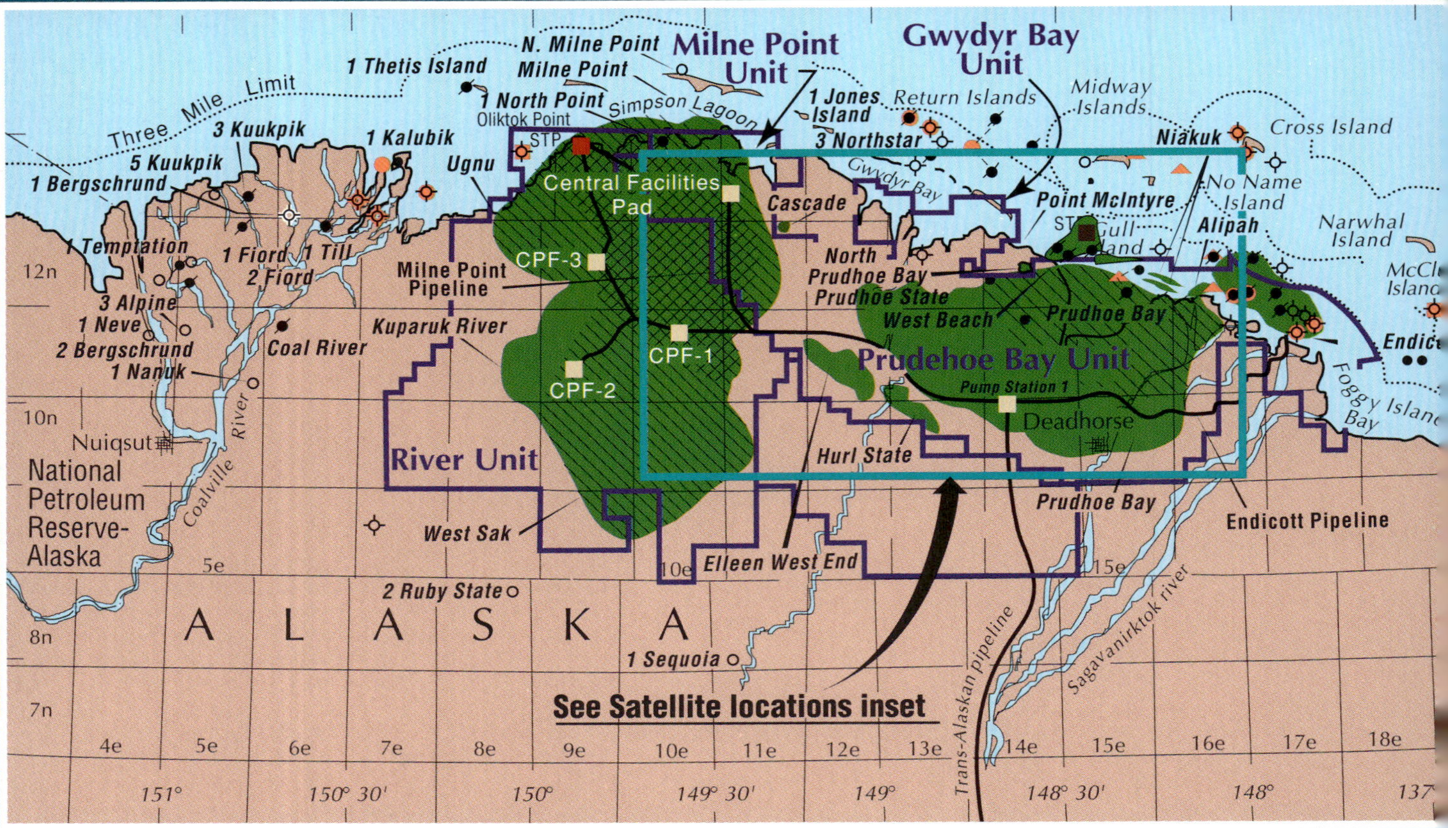
N. Milne Point
Milne Point
Milne Point Unit
Gwydyr Bay Unit
1 Thetis Island
1 North Point
Oliktok Point
Simpson Lagoon
1 Jones Island
Return Islands
Midway Islands
Three Mile Limit
3 Kuukpik
5 Kuukpik
1 Bergschrund
1 Kalubik
Ugnu
STP
Central Facilities Pad
3 Northstar
Gwydyr Bay
Niakuk
Cross Island
No Name Island
Narwhal Island
McClure Island
Point McIntyre
Alipah
Cascade
1 Temptation
1 Fiord
1 Till
2 Fiord
3 Alpine
1 Neve
2 Bergschrund
1 Nanuk
Coal River
Milne Point Pipeline
CPF-3
Kuparuk River
North Prudhoe Bay
Prudhoe State
West Beach
Prudhoe Bay
CPF-1
CPF-2
Prudhoe Bay Unit
Pump Station 1
Deadhorse
Foggy Island Bay
Endicott
Nuiqsut
River
National Petroleum Reserve-Alaska
Coalville
River Unit
Hurl State
Prudhoe Bay
Endicott Pipeline
West Sak
Elleen West End
2 Ruby State
ALASKA
1 Sequoia
See Satellite locations inset
Trans-Alaskan pipeline
Sagavanirktok river
12n
10n
8n
7n
4e
5e
6e
7e
8e
9e
10e
11e
12e
13e
14e
15e
16e
17e
18e
151°
150° 30'
150°
149° 30'
149°
148° 30'
148°

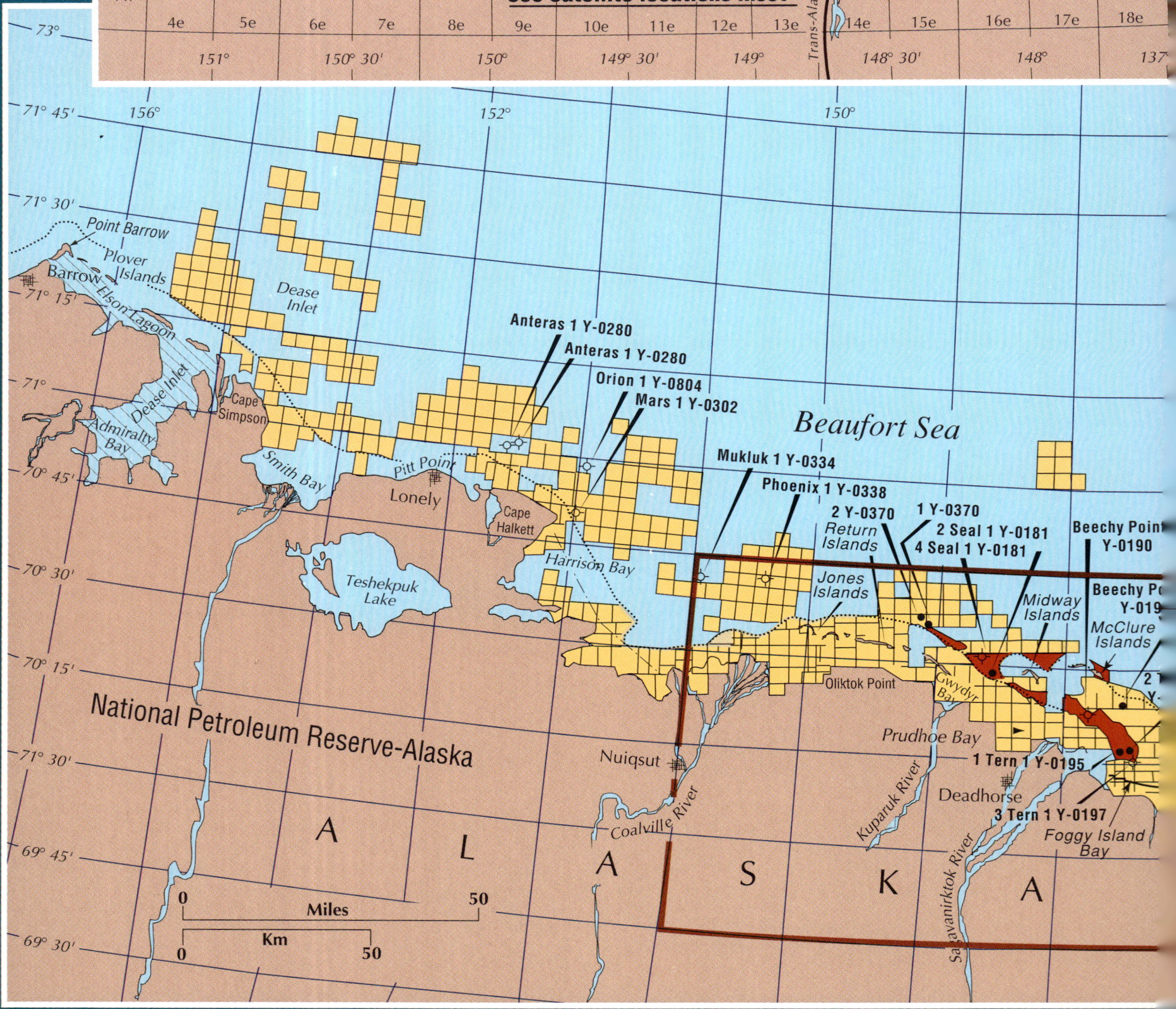
73°
71° 45'
156°
152°
150°
71° 30'
71° 15'
71°
70° 45'
70° 30'
70° 15'
71° 30'
69° 45'
69° 30'
Point Barrow
Plover Islands
Barrow
Elson Lagoon
Dease Inlet
Dease Inlet
Admiralty Bay
Cape Simpson
Smith Bay
Pitt Point
Lonely
Cape Halkett
Harrison Bay
Teshekpuk Lake
Antaras 1 Y-0280
Antaras 1 Y-0280
Orion 1 Y-0804
Mars 1 Y-0302
Beaufort Sea
Mukluk 1 Y-0334
Phoenix 1 Y-0338
2 Y-0370
1 Y-0370
Return Islands
2 Seal 1 Y-0181
4 Seal 1 Y-0181
Beechy Point Y-0190
Beechy Po Y-019
Jones Islands
Midway Islands
McClure Islands
Oliktok Point
Gwydyr Bay
Prudhoe Bay
1 Tern 1 Y-0195
Deadhorse
3 Tern 1 Y-0197
Foggy Island Bay
National Petroleum Reserve-Alaska
Nuiqsut
Coalville River
Kuparuk River
Sagavanirktok River
ALASKA
Miles
0
50
Km
0
50

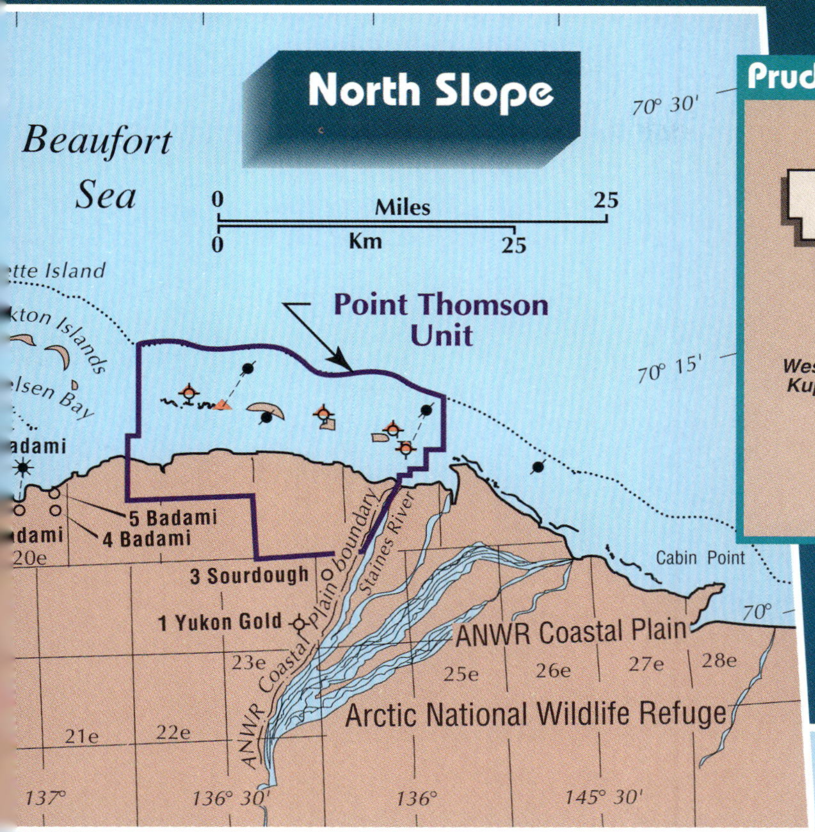
North Slope
Beaufort Sea
Miles
0
25
Km
0
25
70° 30'
70° 15'
70°
Point Thomson Unit
5 Badami
4 Badami
3 Sourdough
1 Yukon Gold
Staines River
ANWR Coastal Plain boundary
Cabin Point
ANWR Coastal Plain
Arctic National Wildlife Refuge
20e
21e
22e
23e
25e
26e
27e
28e
137°
136° 30'
136°
145° 30'

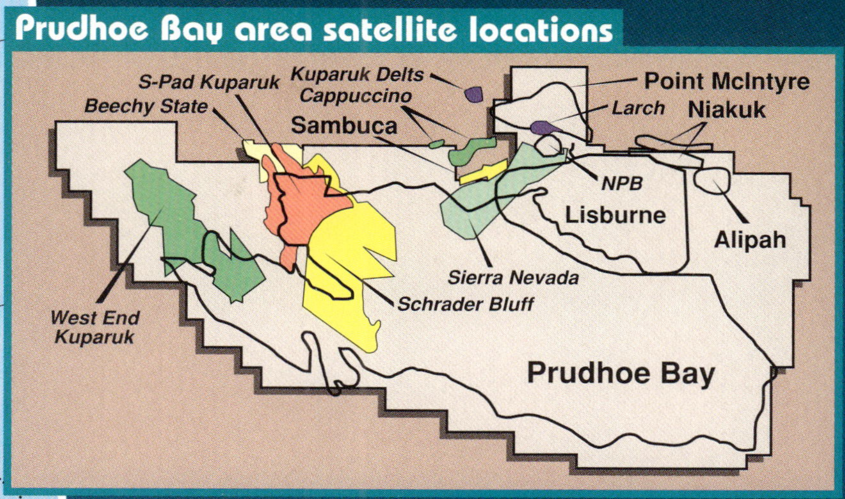
Prudhoe Bay area satellite locations
S-Pad Kuparuk
Kuparuk Delts
Cappuccino
Point McIntyre
Beechy State
Larch
Niakuk
Sambuca
NPB
Lisburne
Alipah
West End Kuparuk
Sierra Nevada
Schrader Bluff
Prudhoe Bay

N
Beaufort Sea planning area
Alaska

Alaskan North Slope/Beaufort Sea
144°
141°
Arctic Ocean
Belcher 1 Y-0924
Kuvlum 1 Y-0866
Corona 1 Y-0871
2 Y-0849
Aurora 1 Y-0943
Jago Lagoon
Barter Island
Katovik
Kaktovik native lands
1 KIC Jago River
Demarcation Bay
Demarcation Point
Katakturuk River
Aichilik River
Arctic National Wildlife Refuge Coastal Plain

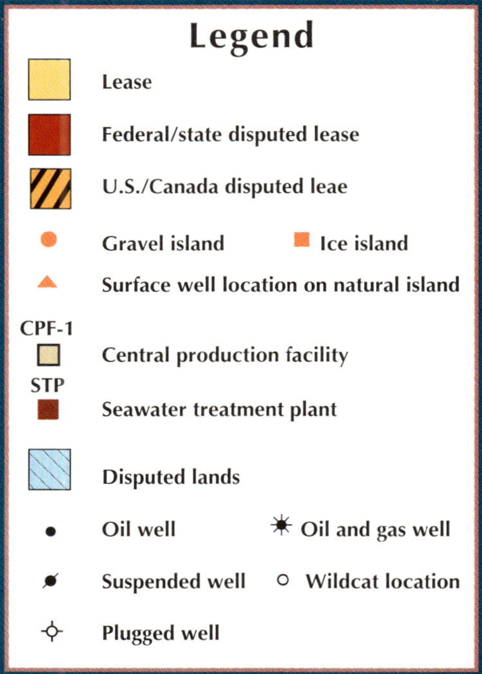
Legend
Lease
Federal/state disputed lease
U.S./Canada disputed leae
Gravel island
Ice island
Surface well location on natural island
CPF-1
Central production facility
STP
Seawater treatment plant
Disputed lands
Oil well
Oil and gas well
Suspended well
Wildcat location
Plugged well

CHINA

CAPITAL: Beijing
MONETARY UNIT: Yuan Renminbi
REFINING CAPACITY: 2.867 million b/cd
PRODUCTION: 3.127 million b/d
RESERVES: 24 billion bbl

China will require at least $20 billion in foreign investment to meet energy production targets set under its current 5-year plan.

Zhao Xizheng, China's vice-minister of power, said central and local governments are expected to raise 80% of the funds needed for the program.

State planners said China must improve its energy efficiency and production if it expects to achieve its goal of 8%/year economic growth.

Production of coal, which represents nearly 75% of China's energy consumption, was expected to reach 1.45 billion tons/year by 2000.

Oil and gas production also were expected to increase, although China will remain a net importer of oil, and its use of natural gas, 2% of energy consumption in 1996, will remain small.

The Asian Development Bank was helping advise the Chinese government on how to change its legal and regulatory framework to attract foreign investment needed to modernize the country's energy sector.

The nation also is concerned about the environmental impacts from meeting its economic goals. It is sharpening its focus on detrimental effects of oil and gas exploration and production. Upstream companies already face a complicated planning and permitting procedure.

China has estimated that pollution creates $100 billion/year in economic losses, half of them in the agriculture industry.

The central government said in 1996 it would revoke state funding for all small industries designated as environmental hazards.

China has estimated there are 24 million small, unregulated mines, mills, and factories operated for profit by local authorities such as village councils.

In an unprecedented move, the National Environmental Protection Agency ordered the closure of more than 70,000 small-volume paper mills, mines, tanneries, refineries, printing and dyeing factories, chemical plants, and other enterprises deemed environmental hazards due to outdated equipment and "low technological standards."

Crude outlook

China is the world's fastest growing oil consumer, but oil analysts say it needs to reform policies in its huge energy sector to attract more foreign investment and avoid massive import bills in the future.

The health of the nation's oil industry is critical to the government's goal of sustained economic growth well into the next century. Without enough oil and the right price, China's reforms will suffer.

But many of the nation's oil firms carry huge overheads, are dependent on large government subsidies, or are laden with debt.

Foreign oil firms are anxious to enter the promising Chinese market, but their investments are delayed by government indecision and red tape.

Ye Qing, China's oil minister, said the State Planning Commission is unlikely to decontrol the nation's oil industry soon, but the trend is towards decentralization.

Fereidun Fesharaki, of the East-West Center, Honolulu, in 1996 said, "China has to enter the second phase of its oil reforms within the next 2 years. This time it ought to emphasize getting investments in the downstream, not just price reforms."

China's demand for petroleum products was expected to reach 3.2 million b/d at the beginning of 1997, compared with 3 million in 1995. Analysts said demand would grow 5%/year until 2000.

The nation's oil refining capacity of 3.5 million b/d is inadequate, but the government has decided not to build new plants, only revamp and expand some large existing ones. The work will add about 600,000 b/d of capacity, but analysts say only two thirds of that is likely to be on stream by 2000.

They say China will need to import 600,000 b/d of crude oil and 600,000 b/d of products by 2000, draining its hard currency reserves.

Fesharaki said China's oil industry needs not only refinery expansions to keep pace with demand, but also sophisticated technologies to shift production to gasoline and diesel fuel.

Chinese refineries are operated like communes and provide jobs for 10,000-20,000 workers and their dependents. Maoming refinery in Guangdong, the second largest refinery in China, employs 25,000 persons and supports a commune population of more than 80,000. A typical refinery elsewhere in Asia employs about 500.

China also has been reluctant to open its retail oil market to foreign firms, and companies with service stations have found their financial returns to be erratic because they have to buy products at controlled prices.

Despite a potential domestic customer base of 1.2 billion people, Chinese planners are forcing foreign firms involved in joint ventures to export much of their production.

Fesharaki said, "No one of sound mind will invest in an export-oriented refinery in China. Investors enter the market hoping to get a foothold in the Chinese retail market."

While the lack of access to China's retail market is an obstacle to refinery investments, analysts say the government's erratic price reform program is a bigger deterrent.

In May 1996 China set refined product prices higher than

Chevron's gas exploration acreage off China Fig. 1

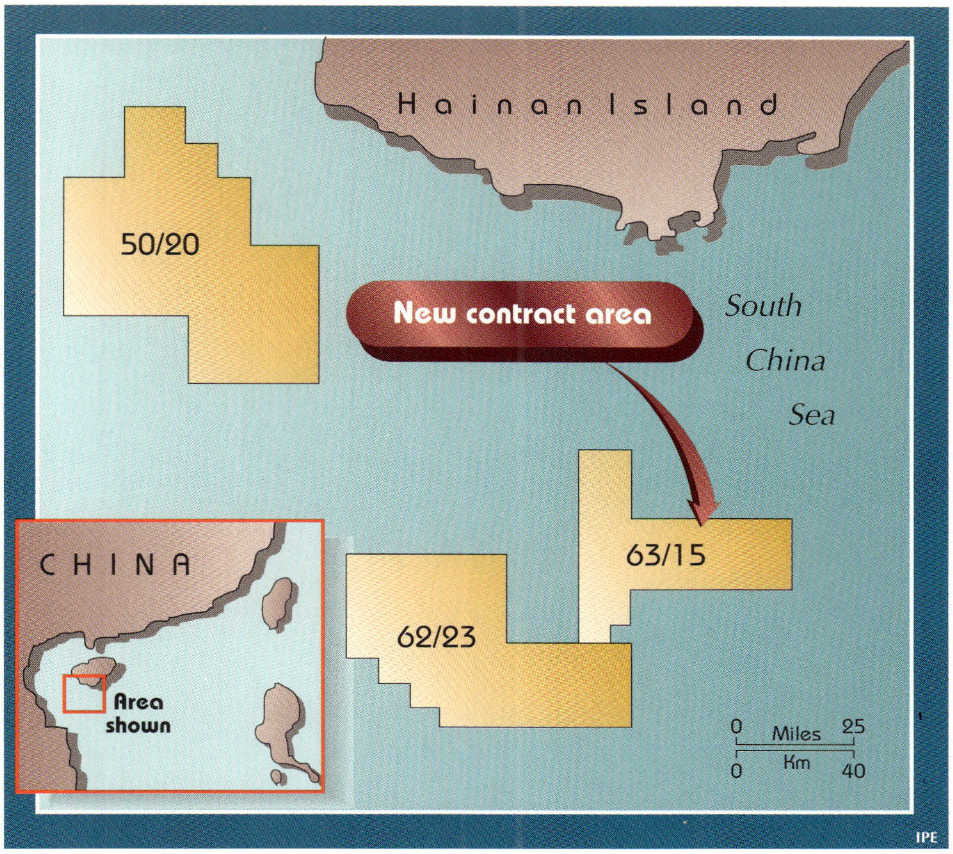

Motor vehicle growth in China Fig. 2

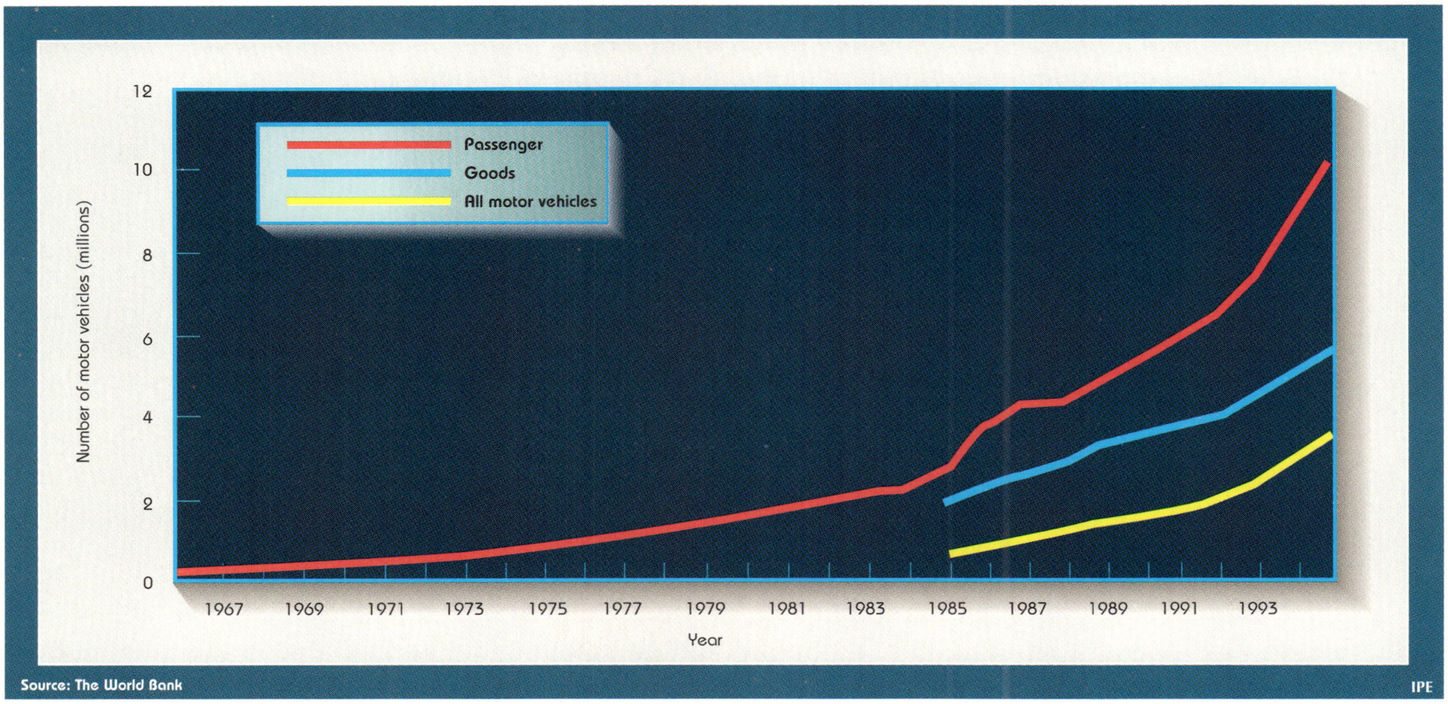

Source: The World Bank

IPE

world levels then slashed them without warning 3 months later.

Analysts said if China wants to attract the foreign investments it needs in refineries, it must permit product prices to rise to international levels, create transparency in its policy making process, allow a fair return on investment, broaden access to the domestic market, accommodate foreign management control of foreign investments, and and provide for freer competition with the state refineries.

Elf optimistic

China's gas industry is easily the world's oldest.

The Chinese produced natural gas in the Sichuan basin as early as the third century B.C., when it was piped through bamboo trunks and used for salt refining and cooking.

Despite China's industrial progress, natural gas has never lived up to its promising start. It remains a poor relation of oil and coal. The latter is China's most plentiful hydrocarbon fuel.

In a 1996 report on its Asian exploration ambitions, Elf Aquitaine SA said much of the exploration potential in Asia lies in gas.

It said China could become a significant gas-producing country, after having been a big coal producer.

Although Elf has had little success in Asia in the past, prospects in China are luring the company back to the region. It opened exploration and production offices in Beijing to facilitate onshore and offshore exploration projects in a number of sectors.

Because of an anticipated shortfall in gas production, and urbanization of coastal areas, Elf's Antargaz unit intends to import liquefied petroleum gas into China.

Antargaz was negotiating to start construction of an LPG import terminal in China with capacity to handle 2-3 million tons/year for the first few years. It also was establishing market presence in China by selling lubricants.

Elf said a very long term view is needed for China. Besides E&P, LPG, and lubricants, it wanted to gain a foothold in China for chemicals, while its Sanofi pharmaceuticals division was pursuing healthcare opportunities. The company said more than half its 52 Asian prospects are in China.

Gas potential

Wood Mackenzie Consultants, Edinburgh, said China has to take steps to guarantee energy supplies to support its booming economy, and gas is expected to form a major element of the government's energy policy.

It said China's government believes that large resources of natural gas remain to be found offshore and in the country's remote northwestern region.

It said a large supply of natural gas could help China address four pressing needs: diversification of energy supplies, reduction of atmospheric pollution caused by coal-fired power stations and boilers, fuel supplies for combined-cycle gas turbines, and reduction of costs for transporting coal from northern China to coastal provinces.

Wood Mackenzie estimates Chinas proved and probable gas reserves at 35 tcf—39% in the Sichuan basin, 17% in the onshore Ordos basin, and 27% offshore.

In 1994, China's gas production amounted to 1.6 bcfd. Production is expected to reach 2.6 bcfd by 2000 and 4.1 bcfd by 2010.

China's gross production grew at roughly 10% /year in the 15 years through 1996 and was expected to grow by 6-10%/year during the following 15 years.

Natural gas provides less than 2% of China's primary energy. China's gas consumption was about 2 bcfd in 1996.

Wood Mackenzie estimated that if the gas portion of total energy demand rises to 3% by 2010, total gas consumption would then reach 5.7 bcfd.

Much of the impetus for China's growing gas demand is expected to come from electricity generation. By 2010, power plants are expected to consume 40% of China's gas, compared with 11% in 1996.

Wood Mackenzie predicted residential and commercial use would grow, especially due to environmental concerns in large cities, and the industrial and petrochemical sectors would use large volumes, but at a slower rate of growth than in other sectors.

It said China will need to discover and develop or import a further 15-30 tcf each 10 years to meet predicted gas demand.

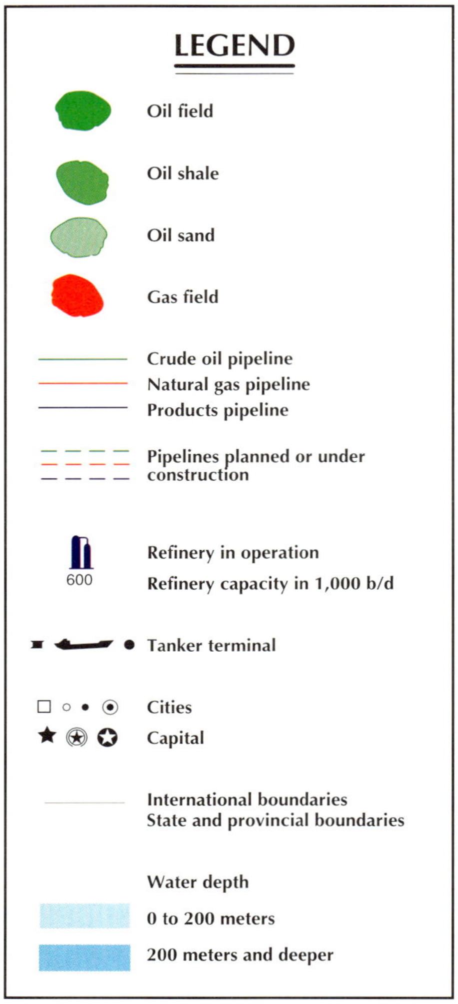

Gas discoveries on that scale are thought most likely in the far northwest in the Tarim, Junggar, and Qaidam basins; offshore in the East and South China Seas, and in northern China in the form of coalbed methane.

Wood Mackenzie said although there have been successes in the Qaidam basin, drilling in the northwestern basins and offshore has proved disappointing.

It predicted that, if one major new gas province comes on stream in the next few years, China's gas production could top 4.5 bcfd by 2010 and reach 6 bcfd by 2015.

It said gas imports will be required during 2005-15, and at least 1 bcfd of imported gas is likely to be required by 2010, mostly in the coastal provinces.

Wood Mackenzie said imports are most likely to take the form of LNG, requiring one to four major LNG terminals by 2015.

Traffic problems

The World Bank notes China's cities are confronting increasing pollution and traffic congestion.

A report, "China's Urban Transport Development Strategy," said numbers of cars, trucks, and motorcycles have risen sharply in cities.

Hou Jie, construction minister, said, "Despite considerable efforts made in recent years, urban transport infrastructure and services are still deficient, and the problem will

Bohai block

Fig. 3

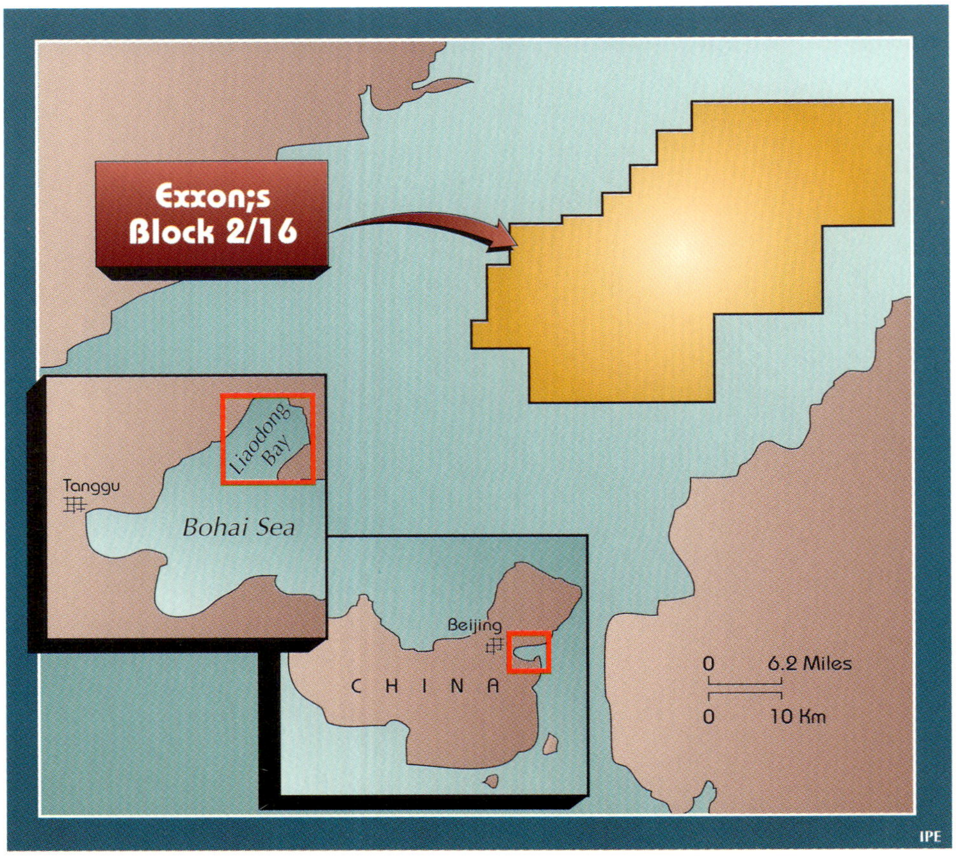

likely become worse.

"Achieving (a major improvement) will be especially challenging and will not be possible without further policy and management reforms."

Motor vehicle ownership is increasing at a faster rate than road space is being made available. Motor vehicles in some cities grew at a rate of 15-20%/year, but the cities are still operating under their old policies.

The World Bank report said managing the growth of motor-vehicle traffic volume should be the priority because expanding streets and roads will be too expensive and cannot accommodate the rapid traffic growth.

Planners also want to encourage use of the bicycle, which will remain a popular means of transportation in Chinese cities.

The study said building subway systems would be too expensive.

It said the motor vehicle pollution is increasingly serious because many vehicles are equipped with outdated engines, and gasoline is still almost entirely leaded.

Onshore activities

China is turning more to tertiary recovery to maintain production from its major onshore oil fields

China National Petroleum Corp. (CNPC) signed a cooperative agreement with Enron Oil & Gas Co., Houston, to evaluate prospects for further development and improved recovery in the Sichuan basin.

The pact calls for a 13 month study of the 19,000 sq km Chuanzhong Block, which contains several fields producing crude oil and natural gas. It is in the center of one of China's oldest oil and gas producing areas.

Production from the block totaled 936,000 bbl in 1995, and the government wanted Enron's help in expanding it to 2 million bbl/year.

Also, CNPC said it would use polymer flooding at six fields to boost production to 200,000 b/d by 2000. Three of the fields, Daqing, Shjengli, and Liaohe, are among the country's largest.

Pilot projects in the six fields have indicated that polymer flooding could improve output by 10%.

CNPC planned to develop Sha'anxi gas field in the province of the same name. Production was due to begin in 1997 at the rate of 2 billion cu m/year, rising to 3 billion cu m/year by 2000.

Texaco Inc. agreed in production sharing contracts with CNPC to explore two contiguous tracts covering a combined 5.4 million acres in South Central China's Sichuan basin.

Texaco planned to begin acquiring seismic data on the acreage in 1996, with exploratory drilling slated for 1997.

CNPC completed development of 14,000 b/d Xiaoguai field in the western Xinjiang Uygur region. Reserves are 42 million bbl. Production was to have been doubled within 2 years.

South China Sea

China National Offshore Oil Corp. (Cnooc) opened the nation's second largest offshore gas field, Dongfang, near the southern island province of Hainan in the western part of the South China Sea.

Dongfang has confirmed reserves of 2.8 tcf, and the operator says it could contain 3.5 tcf.

The nation's largest offshore gas field, Yacheng, began production in January 1996. It has reserves of 2.9 tcf.

China also began production in 1996 of Liuhua oil field, the largest in the South China Sea. It is in contract area 29/04 in the Pearl River Delta basin.

The field is expected to produce 50,000 b/d and could climb to 65,000 b/d. The $620 million project was developed by Amoco, Kerr-McGee, and Cnooc. The latter holds a 51% interest and the two American oil firms 25.5% each.

Chevron Overseas Petroleum Inc. (COPI) expanded exploration for gas off China's Hainan province.

COPI affiliate Chevron Overseas Petroleum Ltd. signed a production sharing contract with Cnooc to explore for gas on 2,030 sq km contract area 63/15 in the South China Sea about 70 km south of the island province.

The deal increased Chevron's gas exploration portfolio in the area, where ARCO and partners were developing a world class gas field, Yacheng 13-1, and have laid pipelines to Hainan and mainland China to deliver Yacheng gas to market. Yacheng 13-1 started production in early 1996.

The new contract area, in which Chevron holds a 100% interest, adjoins one of two blocks Chevron owns south of Hainan. It acquired contract areas 62/23 and 50/20 early in 1995.

Chevron said it believes contract area 63/15 has the potential for significant gas accumulations.

Chevron began a 623 sq km 3D seismic survey in 1996 on contract area 63/15 and planned to integrate the data gathered with data covering contract areas 62/23 and 50/20. Chevron planned to spud a wildcat on the block in 1997.

In the event of a commercial discovery, Cnooc will back into an equity interest of the block, usually 51%.

In 1995, in conjunction with Cnooc and its other partners in the CACT Operators Group (formerly ACT), Chevron

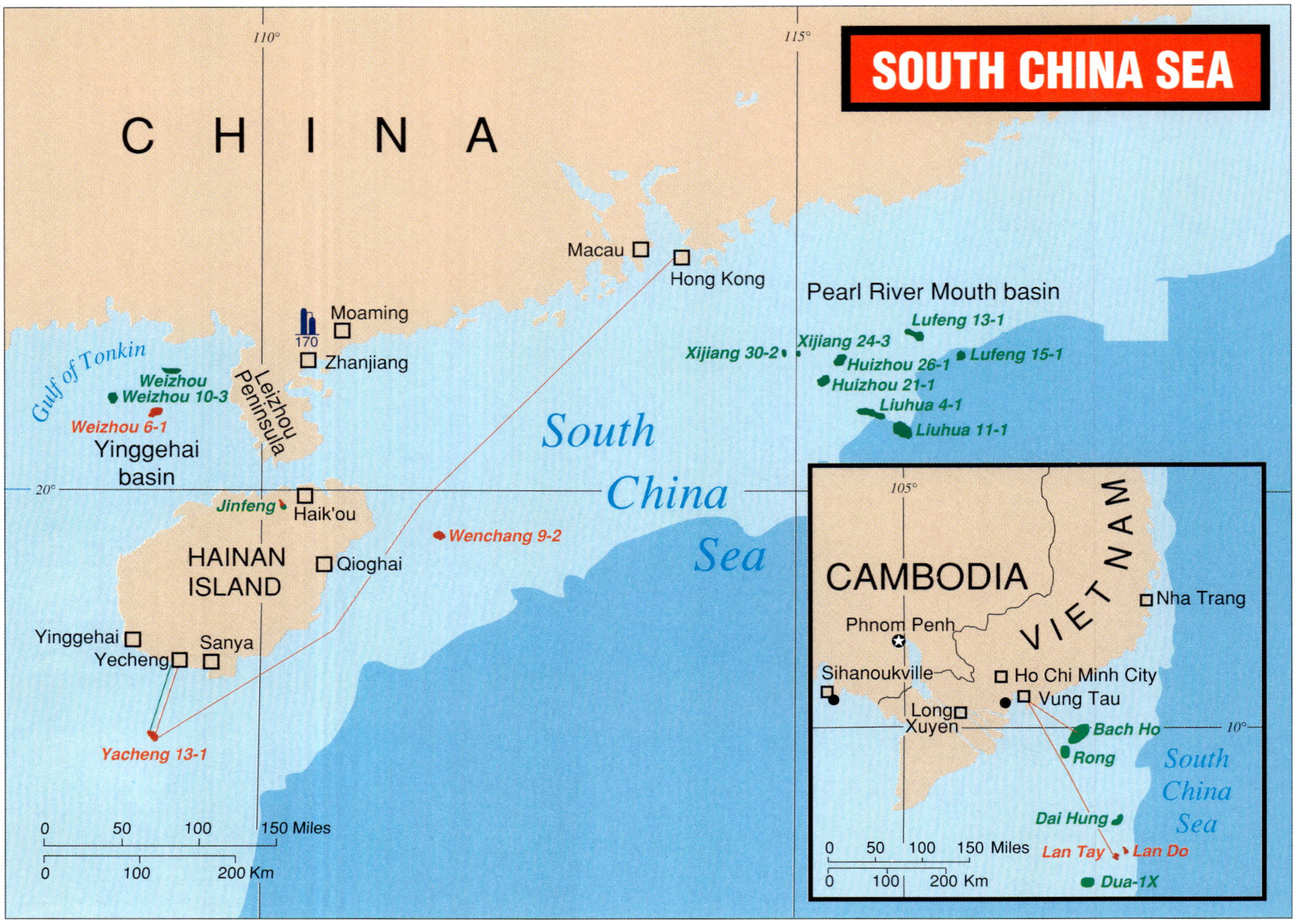

brought the two newest Huizhou oil fields into production in the South China Sea.

This boosted CACT production in the Pearl River Mouth basin to a record 120,000 b/d, making the group the biggest oil producer off China.

Other projects

Chevron, Agip SpA, and Texaco Inc. formed ACT Operators Group in 1983 to develop hydrocarbon resources in the Pearl River Mouth basin.

ACT drilled its first well in 1984 and its first commercial discovery in 1985. That discovery, Huizhou 21-1 oil field, went on stream in 1990. It was followed by oil field discoveries Huizhou 26-1 in 1991 and Huizhou 32-2 and 32-3 in 1995.

Effective Jan. 1, 1996, Cnooc joined ACT in operation of the offshore fields, and the new joint operating group changed its name to CACT Operators Group. Agip, Chevron, and Texaco each holds a 16.33% interest in the Huizhou oil fields, with Cnooc holding the remaining 51%.

Also, the CACT group agreed to conduct an 18 month seismic survey on a 625 sq km tract in the Pearl River Mouth basin.

The 16/19 survey area is a west offset to contract area 16/08, where the group is producing from four Huizhou oil fields.

If the seismic surveys confirm 16/19's exploration potential, Agip, Chevron, and Texaco will have an option to negotiate a petroleum contract with Cnooc.

Norway's Statoil was drilling five wells in Lufeng 22-1 oil field in the South China Sea.

Statoil took over operatorship of the 35 million bbl field in 1995 from Ampol Exploration Ltd., Sydney. The company plans to use a production and storage ship to recover oil through subsea wells for export by shuttle tanker.

ARCO China Ltd. started gas sales to Hong Kong from two platforms in Yacheng 13-1 field in the South China Sea off Hainan Island through a 778 km pipeline, capping an 11 year, $1.2 billion project.

Yacheng 13-1, China's biggest offshore gas field with reserves of 3.4 tcf, will deliver 277 MMcfd to feed a Hong Kong power plant.

Plans called for delivering 53 MMcfd to a power plant and chemical plants on Hainan Island through a 91 km pipeline from the field.

Shanghai Petroleum and Gas Corp. planned to develop acreage in the Pinghu oil and gas field in the East China Sea.

The field, about 400 km southeast of Shanghai, has reserves of 2 tcf and 20 million cu m of crude and condensate.

Plans called for moving the gas to shore to provide 85 bcf/year to the city of Shanghai.

Bohai Sea

An Exxon Corp. unit acquired a large exploration block in China's northern Bohai Sea.

Esso China Upstream Ltd. agreed to explore Block 2/16 in Liaodong Bay, 400 km northeast of Beijing.

Esso holds a 100% interest in the block, which covers about 2,625 sq km in 10-25 m of water. It planned a 3D seismic survey before exploratory drilling.

A Cnooc unit operates nearby Jinzhou 20-2 oil and gas

Phillips project area Fig. 4

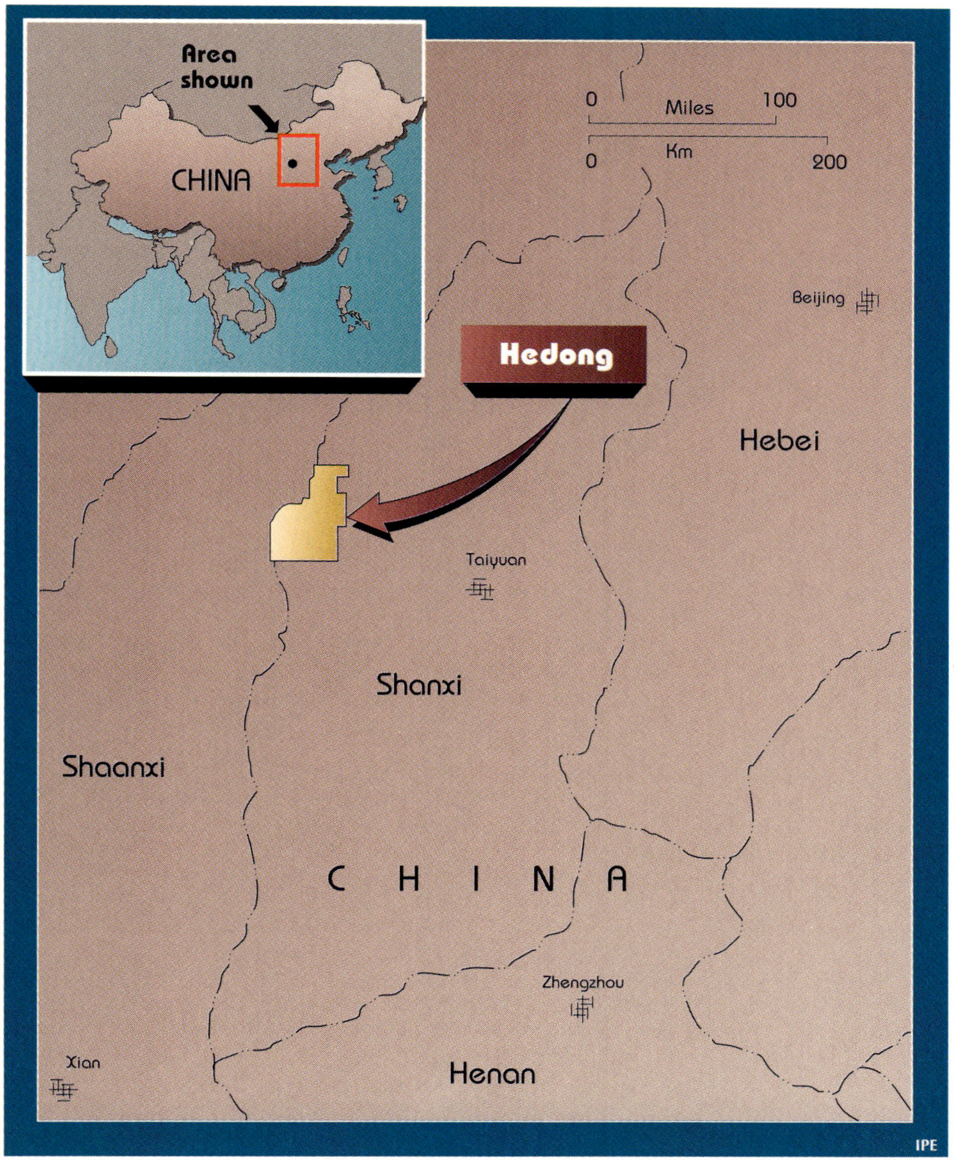

IPE

field and Suizhong 36-1 oil field in the northern Bohai Sea. In the southern Bohai Sea, a Japanese group together with Cnooc produces oil from three fields.

A number of exploration blocks have been awarded foreign oil and gas companies in the Bohai Sea region in recent years.

A unit of Kerr-McGee Corp. signed a contract with Cnooc to explore an area of about 415,000 acres in Bohai Bay and drill two holes.

Kerr-McGee China Petroleum Ltd. will operate contract area 05/36, just east of Kerr-McGee's three existing operated blocks, 04/36, Getuo, and Laopu, about 100 miles southeast of Beijing, in average water depths of 75 ft.

Interests are Kerr-McGee 65% and Huffco China 35%.

Apache Corp. said its D-2 exploratory well on the Zhao Dong Block in Bohai Bay tested oil at the rate 11,571 b/d.

Including the D-2, Apache and its partners in 1996 had completed five wells on the Zhao Dong Block since operations began there in 1994. The combined test rates were about 24,400 b/d.

The D-2 had 225 ft of net pay and was tested in six zones perforated between 3,283 and 5,445 ft in the Minghuazhen and Guantao formations and a lower Tertiary-age sand. It was drilled to a total depth of 7,501 ft.

The D-2 is a wildcat in the Guantao and deeper formations and an appraisal of the shallower Minghuazhen formation discovered in the D-1 well.

The exploratory tests in the Guantao registered a combined rate of 4,860 b/d. The deepest formation tested, a lower Tertiary sand, had the highest flow rate, 4,370 b/d of 27° gravity oil and 774 Mcfd on an open choke with 147 psi of flowing tubing pressure. Perforations were between 5,396 ft and 5,445 ft.

Apache is the operator of the Zhao Dong Block with a 50% working interest. XCL Ltd. holds the remaining 50%.

Refining/Marketing

Chen Jinhua, the state planning commission chairman, said China would look at proposals for refinery projects from foreign oil companies on a case by case basis.

But he said China was using only about 70% of its current refining capacity and wanted to prevent duplication of facilities.

The planning commission said it would not approve additional capacity, particularly from small scale refineries, before the year 2000.

Officials said there were at least 116 refineries operating in China in 1995, and many of them were poorly designed and make inferior products. They are operated by CNPC, China Petrochemicals Corp., the People's Liberation Army, and local governments.

Until 2000, the planning commission wants to focus on updating and expanding existing refineries to produce cleaner fuels, rather than building new ones.

The only exceptions to the policy will be the Concord Group's planned 100,000 b/d Ningbo refinery in eastern Zhejiang province and Hohbond International's 120,000 b/d refinery at Hainan.

The planning commission told South Korea's Yukong that it will postpone its proposed 100,000 b/d refinery in Southern Guangdong province until 2000.

Shell's 120,000 b/d refinery and petrochemical complex planned for southern Guandong province apparently will proceed because it was deemed a project that already was approved.

The $6 billion project also would produce 600,000 tons/year of ethylene. Shell is a 50% owner with Cnooc and other Chinese interests.

The size of the refinery was scaled back from 360,000 b/d; it now will use less heavy Chinese crude and more light crude from the Middle East.

Mobil Corp. said it was continuing discussions with Chinese officials on possible oil refining projects, but talks were not encouraging.

In early 1997 Mobil opened a $45 million lubricants plant in the northern port city of Tainjin.

ARCO increased its 9.9% interest in China's Zhenhai Refining and Chemical Co. to 20% by investing $128 million. It bought its initial interest for $70 million in 1994.

Zhenhai operates a 160,000 b/d refinery about 100 miles south of Shanghai and is the country's third largest refiner.

Jingmen General Petrochemical put a new cat cracker on stream at its 54,000 b/d refinery in Hubei province. It plans to double the plant's capacity by 2000.

Fortune Oil plc, London, opened 10 modern gasoline stations in China and expected to open 15 more by the end of 1997.

Total cost is pegged at $20 million for the 25 stations in the cities of Shunde, Zhuhai, Zhongshan, Zhaoquing, Panyu, and Guangzhou.

Fortune said bureaucratic problems delayed its efforts to open stations. It said 16 government departments must approve a permit to open a gasoline station in China.

Petrochemicals

Analysts predict China's petrochemical demand will be greater than Japan's in 2000: 8 million tons/year of ethylene equivalent products vs. Japan's 6.2 million tons/year.

Chinese state planners want to more than double ethylene production capacity to about 5 million tons/year by 2000 from the current 2.36 million tons/year.

China National Petrochemical Corp. is expanding ethylene capacity at its Daqing petrochemical complex in Heilongjiang province. Output was to rise to 480,000 tons/year by July 1999 from 300,000 tons/year in 1996.

Shanghai Petrochemical Co. Ltd. (SPC) was acquiring Shanghai Jiushi Co.'s Jin-Yang acrylic fiber plant at Shanghai. The plant produced 25,800 tons of acrylic fiber in 1995.

Shanghai Chlor Alkali Chemical Co. Ltd. let contracts for construction of an ethylene dichloride (EDC) plant at its vinyl chloride monomer and polyvinyl chloride (PVC) complex in Shanghai. The unit includes an EDC degasser and a PVC dryer. Completion was due in late 1997.

China National Petrochemical let contract to Brown & Root Inc. for process technology and design and technical services for an expansion of ethylene capacity at its Daqing petrochemical complex in Heilongjiang province.

The revamped plant will use Brown & Root ethylene technology featuring front-end, heat-pumped depropanization integrated with cracked gas compression and a front-end acetylene hydrogenation system to boost capacity by July 1999 to 480,000 tons/year from 300,000 tons/year.

Dongfang Eastern Chemical Works's ethylene plant in Zhang Xinghuang completed performance tests after a year of operation.

Located 28 km east of Beijing, the Dongfang complex includes a 150,000 ton/year ethylene plant, 40,000 ton/year butadiene extraction plant, a 120,000 ton/year, two-step pyrolysis gasoline hydrogenation unit, a waste-water treatment plant, and associated utilities, storage, loading, and unloading facilities.

Dongfang will use products from the plant to produce acrylic ester to meet increasing demand for home electronics, automobiles, construction materials, clothing, and other consumer products.

Shanghai Petrochemical Co. and Phillips Petroleum Co. formed a joint venture, Shanghai Golden Phillips, to build a 100,000 ton/year linear polyethylene resins plant and a 10,000 ton/year plant to provide feedstock for manufacturing polyethylene pipelines at Jinshanwei, Shanghai.

Total investment will be $100 million. Both projects were scheduled for completion in 1998.

Chlor Alkali Chemical Co. Ltd. let contract for engineering and equipment for an ethylene dichloride plant being built at its vinyl chloride monomer and polyvinyl chloride complex in Shanghai. Completion was due in late 1997.

Phillips and Shanghai Petrochemical Co. signed an agreement to study feasibility of expanding the latter's 220 million lb/year high density polyethylene plant due completion at Shanghai in 1998.

Phillips has a 40% interest in that project, which uses Phillips technology, and Shanghai 60%.

Phillips will study expanding the plant by 440-550 million lb/year, holding a 40-50% interest in the additional capacity.

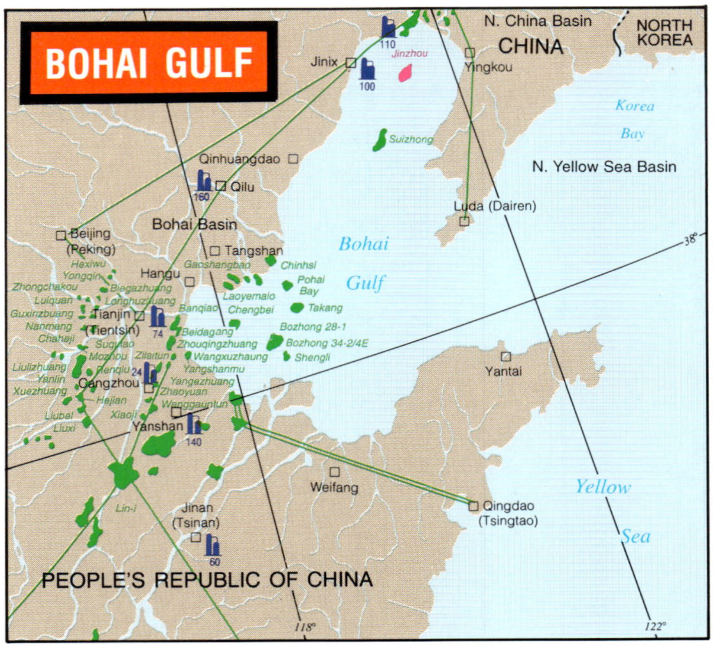

BP Chemicals and Shanghai Petrochemical Co. Ltd. plan to build a $2.5 billion plant in Shanghai capable of producing 650,000 tons/year of ethylene. A 2 year feasibility study was planned. The firms each will own 50% of the venture.

Other projects

Caltex China Ltd. and Shantou Ocean Enterprises were building an import terminal at Shantou in Guangdong Province.

Plans called for two underground caverns, each with capacity of 690,000 bbl, providing China's first mined cavern for LPG storage. Completion was planned for 1998.

Tangshan International Petroleum Gas Co., a joint venture of the Jingtang Port Office and Arab investors, planned to build an LPG terminal at the northern city of Tangshan. Total storage capacity would be 500,000 cu m.

Amoco and several Chinese firms were building an LPG terminal in eastern China's Jiangsu Province. The $20 million project, due completion in early 1997, would distribute 500,000 tons/year of LPG to the Yangzi River Delta region through pipeline and barges. It will import LPG from the Middle East.

China Energy Investment Co. Ltd. planned to build a 1,050 mw gas-fired power plant at Shenzhen. It will consist of three 350 mw combined-cycle gas turbines and was due completion in late 1999.

Phillips will operate a joint venture coalbed methane project on the 781,000 acre Hedong concession in Shanxi province, about 120 miles west of Taiyuan.

Phillips will hold a 65% interest, Chinese partners 30%, and the U.S. firm CBM 5%. Seismic and drilling operations began early in 1997.

Phillips operates Xijiang oil fields in the South China Sea and a Bohai Bay exploration permit, but the coalbed methane project is its first one onshore.

China could become Venezuela's best customer for the heavy boiler fuel Orimulsion.

Venezuela sent 140,000 tons of Orimulsion to China for a test burn in December 1996. The two countries were joining in a feasibility study to build a production plant in Venezuela. The study was due completion in 1997.

China was building a 303 gas pipeline in central Sha'anxi province, to move gas from the Sha'anxi-Gansu-Ningxia basin to Xi'an. IPE

"It is well known that Romania is a country of an old oil and gas tradition. The prestige Romania has gained in these fields, as well as a century old experience, is now fundamental to all activities developed by our company.

In all our partners' countries where contracts are performed, ***ROMPETROL S.A.*** opens offices staffed with highly qualified specialists entrusted with the coordination and supervision of the good execution of the jobs undertaken on cooperation contract basis.

ROMPETROL S.A. is always ready to turn to account in favour of its partners, the experience accumulated and guaranteed by its activity in many countries of the world."

109, CALEA VICTORIEI, BUCHAREST, COD 70176,
TEL:40 1 3129540, TELEX:10155 ROMPER;
FAX 40 13122490; 40 1 3120687

ASIA PACIFIC

AUSTRALIA

CAPITAL: Canberra
MONETARY UNIT: Dollar
REFINING CAPACITY: 771,250 b/cd
PRODUCTION: 506,200 b/d
RESERVES: 1.6 billion bbl

The Timor Sea area jointly administered by Australia and Indonesia emerged as a world-class gas province, now complete with its own liquefied natural gas export scheme.

Phillips Petroleum Co. proposed a $1.9 billion (Australian) LNG development based in Darwin for the Bayu/Undan discovery in the Timor Gap Zone of Cooperation Area (ZOCA) between Australia and Indonesia.

Approval by BHP Petroleum Pty. Ltd. through a unitization process is needed before any final plans take effect because Bayu/Undan straddles the permit boundary between the BHP-operated and Phillips-operated parts of the field.

There were hopes the two would reach agreement on development options by mid-1997.

Late in 1996, BHP and partners were awarded four new production sharing contracts in the Timor Gap.

In two of the blocks—ZOCA 95-15 and 95-17—BHP has 100% interest. In ZOCA 95-19 and 16-20, BHP has an equal one-third interest with Woodside Petroleum Pty. Ltd. and Shell Development (Australia) Ltd., with Shell as operator in both. BHP is involved in six Timor Gap permits, including those with the Kakatua and Elang oil discoveries and Bayu/Undan field.

The work programs for the four new areas include four wells during the next 3 years on ZOCA 95-19, one slated for 1997.

This permit lies in the northeast corner of the Timor Gap opposite the recent discoveries but adjacent to Woodside's Troubadour and Sunrise gas/condensate finds made in the 1970s.

New bidding round

Australia opened a bidding round for 38 offshore areas in 10 regions, including acreage near discoveries in the Bonaparte and Carnarvon basins.

Included in the offering was prospective acreage in the central part of world-class Gippsland basin off Western Australia and lightly explored blocks off Victoria and the island of Tasmania.

Operators working in 1995 on Australia's North West Shelf gauged significant oil and gas discoveries. The Corallina prospect in the northern Bonaparte basin confirmed expectations for the region raised by discovery in 1994 of Laminaria field. Also in Bonaparte, delineation was under way on the Bayu and Undan gas discoveries.

Discoveries in 1995 in the Carnarvon basin included Perseus gas field on the Rankin platform, where reserves are estimated at several trillion cubic feet. Carnarvon's exploration record includes oil strikes at Blencathra, Wonnich, and Agincourt.

Australia in its 1996 offshore tender was seeking work program bids on acreage in proven producing areas, as well as in frontier areas, in water depths ranging from extremely shallow to as deep as 2,000 ft.

Queensland oil shale

A Canadian-Australian combine agreed to proceed with an oil shale development program in Queensland, Australia.

Phased development at the port city of Gladstone could produce an ultimate 85,000 b/d of oil from the Stuart deposit on Queensland's Coral Sea coast.

In the first phase, combine member Suncor Inc., Calgary, will spend $7 million (Canadian) to conduct preliminary engineering and complete project negotiations. Its partners are Australia's Southern Pacific Petroleum NL and Central Pacific Minerals NL, Sydney, which will contribute $3 million to the first-phase study.

Suncor will operate the project with a 50% interest. Its Australian partners will share the remaining 50%.

Suncor, one of two producers in Alberta's Athabasca oil-

sands region, said the Stuart deposit could hold the equivalent of 3 billion bbl of shale oil. The Australian project is Suncor's first venture outside Canada.

The Queensland project involves scaling up from an earlier pilot plant to a Stage 1 demonstration plant expected to produce 4,500 b/d at a capital cost of $217 million (Australian), including $17 million for contingencies. The program will be entitled to research and development tax benefits.

Suncor holds the right to acquire an option for $3.5 million to purchase a 22.4% interest in Southern Pacific and Central Pacific. The option can be exercised within 6 months after the plant begins operation.

Stage 2 calls for scale-up to a commercial module of 14,800 b/d. Full commercial operations will occur at Stage 3, which involves replication of commercial modules to produce 65,000-85,000 b/d and an upgrade to allow a greater range of products.

The agreement anticipates building of a second full-size commercial unit on which, after a defined period, Suncor will pay its Australian partners a royalty on revenues from its 50% share of production. Royalty will be based on a sliding scale between 2% at a West Texas intermediate crude oil price of $20/bbl and 5.5% at more than $35/bbl, both in 1995 U.S. dollars.

To secure development within a reasonable period, either Suncor or Southern Pacific-Central Pacific may proceed, under certain conditions, with development without the other.

Bechtel Corp., San Francisco, agreed in principle to build the plant. It is working toward detailed engineering design and a cost estimate that will corroborate its estimate for a fixed-price construction contract with performance guarantees.

The Australian companies said the Stuart deposit could be capable of producing 200,000-250,000 b/d at full development. They called the development agreement with Suncor "the first crucial step" in development of their resources, which they estimate at 20 billion bbl of shale oil.

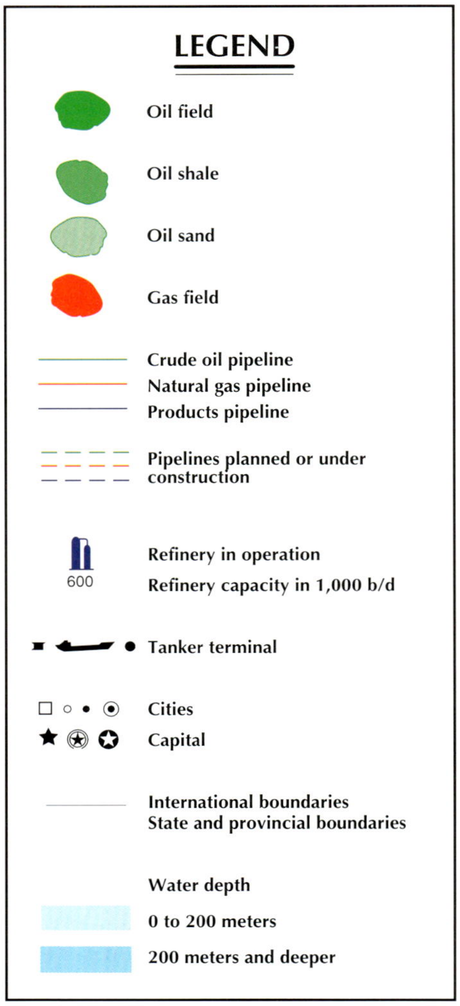

BANGLADESH

CAPITAL: Dhaka
MONETARY UNIT: Taka
REFINING CAPACITY: 31,200 b/cd
PRODUCTION: 1,000 b/d
RESERVES: 5 million bbl

The government of Bangladesh expected to open a new exploration licensing round by yearend 1996, following approval of a new model production sharing contract.

Initial interest in new licenses from international companies was high, and a number of new contracts are expected to be signed in 1997, said Wood Mackenzie Consultants Ltd., Edinburgh.

State firm Petrobangla was expected to give companies 90 days to submit bids once the exploration round is announced. It was not known whether the round would include rights to undeveloped or partially developed fields.

"If subsequent drilling is as successful as it has been in the past," said Wood Mackenzie, "then the future for the oil and gas sector in Bangladesh appears very promising."

Five licenses were awarded foreign firms as a result of 1993 reforms to petroleum legislation: Blocks 15 and 16 offshore to Cairn, and land Blocks 12, 13, and 14 to Occidental Petroleum Corp.

The Oxy license areas contain a number of gas/condensate fields operated by Petrobangla, said the analyst. One includes the Jalalabad discovery, which Oxy has a license to develop.

Cairn has drilled two wells in Sangu field and acquired seismic data on Block 15 with the aim of drilling a new pool wildcat in early 1997. This license includes rights to an existing discovery, Kutubdia, in the bay.

Oxy was said to have applied to drill an exploration well in the Moulavi Bazar prospect on Block 14 and was expected to spud the well in 1997.

Petrobangla has drilled a number of wells, most notably making the Shahbazpur discovery in 1995, which has estimated reserves of 400 bcf of gas.

Wood Mackenzie reckoned remaining total reserves in Bangladesh amount to 60 million bbl of liquids and 10.6 tcf of gas. Production was estimated at 4.5 million bbl of liquids and 3 tcf of gas.

Most of the fields are in the eastern fold belt and have stacked Miocene and Pliocene reservoirs.

Petrobangla began producing the country's only oil field, Sylhet, in 1987. However, wax buildup in the export pipeline led to the field being shut in during July 1994, and there is no sign of Sylhet being put back on stream.

Associated liquids production amounts to about 1,500 b/d, said Wood Mackenzie, but in 1998 Petrobangla's Kailastila field is expected to begin raising output from 600 b/d to a plateau of 2,000 b/d in 2005.

Also, Oxy is expected to bring on stream Jalalabad field in 1997, with the aim of reaching plateau liquids production of 1,000 b/d by 1999.

"Gas production has been gently but continuously increasing since 1985," said Wood Mackenzie. "In 1994 gas production was boosted when Petrobangla's Rashidpur field was brought on stream. Initial production of 25 MMcfd quickly rose to just less than 100 MMcfd by end 1995."

From a total 330 MMcfd in 1985, gas production is expected to reach a peak of more than 1.2 bcfd in 2001 as Cairn and Oxy complete developments.

"Petrobangla has plans to bring several other fields on stream over the next 2 years, including Belabo, Fenchuganj, Beanibazar, and possibly Shahbazpur," the analyst said.

The gas and gas/condensate reservoirs are mainly the Lower Miocene Bhugan and lower Middle Miocene Boka Bil formations. Both formations make up the Surma Group.

"It is expected that Occidental will bring Jalalabad field on stream during 1997, followed by Cairn with Sangu field in 1998. Both Occidental and Cairn are considering independent power projects."

A serious power generation shortage is developing in Bangladesh, but successful exploration could lead to available gas supply outstripping total domestic gas demand.

"So an alternative market would need to be developed," concluded Wood Mackenzie. "One possible solution would be to export gas to the east coast of India or across the Bangladesh/India border to Calcutta. However, for this to happen, a number of political hurdles would need to be cleared."

Unocal energy project

Unocal Corp. proposed an energy project to the government of Bangladesh that could involve development of gas resources and construction of a gas-fired power plant.

As a first step, Unocal signed an agreement for a joint technical study with state-owned Petrobangla to delineate Shahbazpur gas field in southern Bangladesh on the Bay of Bengal.

Unocal's proposal calls for a multiphase, integrated project.

The first phase, bearing a price tag of $250 million, would include delineation and development of Shahbazpur gas field to produce 30 MMcfd and construction of a 40 km gas transmission line to Barisal and a 150,000 kw power generating plant. Start-up could occur in 1999 if technical, contractual, and financial details are resolved.

John G. Vandermeer, president of Unocal Asia-Pacific Ventures Ltd., Singapore, called the proposal "an exciting project that links a known natural gas resource with a ready, growing market."

From Barisal, electricity from the proposed power plant could tie into the Bangladesh grid. The plant in the first phase could be expanded to 300,000 kw, depending upon Unocal's power sales contract that would be negotiated.

Petrobangla found Shahbazpur field in 1995. At that time, it estimated the field could contain about 400 bcf of recoverable gas.

The second and third phases of the proposed project would include a fertilizer plant and a cement plant. These additional projects that use gas would hinge on available gas resources and results of further feasibility studies.

INDIA

CAPITAL: Delhi
MONETARY UNIT: Rupee
REFINING CAPACITY: 1 million b/cd
PRODUCTION: 673,000 b/d
RESERVES: 4 billion bbl

India continues to lag behind its huge potential as a major player on world energy markets.

All forecasts point to strong growth rates in oil and gas demand continuing well into the next century.

Government estimates see India's refined products demand soaring to 3 million b/d by 2010 from 1.4-1.6 million b/d in fiscal 1996-97. If India's natural gas demand growth continues at its current rate, it would double every 5 years, the government predicts.

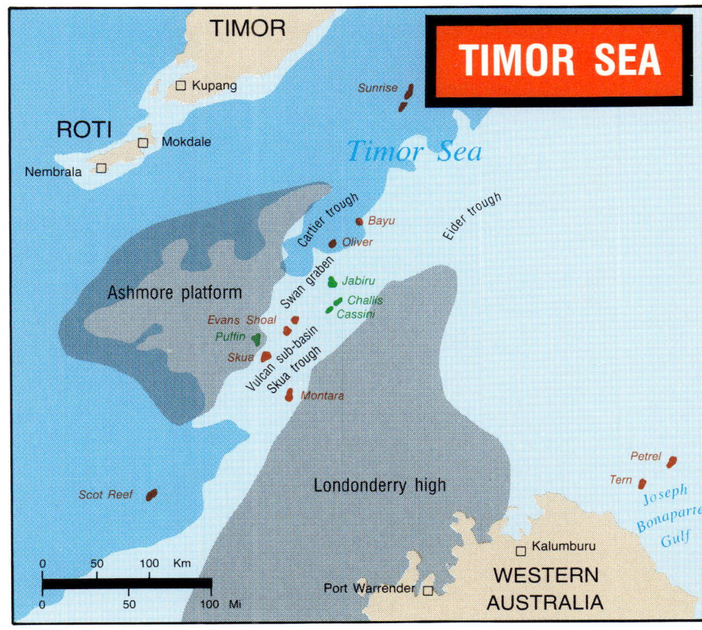

However, although it is the world's second largest country in terms of population—possibly overtaking leader China in the next century—India's energy intensity is among the lowest, lagging behind countries less-developed.

Per capita consumption of energy in India of about 1.7 bbl of oil equivalent (BOE)/year is much lower than the world average of 11.6 BOE/year. At the top end of the scale are the U.S. and Canada, where per capita energy consumption is more than 35 times that of India. Even China, often cited for its untapped energy consumption potential, consumes about 3% more per capita than does India.

At the same time, India is moving slowly to privatize and deregulate its energy sector. It is trying to attract foreign capital to a sector in need of investments the government estimates at as much as $120 billion by 2010. About $60-80 billion of that sum will be needed for upstream projects in order for India to approach oil and gas self-sufficiency.

That's not out of line with private sector projections for petroleum sector investment needs. ABN-Amro Bank NV of Netherlands estimates combined investment needs in India for upstream and downstream oil and gas projects at $28-48 billion by 2000 and $90 billion by 2010.

Scant success to date

Despite the potential, India's attempts to attract private sector investment in its energy sector, particularly in oil and gas, have seen scant success.

Although foreign companies have shown only limited interest in India's exploration offerings—mostly because of what they see as inadequate terms and less than prime acreage—their interest remains strong in participating in India's downstream.

Companies have submitted proposals covering a combined 1.3 million b/d of added refining capacity in India. Of that total, more than 1 million b/d is grassroots capacity to be added mainly by joint ventures with foreign companies.

Because of political infighting over regulatory and fiscal reforms, however, many of these proposals—notably the foreign joint venture projects, some of which date back to the 1980s—are being held in abeyance.

Investors' reluctance is underpinned by rough and tumble national and local politics that make it difficult for energy projects to get off the ground in India. Provincial politics almost scuttled a megaproject promoted by Enron Corp. that

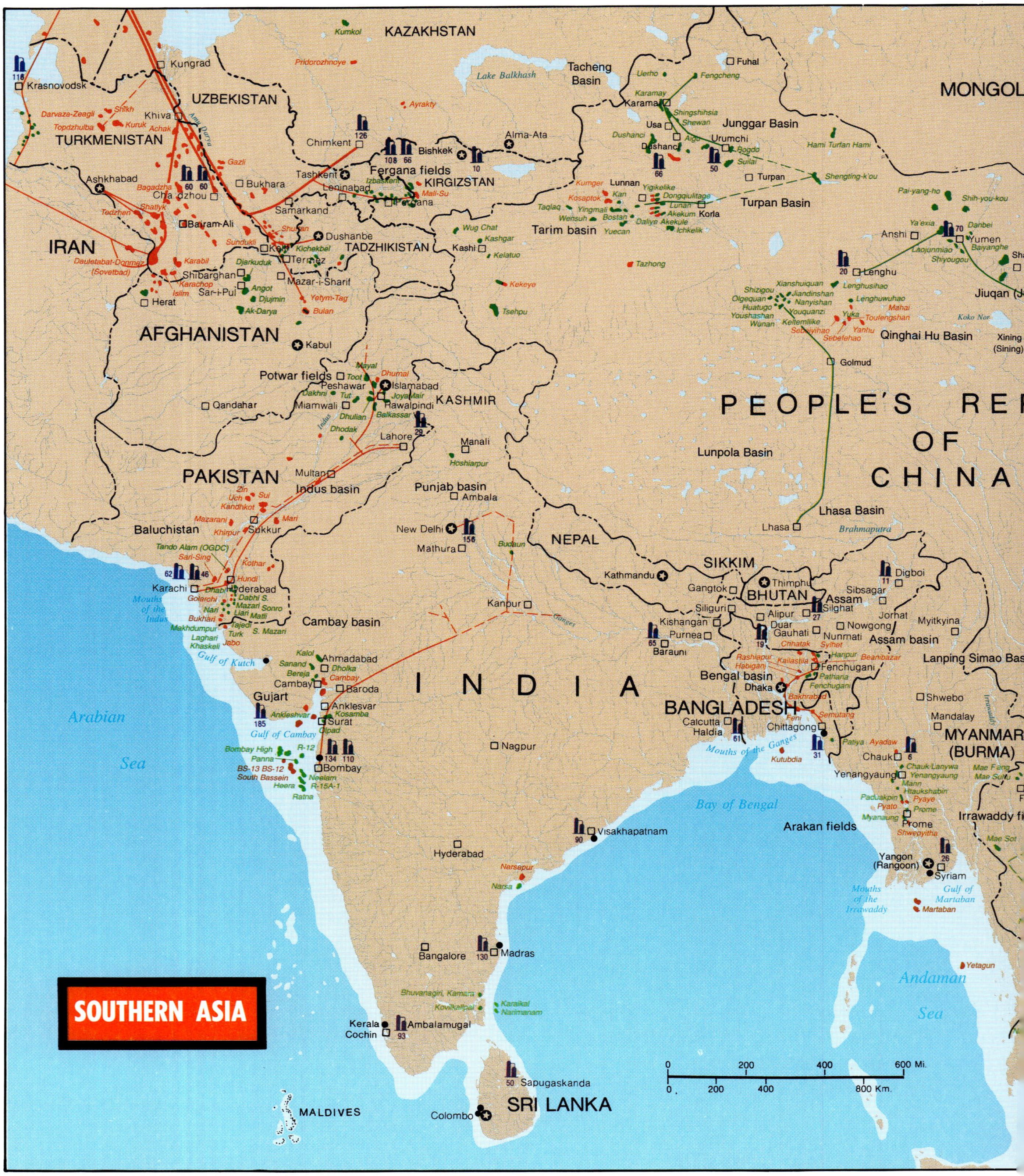

combined a major electrical power plant with South Asia's first liquefied natural gas receiving terminal.

Another negative factor for investors is the seemingly intractable—from a political standpoint—problem of removing heavy subsidies for domestically consumed petroleum products in India. New Delhi knows any petroleum sector deregulation and privatization effort will remain hamstrung by such subsidies, yet any attempt to scrap subsidies will prove politically explosive in this poverty-ridden nation.

Until recently, the petroleum industry in India was highly regulated, with the government exercising virtually total control.

However, a number of factors have spurred calls for a change in the attitude of the Indian government, notably the country's ever-growing tab for imports of crude oil and refined products.

Need for reforms

The Indian government has long been acutely aware of the need for significant investment in the country's petroleum industry.

That awareness led to the petroleum sector being placed among the first industries in India targeted for economic reform this decade.

The petroleum reform process began about 5 years ago, when the leading state owned oil and gas producing company, Oil & Natural Gas Commission (ONGC), began a gradual divestment of many areas that was to accompany its transformation from a government agency to a full-fledged, independent operating company designed along private sector lines.

At the same time, oil and gas exploration and development, for years confined to public sector firms ONGC and Oil India Ltd. (OIL), was opened to foreign oil companies.

The restructuring of the petroleum sector in India began in earnest when the Asian Development Bank (ADB), supported by the World Bank, laid down severe conditions for grants of loans to the Indian government. The loans were ostensibly meant for restructuring the petroleum sector but instead were used to help the country weather its serious balance of payments problem.

ADB insisted that ONGC be restructured, many oil field services be handed over to the private sector, and the government gradually divest its equity stake in the oil and gas industry. The liberalization of terms for oil and gas exploration by the private sector and foreign companies also was among conditions attached to ADB funding.

Ironically, much changed in the hydrocarbon sector after another 2 years, when the ADB loans were no longer needed.

Many new onshore and offshore areas were opened for exploration by the private sector, and oil fields discovered but not developed by ONGC and OIL were offered to other companies for development.

Crude, refining capacities

India has relatively small oil reserves, estimated at about 0.5% of the world total.

India's reserves to production ratio is about 22 years. Projections called for average production of 740,000 b/d in fiscal 1995-96.

Indian refining capacity remains below domestic needs. Combined throughput capacity of India's 13 refineries at the end of fiscal 1994-95 was 1.128 million b/d.

Imports of refined products thus will remain strong. India imported 277,800 b/d of products in fiscal 1994-95.

Because of this shortfall, India's position as a net importer of crude oil and refined products means that more than one third of the country's foreign exchange goes for petroleum imports.

Demand estimates suggest that India could support addition of at least 500,000 b/d of refining capacity, government officials contend.

Self-sufficiency

The long emphasis on oil self-sufficiency has kept New Delhi focused on the urgency of finding more oil fields.

The dilemma of an ever widening domestic crude supply/demand shortfall led to a novel proposal voiced at an oil and gas conference organized by Tata Energy Research Institute (TERI) in New Delhi.

This proposal holds that India should now focus on becoming a powerful oil consumer like Japan instead of trying to raise indigenous production.

This idea is not likely to find much favor with the Indian government, which is committed to searching for more oil either through operations of national oil companies or attracting foreign participation.

The Petroleum Ministry went so far as to ask state-owned refining companies Indian Oil Corp. (IOC), Hindustan Petroleum Corp. Ltd. (HPCL), and Bharat Petroleum Corp. Ltd. (BPCL) to form a joint exploration company that would supplement the exploration efforts of ONGC and OIL.

That initiative was later scrapped, but the same companies have been asked to set up joint ventures with private parties for exploration.

Meantime, New Delhi is evaluating various policy options for devising a new oil and gas exploration policy it hopes will attract significantly more exploration risk capital from a broad spectrum of international companies.

Downstream interest

Because of the prospect for market growth, all the majors that left India after the nationalization of oil companies in the

MYANMAR (BURMA)
THAILAND
CAMBODIA
LAOS
VIETNAM
MALAYSIA
MALAYA
SINGAPORE
BRUNEI
SARAWAK
SUMATRA
KALIMANTAN (BORNEO)
INDONESIA
JAVA
HAINAN DAO
NATUNA ISLAND (INDONESIA)
KEPULAUAN LINGGA
BANGKA
BELITUNG
MADURA
BALI
ANDAMAN ISLANDS
NICOBAR ISLANDS
SIMEULUE
NIAS
SIBERUT
SIPORA
PAGAI UTARA
PAGAI SELATAN
ENGGANO
Bay of Bengal
Gulf of Martaban
Andaman Sea
INDIAN OCEAN
Gulf of Thailand
Gulf of Tonkin
South China Sea
Java Sea
Strait of Malacca
Sunda Strait
Noakhali
Patuakhali
Chittagong
Patiya
Shahbazpur
Mandalay
Ayadaw
Yenangyaung
Chauk/Lanywa
Mann
Htaukshabin
Paduakpin
Pyaye
Pyato
Prome
Myanaung
Shwepyitha
Yangon (Rangoon)
Martaban
Yetagun
Mae Fang
Mae Suhn
Chiang Mai
Nan
Vientiane
Uttaradit
Loei
Mae Sot
Sirikit
KDN-1
Pru Krathiarn
Bung Ya
Phu Horm
Nam Phong
Chonnabot
Khon Kaen
Sisaket
Sawng Neung
Saraburi
Kanchanaburi
Bangkok
Sri Racha
Rayong
Phnom Penh
Sihanoukville
Nang Nuan
Khanom
Si Thammarot
Kaphong
Surat
Pladang
Pakarang
Dara
Erawan
Baanpot
Tantawan
Platong
Platong S.
Trat
Satun
Jakrawan
Funan
Bongkot
Songkhla
Bua Ban
17-B-1
Pilong
Lawit
Damer
Bintang
Noring
Bedong
Tujoh
Jemeh
Sepat
Inas
Bujang
Tangga
Larut
Bubu
Lerek
Tabu
Barat
Besar
Angsi
Duyong
Kakap
Belumut
Sotong
Telebuk
Kerisi
Belanak
Malong
Tembang
Pulai
Udang
Sembilang
Buntal
Kepiting
Natuna
Bursa
Dua-1X
Dai Hung
Bach Ho
Rong
Hanoi
Hai Phong
Tien Hai
Weizhou 11-1
Weizhou 10-3
Weizhou 6-1
Haik'ou
Jinfeng
Wenchang 9-2
Yacheng 13-1
Macau
Hong Kong
Moaming
Lufeng 13-1
Lufeng 15-1
Xijiang 24-3
Xijiang 30-2
Huizhou 21-1
Huizhou 26-1
Liuhua 4-1
Liuhua 11-1
Hue
Da Nang
Nha Trang
Ho Chi Minh City
Vung Tau
Long Xuyen
Kutaradja
Julu Rayeu
Serang Jaya
Perlak
Pangkalanberandon
Belawan
Medan
Meulabah
Pinang
Kerteh
Kuala Lumpur
Port Dickson
Singapore
Batam
Sibolga
Dumai
Pinang
Bangko
Buaya
Menggala
Mandar
Duri
Libo
Minik
Langgak
Minas
Topaz
Zamrud
Mellbur
Pekanbaru
Lirik Fields
N. Palai
S. Palai
Andan
Lirik
Binio
Sago
Molek
Bukittinggi
Djambi
Setiti
Tempino
Bedjubang
Limau Fields
Suban Burong
Sumpal
Dayung
Keban
Bentayan
Sembar
Sungei Gerong
Palembang
Muraraenim Fields
Tanjung Laban
Benakat
Sambar
Kampong Minyak
Taham
Langu
T. Djimar
Ogan Timur
T. Tiga
Batukeras
Telukbetung
Intan
Indri
Windurl
Sundari
Karmila
Krisna
Cinta
Nora
AV
AA
Rama
KN
Ardjuna
HZE
MB
E
F
Arimbi
Jakarta
Sidong
Cirebon
Jatibarang
Randegan
Bandung
Rembang
Ledok
Nglobo
Petak
Camar
Semarang
Candi
Banyubang
Kendangan
Cepu
Kawengan
Surabaja
Waron
Cilacap
Jogjakarta
Wonokromo
Singaradja
Pontianak
Kuching
Bintulu
Temana
Patricia
J4
W. Bayan
C2
D12
E8
F28
F6
M4
B23
M1
M3
Jintan
Serla
F27
Bijan
F14
B11
B12
Magpie
Iron Duke
Samarang
Kecil
Glayzer
Miri
Kuala Belait
Seria
Bandar Seri Begawan
Labuan
Mamburungan
S.W. Emerald
Tembungo
Erb W.
Kinarut
Barton
S. Furious
St. Joseph
Kudat
Kota Kinabalu
Sangkulirang
Kerindingon
Semberah
Badak
Sanga-Sanga
Pamaguan
Kerendan
Balikpapan
Louise
Sanggur
Bangkerak
Mutiara
Sepingg
Wailawi
Kambatin
Tandjung
Tapian Timur
Warukin Tengah
Warukin Selatan
Palangkaraya
Bandjarmasin
31
6
26
61
166
207
123
4
75
80
105
114
227
255
405
270
47
285
45
8
240
170
20°
15°
10°
5°
0°
5°
10°
95°
100°
105°
110°
115°
0 50 100 150 200 250 miles
0 100 200 300 400 kilometers
MALAYSIA-INDONESIA

ung
PACIFIC
OCEAN
ON
PHILIPPINES
zon City
nila
angas
Philippine
Sea
LEYTE
PANAY
Bacolod
Tabango
Tacloban
103
Cebu
EGROS
BOHOL
MINDANAO
Davao
Champion
Samarang Kecil
Pelican
Glayzer
Iron Duke
Petrel
SABAH
Magpie
Osprey
Egret
Bandar Seri Begawan
Fairley
Fairley Baram
Ampa
S.W. Ampa
Baram
Tali
Seria
W. Lutong
BRUNEI
Kuala Belait
Rasau
SARAWAK
elebes
Sea
Manado
Soasiu
Molucca
Sea
1-X TBM
Kasim
Jaya
Walio
Salawati
Sele
Sorong
Klamono
Wiriagar
Manokwani
Mogo
Wasian
Steenkool
Bismarck
Sea
Ceram Sea
Bula
Fakfak
Hollandia
BURU
CERAM
Ambon
IRIAN JAYA
Wewak
Kendari
PAPUA
NEW GUINEA
Banda
Sea
Madang
Elvala
Ketu
Elevala
Juha
Hides
Agogo
Iagifu
S.E. Hedinia
2XGobe
4XGobe
S.E. Gobe
Bwata
Barikewa
Kuru
Omati
Puri
Mt. Hagen
Goroka
Lae
ARU
Lake Murray
Kikori
Baimuru
Uramu
Solomon
Sea
Sea
TANIMBAR
Gulf
of
Papua
Pasca
Dili
Ossulari
Aliambata
Matai
TIMOR
Arafura
Sea
Pandora-B1X
Pandora-1X
Port Moresby
Kupang
Roti
Bayu
Jabiru
Challis
Cassini
Puffin
Timor
Sea
Darwin
Gulf
of
Carpentaria
Coral
Sea
Bonaparte
Gulf
AUSTRALIA
125°
130°
135°
140°
145°

early 1970s have returned eager to invest in the liberalized economy. Leading the charge are Exxon Corp., Mobil Corp., Royal Dutch/Shell Group, and Caltex.

These companies have formed joint ventures in lubricants production and marketing with public sector firms IOC, HPCL, BPCL, and IBP Co. Ltd.

Oil majors were represented at the New Delhi conference, but their hopes of an early decision on dismantling the administered price mechanism were dashed at the outset when Finance Minister Manmohan Singh ruled out deregulation in the immediate future.

The upshot to prospective downstream investors is that most are awaiting some decision moving toward deregulation. First steps would include proposals to reduce tariffs on petroleum products to make refining more attractive.

INDONESIA

CAPITAL: Jakarta
MONETARY UNIT: Rupiah
REFINING CAPACITY: 804,745 b/cd
PRODUCTION: 1.5 million b/d
RESERVES: 5 billion bbl

Indonesia's state-owned Pertamina opened its 1996 tender of acreage for exploration and development through joint ventures with foreign partners.

Included in the offering were three tracts in Indonesia's eastern frontier on which Pertamina was seeking production sharing contracts (PSCs). The blocks qualify for incentives Pertamina introduced in December 1993 to boost interest in underexplored areas.

That incentive package was available for onshore and offshore acreage in eastern Indonesia—except for tracts in the Salawati, Bintuni, and Seram basins—and for frontier acreage in western Indonesia.

Although geological data are sparse in eastern Indonesia, companies working in the geologically complex region have reported pre-Tertiary discoveries at several sites.

Also in its 1996 tender, Pertamina was seeking PSCs on three tracts in western Indonesia.

The company, in addition, was offering 23 areas for exploration through direct negotiations, including 22 blocks for PSCs and one for a joint operating agreement (JOA), and two tracts for development through technical assistant contracts (TACs).

Frontier tracts

Two of the eastern frontier tracts—Sabo and Rabe offshore blocks—included in Indonesia's 1996 tender are in the Southeast Timor Sea region, about midway between Timor Island and the Indonesian-Australian Zone of Cooperation (ZOC) in Timor Gap.

Sabo covers an area of about 4,570 sq km and Rabe 6,500 sq km.

The third frontier tract in eastern Indonesia, Kaimo, covers 10,000 sq km onshore in Irian Jaya, near the Arafuru Sea coast.

Terms covering exploration and development on the eastern frontier tracts allow contractors to retain 35% of net oil production and 40% of net gas production. Earlier incentives allowed companies:

- 20% of net oil production on frontier acreage and 25% of net oil produced in more than 1,500 m of water.
- 40% of net gas produced on frontier acreage and 45% of net gas produced in more than 1,500 m of water.

Limited seismic data and geophysical reports on Sabo and Rabe are available.

Included in data packages for the Southeast Timor Sea are 1,530 line-km of regional seismic data collected by Pertamina in December 1992.

Pertamina said Paleozoic and Mesozoic depocenters in the Indonesian Timor Sea indicate the possible existence of hydrocarbon kitchens.

In addition, the Geco-Prakla unit of Schlumberger in 1995-96 acquired 3,408 line-km of 2D seismic data whose grids merge with about 2,000 line-km of seismic data on the Australian Timor Sea.

Geco-Prakla acquired the data in cooperation with Indonesia's Directorate General of Oil & Gas.

Similarities with ZOCA

Pertamina said available evidence shows strong geologic similarities between areas covered by Sabo and Rabe and ZOC Area A (ZOCA).

Phillips ZOC unit of Phillips Petroleum Co. and partners said the 2 Bayu appraisal on ZOCA Block 91-13, about 185 miles northwest of Australia, cut a thin, productive hydrocarbon section above 10,417 ft total depth, extending the eastern flank of Bayu gas/condensate field. Partners plugged the $6.5 million hole without testing.

Phillips and its partners in mid-1996 planned to spud their 4 Bayu appraisal well, with a fifth well planned in fourth quarter 1996.

Partners were studying several scenarios for developing Bayu, including a program based on an onshore liquefied natural gas facility using Phillips technology.

Pre-Tertiary highlights

Companies working in eastern Indonesia have established oil production from Tertiary pay in the Salawati, Bintuni, and Seram basins.

Pre-Tertiary formations also appear productive in the eastern frontier, where PSC contractors were appraising discoveries at Seram Island and Irian Jaya.

The Kufpec (Indonesia) Ltd. unit of Kuwait Foreign Petroleum Corp. and partner ARCO Indonesia Oil & Gas Co. in fourth quarter 1996 planned to spud their 2 Oseil appraisal well on the 1.883 million acre Seram block.

ARCO is operator of the Wiriagar Deep play involving two PSC areas onshore and offshore Irian Jaya.

ARCO and partners were delineating the Mesozoic Wiriagar Deep discovery with a series of wells on the Berau block, mostly off Irian Jaya in Bintuni Bay. The program was appraising intervals at 6,000-10,000 ft indicated in late 1994 at 1 Wiriagar Deep wildcat. The discovery flowed 90 MMcfd of gas from Triassic sandstone on the Wiriagar block, an onshore tract in western Irian Jaya adjacent to Berau.

Atlantic Richfield Wiriagar Inc. holds an 80% interest in the Wiriagar PSC and the KG Wiriagar Petroleum Ltd. unit of Japan's Kanamatsu Co. the other 20%. Partners on the Berau block are operator Atlantic Richfield Berau Inc. with a 48% interest, KG Berau Petroleum Ltd. 12%, Occidental Berau of Indonesia Inc. 22%, and Nippon Oil Exploration (Berau) 18%.

On Berau, partners logged a flow of more than 100 MMcfd of gas from six intervals on drillstem tests of the 2 Wiriagar Deep appraisal well. Early in 1996, the 3 Wiriagar Deep flowed about 35 MMcfd of gas, again on drillstem tests of multiple zones.

Berau partners planned to spud two more offshore appraisals on the block in 1996.

Pertamina also lists as significant Mesozoic discoveries in eastern Indonesia the 1 Loku wildcat in the Maluku Sea and the 1 South Onin wildcat off Irian Jaya. The 1 Loku flowed 1.7 MMcfd of gas on tests of Permo-Triassic fractured granite basement, and 1 South Onin flowed 3.5 MMcfd of gas from Cretaceous Upper Kemblengan sandstone, the state company said.

JAPAN

CAPITAL: Tokyo
MONETARY UNIT: Yen
REFINING CAPACITY: 5 million b/cd
PRODUCTION: 14,000 b/d
RESERVES: 50 million bbl

Japan's downstream oil industry was in turmoil in 1996 following a deregulation step early in the year that allowed import of petroleum products by non-refiners.

That move, together with a sharp drop in refining margins, falling retail gasoline prices, and a service station sector on the brink of collapse, pointed to massive changes in the way the country's refiners and marketers do business.

The trouble began in autumn 1994, when the government of Prime Minister Morihiro Hosokawa disclosed plans to scrap the Provisional Law on the Importation of Specified Petroleum Products (Plispp), which had been introduced 10 years earlier.

The immediate effect of the news was a sharp fall in the retail price of gasoline, which by the end of that fiscal year had dropped to 117 yen/l. from 123 yen/l. the previous April. This was disaster for the domestic operations of Japanese oil companies, nearly all of which are downstream.

As a result of declining gasoline prices, the aggregate fiscal 1994 profit for the country's top publicly listed seven refiners—Nippon Oil, Showa Shell Sekiyu KK, Mitsubishi Oil Co., Tonen Corp., Cosmo Oil Co., General Sekiyu KK, and Japan Energy Corp.—fell 23%.

As retail prices continued to plunge, reaching 107 yen/l., refining and marketing profits also continued to fall. In fiscal 1995, the seven oil giants saw an additional 46% decline in their aggregate pretax profit. Nippon Oil, for example, posted its first operating loss in 9 years. Moreover, the drop in combined profits for the entire refining/marketing sector—including nonlisted companies—was even steeper at about 55%.

A new price system in Japan attempted to align wholesale prices of three major petroleum products—gasoline, fuel oil, and kerosine, possibly offsetting declines in gasoline prices with increases in prices of the other products.

However, the new pricing system, on which many Japanese oil companies were basing their fiscal 1996 profit predictions, was not working as well as had been hoped. While gasoline retail prices continued to fall, the implementation of price hikes for diesel and kerosine proved difficult. This was particularly true of diesel prices, with oil majors facing stiff resistance against price hikes from the country's powerful road transportation lobby groups.

Restructuring

Most of the country's oil companies were restructuring as a result of the upheaval in their market.

Nippon Oil Co. and its wholly owned subsidiary Nippon Petroleum Refining Co. planned to cut combined staff levels from 4,286 to about 3,700 by the end of fiscal 1999.

Japan Energy Corp, meanwhile, started a program that included cutting its headquarters staff by half during 5 years. It also planned not to hire new graduates in spring 1997 for the first time in its history. In 1996, it hired just 40 new graduates, compared with 440 in 1993.

Other oil majors, such as Showa Shell, Esso, and Mitsubishi Oil were implementing early retirement programs, aimed particularly at middle management.

Five major Japanese refiner/marketers—Showa Shell Sekiyu KK, Cosmo Oil Co., Japan Energy Corp., General Sekiyu KK, and Mobil Sekiyu KK—planned to integrate their oil storage complexes in Kochi Prefecture on the southern island of Shikoku by summer 1997 in a bid to trim distribution costs.

Showa Shell and General Sekiyu will close their tank farms in Kochi, while Japan Energy will halve the capacity of its storage. Cosmo Oil and Mobil Oil will expand their facilities.

The combined storage capacity will total half the current 40,000 kl. when the integration is complete. Operation of the facilities will be consigned to a Japan Freight Railway Co. affiliate specializing in transportation of oil products.

Mitsubishi Oil, Mobil Sekiyu, and General Sekiyu KK, meanwhile, were interconnecting their tank farms at Takamatsu, also on Shikoku Island.

Storage facility integration by Japan's oil companies appeared likely to increase.

According to some estimates, the number of service stations in Japan will shrink to 40,000 from 60,000 in 1996 within a few years. And Japanese companies are expected to shrink their vast wholesale networks and begin selling directly to retail outlets.

Consolidation of Japanese marketing operations was likely.

KOREA, SOUTH

CAPITAL: Seoul
MONETARY UNIT: Won
REFINING CAPACITY: 2 million b/cd
PRODUCTION: N.A.
RESERVES: N.A.

BP Chemicals Ltd. continues its global acetyls expansion with a plant start-up in South Korea involving BP technology.

At Ulsan, Asian Acetyls Co., an equal joint venture of BP, Union Carbide Corp., and Samsung, started production at a 150,000 metric ton/year vinyl acetate monomer plant.

Hanwha Energy Co. Ltd. expanded sulfur recovery capacity at its Inchon refinery using an oxygen injection system provided by TPA Inc., Dallas.

The oxygen enrichment technology increased sulfur recovery capacity to 72 metric tons/day from 35 tons/day, well above the guaranteed capacity of 60 tons/day.

Tongyang Nylon Co., Seoul, chose Union Carbide Corp.'s Unipol process for a planned 110,000 metric ton/year polypropylene plant at its Ulsan petrochemical complex.

The unit was scheduled for completion in 1997. The plant will be designed to produce polypropylene homopolymers, random copolymers, and impact copolymers.

Tongyang operates an 80,000 ton/year polypropylene plant at Ulsan, which started up in 1991, using another technology.

MALAYSIA

CAPITAL: Kuala Lumpur
MONETARY UNIT: Ringgit
REFINING CAPACITY: 330,000 b/cd
PRODUCTION: 650,000 b/d
RESERVES: 4 billion bbl

The Malaysia-Thailand Joint Development Area (JDA) of the Gulf of Thailand likely will produce first the Cakerawala find, for which a field development plan was expected by yearend 1996.

Wood Mackenzie Consultants Ltd. said Cakerawala is the most significant of three finds made so far on Block A-18 by the Carigali-Triton Operating Co. (CTOC) joint venture of

Triton Energy Ltd., Dallas, and Malaysian state firm Petroliam Nasional Bhd. (Petronas).

On Block B-17, operated by the Carigali-Pttepi Operating Co. (CPOC) joint venture of Petronas and Thai state firm Petroleum Authority of Thailand (PTT), two gas finds have been made, Muda and Tapi, the first of which is slated for production by the end of 2000.

"The reserves estimate for the JDA is considered to total around 6-7 tcf of natural gas," said Wood Mackenzie, "with associated condensate and black oil."

On Block A-18, the analyst reckons CTOC has proven reserves of 4 tcf of gas in the Cakerawala, Suriya, Bulan, and Bumi reservoirs. These also have total reserves of 30-35 million bbl of oil.

CTOC is expected to develop Block A-18 discoveries in stages, starting with Cakerawala. Wood Mackenzie initially envisages a central processing and production platform with two or three satellite wellhead platforms.

The analyst sees gas exports by pipeline via a planned riser platform in Erawan field off Thailand as the most likely approach, while liquids produced in later development are expected to be loaded into a floating storage unit for tanker export.

"Production from phase one development of Cakerawala could start in 2000," said Wood Mackenzie, "assuming a gas sales contract can be agreed during 1996.

"Production rates from the field are likely to plateau at around 300-400 MMcfd by early next century. Associated liquids production is expected to reach around 5,000 b/d."

The analyst said a memorandum of understanding between the Malaysian and Thai governments lays the foundation for gas sales negotiations: "It appears that PTT and Petronas will jointly be the buyers, although the end market for initial sales will most likely be Thailand."

Estimated reserves for Block B-17 are tentative, based on only one well in each of the Muda and Tapi finds, said Wood Mackenzie.

Gas reserves are pegged at 1.5 tcf for Muda and 1 tcf for Tapi. Block B-17 development is expected to be similar to Block A-18.

MONGOLIA

CAPITAL: Ulaanbaatar
MONETARY UNIT: Tughrik
REFINING CAPACITY: N.A.
PRODUCTION: N.A.
RESERVES: N.A.

Snyder Oil Corp.'s SOCO International Inc. expressed encouragement about its exploration results in northeastern Mongolia, where it planned to complete two oil discovery wells.

The Fort Worth operator planned to complete the 19-2 well and the 21-1 well in the Tamtsag-Hailar basin from oil pay in a conglomeratic sandstone in the upper part of the Lower Cretaceous-Upper Jurassic Tsagaantsav formation.

SOCO International, operator and major shareholder of SOCO Tamtsag Mongolia Inc. (Sotamo), has installed storage tanks at the 19-2 well and planned to begin oil export sales to China. It also planned to develop sources of winterized equipment to support year-round exploration and development operations, said John C. Snyder, SOCO chairman.

"We have acquired over 3,000 km of seismic data and drilled four exploratory wells, two of which are apparent discoveries," Snyder said.

The company controls more than 40,000 sq km, an area one-third the size of Louisiana.

Indicated discoveries

From its early frontier exploration efforts SOCO believes the Tamtsag basin, a major rift basin with numerous large structures, will become a major producing province, Snyder said.

It planned to complete the Sotamo 19-2 well, drilled in 1995, as a low-rate, pumping oil well. SOCO stimulated and swabbed the well in the summer of 1996 trying to clean out lost circulation material that caused severe formation damage to Tsagaantsav in a porous interval below 8,860 ft. The well has produced 41° gravity crude at various rates from perforations at 8,865-8,944 ft.

The 21-1 well, drilled in mid-1996 about 60 miles east of the 19-2, was suspended to await delivery of completion and production equipment. SOCO cored 26 ft of oil-saturated conglomeratic sandstone of 18% porosity in Tsagaantsav. It recovered about 886 ft of estimated 32° gravity oil on a 96 hr drillstem test at 6,274.6-6,307.4 ft.

SOCO identified a number of prospects and well locations updip from the 21-1 well that it planned to drill.

The 22-1 well, drilled in June-July 1996 to TD 8,589 ft, found no oil shows in the Lower Cretaceous-Upper Jurassic interval but encountered 2,100 ft of 28% porosity sandstone above basement.

PAKISTAN

CAPITAL: Islamabad
MONETARY UNIT: Rupee
REFINING CAPACITY: 137,325 b/cd
PRODUCTION: 54,000 b/d
RESERVES: 208 million bbl

Pakistan's Economic Coordination Committee directed gas reserves totaling 270 bcf in Miano gas field, Khanpur district, to be allocated to Sui Southern Gas Co. Ltd.

The gas, found by the Hardy Oil & Gas (U.K.) PPL-Pakistan Oil & Gas Corp. joint venture, will feed diammonium phosphate fertilizer units of Fauji Fertilizer Co. Ltd. and Al Noor Fertilizer Ltd.

Deliveries will be made via a 35-km line to be laid to the existing Karachi pipeline.

National Refinery Ltd., Karachi, will build three crude oil storage tanks at its Karachi complex to increase oil storage capacity by 45,000 metric tons and improve inventory levels to 22 days from 17 days. Project cost is estimated at $2.5 million.

NRL increased its OP-V berth crude tanker capacity to 75,000 dwt from 45,000 dwt, necessitating the increased storage capacity.

A joint venture of Pakistan's state-owned Petroleum Refinery & Petrochemical Corp. (Perac) and Crescent Refining & Marketing Co., Sharjah, established 3 years ago to build a hydrocracker at Perac's 32,000 b/d Karachi refinery, dissolved due to lack of financing.

Cost estimates for the project since the joint venture was signed increased to more than $800 million from $396 million.

Kuwait and Pakistan finalized a $1.2 billion plan to construct a 90,000 b/d, jointly operated refinery in Pakistan's Baluchistan province.

Kuwait Petroleum Corp. and Pakistani State Oil each is to hold a 26% stake in the project, with remaining shares to be offered to private investors. Kuwait aims to boost its foreign refining capacity in Asia to 400,000 b/d.

Pakistan's Oil & Gas Development Corp. and Polish Oil & Gas Co. signed a memorandum of understanding for joint exploration in the Bitrism district of Pakistan's Sindh province. They plan to collect and interpret seismic data and drill 13 exploratory wells.

Japan

Location	No. Refineries	Location	No. Refineries
Chiba	3	Mizushima	2
Sakaide	1	Okinawa	3
Sakai	2	Toyama	1
Yokkaichi City	2	Funakawa	1
Chita	2	Nigata	2
Hyogo	1	Muroran	1
Tokuyama	1	Nigishi	1
Tomakomai	1	Yokohama	1
Kashima	1	Yamaguchi	1
Marifu	1	Ehime	1
Osaka	1	Owasi	1
Kawasaki	5	Sendai	1
Oita	1	Wakayama	2

JAPAN

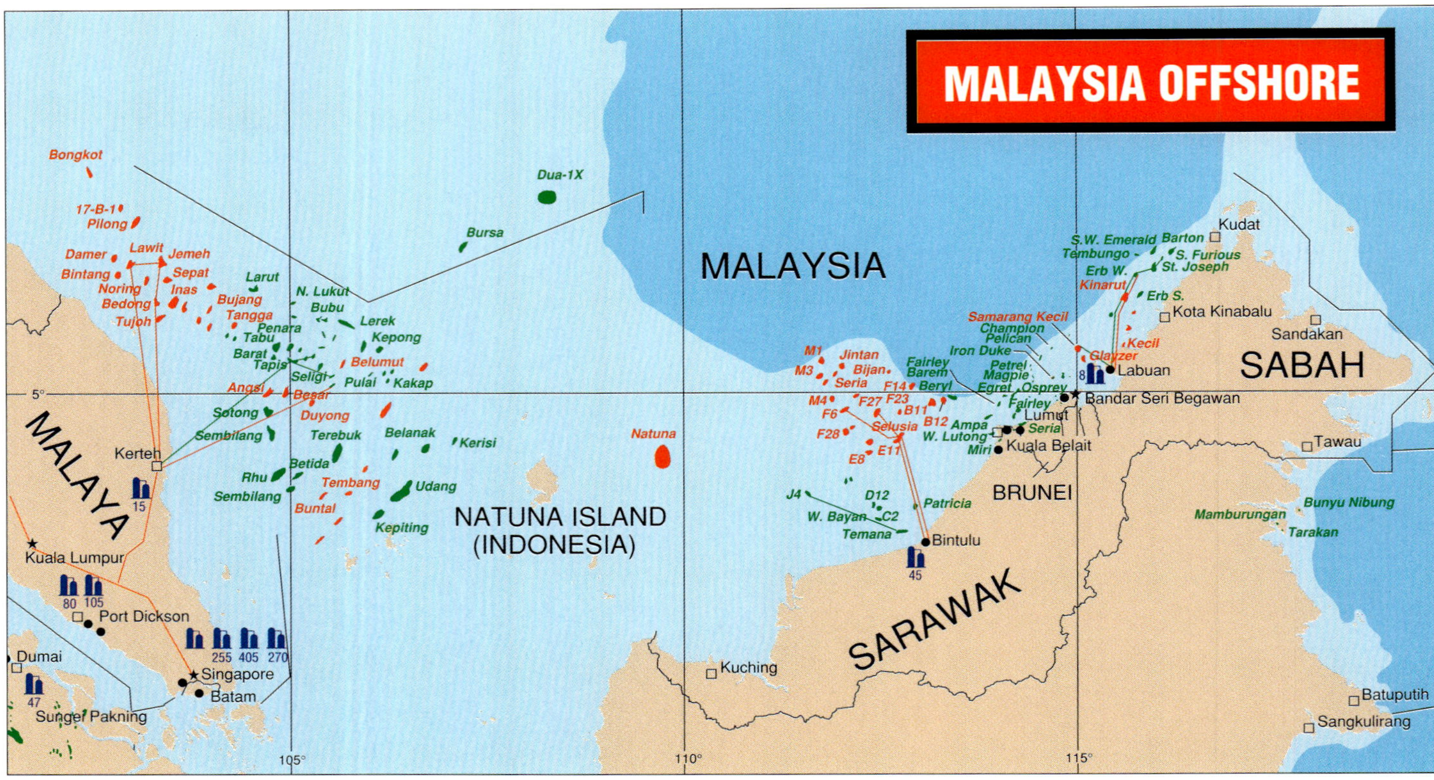

PAPUA NEW GUINEA

CAPITAL: Port Moresby
MONETARY UNIT: Kina
REFINING CAPACITY: N.A.
PRODUCTION: 100,000 b/d
RESERVES: 275 million bbl

International Petroleum Corp. (IPC) and Chevron Corp. agreed to join forces in developing a proposed major natural gas pipeline system linking Papua New Guinea and northern Queensland, Australia.

IPC estimated project development cost at $1.3 billion. Tentative plans called for the project to begin in early to mid-1997, with start-up scheduled in late 1999 or early in 2000.

IPC and a Chevron Corp. unit earlier signed a cooperation agreement to study feasibility of laying a New Guinea-Australia pipeline from Pandora gas field in the Gulf of Papua to Queensland.

When completed, the onshore-offshore pipeline system will total 2,055 km.

IPC, Vancouver, B.C., is operator of Pandora gas field and developer of the Pandora-Queensland gas pipeline project. It is majority interest owner in the PPL 82 joint venture (JV), which consists of IPC 48.189%, Ampolex Ltd. 16.3636%, Command Petroleum Ltd. 12.7273%, Claremont Petroleum NL 6.3636%, Pacarc Energy NL 6.3636%, Secab Niugini 5%, and OSL 5%.

Chevron is operator of Papua New Guinea's Kutubu oil field development and crude oil export project, as well as developer of a proposed Kutubu-Queensland pipeline.

Project highlights

IPC said the PPL 82 JV will contribute its work developing the Pandora-Queensland pipeline, and Chevron will contribute its work on the Kutubu-Queensland pipeline.

A Chevron unit, to be designated later, will take over as project developer.

Pipeline origination point in Papua New Guinea will be the Chevron group's Lake Kutubu area fields in the Papua Highlands.

First segment of the 18 in. main transmission line will consist of 170 km onshore pipeline parallel to an existing field oil export line. The gas line will link with a 100 km subsea segment and connect with a Chevron marine terminal in the Gulf of Papua.

At that point, 135 km of subsea line will be laid to Pandora offshore gas field, off Port Moresby, Papua New Guinea. From Pandora field, 340 km of subsea line will be laid under Torres Strait to near Injinoo onshore, at the tip of Cape York, North Queensland. At Injinoo, the gas will be processed and compressed for further transport after liquids are stripped. The next leg will extend 895 km to Mareeba.

A 16 in. final leg will extend 320 km to terminus at Townsville, Queensland.

A 95 km lateral will connect Weipa, Queensland, to the main line.

First refinery

Papua New Guinea's first refinery moved closer to fruition with project participants signing a memorandum of understanding.

The $250 million refinery at Motukea would have capacity of about 40,000 b/d and start up by mid-1997.

Partners are Australia's PNG Oil Refineries Ltd. and Barclay Mowlem Construction Ltd. and Japan's Chiyoda and Sumitomo Corp. Sumitomo was arranging financing. Construction was awaiting approval of an environmental management plan.

PHILIPPINES

CAPITAL: Manila
MONETARY UNIT: Peso
REFINING CAPACITY: 323,050 b/cd
PRODUCTION: 3,000 b/d
RESERVES: 213 million bbl

Bataan Polyethylene Corp. (BPC) plans to build the Philippines' first polyethylene plant, a $200 million, 200,000 metric ton/year project at Limay, Bataan, slated to start up in 1998.

BPC is a venture of Bataan Polyethylene Holding Corp. 50%, BP Chemicals Ltd. 30%, and Philippines National Oil Co. and Japan's Sumitomo Corp. 10% each. The venture also agreed with state-owned refiner/marketer Petron and Petroleum Corp. of Asia Pacific (Petrocorp) to study feasibility of building a naphtha cracker at the site to provide feedstock for the polyethylene unit and a 160,000 ton/year polypropylene plant Petrocorp expected to bring on stream by yearend 1996.

Pilipinas Shell Petroleum Corp. and Occidental Petroleum Corp. offered to convert the mothballed Bataan nuclear power plant in the Philippines into a 1.2 million kw gas-fired station. Conversion is expected to cost $1.5 billion.

Shell and Oxy plan to supply the plant with gas from their Malampaya/Camago gas fields off Palawan Island. Malampaya and Camago are earmarked for development to provide gas for a number of electricity generation projects.

Petron Corp. selected UOP's CCR platforming process for a 17,000 b/sd catalytic reforming unit to be built at its 147,250 b/d refinery at Limay.

The unit will produce a high octane component for blending unleaded gasoline.

TAIWAN

CAPITAL: Taipei
MONETARY UNIT: New Taiwan Dollar
REFINING CAPACITY: 770,000 b/cd
PRODUCTION: N.A.
RESERVES: N.A.

Chinese Petroleum Corp., Taipei, let a $20 million contract to Tenneco Energy, Houston, and partner CTCI Corp., Taipei, to design Taiwan's first offshore gas pipeline.

The 190 mile pipeline will transport gas from the Yung-An liquefied natural gas receiving terminal on the southern end of the island to markets in the north. Construction is to begin in 1998, with start-up set for 1999.

Formosa Plastics Group was considering building its own tanker fleet to supply the huge petrochemical complex the group is building at Mailiao in northern Taiwan.

FPG tentatively decided to order six to eight 200,000 dwt crude oil tankers at a total cost of about $436 million.

While it would be more expensive to set up its own fleet than to commission shipping companies to transport the crude oil required by the new complex, FPG officials apparently feel the company would be better able to handle risks involved in the transportation of large volumes of crude oil if it had its own fleet.

FPG owns and operates a fleet of 11 petrochemical vessels, each with a loading capacity of 30,000 metric tons.

Tuntex Distinct Corp., Taiwan, plans to build a $2 billion liquefied natural gas storage terminal in northern Taiwan.

The first of three stages is to be completed by 2002 at a cost of $1.5 billion (U.S.). When completed in 2007, the terminal will have capacity for as much as 6 million metric tons/year of LNG.

Chinese Petroleum Corp. and Taiwan Power Co. were reported to be interested in the project, and each could take 10-20% interest.

Taiwan's Chi Mei Corp., which disclosed plans to move into upstream petrochemicals, will postpone plans to set up a styrene monomer plant in the U.S.

It cited soft prices in the decision to temporarily shelve a project involving construction of $200 million, 500,000 metric ton/year SM plant either in Texas or Louisiana.

Sources in Taipei say another factor contributing to the decision was the commencement of a joint venture of Chi Mei and South Korea's Samsung Group to build a 350,000 ton/year SM plant.

Taiwan's Council for Economic Planning and Development (CEPD) took steps to end Taiwan's ban on imports of fuel oil and permit establishment of private refineries.

The move will end CPC's long monopoly on fuel sales in Taiwan. CEPD also recommended CPC follow international practice and offer higher discount rates to its larger customers than its current ceiling of about 8%.

THAILAND

CAPITAL: Bangkok
MONETARY UNIT: Baht
REFINING CAPACITY: 558,250 b/cd
PRODUCTION: 51million b/d
RESERVES: 295 million bbl

The southern Gulf of Thailand is shaping up as a hot exploration and development play.

Carigali-Triton Operating Co. (CTOC) in 1996 moved ahead with plans to develop gas discoveries in the Malaysia-Thailand Joint Development Area (JDA) in the southern Gulf of Thailand.

CTOC deferred further appraisal of Block A-18's Cakerawala field in favor of finishing design by yearend 1996 of the field's development program. CTOC officials expected by yearend to have concluded a sales contract for Cakerawala gas output (see Malaysia).

Elsewhere in the southern Gulf of Thailand, the upstream arm of state-owned Petroleum Authority of Thailand (PTT), PTT Exploration & Production plc (Pttep), was seeking coventurers for its gas-prospective concession block near Bongkot, one of the largest gas fields in the gulf.

A group led by Total hammered out an agreement to boost gas deliveries from Bongkot field, enhancing the attractiveness of the Pttep block.

JDA gas accord

Malaysia-Thailand Joint Authority (MTJA) and its two production-sharing contractors signed a memorandum of understanding to sell natural gas discovered on JDA acreage to the Thai and Malaysian state oil concerns.

The memorandum of understanding lays the guidelines and groundwork for MTJA and its contractors Pttep and Petronas Carigali to negotiate for the sale of natural gas from Blocks B-17 and C-19 to PTT and Petronas.

That followed a letter of intent that called for PTT and Petronas to purchase gas from several JDA gas-related joint ventures.

But the latter memorandum deals specifically with gas from B-17 and C-19, two of three blocks lying in the JDA. The other is Block A-18.

According to Pttep, the memorandum sets forth 2000 as the target date for bringing natural gas from Blocks B-17 and C-19 into production. The gas delivery rate has not been specified and depends on further confirmation of gas reserves on the blocks.

So far, Pttep-Petronas Carigali joint venture has discovered two gas fields on Block B17, Muda and Tapi. The 1 Muda wildcat, about 290 km east of Thailand's Songkhla coast, is the most productive exploratory well drilled in the JDA. It flowed on test natural gas from a number of zones at combined rates of about 70 MMcfd and 726 b/d of condensate.

Early in 1996, Pttep-Petronas Carigali completed an additional 3D seismic campaign of 1,100 sq km. As part of its continuing exploration program, the venture also plans to drill one wildcat and two appraisal wells.

Although PTT and Petronas were described as "potential buyers" of the B-17 and C-19 gas in the memorandum, PTT appeared keener to purchase the gas and transport it via pipeline to Thailand to meet soaring domestic gas demand, especially for power generation.

Gas supply hunt

PTT has been looking for natural gas supplies from neighboring countries including Myanmar, Malaysia, Cambodia, and Viet Nam, as well as domestic fields to meet Thailand's burgeoning gas demand.

Gas discovered in the JDA is split equally between Thailand and Malaysia through MTJA. MTJA is vested with the exclusive rights of exploring for and developing petroleum resources in the JDA under a memorandum of understanding the Thai and Malaysian governments signed in 1979. That agreement ended decades of disputes over which nation owned petroleum deposits underlying the territorial claims.

Malaysia and Thailand are becoming optimistic of a gas development boom in the JDA, following what appeared to be promising gas finds. Through the latest appraisal drilling, about 6-7 tcf of gas reserves is believed to be contained in the once-disputed waters.

That led the two to sign the letter of intent to establish a gas supply deal and principles for other joint venture projects involving the utilization of JDA gas, such as power generation and petrochemicals, subject to approval from their respective governments.

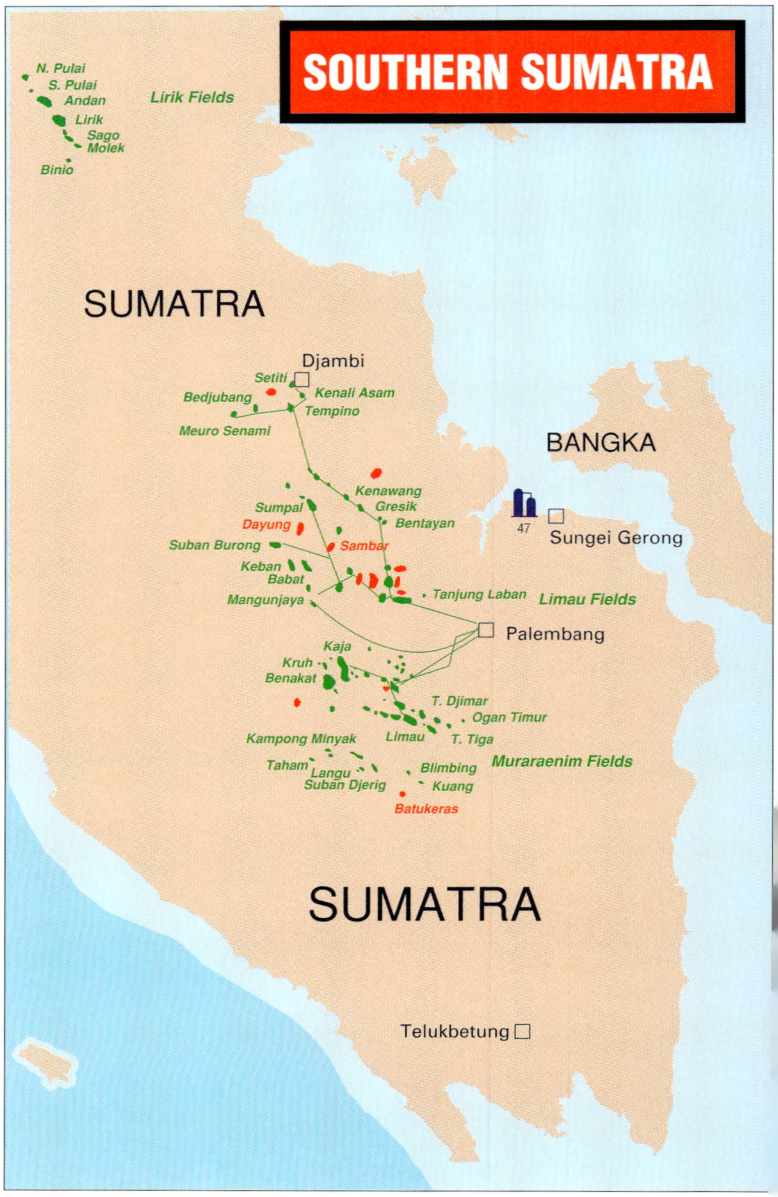

These "strategic alliances" will not be restricted to Thailand but can expand to Malaysia and other countries in Southeast Asia.

While exploration is continuing in the JDA, PTT and Petronas officials have estimated discoveries made to date could support gas production at the rate of 300-500 MMcfd.

Block partners sought

A company source said Pttep's partners in the Bongkot development project—Total, British Gas plc, and Norway's state-owned Den norske stats oljeselskap (Statoil)—are the most likely candidates for partnership in Block B-13/38, now wholly owned by Pttep.

Although other international candidates for partnership were not ruled out, Pttep was focusing on this trio because of their working and equity relationships in Bongkot as well as their experience and knowledge of the geological condition in the general area of Bongkot, the source said.

Pttep had not decided on the size of stake in the 655 sq km tract it wanted to allocate to its potential partners, depending on negotiations.

But one possibility was to follow the same arrangement as in the Bongkot scheme. That called for Pttep to reduce its stake in B-13/38 to 40% while allowing Total to retain a 30% share and assume the operatorship, with interests for British

Gas of 20% and Statoil 10%.

The idea is to ensure that exploration for and development of gas reserves on B-13/38, south of Bongkot, is carried out in concert with Bongkot development, whose facilities could accommodate the new production.

Based on previous geological studies and exploration work undertaken in Bongkot, now producing 350 MMcfd, Pttep believes there is good potential for hydrocarbon accumulation on Block B-13/38.

Bongkot sales accord

The Total group reached an accord to boost natural gas delivery from Bongkot to PTT by 57% from the current contract level.

The agreement followed tough negotiations in which the concessionaire group demanded a higher gas tariff to justify millions of dollars in additional investment required for increasing gas production under Phase III development.

According to PTT, the group is due to increase Bongkot gas delivery from 350 MMcfd in the current contract year to 550 MMcfd in mid-1998.

Pttep, which has a 40% interest in Bongkot, said the increase in gas production results from another gas discovery on the block, south of Bongkot, and the Ion Suk structure east of Bongkot.

The agreement sets the stage for further development of Bongkot, by far the country's single largest gas field.

Processing activity

Shell Co. of Thailand Ltd. inaugurated its $2 billion, 145,000 b/d Rayong refinery at Mab Ta Phut, Thailand.

Rayong, Thailand's fourth refinery, was developed by a venture of Shell 64% and PTT 36%. Construction began in August 1993, and the plant was completed for start-up in December 1995.

Products include liquefied petroleum gas, unleaded gasoline, jet fuel, low sulfur diesel, and fuel oil.

VIET NAM

CAPITAL: Hanoi
MONETARY UNIT: Dong
REFINING CAPACITY: N.A.
PRODUCTION: 177 million b/d
RESERVES: 600 million bbl

Chinese Petroleum Corp. (CPC) signed a letter of intent with Taiwanese and Vietnamese partners to build a $35 million crude oil-based petrochemical plant in Viet Nam's Mekong Delta.

Plant will produce a range of lubricants, liquefied petroleum gas, and other derivatives.

CPC will hold a 45% stake in the venture, to be located in Can Tho Province, about 120 km from Ho Chi Minh City. Two other Taiwanese companies, Yi Jinn Industrial Ltd. and Technical Consultant Co., will hold 15% and 10% interests, respectively, with the remaining 30% being held by Viet Nam's Can Tho Agricultural & Stocks Product Co.

Enron Corp. was chosen to negotiate with state-owned Petrovietnam to jointly develop, own, and operate a $161 million, 96 MMcfd gas processing plant south of Ho Chi Minh City in Ba Ria-Vung Tau province.

Under a heads of agreement, Enron is to hold a 49% interest and Petrovietnam 51% in the project. Petrovietnam will deliver gas to the plant from Bach Ho oil and gas field off southern Viet Nam.

Dry gas will be sold for domestic power generation and industrial use. Condensate and natural gas liquids will be sold locally or exported through a terminal that is also part of the project.

In upstream activity, Petrofina SA was evaluating commerciality of an oil and gas discovery off Viet Nam.

Its 46-DD-1X wildcat on Block 46 in the Malay basin about 130 km southwest of Nam Can flowed 22 MMcfd of gas and 3,000 b/d of oil from two Miocene intervals at undisclosed depths.

Petrofina holds 75% interest in the block and Japan's Sodec 25%. Petrovietnam may acquire as much as a 15% stake if partners opt to develop the field.

Unocal Vietnam Exploration Ltd. signed a production sharing contract with Petrovietnam for exploration of gas-prone Block B off Southwest Viet Nam.

The block covers more than 1.3 million acres in the northern Malay basin in 180-215 ft of water 300 miles west-southwest of Vung Tau. Under a 3 year work program, seismic surveys are expected to take 9 months to complete and analyze. The first wildcat was to be spudded in 1997.

Interests are operator Unocal 45%, Repsol SA 30%, and Mitsui Oil Exploration Co. Ltd. 25%. Petrovietnam has an option to acquire a 15% interest in the block. IPE

IRAN

CAPITAL: Tehran
MONETARY UNIT: Rial
REFINING CAPACITY: 1,242,000 b/cd
PRODUCTION: 3.675 million b/d
RESERVES: 93 billion bbl

Despite U.S. isolation efforts, Iran in 1996 was asking international companies for financial and technical help with a number of large oil and gas projects.

Several of the projects would revive prerevolutionary ambitions to make economic use of gas reserves estimated at 740 tcf.

Plans of the 1970s to end flaring of associated gas by 1980 stalled after the Islamic revolution of 1978-79 and died in the 8 year war with Iraq that followed. Although domestic gas markets have grown, major reinjection and export plans foundered after the revolution, and much associated gas production, especially offshore, is still flared.

Since the end of the war with Iraq, National Iranian Oil Co. (NIOC) has had to rebuild heavily damaged oil production and processing facilities and spend heavily just to maintain production of crude. The state-owned company now faces huge capital needs it cannot satisfy from oil sales alone, a fractured domestic political system with factions still violently opposed to non-Iranian influences, and an increasingly hostile U.S.

South Pars field

NIOC seeks international partners for the second and third of three planned phases of development of giant offshore South Pars gas/condensate field.

South Pars is an extension into Iranian territory of Qatar's North field. NIOC claims reserves of 100 tcf.

Each of the three phases of South Pars development is designed to produce 1 bscfd of gas from 20 wells.

NIOC expects the second and third phases each to involve two drilling platforms linked to a central production platform connected by pipeline to Assaluyeh, 97 km away.

Offshore processing would include gas dehydration and condensate dewatering. Production probably would be carried ashore as a gas/condensate mixture through a 32 in. pipeline, entering at 1,900 psi and arriving onshore at an estimated 1,515 psi.

Onshore facilities in NIOC's scheme would handle condensate stabilization, acid gas removal, dehydration, LPG recovery, and sulfur recovery. Some Phase 1 facilities could be used in the later phases. Sales gas pressure will be about 1,450 psi.

First phase development is under way, similar in design to plans for later phases.

Outlet gas from the first phase will enter the Iranian transmission network at Kangan. Pentanes and heavier liquids, LPG, and sulfur in flake form are to be exported.

The first-phase offshore complex comprises four platforms: a facilities and accommodation unit, central production facilities, a drilling platform, and a flare unit. A second drilling platform attaches to the complex as a satellite.

Gas and condensate are separated and treated offshore in the first phase and piped ashore independently.

Salman-Dalan development

With international participation, NIOC hopes to develop nonassociated gas from the Permian Khuff reservoir, which it calls Dalan, underlying offshore Salman oil and gas field.

Salman is the Iranian extension of Abu Dhabi's Abu Al Bukhoosh field. Total-Abu Al Bukhoosh operates the Abu Dhabi side of the field. NIOC produces oil and gas from Salman field, formerly called Sassan.

NIOC claims that 70% of the Dalan reservoir lies in Iranian waters and estimates gas in place on its side at 6.4 tcf.

The company wants to produce 500 MMscfd from five Dalan wells at first, rising to 12 wells as flow rates decline during the 20 year reservoir life.

Balal field

The Balal field project would involve development of a 1967 discovery by Lavan Petroleum Co. (Lapco), a combine of Atlantic Richfield Co., Murphy Oil Corp., Sun Oil Co., and Union Oil Co. of California. The field was originally named Bahram.

Lapco planned to develop the field and had laid a 14 in. pipeline to Lavan Island, 98 km to the northeast.

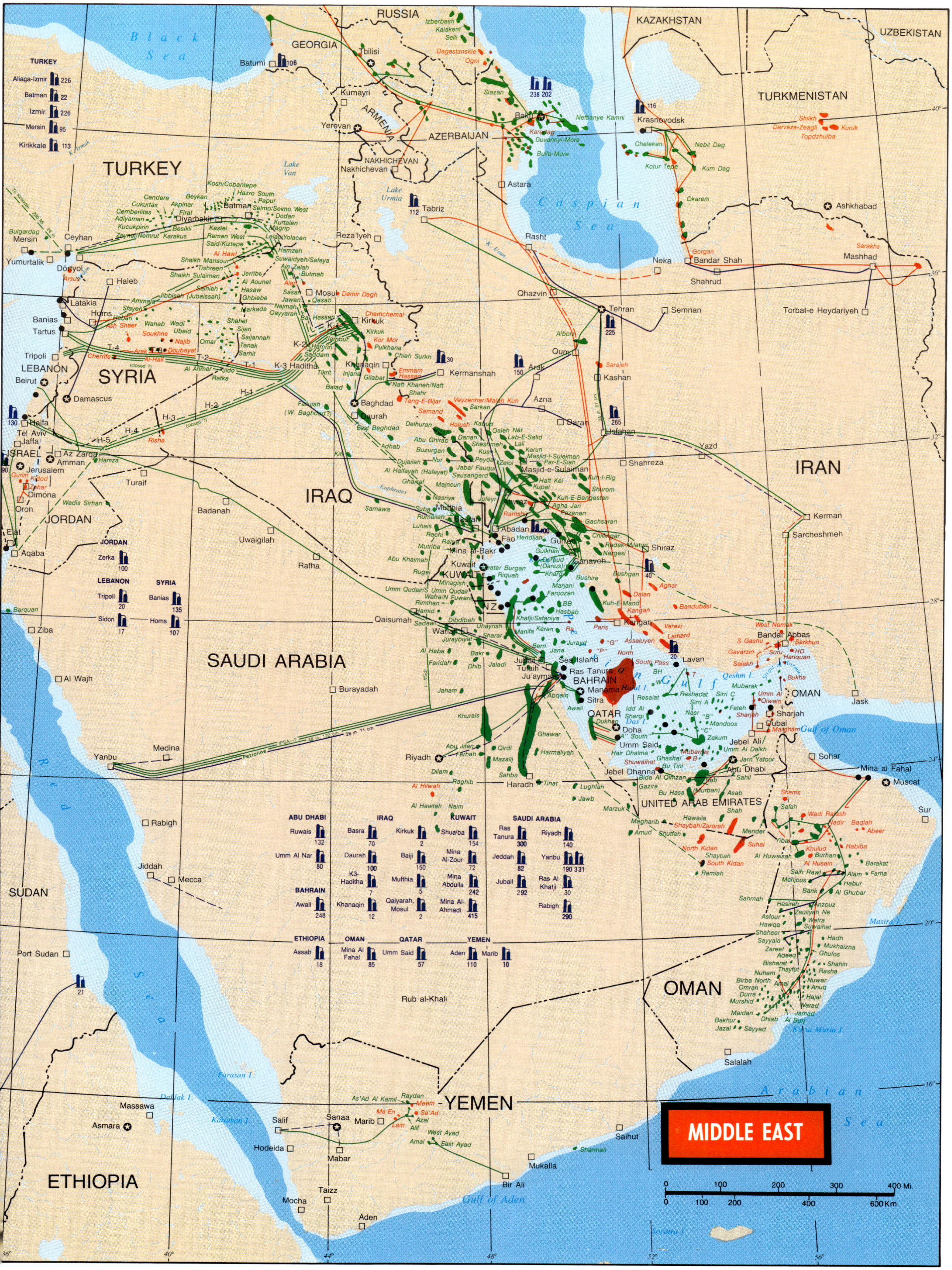

MIDDLE EAST
RUSSIA
GEORGIA
KAZAKHSTAN
UZBEKISTAN
TURKMENISTAN
AZERBAIJAN
ARMENIA
TURKEY
SYRIA
LEBANON
ISRAEL
JORDAN
IRAQ
IRAN
KUWAIT
BAHRAIN
QATAR
SAUDI ARABIA
UNITED ARAB EMIRATES
OMAN
YEMEN
SUDAN
ETHIOPIA
Black Sea
Caspian Sea
Red Sea
Arabian Sea
Gulf of Aden
Gulf of Oman
Rub al-Khali
Tbilisi
Batumi
Yerevan
Baku
Krasnovodsk
Ashkhabad
Tabriz
Tehran
Baghdad
Kirkuk
Mosul
Basra
Kuwait
Riyadh
Jiddah
Mecca
Medina
Yanbu
Damascus
Beirut
Amman
Aqaba
Haifa
Tripoli
Latakia
Homs
Abadan
Shiraz
Isfahan
Kerman
Mashhad
Bandar Abbas
Manama
Doha
Abu Dhabi
Dubai
Muscat
Sanaa
Aden
Salalah
Port Sudan
Massawa
Asmara
Hodeida
Mukalla
0 100 200 300 400 Mi.
0 100 200 400 600 Km.

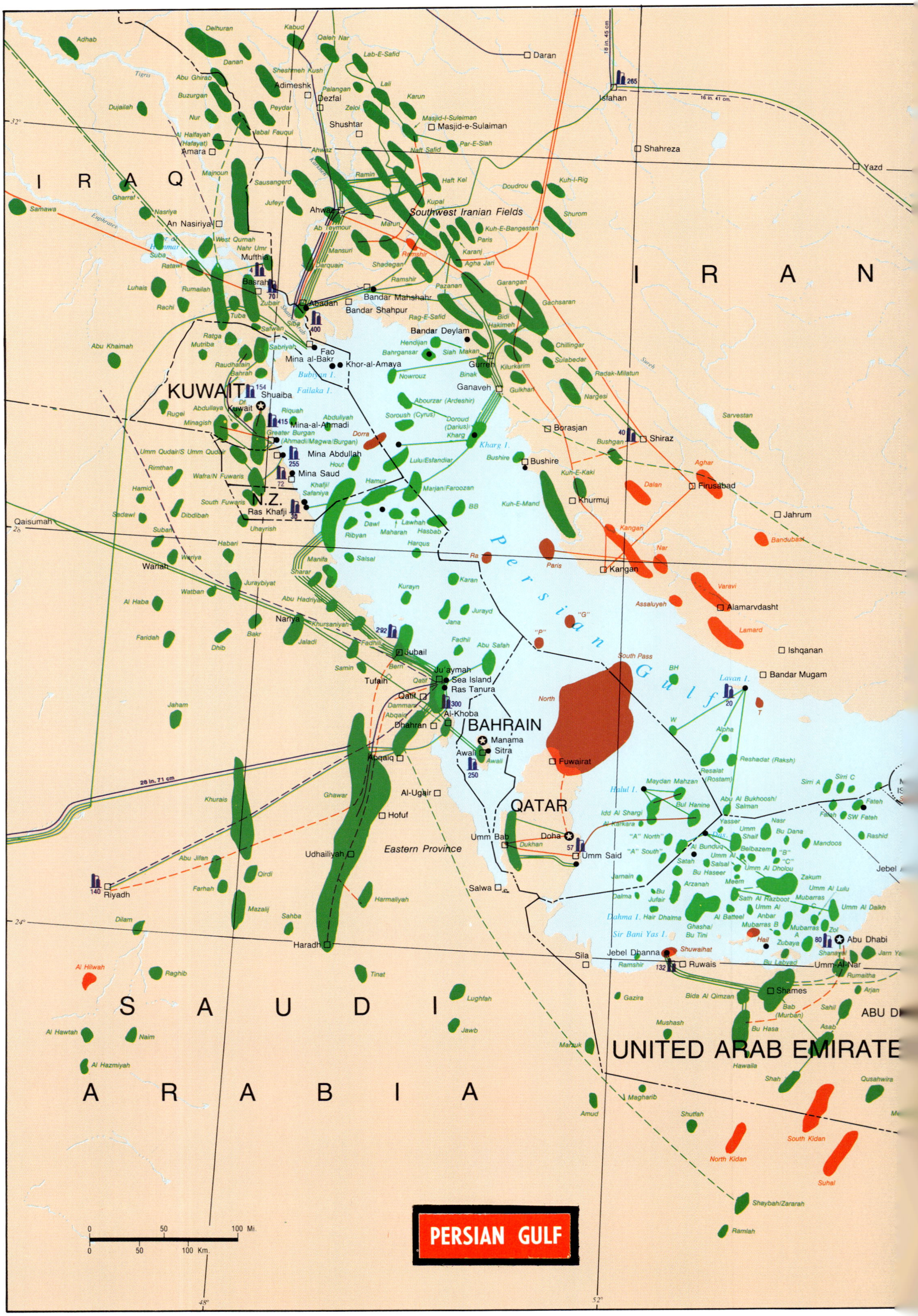
PERSIAN GULF
IRAQ
IRAN
KUWAIT
N.Z.
BAHRAIN
QATAR
SAUDI ARABIA
UNITED ARAB EMIRATES
Persian Gulf
Southwest Iranian Fields
Eastern Province
Daran
Isfahan
Shahreza
Yazd
Dezfal
Shushtar
Masjid-e-Sulaiman
Amara
An Nasiriya
Basrah
Abadan
Bandar Mahshahr
Bandar Shahpur
Bandar Deylam
Fao
Mina al-Bakr
Khor-al-Amaya
Gurreh
Ganaveh
Borasjan
Shiraz
Bushire
Khurmuj
Firusabad
Jahrum
Kangan
Alamarvdasht
Ishqanan
Bandar Mugam
Shuaiba
Kuwait
Mina-al-Ahmadi
Mina Abdullah
Mina Saud
Ras Khafji
Qaisumah
Wariah
Nariya
Jubail
Ju'aymah
Sea Island
Ras Tanura
Tufain
Qatif
Dhahran
Al-Khoba
Manama
Sitra
Awali
Fuwairat
Abqaiq
Al-Ugair
Hofuf
Udhailiyah
Haradh
Riyadh
Umm Bab
Doha
Umm Said
Salwa
Sila
Jebel Dhanna
Ruwais
Abu Dhabi
Umm Al Nar
Shames
Ghawar
Safaniya
South Pass
North
Ahwaz
Agha Jari
Gachsaran
Kharg I.
Lavan I.
Halul I.
Das I.
Dahma I.
Sir Bani Yas I.
Zakum
Bab (Murban)
Bu Hasa
Asab
Sahil
Shah
North Kidan
South Kidan
Suhal
Shaybah/Zararah
Ramlah
Khurais
Abu Jifan
Mazalij
Harmaliyah
Al Hilwah
26 in. 71 cm
16 in. 41 cm.
18 in. 45 cm
0 50 100 Mi.
0 50 100 Km.

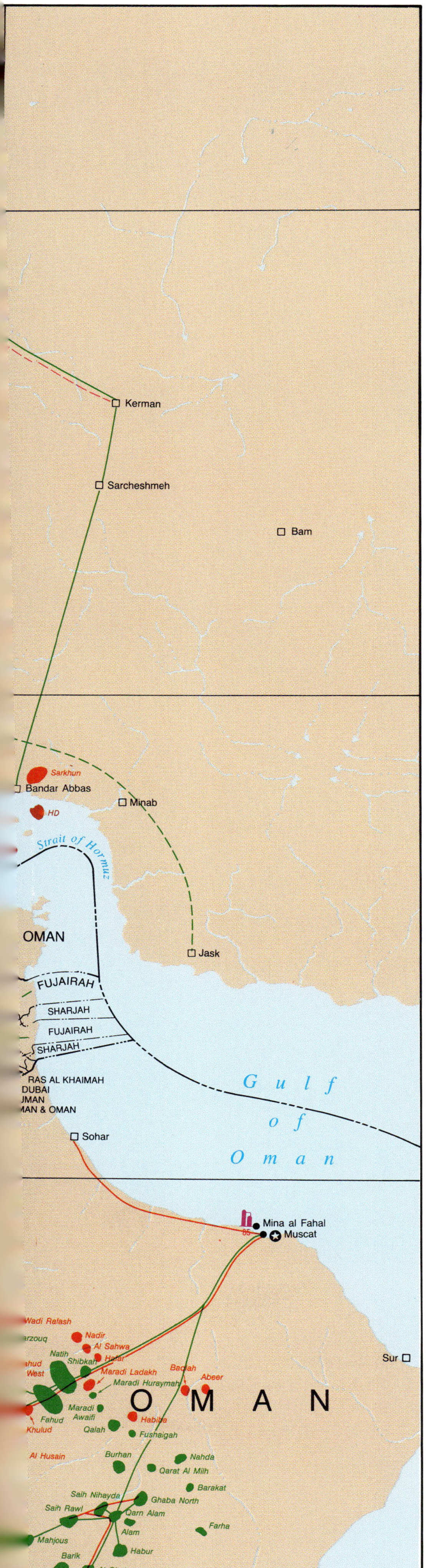

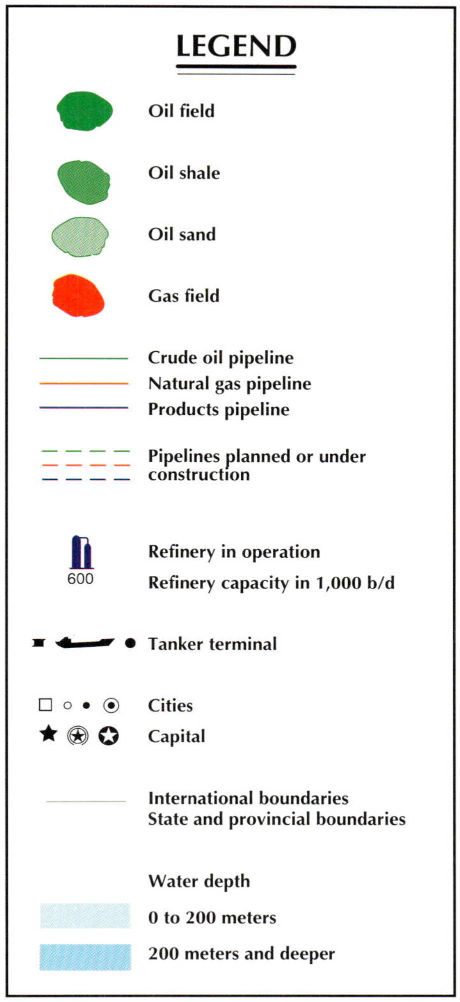

NIOC estimates field reserves at 117 million st-tk bbl in the Arab/Hith formation and 17 million st-tk bbl in the Khatia formation.

Development would involve drilling of five wells, which would produce at a total target rate of 40,000 b/d for 4 years and at a declining rate for 11 more years. NIOC says gas lift or electric submersible pumps (ESPs) would be required, along with water injection of perhaps 50,000 b/d.

Subject to further engineering work, a development program might involve a 12-16 slot drilling platform from which the production and water injection wells would be drilled, a production platform, a tripod flare platform, and an accommodation platform for 60 workers.

After single-stage separation on the platform, oil would move to Lavan Island through the pipeline already in place. Final processing would occur in facilities now handling oil from Salman, Reshadat (formerly Rostam), and Resalat (formerly Rakhsh) fields.

Soroosh field

Farther north, NIOC hopes to refurbish and resume production from an offshore field shut-in since Iran's war with Iraq.

Soroosh field, in 150 ft of water 80 km west-southwest of Kharg Island, produced 86.3 million bbl of crude during 1967-79. It was shut in when a storage barge moved into dry dock.

Most production facilities, heavily damaged in the war, require replacement or refurbishment.

With international involvement, NIOC wants to restart the field and eventually produce 60,000 b/d.

The field has 14 wells. They produced 19° gravity, low GOR crude via ESPs from two zones of the Burgan sandstone found at depths between 6,710 ft and 7,500 ft subsea. A third Burgan zone in the field holds very heavy crude.

The original production scheme involved satellite production equipment linked to a main production platform, which handled gas separation. Crude moved from there through a 16 in. pipeline to the Pazargad storage barge for final desalting and storage.

Crude moved from the barge via 20 in. pipeline to a multibuoy mooring system for loading aboard tankers.

The project NIOC envisions includes inspection and refurbishment of eight, three- and four-legged well protector platforms and of the six pile production platform. Also needing inspection and repair are five subsea flow lines between satellite wells and the main production platform and a 16 in. subsea pipeline between the production platform and barge.

Dorood gas injection

Another production project would use associated gas now flared in offshore fields near Kharg Island for injection in Dorood field, which lies under the island.

Subject to results of miscibility studies, NIOC estimates that injection of 400 MMscfd of gas could boost ultimate oil recovery from Dorood field by 200-600 million bbl. The project also would boost liquid recoveries at existing and new facilities.

Associated gas for the project would come from Aboozar, Foroozan, Nowrooz, and Dorood fields.

NIOC is revising a reservoir simulation study for Dorood field and will conduct a feasibility study before opening the project to international bidding. It assumes the project would take 4 years to complete.

Related to the planned Dorood gas injection scheme is a project under way to expand the Kharg Chemical Co. (Khemco) plant on Kharg Island and add methanol to its product slate. The plant now has design capacities to process 150 MMscfd of gas feed and recover 3,800 b/d of propane, 2,200 b/d of

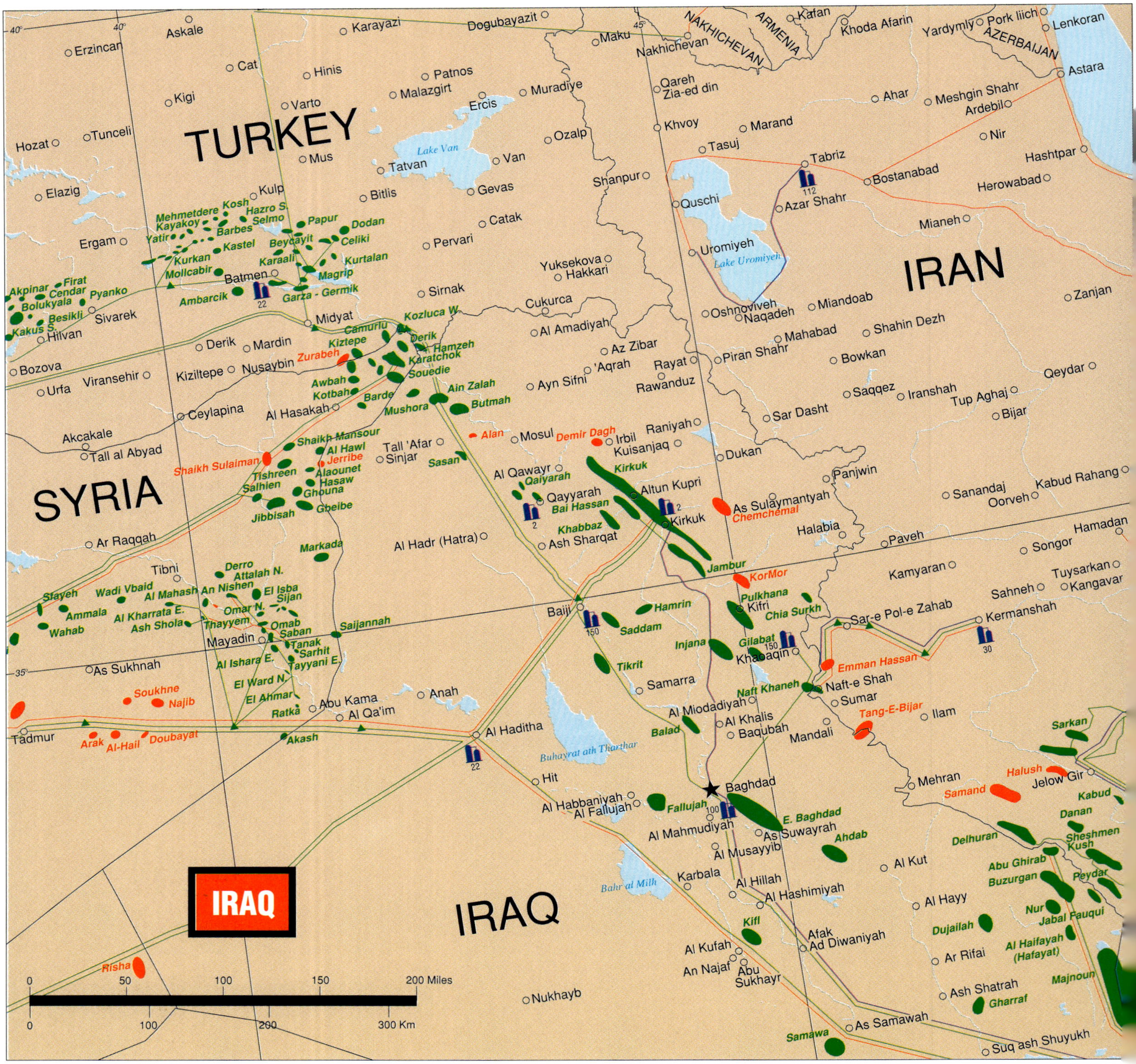

butane, 1,000 b/d of heavier liquids, and 600 tons/day of sulfur.

The plant currently processes 120 MMscfd of associated gas, mostly from Dorood field, and produces 2,700 b/d of propane, 1,900 b/d of butane, 3,100 b/d of heavier liquids, and 422 tons/day of sulfur.

After expansion, the plant will be able to process 200 MMscfd of rich gas and produce 4,600 b/d of propane, 3,200 b/d of butane, 5,100 b/d of heavier liquids, and 700 tons/day of sulfur. It also would yield 70 MMscfd of feed for a methanol plant.

IRAQ

CAPITAL: Baghdad
MONETARY UNIT: Dinar
REFINING CAPACITY: 347,500 b/cd
PRODUCTION: 600,000 b/d
RESERVES: 112 billion bbl

Companies were scrambling for contracts with Iraq as Baghdad accepted U.N. terms on the long-delayed oil-for-aid program and began limited exports of crude oil through Turkey.

Iraq claimed to have initial deals with 50 firms from Europe, Southeast Asia, and South America to purchase oil. Baghdad said late in 1996 it hadn't signed any deals with U.S. or U.K. companies.

If President Saddam Hussein abided by U.N. conditions, Iraq was to be allowed to sell $2 billion of oil through mid-1997 to pay for food and medical supplies. That translates to 550,000-800,000 b/d, depending on prices. At prices prevailing late in 1996, exports would have been at the lower end of the scale. Under the U.N. deal, Iraq could send as much as 350,000 b/d through Mina al-Bakr on the Persian Gulf and perhaps 450,000 b/d via pipeline through Turkey.

Deals with Baghdad

Middle East Economic Survey (MEES) reported that Iraq's national assembly approved a production-sharing agreement with China National Petroleum Corp. for development of Al-Ahdab field. MEES said the deal calls for a 4-year development plan, beginning with analysis of seismic data and leading to estimated production of 80,000 b/d.

French and Russian companies had secured agreements for Iraqi field developments once sanctions against Iraq are lifted. France and Russia supported not only the oil-for-aid program under U.N. Resolution 986 but also total lifting of the trade embargo, imposed after Iraq invaded Kuwait in 1990.

JORDAN

CAPITAL: Amman
MONETARY UNIT: Dinar
REFINING CAPACITY: 100,000 b/cd
PRODUCTION: 100 b/d
RESERVES: 300,000 bbl

Anadarko Jordan Co. has signed a production sharing agreement (PSA) covering the 4.2 million acre Safawi block in Northeast Jordan.

The company, a wholly owned unit of Anadarko Petroleum Corp., Houston, agreed to spend at least $5 million during the first 2½ years of exploration. It planned to drill two stratigraphic holes during 1996.

Anadarko owns a 100% working interest in the project but may take partners.

KUWAIT

CAPITAL: Kuwait City
MONETARY UNIT: Kuwaiti dinar
REFINING CAPACITY: 824,000 b/cd
PRODUCTION: 1.818 million b/d
RESERVES: 94 billion bbl

Kuwait Oil Co. (KOC) renewed its agreement with British Petroleum Co. plc under which BP provides technical advice and assistance in Kuwaiti oil production operations.

BP first started work for KOC in 1992 on a 3 year program of projects including assessment of reservoir damage sustained during the Persian Gulf War of 1990-91.

BP has been working closely with KOC to increase oil reserves and plan future field developments, while advising on technical and organizational matters.

The new 3 year deal was said to involve BP in technical support for KOC's reservoir management, drilling, and organizational development.

Exxon Exploration Kuwait Inc. signed a technical study agreement with KOC to jointly evaluate the Karaa Al-Marou discovery in west-central Kuwait, about 40 miles west of Kuwait City.

The study will include integrated evaluation of the discovery, its geologic trend, appraisal options, and hydrocarbon potential estimates of the Karaa Al-Marou trend.

Reserves are estimated at 350 million bbl.

KOC let a $390 million contract to China's state-owned China Petroleum Engineering Construction Co. for two oil gathering centers.

The centers will serve Minagish and Umm Gudair fields in western Kuwait and have combined capacity of 410,000 b/d.

The project is part of Kuwait's plan to hike oil production capacity to 3 million b/d from 2.5 million b/d by 2000.

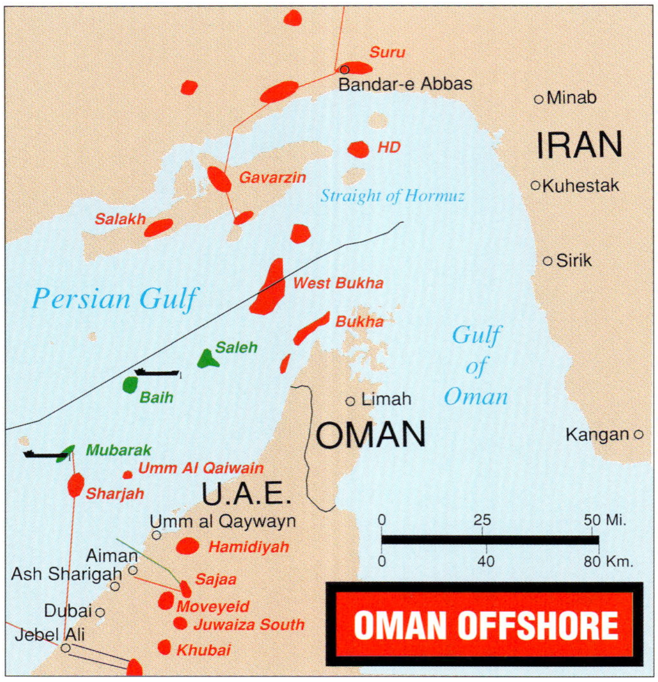

OMAN

CAPITAL: Muscat
MONETARY UNIT: Omani riyal
REFINING CAPACITY: 85,000 b/cd
PRODUCTION: 883,000 b/d
RESERVES: 5.138 billion bbl

Oman and Petroleum Development Oman (PDO)—a combine of the Omani government and Royal Dutch/Shell, Total SA, and Partex—agreed on a $1.4 billion gas field development project.

Much of the gas will be earmarked for Oman's liquefied natural gas export project.

The development project will involve Saih Rawl, Barik, and Saih Nihayda gas fields in Central Oman and construction of a gas processing station at Saih Rawl, a gathering station at Barik, and a 356 km pipeline to the coast.

Construction work was expected to start in mid-1997 and be completed in April 1999.

Oman's LNG project, with capacity to export 6.6 million metric tons/year of LNG, had a contract with Korean Gas Corp. to deliver 4.1 million metric tons/year of LNG to South Korea for 25 years beginning in 2000.

The Omani government allocated about 7 tcf of proved gas reserves to the South Korean LNG contract.

Oman LNG was reported to be negotiating an LNG sales contract with Petroleum Authority of Thailand. The deal was likely to involve 1 million metric tons/year to be exported to Thailand beginning in 2003, rising to 1.7-2.5 million metric tons/year in 2005.

A unit of Phillips Petroleum Co. in mid-1996 was poised for an immediate start on exploration of a 4.5 million acre block in southern Oman. Phillips Petroleum Oman Ltd. was to conduct the program under an exploration/production sharing contract covering a 100% interest in Block 36.

The tract lies flush with the borders of Saudi Arabia and Yemen and flanks the Rub Al Khali basin of Saudi Arabia and the United Arab Emirates.

Phillips intended to conduct an aeromagnetic survey by yearend 1996 and begin acquiring seismic data early in 1997. It also is committed to drill five wells during a 9 year exploration phase of its contract.

Oman suspended plans for a $10 billion subsea gas pipeline to India after spending about $70 million far on feasibility studies.

Trade and Industry Minister Maqbul ibn Ali ibn Sultan said no more money would be spent on the "unprofitable project." He cited insufficient gas reserves and "technological problems" associated with laying the line under the Arabian Sea in waters as deep as 9,900 ft.

QATAR

CAPITAL: Doha
MONETARY UNIT: Riyal
REFINING CAPACITY: 57,500 b/cd
PRODUCTION: 480,000 b/d
RESERVES: 3.7 billion bbl

Qatar expected in 1996 to spend about $18 billion by 2000 to boost oil production capacity, develop North gas field, and expand refining and petrochemical industries. Much of the money will come from foreign investors.

Qatar's energy and industry ministry said the country aims to ramp up production capacity to at least 700,000 b/d by 2000. Qatar's OPEC oil production quota in 1996 was 378,000 b/d.

Occidental Petroleum of Qatar increased oil production in Idd al Sharqi North Dome field (ISND) to 85,000 b/d in 1996 from 20,000 b/d in 1994.

It hiked gas output to 125 MMcfd after upgrading compression and treatment facilities. Since signing a production sharing agreement with Qatar General Petroleum Corp. (QGPC), Oxy had drilled 15 wells into the Shuaiba reservoir. ISND output is expected to reach 100,000 b/d by 2000.

Meantime, a report by the Organization of Arab Petroleum Exporting Countries says Qatar's spending could include more than $8.5 billion for the Ras Laffan and Qatargas LNG ventures and $3.9 billion for an LNG deal being discussed with Enron, all based on massive North gas field.

Ras Laffan Liquefied Natural Gas Co. in 1996 disclosed the award of a $1 billion contract for engineering, procurement, and construction of a gas liquefaction plant in Qatar's Ras Laffan industrial area on the Persian Gulf coast.

The contract went to a joint venture of JGC Corp. of Japan and M.W. Kellogg of the U.S. for an LNG export plant with a capacity of about 5 million metric tons/year. Work was scheduled to get under way in 1996, with first LNG shipments to Korea Gas Corp. of South Korea scheduled in August 1999.

Ras Laffan LNG is a venture of QGPC 70% and Mobil QM Inc., a unit of Mobil Corp., 30%.

Meanwhile, a project by Qatar Liquefied Gas Co. was expected to be commissioned during 1996 and produce 10 million metric tons/year of LNG.

SAUDI ARABIA

CAPITAL: Riyadh
MONETARY UNIT: Riyal
REFINING CAPACITY: 1,655,700 b/cd
PRODUCTION: 7.841 million b/d
RESERVES: 259 billion bbl

Saudi Basic Industries Corp. (Sabic) and 50-50 partner Mobil Corp. in 1996 unveiled plans for a big expansion of their Yanbu petrochemical complex on Saudi Arabia's Red Sea coast.

The $2 billion project will more than double capacity of the partnership's Saudi Yanbu Petrochemical Co. (Yanpet). Construction was to begin in 1997, with start-up set for early 2000.

Construction will include an 800,000 metric ton/year ethylene cracker, 535,000 ton/year polyethylene plant, 410,000 ton/year ethylene glycol plant, and 260,000 ton/year polypropylene unit.

The new cracker will use propane and light naphtha as feedstock to produce ethylene. The process will produce a significant volume of propylene, which will be converted to polypropylene in an addition to the venture's product slate.

Ibrahim A. Ibn Salamah, Sabic vice-chairman and managing director, said the expansion project will make Yanpet one of the largest petrochemical complexes in the world, with capacity to produce more than 1.6 million tons/year of ethylene and 2 million tons/year of derivative products.

Yanbu's present cracker uses ethane feedstock to produce more than 800,000 tons/year of ethylene. Other units in the complex produce a total 350,000 tons/year of ethylene glycol and 610,000 tons/year of polyethylene.

Mobil participates in the complex through Mobil Yanbu Petrochemical Co. Inc.

Sabic and Mobil formed their joint venture in 1980 and began operations in 1985.

Elsewhere, in eastern Saudi Arabia:

- Sabic will build a world scale ethylene glycol plant at its Al Jubail complex. The 497,000 ton/year plant will take Sabic's ethylene glycol production capacity to more than 2 million tons/year by 2000.

The company will also debottleneck two linear low density polyethylene plants at Al Jubail to raise combined capacity to 750,000 tons/year, bringing Sabic's ethylene production capacity close to 3 million tons/year. The projects are part of a plan to raise Sabic's total petrochemical capacity to 25 million tons/year by 2000 from the current 20 million tons/year.

- Chevron Chemical Co. and Saudi Industrial Venture Group formed a 50-50 venture to build and operate a $650 million petrochemical complex at Al Jubail.

Construction of a 480,000 ton/year benzene plant and 200,000 ton/year cyclohexane plant is scheduled for completion in mid-1999. The complex will use Chevron technology to manufacture benzene from a natural gasoline feedstock supplied by Saudi Aramco and Institut Francais du Petrole technology to manufacture cyclohexane from the benzene.

- Saudi Methanol Co. (Ar-Razi) and a group of Japanese companies signed a $160 million loan agreement with Export-Import Bank of Japan to finance construction of an 850,000 ton/year chemical-grade methanol plant at Ar-Razi's complex at Al Jubail.

Mitsubishi Heavy Industries Co., Tokyo, is performing engineering, procurement, and construction. The plant will use Mitsubishi Gas Chemical Co. technology. Start-up was scheduled for mid-1997.

UNITED ARAB EMIRATES

CAPITAL: ABU DHABI
MONETARY UNIT: Dirham
REFINING CAPACITY: 212,800 b/cd
PRODUCTION: 2.217 million b/d
RESERVES: 97.8 billion bbl

Abu Dhabi National Oil Co.'s (Adnoc) $1.35 billion Bab/Habshan gas gathering and injection complex started up in 1996 as a key element in a massive investment program Abu Dhabi is undertaking to bolster its oil and gas production and expand its downstream presence.

The emirate plans to hike production capacity of crude oil by 50% and condensate by 300% by 2003 and sharply expand its refining and petrochemical capacity. Overall spending upstream and downstream is earmarked at $10 billion over 5 years.

Habshan complex

Habshan, touted as the world's largest onshore natural gas complex, is 150 km south of Abu Dhabi City near the Persian Gulf coast. New facilities integrate into the complex production from giant Bab oil and gas field's Cretaceous Thamama F, B, and C reservoirs, raising the site's gas processing capacity by more than 960 MMcfd to 1.7 bcfd.

At the same time condensate production jumped to 131,000 b/d from 5,000 b/d, and recovery began at an average 5,000 metric tons/day of natural gas liquids and 1,800 tons/day of sulfur. Condensate is transported via pipeline and LPG and sulfur via truck to the Ruwais refinery on the coast for export.

The sale of condensate alone—exempt from OPEC quotas—is expected to pay for the entire project in 2 years even if crude oil prices were to drop as low as $13/bbl. Total revenues from the plant are expected to generate $600 million/year.

A combine of Technip 60% and Bechtel 40% completed the turnkey contract for Adnoc.

Under first-phase Bab development, 40% of the gas produced is being reinjected into the oil reservoir for pressure maintenance. In a second stage, the gas will be recovered to generate electricity and be used as feedstock for Abu Dhabi's first venture into petrochemicals, to be based in Ruwais.

Phase 2 also calls for three or four gas processing trains to handle another 1 bcfd of gas as well as 1,800 tons/day of NGL, 30,000 b/d of condensate, and 850 tons/day of sulfur.

Sharjah redevelopment farmout

Enterprise Oil plc, London, acquired a farmout of a redevelopment program for Mubarek field off Sharjah.

Mubarek is operated by the Buttes Gas & Oil Co. International (BGOI) unit of Crescent Petroleum Co., Sharjah.

Mubarek was discovered in 1972 and brought on stream in 1974. It has yielded 83 million bbl of crude oil from its Ilam/Mishrif reservoir. Mubarek oil production averaged about 4,000 b/d in 1994 and has fallen since then.

Enterprise will spend $25 million for a 3D seismic survey of the field and drilling at least two wells, in return for a 40% share of output from the new wells drilled.

Enterprise sees the project as a low risk exploration and production venture, with Mubarek field wells typically producing 20,000 b/d of oil in the past.

Enterprise expected the drilling program to be complete by yearend 1997. BGOI remains operator.

Mubarek has two Cretaceous main reservoirs: Ilam/Mishrif, containing 36° gravity oil and associated gas, and the lower Thamama reservoir, which produces gas and condensate.

The Enterprise farm-in covers geological structures down to and including the Ilam/Mishrif formation. Crescent retains control of the Thamama reservoir.

Mubarek's crude oil and condensate is pumped to a floating storage unit for tanker export. Gas is exported via an offshore gathering platform and 16 in. pipeline to Dubai. New production would be processed through these facilities.

YEMEN

CAPITAL: Sanaa
MONETARY UNIT: Rial
REFINING CAPACITY: 120,000 b/cd
PRODUCTION: 338,000 b/d
RESERVES: 4 billion bbl

Yemen's parliament in 1996 ratified an LNG project agreement with Total.

The French company plans to produce 5 million metric tons/year of LNG starting in 2001 at a cost of $3 billion. Total was talking with potential LNG buyers and competing bidders Exxon, Hunt, and Yukong to share project risks. Total holds a 70% interest in the project, Yemen's General Gas Corp. 30%.

Elsewhere, Coplex Resources NL, Hobart, Tasmania, agreed to acquire from Shell Oil Co. unit Pecten International an added 25% working interest in the North Sanau block in Yemen in exchange for a royalty interest of as much as 0.865%, or $5 million, in Philippines license GSEC 72 in Manila Bay. This boosts the Coplex interest in North Sanau to 37%. IPE

LATIN AMERICA

ARGENTINA

CAPITAL: Buenos Aires
MONETARY UNIT: Austral
REFINING CAPACITY: 665,000 b/cd
PRODUCTION: 721,000 b/d
RESERVES: 2.4 billion bbl

Gasoducto GasAndes SA partners in 1996 were mounting a sizable lead in the race to transport Argentine gas to emerging markets in Chile.

Crews by early in the year had begun construction along the GasAndes pipeline route in Chile and Argentina. Workers were trying to complete pipelaying in the high country on either side of the international border before winter.

Meantime, sponsors of the competing Gasoducto Transandino (TransGas) project pushed back to July 1996 the planned start of construction for their proposed $689 million gas pipeline. Under the revised timetable, gas was to begin flowing by yearend 1997 along the 750 mile TransGas trunk line from Loma La Lata, Argentina, to a point near Concepcion, Chile.

GasAndes sponsors proposed a $350 million project to lay a 24 in. pipeline along a 290 mile pipeline to ship gas to Santiago, Chile, from La Mora, Argentina. GasAndes is to link at La Mora with Transportadora de Gas del Norte (TGN), one of Argentina's two main gas transmission lines.

GasAndes plans to transport gas for Santiago's gas distribution system and four 350,000 kw gas-fired power plants. Sources reported the TransGas group had agreed to transport gas for a multiphase 1 million kw power generation plant proposed by a U.S.-Canadian group.

Sponsors of both projects continued to dispute skeptics who said both pipelines are not needed to serve Chile's future gas markets.

Later in 1996, units of NOVA Corp., Calgary, and CMS Energy Corp., Dearborn, Mich., proposed an Argentina-Chile integrated gas pipeline/power project.

NOVA Gas International and CMS Gas Transmission & Storage plan a $700 million project to transport gas from Northwest Argentina's Noroeste basin that will fuel a proposed 400,000 kw combined cycle power plant at the line's terminus and serve other customers.

Construction of the 820 km, 20 in. Atacama pipeline was to begin in mid-1997 with commercial start-up slated for early 1999.

The line will extend from the Noroeste basin to Mejillones, with possible laterals to Antofagasta, Tocopilla, and Calama in northern Chile.

Project sponsors were in talks with several major industrial firms in northern Chile for sale of gas to be transported by the Atacama pipeline.

Falklands activity

The government of the Falkland Islands awarded seven exploration licenses covering areas to the north of the islands totaling 12,800 sq km.

Bidders in the round applied only for acreage to the north of the South Atlantic islands, where a number of large targets have been identified by loose-grid seismic data acquired ahead of the licensing round.

Falklands government said no bids were received for acreage to the south because of the area's deep water and paucity of geological information.

In 1995, the Falklands government offered more than 44,000 sq km of virgin offshore territory to international bidders, divided into 19 tranches covering 215-250 sq km.

Acreage allocations are:

- Tranche A to operator Amerada Hess (Falkland Islands) Ltd., Fina Exploration Atlantic BV, Murphy South Atlantic Oil Co., Teikoku Oil Co. Ltd., and Argos Evergreen Ltd.
- Tranche B to operator Shell Exploration BV and Agip Exploration BV.
- Tranches C and D to operator Lasmo International Ltd., Desire Petroleum Ltd., Malvern, U.K., and Clyde Expro plc, Ledbury, U.K.
- Tranche F to operator International Petroleum Corp., Vancouver, B.C., and Sands Petroleum AB.
- Tranches I and L outright to Desire Petroleum.

Operators are expected to spend a total $150 million on seismic acquisition and drilling the next 5 years and at least $120

SOUTH AMERICA
Caribbean Sea
PACIFIC OCEAN
ATLANTIC OCEAN
COSTA RICA
PANAMA
COLOMBIA
VENEZUELA
GUYANA
SURINAME
FRENCH GUYANA
ECUADOR
PERU
BRAZIL
BOLIVIA
PARAGUAY
CHILE
ARGENTINA
URUGUAY
ARUBA
CURACAO
GRENADA
TRINIDAD and TOBAGO
ST. JOHN'S
Fort de France
BARBADOS
Bridgetown
Port of Spain
Puerto la Cruz
Caracas
Maracaibo
Santa Marta
Barranquilla
Cartagena
Pto. Limon
Colón
Panama
Barrancabermeja
Cantimplora
Tibu
S. Cristobol
S. Silvestre
Ciudad Bolivar
Georgetown
Paramaribo
Cayenne
Bogota
Tulua
Cali
Tumaco
Esmaraldas
Quito
Guayaquil
Tumbes
Talara
Bayovar
Iquitos
Concordia
Pucallpa
Lima
La Pampilla
Conchan
Manaus
Belem
Sao Luis
Fortaleza
Aracaju
Salvador
Brasilia
Belo Horizonte
Betim
Campos
Rio de Janeiro
Duque de Caxias
Sao Sebastiao
Santos
Sao Paulo
Cubatao
Maua
Curitiba
Apucarana
Sao Francisco do Sul
Sao Mateus do Sul
Laguna
Canoas
Porto Alegre
Rio Grande do Sul
La Paz
Cochabamba
Pto. Villarroel
Santa Cruz
Sicasica
Oruro
Sucre
Camiri
Arica
Corumba
Campo Grande
Aquidauana
Villa Elisa
Asuncion
Formosa
Resistencia
Corrientes
Jujuy
Salta
Metan
Campo Duran
Cordoba
San Lorenzo
Plaza Huincul
Mendoza
San Luis
Campana
Buenos Aires
La Plata
Dock Sud
Montevideo
Las Flores
Concon
Valparaiso
Santiago
Concepcion
Cnl. Pringles
Bahia Blanca
Punta Alta
Puerto Rosales
San Antonio
Comodoro Rivadavia
Santa Cruz
Rio Gallegos
Falkland Islands (Islas Malvinas)
TIERRA DEL FUEGO
Punta Arenas
Rio Grande
Ushuaia
Amistad
SANTA ELENA FIELDS
BREA-PARINAS FIELDS
Aguaytia
Aguas Calientes
Carmisea
Jurua
Southwest Urucu
Rio Urucu
Nova Olinda
Karanambo
HAMACA
CERRO NEGRO FIELDS
MACHETE FIELDS
ZUATA FIELDS
Volcanera
Cupiagua
Cisiana
Apiay Complex
Chichimene
Castilla
Andalucia
San Francisco
Dina
Tello
Hato
Sinco
Palmita
Silvestre
Punzan
Grico
Lechoso
Teak
Radix
Penal-Barrackpore-Wilson
Balata-Bouvallius
Southeast Galeota
E. Queens Beach
Quarry-Coora-Quinam
Tambaredjo/Jossikreek
Surubi
Colpa
Tita
Rio Grande
Tatarenda
Boyuibe
Monteagudo
Yuelta Grande
Buena Vista
Tigre
Caigua
Sanandita
Madre Jones
Campo Duran
Lomitas Tranquilas
Toro
Bermejo
Ramos
Rio Pescado
Caimancito
Tremembe
Irati
Merluza
Perimbo
Sao Gabriel
Tupungato
Lumunta
Cacheuta
Refugio
Colorados
Barrencas
El Sosneado
Colonia
Catriel
El Medanito
Guanco
Plaza Huincul
Challaco
Cerro Bandera
Barda Gonzales
Rivadavia
Las Flores
Anticlinal Grande
Cerro Dragon
Cerro Tortuga
Comodoro
Canadon Grande
Canadon Seco
Caleta Olivia
Pico Truncado
1-CES-8
Atum
Curima
Xareu
Espada
Pescada
Fazenda Belem
Ubarabano
Canto do Amaro
Agulha
Guamare
Serraria
Lorena
Faz. Pocinhos
Estreito
BRAZIL
Tabuleiro dos Martins
Pilar
Furado
Maceio
C. S. Miguel dos Campos
S. Miguel dos Campos
Cavala
Brejo Grande
Carmopolis
Mero
Sirizinho
Riachuelo
Tigre Robalo
Aracaju
Camorim
Atjalaia
Caioba
Sul
Dourado
Guaricema
Faz. Alvorada
Faz. Balsamo
Comceicao
Aracas
Malombe
Buracica
Imbe
Panelas
Santana
Miranda Norte
Casarongongo
Miranda
Taquipe
Agua Grande
Dom Joa
Jacuipe
Candejas
Gexis
Pirapema
Aratu
Salvador
Itaparda
Lobato
BRAZIL
Campos
22 in
12 in
24 in
12 in
18 in
366
Salema
Albacora
Vermelho
Pargo
Moreia
Carapeba
Garoupinha
Marlim
Marlim Leste
Parati
Namorado
Anequim
Complexo
Corvina
Marlim Sul
West Enchova
Cherne
Badejo
Marimba
Linguado
409
Pampo
Enchova
485
493
Bicudo
Guarajuba
0 100 200 300 400 Miles
0 200 400 600 Km

SOUTH AMERICA, SOUTHERN PORTION

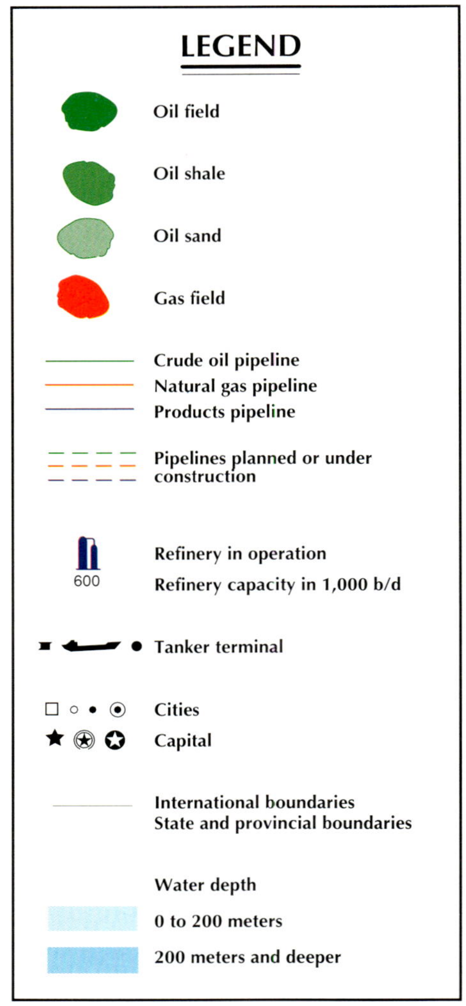

million on further exploration thereafter.

Successful bidders have committed to drill a total of seven wells during the first phase of exploration, with a further five conditional wells. Four more wells have been committed to under second-phase exploration.

Tranches A, B, and C are believed to hold the hottest prospects and to have the bulk of drilling commitments. Some tranches carry two obligation wells plus one conditional well, while the more southerly licenses carry only conditional drilling requirements.

All the largest targets identified in seismic data are expected to be drilled within the next 3-4 years, while a number of smaller targets are likely to be drilled later.

A seismic survey to gather about 10,000 line-km of detailed data was expected to begin in 1997, and 3D seismic data acquisition also was planned.

In addtion, the U.K. and Argentine governments agreed to open for exploration disputed territorial waters southwest of the Falkland Islands in the South Atlantic Ocean.

Their "special cooperation zone" covers 18,000 sq km and lies roughly half in Falklands waters and half in Argentine territory.

A U.K./Argentine agreement for joint exploitation of any hydrocarbons in this area was key to Argentina letting the recent Falkland Island licensing round go ahead.

The two government delegations met in London late in 1996 and agreed to allow airborne and seismic surveys of the cooperation zone, beginning in February 1997.

Two applications to conduct surveys were received, and results of the surveys were expected to be available by mid-1997.

In a joint declaration, the two governments said they would aim to open the cooperation zone for licensing by yearend 1997.

BOLIVIA

CAPITAL: La Paz
MONETARY UNIT: Boliviano
REFINING CAPACITY: 48,000 b/cd
PRODUCTION: 28,000 b/d
RESERVES: 132 million bbl

After a series of false starts, delays, and violent protests, the

50% partial privatization of Bolivia's state-owned petroleum company, Yacimientos Petroliferos Fiscales Bolivianos (YPFB) was finally achieved in 1996, a year behind schedule.

The initial results of the so-called "capitalization" program were unveiled at year's end. YPFB's exploration, production, and pipeline operations were acquired by three winning bidders that put up total investment bids worth $835 million.

The amount received for YPFB is the highest offered for any of Bolivia's five state companies privatized to date and sets the capital market value of the company at almost $1.7 billion.

The two upstream units for exploration and production and one transportation division belonging to YPFB were sold as separate entities to three international bidding groups from a field of six contenders.

The winners were Amoco Corp.; a group of three Argentine companies led by YPF SA; and a combine of Enron Corp. and Shell International Overseas Holdings.

The Argentine group of YPF SA, Perez Companc, and Pluspetrol bought its 50% interest in the upstream unit Empresa Petrolera Andina for $264.8 million, beating rival bidder Amoco (Bolivia) Petroleum with $242.4 million.

Amoco, however, topped bids for the second upstream unit, Empresa Petrolera Chaco, with $306.7 million, ahead of runner-up Repsol Exploration, which bid $280.1 million.

YFB's pipeline unit Transportadora de Hidrocarburos went to Enron-Shell in a joint venture bid for $263.5 million, well ahead of rivals NOVA Gas, which bid $213.1 million, and Williams International Pipeline Co.'s offer of $200 million.

The sales leave a rump YPFB holding on to its refining and domestic marketing operations alongside some technical and maintenance units.The government's remaining 50% stake in the privatized industries is being used to capitalize individual pension accounts for all adult Bolivians, which would have been jeopardized had the YPFB sale not gone ahead.

Uncertainty surrounding the sale affected investor confidence, and from an original field of 25 prequalified companies, only six remained to bid in the highly controversial sale. Political and social unrest caused by opposition protests from oil workers, politicians, pensioners, and civic groups was only half the reason so many companies dropped out.

A drawn-out renegotiation of the 1994 joint venture contract signed between YPFB and Enron Development Corp. for Bolivia's gas sale contract to Brazil created considerable last-minute uncertainty for many bidders that eventually turned elsewhere to other opportunities in the region.

Other Bolivian activity

Mexico's Protexa and Bolivia's YPFB agreed to build the Carrasco-Valle Hermoso pipeline in Bolivia's Coche- bamba province.

The 225-km pipeline will convert the province into an important oil-producing region, enabling start-up of production of 19,000 b/d. Protexa is investing about $326.3 million and YPFB $6.6 million in the project.

Bolivia and Brazil set definitive terms covering gas exports from Porto Alegre, Bolivia, to industrial markets in southern Brazil to begin in 1999 via the proposed $1.9 billion, 1,926 mile gas pipeline system to Sao Paulo.

Terms of the 20 year pact signed by Bolivia's YPFB and Brazil's Petroleos Brasileiro SA call for gas volumes to rise from 565 MMcfd to as much as 1.13 bcfd, depending on demand.

BRAZIL

CAPITAL: Brasilia
MONETARY UNIT: New Cruzado
REFINING CAPACITY: 1.3 million b/cd
PRODUCTION: 690,000 b/d
RESERVES: 4.8 billion bbl

Soaring demand for refined products was expected to boost Brazil's oil import bill by 22% in 1996.

Officials of state petroleum company Petroleo Brasileiro SA said that the tab for imports of refined products by the company was to increase by yearend 1996 to $6.3 billion from $5.18 billion in 1995.

Aurilio Fernandes Lima, Petrobras director, said, "This increase is mainly due to an expansion of domestic oil products consumption, particularly of gasoline. This year (1996) we are consuming 17% more gasoline than last year."

The other factor was the increase in international oil prices in 1996.

Refineries lagging

Lima noted that the increase in refined products imports was unrelated to routine maintenance turnarounds at Brazil's refineries.

"The 10 Brazilian refineries and one asphalt plant are operating normally," he said.

However, the rising demand for refined products imports points to a need to continue upgrading and expanding Brazil's refining capacity.

"Petrobras needs to invest around $800 million/year to expand its refining infrastructure," Lima said.

However, these investments are on hold until Brazil's post-monopoly regulatory framework is approved by Congress.

Lima cited Petrobras's project to double products output at its Mataripe, Bahia state, refinery, at a cost of about $362 million.

The refinery was expected to produce 268,000 b/d of refined products beginning in January 1997.

Rising imports

From January to September 1996, Brazilian crude oil and products imports totaled $4.27 billion.

In September alone, Brazilian oil imports totaled $665 million, a jump of 70% from 1995.

At yearend 1996, Petrobras' maximum output of refined products was 1.4 million b/d, and consumption in September 1996 reached a record 1.6 million b/d.

Much of the increase has come in diesel imports. "We are going through a harvest period, which increases diesel consumption," Lima said.

Argentina is the main exporter of crude oil to Brazil, surpassing Saudi Arabia. From January to August (last data available), Argentine crude oil exports to Brazil totaled $550.3 million, an increase of 34% from the same period a year earlier.

Argentina is the source of almost 30% of Brazil's crude oil imports, while Saudi Arabia accounts for 27%. The Middle East as a whole supplies about 46% of Brazil's oil.

Pipelining activity

Petrobras called for international bids to lay 280 km of dual 14-in. pipelines to handle growing production of oil and gas in Brazil's Amazonas region.

The project is part of a larger, $391 million effort to increase production in the Amazonas region to 45,000 b/d of oil and 210 MMcfd of gas from 20,000 b/d and 70 MMcfd.

Much of this outlay is earmarked for expansion of the Arara oil and gas complex, scheduled to be completed by first quarter 1998.

The Urucu-to-Coari crude/gas dual pipeline system is another step in efforts to implement the approved further development of Urucu and East Urucu oil and gas fields in the Amazonas region.

At the pipeline terminus, near the town of Coari, Petrobras will build the Polo Arara terminal on the Solimoes River, including crude and gas transshipment facilities.

Petrobras' main obstacle in the Amazon is the river system itself, the principal means of transportation in the region. The levels of Amazon tributaries vary widely from June to November, when rainfall is less frequent.

From Porto de Urucu river terminal to the state capital of

Manaus, flotillas of barges and river boats take 8-9 days to cover about 900 km.

The oil is currently carried from Urucu by a 10-in., 51-km pipeline to a terminal on the banks of the Tefe River. From there, it is taken by barge to a storage tanker anchored close to the town of Tefe, and from there, shuttle tankers transport it to the Manaus refinery for processing.

This is not a feasible option for larger volumes, because of the shallowness of the river during the dry season.

With the installation of the new pipeline, it will take only 16 hr for the crude oil to travel the stretch from Coari to Manaus by oceangoing vessels. Initially, the gas will be processed, with its liquid petroleum gas recovered and marketed. Later, the gas is to be liquefied and shipped out by cryogenic LNG barges to gas-fired thermal power plants in the cities of Manaus, Porto Velho, and elsewhere in the region.

Located about 600 km from Manaus and 500 km from Porto Velho, the capital of Roraima state, the Rio Urucu region produces a sulfur-free, extremely light 47° gravity oil that yields healthy cuts of the naphtha, gasoline, and diesel that are in short supply throughout the Amazon region. In addition to yielding LPG, Rio Urucu natural gas can also be used to generate electric power, replacing fuel oil in the environmentally sensitive rain forest.

In addition to the pipeline, the project involves adding to facilities that will enable Petrobras to increase capacity for production, transportation, and marketing of Amazon oil and gas.

Extending the gathering system, expanding primary oil and gas processing capacity, building a gas processing plant, and increasing gas compression for injection and transportation also are part of the project.

The new natural gas processing plant will have capacity of 210 MMcfd and produce as much as 1,378 cu m/day of LPG, which will be stored in two 3,200 cu m tanks for later shipment along a multiproduct pipeline to the Solimoes river terminal.

The existing natural gas processing plant has a capacity of 21 MMcfd and produces 180 cu m/day of LPG that is transported through a 4.5-in. pipeline to the Tefe river terminal for sale to local distribution companies.

Refinery changes

Expanding oil supplies from Urucu were prompting changes at the Manaus refinery.

A new atmospheric distillation unit will be installed at the refinery to increase crude throughput capacity to 50,370 b/d from 15,870 b/d. The added capacity is to come on stream in April 1998, keeping pace with expanding processing requirements for Urucu oil.

This will be timed to coincide with completion of the new Arara complex, to avoid having to process this oil at other refineries at a higher cost.

Construction of this new unit was triggered by the fact that Urucu oil yields cuts of 60% diesel, 30% naphtha, and 10% atmospheric residue.

Increased drilling

Petrobras was to have started in late 1996 a $100 million program to drill 20 wells as part of the overall program to expand production of oil and gas in the onshore Urucu and Jurua regions of the Upper Amazon.

But even before this drilling program was to start, Petrobras reported a significant gas strike in the region.

Its 1 Copaca wildcat flowed on test about 9.3 MMcfd of gas.

Petrobras' preliminary evaluations estimate potential reserves at more than 35 bcf.

More importantly, the find may open a new play, 60 km from the natural gas province of Jurua and 100 km northwest of the oil and gas producing Urucu region.

If this turns out to be an indication of a hydrocarbon-bearing trend extending all the way from the two producing areas, the proved natural gas reserves in the region—a total of 2.9 tcf, or one fourth of Brazil's total—could increase significantly.

The Amazon region has a sedimentary area prospective for hydrocarbons that covers more than 1.8 million sq km.

In addition to the producing Solimoes basin, other Amazon region basins of interest are Acre, Amazonas, Parnaiba, Tacutu, Marajo, Sao Luiz, Braganca-Viseu, and Barreirinhas.

Of special interest for oil potential is the deepwater portion of the mouth of the Amazon River.

Possible deepwater record

Petrobras's possible record deepwater strike in the Campos basin off Brazil may be another supergiant oil field.

Petrobras more than doubled its estimate of the oil reserves found by its 1-RJS-436 wildcat in 1,853 m (6,078 ft) of water off Rio de Janeiro state. Petrobras claimed it as a possible record water depth for a commercial oil strike.

Initially, Petrobras estimated the find's potential reserves at 400-600 million bbl. Subsequent flow tests of intervals at 3,370 m and 3,395 m indicated a potential productive capacity of 10,000 b/d of 31° gravity oil.

Roberto Alfradique, a top aide to Petrobras E&P Director Antonio Carlos Agostini, said that production test data and updating of seismic data suggest the field, dubbed Roncador, could contain as much as 1.3 billion bbl of oil.

COLOMBIA

CAPITAL: Bogota
MONETARY UNIT: Peso
REFINING CAPACITY: 249,000 b/cd
PRODUCTION: 575,000 b/d
RESERVES: 2.8 billion bbl

Colombia plans to play a growing role in international oil markets while expanding and privatizing its domestic gas and electricity industries.

Officials intend to curb the government's spending on energy development while increasing its energy revenues. Their plans imply growing participation in energy projects by private companies.

Despite its political uncertainties, Colombia has strong sovereign credit and one of South America's most stable economies. Its economy in 1995 grew by 5.5% and has shown sustained strength in this decade.

Officials believe the country's financial reputation and

range of opportunities will attract the estimated $27 billion needed through 2000 for new infrastructure, including big expansions of oil, gas, and power facilities.

Also certain to help attract investment capital is the country's new standing as a world-class oil and gas province. Discovery of Cusiana oil field in 1989 and of Cupiagua oil field in 1992 added 2 billion bbl of oil and 3 tcf of gas reserves, effectively doubling Colombia's totals. Exploration near the giant Cusiana-Cupiagua complex, in the eastern foothills of the Andes about 100 miles northeast of Bogota, has turned up an estimated 10 tcf of gas and 1 billion bbl of oil in Volcanera field and two discoveries overlying it, Florena and Pauto Sur.

Colombia has seized the opportunity provided by Cusiana-Cupiagua to quickly boost oil output. Production during phase two development of the fields, under way since mid-1995, was to reach more than 500,000 b/d by the end of 1997. Cusiana-Cupiagua operator BP Exploration Co. (Colombia) Ltd. and partners since mid-1995 have been producing 180,000-185,000 b/d of oil from phase one facilities.

Oil output countrywide by the end of the century, by some estimates, could surpass 900,000 b/d. In addition, the large gas reserve additions at Cusiana, Volcanera, and other areas will help Colombia boost domestic electricity markets.

Colombia's critics say that, despite its laudable economic stability and improving oil and gas prospectivity, political impediments could interfere with progress toward its lofty energy goals.

Proponents of the expansions maintain the government's energy reforms will come surely but slowly—slowly because a democracy must build national consensus before trying to implement major energy reforms.

Whatever the future holds for Colombia's energy industries, foreign companies in growing numbers are apparently concluding that opportunities in the country outweigh the risks.

Gas pipeline construction

Colombia's gas industry deregulation was entering the final stages.

Officials since 1991 have been laying plans to expand the role of gas in domestic energy markets.

The so-called gas massification plan contemplates spending of more than $3 billion on gas transportation and distribution pipelines, compressed natural gas stations, and customer hardware conversions to double gas consumption by during 1996-2000 to 800 MMcfd. Most of the needed capital is to come from private sources.

The plan essentially would create a national gas pipeline grid by linking Colombia's Atlantic Coast with interior markets, the latter of which are being interconnected by a series of pipeline construction and conversion projects. An estimated 1,400 km of trunk lines and 1,000 km of distribution pipelines are to be built and about 900 km of oil pipelines converted to gas service.

A group led by Enron Corp., Houston, in February 1996 finished and placed into service the $215 million gas trunk line connecting Colombia's coastal and interior gas markets. The 18 in. Centragas pipeline runs 575 km from Ballena on Colombia's Caribbean coast to Barrancabermeja in central Colombia.

Ecopetrol controls the Centragas system's entire 150 MMcfd of capacity through a 15 year contract. Under Colombian law, Ecopetrol is the only company authorized to transport gas on the emerging national grid.

Earlier in 1996, units of TransCanada PipeLine Ltd., Calgary, and BP began a $310 million construction program to develop Colombia's second large diameter gas trunk line. TransGas de Occidente's 345 km, 20 in. main line by yearend 1996 was to have begun transporting gas from Mariquita, northwest of Bogota in Tolima Department, to Cali in Cauca Department. The system also includes about 420 km of 2-8 in. distribution laterals to serve some 47 Cauca Valley communities.

Other trunk lines to form segments on Colombia's national gas grid are in various stages of development under build-operate-transfer (BOT) schemes. Officials created the BOT framework to overcome investment restrictions of the government and help distribute risks among public and private players.

Tying gas to power

Colombia is amassing the gas supplies it will need to serve growing domestic demand.

In addition to the estimated 13 tcf of proved and probable gas reserves likely to be added at Cusiana-Cupiagua and Volcanera, Florena, and Pauto Sur, at least two other fields appear likely to play key roles in the country's growing gas markets.

A unit of Texaco Inc. has agreed with Ecopetrol to prolong production of Chuchupa field in Guajira Department in coastal northeastern Colombia, possibly doubling field output by 2004 to 600 MMcfd.

The new agreement extends Texaco's existing association contract to 2016 from 2004 and changes the terms to a build-operate-maintain-transfer pact after 2004.

Texaco reportedly plans to install a second Chuchupa offshore platform, drill as many as six horizontal wells, and lay a 12 mile gas line from the new platform to facilities onshore. Drilling was set for third quarter 1996, with pipeline and platform installation to occur in the fourth quarter.

Texaco's Guajira fields contain more than 3 tcf of proved gas reserves.

Meantime, Ecopetrol in May 1996 declared the commerciality of Opon field, under development in north-central Colombia by a group led by Amoco Colombia Petroleum Co. The announcement cleared the way for Opon production to start by late 1996 or early 1997.

Reform in the oil sector

Reform in Colombia's oil sector has been shaped by the Cusiana-Cupiagua success.

In an effort to attract multinational companies to Colombia's oil and gas industry, the government in 1994 began revising terms offered through association contracts between Ecopetrol and foreign companies. Officials among other things aimed to increase incentives for firms to undertake exploration of smaller fields in Colombia.

Foremost among the changes was creation of a profitability component—the so-called R factor—which adjusts Ecopetrol's profit share to 50-75%, depending on the ratio of the partner's cumulative income to its cumulative exploration and development costs at a field. Officials also provided that as much as 50% of dry hole direct drilling costs could be reimbursed, with limitations, in any field that eventually became commercial.

In 1995, the government introduced another round of reforms:

- Opening to private foreign and domestic companies areas previously reserved for Ecopetrol.
- Allowing renegotiation of expiring association contracts.
- Adding joint venture and shared risk contracts to the types of joint agreements available in partnership with Ecopetrol.

CUBA

CAPITAL: Havana
MONETARY UNIT: Peso
REFINING CAPACITY: 301,000 b/cd
PRODUCTION: 28,000 b/d
RESERVES: 100 million bbl

Cuba faces a growing energy crisis likely to be exacerbated by U.S. sanctions.

The Helms-Burton Act seeks to block international companies from profiting from the use of U.S. assets expropriated by Cuba in the 1959 revolution, targeting those with U.S. subsidiaries.

The law had been adrift in the U.S. Senate until Cuban jet fighters in February 1996 shot down in international airspace two aircraft flown by Cuban dissidents. The resulting public outrage in the U.S. led to its swift passage and enactment.

However, just when the law was to take effect in July 1996, President Bill Clinton suspended its implementation for 6 months with the promise of an extension if allies joined U.S. efforts to isolate the government of Fidel Castro.

Cuba was struggling to adapt to a sharp cutback in subsidized oil supplies that began with collapse of the Soviet Union in 1989.

Price increases hurting

Adding to Cuba's energy woes were 1996 increases in international oil prices.

Interviewed by a Cuban newspaper, Cuba's Deputy Economy Minister Jose Gonzalez, said, "This situation hurts us a great deal, since prices are going up for the products we need most and, in many cases, we are obliged to sell our products (domestically) at approximately the same prices."

Earlier in 1996, Cuba projected its average 1996 petroleum costs at $135/metric ton, but prices rose to $175/ton during the year.

Cuba's fuel rationing system assigns highest priorities to government operations (especially the military), electric power generation, and the sugar, nickel, and tourism industries.

Cuba's oil supply, imports

Cuba expected to produce a total of about 11 million bbl of crude oil in 1996, about the same as in 1995, according to Juan Fleites, general manager of Cupet Comercial SA, a subsidiary of Cuba's national oil company Cupet.

Exploration efforts by about 10 international oil companies working with Cupet, plus the increased use of enhanced recovery, failed to raise output, leaving the Caribbean nation heavily dependent on imported refined products and severe fuel shortages.

Cuba has to spend about 40% of its export revenues on petroleum imports.

According to Cupet, the country requires about 54.75 million bbl/year of crude and products. With domestic output of both stagnating, Cuba must import 43.8 million bbl/year.

Prior to the demise of the Soviet Union, Cuba used 73-87.6 million bbl/year of crude and products. Since then, the country has heavily rationed the use of petroleum, made efforts to apply energy conservation, and watched its economy crash due to extreme shortages of refined products.

The Soviets formerly supplied Cuba with crude and refined products under highly favorable terms.

Exploration efforts

Cupet was not exploring in 1996, but foreign companies working under production-sharing agreements were conducting seismic work and drilling three wildcats onshore, an official with the state company said.

The government had contracts for exploration for seven onshore and 15 offshore blocks.

Cuba's last discovery was Cupei 1X, an offshore well completed at yearend 1995. Cupet said the well flowed on test at a rate of 3,700 b/d of 16° gravity crude.

The Helms-Burton Act has not yet forced any foreign oil companies to leave Cuba, a U.S. official said. France's Total pulled out in 1995 after working under a risk contract for about 5 years, and a Canadian company, Talisman Energy Corp., sold its Cuban interests in 1994 because its exploration results were disappointing.

Companies from Canada, the U.K., and a few other countries reportedly were exploring in Cuba under production-sharing agreements. But the companies—and the Cuban government—feared sanctions under the Helms-Burton Act.

Cupet said that it was looking for foreign companies to explore 12 other blocks under production-sharing agreements.

It was also seeking partners to add vacuum distillation and cat cracking units to its Cienfuegos refinery, a project started by the Soviets in 1985 and never completed. However, the political tensions between Washington and Havana and the threat of sanctions under Helms-Burton made any new agreements unlikely.

ECUADOR

CAPITAL: Quito
MONETARY UNIT: Sucre
REFINING CAPACITY: 148,000 b/cd
PRODUCTION: 387,000 b/d
RESERVES: 2 billion bbl

Oil and gas companies operating in Ecuador were pressing exploration and development but maintaining a watchful eye

115°
110°
105°
100°
95°
UNITED
Texas
BAJA CALIFORNIA NORTE
BAJA CALIFORNIA SUR
Gulf of California
Nogales
Nogales
Cananea
Magdalena
El Paso
Ciudad Juarez
SONORA
Hermosillo
Guaymas
Navojoa
Celuiosa de Chuhuahua
Chihuahua
Delicias
CHIHUAHUA
Cuidad Camango
Jimenez
COAHUILA
Rio Grande
Ulua
Buena Suerte
Monclova
Nuevo Laredo
Laredo
Lampazos
Corpus Christi
La Presa
Arcos
Sta. Rosalia
Lojitas
Culebra
Canbr
Carretas
Reynosa
Macallen
235
Brownsville
Mission-Trevino
Cadereyta
Reynosa
Brasil
Fortuna
Matamoros
Matamoros
Primavera
Cabeza
Ramirez
S. Bernardo
18 de Marzo
Benavides
Chapul
San Fernando
Pobladores
Huizache
Topolobampo
SINALOA
DURANGO
Gomez Palacio
Monterrey
Culiacan
La Paz
MEXICO
NUEVO LEON
TAMAULIPAS
Lerma
Durango
ZACATECAS
Ciudad Victoria
Mazatlan
SAN LUIS POTOSI
Zacatecas
195
Barcodon
Pacfic Ocean
Chicura
Canuch
Jayabo
NAYARIT
Tepic
San Blas
AGUAS
San Luis Potosi
Ebano Panuco Fields
Ciudad Madero
Tampico
Tamaulipas-Constituciones
Arenque
Cabo Nuevo
Arrecife Medio
Isla de Lobos
TUXPAN
Lagos
GUANAJUATO
QUERETARO
Golden Lane Fields
Tiburon
Esturon
Marsopa
Tuxpan
Puerto Vallarta
JALISCO
Guadalajara
Guanajuato
Queretaro
HIDALGO
320
Bagre
Escuala
Poza Rica
Lago de Chapala
Salamanca
La Barca
240
Tula
Pachuca
Ponche
VERACRUZ
Morelia
MEXICO
TLAX
Jalapa
Manzanillo
Colima
COLIMA
Texoman
MICHOACAN
Mexico City
Toluca
D.F.
Tlaxcala
Veracruz
Miralejos
Remudauer
Cuernavaca
Puebla
Capite
M. Piancho
Mirador
Mecayuman
Coapo
MORELOS
PUEBLA
Angastura
Novillo
Azcapotzelco
Mata Verde
GUERRERO
Mina
Chilpancingo
OAXACA
Oaxaca
Acapulco
Tehuantepec
330
Xicalango
Xicalango
TABASCO
Dos Bocas
Santa Ana
Tupilco
Mecoacan
Cunduacan
El Golpe
El Golpe
Ojiacaque
Puerto Ceiba
Tepotzingo
San Roman
Mango
Usumacinto
Ixhuation
Luna
Ceiba
Cantemoc
Coatzacoalpos
La Venta
Villahermosa
Samaria
Nanchital
Tanaya
La Venta
A.J. Bermudez
Iride
Tasajeras
Zaragoza
Cuichapa
5 Presidentes
Cardenas
Villahermosa
Bitzal
Pajaritos
Minatitlan
Nuevo Teape
El Plan
Ciudad Pemex
El Cobo
El Plan
Cactus
Jose Colomo
Los Soldados
Paredon
Chilapilla
200
Tepate
Cactus
La Central
Tecuanapa
Sitio Grande
Vernet
Paredon
Rio Neevo
Mundo Nuevo
Cacho Lopez
Sitio Grande
F. Nacional
Artesa
Sarlat
Giraldas
Sebancuy
Agave
Copano
Agave
Sabancuy
VERACRUZ
Zapatero
Sunuapa
C. Nanchital
CHIAPAS
Presa Nezahualcoyotl

on a new government.

This posture stems from widespread review of service contracts by the new government of President Abdala Bucaram—and comes on the heels of a reported agreement between the government and YPF SA unit Maxus Energy Corp., which had been embroiled in a contractual dispute.

Service contracts under review in 1996 were held by Oryx Ecuador Energy Co., Occidental Exploration & Production, ARCO Oriente Inc., Elf Aquitaine, and Tripetrol SA. But industry officials said the review was not confined to those companies.

The new government of President Bucaram, which took office in August 1996, deems Ecuadorian economic development a priority—notably foreign investment. But efforts to end state subsidies of petroleum products were politically unpopular.

Upstream projects on track

Upstream projects were moving ahead. Action centered on the Oriente jungle, where wildcats were drilled or planned on Blocks 11, 15, 19, and 21.

Santa Fe Energy Resources Corp. unit Petrolera Santa Fe (Ecuador) Ltd. was drilling its first test as part of a four-well primary term obligation in Block 11 in the North Central Oriente basin.

Oryx planned a wildcat on Block 21 late in first quarter 1997 and continued to build production levels from five fields on Block 7, acquired from British Petroleum Co. plc.

ARCO and partner Agip Petroleum (Ecuador) Ltd. were continuing with previously disclosed plans on detailed engineering and environmental impact studies on a pipeline to move Villano field production to market from Block 10.

Oxy planned a wildcat in Block 15 in fourth quarter 1996.

Triton Energy Ltd. and partners planned to drill two exploratory wells on Block 19 in 1997.

Maxus situation

Maxus faced ouster from Ecuador and possible nationalization of its interests if it and the government could not agree on new contract terms.

According to South American press reports, the government will pay Maxus $108 million as compensation for expenditures Maxus incurred as part of field development work in Ecuador under a service contract signed in 1986. The new participation contract was to be reviewed by officials of the comptroller's office, military commanders, and the Ecuadorian attorney general before final approval.

Various press reports indicated Maxus would pay the government a royalty of 18.4% of gross revenues or, alternatively, 29% of gross production.

Among its Ecuadorian interests, Maxus owns a 35% interest in the 511,000-acre Block 16, about 160 miles southeast of Quito. It operates five fields with combined production totaling 35,000 b/d.

Political scene

President Bucaram, leader of the Roldosista Party, announced a slate of measures aimed at boosting foreign investment in all economic sectors.

The new administration appears to favor oil policy constructed along the lines of a recent National Council on Modernization (Conam) proposal to modify current policy.

The Conam energy proposals under review and discussion include:

- Authorizing construction of private pipelines to carry heavy oil production from fields in the southern Oriente region, in addition to expanding the trans-Ecuadorian Lago Agrio-Balao pipeline.
- Constructing new refineries with private investment.
- Adopting new forms of contracts to foster exploration and production, such as the concession and association contracts that were used previously.
- Reorganizing the state oil company Petroleos del Ecuador (Petroecuador) into a centralized entity by combining the services that are now provided by affiliates Petroproduccion, Petrocomercial, and Petroindustrial.

Santa Fe test

Santa Fe was drilling ahead with its 1 Cristal at yearend 1996, targeting Cretaceous pay in the main Hollin and Napo sections. In mid-October, the well was drilling below 8,000 ft.

In June 1996, Santa Fe completed interpretation of 940 km of high-quality 2D seismic and selected the initial drilling locations from "first-pass" data interpretation.

Santa Fe's seismic gathering work was carried out so as to have minimal environmental impact, the company said. Paths cleared did not exceed 1.2 m, and the company avoided cutting trees that exceeded 1 ft in diameter.

A second test was planned 10 miles southeast of 1 Cristal immediately following the first well.

Santa Fe is obligated to drill 4 exploratory wells in a 4-year primary term contract. Two remaining wells were planned in 1997.

Oryx sets brisk pace

Oryx and partners remained active on productive Block 7 and on Block 21, awarded in 1995 as part of the mid-1994 seventh bid round.

Oryx's 1 Yuralpa Centro, an 8,500 ft test, targeting the Cretaceous main Hollin or pre-Hollin—whichever is encountered first—was to tap an identified structure in an area drilled by Texaco Inc. on the southeast flank of the structure.

On Block 7, the company increased net production after drilling eight of 10 planned wells in a 1996 development drilling program. Oryx boosted production of 23.5° gravity blended crude from five fields to an average rate of 8,600 b/d from a rate of 7,000 b/d net at the beginning of 1996.

Gross production averaged 25,500 b/d from five fields: Coca-Payamino, a unitized field owned by Oryx 46% and Petroproduccion 54%; and from Gacela, Lobo, Jaguar, and Mono fields, all 100% Oryx-owned.

Coca-Payamino, Gacela, and Mono fields produce from multiple horizons. Jaguar produces from the main Hollin, and Lobo produces from the Napo (U), found at about 9,000 ft.

Coca-Payamino is the largest of the five fields. It has a total of about 30 producing wells that yield about 15,500 b/d gross from the main Hollin, encountered at about 9,500 ft, as well as from the upper Hollin, Napo (U), and basal Tena zones. Five wells are producing in Gacela, six in Mono, three in Jaguar, and one in Lobo.

Oxy, Triton plans

Oxy planned a test of the Yuturi prospect on Block 15. In the unexplored extreme southeastern corner of Block 15, where Oxy had gathered 2D and 3D seismic data, the company was to have spudded the 1 Eden wildcat in fourth quarter 1996.

The well is part of an obligation calling for 600 km of seismic and 4 wells during a 3-year exploration term.

In an agreement signed with the government, Oxy was granted a minimum 7-year extension to develop new discoveries.

Oxy, the first foreign company to sign a service contract with the government, has been developing Block 15 since its initial plan of development was approved in July 1992. Average 1996 net production totaled about 17,000 b/d.

On Block 19, awarded in the seventh bid round, Triton and partners had acquired 400 km of 2D seismic, and data interpretation was under way in 1996. The block covers 494,200 acres. Triton did not disclose details of the two exploratory wells planned for the block.

ARCO-Agip work

ARCO and partner Agip Petroleum (Ecuador) Ltd. planned a pipeline to transport crude from Villano field on Block 10.

A 105-mile secondary pipeline is planned to transport crude oil from Villano field—where the companies expect to recover 160 million bbl of 21° gravity oil—to the Trans-Ecuadorian Pipeline System.

An agreement with the government of Ecuador amends the existing ARCO-Agip service contract. The government will reimburse the partners for their exploration, development, and production costs after development is completed and production begins.

Plans call for the pipeline to be operational by 1999. It will have a capacity of 80,000 b/d, but initial shipments will be 30,000 b/d, ARCO said. Excess capacity will be reserved for other field developments or to allow partners to ramp up Villano production levels.

Trunk pipeline plans

Authorities and production-sharing contractors in 1996 wanted to boost pipeline capacity of the Trans-Ecuadorian Lago Agrio-Balao trunk line under a phased, build-operate-transfer (BOT) approach.

Capacity in the Lago Agrio-Balao trunk line is limited to 380,000 b/d.

A tender was being prepared for first-phase expansion by Petroecuador, and about 45 companies submitted prequalification documents.

Second phase, requiring a 120,000-150,000 b/d loop line, will be constructed by private companies under a BOT scheme.

Another plan, which has been under preliminary discussion with the government of Ecuador but was in question, is a new 180,000 b/d heavy crude pipeline to carry oil from the southeastern Oriente region.

The proposed pipeline, which would be built by a group of companies, would parallel the existing Trans-Ecuadorian pipeline.

Project cost is estimated at $400-500 million, and construction would take about 2 years.

The government said in early October 1996 it wanted to seek competitive bidding on the pipeline, and Ecuadorian Energy Minister Alfredo Adum said other companies will be asked for bid proposals.

What that action means for this proposal remains to be seen. A spokesman for Enron Development Corp. (EDC), one of the group members engaged in the talks, said EDC may or may not take part in the bidding process because the project was "up in the air."

MEXICO

CAPITAL: Mexico City
MONETARY UNIT: Peso
REFINING CAPACITY: 1.5 million b/cd
PRODUCTION: 2.7 million b/d
RESERVES: 49 billion bbl

Mexico's state-owned petroleum company Petroleos Mexicanos was grappling with a host of woes in 1996 amid creeping privatization.

Pemex roller-coastered from tragedy to triumph, coming under increasing political and public scrutiny as it coped with the Mexican government's efforts to liberalize investment in the energy sector.

On the bright side, there were huge pre-tax profits for the company, making it a powerful generator of income for the cash-strapped federal government.

But setbacks stalked the company, with at least three major, widely reported incidents that shook confidence in Pemex and caused people to question its role in Mexico.

Not since April 1993—when an underground gasoline spill leaked into sewers and ignited, devastating a colonial area of Guadalajara and killing more than 200 people—has Pemex been under such intense pressure and scrutiny. The incidents:

- In October 1995, powerful Hurricane Opal twice slammed into Pemex's key producing area in Campeche Sound, killing oil workers and damaging equipment. Production—which dropped from 2.728 million b/d to 712,000 b/d—did not return to normal levels until December 1995.
- In February 1996, angry protesters blocked 69 oil wells for 2 weeks in the southern state of Tabasco, causing Pemex to lose more than $10 million in revenue. With international attention focused on them, the protesters complained about political irregularities in the state and pollution allegedly caused by Pemex.
- On July 26, a series of explosions crippled the Cactus natural gas processing plant, killing half a dozen workers and knocking off-line more than 30% of the nation's natural gas supply.

Few Mexicans know much about the traditionally secretive Pemex, other than the school textbook story about its nationalization in 1938 by President Lazaro Cardenas.

Meanwhile, the state company is being pushed to produce more oil, generate more revenue, and comply with a variety of political and economic situations that are rattling officials at their Mexico City headquarters.

Starving the "goose"

Observers, as well as Director General Lajous, are worried the "goose that laid the golden egg" is being starved.

Pemex's tax rate is 67%, the highest for any company in the country.

"Like any business, we would like to pay lower taxes and have more money available for expansion," Lajous told reporters at the end of February 1996.

An industry observer was more blunt. "The federal government must stop bleeding Pemex," said Juan Quintanilla, deputy director of the Programa Universitario de Energia at the Universidad Nacional de Mexico.

Quintanilla, a noted analyst on Pemex and domestic energy policy, said that instead of paying such a high percentage of profits to the federal treasury, Pemex should be able to invest in modernization, increasing its potential to produce more value-added products, and ultimately generate additional revenue.

Safety

Pemex's safety record was the focus of a great deal of scrutiny, particularly after the devastating series of explosions at the Cactus gas processing complex in the southern state of Chiapas.

"There has been an abandonment of the oil industry in the country, not only in terms of investigation and exploration, but also crucial activities that have to do with maintenance," said Alejandro Encinas, a member of the opposition Democratic Revolutionary Party.

Pemex officials were quick to develop a series of responses to the growing public outcry over the Cactus explosion, as well as to the potential for similar disasters elsewhere.

Pemex officials presented statistics that purported to show that Pemex's incidence of industrial accidents, based on injured workers, was only half the level of those reported by the U.S. Gas Processors Association (GPA). However, those numbers covered only Pemex's record for the first 6 months of 1996, whereas the GPA data covered 1992-95.

Even then, the numbers showed that Pemex accidents tended to be more serious than those of its U.S. counterparts.

Pemex pledged to earmark more funds for safety and maintenance but would not specify how that money would be spent.

Secondary petrochemicals

In a political about-face, Mexico decided to seek 49% private investment in its "secondary" petrochemical plants—instead of the politically controversial outright sale of the plants to investors.

At the same time, however, the plan also opened this sector of the petroleum industry to foreign companies to build and operate their own, 100% privately owned secondary petrochemical plants. This will mark the first time private investment has been allowed in Mexico's petroleum operations sector since March 1938.

Mexico expected to create 10-15 public-private companies early in 1997 that would manage the secondary petrochemical plants, Energy Secretary Jesus Reyes Heroles said. The government will hold a 51% share.

"The most important thing is to ensure that this sector gets what it requires—as much new investment as possible," Reyes Heroles said.

Since 1992, Mexico had 61 secondary petrochemical plants in the process of privatization, a cornerstone of the current and past administrations' economic policy.

The original plan, which was to generate as much as $3 billion for the government, fell victim to nationalist sentiments and opposition by the government-aligned Institutional Revolutionary Party, among other opponents.

Secondary petrochemicals, by the government's description, intermediate petrochemicals derived from olefins and aromatics are currently produced only by Pemex. A sizable number of private firms produce petrochemicals further downstream as well as specialty chemicals in Mexico.

The administration, which will propose changes to Article 27 of the Mexican constitution, would allow private companies to set up operations and compete with the government in the area of secondary petrochemicals.

The Energy Secretariat, the Federal Competition Commission, and the Commerce Secretariat are to establish regulations governing these private-sector operations.

Any new plants—as well as those incorporated in the public-private partnership—would still have to obtain feedstocks from Pemex.

Nonetheless, the government's decision not to sell the current state-owned secondary petrochemical operations was seen as a means to placate the feverish opposition and regain points with the public.

PERU

CAPITAL: Lima
MONETARY UNIT: Inti
REFINING CAPACITY: 182,000 b/cd
PRODUCTION: 124,000 b/d
RESERVES: 808 million bbl

The privatization of Peru's petroleum industry marked a new turning point with the sale of Petroleos del Peru SA's (Petroperu) last oil field.

Petroperu's privatization committee sold the Talara basin's Block X on the northern coast to Perez Companc SA, Buenos Aires.

It sold for an unexpectedly high $202 million—more than triple the minimum bid of $65 million.

Also auctioned in 1996 were a 50% interest in the 102,000 b/d La Pampilla refinery at Lima, Petroperu's lubricants business, and northern jungle Blocks 8 and 8X. A fifth unit, the Talara refinery, was slated for auction by yearend 1996, but those plans were delayed.

In other activity, Peru's government signed contracts for 13 blocks, and negotiations were under way for another four blocks. Among the largest, signed in May 1996, was a contract with units of Royal Dutch/Shell Group and Mobil Corp., under which the companies will spend $2.7-2.8 billion to develop the giant Camisea gas fields in the central southern jungle.

Perupetro SA, the state's regulatory agency, signed contracts with other firms for development of oil and gas fields in the northern and central jungles.

Recent developments

Among other developments:

• Perupetro signed contracts with units of Denver-based Advantage Resources International and Barrett Resources Corp. for Blocks 55A, 55B, and 55C in the northern jungle and with a unit of Occidental Petroleum Corp. for an exploration license in Peru's northern jungle Block 72.

• Pluspetrol SA, Buenos Aires, and partners took over operation of Petroperu's former northern jungle Blocks 8 and 8X and signed an exploration license with Perupetro for the first stage of development in the central jungle's Block 79, near the Aguaytia gas fields.

• Shell Prospecting & Development (Peru) BV, operator of the Camisea fields, announced plans to drill appraisal wells starting early in 1997. In addition, Shell and partner Mobil Exploration & Producing Peru Inc. awarded exclusive rights to a group of U.S. firms to build and operate a 600-Mw power plant fueled by gas from the Camisea fields and selected contractors for the preliminary design of a gas plant, a fractionation plant, and pipelines connecting the fields to Lima.

• Mobil Oil del Peru won the auction held by Petroperu's privatization committee for Petrolube SA, the company's lubricants business.

• Refinadores del Peru SA, a new company formed by a group led by Spain's Repsol SA, formally took over operations of the La Pampilla refinery and disclosed investment plans.

Block X Sale

Auction winner Perez Companc is no newcomer to Block X. The company operated the Laguna Zapatal fields on the block during 1984-88 under contract to Petroperu to reactivate shut-in oil wells in the area. Perez Companc is now committed to invest a minimum of $25 million on Block X the next 5 years. It was slated to take over operation in mid-December 1996.

The block lies along the northern coast of Peru, covering about 96,330 acres. It contains proven reserves of 46.4 million bbl, but local geologists believe the fields could produce another 200 million bbl. The block has more than 1,200 producing wells, many yielding only a few barrels a day. The oil, at 30-35° gravity, is lighter than jungle production and is transported via pipeline to the north coast refinery. The field's production in September 1996 averaged 16,000 b/d.

Camisea area action

Shell and Mobil are developing the Camisea fields under a contract in which Shell holds a 57.5% interest.

Shell discovered the world-class natural gas fields in the mid-1980s. Camisea is 500 km east of Lima, across the Andes, in the Ucayali basin. The area includes Cashiriari, San Martin, and Miyapa fields. Estimated reserves are 11 tcf of natural gas and 600 million bbl of condensate.

Shell planned to drill three appraisal wells starting in February 1997. The wells were to be drilled about 100 days apart, starting in the Cashiriari field, moving to the San Martin field, and then back to the Cashiriari field.

The license agreement provides 2 years to evaluate options for developing the reserves. As part of the project, Shell also is studying potential size of the gas market in Lima. "We see the market as industrial," a company official said, adding that there would have to be demand of at least 200 MMcfd to justify full development.

Shell was in the early stages of previewing design options for future facilities, which would include one natural gas and one condensate pipeline—each about 500 km—between the Camisea area and Lima, a fractionation plant, and a gas plant.

Advantage/Barrett plans

Advantage Resources Selva LLC, a unit of an established player in Peruvian exploration, will team with Barrett Resources (Peru) Corp., a newcomer to Peru, in exploring northern jungle blocks 55A, 55B, and 55C. The blocks cover more than 812,000 acres.

The companies will be working in areas where Amoco Corp., Phillips Petroleum Co., and Union Oil Co. of California (now Unocal Corp.) in the early 1970s drilled dry holes and several wells with shows of heavy oil.

One prevously mapped feature where early efforts will focus could contain 50-80 million bbl of oil.

Work in the first 9 months were to include reprocessing and interpreting 2,000 line-km of seismic data and production engineering studies with new simulation methods on the wells. The second 15-month period will include the acquisition of 400 km of 2D seismic and drilling one exploratory well. The companies are expected to invest about $25.9 million during the minimum 4-year work period.

Oxy efforts

Occidental Petrolera del Peru added a third area to its active roster in the Andean nation when it acquired exploration and development rights on the nearly 2 million-acre Block 72 in the northern jungle.

The contract's exploration stage includes acquiring 100 line-km of 2D seismic data, reprocessing and interpreting 100 km of existing seismic surveys, and drilling five exploratory wells.

Perupetro estimates a minimum $44.5 million investment by the Oxy unit. If successful, Oxy will pay royalties beginning at 18% on the first 40 million bbl of oil, rising gradually to 40% for output exceeding 250 million bbl.

Oxy continues producing oil from declining fields on northern jungle Block 1AB. Through September 1996, output averaged 52,957 b/d, or 44% of Peru's production of 119,754 b/d.

Occidental also is the operator in exploring northern jungle Block 54, in association with Pluspetrol. It withdrew from Block

4, also in the northern jungle, after completing a 2-year exploration program that ended with a dry hole.

Pluspetrol group

Pluspetrol, the operator with 60%, and its partners Korea Petroleum Development Corp. (Pedco), Daewoo Corp., and Yukong Ltd., all of Seoul, took over the operation of Petroperu SA's former northern jungle Blocks 8 and 8X.

The companies won Petroperu's 20 and 25-year contracts for the blocks in a tender held at the same auction as the La Pampilla refinery.

As part of the deal on the northern jungle blocks, the Argentine and South Korean companies also acquired the oil field assets, which include 49 million bbl of proven oil reserves and an average 27,000 b/d of crude oil production. They will pay 25.5% royalties to the government on oil production.

Block 8, in the Maranon basin, is formed by the oil fields that Petroperu found and developed after it started its jungle operations in 1971. Block 8X is made up of the rest of the area where Pluspetrol will continue Petroperu's earlier exploration.

The new operator's expenditure will include maintenance and renewal of installations and equipment, drilling of development wells to maintain and increase production in Block 8, and seismic studies and drilling exploratory wells on Block 8X. It also will cover environmental remediation costs, especially in the Yanayacu fields, located in the Pacaya Samiria national ecological reserve. The cost of remediating environmental damage by earlier oil operations will be covered from privatization funds.

On another front, Pluspetrol will spend a minimum $29 million on the first stage of an exploration and development licensing contract signed with Perupetro for the central jungle's Block 79 in the Ucayali basin, near the Aguaytia gas fields.

The 7-year program includes a 400-km seismic study and five exploratory wells.

Also in the Ucayali basin, Anadarko Petroleum Corp., Houston, estimates that it will spend $57 million on exploration and development of Block 84, for which it signed a license with Perupetro.

The 30-year contract can be extended to 40 years, if there is a gas find, and includes minimum work of a 600-km seismic study and drilling five exploratory wells.

Downstream privatization

Petroperu also moved ahead in its privatization of downstream assets in 1996, awarding the bid for Petrolube SA, the company's lubricants business, to Mobil Oil del Peru (Cia. Comercial).

Mobil won the lube operation with an offer of $18.85 million, two and a half times the $7.5 million base price. The purchase includes a 300,000 bbl/year lubes blending plant, a grease plant, and the brand name.

Mobil intends to continue marketing Petrolube products and will produce Mobil and Petrolube lubricants at the same plant. The company said both brands combined cover almost half the country's market.

Mobil already has a lube blending plant at Callao with capacity of 160,000 bbl/year. Mobil also has a 9% share in the group led by Repsol that bought a 60% stake in Petroperu's La Pampilla refinery.

Meanwhile, Refinadores del Peru SA, the new owners of the 60% stake in the refinery, formally took over operations, changing the company's name to Refineria La Pampilla SA, Relapasa. Empresa Repsol SA, the Peruvian subsidiary of Repsol, is the technical operator. Relapasa will continue to supply all domestic and foreign clients interested in its oil products.

The new owners of La Pampilla must invest a minimum $50 million upgrading the refinery the next 5 years, starting with $5 million the second year. The companies will first let contract for an engineering study to decide where to begin.

Petroperu's privatization committee will contribute $37 million to environmental remediation programs at La Pampilla the next 5 years. After that, it will be the responsibility of the new owners.

TRINIDAD & TOBAGO

CAPITAL: Port of Spain
MONETARY UNIT: Dollar
REFINING CAPACITY: 245,000 b/cd
PRODUCTION: 129,000 b/d
RESERVES: 551 million bbl

Major construction work on Trinidad and Tobago's Atlantic LNG project, the first grassroots liquefied natural gas export project in the Western Hemisphere in more than 25 years, was under way at yearend 1996.

The project, conceived in 1992, calls for building a single-train, $1 billion LNG complex at Point Fortin, in Trinidad.

It is designed to produce 3 million metric tons/year of LNG, with first shipments projected for mid-1999.

The plant's entire output will be exported to markets in the Northeast U.S. and Spain, and the project is being laid out with space for additional LNG trains.

Atlantic LNG Co. of Trinidad & Tobago, the joint venture that will build and operate the plant, has these partners: Amoco Trinidad (LNG) BV, a unit of Amoco Corp., 34%; British Gas Trinidad LNG Ltd., a unit of British Gas plc, 26%; Repsol International Finance BV, a subsidiary of Spain's Repsol SA, 20%; Cabot Trinidad Ltd., a unit of Boston-based Cabot Corp., 10%; and the National Gas Co. (NGC) of Trinidad & Tobago, a government-owned concern, 10%.

Bechtel is the prime contractor for the project, with responsibility for engineering, procurement, construction, start-up, and initial operating services.

Atlantic had already carried out site preparation and some design/engineering work, and orders had been placed for equipment.

Atlantic signed an agreement with Phillips Petroleum Co. to use its Optimized Cascade LNG process, and financing of $600 million was being arranged by ABN Amro Bank N.V., Barclays Bank plc, and Citibank N.A.

Economic effects

The project ranks as the largest single investment ever made in the Caribbean islands and will have a major effect on the economy of Trinidad and Tobago, a republic of only 1.3 million people.

At its construction peak, the project will employ about 2,000 people, the great majority from Trinidad.

However, the plant will be highly automated and will have only 100-150 workers after it goes into commercial operation.

Atlantic, set up in 1995, estimates that the project will have a direct economic benefit of about $6 billion to the island republic during its first 20 years, including taxes and royalties, plus a ripple effect on the general economy.

Small scope, short fuse

Atlantic's investors kept the project's size and development costs relatively small in comparison with other LNG projects under consideration internationally.

If the project goes on stream in 1999, as planned, it will have a 7-year development cycle, compared with a world average of 14 years or more. The future plant's natural gas requirements (as much as 475 MMcfd) will be met by Amoco's Trinidad operating unit, Amoco Trinidad Oil Co. (ATOC), under a 20-year supply agreement, with an option to extend under certain conditions.

The gas will come from fields in the Atlantic Ocean off Trinidad's southeastern coast and will be carried to the Point Fortin facility in the west by subsea and onshore pipelines.

Amoco plans to lay a total of 172 miles of pipelines—112

miles of subsea and onshore lines for natural gas and 60 miles for condensates—linking the offshore fields to the plant site.

LNG buyers

Cabot and Repsol affiliate Enagas SA, also a Spanish company, will take 100% of Atlantic LNG's output under another 20-year contract that may be extended under certain conditions.

The two companies see windows of opportunity for LNG in their respective markets, and they contend the Atlantic project will provide them with a competitive advantage over planned gas pipelines and competing fuels.

Cabot LNG Corp., which has been importing and distributing LNG in the U.S. Northeast for 25 years, will purchase 60% of overall production and Enagas the remaining 40%.

Repsol is an integrated oil, gas, and petrochemical company that works in Spain and internationally. It owns 45% of Gas Natural, Spain's largest natural gas distributor, which in turn holds 91% of Enagas, the largest importer and wholesaler of natural gas in Spain.

Phillips process

Phillips's Optimized Cascade LNG process was chosen over Air Products & Chemicals Inc.'s LNG technology.

The only commercial application of the Phillips Cascade system up to now has been at the Kenai LNG plant in Alaska, a joint venture of Phillips and Marathon Oil Co. that went on stream in 1969 with a nameplate capacity of 1.56 million tons/year.

Prior to the Atlantic project, Kenai was the last grassroots LNG export project to be built in the hemisphere.

The plant will use five GE Frame 5 gas turbines for its drivers and have an air cooling system. It will also have several smaller turbines to improve reliability and flexibility and maintain a high level of efficiency.

Other spending

Aside from the $1 billion investment estimate for the LNG plant, loading facilities, and marine terminal (a port will have to be dredged at Point Fortin), partners estimate that $300-400 million or more will be part of the overall project outlay.

Most of these additional investments cover what Amoco will have spent for exploration, development, and production in Trinidad's offshore gas fields, as well as pipeline construction.

Also, Cabot will invest in refurbishing and upgrading its LNG tanker and in raising regasification capacity at its Everett, Mass., terminal.

Amoco project work

Amoco Trinidad is developing two of its offshore gas fields—East Mayaro and South SEG (southeast Galeota)—to supply the Point Fortin LNG plant with as much as 475 MMcfd of gas for 20 years starting in 1999.

It plans to drill 65 wells in these two fields the next few years, with 12 wells to be drilled in East Mayaro during 1997-98.

Overall, 40 wells are scheduled for East Mayaro and 25 for South SEG. Wells will be drilled directionally from platforms.

Amoco plans to install two platforms at the outset and may add another later.

Initial separation of natural gas liquids will be carried out on the platforms.

Atlantic intends to sell its mixed NGL stream to Phoenix Park Gas Processors Ltd. (a joint venture of Conoco Inc., NGC, and Pan West Engineers & Constructors) on a netback basis.

Pipeline work

The LNG project will require construction of two subsea pipelines.

A 14-in. condensate line will extend from the offshore platforms about 60 miles to Galena Point. Most of the condensate pipeline will be offshore.

To carry natural gas to the plant at Point Fortin, Amoco will lay about 112 miles of pipeline: 62 miles of 40-in. subsea line and 50 miles of 36-in. line onshore.

The offshore pipelines will be built, owned, and operated by Amoco Trinidad. The onshore segment of the gas pipeline will be built by Amoco Trinidad on behalf of owner NGC, and Amoco will operate the line.

Amoco Trinidad E&D

Amoco has invested more than $1.5 billion for exploration, development, and production in the gas and oil fields off Trinidad's eastern coast since the mid-1960s.

The company expects substantial future capital outlays for offshore development and production, platforms, pipelines, and other facilities to provide the LNG plant with natural gas.

Amoco estimates its capital investments in Trinidad the next 2 decades at $1.2 billion.

During 1976-93, Amoco drilled about 40 exploratory wells in the Atlantic east of Trinidad, with only four discoveries (two crude oil and two gas).

"But 1994 to early 1995 was the big turnaround for us," said Larry Tiezzi, Amoco Trinidad's exploration manager.

The company drilled six exploratory wells, finding gas with three during its 1994-95 exploration program.

Since then, under its 1995-96 exploration program that started in October 1995, the company has drilled eight more wells, discovering large volumes of gas with six. One well was a dry hole and another, a discovery, is still being tested. The eighth well, La Novia, located 35 miles offshore, completed the company's 1995-96 drilling program for Trinidad.

Of its total reserves of 10 tcf, Amoco Trinidad has added about 7 tcf of natural gas and more than 100 million bbl of crude to its reserves in Trinidad since 1994.

This accounts for a major share of the island's proven and probable natural gas reserves, estimated by the government at 18.1 tcf by yearend 1995 vs. 13.9 tcf in 1994.

Trinidad potential

Trinidad's natural gas reserves figure as a major reason for the project's feasibility.

NGC calculates that the country's estimated reserves will cover 28 years of production, including domestic consumption and the LNG plant requirements.

International companies believe the island republic has additional commercial reserves off the eastern coast and in the north coast offshore, some of which have already been identified.

Trinidad's Ministry of Energy and Energy Industries issued a public call for bids on nine deepwater blocks to the east and northeast of the main island.

This was the first time the country had sought offers for deepwater blocks.

The most recent oil and gas discoveries were drilled in water depths of 200-350 ft from 35-53 miles offshore in the Atlantic.

Amoco's 1 Corallita, the well located farthest offshore, was drilled to 15,124 ft TD and flowed 60.4 MMcfd of gas.

This was the most expensive Trinidad well to date, costing about $13 million. Other wells in the current program cost $8-9 million each.

Another discovery, 5 East Mayaro, drilled to 13,315 ft in 290 ft of water, tested at 34.9 MMcfd of gas and 3,400 b/d of crude.

Amoco's 5-X East Mayaro, 45 miles offshore, tested at 64 MMcfd of gas and 3,700 b/d of crude and condensate.

There are more than 20 oil and gas fields east of Trinidad, and Amoco has discovered most of them. Even though Amoco has drilled as deep as 18,000 ft, it has mostly worked in Pleistocene to modern structures.

The basin east of Trinidad where Amoco and other companies are drilling offers excellent source rock, good quality reservoir rock, and multiple pay zones.

Gas market

NGC says that natural gas demand in Trinidad and Tobago grew from 150 MMscfd in 1978 to 593 MMscfd at yearend 1995, an average increase of 8.4%/year.

Using a "moderate growth scenario," NGC predicts that natural gas demand in Trinidad and Tobago will rise to 1.6 bscfd by 2000, including the LNG project, petrochemicals, additional light and heavy industrial requirements, plus other domestic demand.

And excluding a second LNG train, NGC projects natural gas demand will jump to as much as 1.8 bscfd by 2005.

NGC says the country's domestic gas requirements by 2000 will be met by Amoco, British Gas, and Enron, as well as NGC's own operations.

The Atlantic LNG project is by far the largest of several natural gas-related projects that are expected to bring the island investments of $3 billion through 2001-2002.

Other major projects are being planned or carried out with the help of international investors in methanol, ammonia, other petrochemicals, and iron carbide and hot-briquetted iron.

VENEZUELA

CAPITAL: Caracas
MONETARY UNIT: Bolivar
REFINING CAPACITY: 1.2 million b/cd
PRODUCTION: 2.6 million b/d
RESERVES: 65 billion bbl

Venezuela's long-range program to rejuvenate its marginal oil fields continued to gather momentum with disclosure of its third operating agreement round and new initiatives to encourage participation.

The Ministry of Energy and Mines, Petroleos de Venezuela SA (Pdvsa), and Pdvsa units Corpoven SA, Lagoven SA, and Maraven SA said the planned operating-agreement round would involve 20 inactive and producing marginal field areas covering 7,800 sq km (1.9 million acres) in Venezuela's eastern and western basins.

Pdvsa said the areas could contain 2-3 billion bbl of oil reserves.

"The third round represents the next stage of the highly successful process, started in 1991, of reactivating fields and incorporating them into Venezuela's mainstream production," said Energy and Mines Minister Erwin Arrieta.

Through 2006-2011, Venezuela hopes to generate as much as $12 billion in added investment in its upstream sector. It plans to increase its production capacity to more than 6 million b/d as part of a continuing upstream development plan.

Pdvsa hopes production from the 20 fields offered will yield 300,000 b/d. Production from the 15 fields in the first two bid rounds totals about 450,000 b/d, Pdvsa said.

What's involved, terms

The 20 areas offered cover both onshore and offshore acreage and include Lake Maracaibo acreage.

The areas contain more than 3,000 wells, 700 of which are producing mostly light and medium oil at combined rates of 66,000 b/d.

Fields offered in western Venezuela are: Ambrosio, Bachaquero South West, Cretacico Sur, La Concepcion, Mene Grande, Intercampo North, B-2X.70/80, B-2X.68/79, LL-652, Cabimas, and La Vela Costa Afuera.

Offered eastern fields are: Acema, Boqueron, Caracoles, Casma Anaco, Dacion, Kaki, Maulpa, Mata, and Onado. Bidding was expected to take place in May 1997.

Five fields were reserved for Venezuelan companies or groups of companies that have a Venezuelan operator. They are: Acema, Casma Anaco, Kaki, Maulpa, and Mata. The Minister of Energy & Mines said he hopes this will encourage greater domestic participation in Venezuela's exploration and production sector.

Also, the ministry wanted to encourage participation by Venezuelan companies whose activity had been limited to engineering and other services, companies entering the oil sector for the first time, and entrepreneurial and start-up companies.

Under each of the operating agreements, the successful company or group will be required initially to evaluate and then present a plan to undertake, on behalf of the affiliate, the rehabilitation, reactivation, and continuing development of the area involved.

Initiatives

Pdvsa said two initiatives will be introduced in the third round.

First, the five fields reserved to Venezuelan companies are an attempt to form the core of a new, emerging exploration and production sector, according to Claus Graf, Pdvsa vice-president.

"While these operators will be free to form joint ventures with international companies in bidding for these areas, this will provide a significant new opportunity not only for existing Venezuelan oil and service companies, but also for new ventures formed especially for this round," Graf said.

Second, a new investment vehicle will be offered to encourage direct participation by the Venezuelan public.

Graf said the new vehicle was to be organized through a new Pdvsa unit, Soc. de Fomento de Inversiones Petroleras (Sofip).

Graf said Sofip will have the opportunity to participate in all the areas as a 10% working interest partner alongside winning consortium members.

First round awards

At midyear 1996, Venezuela began awarding acreage offered earlier in the year in the country's first oil and gas bidding round since it reopened to foreign investment in 1993.

In all, Venezuela awarded profit sharing contracts (PSCs) covering exploration activity on eight tracts with a combined area of 18,000 sq km.

The PSCs are expected to require initial investment of $1-2 billion during 5-9 years. On acreage where operators achieve commercial production, the agreements could be extended for 3 decades or more.

Undiscovered oil resources on the newly assigned areas are estimated at 7-23 billion bbl. Pdvsa, through its Corp. Venezolana del Petroleo SA (CVP), unit retains the right to acquire as much as 35% interest in areas marked for development.

Among the winning bidders:

- A group led by Mobil Exploration & Development Venezuela Inc. won the right to explore La Ceiba block, a hotly contested 445,000 acre tract on the southeastern shore of Lake Maracaibo.
- A combine of Enron Oil & Gas Venezuela Ltd. (EOG) and Inelectra SA, one of Venezuela's largest construction and engineering companies, offered the highest bid for the 268,000 acre Gulf of Paria East tract off Venezuela and near Trinidad.
- Louisiana Land & Exploration Co. (LL&E), New Orleans, Norcen Energy Resources Ltd., Calgary, and Benton Oil & Gas Co., Oxnard, Calif., received a PSC on Delta Centro block, a 526,000 acre tract in the Orinoco River delta marshlands of Venezuela's Delta Amacuro state.
- Other high bidders and their tracts included British Petroleum Co. plc, Amoco Corp., and Maxus Energy Corp. on the Guarapiche block; Conoco Venezuela on the Gulf of Paria West block; Elf Aquitaine and Conoco on Guanare block; Amoco on Punta Pescador block; and Perez Companc on San Carlos block.

La Ceiba plans

Details of the PSCs governing exploration and development on the profit sharing tracts were beginning to emerge.

Mobil and partners Veba Oel and Nippon Oil won rights to explore the La Ceiba tract by committing to a $50 million work program on the concession in the next 3_ years. The group agreed to collect 2D and 3D seismic data and drill three wildcats to at least 18,000 ft during the period.

Under an accelerated program, the partners expectd to begin seismic work in fourth quarter 1996 with the first well to spud early in 1997.

Paria East concession

EOG and Inelectra agreed to an initial exploration term of 4 years on the Gulf of Paria East block.

The PSC on the acreage requires partners to acquire 300 sq km of 3D seismic data and 1,000 line-km of 2D, plus drill two wells. If production is achieved on the acreage, the agreement with CVP could be extended for as long as 35 years.

Previous drilling within the Paria East concession area confirmed the presence of hydrocarbons on the acreage. Located off the eastern Venezuelan state of Sucre in water as deep as 80 ft, Paria East is adjacent to Trinidad's Soldado field.

EOG or an affiliate is expected to become operator of the tract with 90% interest. Inelectra holds the remaining 10% interest in the concession.

EOG Chairman, Pres., and Chief Executive Officer Forrest E. Hoglund said partners expected to begin acquiring 3D seismic data in fourth quarter 1996.

Other exploration plans

LL&E, Norcen, and Benton agreed to acquire and process 1,300 km of seismic data on Delta Centro block and drill three wells during a 5 year exploration period. The partners have an option to extend exploration for another 4 years.

The group planned to begin gathering seismic data in fourth quarter 1996 in the southwestern part of the tract, pending approval of environmental permits. Exploratory drilling was to begin in second half 1997.

LL&E and Norcen each hold 35% interest in the acreage and Benton 30%.

On other exploration tracts:

- Conoco Venezuela hoped to begin drilling on Guanare block in fourth quarter 1997 and to start production in 1998-99.
- BP, operator of the Guarapiche block, said its group expects to spend about $60 million on the tract during 2-3 years. Exploratory drilling was to begin by fourth quarter 1997.

Heavy oil deal

ARCO and Corpoven agreed to form a joint venture to undertake a $3.5 billion heavy oil project in Venezuela.

Partners by 2006 expected to be upgrading as much as 200,000 b/d of 9° gravity crude from Venezuela's Orinoco belt. The upgraded 25° gravity oil will have characteristics similar to crude produced on Alaska's North Slope.

Corpoven Chairman Guillermo Archila and ARCO Chairman Mike R. Bowlin set terms and conditions of the deal in a memo of understanding. The strategic association is a first for Corpoven.

The Venezuelan government's executive branch was to present the plan for approval to the next session of the National Congress.

The deal calls for partners to produce extra-heavy crude from the Hamaca zone south of El Tigre in Anzoategui state and transport the crude by pipeline to an upgrading plant to be built at Jose.

The estimated cost of the three-phase project includes drilling and construction of field, transportation, and upgrading facilities.

Processing activity

Mobil Chemical Corp. formed a 50-50 joint venture with Pequiven, the petrochemical unit of Pdvsa, to develop a $1.5 billion grassroots olefins complex at Jose.

The project includes an 830,000 metric ton/year ethane-based ethylene cracker and related facilities to produce 480,000 tons/year of polyethylene and 430,000 tons/year of ethylene glycol. Pdvsa's Corpoven unit will supply the cracker with associated gas from eastern Venezuela's San Joaquin field.

Mobil and Lagoven formed a 50-50 joint venture to produce heavy crude oil from the Orinoco belt, upgrade it in Jose, and complete processing in Mobil's 180,000 b/d refinery in Chalmette, La..

Pequiven also plans to build a $120 million, 120,000 metric ton/year polyvinyl chloride resins plant to supply Venezuelan and other Latin American markets.

The plant, to be built by Jantesa SA, Venezuela, and Technipetrol, Italy, was targeted for completion by August 1998.

Lagoven let contract to a combine of M.W. Kellogg and Venezuela's Inelectra to build a naphtha catalytic cracker and a tertiary amyl methyl ether (TAME) unit at its Amuay refinery in Northwest Venezuela. IPE

ALGERIA

CAPITAL: Algiers
MONETARY UNIT: Dinar
REFINING CAPACITY: 465,000 b/cd
PRODUCTION: 764,000 b/d
RESERVES: 9 billion bbl

Algeria planned a conference late in 1996 aimed at ending the country's civil strife, a welcome sign to petroleum companies and employees that have been targets of violence there in recent years.

Meanwhile, BP Exploration Operating Co. Ltd. was to begin exploration work ahead of a major gas development in southern Algeria, away from the violence in the north.

Algeria's government and most legal opposition parties were to meet in Algiers with a view to agreeing to a rejection of violence and a ban on using Islamic fundamentalism as a lever to attaining power.

Algeria's army canceled elections in 1991, and since then government forces and Islamic fundamentalist groups essentially have been at war.

The civil violence was mostly confined to northern Algeria, particularly around Algiers. The country's oil and gas hub is Hassi Messaoud about 600 km southeast of the capital.

BP's In Salah license area lies 1,200 km south of Algiers. The company was completing construction of offices at Hassi Messaoud, near the offices of partner Sonatrach, and one at In Salah.

"There are lots of expats already in the Hassi Messaoud area," a BP official said, "and there have been no problems reported there or at In Salah." BP has an office in Algiers, used mainly for meetings.

BP and Sonatrach planned to begin acquiring seismic data on the In Salah block and expected the program to take 2-2½ years. BP has committed to drilling nine wells, with the first to spud in 1997.

BP and Sonatrach concluded the In Salah development deal late in 1995. The $3.5 billion plan is Algeria's first major agreement with a foreign major in many years and is expected to lead to exports of 350 bcf/year of gas to southern Europe early next century.

Other industry activity

Algeria's Sonatrach assigned an exploration permit to Italy's Agip SpA covering the 591 sq km Wadi el Teh tract in Block 440 about 250 km southwest of Hassi Messaoud in Algeria's Ghadames basin.

Agip agreed to spend about $28 million during the pact's initial 4 year exploration period to drill three wells and collect seismic data over a 220 sq km area.

Algeria provisionally approved development plans by a group led by Anadarko Petroleum Corp., Houston, for Hassi Berkine and Hassi Berkine South fields on Block 404 in Southeast Algeria.

That allows partners to proceed with design and construction of first phase facilities. Interests are operator Anadarko Algeria Corp. 50% and Lasmo Oil (Algeria) Ltd. and Maersk Olie Algeriet AS 25% each.

Sonatrach let a $260 million contract to SNC Lavalin Group Inc., Montreal, to expand the Rhourde Nousse natural gas complex.

The project, to be completed in 1999, involves adding a gas gathering network, treating unit, and liquid petroleum gas extraction unit to existing facilities. Rhourde Nousse's increased output will target mostly European markets and will be transported via the Maghreb-Europe pipeline.

ANGOLA

CAPITAL: Luanda
MONETARY UNIT: Kwanza
REFINING CAPACITY: 32,100 b/cd
PRODUCTION: 621,000 b/d
RESERVES: 5.4 billion bbl

Angola planned to invite foreign participation in downstream oil and gas projects for the first time, following the success of offshore production ventures.

AFRICA
Atlantic Ocean
Indian Ocean
Mediterranean Sea
Black Sea
Caspian Sea
Red Sea
Gulf of Aden
Gulf of Guinea
Bight of Biafra
Strait of Gibraltar
Bay of Biscay
Adriatic Sea
Ionian Sea
Aegean Sea
Cape Bonn
Mozambique Channel
Cape of Good Hope
Lake Chad
Lake Tana
Lake Albert
Lake Victoria
Lake Tanganyika
Lake Malawi
Lake Kariba
PORTUGAL
SPAIN
FRANCE
CORSICA
SARDINIA
ITALY
SICILY
FORMER YUGOSLAVIA
ALBANIA
GREECE
CRETE
ROMANIA
BULGARIA
TURKEY
CYPRUS
RUSSIA
GEORGIA
ARMENIA
AZERBAIJAN
SYRIA
LEBANON
ISRAEL
JORDAN
IRAQ
IRAN
SAUDI ARABIA
YEMEN REPUBLIC
MOROCCO
ALGERIA
TUNISIA
LIBYA
EGYPT
WESTERN SAHARA
MAURITANIA
MALI
NIGER
CHAD
SUDAN
ERITREA
DJIBOUTI
ETHIOPIA
SOMALIA
SENEGAL
GAMBIA
GUINEA-BISSAU
GUINEA
SIERRA LEONE
LIBERIA
IVORY COAST
GHANA
TOGO
BENIN
BURKINA FASO
NIGERIA
CAMEROON
CENTRAL AFRICAN REPUBLIC
EQUATORIAL GUINEA
GABON
CONGO
ZAIRE
CABINDA
UGANDA
KENYA
RWANDA
BURUNDI
TANZANIA
ANGOLA
ZAMBIA
MALAWI
MOZAMBIQUE
ZIMBABWE
NAMIBIA
BOTSWANA
SWAZILAND
LESOTHO
REPUBLIC OF SOUTH AFRICA
MADAGASCAR
Lisbon
Madrid
Trieste
Belgrade
Bucharest
Sofia
Rome
Tirana
Istanbul
Ankara
Athens
Tehran
Nicosia
Beirut
Damascus
Baghdad
Amman
Jerusalem
Kuwait
Manama
Doha
Riyadh
Hilwah
Ceuta
Rabat
Mohammedia
Casablanca
Safi
Essaouira
Kachouie
Djebel-Jeer
Sidi Ghalem
Sidi-Kacem
Sidi Ifni
Tarfaya
Las Palmas
Oran
Arzew
Algiers
Skikda
Bejaia
Bizerte
Tunis
Elyssa
Hassi Messaoud
El Golea
Bel Rhazi
Touat
Ilatou
SBAA
Azzene
In-Salah
Reggane
Amasralad
Le Camp
In Amenas
Tripoli
Sider
Tobruk
Farrud
Umm Farud
Amal
Nafoora
Augila
Defa
Messla
Sarir
Alamein
Abu-Qir
Alexandria
Cairo
Abu Gharadig
Ramadan
Ras Garib
Suez
Midyan
Gelson
Mango
Port Sudan
Jizan
Sanaa
Ma'bar
Aden
Asmara
Assab
Djibouti
Khartoum
Kassala
Kosti
Malut
Adar
Unity
Talin
Sheraf
Muglad
Tabaldi
Abu Gambre
Bentiu
Addis Ababa
Mogadishu
Nouakchott
Bamako
Niamey
Ouagadougou
Bissau
Conakry
Freetown
Monrovia
Abidjan
Espoir
Panthere
Belier
Belia
Foxtrot
Saltpond
Accra
Lome
Porto Novo
Lagos
Kano
Kaduna
Makurdi
N'Djamena
Bangui
Yaounde
Sao Tome
Libreville
Cape Lopez
Port Gentil
Tschengue
Rembo-Kotto
Asswe
Sette-Cama
Gamba-Ivinga
Mossaka
Brazzaville
Kinshasa
Pointe Noire
Nkossa
Emeraude
Cco
Essungo
Mavanga
Sulele
Guntala
Maleva North
Luanda
Benfica
Tobias
Lobito
Kampala
Nairobi
Mombasa
Kigali
Bujumbura
Zanzibar
Dar es Salaam
Kilwa
Songo-Songo
Ndola
Lusaka
Lilongwe
Harare
Mutare
Beira
Pande
Thohoyandou
Gaborone
Windhoek
Walvis Bay
Luderitz
Kudu
Pretoria
Johannesburg
Maputo
Mbabane
Sasolburg
Maseru
Durban
Umtata
Mossel Bay
Cape Town
F-A
Tamatave
Antananarivo
2 Lines
58
310
34
129
26
60
90
30
120
7
8
220
29
94
68
141
99
62
43
21
104
118
150
60
54
10
15
42
17
85
24
32
106
86
156
65
0
300
600 Mi.
0
200
400
600 Km.

WEST AFRICA
GHANA
TOGO
BENIN
NIGERIA
CAMEROON
EQUATORIAL GUINEA
GABON
CONGO
CABINDA
ANGOLA
Gulf of Guinea
Bight of Biafra
Kaduna
104
Bida
Baro
Yola
Ilorin
Ibadan
Makurdi
Donga
Porto Novo
Lagos
Lome
Seme
Accra
26
Tano
118
Warri
Meren
Okan
Forcados
Oguta
M'Bede
150
60
Alesa-Eleme
Ea
Pennington
Brass
Ekulama
Okubie
Idol
Kole
Victoria
Douala
Malabo
Yaounde
42
Kribi
Ebolowa
Campo
Bata
Oyem
Sao Tome
Libreville
17
Booue
Cape Lopez
Lopez
Clairette
Tchengue
Anguille
Ozouri
Torpille
Loanda
Lambarene
Odombo
Ikenge
Omboue
Mossaka
M'Bassou
Gamba
Ivinga
Lucina
Tchibala
Mwengui
Mayumba
Tchibala S.
Lucine
M'Baya N.
M'Baya S.
Madingo
Yanga-Sendji
Pointe Noire
21
Loango
Pointe Indienne
Sendji
Yenga
Nkossa
Emeraude
Takula
Malongo
W. Malongo
Cabinda
Brazzaville
Kinshasa
Mibale
Essungo
GCO
17
Moanda
Matadi
Lele
N'Zombo
Quinguila
Cabeca Da Cobra
Guntala
Mavanga
Maleva North
Sulele
Nzeto
Ambriz
E. Lombo
32
Barra do Dande
Luanda
Cauaco
Luanda
Benfica
Uacongo
Mulenvoss
Barra do Cuanza
Tobias
Galinda
Lobito
GABON
Konzi
17
Gongue
N. Tombenyoni
Assala
Cape Lopez
Pointe Weze
Mporaloko
Lopez N.
Lopez S.
Clairette
Port Gentil
Port Gentil
Alewana
Anguille NE
N'Tchengue
Grand Anguille
Loanda
Anguille
N'Tchengue Ocean
Bilape
Anguille SW
M'Begga
Octopus
Arimba
Ozuri
Pageau
Doree
Girelle
Torpille NE
Pelican
Torpille
Baudroie Nord
Olende
Obando
M'Polunie
Chikawar
Baudroie
Baliste
Rembo Kotto
Hylia
Grondin
Ayol
Batanga
Odombo
Breme
Ongindjo
Gonelle
Barbier
Gombe
Mandaros
Assewe
Ikenge
25 Mi.
40 Km.
Omboue
Avocette
Coucal
Autour
Rabi Koung
Niungo
100
200
300 Mi.
400 Km.

Rosario Jacincta, deputy general manager of state oil and gas firm Sonangol, told delegates at the sub-Saharan Oil & Minerals Conference how the country's sustained peace, after years of civil war, makes it possible to try to attract foreign investment in onshore projects.

Angola's oil production was expected to average 750,000 b/d in 1996, due in part to successful offshore development projects.

There are major opportunities for deepwater exploration in Angola, Jacincta said. He reported "strong interest" in deepwater prospects off Cabinda, where Sonangol has completed mapping several blocks that will be offered for bidding. Onshore, there are exploration and development opportunities in the Soyo and Cabinda areas.

Jacincta said BP Exploration Operating Co. Ltd., Elf Aquitaine SA, Petrofina SA, Repsol SA, and Texaco Inc. were negotiating for projects. "Sonangol is getting ready for onshore licensing and has prepared data to encourage exploration and development of new regions," he said.

Downstream, the government was placing priority on regeneration of infrastructure as part of a national reconstruction plan.

Sonangol intends to use associated gas, currently flared or reinjected, to produce liquid petroleum gas for sale in local markets.

The company also planned to expand its aging 20,000 b/d refinery and was looking to build a new plant with 150,000 b/d of crude distillation capacity.

Angola's marketing sector is being readied for entry by foreign firms, while Sonangol has plans to build grassroots methanol and ammonia plants to utilize gas reserves further.

Angola produced about 38 billion cu m of gas in 1995, said Jose Mangueira, national director for petroleum in the Ministry of Petroleum. More than 50% was flared because there is no viable commercial option.

In other activity, Sonangol awarded an offshore production

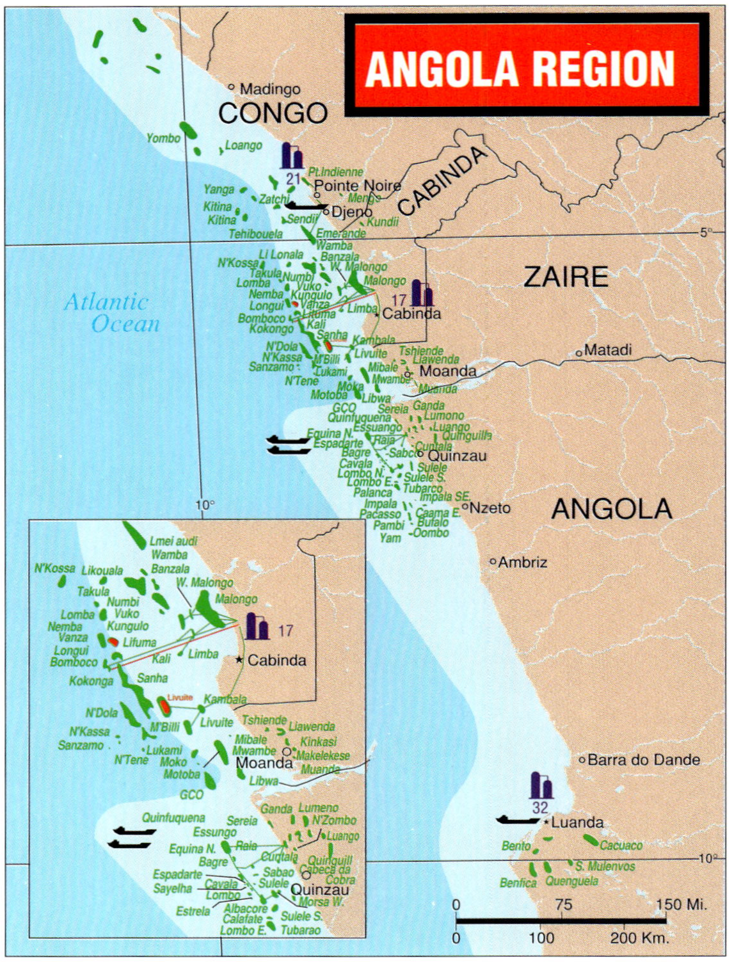

New oil production exepcted off West Africa in 1996

Field	License	Operator	Peak production (b/d)	Estimated reserves (million bbl)
ANGOLA				
Numbi Northeast	Cabinda A	Chevron	11,000	20
Nemba South	Cabinda B	Chevron	55,000	205
Lombo North	Block 2/85	Texaco	4,000	6
Cavala	Block 2/85	Texaco	2,700	4
Calafate	Block 2/85	Texaco	4,000	6
Bagre	Block 2/85	Texaco	12,000	35
Estrela	Block 2/85	Texaco	12,000	30
Oombo	Block 3/91	Elf	19,000	48
Kiame	Block 4	Ranger	12,000	15
CAMEROON				
South Asoma	PH59	Pecten	2,300	1
Lipenja	Lipenja-Erong	Pecten	4,500	8
CONGO				
Nkossa	Nkossa	Elf	110,000	440
EQUATORIAL GUINEA				
Zafiro	Block B	Mobil	40,000	105
GABON				
Ekouata	Ekouata Marin	Vaalco	3,900	7
ZAIRE				
Lubi	Offshore	Chevron	800	1

Source: Wood Mackenzie Consultants Ltd.

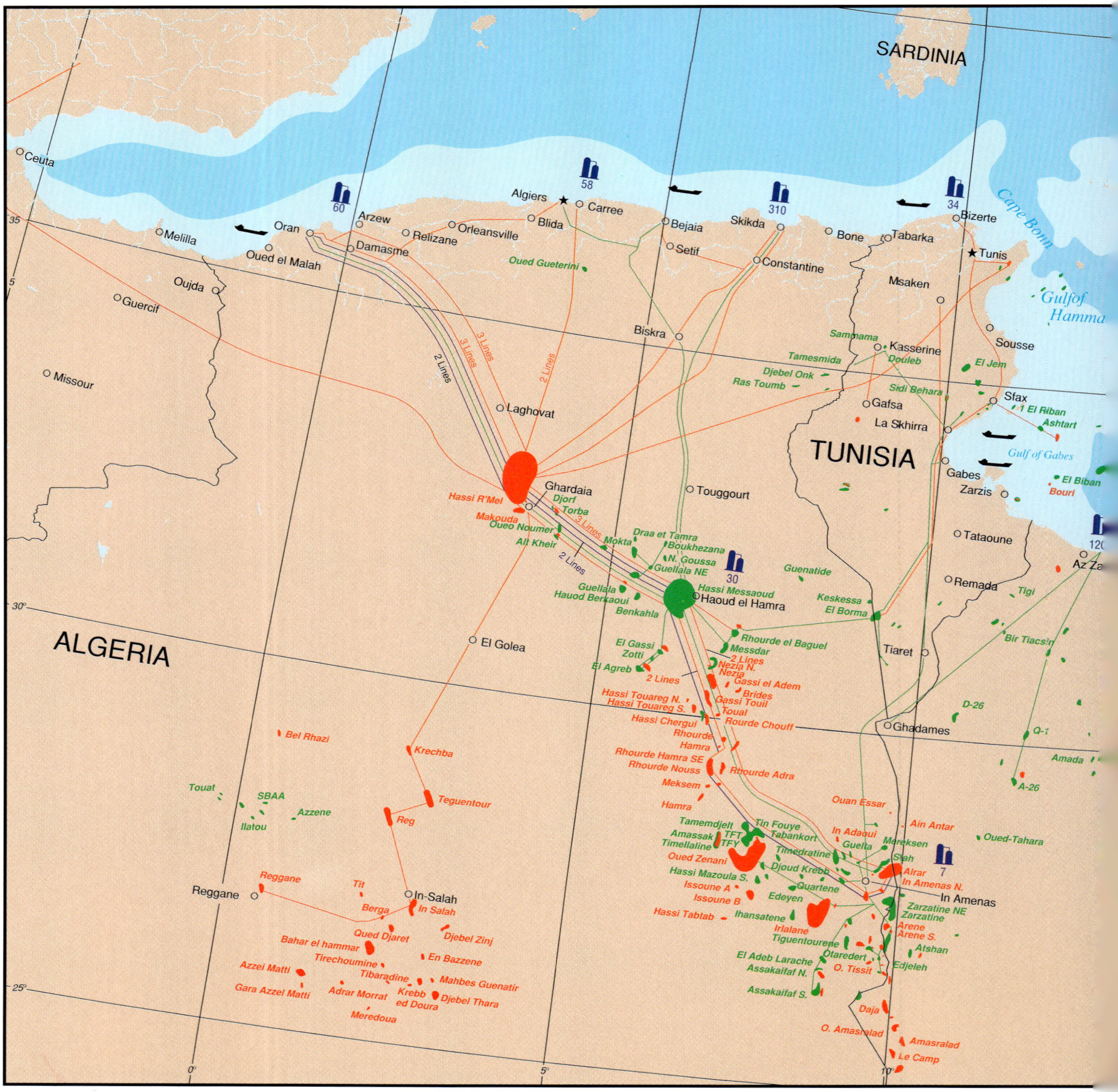

sharing contract to operator Amoco Angola BV and 50-50 partner Shell Exploration & Production Angola BV.

Work involves exploration and development in as much as 1,700 m of water on Block 18, covering 5,000 sq km about 75 km northwest of Luanda. Exploratory drilling was planned in late 1997 or in early 1998 on the block, where 3D seismic has been acquired.

In addition, Elf Angola let a $14 million contract to Stolt Comex Seaway SA, Aberdeen, for installation and commissioning of 46 km of pipelines in fields off Angola. The contractor was to lay pipelines late in 1996 serving Buffalo, Palanca, Pacassa, Impala, and Cobo fields.

The contract calls for laying five 4 in., two 6 in., and two 8 in. pipelines in 40-100 m of water. The Seaway Falcon ship will lay the pipe, and Seaway Harrier will construct pipeline crossings, install risers and spool pieces, and perform tie-in and testing.

CHAD

CAPITAL: N'Djamena
MONETARY UNIT: CFA franc
REFINING CAPACITY: N.A.
PRODUCTION: N.A.
RESERVES: N.A.

Esso Exploration & Production Chad Inc. signed a memorandum of understanding (MOU) with Chad that could lead to

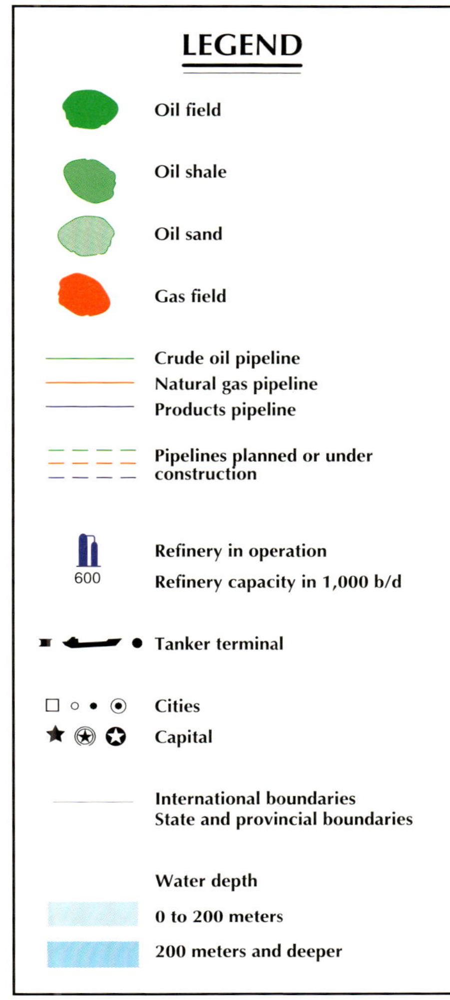

that country's first commercial oil production.

In 1995, operator Esso and partners signed a framework agreement with the governments of Chad and Cameroon covering a proposed pipeline to move crude from landlocked Chad to the Atlantic coast for export.

The MOU addressed key financial, legal, and operating terms under which the project, in southern Chad's Doba basin, would be developed. Project area, about 350 miles south of N'Djamena, is estimated to contain 900 million bbl of reserves.

Esso said the cost of developing oil reserves in Kome, Miandoum, and Bolobo fields and the infrastructure needed to transport them is expected to total about $3 billion.

Interests are Esso and Ste. Shell Tchadienne de Recherches et d'Exploitation 40% each and Elf Hydrocarbures Tchad 20%.

Remaining hurdles include final government ratification of terms, as well as obtaining project financing. In the interim, Esso said, the group will invite proposals from potential bidders for the major engineering, procurement, and construction contracts.

What's planned

Esso said about 300 wells would be drilled, with production to peak at 200,000-250,000 b/d of oil as early as 2000. Production would be gathered into a central treating complex.

Oil would be transported about 650 miles via a 30-in. pipeline across Chad and neighboring Cameroon to the Atlantic coast. Chad and Cameroon signed a treaty establishing a basis for construction and operation of the planned pipeline.

Commercial tankers would load oil at an offshore terminal near Kribi, Cameroon.

Second project

The MOU also outlined a second potential project in Chad that calls for development of Sedigi field, north of Lake Chad, and a pipeline to supply a proposed refinery at N'Djamena to be operated by Ste. d'Etude et d'Exploitation de la Rafinnerie du Chad.

The plant would produce fuel for transportation, power generation, and other uses.

In the late 1970s, plans were put forth to build a 2,700 b/d refinery to process Sedigi field oil.

Conoco Inc. and partners discovered the field in the late 1970s.

CONGO

CAPITAL: Brazzaville
MONETARY UNIT: CFA franc
REFINING CAPACITY: 21,000 b/cd
PRODUCTION: 175,000 b/d
RESERVES: 1.5 billion

Exploratory drilling off the Congo will see a resurgence the next few years as a result of a spate of license awards following the country's 1994 introduction of production sharing contract legislation.

This is the view of Wood Mackenzie Consultants Ltd., Edinburgh, which noted in 1996 that seven exploration licenses had been awarded, adding to three older licenses still in effect.

Only two new field wildcat wells were drilled off the Congo each in 1994 and 1995, said the analyst, with a further two expected in 1996. But 1997 and 1998 are expected to see at least six wildcats drilled each year.

"The potential for significant new discoveries in Congo," said Wood Mackenzie, "especially in the deeper water areas, has been indicated by the success of Elf's 1 Moho Marine well."

Elf Congo is thought to have discovered Congo's largest oil field yet with this well. Wood Mackenzie estimates Moho reserves at 400 million bbl of oil and said 600 million bbl could eventually be confirmed.

Increased activity

The analyst said licensing activity has been relatively high in the preceding couple of years, with award of seven new blocks attributed to revised fiscal terms and an increase in perceived potential of pre-salt and deepwater plays.

"Most offshore acreage is now under license," said Wood Mackenzie. "By contrast, almost all onshore acreage is open."

The trough of exploration activity follows a peak of 18 wildcat wells drilled in 1992. Moho discovery was made in November 1995.

Deepwater acreage off Congo is seen as particularly attractive, boosted by Elf's Moho find in 800 m of water. Three of the blocks awarded—Marine IX, Mer Profonde Nord, and Mer Profonde Sud—are in as much as 2,000 m of water.

Four blocks—Marine IV, Marine X, Marine XI, and Marine XII—have pre-salt plays as the main attraction, said Wood Mackenzie.

"All four blocks have previously been relatively well explored in terms of post-salt potential," said the analyst. "All production off Congo is from post-salt reservoirs.

"As with the deepwater arena, the rise in interest in pre-salt potential is a result both of new play concepts and better technology. In the case of the pre-salt, technological improvements are allowing better seismic imaging of targets."

Wood Mackenzie said 11 commitment wells are to be drilled on the seven licenses, while Elf and Agip are planning exploratory and appraisal drilling within their development licenses and on the three oldest exploration licenses.

"In 1997," said the analyst, "we predict six wildcats and four appraisal wells will be drilled, all offshore, and a similar number, perhaps even more, is expected in 1998."

Little unlicensed offshore exploration acreage remains, said Wood Mackenzie. Only the nearshore Marine III license is available, having been relinquished by Elf in October 1995.

One small discovery was made on Marine III Block, known as Tilapia. The government hopes to reoffer this acreage under special marginal-field terms.

Onshore acreage open

Apart from development licenses for two minor fields, Elf's Pointe Indienne and Mengo, all the Congo's onshore acreage is open, for the first time in many years.

The three Kayes blocks were licensed in 1988 to groups led by BP Exploration Operating Co. Ltd., Chevron Corp., and Conoco Inc. These were relinquished, after disappointing results, in 1992.

Elf relinquished its onshore La Loeme permit after 22 years in September 1995, keeping the areas around the two small fields. Elf also made the small Kouakouala find here, and the government hopes to attract other companies to develop it.

In addition, said Wood Mackenzie, the government has delineated two onshore blocks, La Noumbi and Le Kouilou, which together contain most of Congo's coastal area.

Rising production

Elf's N'Kossa field, brought on stream in June 1996, is Congo's largest field to date. It has estimated reserves of 500 million bbl of liquids and is expected to reach plateau production of 122,000 b/d in 1998-99.

Congo's total oil reserves are estimated at 1.645 billion bbl, and production in 1996 was expected to average 201,000 b/d, boosted by N'Kossa from a level of 169,000 b/d.

Wood Mackenzie said Agip SpA is developing Kitina and Kitina Sud fields, with estimated reserves totaling 125 million bbl of oil. These are due on stream at yearend 1997.

"These developments should help raise Congo's oil production to a new peak of around 310,000 b/d in 1999," said Wood Mackenzie. "Longer term, production will depend very much on the eventual size and development scenario of Moho."

The analyst expects Elf to undertake a phased development of Moho. First production is anticipated in 2001, with a slow buildup in production to about 120,000 b/d in 2006.

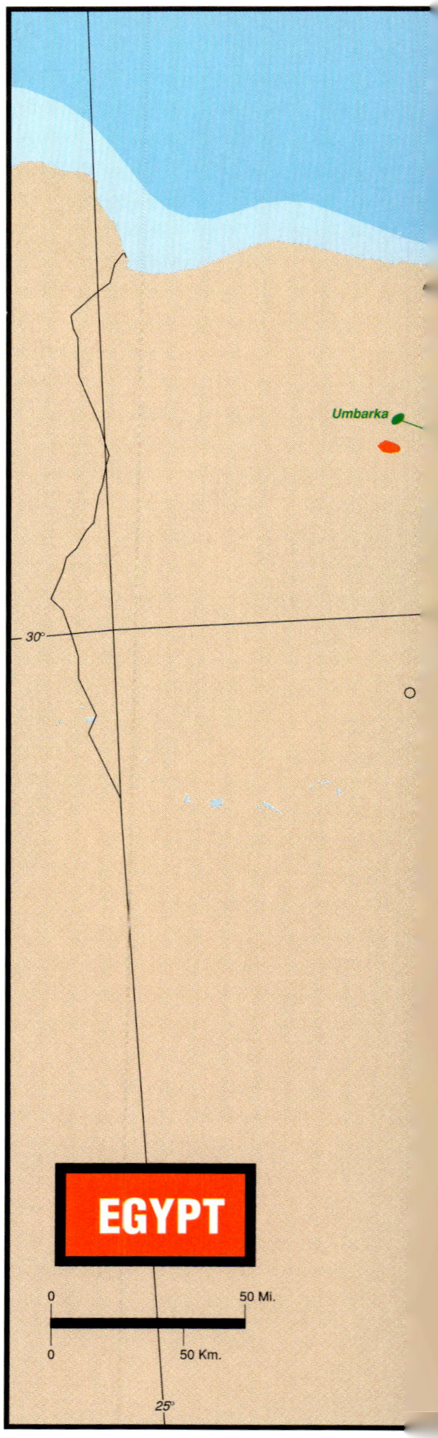

COTE D'IVOIRE

CAPITAL: Abidjan
MONETARY UNIT: CFA franc
REFINING CAPACITY: 64,000 b/cd
PRODUCTION: 11,000 b/d
RESERVES: 100 million bbl

Santa Fe Energy Resources Inc., Houston, signed an exploration contract with Cote d'Ivoire in 1996 to explore, develop, and produce oil and gas on the CI-24 block in the offshore portion of the Abidjan margin.

The contract provides for three exploration periods totaling 5 years and a 20-year production period. Drilling is to begin in 1998. Early exploration will focus on interpretation of 3D seismic acquired by state-owned oil company Petroci.

Operator and majority working interest owner is Santa Fe unit Santa Fe Energy Resources of Cote d'Ivoire. Petroci holds the remaining working interest.

United Meridian Corp., Houston, placed its A-3 Lion dual-oil completion delineation well on production in Block CI-11 off Cote d'Ivoire.

Estimated initial production was 4,000 b/d. When tie-ins are completed, Lion field oil production will total about 19,000 b/d.

On test, the well flowed at a rate of 42 MMcfd of gas and 11,960 b/d of oil from three zones, including two previously untapped, shallower sands.

Operator UMC holds a 25% working interest in the block.

International operations of Phoenix Resources Cos. Inc., Oklahoma City, center on Egypt's Western Desert. Here construction of storage tanks is under way to transfer production into the Sumed crude oil pipeline. Photo by Josef Polleross, courtesy of Phoenix.

UMC and Shell Exploration Africa BV signed a production sharing contract with Cote d'Ivoire for the country's first deepwater block.

The contract covers the 512,000 acre block CI-105, also known as Etente, which lies in 1,500-6,000 ft of water. Several prospects and leads were identified on the block by existing 2D seismic data.

EGYPT

CAPITAL: Cairo
MONETARY UNIT: Pound
REFINING CAPACITY: 546,060 b/cd
PRODUCTION: 922,000 b/d
RESERVES: 3.7 billion bbl

In Egyptian downstream activity, Midor, the Egyptian-Israeli group, let contract to Italy's Technipetrol SpA and France's Technip for procurement and construction of a $1.2 billion, 100,000 b/d refinery at Alexandria.

Scheduled to come on stream at yearend 1999, the project will give Egypt its first private sector refinery. The refinery, which will feature UOP's hydrocracking process, is intended to be the first in the region to meet European environmental standards.

Egyptian General Petroleum Corp. (EGPC) and Phillips Petroleum Co. signed a letter of intent for construction and operation of a 330 million lb/year high density polyethylene plant near Alexandria, Egypt.

Phillips would be the plant's majority owner. The plant would use Phillips' proprietary polyethylene technology and feedstock from an ethylene cracker to be built at the same site by a unit of EGPC.

Construction is projected to start in 1998, with first output in 2000.

Upstream, EGPC awarded Pennzoil Exploration & Production Co. the 34-sq km North July block in the central Gulf of Suez, site of a 3D survey.

The work program was to begin in 1997, subject to parliamentary approval.

Three wells on the block tested at a combined rate of 8,000 b/d from Miocene Rudeis sands. Pennzoil, with interests in the southeastern Gulf of Suez, Southwest Gebel El-Zeit, and West Feiran blocks, was conducting a seismic survey on the concessions.

Pennzoil planned to drill the first of five wells on the three blocks in 1997.

Apache Corp., Houston, found oil on its Qarun concession in Egypt's Western Desert. The 1X SW Qarun wildcat, about 3 miles southwest of Apache-operated Qarun "A" field, opened the SW Qarun pool.

The Kharita zone flowed on test at a rate of 2,600 b/d of 40° gravity crude through a 1 in. choke at 58 psi flowing tubing pressure from perforations at 9,933-53 ft. The Lower Bahariya zone flowed on test at a rate of 1,100 b/d of 36° gravity crude through a 1 in. choke at 44 psi flowing tubing pressure from perforations at 9,160-9,350 ft.

Interests are operator Apache 75% and Global Natural Resources Inc. 25%.

EQUATORIAL GUINEA

CAPITAL: Malabo
MONETARY UNIT: CFA franc
REFINING CAPACITY: N.A.
PRODUCTION: 7,000 b/d
RESERVES: 12 million bbl

Equatorial Guinea joined the ranks of commercial oil producers in 1996.

Units of Mobil Corp. and United Meridian Corp., Houston, started production from Zafiro field off Equatorial Guinea.

Zafiro field is on the 547,000 acre Block B off Bioko Island in the Gulf of Guinea.

The 1 Zafiro well came on line flowing 7,000 b/d of oil less than 18 months after the field's discovery.

Operator Mobil Oil Equatorial Guinea Inc. holds 75% interest in Block B and UMC Equatorial Guinea Corp. 25%.

Production update

Partners installed flowlines to five wells in the field and planned to drill, complete, and connect three more Zafiro/Opalo development wells to production facilities.

Partners expected oil production of about 40,000 b/d by yearend 1996 from the eight subsea wells.

The Mobil-UMC combine credited the speed of Zafiro field's development to an aggressive drilling program and a development scheme based on subsea production facilities tied back via flexible risers to a floating production, storage, and offloading (FPSO) system.

Zafiro Producer FPSO, formerly a 1,087 ft, 268,000 dwt crude oil tanker, was converted earlier in 1996 to FPSO service at PMB-Bechtel's Pelican Island fabrication yard, near Galveston Island at the mouth of the Houston Ship Channel. Oceaneering Production Systems, a unit of Oceaneering International Inc., Houston, was the main contractor on the

Lightly explored regions open for licensing in southern Africa

COUNTRIES IN SOUTHERN AFRICA ARE OPENING relatively unexplored regions for licensing to foreign firms.

That was evident as energy ministers and senior officials from Zaire, Senegal, Ethiopia, and Equatorial Guinea outlined exploration prospects during the Sub-Saharan Oil & Minerals Conference in Johannesburg in 1996.

Zaire

Mpetshi Ilonga, Zaire's minister of energy, said his country is optimistic about oil potential in its three sedimentary basins, which cover about half of Zaire.

His government is trying to attract major companies for exploration and production. It has been collecting data on prospectivity through state firm Petrozaire.

Zaire's coastal basin covers 6,000 sq km, of which 1,000 sq km is offshore. Exploration of this basin began in 1956, with discoveries onshore and offshore placed on production by Petrozaire in the 1970s.

All of Zaire's crude oil is exported because it is comparatively heavy and thus unsuitable for the country's unsophisticated refinery, which uses oil from Middle East.

The Tanganyika basin's graben play also has yielded discoveries. Ilonga said the government is eager to persuade international participants to explore further and develop finds in this region.

Zaire's Central basin has been explored with aerial and gravimetric surveys during the last 10 years. The government plans to split the area into blocks to offer to oil companies.

"Here we have proven these are rocks that could have generated hydrocarbons," Ilonga said. "The potential of the Central basin requires us to create concessions for oil companies."

Ilonga said Chevron Corp., Mobil Corp., Royal Dutch/Shell, Elf Aquitaine SA, and Agip SpA are among majors working and considering projects in Zaire.

Senegal

Magued Diouf, Senegal's minister of energy, mines, and industry, said his government is updating its mining and petroleum codes as a prelude to courting international companies.

Senegal's Coastal basin features a mid-Jurassic play, while to the south is an offshore region said to be similar to the Gulf of Mexico. The Eastern basin is characterized by pre-Cambrian metamorphic rocks.

Diouf said the first indications of Senegal's oil potential surfaced in 1917, but it was not until the 1950s that exploration began. That led to oil and gas strikes in Southeast Senegal, about 50 km from Dakar.

State firm Petrosen is looking for partners for frontier exploration. The government has created 16 license blocks—seven onshore and nine offshore.

Diouf said the onshore area is a Paleozoic play, while the offshore blocks feature Mesozoic structures.

The onshore area has been lightly explored. An 80,000 sq km area has so far been probed by nine wells and 5,000 line km of seismic data.

The offshore area also is lightly explored. Seismic data are old, and 14 wells to date have penetrated no deeper than 2,500 m below the seabed.

Senegal is offering two exploration approaches to foreign firms.

For northernmost onshore concessions and offshore blocks, the government hopes to attract partners to acquire seismic data. For other, less risky zones onshore, the government is looking for partners to drill four wells targeting separate structures identified by seismic data collected in 1995-96.

Ethiopia

Abiy Hunegnaw, head of petroleum operations for Ethiopia's Ministry of Mines & Energy, pointed out that his country's hydrocarbons exploration history goes back 40 years, although no production had occurred.

About 27,000 line-km of seismic data has been acquired and 34 wells drilled. One discovery in the Ogaden basin holds estimated reserves of 68 billion cu m of gas, plus condensate, and is being readied for development.

First-phase development is to involve production of liquids for local sale, with gas being reinjected. Second-phase production will recover gas for pipeline supply to nearby cities.

The government is offering exploration acreage in Ethiopia's Ogaden and Blue Nile basins. On offer are 14 blocks centered around the gas/condensate discovery.

Most available data, raw and processed, involves the Ogaden basin, where a seismic survey was completed in 1995.

To the north, in the Blue Nile basin of Ethiopia's central highlands, aeromagnetic and gravimetric data are said to show possible source and reservoir rocks similar to those in the Ogaden basin.

Hunegnaw said, "Oil seepages have been seen here, but there has not been much exploration to date. This is really a virgin area being promoted."

Farther north and even less explored, Hunegnaw said, surveys indicate potential source rocks in the Medele basin.

Under a 1994 production sharing law, contractors are invited to take 25-85% of concessions. Many terms, including seismic survey and drilling obligations, are open to negotiation.

Equatorial Guinea

Juan Olo Mba Nseng, Equatorial Guinea's minister of mines and energy, reported success with offshore exploration north of Bioko Island.

There, units of Mobil Corp. and UMC Petroleum Corp. are moving to begin production from the country's first commercial oil field, Zafiro.

Nseng told delegates the government plans to invite onshore exploration by foreign firms. He said, "The basin of the River Muni has hydrocarbons potential larger than that north of Bioko Island, yet only five wells have been drilled."

Flares signal the discovery of Zafiro field on Block B off Equatorial Guinea by units of Mobil Corp. and United Meridian Corp., Houston. The strike flowed more than 10,500 b/d of oil. Production start-up was due in second half 1996. Photo courtesy of United Meridian.

conversion.

The FPSO left for Equatorial Guinea in June 1996. The unit can process as much as 80,000 b/d of oil and has storage for about 1.5 million bbl of oil.

Partners offload production from the unit through a floating hose to export tankers.

Estimated total initial development costs of Zafiro field are about $133 million.

Zafiro activity roundup

Mobil and UMC said the 1 Amatista delineation well had extended the Zafiro and Topacio discoveries in the Qua Iboe formation, marking the eighth consecutive successful well drilled in the Zafiro/Opalo/Topacio complex.

Partners cased the well to 6,600 ft and suspended operations temporarily, pending installation of completion equipment and flowline.

The 1 Amatista is halfway between the Zafiro and Topacio discoveries in a downdip extension that shows Zafiro and Topacio are parts of the same field.

In addition to encountering an oil/water contact in the main field pay zone, 1 Amatista found two other shallower sands within the oil column, which were gas-bearing in previous wells.

Partners deepened 1 Amatista to 11,378 ft to test the Isongo formation. While no productive sands were seen, thick reservoir-quality sands with minor oil and gas shows were found.

The Atwood Eagle drilling rig, which drilled 1 Amatista, was moved 17 miles southwest to drill 1 Azurita, a Qua Iboe exploratory well.

The Aleutian Key drilling rig spudded the 6 Zafiro development well in Zafiro field.

Mobil in May 1994 acquired an interest in Block B from UMC and became operator in January 1995 after completing the first wildcat.

Partners discovered the Zafiro oil accumulation in March 1995 and declared the field commercial in October 1995.

GABON

CAPITAL: Libreville
MONETARY UNIT: CFA franc
REFINING CAPACITY: 17,300 b/cd
PRODUCTION: 364,000 b/d
RESERVES: 1.3 billion bbl

Gabon in 1996 let an exploration and development contract to the Santa Fe Energy Resources of Gabon (Mondah Bay) unit of Santa Fe Energy Resources Inc., Houston, covering the 600 sq mile onshore-offshore Mondah Bay block in Gabon's Atlantic Salt basin.

The pact includes a 2 year exploration period with a 3 year optional extension and a 20 year production period. Santa Fe Gabon planned to drill the first of several offshore prospects in less than 100 ft of water, targeting objectives at less than 5,000 ft, in 1997.

The country let an exploration and production permit to Chauvco Resources Ltd., Calgary, for a 561 sq mile onshore tract that includes the 1991 Remboue discovery.

Undeveloped reserves in the permit area are estimated at 10-15 million bbl, with some upside potential likely through further delineation. Chauvco's permit includes a 3 year exploration period with an option for 2 more years.

Gabon awarded an exploration and production sharing contract to the Marathon Petroleum Akoumba Ltd. unit of

Marathon Oil Co. for the 636,000 acre Akoumba Marin permit, an offshore tract in the North Gabon basin.

The company has 100% interest in the block, where water depths range from 600 ft to more than 6,000 ft.

Amoco Gabon BV and Phillips Petroleum Gabon Ltd. agreed in a production sharing contract with Gabon to explore the 2.4 million acre Gryphon Marin block off southern Gabon in the Atlantic Ocean.

Amoco is operator.

GHANA

CAPITAL: Accra
MONETARY UNIT: Cedi
REFINING CAPACITY: 26,600 b/cd
PRODUCTION: 6,000 b/d
RESERVES: 16.5 million bbl

The U.S. Export-Import Bank approved financing to support $326 million in sales of U.S. oil and gas production equipment and services for an offshore gas field development project in Ghana.

It approved a $253 million, long term guarantee to finance support of capital equipment and services by U.S. suppliers to develop the Tano offshore fields and build pipelines to a barge-mounted, 130,000 kw power plant to be installed near the village of Effasu.

The bank also approved a $62.5 million direct loan to support long term operations and maintenance services for the gas field system and power plant.

Principal U.S. suppliers include Continental Engineering & Construction Co., Lafayette, La., Westinghouse International Service Co., Orlando, Fla., and a number of oil and gas firms in Louisiana and Texas.

Martin Kamarck, Ex-Im Bank chairman, said, "This transaction opens doors for U.S. exporters in the oil and gas industry in West Africa. This project will be the first offshore gas development in Ghana, which has considerable reserves and a great need for power to develop its infrastructure."

The bank said the Tano gas fields are part of the greater Ivory Coast geological basin system, which is marked by small to medium-size fields mainly holding gas reserves.

In other activity, affiliates of Hunt Oil Co., Dallas, agreed with Ghana National Petroleum Corp. to conduct exploration and production in Ghana's western offshore Cape Three Points basin, which lies between the Tano and Saltpond basins.

Seismic work was to get under way immediately.

MOZAMBIQUE

CAPITAL: Maputo
MONETARY UNIT: Meticais
REFINING CAPACITY: N.A.
PRODUCTION: N.A.
RESERVES: N.A.

BP Exploration Operating Co. Ltd. signed an agreement with the government of Mozambique for exploration of an 80,000 sq km tract in the delta area of the Zambeze river.

During 6 months of initial surveys covered by the deal, BP planned to study existing geological, geophysical, and geochemical data to see if it can prove the existence of seabed oil seeps.

Seismic surveys in the delta's shallow waters during the 1980s proved inconclusive, but BP's tract extends to water depths as great as 2,000 m.

During the initial period BP and Mozambique's government will negotiate a production-sharing contract covering half of the exploration deal area.

If early indications are encouraging, BP will acquire seismic data the subsequent 2 years.

If this proves positive, 3D seismic surveys and drilling will follow.

Meanwhile, a group led by a unit of Scimitar Hydrocarbons Corp., Calgary, was fielding seismic crews for an exploration program on a large tract in Mozambique.

Scimitar Production International Ltd. (SPIL) and partners by late summer 1996 expected to begin acquiring seismic data over a large part of the Buzi-Divinhe block, a 2.1 million acre tract extending south from a point north of the coastal city of Beira to within about 45 km of Pande gas field.

The seismic program was the first field work under a production sharing agreement (PSA) signed Dec. 15, 1995. Effective Jan. 1, 1996, the PSA included a 21 month initial exploration period with an optional 12 month extension.

Buzi-Divinhe operator SPIL and Zarara Petroleum Resources Ltd. each holds 50% interest in the PSA. The government of Mozambique and state company Empresa Nacional de Hidrocarbonetos (ENH) are coventurers in the agreement.

SPIL retains the right to earn another 25% interest in the agreement by fulfilling certain work commitments.

Buzi-Divinhe PSA overview

The Buzi-Divinhe PSA stems from a memorandum of understanding concluded Oct. 24, 1994.

PSA partners in the first exploration period are to:

- Review, reprocess, and reinterpret existing data on PSA acreage.
- Acquire, process, and interpret new seismic.
- Mark potential drilling locations and plan a logistical program.

The group in second-phase exploration, beginning as early as mid-1997, may opt to drill an exploratory well, pending results of seismic and other preliminary work. Officials also are evaluating an early production program for Buzi gas/condensate field in the northern part of the tract.

Information was scant on Buzi-Divinhe geology, but officials said the group's exploratory program is targeting some of the same Grudja intervals encountered at Pande and other points south.

Grudja wells on the Buzi-Divinhe tract will focus on formations at 4,000-6,000 ft, with shallower and deeper secondary targets.

One of the primary zones targeted by SPIL and partners—Maastrichtian Lower Grudja D-6 horizon—produces gas in commercial volumes at Pande and has demonstrated wider than expected pay with excellent productivity potential.

Another primary target, Lower Grudja G-9 strata, provides productive intervals at Buzi field. Previous exploration in Mozambique also has reported G-9 strata at 1.5 tcf Temane gas field south of Pande.

NIGERIA

CAPITAL: Abuja
MONETARY UNIT: Naira
REFINING CAPACITY: 433,250 b/cd
PRODUCTION: 1.9 million b/d
RESERVES: 15.5 billion bbl

Shell Petroleum Development Co. of Nigeria Ltd. proposed a capital budget of $1.63 billion in 1996 by partners in a venture that accounts for almost half of Nigeria's oil production.

However, the company feared spending could be curtailed because state-owned Nigerian National Petroleum Corp. (NNPC), a partner, appeared unable to raise its share of the cash.

Shell owns a 30% interest and operates the onshore production venture, with NNPC holding 55%, Elf Nigeria Ltd. 10%, and Agip SpA 5%.

Brian Anderson, Shell Nigeria chairman and managing director, said the venture's 1996 budget had not been approved by the Nigerian government.

"We expect the budget to be cut to $1.3 billion," Anderson said, "but the shortfall could be even more. Last year's proposed budget was $1.5 billion, but only $1 billion was spent because NNPC couldn't fully pay its share."

Anderson came under fire at the meeting from protesters who criticized, among other things, Shell's treatment of communities in oil producing areas.

Anderson warned that if NNPC did not provide its share of the venture's budget, some spending would have to be deferred.

He said the government's revenue from oil exports in 1996 was expected to amount to $7 billion.

Anderson said the venture spent $150 million in 1995 on projects to improve its environmental performance and another $22 million on community projects. The budget in 1996 included $90 million for environmental projects and $30 million for community projects.

Shell is sponsoring a survey of the environmental and social problems of the Niger Delta.

The Shell combine produces 930,000 b/d of oil from 94 onshore fields. It is upgrading producing facilities and pipelines in a $2 billion program due to be complete in 1998.

The venture also is working to reduce gas flaring in its oil fields by 20% by 1999.

Some oil wells that produce large volumes of gas have been shut in, and some flared gas will be diverted to feed the much delayed Bonny Island liquefied natural gas export project.

A further 10% reduction in gas flaring from the venture's fields, estimated to amount to 1 bcfd, will come from gas sales to an aluminum plant due on stream in 1999.

In other 1996 Nigerian activity, Abacan Resource Corp., Calgary, was drilling the 2 AJE appraisal well after a production test of its Benin basin 1 AJE wildcat on OPL Block 309 in 328 ft of water, about 19 miles off Nigeria near the Benin border.

The 1 AJE flowed 5,500 b/d of oil and condensate with associated gas from Turonian perforations. Abacan said seismic identified the deeper Abbian and Ise formations. Abacan said the 1 AJE could open a new Nigerian exploration area.

Shell Petroleum Development planned to build a $300 million pipeline to deliver gas to the delayed Aluminium Smelter Co. of Nigeria plant.

The smelter, which will use gas from oil fields that currently flare associated gas, is expected to start up in 1997, 7 years after construction began.

NNPC expected to approve a proposed $318.43 million contract for construction of a gas treating plant to a group of Japanese and Italian companies.

The plant, slated for start-up May 1, 1999, will provide enough treated dry gas to supply 53.33% of the 931 MMcfd of gas required by Nigeria's proposed $3.8 billion Bonny liquefied natural gas export project.

Nigeria approved proposals by local investors to build the country's first privately owned refineries, each export-oriented.

Brass Oil Refinery Ltd. would build and operate a 200,000 b/d refinery in Rivers state, and Qua Petroleum Refinery Ltd. would build and operate a 100,000 b/d refinery at Ibino, Akwa Ibom state.

The investors are taking advantage of new government incentives encouraging private domestic involvement in Nigeria's petroleum industry.

SOUTH AFRICA

CAPITAL: Pretoria/Cape Town
MONETARY UNIT: Rand
REFINING CAPACITY: 414,150 b/cd
PRODUCTION: 10,000 b/d
RESERVES: 27 million bbl

South Africa's Sasol Ltd. plans to upgrade its synthetic fuel plant at Secunda in an 820 million rand ($185 million) project due for completion in 1999.

At Secunda, 180 km southeast of Johannesburg, Sasol produces 150,000 b/d of synthetic crude oil from low grade coal using the Fischer Tropsch gas/syncrude process.

Sasol will replace 16 reactors at the plant with six new ones. The new units will be fluidized bed reactors, said to be vastly superior in performance to existing circulation bed reactors.

A 10,000 b/d fluidized bed syncrude unit has been in commercial operation at Secunda since June 1995. Because it involves only one free-standing pressure vessel, it is said to be easier to operate and maintain.

Sasol said the new reactors are being installed to maintain present production volumes while increasing yields by 30% and lowering production costs. The first will be commissioned in May 1998.

There is a provision to expand production if demand for syncrude increases, but this would also require debottlenecking of downstream units.

Hannes Botha, managing director of Sasol Synthetic Fuels, said, "The new SAS reactor technology will enable us to reduce our operating costs. It will eliminate replacement of high wear components.

"The system uses significantly less catalyst and is easier to operate and maintain. Recovery of energy is more efficient, and an additional 1,000 tons/hr of steam will be generated.

"It is foreseen that this project will significantly contribute to lowering the cost of production of synthetic crude oil in the longer term. This transformation process is aimed at countering the effect of the reduction in our tariff protection."

South Africa's new government is reducing price protection for synthetic fuel producers as the country opens its doors to international trade after years of trade boycotts.

Sasol, along with Haldor Topsoe AS of Denmark, has begun marketing a development of the Fischer Tropsch process to produce diesel fuel from natural gas.

ZAIRE

CAPITAL: Kinshasa
MONETARY UNIT: Zaires
REFINING CAPACITY: 17,000 b/cd
PRODUCTION: 28,000 b/d
RESERVES: 187 million bbl

Global Industries Inc., Houston, was using the Cheyenne derrick/lay barge off Zaire to lay six pipelines as large as 20 in. with combined length of 16 miles for Zaire Gulf Oil Co.

The Cheyenne also was to install a four pile platform for Zaire Gulf. IPE

COMMONWEALTH OF INDEPENDENT STATES

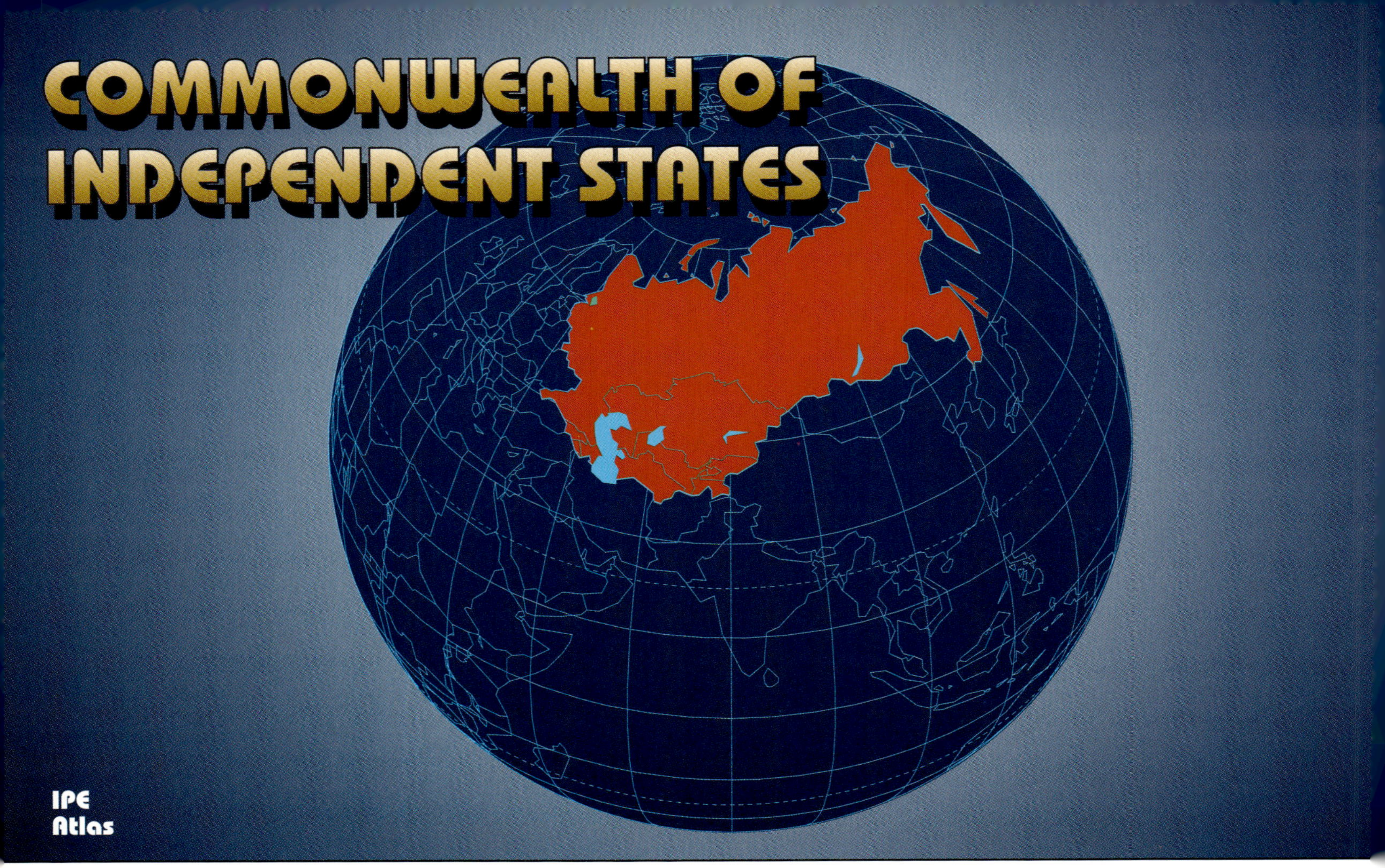

C.I.S.

CAPITAL: Minsk, Belarus
MONETARY UNIT: Ruble
REFINING CAPACITY: 10,100,520 b/cd
PRODUCTION: 7.044 million b/d
RESERVES: 57 billion bbl

Crude oil production in the Commonwealth of Independent States (C.I.S.) appeared to be flattening in 1996. Alhough it continued to decrease, the rate of change was not nearly as great as it had been in the early 1990s. Through the third quarter, the year's production totaled 259.7 million metric tons (an average of 6.944 million b/d), compared with 260.2 million tons (6.958 million b/d) for the same 9 months of 1995.

Gas production in the first 9 months of 1996 increased to 537.4 billion cu m from 516.3 billion cu m the same time in 1995.

Offshore accent

Oil and gas exploration and development in the C.I.S. after the turn of the century will focus increasingly offshore.

So said Vladislav P. Chtcherbakov, first deputy chairman of Russia's Committee on Geology & Use of Mineral Resources, at the 1996 Offshore Technology Conference (OTC) in Houston.

With 3.6 million sq km of prospective area offshore—from the Barents Sea north of the Arctic Circle around Bering Strait to the Sea of Okhotsk off Sakhalin Island—Chtcherbakov estimated potential hydrocarbon resources on Russia's continental shelf could exceed 100 billion tons of oil equivalent (TOE), most of it gas.

Yet officials of western companies who also spoke at OTC said roadblocks remain to restoring vitality to upstream oil and gas activity in the C.I.S. despite the area's huge potential.

Describing the C.I.S. as one of the most enigmatic parts of the world, T. Don Stacy, chairman and president of Amoco Eurasia Petroleum Co., said capital spending by foreign companies during 1996 on upstream Russian oil and gas projects would be relatively small. That's because many companies were waiting on clarification of production sharing legislation passed late in 1995.

"Although there is a dire need for stable investment in Russia's oil and gas industry, the production sharing agreement (PSA) law as it exists does not contain everything needed to encourage investment," Stacy said.

Meantime, K. Terry Koonce, president and chief executive officer of Exxon Ventures (C.I.S.) Inc., Moscow, said cumulative outlays needed to fund all upstream oil and gas joint ventures currently being pursued in the C.I.S. by foreign companies could amount to as much as $150 billion in the next 15 years.

If all projects being discussed publicly unfold as proposed, Koonce said, C.I.S. production by 2010 could be restored to the historic peak of about 12 million b/d. But if adequate technology and capital are not concentrated on C.I.S. exploration and development, production could continue to decline 3-4%/year to about 4 million b/d by 2010.

Russia

In Russia, largest oil and gas producer in the C.I.S., oil production during the first three quarters of 1996 totaled 225.8 million tons (6.038 million b/d), compared with 229.7 million tons (6.142 million b/d) during that period the prior year.

Russian gas production for the first 9 months in 1996 increased to 441.3 billion cu m from 436.5 billion cu m during the same 1995 period.

Despite difficulties, Chtcherbakov said progress toward a market economy is visible in Russia.

Among recent positive factors, Russia organized 10 vertically integrated oil and gas companies for operations ranging from exploration through refining. But even those operations suffer because of Russia's lack of clear investment laws to the extent that state-sponsored exploration has practically dried up, Chtcherbakov said.

Foreign investors have taken up some of the slack from lagging state spending, he said, but a lack of legal framework stalled talks on many deals involving foreign partners.

Regarding Russia's offshore hydrocarbon resources, Chtcherbakov said about 70% of the country's offshore gas is in the western Arctic, while oil reserves are concentrated in the Barents, Pechora, East Siberian, Kara, and Okhotsk seas.

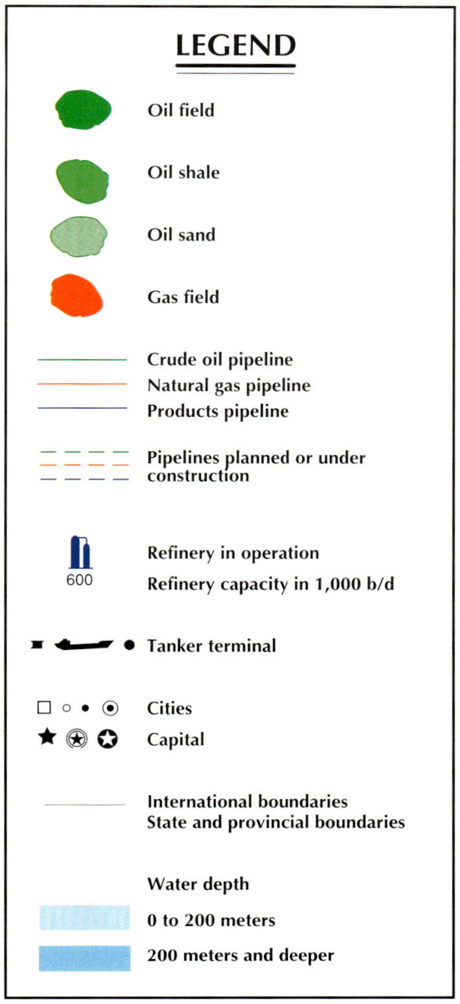

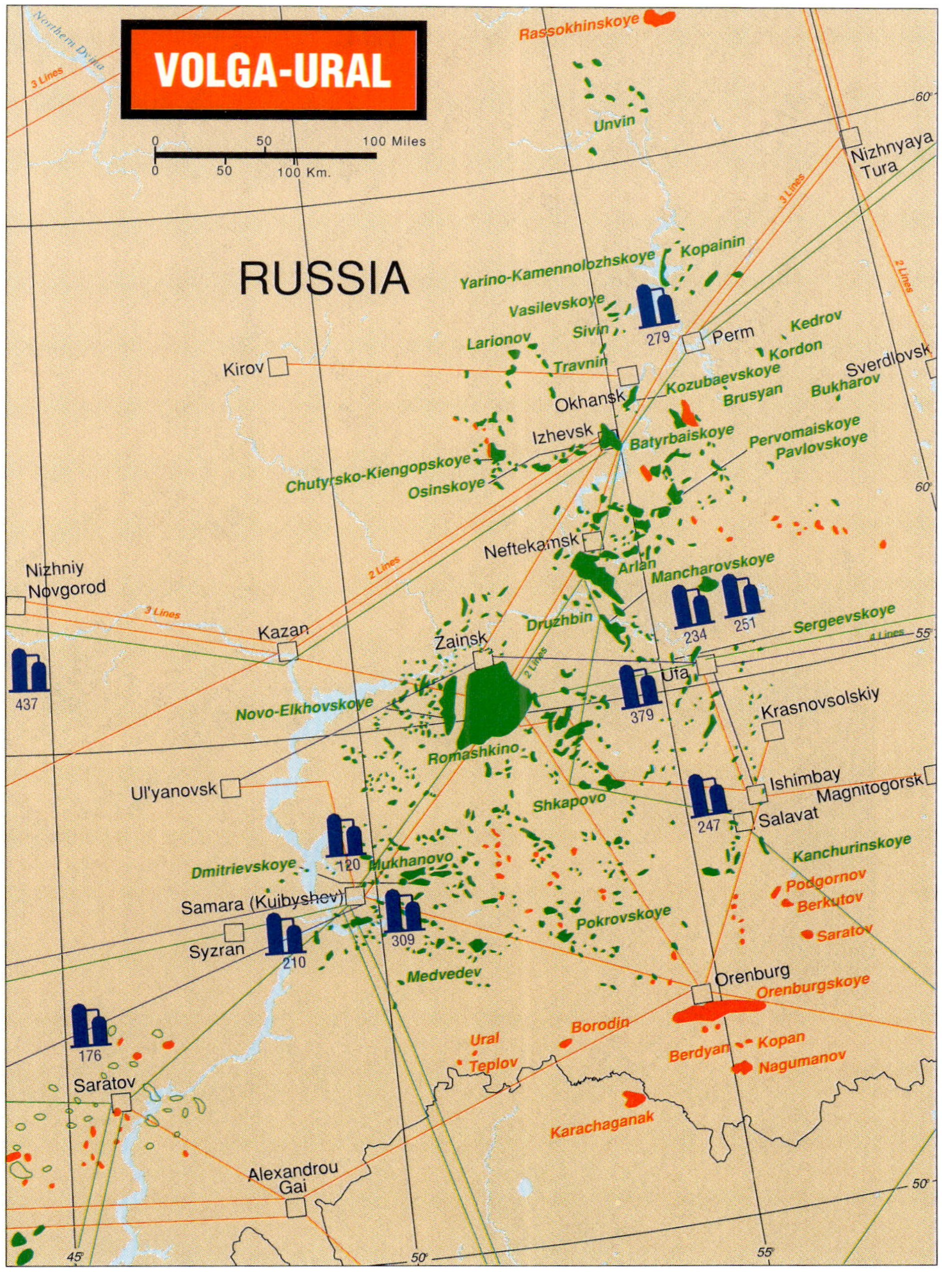

Despite high potential, Chtcher- bakov said, the only offshore 3D seismic data were collected in 1996 near Sakhalin Island.

Similarly, only 110 oil and gas wells have been drilled off Russia, including 66 at Sakhalin and 35 in the western Arctic. The vast area from the Kara Sea to offshore Magadan has had no exploratory drilling, but Chtcherbakov said existing data have revealed 40 offshore basins.

Offshore strategy

Chtcherbakov said Russia's strategy for offshore development includes attracting a wide range of private and foreign companies with competitive acreage tenders, providing state support for Russian companies, and promoting Russian businesses onshore.

The most important development in 1995, he said, was discovery of a vast petroleum province in the Barents and Kara seas with total combined hydrocarbon resource potential estimated at 70 billion TOE.

The largest fields found in the Barents-Kara Sea region include:

- Shtockmanskoye gas/condensate field, with Jurassic gas reserves estimated at 3 tcf.
- Leningradskoye and Rusakovskoye gas/condensate fields, each with Cretaceous gas reserves of 4-6 tcf.
- Prirzolmnoye field in the Pechora Sea.

Chtcherbakov said Far East Russia's estimated 20 billion TOE could provide a base for significant economic development in the region. The main goal there will be to increase production in Sakhalin's northern offshore areas to about 25 million tons/year.

Secondary objectives in the Pacific region include exploration and development of offshore prospects in the North Priokhotye and Western Kamchatka areas. Chtcherbakov said offshore work at Anadyr and Khatyr must occur as exploration continues in the Chukchi and East Siberian seas.

E&P off Sakhalin Island

Only weeks after winning an agreement covering E&P off Sakhalin Island following 5 years of negotiations, Exxon Corp. and partners disclosed plans for work to kick off a $15 billion project to develop three giant oil and gas fields off the Far East Russian outpost.

Exxon, Japan's Sodeco combine, and two Russian firms will spend $30 million to conduct a 3D seismic survey and drill a well, getting a $200-300 million initial appraisal phase off the ground. The group in mid-1996 signed a contract with the Kremlin and local officials for the project, which involves developing reserves pegged at 2.5 billion bbl of oil

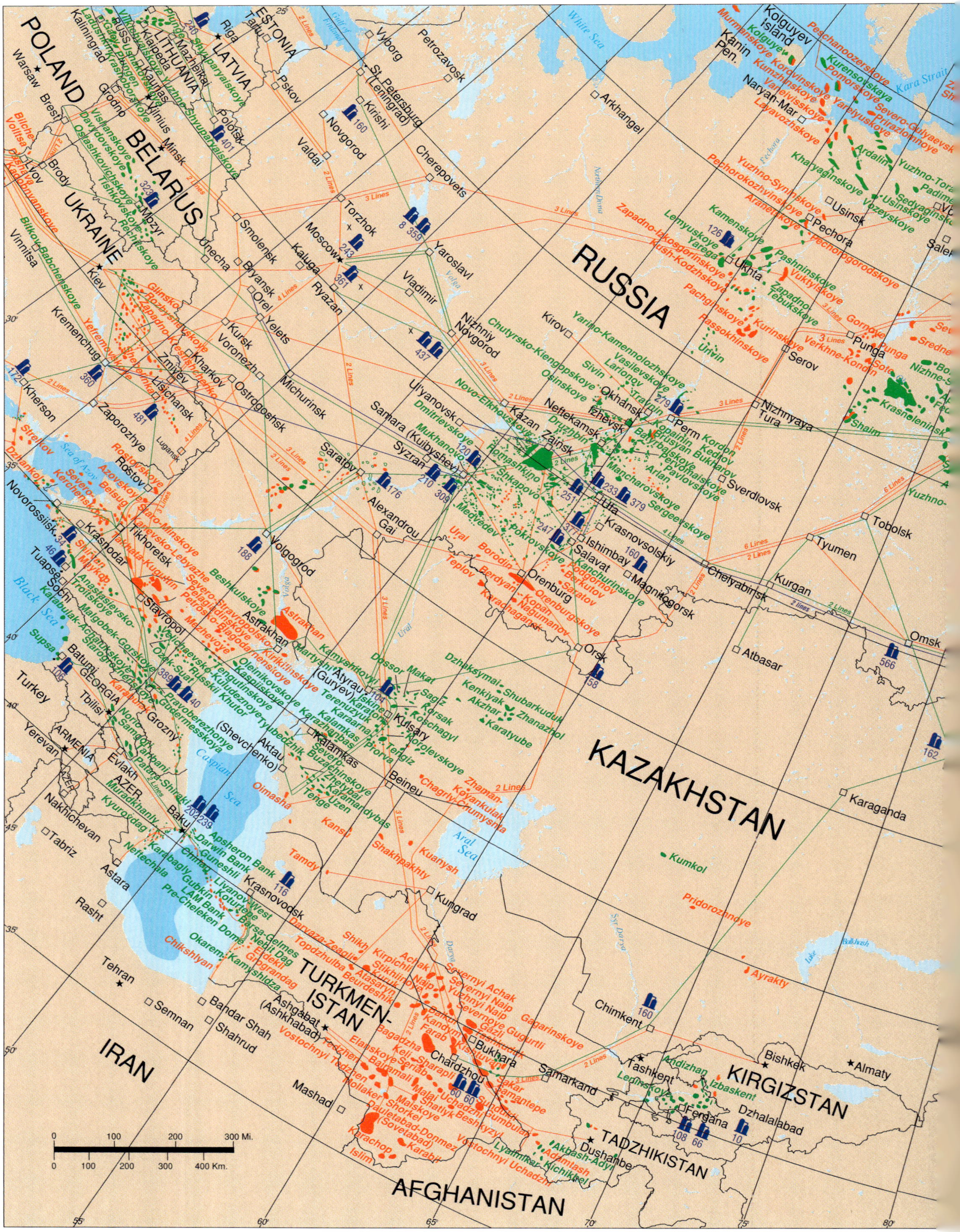
POLAND
LITHUANIA
LATVIA
ESTONIA
BELARUS
UKRAINE
RUSSIA
KAZAKHSTAN
TURKMEN-
ISTAN
KIRGIZSTAN
TADZHIKISTAN
AFGHANISTAN
IRAN
GEORGIA
ARMENIA
AZER.
Turkey
White Sea
Black Sea
Sea of Azov
Caspian
Sea
Aral
Sea
Kara Strait
Kolguyev
Island
Kanin
Pen.
Warsaw
Kaliningrad
Riga
Tallin
Vilnius
Minsk
Kiev
Moscow
St. Petersburg
(Leningrad)
Arkhangel
Naryan-Mar
Pechora
Usinsk
Ukhta
Kirov
Perm
Kazan
Ufa
Orenburg
Samara (Kuibyshev)
Saratov
Volgograd
Astrakhan
Rostov
Krasnodar
Stavropol
Grozny
Tbilisi
Yerevan
Baku
Tabriz
Tehran
Krasnovodsk
Ashgabat
(Ashkhabad)
Mashad
Bukhara
Samarkand
Tashkent
Dushanbe
Bishkek
Almaty
Chimkent
Karaganda
Omsk
Tyumen
Tobolsk
Chelyabinsk
Kurgan
Sverdlovsk
Orsk
Aktau
(Shevchenko)
Atyrau
(Guryev)
Kungrad
Chardzhou
Fergana
Dzhalalabad
0
100
200
300 Mi.
0
100
200
300
400 Km.

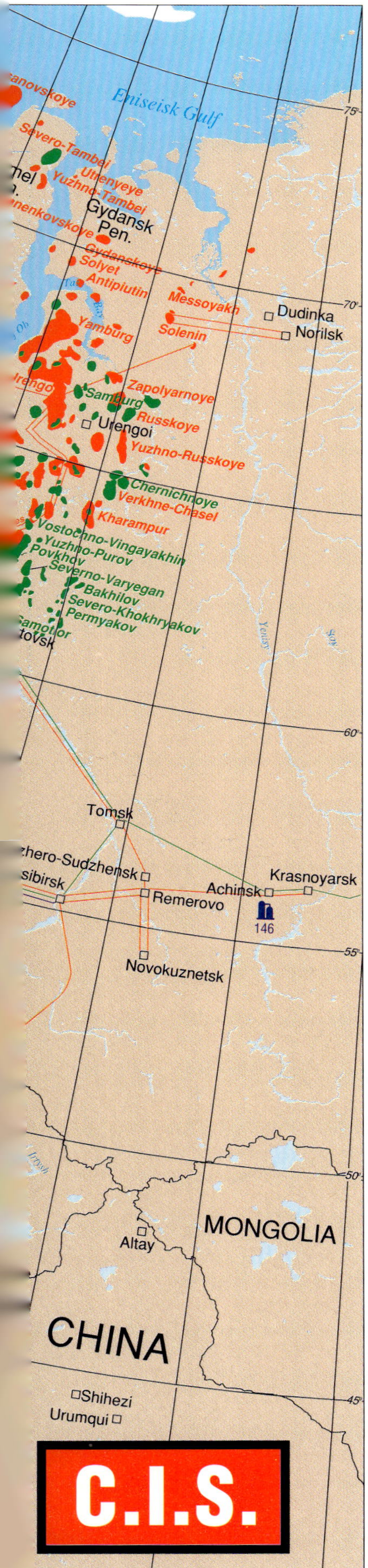

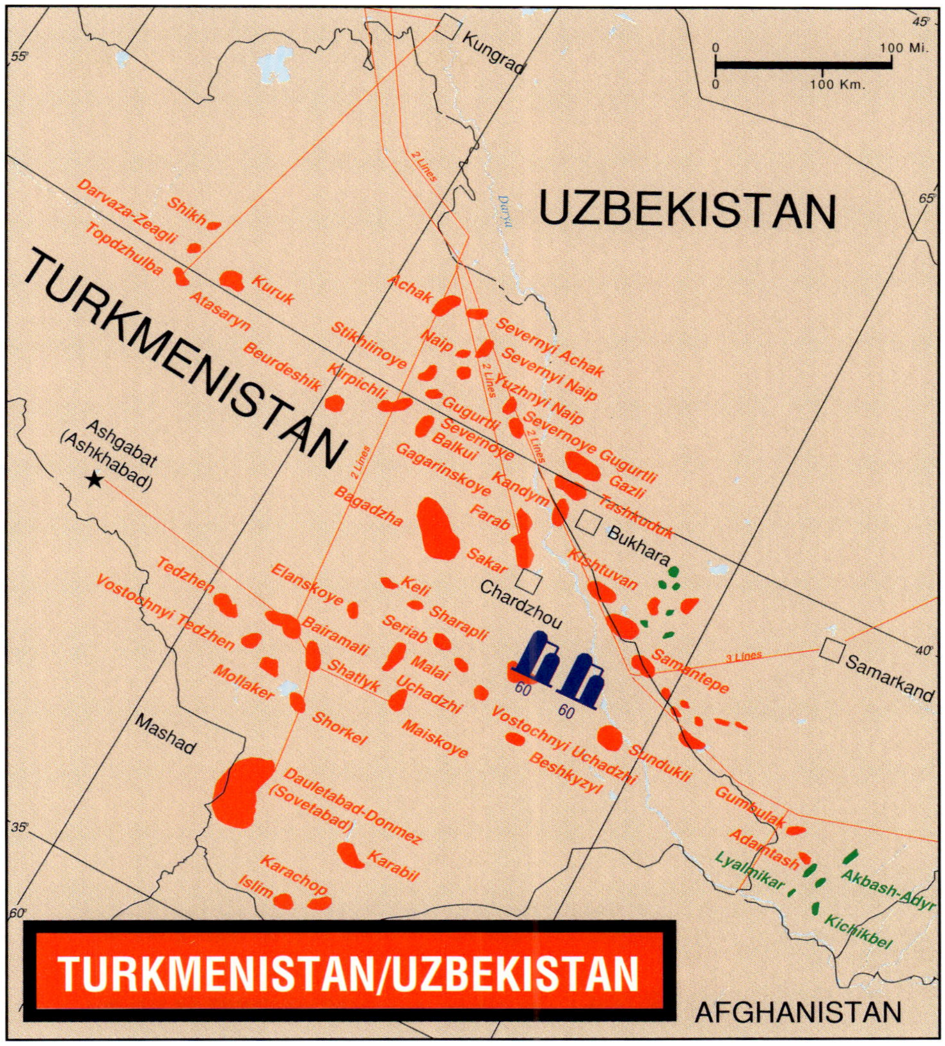

and 15 tcf of gas.

Exxon Corp. unit Exxon Neftegas Ltd., operator of the Sakhalin I Consortium, updated progress on 1996 results and unveiled plans for 1997 under the appraisal program.

Exxon said the group plans to drill three additional appraisal wells in Arkutun-Dagi field, as well as acquire additional 3D seismic on Chayvo, a second offshore field in the Sakhalin I area. Seismic was to be shot from mid-June to mid-October 1997 when pack ice is not present.

The first well drilled under a June 10, 1996, production-sharing agreement in Russia, 5 Dagi, was drilled to a total depth of 8,200 ft in the Sea of Okhotsk.

Results confirmed oil reserves in the central portion of the field, Exxon said, without disclosing specific test results.

Two wells planned during 1997 were to drilled with the Rosneft-Sakhalinmorneftegas Okha jack up under contract to the group.

The group planned to hire another rig to drill the third well.

Design studies for the first phase of development of the Arkutun-Dagi field were also planned for 1997.

Under consideration was a 40-slot, ice-resistant platform to be set in about 150 ft of water to develop oil reserves in the central portion of the field.

Phase one development also was to include provisions for oil export and domestic sales.

Environmental, ice, and soil data gathering and studies were to be undertaken during 1997 to finalize platform substructure design criteria and provide data required to support a field development plan.

In addition to Exxon, with a 30% interest, other interest owners in the group are Japan's Sakhalin Oil & Gas Development Co. Ltd. 30%, Sakhalinmorneftegas-Shelf 23%, and Rosneft-Sakhalin 17%.

Azerbaijan

Azerbaijan in 1996 moved toward a planned increase in offshore oil production and made progress on several large contracts for further development.

The parliament ratified a contract

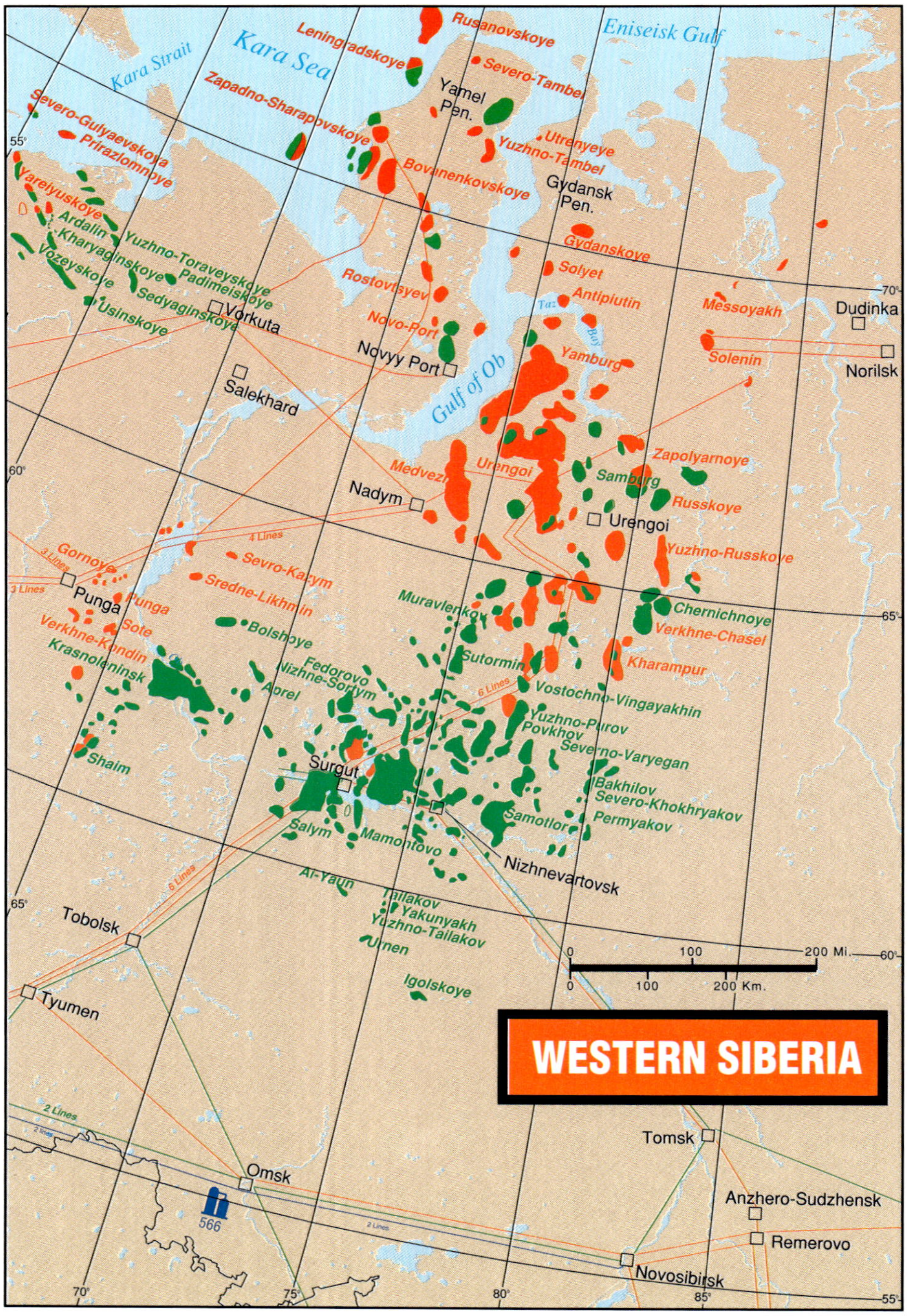

between State Oil Co. of Azerbaijan Republic (Socar) and a foreign group to develop giant Shah Deniz oil field in the Caspian Sea at a cost of $4 billion.

The group consists of Russia's Lukoil, British Petroleum Co. plc, Norway's Den norske stats oljeselskap, Turkey's TPAO, Elf Aquitaine, and Iran's partly state-owned Ocean Industries Engineering & Construction. Shah Deniz is thought to contain a resource of about 17.5 tcf of gas, 1.5 billion bbl of condensate, and 1.4 billion bbl of crude oil. Start-up is projected for 2002 under a 35-year contract. The project will enable Azerbaijan to become a significant natural gas exporter.

In December 1996, Socar was preparing to sign a $1.5 billion contract with a group involving Unocal, Amoco, Itochu, and Delta Nimir for operation of Dan-Ulduzu and Azhrafe fields in the Apsheron ridge of the Caspian Sea. It also was reported to have signed a memorandum of understanding with Conoco to rehabilitate wells and further develop Guneshli field.

Azerbaijan International Operating Co. (AIOC), a London-based consortium of international oil companies, was developing Azeri, Chirag, and the deepwater portion of Guneshli fields and planned to begin production in 1997.

In a development crucial to future increases in Caspian Sea production, AIOC signed a transportation agreement allowing Azeri crude oil to begin reaching world markets about mid-1997.

The agreement with Russia's Transneft oil pipeline company set a tariff of $15.67/metric ton for shipments of AIOC's fields, about 120 miles off Azerbaijan in the Caspian Sea.

Transneft will transport AIOC's crude through a 1,250 km northern route from a point near Baku by way of Tikhoretsk, Russia, to the Russian Black Sea port of Novorossiisk. The northern route main line will consist mostly of a reversed oil pipeline.

Russian and Azerbaijani officials on Jan. 18, 1996, in an intergovernmental agreement set the framework under which the oil pipeline could proceed.

Meantime, talks continued on a proposed western pipeline route that would transport AIOC crude through Georgia to the Black Sea port of Supsa. Negotiators also were working on pipeline proposals that would allow exports of Caspian oil to bypass the Black Sea. Those alternatives would avoid increasing oil shipments to the Mediterranean Sea through the environmentally sensitive Bosporus Straits through Istanbul.

With the transportation agreement with Transneft in place, AIOC Executive Vice Pres. E.R. McHaffie said the multinational group of companies immediately stepped up offshore development spending in its three fields and began work on northern route components. McHaffie unveiled the plan at an early 1996 meeting in Houston sponsored by Cambridge Energy Research Associates.

AIOC partners agreed in 1995 to a $7.95 billion development program for its Caspian Sea tract. The plan included minimum obligatory spending of $150 million through mid-1997 to appraise the acreage. Activity funded by the appraisal program includes collecting 3D seismic data over the area, surveying the seabed, compiling baseline environmental data, analyzing an existing platform in Chirag field, and evaluating possible export routes for early production from the area.

AIOC also expected to spend $350 million through mid-2000 to refurbish the Chirag platform, equip it for drilling, and drill 20 wells from the structure. With costs of past and future bonuses, operating costs in advance of first production, and general administrative expenses, total early oil phase spending could amount to as much as $1 billion, McHaffie said.

Main development in the three fields was to occur in three phases costing $2.1 billion, $1.85 billion, and $3.5 billion, respectively.

AIOC estimates reserves of its Caspian Sea acreage at about 3.8 billion bbl of oil, Caspian regional reserves at 12 billion bbl, and undiscovered regional resources at another 37 billion bbl.

AIOC expects production from Guneshli, Chirag, and Azeri fields to peak in 2010 at about 700,000 b/d. With other

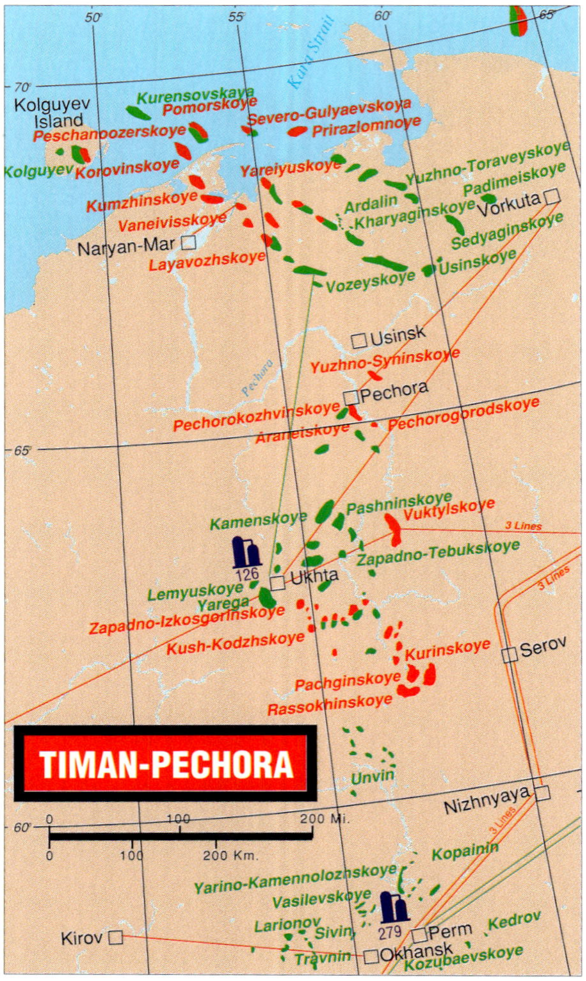

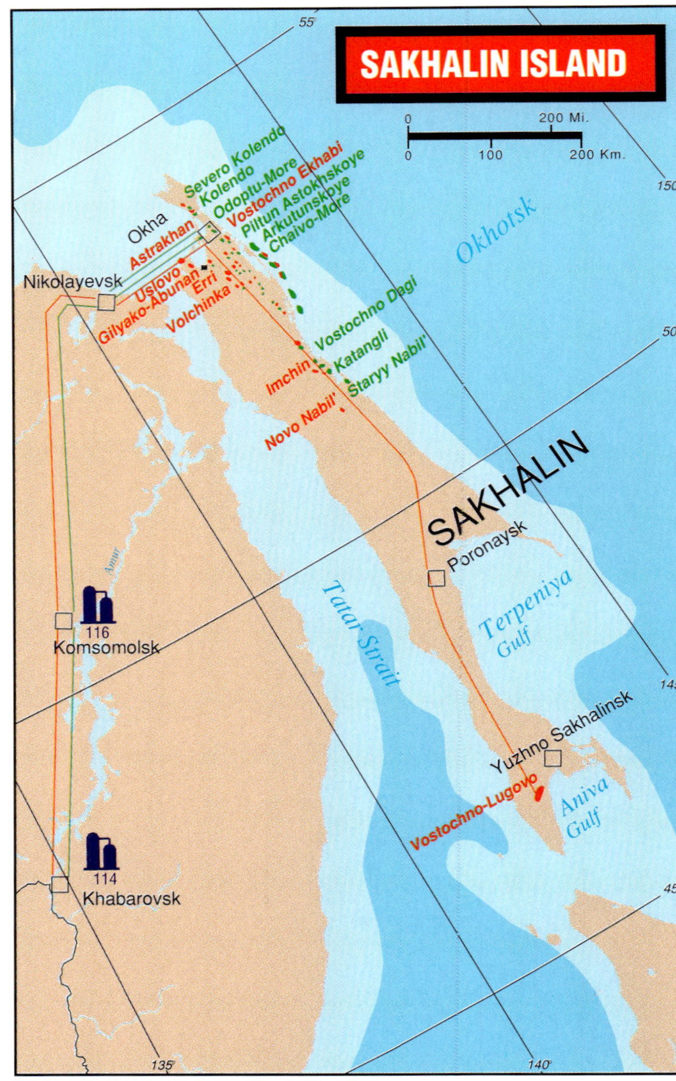

upstream projects advancing around the Caspian, oil volumes from the region over time should be great enough to warrant multiple export pipelines, McHaffie said.

To export oil on the agreed northern route, AIOC plans to bring oil ashore at Sangachal, Azerbaijan, south of Baku through an existing, idle pipeline as far as Guzdek, Azerbaijan. From Guzdek, AIOC will lay a short pipeline to an existing, southbound oil pipeline between Tikhoretsk and Baku. AIOC will reverse the crude line's flow to ship oil through Tikhoretsk to Novorossiisk.

To move oil on the 950 km western pipeline route still being negotiated, AIOC at first would use the same pipeline to bring oil ashore at Sangachal. Crude then would move south from Sangachal to Kazi Magomed, Azerbaijan, where it would enter an existing pipeline to be shipped as far as Kazakh, Azerbaijan, near the Georgian border.

AIOC would have to lay 117 km of 500 mm pipeline between Kazakh and Tblisi, Georgia, where another existing oil pipeline would carry crude about 352 km to a new oil terminal to be built at Supsa.

AIOC will rehabilitate all existing pipelines to be adapted for the western route.

At least 1,100 leaks are to be repaired on the Tblisi-Supsa segment.

Kazakhstan

Kazakhstan moved to relieve the the transportation constraints on its crude oil production in 1996.

In an important development, the proposed 900-mile crude oil pipeline to move oil from Kazakhstan via Russia to the Black Sea for shipment to world markets moved closer to reality.

Mobil Corp. signed an agreement in Moscow as 1997 approached to restructure the Caspian Pipeline Consortium (CPC). Action follows the signing of a protocol in 1996 to restructure CPC.

The latest agreement permits Mobil to exercise its right to acquire a 7.5% equity interest in the planned pipeline project.

Also, the agreement enables Mobil and seven other producer companies to purchase a 50% equity interest in the CPC pipeline from its founding members in exchange for 100% funding of the initial pipeline construction cost.

"It is a major step toward the implementation of the transportation system, which will support full development of Kazakhstan's Tengiz oil field," said Lucio A. Noto, Mobil chairman and chief executive officer.

The system will support other Kazakh and Russian oil.

After closing, equity interests will include the governments of Russia 24%, Kazakhstan 19%, and Oman 7%, and Chevron Corp. 15%, Lukoil 12.5%, Mobil and Russia's Rosneft 7.5% each, Agip SpA and British Gas plc 2% each, and state-owned Kazakh Munaigaz and Oryx Energy Co. 1.75% each.

Terms call for producer companies to fund the project at twice their shares of equity for the initial construction of the pipeline project.

The overall project involves the rehabilitation and upgrading of the existing pipeline from Tengiz to Komsomolsk, con-

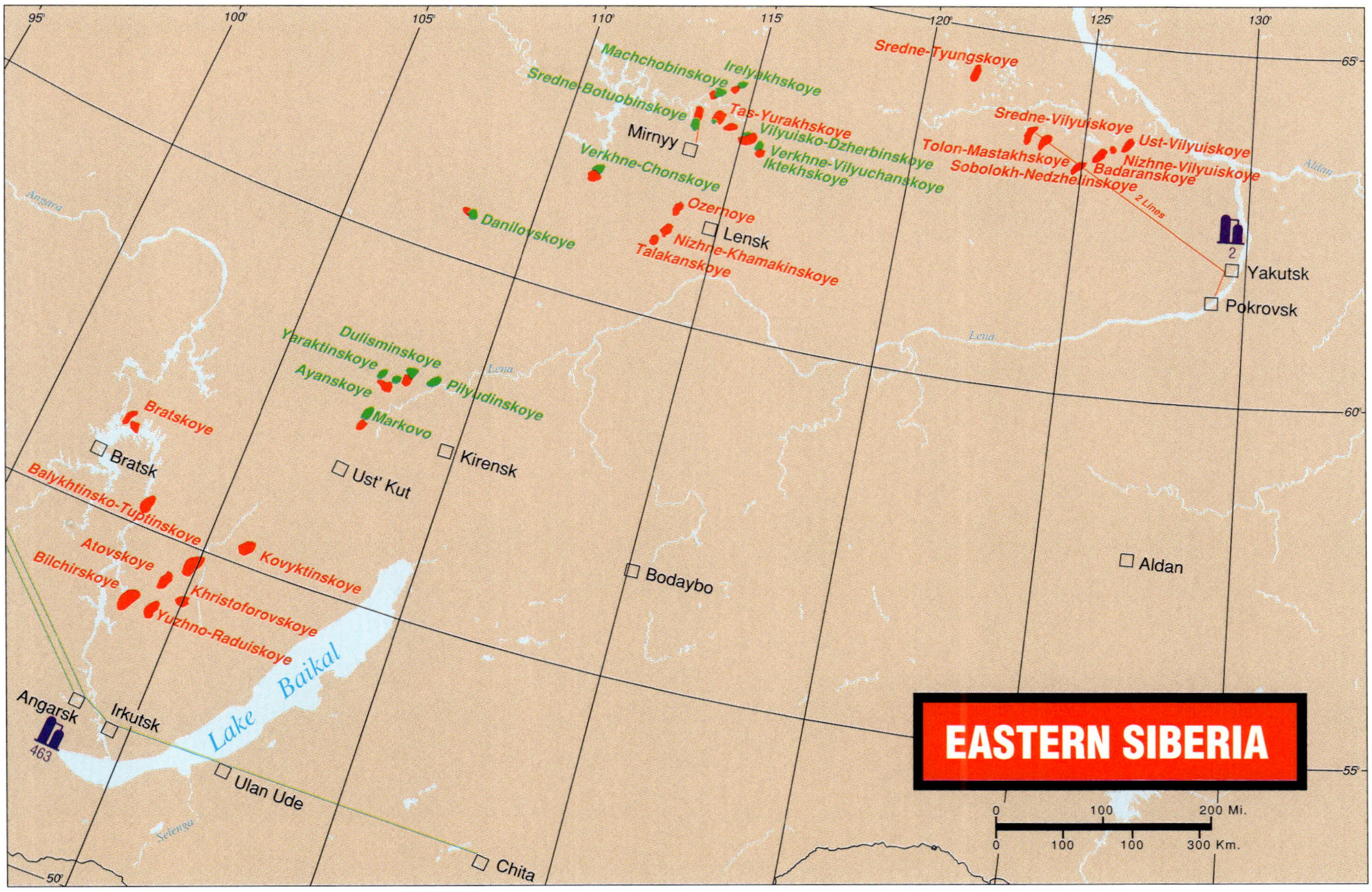

struction and completion of a pipeline from Komsomolsk to the Black Sea, and a new single-point mooring system and offshore loading complex at or near Novorossiisk.

When complete, the pipeline will allow Tengiz field production to exceed 200,000 b/d by the turn of the century and to reach about 800,000 b/d by 2010, Mobil said. The company has a 25% equity interest in Tengiz. Production at the end of 1996 was about 150,000 b/d.

The pipeline, to be commissioned by late 1999, will provide export capacity of 580,000 b/d of Russian and Kazakh oil.

Estimated capital expenditures for initial construction is $2.1 billion during the next 3 years. The total does not include pipeline assets valued at about $600 million contributed by the founding CPC members.

After completion of initial construction, the pipeline is expected to undergo a phased expansion, Mobil said, to accommodate a projected 1.4 million b/d level of Russian and Kazakh exports.

The expansion is projected to cost $2 billion, with completion set around 2010.

Separately, Kazakhstan at yearend was completing a swap agreement with Iran that eventually will provide an outlet for 120,000 b/d of crude.

Under the arrangement, initially involving 40,000 b/d of crude, Kazakhstan oil will move across the Caspian Sea to Iran, which will refine it at Tehran and Tabriz. Iran will deliver equivalent volumes of its crude on Kazakhstan's behalf at its Persian Gulf ports.

Officials of both countries said at yearend 1996 that they were close to signing the deal, which had been delayed by negotiations over crude quality.

Turkmenistan

Prospects for resumption of natural gas exports to western Europe from Turkmenistan rose during 1996 via creation of the joint stock company Turkmenrosgaz.

The new venture joins Turkmenistan's Turkmengazprom and Russia's Gazprom. It was formed following a 1995 meeting between Turkmen President Niyazov and Russian President Yeltsin. Owners are Turkmengazprom 51%, Gazprom 45%, and Itera 4%.

Turkmenrosgaz is empowered to handle all gas exported to Russia, other C.I.S. and non-C.I.S. countries, and also to explore for and develop new gas fields.

The venture calls for delivery of as much as 125 billion cu m/year of Turkmen gas across Russia, a level it will be unlikely to meet soon.

Turkmenistan produced only 31 billion cu m during 1995 and planned to produce 65 billion cu m in 1996. Its best year was 1989, when it produced 89.9 billion cu m.

Turkmenrosgaz hoped to deliver 23 billion cu m to Ukraine in 1996 and increase deliveries to Russia above the 12 billion cu m mark it achieved during 1992-93. For 1996, Turkmenistan planned to export a total of 38 billion cu m, earning $1.9 billion from sales to C.I.S. countries at an average price of $50/thousand cu m (Mcm).

The agreement for the creation of Turkmenrosgaz includes a guarantee that at least 30 billion cu m/year will be delivered via pipeline. Gazprom will buy gas at the Turkmen-Uzbekistan border for $42/Mcm and sell it to other countries through Itera and other companies including Gazprom unit Gazeksport. The agreement further requires Gazprom to increase its sale of Turkmen gas to foreign markets in the near future and also to establish a flexible pricing policy.

Turkmenrosgaz plans to invest $300 million/year, initially

to renovate Turkmenistan's pipelines and compressor stations. It's mainly concerned with the Central Asia-Centre corridor of four gas pipelines of 40-56 in. diameter. Each one is badly corroded, with long sections unable to move gas at 1,100 psi design pressure. There have been regular interruptions to flow.

The Central Asia-Centre corridor of pipelines enters Russia from Kazakhstan at Aleksandrov Gai in Saratov Province, where the gas is acquired by Gazprom's Yugtransgaz subsidiary.

However, the company's pipelines have been operating at less than half their capacity because of the sharp reduction in the flow of gas from Turkmenistan.

Yugtransgaz moves Turkmen gas for Ukraine and Caucasus republics as well as Russia. Part of the reduction in flow has been caused by periodic disputes between Turkmenistan and these countries over nonpayment.

Uzbekistan

Uzbekistan in 1996 began seeking foreign partners for a long list of high priority oil and gas exploration and development projects.

Potential investors may propose joint ventures (JVs), production sharing schemes, or other forms of joint activity on a wide range of upstream prospects.

State company Uzbekneftegaz (UNG) invited companies to:

- Explore for and develop new oil and gas reserves.
- Develop oil reserves beneath gas caps in certain existing fields.
- Implement redevelopment and secondary recovery programs in specified producing fields.
- Develop oil and gas fields discovered by previous activity.

A delegation of Uzbek officials led by Uzbekistan President Islam Karimov visited Houston in mid-1996 to brief prospective partners on oil and gas opportunities available in the country.

The U.S. Trade and Development Agency (Ustda) organized the conference with help from the Greater Houston Partnership, a local business promotion organization.

Uzbekistan since gaining independence from the former Soviet Union in 1991 has created a legal environment that guarantees the rights and protects capital investments of foreign partners. The country also has instituted a favorable tax regime.

At the same time, Uzbekistan has distinguished itself as the only former Soviet republic to increase oil output since becoming independent.

UNG earlier in 1996 ramped up oil output to 160,000 b/d, a level at which it became self-sufficient in oil.

About 60% of Uzbekistan's total area of 447,400 sq km is prospective for oil and gas. Through mid-1996, UNG had discovered and delineated 162 fields, 74 of which had been brought into production.

To demonstrate Uzbekistan's oil and gas potential, Karimov told companies attending the Ustda meeting in Houston he was releasing all available data describing the country's hydrocarbon resources. The information included previously secret geological data and maps developed by the former Soviet government at a time when Uzbekistan's oil and gas output mainly was directed to meet demand in the Urals and other Soviet industrial areas.

"We are willing to open every door to you," Karimov said. "My goal is to reshape Uzbekistan into a model of the western economy through cooperation with the U.S."

The government's emphasis on developing energy resources—coupled with Uzbekistan's history of strong well productivity, extensive pipeline network, refining industry expansion and modernization, and revised foreign investment rules—should enable efficient companies to earn high returns, Karimov said.

Companies from 70 countries are working in Uzbekistan, but Karimov said the country especially wants to develop relationships with U.S. businesses. IPE

EUROPE

AUSTRIA

CAPITAL: Vienna
MONETARY UNIT: Schilling
REFINING CAPACITY: 210,000 b/cd
PRODUCTION: 21,300 b/d
RESERVES: 76.486 million bbl

OMV AG, the state oil company, increased the volume of gas it imports from Russia's Gazprom by 17.5 bcf/year to 192.5 bcf/year.

The Austrian firm also imports 52.5 bcf/year from Norway. Along with OMV's 31.5 bcf/year share of Austria's gas production, the added Russian imports will secure Austria's gas requirements well into the next century.

OMV said it had three oil and gas discoveries in the Vienna basin north of that city in 1996, all the results of 3D seismic. It planned six more exploratory wells in 1997.

The company completed a 20 km section of its Penta West gas pipeline from Mauerkirchen to Burghausen, Germany. The $17 million section has initial capacity of 17.6 bcf/year.

The Penta West pipeline is due completion in 1998, when it will extend 80 km from Oberkappel, Austria, to Burghausen, with capacity to carry 245 bcf/year of Russian gas.

OMV and Bayerwerk AG plan to extend the pipeline system into northern Italy, moving Norwegian or Russian gas to the growing Italian market.

The Austrian firm wants to establish Austria as a transit hub between Eastern and Southeastern Europe. But it has deferred participation in a joint venture for an LNG terminal on the Croatian coast in the Adriatic, which would feed the Austrian pipeline network. OMV explained the project was not economic.

The Austrian government sold more stock in OMV in 1996, reducing its share of the company from 49.9% to 35%. About 40% of the shares were sold to Austrian investors. Abu Dhabi's International Petroleum Investment Co. retained its 19.6% share of OMV.

Plans were dropped to merge OMV's polymers division with the Spanish firm Repsol SA's operations. Repsol explained that the two firms could not agree on a business strategy outside of Europe, but they may consider merging only their polypropylene operations.

BELGIUM

CAPITAL: Brussels
MONETARY UNIT: Franc
REFINING CAPACITY: 629,750 b/cd
PRODUCTION: 0
RESERVES: 0

Belgium worked in 1996 toward its goal of becoming a major transportation hub in the growing European gas trade.

That role was assured in 1996 when construction began on the Interconnector gas pipeline. The 240 km, 40 in. pipeline is due completion in October 1998.

The 700 bcf/year line, managed by Interconnector (U.K.) Ltd., will link Bacton, U.K., with Zeebrugge, Belgium, allowing the export of British gas to the European continent for the first time.

The landing at Zeebrugge would allow easy links to other major distribution pipelines serving western Europe. The line could be used to import 315 bcf/year of gas from the continent as Britain's reserves are depleted.

British Gas, the largest shareholder in Interconnector with a 40% interest, signed a contract to supply 700 bcf/year to Germany's Wingas GmbH, Kassel, through the new line.

Distrigaz SA, the Belgian gas firm, will move the gas from Zeebrugge through the national gas grid to Aachen on the German border. Distrigaz said it may have to build new pipeline links to Aachen.

From Aachen, Wingas will transport the gas through its Wedal gas trunkline, which was under construction and which will join the existing Midal pipeline system.

Belgium's role as an international conduit for gas began in 1967 with deliveries of Dutch gas to France and grew with the addition of Norwegian gas from France in 1977 and Norwegian supplies for France and Spain via Zeepipe in 1993.

Location No. Refineries
United Kingdom
South Killingholm 1
Fawley 1
South Humberside 1
Ellesmere Port 1
Croyton 1
Port Clarence 1
Shell Haven 1
Stanlow 1
Scotland
Grangemouth 1
Dundee 1
Wales
Milford Haven 3
Llandarcy 1
Pembroke 1
Belgium
Antwerp 4
France
L'Orcher 1
La Mede 1
Mardyck 1
Reichstett-Vandenheim 1
Donges 1
Feyzin 1
Grandpuits 1
Fos sur Mer 1
Port Jerome 1
Notre Dame de Gravenchon 1
Berre l'Etang 1
Petit Couronne 1
Dunkirk 1
Lavera 1
Netherlands
Rotterdam 2
Pernis 2
Amsterdam 1
Vlissingen 1
Location No. Refineries
Italy
Livorno 1
Porto Marghera 1
Sannazaro, Pavia 1
Taranto 1
Falconara, Marittima 1
LaSpezia 1
Augusta, Siracusa 1
Frassino, Mantova 1
Busalla 1
Prilo Gargallo 1
Rome 1
Milazzo 1
Gela 1
Sarroch 1
Trecate, Novara 1
Priolo 1
Cremona 1
Germany
Location No. Refineries
Merseburg 1
Hamburg 1
Heide 1
Wesseling 1
Burghausen 1
Godorf 1
Harburg Grasbrook 1
Neustadt 1
Neustadt-Donau 1
Location No. Refineries
Karlsruhe 2
Harburg 1
Zeitz 1
Leuna 1
Woerth 1
Schwedt 1
Vohburg/Ingolstadt 1
Geisenkirchen 1
Lingen 1
Salzbergen 1
Wilhelmshaven 1
NORWAY
SCOTLAND
UNITED KINGDOM
N. IRELAND
IRELAND
WALES
ENGLAND
DENMARK
NETHERLANDS
BELGIUM
LUXEMBOURG
GERMANY
FRANCE
SWITZERLAND
PORTUGAL
SPAIN
ANDORRA
CORSICA
SARDINIA
MOROCCO
ALGERIA
TUNISIA
North Sea
North Atlantic Ocean
English Channel
Bay of Biscay
Mediterranean Sea
Ligurian Sea
Gulf of Cadiz
Strait of Gibraltar
Livorno 84
Sannazzaro, Pavia 200
Taranto 84
Porto Marghera 80
Falconara, Marittima 77
LaSpezia 33
Augusta, Siracusa 182
Milan 80
Italy
Frassino, Mantova 50
Busalla 46
Priolo Gargallo 235
Naples 100
Milazzo 160
Rome 81

BULGARIA

CAPITAL: Sofia
MONETARY UNIT: Lev
REFINING CAPACITY: 300,000 b/cd
PRODUCTION: 1,000 b/d
RESERVES: 15 million bbl

Agropolychim plc, Devnya, Bulgaria, let an engineering and procurement contract to Jacobs Engineering Group Inc., Pasadena, Calif., for Agropolychim's continuing project to improve ammonia plant efficiency.

Jacobs will reengineer and refurbish two fired heaters to incorporate combustion air preheat for conversion to a forced-draft burner system.

Elsewhere, Bulgaria reportedly decided to close its Plama base lubricants refinery permanently if a buyer couldn't be found.

The plant shut down in November 1995 when it ran out of cash to buy crude oil.

Government officials say a buyer would have to pay the refinery's debts, estimated at $45 million.

The plant produced 80% of Bulgaria's lubricants.

CZECH REPUBLIC

CAPITAL: Prague
MONETARY UNIT: Koruna
REFINING CAPACITY: 187,139 b/cd
PRODUCTION: 2,000 b/d
RESERVES: 6 million bbl

Czech state firm Transgas and Norway's Gas Negotiating Committee agreed to a 20 year gas sales contract on behalf of Norwegian gas producers.

Norway's Den norske stats oljeselskap AS said deliveries are to begin during 1997 and reach a plateau of 105 bcf/year in 2002.

Before sales can begin, Transgas must find a supply route through Germany, and the Czech government must approve the deal.

Meantime, Marine & Mercantile Securities plc (M&M), London, entered a venture with Energie Kladno AS, Kladno, Czech Republic, to develop coalbed methane resources in established coal fields.

The Czech company was formed by privatizing a state concern. It holds eight coalbed methane licenses covering a total of 942 sq km.

M&M and Energie Kladno, operating under the name Eurogas AS, plan a $3 million program to evaluate five existing wells and drill more wells. Energie Kladno estimates coalbed methane reserves on its licenses at 1.8 tcf. M&M hoped to begin gas production there in 1997.

DENMARK

CAPITAL: Copenhagen
MONETARY UNIT: Krone
REFINING CAPACITY: 189,100 b/cd
PRODUCTION: 205,800 b/d
RESERVES: 957.1 million bbl

Denmark's Energy Ministry was beginning preparations for a fifth offshore licensing round while moving toward an open-door policy for the least prospective Danish waters.

The government planned to offer all unlicensed acreage in the nation's Central Graben area in the fifth round. Other blocks were to be near acreage offered in the fourth licensing round, in which foreign companies were allowed to bid for the first time.

The Energy Ministry planned to propose the blocks for the fifth round in mid-1997, with submissions by companies on Jan. 1, 1998, and the awards to follow in May of that year.

It said terms for the fifth round licenses would be similar to the fourth round terms, which featured a reduction in state participation after commercial discoveries are made.

Meanwhile, the ministry planned to open bidding on a permanent basis in 1997 on all Danish acreage outside the Central Graben area, where all Denmark's commercial discoveries have been made so far.

Kuwait Petroleum Corp. planned to close its 59,000 b/d refinery at Stigsnaes in early 1997. It explained the plant had limited conversion capacity and lacked the economies of scale for heavy fuel upgrading investments.

KPC will meet its Danish products requirements by purchases from Neste Oy, the Finish firm, and will use the Stigsnaes refinery as an import terminal.

Venezuela's Bitor will supply Danish electricity generator SK Power 1 million metric tons/year of Orimulsion boiler fuel for use at its Asnaes plant on the island of Zeeland.

The plant has tested use of 900,000 metric tons of the heavy oil/water emulsion fuel. The contract was to begin in 1997 and run for 7 years.

The Danish-German Deudan gas pipeline was being expanded at a cost of $65 million. The work, along a 31 mile stretch, will enable deliveries to be increased from 1 billion cu m/year to 2.5 billion.

Protectorates

The hydrocarbon planning commission of the Faroe Islands, a Danish pro-

EASTERN EUROPE
Copenhagen
Malmo
Baltic Sea
BORNHOLM
RUGEN
Reinkenhagen
Kolberg
Rostock
Gdansk
60
KALINGRAD
Kalingrad
Krasnoborskoye
Ushakovskoye
Kaunas
Vilnius
LITHUANIA
Molodechno
Baranovich
Grodno
BELARUS
Davydovskoye
Vishanskoye
323
Mozyr
Minsk
2 Lines
Unecha
Stettin
Schwedt
230
Bromberg
3 Lines
260
Glinik
Plock
Warsaw
Brest
Kobrin
Pinsk
Ovruch
Berlin
Vestrup
Rudersdorf
Poznan
Frankfut-an-der-Oder
Staakow
Guben
Grunberg
Cottbus
Magdeburg
GERMANY
Lodz
POLAND
Radom
Pulawy
Kovel
Lutsk
Rovno
Dubno
Kiev
UKRAINE
Berdichev
Staro-Konstantinov
Vinnitsa
Leipzig
100
12
Jena
Dresden
Zeitz
Gera
Zaluzi
Litvinov
68
Kralupy
5
20
Pardubice
Kolin
Prague
Pizen
As
Waidhaus
CZECH REPUBLIC
Trebio
Brno
Kielce
Sandomierce
Rozwadow
Partinia
Lubaczow
Jaroslaw
Brody
Ternopol
Lvov
Grobla
Trzebina
Bochnia
Oswiecim
Jasto
Tarnow
Jedicze
Czechowice
Rudki
Borislav
Stryy
Dashava
Kradobnensk-Kalusz-
Drogobich
78
Starynj
Bitkov
74
Dolina
Nadvornaya
Chernortsy
Kosov
Krasnoilsk
MOLDOVA
Ostrava
Pribor
Zukow
Stahavo
Gorlice
Smilov
Mikova
Olka
Lugskoye
Uzhgorod
Strazske
Martin
SLOVAKIA
Zvolen
Salushsk
Kosmachskoye
Vacenovice
Ianzhor
Hodonin
Stefanov
Znojmo
Neustadt-Donau
Vohburg/Ingolstadt
Ingolstadt
114
105
72
125
Burghausen
Linz
Munich
Salzburg
Malacky
Wysok
115
Nirta
Sala
Bratislava
210
Vienna
Schwechat
Gyor
Komarom
Sopron
Szony
Sahy
Fedemes
Mezokeresztes
Miskolo
Demjen
61
Leninvaros
Nyirbogdany
Satu-Mare
Baia-Mare
Debrecen
Hajduszoboszlo
Nadudvar
Biharnagybajom
Oradea
ROMANIA
Iasi
Ugeny
Kishinev
Odessa
Bicaz
Stanesti
8
Zemes
Cucacesti
Bacau
Gheorghiu-Dej
Sarmasel
Teleac
Cluj
Zaul-de-Cimpie
Bogota
Tauni
Saros
Bazna
Miercurea
Singeorgiu
Noul-Sasesc
33
87
Budapest
Szazhalombatta
161
Szandaszolos
Szombathely
Kecskemet
AUSTRIA
Graz
10
Lovaszi
Budafap
Zalaegerszeg
Nagylengyel
HUNGARY
Pusztafoldvar
Battonya
Ulles
Szeged
Arad
Sibiu
9
Brasov
Galati
Boldest Moreni
Reni
Izmail
Buzau
Faurei
110
Lebada
Lendava
12
Legrad
Nagykanizsa
Molve
Petisovci
Veliki Otok
Lepavina
Hampovica
Dugo Selo
Babocsa
Cabuna
Pecs
Algoye
Novi Knezevac
Mokrin
Timisoara
Srpska Crnja
Gura-Ocnitei
Frasinu-Mislea
Cimpina
Gura
Ploiesti
56
69
104
11
Midia
Navodari
Constanta
Tarvisio
SLOVENIA
Trento
Pordenone
Udine
Ljubljana
Zagreb
8
Gakovo
Pepelana
Jezevo
Zutica
Voloder
Benicanci
Bizovac
Sombor
Ada
Begejci
Medja
Boka
Velebit
Srbobran
Novi Sad
Resita
Gospodjinci
Ticleni
Bilteni
77
Pitesti
Treviso
Trieste
Koper
Rijeka
Venice
Gulf of Venice
Porto Margjera
80
150
Ivanic Grad
Struzec
Lipovljani
Janja Cipa
Obod
Jamarica
Nova Gradiska
Sisak
143
Bosanski Brod
60
Pancevo
107
Belgrade
Nikolinki
Mramorak Selo
Turnu-Severin
Craiova
Borzetsi
Leonardi
Budisterni
Bucharest
Giurgiu
Ruse
Tollokhin
Kavarna
Varna
Tjulenovo
Staro Orjachovo
Ferrara
Pula
Gospic
BOSNIA HERZEGOVINA
FORMER YUGOSLAVIA
Gigen
Pleven
Devetak
Gorni Dabnik
Beli Izvor
Chiren
Vraca
BULGARIA
Otmanli
Burgas
Bologna
Forli
Cesena
Rimini
San Marino
Florence
CROATIA
Sinj
Split
Sarajevo
Aleksinac
Nis
SERBIA
Pristina
Sofia
Stara Zagora
Falconara
Ancona
77
ITALY
Adriatic Sea
MONTENEGRO
Plovdiv
Karacakoy
Istanbul
Sea of Marmara
Bellante
Dubrovnik
Skopje
51
Shkoder
Cellino
Rospo
Allano
Lanciano
San Stefano
Valle Cupo
Chieufi
Cupello
S. Salvo
Vasto
Termoli
Civitavecchia
ALBANIA
MACEDONIA
Philippi
Alexandroupolis
Kavala
Prinou
S. Kavalla
Bandirma
Rome
Fiumicino
Larino
Foggia
Gulf of Manfredonia
Ripi
Tirana
Cerrik
Thessaloniki
66
Balikesir
Burhaniye
Petroliard-Farnesina
Monte Stillo
Candela
Pietralunga
Giovinazzo
Ballaj
Divjaka
Seman
Kucove
Bubullima
Marinze
Fier
Panaja
Cakran
Gorisht
Vlore
Ballsh
Stalin
Terracina
Gaeta
Benevento
Monopoli
Fasano
Naples
100
84
Taranto
Drashovice
Grottole
Pomarico
Accettura
Ferrandina
Nova Siri
Pisticci
Rotondella
Finiq
Larissa
TURKEY
Izmir
Tyrrhenian Sea
Sibari
Gulf of Taranto
GREECE
Agean Sea
Arta
Soke
Crotone
Luna
San Leonardo
C. Cimiti
Vibo Valentia
Lavinia
Delfi
108
121
Aspropyrgos
Athens
Gulf of Corinth
Corinth
100
0 50 100 150 Mi.
0 50 100 150 200 Km.
Rosarno
Bagnara
Milazzo
Messina
Palermo
160
Gaglioano
San Nicola
SICILY
Mazara del Vallo
Marsala
Marinella
Bronte
55°
50°
45°
40°
30°
15°
20°
25°

tectorate, invited 30 international oil groups to submit nominations for offshore tracts.

The first round of bidding, expected to be held in mid-1997, could offer part of 200,000 sq km around the islands.

Five international oil companies had applied to Denmark's Raw Materials Administration for exploration licenses in the Fylla area off western Greenland.

The applicants are Statoil, Total, Elf, Phillips Petroleum, and Dansk Olie og Naturgas A/S (DONG). The awards will be made by the Greenland and Danish authorities.

Seismic surveys west of Greenland have indicated large geological structures, which are believed to be gas-prone, about 100 miles offshore from Nuuk, Greenland's capital. The seabed in the area slopes steeply, with water depths of 200-1,000 m.

FINLAND

CAPITAL: Helsinki
MONETARY UNIT: Markka
REFINING CAPACITY: 200,000 b/cd
PRODUCTION: 0
RESERVES: 0

Ample Russian natural gas supplies attracted projects to Finland in 1996.

Gasum Oy, a venture of the Finnish firm Neste Oy and Russia's Gazprom, signed an additional gas supply contract with Russia's VEP Gazexport to increase imports from Russia by 10%.

Gasum imported 115.5 bcf of Russian gas in 1995 and expects demand to build to about 140 bcf by 2000.

Neste is a 75% partner in Finland's natural gas distributor Gasum Oy, along with Russia's Gazprom. Gasum operates a gas pipeline from Russia to southern Finland which was moving about 3.2 billion cu m/year.

Gasum plans to double capacity of the pipeline so it can take imports of about 4 billion cu m/year by 2000. And it continues to examine proposals for establishing a gas pipeline link with Sweden or Norway.

Neste Oy also planned to build a $70 million, 70 mw natural gas-fired power plant to supply its Porvoo refinery. It will operate on Russian gas.

And Vattenfall, the Swedish state power group, was considering building two gas-powered electric generating plants in eastern Finland to operate on Russian gas.

If the firm decided to proceed with the plants, which would be about 400 mw each, it was to have launched an environmental impact study in mid-1997.

Borealis AS, the petrochemical joint venture of Neste Oy and Norway's Statoil, began work on an expansion of cracker capacity at its Porvoo ethylene plant. The $88 million project was to raise ethylene capacity 25% to 290,000 metric tons/year and propylene capacity 20% to 170,000 tons/year. Completion was due in mid-1997.

Neste Oil was building a lube base oil plant at its Porvoo refinery, with initial capacity to produce 50,000 metric tons/year for use in lubricants blending. The $52 million plant was to start up in late 1997.

Conoco's Jet Finland subsidiary opened an $8 million oil import terminal at Turku on Finland's southwestern coast, enabling it to import products from the U.K. rather than buy them from Neste Oy.

FRANCE

CAPITAL: Paris
MONETARY UNIT: Franc
REFINING CAPACITY: 1,785,580 b/cd
PRODUCTION: 43,600 b/d
RESERVES: 117.312 million bbl

French state gas officials were objecting to adoption of a European Union gas deregulation directive critical of their closed distribution industry.

EU staff was working on the directive, but French gas officials said it was unnecessary and should recognize that France is totally dependent on gas imports and needs to safeguard it security of supply and distribution.

But Gaz de France and Electricite de France did begin to separate about 3,000 persons in their commercial and other staff into two groups to increase competition. They had shared staff since 1946, when the two companies were established.

Also, the International Energy Agency issued a report urging

France to decontrol its electricity and gas monopolies and to reform its energy taxation system.

The report said France should deregulate both industries and drop oil-product taxes that distorted markets.

And the oil industry issued a study critical of tax preferences for electricity and natural gas.

Its study said those market "distortions" cost industry 60-80 billion francs/year and cost the French public the equivalent of 1.4-1.8% of GNP. The study advocated tax neutrality for all forms of energy.

Meanwhile, France's draft clean air law proposed only "minimal" volumes of oxygenates in gasoline and fuel oil in the year

2000, for fear that French taxpayers would have to subsidize the agricultural products of other European countries in the open market. The draft law also called for tax incentives for vehicles fueled by electricity or gas.

The French parliament approved the NorFra gas pipeline, which is proposed to carry gas from Sleipner field in the Norwegian sector of the North Sea to landfall in Belgium and then on to Dunkirk.

The 42 in., 872 km pipeline would be completed in 1998 and would carry 14 billion cu m/year of gas by 2000. Norwegian producers would own the pipeline, and Gaz de France would operate a terminal at Dunkirk and a 185 km pipeline between that city and Gournay sur Aronde.

Esso-Rep, the exploration subsidiary of Esso SAF, planned to sell its interests in six aging oil fields in the Paris basin and six in Aquitaine. In 1995 Esso-Rep's share of production from the fields amounted to about 5,000 b/d.

The French government sold all but 1% of its 5% interest in Total for $620 million. It owned 35% of Total for many years until 1992, when it sold all but 5%.

Refining

The French industry ministry proposed that refiners add $1 billion of hydrocracking capacity to plants along the Mediterranean and in Normandy.

The ministry said the industry's downstream problems are rooted not in excess capacity but in an imbalance in the product slate. It said refineries make too much heavy fuel oil and gasoline and not enough diesel and heating oil.

It said refiners made large investments in the last 5 years to meet toughened environmental standards, but a product imbalance developed as heavy fuel oil demand slipped, gasoline production exceeded demand, and diesel and heating oil did not meet demand.

Meanwhile, Industry Minister Franck Borotra was negotiating with BP, Esso, Shell, and Total for closure of some capacity at the Fos-Berre-Lavera complex in southeastern France, where refinery utilization averages only 70%.

Those refiners were resisting closures because margins were positive, although slim, and supplies of sweet crude remained ample.

Shell said it was seeking a partner for its 125,000 b/d refinery at Berre, Total said it had 60,000 b/d of excess capacity in northern France, and BP said it might close or sell its 190,000 b/d Lavera refinery.

Mobil Oil Corp. spent $48.5 million to expand capacity of a lube oil blending plant at Notre Dame de Gravenchon in Normandy to 6,000 b/d from 4,000 b/d.

Total claimed two firsts with the start-up of the Nord ethyl tertiary butyl ether (ETBE) unit at its Dunkirk refinery.

It said the $30 million, 50,000 metric ton/year unit is the world's first grassroots, purpose-built ETBE unit and the first instance of a venture between oil and agricultural interests to produce ETBE.

The unit uses as feedstock ethanol derived from wheat and beets. Total owns 40% of the unit, Eridania Beghin-Say 23%, Bio-Ethanol Nord-Picardie 17%, and two French farm associations 10% each.

GERMANY

CAPITAL: Bonn
MONETARY UNIT: Deutsche Mark
REFINING CAPACITY: 2,108,300 b/cd
PRODUCTION: 56,500 b/d
RESERVES: 385.35 million bbl

The German Economics Ministry drafted a law to liberalize Germany's natural gas sector. The Bundestag was expected to consider the legislation during 1997, but passage was far from certain.

The draft law would have allowed third-party access to pipelines, banned marketing agreements that allocate sales territories, and allowed trunk lines to compete with local distribution firms, which are monopoly suppliers.

Most major pipelines opposed the draft law. They said it would endanger long-term supply contracts for imported gas.

Germany took delivery of its first gas supplies from super-giant Troll field off Norway in 1996.

Verbundnetz Gas AG (VNG) took delivery of the gas at Leipzig, which also marked the first delivery of Norwegian gas to the former East Germany. VNG said the contract calls for delivery of about 80 billion cu m of gas worth nearly $8 billion until the year 2016.

Deliveries are due to begin at 1.5 billion cu m/year and rise to 4 billion cu m/year on Oct. 1, 1998, about a quarter of VNG's annual needs. The gas will come from Troll and Sleipner fields initially, and from Oseberg and Asgard fields after 2000.

Wingas GmbH has completed a 20-year pact with Belgium's Distrigaz SA, enabling Wingas to receive 35 bcf/year of gas from U.K. via the Interconnector pipeline being built from Bacton, U.K., to Zeebrugge, Belgium.

Gas began flowing in late 1995 through the 180 mile Norddeutsache Ergas Transversale (Netra) pipeline.

Netra moves gas from Etzel, Germany, near Norway's Emden terminal for North Sea pipelines, through Wardenburg and Achim, Germany, to Salzwedel in the eastern part of the country. From there, it links with other gas lines recently laid in the region.

Netra gets gas from Emden through a 42 mile pipeline. With more compression, the $720 million, 1,200 mm Netra line could handle up to 630 bcf/year.

The Economic Union Court of Justice was expected to rule on a division of territory by Ruhrgas and Thyssengas. The pact allocated Thyssengas exclusive marketing rights in Germany near the Benelux border, and the rest of Germany to Ruhrgas.

The German cartel office ruled in 1994 that the agreement violated European Commission competition rules and ordered it to be scrapped. The two companies appealed, claiming the demarcation was in the public interest.

RWE AG, the parent firm of RWE-DEA, bought 50% of Thyssengas from the utility Bayernwerk AG in exchange for RWE's 25% share of Munich utility Isarwerke GmbH and a small share in another firm.

Esso and Shell each hold 25% of Thyssengas, which operates a 1,420 mile pipeline network, mostly in North Rhine-Westphalia.

Three companies opened a 500 million cu m underground gas storage field at Breitbrunn, 47 miles south of Munich.

RWE-DEA, Ruhrgas, and Mobil Erdgas-Erdoel will use the 10,000 ft deep reservoir to store Russian gas needed to meet peak winter demand. They plan to double storage at the field in the future.

Refining woes

BP and Mobil won approval from the European Commission to combine their marketing and refining operations in Germany. BP will operate and have a 70% interest in the refineries and service stations. Mobil will operate and have a 51% interest in the lubricants part of the venture in each country.

Esso AG plans to combine its Karlsruhe refinery in southwestern Germany with a neighboring plant owned by Oberrheinische Mineralolwerke GmbH (BMW).

The Esso plant is rated at 152,000 b/d and OMW's at 179,000 b/d. It will cost about $30 million to fully integrate the refineries by late 1997.

The combined refinery will process crude and other feedstock supplied by partners in proportion to their shares: DEA Mineraloel AG 32.25%, Esso 25%, Ruhroel GmbH 24%, and Conoco 18.75%.

The government privatization agency BVS plans to dismantle the 67,000 b/d Zeitz refinery in the former East Germany. The grounds will be cleaned and used for an industrial park.

Meanwhile, BVS alleged that Elf inflated the cost of the Leuna

AND THEY LIVED
HAPPILY
EVER AFTER.
HEEREMA
HERMOD
FULL
SERVICE
AHEAD

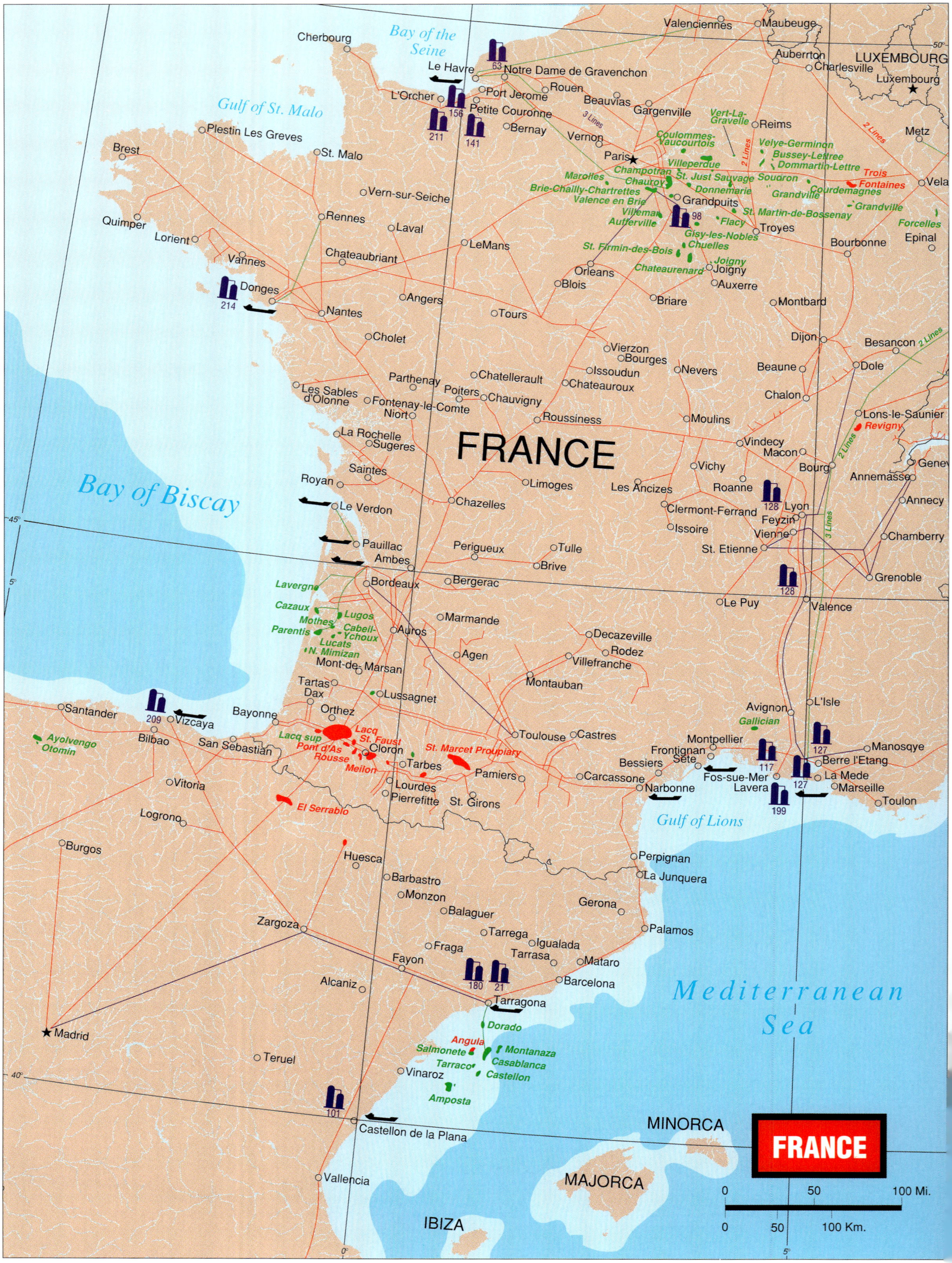
FRANCE
Bay of Biscay
Bay of the Seine
Gulf of St. Malo
Gulf of Lions
Mediterranean Sea
LUXEMBOURG
MINORCA
MAJORCA
IBIZA
Cherbourg
Le Havre
Notre Dame de Gravenchon
L'Orcher
Port Jerome
Petite Couronne
Rouen
Bernay
Beauvais
Gargenville
Vernon
Paris
Valenciennes
Maubeuge
Auberrton
Charlesville
Luxembourg
Reims
Metz
Brest
Plestin Les Greves
St. Malo
Quimper
Lorient
Vannes
Rennes
Vern-sur-Seiche
Laval
LeMans
Chateaubriant
Donges
Nantes
Angers
Tours
Orleans
Blois
Troyes
Grandpuits
Joigny
Auxerre
Briare
Montbard
Dijon
Besancon
Dole
Beaune
Chalon
Bourbonne
Epinal
Cholet
Vierzon
Bourges
Issoudun
Chateauroux
Nevers
Moulins
Les Sables d'Olonne
Parthenay
Poiters
Chatellerault
Chauvigny
Fontenay-le-Comte
Niort
Roussiness
La Rochelle
Sugeres
Saintes
Royan
Le Verdon
Pauillac
Ambes
Bordeaux
Bergerac
Perigueux
Chazelles
Limoges
Tulle
Brive
Vichy
Les Ancizes
Clermont-Ferrand
Issoire
Roanne
Vindecy
Macon
Bourg
Lons-le-Saunier
Annemasse
Geneva
Annecy
Lyon
Feyzin
Vienne
St. Etienne
Chamberry
Grenoble
Le Puy
Valence
Marmande
Auros
Agen
Decazeville
Rodez
Villefranche
Montauban
Mont-de-Marsan
Tartas
Dax
Lussagnet
Orthez
Bayonne
Santander
Vizcaya
Bilbao
San Sebastian
Oloron
Tarbes
Lourdes
Pierrefitte
St. Girons
Pamiers
Toulouse
Castres
Carcassonne
Narbonne
Bessiers
Sete
Frontignan
Montpellier
Fos-sue-Mer
Lavera
Avignon
L'Isle
Manosqye
Berre l'Etang
La Mede
Marseille
Toulon
Vitoria
Logrono
Burgos
Huesca
Barbastro
Monzon
Balaguer
Perpignan
La Junquera
Gerona
Palamos
Zargoza
Tarrega
Igualada
Fraga
Tarrasa
Mataro
Barcelona
Fayon
Alcaniz
Tarragona
Madrid
Teruel
Vinaroz
Castellon de la Plana
Vallencia
Lacq
Lacq sup
St. Faust
Pont d'As
Rousse
Meilon
St. Marcet Proupiary
El Serrablo
Revigny
Trois Fontaines
Lavergne
Cazaux
Lugos
Mothes
Cabeil-Ychoux
Parentis
Lucats
N. Mimizan
Ayolvengo
Otomin
Gallician
Vert-La-Gravelle
Coulommes-Vaucourtois
Villeperdue
Champotran
Chauroy
St. Just Sauvage
Soudron
Marolles
Brie-Chailly-Chartrettes
Valence en Brie
Donnemarie
Villemau
Aufferville
Flacy
St. Martin-de-Bossenay
Gisy-les-Nobles
Chuelles
St. Firmin-des-Bois
Joigny
Chateaurenard
Velye-Germinon
Bussey-Lettree
Dommartin-Lettre
Courdemagnes
Grandville
Forcelles
Dorado
Angula
Salmonete
Montanaza
Casablanca
Tarraco
Castellon
Amposta
2 Lines
3 Lines
63
156
211
141
214
98
128
209
117
127
199
180
21
101
FRANCE
0
50
100 Mi.
0
50
100 Km.

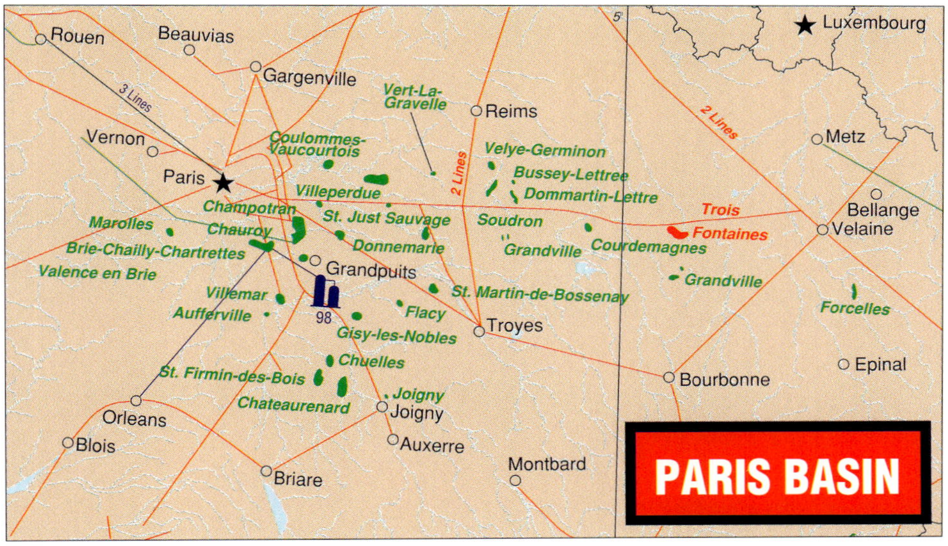

refinery it is building nearby. BVS, which was to have a 33% interest in the plant upon its completion, said the cost should be $1.3 billion, while Elf said it will be $2.2 billion.

The 175,000 b/d refinery, the first to be built in Europe in 15 years, was due completion in late 1997. Elf has a 42.7% interest.

Elf and Dow Chemical planned to build a 16 in. dual use pipeline 430 km from the Baltic seaport of Rostock to the Bohen ethylene plant operated by BSL Olefinverbund (80% owned by Dow) and on to the Mider refinery.

The $300 million line and the refinery would supply naphtha to the ethylene plant and could provide crude for the refinery.

The mothballed Erdolwerk Frisia refinery at the port of Emden will be dismantled and shipped to Asia. A group of Singapore investors bought the bankrupt 48,000 b/d refinery. Lower Saxony has estimated it will cost about $65 million to clean the grounds where the refinery was located.

In 1995 Mobil had sold its closed 100,000 b/d refinery at Woerth near Kalsruhe. It was being dismantled so it can be shipped to India and rebuilt.

The 170,000 b/d Beta refinery at the port of Wilhelmshaven filed for bankruptcy following cancellation of its crude processing contracts by half-owner Louis Dreyfus Energy Ltd. The other owner, Tusculum, a subsidiary of Carlyle Development Corp., continued operating the plant.

Deutsche Shell, Esso AG, and Aral opened a $70 million, 120,000 cu m product tank farm at Rhasa near Dresden. The terminal was to be expanded another 65,000 cu m by late 1997.

GREECE

CAPITAL: Athens
MONETARY UNIT: Drachma
REFINING CAPACITY: 395,500 b/cd
PRODUCTION: 8,000 b/d
RESERVES: 12 million bbl

The European Investment Bank approved a $254 million loan to help the state-owned Public Gas Corp. of Greece complete construction of a gas transmission and distribution system.

Public Gas began work on the project in 1990, which is due completion in 1999. It includes construction of an LNG terminal to receive Algerian gas, as well as a pipeline running from Kula on the Bulgarian border to Athens.

The Greek government still plans to build a 600,000 b/d pipeline with Russia and Bulgaria linking the Bulgarian port of Burgas to the Aegean Sea port of Alexandroupolis.

The 300 km, $670 million line would enable Russian oil exports to bypass the congested Bosphorus Straits. Storage at both terminals would cost $306 million.

Russia shipped about 734,000 b/d of oil across the Black Sea and through the Bosphorus in 1995. Turkey wants any export line to cross its own territory.

Saudi Aramco bought 50% of Greek refiner Motor Oil Hellas and its marketing and distribution subsidiary Avinoil from the Vardinoyannis Group.

The Saudis will supply all the sour crude needs of Motor Oil Hellas' 100,000 b/d refinery at Cornith, about 40 miles west of Athens. The sale was estimated at about $200 million.

Public Petroleum Corp. received 10 offers in a 1996 licensing round, eight for onshore blocks and two for offshore tracts. It had offered six blocks in western Greece totaling 750 sq km onshore and 1,500 sq km offshore in the Ionian Sea. It was continuing talks with the oil companies.

Greece planned to take about 50% of gross profits from the exploration blocks through a sliding royalty and a 40% tax on net income.

Offshore tracts will carry a 7-year exploration stage and onshore tracts 6 years. DEP-EKY, the state exploration and production company, will be a 12% fully paying partner in all blocks.

Meanwhile, Denison Mines Ltd. reported a discovery in the Prinos area of the Aegean Sea.

The well, near Prinos North field, flowed 3,500 b/d of high sulfur crude. Denison has a 45% interest in the area and a 69% interest in the larger Prinos field.

HUNGARY

CAPITAL: Budapest
MONETARY UNIT: Forint
REFINING CAPACITY: 232,000 b/cd
PRODUCTION: 30,500 b/d
RESERVES: 120 million bbl

Hungary's efforts to privatize industry, establish a market economy, and participate in European energy and economic cooperatives advanced on several fronts during 1996.

Hungary was accepted for membership in the Organisation for Economic Cooperation & Development (OECD). Hungary saw OECD membership as the key to entering the European Union (EU). It was tightening petroleum product specifications to meet EU environmental standards.

Also, construction was under way on a strategic storage system that will meet requirements of the International Energy Agency (IEA).

Hungarian officials hoped that a second round of acreage awards during 1997 would attract more international bidding and eventually add to petroleum resources. And Hungarian energy companies were struggling to restructure so they could compete not only in the home market but outside Hungary, too. More crude from abroad, mostly Russia, will be needed to supplement domestic energy supplies.

MOL operations

During 1995, state-owned oil company Magyar Olajes Gazipari Tr (MOL) produced 4.8 billion cu m of natural gas and 1.6 million metric tons of crude. It processed 8.3 million metric tons of oil and other feedstock in its three refineries.

Domestic sales of oil products totaled 5.4 million metric tons, export sales 2.1 million tons. As Hungary's natural gas wholesaler, MOL sold 11.5 billion cu m of gas, up 10% from 1994.

MOL's operating profit improved in 1995 by threefold over the previous year, reaching 9.6 billion forints ($71 million). Revenues grew 28% to 355 billion forints ($2.63 billion).

Natural gas distribution companies in Hungary were sold late in 1995 to Germany's Ruhrgas, Gaz de France, and Italy's ENI (SNAM/Italgas). Thirty bidders bought data packages.

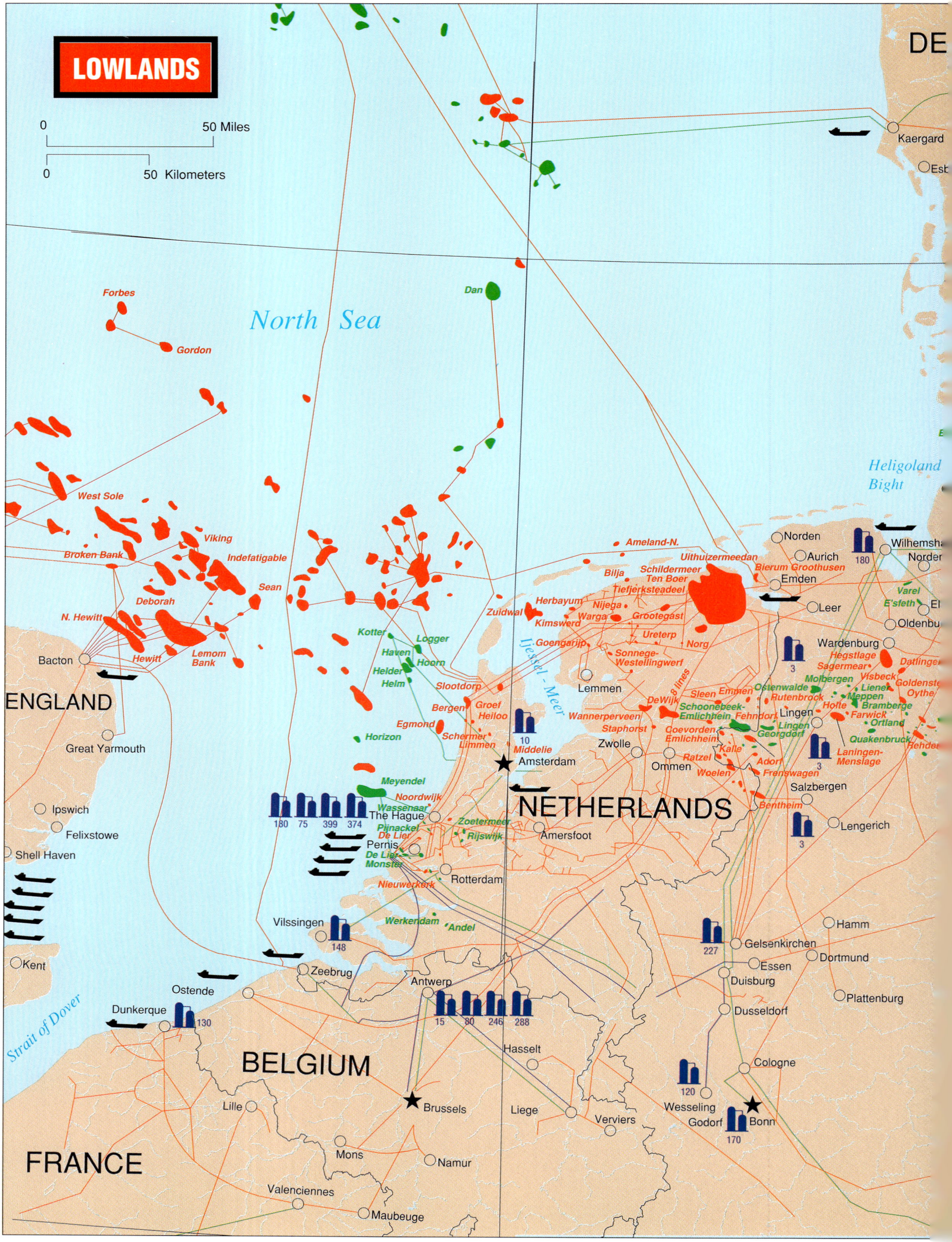

LOWLANDS
0
50 Miles
0
50 Kilometers
DE
Kaergard
North Sea
Forbes
Gordon
Dan
West Sole
Viking
Indefatigable
Broken Bank
Sean
Deborah
N. Hewitt
Hewitt
Lemom Bank
Bacton
ENGLAND
Great Yarmouth
Ipswich
Felixstowe
Shell Haven
Kent
Strait of Dover
Heligoland Bight
Norden
Aurich
Wilhemsha
Norder
180
Emden
Leer
Oldenbu
Varel
E'sfeth
Wardenburg
Ameland-N.
Uithuizermeedan
Schildermeer
Ten Boer
Bierum Groothusen
Bilja
Tiefjerksteadeel
Herbayum
Nijega
Warga
Grootegast
Kimswerd
Zuidwal
Ureterp
Norg
Goengarijp
Sonnege-Westellingwerf
Ijessel - Meer
Lemmen
Kotter
Logger
Haven
Hoorn
Helder
Helm
Slootdorp
Groef
Heiloo
Bergen
Egmond
Schermer
Limmen
Horizon
10
Middelie
Amsterdam
Wannerperveen
Staphorst
Zwolle
Ommen
8 lines
DeWijk
Sleen
Emmen
Schoonebeek-Emlichheim
Fehndorf
Coevorden
Emlichheim
Ostenwalde
Rutenbrock
Lingen
Georgdorf
Kalle
Adorf
Ratzel
Woelen
Frenswagen
Bentheim
Salzbergen
Lengerich
3
Hegstlage
Sagermear
Molbergen
Visbeck
Liener
Meppen
Hofte
Bramberge
Farwick
Ortland
Quakenbruck
Laningen-Mensiage
Datlinge
Goldenst
Oythe
Hehde
Meyendel
Noordwijk
Wassenaar
Pijnacker
De Lier
The Hague
Pernis
De Lier
Monster
180
75
399
374
Zoetermeer
Rijswijk
Amersfoot
NETHERLANDS
Rotterdam
Nieuwerkerk
Werkendam
Andel
Vilssingen
148
Zeebrug
Ostende
Dunkerque
130
Antwerp
15
80
246
288
BELGIUM
Hasselt
Brussels
Liege
Verviers
Lille
Mons
Namur
FRANCE
Valenciennes
Maubeuge
227
Gelsenkirchen
Hamm
Essen
Dortmund
Duisburg
Dusseldorf
Plattenburg
Cologne
120
Wesseling
Godorf
Bonn
170

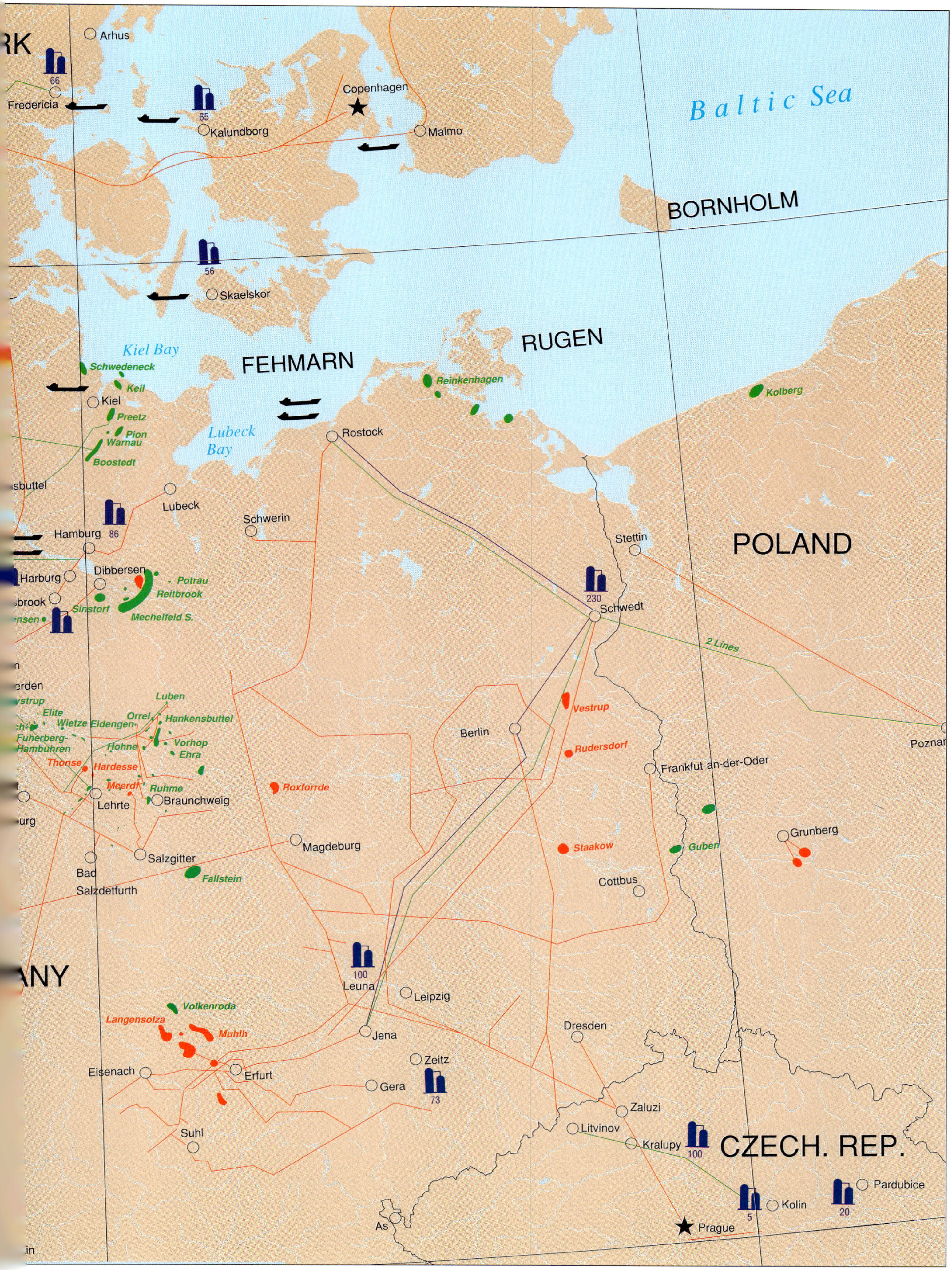
Baltic Sea
BORNHOLM
RUGEN
FEHMARN
POLAND
CZECH. REP.
Kiel Bay
Lubeck Bay
Arhus
Fredericia
66
65
Kalundborg
Copenhagen
Malmo
56
Skaelskor
Schwedeneck
Keil
Kiel
Preetz
Pion
Warnau
Boostedt
Reinkenhagen
Kolberg
Rostock
Lubeck
Schwerin
Hamburg
86
Harburg
Dibbersen
Potrau
Reitbrook
Sinstorf
Mechelfeld S.
Stettin
230
Schwedt
2 Lines
Luben
Elite
Wietze
Eldengen
Orrel
Hankensbuttel
Fuherberg-Hambuhren
Hohne
Vorhop
Ehra
Thonse
Hardesse
Meerdf
Ruhme
Lehrte
Braunchweig
Roxforrde
Vestrup
Berlin
Rudersdorf
Frankfut-an-der-Oder
Poznan
Grunberg
Guben
Staakow
Cottbus
Magdeburg
Salzgitter
Bad Salzdetfurth
Fallstein
100
Leuna
Leipzig
Volkenroda
Langensolza
Muhlh
Jena
Dresden
Zeitz
Gera
73
Eisenach
Erfurt
Zaluzi
Litvinov
Kralupy
100
Suhl
5
Kolin
20
Pardubice
As
Prague

All gas for these systems must still be bought from MOL, which in turn buys it from Russia's Gazprom.

Domestic prospects

Hungary's oil and gas resources are limited. That is why energy strategy includes offering licenses to foreign explorers, exploring abroad for equity crude, and using 3D seismic technology to take another look at mature regions at home.

In 1996, exploration was under way in areas awarded in 1994 to Mobil Corp., Occidental of Hungary, Coastal Oil & Gas Corp., and Blue Star Corp. The government was considering three areas for a second licensing round in 1997:

- An area adjacent to the Blue Star/Coastal concession in Central Hungary.
- An area near the Lake of Velence about 50 km from Budapest.
- An area in the Nyirseg Area near the Ukrainian border.

Main elements of a concession agreement are a 4 year exploration term that can be extended for 2 years and a production period of 35 years that can be extended by 17½ years. The foreign partner must guarantee that it can restore the area.

Product upgrading

The Hungarian Petroleum Association has been pushing for better petroleum product quality and new quality standards. One of the association's early efforts was to urge an inspection program to sample the quality of petroleum products.

Currently, 92 RON and 98 RON leaded gasoline are sold in Hungary. EU rules state that only one leaded grade can be sold, and it must be 95 RON or higher. Because Hungary is working toward EU membership, it eliminated the 92 RON leaded grade effective July 1, 1996.

MOL was working to upgrade capacity as new product specifications evolve.

To meet a reduced sulfur limit the company undertook a hydrodesulfurization project at the Danube refinery near Budapest, Hungary's biggest.

The Danube refinery has a 1 million ton/year UOP FCC plant, visbreaking, and mild hydrocracking following the FCC. Further upgrading, perhaps with a new FCC unit, was in the planning stage.

Strategic storage

In 1996, Hungarian production filled only about one fourth of the country's petroleum consumption. The country had only two sources of crude oil imports: the Friendship (Druzhba) and Adriatic pipelines. The Adriatic pipeline has not been reliable. Some shipments can be made on the Danube, but it is an economic option only for petroleum products, not crude.

Act 49 of the 1993 Stockpiling Law established the Association of Crude Oil & Products Stockpiling and charged it with developing storage facilities and capacity that meet European standards.

IRELAND

CAPITAL: Dublin
MONETARY UNIT: Irish Pound
REFINING CAPACITY: 65,000 b/cd
PRODUCTION: 0
RESERVES: 0

The Irish government offered 615 full blocks and 35 partial blocks for exploration in the Rockall Trough area off western Ireland.

Rockall Trough is a large northeast-southwest trending Mesozoic to Cenozoic sedimentary basin lying 100-650 km offshore. It is bounded on two sides by shallow platforms: the Erris and Slyne and Porcupine Ridges on the southwest and Rockall Bank on the northwest.

The frontier blocks totaled nearly 150,000 sq km. Companies were asked to apply for licenses by mid-1997, with awards to follow in late 1997.

Water depths ranged from more than 2,500 m at the center of the trough to about 500 m on the margins.

Irish National Petroleum Corp. began operating its 56,000 b/d Whitegate refinery on a commercial basis beginning Jan. 1, 1997. At that time, the government no longer required retailers to buy 20% of their products from the plant. Until Jan. 1, 1996, the requirement had been 35%.

Major retailers in Ireland said they would continue buying from the refinery if its prices were competitive.

Ireland and Northern Ireland governments and gas companies are studying the feasibility of building a natural gas pipeline to link the networks in the north and south of the island.

A gas pipeline has been built to take gas from the U.K. supply grid in Scotland to a point north of Dublin.

A separate link is being completed to take gas from Scotland to supply a power plant in Ballylumford and a residential supply grid for Belfast.

The Irish government blocked plans by Statoil, the Norwegian state oil company, to take over Conoco's Jet service station chain. It said the 257-station acquisition would reduce retailing companies in Ireland to five firms and would have given Statoil 430 outlets and 25% of the market.

Statoil plans to invest $60 million to explore around the Connemara oil discovery on acreage it acquired in a $313 million takeover of Aran Energy.

Statoil planned to drill more wells in 1997 and even to begin limited production by the end of the year with a production, storage, and offloading ship. If Connemara is developed, it would be the first oil field in Irish waters.

Connemara lies in 365 m of water on Block 26/29 in the Porcupine basin off Southwest Ireland. BP made the discovery in 1982 but decided not to develop it because of low recovery rates.

ITALY

CAPITAL: Rome
MONETARY UNIT: Lira
REFINING CAPACITY: 2,261,818 b/cd
PRODUCTION: 101,300 b/d
RESERVES: 684.6 million bbl

The Italian government advanced privatization of Enti Nazionale Idrocarburi (ENI), the national oil firm and the eighth largest petroleum company in the world.

In two sales, it reduced its holdings in ENI to 70%. More sales were planned, depending on market conditions.

The government planned to lower the maximum benzene level in gasoline from 3% to 1.4% effective July 1, 1997.

ENI plans to invest more than $3.5 billion in North Africa in the next 3 years. It said E&P projects in Egypt and Algeria will push its North African oil and gas production to 236,000 b/d and 153 MMcfd of gas by 1999.

Agip SpA tested the first horizontal well in its Monte Alpi oil field in Italy's southern Apennines.

The 5 Monte Alpi flowed 3,700 b/d of 37° gravity oil through a half-in. choke. The well is believed capable of producing 8,000 b/d. Agip is operator with 60%, and Enterprise Oil has 40%.

Italy awarded three new onshore permits in the southern Apennines to a combine consisting of Triton Energy Ltd., Union Texas Adriatic Inc., and Canada Northwest Italiana SpA.

Agip SpA planned to build a 100,000 b/d crude oil pipeline from the Monte Alpi and Tempa Rossa fields, extending 140 km to Taranto.

At Trecate field, Agip will test a prototype pressure-boosting unit in an effort to increase production from marginal wells. The British-designed unit uses output from high-pressure wells to boost the flow from low-pressure wells in the same area.

Kuwait Petroleum Corp. bought a 50% interest in Agip's 300,000 b/d Milazzo refinery and 330 service stations. An extensive upgrade at the refinery was due completion in 1997. For KPC, the deal replaces its 85,000 b/d Naples refinery, closed in 1993.

ISAB Energy let a $730 million contract to build an integrated gasification/combined-cycle cogeneration power plant next to its Priolo Gargallo, Sicily, refinery to convert high sulfur heavy oil residue into synthetic gas to generate electricity and steam.

Anonima Petroli Italiana (API) let a $470 million contract for a 260,000 kw integrated gasification/combined-cycle power plant at its Falconara refinery. The plant will gasify 440,000 metric tons/year of visbreaker tar to fuel gas turbines that will supply steam and power to the refinery.

MALTA

CAPITAL: Valletta
MONETARY UNIT: Pound
REFINING CAPACITY: 0
PRODUCTION: 0
RESERVES: 0

Malta is planning a new offshore licensing round under relaxed fiscal terms.

The island nation revised its model production sharing contract to lower the income tax to 35% from 50% and to boost the share of net annual production availabale for cost recovery to 75%.

For several years, Malta has sought its first oil production. The island lies on a trend between the two largest producing fields in the Mediterranean: Sicily's Vega field and Libya's Bouri field.

Several international oil companies have drilled wildcats on acreage around Malta, but none have announced discoveries.

East of the island, Texaco Exploration Malta Inc. holds concessions in the strait between Malta and Sicily near Italy's Vega oil field.

NETHERLANDS

CAPITAL: Amsterdam
MONETARY UNIT: Guilder
REFINING CAPACITY: 1,186,500 b/cd
PRODUCTION: 60,000 b/d
RESERVES: 88.057 million bbl

Nederlandse Aardolie Mij. BV (NAM) made a gas discovery in the environmentally sensitive Waddenzee region, which it earlier had predicted might contain 200 billion cu m of gas.

The Waddenzee area, an area of shallow water and mudflats between the Dutch coast and the Friesian island chain, attracts millions of migratory birds yearly.

The discovery well was directionally drilled from the Dutch coastline. A second horizontal well was planned during 1997. NAM also holds a permit to drill six horizontal wells from an offshore rig.

The company said if the field is developed, it will be produced from the Dutch coast or Ameland Island, but not from a facility in the Waddenzee itself.

Gasunie, the Dutch state distribution company, signed a 20-year contract with Gazprom for access to 4 billion cu m/year of Russian gas.

Gasunie also signed a contract with Amoco Netherlands BV to use the latter's onshore Alkmarr gas field for underground storage. Amoco will convert the largely depleted field so that it can deliver up to 24 million cu m/day of gas at peak demand periods.

The $190 million project was to be completed in time for the 1997-98 winter. Gasunie increasingly needs to store gas since production is declining from giant Groningen gas field.

Texaco closed its Pernis refinery but kept part of it in operation as a terminal. It operates the plant and one at Europort with BP; together, the units have 399,000 b/d of capacity.

BP also plans to close its section of the Pernis plant. The firms said the closures will result in only a 20,000 b/d drop in their joint refining operations.

NORWAY

CAPITAL: Oslo
MONETARY UNIT: Krone
REFINING CAPACITY: 307,000 b/cd
PRODUCTION: 3,085,700 b/d
RESERVES: 11.234 billion bbl

Norway, western Europe's pacesetter in oil production, is focusing on natural gas as its principal hydrocarbon export.

The International Energy Agency predicts that investments in Norwegian oil prospects will continue to drop from the 1993 peak because there are fewer and smaller oil fields to be developed.

But IEA said gas projects should offset that. "Gas constituted about 18% of Norway's total petroleum production in 1993. The relative share of gas in total petroleum production and revenues will increase over time due to increased gas sales and to an expected drop in annual oil production."

Norway expects to increase gas exports to continental Europe by 2005 to 2.17 tcf/year from the current 1.05 tcf.

IEA estimates gas reserves discovered off Norway total more than 2.8 trillion cu m, and production at current levels could be maintained for more than 100 years.

With undiscovered resources estimated at more than 2.4 trillion cu m of gas, EIA said, Norway could become a bigger gas supplier in the future.

Norway's operators have begun construction of more offshore trunk lines to carry gas to continental Europe at the turn of the century.

They will bring the nation's total gas export capacity to 72 billion cu m/year.

The three existing trunk lines will be joined by two new lines. Norwegian fields then will be connected by three lines to Emden, Germany, one to Zeebrugge, Belgium, and one to Dunkirk, France.

Den norske stats oljeselskap AS (Statoil) plans to expand the Kaarsto gas terminal, where it will process gas from Aasgard fields for export. The 12 million cu m/year plant is due completion in late 2000.

Statoil completed the Haltenpipe gas pipeline from Heidrun platform in the Norwegian North Sea to Tjeldbergodden in Central Norway. The line will carry gas from Heidrun field to a new methanol plant due completion in mid-1997.

Statoil also planned to build an LNG plant at Tjeldbergodden with initial capacity of 7,500 tons/year. The LNG will be used to fuel ferries and buses.

In its 15th offshore licensing round, Norway offered foreign firms operatorships of more than half the exploration licenses. In all, it offered 18 production licenses covering 33 blocks in the Norwegian Sea and 13 in the North Sea, as a result of applications filed in February 1995.

For years, the government had favored Statoil, Norsk Hydro, and Saga as operators when it issued licenses.

Norway's Ministry of Industry and Energy offered 45 blocks in the Barents Sea for exploration. It expected to make awards in mid-1997.

Industry has drilled 53 holes in the Barents and found significant gas deposits, but they were not commercial because of the distance from markets.

In the latest round, the government loosened its licensing terms. Companies also pooled their exploration results in efforts to improve their bids.

POLAND

CAPITAL: Warsaw
MONETARY UNIT: Zloty
REFINING CAPACITY: 352,000 b/cd
PRODUCTION: 5,000 b/d
RESERVES: 40 million bbl

Texaco Inc. and Tenneco Energy, though a joint company, began exploring a 1.18 million acre concession in Central Poland,

southwest of Warsaw.

The partners aimed to explore Permian Rotliegendes gas intervals at 3,500-5,000 m on the eastern end of the southern gas basin, which extends from the North Sea across Netherlands and Germany and into Poland.

Work on the Texaco-Tenneco acreage proceeded under a license granted Mar. 1, 1996. That followed acceptance by Gminas—local Polish political units—of a two-phase, 6 year exploration program agreed to in an earlier contract between Texaco-Tenneco joint company Wielkopolska Energia SA (Wpesa), Warsaw, and Poland's Ministry of Environmental Protection, Natural Resources and Forestry. Sixty-six Gminas in Wpesa's concession area had to approve the program for the deal to advance.

Wpesa's concession covers Blocks 229, 249, 250, 270, and 271.

Wpesa seismic contractor Geofyzika Torun, based in Torun, Poland, began acquiring permits for a 1,000 line-km, 2D seismic survey through the heart of the acreage.

Terms of the work program require Wpesa to collect, process, and interpret the 2D data within 3 years. Drilling could follow in phase two of the exploration period if new 2D data firm up prospects indicated by older regional seismic.

Wpesa's Polish acreage is squarely within the eastern extension of the southern gas basin, with Rotliegendes gas production across the length of the trend from the same types of traps and seals, according to Frederick Frankel, Texaco's exploration coordinator for Poland.

Frankel said source rocks for Rotliegendes gas are Carboniferous coals and shales, overlain directly by fluvial, eolian Rotliegendes reservoir sands. Rotliegendes formations, in turn, are overlain immediately by thick Zechstein evaporites, thousands of feet thick in some places, deposited in four cycles.

Most gas from the trend is produced along the southern edge of the basin from reservoirs in eolian dune type facies at the top of the Rotliegendes.

The Rotliegendes on Wpesa's blocks underlies thick Zechstein sediment between Carboniferous gas-generative formations and areas in Poland of shallow Rotliegendes gas production.

Baltic license area

Poland assigned an exploration license on a large onshore tract in the eastern Baltic region to a unit of Frontier Exploration Co., Salt Lake City, Utah.

Frontier Poland Exploration & Producing Co. Ltd. formally received the 2 million acre tract late in 1995 after approvals of the deal by local governments in the region.

Frontier was the first U.S. independent operator to sign such an agreement under Poland's 1994 mining law. The license requires the company to pay a 6% fixed oil or gas royalty, 60% of which is to remain with local government entities.

The company planned to focus exploration first in the heart of the license area, where structures with porosity of 10-20% occur at 2,200-3,000 m.

Other action

In other developments:

- Russia's Gazprom signed a 25 year gas supply agreement with Poland. The agreement will increase Poland's imports of Russian gas to 490 bcf/year from 210 bcf/year as of late 1996.

New gas supplies are expected to come from the Yamal Peninsula in western Siberia, once a 4,000 km pipeline has been built to take gas to Poland and Germany.

- Exxon AG and Shell Exploration Orient BV agreed to form a company for oil and gas exploration in Central Poland.

The new company, Polish Petroleum Development Co. Sp. z.o.o. (PPDC), needed approval from Polish authorities. PPDC will continue discussions started in 1993 with Polish officials on exploration opportunities and concession arrangements in the Polish Trough, about 150 miles west of Warsaw.

- Petrochemia Plock SA let contract to Fluor Daniel International Ltd., Uxbridge, U.K., to revamp a crude distillation unit at its Plock refinery. Completion was scheduled for spring 1997.

Petrochemia was carrying out a multimillion dollar expansion at Plock to prepare for deregulation of Poland's oil and gas industry and begin producing unleaded and low sulfur fuels.

The new unit was intended to improve yields and quality of products, reduce waste heat, and cut emissions. Sixty-six pieces of equipment were to be renewed and 40 modified, while process control equipment will be replaced.

- Konsorcjum Poludnie SC, a consortium of 32 Polish companies, let contract to Fluor Corp. for a feasibility study of a grassroots refinery and petrochemical complex in southern Poland.

PORTUGAL

CAPITAL: Lisbon
MONETARY UNIT: Escudo
REFINING CAPACITY: 304,172 b/cd
PRODUCTION: 0
RESERVES: 0

Privatization of Portugal's energy industry remains on track.

The centerpiece of that campaign, continued privatization of state-owned Petrogal, received a boost when private shareholders approved a 5 year plan for revitalizing the troubled company.

The third phase of Petrogal's privatization, an international share offering, was planned for sometime in 1997.

Portugal is intent on privatizing a number of industries nationalized in the 1970s and by late 1996 had sold more than $8 billion of assets since 1989.

SAIPEM

In addition to Petrogal, plans called for selling the government stake in petrochemical producer Cia. Nacional de Petroquimicas (CNP) and fertilizer company Quimigal Adubos.

Borealis AS, a joint venture of Norway's and Finland's state oil companies, bought CNP.

CNP owned a cracker at Sines with capacity to produce 330,000 metric tons/year of ethylene and 150,000 tons/year of propylene.

The purchase replaced a long-term lease dating from 1989 under which Borealis operated the cracker. The plant provides feedstock to Borealis' polyolefins complex at Sines.

The privatization of Portugal's two main natural gas companies, Transgas and Gas de Portugal (GDP), was not expected until completion of an internal pipeline network in 1997.

Portugal is building a gas trunk line from Setubal, south of Lisbon, north to Braga. Along the way, the nation's four regional gas distributors are building a network of low pressure lines.

The Setubal-Braga pipeline will be fed by imports from Algeria through the Europe-Maghreb pipeline, and by gas from northern Europe via connections with the Spanish pipeline grid.

Saudi Arabian Oil Co. (Saudi Aramco) was negotiating with Petrogal to acquire a substantial stake in the company. Currently, the government owns 55% of Petrogal, and private investors have the balance.

Petrogal has three refineries with total capacity of 265,000 b/d, and the deal would involve Aramco's supplying feedstocks.

ROMANIA

CAPITAL: Bucharest
MONETARY UNIT: Lei
REFINING CAPACITY: 558,770 b/cd
PRODUCTION: 136,000 b/d
RESERVES: 1.606 billion bbl

Romania's efforts to reorganize its oil and gas industry raised controversy in 1996.

Private sector oil importers and processors in Romania complained that the National Oil Co. of Romania (NOC), formed in August 1996 out of various state oil firms, threatened their independence.

Traders, including General Consulting Procurement (GCP) and General Trade & Investment (GTI), formed their own oil company, Petrogas, with start-up assets of more than $150 million vs. NOC's almost $300 million.

Founders of Petrogas claimed they were endangered by firms such as Compet, which runs most of Romania's oil pipelines, and Rafirom, which handles most of Romania's refining. Private firms do their importing, transporting, and processing through such firms, with almost no facilities of their own.

Petrogas founders told Bucharest of their plans to buy a stake in NOC.

Observers questioned the free-market credentials of Petrogas. Heads of GCP and GTI were close friends with members of parliament, and the firm's investors also appeared to be linked more by personal connections with public officials than any grouping logically built around oil importing. And foreign private investors—Amoco, Enterprise Oil, and Shell—exploring for hydrocarbons under established concessions had not joined in with Petrogas' criticism of NOC.

Blocks offered

Romania's National Agency for Mineral Resources (NAMR) in mid-1996 kicked off a series of presentations of details of 15 blocks offered for exploration in the country's first licensing round.

Bids were required late in 1996 with a view to negotiations between NAMR and shortlisted bidders taking place in January-April 1997 and signing of contracts by the end of May 1997.

Marketing of data packages and presentations to potential bidders were handled by Geoquest Reservoir Technologies Ltd., Henley-on-Thames, U.K.

Fifteen blocks were offered, all onshore except one that covers onshore and Black Sea acreage. NAMR said the blocks are underexplored.

NAMR said, "This is due to the paucity of seismic data in some areas—for example, on the eastern Carpathian blocks—and to the historical focus on discovery and development of Romania's prolific shallow reserves.

"Exploration will now focus on the deeper and prospective Paleogene, Mesozoic, and upper Paleozoic sections. Deep drilling has encountered significant source rock horizons in the older stratigraphic section."

SLOVAKIA

CAPITAL: Bratislava
MONETARY UNIT: Koruna
REFINING CAPACITY: 115,000 b/cd
PRODUCTION: 1,000 b/d
RESERVES: 9 million bbl

State refiner and petrochemical producers Slovnaft AS of Bratislava let an engineering, procurement, and construction contract to Fluor Daniel International Ltd., Uxbridge U.K., and joint venture partner Mitsubishi Heavy Industries Ltd., Tokyo, to provide a residue hydrocracking plant.

The unit will use ABB-Lummus Global technology and is scheduled for completion in December 1998. It will convert high sulfur fuel oil to low sulfur fuels and heating oil.

Engineering will be carried out at Fluor Daniel's Haarlem office in the Netherlands.

Three 1,200 metric ton reactors will be delivered from Japan to Bratislava via the Danube River.

SPAIN

CAPITAL: Madrid
MONETARY UNIT: Peseta
REFINING CAPACITY: 1,295,650 b/cd
PRODUCTION: 16,300 b/d
RESERVES: 30 million bbl

Spain received its first gas through the $2.3 billion Maghreb pipeline from Algeria across Morocco and the Strait of Gibraltar to Cordoba.

Capacity of the line, about 1 bcfd, can be doubled with the addition of compression pumps. Most of the line diameter is 48 in., but twin 22 in. lines were laid across the strait.

Although the 865-mile line from Hassi R'mel field will initially serve the Spanish grid with 282 bcf/year, it will be linked with the new Portuguese gas distribution network in 1997.

Officials said Algerian gas would provide 12% of Spain's energy consumption in 2000. Algeria wants to double gas exports by 2000 and expects the pipeline to carry 706 bcf/year then.

Meanwhile, Gas Natural SDG plans to triple gas underground storage capacity in Spain over the next 5 years. It plans to build at least four 1 billion cu m storage facilities in northern Spain to complement two existing ones.

The Spanish government began the process of selling its remaining 10% in Respol SA and planned to offer the 30 million shares on the market in 1997 for about $1 billion.

It also planned to sell its 3.6% share in distributor Gas Natural and its 9% holding in pipeline operator Enagas during 1997.

Repsol SA brought the 5,000 b/d Rodaballo oil field on stream in the Mediterranean Sea.

The field, in the Angula concession 28 miles off Tarragona, is near Casablanca field, where it will be tied into processing facilities.

Repsol planned to build a crude and products terminal at Cartagena in southeastern Spain and a 217 mile, 170,000 b/d pipeline linking it with its Puertollano refinery near Madrid. The

$200 million project was due completion in late 1997.

BP Oil Espana let an $11 million contract for construction of two 45 metric ton/day sulfur recovery units at its 102,000 b/d refinery in Castellon de la Plana. Start-up was scheduled for mid-1997.

SWEDEN

CAPITAL: Stockholm
MONETARY UNIT: Krona
REFINING CAPACITY: 427,000 b/cd
PRODUCTION: 0
RESERVES: 0

Swedish refiner and retailer OK Petroleum changed its name to Preem Petroleum. Upstream operations were spun off into a second new firm, Svenska Petroleum Exploration.

Preem/Svenska is the largest oil company in Sweden, with an 18% retail market share, 450 service stations, a 106,000 b/d refinery at Gothenburg, and 78% of the 200,000 b/d Scanraff refinery at Lysekil.

The OK union owns 52% of Preem/Svenska, the Swedish government 24%, and Neste Oy 24%.

Sydgas planned to build a 400,000 cu m gas storage facility at Susegaarden on the southwestern coast. The $35 million cavern will be blasted from solid rock. Completion is due in 2001.

Sweden's National Stockpile Agency is selling 45 oil storage caverns scattered around the country. The caverns, as large as 100,000 cu m, were created to stockpile oil and products during the Cold War.

TURKEY

CAPITAL: Ankara
MONETARY UNIT: Lira
REFINING CAPACITY: 683,095 b/cd
PRODUCTION: 68,800 b/d
RESERVES: 260.046 million bbl

Turkey scrambled for energy supplies in 1996. It was the fastest growing market for electricity in Europe, with demand projected to jump 5%/year to 170 billion kw-hr by 2010.

Electricity production was about 93.1 billion kw-hr in 1996, but Turkey bought supplemental electricity from Iran and was negotiating with Bulgaria and Georgia.

It even was considering revamping a 30-year-old plan to build a $5 billion nuclear power plant on the Mediterranean coast.

Turkey fuels much of its power generation with gas, and during 1995 the energy ministry launched negotiations with natural gas producing nations in the region—including Russia, Iran, and Egypt—although imports would require massive investments in infrastructure. Also during the year, Turkey bought LNG shipments from Algeria and Qatar.

In mid-1996 it signed a $23 billion deal to buy Iranian gas, starting with 105 bcf/year in 1999 and rising to 350 bcf/year in 2005. Energy and Natural Resources Minister Recai Kutan said Turkey needed the Iranian gas to avert shortages in 4 years.

The deal will require construction of a $1.2-2 billion, 890 mile pipeline between Tabriz and Ankara, of which 720 miles will be in Turkey. Laterals will expand the total network to about 1,250 miles of pipe. Construction was due to begin in the spring of 1997.

Turkey also agreed to increase its purchases of Russian gas from 6 billion cu m/year to 20 billion by 2010. Under the deal, the gas pipeline carrying Siberian gas through Ukraine and Bulgaria will be expanded to 14 billion cu m/year, and a second line would be built to carry 10 billion cu m/year through Georgia to Erzerum in eastern Turkey.

Turkey still wants to be the main export route for Caspian Sea crude. It insists oil from increased production from the Caspian cannot pass through the crowded Bosphorus and Dardanelles straits for safety reasons and should be routed across Turkey to the Mediterranean port of Ceyhan.

Botas Petroleum Pipeline Corp. signed a preliminary deal with Amoco Egypt Oil Co. and Egyptian General Petroleum Corp. to buy up to 7.3 million metric tons/year of LNG from Nile Delta fields. A liquefaction plant would be built on Egypt's Mediterranean coast and a regasification plant near Izmir, Turkey.

Turkey spent most of 1996 waiting for the United Nations and Iraq to come to terms on limited exports of Iraqi crude. Restart of the 40-in., 450,000 b/d Kirkuk to Ceyhan pipeline occurred Dec. 10.

UNITED KINGDOM:

CAPITAL: London
MONETARY UNIT: Pound
REFINING CAPACITY: 1,940,990 b/cd
PRODUCTION: 2,663,000 b/d
RESERVES: 4.517 billion bbl

Britain's natural gas industry has undergone a radical transformation in the last decade, with competitive suppliers taking the place of British Gas, a formerly state-run utility.

The government's Office of Gas Supply (Ofgas) has been pushing to open the domestic gas market. So far, about 10 major firms are marketing gas in the U.K.

The government published operating rules and licensing terms for independent gas suppliers' use of the British Gas system. And Ofgas has been forcing gas firms to enable customers to choose gas suppliers.

British Gas in 1996 dropped a lawsuit to recover $1.5 billion in taxes paid under the 1981 Gas Levy Act. And it accepted proposals by Ofgas for a new domestic tariff formula and a reduction in charges to customers for billing.

To respond to new market pressures, British Gas split into two companies. Transco International received the transportation and storage businesses, along with most of the exploration and production assets and the power generation business.

British Gas Energy mainly was given the supply and trading business, which will face intense competition from new suppliers. It also got the Morecambe Bay producing gas fields with reserves of 6.6 tcf of gas.

In the 17th offshore licensing round, planned for 1997, the U.K. Industry and Energy Ministry planned to offer much of Britain's frontier exploration areas. But it said subsequent rounds would be smaller annual events that would feature relinquished acreage. It was asking operators to relinquish blocks they had not explored and had no firm plans to drill. It also was considering changing licensing regulations for mature areas.

A major oil spill occurred in February 1996 outside Milford Haven harbor. The Sea Empress oil tanker grounded entering the harbor mouth and spilled 70,000 metric tons of crude during a bungled salvage operation.

The 28 companies that own the Sullom Voe oil terminal in the Shetland Islands accepted the local council's offer of a 50% reduction in rent on the land. Oil firms have used the terminal since the 1970s but had told the council they would not renew their lease after 2000 because the high rent made the facility uneconomic as production volumes declined from North Sea fields.

BHP Petroleum boosted production from its four Liverpool Bay fields to 35,000 b/d from 15,000 b/d after installing gas flaring equipment. The first cargo of crude from the fields was shipped in March.

Elf Oil, Gulf, and Murco Petroleum announced that they would form a new refining company to operate the 108,000 b/d Milford Haven refinery in South Wales, formerly owned by Elf and Murco, and close Gulf's nearby 115,000 b/d refinery. Gulf will sell its 50% interest in the 180,000 b/d Pembroke refinery to its partner, Texaco. IPE

North Sea action keys on small fields, cost control in new areas

North Sea operators are continually searching for new ways to develop small finds near existing infrastructure and to develop discoveries in new areas at low cost.

Floating production systems and subsea technology are vital parts of many of Northwest Europe's recently sanctioned field developments, for both large and small reservoirs.

In field developments through 2005, operators will concentrate on squeezing much more oil out of every dollar spent.

In the past 20 years oil firms spent their money on fixed platforms and topsides and their associated installation and hook-up techniques and equipment.

The next decade will see a greater variety of field developments. There are many more projects than in the past decade, most of them much smaller in size, with shorter lead times and with a larger share of marine and subsea costs and a lower share of shore-based services and asset costs.

Smith Rea Energy Analysts Ltd., Canterbury, U.K., predicts floating production units will dominate future field developments in the North Sea.

It said 77% of oil output capacity of new fields brought on stream in 1995 in Northwest Europe relied on mobile production units, while demand for floaters is growing worldwide, particularly floating production, storage, and offtake (FPSO) units.

Smith Rea expects 76 floaters to be in use around the world by 2001. The number of contractors capable of building floaters was also said to have doubled in 12 months.

It said continued technical progress and changing commercial attitudes have made the mobile production unit the preferred option not only for marginal fields but also for larger fields of widely differing sizes and characteristics.

Smith Rea said recent advances in drilling technology, including horizontal and extended-reach drilling and multilateral completions, may have had more effect on industry economics in the 1990s than industry cost-cutting initiatives.

It said technological breakthroughs not only saved billions, they increased commercially recoverable reserves in existing fields by more than 2.2 billion bbl and allowed development of fields with reserves of 2.5 billion bbl.

It said the gross production value of the 4.8 billion bbl at 1996 prices is $81 billion, much of which is likely to accrue before the turn of the century.

North Sea operators completed a number of large and some small developments in 1996, and in most of them an innovative approach was required to make them viable.

Troll example

In North Sea action during 1996, Den norske stats oljeselskap AS (Statoil) took over operatorship of the giant Troll gas field development in Norway from Norske Shell AS. Troll has begun to supply up to 24 billion cu m/year of gas to European customers.

Troll field has estimated reserves of 1.2 billion bbl of oil and 1.3 trillion cu m of gas, but development was viable only because of new technologies.

Troll's western oil province contains the bulk of the field's liquids in a large but thin reservoir. Without horizontal drilling, the field would not have been viable.

Troll West was brought on stream with a production semisubmersible by Norsk Hydro AS. Troll East gas was developed with the world's tallest and heaviest platform, at 430 m tall and 1.05 million metric tons in weight the largest man-made object ever to be moved.

The platform will produce from 39 wells, each capable of yielding up to 3.4 million cu m/day of gas though normally restricted to 2.8 million cu m/day. Production capacity of the platform is 100 million cu m/day of gas.

Gas is piped ashore to an 89 million cu m/day terminal at Kollsnes for treatment prior to export via pipeline to Europe.

Norsk Hydro AS, operator of Troll West oil field, planned to install a third platform in supergiant Troll.

Statoil said the Troll C platform will be designed to produce 125,000 b/d of oil and 320 MMcfd of gas, while capacity on Troll B will be expanded to 250,000 b/d.

Hydro wanted to begin production from Troll C in mid-1999. It expected the semisubmersible and 56 subsea wells to cost $2.3 billion.

Troll C semisubmersible platform will be installed in the northeastern part of the field's central gas province.

Andrew, Harding fields

In the U.K. sector, innovative contracting allowed BP Exploration Operating Co. Ltd. to begin oil production from a conventional platform on Andrew field in Block 16/28 in mid-1996. First oil was achieved only 6 weeks after platform deck installation.

Production, along with the Cyrus subsea satellite, was about 60,000 b/d in late 1996.

Andrew has estimated reserves of 119 million bbl of oil and condensate and 134 bcf of associated gas. The field was discovered in 1974 in 116 m of water.

Cyrus field, which had earlier produced through a production ship, was tied in as a two-well subsea satellite of the platform.

The contracts gave the companies that designed, built, and installed the platform a share in any cost savings made during construction.

BP and the contractors estimated Andrew would cost $560 million, vs. the $675 million BP had estimated earlier. By the time Andrew began production, BP said total development cost was $435 million.

Oil will move to shore through a 16 km, 10 in. pipeline to BP's Forties export network. Gas will move through a 44 km, 8 in. pipeline into the Central Area Transmission System operated by Amoco (U.K.) Exploration Ltd.

In April 1996 BP began oil production from the U.K. North Sea's Harding field, using a platform comprising a jack-up production unit mounted on a concrete storage base.

Harding is in 110 m of water on Block 9/23b and has estimated reserves of 185 million bbl of oil and 200 bcf of gas. Development cost was $650 million.

Production rose to about 60,000 b/d by early 1997. The 23,000 metric ton heavy-duty jack-up has capacity to produce 64,000 b/d of oil.

The jack-up sits on a T-shaped concrete gravity base, which weighs 90,000 metric tons. The base has capacity to store more than 500,000 bbl of oil, which is pumped for export to a shuttle tanker moored 2 km away.

BP said Harding's Central and South reservoirs have been developed, while a further 15-40 million bbl of oil lies in satellite development prospects on the same block.

Field partner Ranger Oil Ltd. said the development cost of $3.50/bbl makes Harding one of the most economical fields in the U.K. North Sea. Ranger said operating costs are expected to be less than $3/bbl once full production is achieved.

Beaufort, Davy fields

Also in the U.K. North Sea, Amoco began production from Beaufort gas field, which is in Blocks 49/23 and 49/28 of the southern basin.

Amoco developed the field using a single extended reach well drilled from nearby Bessemer platform by a jack up rig. Development cost was $9 million.

Beaufort is expected to produce as much as 30 MMcfd of gas during a 4 year life. Gas is exported via Bessemer by pipeline to Amoco's Indefatigable 49/23AT platform and on to Bacton terminal.

Amoco said advanced drilling technology enhanced its capability to develop small fields, while maximizing use of existing North Sea infrastructure.

Beaufort partners are operator Amoco 30.77%, British Gas Exploration & Production Ltd. 30.77%, Amerada Hess Ltd. 23.08%, and Enterprise Oil plc 15.38%.

Last year Amoco brought on stream Davy and Bessemer fields as satellites of Indefatigable. Davy and Bessemer platforms were

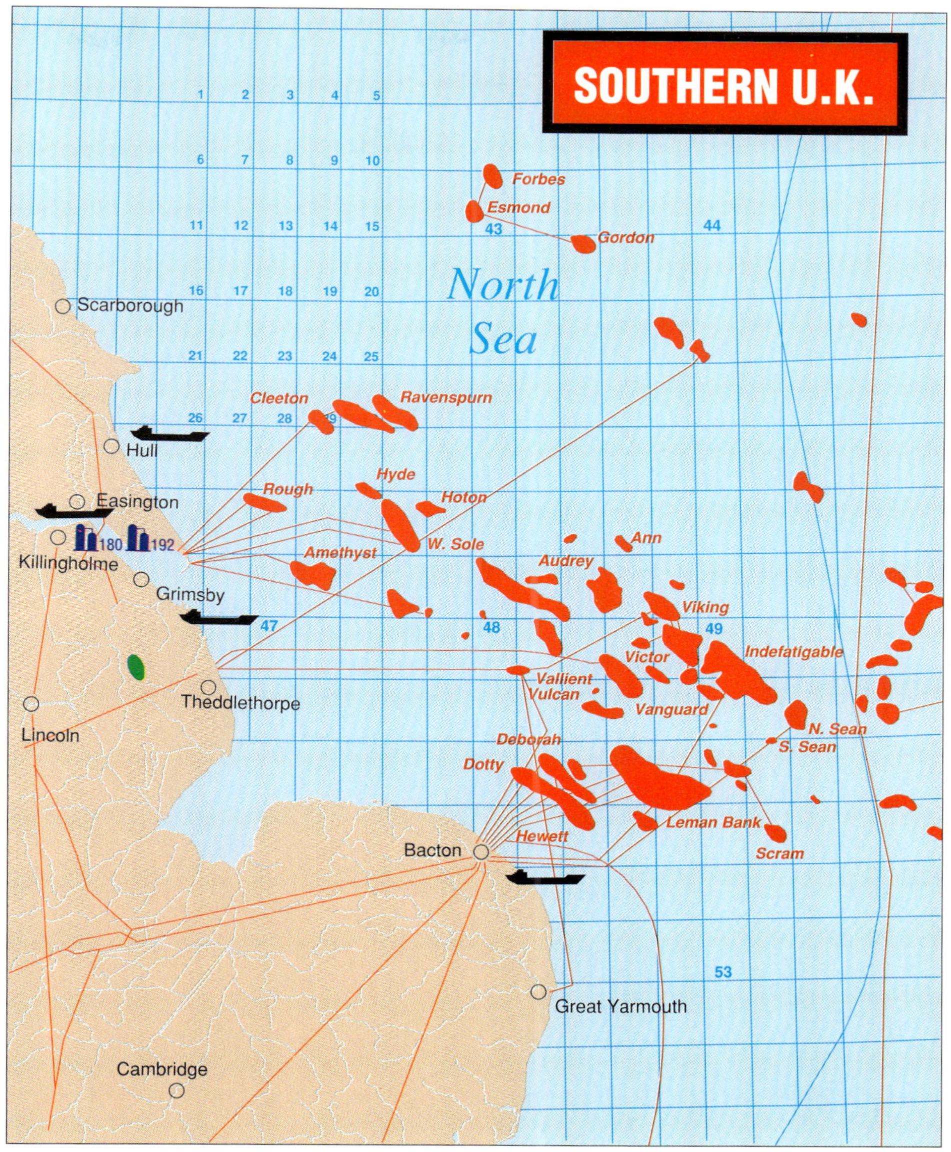

the first monotowers installed in the U.K. North Sea.

Mobil North Sea Ltd. used the design to develop Galahad field. Amoco is considering development of other finds near Indefatigable under the same concept.

BP also began production from South Magnus field in the northern U.K. North Sea area. The field, on Block 211/12a, was developed with a subsea well tied back to Magnus platform 7 km to the north.

Production started in mid-1996 at a rate of 17,000 b/d of oil. South Magnus has estimated reserves of 20 million bbl of oil, and gas equivalent to 6 million bbl of oil. Production is expected to settle to around 14,000 b/d and to last 10 years.

Aasgard fields

Norway had its own giant floater project under way in 1996. Statoil's Aasgard fields in the Norwegian Sea will be developed with an oil production ship and a gas production semisubmersible.

For well workovers and completions, Statoil considered using a twin-hull drilling vessel that it expected to reduce overall development costs of Aasgard fields. The small waterplane area twin-hull (Swath) concept was developed by naval architects Kverndokk & Eldoey of Aalesund, Norway, and was based on a catamaran hull first designed in the 1940s.

Statoil planned to use a Swath vessel for a variety of well operations in water depths to 1,500 m but scrapped the idea when the Swath hull design fell short of stability requirements during wave-tank tests. The operator was considering semisubmersible designs for a completion and maintenance vessel.

Statoil let contracts for construction of the world's largest oil production ship and gas production semisubmersible for the Aasgard fields. The project involves the Smoerbukk, South Smoerbukk, and Midgard discoveries with combined reserves estimated at 800 million bbl of oil and 7 tcf of gas.

The oil production vessel will be able to produce 200,000 b/d of oil, process 15-16 million cu m/day of gas, and store 150,000 cu m of oil. It will be 276 m long, 45.4 m wide, and have a draft of 26.6 m.

Gullfaks

Statoil announced plans to develop three discoveries near its Gullfaks field in the Norwegian North Sea as subsea satellites of Gullfaks A platform.

Statoil's South Gullfaks, Rimfaks, and Delta discoveries, with combined reserves estimated at 260 million bbl of oil, will be developed with a total of seven subsea templates and 23 wells.

Total development cost is estimated at $1 billion. First oil production is slated for late 1998, with peak output of 125,000 b/d expected to coincide with declining flow from Gullfaks.

New processing modules will be installed on Gullfaks A platform, and processed oil will be stored for shipment along with oil from Gullfaks A and B platforms.

Gullfaks A is a concrete platform with oil storage facilities in its base. Oil is exported in shuttle tankers, which receive production through loading buoys. Associated gas from the satellites will be reinjected.

Oseberg

Norsk Hydro AS put innovative lateral wellbore technology to work in Oseberg oil field in the Norwegian North Sea.

Hydro's C-12 well on Oseberg Platform C used a multilateral well that provided full bore reentry access to a lateral while maintaining integrity of the main wellbore. The system allows commingling of production streams.

Hydro chose lateral drilling because of the small number of well slots on Platform C and the need to reach remote portions of the field's reservoirs.

Hydro said three wells in Oseberg field will be multilaterals. The company intends to use the technology in other fields.

Hydro developed Oseberg field, on Blocks 30/6 and 30/9, with bridge-linked Platforms A and B over the southern part of the reservoir and Platform C over the north.

Oseberg held estimated oil reserves of almost 2 billion bbl when production began in December 1988. By the end of 1994, reserves were estimated at more than 1 billion bbl.

Production averaged 500,000 b/d in 1995.

The field's gas reserves of 89 billion cu m have not been tapped. Norway has approved a plan to begin Oseberg gas production in 2000.

Hydro also plans to develop the Oseberg East discovery 27 km northeast of Oseberg field center. It has estimated reserves of 145 million bbl of oil.

Hydro planned to use a steel platform with first-stage processing, drilling, and accommodation facilities. The $500 million development is expected to lead to first oil in October 1998. Production will be piped to Oseberg center for final processing and transport to the Sture terminal near Bergen.

NORTH SEA
0 50 100 150 Miles
0 50 100 150 200 Km
Atlantic Ocean
OUTER HEBRIDES
I. OF SKYE
INNER HEBRIDES
I. OF MULL
SCOTLAND
ORKNEY
Stornoway
Ullapool
Nigg Bay
Moray Firth
Inverness
Mallaig
Kirkwall
Flotta
Wick
Beatrice
St. Fergus
Peterhead
Cruden Bay
Aberdeen
Dundee
Firth of Tay
Glenrothes
Milton of Balgonie
Grangemouth
Firth of Forth
Edinburgh
Finnart
Ardyne Point
Glasgow
Ardrossan
Firth of Clyde
North Channel
Moffat
Carlisle
Newcastle
Port Clarence
Tees
Middlesbrough
Darlington
Sullom
Clair
Victory
Londonderry
N. IRELAND
Belfast
Donegal Bay
Sligo
Ballina
Galway
Galway Bay
IRELAND
Ballough
Dublin
Arklow
Limerick
Foynes
Tralee
Wexford
Waterford
Bantry
Cork
Whitegate
Kinsale Head
Celtic Sea
St. George's Channel
I. OF MAN
Irish Sea
Solway Firth
Morecambe
Barrow
Lancaster
Heysham
Preston
Formby
Liverpool Bay
Liverpool
Holyhead
Stanlow
Eastham
Ellesmere Port
Manchester
Bradford
Hull
Easington
Killingholme
Gainsborough
Egmanton
Duke's Wood
Farley
Rungar
Cropwell Butler
Lincoln
Nottingham
Birmingham
ENGLAND
Cardigan Bay
Aberystwyth
WALES
Milford Haven
Angle Bay
Pembroke
Llandarcy
Neath
Cardiff
Bristol
Bath
Bristol Bay
Northampton
Oxford
Dunstable
Reading
London
Humby Grove
Bletchingley
Baxters Copse
Fawley
Southampton
Horndean
Portsmouth
Bournemouth
Weymouth
Wytch Farm
Kimmeridge
Lyme Bay
Exeter
Plymouth
Cherbourg
Bay of the Seine
Le Havre
Caen
Lisieux
Plestin Les Greves
Gulf of St. Malo

Gulf of Bothnia
NORWAY
SWEDEN
Gaule
Mongstad
Kollsnes
Sotra
Bergen
Troll
Oslo
Stockholm
Dalaro
Nynasham
Orebro
Slagentangen
Vall oy Tonsberg
Karsto
Kopervik
Stavanger
Sola
Arendal
Mandal
Lysekil
Goteborg
Skagen
North
Sea
DENMARK
Arhus
Fredericia
Kaergard
Esbjerg
Kalundborg
Copenhagen
Malmo
OLAND
Baltic
Sea
BORNHOLM
Skaelskor
Kiel Bay
FEHMARN
RUGEN
Reinkenhagen
Kolberg
Kiel
Heide
Lubeck Bay
Rostock
Heligoland
Bight
Brunsbuttel
Cuxhaven
Lubeck
Schwerin
Norden
Wilhelmshaven
Hamburg
Harburg
Nordenham
Grasbrook
Emden
Leer
Wardenburg
Bremen
Verden
Stettin
Schwedt
POLAND
2 Lines
Vestrup
Rudersdorf
Berlin
Frankfut-an-der-Oder
Poznan
Roxforrde
Staakow
Guben
Grunberg
Cottbus
Magdeburg
Salzgitter
Beckedorf
Lehrte
Meerdf
Buckeburg
Herringhausen
Lengerich
Salzbergen
Lingen
Lemmen
Zwolle
Ommen
Amsterdam
NETHERLANDS
The Hague
Rotterdam
Groningen
Schoonebeek
Zuidwal
Ijssel Meer
Indefatigable
Leman Bank
Hamm
Gelsenkirchen
Dortmund
Essen
Duisburg
Plattenburg
Dusseldorf
Cologne
Wesseling
Bonn
Zeebrug
Antwerp
BELGIUM
Brussels
Hasselt
Liege
Verviers
Mons
Namur
Maubeuge
Charlesville
LUXEMBOURG
Luxembourg
Auberrton
Reims
GERMANY
Eisenach
Erfurt
Suhl
Leipzig
Jena
Zeitz
Gera
Dresden
Breslau
Zaluzi
Litvinov
Kralupy
Kolin
Pardubice
Prague
CZECH REP.
Plzen
Waidhaus
Frankfurt-am-Main
Trebio
Brno
Hodonin
Murchison
Statfjord
Gullfaks
Brent
Ninian
Columba
Huldra
N. Alwyn
Oseberg
Brage
Alwyn
Bressay
Odin
N.E. Frigg
E. Frigg
Frigg
Heimdal
Balder
Forth
Gudrun
Tiffany
Miller
Sleipner
Maureen
N. Everest
Brisling
Bream
Ula
Cod
Albuskjell
Flyndre
Tor
S.E. Tor
W. Ekofisk
Ekofisk
Eldfisk
Auk
Duncan
Edda
Valhall
Argyll
Hod
Bent
Tyra W.
Tyra
Adda
Roth
Dan
Anne
Kotter
Logger
Helder
Helm
154
90
28
53
200
12
106
81
66
65
56
80
180
98
78
230
10
3
399
374
75
148
15
246
288
227
120
170
100
73
5
20

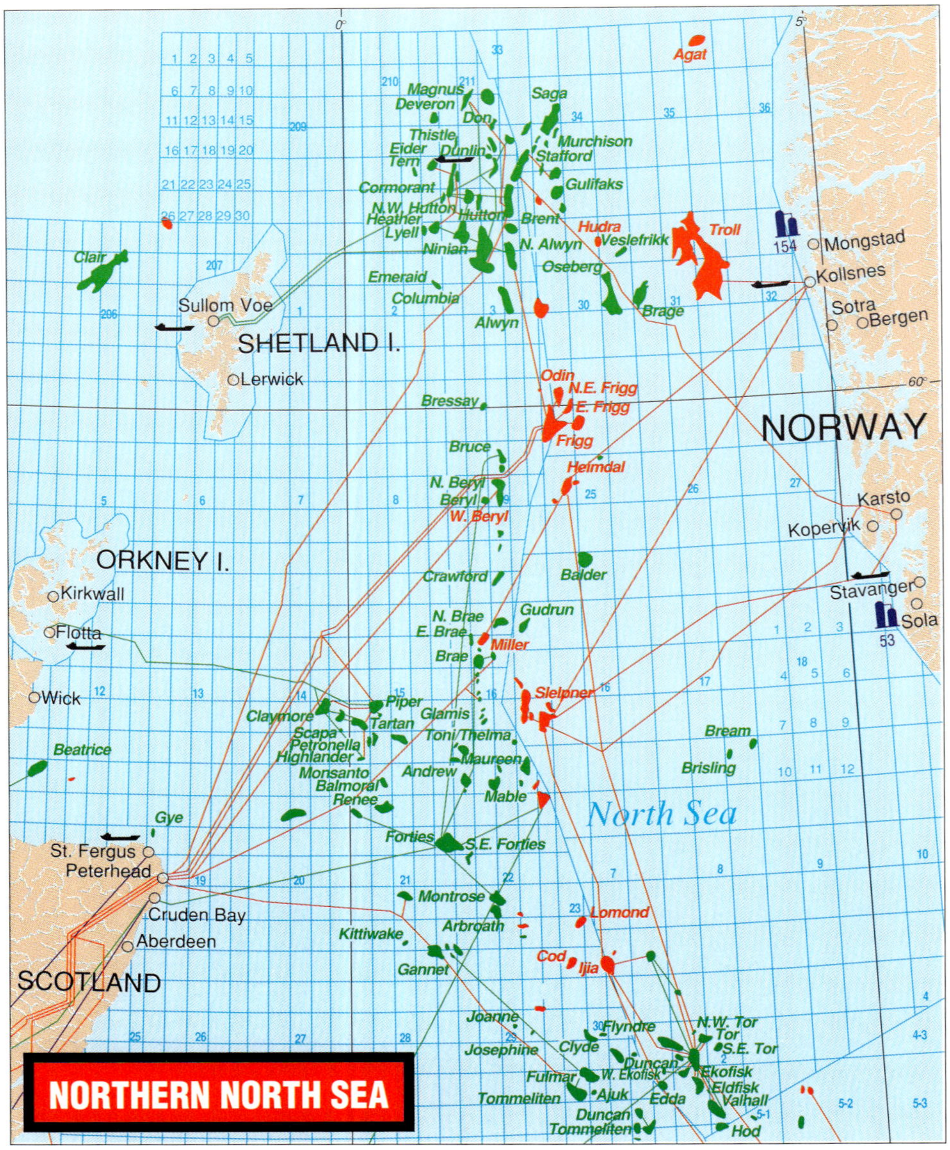

Varg, Yme fields

Saga Petroleum AS plans a $460 million development for its Varg discovery, which is in Norwegian Block 15/12, with first oil due in second quarter 1998. The plan calls for a wellhead platform and production ship to produce and process oil prior to export by shuttle tanker.

Saga views its Varg plan as a model for development of other small North Sea fields far from infrastructure.

Varg, formerly known as Fenris, has reserves estimated at 5.2 million cu m, although Saga said drilling might raise the figure to 9.1 million cu m of oil.

Saga has made its investment decision based on the higher reserves estimate, although the field's structures are complex with many faults.

The production vessel will be able to produce 9,000 cu m/day of oil and 1.5 million cu m/day of associated gas. Gas will be used to generate electricity on board the vessels and platform and for reinjection.

The platform was due to be installed in the summer of 1997. Varg partners are operator Saga 35% and Statoil 65%.

Statoil began production from Yme oil field, the smallest stand-alone field development in the Norwegian sector to date.

Yme, in North Sea Block 9/2, holds estimated reserves of 36 million bbl of oil. It was developed with a storage tanker and a jack up drilling rig converted for production. Production was 50,000 b/d.

A smaller satellite, with estimated reserves of 11 million bbl of oil, was discovered after development had begun. Yme Beta East field was brought into production through Yme platform facilities.

Other Norwegian, Danish fields

Esso Norge AS plans two separate developments in a North Sea area far from pipelines.

Its Jotun, Jotun East, and Jotun South discoveries have total estimated reserves of 200 million bbl of oil. Esso believes it will be possible to produce the three from one installation.

Three main options were under study in 1996: a production, storage, and offloading ship with subsea wellheads; a production, storage, and offloading ship linked to a wellhead platform; and a wellhead platform in the field tied back to a new platform in Heimdal field, where Elf Petroleum Norge AS is operator.

First oil production from the finds is scheduled for late 1998 or early 1999.

Esso also plans to develop the Balder discovery, 25 km south of Jotun, with 15 subsea wellheads tied back to a production, storage, and offloading ship.

The 1974 discovery on Block 25/11 has estimated reserves of 170 million bbl of oil. Its complex reservoir and distance from infrastructure have delayed development.

The $770 million project was due on stream in early 1997 and is expected to produce about 75,000 b/d of oil at plateau through the subsea wells tied back to the ship. The vessel can store 380,000 bbl of oil and will be unloaded by shuttle tankers.

Norsk Hydro AS and partners let contracts for the $1.12 billion development of Visund field on Block 34/8 in the Norwegian North Sea.

A floating production platform will be towed to the field and linked by an oil pipeline to the Gullfaks field Platform A about 27 km away.

Statoil began commercial gas production from West Sleipner field on Norwegian North Sea Block 15/6 in late 1996.

Production from West Sleipner's estimated 4.5 tcf of gas reserves will be moved to East Sleipner field and then to continental Europe. The field's condensate reserves, estimated at 246 million bbl, will be used as feedstock for Statoil's Kalundborg refinery in Denmark.

In Danish waters, Amerada Hess reported its South Arne oil discovery is commercially viable. South Arne, in Danish North Sea Blocks 5604/29 and 30, flowed almost 2,500 b/d.

Amerada Hess was studying whether to use a platform or a floating production unit, either with a gas pipeline to shore. It hoped to begin production in 1998.

Elgin, Ninian fields

In the British sector, Elf Exploration U.K. plc let contracts for design of a platform for its planned Elgin/Franklin development.

The design will use low-cost fabrication techniques, capability for full onshore commissioning, and onboard installation facilities which allow the platform to be installed without the need for heavy-lift crane barges.

Elgin and Franklin gas/condensate discoveries lie on Blocks 22/30c and 29/5b respectively. Elf plans to begin production in 2000, using a central processing complex in Elgin and a smaller platform in Franklin.

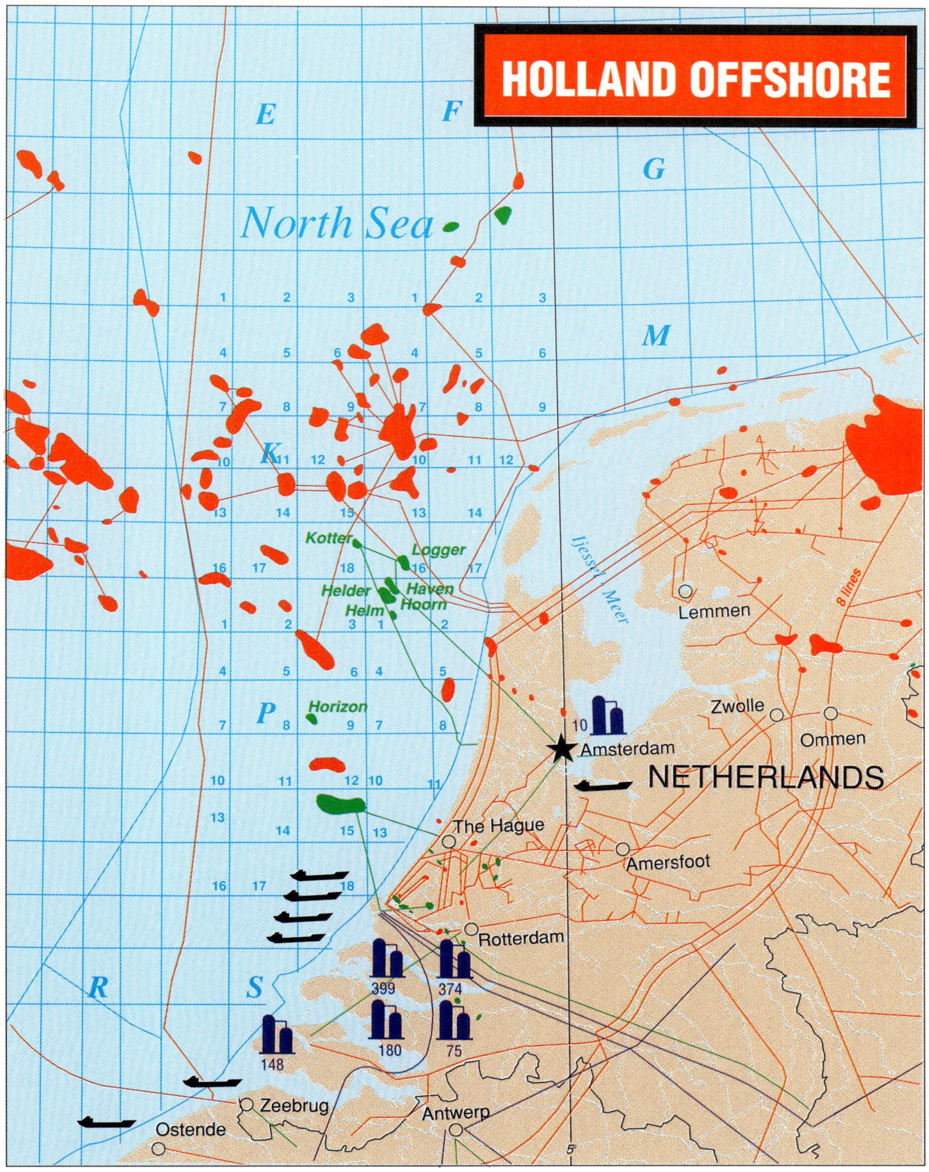

Elgin reserves are pegged at 125 million bbl of condensate and 550 bcf of gas, and Franklin at 75 million bbl of condensate and 700 bcf of gas.

Elf originally planned to begin producing the fields in 1998. However, low gas prices following Britain's gas market liberalization forced Elf to sell the gas through the planned Interconnector pipeline from the U.K. to Belgium.

Ownership changed significantly for several major U.K. North Sea fields in 1996.

Chevron U.K. Ltd. sold its interests in Ninian, Hutton, Lyell, and Murchison fields, and the Columba B discovery to a combine of Oryx Energy Co. and Ranger Oil (U.K.) Ltd. for $140 million.

Oryx was operator of Hutton, Lyell, and Murchison, and took 65% of the new assets with Ranger 35%. Ninian oil production exceeded 1 billion bbl in 1994. In early 1996 it had remaining reserves of 50 million bbl of oil.

Ninian was producing 55,000 b/d and had about 10 years more life. Ninian facilities are also used to produce two subsea satellites, Lyell and Strathspey, and Columba D reservoir through an extended reach well from Ninian South platform.

Oryx took over operatorship of Hutton, Lyell, and Murchison from Conoco (U.K.) Ltd. in January 1995 and cut operating costs more than $1/bbl.

Before the sale, Chevron drilled an extended-reach well from the Ninian South platform in U.K. North Sea Block 3/8a to develop the Columba B field.

Columba B is the fifth satellite of the aging Ninian complex. It has estimated reserves of 10 million bbl of oil. The development well will have a total measured depth of 16,500 ft.

Judy/Joanne

Phillips Petroleum Co. U.K. Ltd. placed development of Judy and Joanne fields in the U.K. sector back on track by choosing to reinject gas originally intended for sale to Enron Europe Ltd.

The U.K. Department of Trade & Industry approved Phillips's plan to install an $82 million gas reinjection plant on Block 30/7a Judy platform, which was expected to enable oil production to start Apr. 1, 1997.

Phillips had intended to place Judy and Joanne gas on stream early in 1996, but Enron decided to take no gas for the first year of its purchase contract.

Phillips delayed gas development because associated gas had been sold to Enron and oil production could not proceed without gas production under the existing platform configuration.

Judy and Joanne originally were expected to produce about 65,000 b/d of oil and as much as 260 MMcfd of gas.

Now Phillips expects to start liquids production at 30,000-40,000 b/d, with gas reinjected for later delivery to Enron. The new plant is believed to have capacity to reinject 200 MMcfd of gas.

Although early production will be lower than intended, Phillips said the reinjection project is expected to increase ultimate hydrocarbon recovery by more than 5%. Judy and Joanne's combined reserves were earlier estimated at 97 million bbl of liquids and 796 bcf of gas.

Phillips had a four well program under way to probe satellite reservoirs within development reach of the Judy platform. Phillips completed work on the fields' production, processing, and transportation facilities.

Partners in Judy and Joanne are operator Phillips 36.5%, Agip (U.K.) Ltd. 33%, and British Gas Exploration & Production Ltd. 30.5%.

Kerr-McGee Oil (U.K.) plc was considering development of the Janice discovery in U.K. North Sea Block 30/17a with a production, storage, and offloading ship. Janice is in 80 m of water and has estimated reserves of 20 million bbl of oil.

Windermere, Curlew

Wintershall (U.K.) Ltd. planned to develop its Windermere gas discovery in U.K. Block 49/9b as a satellite of Markham field. Markham, astride the U.K.-Netherlands boundary, is operated by Lasmo Nederland BV.

Wintershall's Windermere field, with estimated reserves of 100-125 bcf of gas, will be developed with a simple unmanned platform. Production was slated for early 1997.

Lasmo said gas will move through an 8 in. pipeline to Markham ST-1 platform in U.K. Block 49/5. From there it will pass through a 12 in. in-field pipeline to the Markham processing platform in Dutch North Sea Block J6, and from there to Den Helder terminal.

Windermere will be the second third-party field development to use Markham facilities. Earlier in 1996, Elf Petroland BV placed on stream small J3-Charlie field using a single well drilled from Markham's Dutch platform.

Shell U.K. Exploration & Production received government approval for a $450 million fast-track development of Curlew oil and gas fields in the U.K. North Sea with a converted tanker as an FPSO.

Curlew consists of two accumulations on Block 29/7, one discovered in 1990 and the other in 1994. Shell/Esso estimated combined reserves at 71 million bbl of oil and condensate and 244 bcf of gas.

First production was slated for late 1997. Peak output will be 45,000 b/d of oil and 100 MMcfd of gas. The ship will store 560,000 bbl of oil.

Shuttle tankers will carry the oil, while gas will flow through the nearby Fulmar pipeline to St. Fergus terminal, north of Aberdeen.

Other U.K. fields

Amoco was developing its Arkwright oil discovery in U.K. North Sea Block 22/23a, at a cost of $87 million.

Arkwright involved tieback of three wells via a subsea manifold to its Arbroath platform 7 miles away. Production of 12,000 b/d was to begin in early 1997. Reserves are estimated at 10 million bbl. Arkwright's oil will be shipped to Cruden Bay terminal, north of Aberdeen. Owners are Amoco 30.77%, Amerada Hess 28.2%, and Enterprise Oil plc 41.03%.

Amerada Hess began oil production from Fergus field on Block 39/2. It is the most southerly producing oil field in the U.K. North Sea.

Fergus is a single well subsea satellite of Amerada's Fife field 4 miles northwest, which is being produced through the Uisge Gorm production storage and offloading ship.

Amerada said Fergus production reached 15,000 b/d. Reserves are 6 million bbl of oil. Fife was producing about 34,000 b/d of oil.

Amerada Hess received U.K. approval to develop Durward oil field on North Sea Blocks 21/6 and 21/11. Durward will be developed with five producers and four water injectors tied back to an FPSO system via two subsea manifolds.

Conoco and Chevron U.K. expected to begin production at Britannia field in late 1998. It is the U.K.'s largest undeveloped gas field, with reserves of 2.6 tcf of gas and 140 million bbl of condensate.

Marathon Oil U.K. Ltd. formed a 5-year alliance with AMEC Process & Energy Ltd., London, to help develop other fields as satellites of Brae field on U.K. Block 16/7a.

Marathon had several prospects in the Brae area, and planned to drill the Web prospect from nearby Brae East field platform on Block 16/3a.

West Brae will be developed with one water injection well and three horizontal wells tied back to Marathon's Brae A platform, about 5 miles away.

Mobil North Sea Ltd. started production from Nevis oil and gas field, following a $90 million subsea development in 340 ft of water on Block 9/12.

Nevis production began from the southern sector of the reservoir, with reserves of 50 million bbl of oil, 1.8 million bbl of condensate, and 175 bcf of gas.

Production was expected to settle at 13,500 b/d of oil and 11 MMcfd of gas. Oil and gas are moved to Mobil's Beryl Alpha platform 5 miles west for processing and transport to shore.

Nevis also will be a phased development. Early production is from two wells. As many as eight subsea wells may be required in the northern part of the reservoir to take output to 23,000 b/d of oil and 53 MMcfd of gas in 2003.

Production was to begin in late 1997 and climb to 25,000 b/d in 1998. Estimated field reserves are 30 million bbl of oil.

The Shell Expro joint operating venture of Shell U.K. Ltd. and Esso Exploration & Production U.K. Ltd., towed the Anasuria production, storage, and offloading ship out to location in Guillemot, Teal, and South Teal fields on Block 21/25.

The ship can process 55,000 b/d of oil and 30 MMcfd of gas. Oil storage is 850,000 bbl, and water injection capacity is 85,000 b/d.

Shell Expro began subsea production through two wells with water injection through a third. It planned eight producing and four injection wells.

Total reserves in Guillemot, Teal, and South Teal fields are estimated at 92 million bbl of oil and 47 bcf of gas. Development will cost $750 million.

More projects

Shell Expro was planning to develop U.K. North Sea Gannet E and F discoveries and set a world record distance for deployment of an electrical submersible pump (ESP).

Gannet E will be developed with a single subsea well tied back to Gannet platform 14 km away. The ESP is required by Gannet E's heavy crude.

Develoment of Gannet E and F will cost $135 million.

Shell/Esso said success of the pumping system will have major implications for development of many small oil fields which, because of the characteristics of the oil or the particular geology, are difficult to produce and far from infrastructure.

Gannet E and F are both 14 km from Gannet platform and about 8 km apart. Production was expected to begin in July 1997, with both structures developed with single wells tied back by a common subsea pipeline.

Gannet E has estimated reserves of 23 million bbl of oil. Production is expected to peak at 8,000 b/d and to last 9 years.

Gannet F contains much lighter crude oil than does E and so does not require an ESP. Estimated reserves are 19 million bbl of oil, with peak output expected to be 12,000 b/d and field life 16 years.

Shell Expro began gas production in late 1996 at Schooner field. Initial output was 130 MMcfd; peak output will be 170 MMcfd. Schooner is in 70 m of water on Block 44/26a and has reserves of 600 bcf of gas.

Schooner was developed at a cost of $393 million, with an unmanned platform connected by a 17-mile, 16-in. pipeline to Murdoch platform.

Conoco started early oil production from Banff field on Block 29/2a, with a converted semisubmersible producing into a shuttle tanker.

Banff field reserves are 20-110 million bbl of oil. Conoco said early production would help it decide on a full-scale development plan.

Early production from Banff was expected to peak at 35,000 b/d of oil. Full field development was to begin in 1998.

Conoco also was developing Boulton gas field in 37 m of water on North Sea Block 44/21a. It will use an unmanned platform linked by pipeline to processing and export facilities on Conoco's Murdoch platform 11 km east.

Boulton gas reserves are 165 bcf. Production was expected to begin in second quarter 1998 and to peak at 90 MMcfd.

The field, discovered in 1984, will be developed with two wells drilled in mid-1997, one of them a dual-lateral.

Discoveries

Enterprise Oil plc found gas with its 53/5b-5 well in the U.K.'s southern North Sea. The 9,500 ft hole flowed 12.6 MMcfd from the Rotliegendes. The strike is 6 km southeast of Davy field, which is tied back to the Indefatigable complex.

Amerada Hess had an oil discovery on Block 20/5c-6, which flowed 8,647 b/d of light hydrocarbons through a 2 in. choke.

The discovery is 25 km southwest of Amerada's Ivanhoe/Rob Roy fields and 12 km northwest of Buchan field, operated by BP.

Saga Petroleum AS found oil and gas on Norwegian North Sea Block 34/7 near Tordis field.

The hole flowed on test 6,604 b/d of oil and 3.7 MMcfd of gas through a 40/64 in. choke. The discovery was in 187 m of water. Saga was considering development by subsea tieback to Tordis, itself a subsea satellite of Gullfaks field.

Statoil gauged what appears to be the largest oil strike off Denmark in almost 20 years. License partner Enterprise Oil plc, London, said preliminary estimates indicate Statoil's 1 Siri wildcat in Block 5604/20 of the North Sea is Denmark's biggest discovery since Skjold field was found in 1977.

Statoil's 1 Siri discovery flowed at a maximum rate of 5,988 b/d of oil, along with associated gas, Enterprise reported. Statoil said the discovery, drilled to 2,200 m by the Deepsea Bergen semisubmersible in 60 m of water, is thought to hold reserves of 150 million bbl of oil.

Enterprise said the find is the first off Denmark outside the Viking graben area and confirms a new exploration model. Although the strike is not near infrastructure, Statoil said it appears to be large enough to support a stand-alone development.

License partners are operator Statoil 50%, Enterprise and Dansk Olie & Gasproduktion AS 20% each, and Denerco KS 10%.

Brent spar

Shell U.K. Exploration & Production got more bad news about its Brent spar loading buoy in 1996.

Structural analysis showed offshore dismantling of the spar will be trickier than expected and another solution must be found.

The U.K. government had approved a plan to dump the buoy in deep water off Northwest Britain in 1995, but international protests forced Shell/Esso to abort the operation.

Shell said previous plans for offshore dismantling of the spar for onshore disposal are not feasible because likely stresses in the structure during dismantling are higher than previously estimated.

Engineers said the spar is strong while floating and could stay in the North Sea for another 20-30 years.

The problem will be trying to get it out of the water. The outside pressure on the walls after its ballast water is pumped out would create problems.

Engineers said new techniques have shown that when the spar was installed in the 1970s, it was highly stressed and close to the point of failure. So the installation process cannot be reversed to dismantle the spar. The consultants said previous dismantling proposals are not feasible.

Shell had been considering dismantling the spar either by raising it higher in the water in its vertical position and removing it slice by slice from the top or rotating it into a horizontal position for loading onto a barge or for towing.

Shell said that during deballasting the spar's outer walls soon would reach their safety limit and could collapse. Even if its two damaged tanks were repaired first, deballasting would still be risky.

Now the company believes buoyancy aids will be needed to reduce stresses during dismantling. It is considering use of a crane, air bags, compressed gas, or polystyrene balls.

Abandonment issues

Unocal U.K. Ltd. could be the next company to fall foul of environmental campaigners over platform abandonment if it proceeds with announced intentions for its Heather field platform.

Unocal said it plans partial removal of Block 2/5 Heather platform in a $45-75 million decommissioning program. This will involve removal of most of the topsides and toppling much of the jacket to yield clearance of at least 55 m below sea level.

Heather's drilling, production, and quarters platform measures 236 m from seabed to top of derrick and has topsides weighing 12,200 metric tons and a 17,300 metric ton steel jacket.

Heather began production in 1978. It produced about 7,500 b/d of oil in 1996, but production was not expected to be viable beyond 1998.

Unocal hopes to prolong the platform's life. It plans to drill on Block 2/4, which contains the West Heather prospect, and if it proves to be commercial, Heather platform would be used to produce it.

A number of U.K. operators have proposed platform abandonment plans since environmental campaigners and European government pressure forced Shell to abort its plan to dump its Brent spar in deep water.

However, these all will involve complete removal because they are in less than 55 m of water. Heather's abandonment proposal is the first since Brent spar to involve dumping.

International Maritime Organization rules require all platforms in less than 75 m of water to be completely removed, although the limit is expected soon to be relaxed to 55 m.

Under the 55 m clearance limit, about 30% of the North Sea's 420 or so platforms would be eligible for partial removal or dumping.

Pipelines

Wood Mackenzie Consultants Ltd., Edinburgh, said there was so much spare capacity in U.K. North Sea oil pipelines in 1996 that construction of additional offshore pipelines was unlikely in the short term.

The region's Norpipe, Flotta, Sullom Voe Brent and Ninian, and Beatrice export systems have combined capacity of 3.65 million b/d of oil.

However, the five lines moved only 1.45 million b/d from offshore fields to onshore terminals in 1996. Only the Forties pipeline was operating at full capacity, 1 million b/d, with a 15% capacity expansion planned.

The spare capacity offers an opportunity for use in future field development projects. Such projects are generally expected to be much smaller than the fields for which the pipelines were built.

However, future North Sea gas field developments of the future are likely to require new pipelines. The U.K. is expected to have gas export pipelines to Ireland, Northern Ireland, and Belgium in place by 2000.

Wood Mackenzie said the three systems could be able to export almost 2.9 bcfd from mainland U.K. by early next century, with the U.K.-continental Europe interconnector making up 1.94 bcfd of this capacity. If this capacity were fully utilized, it would be equal to 40% of 1996 U.K. gas demand.

Meanwhile, Shell U.K. Exploration & Production finished a pipeline in 1996 to take oil ashore from a number of U.K. North Sea oil fields that relied on tanker-loading.

A 16-km long, 24-in. diameter pipeline runs from the Fulmar platform to the Norpipe line operated by Phillips Petroleum Co. U.K. Ltd. Cost was $112.5 million.

The link will have capacity to carry 140,000 b/d of oil and will enable output from Shell/Esso's Fulmar, Gannet, and Auk platforms, along with BP's Clyde field, to join oil from Phillips's Ekofisk complex in the Norwegian sector on its way to a U.K. oil terminal at Teesside. IPE

Chronology of events for 1996

JANUARY

THE MARKET: Gulf of Mexico storms force Mexico to suspend exports as winter cold grips the Northern Hemisphere. The near-month price for futures contracts covering light, sweet crude on the New York Mercantile Exchange averages $18.07/bbl in the last week of the month. The Nymex natural gas contract price averages $2.31/MMBTU.

POLITICS: Saudi Arabia's King Fahd, recovering from a stroke, temporarily gives control of the government to Crown Prince Abdullah.

ENERGY POLICY: The European Commission agrees on guidelines, spelled out in a white paper by Commissioner Christis Papoutsis, for a unified energy policy for European Union members and calls for adoption of a policy within 5 years.

PRODUCTION: ARCO China starts pipeline gas sales to Hong Kong from two platforms in Yacheng 13-1 field off Hainan Island in the culmination of an 11 year, $1.2 billion project.

LNG: Yemen's parliament approves an agreement with Total for construction of a $3 billion LNG facility able to produce 5 million metric tons/year...A group led by Enron adjusts plans for its proposed, LNG-based power project in Dabhol, India, the original and larger version of which was rejected by an incoming state government in Maharashtra.

REFINING: Sharjah Oil Refining Co. plans a 40,000 b/d refinery in Sharjah, targeting start-up by the end of 1997...BP announces a plan to sell its refineries in Lima, Ohio, and Lavera, France, and to cut capacity of the Nerefco refinery it shares with Texaco in Rotterdam...World Trade Organization upholds Venezuela's challenge to U.S. environmental standards for imported gasoline...Lagoven of Venezuela begins a $1.1 billion, 10 year program to upgrade and expand its 635,000 b/d Amuay refinery.

EXPLORATION: Venezuela opens its first round of bidding for exploration acreage since nationalizing its oil industry in 1976.

COMPANIES: Chevron and NGC begin merger talks leading to creation of North America's largest marketer of natural gas and gas liquids.

FEBRUARY

THE MARKET: Severe winter weather in the U.S. raised January demand by 5% from the level a year earlier, API reports. The near-month Nymex crude price averages $18.81/bbl in February's last week, the gas price $2.54/MMBTU.

GOVERNMENT: U.S. President Clinton signs a bill allowing the federal government to sell its 78% interest in Elk Hills Naval Petroleum Reserve in California.

EXPLORATION: Cairn Energy of Scotland makes Bangladesh's first offshore gas strike, testing 50 MMcfd in its Sangu wildcat.

THE INDUSTRY: Capital and exploration spending in the U.S. by U.S. oil and gas companies is projected at $33.4 billion in 1996, the second straight year of increase, according to an annual survey by Oil & Gas Journal.

COMPANIES: BP and Mobil announce a plan to combine their European refining and marketing operations, combined assets of which total $5 billion.

SPILL: The Sea Empress tanker hits rocks outside the harbor of Milford Haven, Wales, spilling 65,000 metric tons of crude.

MARCH

THE MARKET: Winter lingers in the Northern Hemisphere. The Nymex crude price closes the month at $22.78/bbl, the gas price at $2.64/MMBTU.

REFINING: Powerine Oil Co., with new owners, prepares to reopen a 49,500 b/d refinery at Santa Fe Springs, Calif., shut down in July 1995...Parco, a joint venture of the governments of Pakistan and Abu Dhabi, plans a 100,000 b/d refinery at Mahmood Kot in Central Pakistan.

PIPELINES: Azerbaijan International Operating Co. signs an agreement allowing export of crude from its Caspian Sea fields through existing Russian pipelines to the Black Sea port of Novorossiysk; a second route, involving new pipelines through Georgia, is planned.

GOVERNMENT: U.S. DOE sells 5 million bbl of crude oil from the Weeks Island, La., Strategic Petroleum Reserve site to pay for closing of the facility, which has leaks in the salt formation above its storage chambers...EPA issues a final rule lifting the cap on ethanol blended with gasoline to 10 vol % from 7.7 vol %...California refiners on Mar. 1 begin delivering so-called "Phase II" reformulated gasoline (RFG), specifications for which are stricter than those for federally mandated RFG...Canada approves a federal budget with provisions designed to help the oilsands industry.

LNG: Ras Laffan Liquefied Natural Gas Co. lets a $1 billion contract to a joint venture of JGC Corp. and M.W. Kellogg for engineering, procurement, and construction of a 5 million ton/year LNG plant in Qatar.

ELECTRICITY: Nymex begins trade of an electricity futures contract.

APRIL

THE MARKET: Rising gasoline prices in the U.S. revive calls in Congress for a "windfall profit" tax on oil. The Nymex crude price closes a volatile month at a weekly average of $22.74/bbl, the gas price at $2.26/MMBTU.

GOVERNMENT: Japan allows a long-standing law that limits imports of petroleum products to expire, opening its wholesale and retail markets to competition from abroad...U.S. EPA approves a request by Colorado for relaxation of the summertime volatility limit for gasoline sold in the Denver-Boulder area, agreeing with the state that the tougher standard wasn't needed to bring the region into compliance with ozone pollution limits...President Clinton orders sale of 12 million bbl of crude from the SPR in an effort to blunt the runup in oil prices. His Republican challenger in November elections, Sen. Bob Dole of Kansas, proposes repeal of the 4.3¢/gal gasoline tax increase imposed early in Clinton's term...Britain begins a pilot program under which 500,000 residential gas buyers in Southwest England's Devon, Somerset, and Cornwall receive a choice of gas supplier...Clinton formally ends the 23 year old ban on export of crude from Alaska's North Slope by declaring exports to be in the U.S. national interest...FERC Order 888 provides open access to electricity transmission systems and allows recovery in utility rates of costs stranded by deregulation.

EXPLORATION: A Central Gulf of Mexico lease sale attracts a record high 1,381 bids for 924 federal tracts out of 5,649 offered.

REFINING: Total says start-up of the 50,000 ton/year Nord ethyl tertiary butyl ether unit at its Dunkirk, France, refinery is the world's first grassroots, purpose-built unit of its kind and the first venture in which oil and agricultural interests have jointly produced ETBE.

MAY

THE MARKET: The U.N. and Iraq, after months of negotiation, agree to resumption of Iraqi oil exports to raise as much as $2 billion for humanitarian purposes. The question: When? The Nymex crude price slips to an average of $20.39/bbl in the last week of the month. The Nymex gas price climbs to $2.42/MMBTU.

GOVERNMENT: Canada's parliament reintroduces a bill to ban the gasoline octane booster MMT.

EXPLORATION: Romania begins its first licensing round, soliciting bids for 15 mostly onshore blocks.

ALTERNATIVE FUEL: Sasol of South Africa plans to upgrade its coal-based synthetic fuel plant at Secunda by replacing 16 circulation-bed reactors with six fluidized-bed reactors.

PRODUCTION: Shell and Mobil sign a contract with Peru's government to develop the giant Camisea complex of gas and condensate fields in the country's central southern jungle.

JUNE

THE MARKET: In anticipation of restart of oil exports by Iraq, OPEC raises its group quota to 25 million b/d from 24.5 million b/d for the rest of the year...In the U.S., gasoline prices subside after 3 months of controversial increases...Crude prices spurt at month's end in response to a car-bomb explosion that kills 19 and injures hundreds at a U.S. military housing complex near Dhahran, Saudi Arabia...By month's end Nymex futures prices exceed $21/bbl for crude oil and $2.60/MMBTU for natural gas.

PIPELINES: Alyeska plans to place two of the Trans-Alaska Pipeline System's 10 pump stations on stand-by status to adjust to a throughput decline to 1.5 million from as much as 2.1 million b/d.

EXPLORATION: A group led by BP Exploration enters an agreement with State Oil Company of the Azerbaijan Republic to explore the Shakh Deniz prospect in the Caspian Sea.

OPEC: Gabon withdraws from OPEC.

PRODUCTION: Statoil takes over as operator of giant Troll oil and gas field's gas platform in the Norwegian North Sea and onshore treatment plant from development operator Norske Shell, following start of gas flow May 28.

MERGERS: El Paso Energy Corp. agrees to merge with Tenneco Energy in a $4 billion transaction that will create the only pipeline system in the U.S. able to ship natural gas to either the East or West Coast.

JULY

THE MARKET: The Nymex crude price slumps toward the end of the

month to $20.67/bbl. The gas price falls to $2.29/MMBTU.
LNG: Atlantic LNG Co., major interest holder in which is Amoco Corp., schedules construction of a 3 million ton/year LNG plant in Trinidad & Tobago and discloses contracts to sell output in the U.S. and Spain...Petroleum Development Oman receives bids for upstream work linked to Oman Liquefied Natural Gas's plans for a 6.6 million ton/year LNG project.
PRODUCTION: Start-up of the Mars tension leg platform in the Gulf of Mexico by Shell and BP sets gulf records for water-depth (2,490 ft) and single-well sustained flow (15,000 b/d).
GOVERNMENT: The European Commission agrees to tighten vehicle emission standards and fuel specifications in a program to reduce emissions from road transport by as much as 70% by 2010...President Boris Yeltsin wins reelection in Russia...U.S. Senate approves a bill imposing economic sanctions on foreign firms investing more than $40 million/year in the energy sectors of Iran or Libya...U.S. Undersecretary of State Timothy Wirth, at a U.N. conference on climate change, shifts the U.S. position on climate change by urging all nations to adopt internationally enforceable standards on emissions of greenhouse gases.
HEAVY OIL: Venezuela's Congress approves a $1 billion joint venture with Conoco, Statoil, and the Venezuelan firms Bitor and Jandis to build three Orimulsion production modules in Eastern Venezuela.
GAS PROCESSING: An explosion damages two 500 MMcfd units at Pemex's Cactus gas processing complex in Chiapas, idling more than one fourth of Mexico's gas processing capacity.

AUGUST

THE MARKET: Despite signs that Iraq will resume limited exports of oil, oil prices remain above $22/bbl as inventories worldwide stay low. The Nymex oil price ends the month at about $22.40/bbl, the gas price slightly above $2/MMBTU.
GOVERNMENT: President Clinton signs the Iran-Libya Sanctions Act into law.
PRODUCTION: BP Exploration, 3 years after becoming field operator, and partner Oxy U.S.A. increase production of Alaska's Milne Point field to 65,000 b/d and triple the field's reserves estimate to 330 million bbl, based on extensive drilling...Petro-Canada and partners file a plan for the $2 billion development of Terra Nova oil field on the Grand Banks off Newfoundland.
TRANSPORTATION: In defiance of new third-party sanctions enacted by the U.S., Turkey signs a 23 year, $23 billion agreement to buy natural gas from Iran...Separately, National Iranian Oil Co. and Kazakhstan agree to a swap of 40,000 b/d of crude, with Iran taking Kazakh oil at its Caspian Sea ports and delivering like volumes on Kazakhstan's behalf in the Persian Gulf.
REFINING: State-owned companies of Kuwait and Pakistan finalize plans to build a 90,000 b/d, $1.2 billion refinery in Pakistan's Baluchistan province, where Pakistan also says it has plans with Iran for a similar facility...Kuwait Petroleum Corp. shuts its 59,000 b/d refinery at Stigsnaes, Denmark, and begins converting it into an import terminal...BP and Mobil win European Union approval for their plan to merge European refining and marketing operations.
HEAVY OIL: ARCO and Venezuela's Corpoven agree to form a joint venture for a $3.5 billion project to upgrade as much as 200,000 b/d of 9° gravity crude from the Orinoco belt.

SEPTEMBER

THE MARKET: Prices leap as Iraqi President Saddam Hussein chills the U.N. deal for limited exports by attacking Kurdish strongholds in northern Iraq. The U.S. responds with isolated missile attacks that cause little damage...EIA reports U.S. inventories of distillate at the end of August totaled 19.7 million bbl, 16% less than the 5 year average for the month. The Nymex crude price settles by month's end at $24.13/bbl, the gas price at $2.02/MMBTU.
HEAVY OIL: Mobil and Lagoven sign a $2.3 billion deal to transport and upgrade 8° gravity Orinoco heavy oil for use in Mobil's Chalmette, La., refinery, in which Lagoven will take a 50% interest.
GOVERNMENT: The U.S. Minerals Management Service, having alleged that specified producers undervalued crude oil produced on federal land in California, begins a nationwide audit of royalty payments...The U.K. Office of Gas Supply plans to give 1.5 million residents of Dorset, Avon, Kent, and East and West Sussex choice of gas suppliers...Japan's Ministry of Trade and Industry seeks $63 million in government funds to help service station owners develop new lines of business in response to deregulation of the refining and marketing business.
PRODUCTION: Norsk Hydro raises its reserves estimate for Troll field in the Norwegian North Sea to 1.2 billion bbl of oil from 1 million bbl...Equatorial Guinea becomes a commercial oil producer as Mobil and United Meridian start flow at 7,000 b/d from the first well in offshore Zafiro field.
REFINING: Kyrgoil Corp., Calgary, starts up Kyrgyzstan's first refinery, a modular 10,000 b/d unit built by Petrofac International Ltd. of Tyler, Tex., and assembled at Jalabad...Ultramar and Diamond Shamrock agree to a merger that will create an independent refiner with revenues of $8 billion/year and total crude capacity of 475,000 b/d.

OCTOBER

THE MARKET: Tight supplies, especially of distillate heating oil, and unrest in Iraq push crude prices up. The Nymex crude price ends the month at $25.17/bbl. The gas price rises to a weekly average of $2.56/MMBTU at month's end as the heating season gets under way in the Northern Hemisphere.
REFINING: Shell, Texaco, and Saudi Aramco consider forming a refining and marketing alliance to operate a combination of their U.S. downstream assets.
PIPELINES: Pakistan and Iran begin a feasibility study for a $3.5 billion, 1.6 bcfd pipeline to carry natural gas from Iran to Pakistan after the latter withdraws from plans to lay a subsea line to India...International Petroleum Corp. and Chevron agree to jointly develop a natural gas pipeline system linking Papua New Guinea and northern Queensland, Australia.
PRODUCTION: EIA says U.S. oil reserves fell 0.5% in 1995 to 22 billion bbl, while gas reserves rose 1% to 165 tcf.
LNG: Significant civil work begins on the Atlantic LNG Co. project in Trinidad & Tobago.

NOVEMBER

THE MARKET: OPEC ministers extend their group's production quota of 25 million b/d until June 1997. The Nymex crude price ends the month at $23.62/bbl, the gas price at $3.52/MMBTU.
RUSSIA: Demand in the West for shares in the first international offering by Russia's Gazprom exceeds expectations, with prices set at $15.75/share, triple the level in Moscow.
PIPELINES: Spain receives its first gas transported through the $2.3 billion, 1,400 km Maghreb pipeline from Algeria across the Strait of Gibraltar to Cordoba.
REFINING: Elf Oil (U.K.), Gulf Oil (Great Britain), and Murco Petroleum plan to merge their downstream assets into a new firm and close one of two refineries involved, the 115,000 b/d Gulf refinery in Milford Haven, Wales.
GOVERNMENT: Democrat Bill Clinton wins reelection as President of the U.S., while both houses of Congress remain under Republican control.
COMPANIES: Texaco makes as much as $176 million available in compensation and agrees to let a task force on "equality and tolerance" have a say in its personnel policies following disclosure of a tape-recorded conversation among top executives that included apparent racial slurs...Tosco Corp. signs a letter of intent to buy Unocal Corp.'s West Coast refining and marketing division for $1.4 billion...Duke Power Co. of Charlotte, N.C., and PanEnergy Corp., Houston, agree to merge in a deal valued at $23 billion.
LNG: Amoco Egypt, Egyptian General Petroleum Corp., and Botas Petroleum Pipeline of Turkey sign a memorandum of understanding for a project to liquefy natural gas produced in Egypt's Nile delta and ship it to Turkey...Phillips Petroleum Co. proposes a $1.9 billion (Australian) LNG project in Darwin based on gas from the Bayu/Undan discovery in the Timor Gap Zone of Cooperation Area shared by Australia and Indonesia...The Cristobal Colon LNG export project in Venezuela goes on indefinite hold due to poor economics.

DECEMBER

THE MARKET: Iraqi oil exports finally resume under the oil-for-food deal between Baghdad and the U.N. Oil prices fall but quickly stabilize as unusually cold weather sweeps across Europe and North America. Nymex crude at times exceeds $26/bbl, while gas tops $4.50/MMBTU. By month's end the crude price settles at about $25/bbl, the gas price at $3.64/MMBTU.
RUSSIA: Moscow reports signing of a protocol covering a long-negotiated, $20 billion production sharing contract covering 2,847 sq miles north of the Arctic Circle with Timan Pechora Co., which includes Amoco, Exxon, Texaco, and Norsk Hydro.
CASPIAN: Azerbaijan lets contract worth a potential $1.5 billion to an Amoco unit and partners for exploration of the Dan Ulduzu and Ashrafi prospects in the Caspian Sea.
LNG: Coastal and Indonesia's Pertamina form a venture to develop LNG import capability and conduct related activity in India...PacRim LNG Inc. of Calgary plans a $1.4 billion (Canadian) liquefaction plant on the northwest coast of British Columbia...Qatar's Ras Laffan LNG facility sends its first shipment of LNG to Japan.
GOVERNMENT: Bolivia completes the 50% privatization of Yacimientos Petroliferos Fiscales Bolivianos.
REFINING: Yukong Ltd. claims the world refinery-size record when addition of a fifth crude distillation unit raises capacity at its Ulsan, South Korea, plant to 810,000 b/d from 610,000 b/d.

Offshore decommissioning a growing challenge for operators

Removal of production equipment from depleted offshore fields has developed into a complex technical, economic, and political issue for oil and gas companies.

Industry representatives say they have the technical ability to deal safely with abandonment—or decommissioning, as they increasingly call it. But their methods and plans do not always win the approval of governments and environmental activists.

In two mature offshore producing areas—the North Sea and the Gulf of Mexico—the challenge was nothing new in 1996. Operators in both regions had performed a number of successful decommissionings and faced the need for many more. What was new in 1996, at least in some jurisdictions, was the growing need of oil and gas companies to deal with government agencies and pressure groups with contrary views about how field shut-downs should proceed.

Shell Expro is considering 30 proposals for dismantling of Brent Spar, which in late 1996 was moored in a Norwegian fjord awaiting preparation and approval of a new decommissioning plan following the aborted dumping program of 1995.

North Sea

After the dumping of the Brent Spar loading buoy was aborted in 1995, when the environmentalist group Greenpeace mounted an international protest, the derelict structure dominated North Sea debate on abandonment.

The buoy in 1996 was moored in a Norwegian fjord, while operator Shell U.K. Exploration & Production looked for a less controversial disposal plan. Meanwhile, other, smaller abandonments have gone ahead.

The Norwegian and U.K. governments maintain that deep-sea disposal of platforms remains a viable option, but the abandonments approved through 1996 showed how the governments differ in approach.

International Maritime Organization (IMO) requires all platforms in less than 75 m of water to be completely removed, though the limit is expected soon to be relaxed to 55 m. Under the 55 m clearance limit, about 30% of the North Sea's current 420 or so platforms would be eligible for partial removal or dumping.

Small scale projects

Offshore Denmark, no abandonment plans have been put forward, while offshore Netherlands, where the water is shallow, and in the U.K.'s shallow Southern Gas basin, a handful of complete platform removals have taken place.

Wintershall Noordzee BV removed three small steel platforms from K13 gas field in 1989. In the same year Unocal Netherlands BV removed a platform from Helder oil field.

With offshore production from the Netherlands in decline, three to five platforms a year are anticipated to require removal in the near future. All will be completely removed.

Before Brent Spar, Norway's only abandonment was by operator Norsk Hydro AS, which developed Mime field as a single well subsea satellite of Cod field, which links into the Ekofisk complex.

Mime production ceased in 1994, and the well was plugged and abandoned and subsea equipment removed.

Before and after the Brent Spar furor, U.K. operators decommissioned a number of small oil and gas fields. In 1996 Lasmo plc killed and cemented two wells and brought their subsea wellheads to shore from shut-in Staffa field on U.K. Block 3/8b. The company also removed a 10 km long pipeline which tied the field back to the Ninian Southern platform.

Staffa was brought on stream in March 1992. Output peaked at 11,000 b/d, and the field produced almost 4 million bbl of oil before it was shut in during November 1994 after the export pipeline clogged.

Midland Scottish Energy Ltd. abandoned U.K. North Sea Emerald field in February 1996. At Emerald, a converted semisubmersible recovered oil through nine subsea producers and injected water through two wells.

Nowsco U.K. Ltd., Aberdeen, flooded the export line gas lift and umbilical system; cleaned subsea pipelines, subsea manifolds, and production umbilicals; killed the wells; and pumped nitrogen through the topsides.

Risers were then cut, and the rig was removed to Invergordon for refurbishment. The field's Ailsa Craig storage tanker is also being marketed.

Before Brent Spar, BHP Petroleum Ltd. decommissioned the production semisubmersible developments in Crawford and Argyll/Duncan/Innes fields and a platform in Forbes field.

Forbes was a satellite of Esmond field, which was itself decommissioned by BHP in 1996 along with its other satellite, Gordon.

Esmond's central production platform and adjacent wellhead platform and Gordon's satellite production platform were removed by Heeremac VOF of Leiden, Netherlands.

Production from Esmond and Gordon gas fields ceased in March 1995, and Heeremac began heavy lifts to dismantle the platforms in April 1996 using the DB102 crane barge.

Two decks and the accommodation unit of Esmond's topsides were removed first and taken by barge to the Able U.K. Ltd. yard in Middlesbrough to be broken into scrap for recycling.

In early June 1996, DB102 removed the remaining deck sections and jackets. Esmond's platforms stood in 33 m of water, and Gordon stood in 19 m, so complete removal of jackets was required.

Northeast Frigg

In early 1996, Norway's Ministry of Industry & Energy approved Elf's abandonment plan for Northeast Frigg field.

Northeast Frigg, on Block 25/1, was developed with a six well subsea manifold tied back to the Frigg TCP2 platform with a 150 m articulated control tower to govern well operations.

In January, Elf let a 95 million kroner ($15 million) contract to

Kvaerner Installasjon AS and Stolt Comex Seaway AS of Stavanger to remove and abandon the facilities.

In July, Elf removed NE Frigg's articulated control tower and flare column and moored the tower in the fjord outside Tau, near Stavanger, 200-300 m from where the deck and tower will be reused.

The wellhead template will be resmelted, and flow lines and cables will be scrapped. The quarters and work deck were moved to a nearby safety training center.

In the nearest approach to acceptance of platform dumping offshore Norway to date, the government agreed the steel articulated column could be laid on a bed of rock to form a breakwater at a new marina at Tau.

In the U.K. sector, Elf Norge was given the green light by U.K. Department of Trade & Industry (DTI) to remove a flare column in the U.K. part of Frigg field.

Though this stands in 107 m of water and could theoretically be dumped at sea according to DTI guidelines, removal and towing to shore for dismantling was said to be straightforward.

Conoco removed four platforms in Viking A field in the U.K.'s shallow Southern Gas basin using the Stanislav Yudin crane ship. Only a riser platform remains in Viking A.

Viking & Leman

Throughout the summer of 1996 and finishing Oct. 1, Conoco (U.K.) Ltd. removed four of five platforms in North Viking A gas field on U.K. Block 49/12.

Viking A, part of a 14 platform development which includes South Viking field on Block 49/17, ceased production in 1991. One platform, Viking AR, has been used as a riser platform since then and will be retained.

The four platforms which were removed had not been upgraded under new U.K. offshore safety regulations, implemented in the wake of the Piper Alpha platform blast of 1988.

The platforms weighed a total of 8,600 metric tons. The Stanislav Yudin heavy lift vessel took the platforms to shore in 22 lifts of more than 50 metric tons and 24 of less. The pieces were taken to Swan Hunter yard on Tyneside, where Conoco expects 99% of their materials to be recycled.

Around the same time, Shell U.K. Exploration & Production, the Shell U.K. Ltd./Esso Exploration & Production U.K. Ltd. combine, decommissioned Leman BK compression platform, one of 15 platforms in Leman gas field in the southern North Sea. Its function was taken on by another compression platform, Leman AK.

Leman BK abandonment was estimated to have cost £11 million ($17 million). The platform weighed more than 6,000 metric tons, of which 4,600 metric tons is topsides.

The DB 102 heavy lift vessel, operated by Heeremac and McDermott Marine Construction Ltd., London, removed three platform modules, a module support frame, then the jacket.

A Shell official said topsides were removed in early October and taken to the Able yard on Teesside for dismantling and recycling. The jacket was removed and taken to Able's yard later in the month.

Sensitive to public opinion after the Brent Spar outcry last year, Shell/Esso published a list of potential contaminants on board the platform, including about 50 metric tons of heavy metals, almost 1 metric ton of halon and freon compounds, and 3,300 l. of oils.

Odin

After Norway's Ministry of Industry & Energy approved use of the Northeast Frigg tower in building a marina, North Sea operators had hopes of being given leeway for dumping some structures despite Brent Spar.

Odin field operator Esso Norge AS submitted a decommissioning plan in March 1995, which proposed removing the platform's topsides and toppling the steel jacket to make an artificial reef.

But the Norwegian ministry surprised the industry in March 1996 by insisting that the Odin platform, which stopped producing in August 1994, be completely removed.

A U.K. oil industry official said the decision was a setback to Britain's attempts to persuade environmental pressure groups that deepwater disposal is still a viable option after last year's Brent Spar battle.

Norway's ministry said the Odin platform had to be taken to shore for dismantling and recycling, with total decommissioning costs estimated at 245 million kroner ($40 million).

The Odin platform was a conventional steel structure with topsides weighing 7,600 metric tons and a steel jacket of 6,000 metric tons, installed on Block 30/10a in 103 m of water. It had produced some 30 billion cu m of gas over 10 years, with output being exported via the Frigg complex.

"Esso originally proposed to topple the platform and use it as a fish reef," said the ministry, "and that future responsibilities be transferred to the state.

"Due to the uncertainty connected with leaving the installation in place, the government did not consider this a viable option in the case of Odin. This does not, however, rule out the possibility of offshore disposal in the future."

Karl Otto Gilje, chief executive officer of Esso Norge, said: "The plan we presented in March 1995 was well-researched and contained a careful analysis of all practical alternatives.

"While we made our preference for the artificial reef alternative clear, the review process was both rigorous and consistent with national and international rules governing platform decommissioning."

Esso let contract to a joint venture of Aker AS of Oslo and Saipem SpA of Milan for removal and disposal of the Odin platform. Recycling and scrapping work is being carried out at Aker's Stord yard in Norway.

Aker and Saipem set up an alliance in autumn 1994 in anticipation of a growing demand for abandonment work to use Saipem's S-7000 heavy lift vessel; this was its first contract.

In October 1995, Saipem removed the Odin platform's five modules in two consignments, which were loaded onto the S-7000 for removal to Stord. Aker is working on opportunities for reusing the modules and equipment from the platform in new projects.

Brent Spar

As the smaller abandonments went ahead, Shell/Esso continued with studies into alternatives for disposal of Brent Spar.

Meanwhile, the U.K. government continued to claim that deep-sea dumping is still an abandonment option, despite environmental protesters' disruption of the Brent Spar dumping operation.

Northeast Frigg field's control tower being towed from the field. The abandonment contract was carried out for operator Elf Norge by an alliance of Kvaerner and Stolt Comex Seaway.

Industry & Energy Minister Tim Eggar, who later resigned from government, said: "Our policy on decommissioning redundant oil and gas structures remains the same — each case is considered to establish the best practicable environmental option so as to safeguard the interests of the environment and other users of the sea.

"In the Leman BK case Shell has concluded, and government agreed, that the best option is to bring it ashore. Most redundant North Sea installations are likely to be treated in the same way. For those larger, heavier installations in the northern parts of the North Sea, deep-sea disposal will remain an option on environmental and technical feasibility grounds."

Despite government's stance, operator Shell/Esso gave its first public hint that onshore disposal is more likely. Graham Dunlop, senior project engineer on the Brent Spar decommissioning project, told an Institute of Petroleum conference in early 1996 that the spar posed unprecedented challenges for Shell and an opportunity to learn and change.

"The spar is like an iceberg," said Dunlop. "Most of its bulk, mainly the six huge storage tanks, is beneath the water's surface. At 14,500 metric tons, its huge tanks displace 66,500 metric tons of water. Apart from the waters north of Orkney, most of the U.K. North Sea is too shallow to accommodate it.

"Herein lies the fundamental issue. Removing the spar from the water, or just raising it higher, without posing undue risk to people or the environment, requires an exceptional feat of civil engineering."

Dunlop said that while the spar is robust and still fit to act as an oil storage buoy, calculations have shown that the original construction process — an exceptional feat of engineering in its own time — cannot readily be reversed.

"Raising it out of the water in its vertical position, or attempting to rotate it to the horizontal, both pose a significant risk to its structural integrity," said Dunlop.

"This is mainly due to its design and the need to maintain, during movements of this kind, the balance of internal and external pressures which stop the tank walls from buckling and imploding.

"This challenge is further complicated by the fact that two of the spar's six storage tanks were damaged during operation. Any future solution will have to balance benefits carefully with these risks."

Spar hitch

In midsummer 1996, Shell/Esso revealed that new structural analysis showed offshore dismantling of the derelict Brent Spar loading buoy will be trickier than first expected and that a new solution must be found.

At the same time, the company announced a list of contractors working on outline proposals for disposal of the spar.

Shell said previous concepts for offshore dismantling of the spar for onshore disposal are not feasible because likely stresses in the structure during dismantling are higher than previously estimated.

Engineering consultant W.S. Atkins Consultants Ltd., London, was commissioned by Shell/Esso to carry out an independent assessment of the spar structure using finite element analysis.

Eric Faulds, decommissioning manager at Shell Expro, said: "The analysis showed that, while the spar is floating it is strong and could stay in the North Sea for another 20-30 years.

"The problem will be trying to get it out of the water. The outside pressure on the walls after its ballast water is pumped out would create problems for the contractors."

W.S. Atkins has showed, with techniques not available when the spar was installed in the 1970s, that it was highly stressed and close to the point of failure during the installation process.

This means the installation process cannot simply be reversed to dismantle the spar. The consultant said previous concepts for offshore dismantling are not feasible, and new solutions will have to be found.

Shell said: "Raising the Spar from the sea presents a huge engineering challenge in overcoming major structural limitations and safety risks."

Before the Atkins study results were known, Shell was considering dismantling the spar either by raising it higher in the water in its vertical position and removing it slice by slice from the top or rotating it into a horizontal position for loading onto a barge or for towing.

Shell said that during deballasting the spar's outer walls would soon reach their safety limit and could collapse. Even if its two damaged tanks were repaired first, deballasting would still be risky.

Now the company believes buoyancy aids will be needed to reduce stresses during dismantling.

Shell/Esso subsequently invited suggestions for disposal of the spar and asked 21 contractors to prepare outline disposal plans for the Brent Spar loading buoy, bearing in mind the new findings.

The 21 contractors were required to submit outline plans by July 31, after which Shell/Esso aimed to select a short list of about six different contractors to develop their disposal plans fully.

Heinz Rothermund, managing director of Shell Expro, said the aim of the "long list" was to utilize the ingenuity of contractors in the disposal task. The short list is intended to feature several different disposal options.

"Whatever solution we propose needs government approval and must be at least as good or better than the original deepwater disposal plan," said Rothermund. "The emphasis is on getting it right and not rushing it.

"The Best Practicable Environmental Option (BPEO) will be determined on a balance of safety and the risks to human life, technical feasibility, economics, environmental impacts of all kinds, and widespread acceptability."

Faulds said, "We would not like to arrive at a short list of six very similar onshore scrapping options, for example, or six fish-farm ideas.

"We are looking for a spread of realistic disposal options which can compete strongly with each other, and with deep-sea disposal, to determine the BPEO."

Suggestions

Faulds said the company had received more than 100 ideas

of how to dispose of or reuse the spar.

"Many were fascinating," said Faulds, "but not practical. Many people making suggestions hadn't appreciated how large Brent Spar is."

One suggestion was refurbishing the spar as a floating hotel: "This would pose a few problems because it would have to be far from shore, because the spar would need to be in water 150 m deep."

Another idea was to convert the spar into a casino for operation outside the reach of U.K. tax authorities: "The government is unlikely to approve a tax-dodging scheme."

Wind and wave power schemes were also popular: "But these may not be feasible. There were also many suggestions for artificial reefs and fish farms, and these are being pursued by a Norwegian contractor."

Schematic of the Maureen field platform offshore the U.K., which operator Phillips reckons could be used for at least a further 25 years in another field development.

Rothermund said: "It is possible an uncontroversial solution will emerge. But we may need to balance the safety risk with environmental risk.

"In the meantime we want to share information and obtain feedback. Anyone is welcome to join the debate."

Two contractors dropped out of the Brent Spar ideas program. In July, Shell/Esso revealed 30 initial proposals by 19 contractors and consortia.

A Shell official said that, of the 30 options proposed by the 19 contractors and consortia, 19 are for onshore scrapping, while 11 are nonscrapping schemes.

The official said all have picked up on the buoyancy requirement. Some proposals referred to a need for buoyancy, he said, while others refer specifically to use of pontoons and semisubmersible crane vessels, for example.

The contractors and consortia submitted outline proposals for disposal of Brent Spar as follows:

- John Wood Group plc, Aberdeen and Maritime GMC, Stavanger, proposed removing Brent Spar topsides for use possibly as an onshore training unit and cutting the column into sections for placement as a foundation for a new quay at Mekjarvik harbor in Norway.
- Rhodes Offshore Partners Inc., Toronto, suggested towing the spar to the deepwater Bull Arm yard in Newfoundland, where it would be dismantled offshore for recycling onshore.
- ROS Holland BV, Ijmuiden, Netherlands, proposed floating and turning the buoy into a horizontal position to be carried onshore for recycling. Options include reuse of topsides for training and offshore dismantling using pontoons.
- Hollandsche Staalbouw Maatschappij BV, Gouda, Netherlands, suggested dismantling the buoy offshore, including cutting its storage tanks into nine smaller units to be reused as storage tanks at a Shell refinery.
- Brown & Root Ltd., London, would like to up-end the buoy to a horizontal position and tow it to a decommissioning facility at its Nigg yard in Scotland for recycling.
- Kvaerner Installasjon AS of Oslo, Stolt Comex Seaway Ltd. of Aberdeen, and Seaway Heavy Lifting Ltd. of Zoetermeer, Netherlands, suggested towing the spar to the Hanoeytangen yard near Bergen for offshore dismantling. Options include use of topsides as a training unit, resmelting steel in the main body, and reusing bottom ballast as rock fill in Norway.
- Mayer Parry Recycling Ltd. of Erith, U.K., suggested towing the buoy from Norway to a site near the Loch Kishorn dry dock in Scotland. There it would be up-ended for floating into the dock for onshore dismantling and recycling.
- Costain Land & Marine Engineering Ltd., Bromborough, U.K., proposed to remove topsides at the buoy's current site then tow the remainder to Loch Kishorn for offshore dismantling prior to onshore disposal and recycling.
- Thyssen Stahlunion GmbH, Dusseldorf, submitted two plans: vertical dismantling of the buoy offshore, using clamps or climbing jacks to increase buoyancy, followed by disposal onshore; and reuse of the spar as a water desalination plant offshore Norway.
- Amec Process & Energy Ltd., London, suggested offshore dismantling with use of some parts for construction projects, or up-ending it for return to shore on Tyneside, U.K., for dismantling and recycling.
- Umoe Haugesund AS of Haugesund, Norway, would tow the buoy to its fabrication yard for removal of topsides using a semisubmersible crane vessel and deballasting while the crane vessel lifts it into a horizontal position for dismantling onshore.
- Jan De Nul BV of Aalst, Belgium, proposed removal of topsides offshore followed by controlled burial of the spar's main body in the seabed in a trench dug by Gerardus Mercator, the world's largest dredger.
- Hollandia BV of Krimpen, Netherlands, suggested refurbishing the topsides and converting the buoy to a floating power station with three windmills each generating 3,000 kw of electric power.
- Ramboell/Monberg & Thorsen AS Consortium had two suggestions: reuse as a fixed offshore platform for accommodation or drilling; and onshore scrapping after maneuvering the spar into a horizontal position for transport to shore.
- McAlpine Doris JV of Hemel Hempstead, U.K., suggested up-ending the buoy into a horizontal position with inert pressurized gas for buoyancy, followed by onshore dismantling for reuse in coastal civil engineering works and sectioning of storage tanks for reuse.
- The U.K.'s Cammell-Laird, NNC Ltd. and VSEL proposed transporting the Spar to docks at Birkenhead, U.K., for raising to a horizontal position with buoyancy aids and heavy lift equipment prior to onshore dismantling.
- Heeremac suggested using its fleet of cargo barges and crane vessels, one with lift capacity of 12,000 metric tons, to raise the spar to a horizontal position by one of three methods for dismantling onshore, or dismantling it offshore in a vertical position.
- Aker and Saipem would tow the buoy to Aker's Stord yard in Norway for vertical dismantling while afloat into sections suitable for recycling.
- Taylor Woodrow Civil Engineering Ltd. of Southall, U.K., proposed maneuvering the buoy into a horizontal position with compressed air for buoyancy, with disposal onshore at Hunterston yard, Scotland.

Faulds said: "We are not making any judgment or indicating a preference for any of the concepts at this early stage. Over the next few months our task is to review the documents in detail, clarify the proposals with the contractors, and select a range of options for the short list."

Shell/Esso expects to announce the short-listed proposals early in 1997. Short-listed contractors will be asked to produce detailed proposals, which will be further analyzed before Shell/Esso submits its preferred disposal option to the U.K. government later in 1997.

Future abandonments

A Norwegian Petroleum Directorate (NPD) official said major abandonments ahead off Norway are Frigg and Ekofisk fields, both multiplatform complexes.

Ekofisk operator Phillips Petroleum Co. Norway expects to shut down most platforms in the field in 1998 after subsidence in the area required installation of new ones under a massive redevelopment plan.

The NPD official said there have been no discussions so far with Phillips and Frigg operator Elf over abandonment options. Phillips has said it hopes to leave Ekofisk platforms in place until the field is fully depleted, around 2030.

Also offshore Norway, Den norske stats oljeselskap AS (Statoil) expects production from Tommeliten gas field, a small subsea satellite of the Edda platform, to cease in 1997 or 1998. Statoil hopes to reuse templates and pipelines installed during development.

Mackay Consultants of Inverness, Scotland, recently listed U.K. fields it expects to cease production by 2000. During 1996, Deveron, Hamish, and Leven were expected to be shut down.

In 1997, Mackay expects Don and Northwest Hutton fields will cease production, while Heather, Highlander, Maureen, Montrose, and Petronella are expected to stop in 1998.

In 1999, Mackay expects Blenheim, Carnoustie, Chanter, Kittiwake, and Ness fields to cease production.

"Most of these are small fields," said Mackay, "but they include three relatively large ones — Northwest Hutton, Heather, and Maureen — which have played important roles in development of the U.K. sector of the North Sea.

"Their decommissioning therefore will represent something of a turning point in the history of North Sea oil industry. Their platforms will be the first large ones to be decommissioned."

Heather

The next Greenpeace onslaught could come when Unocal U.K. Ltd. attempts to abandon its Heather platform. Despite Shell's experience with Brent Spar, Unocal announced in March 1996 a controversial plan for Heather.

Heather's drilling, production, and quarters platform measures 236 m from seabed to top of derrick and has topsides weighing 12,200 metric tons and a 17,300 metric ton steel jacket.

Unocal has said it plans a partial removal of the Block 2/5 platform in a £30-50 million ($45-75 million) decommissioning program. This will involve removal of most of the topsides and toppling much of the jacket to give clearance of at least 55 m below sea level.

"The remainder of the platform," said Unocal, "most of which has already been in the marine environment for the last 20 years, will be decommissioned safely by controlled toppling — that is, lifting and placing on the adjacent seabed with little or no environmental impact.

"The total removal option was extensively evaluated. Operational complexities associated with this method result in higher exposure to safety hazards for our workforce.

"Furthermore, total removal does not eliminate environmental impacts. Overall, total removal results in onshore impacts, achieves little additional environmental benefit, results in higher exposure to safety hazards, and escalates costs to at least £85 million ($127.5 million)."

Heather was brought into production in 1978. A Unocal official said Heather field currently produces about 7,500 b/d of oil, but continued production is not expected to be viable beyond the end of 1998.

"We know Greenpeace is totally opposed to this approach to decommissioning," said the Unocal official, "but our viewpoint is that whatever we leave behind will be clean steel."

Unocal intended to be ready to submit an abandonment plan to DTI in the third quarter 1996, but submission could not happen without DTI's publishing its own decommissioning requirements first.

The official said that, given that it would take 2 years for a complete decommissioning program, abandonment of the Heather platform could take place before the end of 1999.

However, Unocal has hopes of prolonging the platform's useful life. The company was awarded an exploration license for Block 2/4 in 1995, in which lies the West Heather prospect. If this proves to be a commercial find, the Heather platform could be used to handle its output.

N.W. Hutton/Maureen

Amoco (U.K.) Ltd. is expected to stop producing from Northwest Hutton field in Block 211/27a around 1998. The company has not put forward an abandonment plan and has said only that it is working to extend production for as long as possible.

Phillips U.K. is operator of Maureen field on Block 16/29a, where the water is 96 m deep. The field produces through a steel platform and a short pipeline link to a tanker-loading column.

Phillips said the Maureen platform is unique since it was designed to be floated off its site for deployment in another field once Maureen has been depleted.

The platform's triangular gravity base, with three massive tanks, was the world's first steel platform to combine flotation, ballasting, and oil storage.

Two studies show the platform can be refloated, and it is said to have enough working life remaining to be reused on its own or as part of a larger development scheme.

Maureen platform's three storage tanks can each hold 220,000 bbl of oil. Topsides were designed for 80,000 b/d production, though output peaked at 102,000 b/d in 1984, a year after first oil.

In late 1996, production was about 9,000 b/d of oil, and the field will become uneconomic when production falls to 5,000 b/d. This is expected before 2000.

The platform's current certificate of fitness expires in September 1998, but Phillips reckons there is plenty of useful life yet in the Maureen platform.

David Brown, Phillips' exploitation and development manager, said: "The lowest remaining fatigue life for any structural member is still in excess of 25 years. All major structural members have a life in excess of 35 years."

Phillips has recently completed studies which confirm the platform can be safely removed from the seabed. To refloat the platform, water would first be pumped from the topsides to the undersides of the storage tank skirts through existing pipes to loosen the skirts' hold in the seabed.

Then air would be blown into the storage tanks to give buoyancy: "There would be no surge, and stress levels generated during the refloat can be maintained at acceptable levels, with the deck in place."

Brown said Maureen could serve as a host platform for satellite developments or subsea wells, be bridge-linked to a gas processing platform, or be split to become a storage unit and topsides for another jacket.

"The most suitable option," said Brown, "would be to continue to use the existing process and facilities without further modifications. In this mode the platform could continue to work as a drilling, production, quarters, and storage facility."

The company has no developments under way which could utilize the platform, though it is considering using it as a means of paying to farm-in to another operator's license.

Meanwhile, Phillips has begun touting the platform to oil producers worldwide. In case a buyer cannot be found, the company also invited tenders from contractors for onshore disposal and recycling.

"The main limitation on reuse is water depth," said Brown. "For the North Sea the range is 90-98 m of water. This can be increased to 125 m through the use of concrete plinths, gravel islands, or new leg sections.

"Outside the North Sea, where wave heights are not so severe, the platform could be used in even deeper water."

Issues unresolved

While Norway's government appears to be against dumping of platforms though not ruling it out in theory, the U.K. government continues to support inclusion of dumping as a valid option.

In the 1996 Energy Report, an annual DTI review of the entire U.K. energy industry, the ministry hinted it may make life difficult for Shell Expro as it seeks approval for a new disposal plan for Brent Spar:

"The government will consider any suggestions put forward by Shell, but any new proposals will need to address those issues which had originally led to the conclusion that deep-sea disposal was the best option."

Following the media hammering the U.K. oil industry took after the Brent Spar fight, U.K. Offshore Operators Association appointed a public relations consultancy to publicize its plea for a scientific approach to abandonment rather than an emotional response as demonstrated by the Brent Spar antidumping campaign.

Paul Horsman, head of Greenpeace's international oil campaign, said: "It is disappointing to see that the industry's response in the U.K. has been simply to see the issue as a PR battle, and all they have to do is convince the public by more glossy leaflets and adverts.

"This is not the response we want to see. It is negative and looks backwards and not forwards. The challenge to industry is to accept the situation that dumping redundant installations at sea is not acceptable and to start to work to find the best solutions with us. We do not mind cheap solutions as long as the environment is protected."

Rick Le Coyte, of Greenpeace's U.K. oil campaign, said that since Brent Spar no company has gone further than timidly suggesting that disposal of platforms jackets at sea is a preferred option.

"We will continue to campaign against dumping at sea of any industrial waste," said Le Coyte, "and that includes oil and gas installations."

Meanwhile, U.K. operators were left to wait on DTI guidelines for platform abandonment. A DTI official said that since draft guidelines were published in 1995 "other things have had to be considered."

The official said there had been lots of input on many topics, including the Brent Spar experience, and guidelines are taking longer than expected.

In May 1996, Eggar, the former industry and energy minister, announced publication of a report on abandonment he had commissioned from the Natural Environment Research Council.

"I welcome the conclusion of the report," said Eggar, "that the global impacts on the environment and on human health of the sea disposal of a structure such as the Brent Spar would be very small, roughly equivalent to the impacts associated with the wreckage of a fairly large ship."

Given the U.K.'s success with handling the grounding of the Sea Empress tanker in South Wales in February 1996 — bungled salvage attempts and inadequate rescue services turned a potentially minor incident into Britain's biggest ever oil spill — these were not viewed as words of comfort.

After Greenpeace's mauling of Shell/Esso in 1995, the oil industry was surpised when the campaign group lent its support to 22 of the 30 disposal options currently under review.

At a Greenpeace conference in September, Chris Rose, the group's communications and programs director, said it objected in principle to only one of the proposals.

Greenpeace said it could not back the suggestion by dredging contractor Jan de Nul to bury the main body of the derelict structure in a seabed trench. Another seven suggestions were said to be lacking in detail or likely to cause other problems and so could not be supported by Greenpeace. These were proposals by Wood-GMC, Aker, AMEC, Brown & Root, UMOE Haugesund, Land & Marine Engineering, and Taylor Woodrow.

Rose said Shell/Esso's options showed there is no engineering obstacle to bringing oil installations onshore for recycling.

Jetting out a mud plug is often required before explosives can be run down the piles of offshore structures. Seen here is Unocal's High Island A-341 jacket, toppled in place in 239 ft of water. Photo courtesy of Unocal Corp.

"Based on Shell's options," said Rose, "it seems clear that the spar is heading back to land. The signs are that Shell is now following the logic of environmental responsibility and public opinion. Governments should rule out all dumping as an option."

Rose said Greenpeace plans to contact all the contractors on Shell's list to encourage them to propose onshore handling of 70 U.K. North Sea facilities expected to be decommissioned in the next 10 years.

Wood Mackenzie Consultants Ltd., Edinburgh, has calculated that U.K. offshore operators will have to spend a total £8.7 billion ($13 billion) to decommission fields currently in production, under development, and expected to be developed.

The analyst sees the peak period for U.K. abandonment activity as 2007-18, when most U.K. fields will be decommissioned. Shell U.K. Ltd. was said to be the operator facing the biggest abandonment bill, amounting to £1.2 billion ($1.8 billion) in 1996 terms. However, a significant amount of this will be clawed back in tax relief.

Shell, Esso, and BP Exploration Operating Co. Ltd. together account for 40% of total U.K. abandonment costs, said Wood Mackenzie.

"Although more than 20 facilities have been decommissioned to date, we can expect a further 14 fields to cease production before the year 2000. Of these, seven will be subsea developments, three platforms, three floaters, and one an extended reach well development."

Gulf of Mexico

As oil and gas fields deplete in the Gulf of Mexico, operating companies face the prospect of spending $1.4-3.3 billion to decommission and remove offshore production facilities. As shown in Fig. 1, costs depend on the method used. These estimates do not include the platforms still being installed

Since 1988, about 100 structures/year have been decommissioned in the Gulf of Mexico, with a high of 181 in 1993 (Fig. 2).

According to U.S. Minerals Management Service (MMS) records, during 1973-95 operators removed 1,363 platforms.

About 3,800 structures remain on the Outer Continental Shelf (OCS) of the Gulf of Mexico. Another 900-1,000 structures lie in shallow, state-controlled waters not included in MMS statistics.

OCS structures vary from simple shallow-water caissons to Shell Offshore Inc.'s Mars tension-leg platform, installed in 2,945 ft of water. The conventional fixed platform installed in the deepest water, 1,350 ft, is Shell's Bullwinkle.

PLATFORM ABANDONMENT

MMS requires operators to remove structures within 1 year of termination of a lease.

Future production

The steady clip of platform scrapping does not mean that Gulf of Mexico production will decline substantially in the near future. Expectations are that new plays, such as subsalt and deepwater, will continue to boost production.

Shell estimates that by 2000 its deepwater projects alone will produce over 600,000 b/d of oil equivalent.

The Gulf of Mexico OCS currently produces about 900,000 b/d of oil and condensate and 13 bcfd of gas.

In the 743 active fields in federal waters at the beginning of 1995, MMS estimates proved reserves remaining were 2.52 billion bbl of crude and condensate and 29.3 tcf of gas. Originally, the estimated recoverable reserves in 876 fields were 11.86 billion bbl and 141.9 tcf. Of those fields, 133 have been depleted and abandoned.

Decommissioning process

Requirements for protecting the environment and fisheries complicate platform decommissioning and removal. Typical work encompasses:

- Debris survey.
- Diving.
- Pipeline removal.
- Well plugging and abandonment.
- Severing piles and conductors.
- Decommissioning facilities.
- Platform removal.
- Trawling for debris.
- Sales of salvaged material.
- Disposal of structures as artificial reefs.
- Obtaining appropriate permits and submitting required reports.
- Having on board a National Marine Fisheries (NMFS) observer.

Severing structures

One controversy surrounding fixed structure removal involves explosives for severing piles. Currently, explosives are used in two thirds of the removals. But for structures in more than 150 ft of water, this share jumps to 90-95%.

Mechanical cutters work but are said to be troublesome. Failures are a problem. Blades dull, and it is difficult to return to a previous cut. Diver safety is another major consideration in using mechanical cutters or torches.

In 1994 the U.S. General Accounting Office published a report concluding that MMS regulations were discouraging nonexplosive methods that would be less destructive on fish populations.

In response, MMS requested that the National Research Council (NRC) study the problem. In 1996, NRC's Marine Board concluded that for most Gulf of Mexico platform removal explosives are both more economical and safer than other currently available methods for severing fixed structures.

Some conclusions in the Marine Board report are as follows:

- The NMFS observer program seems to have worked well. No marine mammals and only one turtle have been injured since the program started. The report did recommend that the predetonation observation period be shortened to 24 hr from 48 hr.
- Concern over the effects of explosives on fish appears to have grown because almost all fish resident during platform removal with explosives are killed. But no evidence exists that this kill significantly impacts total fish populations. Study continues.
- The 50 lb/charge and eight-detonation limit stipulations are weaknesses in MMS's permits. Because explosives are inexpensive, the 50-lb charge is often the minimum as well as a maximum. The eight-explosion limit may also increase fish kill if the removal requires more than eight explosions. Fish may return to the site after the initial explosion.
- The private sector is developing nonexplosive techniques, but one obstacle is MMS's requirement that platforms be severed a least 15 ft below the mudline. The report recommends that this be raised to 3 ft below the mudline.

New nonexplosive techniques include laser cutting, pyrotechnic cutting, cryogenics, chemical cutters, cutting with remotely operated vehicles, bubble curtains to attenuate the blast pressure, acoustic devices to keep fish away from platforms, and incorporating in the original platform design ways to make it easier to remove the structure.

Fig. 1

Removal cost of 3,093 existing platforms

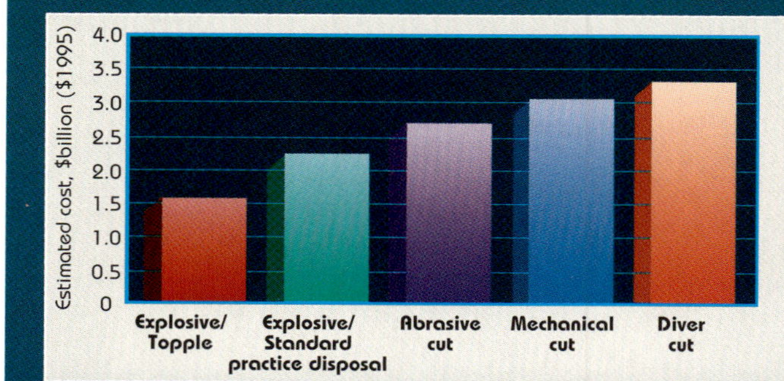

Source: Pulsipher, et al. IPE

Fig. 2

Platform installation and removal

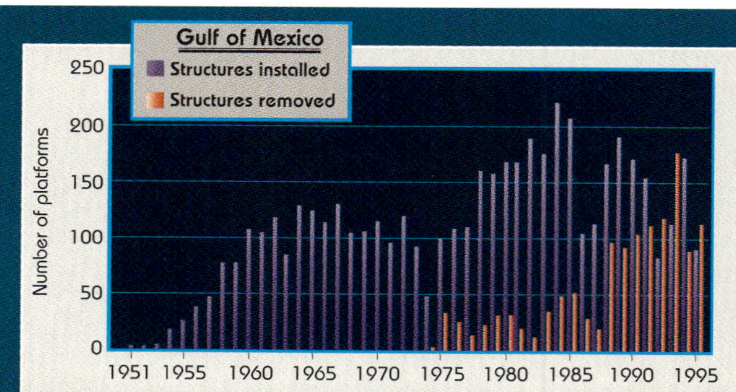

Source: U.S. Minerals Management Service IPE

Fig. 3

Artificial reef sites off Texas

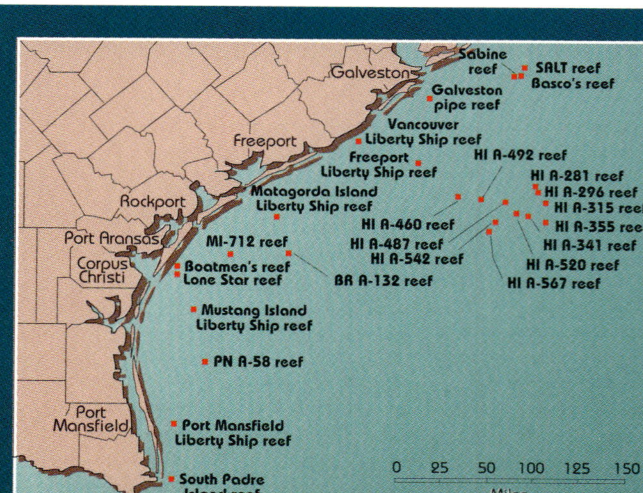

Source: Texas Parks & Wildlife Department IPE

Rigs-to-reefs sites off Louisiana

Fig. 4

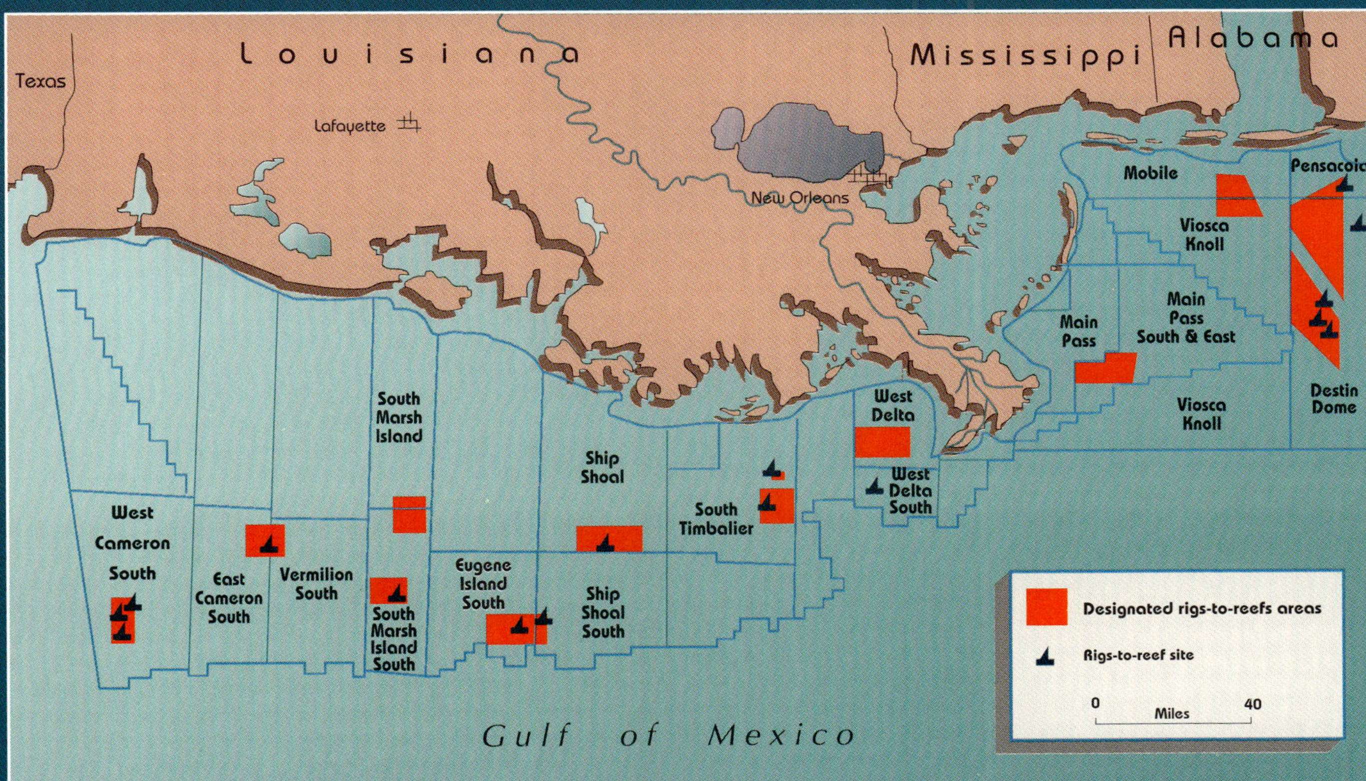

Source: U.S. Minerals Managment Service

IPE

Structure disposal

Once a fixed structure is severed it can be taken to shore for scrapping or refurbishment. But with appropriate permits and economics, the structure also can be toppled in place or disposed of at another location to form an artificial reef.

Unlike the controversial proposal for ocean disposal of Shell's Brent Spar in the North Sea, Gulf of Mexico structures have not been used for oil storage and, therefore, can be regarded as clean. Most environmentalists, government agencies, and fisherman support disposal of platforms to form artificial reefs.

Smaller structures are not appropriate for reefs. One breakdown shows that as deeper-water structures are removed, a greater percentage of them are being included in the rigs-to-reefs programs, as follows:

- In less than 20 ft of water, none of the 168 removed structures were converted to reefs.
- In 20-100 ft of water, 7 of 753 removed platforms formed reefs.
- In 100-200 ft of water, 63 of 152 removed platforms formed reefs.
- In 200-400 ft of water, 32 of 38 removed platforms formed reefs.

No structures have been removed in over 400 ft of water.

The industry hopes that more reef sites are created so that platforms will not have to be transported long distances for disposal.

The most active rigs-to-reefs programs are offshore Texas and Louisiana.

Texas reefs

Fig. 3 shows the artificial reefs off Texas. The first reefs in the 1960-80s were concrete pipes, barges, and World War II Liberty ships.

The first platform offshore Texas converted to an artificial reef was Transco Corp.'s four-pile structure at High Island A-492 in 195 ft of water. Transco signed the deed of donation on Jan. 1, 1990.

Since then, through March 1996, 36 structures have been donated, and Texas has received $3.8 million in contributions for maintenance.

Two recent platforms made into reefs, Union Pacific Resources Co. North Padre Island A-58 four-pile jacket in 252 ft of water, and Oxy USA Inc.'s High Island A-355 eight-pile jacket in 305 ft of water, had only the top portion of the jacket severed. The remaining structure was left intact.

Union Pacific's platform was cut at –86 ft and Oxy's at –91 ft. The tops from both platforms will be refurbished and reused.

For deeper-water structures, the flexibility of partial removal can significantly reduce decommissioning costs. The Marine Board report on decommissioning does point out that shrimpers are prime opponents of partial removals in water shallower than 300 ft. Shrimpers fear a decrease in trawlable waters.

Louisiana program

In Louisiana, nine main sites for reef disposal have been created (Fig. 4). These sites cover about a three by six block area. Some already have six to eight decommissioned structures, and all except two have at least one structure.

From the program's beginning in 1986 until March 1996, 58 structures had been added to the rigs-to-reef program.

Industry had contributed about $7 million to the maintenance program, which is a model for other states.

In this program the operator donates to the state 50% of the costs saved by converting the platform structure to a reef. The money is then used for long-term reef maintenance such as expenses for marker buoys and monitoring.

The state assumes all liabilities for the reef. IPE

The Sedco Explorer semisubmersible and Dicto tanker conduct a long term test of Clair field for BP Exploration.

U.K. operators work to open up new West of Shetland play

An exciting offshore play has opened to the west of the Shetland Islands off northern Scotland, and U.K. operators pushed hard in 1996 to start commercial oil production from the region early in 1997.

West of Shetland offshore work has presented major challenges. Most obviously, sea and weather conditions are even more hostile than in the North Sea so all work has to be achieved within a summer weather window.

Also, the seabed slopes rapidly downwards with distance from the islands westwards towards the Atlantic Ocean, so the West of Shetland area is in most parts a deepwater play.

The geology of the region is also a major challenge. The West of Shetland area contains the U.K.'s largest find in terms of oil in place: the 1977 Clair discovery by operator BP Exploration Operating Co.

Clair has estimated oil in place of more than 4 billion bbl. Yet the find has remained undeveloped because BP and other license partners were not until 1996 able to produce oil consistently enough during well testing to justify production.

Discovery of Clair led operators to think there might be more oil to be found west of the Shetlands, but it was not until 1993 that news of a major discovery, again by BP, sparked exploration fever among U.K. companies.

BP followed this find by another of almost identical size, and further discoveries by Amerada Hess Ltd. led to growing optimism about a potentially massive play.

Since 1993 West of Shetland exploration activity has been running high, with Shell U.K. Ltd, BP, Conoco (U.K.) Ltd., Kerr-McGee Oil (U.K.) plc, Esso Exploration & Production U.K. Ltd., and Total Oil Marine plc among companies drilling recent wells.

However, none of the companies have disclosed well results recently, and all wells west of the Shetlands have been declared tight holes for some time. This has led to speculation that the West of Shetland play may already be played out.

Early exploration

West of Shetland acreage was first licensed in the U.K.'s third offshore round of 1970, and first licenses covering the West of Shetland basin area were granted in the sixth offshore round of 1978-79.

Esso spudded the first West of Shetland wildcat in 1972, on Block 206/12. Since then Smith Rea Energy Analysts Ltd., Canterbury, U.K., reckoned more than 20 operators have drilled there, with BP and Shell accounting for more than half of the wells.

Tom Fyfe, deputy asset manager in BP's Atlantic Margin program, said that by the end of 1995 a total of 133 wells had been drilled West of Shetland: 93 exploration and 40 appraisal wells. Exploration in the area had by then cost more than $2 billion in total.

Clair field was the region's first big strike, made in 460 ft of water. It was followed in 1977 by a noncommercial gas discovery by Elf Exploration U.K. plc on Block 206/11 and discovery by Texaco Britain Ltd. of Victory on Block 207/1, with estimated reserves of 300 bcf of gas.

During 1984-86 four noncommercial gas discoveries were made: by BP on Block 205/10; by British Gas plc on Block 214/30; by Chevron U.K. Ltd. on Block 214/27; and by Shell on Block 206/1.

Amerada Hess made a Block 205/26a discovery in October 1990, later named Stronsay and subsequently estimated to have oil reserves of 100-250 million bbl.

But it was a BP strike in October 1992, with its 204/24a-2 well, which hit the headlines and put back into U.K. exploration the excitement which had been missing since the early 1980s.

Exploration fever

This find was named Foinaven. At the end of testing of an appraisal well in March 1993, it was announced to have estimated reserves of 250-500 million bbl of oil—the largest U.K. discovery since Amerada found Scott on Block 15/21 in January 1984.

The Ocean Alliance semisubmersible, working in 1,600 ft of water, drilled and tested this second well into the Foinaven structure. An earlier well, 204/24a-1, was drilled in 1990 and cut a thin oil and gas column but was not tested.

John Browne, chief executive of BP, said at the time: "This discovery has the potential to open a significant new play in the West of Shetland province, although there is substantial work to be done to evaluate its size."

As the U.K. oil industry looked with new eyes at West of Shetland potential, speculation began to mount over another BP well, the 204/20-1 well drilled by the Ocean Valiant semisubmersible in 1,300 ft of water, and completed in late October 1993.

In early February 1994 BP completed well testing and disclosed that it had made another discovery with estimated reserves of 250-500 million bbl of oil. This find was named Schiehallion.

Later in 1994 Amerada Hess confirmed that the Schiehallion discovery extends into a block it operates. Amerada's 205/25a-2 well was said in October 1994 to have flowed hydrocarbons from several horizons.

Drilled by Sonat's Arcade Frontier semisubmersible in 1,140 ft of water, the well flowed a maximum 5,300 b/d of 27º gravity oil, with a GOR of 320:1.

By this time Amerada had also decided its Stronsay find, some 30 km south of Schiehallion in only 410 ft of water, is two separate structures in different formations.

These were named as Solan for the Jurassic reservoir and Strathmore for the Triassic. Amerada tentatively estimated combined reserves at 100-250 million bbl of oil and slated further appraisal drilling.

A wellhead takes shape for one of the 22 subsea wells to be drilled from two drill centers during development of BP Exploration's Foinaven field.

Disappointments

In August 1995 Mackay Consultants of Inverness, Scotland, reported that Amerada Hess had returned disappointing results from further appraisal drilling in Solan and Strathmore.

"We understand the Strathmore appraisal 204/30a-3 was abandoned untested," said Mackay, "having intercepted only poor quality oil shows. In May, Amerada Hess abandoned the Solan appraisal 205/26a-26 as a dry hole."

Amerada Hess did not disclose well results and did not comment on the report other than to say that they showed the Solan and Strathmore reservoirs are complex.

In mid-1994 Smith Rea said that, disregarding oil and gas shows, there have been 10 oil or gas discoveries west of the Shetlands, of which five are considered significant.

At that time, 37 of the region's wells remained tight holes, and that total has been growing rapidly, though there has been nothing in the way of discovery announcements since then.

In November 1996 Ian Blood, Conoco's head of exploration in U.K., reportedly said the West of Shetland province has not lived up to expectations.

Blood was quoted as saying: "Obviously the lack of any follow-up success, since BP's Foinaven and Schiehallion finds, has been a disappointment."

The report said Blood believed it was still early for the West of Shetland province, with work on huge frontier tranches of acreage only beginning: "I still expect to see a lot of healthy activity in the region in the coming years."

While exploration teams scratch their heads, however, BP has been working to bring Foinaven and Schiehallion discoveries into production, using development concepts which increasingly appear to be typical for remote, deepwater finds.

Foinaven development

In July 1994 BP pushed the button to begin development of the Foinaven discovery, with a production, storage, and offloading (FPSO) ship linked to two clusters of subsea wells, and export by two shuttle tankers. Production start-up originally was slated for late 1995 or early 1996.

BP let contract to a combine of McDermott International Inc. and Golar-Nor Offshore AS to convert the Anadyr support vessel to a floater with capacity to produce 80,000 b/d of oil, to store 300,000 bbl of oil, and to inject 120 MMcfd of gas and 165,000 b/d of water.

In October 1994 BP shipped to its Rotterdam refinery the first cargo of oil produced west of the Shetlands. This followed an extended well test by the Ocean Guardian semisubmersible rig, linked to the Vigdis Knutsen tanker.

BP said the test ran from Aug. 15 to Sept. 29, with the Foinaven 204/24a-4 well flowing up to 20,000 b/d of 26º gravity oil at an average rate of 17,800 b/d. The total shipment amounted to 437,000 bbl of oil.

During 1996, however, it became apparent that BP had run into problems with Foinaven. A fault with one of two subsea manifolds was discovered during offshore testing, and there was an earlier strike at the Astano yard in Spain, where the Petrojarl Foinaven production/storage ship was built.

These problems forced BP to put back its expected start-up date for Foinaven to spring 1997, because the 1996 weather window for offshore commissioning was missed.

The Ocean Guardian semisubmersible conducted an extended well test of Foinaven field for BP Exploration.

BP had installed the first of two manifolds on the seabed, but this had to be recovered for examination, after cracks appeared on hubs during leak testing in May.

A team of experts established that the cracks were caused by a combination of overall stresses in the hub connections, and hydrogen embrittlement induced by the cathodic protection system.

The problem was said to have been overcome by reducing stress levels in the metal and local shielding of the cathodic protection system. Meanwhile, BP set out to install the second manifold in place of the first.

Dave Brookes, subsea manager on Foinaven, said: "We are now satisfied that the hub stress levels are such that there will be no repetition of cracking. As a precaution, everything will be hydro-tested over an extended period, and we are confident that the system is now fit for full field life."

BP estimated that the manifold problem set back subsea work by 3 months, enough to delay first production until 1997.

Meanwhile, flexible risers and umbilicals were installed in another part of the field, and the flexible connectors removed for examination were relaid by the Iolair and Semi 1 construction vessels.

The Petrojarl Foinaven sailed to the field in late 1996 after completing sea trials. The ship started pulling risers as soon as it was anchored.

Schiehallion development

In August 1995 BP reported healthy results from an extended test of the 204/20-5 appraisal well in Schiehallion field. The test was performed by the Henry Goodrich semisubmersible producing into the Savonita tanker.

The well flowed up to 20,000 b/d of 26º gravity oil at an average stabilized rate of 18,000 b/d. A total of 714,000 bbl of oil was produced and shipped, as with Foinaven, to BP's Rotterdam refinery.

In April 1996 BP received DTI approval for development of the Schiehallion discovery and the nearby Loyal find. Like Foinaven, Schiehallion development involves an FPSO, but this time BP will own and operate the vessel.

When government sanctioned Schiehallion development, BP had already begun work on a £900 million ($1.35 billion) project involving an FPSO producing from 29 seabed wells completed in four clusters.

Schiehallion and Loyal lie in 375 m of water on U.K. Block 204/20 and have estimated reserves of 340 million bbl of oil and 85 million bbl of oil, respectively.

As is increasingly common with the current trend for fast-track developments, BP let the first of a long series of contracts more than 9 months before the DTI's approval of the project.

In June 1995 the operator let contract to Atlantic Frontier Alliance, comprising Brown & Root Ltd. of Aberdeen, Single Buoy Moorings Inc. of Marly in Switzerland, and Harland & Wolff Ltd. of Belfast, to design and build the ship.

Announcing the approval, then Minister for Industry & Energy Tim Eggar said the Schiehallion ship will be the world's largest newbuild FPSO vessel, with a hull volume of 279,000 cu m.

"Not only will the vessel have a storage capacity of nearly a million bbl of oil, and the ability to process around 140,000 b/d of oil," said Eggar, "it will have been constructed in the shortest ever time for such a vessel."

Schiehallion is expected to begin production in early 1998.

Clair tests

Despite all the drilling and testing to date in Clair, the complexity of the reservoir has meant that BP has been able to quote oil reserves of only 100-300 million bbl out of more than 4 million bbl in place.

But after almost 10 years if head-scratching, it appears BP

has finally cracked the code for Clair, and the proof came with an extended well test carried out during late summer of 1996.

In May 1996 BP announced preparations for an extended well test in the Clair oil discovery, in a bid to prove commerciality of this large but complex reservoir.

Clair lies on Blocks 206/7a, 206/8, 206/9, 206/12, and 206/13, where water depth is up to 150 m. Since its discovery in 1977 ten appraisal wells had been drilled, but none has flowed sufficiently to deem Clair viable.

A BP official said in May 1996 that the Sedco Explorer semisubmersible was anchoring in the field and was expected to re-enter an earlier well for ambitious testing.

If the test was successful, BP was expecting to look at development options for Clair, particularly at a floater as in Foinaven and Schiehallion developments, and perhaps a platform long term.

The well to be re-entered was 206/8-10, a high angle well drilled into the core of the reservoir in 1995. Extended well testing was planned to take place in 1995, but the well was suspended without testing.

A strike at the Astano yard in Spain during construction of the Petrojarl Foinaven FPSO was one of the factors delaying production start at Foinaven field.

BP said delays and deteriorating weather caused the well to be suspended without testing, before the onset of winter. In 1996 BP set out to resume work with a 45 day extended well test.

"The objective of this test," said BP, "will be to try and produce some 15,000 b/d and maintain this over an extended period.

"If such production can be maintained, the partners may decide to extend the test beyond 45 days and attempt to produce up to 2 million bbl from the reservoir, equivalent to three tanker cargoes."

The best flow rate from Clair to date was then a maximum of 7,300 b/d with the 206/8-9z well drilled in 1992. A second well that year, aimed at demonstrating repeatability, flowed at only 2,545 b/d maximum.

The BP official said that, since these earlier tests, analysis of 3D seismic data from Clair has enabled geologists to map fractures in the reservoir.

They had worked out which fractures can act as conduits to boost oil flow and which can restrict flow. This information was used to plot the course of the 206/8-10 well.

"If the 1996 work program is a success," said BP, "the partners may decide to bring forward some form of early production scheme before the end of the century.

"Although no decisions have been taken, an early production system would help to ensure that all the commercial and geological risks are fully understood before plans for more permanent development are considered."

In October 1996 BP completed its extended well test in Clair with results as anticipated. Arthur Andersen & Co., London, reported that the well flowed at more than 15,000 b/d, though BP did not confirm this officially. Produced oil was offloaded into a shuttle tanker for marketing in Europe.

A BP official said that Clair's core area, the site of this well, had always flowed best, but that any further appraisal would need to check out the more difficult areas of the reservoir.

License partners were expected to meet within the following few weeks to agree on a program for further work in Clair. The official said an early production scheme, as being developed in nearby Foinaven and Schiehallion fields, was thought unlikely at the moment.

The partners were expected to limit their considerations to further appraisal wells or an extended well test in the reservoir's flank area, with appraisal drilling in 1997 thought to be the most likely outcome.

Clair license partners are: operator BP 25.77%, Amoco (U.K.) Ltd. 3.34%, Chevron U.K. Ltd. 22.65%, Conoco (U.K.) Ltd. 11.68%, Elf Caledonia Ltd. 7.18%, Enterprise Oil plc 14.38%, and Esso Exploration & Production U.K. Ltd. 15%.

Future developments

Amerada has looked into development of Solan and Strathmore jointly with second phase development work in Schiehallion. However, the disappointing test results, and the fact that the finds have joined Clair in the "complex" category, have made the company's plans tentative.

In August 1996 Phillips Petroleum Co. U.K. Ltd. completed a study of West of Shetland development options using spar platforms, even though it has no acreage in the region.

A Phillips official said the company is intending to bid aggressively for West of Shetland acreage to be offered in 1997 in U.K.'s 17th offshore licensing round.

Phillips commissioned a study by McDermott Marine Construction Ltd. into development options for various imaginary discoveries west of the Shetlands, in water up to 5,300 ft deep.

McDermott said it looked into development of fields with production rates of 40,000-150,000 b/d of oil and 130-1,220 MMcfd of gas.

It investigated exports by pipeline and also alternatives for gas conversion into liquids for export by shuttle tanker.

McDermott concluded that the spar platform concept would be the most cost-effective way to support envisaged riser systems and production facilities.

Smith Rea has said West of Shetland production could build to 500,000 b/d of oil from as many as seven fields by 2005, by which time the area could be contributing one third of U.K.'s total oil output.

The analyst said: "Phased development, beginning with early production, and perhaps extended well tests, will probably give way to area development schemes culminating in the construction of a fixed infrastructure." IPE

The 95,000 dwt M/T Patriot, Conoco Inc.'s first double-hull tanker, unloads a cargo of Venezuelan crude at Conoco's Clifton Ridge terminal at the Port of Lake Charles, La.

Rising oil demand brightens outlook for tanker market

Rising oil demand, an aging tanker fleet, and concerns over safety and the environment will drive new vessel construction between 1997 and the end of this century.

Because of their size and economies of scale, very large crude carriers (VLCCs), or tankers larger than 200,000 dwt, are expected to maintain their dominance of long-haul international trade routes. This stems from increasing oil demand and strong world economic growth, notably in Southeast Asia (Table 1).

Scrapping, meanwhile, will make room for newbuilding, with about 57% of the 1994 VLCC fleet expected to be scrapped by 2003.

Those were some of the predictions contained in an Oil & Gas Journal article at the start of 1996 based on data supplied by Drewry Shipbuilding Consultants Ltd., London. Drewry pointed to a changing, but positive, tanker scene: "The environment of shipping is changing. It is an opportunity for innovative companies to set the course and prosper by investing in quality," Drewry said.

The firm said rising oil demand, coupled with environmental and safety standards, will be major influences on tanker building for the next 10 years. The driving force behind increased environmental and safety awareness was passage of the U.S. Oil Pollution Act of 1990 (OPA90), whose double-hull and stiff liability provisions started having an impact on tanker construction and operation during the mid-1990s.

OPA90 mandated that aged tankers and those of single-hull construction be phased out of U.S. trades. The maximum allowed age, 28 years, for single-hull tankers trading to the U.S. will be reduced by 1 year annually through 2000, when the maximum allowed age will be 23 years.

And by 2010, no single-hull tankers larger than 30,000 dwt will be allowed to trade in U.S. waters. However, there are two exceptions that will be in force until 2015: vessels using the Louisiana Offshore Oil Port (LOOP) and those that lighter more than 60 miles offshore.

During 1996, according to Clarkson Research Studies, London, the total number of double-hulled VLCCs grew gradually, increasing to 46 at the beginning of September 1996 from 34 at the end of 1995. The total deadweight tonnage represents nearly 11% of the total VLCC fleet, or 13.5 million dwt.

In addition, OPA90 requires that all U.S. trade vessels must prove they can meet the cost of cleanup in case of an oil spill. Certificates of Financial Responsibility (COFRs) are required in the form of bank guarantees.

OPA90 has a complicated requirement covering minimum vessel liability. Specifically, language in the act stipulates "the greater of": $1,200/gross ton or $10 million for vessels more than 3,000 gross tons; or $2 million for vessels 3,000 gross tons or less. As a result, liability for VLCCs and ULCCs can easily total in the hundreds of millions of dollars.

Additional pressure on the aging fleet comes from the International Maritime Organization (IMO), whose rules will phase out single-hull tankers in international waters at age 25. IMO rules also require double hulls or equivalent designs for newbuilding. And, in 1997, a new IMO Convention on Standards of Training, Certification, and Watchkeeping is scheduled to be implemented, updating the 1978 convention.

As a result of OPA90 and IMO regulations, the rate of scrapping of older tankers is expected to increase markedly.

In Drewry's comprehensive shipping report, "The Tanker Market - Supply, Demand, and Prospects for Recovery, 1995-2000," the consulting firm said the world's tanker fleet will be affected by the following factors:

In spite of short- and medium-haul imports, accounting for much of the incremental growth in oil demand in 1994 (plus 1995 and 1996 forecast growth), increases in supplies from the OPEC countries will maintain their share of the global market (Fig. 3).

The age profile of the fleet means that substantial fleet renewal will be required toward the end of the decade, as increasing numbers of VLCCs are demolished for both technical and economic reasons.

Surplus tonnage in the tanker market will be concentrated in the VLCC and Suezmax sectors, but technical and economic factors mean that the surplus should be eradicated by 2000.

Given the lack of speculative newbuilding orders, a cyclical peak in freight rates is projected for 1999, while rates for VLCC and Suezmax tankers are likely to fall short of the level needed to encourage speculative rather than commercial newbuilding.

VLCCs, ULCCs

Demand for VLCCs and ULCCs will be driven by crude oil exports from the Middle East, primarily on destinations east of Suez, according to Drewry.

"The emphasis on incremental crude supplies in the medium term remains with the Middle Eastern producers and, as such, will provide slow but steady demand growth for VL/ULCC tonnage.

"In the near term, the existing overhang of scheduled deliveries will quickly dissipate, and by 1997 the continued demolition of tonnage for technical/economic reasons will likely bring the market quickly back into balance," Drewry said.

The VLCC fleet is aging, but many VLCCs built in the 1970s continue to trade. In general, the vessels can be expected to go to demolition at the age of 20, and Drewry forecast a supply-demand balance point will be reached around 1998-99, when time charter-equivalent earnings could reach $30,000/day.

Regarding demolition, Drewry said technical factors, including fuel inefficiency and capacity constraints, are being aided by the economics of upgrading these vessels to pass enhanced special survey requirements.

"Once again the issue is when, rather than if, the VLCC will reach a balanced point between supply and demand," Drewry said.

The health of the VLCC market's freight rates will rely on sustained scrappings, according to the report. Drewry predicted that freight rates would rise sharply, to a forecast level of $35,000/day in 1999 from a level of about $23,000/day in the first half of 1995. It based the prediction on market weakness in 1994 and a lack of speculative orders subsequently. After 1999, however, rates should ease slightly, Drewry added.

The forecast increase was based on 12 month time charters covering vessels built in the 1990s.

Drewry said that VLCCs get more than their share of attention in the trade press, overshadowing other areas of significance in the international tanker market, so "that it is often difficult to put the various segments of the market clearly into focus."

But, Drewry said, "The fundamental picture emerging in the tanker market is one of a contracting surplus of tonnage that seems certain to produce a cyclical peak in freight rates before the end of the decade."

Table 1

Forecast tanker demand by size category*

Year	10-45,000 dwt	45-90,000 dwt	90-175,000 dwt	175,000+ dwt	Total
	Million dwt				
1995	31.5	42.8	45.8	94.3	214.4
1996	31.7	43.3	46.4	98.5	218.9
1997	31.9	43.9	46.9	102.6	225.3
1998	32.1	44.5	47.4	106.7	230.7
1999	32.0	44.8	47.8	110.8	235.4
2000	32.0	45.1	48.0	114.8	239.9

*Excludes combined carriers.

Source: Drewry Shipping Consultants

Product tanker, 'niche' markets

The product tanker market remains favored, according to Drewry, and intraregional trade in Asia is set to be boosted by market deregulation and China's need for imports.

Drewry said other factors supporting predictions for the product tanker trade included environmental considerations in Europe and North America, which could limit debottlenecking and upgrades of existing units. And, Drewry said, "Substantial medium- and long-haul arbitrage movements of refined products should also remain a feature of the spot charter market."

Drewry said against this background limited growth is foreseen in the product tanker fleet in spite of attractive rates for newbuilding.

According to the consulting firm, "The niche Panamax tanker market could offer strong returns from spot charters." Saying that during the first half of 1995 there was a flurry of activity in this sector, Drewry pointed to Middle Eastern long-haul, clean-market movements overshadowing dirty trades in fuel oil and crude in draft-restricted Black Sea and Mediterranean ports.

It said the 50,000-80,000 dwt Panamax fleet is relatively young and has "a virtually nonexistent orderbook, with many recent additions being made from yards outside of South Korea and Japan."

Aframax, Suezmax outlook

As 1996 was drawing to a close, Oil & Gas Journal reported the latest predictions by the London consulting firm. Drewry forecast that VLCCs and the smaller 60,000-100,000 dwt Aframax class tankers would be the primary vessels plying international trades for the foreseeable future, while the Suezmax class tanker market would be squeezed.

That could result in more prevalent Suezmax usage in the restricted trades, in areas such as the Mediterranean, Black Sea, and Far East where premium-type vessels are not required. Some Suezmax vessels are used by a few major oil companies, however, in the North American trades to-from the U.S. West Coast, as well as on the East Coast of Canada.

Suezmax tankers — also known as "million-barrel tankers" — get their popular name from their ability to pass through the Suez Canal fully laden; a VLCC cannot pass through the canal with a full oil cargo. Suezmax tankers typically are 140,000-150,00 dwt.

Late in 1996, Drewry said VLCCs were eating into the markets traditionally held by the million barrel tankers, especially in the trades from West Africa to North America.

"Originally designed as a servant of the Middle East,"

Global bulk shipping markets

Fig. 1

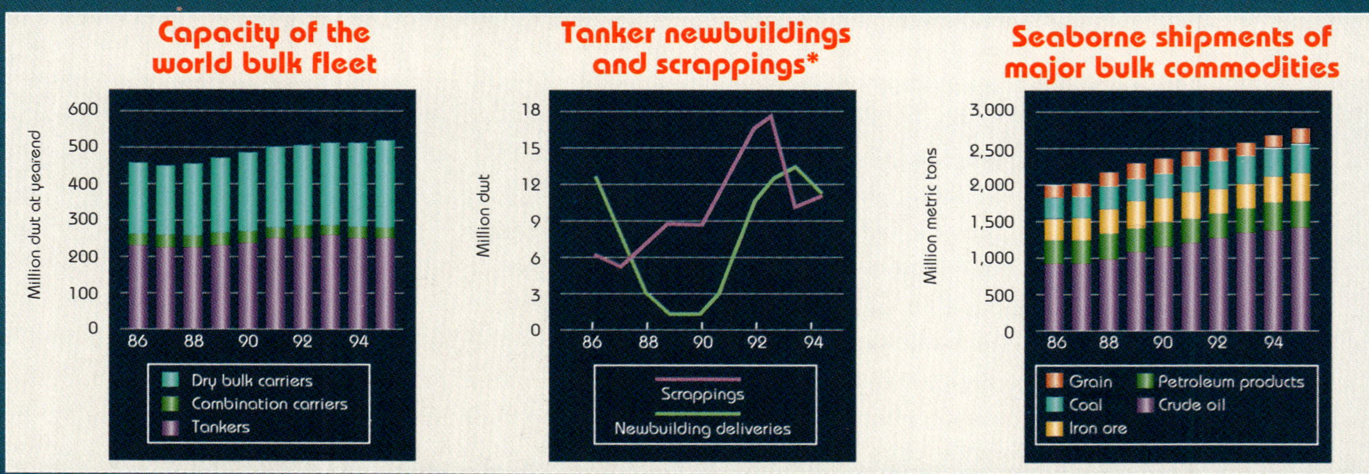

*Scrappings include losses.
Source: Overseas Shipholding Group Inc.

IPE

Drewry said, "it (the Suezmax class) failed to gain a significant market. The Suezmax tanker has neither the trading flexibility of an Aframax tanker nor the economies of scale of the VLCC, yet it is subject to compliance with OPA90 for much of its trade."

Drewry said many Suezmax vessels have been purchased by Greek independents that benefit from that class of tanker's price softness in the early 1990s. A total of 46% of the Suezmax tankers sold during 1990-95 were purchased by Greek shipping interests, and most tankers were 16-20 years old.

Drewry predicted a sustained period of evenly balanced demand and supply "should maintain a firm tone" in the Aframax market, and increasing exports of crude oil from the North Sea, Caribbean, and Black Sea should maintain and prolong the growth in demand for popular Aframax tonnage.

It pointed to the strength of time charter rates throughout 1994 and during the first 6 months of 1995 in making that assessment.

Specifically, in Caribbean vs. Mediterranean spot markets, the firm said, "there is an apparent distinction between modern vessels able to obtain premium rates in the Caribbean over more-aged vessels that are frequently found in the Mediterranean."

International market assessment

An analysis by the Overseas Shipholding Group Inc. (OSG), New York City, showed that as 1995 ended international tanker markets were continuing to operate under pressure, as trade increased and the world tanker fleet declined (Fig. 1).

OSG said the major oil companies continued reducing their tanker ownership because of increased environmental concerns and decreased control of oil supply sources. Majors' ownership in the world tanker fleet totaled 7% in 1995 compared with 20% in 1987, 2 years before the Exxon Valdez incident (Fig. 2).

Independents at yearend 1995 controlled about 73% of the world fleet vs. 58% in 1987; the average vessel age was 13 years.

Oil demand in the major importing regions of the world increased 2% in 1995, while oil demand in Asia rose by 8%, accounting for the majority of the demand growth in the major oil-importing regions of the world.

OSG noted that developing-Asia's share of world oil demand has been steadily increasing, reaching 16% in 1994 with further increases expected during 1996.

In 1995 as in 1994, OSG said, the average length of a voyage declined between oil-producing nations and oil-consuming nations. That reflected greater short-haul shipments from the North Sea and the Caribbean, OSG said, at the expense of long-haul Middle Eastern shipments (Fig. 3). This had the effect of decreasing tonnage requirements for tankers.

OSG predicted that, during the next few years, production from sources outside the Middle East will grow, which will increase short-haul shipments. A significant portion of the volumes likely would be exported via pipeline from the Mediterranean on short-haul routes. An added major factor would be resumption of Iraqi oil exports.

OSG said the highly versatile, shallow-draft Aframax tankers stand to gain the most benefit from increases in short-haul movements from the North Sea and the Caribbean, in part because of their ability to access many ports.

In 1995, OSG said, the world tanker fleet declined for the second consecutive year, falling a modest 1 million dwt to 261 million dwt by yearend. It said nearly all of the sales for scrap occurred during the first half of 1995, before stronger freight rates discouraged shipowners from selling older tonnage.

Most of the tonnage scrapped was in the VLCC segment, where 57% of the fleet was at least 15 years old. The advanced age of the VLCC fleet, combined with mandated deletions due to U.S. and international regulations, should keep scrapping levels relatively high in the coming years, according to OSG.

At yearend 1995, international tankers in layup fell to 3 million dwt, the lowest level since 1991.

Newbuilding prices stabilized in 1995, and prices for second-hand vessels firmed. The year also saw improvement in freight rates.

Newbuilding deliveries of about 11 million dwt were slightly greater than the previous year, while contracting for new ships fell to 7 million dwt from 12 million dwt in 1994. As a result, OSG said, "The newbuilding orderbook for delivery over the next 3 years declined 4 million dwt to 20 million dwt, its lowest yearend level since 1988."

Of the total, OSG said, 11 million dwt were scheduled for delivery during 1996.

In mid-1996, OSG reported international tanker market rates averaged above levels seen at the same period in 1995, reflecting a 3% increase in oil demand in the major oil-importing regions.

Newbuilding deliveries were down, and the size of the international tanker fleet from the end of March 1996 was 263 million dwt.

Clarkson's view

In its Autumn 1996 "Shipping Review & Outlook," Clarkson Research Studies said 1996 was proving to be a "fascinating year" for a variety of reasons.

Clarkson said contracting for tankers during the second and third quarters of 1996 "confirmed the upturn of the beginning of the year. By the end of August...7.6 million dwt of tankers had been ordered already, beating the 7.4 million dwt ordered in the whole of 1995 and an annualized 54% overall."

It said all tanker types except for Suezmaxes were witnessing an increased level of ordering, "indicating that the market may finally have bottomed out."

Among the principal findings in its half-yearly review, Clarkson reported:

Supply growth in the dry bulk market "is so far ahead of any reasonable demand forecast that the gap can only be closed by scrapping, which means low freight rates."

VLCC and Suezmax markets just held on to gains achieved during the previous 6 months of the year, averaging about $20,000/day, while rates for Aframax tankers fell by 6%, and clean products' rates fell by 12%.

The OECD economic outlook is improving, "so the next 12 months should be reasonably good for sea trade" with growth of about 2% expected in 1996 and 3% in 1997.

Clarkson said the tanker market outlook was becoming very positive.

"For once, supply is under control. The market must absorb 6.6 million tons of deliveries in 1997, but scrapping is running at 7.7 million tons/year, so the fleet should start to edge downwards. Better still, we expect the oil trade to grow by 3.7% in 1996 and 3.1% in 1997."

For crude tankers, Clarkson noted that short-haul production continued to increase during 1996, adding that "rising demand and tighter availability of modern tonnage...helped strengthen rates across the crude tanker size ranges. Over the last 6 months," the London firm said, "VLCC rates firmed 22%. Suezmax rates were 24% higher," and rates for Aframax tankers rose 11% from the same period the year before.

It reported that, at the beginning of September 1996, the 436 vessel VLCC fleet stood at 125.3 million dwt, 1% higher than in 1995, and the Aframax fleet also increased, expanding 1.5% to 41.8 million dwt. But the Suezmax fleet contracted by 1.3% vs. 1995

The VLCC orderbook continued to decline during 1996. In its 6 month report, Clarkson said at 6.1 million dwt, the orderbook "is now at its lowest level" since first quarter 1987 and only half of the 12.3 million dwt that were on order at the same time in 1995. Of the 6.1 million dwt total, 2.3 million dwt was scheduled for delivery during the remainder of 1996; 1.7 million dwt in 1997; and 2 million dwt in 1998.

According to the report, there was an annualized increase of 14% on newbuilding, with 29.9 million dwt of contracts placed during the first 8 months of the year.

U.S. deepwater port plans

Two deepwater port projects have been planned for some time on the Texas Gulf Coast, but one was on hold and the other was moving slowly in 1996.

On the Upper Texas Coast, Blue Dolphin Energy Co., Houston, planned a deepwater facility in about 120 ft of water about 45 miles off Freeport, Tex. The facility, called Petroport, would handle an initial 1.2 million b/d of imported crudes and crudes produced from the U.S. Outer Continental Shelf.

Blue Dolphin officials said the project will benefit from changes in the U.S. Deepwater Port Act signed into law late in 1996 by Pres. Clinton. The changes will allow Petroport, if it reaches fruition, to handle OCS crudes.

Backers say enactment of the new provisions gives the project added impetus as the company proceeded with plans late in 1996 to begin the application process and detailed engineering work.

Assuming the project moves ahead, Blue Dolphin officials

Fig. 2
Percentage of world tanker fleet ownership

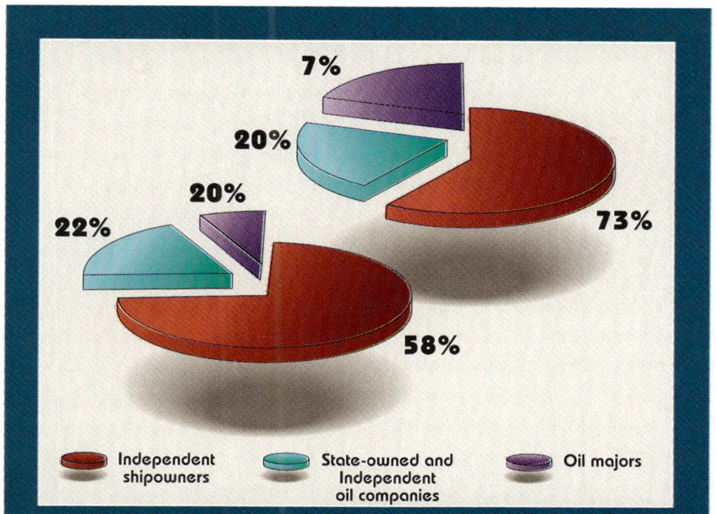

Source: Overseas Shipholding Group Inc.
IPE

foresee Petroport could be operational late in 2000. During 1996, officials completed an economic study on the project's viability, and results were being analyzed late in the year.

Cost of the project in current dollars totals $400-450 million, Blue Dolphin said.

On the Lower Texas Coast off Corpus Christi, a planned deepwater port known as Safeharbor was on hold late in 1996 while oil companies assessed their future needs. Officials completed a project study in midyear and solicited comments from oil companies on their projected crude-handling requirements in the next 5-10 years. The project was awaiting their responses at yearend.

The facility is planned in about 100 ft of water about 20 miles southeast of Corpus Christi. Optimally, crude could be offloaded through a single buoy, with an initial throughput of about 300,000 b/d to shore via a 42-in. pipeline. Maximum throughput with that offloading scheme could be increased to handle as much as 600,000 b/d, however, officials said.

When the $100-125 million (current dollars) project was first proposed, planning was based on offloading 150,000-300,000 dwt tankers carrying long-haul shipments of imported crudes. Now, with a changing mix of crude and crude supplies and the outlook for more short-haul traffic from Latin America and the Caribbean in 150,000-200,000 dwt vessels, dynamics of the project have changed.

LOOP

Although it continued to face pressure in 1996, the Louisiana Offshore Oil Port (LOOP) had increasing throughput levels. LOOP's average throughput from January through October 1996 was 840,000 b/d. By comparison, during the first 6 months of 1995, throughput averaged 617,000 b/d.

LOOP, which opened in May 1981, has three single point moorings that receive oil for movement to its marine terminal through a 56 in. submarine pipeline.

Officials of New Orleans-based LOOP, the nation's only deepwater oil port, acknowledged that the short-haul trend reported in 1995 was continuing in 1996. The facility was originally designed to handle 170,000-318,999 dwt VLCCs and ULCCs as large as 700,000 dwt, but increasing deliveries are being made by smaller tankers.

LOOP officials admit that the port is at a disadvantage when competing for short-haul volumes because it can't handle smaller vessels as efficiently as larger ones. And its fee structure is designed around larger vessel traffic.

Major worldwide trade movement

Fig. 3

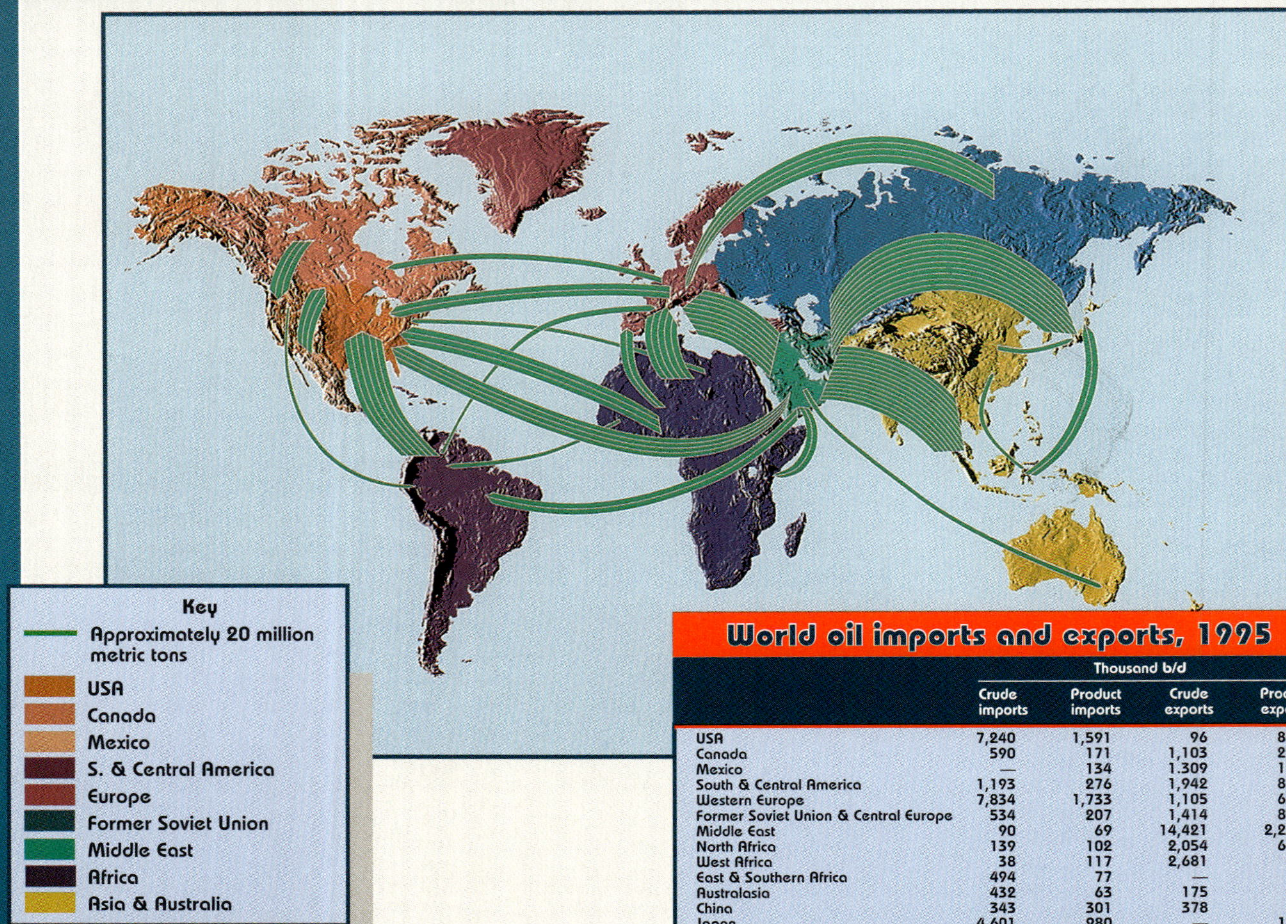

World oil imports and exports, 1995

	Thousand b/d			
	Crude imports	Product imports	Crude exports	Product exports
USA	7,240	1,591	96	853
Canada	590	171	1,103	299
Mexico	—	134	1.309	113
South & Central America	1,193	276	1,942	855
Western Europe	7,834	1,733	1,105	617
Former Soviet Union & Central Europe	534	207	1,414	899
Middle East	90	69	14,421	2,230
North Africa	139	102	2,054	642
West Africa	38	117	2,681	42
East & Southern Africa	494	77	—	6
Australasia	432	63	175	84
China	343	301	378	69
Japan	4,601	980	—	157
South Asia	685	604	—	31
Other Asia	3,769	1,380	1,036	803
Unidentified*	201	251	470	357
Total	28,183	8,056	28,183	8,056

*Includes changes in the quantity of oil in transit, movements not otherwise shown, unidentified military use, etc.
Bunkers and intraregion shipment (for example, between countries in Western Europe) are not included.
Source: BP Statistical Review of World Energy, 1996

IPE

Crudes offloaded at mainland marine terminals and ports at rates of 25-30¢/bbl can significanlty erode profitability when contrasted against LOOP's average VLCC average charge of 37¢/bbl.

LOOP has a two-tier fee structure using an A rate and B rate for the level of service provided. The former is 60¢/bbl and 60 days of minimum storage. The latter is an hourly offloading charge of $8,000/hr, plus a declining fee scale based on the volumes discharged per vessel.

For the first 500,000 bbl offloaded, the fee is 26¢/bbl, plus the $8,000 hourly charge; for the second 500,000 bbl offloaded, the charge drops to 23¢/bbl, plus the $8,000 hourly charge. For volumes exceeding the first 1 million bbl offloaded, the charge reduces to 20¢/bbl, plus the $8,000 hourly fee.

LOOP's highest daily throughput level was 1.8 million bbl in June 1992.

LOOP's supply source percentage breakout during 1996 reflected changing crude supply patterns, burgeoning South American and African crude supplies, and increasing U.S. reliance on imports from the Persian Gulf: Middle East, 55%; Africa, 23%; Latin America, 19%; and North Sea, 3%. This contrasts with the percentages reported after the facility opened: Mexico, 35%; Persian Gulf, 35%; North Africa, 17%; and North Sea, 13%.

U.S. flag markets

Contraction continued in the U.S. flag fleet during 1995 in spite of a major change in federal law that, for the first time, allowed export of Alaskan North Slope oil as long as transport was in U.S. flag vessels.

The principal source of employment for U.S. flag crude carriers has been shipping Alaskan crude oil to ports in the Lower 48 states.

Pres. Clinton signed a law that lifted the ban on exporting Alaskan North Slope oil. But declining Alaskan production hurt the long-haul tanker trade, which requires more tonnage than do closer shipments to the U.S. West Coast.

Alaskan crude shipments declined as production fell 4% to 1.57 million b/d in 1995, OSG reported. As a result, long-haul volumes destined for Gulf Coast and East Coast ports fell by one third from an already low 1994 level.

Production continued to fall as 1996 began. During the first quarter, production from Alaska fell 5% compared with the same period in 1995. IPE

Seismic technology gains role in reservoir characterization

Seismic technology in 1996 was advancing along a front where only a few years earlier progress had been slow: proving itself to be an important tool for reservoir characterization.

This technological movement widened the role of seismic data in development planning for oil and gas fields and for monitoring reservoir performance during production. It both took advantage of and supplemented the strong gains seismic technology had made since the early 1980s in imaging and structural interpretation. It thus expanded the applicability of seismic technology—once largely confined to exploration—to the full spectrum of upstream oil and gas operations.

Central to the burgeoning seismic role was widespread use of 3D methods. By 1996, 3D seismic had come to dominate geophysical work. Since the early 1980s, when the swing to 3D began to gain momentum, geophysicists had made dramatic improvements in 3D acquisition, processing, interpretation, and imaging techniques. By the mid-1990s, they had added a fourth dimension—time—to 3D seismic to detect changes in reservoirs between intervals of production.

But a place for seismic in development work also depended on technological gains in the modeling of reservoirs and their processes. Somewhat as seismic had done in the 1980s, statistical modeling of reservoirs was moving from the area of research into actual oil-company practice in the mid-1990s. The modeling techniques blend—or integrate—data from a variety of sources and disciplines to produce visual representations of reservoirs and of fluid flows within them.

Improving resolution

The fundamental—although not the only—advantage of blending seismic data into the reservoir model is improvement in lateral resolution of the 3D statistical volume on which the model is based. This concept is crucial to an understanding of the technological trend.

Without seismic inputs, most statistical components of reservoir models come from wells. Measurements from well logs and core cuttings provide data on rock properties, fluid content, and facies depths. From such data, technicians can build conceptual geological models, which are static representations of lithologies and structures. A traditionally discrete step then simulates fluid flows and pressure and temperature changes through the geologic model to produce a dynamic, engineering model.

Well data have great vertical resolution but poor lateral resolution. That is, they can distinguish changes of the measured property that occur over a very small change in depth. But the measurements pertain only to the vicinity of the well bore in which they are taken. In the absence of supplementary data, characteristics of reservoirs between well bores must be estimated. The random nature of lateral changes in the subsurface makes such estimates very coarse.

Seismic surveys help fill the data gaps between wells. Their lateral sampling depends not on the distance between wells but rather on the distance between recording lines and other acquisition parameters—down to certain limits. They thus can be designed to fit the measurement needs of the modeling problem.

Limitations of seismic

So why don't companies just build reservoir models from seismic data? There are several answers.

While seismic data provide lateral resolution not achievable with well data, their vertical resolution cannot approach that of well measurements. The basic limitation is wavelength of the seismic signal. Vertical subsurface changes that occur within about one-fourth of the acoustic wavelength cannot be distinguished in seismic data. Wavelength varies, depending on frequency and velocity of the seismic energy, so resolving power of seismic data varies as well. Resolution for a shallow subsurface bed through which sound with a dominant frequency of 60 Hz travels at 6,000 ft/sec would be about 25 ft. At greater depth, vertical resolution can be several hundred feet. By contrast, resolution of some well measurements can be less than 1 ft.

Fig. 1

Eugene Island 330 field

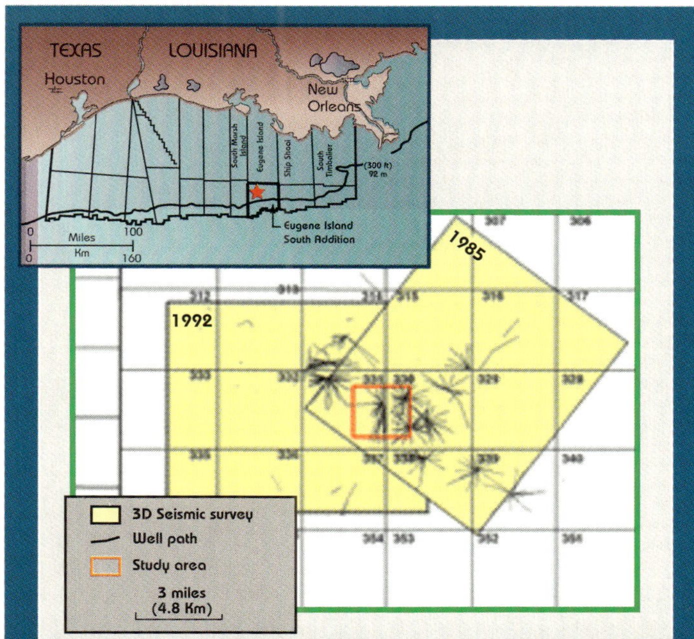

*Reservoir characterization of the LF reservoir used inverted acoustic impedance from the 1992 seismic survey because of its better data quality.

Fig. 2

Structure map of LF sand top

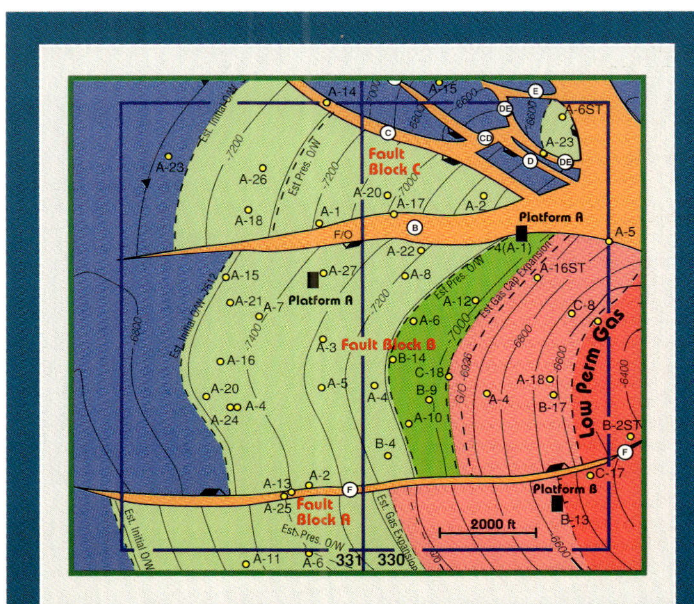

*Interpreted from wireline logging data by Pennzoil Exploration & Production Co. Gas caps are coded in red, water in blue, and oil in green. The low peremeability gas cap surrounding the crest of the structure is coded in purple. The estimated present gas-oil and oil-water contacts refer to 1992. The initial contacts refer to 1972. IPE

Fig. 3

Drainage from 4D impedance data

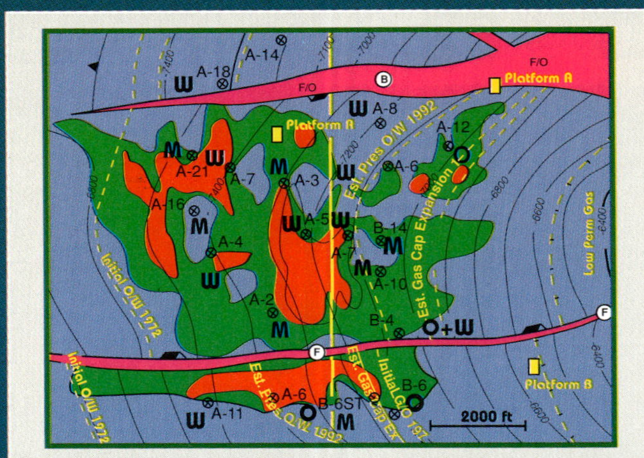

*LF reservoir. Water is shown in light blue, oil in green, decreased impedances (possible gas caps) over time in red.

IPE

Fig. 4

LF reservoir constructed from...

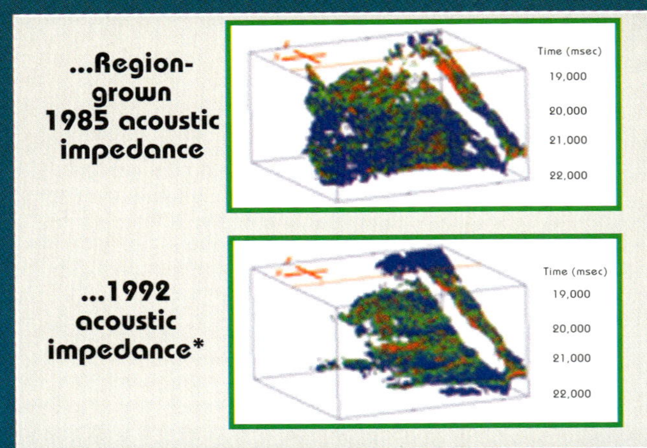

*Using 4D seismic reservoir-building algorithm. The region-growing lgorithms were applied to extract low impedance regions (LIRs) within the acoustic impedance volumes.

IPE

Fig. 5

Region-grown impedances differences*

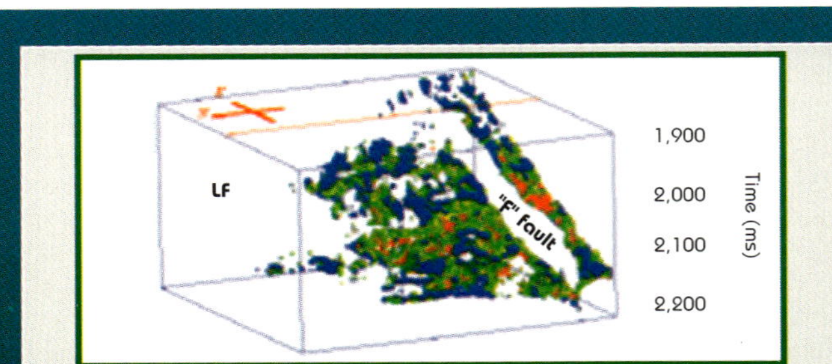

*Of the LF reservoir between the 1985 and 1992 seismic volumes. Red denotes areas with decreased impedances from 1985 to 1992. Blue denotes areas with increased impedances. Green and yellow denote areas with unchanged (<10%) impedances. View is of the outer surface of the reservoir.

IPE

Furthermore, seismic surveys directly measure only strengths, locations, and times of reflected and refracted sound waves. Properties of subsurface rocks must be deduced from measurements of seismic amplitudes, positions, and times. Errors are inevitable. But the deductions profit greatly from calibration with rock properties assessed by well logs, which is why well control has always been critical to seismic interpretation.

Integration of seismic and well data thus enables the lateral resolving advantages of seismic measurements to complement the vertical resolving advantages of measurements taken at the well. Combination of the data through modern and computationally intensive modeling techniques is giving the industry new understanding about how reservoirs look and behave.

The use of seismic methods in reservoir characterization thus evolved from advances on two separate technological tracks: 3D seismic and geostatistical approaches to reservoir characterization.

The 3D advantage

The easiest way to express the advantages of 3D seismic over 2D seismic is to say that the three dimensional character of nature dooms two dimensional representations to eternal insufficiency. Yet even 3D data are often depicted in 2D vertical sections or horizontal slices through the data volume. What's important is that the 2D representations of data acquired and processed in three dimensions are more accurate and better-resolved than their counterparts for 2D data.

The key is a processing step called migration. This step essentially attempts to position reflections from nonhorizontal rock layers properly in both time and space relative to surface locations. The corrections account for reflecting horizons with significant dip—or variations from horizontal. They also improve the lateral resolution of the data.

Migration in 2D seismic data has serious limits. It assumes that all reflected energy recorded in the vertical section comes from points in the same vertical plane in the subsurface. Because sound expands in three dimensions as it moves through the subsurface, this assumption about point to point reflection cannot be valid.

Reflected energy recorded at a point on the surface—a geophone array—doesn't come from a single point on the subsurface reflector. Rather, it comes from an area on the reflector, the size of which depends on a variety of things but that generally increases with depth. The reason: Source energy spreads out in all directions as it penetrates the subsurface; reflected energy behaves the same way in the reverse direction. Even if reflectors were all horizontal, therefore, some recorded energy would come from outside the plane of the vertical section. Where the subsurface reflectors dip, unmigrated reflections on a given vertical section actually come from somewhere updip of their recorded positions.

Migration in 2D can make positional corrections only along the horizontal axis of the vertical section: the direction of the receiver line. This correction shrinks the reflection-producing area on subsurface horizons in this direction. It thus improves lateral resolution of the data along the receiver line, so that resolution becomes the distance between traces. But the correction has no effect on the reflection-producing area to the sides of the vertical recording plane. For this reason, lateral resolution of 2D seismic data in the direction perpendicular to receiver lines can be greater than the spacing between lines. This is a significant limitation. It also means that even after migration, a vertical section contains large amounts of out-of-plane reflection data.

Migration in 3D makes positioning corrections in two perpendicular directions. This not only does a much better job of correcting for dip than 2D migration can do but also collapses the reflection-producing area of subsurface reflectors laterally as well as longitudinally. The lateral resolution of 3D data thus greatly exceeds that of 2D data. Vertical sections from a 3D-migrated data volume contain lower percentages of out-of-plane reflections than do those from 2D-migrated sections, so their "signal-to-noise ratios" are much better.

Because 3D migration can improve resolution laterally as

Effective oil saturation map* — Fig. 6

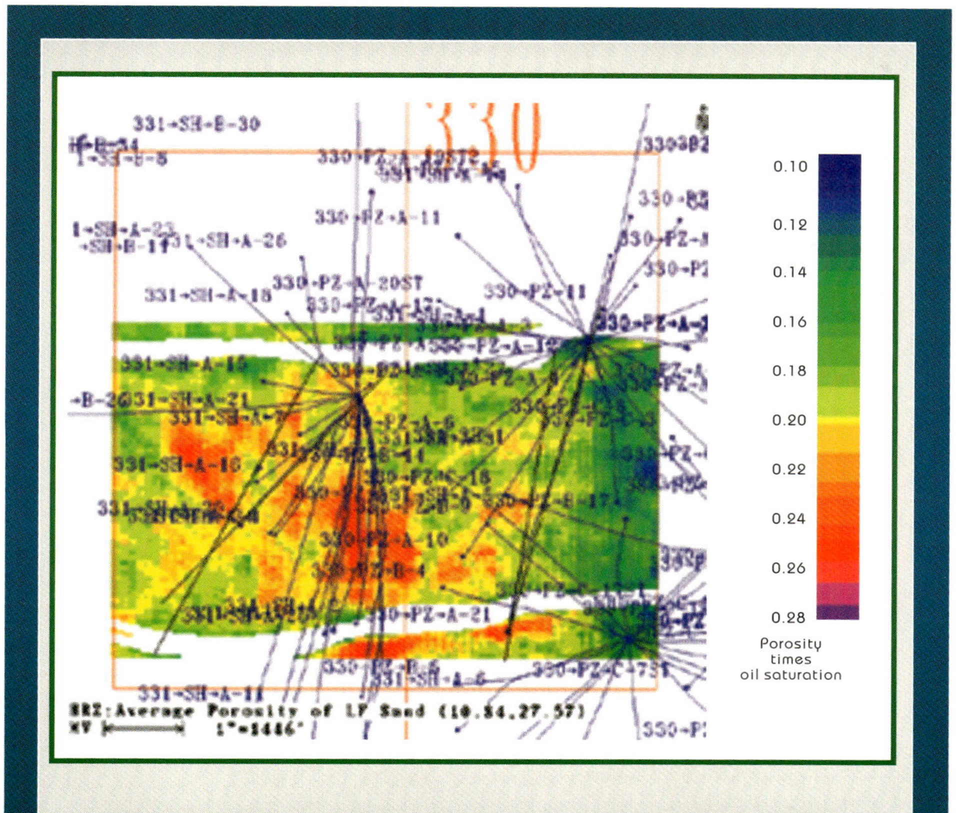

*Effective oil saturation is essentially the product of porosity times oil saturation.

IPE

well as longitudinally, 3D surveys can be designed with crisscrossing lines just tens of feet apart to provide much finer sampling than is possible with 2D data. The effect is to bring reflecting horizons in map view—looking down from above rather than from the side as in vertical sections—into much better focus than is achievable with 2D data and to show much greater detail. The finer sampling achievable with 3D over 2D moves the technology toward the requirements of reservoir engineering.

Reservoir characterization

Modern work in reservoir characterization can be roughly described as an effort to integrate the static geologic model and dynamic, fluid-flow simulation of the engineering model of the reservoir.

In a May 20, 1996, article in Oil & Gas Journal, Gautam S. Shiralkar and coauthors, all from Amoco Exploration & Production Technology, described the traditional approach as a hand-off from geologists to reservoir engineers. The engineers receive the geologic model, which tends to focus on lithological and structural information, and use porosity, production, and pressure information to simulate fluid flows. In a process called "history-matching," engineers compare production histories to the forecasts of their simulations. The reservoir parameters of the simulation best matching historic production are taken to be the best description of the reservoir.

The history-matched reservoir model, according to Shiralkar et al., suffers from "non-uniqueness." Several very different reservoir descriptions can produce very similar reservoir performances over the historic data period but very different predictions about future performance. This type of modeling also must assume reservoir homogeneity that doesn't exist in nature.

The alternative approach under development in the 1990s employed a technology called geostatistics. The reservoir model in this technology comprises millions of spatially defined cubes, each assigned values for particular characteristics such as lithology, porosity, permeability, and pressure. Computer visualization methods color-code the characteristics and values to create a manipulable 3D image of the reservoir.

Geostatistical methods generate a range of possible reservoir descriptions, called realizations. Simulations of flow through these descriptions thus produce a range of possible reservoir performances. The simulations that best match actual field performance are assumed to be those based on realizations best matching the actual reservoir.

Industry technicians using geostatistical methods for characterizing reservoirs can integrate geophysical data into their quantitative models. Furthermore, seismic data have become important ways of tracking actual reservoir performance for comparison with geostatistical realizations.

Seismic inversion

Seismic data, however, do not translate directly into terms useful in reservoir descriptions. They are, after all, only measurements of sound. Before they can be incorporated in reservoir modeling, they must be cast in terms descriptive of the reservoir.

The basic process for doing this is not new. Called seismic inversion, it has long been part of the production of synthetic seismograms and other seismic modeling.

Inversion translates sonic reflection strength—or amplitude—into a rock-layer description called acoustic impedance (AI). This is a measure of the relative ease with which sound passes through a particular rock layer. It's calculated as the product of density times sonic velocity in the layer under study.

Seismic reflections occur at boundaries between rock layers with differing AIs. The strength of a reflection, recorded at the surface as amplitude, is a function of the AI contrast at the reflecting horizon. Seismic interpreters, therefore, can infer AI values from seismic amplitude data. AI values then can be reduced to density and velocity data. These data can be correlated with density and sonic data from well logs and assist with the inference of reservoir characteristics such as lithology, porosity, and fluid content.

Geophysicists use a variety of mathematical techniques called algorithms to invert seismic data. Accuracy of the process depends greatly on adequacy of the algorithm, of course. Work in development and improvement of inversion algorithms has been an area of much work and progress and will continue to be.

Noninversion techniques

AI values thus provide a useful way to blend with petrophysical and geologic data the information contained in seismic amplitudes. But they were not the only method geophysicists were developing in 1996 to evaluate rock and reservoir properties with seismic data.

Amplitude variation with offset (AVO), for example, can imply densities, sonic velocities, and fluid content of intervals on either side of a reflecting horizon. AVO had proven to be useful in a number of areas in 1996 and was an area of active research.

Another seismic method under study as a reservoir characterization tool was cross-well tomography, in which seismic

Integration of seismic data improves

INTEGRATION OF SEISMIC STRUCTURAL and stratigraphic data with reservoir and simulation models based on well data helped Saudi Arabian Oil Co. (Saudi Aramco) understand unexpectedly rapid water encroachment in part of the world's largest onshore oil field.

Information from a recent 3D seismic survey showed the Arab D carbonate reservoir on the eastern flank of Ghawar field in Saudi Arabia to have faults and related fractures that did not appear on interpretations based on well control. Existence of the fractures helped explain faster-than-expected sweep of injected water through part of the reservoir. Before the seismically defined structures entered the interpretation, reservoir and simulation models could account for the water encroachment only by postulating the existence of zones extreme permeability (k), in places exceeding 250 darcies.

Models incorporating the conductive faults and fractures more accurately predicted actual fluid flows than did the earlier models. They enabled Saudi Aramco to plan for the drilling of wells to recover oil that otherwise would have been bypassed.

Saudi Aramco's A. Valle, J.J. Faulhaber, T.H. Keith, and P.T. Hsueh described the integration project in an article in the Fall 1996 issue of the Saudi Aramco Journal of Technology.

The project focused on a 15 km by 15 km area of Ghahwar field producing via peripheral water injection. Rapid

Fig. 1

Permeability model before integration*

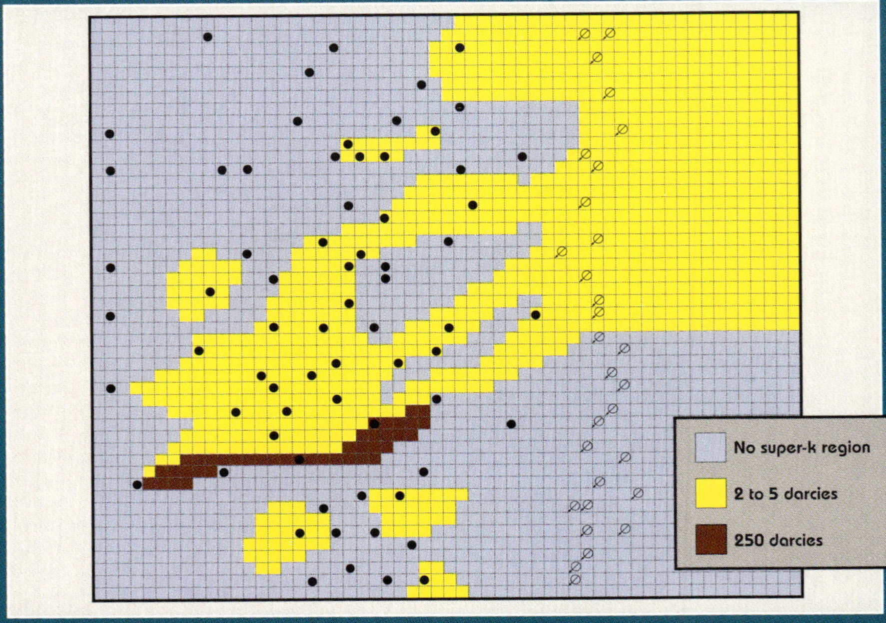

*Final dolomitic super-k description, previous fine-grid model.
Source: Saudi Aramco Journal of Technology

IPE

Fig. 2

Two views of top, Zone 2A*

Fig. 2a

Structure from well control

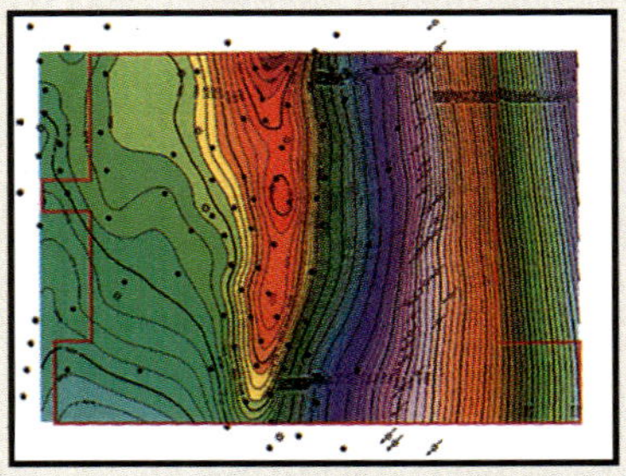

Fig. 2b

Structure and faults from 3D seismic

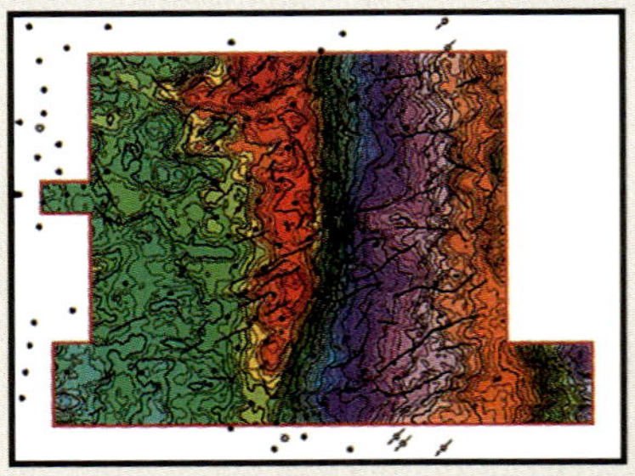

*Arab D reservoir, eastern flank, central Ghawar field.
Source: Saudi Aramco Journal of Technology

IPE

energy generated at varying depths in one well bore is measured by receivers inside a different well.

While both AVO and cross-well tomography held great promise in 1996, neither was considered to be widely applicable. A problem with AVO, for example, is that a range of subsurface characteristics often can produce a single AVO effect. An AVO pattern evident in a seismic data set therefore can mean a number of different things. And cross-well tomography depended on the existence of handily spaced wells, as well as further development of interpretation techniques.

An advantage of AI values is that they can be extracted from any seismic data set with clear and consistent amplitude values.

4D seismic

A seismic-based method of reservoir description called 4D seismic, under development since the late 1980s, was coming into its own in 1996.

The technique uses 3D seismic data to detect changes in the reservoir due to fluid flows over time—the fourth dimension. It essentially involves identical 3D surveys shot at intervals of months or years. Changes in acoustic responses that occur from one survey to another can be related to changes in reservoir properties, such as fluid content, pressure, and temperature, resulting from production.

In some reservoirs, for example, it is possible to detect

Ghawar field model

Final reservoir characterization–integrated model

Fig. 3

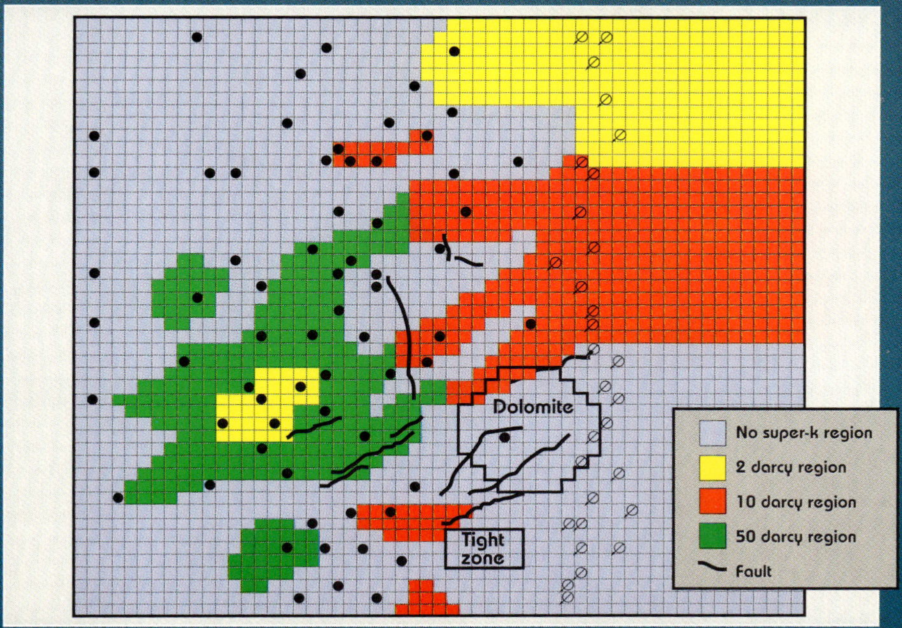

Source: Saudi Aramco Journal of Technology

IPE

water-front advance westward through the area had been attributed to high horizontal permeabilities resulting from vugular porosity and coupled with relatively low vertical permeability in dolomite in the middle of the reservoir. Water traveled through the superpermeable dolomite, bypassing oil above and below the high-k level.

Before the 3D seismic data became available, reservoir and simulation models came from studies of 20 cored wells, analysis, and log and reservoir-performance data. They included detailed geocellular models of porosity and permeability as well as a discrete geocellular model showing the occurrence of superpermeability through the reservoir (Fig. 1). Problems in matching computed and observed injection-flank pressures represented one sign that something was missing from the interpretation.

Postulation of an area of extreme permeability (250 darcies) needed to match computations with field observations signalled the existence of faulting in the area. No such faulting appeared on horizon maps derived from well data, however (Fig. 2a). Complexity of the area became apparent in horizon maps derived from 3D seismic data (Fig. 2b).

In addition to faulting, the seismic data showed that the structural flank dipped much more than had been assumed between the water-injection wells and first line of producers. They further showed a trough corresponding to the area previously assigned extreme permeabilities.

Evaluation of pressure-buildup test data for wells in the 3D seismic survey area helped identify reservoir heterogeneities such as faults and fractures and rapid changes in porosity and permeability. In the integration of seismic data into previous models, fractures were inferred from seismically defined faults, although not all of the faults were associated with conductive or sealing fractures.

The interdisciplinary team that conducted the integration work used what Valle et al. described as a simplistic approach to modeling the fractures; they depicted them as columns of grid blocks having high vertical and horizontal permeabilities. The team assigned the faults steep gradients rather than abrupt displacements in layer depths. The authors said the team planned later to use a more rigorous simulation approach involving a dual porosity/permeability model.

After integration of the seismic data, history-matching defined fracture lengths and areal extent of reservoir features, including a massive tight dolomite in the southeastern part of the study area. The tight area reduces displaceable pore volume, forcing water to advance through more-permeable dolomite-free layers.

Fig. 3 shows how the final reservoir characterization accounts for northeast-southwest trending faults and the tight dolomite and does not require extreme assumptions about permeability.

The 10 km northeast-southwest fault was believed to be associated with a major fracture allowing water to flow easily toward the center of the field. It was that flow that required earlier models to assume unreasonable values for permeability.

Fluid-saturation models based on the integrated reservoir characterization predicted accumulations of oil behind the flood front. Saudi Aramco planned to drill two wells based on the predictions.

Although seismic information in this study was mostly structural, the Saudi Aramco authors said inversion of the 3D data might in the future help to identify horizons and other features between wells.

changes in acoustic impedance that occur after water displaces oil as production advances. Sequential seismic surveys thus can track movement of the oil-water contact over time. Movement of a gas-oil contact similarly can be monitored as a gas cap expands. Engineers can compare seismically monitored fluid-flow information with simulation data to adjust the reservoir model and manage production—the benefit being, of course, improved recovery rates.

Since 4D seismic depends on comparison of identical 3D seismic surveys, a crucial factor is accuracy of positioning of seismic sources and receivers. For the time-lapse data to be comparable, these locations must be identical from survey to survey. Modern acquisition technology enables crews to accurately locate sources and receivers, so replicating surveys with the stationary cables employed onshore is not a great problem. For the moving receiver lines (or streamers) common in marine surveys, however, replicating locations can be a challenge.

A solution can be ocean-bottom cable (OBC) technology. As the name implies, the cable in this technique lays on the seabottom and doesn't move while its receivers collect data. The method makes duplicating source and receiver locations between surveys much easier than it is with normal marine surveys. In some cases, companies simply leave the cables in place between surveys.

Drainage from well into the LF reservoir, EI 330

Fig. 7

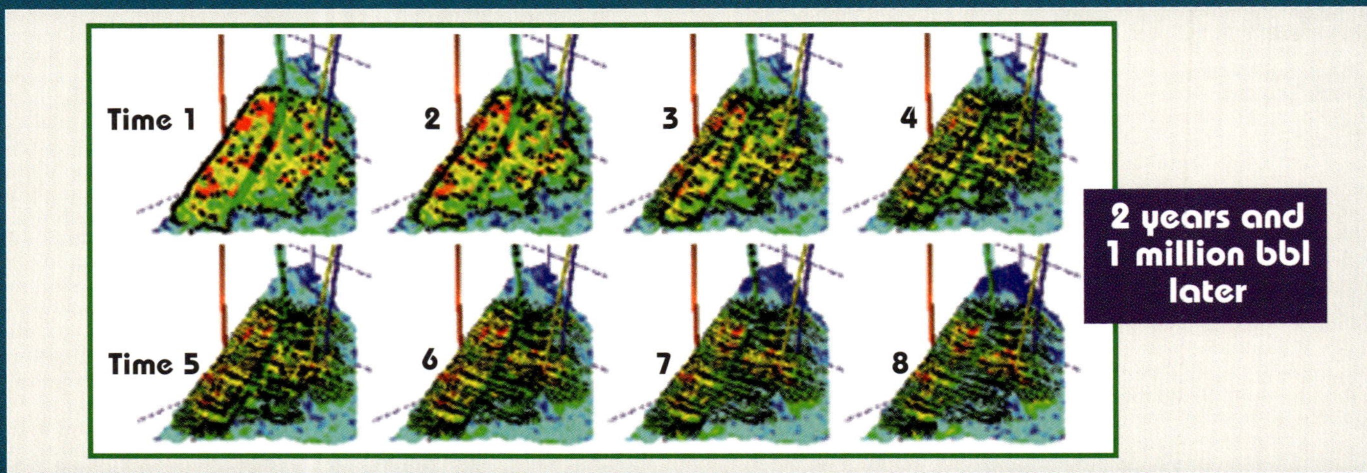

IPE

OBC technology further makes possible the acquisition of data on the transverse motion of sub-seabottom rocks in addition to the normal data on compressional motion. Transverse motion—represented as "shear waves"—doesn't occur in liquid, so normal marine data are for compressional waves only. Since comparisons between shear wave and compressional wave data are useful in AVO and other methods of deducing rock properties, OBC technology offers another potential advantage in the monitoring of reservoirs on production.

Applying the technology

Although 4D seismic techniques are complex and far from perfected, a number of success stories had been reported by 1996.

One well-documented application of the technology was under way in South Eugene Island Block 330 field in the Gulf of Mexico off Louisiana (Fig. 1). Wei He, Roger N. Anderson, and other authors from 4D Technology Inc. and the Lamont-Doherty Earth Observatory at Columbia University, Palisades, N.Y., reported on the 4D seismic work in the May 20, 1996, issue of Oil & Gas Journal.

Reservoir monitoring with 4D seismic showed a drainage pattern of the field's LF reservoir quite different from the gravitational pattern assumed when the field began production in 1972 (Fig. 2). By 1992, downdip wells had watered out in conformance with expectations of a systematic, updip migration of the oil-water contact.

Inversion and comparison of seismic data acquired in 1985 and 1992 revealed much more water fingering than had been expected, however, which meant significant volumes of oil had been bypassed by the water sweep. Potential volumes of unswept oil appeared as high-amplitude, low-impedance zones downdip of the apparent oil-water contact (Figs. 4, 5). The timing of watering-out of some of the wells proved to be consistent with the irregular sweep indicated by the 4D, AI analysis.

Interpreters used geostatistics to link AI changes with well log data to model porosity and lithology changes over time and map "effective oil saturation"—essentially porosity times oil saturation (Fig. 6). They were able to relate effective oil saturation with bypassed hydrocarbon locations to predict where new wells might be drilled (Fig. 7). A horizontal well targeted with 4D technology had produced more than 1 million bbl of oil equivalent for 2 years at the time the authors wrote.

Work patterns and computers

The new role of seismic in reservoir characterization contributed to a revolution in oil company work patterns that was well under way by 1996.

Old work sequences defined by industry discipline—such as geophysics, geology, petrophysics, and engineering—had been replaced by interdisciplinary teams. Often joined by financial experts, teams of technicians in these once-isolated specialties formed around fields, regions, or basins, responsible for extracting maximum economic advantage from related company assets.

The strong tendency in most oil companies, therefore, was to work on development and production problems while exploration was still in progress—sometimes before spudding of the first wildcat. This practice, most companies believed, kept a strong economic perspective at work in exploration and development decisions that might, in an earlier time, have been made department by department within inappropriately narrow parameters.

This revolution in upstream management certainly accommodated growth in seismic's role in reservoir characterization.

But the change would not have been possible without the burgeoning computational capacity afforded by zooming computer technology. Indeed, many oil company managers conceded that interdisciplinary teamwork depended on the ability to put data of many types from many sources on commonly accessible data bases manipulable in nearly real time.

The needed computing capacities thus are huge. And they grow with each new technology and application. In the late 1980s and early 1990s, so-called supercomputers provided the required computational power. But their limits quickly came into view, generally having to do with speed of data transfer between computer memory and processing areas.

The solution in the mid-1990s was massively parallel processing, which used a number of computers to work simultaneously on computationally intensive problems, such as reservoir characterization. So-called "data parallelism," essentially the performance of similar operations on many elements of a problem at once, made parallel processing scalable; that is, adding processors increases computing power.

Massively parallel computing thus solved a computing bottleneck—at least temporarily—that might have discouraged use of the sophisticated reservoir characterization and seismic integration technologies that were rapidly becoming part of the upstream industry's tool chest in 1996. As the techniques develop and computing requirements grow, advances in computer technology will become as critical to future progress as the scientific and engineering achievements that surely lie ahead. IPE

Stratigraphic charts

The six stratigraphic charts presented here cover important basins from various parts of the world. The columns are from the Australia-Indonesia Timor Gap Zone of Cooperation Area in the Timor Sea, eastern fold belt of Bangladesh, Nile delta in the Mediterranean Sea off Egypt, Papuan basin of Papua New Guinea's Southern Highlands, Marañon basin of northeastern Peru, and the Carpathian foredeep of Ukraine.

Timor Sea

Several discoveries in and adjacent to the Australia-Indonesia Timor Gap Zone of Cooperation Area made the eastern Timor Sea one of the world's hottest exploration theaters in the mid-1990s.

The discoveries are Laminaria/Corallina in AC/P8, Elang, Kakatua, and Bayu/Undan in ZOCA 91/12 and 91-3, and Buffalo in WA-260-P.

However, the size of many of the discoveries tended to be limited, and operators faced a crossroads in 1996 as to whether to undertake marginally commercial development projects and continue exploration of ever riskier prospects or begin to relinquish acreage.

The Laminaria discovery well came in during October 1994 with a maximum flow rate of 7,507 b/d of 59° gravity crude with a GOR of 175 scf/st-tk bbl from the Callovian-Oxfordian aged Laminaria formation. Zones at 3,213-3,264.5 m deep were tested at the well, in 361 m of water.

Before drilling, the prospect was expected to have Upper to Middle Jurassic Flamingo and Plover sandstone reservoirs, sealed by Flamingo Group shales, authors with Woodside Offshore Petroleum Pty. Ltd. group wrote in the Australian Petroleum Production & Exploration Journal (Fig. 1).

The Laminaria prospect was initially thought to be a large complex horst block produced by major east-west faults discernible on 2D seismic lines at Aptian level. Data from a 3D seismic survey and more wells led to its reinterpretation as a series of tilted fault blocks, oriented east-northeast to west-southwest and dipping to the southeast.

The Corallina discovery on AC/P8 flowed 8,000 b/d. It is 9 km from Laminaria and thought to be connected.

A significant late 1996 discovery was BHP Petroleum Pty. Ltd. 1 Buffalo in 89 ft of water 4 miles southeast of the Laminaria East discovery. The Buffalo well flowed 11,770 b/d of 53° gravity oil and 328 Mcfd of gas through a 52/64 in. choke from Jurassic Elang intervals at 10,849-941 ft.

The Phillips Petroleum Co./BHP Bayu/Undan gas/condensate field is 350 km east-southeast of Kupang, Timor. The discovery well, Phillips Bayu-1, encountered 155 m of gross gas/condensate column in Middle Jurassic sandstones at 2,954.5 m in early 1995. This and a second well confirmed existence of a large field most likely covering 160 sq km, wrote Deidre M. Brooks and others in the APPEA Journal.

The sandstone reservoir consists of late Oxfordian to Callovian shallow marine, deltaic to shoreface, coarsening upward parasequences overlying Callovian to Bajocian marginal marine to coastal plain sediments. The closure is the culmination of the Flamingo high, which has been viewed as having significant hydrocarbon potential since the Arco Flamingo-1, a few miles west of Bayu/Undan, recovered gas from shallower Berriasian sandstones in 1971. Flamingo-1 was the only well in Area A before 1991.

Pyrolysis/gas chromatograph data indicated that the Echuca Shoals formation is the source of Bayu/Undan condensate. If this is correct, the most likely source kitchen is inferred to be the Malita graben to the east, or possibly the southern Flamin-

Fig. 1

Northern Bonaparte basin (Timor Sea)

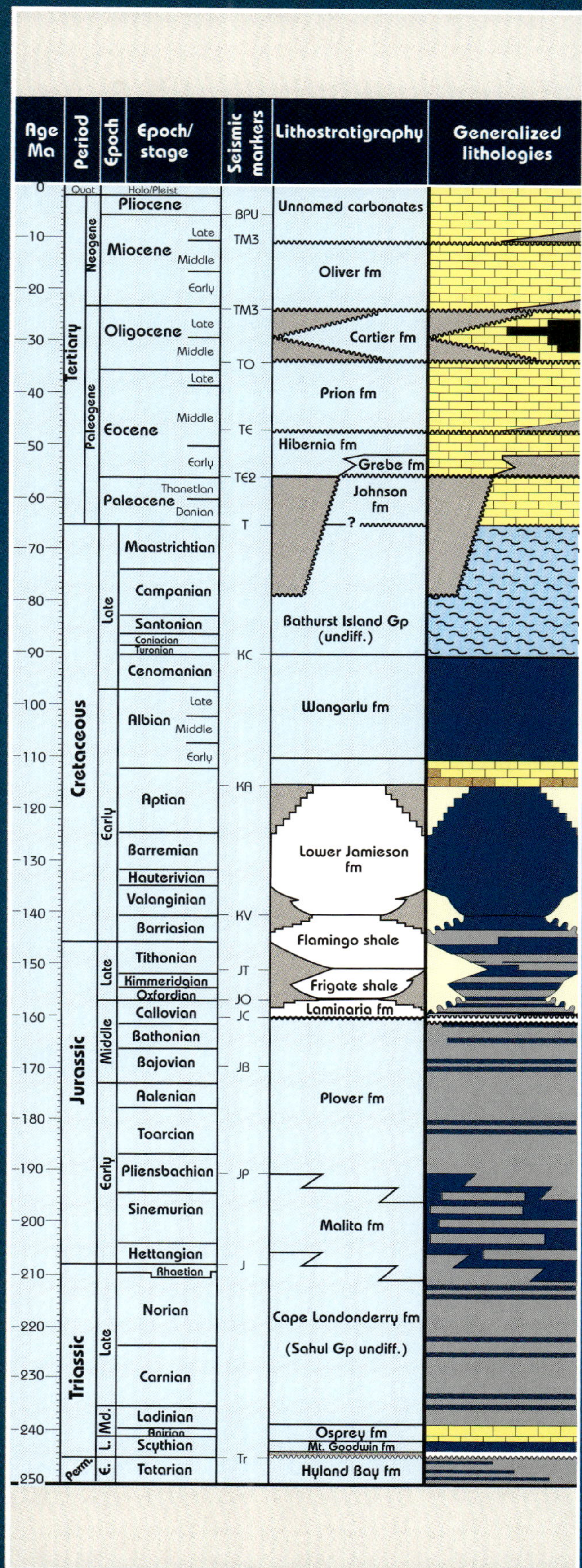

Source: After Smith, APPEA Journal 1996 (age scale based on Harland et al, 1990)

IPE

go or Sahul synclines, but not a depocenter north of the field, the authors wrote.

Bayu/Undan reserves are estimated at 3-5 tcf of gas and 150-250 million bbl of condensate.

First of the modern Timor Gap discoveries was BHP's Elang field, 18 km northwest of Bayu/Undan field, in early 1994. The Elang discovery well recorded the first significant oil flow in the eastern part of the northern Bonaparte basin.

The discovery well flowed 5,800 b/d of 56° gravity oil from marine sandstone of the Late Jurassic (mid-Callovian to Oxfordian) Montara beds. Previous oil discoveries in the western Timor Sea have been from older Triassic-Middle Jurassic sandstones although Montara-1, a noncommercial discovery, recorded a significant flow from the "Montara formation," wrote Ian Young and others in the APEA Journal 1995.

Elang reserves were initially estimated at 15-20 million bbl of oil.

BHP's Kakatua 1, drilled in December 1994, flowed at a combined stabilized rate of 9,000 b/d of 53° gravity oil. Kakatua reserves are estimated at 5-10 million bbl. Kakatua is 12 km west of Elang field. A smaller discovery, West Elang, was thought questionably commercial at 1-2 million bbl.

An Elang/Kakatua development plan envisioning recovery of 17 million bbl of reserves was moving forward in late 1996. The field area is in about 80 m of water.

Exploratory drilling in the ZOCA peaked in 1994 with 11 wildcats and one appraisal well. Five wildcats and three appraisal wells were drilled in 1995; 1996 looked like six wildcats and six appraisals and 1997 nine wildcats and three appraisals.

Fig. 2

Bangladesh composite stratigraphy

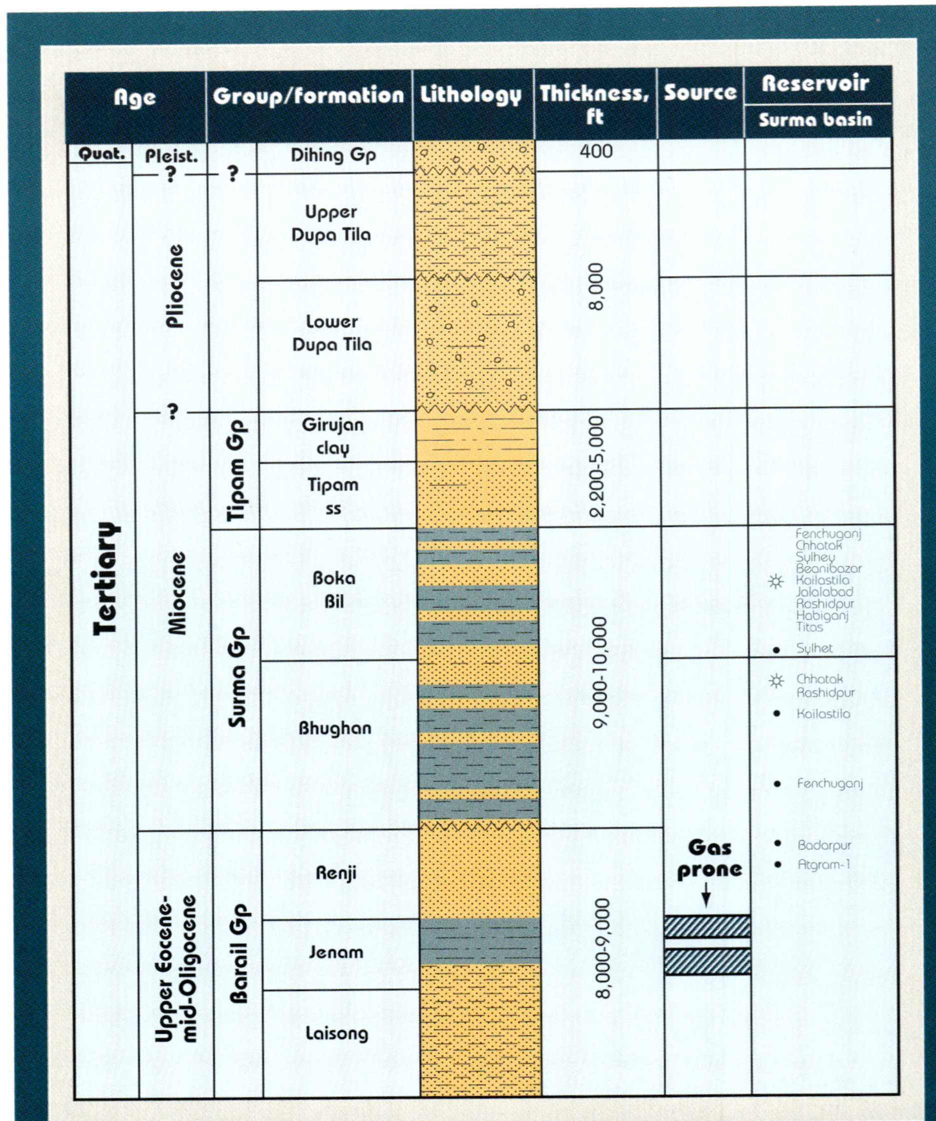

Source: Occidental Petroleum Corp.

IPE

Exploration quickens in Bangladesh

Reservoirs in Bangladesh's main producing area, the eastern fold belt, are stacked Miocene fluvial and deltaic sandstone reservoirs. Reservoir porosities of 20-22% are common at depths of 1,096-3,020 m.

Bangladesh has about 20 relatively small fields or discoveries. Most lie on the eastern foldbelt along a gas pipeline that extends from Chhatak and Sylhet along the India border in northeast Bangladesh past Dhaka and ending at Chittagong on the Bay of Bengal.

The gas and gas/condensate reservoirs are the Lower Miocene Bhughan and lower Middle Miocene Boka Bil formations, which make up the Surma Group (Fig. 2).

Small volumes of paraffinic oils have been discovered at Kailastila, Sylhet, and Fenchuganj in the Surma basin. Murphy reported in 1988 that the national oil company discovered oil at Haripur village in Sylhet gas field in December 1986. Oil was also found at Fenchuganj 40 km south of Sylhet.

The Sylhet and Fenchuganj oils are typical of paraffinic, low sulfur oils found in Assam, Burma (Myanmar), and other parts of Southeast Asia, Murphy wrote. Sylhet produced 28° gravity oil from 2,020 m, deeper than the Sylhet gas reservoirs in Boka Bil. Fenchuganj produced 17.2° gravity oil from 3,068 m.

In the Bay of Bengal, Unocal discovered Kutubdia gas field in 1978. The discovery well produced gas and small amounts of condensate from Late Miocene-Pliocene siltstone with 17% porosity and 35% water saturation at 8,730-60 ft. The zone flowed 17.9 MMcfd of gas.

Logs suggested the possibility of two additional gas sands at 9,573-9,638 ft and 10,457-488 ft, but the two zones were not tested. TD is 11,500 ft.

Cairn Energy plc, Edinburgh, in early 1996 tested the Sangu-1 gas discovery on Block 16 about 40 km southwest of Chittagong. It flowed 50 MMcfd of gas from a main gas bearing zone of undisclosed age and a further 32 MMcfd from a shallower formation. The gas is 96% methane with no hydrogen sulfide, little carbon dioxide, and no liquids potential.

Cairn said other gas bearing zones were not tested. Water is 20-40 ft deep in the area. The field will probably being delivering gas in 1998.

Northwest of Sangu, on Block 10 on an island at the mouth of the Ganges River, Unocal has proposed to develop Petrobangla's 400 bcf Shahbazpur field, discovered in 1995.

Development would involve a 40 km, 30 MMcfd gas pipeline to Barisal, southwest of Dhaka, and a 150 mw power station with start-up as early as 1999.

Petrobangla plans to start gas production from Belabo,

Fenchuganj, and Beanibazar fields during 1996-97, and Occidental should start Jalalabad field in 1997.

Nile delta becoming large gas province

More gas and gas/condensate reservoirs are being discovered as operators intensified exploration in Egypt's Nile delta to support domestic gas demand, shipments on the planned "Peace" pipeline to Israel, Palestine, and Jordan, and LNG shipments to Turkey.

Three reservoirs have been found gas-productive offshore (Fig. 3). The oldest are Serravallian (Middle Miocene) sands. Temsah gas/condensate field and the Akhen gas/condensate discovery are examples.

The sands have porosities of 20% to more than 30% with excellent permeabilities. DSTs of 30-40 MMcfd on 5/8 in. chokes are common. These sands are at about 4,000 m.

Reservoir characteristics are also excellent in the Baltim fields, which produce from the Abu Madi formation of Upper Messinian, latest Miocene. These sands are 3,300-3,500 m deep.

The third play is for dry gas in Pliocene age sands in the Kafr el Sheikh formation. The Nile delta, a continental margin, becomes a true delta in Pliocene with largely focused sediments with sand from an integrated river. Wells encounter Pliocene sediments at 500-3,300 m.

Kafr el Sheikh is productive in the Akhen discovery well and in Denise, Denise South, Ha'py, and Seth gas fields. Amoco expects Pliocene to be a significant play in the delta, but it has proved difficlut to drill.

Kafr el Sheikh contains much sediment deposited very quickly. Deeper Pliocene has severe overpressuring with gradients of 0.8 psi/ft, while Miocene Abu Madi is normally pressured, and deeper Temsah is overpressured at 0.6 psi/ft. Multiple casing strings to control pressures are common, and the lowermost portion of the Akhen discovery is a 6 in. hole.

Many shows recorded in Papua New Guinea

The only formations producing in the Papuan basin as of late 1996 were the Cretaceous Toro formation and the Cretaceous Digimu and Jurassic Iagifu members of the Imburu formation.

However, hydrocarbon shows have been recorded in numerous other formations in the basin (Fig. 4). Here is a listing by well, formation, and type of hydrocarbon show, according to the Petroleum Division of the Department of Mining and Petroleum in Port Moresby:

Puri 1X, oil in Miocene Puri/Yala limestones.

Elevala 1X, gas and condensate in Cretaceous Elevala sandstone.

Pasca, gas in the Miocene Pasca formation.

Pandora, gas in the Miocene Pandora formation.

Menga 1X, oil in the Giero member of the Ieru formation and the Jurassic P'nyang formation.

Uramu 1A, gas in the Miocene Uramu formation.

North Paibuna 1X, oil and gas in the Jurassic Koi-Iange member of the Imburu formation.

Makas 1X, oil and gas in undifferentiated Ieru sands.

Marañon basin Peru's largest producing area

The inland Marañon basin covers about 49.5 million acres inland south of Iquitos between Peru's borders with Ecuador and Brazil. At well over 100,000 b/d of oil it is Peru's largest basin both in area and production, but geologically it is still considered underexplored.

The stratigraphic chart shows reservoirs of Cretaceous, Triassic, and Carboniferous age, but only Cretaceous contains significant reserves (Fig. 5). Paleozoic prospects are considered to be significant in the basin.

The basin has hosted more than 30 discoveries out of fewer than 100 exploratory wells, but only 17 fields are on production. These fields have yielded around 500 million bbl of oil since 1971. Estimated ultimate recovery from Marañon is some 750 million bbl.

The main production is from Cretaceous zones. Oil has been tested or produced from several Cretaceous sandstone reservoirs, with commercial production from the Upper Cretaceous Chonta and overlying Vivian formations.

Vivian is the primary producing formation, with more than half the basin's total, and most of the rest is in Chonta.

The formations, at depths of 7,000-14,000 ft, produce 10-42°

Fig. 3

Nile Delta formations

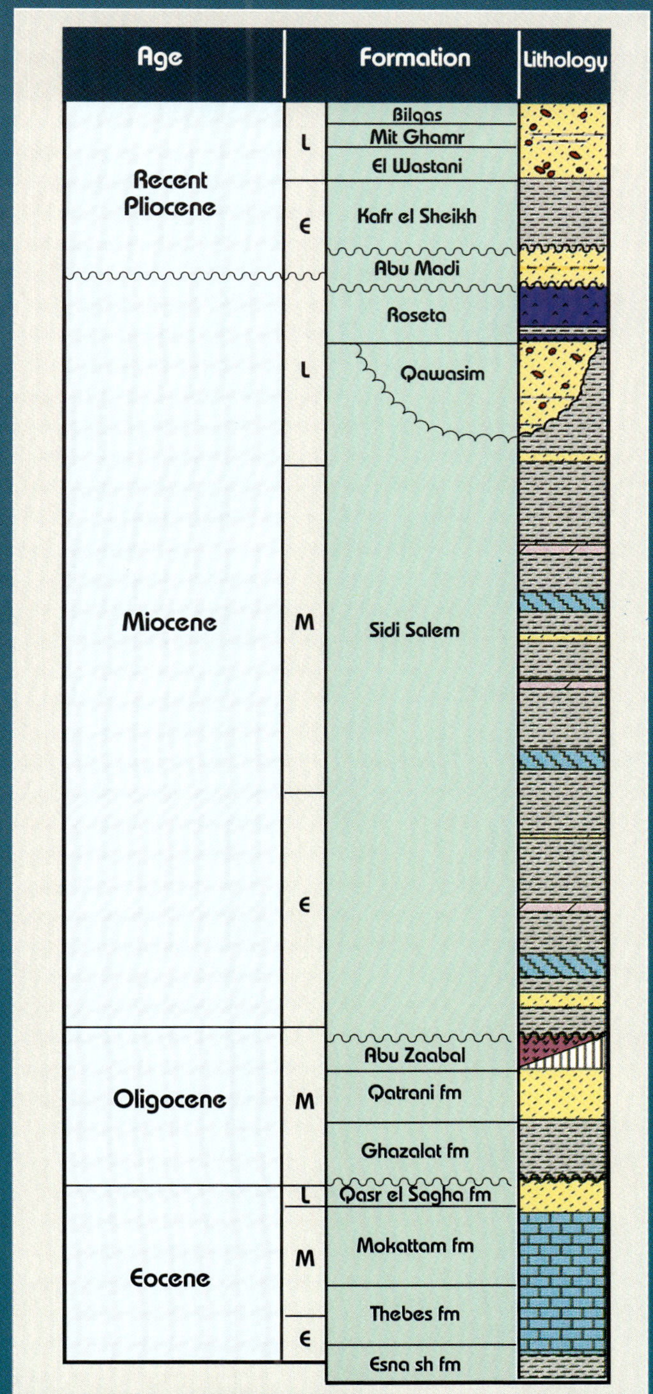

Source: Amoco

IPE

Papuan basin, Papua New Guinea

Fig. 4

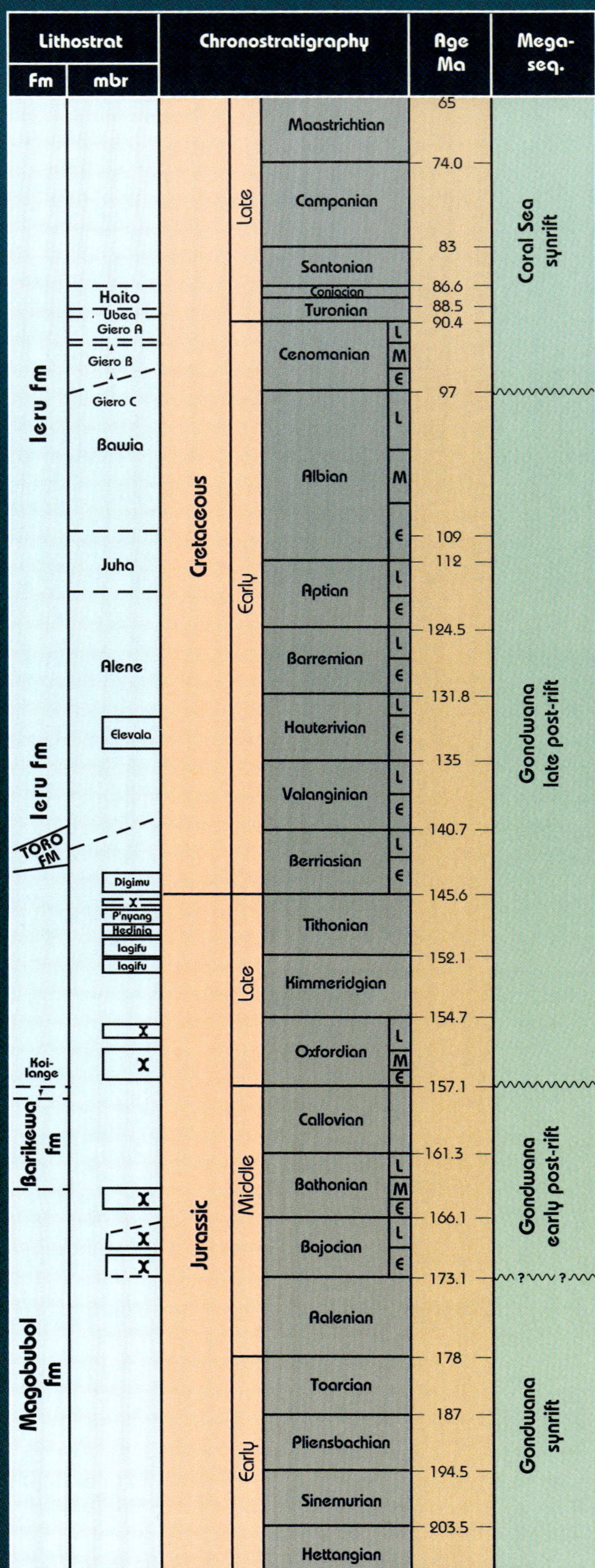

x= Unnamed sandstone members
Source: British Petroleum Co. plc after T.D. Varney, Febuary 1992

IPE

gravity crude oil. Production comes from about 150 wells in 17 fields.

Cushabatay contained 45° gravity oil in Occidental's Tambo South field, discovered in 1982. It is estimated to hold about 4 million bbl of reserves.

Carpathian area produces oil, gas in Ukraine

The Dnieper-Donets and Carpathian provinces account for most of the production in Ukraine.

The part of the Carpathian province lying in Ukraine covers about 20,800 sq km in the country's far west, according to extensive background information compiled by Gustavson Associates Inc., Boulder, Colo. Oil has been produced in the region for centuries from seeps and hand-dug pits, but no mechanical drilling occurred until 1854. Dolina oil field was discovered in 1860. The first gas production was found in 1920.

No important discoveries have been made the past five decades, and since its separation from the former Soviet Union in the early 1990s Ukraine has been seeking help from western exploration companies to prop up sagging production.

Reservoir rocks in the pre-Carpathian depression are almost exclusively clastic in nature. They consist of calcareous and quartzose sandstones, conglomerates, and very sandy marls in the Oligocene, Miocene, and Pliocene intervals (Fig. 6).

The most prolific producing intervals are within the Pliocene, and two main producing zones can be identified. Lower Pliocene Meotian sands, deposited under brackish to fresh water conditions, form the main reservoirs in numerous fields. Their reservoir characteristics are generally excellent but deteriorate gradually with depth. Porosities average 25-30%, and permeabilities average 200 md to a depth of about 2,000 m. Net effective thickness of these sands is 85 m. They are sealed by Pontian marls and contain about 7.3 million bbl of recoverable oil per square kilometer.

The second main group of Pliocene reservoirs is in the Upper Pliocene Dacian sands. The distribution of these lacustrine sands is more irregular than those of the Meotian, but they exhibit somewhat more favorable reservoir characteristics, especially in terms of thickness. They provide 29 million bbl of recoverable oil per sq km.

It is possible, Gustavson reckons, that Mesozoic and even Paleozoic carbonate rocks, where not excessively buried, may act as reservoirs in the pre-Carpathian depression. Upper, unaltered portions of the metamorphic basement even have reservoir qualities in the North Dobrogea area.

The Paleozoic section ranges from 500 m to nearly 2 km thick. The main play is in Cambrian and Devonian clastics, mainly sandstones. These reservoirs are described as being of rather poor quality and occurring at great depths, yet having considerable hydrocarbon potential.

Most of the province's oil and gas fields are grouped in the northwest-southeast trending Lvov Paleozoic trough and pre-Carpathian trough units.

Two main hydrocarbon-bearing zones are recognized among the several thrust sheets that comprise the pre-Carpathian depression as it exists in Ukraine. These are the inner zone, which is mainly oil prone, and an outer zone that is gas prone. The inner zone is one of high-angle thrusts—a transitional belt between the nappes on the south and west, and the outer zone of normal or block faults and the gently folded platform.

Among the most important oil and gas fields are Dolina, Bitkov, Rudkov, and Borislav. Borislav field, discovered in the 1860s, has produced 220 million bbl of oil. Large gas fields, such as Bilche-Volista (1.3 tcf), were discovered in the late 1940s and early 1950s. Cumulative production from the Ukrainian Carpathians is estimated to be 700 million bbl of oil and 8 tcf of gas.

Most oil accumulations in the depression have no primary gas cap but are rich in dissolved gas. Exceptions are those fields

Marañon basin, Peru

Fig. 5

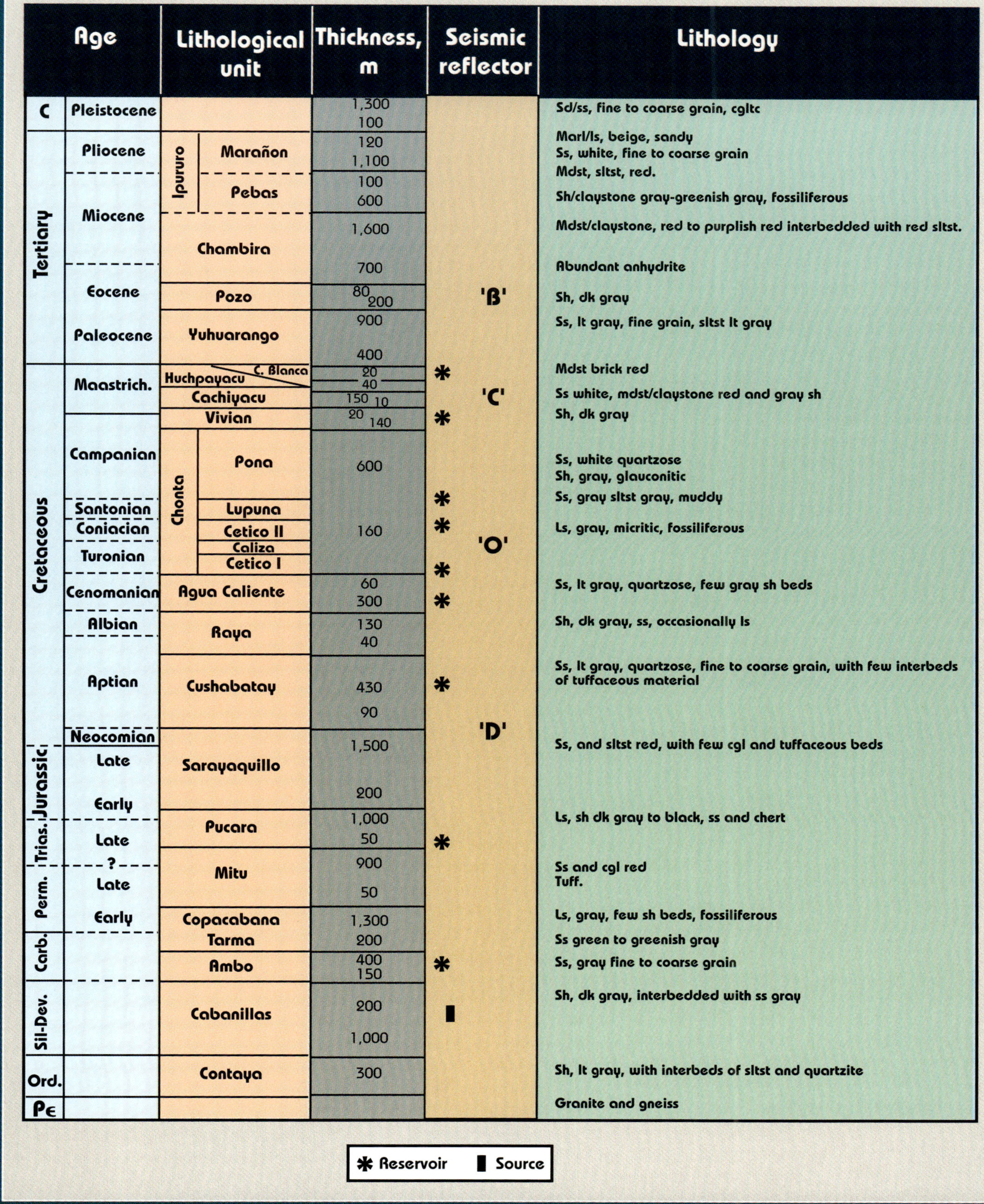

Source: Perupetro SA

IPE

Ukraine Carpathian Foredeep Tertiary

Fig. 6

Period		Epoch	Age		Thickness ft	Generalized lithologic descriptions	Facies	Hydrocarbon accumulations
Quaternary					100-6,000	Clg, pebbles, sds, and marls	Fluviatile	
Tertiary	Neogene	Pliocene	Levantine		1,500	Sds, clays, marls, and lignites	Lacustrine	• ☼
			Dacian		600-1,200	Sds, marls, and lignites	Lacustrine	• ☼
			Pontain		1,000-3,500	Marls in west; marls and sds in north and east	Brackish with fresh-water intercal.	• ☼
			Meotain		350-2,000	Ss and marls	Brackish with fresh-water intercal.	• ☼
		Miocene	Sarmatian	Kersonian	1,500-2,000	Ss and ls	Brackish	•
				Bessarabian		Ss, sds, marls	Brackish	
				Volhynian		Marls, sds	Brackish	•
				Buglovian		Marls	Marine, Brackish	
			Tortonian	Late	300-600 300	Marls, sdy complex with Spirialis Shls with Radiolaria	Marine	
					1,800	Breccia with rocksalt mass	Lagoonal	
				Early	30-300	Tuffs with Globigerina	Marine	
			Helvetian	Late	5,000	Marls, gypsum, sds	Marine, Lagoonal	
				Early	1,500	Clg, red ss, and marls	Marine, Lagoonal	•
			Burdigalian		1,800-3,000	Clg, marls, and sds	Marine	
	Paleogene	Oligocene	Aquitanian		300	Marls, breccia, salt, gypsum	Lagoonal	
			Late		165-200	Upper Menilites and diatomites	Marine, euxinic	
					1,650	Upper Kliwa ss	Marine	•
			Middle		650-820	Podul Morli beds(calcareous curbicortical ss with heiroglyph)	Marine	
			Early		1,500	Lower Kliwa ss	Marine	•
					390-650	Disodilic shls	Marine, euxinic	
					65-130	Lower Menilites	Marine, euxinic	
		Eocene	Late		6,000	Marls and ss	Marine	

• Oil ☼ Gas

Source: From Gustavson Associates Inc.

IPE

in the inner zone of the depression, which are more often than not poor in dissolved gas. Towards the exterior, on the line of diapiric folds, the oil fields are rich in dissolved gas or have a primary gas cap. Reservoir pressures are generally hydrostatic with local overpressured anomalies.

Future exploration is not likely to uncover new structural features but might unearth additional reserves in deeper pay zones in existing fields or subtler stratigraphic traps.

Most of the hydrocarbons are thought have been generated from Oligocene source rocks deeper than 13,000 ft. This implies that subthrust structures—deep but well within reach of western deep drilling practices—are prospective. Lower Cretaceous sands have yielded gas shows at depths of almost 22,000 ft. The Borislav-Pokutian zone of the foredeep has yielded oil at depths of about 19,000 ft. The subthrust structures below 15,000 ft have not been adequately tested.

The use of 3D seismic, a technology not applied by the Ukrainians, is the best method for searching for these structures, but this will present logistical problems in the heavily forested mountains. IPE

The 24-in., 785-mile Express crude oil pipeline follows the contours of the rolling landscape near the South Saskatchewan River crossing in Alberta, Can. Photo courtesy Express Pipeline.

Production, import changes shift U.S. patterns of crude supply

Increasing levels of oil imports and dwindling production in specific areas changed U.S. crude oil supply patterns during 1996.

As the year drew to a close, monthly production of crude oil in the Lower 48 was increasing slightly, while production from Alaska decreased.

At the same time, crude oil and product import levels were increasing. On an annual basis, the long term U.S. production decline showed little sign of abating as 1996 was ending.

According to the American Petroleum Institute (API), imports of crude in October 1996 totaled 7.8 million b/d, an increase of about 10% vs. the same period in 1995. Product imports were more than one-third higher than at the same time a year earlier.

Crude oil production during October was just less than 1% above the previous year's levels, reflecting a 120,000 b/d increase in production from the Lower 48 and a decline in Alaskan output of 60,000 b/d.

API said the increase for October 1996 marked the third consecutive monthly increase in Lower 48 production, "most likely reflecting new offshore production in the Gulf of Mexico."

Total U.S. crude oil production was 6.48 million b/d, highest since March 1996. Alaskan production was 1.4 million b/d. The remainder of the country produced an average of about 5 million b/d.

Crude oil production on a year-to-date basis was just 2% lower than the same time in 1995, according to API, with most of the decline in Alaska.

Crude imports from Canada during January-October averaged 1.028 million b/d vs. 1.031 million b/d in 1995, according to API.

The longer term trend of year-by-year increases in Canadian imports into the U.S. is expected to continue, boosted by new pipeline capacity that was to have gone on stream late in 1996.

With existing pipeline projects, possible line expansions, and actual or contemplated line reversals, future incremental supply from Canada could total between 700,000 b/d to 1 million b/d or more by the turn of the century or shortly after, filling foreseen gaps in crude supply in the U.S. Midwest, Midcontinent, and Rocky Mountain areas.

Purvin & Gertz assessment

Crude oil supply patterns for refiners in the Midwest and Rocky Mountain regions in Petroleum Administration for Defense Districts II and IV (PADDs II and IV) were in a state of transition in 1996 as regional crude oil production continued to decline rapidly.

In PADD III the situation in 1996 was markedly different: Forecast increases in production from the Gulf of Mexico during the next 10 years will offset declines predicted to occur in other PADD III areas.

Those were among the major conclusions reached in an exclusive report on changing crude supply patterns prepared late in the year for Oil & Gas Journal by authors Robert J. Hewitt, Kenneth D. Miller, Blake T. Eskew, and Steven J. Kelly of the Houston, Philadelphia, and Calgary offices of Purvin & Gertz Inc., international energy consultants.

According to their assessment, inland refiners were becoming increasingly dependent on deliveries of imported crude from Canada and offshore sources.

Meanwhile, numerous pipeline projects were under way to deliver increased import volumes from both of those sources to forestall any regional shortfalls. However, as new refinery supply patterns emerged, crude price relationships between the major North American markets — the Gulf Coast; Cushing, Okla.; and Edmonton, Alta. — were continually adjusting to reflect evolving regional supply balances.

U.S. crude production

Purvin & Gertz said between 1985 and 1995 crude oil production in the United States decreased to 6.6 million b/d from 8.9 million b/d, an average annual decline rate of 3.0%/year. New production from the Gulf of Mexico will arrest this decline through 2000, but by 2005 total production is projected to fall to about 6.1 million b/d (Fig. 1).

In PADDs II and IV, the inland refinery districts, crude production has fallen more sharply. The annual decline rate has averaged 5.5%/year since 1985 and is projected to exceed 4%/year throughout the next decade. As a result of these dwindling local crude supplies, inland refiners satisfied just 27% of their 1995 crude needs with in-PADD production, down from more than 50% 10 years earlier.

By 2005, Purvin & Gertz projects this coverage ratio will fall to only 16%. Combined crude production in PADDs II and IV will sink to an estimated 631,000 b/d from 1.7 million b/d in 1985.

The outlook for crude oil production in PADD III is more upbeat. Spurred by improvements in seismic data interpretation and supported by rapid advances in drilling technology, production from the Gulf of Mexico is projected to almost double during the next 10 years.

This surge will more than offset continuing declines in West Texas and in other mature producing areas in PADD III (Table 1).

In PADD V, according to Purvin & Gertz, crude oil production is projected to decrease by 2005 to less than 1.7 million b/d from 1995's 2.5 million b/d. Policies and regulations governing exploration, production, and transportation activities in both Alaska and California will limit future crude oil production in PADD V.

Fig. 1

Outlook for U.S. crude oil production

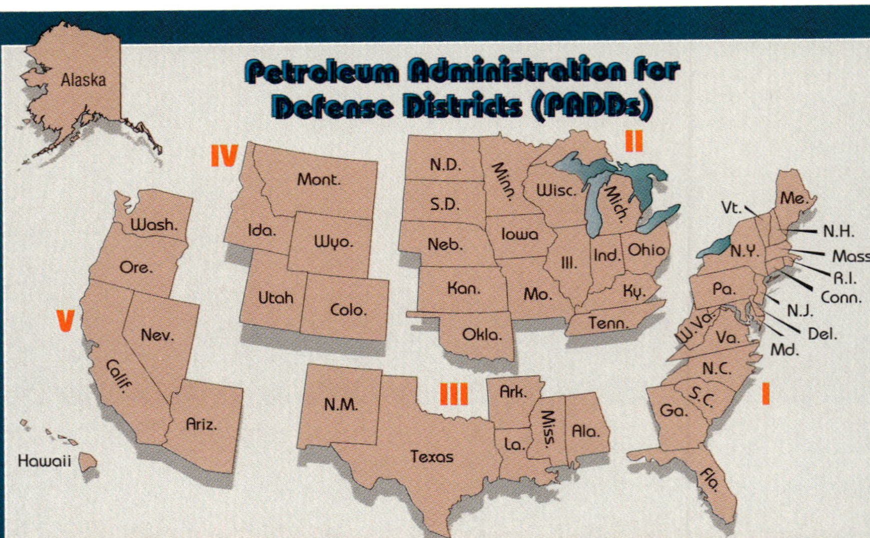

PADD	1985	1990	1995	2000	2005
			1,000 b/d		
I	57	30	27	27	26
II	1,052	742	571	460	377
III	4,238	3,364	3,120	3,833	3,769
IV	628	498	393	312	254
V	2,944	2,777	2,522	2,105	1,658
Total*	**8,920**	**7,410**	**6,633**	**6,737**	**6,084**

*Columns may not add due to rounding.
Source: Purvin & Gertz Inc.

IPE

Crude oil imports

Imported crude's share of U.S. supply will continue to grow (Fig. 2). By 2005, U.S. refinery runs are projected to increase to 15.5 million b/d from 12 million b/d in 1985.

During this same period, total crude imports will have risen to 9.4 million b/d from 3.2 million b/d. In relative terms, while refinery runs increase by 22%, crude imports must triple. Imported crude's share of total crude supply moved up from 27% in 1985 to 52% in 1995 and will climb further to 60% by 2005, according to Purvin & Gertz.

Roughly 80% of crude oil imports were received by East Coast, Gulf Coast, and West Coast refineries in 1996. The remaining imports went to inland refiners. And these volumes are split between Canadian and offshore receipts (Fig. 3). A dynamic balance exists between these "Northern" and "Southern" sources of crude imports for inland refiners, and the economic balance point will be shifting with each new change in regional crude supplies (Table 2).

Canadian crude outlook

Canada's crude exports to the U.S. have risen steadily with production. Canadian production in 1995 approached 2 million b/d, up 25% since 1985 (Table 3).

Essentially all of 1995 production originated in the western provinces. Canada's demand for domestically produced crude in 1996 was about 900,000 b/d; refineries in the Atlantic provinces and in Quebec process imported crudes. Canadian crude exports to the U.S. in 1995 exceeded 1 million b/d, up by 570,000 b/d from the 1985 level.

By 2005, Purvin & Gertz said, total Canadian crude production may exceed 2.3 million b/d. A substantial portion of this increase will be heavy crude. In the near term, total production of Canadian heavy will likely be constrained by refinery processing capabilities rather than supply limits.

In response to these increasing supplies, a number of pipeline expansion projects were under way late in 1996. Interprovincial Pipe Line Inc. (IPL), Edmonton, Alta., was scheduled to complete an expansion project late in 1996 that would increase delivery capability into northern PADD II by 120,000 b/d.

A new bypass connection between IPL's Westspur (Saskatchewan) system and the Portal pipeline is also part of this expansion, which will allow IPL to divert up to 50,000 b/d of crude around a capacity-limited line segment at Cromer, Man., for delivery into Clearbrook, Minn.

With production and exports expanding further, IPL has announced a phase two expansion, expected to be completed in 1998, which will add 170,000 b/d of export capacity destined for PADD II.

Table 1

PADD III crude oil production

	1985	1995	2005
		(Thousand b/d)	
West Texas/ New Mexico	1,798	1,222	949
Louisana Gulf Coast	1,307	1,227	2,418
Other PADD III	1,133	671	403
Total:	**4,238**	**3,120**	**3,770**

Source: Purvin & Gertz Inc.

Express pipeline

Alberta Energy co. Ltd. (AEC) and TransCanada Pipelines have formed a joint venture to construct a new "Express" pipeline from Hardisty, Alta., to Casper, Wyo. Construction of the pipeline was to be complete by yearend 1996.

The initial capacity of this 775-mile, 24-in. pipeline will be 172,000 b/d, AEC said late in November. During 1996, Express was determining the level of interest in a further 100,000 b/d expansion.

At Hardisty, the pipeline could receive many crudes directly, including Hardisty Light, Bow River, Lloydminster Blend,

U.S. oil supply, imports Fig. 2

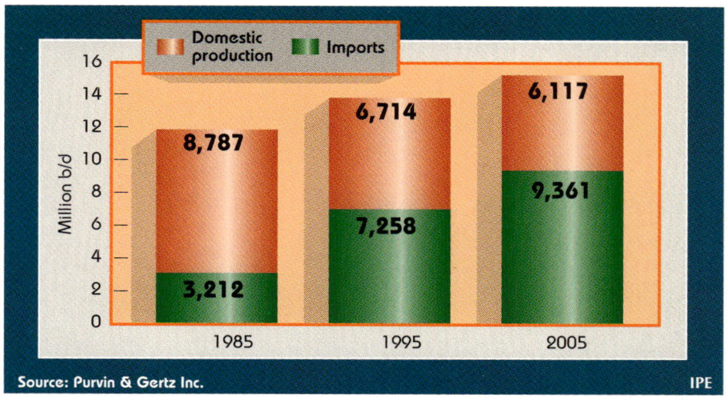

U.S. inland oil imports Fig. 3

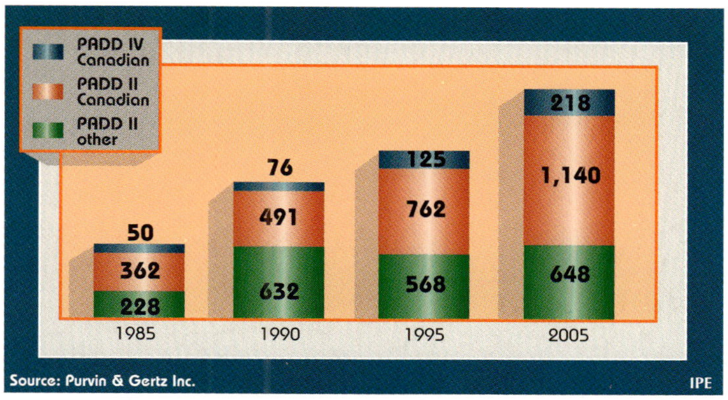

Midcontinent/gulf price spread volatility Fig. 4

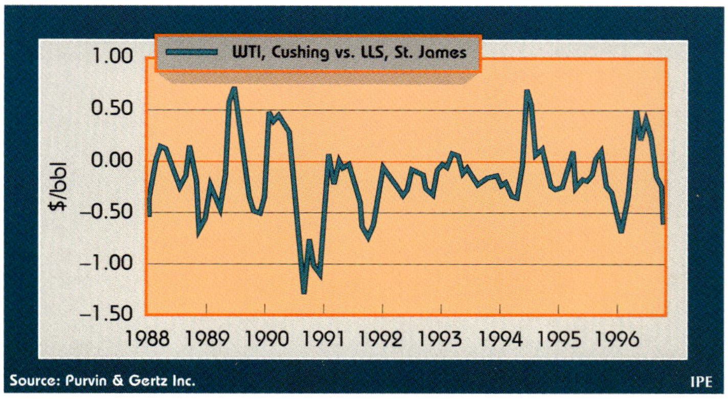

Outlook for inland/gulf price spread Fig. 5

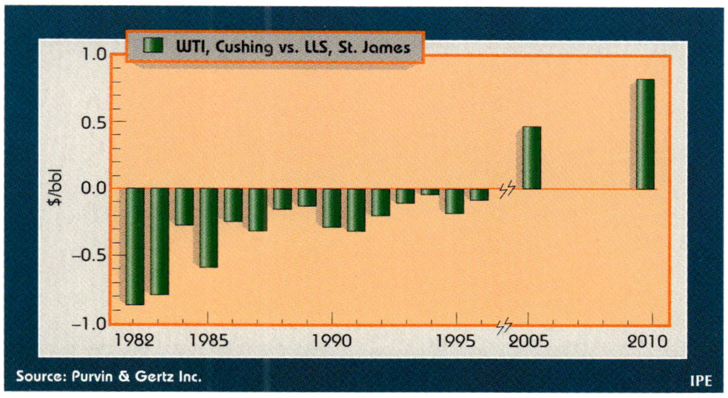

and Bi-Provincial synthetic crude. It could also receive crudes delivered from Edmonton on IPL, notably Mixed Sweet and Ft. McMurray synthetic crudes.

The pipeline will supply PADD IV with Canadian crude oil but will not initially be connected to refineries at Billings, Mont. It will, however, be connected to the existing major crude oil trunk lines at Casper, Wyo. From Casper, crude oil could be delivered through existing pipelines to Denver; Cheyenne, Wyo.; and Salt Lake City, Utah.

At Casper, Express will be able to deliver crude to PADD II via the Platte pipeline, which was purchased by Express early in 1996. Platte delivers crude to Wood River, Ill., and to connecting pipelines in Kansas. A combined Express/Platte tariff was being developed, which would be competitive with the existing IPL/Lakehead/Mobil tariff to Wood River. Express will feature a unique toll design, in which tariffs will vary depending on the term of delivery contracts signed by shippers.

The Express/Platte system will expand crude supplies to both PADDs II and IV. Several other pipeline debottlenecking projects were under way (Cenex; Amoco/Conoco; Bow River/Milk River; and Wascana/Texaco/Butte). They collectively may add 150,000- 200,000 b/d of crude delivery capacity to PADD IV.

Sarnia-Montreal pipeline reversal

Reversal of IPL's Line 9 would initially allow Ontario refiners new access to 120,000-150,000 b/d of crudes originating either from international trade or new East Coast production from Hibernia and Terra Nova fields.

Initial steps leading to this reversal were under way in 1996. In June the Canadian government relinquished its option to acquire Line 9, so IPL now has outright ownership.

A price "trigger" agreement negotiated between refiners and West Canadian producers as a condition for reversal was satisfied. This agreement stipulated that a deemed cost for Brent crude be less than the delivered cost of Western Canadian Mixed Sweet (quality-adjusted) for 5 of 7 consecutive months.

Accordingly, IPL was negotiating facilities-support agreements with prospective shippers and preparing to submit filings to Canada's National Energy Board to initiate review of proposed tariffs, operating mode, and shipper access. Given the contractual and procedural steps required, reversal probably cannot take place any sooner than mid-1998.

After this time, any reversal decision will hinge on negotiated shipper agreements and on supply economics. Following reversal, Canadian exports to the U.S. will increase, as Western Canadian crude is backed out of Ontario and diverted south into PADD II.

U.S. pipelines have positioned themselves to handle increased Canadian imports. In April 1994, Mobil reversed its Patoka-Chicago line to extend the southern range for Canadian imports. More than 50,000 b/d of Canadian crude has moved south via this route, and higher volumes are possible depending on the crude type.

While significant reversal flows may not occur until after 2000, future shipments on Line 9 could exceed initial start-up estimates. The Portland pipeline will deliver offshore crudes into the IPL system at Montreal. Until mid-1998, only one of Portland's two active lines is available for crude service. This line had a capacity of 245,000 b/d in 1996 and could be expanded to almost 400,000 b/d.

The second line was in natural gas service but could be returned to crude, increasing Portland's potential capacity to almost 600,000 b/d. The delivery capacity of a reversed Line 9 is estimated at 300,000-350,000 b/d, so it could be fully utilized given sufficient refinery demand.

Table 2

Crude imports for PADDs II and IV

	1985	1990	1995	2005
Thousand b/d	640	1,199	1,456	2,007
% of total supply	20	35	40	52

Source: Purvin & Gertz Inc.

Table 4

PADD II crude oil balance

Production	1985	1995 (Thousand b/d)	2005
Crude runs	2,737	3,167	3,390
Production	1,052	571	377
Net transfers in	1,134	1,200	1,224
Canadian imports	362	762	1,140
Other imports	228	569	648
% imports	22	42	53

Source: Purvin & Gertz Inc.

Table 3

Canadian crude balance

Production	1985	1995 (Thousand b/d)	2005
Western-light crudes	1,228	1,302	1,072
Western-heavy crudes	346	644	1,055
Eastern	0	21	226
Total:	**1,574**	**1,968**	**2,353**
Crude Runs	1,363	1,518	1,606
Net available for export	211	450	747
Imports to Atlantic/Quebec	264	594	590
Exports potential before Line 9 reversal	475	1,044	1,337

Source: Purvin & Gertz Inc.

Table 5

PADD IV crude oil balance

Production	1985	1995 (Thousand b/d)	2005
Crude runs	432	458	469
Production	628	393	254
Net transfers in	(258)	(68)	(29)
Canadian imports	50	125	218
% imports	12	27	47

Source: Purvin & Gertz Inc.

PADD II crude balance

During 1995, PADD II refiners imported 42% of their crude supplies. Approximately 24% of their supplies were Canadian imports, while 18% moved up through various pipeline systems (primarily Capline) from the Gulf Coast.

By 2005, regional crude production will furnish only 11% of the projected crude runs, so imports will be growing steadily (Table 4). In addition to new Canadian supply options for the Midwest, several other pipeline projects have been implemented to increase import capacity through Gulf Coast ports into both the Midwest and the Midcontinent refining regions.

The Seaway pipeline system began operating in May 1996. This ARCO/Phillips joint-venture pipeline has the capacity to deliver up to 270,000 b/d of imported crude through its Freeport, Tex., terminal to Cushing, Okla.

And Mobil has reversed its Beaumont-Corsicana-Ringgold, Tex., pipeline system, providing 250,000 b/d of new capacity for northward movement of domestic and imported crude.

Up to 100,000 b/d could be routed indirectly into Midcontinent markets (Cushing), and up to 200,000 b/d can move through Mobil's existing system into the Midwest. Purvin & Gertz's PADD II balances indicate that sufficient pipeline capacity will be available to deliver the required crude supplies.

The balance point, where competing Canadian and Gulf Coast imports meet, may well be determined by competing delivery costs rather than deliverability limits, according to the Purvin & Gertz report.

Crude quality will also be an important consideration, given that much of the new West Canadian supply will be heavy. IPL announced its intention during 1996 to construct a new connection to BP Oil's Toledo, Ohio, refinery. This line would support BP's partial conversion of that facility from light-sweet to heavy-sour processing. Initial capacity would be 85,000 b/d, expandable to 110,000 b/d.

PADD IV crude balance

PADD IV refiners processed 125,000 b/d of Canadian crude during 1995 (27% of runs). As production declines, the share of runs provided by imports is projected to reach 47% by 2005, Purvin & Gertz said (Table 5).

The Express pipeline project, together with the other northern expansion projects identified, should provide PADD IV refiners ample access to the crude supplies they need. PADD IV's growing requirements will contribute to Canada's increasing share of U.S. imports (Fig. 3).

Crude pricing implications

The changing inland U.S. crude balance has affected crude oil markets throughout the world through its influence on the pricing of West Texas Intermediate (WTI). WTI is deliverable under the Nymex light, sweet crude oil contract, which is the pricing basis for the majority of foreign contract crudes delivered to the U.S. market.

The delicate balance in the Midwest and Midcontinent markets has increased volatility in WTI pricing over the years, causing erratic variations in the prices paid for crudes solely indexed to this benchmark.

Wide swings have occurred in the pricing of WTI at Cushing relative to the Gulf Coast market, which is more accurately reflected in the pricing of Light Louisiana Sweet (LLS) (Fig. 4).

The volatility in the short term differential is largely a result of seasonal shifts in the price parity point for WTI, and Purvin & Gertz said the longer term path in the relationship will be affected by the evolving inland balances and logistical constraints.

During the next few years, the Cushing market will be kept relatively depressed by increasing supplies of Canadian crude. In particular, said Purvin & Gertz, the reversal of the Sarnia-Montreal pipeline will result in North Sea crude's displacing Canadian sweet crudes from Ontario, forcing Canadian crude into the Midwest and backing out domestic and offshore crudes.

Beyond the end of the decade, the continuing decline of inland production will tighten the balance, in spite of the increased availability of Canadian crude. The need for offshore imports, particularly in the Midcontinent, will result in stronger prices for WTI and Canadian crudes (Fig. 5). IPE

Worldwide growth in demand for natural gas boosts LNG trade

World demand for natural gas is increasing, intensifying competition for and international trade in liquefied natural gas.

By the end of 1996, numerous export schemes had been proposed or put in motion. In 1997 and beyond, project economics and market demand will continue to dictate which projects reach fruition.

Industrial growth, environmental issues, and energy security in particular regions and countries will increase the need for LNG in various market niches, especially power generation. LNG becomes especially attractive as a fuel where there is no transportation infrastructure linking sources of supply to gas-hungry end-use markets, and where pipeline capacity isn't sufficient to move volumes needed to satisfy demand.

The Institute of Gas Technology (IGT) reported that during 1970-95 the share of natural gas in world primary energy consumption increased significantly. In 1995, natural gas claimed almost a 24% share of world energy consumption compared with 17% in 1970.

In its 1996 report, "An Overview of the Global LNG Industry - Markets, Projects, Economics," by Colleen Taylor Sen, Ph.D., associate director, LNG Resources, IGT said that during 1970-95 the amount of gas traded internationally grew by a factor of 8 to about 18% of world production, or some 400 billion cu m, from a 1970 level of only 4.4% of world production.

Approximately one fourth of that growth IGT attributed to LNG, with consumption of LNG increasing almost 8%/year since 1980 (Fig. 1). In 1995 alone, LNG consumption increased 4.7% to 92 billion cu m.

IGT said the fastest growing region in terms of gas demand is Latin America, where overall demand in 1995 increased 7.5% to 3.6 tcf. In Asia, it increased to 217 billion cu m, or 6.3%, while consumption in western Europe rose 5%.

Fig. 1

Growth of international LNG trade

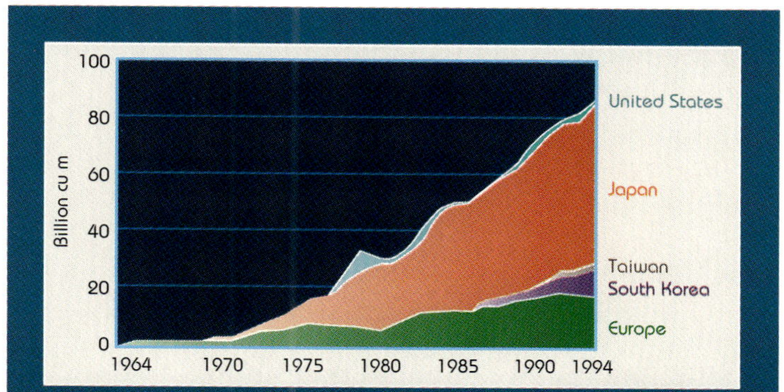

Source: Cedigaz, 1995

IPE

Fig. 2

Asian LNG supply and demand outlook

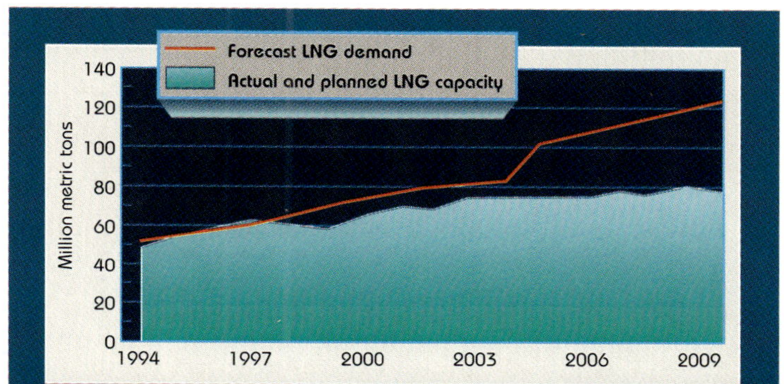

Source: International Energy Agency

IPE

Regional demand

The largest concentrations of LNG supply and demand are in the Far East. In 1995, 77% of the world's LNG was consumed by Japan (63%), followed by Korea (10%) and Taiwan (about 4%); Europe consumed the majority of remaining supply (Table 1).

At yearend 1996, LNG demand in Asia showed no sign of letting up. According to France's Cedigaz, Pacific Rim deliveries in 1995 totaled 70 billion cu m, or 52.5 million tons/year. They accounted for 76% of total volumes traded worldwide, and Japan accounted for two thirds of all demand.

Cedigaz states that Japan will remain the largest import market for LNG for some time, and that growth in Korea will be strong, attaining an import level of 16 million metric tons/year by 2000 and more than 21 million metric tons/year in 2010.

Table 1

LNG importing countries, 1995

Importing country	Million metric ton	Billion cubic meters of gas	%
Japan	42.373	53.169	62.79
Korea	6.971	10.33	10.33
Spain	5.563	7.039	8.24
France	5.103	6.457	7.56
France/Belgium	0.716	0.90	1.06
Belgium	3.046	3.855	4.51
Taiwan	2.442	2.090	3.62
Turkey	0.895	1.133	1.33
U.S.	0.379	0.480	0.56
Total	**67.488**	**85.400**	**100**

Source: Group Internationale des Importateurs de Gaz Naturel Liquéfié (G.I.I.G.N.L.)

In its "Asia Gas Study," the International Energy Agency (IEA) forecast that Asian LNG demand by 2010 will more than double from its 1994 level, and imports from outside the region could represent as much as 40% of total imports. Moreover, IEA said, regional LNG trade could triple during the period (Fig. 2).

Currently, Asia is viewed as principally self-sufficient in natural gas, and as a whole the region is a net LNG exporter; however, No. 1 LNG importer Japan is the exception because of its LNG volumes from Abu Dhabi and Alaska's Kenai facility. But, as is shown in Fig. 2, Asian demand could begin to outstrip supply beginning as early as 1997.

By 2010, IEA noted, as much as 40% of Asian gas, or about 48 million metric tons/year, could come from outside Asia, including supply sources such as the Middle East.

According to Cedigaz's estimates, as much as 27 million metric tons/year of new liquefaction capacity may be needed in Asia alone by 2010 at a cost of $11 billion, plus as many as 25 new LNG carriers costing $6 billion. Most of the vessels will be built in Asia.

Indonesia and Algeria continued their export trade dominance in 1996 (Fig. 3).

Future significant Middle East LNG supply sources include Qatar and Oman, both of which were moving ahead with large-scale projects in 1996. Abu Dhabi, with one liquefaction plant yielding in excess of 4 million metric tons/year, is the region's only exporter currently, with contract LNG volumes dedicated solely to Japan.

IEA said that while gas supply security is not yet viewed as a major issue in Asia, it could become so in the future as consumption rises and the gas share of total world primary energy supply increases. Asia's share of total world primary energy supply is projected to increase to 21% in 2010 from 17% in 1990, and natural gas's share is projected to rise to 15% from about 10%.

IEA predicts that annual average gas demand growth in Malaysia, Indonesia, and Brunei will be 8-10% through 2010.

Table 2

LNG exporting countries, 1995

Exporting country	Million metric ton	Billion cubic meters	%
Indonesia	24.457	30.949	36.24
Algeria	13.243	16.758	19.62
Malaysia	9.391	11.883	13.92
Australia	7.005	8.863	10.38
Brunei	6.083	7.698	9.01
Abu Dhabi	4.879	6.174	7.23
U.S.	1.337	1.692	1.98
Libya	1.093	1.383	1.62
Total	**67.488**	**85.400**	**100**

Source: Group Internationale des Importateurs de Gaz Naturel Liquéfié (G.I.I.G.N.L.)

Trade patterns

According to the Society of International Gas Tankers & Terminal Operators Ltd. (Sigtto), worldwide LNG shipments by ocean-going vessels in 1995 increased about 2% to 1,648 voyages from 1,619 voyages in 1995. Total deliveries were about 149.8 million cu m in 1995 vs. 144.3 million cu m the previous year.

Siggto said of the voyages completed during 1995, 611 were to European receiving terminals compared with 596 in 1995. The Far East accounted for 1,030 voyages in 1995, up 27 from the prior year. But the U.S. was down significantly, with only seven total voyages for deliveries to Lake Charles, La., and Everett, Mass. The year 1994 saw 20 shipments to the U.S.

The active LNG vessel fleet in 1995 grew by eight to 86, with seven new ships built and one returned to service after being idle in 1994. Two new ships each were built for Petronas, Korea, and Abu Dhabi and one for the North West Shelf project in Australia.

A total of 26 ships were on order in 1995, representing a 30% increase in total active fleet vessels.

Indonesian LNG exports

Indonesia is currently the world's largest exporter of LNG (Table 2). Its LNG supply dominance is not expected to decline, with major plans announced in 1996 by Mobil Corp. and Coastal Corp.

Since 1978, Mobil has operated the giant PT Arun liquefaction plant — the world's largest — in North Sumatra in a joint venture with state-owned oil company Pertamina. Late in 1996, Arun field was producing a total of 2.3 bcfd of gas for liquefaction into more than 12 million metric tons/year of LNG.

In a presentation to the Second Annual Middle East Gas Summit in Abu Dhabi in October 1996, Daniel Nelson, Mobil's executive vice-president—LNG Venture Development, said during 20 years of operation the (Mobil-Pertamina LNG) joint venture has not missed a single cargo in more than 2,700 deliveries, and in those two decades has shipped approximately 160 million tons of LNG.

Mobil agreed in principle with Pertamina in 1996 to acquire a 26% interest in the Natuna field gas development under study by Esso Exploration & Production Natuna Inc. Natuna, Indonesia's largest field, has estimated gas reserves of 210 tcf, including 60 tcf of methane and heavier hydrocarbons and much of the rest carbon dioxide.

Coastal and Pertamina will team to develop LNG import projects and conduct related work in India.

Algeria's efforts

Late in 1996, No. 2 LNG exporter Algeria was ready to begin supplying incremental volumes of gas to Europe.

According to IGT, European natural gas demand is projected to rise at a rate of more than 12%/year during 1994-2010, primarily because of mounting power generation needs. Cedigaz projects LNG consumption in southern Europe could be 6-7 times recent levels by the end of the period (Table 3). Demand increases could be seen in Turkey, a significant LNG and pipeline importer of gas, and also in Central Europe to meet rising gas demand, especially after 2000.

And, late in 1996, Egypt, Turkey, and Amoco Corp. signed a memorandum of understanding calling for LNG exports of as much as 7.3 million metric tons/year to Turkey, with first deliveries slated for 2000. A plant to be built on the Egyptian coast would liquefy gas produced by Amoco Egypt Oil Co. from Nile Delta fields.

LNG imports constitute only 11-12% of total gas imports to western Europe, a net importer of gas. Until 2000, IGT said, most incremental gas supplies needed will come under existing contracts or contract extensions.

But, by 2010, contracts and anticipated extensions will supply only about 70% of projected western European demand (Table 4).

As a result, about 155 billion cu m by 2010 would need to be filled by new sources — including Algerian volumes provided by LNG carriers, traditional pipeline deliveries, or both, as well as pipeline deliveries from Russia and Central Asia.

Algeria's goal is to double its overall gas exports to 60 billion cu m/year by the end of this century. If Algeria is successful, its production could approach, or surpass, 75 billion cu m/year level, giving it the ability to supply much of the incremental demand foreseen in western Europe and allowing it to gain greater global gas and LNG market share.

During 1996, Algeria's state-owned oil company Sonatrach was investing $2.4 billion to raise efficiency and increase production capacities at its LNG complexes at Skikda and Arzew, and at the smaller Camel complex. Capacity at Skikda's GL1K complex is expected to reach 7.9 billion cu m/year in 1997, and Arzew's GL1Z and GL2Z trains were to attain or surpass their combined original design capacities of more than 21 billion cu m/year.

Camel, the world's first gas liquefaction plant when it was placed into service in 1964, will receive upgrades, but its capacity of 600 million cu m/year will be kept in reserve until after 2000.

Qatar's projects

In 1996, Qatar had three projects in various stages of development or planned to supply Asian markets with LNG produced from volumes extracted from its ultragiant North field: Qatargas, Ras Laffan (also known as the Rasgas project), and a project planned by Enron Corp.

Qatar is viewed as a major LNG exporter of the future. North field reserves are placed at 380 tcf recoverable, representing about 9% of world natural gas reserves.

Qatargas, closest of the three projects to completion, is operated upstream by Total and downstream by Mobil. Qatar General Petroleum Corp. (QGPC) holds a majority interest.

Chiyoda of Japan is constructing the first two liquefaction trains under a $1.8 billion contract with a planned 1997 start-up.

Chubu Electric Power Co. Inc., Tokyo, has contracted for 4 million metric tons/year, and a group of seven gas and power utilities will receive 2 million metric tons/year.

Late in 1996, the first two trains of the Qatargas project were in late stages of development, each with a capacity of 2.2 million metric tons/year. Completion was set for late in 1996, and initial deliveries were scheduled to begin in January 1997.

Ras Laffan, Qatar's second greenfield project, is scheduled for initial start-up in 1998. Operated by Ras Laffan Liquefied Natural Gas Co. Ltd., the project will liquefy volumes produced in North field for transport to buyers in Asian and Turkish markets. Rasgas is a joint venture between QGPC with a 70% interest and Mobil QM Gas Inc. 30%.

JGC Corp., of Japan, and M.W. Kellogg Co. are constructing the first of two trains, which will have a 2.5 million metric tons/year design capacity each. First deliveries are set for mid-1999 to the Far East and, potentially, other customers later. Additional trains may be added subsequently.

Korea Gas Corp. (KGC) has an agreement to buy 2.4 million metric tons/year, and Rasgas was courting numerous other buyers for the 2.6 million metric tons/year uncommitted in 1996. LNG will be shipped to Korea in four 138,000 cu m carriers to be built in Korean shipyards.

KGC also planned to buy 3.5 million metric tons/year from Pac-Rim LNG Inc., Calgary, in a project in British Columbia advancing late in 1996.

The third Qatari project was to begin construction early in 1997 by Enron. Exports totaling 5 million metric tons/year are planned to India, Israel, and Jordan.

FIG. 3

World trade in natural gas and LNG, 1995

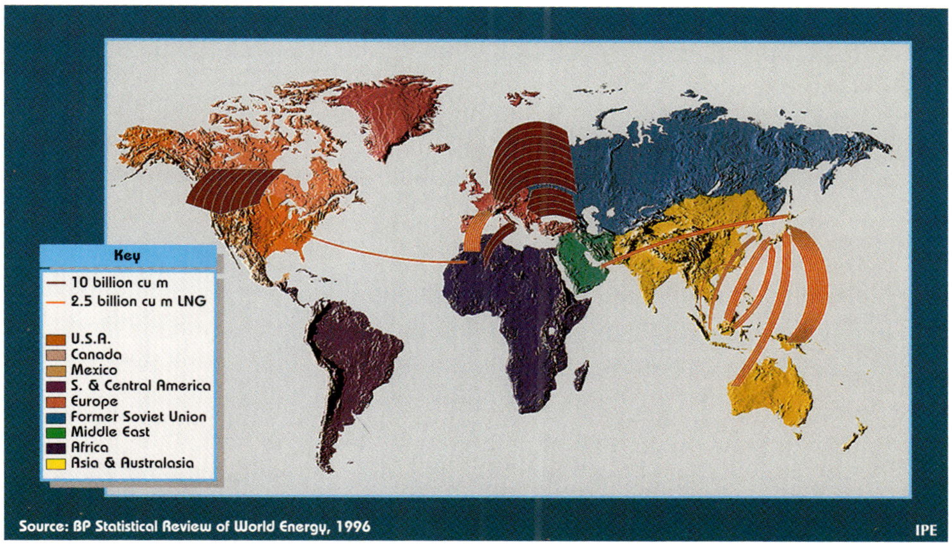

Source: BP Statistical Review of World Energy, 1996

IPE

Enron has an agreement with QGPC to form Qatar-Enron Liquefied Natural Gas Co., and discussions continued in 1996 on constructing an LNG plant in Qatar. About 2 million metric tons/year are envisioned for Enron's planned $2.5 billion Dabhol power station at Maharashtra, India, while Israel could take 2 million metric tons/year and Jordan 500,000 metric tons/year.

Oman plans shipments

Oman was moving ahead in 1996 with plans for first shipments of LNG to Korea by 2000. Late in 1996, Oman LNG Co. signed a 25 year contract with Korea Gas Corp. to supply 4.1 million metric tons/year to Korea as part of a project totaling about $6 billion. Oman's planned liquefaction complex at Al-Ghalilah, near the southern port of Sur, will have two trains, each with a design capacity of 3.3 million metric tons/year.

Three gas/condensate fields will be developed, treatment installed, and a 370 km feedgas pipeline laid to the plant. Commissioning is planned in 1999.

Oman was obtaining financing late in 1996 to build the liquefaction plant. It held a funding agreement placed at about $1.4 billion to be used to increase gas production from the sultanate for the LNG project. Royal Dutch/Shell Group, Total, and Partex — which already together hold 40% of Petroleum Development Oman — will operate the production facilities for 25 years and supply gas to the LNG plant, as well as to other projects within Oman.

Also, Oman LNG LLC signed a letter of intent in 1996 with the Petroleum Authority of Thailand to supply about 2 million metric tons/year beginning by about 2003.

Trinidad & Tobago project

Atlantic LNG Co. of Trinidad & Tobago was moving ahead in 1996 with a $1 billion, 3 million metric ton/year LNG plant to supply markets in Spain and the Northeast U.S. — the first greenfield LNG plant to be built in the Western Hemisphere in more than 25 years. The complex will be built with one train only; however, it has been designed, planned, and located so that additional production trains can be added as demand for LNG increases.

Atlantic LNG has sold 100% of the LNG to Cabot LNG Corp. and Spain's Enagas. First deliveries are to begin in mid-1999. Commercial deliveries are expected to be under way by October 1999.

Amoco Trinidad Oil Co. will supply gas to the plant at a rate of about 450 MMcfd for an initial contract period of 20 years. The entire project, which includes the development of two offshore gas fields, a pipeline to shore and across the island, and construction of the plant will generate an estimated economic impact of $6 billion during the first 20 years of its life, according to Atlantic LNG.

Shareholders in Atlantic LNG are Amoco Trinidad (LNG) BV 34%, British Gas Trinidad LNG Ltd. 26%, Repsol International Finance BV of Spain 20%, and Cabot Trinidad LNG Ltd. and NGC Trinidad & Tobago LNG Ltd. 10% each.

The LNG will be sold fob. It will be transported by four carriers, three of which will be chartered by Enagas.

Prime contractor for the plant, to be built at Point Fortin, is Bechtel Corp., which will provide engineering, procurement, construction, start-up, and initial operating services.

Atlantic LNG signed a licensing agreement with Phillips Petroleum Co. for use of Optimized Cascade Process technology. And late in 1996, in a separate move, Phillips and Bechtel agreed to form an alliance to expand their roles in world LNG markets.

Northwest Shelf

As 1997 began, project participants were continuing efforts to expand the North West Shelf LNG project in Australia, which has been producing LNG for export since 1989.

A formal proposal, which could lead to a $5 billion expansion of the project, was presented to the eight Japanese power and gas utilities that purchase North West Shelf LNG under a 20 year contract.

The purchasers receive 131 cargoes/year. They are: Tokyo Electric Power Co. Inc., Chubu Electric Power Co. Inc., Kansai Electric Power Co. Inc., Chugoku Electric Power Co. Inc., Kyushu Electric Power Co. Inc., Tokyo Gas Co. Ltd., Osaka Gas Co. Ltd., and Toho Gas Co. Ltd.

The proposal outlined plans for a two-train expansion at the Burrup Peninsula complex, which would almost double the project's existing sales capacity of 7.5 million metric tons/year. Subject to the requirements of Japanese customers, the 7 million-ton expansion could be on stream as early as 2000.

The six equal participants in the project are Chevron Asiatic Ltd., BHP Petroleum (North West Shelf) Pty Ltd., BP Developments Australia Ltd., Japan Australia LNG (MIMI) Pty Ltd., Shell Development (Australia) Pty Ltd., and North West Shelf Group Leader Woodside Petroleum Ltd.

A 14.5 million metric tons/year expanded capacity would entail additional offshore production facilities and LNG shipping. Such an expansion would allow for growth in domestic gas sales and for the extension of existing contracts, as well.

In the past 3 years, the North West Shelf LNG Project has supplemented its income by marketing surplus output to Spain, Turkey, and South Korea.

North West Shelf is Australia's largest natural resource development. The project uses feedgas produced from North Rankin and Goodwyn offshore fields, with combined reserves totaling about 2.5 billion bbl of oil equivalent. The North West Shelf Project produces not only LNG but also condensate, crude oil, and liquefied petroleum gas.

The discoveries of Perseus field and other area fields have stimulated expansion plans. Perseus gas is expected to be central to the proposed expansion.

In 1996, Mobil acquired a controlling interest in Australia's Ampolex Ltd., which is an interest owner in Gorgon and other fields in western Australia. Mobil told a 1996 Abu Dhabi gas conference it will work with partners and key customers "to monetize these reserves in the most economic way possible." It said "delivery of LNG from Gorgon field gas to market by 2003 may be achievable."

LNG dynamics

LNG's advantages in moving gas from remote production areas to growing markets will gain importance as demand increases in the next century.

But LNG projects, because of their huge initial capital requirements, are among the most difficult of energy projects to structure and finance. They depend on long-term commitments by producers and buyers. Buyers asked to make such commitments demand careful attention in contracts to price.

Each of LNG's three main regional markets has a distinct method of price determination. In the U.S., a netback method dominates. In Europe, the price is linked to petroleum products.

Asian contracts use various methods of pricing. Japan links LNG prices to an average of prices of the crudes it imports, with a 6-month time lag and a fixed factor; however, new contracts contain a floor- and ceiling-price formula, known as the "S-Curve." Korea uses a base price 90% of what is paid by Japanese buyers.

New LNG projects require investments in the $5-10 billion range, including access to large reserves and associated field developments, gathering-pipeline systems, liquefaction plant trains, LNG vessels, and facilities for shipping, receiving, and regasification. For extremely large projects, such as Natuna or a new Alaskan project, investment requirements could be twice this range.

LNG demand, according to Mobil, has grown at an average rate of 20%/year for the past 25 years and is projected to double in the next 15 years. Even though LNG represents only 1-2% of the total world energy market, Mobil said LNG is expected to be the fastest growing segment of the natural gas market.

In addition to needing huge outlays of capital, LNG projects require much time from conception to start of production and supply contracts of 20 years or longer.

The financing hurdle

Financing of LNG projects will continue to be a major hurdle, especially for countries in Asia seeking to finance and build adequate supply infrastructure.

IGT's "LNG Observer" said that, according to Enron Corp., more than $1 trillion will be needed by 2010 for energy infrastructure in the Asia-Pacific region, including $19 billion for 19,200 miles of gas and oil pipelines; $63 billion for exploration and production; and $20-28 billion for five to seven LNG projects.

In an article in the Spring 1996 issue of "LNG Observer," Gerald B. Greenwald, a Washington, D.C.-based LNG consultant and project adviser, noted that each LNG project "has its own unique strengths and its own attractiveness to financial markets."

He cited the example of Algeria, the pioneer in the LNG trade, which built extensive supply, liquefaction, and transportation capacity on its own sovereign credit "utilizing financing supplied by national export credit agencies and Eurodollar loans."

Companies, such as Phillips and Marathon Oil Co., used balance sheet financing and self-generated funds to construct their Kenai, Alaska, project. North West Shelf partners followed the same path.

"These balance sheet financings made two positive contributions to past LNG project development," Greenwald said. "The first was access to financial markets of strong borrower credits...The second benefit is lower cost of borrowing.

"An LNG project financed by strong corporate borrowing will bear less interest expense than a stand-alone LNG project, thereby improving the project's economics and its feasibility for development."

Table 3

Outlook for LNG demand in southern Europe

	1995	2000	2010
	(Billion cubic meters)		
Greece	—	0.5	1-2
Italy	—	2.4	10-12
Portugal	—	—	0=2
Spain	7.04	6	7-8
Turkey	1.13	5	8=9
Krk Island (serves several Central European countries	—	—	9-10
Total	**6.27**	**13.5-15.5**	**34-42**

Source: Cedigaz, 1994

Table 4

Projected natural gas supply and demand in western Europe

	1994	2000	2010	% of Total Gas Demand in 2010
	(Billion cubic meters)			
Demand	330	400	500	
Indigeneous production	207	205	220	44
Imports from:				
Norway	27	65	80	16
Algeria & Libya	30	60	70	14
Russia	67	65	100	20
Trinidad & Nigeria	—	2	8	2
Potential shortfall	0	3	22	4

Source: Cedigaz, 1994

Greenwald added that nonrecourse financings are the trend by international energy companies as new greenfield projects emerge. If the project fails, lenders have no right to the non-project assets of the borrower or sponsors.

Allocation of risk—technical, political, and commercial—is another major issue.

Because LNG trade depends on reliability of scheduling and shipping, interruptions can devastate project economics. Political risk is, therefore, a large concern.

Technical risk relates principally to gas reserves, production, facilities, transportation, operations, and environmental liabilities, while commercial risks include sales volumes, price, and insurance covering the scope of facilities.

Greenwald cited the Qatargas project as a possible trend-setter for future LNG trade. He noted that Qatargas obtained 70% of its downstream funds from Japanese financial markets and that the project had a large degree of Japanese content throughout: Japan is an LNG purchaser, contractor, shipbuilder, and vessel operator.

"This concentration of Japanese interests, coupled with the Japanese government's import finance programs and Japan's sizable capital market, enabled the project finance to succeed," said Greenwald.

Today, as finance moves closer to project finance and away from balance-sheet debt, there is greater involvement by multilateral development organizations, such as the World Bank and the European Bank for Reconstruction and Development, and national export credit institutions, in accepting a greater share of project risk.

In spite of the huge costs and complexities involved, LNG projects can provide strong cash flows and earnings for LNG venturers, as well as substantial benefits for host nations. Technology continues to advance, helping to lower costs and improve operating efficiencies. And novel financing mechanisms will continue to be found, further assisting LNG to gain an increasing share of the global energy market. IPE

Salomon Bros. midyear 1996 survey projects strong E&P spending

A Salomon Bros. Inc. 1996 midyear survey forecast that petroleum industry upstream spending would remain strong worldwide during the year, portending a robust 1997.

In the June 1996 exploration and production spending survey by the New York investment firm, 241 companies indicated plans to increase worldwide E&P spending to $67.1 billion in 1996 from $60.2 billion in 1995.

Salomon Bros. said the planned 11.4% increase, following a 9% increase in 1995, represented the strongest back-to-back increases since 1990-91.

In the 1995 yearend survey, 275 companies told Salomon Bros. they would increase their budgets a total of 7.7% for 1996 to a total of $63.9 billion.

U.S. E&P budgets were slated to climb 12.7%, in line with the yearend 1995 estimate of 11.8%, driven by planned increases by independents and majors. The 12.7% aggregate increase in U.S. spending was the largest such gain since the Salomon Bros. December 1987 survey of 1988 spending.

Oil price assumptions increased between the end of 1995 and middle of 1996, with assumptions at midyear of $18.29/bbl for West Texas intermediate vs. $17.48/bbl at yearend. The natural gas price outlook also increased, to $2.01/Mcf at the Henry Hub in the midyear survey from $1.75/Mcf at yearend 1995.

Spending increases by U.S. independents and operators outside North America accounted for the majority of the growth in worldwide spending. In the U.S., independents at midyear said they planned increases in spending totaling 21.5% in 1996, up from 9.3% in the yearend 1995 survey, and almost five times greater than the gain of 4.1% recorded for 1995.

Internationally, spending was projected at midyear to jump 12.4% vs. the 8.6% increase indicated at yearend and comparable to the 14.4% gain registered in 1995. A total of 70% of the companies surveyed at midyear said they expected to increase spending outside North America in 1997, including more than 50% with planned increases exceeding 10%. Only 11% said they expected to reduce spending outside North America.

Spending by the 15 U.S. majors in the midyear survey was below expectations at the beginning of the year. Increases in spending were expected to be 7.2% at midyear, well below the increase of 13.4% reported 6 months previously. Salomon Bros. noted, however, that the lower percentage increase resulted primarily from higher 1995 spending than was estimated at yearend–not actual decreases in spending plans for 1996. In fact, the investment firm said, 1996 spending plans by the majors have been unchanged, essentially, since December 1995 and still represent the most significant increase by the majors in the United States since 1988.

In a reversal of a predicted spending decline, Canadian E&P expenditures were projected at midyear to be 3.2% higher in 1996 instead of a 6.4% decrease projected 6 months earlier. The increases were attributed to higher commodity prices and stronger cash flows among the most often cited reasons, Salomon Bros. said.

Higher prices, cash flows

At midyear, Salomon Bros. said the outlook for 1997 was exceptionally positive. According to the survey, 66% of the 241 companies said they planned to increase spending in 1997, including almost 39% that expected increases greater than 10%.

Salomon Bros. said this represented the strongest indicator of the year ahead in the 9 years that companies have been asked to answer that survey question.

Previously, the strongest year-ahead indication came in June 1994, when 56% of the companies responded that they planned to increase spending.

The 1996 midyear survey showed more than 48% of respondents said they had increased their spending plans–almost four times as many as had reduced planned expenditures. The investment firm said this was the largest number of respondents with increased spending plans since 1990's midyear update and marked the smallest number of planned decreases in the 9 years that companies have been responding to that survey question.

Also, 84% of those surveyed said their actual expenditures would equal or exceed current budgets.

About one third of the respondents said their spending would exceed operating cash flow.

Independent operators

For the 129 U.S. independents surveyed at midyear, 1996 expenditures were expected to increase 21.5% over 1995—more than double the growth cited in the Salomon Bros. yearend 1995 survey.

During the first 6 months of 1996, about 44% of the respondents had increased their spending plans, but only 13% had cut budgets. A firmer price outlook for both oil and gas apparently was a factor in the revisions upward.

Average oil price expectations among independents increased to $18.37/bbl at midyear from $17.37/bbl at yearend 1995, and natural gas prices had risen to $2.01/Mcf from $1.75/Mcf from yearend 1995.

How spending survey results compare

	No. of cos.*	†1995 (Million $)	§1996 (Million $)	% change	No. of cos.*	†1995 (Million $)	§1996 (Million $)	% change
U.S.								
Independents	129	6,876	8,354	+21.5	163	7,600	8,303	+9.3
Majors	15	9,865	10,578	+7.2	15	9,089	10,310	+13.4
Total¶	**144**	**16,327**	**18,402**	**+12.7**	**178**	**16,309**	**18,233**	**+11.8**
CANADA	103	7,268	7,498	+3.2	96	7,052	6,602	–6.4
OUTSIDE NORTH AMERICA	102	36,635	41,194	+12.4	110	35,957	38,041	+8.6
Total¶	**241**	**60,230**	**67,094**	**+11.4**	**275**	**59,318**	**63,875**	**+7.7**

*Column does not add because some companies are counted as many as three times—once in each regional category. †Approximate spending. §Salomon Bros. Inc. estimate. ¶Some dollar columns do not add because of rounding.

Source: Salomon Bros. Inc.

Breakout of exploration/production spending*

Company	*1995 (Million U.S. $)	†1996 (Million U.S. $)
SELECTED INDEPENDENTS, U.S. PROJECTS		
Abraxas Petroleum Corp.	11	12
Adams Resources	5	3
AGIP SpA	54	65
Alamco	6	9
American Exploration	26	36
An-Son Co.	3	3
Anadarko Petroleum	205	300
Apache Corp.	204	250
Arakis Energy Corp.	3	1
Arch Petroleum	6	7
Ashland Oil	49	59
Barnwell of Canada	0	1
Basin Exploration	15	25
Belden & Blake Corp.	25	35
Bellwether Exploration	4	7
Benton Oil & Gas Co.	6	0
Berry Petroleum	9	10
BHP Petroleum	119	120
Box Energy	37	37
BRG Petroleum Inc.	8	10
Burlington Resources	443	420
C. Occidental Petroleum Ltd.	50	81
Cairn Energy USA	29	52
Case, Pomeroy & Co.	5	7
Century Offshore	1	1
Chesapeake Energy	121	250
Chief Petroleum	1	1
Chieftain Intl.	36	61
Clayton Williams Energy	21	27
Clinton Gas Systems	4	5
Coastal Corp.	131	185
Coho Resources Ltd.	32	40
Columbia Gas System	16	15
Columbus Energy	3	3
Comstock Resources Inc.	5	15
Consolidated Natural Gas	171	179
ConVest Energy Corp.	7	14
Cross Timbers Oil Co.	20	40
DDD Energy (Seitel)	20	25
Devon Energy	68	75
Elf Aquitaine	36	38
Energen Corp.	10	25
Enron Oil & Gas	350	350
Enserch Corp.	182	177
Equitable Resources	45	50
Equity Oil Co.	4	5
Evergreen Resources	5	5
Forcenergy Gas Exploration Inc.	52	88
Foreland Corporation	5	6
Forest Oil Corp.	26	35
Global Marine (Challenger Minerals)	5	6
Global Natural Resources	29	18
Goodrich Petroleum	2	7
GulfWest Oil Co.	1	1
Hallwood Energy Partners	15	12
Harken Energy Corp.	3	1
HCO Energy Ltd.	0	1
Home-Stake Oil & Gas Company	1	3
Inland Resources	12	35
J.M. Huber	16	21
JN Exploration & Production L.P.	5	15
Kelley Oil et al.	49	30
Kerr-McGee	265	200
Key Production Co.	12	18
Lomak Petroleum	11	15
Louis Dreyfus Natural Gas	65	75
Louisiana Land & Exploration	130	164
Mariner Energy Inc.	36	40
Maynard Oil Co.	5	5
McFarland Energy	8	6
MCN Corp.	145	100
Midland Resources	5	7
Mitchell Energy & Development	116	131
Montana Power	1	1
Murphy Oil Corp.	69	130
National Fuel Gas	56	92
National Gas & Oil Co.	1	1
Newfield Exploration	84	102
Noble Affiliates	178	165
NOMECO	30	36
Norcen Energy Resources Ltd.	50	50
Nuevo Energy	37	84
Ocelot Energy Inc.	0	0
ONEOK	11	7
Orbit Oil & Gas Ltd.	0	1
Oryx Energy Co.	200	300
Oxford Oil Co.	2	2
PANACO	8	12
Panhandle Royalty Co.	2	2
Parker & Parsley	136	180
Patterson Energy	5	4
Petrofina Group	84	110
Pittencrieff Resources	10	4
Plains Resources Inc.	28	48
Pogo Producing	62	116
Questa Oil & Gas Co.	2	2
Questar Corp.	24	39
Ranger Oil Ltd.	10	11
Rigel Oil & Gas Ltd.	2	4
River Gas Corporation	13	10
Santa Fe Energy Resources	180	164
Seagull Energy	87	110
Snyder Oil	88	82
Sonat	208	225
Southwestern Energy Co.	76	51
St. Mary Land & Exploration	24	31
Stone Energy	37	48
Summit Resources Ltd.	10	12
Swift Energy	36	60
Tana Oil and Gas Corp.	23	23
TGX	1	4
Tidal Resources	2	2
Tom Brown	26	20
Total CSB	46	40
UMC Petroleum Corp.	56	72
Union Pacific Resources Co.	568	752
Union Texas Petroleum Holdings	5	20
United Energy plc	1	7
Upton Resources	3	3
Vastar	414	530
W & T Offshore	16	28
Wainoco Oil Corp.	1	0
Willard Pease Oil & Gas	1	1
Williams Cos.	15	42
Wiser Oil	21	47
YPF SA	58	72
Zilkha Energy	140	225
CANADA		
Abraxas Petroleum Corp.	0	3
Alberta Energy Co. Ltd.	205	285
Amerada Hess Corp.	0	22
Amoco Corp.	450	400
Anderson Exploration	232	195
Apache Corp.	24	49
Arakis Energy Corp.	1	1
Archer Resources	22	29
Ascentex Energy Inc.	3	2
Aztec Resources Ltd.	8	7
Barnwell of Canada	3	5
Beau Canada Exploration	41	39
Berkley Petroleum	18	21
C Natural Resources	156	194
C Occidental Petroleum Ltd.	58	74
Cabre Exploration Ltd.	36	40
Canadian 88 Energy Corp.	28	33
Canrise Resources	7	9
Chauvco Resources Ltd.	32	56
Chevron Corp.	400	300
Cimarron Petroleum Ltd.	19	32
Columbus Energy	0	0
Consolidated Natural Gas	1	3
Crestar	128	125
CS Resources Ltd.	42	51
Discovery West Corp.	26	26
Dorset Exploration Ltd.	27	29
DuPont/Conoco	30	20
Dynamic Oil Ltd.	1	1
Elan Energy Ltd.	45	88
Encal Energy Ltd.	30	73
EnerPlus Group	6	22
Enron Oil & Gas	50	40
Equitable Resources	1	2
Equity Oil Co.	1	1
Forest Oil Corp.	0	20
Gentry Resources	3	3
Grad & Walker Energy Corp.	28	60
Gulf Canada Corp.	328	292
HCO Energy Ltd.	26	25
Highridge Exploration Ltd.	5	5
Imperial Oil Ltd.	241	294
J.M. Huber	6	5
Jordan Petroleum	54	44
Kerr-McGee	20	20
Lexxor Energy Inc.	0	7
Maxx Petroleum	25	34
Mobil Corp.	435	490
Montana Power	1	1
Morgan Hydrocarbons	42	50
Morrison Petroleums Ltd.	89	73
Murphy Oil Corp.	94	100
Newport Petroleum Corp.	18	25
Noble Affiliates	7	5
Noranda	57	100
Norcen Energy Resources Ltd.	224	175
Northstar Energy Corp.	58	60
Numac Energy Inc.	76	69
Ocelot Energy Inc.	53	20
Orbit Oil & Gas Ltd.	12	14
Paloma Corp.	12	7
PanC Petroleum Ltd.	610	475
Paragon Petroleum	20	19
Paramount Resources	18	18
Pembina Corporation	54	46
Pennzoil Co.	49	21
Petro-Canada	150	184
Petrofina Group	1	1
Petromet Resources	28	15
Phillips Petroleum	10	10
Pinnacle Resources Ltd.	49	36
Pittencrieff Resources	3	1
Place Resources Corp.	4	10
Poco Petroleum Ltd.	162	160
Pursuit Resources	4	4
Ranger Oil Ltd.	39	70
Remington Energy	10	18
Renaissance Energy Ltd.	725	700
Rigel Oil & Gas Ltd.	45	82
Rio Alto Exploration	39	33
Santa Fe Energy Resources	1	0
Seagull Energy	5	8
Shell Canada	198	245
Star Oil & Gas Ltd.	16	18
Startech Energy Inc.	15	19
Summit Resources Ltd.	50	48
Suncor	128	130
Syncrude Canada	149	190
Talisman Energy Inc.	180	196
Tarragon Oil and Gas Ltd.	79	73
Texaco	19	15
Tidal Resources	10	9
Tri Link Resources Ltd.	46	55
Triumph Energy	5	9
Ulster Petroleums Ltd.	79	65
UMC Petroleum Corp.	5	6
Union Pacific Resources Co.	12	15
Unocal Corp.	40	50
Upton Resources	8	9
Vermilion Resources	3	10
Wainco Oil Corp.	11	11
Wascana Energy	137	135
Wiser Oil Co.	10	6
OUTSIDE NORTH AMERICA		
Agip SpA	1,857	2,145
Alberta Energy Co. Ltd.	25	25
Amerada Hess Corp.	383	575
Amoco Corp.	1,150	1,400
Anadarko Petroleum Corp.	125	185
Anderson Exploration Ltd.	0	6
Apache Corp.	55	166
Arakis Energy Corp.	47	70
Ashland Oil	41	35
Atlantic Richfield Corp.	900	900
Beach Pettroleum N.L.	3	4
Benton Oil & Gas Co.	68	80
BHP Petroleum	840	870
British Gas plc	1,100	840
British Petroleum	2,335	2,800
C Occidential Petroleum Ltd.	92	221
Chauvco Resources Ltd.	32	47
Chernogorneft	50	80
Chevron Corp.	1,300	1,700
Chieftain Intl	15	4
Clyde Petroleum plc	38	66
Coastal Corp.	20	15
Command Petroleum Holdings NL	43	36
Croft Oil & Gas	3	3
Crusader, Ltd.	11	9
Dansk Olie og Naturgas A/S	9	30
Deminex	270	350
Dragon Oil plc	6	25
DuPont/Conoco	750	1,100
Elf Aquitaine	2,450	2,300
Enron Oil & Gas	100	130
Enserch Corp.	7	10
Enterprise Oil plc	428	633
Equitable Resources	0	3
Equity Oil Co.	3	3
Evergreen Resources	1	1
Exxon Corp.	3,884	4,060
Garnet Resources	8	7
Global Natural Resources	34	35
Goodrich Petroleum	0	0
Gulf Canada Corp.	18	73
Hallwood Energy Partners	2	0
Hardy Oil & Gas	47	60
Harken Energy Corp.	4	4
Intl. Petroleum Corp.	9	17
Kerr-McGee	115	80
Lasmo plc	476	423
Louisiana Land & Exploration Co.	68	51
Lukoil	980	1,000
Maraven SA	700	740
Mobil Corp.	1,410,	1,810
Monument Oil & Gas plc	170	66
Morgan Hydrocarbons	1	2
Murphy Oil Corp.	62	117
Neste Oy	195	160
Noble Affiliates	10	10
Nomeco	65	84
Norcen Energy Resources Ltd.	62	55
Norsk Hydro	754	813
Noyabrskneftegaz	180	200
Nuevo Energy	0	16
Occidental Petroleum Corp.	387	425
Ocelot Energy Inc.	2	4
OMV AG	118	239
Oryx Energy Co.	100	100
PanC Petroleum Ltd.	23	51
Parker & Parsley	32	10
Pennzoil	20	20
Perenco	14	55
Petro-Canada	25	26
Petrofina Group	334	482
Petroleum Co. of Trinidad	77	60
Petronas	7	4
Phillips Petroleum	517	728
Pogo Producing	30	59
Premier Oil plc	46	50
PTT Exploration & Production	32	140
Purneftegaz	70	70
Ranger Oil Ltd.	75	85
Rigel Oil & Gas Ltd.	1	2
Royal Dutch/Shell	3,880	4,000
Saga Petroleum	362	370
Santa Fe Energy Resources	36	51
Seagull Energy	3	5
Shell U.S.	250	250
Statoil	1,250	1,400
Sun Co.	30	30
Svenska Petroleum Exploration AB	32	63
Swift Energy Co.	3	1
Talisman Energy Inc.	140	193
Taurus Petroleum	2	4
Texaco	1,014	1,290
Total CSB	1,242	1,380
Triton Energy Corp.	175	260
UMC Petroleum Corp.	78	93
Unimar	26	24
Union Texas Petroleum Holdings	160	180
Unocal Corp.	424	650
USX-Marathon	183	155
Wascana Energy	11	18
YPF SA	1,588	1,336
Yukong	28	85

*Approximate spending. †Salomon Bros. estimate.

Source: Salomon Bros. Inc.

Breakout of exploration/production spending*

	*1995 (Million U.S. $)	†1996 (Million U.S. $)
MAJORS, U.S. PROJECTS§		
Amerada Hess	195	302
Amoco Corp.	895	1,000
Atlantic Richfield Corp.	800	800
British Petroleum	963	1,000
Chevron Corp.	850	1,000
DuPont/Conoco	315	320
Exxon Corp.	855	890
Mobil Corp.	830	500
Occidental Petroleum Corp.	188	170
Pennzoil Co.	257	240
Phillips Petroleum	329	291
Shell U.S.	1,600	2,150
Texaco	904	1,035
Unocal Corp.	541	480
USX-Marathon	343	400
Total	**9,865**	**10,578**
Change		**+7.2%**

*Approximate spending. †Salomon Bros. estimate. §Companies spending at least $500,000 in either year.

Source: Salomon Bros. Inc.

Several companies cited improved drilling success rates for their increased spending plans, similar to yearend findings.

About 62% of the respondents anticipated that second half 1996 spending would exceed first half 1996 spending; almost 83% expected budgets to be fully spent or surpassed. About 45% of the independents said E&P spending would exceed operating cash flow.

Companies noted higher prices and opportunities in specific operating areas for their spending plans. Vastar said it was taking advantage of a large number of its high-quality projects due to increased cash flow; Union Pacific Resources noted higher prices and better cash flow; Chesapeake Energy cited stronger prices as well as a high drilling success rate; and Chieftain Petroleum pointed to its strong activity levels in the Gulf of Mexico.

How E/P spending plans have changed

	% increase	% no change	% decrease
U.S.			
Independents	44.2	42.6	13.2
Majors	33.3	60.0	6.7
Canada	43.6	47.5	8.9
International	30.4	51.0	19.6
Worldwide	48.5	38.9	12.6

Source: Salomon Bros. Inc.

Major companies

U.S. plans of the 15 majors in the midyear survey remained relatively stable; however, the expected increase in 1996 spending fell to 7.2% from 13.4% as a result of higher than anticipated spending in 1995, the Salomon Bros. survey found.

1995 spending was underestimated at yearend by Amerada Hess, British Petroleum, and Mobil.

Among the majors, five said they anticipated higher budgets than originally stated at yearend 1995, and Mobil expected lower domestic spending than first planned. The anticipated decrease stemmed from Mobil's completing its budget early in the year and allocating more to international operations.

Pennzoil and Texaco cited greater than expected opportunities in the U.S.

All 15 majors said that strong commodity prices in the first half of 1996 had no effect on their spending plans. Among the majors, the average price expectation for natural gas increased to $2.04/Mcf from $1.76/Mcf.

No company expected to spend less than its 1996 planned budget, and one fourth of the respondents anticipated that 1996 spending would exceed their budgets.

All expected 1997 spending to be equal to or greater than 1996 levels, and 42% planned increases.

Canadian outlook

Among the 103 companies in the Salomon Bros. survey with Canadian operations, spending plans at midyear indicated a total increase of 3.2% vs. a reduction of 6.4% indicated at yearend 1995.

About 44% of the companies reported increased budgets for 1996, and only 9% said they cut spending since yearend.

Stronger natural gas prices were cited by Encal, Noranda, Morrison Petroleum, and several others as the primary reason for spending increases although the average natural gas price assumption at midyear had decreased to $1.44/Mcf (Canadian) from $1.63/Mcf at yearend 1995.

Other companies that noted they had materially increased their budgets were Ranger Oil, Renaissance Energy, and Remington Energy. Ranger based its increase on stepped up exploration activity; Renaissance cited increased spending on land, seismic, and drilling; and Remington said it had increased its drilling program.

Those saying they would experience decreases included Norcen Energy, which said it was shifting some spending to the U.S. and other areas outside of Canada, and Discovery West, which blamed lower than expected cash flows.

More than 75% said they expected second half spending would equal or exceed first half levels, while about 72% of the respondents said they expected 1996 spending would match their current budgets.

Of companies responding, 17% said they expected to spend less than they had budgeted.

About 63% of the companies said they expected to increase E&P spending in 1997, while 21% said they expected spending would be flat in 1997.

In addition, 40% said their spending in 1997 would exceed 1996 spending by more than 10%.

International spending

The Salomon Bros. midyear survey found that the 1996 increase in spending outside North America will be close to the 14.4% increment of 1995.

Among the 102 companies with spending outside North America, 1996 E&P spending was projected to be up by 12.4% vs. the 8.6% increase projected at yearend 1995.

During the first half of 1996, about 30% of respondents reported increased spending plans internationally, and 20% said they reduced their budget levels.

Almost 60% of companies responding said they intended to spend their entire budgets this year; 26% said they expected to overspend their budgets; and 15% expected to spend less than their 1996 budgeted amounts.

Oil price assumptions at midyear increased among the respondents in the international category to an average $16.97/bbl (Brent) vs. $16.35/bbl at yearend 1995.

About 50% expected E&P spending to be less than operating cash flow.

During the first half of 1996, the number of respondents with spending plan increases was larger than in any year since 1990 except for the dramatic increase in 1995, Salomon Bros. noted.

Major budget increases were cited by Phillips, Mobil, Statoil, Dupont/Conoco, Chevron, Triton, Canadian Occidental, Apache, Agip, UMC, British Gas, Maraven, and Saga. The most frequently cited reason for the increases: development of recently acquired properties.

Material decreases in spending were cited by Elf, Total, Yukong, Deminex, and USX-Marathon, with reductions due in large part to changes in the exchange rate of the dollar and minor budget refinements. IPE

Geopolitical issues complicate Caspian oil-transport questions

Controversies over transportation of oil and natural gas from the Caspian Sea region festered at the center of a major geopolitical struggle in 1996. The immediate question was how new production from the region should move to markets in Europe and Asia. A much larger issue was which country or alliance would ultimately dominate the resource-rich area—and how it would achieve and exercise control.

Pipeline routing and construction were of course crucial to groups of oil companies preparing to raise production from fields off Azerbaijan and in Kazakhstan. In Azerbaijan, a twin-route compromise, designed to appease both sides of a contest over Russian influence in the region, was at least moving the issue away from stalemate in 1996.

Even before the compromise surfaced, however, geopolitical complexities were demonstrating their ability to obstruct transportation plans. Since collapse of the Soviet Union, the Caspian Sea had been a volatile crossroads of cultural, ethnic, and political influences. Through its interventions in the pipeline issue—including military and insurrectionist adventures in Chechnya and Georgia—Russia had shown its determination to retain de facto control over former satellites in the Caucasus and Central Asia. Iran, with its long coast along the southern Caspian, clearly coveted influence in Central Asia and could claim affinities of religion, ethnicity, and—in the case of Tajikistan—language. The third strong regional force was Turkey, the strongest ethnic and linguistic influence along the southern tier of the former Soviet Union and, until 1996, a model of Muslim secularism offering an alternative to Iranian theocracy.

Caspian issues were far more than a triangular struggle for influence with pipelines at the center, however. In addition to bilateral conflicts within the region, such as Russia's war with break-away Chechnya and Azerbaijan's struggle with Armenia over Nagorno-Karabakh, multilateral questions and interventions from outside the region complicated relationships and jeopardized any project spanning international borders. Ownership of Caspian resources remained subject to question in 1996, essentially pitting Russia and Iran against the emergent littoral states of Azerbaijan, Kazakhstan, and Turkmenistan. And the U.S. remained determined to economically punish Iran for the Islamic republic's alleged support for terrorism, violations of human rights, and opposition to Middle East peace. U.S. opposition to an Iranian role in the export of Caspian oil and gas gave the region's political complexities global proportions.

Platform construction advances at the Shelfprojekstrol yard south of Baku. Photo courtesy of Amoco

In 1996, the multilevel struggle for political influence in the Caspian was far from settled. Yet the stakes were enormous. The region may have the world's third largest concentration of oil reserves, after the Persian Gulf and Siberia. The world's two biggest holders of natural gas reserves, Russia and Iran, have Caspian coasts. And gas reserves of other Caspian states are substantial and largely undeveloped. British Petroleum estimated gas reserves of Kazakhstan in 1994 at 1.8 trillion cu m, for example, and of Turkmenistan at 2.98 trillion cu m.

The Caspian region thus holds potential to be a central factor in future international energy supply and investment opportunity. And it is connected by one of the three contestants for regional influence, Iran, to the world's most important concentration of petroleum reserves, the Middle East.

Regional politics

The Caspian Sea is technically a lake—the world's largest—but not necessarily one for legal purposes. Two of its coastal nations have established but internally troubled governments—Iran and Russia. Flanking the sea are three formerly Soviet satellites groping for nationhood—Azerbaijan on the west and Kazakhstan and Turkmenistan along the whole eastern shore.

The newly independent states in 1996 faced the dual challenges of establishing political order and restoring economic growth. Toward both goals, they needed to increase production of oil and gas. The established Caspian powers, meanwhile, wanted to participate in the economic promise of resource development if not to exert outright control over events outside their borders. Economic desperation made Iranian and Russian claims to the benefits of Caspian resource development especially urgent.

Conflict in Azerbaijan

The overt political struggle in Azerbaijan concerned the future of the mountainous region of Nagorno-Karabakh. Shia Muslim Azerbaijan had controlled the area of mostly Christian Armenians since 1921 under a treaty between Russia and Turkey. Conflict between Armenia and soon-to-be independent Azerbaijan emerged in 1988, escalating into warfare during 1992-94. Armenia, which largely prevailed in the fighting but suffered economic isolation as a consequence, sought either control of or independence for Nagorno-Karabakh. Despite its military setbacks, Azerbaijan in 1996 continued to refuse to recognize claims of independence by Armenians in the disputed province.

The clash between Azerbaijan and Armenia had its roots in the Tatar-Armenian war of 1905 and drew sustenance from the nationalist Azerbaijani Popular Front, which instigated the

Oil export network in Central Asia and the Caucasus

Fig. 1

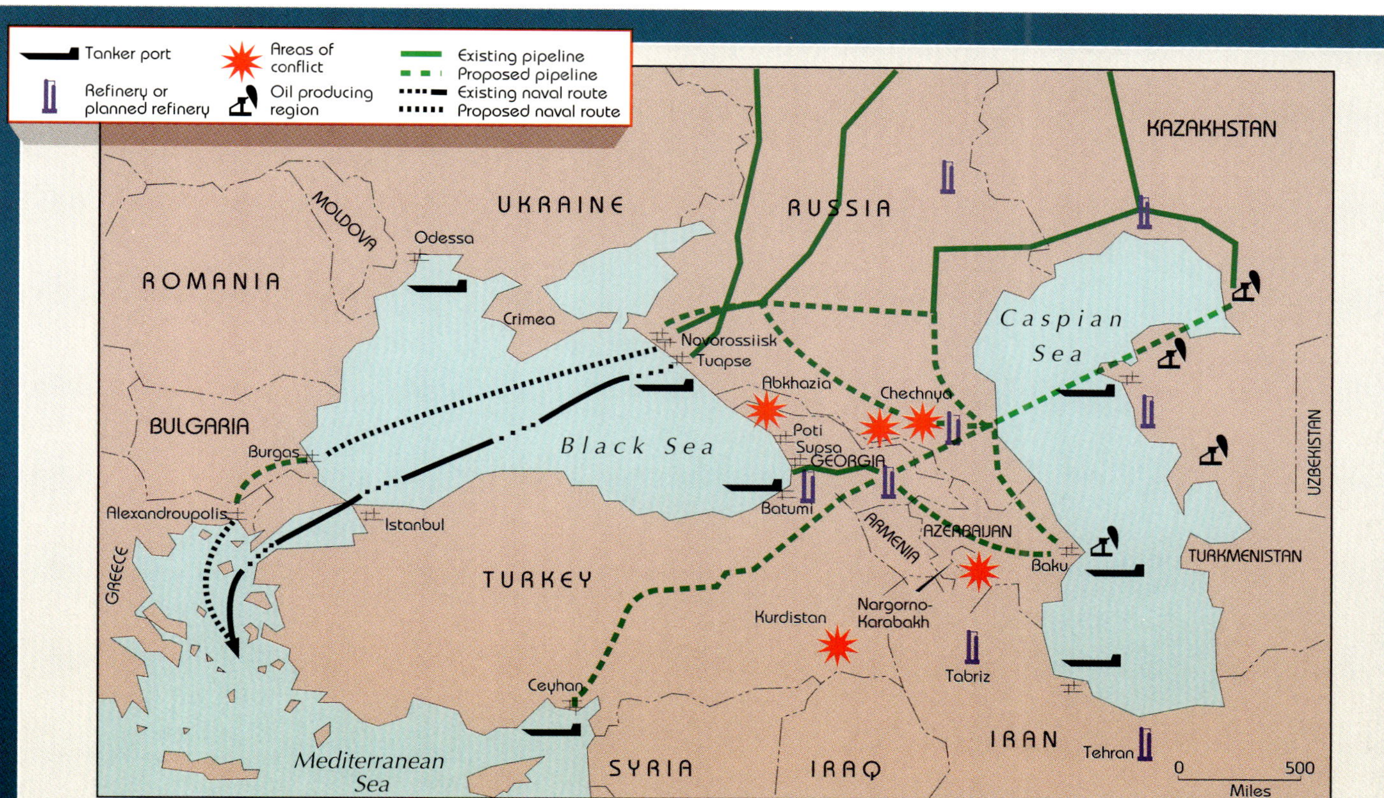

Source: Heritage Foundation

IPE

boycott of Armenia. The organization strongly shaped Azerbaijani politics after dissolution of the Soviet bloc and was able to unseat governments it faulted for not sufficiently resisting Armenian attacks in Nagorno-Karabakh.

Azerbaijanis blamed Moscow for much of the unrest over Nagorno-Karabakh. Russia was known to oppose Azeri President Geidar Aliyev. An early 1996 Heritage Foundation analysis by Arie Cohen said Moscow was suspected of supporting at least two coup attempts against him.

Crucial to Azerbaijan's role in Caspian geopolitics but often overlooked in analyses of the subject was Nakhichevan, an enclave of Azerbaijan on the Iran-Armenia border. Aliyev, a former KGB general and Azeri Communist Party leader, was governor-general of Nakhichevan when former President Abulfaz Elchibey was deposed in a June 1993 coup.

When Azerbaijan was suffering its worst military losses in Nagorno-Karabakh, Iran assisted Aliyev with financial support to Nakhichevan, accepted Azeri war refugees, and denounced Armenia. Iran later considered it an act of betrayal when Aliyev, after becoming president of Azerbaijan, sought friendly relations with the U.S. and in 1995 acceded to U.S. demands that Iran not participate in Azeri oil and gas projects involving American companies.

Georgia's war

Although Georgia has no Caspian coastline, its internal difficulties strongly affect pipeline plans and politics in the region. The country endured a civil war during 1991-93, which ended in victory for President Eduard Shevardnadze after he agreed to join the Commonwealth of Independent States in exchange for Russian support.

Moscow, meanwhile, had supported a separatist group in Georgia's Abkhazia region, where fighting began in 1992. Russia's apparent interest was the Abkhaz coastline on the Black Sea and the Georgian ports of Poti, Supsa, and Batumi, which lie south of the Russian ports of Tuapse and Novorossiysk. Support of the separatists by Moscow began to fade in 1994 as Russia's own separatist problems in Chechnya intensified. Chechen rebels received training in Abkhazia.

Russia's war in Chechnya

Warfare in Russia's break-away region of Chechnya began at the end of 1994 following covert efforts by Moscow to oust Chechen President Jokhar Dudayev. Having declared independence from Russia in 1991, Chechnya under Dudayev had been raising money through oil exports that Moscow considered illegal. Just before open warfare began, Dudayev sharpened divisions between his country's largely Muslim population and the rest of Russia by seeking aid from radical Muslim groups in the Middle East and Asia.

The war in Chechnya was unpopular in Russia and became a key issue in the federation's first presidential election in 1996. Just weeks before the final vote in June, Dudayev was killed in a missile attack. Russian President Boris Yeltsin won reelection.

Central Asian instability

In Central Asian countries along the Caspian, outright hostilities had been fewer in the post-Soviet era through 1996 than in the Caucasus states, but internal instability and Russian ambitions were no less important. These countries faced the challenge of forging national identities despite ethnic tensions exacerbated or created by the influx of Russians during the Soviet era.

In Kazakhstan, nation-building had to progress with a population 38% Russian and a northern neighbor claiming political husbandry over its "near abroad"—the southern tier of its former empire. Under President Nursultan Nazarbaev, Kazakhstan made strong early moves to establish itself as an independent state open to economic reform and foreign capital. After the 1991 coup attempt against Russian President Yeltsin,

AIOC planned to use a refurbished Kaspmorneft semisubmersible for drilling in the Caspian Sea. Photo courtesy of Amoco.

however, it tended to deemphasize independence in favor of friendly ties with Moscow.

Turkmenistan had tried since independence to establish Turkmen as the official language without chasing away the non-native workers it needed for economic growth. Its total population was 10% Russian, although the concentration was much higher in cities.

Turkmenistan's neighbor to the north, Uzbekistan, has a population about 17% Russian and the largest group of Muslims in Central Asia. Although Uzbekistan doesn't have a Caspian coast, it has large potential as an oil and gas producer and is an important factor in the question of hydrocarbon transportation away from the region.

Uzbekistan and Tajikistan, the only Central Asian country with linguistic ties to Iran, have developed friction because of significant ethnic overlaps along their border.

Production and pipelines

Political tensions within and among Caspian countries provide the backdrop against which oil and gas development and transportation projects must take shape, with Russian and Iranian efforts to exert influence nearly constant in regional affairs. Ultimately, therefore, the extent to which Caspian states take advantage of their hydrocarbon potential depends on politics. Whatever the outcome, the potential is large.

At the end of the era of Soviet control, oil reserves in the Caspian region under the Soviet system of estimation were reported at 23.5 million bbl in categories corresponding to proved-plus-provable. Since then, independent governments have increased reserves estimates.

In mid-1994, the Centre for Global Energy Studies in London estimated total reserves in these categories for the Caspian region at 68.23 billion bbl. Of this, 7.5 billion bbl was in Azerbaijan, 49.59 billion bbl in Kazakhstan, 5.24 billion bbl in Turkmenistan, 4.4 billion bbl in Uzbekistan, and 1.5 billion bbl in the Russian littoral republics of Dagestan, Kalmykia, and Astrakhan.

Production potential

Azerbaijan was a leading international oil producer at the turn of the century. While the traditional onshore producing fields of the Apsheron Peninsula peaked during World War II and have all but played out, enormous potential remains offshore. The area all but lay idle during the Soviet era, when Russia emphasized development of giant fields in the Volga-Ural region and Siberia. Azerbaijan nevertheless remained an important supply center for the Russian oil industry.

Two major offshore development projects were in prospect in Azerbaijan in 1996. The more advanced of the two was development of Azeri, Chirag, and southern (deepwater) Guneshli fields by Azerbaijan International Operating Co. (AIOC), a consortium of international companies based in London. With installation of sufficient pipeline capacity, production from the fields was projected to reach 700,000 b/d in 2010 from reserves estimated at 3.8 billion bbl. Under a production sharing contract with the Azeri government, AIOC partners, which include State Oil Co. of Azerbaijan Republic (Socar) and Russia's Lukoil, were to spend $8 billion on field development.

Terms of AIOC's project had undergone several changes, however, so further setbacks were possible. An upset with regional implications occurred in 1994, when Azerbaijan agreed to transfer to Iran one fourth of its 20% share of the consortium. The U.S. government, which asserted an interest because of the participation of American companies—including Amoco, Pennzoil, and Unocal—objected to the move and successfully shut Iran out of the deal. The incident angered Iran, which then joined Russia in opposition to the AIOC project. Although Lukoil held an interest in AIOC, other Russian companies thought they had been excluded, and Russian officials openly opposed AIOC.

Iran's hostility toward Azerbaijan may have eased somewhat in mid-1996, when Oil Industries Engineering and Construction, an Iranian company partly owned by the government, acquired a 10% interest in Azerbaijan's other major offshore project: development of Shah-Deniz field. The $4 billion project was to develop oil and condensate reserves estimated at 1.8 billion bbl and associated gas. The Shah-Deniz consortium, led by British Petroleum and Statoil, had no U.S. members.

In Kazakhstan, the biggest project remained the $20 billion Tengiz field development by Tengizchevroil, a consortium led by Chevron. Under a complete initial phase, the field could produce 85,000 b/d, quickly expandable to 135,000 b/d. But that remained far below the field's potential. Chevron had said the field could be producing 750,000 b/d by 2010.

The constraint was transportation. The only outlet for Tengiz oil in 1996 was a northbound pipeline through Russia, which would allow only about 60,000 b/d to leave Kazakhstan. At first, Moscow said it imposed the limit because of corrosive mercaptans in Tengiz crude. But the limit stayed in place even after Tengizchevroil completed mercaptan-removal facilities in the field.

Kazakhstan's other major development project was Karachaganak field, which was expected to reach peak output of 200,000 b/d of crude oil and condensate sometime after 2000.

With progress slow toward construction of another pipeline, Iran swept into the Kazakhstan production picture in 1996 with a swap arrangement providing an outlet for 40,000 b/d of Ten-

The busy Bosporus Straits through Istanbul figured heavily in decisions about an export route for crude oil from the Caspian Sea.

giz crude. Under an agreement signed in May, Iran was to receive the oil by tanker for processing in its northern refineries and to make equivalent volumes of its own crude available to the Tengiz venture at terminals in the Persian Gulf.

Turkmenistan, meanwhile, had potential to more than double its 3.5 bcfd of natural gas production but, like Azerbaijan and Kazakhstan, lacked outlet transportation capacity. The republic, with huge reserves in Dauletabad and surrounding fields and ambitions to produce 1 million b/d of oil by 2000, had welcomed international capital to joint ventures within its borders in an attempt to encourage exploration and development.

The republic also had warmed its relations with Iran. Its gas fields were linked to a pipeline in northeastern Iran, which could be extended to a connection with the Islamic republic's underutilized export pipeline through Azerbaijan. And in May 1996, Iranian President Ali Akbar Hashemi Rafsanjani inaugurated a rail link to Turkmenistan that revived the historic Silk Road between China and Europe and highlighted traditional ties within the region.

Pipeline progress

With Iran obviously maneuvering for influence in the Caspian region by taking interests in projects to develop oil and gas reserves, Russia in 1996 continued to dominate the vital question of export outlets for Caspian oil.

Its limit on the amount of Tengiz oil it would allow to pass through existing export systems made a new pipeline crucial to future production from Kazakhstan. Plans for such a system emerged from the Caspian Pipeline Consortium (CPC), which originally involved the governments of Russia, Kazakhstan, and Oman. The Russian stake and routing through Russia—bypassing existing Caspian export pipelines through war-torn Chechnya and ending at expanded facilities at Novorossiysk—made the scheme attractive to Moscow.

Financing of the CPC system, however, was a problem. Chevron refused to join the consortium under the unattractive terms it was offered and after Russia failed to provide throughput guarantees. And Oman Oil Co. was understandably reluctant to agree to revision of the favorable terms of its participation. Inevitably, alternative export schemes began to appear, including the swap arrangement with Iran and links to proposed export systems for Azeri production. In early 1996, CPC was restructured to reduce the combined ownership of Russia, Kazakhstan, and Oman to 50%, with the remaining share offered to international investors. This opened the project to equity participation by users of the system.

An option for export of some Tengiz crude was a link across the Caspian to Baku, where the oil could enter whatever pipeline scheme materialized from that point.

In Azerbaijan, export pipeline proposals fell into two crucial categories: those with routes through Russian territory and others. AIOC in 1996 was pursuing both options.

In March, the consortium signed a transportation agreement with Transneft, Russia's oil pipeline company, establishing a tariff of $15.67/metric ton for shipment of Azeri crude through a northern route from Baku through Tikhoretsk, Russia, to Novorossiysk. The scheme required reversal of flow in an existing oil line but little construction. AIOC would bring Caspian oil ashore at Sangachal, Azerbaijan, through an idle pipeline extending to Guzdek. From there it would lay a short line to an existing pipeline between Tikhoretsk and Baku. Flow reversal would be required between Tikhoretsk and Novorossiysk. The pipeline between Baku and Tikhoretsk passed through Grozny, Chechnya, and thus was subject to sabotage. Russia's continued assurances of security for the system depended on the degree of its control over the break-away republic.

AIOC also made headway in 1996 on the principal non-Russian export scheme from Azerbaijan. The route transited Georgia to the Black Sea port of Gupsa. Under the proposal, oil brought ashore at Sangachal would move south to Kazi Magomed and enter an existing pipeline to Kazakh near the

Oil and gas equipment are among products of the Iran Marine Industrial Co. (Sadra) construction yard at Neka on Iran's Caspian coast.

Georgian border. A new 117 km line would link Kazakh with Tbilisi, Georgia, and a connection with an existing line to a new terminal planned at Supsa. The western route would require major rehabilitation of existing lines. Azerbaijan and Georgia signed an agreement for construction of the pipeline in March 1996. Financing, however, was an open question.

Another pipeline issue in the Caspian region was an export outlet for natural gas from Turkmenistan. In 1996 there were two proposals. Unocal Corp. wanted to lay a line through Afghanistan to Pakistan. From there, extensions would be possible to growth markets in India and China. Political unrest in Afghanistan made the project risky.

The other possible outlet for Turkmen gas was an ambitious pipeline all the way across China and eventually to Japan. Mitsubishi of Japan, China National Petroleum Corp., and Esso China were studying the proposal in 1996.

The Turkish factor

Throughout the politics of pipeline construction from the Caspian, Turkey had counterbalanced Russia's efforts to ensure that routes pass through its territory. Ankara's stated concern was growing congestion in the Bosporus Straits through Istanbul.

A March 1994 collision between a tanker and freighter at the Black Sea entrance to the narrow waterway intensified Turkish concern about the increasing traffic that would result from any Caspian export pipeline ending at a Black Sea terminal. The fire resulting from the collision, which killed 30 people, burned for a week.

Although bound by the Montreux treaty of 1936 to allow free passage to all peacetime shipping, Turkey did tighten restrictions over use of the strait after the accident. And it sought even tougher regulations during renegotiations of the treaty in 1996.

New restrictions over shipping through the Bosporus Straits, through which an estimated 40,000 vessels pass each year, also promised to divert some of the flow of Caspian oil into a 1,685 km pipeline Turkey wanted to build from Supsa, Georgia, across its territory to Ceyhan on the Mediterranean. The proposal, depending as it did on completion of the Georgian route from Baku, set Turkey squarely at odds with Russia in the competition over Caspian pipelines.

Earlier in the development of pipeline plans, Ankara even had offered to lay the Georgian pipeline and charge tariffs for its use or to help arrange financing. AIOC refused the offer when Turkey indicated that it expected most production from the consortium's fields to pass through the terminal at Ceyhan, idle since shutdown of a pipeline from Iraq.

The Turkish factor in Caspian politics related to much more than pipeline routes, of course. And it made a major shift in 1996.

Strong ethnic and liguistic influence in Central Asia would have made Turkey a potent factor in the region under any circumstances. And, until 1996, a secularist government in Ankara held the country and its largely Muslim population at a distance from Iran and other Middle Eastern advocates of more-radical forms of Islam.

Elections in March 1996 changed things. The Muslim-oriented Welfare Party headed by Necmettin Erbakan won with only 21% of the votes and was able to form a coalition government in June. As prime minister, Erbakan made no secret of his hopes to turn Turkey away from the moderation of its recent past. Against United Nations sanctions, he traveled to Libya and signed a trade pact with leader Moammar Gadhafi. He also visited Iran and announced that his government had no quarrel with Iraqi President Saddam Hussein.

In September 1996, Erbakan signed a $23 billion, long-term natural gas deal with Iran that included construction of a pipeline from Tabriz to Ankara.

For international powers outside the Caspian region—especially the U.S.—Erbakan's overtures to the Muslim world's maverick states signaled a troubling swing in the geopolitical balance. But Erbakan's government was weak and, late in 1996, appeared likely to succumb to Turkish economic distress.

Global pressures

Political pressures at play in the Caspian region were not confined to the littoral states and their immediate neighbors. With Iran, Russia, and Turkey vying for influence, other countries inevitably considered their interests to be at stake.

Iran's commercial exertions in the region aroused suspicions of the U.S., which wanted to isolate the Islamic republic. It was at U.S. government insistence that Azerbaijan reversed position and precluded Iran's holding an interest in AIOC in 1995. And in 1996, U.S. President Bill Clinton signed a law passed late in 1995 calling for sanctions against countries not honoring U.S. trade sanctions against Iran. The law angered European governments, which demonstrated their defiance by not resisting the Iranian interest in the consortium formed to develop Azerbaijan's Shah-Deniz field.

The U.S. response to that turn of events was, at most, muted. In fact, the U.S. in 1996 had articulated very little in the way of a regional strategy for Caspian issues. Its most active policies had been hostility toward Iran and accommodation toward Russia. If anything, the U.S. maintained a distance from Azerbaijan—in part, perhaps, because of grievances toward that country pressed with some success by expatriate Armenians in the U.S. and elsewhere. And the U.S. chilled its relations with Turkey when Erbakan's Islamist party rose to tentative control of government.

In contrast with sweeping American activism in the Middle East, the piecemeal U.S. approach toward the Caspian region amounted nearly to ambivalence. Yet unilateral U.S. engagement with crucial players in the region made a broadening of strategy at some point inevitable.

Determined European pragmatism in the Caspian region was a clear sign to the U.S. that it would receive no help in its effort to commercially punish Iran. And Russia's uncamouflaged efforts to in some way dominate newly sovereign states along its southern and western frontiers would at some point raise alarms in a U.S. that, in 1996, cared most about its former rival's wary progress toward democracy.

If not European balkiness or Russian expansionism, simple geopolitics seemed certain to eventually widen views in the U.S. and elsewhere about Caspian politics and potential. The region was emerging from Soviet mists as more than a collection of ethnic and sovereign rivalries that could be addressed in isolation. It was moving toward reassertion of its role as a crossroads between the West, the Middle East, and Russia.

Territorial question

Amid all these conflicts in 1996 lay the question of territorial rights in the Caspian Sea. The issue had been scrambled by two events: dissolution of the Soviet Union in 1991 and Azerbaijan's successful appeal for foreign investment in its offshore oil and gas industry. The end of the Soviet Union raised the number of nations with Caspian coastlines to five from two. And the Azerbaijani push for oil and gas development forced the territorial issue.

Before 1991, Russia and Iran treated the Caspian as a shared lake in which they alone held any rights. They based their relationship on the Treaty of Friendship of 1921, which annulled prior Russian agreements by the old Czarist regime. The Treaty of Friendship extended equal sailing rights to both parties and committed Iran to a policy of exclusion of parties outside the treaty.

In 1927, a pact of nonagression and neutrality reaffirmed the Treaty of Friendship and its principles of equality and exclusivity. The countries at this time also began to delineate fishing rights in the Caspian.

The Treaty of Commerce and Navigation in 1940 accorded national treatment for Iranian and Russian merchant vessels in one another's ports and established exclusive fishing zones 10 miles out from the respective coastlines. In 1953, Iran refused to renew the fisheries agreement but agreed not to grant concessions to third parties until at least 1978.

In addition to those treaties and agreements, there were recorded references to a straight-line territorial boundary across the Caspian connecting the points where the Soviet-Iranian land boundaries intercepted the waterline on opposite sides of the sea. Whether that line did constitute an international boundary was a matter of dispute in 1996.

Also subject to question were the degrees to which the former Soviet states on the Caspian should be subject to Soviet treaties predating their independence. In the Almaty Declaration following break-up of the Soviet Union, Azerbaijan, Kazakhstan, Russia, and Turkmenistan committed themselves to the treaties of the Former Soviet Union. Applicability of the declaration and old treaties to Caspian territorial questions, however, was an issue.

Sheet pile driving by Iran Marine Industrial Co. (Sadra) gives shape to a future quaywall along the Caspian Sea.

In general, Iran and Russia favored the former approach of equally sharing Caspian rights and resources among the littoral states and excluding all other interests. They thus rejected Azerbaijan's solo decision to make deals with outsiders for oil and gas work in the Caspian.

The Russian Ministry of Foreign Affairs, in April 1994, wrote to the U.K. government to formally object to wording in a memorandum of energy cooperation with Azerbaijan referring to the "Azerbaijan sector of the Caspian Sea." The Russian ministry insisted that "there exists no division of the Caspian Sea into sectors" and called the sea an "object of common use."

Russia also officially declared the Caspian Sea to be exempt from the 1982 Law of the Sea Convention, which provided for demarcation of territorial seas, exclusive economic zones, and continental shelves. In October 1995, Moscow wrote to the United Nations to assert the "special status" of the Caspian. The sea, it said, was covered by Article 122 of the convention, which excluded lakes or bodies of water with no natural outlets to other seas or oceans. Late in 1996, Russia hinted that it might accept a partitioning of the Caspian out to 45 miles from the coastline, but no official proposals to that effect were known to have been made.

Azerbaijan, quietly joined by Kazakhstan, disputed the Russian and Iranian position. Turkmenistan in 1996 had not taken a strong stand on the Caspian territorial question, although it produced negligible amounts of oil from the sea.

At a conference organized by Iran's Institute for Political and International Studies and Institute for International Energy Studies in December 1995, a Socar official outlined the Azeri position.

The Soviet Union had indeed divided the Caspian Sea into zones for oil and gas work, asserted Socar Director Koshbakht Yousefzadeh. He said that during the 1970s he witnessed the division among what now are the five littoral states. He also said that Iran during that period recognized the sea boundary inscribed by connection of the land boundaries between its territory and that of the FSU. Yousefzadeh also dismissed the Russo-Iranian treaties as relating to marine travel and fishing and not to oil and gas resources.

Differences over territorial issues in the Caspian region thus were sharp in 1996 and could never be fully disengaged from other commercial, political, and ethnic rivalries. How those differences eventually settle out will strongly influence the degree to which the region's rich resource is developed, the manner in which development is carried out, and the country that dominates the region and prospers most from its vast wealth. IPE

Orinoco oil belt essential to Venezuela's growth plans

Orimulsion, an emulsion of extra-heavy crude oil, water, and a surfactant that competes as a boiler fuel with coal and fuel oil, is one of the key components of Venezuela's strategy to exploit its massive heavy oil resource.

Venezuela has pushed exploitation of the Orinoco heavy oil belt to the forefront of its upstream expansion strategy.

Along with its overtures to private petroleum companies, notably foreign multinationals, to invest in the country's conventional upstream oil and gas exploration and development, Caracas also is pursuing an aggressive campaign to increase production of heavy and extra-heavy crude and bitumen in the Orinoco oil belt of eastern Venezuela.

Little wonder: Venezuela's Orinoco resource consists of 1.2 trillion bbl of extra-heavy oil, of which 270 billion bbl is recoverable with current technology. If Venezuela could move that figure into the "proved, economic reserves" category, it would surpass Saudi Arabia in terms of oil reserves.

Venezuela's own conventional oil reserves are put at 64.5 billion bbl, biggest in the Western Hemisphere and ranking the country sixth worldwide. By comparison, the world's biggest reserves of conventional crude oil are in Saudi Arabia and are estimated at 261 billion bbl. Total worldwide conventional crude oil reserves are estimated at 1 trillion bbl.

State-owned petroleum company Petroleos de Venezuela SA (Pdvsa) has a two-pronged approach in its Orinoco strategy: implementing strategic associations with foreign multinationals to exploit and upgrade the extra-heavy crude and bitumen and promoting development of Orimulsion, a bitumen-based boiler fuel meant to compete with coal in electric power plants.

Although Orinoco extra-heavy crude oil and bitumen are considered unconventional oil resources by virtue of their characteristics—typically gravities of 7-10°, sulfur content of 3.2-3.8 wt %, and traces of heavy metals—Pdvsa has largely overcome producing problems in the Orinoco belt by employing the same enhanced recovery techniques used for conventional heavy oil: steam injection, diluents, and chemical additives.

Pdvsa's efforts to step up production, upgrading, and marketing of Orinoco heavy oil have spawned a handful of billion-dollar megaprojects with foreign multinationals that could yield as much as 400,000 b/d of light- and medium- gravity crude oil by the turn of the century.

Pdvsa operating units have agreed to a number of strategic association projects at varying stages of progress that promise to greatly increase Venezuela's production of extra-heavy oil.

Units of Conoco Inc., Total, ARCO, and Mobil Corp. have signed agreements with Corpoven, Lagoven, and Maraven to develop huge reserves of 8-10° gravity crude, upgrade that crude, and market the resulting synthetic light and medium crude.

More problematic are transportation and utilization of Orinoco bitumen, which is what led to the development of Orimulsion. The product—an emulsion of bitumen with water and a surfactant that competes directly with coal and fuel oil in electric power generating plants—is gaining wider acceptance in target markets in the U.S., Europe, Asia, and Latin America.

The Orinoco resource

A 1984 United Nations study found that—based on a definition of heavy oil as being heavier than 20° gravity and less than 10,000 cp viscosity—93% of the world's heavy oil resource is in Venezuela, and most of that is in the Orinoco belt.

The Orinoco oil belt covers an area about 700 km long by 50-100 km wide in Monagas, Anzoategui, and Guarico states along the northern banks of the Orinoco River.

This vast area has more than 1.2 trillion bbl of 6-13° gravity oil in place. Orinoco oil is mobile under reservoir conditions, and shallow wells produce about 100 b/d on rod pump, according to consultant Pantera Petroleum, San Leandro, Calif.

The belt's four areas are Cerro Negro, Hamaca, Zuata, and Machete.

The Cerro Negro area, with about 215 billion bbl of heavy oil in place, is operated by Lagoven SA, one of Pdvsa's three upstream operating affiliates. Corpoven SA operates the Hamaca area, with 220 billion bbl of oil in place. Corpoven's Machete area, farther west and featuring deeper pay, remains undeveloped. Maraven SA, the third operating affiliate, has the Zuata area, with about 500 billion bbl of oil in place.

Producing depths in the heavy oil belt are 750-4,500 ft, and its unconsolidated Tertiary reservoir sands have permeabilities of 1-2 darcies and porosities of 25% or more.

Conoco, Maraven

In a deal signed in November 1995, Conoco agreed to develop a $1.4 billion project with Maraven in the Zuata area to produce 120,000 b/d of 8° gravity crude.

The Zuata heavy crude will be processed at a big coking unit at Jose, near Puerto la Cruz on the Caribbean coast. The $800 million coker will yield 102,000 b/d of 21° gravity synthetic crude.

This synthetic crude will replace Mexican Maya as a feedstock for Conoco's Lake Charles refinery.

In addition, Jose byproduct coke will be exported to the U.S.

Conoco estimates total project investment at $1.4 billion. The 55,000-acre contract area is expected to produce 1.5 billion bbl of extra-heavy oil during the 35-year agreement term.

Total group project

Maraven also has undertaken a strategic association Orinoco project with France's Total and Norway's Den norske stats oljeselskap AS (Statoil) and Norsk Hydro AS.

This project will employ a catalytic process to upgrade

Orinoco strategic associations

Fig. 1

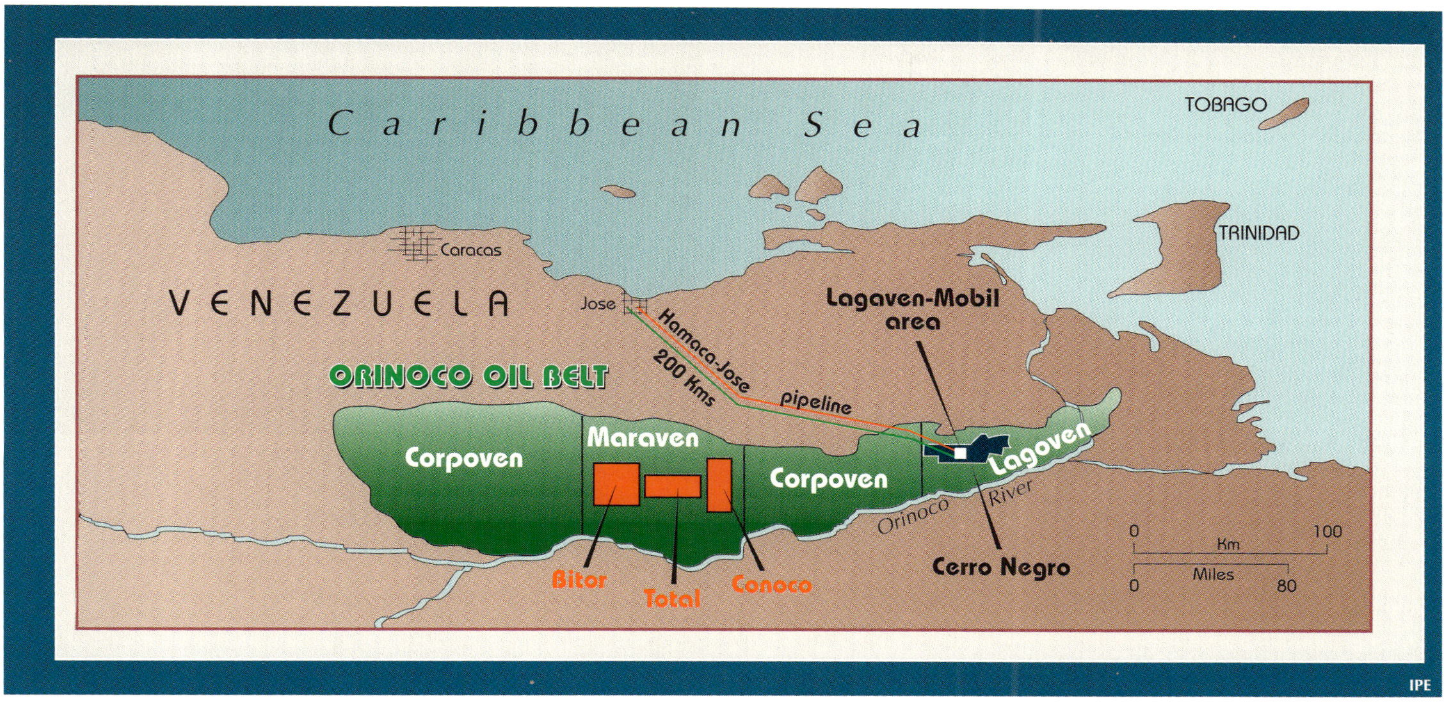

170,000 b/d of Zuata heavy oil.

Japan's Itochu Corp. and Marubeni Corp. were originally partners in the $2.25 billion project but since have pulled out.

About 70% of the capital cost of this project will go for upgrading facilities, according to Pantera.

ARCO/Corpoven deal

ARCO and Corpoven in August 1996 disclosed a three-stage, $3.5 billion heavy oil deal in Orinoco's Hamaca area.

The two companies plan to develop 164,000 b/d of Hamaca crude to be upgraded to a lighter synthetic crude at Jose and exported to refineries in the U.S.

The proposed $2.1 billion upgrader will use the HDH process that Pdvsa research arm Intevep developed.

With this project, says Pantera, Orinoco production can be developed for about $5,000/b/d, with most of the investment earmarked for upgrading the heavy, metals-rich crude.

By 2006, the two partners expect the project to be upgrading as much as 200,000 b/d of 9° gravity crude from the Orinoco. The upgraded 25° gravity oil will have characteristics similar to crude produced on Alaska's North Slope.

The project entails producing extra-heavy crude from the Hamaca zone south of El Tigre in Anzoategui state and transporting the crude via pipeline to the Jose upgrader.

Project costs for all three phases of the project cover drilling and construction of field, transportation, and upgrading facilities.

Under the first phase, ARCO and Corpoven will start up oil production and lay a pipeline from the production area to the Jose upgrader. In the second phase, they will construct the first upgrading module, expected to be on stream by 2001, with an upgrading capacity of about 90,000 b/d.

In the third phase, partners intend to hike crude production and upgrading capacities to allow recovery of about 180,000 b/d of processed oil.

The agreement stems from a letter of intent signed in 1994 that launched a series of feasibility studies of the project.

Late in 1996, Phillips Petroleum Co. and Texaco Inc. joined forces with ARCO and Corpoven in a joint-venture study of the project covering 120,000 acres in the Hamaca region. If it leads to development, Corpoven estimates 2.4 billion bbl of oil could be recovered, with initial production beginning as early as 1999. Initial interests are Corpoven and ARCO 30% each and Phillips and Texaco 20% each.

Where Orimulsion power plant customers are

Operator	Location	Capacity (1,000 kw)
OPERATING		
Kashima Kita	Kashima, Japan	*225
Mitsubishi Kasei	Mizushima, Japan	70
Kansai Electric	Osaka, Japan	156
Powergen	Ince B, U.K.	500
Powergen	Richborough, U.K.	*240
New Brunswick Power	Dalhousie, Canada	*300
SK Power	Asnaes, Denmark	700
COMMERCIAL AGREEMENTS		
National Power	Pembroke, U.K.	*2,00
Florida Power & Light	Manatee, Fla.	*1,600
Hokkaido Electric	Shiriuchi, Japan	350

*Combined capacity of two or more units.

Source: Bitor Europe

Cerro Negro project

Caracas signed a $2.3 billion heavy oil agreement with Mobil in September 1996.

The deal calls for Mobil and Lagoven, beginning early in the next century, to ship 8° gravity Orinoco crude from the Cerro Negro area to Jose for upgrading to 16° gravity feed for Mobil's Chalmette, La., refinery.

In preparation for the project, the partners in summer 1996 processed a shipment of Cerro Negro crude at Chalmette.

Mobil and Lagoven also agreed to develop part of the Cerro Negro area and upgrade 100,000 b/d of extra-heavy crude into a 31° gravity synthetic crude.

Of project costs, $336 million will be earmarked for developing that production volume, but the upgrader will be a $1.5 billion investment. Cerro Negro has the shallowest reservoirs in the heavy oil belt, so development costs there are lower, Pantera noted.

The four Orinoco projects just described will have combined output of more than 550,000 b/d, but they represent development of only a small part of the area of the heavy oil belt, contends Pantera.

Depending on oil prices and capital availability, many more projects could be accommodated, Pantera said.

Orimulsion's promise

Orimulsion, Venezuela's trademark boiler fuel, is fast becoming one of the cornerstones of Pdvsa's growth strategy.

The massive reserves of difficult-to-market heavy crudes and bitumen in the Orinoco belt have posed a major challenge for Pdvsa.

In addition to negotiating strategic associations with foreign oil companies to extract and upgrade the recoverable resources, Pdvsa embarked on a scheme to turn the bitumen into a new fuel that could be used in lieu of more-polluting fuels to burn in electric power generating plants.

It is the extremely high viscosity of Orinoco heavy crudes and bitumen that make their production, transport, and treatment by conventional methods very costly.

Pdvsa's research arm Intevep had considered several production and handling schemes, notably heating and dilution. Both of these methods are energy-intensive processes and require diluents.

Intevep in 1981 signed a research collaboration agreement with British Petroleum Co. plc that led to the development of the Imulsion technology.

Surfactant packages, novel techniques for emulsion formation, mathematical models for pipeline transportation, and processes for breaking these emulsions were the results of extensive laboratory and pilot plant scale work carried out at Intevep's research facilities at Los Teques, Venezuela, and BP's facilities at Sudbury, England.

Successful pilot tests were carried out by Intevep in conjunction with Lagoven in their pilot facilities at Morichal, the field-scale development center for the Orinoco oil belt. They established in November 1985 an experimental, 400 b/d well, a pilot flow station, and main station to adapt and optimize the Imulsion technology to conditions found in the Cerro Negro area, where the average crude gravity is 8.5°.

More than 100,000 bbl of emulsified bitumen was produced at these facilities, allowing further development of the technology at field scale. These emulsions were used to optimize downhole emulsification. The project involved innovative pumping equipment, flowline transportation, degasification, storage, pipeline transportation, desalting, reformulation, and ocean transportation.

In July 1986, based on success of the field test, Lagoven decided to dedicate a commercial production block and dehydration plant to produce and handle 15,000-20,000 b/d of emulsion. The technology also was adapted to winter conditions, and BP performed field scale tests in Canada to validate the technology in temperate and cold climates.

The natural bitumen produced at Cerro Negro was dubbed Orinoco, and its emulsified form became known as Orimulsion.

Bitor created

Once the product received international recognition, Pdvsa created a subsidiary in 1989 known as Bitumenes Orinoco SA (Bitor) to handle the production and international marketing of Orimulsion.

Bitor, which thus far has been viewed by Pdvsa more as a company handling a project than as a fully commercial profit-making operation, has lined up several major contracts for the sale of Orimulsion to customers in the U.S., Canada, U.K., Japan, Denmark, Italy, and Taiwan. Prospective customers include Portugal, Germany, and China.

Bitor's strategy since its creation has been to operate with a negative cash flow as it fulfills its chief goal, which is to make Orimulsion known internationally.

Production facilities shown are in the Hamaca area of the Orinoco oil belt, where ARCO, Corpoven, Phillips, and Texaco plan a $3.5 billion project to recover and upgrade extra-heavy crude oil and market the resulting synthetic crude. Photo by Pablo Krisch, Agencia Condor, courtesy of Petroleos de Venezuela SA.

Orimulsion output has grown steadily. In 1994, output was about 2.7 million tons. It climbed to about 4.7 million tons in 1995. Output in 1996 was estimated at 5 million tons. Bitor's goal is to boost production to more than 20 million tons/year by the turn of the century and about 30 million tons/year by 2005. Bitor's initial capital spending in this effort was put at $2 billion.

With the projected growth in output, Pdvsa launched a project completing the first phase of storage and handling facilities at the Jose port. This project, with capacity for handling about 8.7 million tons/year of Orimulsion, is the first step in moving the product away from the site of production to its point of export. This new infrastructure replaced Orimulsion terminals at Punta Cuchillo and at Bonaire.

The new Jose terminal, which can handle tankers as big as 240,000 dwt, adds 240,000 tons of storage capacity to the 70,000 tons available at Morichal. Also completed was a 310 km pipeline between Jose and Morichal with a capacity of 63,700 tons/day, which allows Orimulsion to be transported directly from the production and emulsification area to the Jose terminal.

Formerly, Orimulsion was pumped south from Morichal through a relatively small-capacity pipeline and then shipped from Punta Cuchillo, a port facility on the southern bank of the Orinoco River, which could handle only tankers smaller than 60,000 dwt. This made it necessary to transfer several loads to larger tankers at a deepwater port at Bonaire in the Caribbean Sea whenever large shipments of Orimulsion had to be exported.

Orimulsion takes off

Pdvsa and Bitor policy-makers have said the economic recovery in major industrial countries, continued growth in energy demand, and the decision of the European Union and the worldwide Customs Cooperation Council in favor of Venezuela's request for a classification exempting Orimulsion from tariff discrimination all have been factors that renewed interest in the product and fostered its entry into new markets.

Orimulsion has passed the test on environmental acceptability in some of the tough markets of the U.S., Canada, and Europe. U.K. authorities have ruled that Orimulsion emissions are comparable to those of other fossil fuels. However, the product in some cases must still face stiff environmental regulations in certain U.S. states before the final go ahead is given for contracts.

The new and growing Orimulsion business in not expected to have any effect on Venezuela's production quota with the Organization of Petroleum Exporting Countries, Bitor executives say. Because it is classified as a natural bitumen, Orimulsion is not governed by OPEC production policies.

Orimulsion sales in 1994 generated about $60 million in revenues. This performance improved substantially in 1995, when revenues from Orimulsion sales were estimated at $130 million, which put Bitor at almost break-even status.

Bitor executives said an expected increase in Orimulsion sales in 1996 would allow their company to report a profit for the first time since its creation in 1989.

Bitor declined to provide details regarding Orimulsion market prices, saying simply that they are competitive with other fuels such as coal and residual fuel oil. The high content of sulfur and metals requires the use of pollution control equipment in power plants burning Orimulsion, and the fuel is priced accordingly.

Upgraded tanker terminal at Jose, Venezuela, will accommodate ARCO/Corpoven group's plans to export as much as 200,000 b/d of blended medium gravity crudes upgraded from Orinoco extra-heavy crude. Photo by Juan Silva, courtesy of Petroleos de Venezuela SA.

While customers find Orimulsion as easy to handle as heavy fuel oil, employing the same kind of storage facilities, the product also is more environmentally friendly than fuel oil or coal, Bitor executives say.

Orimulsion produces far less particulates, ash, and nitrogen oxides than coal, Bitor contends. It also presents no fire hazard and, in the event of a marine spill, creates minimal contamination because it disperses rapidly in seawater, the company claims.

The emulsion contains 29.5% water and has a calorific value of 12,700 BTU/lb.

Opening markets

Bitor's focus since its founding has been on opening markets for Orimulsion.

In its move to establish a broad support network on the international market for Orimulsion, Bitor created subsidiaries that operate in several areas around the world, marketing the product and providing key support services to customers.

The Boca Raton, Fla., based Bitor America Corp. is responsible for marketing Orimulsion in the U.S., Puerto Rico, and Canada.

Bitor America Corp. works in close liaison with Citizens Power and Lehman Bros., which provide special consulting services in the areas, respectively, of power generation and finance. In 1994, New Brunswick's power plant at Dalhousie, N.B., became the first Canadian customer for Orimulsion following the signing of a long-term contract for the supply of 800,000 tons/year of the product to the Canadian province. Subsequently, Bitor America Corp. and Florida Power & Light signed a 20-year contract for the supply of 4 million tons/year of Orimulsion.

Bitor's London-based European subsidiary Bitor Europe Ltd. handles the distribution and sale of Orimulsion in Europe and North Africa, as well as in Turkey, Malta, and Cyprus. This trading affiliate negotiated a 300,000 ton/year supply contract with PowerGen to service a power station at Richborough near London beginning in 1991. A year later, another contract was finalized to supply 1 million tons/year of the product to another PowerGen plant in Northwest England, followed by negotiations to supply as much as 5 million tons/year of Orimulsion to a National Power plant at Pembroke, West Wales.

Taking aim at the explosive growth of the energy markets in Asia and the Far East in particular, Bitor set up another subsidiary in a 50-50 partnership deal with Japan's Mitsubishi Corp., known as MC Bitor. That venture secured three clients in Japan. The Hashima Kita power plant currently consumes 355,000 tons/year of Orimulsion, while Mitsubishi Kasei takes 215,000 tons/year, and Kansai Electric's power plant at Osaka gets 250,000 tons/year.

"The creation of these regional subsidiaries has played a key role in the marketing success enjoyed by the company, since every supply contract negotiated has been the result of painstaking local investigation of markets, of competition, of environmental legislation, and of the prevailing political background, as well as the provision of detailed orientation about the new fuel to potential customers, government entities, and higher economic bodies," said Bitor Vice-Pres. Carlos Borregales.

"Negotiating Orimulsion contracts is difficult," Borregales said. "Negotiations can take 6-10 years" He emphasized that his company offers "guaranteed supplies," given the vast bitumen reserves in Venezuela.

Potential Bitor clients that decide to purchase Orimulsion must also prepare to make a substantial investment in the redesign of their electric generating plants to switch from coal or fuel oil to Orimulsion. This means that contracts with Bitor have to be long term, providing guaranteed supplies at secured prices.

Bitor would have no difficulty meeting long term contracts because Venezuela has vast reserves of natural bitumen and is the sole producer of Orimulsion worldwide.

Studies have shown that converting from coal or fuel oil to Orimulsion makes an electric generating plant far more efficient and less costly to operate, despite the heavy up-front cost of converting the plant—which could run as much as $600 million.

"We are tied to the client. It's a partnership relation between the buyer and the seller, with the contracts basically being long term, about 20 years," Borregales said.

He made it clear that politics does not play a role in the negotiation of contracts. "The government helps Bitor open the possibility of new clients," he said.

Watershed contract

A watershed contract is the one with Taiwan calling for shipment of 3.4 million tons/year of Orimulsion beginning in 2000. It is the largest of its kind in the Asia-Pacific region, has a duration of 25 years, and matches Bitor's biggest sale to date.

Orimulsion MPE-1 plant in the Cerro Negro area of the Orinoco oil belt produces the proprietary Venezuelan boiler fuel.

"The approval constitutes the most significant step forward in the Asia-Pacific region by Bitumenes Orinoco," said company Pres. Jorge Zemella.

Zemella said his company received "with great satisfaction" a report from Taiwan on the outcome of a tender by Taiwan's state-owned power company to select new projects assigned to independent power producers (IPPs).

Zemella said Bitor affiliate MC Bitor Ltd. will "significantly penetrate" the Asian market with the Orimulsion sale to Taiwan.

Orimulsion will be the sole fuel of a power plant to be built by a group led by International Generating Co. (Intergen) , a joint venture of Bechtel Group and Pacific Gas & Electric affiliates, at Lizhe in the Suao region on Taiwan's east coast. Sales will begin in 2000.

The project is one of many proposed under a Taiwanese government initiative to solicit IPPs from the private sector to build power plants to meet Taiwan's soaring electric power demand.

Taiwan's Ministry of Economic Affairs recently chose from the first round of proposals seven groups to build a total IPP capacity of 7.11 million kw. Combined power capacity of 23 projects proposed under the first round totaled 30.3 million kw.

Oil products and natural gas will feed some of the other winning projects.

Among the companies selected in the first round is a combine led by Intergen and including Taiwan Synthetic Rubber Corp., APED, and China Steel.

The group's Lizhe plant will have an installed generating capacity of 1.5 million kw involving two units of 750,000 kw each.

One of the units will begin operations about mid-2000 and the second by the end of that year.

MC Bitor and Mitsubishi Corp. will supply those units about 3.4 million tons/year of Orimulsion for 25 years exported from the Jose terminal.

It will be the largest supply contract of Orimulsion in the Asia-Pacific region. MC Bitor and Intergen were expected to sign the agreement by yearend 1996.

Zemella said, "The approval constitutes the most significant step forward in the Asia-Pacific region by Bitumenes Orinoco, through MC Bitor, in penetrating the electricity segment of the energy market in the Far East."

The market has been dominated by energy sources such as gas, coal, and conventional liquid hydrocarbon fuels.

The next step in marketing Orimulsion in the region is to prepare an environmental impact study to obtain permits from Taiwanese local and regional authorities.

Among other key contracts signed recently are those covering sale of 1.5 million tons/year of Orimulsion to Denmark's SK Power and 500,000 tons/year to Italian electric utility ENEL.

Shown is part of an integrated storage, transport, and loading system, including a 310-km pipeline from the Morichal area of Venezuela's Orinoco oil region to a recently commissioned deepwater export terminal at Jose for exporting Orimulsion. Photo by Pablo Krisch, Agencia Condor, courtesy of Petroleos de Venezuela SA.

Elsewhere, Bitor in 1996 sent the first shipment of Orimulsion to China, a 52,000 metric ton cargo to state-owned China National United Oil Corp. for use in feasibility tests at electric and industrial plants. Under the agreement with the Chinese company, Bitor is scheduled to deliver an additional 150,000 metric tons of Orimulsion.

"Numerous Latin American, European, and Asian countries are currently evaluating the use of Orimulsion for the electricity generating sector as a competing fuel alternative to coal and fuel oil, thanks to its high yield, low operating costs, and compliance with the strictest environmental norms," Zemella said.

Bitor's efforts

Aside from its continuing efforts to secure new customers around the world, Bitor also is engaged in an aggressive campaign aimed at expanding bitumen production facilities at home to meet expected demand for Orimulsion.

New contracts require a substantial increase in production and blending capacity.

A joint venture of Conoco and Statoil with local engineering firms Distral and Jantesa will develop part of the Cerro Negro area to increase production of bitumen devoted to Orimulsion output.

The Cerro Negro area is operated by Lagoven and currently produces about 20,000 b/d used for Orimulsion.

Bitor in 1996 signed a contract with the Conoco/Statoil group to build a second, $320 million bitumen production plant. With a planned productive capacity of about 104,000 b/d, this plant is scheduled to go on stream in 1997. Bitor holds a 40% stake in the venture, while Conoco holds 30%, Statoil 20%, and Jandis 10%. The project first must be approved by Congress before it can proceed.

The company's medium term plans include construction of a third Orimulsion bitumen production plant in 1998 and another by yearend 1999.

One spinoff from the Orimulsion business came last year with the creation of a joint venture known as Orbit Metallurgical Ltd. involving Bitor with a 45% stake, Strategic Minerals Corp. (Stratcor) with 45%, and Reakt Ltd. with 10%.

Orbit will recover vanadium, nickel, and magnesium from the residual ash obtained through electrostatic precipitators after combustion of Orimulsion and manufacture metal products from them. The new company will establish a plant in Germany, with a processing capacity of about 6,000 tons/year of residual ash, and two more plants are scheduled to be built in Europe, one of them in the U.K. IPE

Syncrude Canada has earmarked $1 billion to expand its Fort McMurray, Alta., oilsands complex. Photo courtesy Syncrude.

Canadian oilsands industry poised for major expansion

Canada's oilsands/heavy oil industry is poised for a major expansion that could extend well into the 21st century.

A 1996 report by a Canadian national task force on oilsands concluded a number of factors are coming together to sharply increase investment and production during the next 25 years.

Canadian oilsands operators in June 1996 disclosed projections that there would be more than $25 billion (Canadian) in new oilsands projects during the next 25 years.

By that time, oilsands in northern Alberta could account for as much as half or more of Canada's oil production.

Vast resource

The resource is huge. Depending on which agency provides the estimate, bitumen in place in Alberta alone could total 1.7-2.5 trillion bbl.

Canadian oilsands reserves increased in 1995 from 1994 by 614 million bbl to 2.567 billion bbl. Alberta's estimated surface mine oilsands reserves at yearend 1995 were 2.4 billion bbl, down 125 million bbl from 1994, and in situ oilsands reserves were 1.3 billion bbl, up 181 million bbl.

Canada's National Energy Board (NEB) and Alberta Energy & Utilities Board (AEUB) disagree on the potential resource held in the four major northern Alberta oilsands deposits: Athabasca, Cold Lake, Peace River, and Wabasca,

Together, these four areas cover about 48,000 sq miles.

NEB pegs the resource at about 2.5 trillion bbl. AEUB estimates there are 1.7 trillion bbl of bitumen in place.

The agencies agree on the ultimately recoverable resource: about 300 billion bbl. Under current permits, about 4 billion bbl can be produced, more than the remaining proved reserves of conventional crude oil in western Canada.

Oilsands production costs have fallen sharply in recent years, thanks to technology improvements in recovery and processing techniques. These costs have fallen to the point where oilsands is becoming increasingly competitive with conventional crude oil in Canada, where reserves long have been declining.

New fiscal regime

After much lobbying and research by industry, the federal and provincial governments have introduced a new royalty and fiscal regime intended to boost oilsands investment.

Now investors have clear incentives to commit money to oilsands projects. These policies also will provide generic tax treatment for all new projects. This has been a long-term goal for sponsors of oilsands projects. In the past, such projects' royalty and tax agreements were decided case by case.

The task force report, issued in fall 1995, represented a watershed for the industry by setting forth a case for Canadian oilsands as a national asset that should be utilized to generate long-term economic growth and revenues for the country and provinces as well as provide profits for investors and operators.

But there needs to be a new approach to oilsands development, the task force contended. Future development should occur incrementally in phases rather than as the multibillion-dollar megaprojects that have been the case in the past.

During the next few years alone, companies plan to spend about $5.6 billion on new oilsands development in Alberta, according to provincial Energy Minister Patricia Black.

Fiscal relief

A new federal budget in 1996 provided a spur for oilsands development in Canada.

It included tax measures to support Canadian oilsands development that Syncrude Canada Chairman Eric Newell said sends a clear signal to the industry.

Together with implementation of a standard royalty formula for the oilsands industry, disclosed in 1995, generic tax measures in the 1996 federal budget embrace the principles and put into practice most of the fiscal recommendations of the National Oilsands Task Force, Newell said.

Under federal budget provisions, Ottawa will broaden mining tax rules to include in situ operations and extend accelerated capital cost allowance to smaller projects to improve efficiency or expand capacity.

Newell said, "The oilsands business was the only industrial sector remaining without generic fiscal terms."

Tax and royalty terms for each oilsands project had been negotiated by developers and governments case by case.

"Over $3.4 billion in new projects and expansions have been waiting for these general fiscal terms to be resolved," said task force Chairman Erdal Yildirim.

Changes to resource allowances and a tightening of tax rules on flow-through shares will cost Canada's upstream industry as much as $10 million/year during 1996-97, said Canadian Association of Petroleum Producers.

The association added, however, that the adjustments are rational and will maintain stability of the fiscal regime.

Syncrude's Newell contends that a single fiscal and resource allowance policy was the key element achieved by the task force initiative.

"Investors are quite willing to accept risks around things like crude oil prices, but they think they ought to know what the tax and royalty regime is going to be," he said. "To me, the big thing was to get a generic regime that suits everybody. Then the market decides what goes ahead."

Because of uncertain economics under a murky fiscal regime, two oilsands mine megaprojects—the Alsands group and the Other Six Lease Operations (OSLO) project—were shelved during the 1980s.

The task force warned that the future of the oilsands resource is not assured, despite its role as a secure source of oil offering significant wealth creation.

"Before stakeholders agree to pay the economic and social costs of new development, they must be convinced the prize is worth the investment," the task force report said.

It noted development failures in the 1980s and said the credibility of a strategy for doubling or tripling production depends on demonstrating fresh approaches to and new levers for development.

"The report sent a strong signal to policy-makers that a special focus on oilsands is in the public interest," Newell said. "Time is running out for our domestic conventional light and medium crude, and something has to be done to make up the shortfall.

Alberta oilsands projects*

Project	Investment (Million Canadian $)	Timing	Description†	Production
Amoco				
Primrose	500	Immediate	SAGD heavy oil production	50,000 b/d of heavy oil
Alberta Energy Co. Ltd.				
Cold Lake	13	Immediate	SAGD heavy oil pilot plant	1,000 b/d of heavy oil
Foster Creek	200	1997-98	Commercial heavy oil project	30,000 b/d of heavy oil
Elan Energy Ltd.				
Lindbergh-Elk Point	60	Immediate	SAGD heavy oil plant	Increase production to 22,000 b/d from 14,000 b/d
Gibson Petroleum Ltd.				
UTF	7	1996-97	SAGD bitumen project	Increase production to 4,500 b/d from 2,000 b/d
Gulf Canada Resources Ltd.				
Surmont	30	1996	Phase 1 SAGD heavy oil project	3,000 b/d
	NA	1998-99	Phase 2	Production increases to 20,000 b/d
Imperial Oil Ltd.				
Cold Lake Phases 9-10	250	Immediate	In situ bitumen production	Phases 9-10 increase in situ bitumen production to 120,000 b/d (about 25,000 b/d added)
Cold Lake Phases 11-12 (proposed)	250	1997	In situ bitumen production following completion of Phases 9-10	Phases 11-12 add about 20,000 b/d
Imperial				
Cold Lake	40	Immediate	Heavy oil development below current Cold Lake lease	9,400 b/d of heavy oil
Koch Oil Co. Ltd.				
Cold Lake-Reita Lake	NA	1997-98	In situ bitumen project	50,000 b/d
Shell Canada Ltd.				
Peace River	3	Immediate	SAGD heavy oil project	Production increase
Solvex				
Bitumount	170	1997	Bitumen mine and extraction complex plus minerals extraction plant	14,000 b/d bitumen plus 100,000 metric tons alumina plus 200,000 metric tons synthetic silica from tailings
Suncor Inc.				
Primrose	17	1996-97	Phase 1: SAGD pilot plant	2,500 b/d of heavy oil
Burnt Lake	122	1998-99	Phase 2: commercial plant	Increase production to 12,500 b/d of heavy oil
Suncor				
OSG Steepbank mine	300	2001	New bitumen mine	Increase production to 90,000+ b/d of light sweet crude and custom blends
Suncor				
OSG Fort McMurray plant	300	1998-2001	Upgrader improvements and plant modifications	Increase production to 80,000 b/d of light sweet crude and custom blends
Suncor				
OSG Fort McMurray plant	190	Immediate	Environmental measures	Reduce SO_2 emissions
Syncrude Canada Ltd.				
North mine-Mildred Lake	500	1998	New bitumen mine and debottlenecking of upgrading plant	Production increase to 82 million bbl/year
Syncrude				
Aurora mine	500	2001	New bitumen and remote extraction plant and debottleneck 2	First train starts 2001, second train 2004. Production increase to 94 million bbl/year
Total	**3,452**			

*A number of these projects are in initial stages of development. The list includes only announced projects. Additional projects in the planning stages add to total investment. †SAGD = steam assisted gravity drainage.

Source: National Oilsands Task Force

Long-term outlook

The task force's 25-year outlook found that maximum development of the 300 billion bbl of potentially recoverable oilsands works out to a doubling or tripling of current production levels to 800,000-1.2 million b/d.

One possible hurdle to faster growth would be a sharp drop in crude oil prices.

In its 25-year outlook, the task force report assumed that growth in the price of conventional oil will remain at about $25 (Canadian)/bbl.

It also assumed fossil fuel will continue to be the engine of the global economy through the first half of the next century, especially for transportation.

The task force also made the assumption that exports of Canadian bitumen, crude oil, and transportation fuels will remain free from restrictive government regulations.

Finally, the task force report concluded that R&D will result in technology that will cut supply costs and improve efficiency and sustainable development.

Suncor Inc. plans to expand its oilsands operations in northern Alberta by adding a new mine and implementing a new in situ recovery project. Shown is one of Suncor's three Marion electric cable shovels able to load a 240-ton capacity Haulpak 830E truck in three scoops. Photo courtesy of Suncor.

Growth strategy

The federal government and Alberta both have responded to the task force's finding that oilsands development is in the country's interest, agreeing to royalty and tax initiatives to spur investment.

The task force concluded that a string of smaller scale expansions of existing operations could increase oilsands production by 14.6 million bbl/year. Ultimately, production could build to as much as 1.2 million b/d of bitumen and upgraded crude by 2020, once remote oilsands mines and in situ projects are factored in.

It also saw growth in prospective ancillary industries, such as coke desulfurization and production and metals extraction. Expanded oilsands production could help spark growth in a regional petrochemical industry beyond that near Edmonton.

The task force called for a collaboration on research by industry, government, and academia to cut capital and operating costs for oilsands operations, recommending the Canadian Oilsands Network for Research & Development (Conrad) be used as a model for future research. Conrad coordinates oilsands R&D by the three sectors.

Another benefit of oilsands growth would be a network of hydrogen and nitrogen plants linked to upgraders. These could support other industries as independent suppliers having the advantages of low power costs and Alberta's huge natural gas reserves.

Pipeline development also would be stimulated, with new lines needed to ship bitumen from producing areas to processing plants and from those plants to market.

New oilsands markets could include the U.S. Rocky Mountain region, where reserves of conventional crude oil are declining, along with Washington and California.

Currently, most crude and products derived from bitumen and blended oilsands synthetic crudes move via pipeline to the Great Lakes, U.S. Midwest, and California. Oilsands crude also is transported to Montreal as well as the U.S. Midwest and South.

Oilsands production

Since commercial production of oilsands began in 1967, output has risen sevenfold, more than doubling in the past decade to top 400,000 b/d.

More than 14% of Canada's current supply of petroleum is synthetic or upgraded crude. Deep in situ projects provide another 7.5% of Canadian oil supply.

Syncrude and Suncor mine more than 325,000 b/d of Athabasca bitumen, upgrading it to 280,000 b/d of light, low-sulfur blended crude oil. Oilsands make up 21% of Canada's light and medium gravity crude production.

Alberta in situ production from 16 projects is forecast to jump to as much as 315,000 b/d by 2005 from 150,000 b/d in 1996.

Not all oilsands production comes from Alberta. About 110,000 b/d of synthetic crude is produced at Lloydminster and Regina, Sask., upgraders operated by Husky Oil Ltd. and NewGrade, respectively. Feedstock for these operations is Saskatchewan heavy oil and Cold Lake bitumen.

Still more research is needed, says the task force, if Canada's oilsands industry is to lower the economic threshold for grassroots projects and to make replacement reserves available. The task force noted new technology will help industry trim operating costs for integrated mine operations to $6-7 (U.S.)/bbl and overall supply costs to $15 (U.S.)/bbl by 2010.

Government role

Federal and provincial governments play a key role in Canada's oilsands development, beyond the fiscal relief.

Alberta and Canada's oilsands industry have extended for 5 years funding for a joint heavy oil research project. The core research program run by the Alberta Research Council will receive $10 million from government and $5 million from industry. The program researches recovery technology for heavy oil and bitumen.

Meantime Alberta is seeking buyers for its 10% interest in the shelved OSLO oilsands mining project near Fort McMurray, Alta. OSLO is a $4.1 billion, 77,000 b/d project proposed in 1988 but shelved in 1991 because of an outlook for low oil prices.

Alberta's partners in OSLO are Imperial Oil Ltd. 25%, Canadian Occidental Petroleum Ltd. 20%, Petro-Canada 15%, Gulf Canada Resources Ltd. 20%, and PanCanadian Petroleum Ltd. 10%. The OSLO group sold some of its leases to Syncrude Canada Ltd. in 1995.

Project outlays

In the 6 months following the introduction of the new oilsands royalty/tax framework, operators unveiled plans for oilsands projects worth a combined $3.5 billion (Canadian), including projects in the Athabasca, Cold Lake, and Peace River areas (see table).

Big expansion projects by industry leaders Syncrude Canada, Suncor Inc., and Imperial Oil Ltd. represent the biggest share of the projected project outlays.

Canada's two operating oilsands surface mines in the Athabasca oilsands region will absorb most of that expansion capital.

Syncrude, a venture of 10 companies, has detailed plans to spend a total of $1 billion to expand production.

Syncrude plans to spend $500 million in 1998 to develop a new bitumen mine and debottleneck its upgrader to hike capacity to 82 million bbl/year.

The company also has earmarked $500 million on the Aurora project, a new remote bitumen mine and extraction plant that will boost Syncrude's output to 94 million bbl/year. That project is scheduled to come on line in 2001.

Syncrude operations

Syncrude claims to have the largest surface mine in the world, in terms of ore processed, at its Fort McMurray, Alta., facility.

More than 430,000 metric tons/day of oilsands are delivered to its extraction plant, with production occasionally topping 500,000 tons/day.

The total volume of material moved at For McMurray is more than 1 million tons/day, including overburden and materials mined by draglines. It takes about 2 tons of oilsands to produce 1 bbl of synthetic crude oil.

Syncrude contends that it has achieved major savings on new mines for existing and new oilsands operators by increasing efficiency and lowering equipment purchase costs that result from its gradual switch to a shovel-and-truck operation and slurry pipeline transport of bitumen.

The slurry pipeline system Syncrude developed for bitumen combines transportation with conditioning of the ore en route to bitumen extraction. This method, dubbed hydrotransport, could be the key technology in expansion of oilsands mining, the company said.

Syncrude started a prototype hydrotransport system in late 1993, developed by operations and contract maintenance employees mostly from surplus components. This enabled Syncrude to cut the project's estimated cost to $12 million from the original estimate of $100 million.

The new system allowed a 3.5 million bbl hike in Syncrude's production of sweet blend crude in 1995 with a payback of only 4 months. It also proved the viability of the new technology for future expansions.

In addition, Syncrude has boosted its bitumen extraction rate to 90%. Both of its two upgrading cokers—each with a 70,000 b/d rated capacity—routinely operate at 110,000 b/d. They have extended run lengths to 2 years from 9 months.

After a record year in 1995, Syncrude Canada in first half 1996 recovered a record 34.8 million bbl of oil from its oilsands operation, 200,000 bbl more than in first half 1995. Syncrude had produced 73.9 million bbl of oil in 1995, up from 69.8 million bbl in 1994. At the same time, it cut operating costs to $13.69/bbl from $14.98/bbl.

The company in June 1996 delivered a record 14.1 million tons of oilsands feed to its extraction plant—500,000 tons more than in December 1995—and extracted more than 8.2 million bbl of bitumen, surpassing the high set in August 1993 by about 150,000 bbl.

Canadian Oil Sands Investments Inc., Calgary, in 1996 completed the purchase of a 10% working interest in Alberta's Syncrude oilsands project from PanCanadian Petroleum Ltd. The purchase is being funded through public and private offerings, respectively, of 10 million trust units at $14.15 each and 13 special warrants at $13.65 each.

Suncor's new era

Suncor, which developed the first commercial oilsands plant in 1967, leading the way in truck-and-shovel technology, is poised for a new era of growth.

On tap are a new oilsands mine, an in situ heavy oil recovery project, and a joint venture shale oil research project in Australia.

Suncor plans to spend more than $600 million to bolster productivity at its existing oilsands operation and to develop a new mine. It plans to boost production at its existing oilsands operation to 105,000 b/d by 2001 from 76,000 b/d in 1995.

Suncor also placed a new $190 million sulfur dioxide reduction plant on stream at its Fort McMurray oilsands complex. The technology, designed by Chiyoda Corp., Tokyo, will capture 95% of sulfur dioxide emissions by mixing sulfur with limestone and oxygen to produce inert gypsum.

The company also plans to hold carbon dioxide emissions at a 1990 level despite planned oil production increases to 105,000 b/d from 78,000 b/d.

The company will spend $15 million on the first phase of a steam-assisted gravity drainage (SAGD) project at Burnt Lake, Alta. It estimates potential recoverable oil at the project at 1 billion bbl, assuming the new technology is successful and heavy-oil prices are adequate.

And Suncor is branching out to a sister technology and another country. It will spend initially $7 million to study feasibility of an oil shale project in the Stuart area of eastern Australia. Suncor could spend as much as $65 million to build a pilot oil shale plant at Gladstone, Queensland.

Gulf Canada

Another SAGD heavy oil project is in the works at Gulf Canada Resources Ltd.'s Surmount lease.

Gulf Canada in 1996 spent $30 million on the first phase of its 3,000 b/d Surmount SAGD project. A second phase is to follow in 1998-99 to boost output to 20,000 b/d.

Gulf Canada said if it commercializes its Surmount oilsands pilot, total production of 100,000 b/d by 2006 is possible. Surmount, 60 km southeast of Fort McMurray, could support a number of 20,000 b/d plants.

Gulf holds about 135,000 acres and has drilled 10 vertical wells in 1996 to delineate the project area's resources. The pilot involves testing of SAGD technology. Four SAGD wells were scheduled for late 1996. Steam injection was scheduled to begin in April 1997. Surmount resource estimates are 10 billion bbl original oil in place and 2 billion bbl recoverable.

Gulf Canada Chief Executive Officer John Bryan is enthusiastic about the potential for growth from development of oilsands deposits in the Fort McMurray region. Gulf has increased its holdings in the area since he took over.

"The oilsands are the only oil stream in the world where the revenue stream is going up and costs are going down. And you could call the reserves nearly perpetual," Bryan said. He predicted Syncrude will be producing oil for $9 (U.S.)/bbl by 2000.

"I think they are the best investment you can make in the Canadian oil business today. The oilsands are now competitive with conventional oil producers."

In November 1995, Athabasca Oil Sands Investment Inc., set up by Gulf, bought the Alberta government's 11.74% interest in the Syncrude oilsands operation at Fort McMurray. A $270 million offering of the trust units helped Gulf finance the purchase. Gulf bought $17.6 million of the units and was hired to administer Athabasca Oil Sands and market its share of Syncrude production.

Gulf already held a 9.03% interest in Syncrude, which contributed an average 18,100 b/d of sweet crude to its production in 1995.

Imperial plans

Imperial allocated $540 million in funds for 1996-97 to expand its in situ bitumen production at Cold Lake, Alta. It cited stronger prices for heavy crude, growing North American

Canadian oilsands production growth spurt

Fig. 1

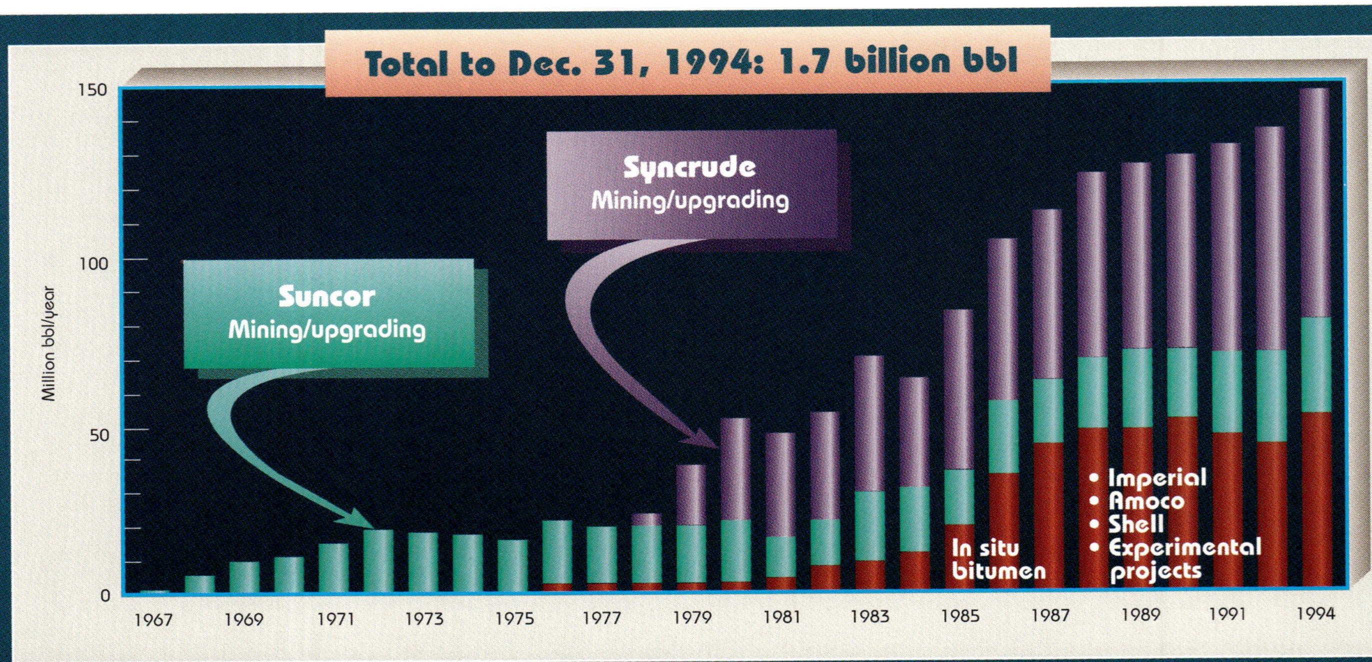

Source: Syncrude Canada from Canadian Association of Petroleum Producers data

IPE

demand for Canadian heavy crude, and continuing cuts in operating costs.

Imperial through 1996 had spent more than $1.2 billion to develop bitumen reserves at Cold Lake.

Imperial Oil Ltd. does not plan to immediately begin commercial development of its South Maskwa and Leming Lake heavy oil leases in Alberta's Cold Lake area.

Imperial had planned to begin drilling 92 directional wells and four horizontal wells from five pads in 1996. Instead, it now plans a series of pilot tests for several years to deal with concerns over casing optimization.

AEUB had imposed more-stringent surface casing requirements in response to concerns that casing failures could contaminate water supplies. Work is under way to ensure Imperial's Cold Lake production still will increase by a targeted 9,400 b/d.

Other expansions

Amoco Canada Petroleum earmarked more than $500 million to expand and further develop its leases at Wolf Lake and Primrose.

The company cited recent steps by Ottawa and the provincial government that have created predictable, long-term fiscal terms and economic certainty to allow expansion of its heavy oil business to continue.

Its plans called for outlays of $175 million in 1996 to further develop its Wolf Lake and Primrose leases, followed by spending of $100 million each in 1997 and 1998. In all, Amoco Canada plans to spend $500 million to increase its heavy oil production to more than 50,000 b/d.

Also at Cold Lake, Alberta Energy Co. Ltd. in 1996 spent $13 million to implement a 1,000 b/d SAGD heavy oil pilot project on its Foster Creek lease. It planned to spend $200 million during 1997-98 to develop a 30,000 b/d commercial-scale heavy oil project.

Shell Canada Ltd. was considering a pilot oilsands project on leases it holds north of the Syncrude plant. Shell was trying to determine the most economic way to conduct the project. It would involve a 500 b/d pilot in 1997-98, a demonstration project calling for 15,000 b/d in mid-2000, and a 30,000 b/d commercial plant about mid-2003.

Shell also was considering trading its leases for a share of Syncrude or pumping future oilsands production directly to its Scotford refinery, near Edmonton.

Bitumen extraction is the focus of two other Athabasca SAGD projects.

Japan Canada Oil Sands Ltd. planned to spend $69 million in 1997 on a bitumen SAGD project involving its oilsands at Hangingstone, Alta.

The project involves reactivating a dormant oilsands project. A SAGD pilot project involving horizontal drilling at Hangingstone, 28 miles south of Fort McMurray, will initially produce 2,000 b/d of oil. If the pilot is successful, additional drilling will increase production to 10,000 b/d by 2000. Construction was planned for early 1997.

And Gibson Petroleum Ltd. slated outlays of $7 million during 1996-97 for a bitumen SAGD project at Fort McMurray, where a joint industry/government program was to expand output to 3,400 b/d from 2,000 b/d.

Solv-Ex Corp., Albuquerque, in 1996 began start-up operations to develop a scaled-down version of an oilsands and minerals extraction project near Fort McMurray, Alta. First phase of the $170 million (Canadian) project is a 5,000 b/d oilsands mine, about one third of project proposed capacity.

Solv-Ex had financing of about $80 million on hand to proceed with initial development and expected the project to be completed by mid-1997.

Koch Exploration Canada Ltd., Calgary, plans a $200 million project to increase production at its oilsands operation at Bonnyville, Alta.

Koch will drill about 140 wells and build a second processing plant to increase output to 40,000 b/d from 14,000 b/d by 1998. Koch began the Reita Lake project in 1993 on leases it acquired from Suncor and Amoco Canada. Koch uses cavity pumps to recover bitumen and sand for processing.

Canadian oilsands operators also are pursuing bitmen projects in other countries. A Jerez Energy International Inc., Calgary, unit in 1996 signed a memorandum of understanding to develop a bitumen property in Nigeria. Jerez Energy (Barbados) Inc. made the deal with Tar Sands Mining International Ltd., Lagos. Jerez said the Alberta Research Council will assist in technical development. IPE

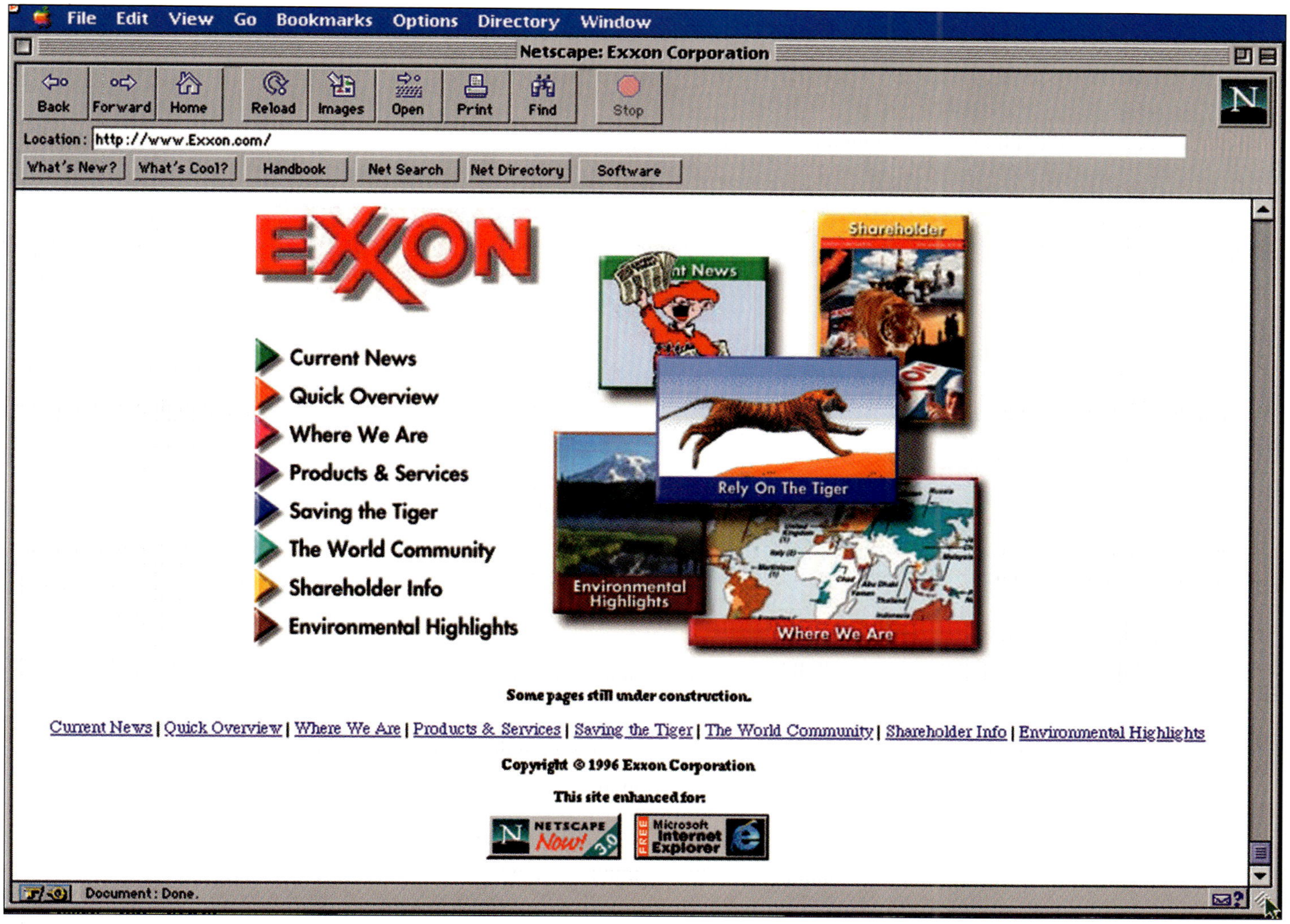

Companies, associations, increase their use of Internet

World Wide Web pages on the Internet are the "1-800" phone numbers of the 1990s, providing companies inexpensive ways to provide information for their customers.

But it's a two-way street. The Internet also is allowing oil companies quicker and more complete access to the information they need from their suppliers, government, and researchers.

The oil industry's use of the Internet has blossomed. In 1996, many oil companies — large and small — established Internet home pages, and firms with existing sites expanded and improved them. But many small and medium-size firms still do not have sites, as well as few large ones.

In almost all cases, Internet pages are being transformed from electronic advertising brochures to sites containing useful data on a company's operations, financial status, offices, and officers.

And sometimes the data doesn't uniquely pertain to the company's operations at all — like a report on West Texas crude prices — but it keeps visitors coming back.

Nearly every oil association and equipment supplier seems to be using home pages on the World Wide Web to keep their members or customers informed. And the 60 oil industry news groups on the Internet remain active.

The federal government, already well ahead of industry, has expanded its presence on the World Wide Web, posting more data, more quickly, than before. State governments also are joining the procession.

Oil Internet growth

Scott Guthery of Schlumberger Ltd. maintains the premier list of Internet home pages. It is at http://www.slb.com.

Guthery, a scientific adviser in the company's technology watch coordination group in Austin, Tex., said oil industry sites jumped from about 600 in late 1995 to 800 in late 1996.

They include home pages for companies, universities, laboratories, research institutions, government agencies, professional societies, libraries, discussion groups, and more.

"It's not growing very quickly any more, about 200 entries in the past 12 months," Guthery said. "All of the standard organizations and geology departments were already listed, and most of the additions have been in oil companies and suppliers."

Guthery said, "Particularly with the commercial sites, we certainly have moved beyond brochures and we're starting to see some solid use of the medium. This is a medium in which the little guys can compete with the big guys."

He said web pages are using more color — although nobody's using background sound yet — and more search engines and forms.

Guthery said the future of the Internet depends on the successful development of microtransactions on the web. "No one

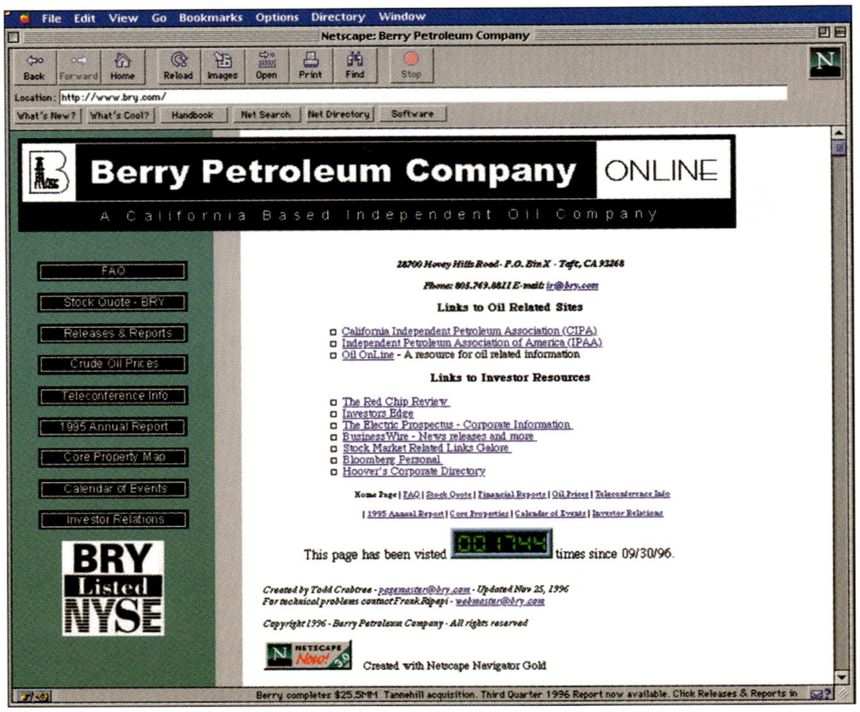

has really solved that problem yet. The missing element still is simple commercial transactions on the web.

"It's fairly clear that the oil industry has discovered the Internet. They've found it's a good way to get information around inside the company, and it's a good way to support company to company cooperation.

"It would be nice to have stronger directories out there. We need a self-serve oil industry Internet address book, which would enable venders to sign themselves up, so producers could instantly access the names of, say for instance, all the consultants that know Permian basin sands."

He said Schlumberger has used the Internet to transmit information from logging trucks to personal computers in oil company offices. "That's been very well received by the industry, as a matter of fact."

Advocacy on the net

Advocacy groups have adapted the Internet to push their causes.

Congress has debated whether to open the coastal plain of the Arctic National Wildlife Refuge for oil exploration, and now it is a hot issue on the World Wide Web.

Leasing proponents have a page, http://www.anwr.com, as do environmentalists against drilling at http://www.igc.apc.org/refuge. Interior Sec. Bruce Babbitt explained his objections to leasing in testimony before Congress but made an appeal to the public on Interior's home page.

Independents for Co-ops, which is lobbying for federal legislation that would allow small producers to aggregate and sell gas without antitrust concerns, is using the Internet as its primary communications tool.

Deborah Siegfried established the page at http://www.gas-coop.com while working as a spokeswoman at Apache Corp.

"This seems to be the perfect medium for communicating information about an issue and keeping people up to date on it," said Siegfried, who left Apache in 1996.

The page explains the need for legislation, has background data on independent producers, and offers a primer on the legislative process. It has a sample letter that producers can download and send their congressmen, along with the legislators' addresses. The page has links enabling producers to check on the status of the co-op legislation at any time.

And it enabled Independents for Co-ops to build an E-mail list of more than 1,100 persons interested in the issue.

Siegfried said, "There always will be people who like information on paper and need to be able to hold it in their hands and file it away. But there also is a huge audience out there which is inclined to get information off the computer.

"If we were to send out as much information on paper that our home page contains, the mailing would be an inch thick, and the cost would be prohibitive. But anyone who wants this data can download it from our page and print it out."

Texaco Inc. found that its new Internet site could be a valuable public relations tool when it was accused of racial discrimination.

It devoted much of its home page to the issue, permitting browsers to read newspaper articles regarding the allegations,

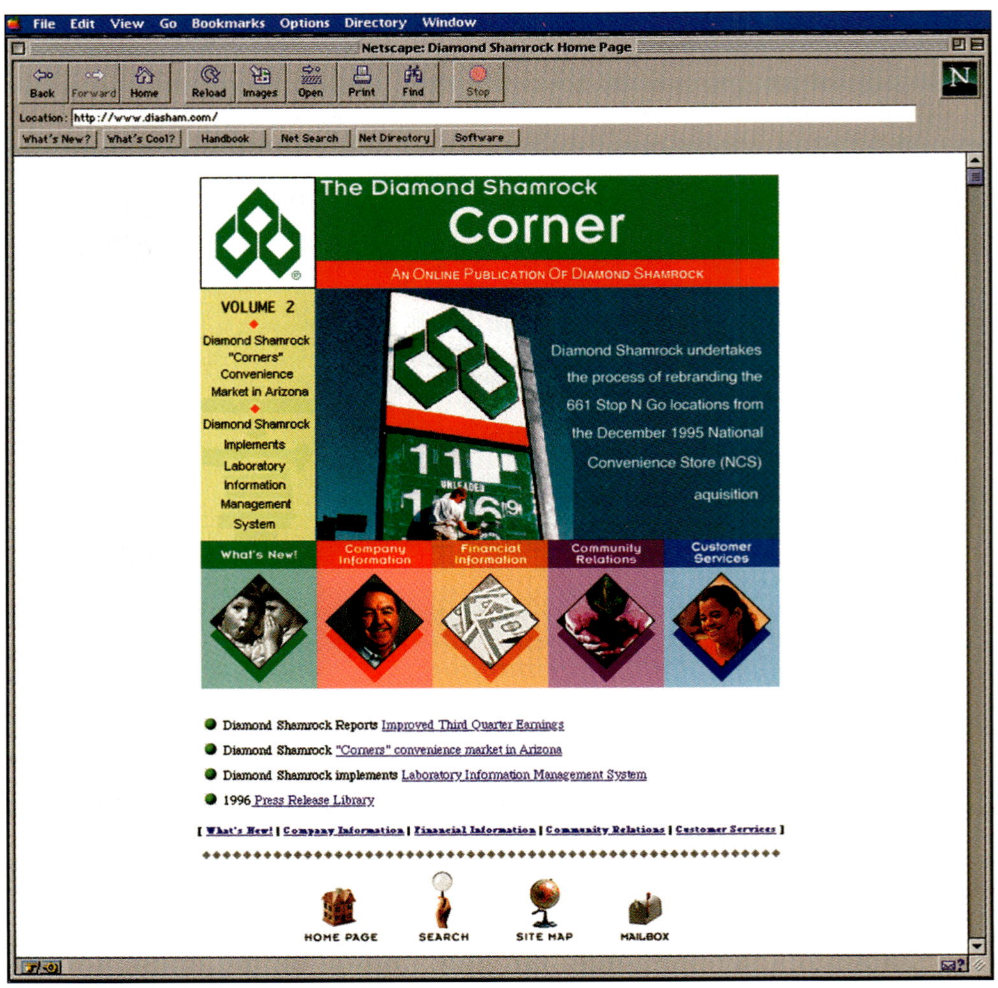

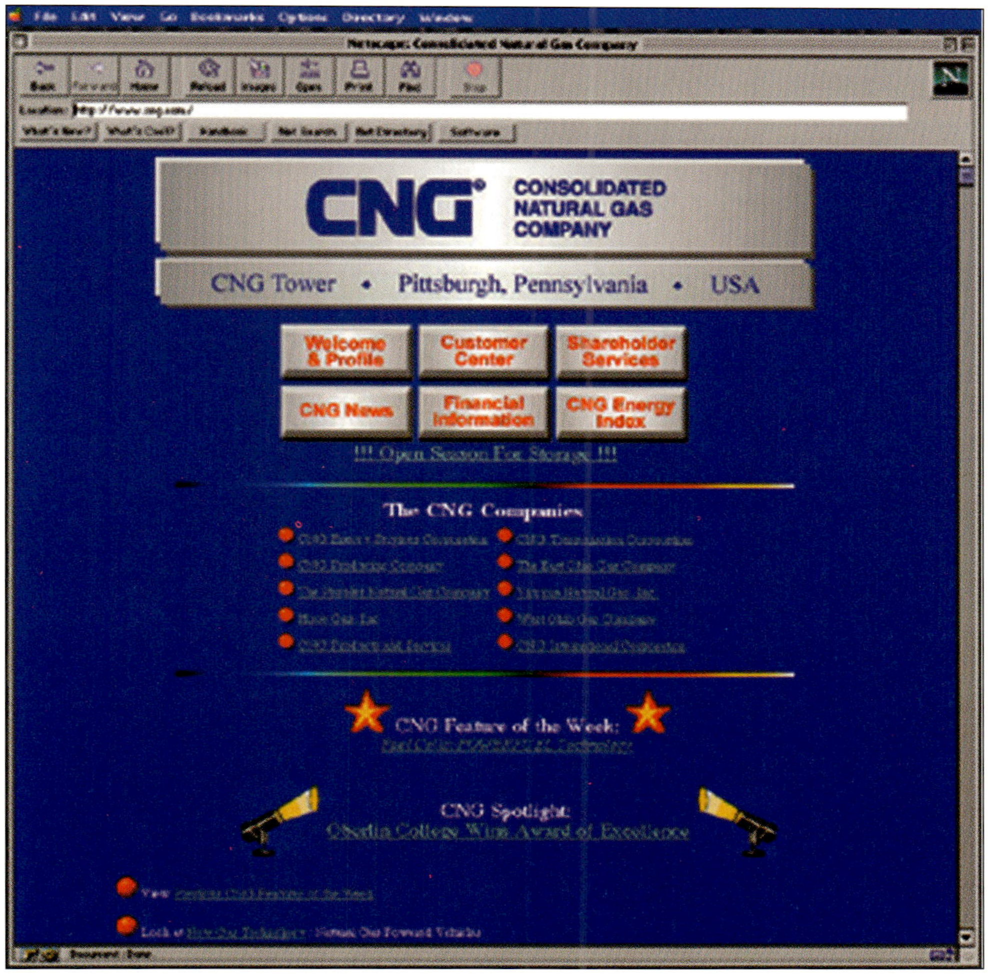

its press releases, a transcript of its video satellite message to employees, and transcripts of press conferences.

Texaco invited its web page visitors to send their opinions to a special E-mail address.

Shell Oil Co. established web pages to publicize its position on disposal of the Brent Spar platform in the North Sea and its environmental protection measures in Nigeria.

When gasoline prices rose in the spring of 1996, the California Energy Commission responded by merging all of its Internet pages regarding the increases into one site on the World Wide Web, along with other data.

Disseminating research

Long term, the oil industry is likely to benefit the most by receiving, rather than sending, information through the Internet.

The nonprofit Petroleum Technology Transfer Council (PTTC) plans to use the Internet as its primary method of communicating drilling and production technology to 8,000 independent producers in the U.S.

Partly sponsored by the Department of Energy, PTTC was established to serve as an information conduit between producers and researchers, making oil people aware of technological breakthroughs while making scientists aware of industry's needs.

The program was designed to offer producers solutions to geologic, geophysical, engineering, environmental, and management problems, with the ultimate goals of reducing finding costs, improving operating efficiency, and boosting oil and gas recovery.

PTTC is decentralized, operating mainly through 10 regional centers that focus on the disparate needs of producers in their areas. But it is heavily reliant on the Internet. Each regional center has its own home page.

For instance, the Central Gulf home page at Louisiana State University contains crude postings by five transporters, Nymex gas prices, field and lease production information, historical oil and gas prices, and state forms that can be downloaded. "Hits" and downloads from the center's home page have jumped by up to 30%/month.

PTTC had always planned to use the Internet to disburse technology, but it has grown so quickly that it will play a larger role in the council's operations than originally planned.

The regional centers issue newsletters and technical reports, and each has an Internet web page connected to PTTC's other nine regional web sites and the council's national page, at http://www.pttc.org/hq/.

The national home page also offers producers links to other Internet locations, a calendar of events, and four technical forums: exploration and development, drilling and completion, production and reservoir, and environment and safety.

The forums are free and interactive. Producers can post detailed questions, respond to the questions of others or post comments and notices.

Deborah Rowell, PTTC president, said, "We have found that all producers don't see the Internet yet as an everyday necessity. But others are beginning to realize that it is and will increasingly become a valuable way for them to access information."

PTTC held a seminar for independent oil producers at a recent Independent Petroleum Association of America meeting, and one of the topics was 3D waterflood applications.

Bob McElroy of Smith Production Co., Jackson, Miss., said, "I was skeptical of this 3D technology because of its cost and complexity. But the speaker showed that even where secondary recovery had failed, a $600 software program and careful well selection could bring more recovery at less cost."

GRI's efforts

The Gas Research Institute, Chicago, operates another significant technology transfer effort for small producers. It distributes GRI research on drilling, completion and stimulation, geophysics, formation evaluation, reservoir geology, gas processing, and more.

GRI has an Internet home page, at http://www.gri.org, where producers can see lists of research and order the results electronically at the click of a mouse.

Rich McBane, webmaster for the Gas Research Institute, said, "We're seeing more and more people coming on line into the Internet and making a lot of use of the information on the Internet.

"For instance, we have a number of advisory bodies that are a part of GRI's organizational structure. About 75-90% of the people serving on those committees have E-mail and access to the World Wide Web. Sure, some of those people are more likely to be connected than most, but a year or two ago there were only a handful connected."

He said the GRI page has seen continual growth in usage. "It's hard to measure. Counting 'hits' can be misleading. But our subscription base has continued to expand.

"An important measure for us is the number of people who come back on at least 2 days a month. A year ago 150-200 came back that often, and now more than 600 do, many of them weekly or even daily."

McBane said since the GRI page was expanded last April more than 25,000 separate individuals have accessed the site.

"Content is king on the Internet. More and more, organizations and companies are realizing that the important thing is what information they provide to the public. The sites really moving in that direction are the ones being used by people."

McBane said GRI's users are seeking data on new technologies that might provide answers to their problems.

"I've never seen a new technology penetrate the American scene like the Internet has. It's been exciting to be on the front edge of it during this growth."

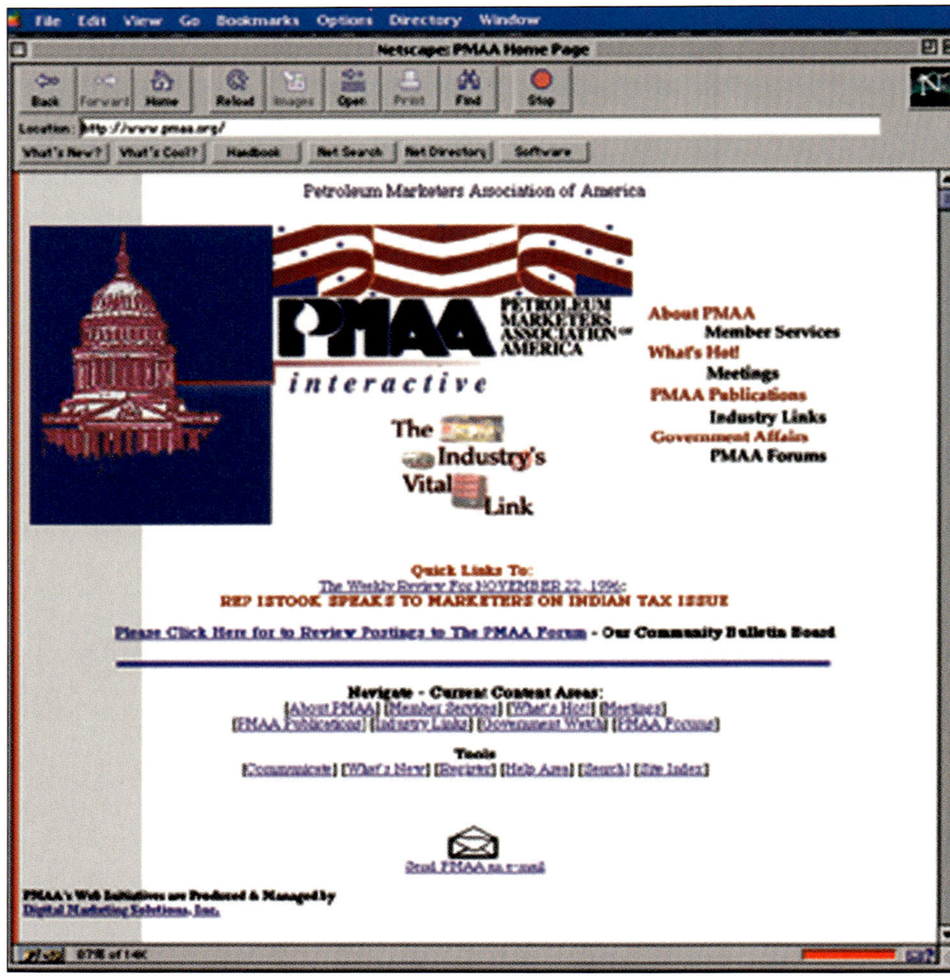

Setting up pages

Roger Staiger, federal relations representative for the Trans-Alaska Pipeline System, established a web page for the pipeline for only $4,000.

"I want it to be useful for external relations. It's so much easier to put out information regarding TAPS on the web site than it is to do mailings."

Staiger said the site contains much background information about the pipeline, including news releases that formerly were only distributed in Alaska. It will contain a schedule of dates when the public can tour the Valdez pipeline terminal. It is at http://www.apsc-taps.com/alyeska.

Charlotte LeGates, public relations director for the Natural Gas Supply Association, added a web page for under $1,000. The address is http://www.ngsa.org.

Her concern was keeping the page focused and not combining public education regarding natural gas with NGSA's policy concerns. "The question of what you're doing with the page should always be clear."

The association also sponsored another page, http://www.naturalgas.org, which is designed to educate the public without company-specific overtones.

NGSA was relatively late to join the list of associations with their own web pages.

LeGates said, "That's partly due to money but also is because our member companies weren't using the Internet much until recently.

"That changed fast. Like the fax machine, one day nobody wanted one, and the next day it's in your car."

LeGates said NGSA expects its web page to save it money. She said, "Some of our member companies are only focused on one or two of our issues. Putting the data on the web site and letting them access it is potentially cheaper than mailing all of the information to everyone."

She said most of the savings are in reduced personnel costs, not necessarily the copying and postage cost.

In her research of Internet sites, LeGates reached some basic conclusions.

"It's important to have things load on the screen quickly. Our logo loads really fast. So you shouldn't use too many colors. And you should avoid the necessity of scrolling by using multiple levels of indices.

"Putting the dates on documents is very important, and it's helpful to make it clear, for downloading purposes, how large documents are. Also, each document you post should have the name and phone number of a person to contact."

Producer orientation

John McGhee, webmaster for the Texas Independent Producers and Royalty Owners Association, said his group operates two web pages.

One, http://www.tipro.org, houses the PTTC Texas outreach program. The other, http://www.energyconnect.com, contains the Tipro site and those of other groups, such as the California Independent Producers Association.

McGhee said, "We've been real aggressive in housing pages for other associations and companies."

Energyconnect is one of the better, and busier, oil industry sites. McGhee said since it registered 258 hits in July of 1995, usage has jumped at least 20%/month to 37,103 in October 1996. About 10-15% of the hits are by Tipro members.

He said, "The Internet model is to give something back to the person accessing the site," and Tipro's sites offer a number of features. One page provides Texas Railroad Commission oil field production data, and another has figures on West Texas crude postings.

A third page provides access to the Energy Department's Advanced Oil and Gas Recovery Technologies database. A search of that database on the subject of offshore horizontal drilling netted 228 papers.

He said Tipro surveyed its membership in January 1996 and found 12% had Internet access. A similar survey in October 1996 found 55% with Internet access.

"There is a presumption among our membership that the Internet will be vital to their businesses, although it may take 10 years to get quite to that point."

The Energyconnect site has a search engine that indexes the contents of all home pages hosed on the Tipro system. McGhee would like to expand that to become a production-related search engine covering the top 200 to 300 sites. IPE

European octane trends — Fig. 1

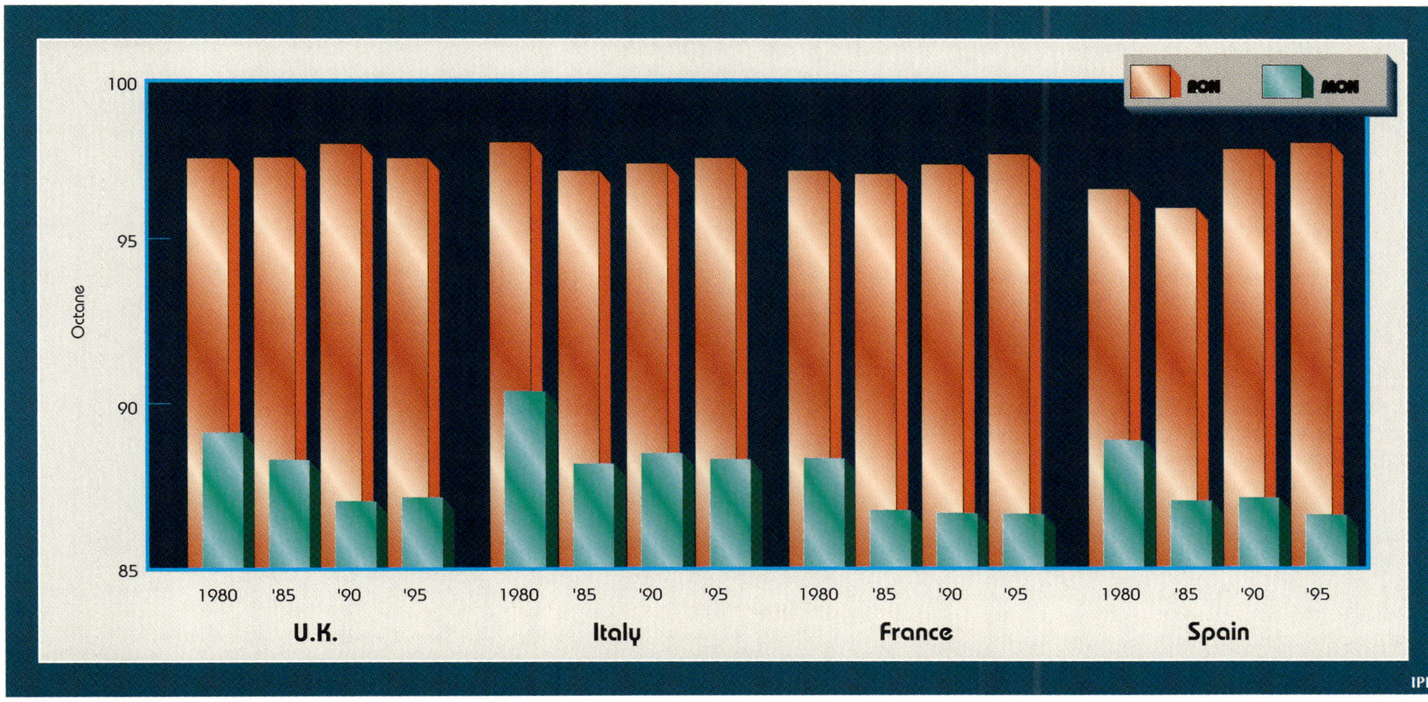

Global fuel quality: Europe and Asia tighten gasoline, diesel specs

Refiners around the world were having to improve the quality of fuels in 1996. In response to government and market pressures, they were reducing lead concentrations, increasing gasoline octane, reducing the sulfur content of diesel fuel, and raising diesel cetane ratings.

In most regions, the only significant refinery construction was in hydrotreating units, which help refiners meet limits on the sulfur contents of gasoline and diesel fuels.

The Far East runs against this trend, with increases in distillation and secondary processing capacities.

Gasoline quality

A survey of fuel quality conducted by Associated Octel Co. Ltd., Milton Keynes, U.K., traced the steady elimination of lead from gasoline.

Thailand and Malaysia eliminated leaded-gasoline production during 1995, following a trend started in the U.S. and Japan. And Singapore, Taiwan, and Korea, started phase-out programs.

Outside the U.S. and northern Europe, aromatics typically replace lead as gasoline octane boosters.

In the U.K., unleaded gasoline contains an average of about 31 vol % aromatics, compared to 26 vol % for leaded gasoline, according to Octel. In France, unleaded grades contain 41 vol% and leaded grades 33.5 vol % aromatics.

Because aromatics raise air-quality and health concerns, some U.K. marketers have stopped selling 98-RON unleaded gasoline. In fact, the British government has reduced tax subsidies on this grade.

For these reasons, 98-RON unleaded will disappear from the U.K. market, predicts Octel.

Increases in isomerization and alkylation capacity in the U.S. and Europe have given refiners in these regions the flexibility to increase octane without raising aromatics concentrations of the pool. As a result, fuel aromatics levels are, in general, declining in these regions, although unleaded gasolines tend to contain higher levels of aromatics than leaded grades.

Relying on catalytic reforming to increase pool octane, refiners outside the U.S. and Europe produce gasolines with aromatics concentrations as high as 40-50 vol % in parts of the Far East and Latin America.

Gasoline octane also varies widely. Gasolines in the U.S., Japan, and Australia, for example, typically are rated at 91-92 RON. European gasolines are rated much higher, at 95-97 RON (Fig. 1).

Gasoline octanes as high as 97-98 RON are common in the Far East, says Octel. There also is a trend toward increased use of premium grades there (Fig. 2). Fig. 2 omits South Asian countries that haven't significantly tightened fuel specifications.

"China's average octane is the lowest in the region," says Octel, "although the Chinese are aiming to improve their gasoline octane, primarily by eliminating the 70 motor octane number (MON) product over the next few years. This will be achieved by increasing catalytic cracking and reforming capacities and by adding lead."

Octel predicts the average octane of gasoline in Far East countries will increase from 90 RON in 1994 to 92 RON by 2000, placing even greater pressure on the region's refineries.

Increased octane requirements have led to greater use of oxygenates, such as methyl tertiary butyl ether (MTBE), in many regions, although the U.S. and Finland use MTBE less to raise octane than to raise fuel oxygen content.

Diesel quality

Diesel demand is increasing in a number of markets because of consumers' perception that diesel-engine vehicles yield benefits in the areas of emissions and fuel economy.

Fig. 2

Asia/Pacific octane trends

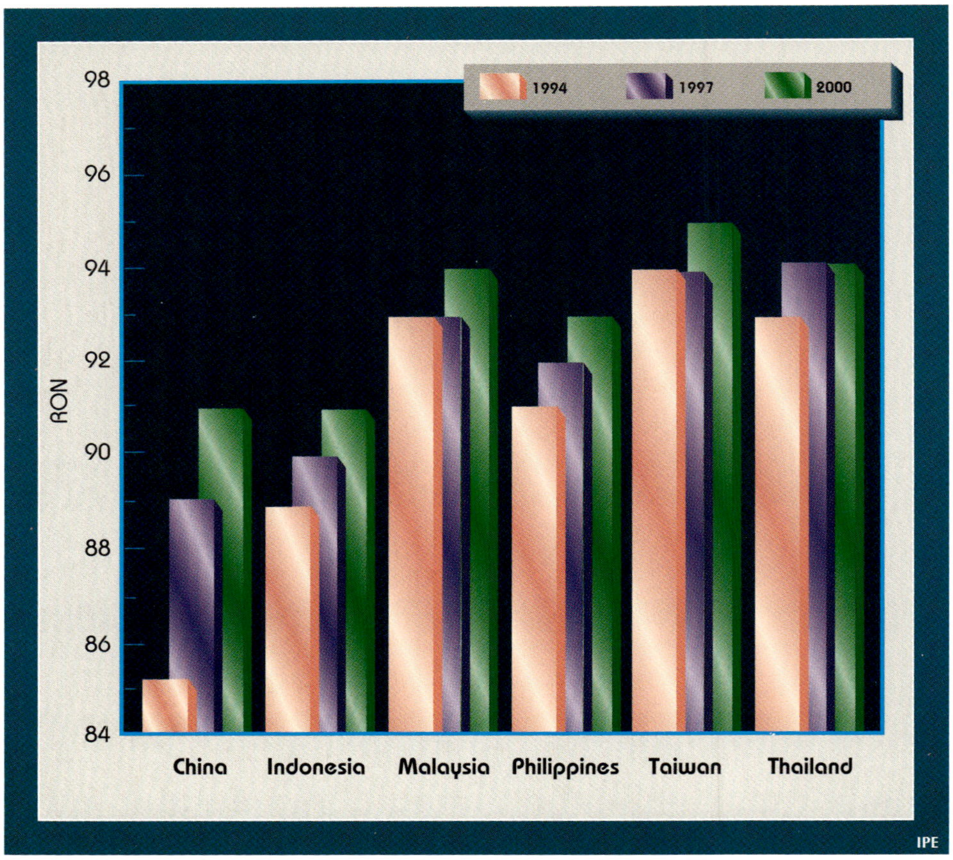

Legislation reducing diesel sulfur concentrations is coming into effect in many countries.

Use of low-sulfur diesel (defined by Octel as 0.05 wt % or less) has been mandatory in the U.S. since October 1993. Germany and Nordic countries introduced the product ahead of the 0.05 wt % limit imposed by the European Union (EU) in October 1996 (Fig. 3).

Sulfur restrictions also have been proposed in Japan, Taiwan, Korea, and Thailand. Other countries in the Asia/Pacific region are expected to follow suit by 2000.

Cetane quality is also an important focus for diesel producers. Research has shown that high diesel cetane can reduce emissions and engine noise.

Cetane index historically has been the preferred measure of diesel quality, says Octel, although cetane number has gained in popularity. In Europe, cetane numbers greater than 50 are now common. In fact, Octel's survey reveals an average cetane number of almost 54 for U.K. diesel during 1995.

Diesel cetane can be increased via crude oil selection, processing scheme, or additive use. In the Far East, diesel cetane numbers depend on crude choice, says Octel. As a result, in many cases, product quality exceeds specifications.

Some marketers in the region, however, are increasing cetane further through the use of cetane-improving additives.

Additive use

Fuel additives have gained widespread acceptance from refiners and marketers. "Performance-enhancing additive packages containing detergents are now used extensively by marketers in Europe, the U.S., and the Far East, as well as by some marketers in South America, to differentiate their products," says Octel.

Historical analysis of Octel's annual fuel quality surveys shows that in 1993 40% of European leaded-gasoline samples collected contained performance additives. By 1995, the percentage had increased to about 75%.

By contrast, about 65% of European unleaded gasolines sampled in 1993 contained additives, compared with 100% in 1995.

Beginning in 1995, all gasoline sold in the U.S. had to contain low dosages of additives. Higher concentrations are likely to be required when the U.S. Environmental Protection Agency finalizes its detergent requirements, predicts Octel.

The U.S. does not require the use of additives in diesel fuel. Some major suppliers use additives to differentiate their product by calling it 'premium' diesel, says Octel.

Europe does not mandate the use of additives in either gasoline or diesel. Still, detergent additives are used widely there.

Table 1

EU gasoline quality, 2000

	Current spec.	Proposed spec.	Predicted avg. without proposal	Predicted avg. with proposal
Rvp (summer), kPa (max.)	<~80	60	68	58
Benzene, vol % (max.)	5.0	2.0	2.3	1.6
Aromatics, vol % (max.)	None	45	40	37
Olefins, vol % (max.)	None	18	11	<11
Sulfur, ppm mass (max.)	500	200	300	150

Source: Concawe, Brussels

Table 2

EU diesel quality, 2000

	Current spec.	Proposed spec.	Predicted avg. without proposal	Predicted avg. with proposal
Cetane number (min.)	49	51	51	53
Polyarom., % mass (max.)	—	11	9	6
Density, kg/cu m (max.)	860	845	843	835
T95*, °C. (max.)	370	360	355	350
Sulfur, ppm mass (max.)	500	350	450	300

* Temperature at which 95% of material is distilled.

Source: Concawe, Brussels

Use of performance additives has increased recently in Latin American and Asian countries. Thailand, Korea, and Argentina, for example, use additives.

These areas currently favor use of U.S.-type performance requirements rather than the more demanding ones found in European countries.

EU 2000

A consortium of European automobile manufacturers and oil companies has undertaken a program to develop a strategy for improving air quality in EU countries. The goal of the 3-year European Auto/Oil Programme is to develop least-cost measures to meet air quality targets for five pollutants: carbon monoxide (CO), volatile organic compounds (VOCs), nitrogen oxides (NOx), particulate matter (PM), and ozone.

The European Commission has adopted two of the proposals resulting from this program. The more costly of the two proposals covers tighter emissions standards for automobiles. The other proposal sets new specifications for EU gasoline and diesel.

Both proposals are scheduled to be implemented by Jan. 1, 2000. The auto emissions proposal is the more costly of the two and is expected to have the greatest benefits, according to Brussels-based Concawe, the oil companies' European organization for environment, health, and safety.

The Auto/Oil Programme will present additional standards in 1997 for light and heavy-duty vehicles (trucks) and for vehicle inspection and maintenance. Other EU initiatives under way will address controls for stationary source emissions.

The changes to EU gasoline and diesel quality are summarized in, respectively, Tables 1 and 2. Also shown are Concawe's projections for average fuel qualities.

"The total cost of the Auto/Oil package is predicted at some 82.5 billion ECU, net present value [European currency units; $108 billion] over 15 years," according to Concawe's 1996 annual review. "Of this, the oil industry's costs in implementing fuels changes will be in the region of 11.5 billion ECU ($15 billion)."

Of the oil industry's investment, 7.2 billion ECU is expected to be spent up-front. This means average capital expenditures of $80 million for every EU refinery.

Concawe also predicted the effects on vehicle emissions of the Auto/Oil measures (Table 3).

The effect of changes in fuels specifications is much less than that of changes in automobile emissions maxima. Of the compounds listed in Table 3, the fuel quality contribution to emissions reductions is proportional only for benzene and particulate matter.

Reductions in allowable benzene levels are expected to decrease benzene emissions by 15-20%, says Concawe. This compares to program costs of about 15% for fuels measures vs. 85% for automotive emissions measures.

Fuel specification changes will contribute only about a 6% reduction to PM emissions. Reductions in NOx and VOCs are only a few percent, at best, says Concawe.

The Concawe report concludes that, "The small fuels effect on these particularly important pollutants means that extreme fuel formulations with steeply higher costs, such as California-style gasoline and Swedish city diesel, are inappropriate for general application across Europe."

The European oil industry concludes, however, that the fuels proposals are a reasonable part of the overall emissions-reduction package, says Concawe. If the bodies reviewing the Auto/Oil proposals are properly informed of the expected results, the EU should adopt the draft legislation in the next year or so, predicts Concawe. IPE

European diesel sulfur trends Fig. 3

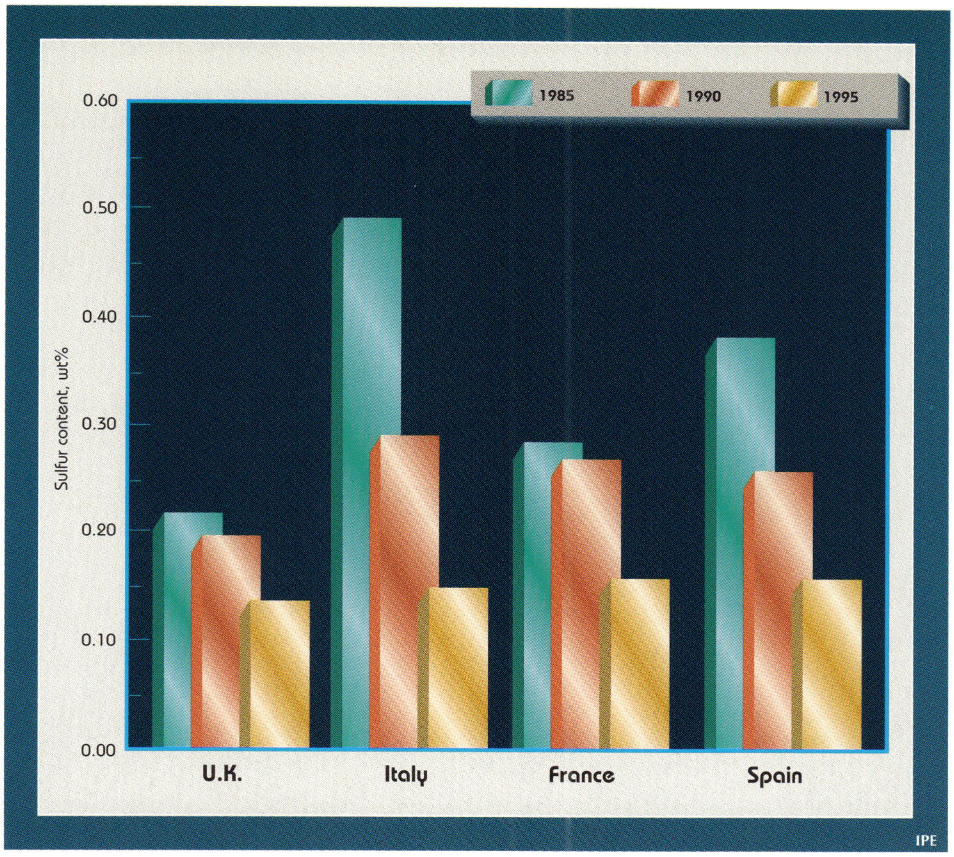

Table 3

Effect of EU auto/oil program on road emissions

	Estimated 1995 emissions, 1,000 mt/y (% of 1990)	Predicted 2010 emissions without program, 1,000 mt/y (% of 1990)	Predicted 2010 emissions with program, 1,000 mt/y (% of 1990)
Urban NOx	1,940 (100)	1,208 (62)	749 (39)
Urban PM	137 (110)	69 (56)	42 (34)
Urban CO	20,224 (80)	11,961 (47)	5,981 (24)
Urban benzene	14 (87)	8 (49)	4 (25)
Total VOCs	3,668 (90)	1,811 (44)	996 (24)
Total NOx	5,581 (95)	3,053 (52)	1,984 (34)

Source: Concawe, Brussels

Construction progresses in 1996 on Delhi Group's Pinnacle Reef project to increase inlet capacity at the Aker treating plant on Delhi's East Texas gathering system. Phase Two of the project, currently underway, will add a total of 275 MMcfd of incremental cpacity in the Pinnacle Reef area.

LPG sales growth through 2010: East to outpace West

LPG sales through the 2010 in the East of Suez region will grow more than twice as rapidly as those in regions west of the Suez Canal.

East-of-Suez sales will grow at more than 4%/year, those elsewhere less than 2%/year, according to a Poten & Partners Inc. study published late in 1996. East-of-Suez sales will reach 92 million tons/year (tpy) by 2010, accounting for 39% of the worldwide total. This share was 31% in 1995 and only 27% in 1990.

LPG sales worldwide will reach 192 million tpy in 2000 and 243 million tpy by 2010. In 1995, they were 163 million tons (Fig. 1).

Concentration

In 1996, about two thirds of the world's LPG sales were in West-of-Suez markets; one-third in markets east of Suez (Fig. 2a), according to the study.

In 1995, 53% of East-of Suez LPG sales went to Japan, South Korea, and Taiwan. In 1990 the figure was 63%.

Market maturity and the lack of competitiveness of LPG with alternative feedstocks for petrochemicals will keep LPG demand growth in these countries modest, at best, said Poten & Partners. The countries will account for only 33% of sales east of Suez by 2010.

In the Middle East, petrochemicals dominate LPG consumption. Saudi Arabia will use 7.6 million tons of LPG in 2000 and 11.3 million tons in 2010. LPG use was 2.6 million tons in 1995 and 1.1 million tons in 1990. Saudi Arabia will account for half of LPG use in the Middle East by 2000.

The most rapidly growing markets are in emerging nations, with China and India leading sales potential (Fig. 2b). Each has low per-capita energy and LPG use.

LPG use in China and India, where sales have been constrained by inadequate infrastructure, will reach a combined 15 million tons in 2000 and 27 million tons in 2010 as foreign and domestic companies invest in LPG terminals and other delivery facilities.

Combined LPG sales in these nations were 9 million tons in 1995 and only 5 million tons in 1990.

Sales in West-of-Suez markets will expand by about 2%/year through 2010 (Fig. 2c). Several factors contribute to the more moderate demand outlook in the West than in the East.

LPG sales, particularly in North America and Europe, are already large. Many of these markets are mature, with little room for expansion of sales in traditional applications. Among important exceptions is Turkey.

Although emerging-market developments are occurring west of Suez similar to those in the East, said Poten & Partners, populations in most nations in Africa, Central Europe, and Latin America are small by Asian standards.

In addition, the more populous nations of Latin America (Argentina, Brazil, Mexico, and Venezuela) already have well-developed LPG markets. Thus, volumetric LPG sales potential is much smaller than in emerging eastern markets.

The most promising market for expanding LPG sales is petrochemical feedstock. Ethylene plants in North Europe and the U.S. are large users of LPG but have feedstock options and are price-sensitive.

The U.S. Gulf Coast can absorb large LPG volumes based on market conditions. The petrochemical plants, vast Mont Belvieu storage, and LPG terminals there can accommodate large quantities of LPG when Mont Belvieu prices include a premium over deliveries cif U.S. Gulf Coast.

Conversely, Mont Belvieu storage is a source of seaborne cargoes when pricing dictates such sales. Poten & Partners expects the Atlantic basin to have ample LPG through 2010 and said that a substantial expansion of price-sensitive sales to petrochemical plants will be required to absorb these volumes.

Another focus of LPG market growth will be in the former Soviet Union (FSU) and Central Europe. Russia, in particular, has significant LPG sales potential when political and economic conditions stabilize. LPG sales in the FSU have collapsed since 1990.

While sales appear to have stabilized, a substantial expansion is unlikely to begin until after 2000. Rising FSU demand will be supplied from production in Russia and the other republics.

Some nations of Central Europe are improving economically. In addition, their LPG industries are attracting foreign companies.

Poland, for example, is emerging as a substantial LPG importer and is diversifying its sources of imports from dependence on overland deliveries from the FSU.

Demand segments

The report noted that LPG market structures contribute to differing trade and price dynamics east and west of Suez (Fig. 3).

LPG sales east of Suez are dominated by residential-commercial customers. These sales primarily take the form of bottled gas to households and often command premium prices (Fig. 3a). They are typically less price-sensitive than other sales.

Emerging-market demands are predominantly for bottled gas.

Relatively tight LPG supply largely precludes development of a large petrochemical market for LPG in the Far East where

LPG will not be priced competitively with alternative feedstocks.

Most growth in LPG use for petrochemical feedstock east of Suez will be in the Middle East, primarily in Saudi Arabia, where the product enjoys a special pricing arrangement. Indeed, the diversion of LPG from export availability will contribute to a tight LPG balance and premium pricing for LPG in the East.

The large concentration of residential-commercial sales causes East-of-Suez LPG purchasers to value security and adequacy of supply.

In addition, a large share of supplies comes from relatively distant markets and is delivered in gas carriers. This has encouraged seaborne trade dominated by term LPG sales and purchase contracts and minimized price competition.

The greater involvement of foreign companies, however, including traders, promises greater competition in supplying emerging markets, said Poten & Partners. Companies supplying these new outlets will compete with those supplying established markets for available LPG supplies.

In contrast to markets in the East, LPG demand is more evenly distributed across end uses in markets west of Suez (Fig. 3b).

A much larger share of the market involves sales to price-sensitive buyers for ethylene feedstock. These buyers can switch between feedstocks, depending on economic considerations.

In addition, there are more sources of domestic LPG supply and a reduced dependence on seaborne imports. Furthermore, sources of seaborne cargoes are usually less distant in the West than East, with delivery times correspondingly shorter.

There is far less concern about supply security, said Poten & Partners, and thus less dependence on term contracts than is typical of transactions east of Suez.

1995 Worldwide LPG production, demand FIG. 1

LPG demand Fig. 2

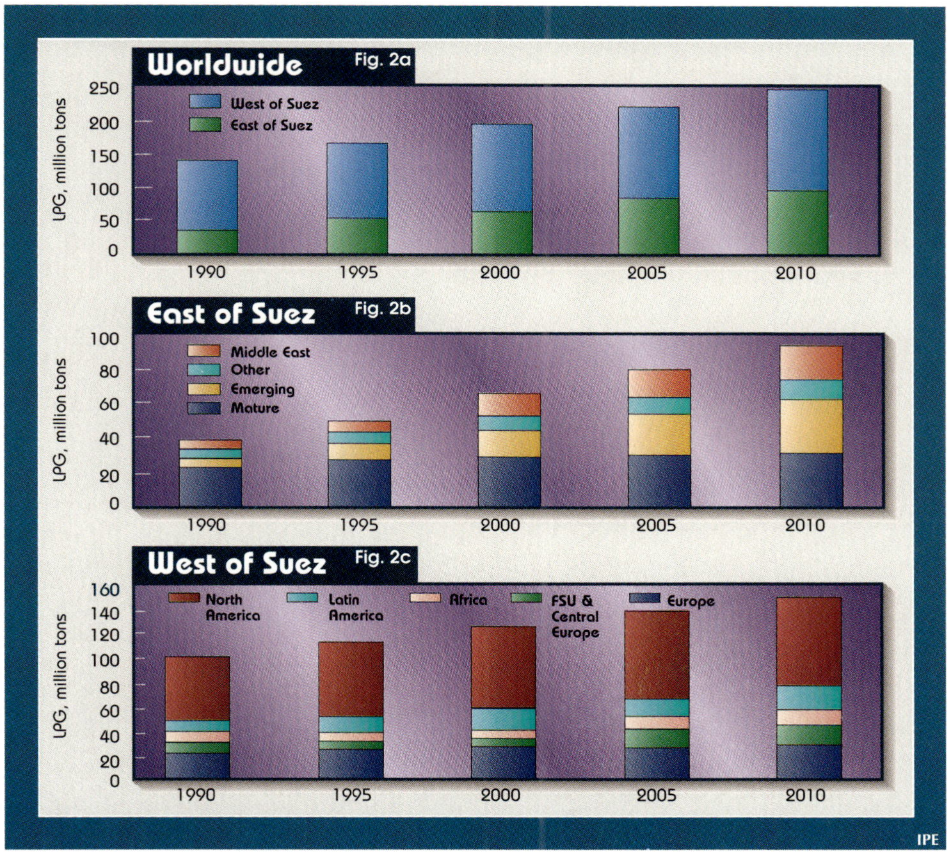

Seaborne balance

East-of-Suez seaborne LPG supplies will be generally tight through 2010. This is demonstrated by the volumes available for export to West-of-Suez destinations after East-of-Suez demands are satisfied.

In recent years, these volumes were as high as 5.6 million tpy but declined to about 3.4 million tons in 1995 (Fig. 4).

The report forecasts availability to fall to about 2.2 million tpy by 2000 and to remain at this low level through 2005 before recovering modestly.

The next few years could see a divergence from this long-term trend as new export supplies become available from Abu Dhabi, Australia, and Malaysia.

Moreover, it is assumed that UN sanctions on Iraq will be lifted and that the 4 million tpy export plant at Khor al-Zubair will be operating.

Starting in 1998, however, an accelerated diversion of Saudi Arabian LPG production from export to domestic use will likely tighten East-of-Suez LPG markets significantly.

After 2000, rising OPEC oil production will boost associated gas-liquids production, which in turn will provide greater LPG seaborne availability, somewhat easing tight supply conditions.

Poten & Partners cautions that, in its forecast, considerable LPG exports are assumed from Iran and Iraq, where energy developments were subject to sanctions in 1996.

From a resource-base perspective, these countries have large LPG export potentials. When these potentials will be realized is uncertain. For example, LPG exports from Iraq's fractionator at Khor al-Zubair in 1996 had been delayed by a decade.

Fig. 5a highlights supply trends expected by Poten & Partners in this trading region.

Rising LPG use in emerging nations is the dominant demand trend. In the mature markets of Japan, South Korea, and Taiwan, LPG demand growth will slow dramatically (Fig. 5b).

Companies importing LPG into China and India will compete with established Japanese and South Korean buyers for available LPG supplies, both contract and spot. Emerging markets will import 25% of available East-of-Suez LPG supplies by 2000 and 42% by 2010. This compares with 14% in 1995 and only 3% in 1990.

This forecast assumes that Chinese and Indian economies remain on their current courses and that foreign confidence in these countries is not seriously shaken. Development of LPG markets in these countries is unlikely to be smooth.

Nearly 3 billion people live in these two nations, however, and energy and LPG consumption per capita are extremely low. Both countries are adopting free-market economic policies and opening their energy industries to private companies, domestic and foreign. A continuation of these policies would result in large LPG import demands.

At the same time, the high cost of LPG will diminish its use in price-sensitive applications in Japan and other mature Far East markets.

Furthermore, expanding availability of pipeline gas, from LNG imports, will curtail LPG use in premium cylinder sales and displace bulk sales, including those to city gas companies for the production of manufactured gas.

End-use demand Fig. 3

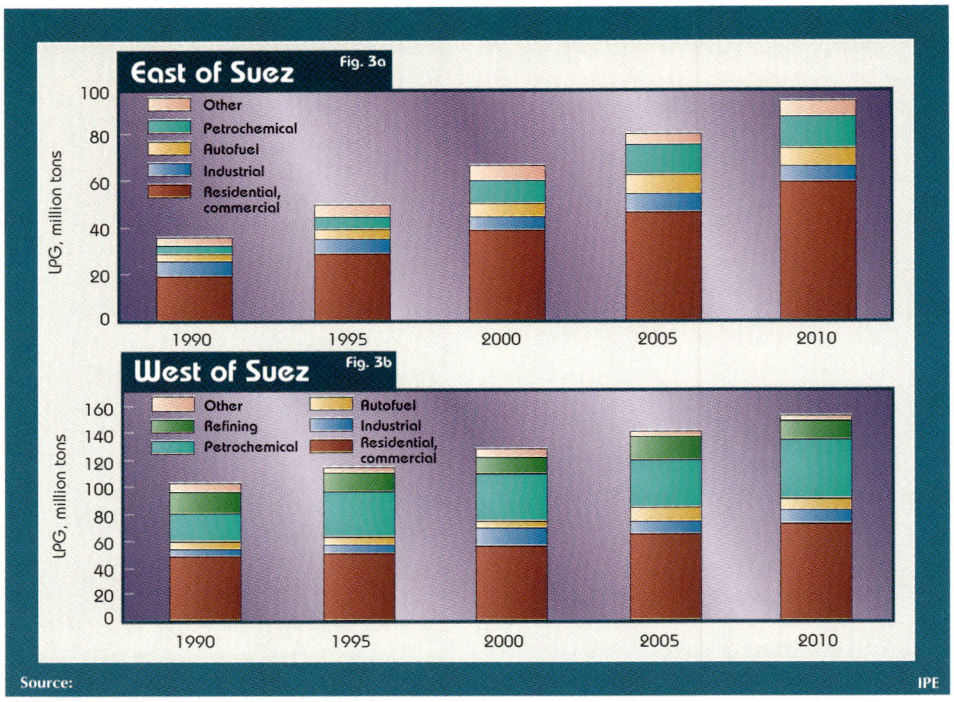

Large-cargo LPG exporters: East of Suez, 1995* Fig. 4

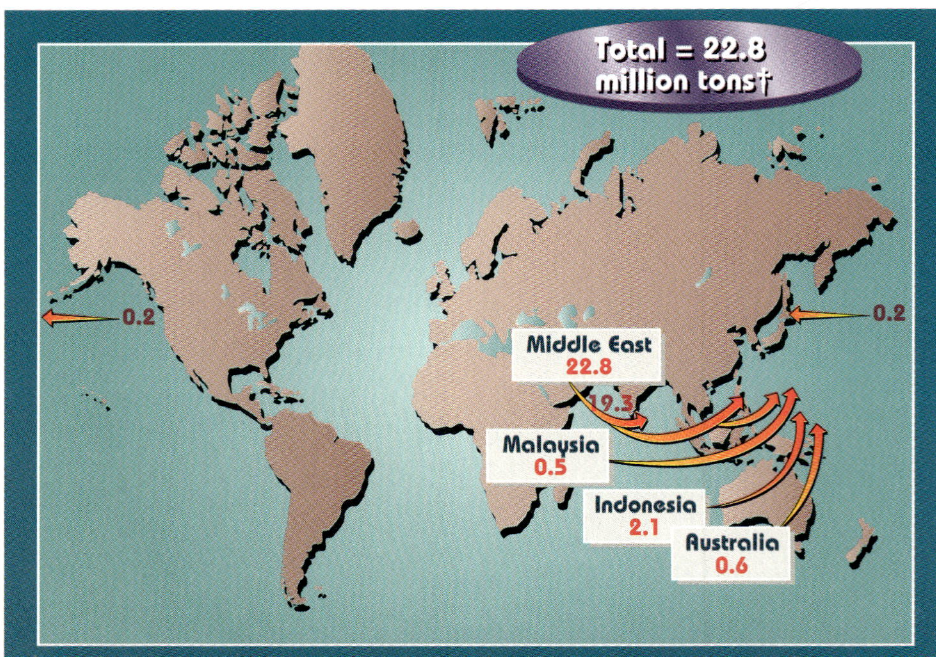

*All volumes in million tons.
†Displayed regional trades exclude selected routes which were less than 0.1 million tons.

Imports in West

West-of-Suez LPG markets depend far less on seaborne imports than those east of Suez. Seaborne imports were about 18.3 million tons in 1995. These accounted for only about 11% of total supplies (Fig. 6).

By contrast, said Poten & Partners, seaborne cargoes accounted for 47% of LPG supplies in markets east of Suez.

Seaborne exports from West of Suez have expanded by 40% since 1990 (Fig. 7). This expansion was centered in the North Sea, where LPG production has doubled since 1990 to 8.1 million tons in 1995. The product primarily found outlets in Northwest Europe, both by further penetrating petrochemical feedstock slates and by displacing longer-haul imports. North Sea producers have also expanded sales to Mediterranean and Transatlantic destinations.

The focus of expansion will shift to Africa and Latin America. Seaborne volumes available from West-of-Suez sources will expand by two-thirds by 2010. These new volumes promise to keep West-of-Suez markets amply supplied, with volumes increasingly destined for price-sensitive petrochemical buyers (Fig. 7a).

Africa is the second most important West-of-Suez source of seaborne LPG volumes after the North Sea. It could emerge as the largest supplier soon after 2000.

Algeria is the main source of African seaborne LPG exports, contributing more than 90% of the total in 1995. Algerian LPG exports will rise from 3.6 million tons in 1995 to 6.0 million tons by 2000 or soon thereafter.

Libya is the other nation in North Africa with considerable LPG export potential. But the country's plans to export up to 1 million tpy have been stymied by international sanctions, said the consulting company.

West Africa is a marginal supplier of LPG to international markets but is set to become an important source from the late 1990s.

Congo will emerge as the next West African LPG exporter after Angola. Nigeria will become as an LPG exporter soon thereafter. The volumes from Nigeria promise to be much larger.

Disposing of these large African volumes could challenge producers. Some potential exists for additional sales to Mediterranean outlets, as markets expand and Middle East supplies shrink.

Much of the incremental African production, however, will have to move to Transatlantic destinations, in competition with Western Hemisphere supplies.

Western sources

Seaborne cargoes originating from Western Hemisphere sources, although only about 2.8 million tons in 1995, will more than double by 2010 (Fig. 7b), said Poten & Partners.

A significant portion of this is in the Caribbean basin small-cargo market. As exports rise, however, an increasing share will move in large-cargo lots.

Venezuela is the largest source of seaborne cargoes in the Western Hemisphere. The country's LPG exports totaled 1.2 million tons in 1995, owing to start-up of the third train at Jose (Accro-I) and the Acogas project.

This was a sharp increase from 331,000 tons in 1993. Corpoven expects LPG exports to exceed 5 million tpy by 2005, a forecast Poten & Partners said may prove to be optimistic.

The vast resource base and the opening of the energy industry to foreign investors, however, ensure that Venezuela will become an increasingly important LPG supplier to regional LPG markets in the future.

Argentina is emerging as an important regional supplier. LPG exports reached 0.5 million tons in 1995. Most of these volumes, however, were delivered overland or by barge to neighboring countries.

If Project Mega (a joint venture between Argentina's YPF and Brazil's Petrobras) proceeds, LPG exports will reach 1 million tpy by 2000 or soon thereafter. This will boost seaborne exports to Brazil.

Mexico is a net LPG importer. In 1995, LPG imports totaled 1.1 million tons, mainly overland from the U.S., while exports reached 0.8 million tons. Imports in 1996 were expected to be even higher, said Poten & Partners, because of an explosion at the Cactus gas-processing complex.

LPG exports included about 0.1 million tons overland to Central America. Seaborne LPG exports will be further curtailed in the future.

Other seaborne LPG exports (Fig. 7b) include cargoes from the U.S. (excluding sales to the Far East), Trinidad, and in the future, Colombia, and Peru.

These two South American nations will likely become substantial LPG exporters, based on processing of Cupiagua and Cusiana gas in Colombia and Camisea gas in Peru.

Largest trading region

Because of high shipping costs for LPG cargoes, Atlantic basin production will be sold in regional markets, with the possible exception of an occasional spot cargo, said the company.

The nations of Western Europe, North Africa, and the Eastern Mediterranean make up the largest seaborne LPG trading region west of Suez (Fig. 8). Seaborne cargoes account for nearly 40% of supplies in this 32 million tpy market.

Net "imports" (Fig. 8) provide a reasonable estimate of seaborne trade in Northwest Europe and the Mediterranean. The estimate includes all regional use of North Sea production (including that in Norway and the U.K.), North African production that is traded internationally, and imports from the Middle

Fig. 5
East-of-Suez seaborne supply, demand

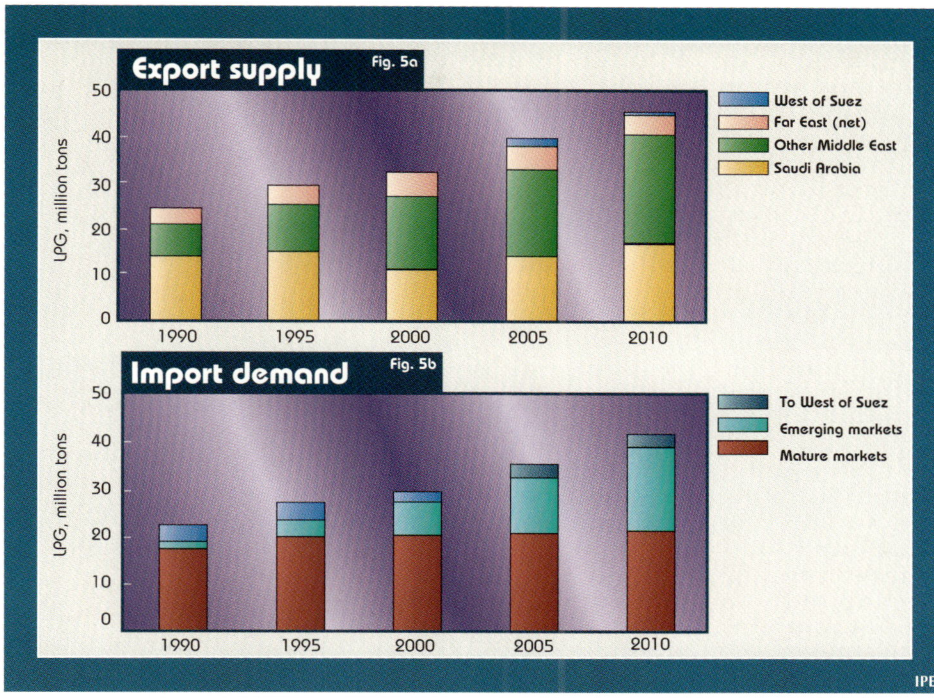

Fig. 6
Large-cargo LPG exporters: West of Suez, 1995*

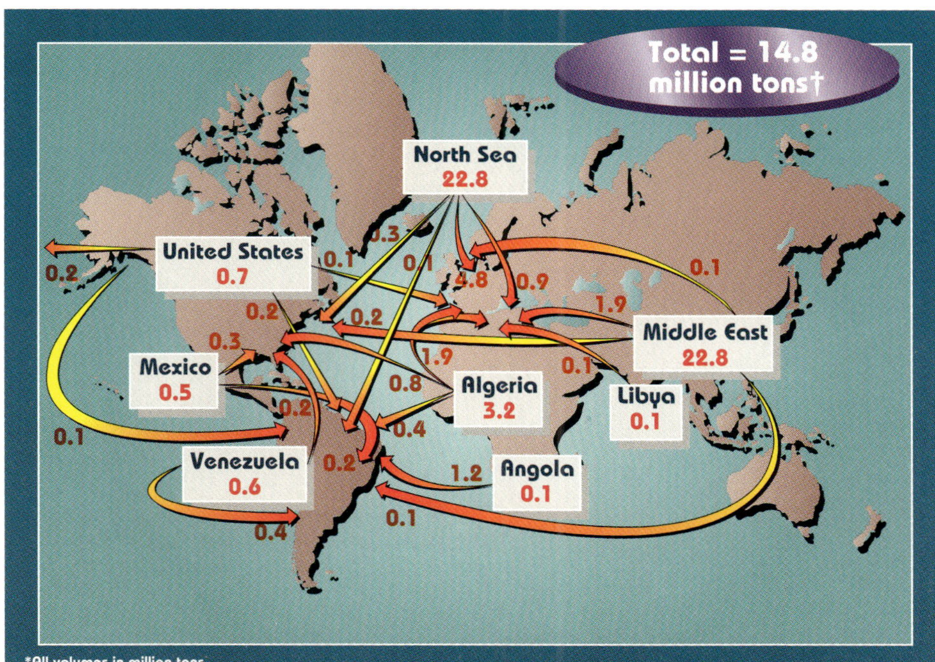

*All volumes in million tons.
†Displayed regional trades exclude selected routes which were less than 0.1 million tons.
IPE

East and elsewhere.

Poten & Partners treats the North Sea as a producing region because LPG produced there is mainly moved to market in gas carriers.

There are two distinct foci of LPG seaborne trade in this region. One is in Northwest Europe, where seaborne trade totaled 7.3 million tons in 1995. The other is in the Mediterranean (including southern Europe and North Africa), where it reached 5 million tons in that year.

Seaborne trade in Northwest Europe is dominated by North Sea LPG production. The doubling of this production in the past 5 years has displaced most long-haul seaborne cargoes into Northwest Europe.

North Sea LPG contributed more than 70% of cargoes delivered in Northwest Europe in 1995, compared with less than half in 1990.

Deliveries to this market from the Middle East have virtually disappeared, down from 1.5 million tons in 1990, and those from Algeria have been nearly halved from 900,000 tons in that year.

North Sea production will dominate seaborne trades in Northwest Europe for the foreseeable future (Fig. 9a). At the same time, rising exports from Algeria will compete strongly with other potential suppliers for sales in Northwest Europe that are not taken by North Sea producers.

Potential seaborne exports from Russia would be destined for Northwest Europe outlets and remain a wild card in the supply outlook. Even without Russian product, this market promises to be amply supplied.

The strategically located Mediterranean LPG market will be increasingly competitive (Fig. 9b). Seaborne cargoes entering this market are mainly supplied by Middle East producers and Algeria. A sizable small-cargo trade supplements LPG trades in large gas carriers.

Algeria is about to realize a near doubling of its LPG exports and will seek to place rising volumes in Mediterranean outlets, as well as in Northwest Europe and Transatlantic markets. At the same time, North Sea producers will seek to maintain and possibly expand sales in these same markets.

Moreover, by 2000 or soon thereafter, more than 1 million tons of new LPG exports will come from West Africa (Nigeria and the Congo). Some of these volumes will be targeted for sales in Europe, particularly in the Mediterranean, though most of this product will likely move to Western Hemisphere destinations.

Fig. 7

Seaborne export supply

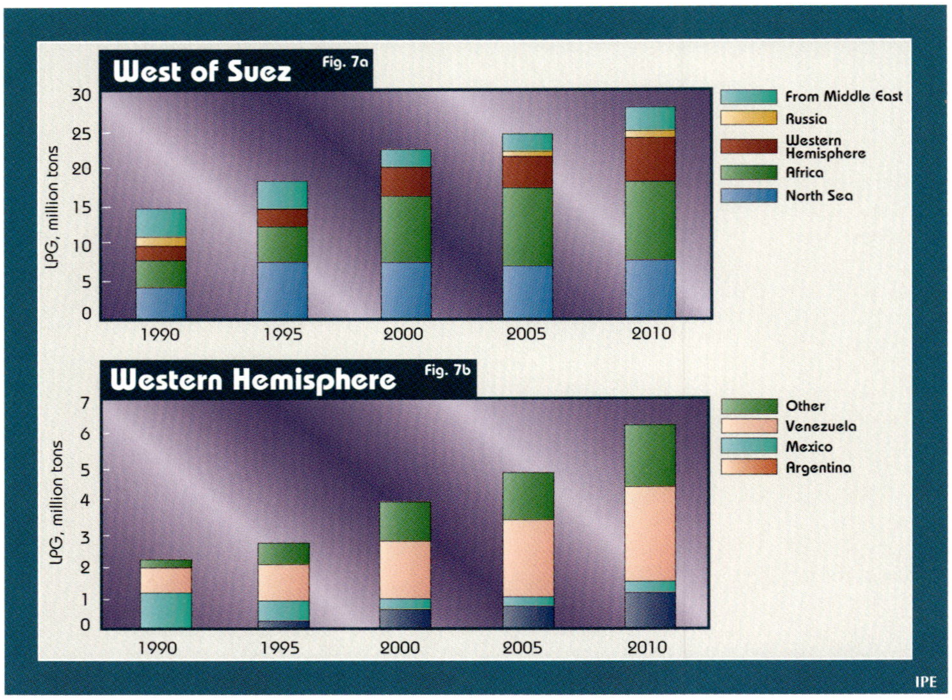

Fig. 8

Net import requirement*

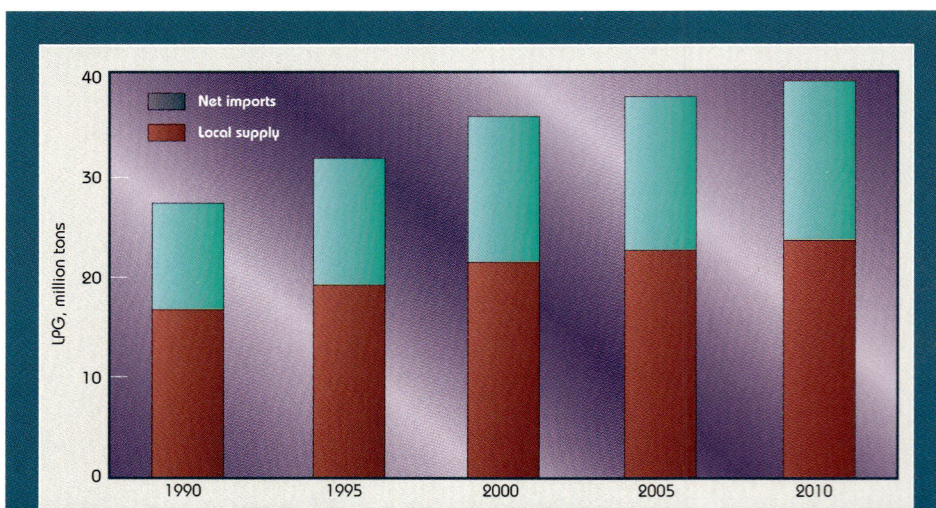

*Europe, North Africa, Eastern Mediterranean

North American supplies

Seaborne cargoes imported in the Western Hemisphere are relatively small compared to sales volume, which totaled 75 million tons in 1995 (Fig. 10a). Most supplies are from regional sources.

LPG production in the U.S. alone totaled 45.7 million tons in 1995. Canada and Mexico also have large energy industries boosting LPG production in North America to 60 million tpy.

In contrast, Middle East LPG production was only half of this in 1995, or 30.4 million tons. LPG production in Latin America is relatively small at 11.4 million tons in 1995. This production is concentrated in Venezuela, Brazil, and Argentina.

There is considerable overland trade between countries in North America where LPG infrastructure is increasingly being integrated.

Well-developed pipeline infrastructure links Alberta, the center of Canadian LPG production, with the U.S. Overland transport of LPG from Canada to the U.S. typically runs 2.0-2.5 million tpy, said Poten & Partners, citing U.S. statistics.

Downstream Mexican LPG and natural-gas businesses are being opened to private company participation, and LPG infrastructure is being built to deliver additional LPG from the U.S. to Mexico. Overland LPG trade from the U.S. to Mexico surpassed 1 million tpy in 1995. Other overland movements are relatively small.

Large domestic production in the largest LPG consuming nations in the Western Hemisphere and the size of overland trade between countries limit the size of seaborne trades, about 6.1 million tons in 1995.

By contrast, LPG seaborne trades east of Suez were about four times as large in 1995, and those in Northwest Europe and the Mediterranean were about twice as large.

The most important destination for seaborne cargoes is Brazil, which imported more than 2 million tons in 1995, mainly in large fully refrigerated cargoes. The main supplier to this market has been Saudi Arabia, followed by Algeria.

Competition for sales in Brazil promises to intensify, said Poten & Partners, as rising Atlantic basin production competes for sales in Western Hemisphere outlets.

The U.S. is the other main destination for large LPG cargoes. The U.S. East Coast requires seaborne imports to meet peak winter demand.

Buyers on the U.S. Gulf Coast can absorb large LPG volumes when international LPG prices are weak relative to those at Mont Belvieu. Volumes either move into storage or are used as feedstock at nearby petrochemical plants (Fig. 10b).

LPG imports on the U.S. Gulf Coast will likely reach nearly 3 million tpy by 2000 and slightly more than 6 million tpy by 2010. The U.S. Gulf Coast could be the destination for rising exports from Africa and Latin America as producers compete for outlets in an amply supplied Atlantic basin seaborne trade region.

Other destinations for large-cargo LPG imports include the nations on the West Coast of South America and Mexico. Energy-industry deregulation and growing participation of private companies are boosting demand for LPG imports.

There is an active small-cargo trade of about 1.5 million tpy. About 1 million tons of this trade occurs in the Caribbean basin. These deliveries command premium prices, providing an attractive market for LPG from Venezuela, Trinidad, and Mexico.

Ample supplies

In the past, the main sources of large-cargo LPG shipments to the Western Hemisphere were the Middle East and Algeria. In recent years, North Sea LPG has become an important supply source for the U.S. East Coast. Angola is a source of modest supplies for Latin America and will soon be joined by Congo and Nigeria (Fig. 10c).

Western Hemisphere markets promise to be amply supplied in the future as new Atlantic basin production looks for sales outlets, said Poten & Partners.

Additional volumes from Algeria and West Africa will compete with rising regional production for sales in Western Hemisphere outlets. Regional producers also plan large increases in export.

Venezuela, the largest regional source of seaborne cargoes, plans a series of gas-processing plants that would boost LPG exports substantially.

The opening of upstream industries has made Argentina an important regional supplier and promises to do the same for Colombia and Peru. IPE

Seaborne export supply — Fig. 9

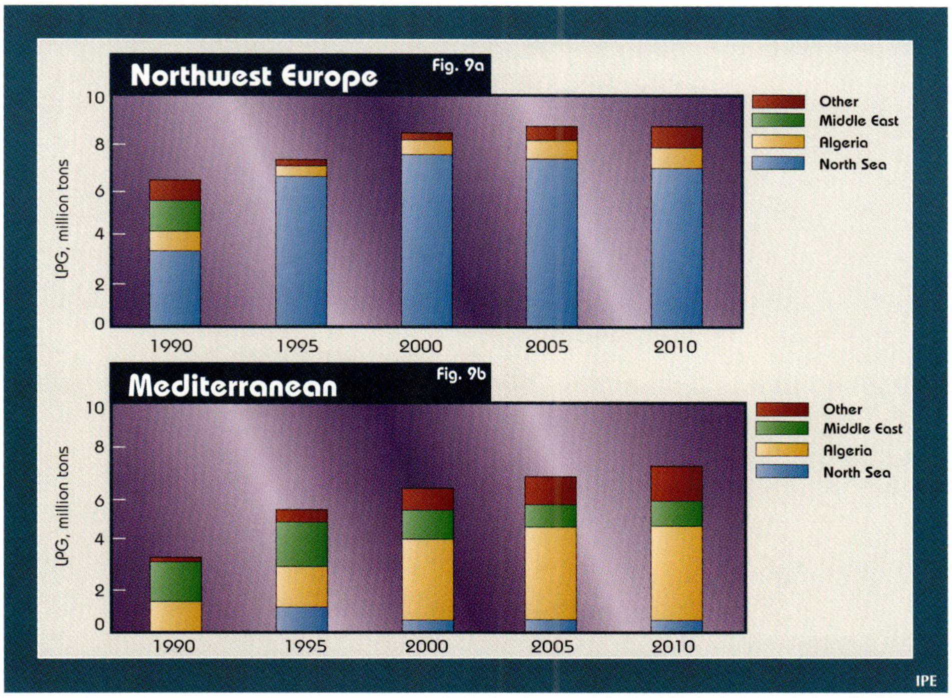

LPG demand — Fig. 10

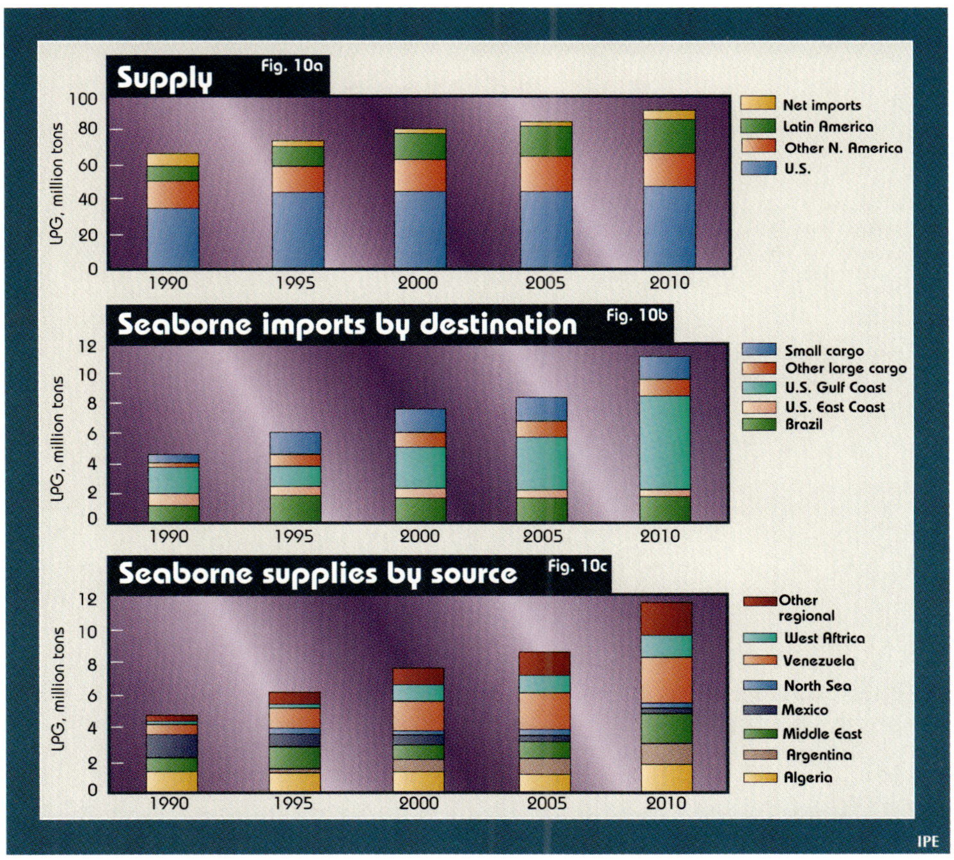

WORLDWIDE GAS PROCESSING

Capacities as of January 1, 1996, and average production

		MMcfd		Production 1,000 gpd (Average based on the past 12 months)								
Country	No. plants	Gas capacity	Gas through put	Ethane	Prop.	Isobut.	Process or unsplit butane	LP-gas mix	Raw NGL mix	Debut. nat. gaso.	Other	Total products
Abu Dhabi	6	1,719.0	1,362.6	....	....	....	....	....	....	546.0	....	546.0
Algeria	4	5,335.2	4,268.2	....	....	....	....	632.8	....	....	5,449.2	6,082.0
Angola	2	200.0	137.0	....	....	....	....	....	199.0	....	....	199.0
Argentina	14	1,488.4	1,498.9	687.7	497.2	....	334.8	....	....	319.8	0.8	1,840.3
Australia	5	3,307.0	1,507.1	430.2	938.4	....	783.0	662.0	....	1,310.0	850.0	4,973.6
Austria	2	67.7	64.7	....	....	....	....	....	....	45.0	41.5	86.5
Bahrain	1	280.0	265.0	....	158.2	....	133.8	....	....	212.7	....	504.7
Bangladesh	2	240.0	178.0	....	....	....	....	....	....	....	8.2	8.2
Bolivia	3	300.0	300.0	....	....	....	....	285.4	....	78.4	....	363.8
Brazil	12	475.7	484.5	2.3	....	....	....	733.9	101.6	159.6	57.6	1,055.0
Brunei	2	1,182.0	967.4	....	13.0	....	....	....	....	400.0	....	413.0
Canada	675	38,958.2	30,482.5	8,008.5	3,684.9	1,687.7	644.7	10,639.9	3,748.9	8,625.5	6,002.3	43,042.5
Chile	2	477.0	381.6	....	39.6	12.9	14.3	....	185.0	19.3	....	271.1
China, Taiwan	4	271.0	47.1	....	11.3	....	9.0	....	1.1	6.1	....	27.5
Colombia	7	333.0	247.3	76.5	58.0	....	63.0	88.8	27.0	63.0	....	376.3
C.I.S.	22	3,071.9	2,457.5	1,270.8	387.2	693.7	2,417.1	8,490.6	....	....	410.8	13,670.2
Denmark	1	597.2	474.2	....	....	....	....	....	....	....	0.1	0.1
Dubai	1	330.0	330.0	....	....	....	....	....	....	....	650.5	650.5
Ecuador	2	41.0	20.5	....	....	....	....	97.1	....	37.3	....	134.4
Egypt	12	1,915.0	1,806.0	....	....	....	....	899.6	1,132.2	575.4	330.0	2,937.2
France	1	570.0	563.0	....	139.0	....	132.0	....	....	270.0	....	541.0
Germany	3	358.0	253.5	....	....	....	....	....	....	....	....	....
Greece	2	30.3	10.4	....	....	....	....	....	....	....	....	....
Hungary	12	946.6	519.9	....	43.7	5.7	42.9	7.9	284.6	571.8	43.7	1,000.3
Indonesia	11	6,419.3	5,870.7	....	1,773.8	838.2	529.4	295.3	1,261.0	....	4,636.4	9,334.1
Iran	4	3,284.2	2,627.4	....	....	....	....	....	....	....	....	....
Italy	17	7,614.0	1,587.0	....	....	....	....	2.7	8.0	7.5	....	18.2
Kuwait	3	1,815.0	1,452.0		1,722.0	....	980.0	....	....	811.8	....	3,513.8
Libya	7	1,851.0	1,227.0	....	....	....	....	37.8	1,494.0	....	551.0	2,082.8
Malaysia	2	282.0	105.0	161.4	23.2	136.3	28.2	....	....	154.1	....	503.2
Mexico	9	4,779.0	3,823.2	....	....	....	....	....	18,819.9	....	....	18,819.9
Netherlands	2	725.0	315.0	....	....	....	....	....	....	....	230.5	230.5
New Zealand	6	1,447.5	679.0	....	9.1	....	16.3	212.9	....	35.2	860.0	1,133.5
Norway	2	950.0	530.8	....	682.0	108.0	256.0	....	175.4	193.0	....	1,414.4
Oman	8	826.0	309.4	....	....	....	....	....	202.0	43.0	....	245.0
Pakistan	12	1,205.0	968.7	....	....	....	....	53.8	64.9	....	9.1	127.8
Peru	2	70.0	37.0	....	3.4	....	1.0	5.6	28.9	....	4.0	42.9
Qatar	3	1,379.0	1,003.0	....	852.0	....	502.0	....	3,021.0	355.0	947.0	5,677.0
Saudi Arabia	5	4,900.0	....	....	....	....	....	....	....	....	....	....
Sharjah, U.A.E.	2	940.0	940.0	....	324.0	....	231.0	....	....	....	1,837.0	2,392.0
Spain	3	428.0	177.0	....	....	....	....	....	....	....	73.0	73.0
Thailand	2	850.0	550.0	....	....	....	....	400.4	8.4	84.0	....	492.8
Trinidad & Tobago	1	650.0	580.0	....	200.0	....	130.0	....	....	115.0	....	445.0
United Kingdom	12	11,740.0	2,774.9	....	....	....	....	....	....	1,572.5	35.1	1,607.6
United States	623	68,964.2	48,354.9	6,629.0	7,865.6	1,220.0	3,302.3	1,476.6	45,542.5	3,814.0	4,687.7	74,537.7
Venezuela	14	2,913.0	2,557.0	213.3	197.4	....	113.4	231.3	3,274.6	171.9	....	4,201.9
Yemen	1	400.0	433.0	....	....	....	....	53.6	305.5	....	....	359.1
Total, excl. U.S.	**925**	**117,962.2**	**77,174.0**	**10,850.7**	**11,757.4**	**3,482.5**	**7,361.9**	**23,831.4**	**34,343.0**	**16,782.9**	**23,027.8**	**131,437.7**
World total	**1,548**	**186,926.4**	**125,528.9**	**17,479.7**	**19,623.0**	**4,702.5**	**10,664.2**	**25,308.0**	**79,885.5**	**20,596.9**	**27,715.5**	**205,975.4**
Canada												
Alberta	622	34,894.0	27,367.5	8,008.5	3,425.7	1,687.7	501.7	10,623.5	3,614.7	8,380.0	5,984.1	42,226.0
British Columbia	20	3,418.1	2,777.4	....	237.5	....	132.9	3.5	30.0	232.7	....	636.6
Northwest Territories	2	219.9	28.3	....	....	....	....	....	....	....	....	....
Saskatchewan	30	356.2	259.3	....	21.7	....	10.1	12.9	104.2	12.8	18.2	179.9
Yukon	1	70.0	50.0	....	....	....	....	....	....	....	....	....
Total Canada	**675**	**38,958.2**	**30,482.5**	**8,008.5**	**3,684.9**	**1,687.7**	**644.7**	**10,639.9**	**3,748.9**	**8,625.5**	**6,002.3**	**43,042.5**
United States												
Alabama	8	773.0	650.4	....	159.3	....	132.8	....	63.4	87.5	539.3	982.3
Alaska	3	8,975.0	8,637.0	....	2.3	....	16.0	....	3,886.1	....	....	3,904.4
Arkansas	3	875.0	525.3	....	....	....	....	....	51.5	....	1.4	52.9
California	25	1,038.4	678.8	....	334.0	56.3	161.5	69.5	196.4	224.7	11.0	1,053.4
Colorado	47	1,268.4	922.0	249.0	189.8	7.4	75.0	29.2	1,010.1	96.3	4.4	1,661.2
Florida	1	90.0	38.0	....	68.0	....	53.0	....	....	24.0	....	145.0
Kansas	16	3,708.6	2,802.8	187.4	829.9	130.7	336.5	1,139.9	1,177.3	259.9	0.9	4,062.5
Kentucky	3	141.0	115.4	....	....	....	....	28.8	153.4	....	....	182.2
Louisiana	68	17,984.1	12,734.4	689.5	719.8	244.4	236.2	0.1	8,740.2	443.3	368.7	11,442.2
Michigan	26	4,697.9	865.9	....	33.0	....	....	2.6	465.2	....	28.3	529.0
Mississippi	5	881.7	209.7	....	7.8	....	8.3	....	11.6	7.6	....	35.3
Montana	5	12.5	6.6	....	17.9	....	10.5	....	....	6.3	2.2	36.9
New Mexico	28	2,771.5	2,121.8	581.0	546.3	46.3	238.9	22.7	4,725.4	208.2	495.6	6,864.3
North Dakota	6	123.9	78.4	....	134.6	....	89.7	....	15.2	81.0	2.1	322.6
Ohio	1	20.0	9.0	....	....	....	....	....	9.3	....	....	9.3
Oklahoma	79	4,007.0	2,748.3	418.3	660.2	73.8	193.9	134.2	5,213.4	218.0	395.2	7,307.0
Pennsylvania	3	20.0	8.3	....	4.7	....	3.0	....	....	4.1	....	11.8
Texas	237	16,233.9	11,501.7	3,689.3	2,884.9	510.6	1,185.1	13.6	18,134.9	1,712.8	2,306.0	30,437.2
Utah	13	617.5	348.6	....	64.0	....	26.8	....	135.6	39.8	1.7	267.9
West Virginia	7	398.9	322.8	269.0	194.0	29.0	60.0	....	356.0	....	....	908.0
Wyoming	39	4,325.9	3,029.7	545.5	1,015.1	121.5	475.2	36.0	1,197.5	400.5	530.9	4,322.2
Total U.S.	**623**	**68,964.2**	**48,354.9**	**6,629.0**	**7,865.6**	**1,220.0**	**3,302.3**	**1,476.6**	**45,542.5**	**3,814.0**	**4,687.7**	**74,537.7**

Nile Delta concessions

Fig. 1

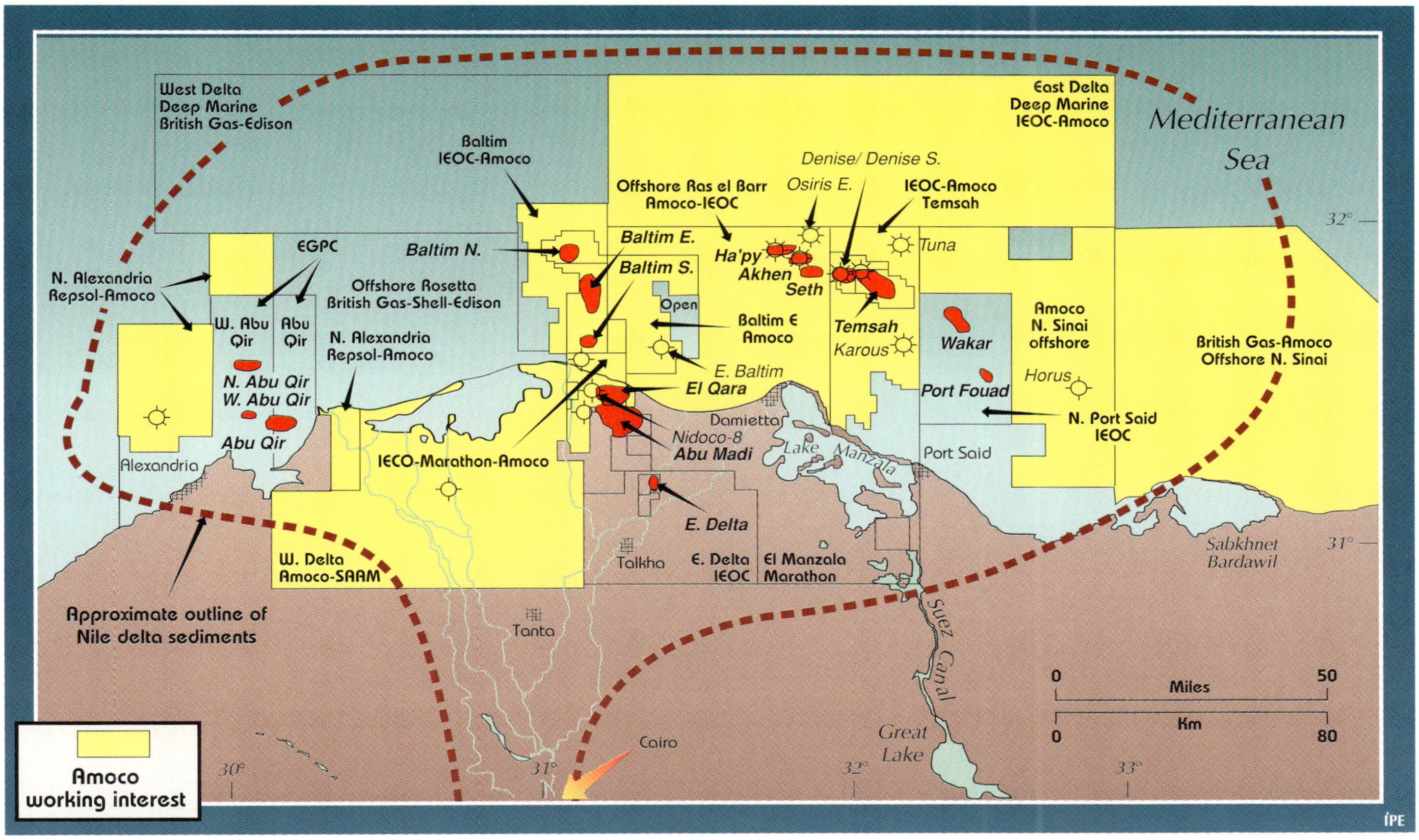

Egypt's three main E&P areas teem with activity

Egyptian exploration and production activity emerged at yearend 1996 from one of its busiest and most productive years in recent history.

All three of the country's main E&P theaters—Gulf of Suez, western desert, and Nile delta—were teeming with operators. Egypt's burgeoning gas industry was the driving force behind some projects, but many oil operations were also in evidence.

Egyptian Minister of Oil Hamdy el-Banbi said Egypt made 32 oil discoveries and signed 14 agreements with international companies during 1996. The agreements call for spending of about $300 million and the drilling of 83 wildcats in areas covering 142,000 sq km across Egypt, he said.

By comparison, Egypt ratified eight concession agreements and amended two prior agreements covering a combined 43,335 sq km in 1995 versus only five agreements and three amendments in 1994.

Twenty of the 1996 discoveries were gas wells, and the other 12 produced oil.

The minister said Egypt's 1996 gas production averaged 1.4 bcfd, up about 65% from 1990 and 2.3 times 1986 production. Larger Nile delta and western desert fields are still to come on production.

Nile delta/Mediterranean fields produce about 65% of Egypt's gas, and the rest comes 50-50 from the western desert and Gulf of Suez. Crude oil production originates 80% in the Gulf of Suez, 11% in the western desert, 5% in Sinai, and the rest in the eastern desert (between the Nile River and Gulf of Suez).

The following is a rundown of major 1996 upstream activity in Egypt's three main areas.

Nile delta gas

Egyptian officials said domestic gas needs come first, but the Nile delta's reserves had grown large enough to support LNG shipments to Turkey as well as a previously discussed pipeline around the eastern Mediterranean to Israel, Jordan, and Palestine.

Amoco Egypt late in 1996 signed a memorandum of understanding with Egyptian General Petroleum Corp. and Turkey's Botas Petroleum Pipeline Corp. to set up two joint ventures to develop the LNG project.

EGPC/Amoco would be responsible for constructing and operating a gas liquefaction plant on Egypt's Mediterranean coast and transporting and selling as much as 7.3 million metric tons/year of LNG to Turkey. Botas would establish a second venture to build and run a regasification plant near Izmir, on Turkey's Aegean Sea coast about 500 miles southwest of Istanbul.

Amoco in late 1996 said the Nile delta had yielded 16 gas discoveries with more than 7 tcf of proved and probable reserves (Fig. 1). Extensive 3D seismic programs revealed additional drilling prospects, and future gas resource potential exceeds 20 tcf, the company said.

In mid-1996, IEOC's Wakar and Port Fouad gas fields began producing. The fields, on the North Port Said concession dating to the early 1980s, were producing about 70

Nile delta discovery is Amoco's Seth 1, a Pliocene gas discovery on the Ras el Barr concession in the Mediterranean. Photo courtesy of Amoco (Fig. 2).

MMcfd through a subsea pipeline with landfall near Port Said.

The only other offshore production was about 175 MMcfd from Abu Qir field, operated by EGPC's General Petroleum Co. unit. Phillips Petroleum Co. discovered Abu Qir just off Alexandria in 1969.

Onshore Nile delta production is about 330 MMcfd from Belayim Petroleum Co.'s Abu Madi field and about 100 MMcfd from Petrobel's Al Qara fields west of Damietta. Abu Madi, a 1967 discovery, is Egypt's first gas field.

Gas discoveries

Amoco and AGIP's IEOC unit reported numerous gas discoveries during the year on various concessions in the Mediterranean portion of the Nile delta gas province (see table).

Most of the delta is under concession. Key operators besides Amoco and AGIP are British Gas, EGPC, Shell, Marathon, Edison Gas, and Repsol.

Late in the year the companies reported three discoveries offshore. AGIP-Amoco's Karous 1 in the central part of the El Temsah concession flowed 16 MMcfd of gas from Pliocene at 1,300 m. Another Pliocene discovery on the concession, Tuna 1, flowed 12 MMcfd of gas from 1,100 m. Both wells were tested on small chokes to limit sand production.

The two discoveries were expected to add about 1 tcf of gas to reserves of the offshore Nile delta basin.

The third discovery, Nidoco 9, is on the West Abu Madi development lease. Petrobel operates on behalf of IEOC, Amoco Egypt, and Marathon Petroleum Nile Delta Ltd.

The discovery well, 3 km offshore, encountered gas and condensate in the Messinian (Late Miocene) Abu Madi formation at 3,400 m. Production capacity was estimated to reach 30 MMcfd of gas plus 500 b/d of condensate. The well cut a 102 ft gas column with net pay of 92 ft at 11,155 ft.

After completion the well was to be tied to the El Qara production facilities.

Amoco in December reported its 12th straight discovery in the Nile delta in partnership with AGIP. The Osiris East 1 on the Ras el Barr concession flowed 35 MMcfd of gas and 2,275 b/d of condensate from Miocene sands below 13,280 ft.

Gas production plans

IEOC/Amoco planned to place several fields on production.

The first was likely to be Baltim South by yearend 1997, the other Baltim fields by 1999, and a combination of fields on the Temsah and Ras el Barr concessions by 2000.

Egypt's gas pipeline grid is mainly developed in populated areas around Alexandria, Cairo, Port Said, and Suez. The grid does not extend to the Sinai, most of northern Egypt, or southern Egypt.

Tentative plans were to lay a pipeline from the Nile delta across northern Sinai to serve Israel, Jordan, and Palestine by about 2000. Intended sales volumes as of 1996 were 250

Amoco Nile Delta discoveries

Discovery	Pay horizon (age)
Baltim E.	Abu Madi sands (U. Messinian of Late Miocene)
Baltim N.	Abu Madi sands (U. Messinian of Late Miocene)
Baltim S.	Abu Madi sands (U. Messinian of Late Miocene)
Temsah	Temsah sands (Serravallian of Middle Miocene)
Akhen	Temsah sands (Serravallian of Middle Miocene) and Kafr el Sheik sands (Pliocene)
Denise	Kafr el Sheik sands (Pliocene)
Denise S.	Kafr el Sheik sands (Pliocene)
Ha'py	Kafr el Sheik sands (Pliocene)
Seth	Kafr el Sheik sands (Pliocene)
Osiris, E.	Temsah sands (Serravallian of Middle Miocene)
Karous	Kafr el Sheik sands (Pliocene)
Nidoco 9	Abu Madi sands (U. Messinian of Late Miocene)
Tuna	Kafr el Sheik sands (Pliocene)

Apache, Shell Western Desert focus area

Fig. 3

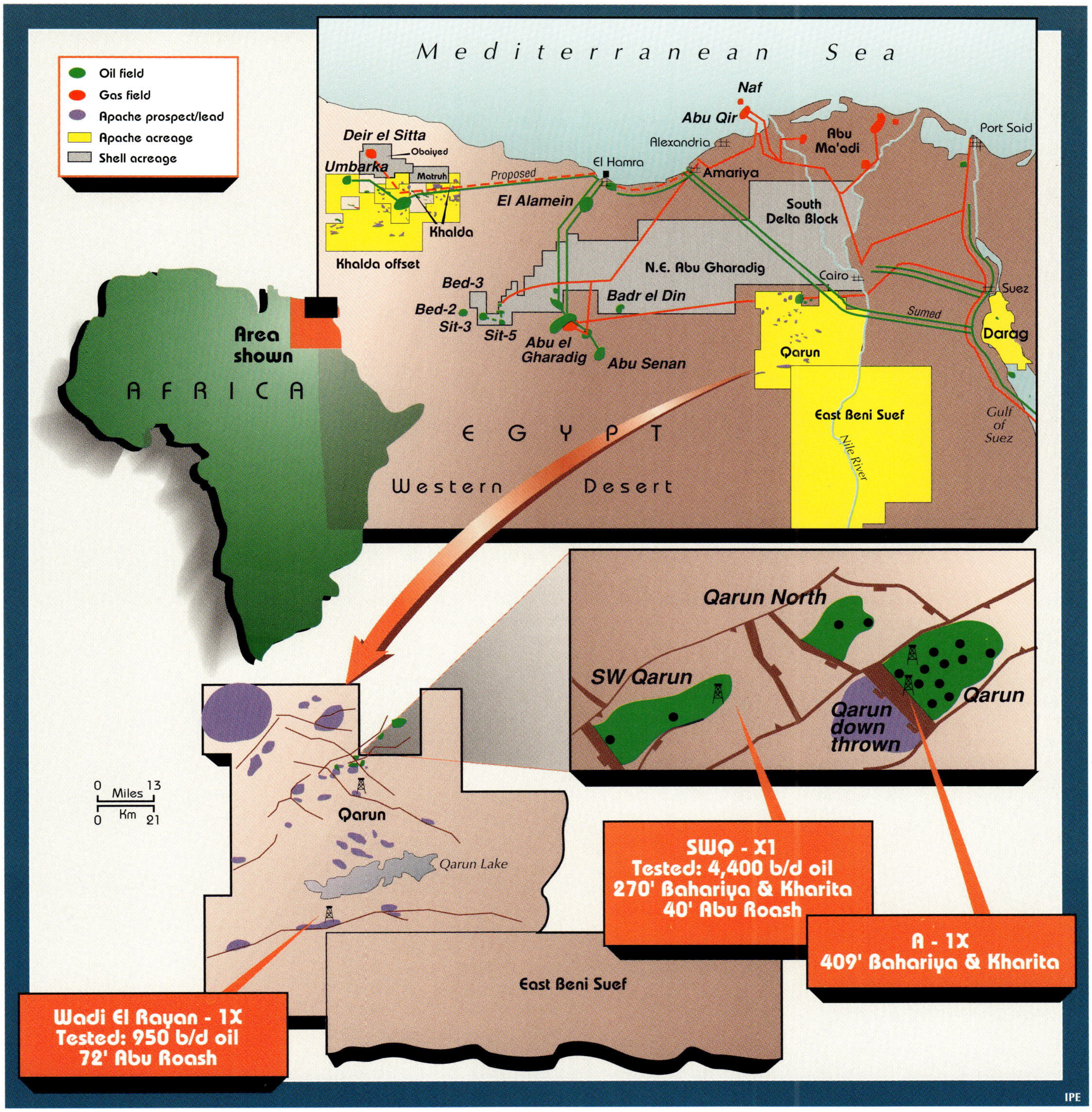

MMcfd each to Israel and Jordan and 50 MMcfd to Palestinian settlements.

Israel burns no gas but intends to generate electricity. Egypt's gas consumption, mainly for electricity, was 1.3 bcfd in 1995.

Egypt's first private pipeline company, Egypt Trans Gas Co., was formed during the year to construct the export pipeline if negotiations succeed. Ownership is the Egyptian government through Egypt Gas 34% and Amoco and IEOC each 33%.

Drilling steady

Drilling perked up in the delta after Egypt began allowing contractors to develop gas in the late 1980s and issued gas concessions in the early 1990s.

Amoco had about 4 million net acres or 34% of the acreage in the delta in 1996. Tracts in which it owns interests cover about two thirds of the delta, eight offshore and one onshore.

Since 1993 through mid-1996 Amoco was involved in about 23 delineation and exploratory wells in the delta, including four 100% owned wells and the rest owned 50-50. All but one

Floor on trip at EDC Rig. 3 in Qarun oil field in the western desert. Photo courtesy of Apache Corp. (Fig. 4).

of the 50-50 wells were with IEOC.

Baltim, Ras el Barr, and Temsah are the most active concessions offshore. Here are the results as of mid-1996:

- Baltim concession, IEOC operator, eight wells drilled with three discoveries, Baltim South, East, and North fields.
- Ras el Barr concession, Amoco operator, three wells drilled with three discoveries, Ha'py, Akhen, and Seth (Fig. 2), and a well drilling on a fourth feature.
- Temsah concession, IEOC operator, 10 wells drilled with three discoveries, Temsah, Denise, and Denise South, and one well drilling.

Temsah field is quite large, at least 20 km long and 4-6 km wide, and will require much delineation drilling, Amoco said.

An AGIP-Amoco task force in Milan was working on development schemes for the companies' fields during 1996. With all in less than 300 ft of water, conventional hardware is likely. Some wells should come on at 40-50 MMcfd.

Condensate may go to Egypt and export markets. The deepest gases in Temsah and Middle Miocene have 40-50 bbl/MMcf, while Late Miocene Abu Madi and deeper Pliocene zones contain 17-25 bbl/MMcf. Shallower Pliocene zones contain almost dry gas.

Western desert

Oil and gas operations were growing in Egypt's western desert, with Apache Corp. of the U.S. becoming a major player.

Apache, which held interests in about 11.3 million gross acres in Egypt at yearend 1996, was preparing to obtain interests in a further 7.7 million gross acres in early 1997. All of that is in the western desert except about 460,000 gross acres on the Darag concession, the most northerly in the Gulf of Suez.

At yearend 1996 contracts were signed for a major gas supply deal from the western desert.

A group that includes Apache, Royal Dutch/Shell, Repsol Exploracion Egipto SA, and Samsung Ltd. planned to build a 315 km, 34 in. pipeline from the western desert to Egypt's national gas grid at Ameriya, west of Alexandria (Fig. 3).

Shell will operate the pipeline, which will transport gas from the Shell group's Obaiyed concession and Apache et al.'s Khalda and Khalda Offset concessions. Capacity is believed to be about 500 MMcfd of gas, with Apache and partners supplying 200 MMcfd of that or a total of 1.8 tcf over the contract life.

The 25 year contract takes effect May 1, 1999. The wellhead contract price, more than $3/Mcf at yearend 1996, is tied to the price of fuel oil and Gulf of Suez blended crude. Apache said its share of future deliveries at yearend 1996 prices represented about $1.2 billion, of which 75% is contracted under take or pay provisions.

Shell drilled five exploratory wells at Obaiyed during 1991-94, three of which were gas/condensate discoveries. During 1995-96 it drilled two successful appraisal wells and two more exploratory wells that effectively delineated the Deir el Sitta field reservoir.

Khalda concession

Apache expected to book about 85 bcf of gas equivalent reserves from 1996 discoveries on the 300,000 acre Khalda concession.

Khalda reserves were estimated in fall 1996 at 255 bcf of gas and 7.7 million bbl of oil. Interests in Khalda are Repsol 50%, Apache 40%, and Samsung Ltd. 10%.

Drilling on Khalda had resulted in several gas/condensate discoveries between existing oil fields in what were previously considered nonprospective graben areas, Apache said. The pays are stratigraphically deeper in some cases, and this deeper gas/condensate province is practically unexplored.

Near yearend Repsol tested the Tut 22X well on Khalda flowing 90 MMcfd of gas and 4,056 b/d of condensate from an undisclosed zone.

The group completed two other hefty discoveries in August

and September 1996. They flowed 40 MMcfd of gas and 1,177 b/d of condensate and 49 MMcfd of gas and 2,119 b/d of condensate, respectively.

The group planned to test in early 1997 an indicated discovery, Shams S-1X, and a late 1996 appraisal, Shams 2X. Shams S-1X had about 300 ft of indicated pay.

Gross production from Khalda at yearend 1996 was 32,000 b/d of oil, including 6,400 b/d net to Apache.

Repsol/Apache planned to escalate exploration on the 2.1 million acre Khalda Offset concession to the south. The offset concession is in an area of tilted fault block plays in Cretaceous, Jurassic, and older rocks.

Four sub-basins

Four sub-basins in the northern part of the western desert each seem capable of producing 300 million bbl of ultimate recovery even without dense exploration, Apache said.

This general assessment is based on field size distributions and the similarity of geological characteristics in the four areas: Shushan sub-basin in the Khalda area, Alamein sub-basin south of El Hamra, Abu Gharadig sub-basin south of Alamein, and Gindi sub-basin southwest of Cairo.

Western desert exploration dates mainly from the 1950s, but the geology was slow to unravel. The desert still has fewer than 800 wells of all types in an area the size of Oklahoma—70,000 sq miles—where tens of thousands of wells have been drilled.

Cretaceous zones have been the big producers, and Jurassic pay was added at Khalda in the mid-1980s.

Shell said Deir el Sitta field on its Obaiyed concession was initially thought to be producing from the Jurassic Khatatba formation. Some uncertainty remained, but the pay zone at 4,000 m was thought in mid-1996 to be Mesozoic-Paleozoic. That could imply Triassic or even Permian production.

Apache's Qarun concession, southwest of Cairo in the Gindi sub-basin, had produced only from Cretaceous zones. But other western desert areas produce from sands that lie just above basement up to the base of the Tertiary section. Apache believes much more of the stratigraphic section is prospective on Qarun.

Qarun concession

Production at Qarun field, about 20,000 b/d in late 1996, was to rise to a gross 35,000 b/d in early 1997. Apache's joint venture company, Qarun Petroleum Co., in November 1996 activated a 30 mile pipeline to the twin 42 in. Sumed oil pipelines from Qarun field (Fig. 4).

Apache began producing Qarun oil in December 1995, trucking it to Tebbin for pipeline shipment to a refinery northeast of Cairo. Concurrently, construction began on production facilities, including two 350,000 bbl tanks, at a Sumed pump station at Dashur southeast of the Giza pyramids.

The Gindi sub-basin had no commercial discoveries when Apache acquired an interest in the 1.9 million acre Qarun area in May 1993.

The Qarun 3 appraisal well in early 1995 had Egypt's largest onshore oil flow—11,957 b/d. By early 1997 Apache had proved 75-80 million bbl of oil reserves in the main, north, and southwest lobes of Qarun field. One of the largest western desert fields, Qarun at yearend 1996 had 20 completed wells with five more being drilled.

Qarun outlook

The northern Qarun discoveries lie among a series of northwest-southeast trends and produce 42° gravity oil from Cretaceous Kharita and Bahariya sandstones at 8,800-9,300 ft. There are indications of shallower Abu Roash pays in the Qarun field complex, and Apache was anxious to test them.

The late 1996 Wadi El Rayan discovery 35 miles south of Qarun field produced 25° gravity oil from 5,550-5,716 ft. That well, the western desert's southernmost producer, is about 19 km west of and on trend with an old Shell well that flowed about 250 b/d of oil from Abu Roash. Apache planned to shoot seismic in the area.

Wadi El Rayan gives increased hope of different kitchen areas and charging mechanisms as well as for new play types on the southern part of the Qarun block, Apache said. It had become convinced of both Jurassic and Cretaceous kitchens in a number of areas in and around the Qarun concession.

Qarun interests are Apache 75% and Seagull Energy Corp. 25%.

Apache fulfilled its Qarun work commitment in 1996 and expected two seismic crews to continue full time there at least through most of 1997 trying to increase the prospect inventory. Apache shot a 3D seismic survey over Qarun A field in 1994 and drilled at least one exploratory well to Jurassic.

The company had used 2D and 3D geophysics, subsurface and surface geology, Landsat, and source rock geochemistry in exploring Qarun.

The Wadi el Rayan discovery is about a mile north of the 6.8 million acre East Beni Suef concession, on which Apache-Seagull 50-50 planned to drill the single commitment well in first quarter 1997.

Gulf of Suez

Government figures for 1996 Gulf of Suez operations were not available as the year ended, but the area continued to dominate Egypt's oil scene (Fig. 5).

The industry drilled 44 wells encompassing 457,789 ft of hole using 17 rigs in the Gulf of Suez in 1995.

Gulf of Suez fields placed on production during 1995 included Gupco's GS-184 field, Magapetco's East Esh el Mallaha field, and Geisum's West Tawilla field.

Gulf of Suez Petroleum Co. (Gupco), the joint company formed by Amoco and EGPC to manage Gulf of Suez and western desert reservoirs, operates fields that produced more than 300,000 b/d of oil at yearend 1996.

Most of the fields are mature, and innovative techniques are needed to maximize recovery and minimize costs in a challenging offshore environment.

Gupco activities

Gupco drilled several wells in Younis (GS-347) field in 1996 that have extended the reservoir limits, resulting in the approximate doubling of the known original oil in place in the field to about 100 million bbl.

The field previously had been thought to be fully developed, but reservoir modeling identified potential for a significant expansion of field boundaries. The development of this relatively remote field, which is now being waterflooded, is unique in that creative techniques such as dumpflooding are being attempted to minimize costs and accelerate response.

Gupco also drilled a previously unpenetrated block in July field during the year.

The well is unique in that the block contained heavy oil and, due to the extremely complex nature of the faulting in the field, its successful completion required extremely detailed mapping and monitoring while drilling using computer visualization.

Water injection at a dually completed offset well has led to an oil rate increase of about 3,000 b/d in just over a month as predicted by reservoir simulation.

Gupco is redeveloping Hilal field following a ship accident that destroyed its production platform in 1994.

Following completion of a multidiscipline field study, two wells were planned in the structurally and stratigraphically complex field, the first wells to be drilled since 1985.

The first of the two wells was a geologic success and was on production at yearend at 5,500 b/d of oil. The second well was drilling.

Following the first discovery of oil in the East Tanka concession in December 1995, Gupco drilled two more discoveries, ET-3 and ET-4. The 3 East Tanka in 203 ft of water flowed 4,884 b/d of 31° gravity oil and 3.7 MMcfd of gas. The well cut 56 ft of net pay in Miocene Asl at 8,592-8,680 ft.

Work to set a platform on the ET-3 discovery was to be completed in 1997. The small stand-alone platform was to be tied into nearby October oil field.

Gulf of Suez oil fields and gas gathering centers

Fig. 5

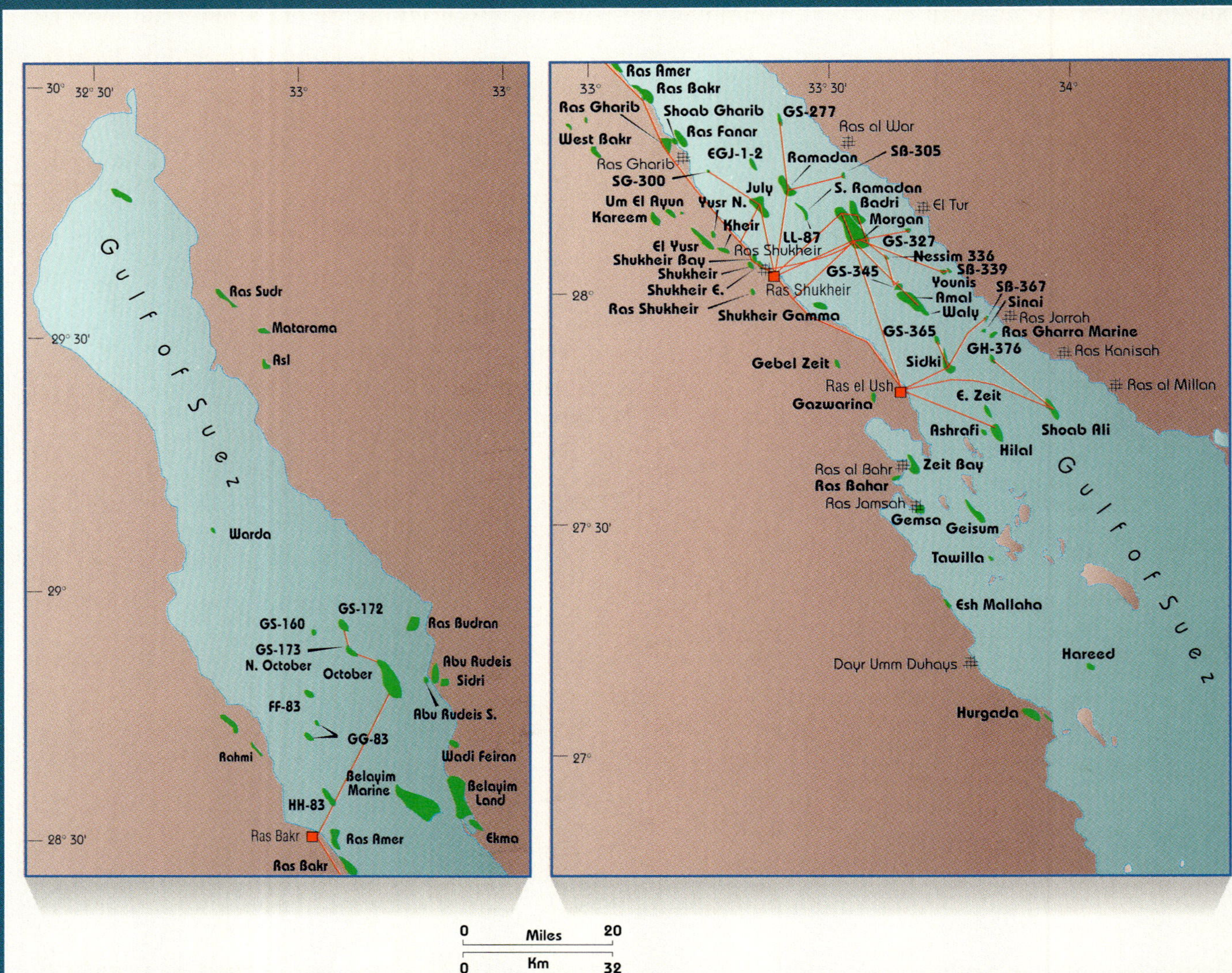

Source: Amoco

IPE

In addition, Gupco was embarking on an active lateral drilling campaign. Several lateral drilling prospects had been identified. The first was to be drilled in October field in early 1997. Gupco also planned to use this technology in July field.

Finally, Gupco set the October K platform in October field. It began producing in December 1996 at 15,000 b/d of oil from three pre-drilled wells. Eight more K platform wells were to be drilled during 1997.

Other companies active

A number of other interesting developments took place in 1996.

AGIP's IEOC and Marathon Petroleum Egypt Ltd. planned to tie back a fault block discovery in Ashrafi field to the main field platform.

The Ashrafi SW-1X, 1 mile southwest of the field, had 269 ft of net pay at 4,770-5,098 ft in Cretaceous Nubia sandstone and 73 ft of net pay across 5,098-5,561 ft in fractured granite basement.

Ashrafi field, in 29 ft of water, began producing in 1992. Cumulative production in 1996 was nearly 30 million bbl of oil. Production was about 20,000 b/d in mid-1996.

Seagull Energy Corp., Houston, acquired Esso Suez Inc. and certain assets of Esso Egypt Ltd. in mid-1996. The acquisition included ESI's East Zeit concession producing 16,000 b/d (Seagull interest 4,000-5,000 b/d) and EEL's 63,000 acre South Hurghada onshore exploration concession 250 miles south of Cairo, which had two oil discoveries and further potential.

Pennzoil planned to start a work program in 1997 on the 34 sq km North July block in the central gulf. Three wells tested at a combined rate of 8,000 b/d from Miocene Rudeis sand, and 3D seismic data were acquired on the block in 1996.

Pennzoil also has southeastern gulf interests in the Southwest Gebel El-Zeit and West Feiran blocks, where drilling was to start in 1997.

Early in the year, Apache became operator with a 50% interest in the 460,000 acre Darag block, largest and northernmost Gulf of Suez concession.

Two of three Darag commitment wells were to be drilled in second half 1997. The block is considered exploratory acreage at the north edge of the Gulf of Suez basin.

Apache planned to conduct 2D seismic and a 110 sq km 3D bottom cable survey in late 1996 surrounding a subcommercial Total well that flowed more than 2,000 b/d of 31-33° gravity oil from Miocene Nukhul in the mid-1980s. IPE

This rear view of the 11,000 b/sd gasifier at Shell Nederland Raffinaderij B.V.'s 374,000 b/d refinery at Pernis, The Netherlands, conveys the magnitude of the upgrade project that was scheduled to start up in May 1997. A 56,000 b/sd hydrocracker was also part of the upgrade project.

Refiners embrace gasification as nearly ideal technology

Gasification has long been used for conversion of coal to a mixture of hydrogen and carbon monoxide called synthesis gas, or syngas. The process is gaining acceptance as a profitable and environmentally beneficial method of converting petroleum feedstocks to syngas.

When fired in a gas turbine, syngas produces electricity with minimal emissions of sulfur dioxide, nitrogen oxides, carbon monoxide, particulates, and volatile organic compounds. Syngas also can be converted to steam or chemicals, or hydrogen can be recovered from it for refinery use.

These features make the technology ideal for refiners in the final years of the 20th century. With low, sometimes negative, margins, refiners are looking to gasification to convert low-value, bottom-of-the-barrel feeds to clean syngas.

David L. Heaven, director of process engineering for Fluor Daniel Inc., Irvine, Calif., said, "The technology is moving from its principal use as a source of hydrogen and carbon monoxide for chemicals production to a broader application as a useful and economic refining tool."

According to Heaven, gasification can solve a number of problems facing refiners, including:

- Increasing availability of heavy, sour, metals-laden crude oils.
- Rising competition among refiners.
- Tightening environmental regulations.

The process can handle a wide variety of feedstocks, including petroleum coke, heavy residues, waste products—even feeds as light as natural gas.

"The environmental performance of gasification is unmatched by competing means of dealing with low-value refinery streams," said Heaven. "The reasons for including a gasifier in a refinery often derive from the combination of crude oil quality trends and increasingly severe restrictions on sulfur dioxide emissions from combustion of heavy fuels."

The need to generate electricity is a common reason refiners add gasifiers, as is production of hydrogen—a useful capability in a period of ever-decreasing fuel sulfur specifications.

"Conventional heavy-resid conversion processes for high-metals stocks—such as coking processes—are no longer the final solution they once were," said Heaven. "Virtually any heavy resid or coke may be processed in gasifiers while meeting environmental regulations anywhere in the world."

Fig. 1 shows the variety of potential products available from a gasification facility integrated with combined-cycle power production.

Italian gasification projects

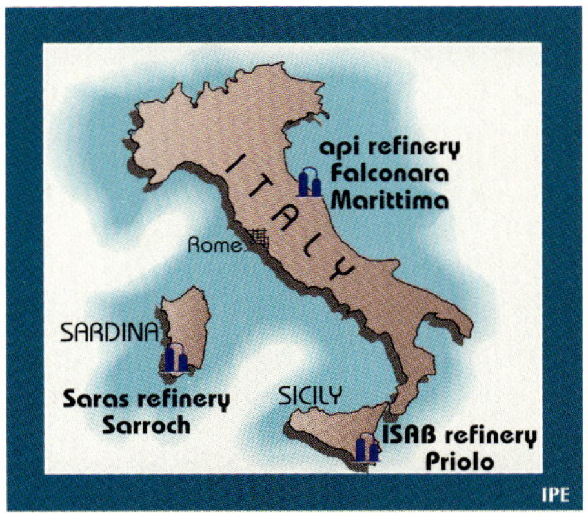

Making the choice

Gasification is usually profitable when used with feedstocks having zero or negative value. The process would rarely be applied to feeds valued at more than \$10/bbl, said Heaven. For this reason, low-sulfur resids and high-sulfur atmospheric resids should not be considered candidates for the process.

Visbreaker tars and low-metals, high-sulfur vacuum resids,

IGCC has a multitude of options

Fig. 1

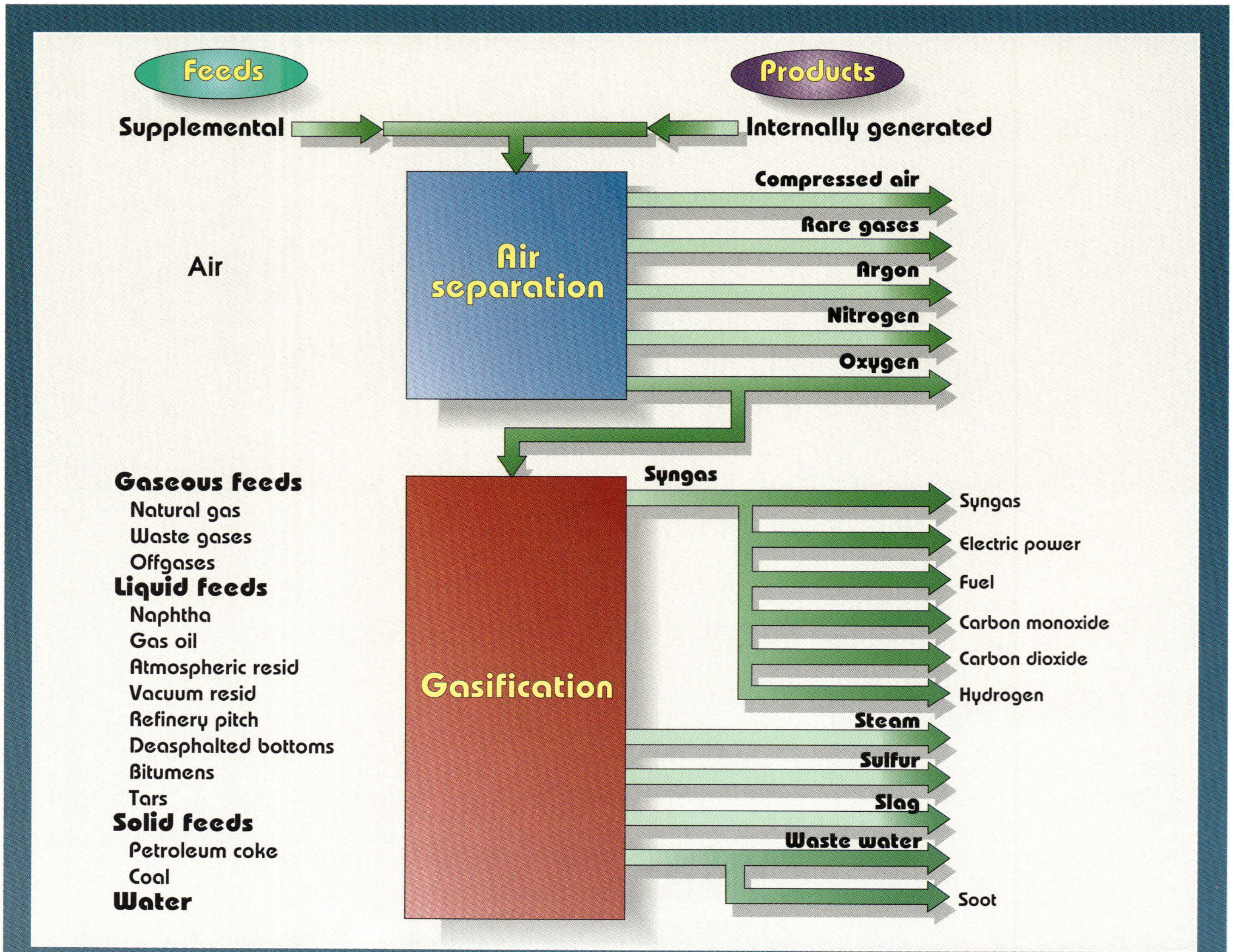

Source: Saras SpA, Sarroch, Sardinia

IPE

Table 1

Typical Syngas compositions

Component	Syngas composition, mole % Heavy oil feed	Coke feed
CO	45.62	47.72
H_2	43.32	30.33
CO_2	8.17	17.88
H_2O	0.27	0.12
CH_4	0.35	0.01
Ar	1.00	0.83
N_2	0.53	1.27
H_2S	0.71	1.76
COS	0.00	0.02
NH_3	0.00	0.00

Source: Fluor Daniel Inc., Irvine, Calif.

on the other hand, often can be processed profitably in a gasifier. Heaven warned that the economics of such projects must be evaluated relative to hydroprocessing technologies.

Vacuum resids containing high concentrations of metals and sulfur make attractive gasification feeds. In addition, technologies such as coking and solvent deasphalting can increase the benefits of a gasifier if installed upstream of it.

While it is possible for a refinery to fully absorb the steam, electricity, and hydrogen produced by a gasifier, product sales will be necessary with most units. Heaven calculated that gasification of 1 ton of coke produces about 1 ton of ammonia, while gasification of 1,000 b/d of heavy oil produces about 32 mw of electricity. Table 1 shows typical compositions for synthesis gas produced from these two feeds.

If hydrogen is the product most desired, the carbon monoxide can be converted almost entirely to hydrogen via the steam shift reaction ($CO + H_2O \rightarrow CO_2 + H_2$). Star Enterprise uses this processing scheme at its refinery in Convent, La., as does Shell Nederland Raffinaderij at its refinery in Pernis, The Netherlands (see photo).

Gasification capacity

According to Dale R. Simbeck, vice-president of technology for SFA Pacific Inc., Mountain View, Calif., 354 gasifiers were operating in 113 facilities around the world in late 1996. These plants produced 10 billion cfd of syngas from a feed slate comprising 47% resid, 42% coal, 8% gas, and 3% coke and refinery wastes. Of the output, said Simbeck, 45% went into chemicals, 26% into liquid fuels, 24% into power, and 5% into gaseous fuels.

The combination of technological advances and deregulation of the power industry is boosting non-utility electricity generation.

"The oil industry could represent the future of power generation, thanks to deregulation," said Simbeck. "In the future, oil refineries could comprise a major segment of the power industry, thanks to gasification-based power generation and the lack of high-value markets for low-quality residues and coke."

A number of gasification projects were under construction in 1996 or had recently started up. The following sections will describe some of them.

A Dutch project

Shell Nederland Raffinaderij B.V. was scheduled to complete a $2.2 billion expansion of its refinery at Pernis, The Netherlands, in May 1997. The upgrade enables the refinery to reduce emissions and meet demand for light, environmentally clean transportation fuels.

Cornerstones of the project are a 56,000 b/sd, single-train hydrocracker and a 1,650 mt/sd, three-train gasification unit. The gasifier produces hydrogen and sulfur-free fuel gas from visbreaker residue. The fuel gas is consumed in a 115-mw cogeneration plant, also part of the upgrade.

For the hydrogen-production options, Shell chose gasification over steam methane reforming (SMR) for several reasons. SMR does not reduce fuel oil production, as gasification does. SMR does, however, diminish crude flexibility, in terms of both sulfur and gravity, said Herman van Wechem, head of refinery technology. For this reason, a more expensive crude diet is required with SMR, as is costly natural gas feed.

Shell's gasification unit is based on the Shell Gasification Hydrogen Process (SGHP), which operates at 50-75 bar and 1,200-1,500° C. (Fig. 2). Feed to the gasifier is heavy, vacuum-flashed, visbreaker residue. About 1,600 mt/sd of oxygen comes from nearby third-party sources.

Shell gasification hydrogen process — Fig. 2

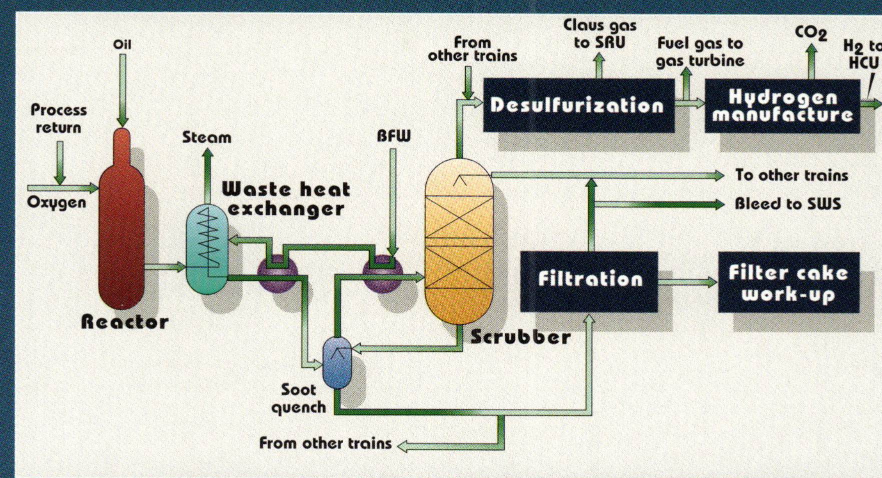

Source: Shell International Petroleum Mij., The Hague — IPE

Integration of hydrogen and utilities — Fig. 3

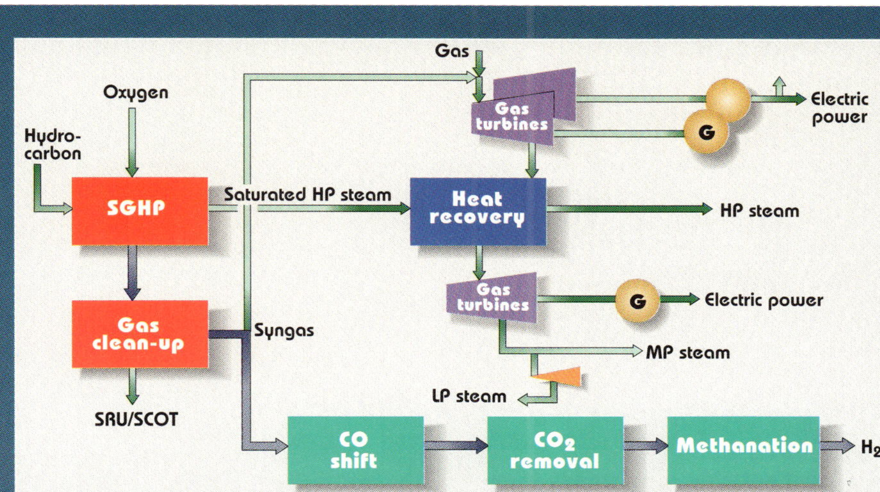

Source: Shell Nederland Raffinaderij B.V. Pernis, The Netherlands — IPE

These streams are fed, along with steam, to gasification reactors equipped with specially designed burners. Here, noncatalytic partial oxidation of the hydrocarbons takes place via an endothermic reaction at 1,500° C. ($C_xH_y + x/2\ O_2 \rightarrow xCO + y/2\ H_2$).

The CO and H_2 products contain contaminants such as H_2S, COS, HCN, nickel, iron, carbonyls, ash, and soot. The syngas flows from the reactor into a waste-heat exchanger, where primary heat recovery takes place.

The stream is cooled to about 340° C. (644° F.) by exchange with boiler feedwater, producing high-pressure (100 bar), saturated steam. Part of the steam is used to preheat the gasifier feeds. The remainder is sent to steam turbines to generate electricity and low-pressure steam.

Shell selected a large, three-train system because, in the event one gasifier goes off line, the hydrocracker's hydrogen requirements can be delivered from the remaining two trains.

"Under normal three-train operation, syngas in excess of the requirement for hydrogen production will be used as gas turbine fuel," said Peter Ladeur of Shell Internationale Petroleum Maatschappij B.V., The Hague.

Shell's gasification process uses a soot-ash quench scrubber to remove solids. Solids-free syngas is treated in a single-train, H_2S-removal unit.

About two thirds of the treated syngas is sent to a hydrogen plant integrated with the gasifier. The hydrogen plant comprises a two-stage CO shift (high temperature and low temperature), carbon dioxide removal, and methanation.

As part of the gasification complex, Shell installed new amine treating, sulfur recovery, and tail gas units. Shell chose Lurgi GmbH's Rectisol process for removal of H_2S from the syngas, and for removal of CO_2 downstream of the low-temperature CO shift.

Acid gas from the Rectisol unit is sent to the refinery's Claus unit. The treated syngas is then reacted with steam in a CO shift unit, where an exothermic reaction takes place ($H_2 + CO + H_2O \leftrightarrow 2H_2 + CO_2$).

The CO_2 in the syngas is removed in another Rectisol unit, and the remaining hydrogen stream is sent to the methanation unit, which converts the last traces of carbon monoxide to methane in an exothermic reaction ($CO + 3H_2 \rightarrow CH_4 + H_2O$).

Two thirds of the syngas product will be converted to

Flow diagram of IGCC plant slated for Sarroch Fig. 4

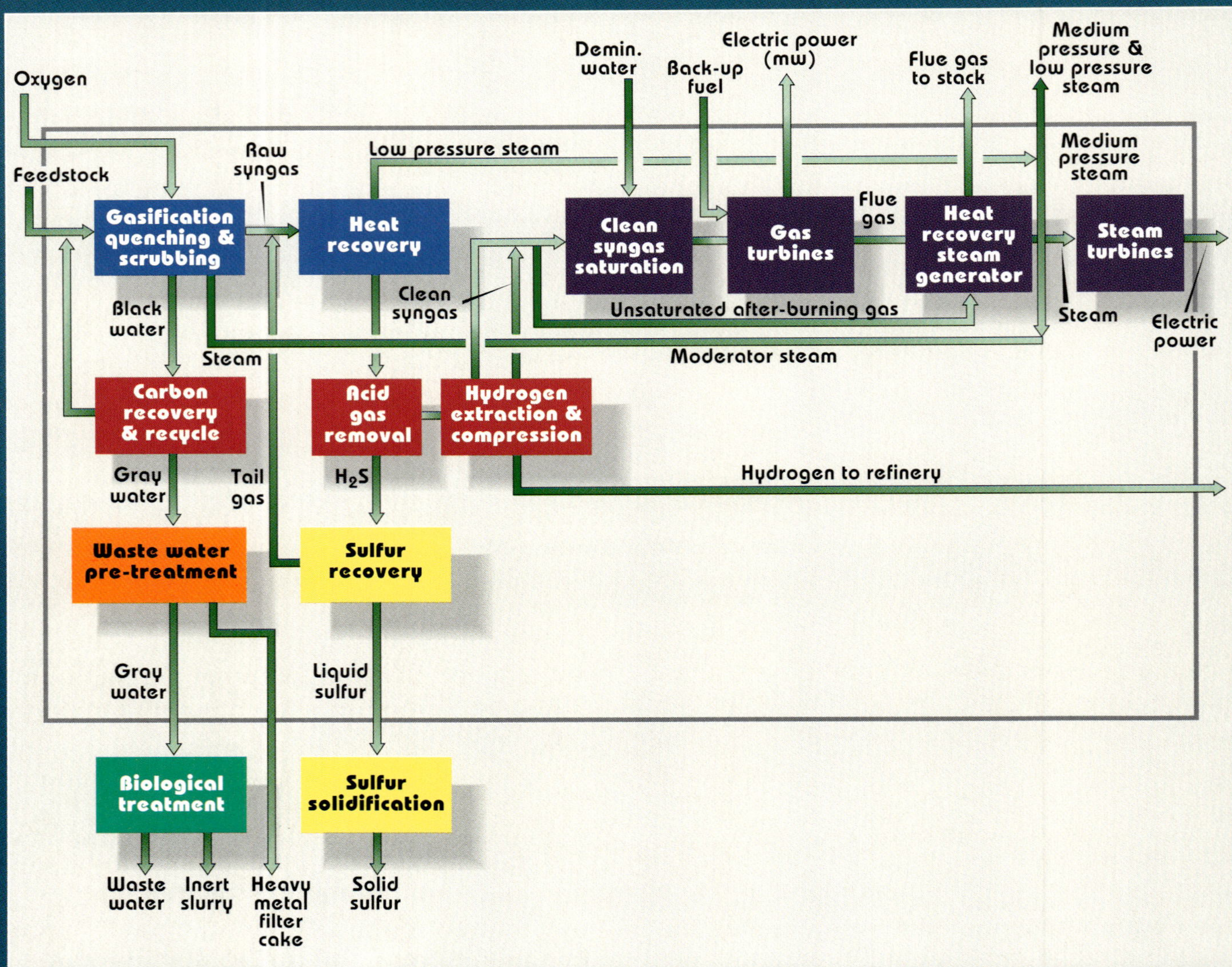

Source: Saras SpA Sarroch, Sardinia IPE

hydrogen. The gasifier will produce 255 tons/day hydrogen, to be used in the new hydrocracker.

The remaining third of the syngas production will be converted to 115 mw of electricity in a combined-cycle plant.

Two gas turbines form the heart of the 115-mw cogeneration plant. A large share of the electricity is exported to the public grid.

Fig. 3 shows the integration of utilities with hydrogen manufacture via gasification.

Table 2 summarizes Shell's projections for the environmental impact of the Pernis upgrade. These data were developed before start-up of the SGHP unit.

Sardinia's unit

A joint venture of Saras SpA Raffinerie Sarde and Enron Corp., Houston, in 1996 was planning a $1 billion integrated gasification combined-cycle (IGCC) plant at Saras' 285,000 b/d refinery in Sarroch, Sardinia. The joint venture, called Sarlux SpA, is headquartered in Milan.

The unit is scheduled to start up in 1999. Fig. 4 shows a flow diagram of the Sarlux plant.

The plant will use the Texaco quench-type gasification process. A flow diagram of Texaco's process is shown in Fig. 5.

Air Liquide will build, own, and operate an air-separation unit off site. Oxygen from this plant will be fed to the gasifier along with the feed.

The unit will gasify 18,000 b/d of visbreaker tar to produce low-pressure steam, hydrogen, and synthesis gas. The synthesis gas will fuel gas turbines to generate 550 mw of electricity. Sarlux estimates that the unit will meet 40% of electricity demand on the island, which is home to 1.6 million people.

The feedstock can contain as much as 6% sulfur and 1,000 ppm combined nickel and vanadium. Saras' manager of strategic planning, Giuseppe Citterio, said that, although there are some limits on the viscosity and gravity of the feed, they basically boil down to the ability to pump the material.

The syngas produced in the gasifier will feed the combined-cycle unit. The turbines will burn more than 600,000 cu m/hr of syngas, comprising 20-25% hydrogen, 25-30% carbon monoxide, and 35-40% water.

Hot exhaust gases from the turbines will be sent to heat-recovery steam generators. Most of this steam will be used to drive steam turbines to produce more electricity. The remainder will be used in the gasification step as a process modifier and in the refinery as process steam.

Acid gases in the syngas (mostly hydrogen sulfide and carbonyl sulfide) are removed in downstream treating units (Fig. 4). Because the syngas is stripped of sulfur before it is combusted, SO_2 scrubbers are not needed.

Electricity produced by the IGCC plant will be supplied to ENEL, Italy's state-owned power company.

Another Italian project

A joint venture company called api Energia SpA began construction on a 280-mw IGCC unit at anonima raffineria di Ancona SpA's 77,000 b/d refinery at Falconara Marittima on Italy's Adriatic coast (see map). Joint venture partners are anonima petroli italiana SpA (api) and ABB Sae Sadelmi SpA. (Anonima raffineria di Ancona is a subsidiary of anonima petroli italiana.)

By the year 2000, three Italian refineries will be generating about 1,300 mw of electricity from gasification of heavy residues, said Roberto del Bravo, ABB Sae Sadelmi SpA, Rome. The electricity will be put on the Italian grid.

The third project in this Italian trio is a 500-mw IGCC plant planned for ISAB SpA's 235,000 b/d refinery at Priolo Gargallo, Sicily (see map). London's Mission Energy is a partner in the ISAB project.

The api Energia IGCC project is valued at more than $1 billion. It will gasify high-sulfur heavy oil produced at the Falconara refinery. The design feedstock is vacuum-visbroken tar from Arabian Heavy crude oil.

The api project also will use Texaco gasification technology. Under normal operating conditions, the unit will process 1,400 tons/day of heavy residues and produce 3,120 tons/day of syngas. The syngas will be mixed with 3,050 tons/day of nitrogen to produce a low-NOx fuel for burning in the gas turbine.

A flow diagram of the api IGCC plant is shown in Fig. 6.

The Texaco-licensed section of api's IGCC project includes:

- One feed preparation section.
- Two quench gasification and scrubbing sections.
- One carbon extraction unit.
- One gray-water treatment section.

The syngas from the gasifiers will be washed with water to remove solid particles of unconverted carbon and metals from the resid feed. The unconverted carbon will be recovered via naphtha extraction. The waste water from this unit will contain metals; it will be treated in the gray-water treatment unit.

The water leaving this unit is treatable in the refinery waste water system. The gray-water treatment unit will discharge a filter cake, from which metals can be recovered.

ABB Lummus Global, Bloomfield, N.J., designed the gas-cooling section of the IGCC plant. This section will recover waste heat and produce steam at three pressure levels. A gas expander will recover pressure energy from the syngas.

A COS hydrolysis reactor will convert COS to H_2S, which can be removed in the acid gas removal section. UOP's Selexol process will be used to remove acid gases. Claus units will recover elemental sulfur from the acid gases.

ABB Power Generation designed the combined-cycle plant, which will comprise a gas turbine, heat recovery steam generated, and steam turbine. The gas turbine will be equipped with low-NO_x burners.

Fig. 7 shows how the addition of the IGCC plant and a 3,000 ton/day gas oil desulfurization unit will affect the refinery's

Fig. 5

Gasification process

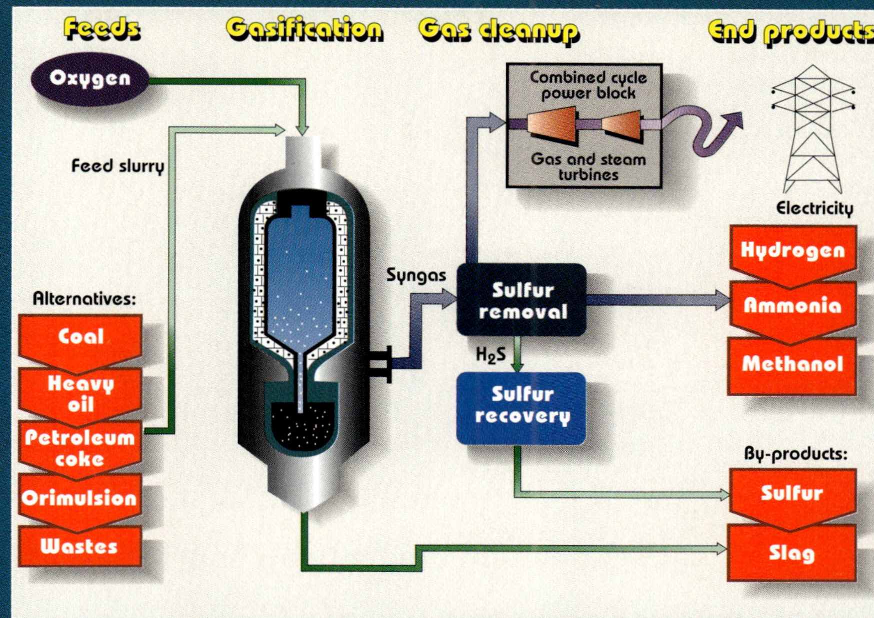

Source: Texaco Inc., White Plains, N.Y.

IPE

Table 2

Projected environmental impact of shell unit

	Before	After
Refinery mass balance, million metric tons/year (mt/y):		
In		
High-sulfur crude	11.3	15.0
Low-sulfur crude	4.5	2.8
Other feedstocks	2.1	0.1
Total intake	17.9	17.9
Out		
White products	12.8	14.0
Fuel oil	3.5	2.1
Sulfur	0.11	0.30
Total output	16.4	16.4
Crude oil properties:		
Avg. gravity, °API	32	31
Avg. sulfur content, wt %	1.55	2.30
Sulfur balance, million mt/y:		
Sulfur in crude, feeds	0.28	0.41
Sulfur recovery	0.11	0.30
Sulfur in products	0.15	0.10
Sulfur emissions	0.02	0.01
S recovery, % of S intake	38	73
Refinery emissions:		
SO_2, 1,000 mt/y	35	24
NOx, 1,000 mt/y	12	7
Particulates, 1,000 mt/y	4.0	1.9
CO_2, million mt/y	5.0	6.1
Global emissions (refinery + products):		
SO_2, 1,000 mt/y	348	206
CO_2, million mt/y	56.6	56.8

Source: Shell Nederland Raffinaderij B.V., Pernis, The Netherlands

yield slate. Diesel production will increase substantially, while production of high and low-sulfur fuel oils will be eliminated. The only fuel oil the refinery will produce will be a "very low sulfur" grade.

Api's IGCC plant is scheduled to start up in second quarter 1999.

A small Kansas gasifier

Texaco Refining & Marketing Inc. started up a small coke-fueled gasifier in June 1996 at its 100,000 b/d El Dorado, Kan., refinery. The unit is unique in that it gasifies not only hydrocarbon fuel but also refinery waste products.

Another interesting characteristic of the plant is that Texaco based its size on utility requirements and coke sales volumes. It produces virtually 100% of the refinery's electricity needs and enough heat to generate 40% of its steam requirements. As a result, Texaco was able to shut down one of the fired boilers used for steam production at the refinery.

The unit is just large enough to handle excess coke production from the refinery. Of the 800 tons/day of coke produced at El Dorado, Texaco was selling about 15% at break-even prices. In addition to this 120 tons/day of coke, 10 tons/day of refinery wastes were deemed suitable for gasification. These wastes include:

- API separator bottoms.
- Acid-soluble oil from the alkylation unit.
- Primary sludge from the waste water treatment unit.
- Phenolic residue.

The refinery's sulfur-recovery and tail gas treating units were not large enough to allow Texaco to increase its use of high-sulfur crudes. Because an air separation plant had to be added to feed the gasifier, oxygen from this unit can be used to enrich the sulfur plant, thus increasing capacity.

Fig. 6

Flow diagram of api IGCC plant

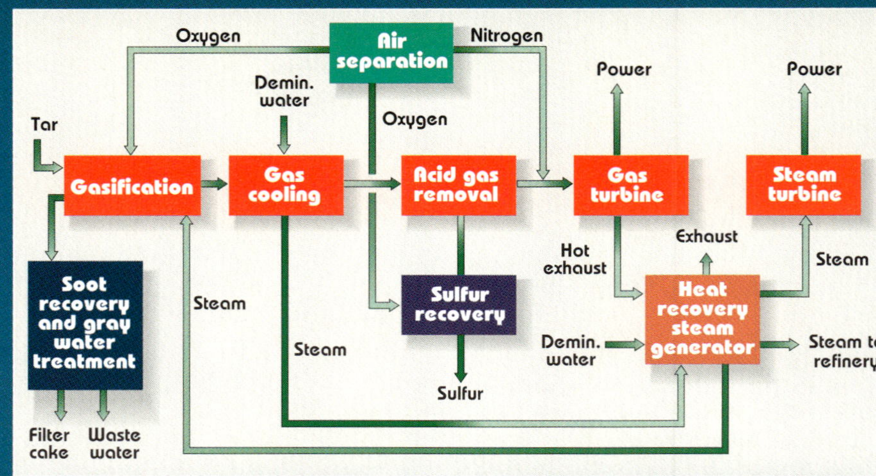

Source: api Energia ApS, Rome

IPE

Fig. 7

Refinery products before and after IGCC plant*

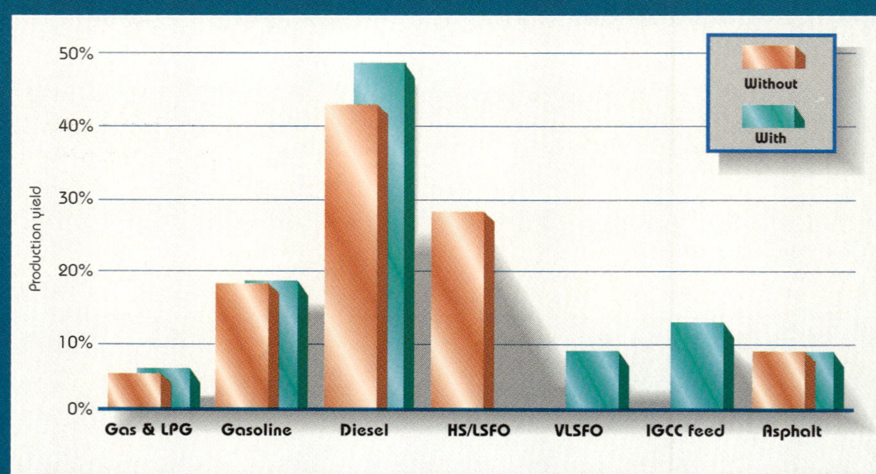

Source: anonima petroli italiana SpA, Rome

IPE

Nitrogen from the air separation plant can now be used for process requirements, which all but eliminated the refinery's purchases of liquid nitrogen.

Syngas from the gasifier is cleaned up with the same general scheme as described for the two Italian projects. The clean syngas is then fed, along with supplemental natural gas, to a gas turbine.

Nitrogen from the air separation plant is added to the mixture to reduce NO_x formation. The turbine produces 40 mw of electricity and 180,000 lb/hr of superheated steam at 600 psi and 150 psi.

The process produces a slag that comprises about 1% of the original coke mass.

Texaco won an important regulatory victory with this unit. Because it processes wastes, the U.S. Environmental Protection Agency (EPA) could have deemed it a waste treatment unit, in which case Texaco would have had to undertake an expensive and time-consuming permitting process.

The Kansas Department of Health & Environment (KDHE) examined the benefits of the unit and sought support from the EPA in designating it a processing facility. In May 1995, EPA formally allowed KDHE to consider the unit a refinery process rather than a waste treatment unit.

At start-up, Texaco expected to save $12-14 million/year in utility costs and $1 million/year in waste shipment and disposal costs. Additional cost savings will come from steam production and a less-expensive crude slate.

Gasification's future

In addition to the units described in detail, Star Enterprise planned to build an IGCC plant at its 140,000 b/d refinery in Delaware City, Del. It will employ the Texaco gasification process. Exxon Chemical Co. also was reported to be planning a Texaco gasifier at its Baytown, Tex., chemicals complex.

Texaco is clearly the leader in gasification unit licensing. At the beginning of 1996, Texaco claimed a total installed capacity of its licensed gasification units of more than 2 billion scfd. Gasification of coal accounts for a large portion of this total.

By 2000, Texaco expected the total installed capacity of its units to exceed 4 billion scfd. This increase was expected to be fueled largely by petroleum-based feedstocks. IPE

The Express Pipeline from near Hardisty, Alta., to Casper, Wyo., was commissioned in 1997. It moves crude oil over 784 miles in a 24-in. line. Photograph by Paul Connor, Calgary.

Need for pipeline construction expected to remain strong

At mid-1997, pipeline operators looking past 2000 were even more optimistic than they had been a year earlier. Steady growth in worldwide demand for crude oil, natural gas, and petroleum products promised to keep pipeline construction active.

As has been the case for several years, demand for natural gas, especially in developing regions and for use in power generation, lies behind several major projects.

In Canada, a major restructuring of pipeline transportation got under way in 1996 and advanced in 1997, pushed by western Canadian gas producers' desire to gain access to strong U.S. Midwest demand. Midwestern demand, coupled with strong markets in the U.S. Northeast, has also pushed several gas-gathering projects in the Gulf of Mexico.

Gas-pipeline projects in Latin America and Europe were moving ahead in 1997 as those areas' economies demanded more and cleaner energy.

The latest Oil & Gas Journal pipeline-construction data evince these trends and derive from a survey of world pipeline operators, industry sources, and published information.

At the beginning of 1997, more than 71,000 miles of crude oil, product, and natural gas pipeline were planned for 1997 and beyond, a jump from plans set a year earlier. Cost of these plans will exceed $68 billion.

Cost estimates are based on U.S. average cost per mile for onshore and offshore gas pipeline construction as determined by Oil & Gas Journal's most recent annual pipeline economics report.

Cost projections assume 90% of all construction to be onshore and 10% offshore. Pipelines of 32 in. OD or larger are assumed to be onshore projects.

South America

A significant gas pipeline in the southern cone of South America started in 1997.

Pipeline construction, 1997 and beyond*

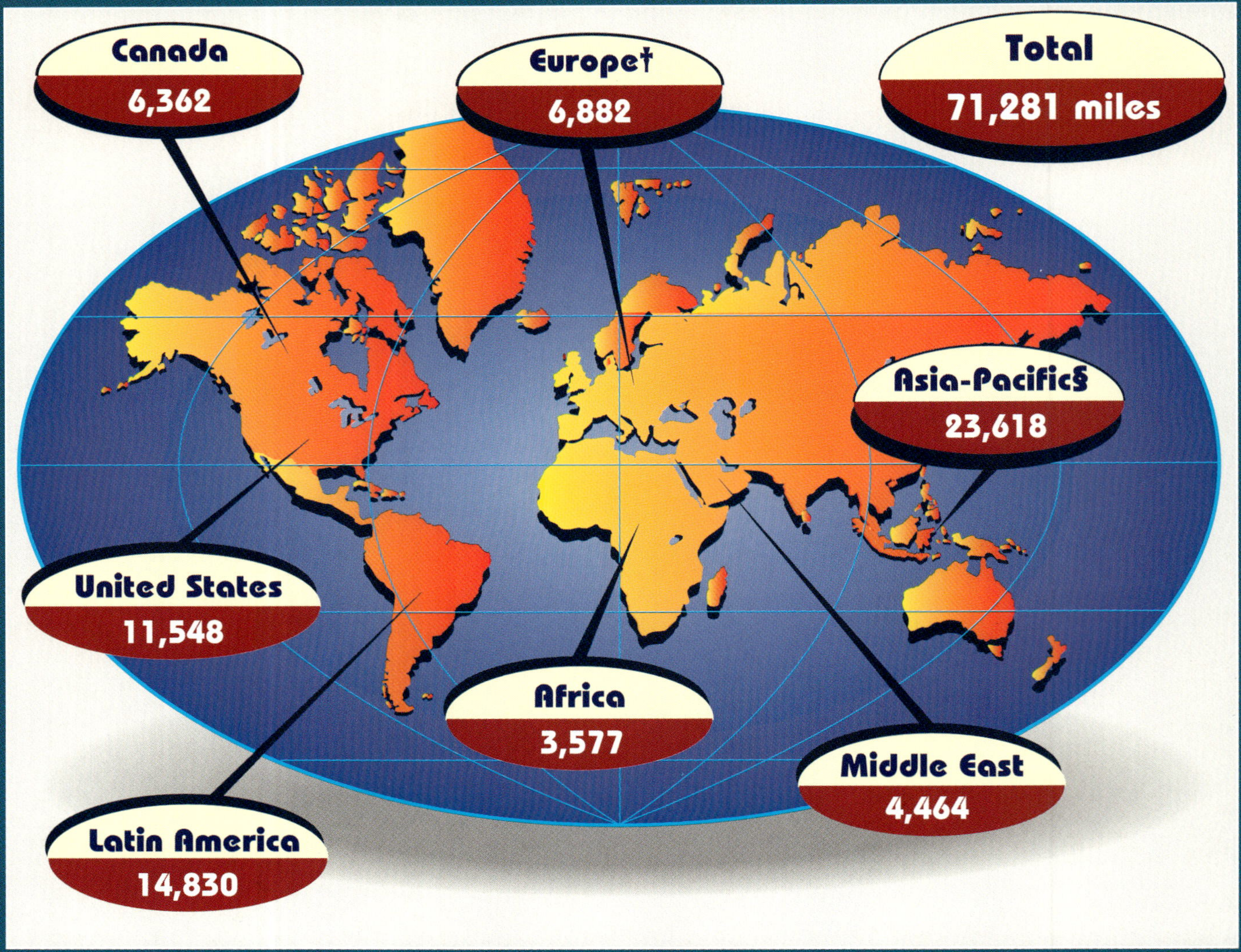

*Projects under way in 1997 and to be completed in 1997 or later. Includes some probable major projects whose installation will begin later than 1997. †Including Russia and former Soviet Republics west of the Ural Mountains. §Including Russia and former Soviet republics east of the Ural Mountains.

IPE

Gasoducto GasAndes SA, Santiago, Chile, completed pipelay on the $350 million, 287-mile, 24-in. line from La Mora, Argentina, to Santiago. The line draws historically antagonistic countries into closer interdependence.

Gas from the line will fuel several power plants supplying electricity to Santiago. In addition, Metrogas SA, Santiago's gas distribution company and a partner in GasAndes, was installing the city's first natural-gas distribution system.

NOVA Gas International, 56.5% interest holder in GasAndes and the pipeline's project manager, said the line's initial capacity will be 124 MMcfd. Capacity will expand to 212 MMcfd in 2000 and 600 MMcfd by 2007.

Plans called for work to start on a 68-mile extension to Quillota, 19 miles from Valparaiso on Chile's Pacific coast when mainline construction was complete.

Another major gas-pipeline project between Argentina and Chile received a setback late in 1996.

NOVA Corp. withdrew from its partnership with CMS Energy Corp., Dearborn, Mich., and Empresa Nacional de Electricidad SA to build the 509-mile, 24-in. GasAtacama pipeline from Argentina's Noroeste basin to Mejillones, Chile.

CMS expected to announce by the middle of 1997 the addition of a major Argentine gas producer as a partner in the project. All permits had been obtained, said CMS.

Its intended market is a proposed 400-mw combined-cycle power plant in Mejillones. The pipeline partners are also partners in the power plant.

The company has said that laterals along the pipeline route are possible to Antofagasta, Tocopilla, and Calma in northern Chile. In a 30-day open season that concluded Jan. 15, 1997, CMS Energy said nominated volumes came to more than 180 MMcfd, about 21% more than the originally planned 150 MMcfd anticipated design of the pipeline.

In Colombia, gas was to begin flowing in 1997 through the 214-mile, 20-in. line built for TransGas de Occidente SA. Partners in the project are TransCanada 34%; BP International 20%; Gas Natural del Oriente 14%; PetroColombia 12%; and Destillados Agricolas, Fluor Daniel, Inversora Arlloz, and Spie-Capag 5% each.

Capacity in the mainline will be about 220 MMcfd, says TransGas' project manager. And more than 260 miles of laterals were being laid to serve 47 communities in addition to the major city of Cali. La Guajira fields in the Mariquita region on the Caribbean coast are supplying the gas.

In nearby Bolivia, with the apparently successful partial privatization of Yacimientos Petroliferos Fiscales Bolivianos (YPFB) in late 1996, the proposed 3,700-km gas pipeline from Santa Cruz to Southeast Brazil took a major step forward.

High bidder for YPFB's pipeline unit Transportadora de Hidrocarburos with $263.5 million was a joint venture of Enron Development Corp. and Shell International Gas Ltd.

The joint effort was viewed as an indication that gas from Shell's proposed Camisea development in Peru may be available to augment supplies headed to Brazil. Previous plans for Camisea included gas and condensate pipelines across the Andes to serve Lima. That remained a possibility.

From Santa Cruz, the Bolivia-Brazil pipeline would extend to Corumba, Brazil, and on to Campinas and Sao Paulo.

The first 2,840 km would consist of 28-in. line; the remainder, of decreasing diameters of 22, 20, 18, 16, and 14 in. In the original contract between the countries, Bolivia was to supply 3.7 tcf/year for 20 years.

European gas demand

Expansion to feed Europe's gas-transmission system is likely to accelerate the next few years.

The European Investment Bank (EIB), Luxembourg, estimated in late 1996 that gas demand could increase to about 390 billion cu m/year by 2000 from the 1996 level of 330 billion cu m/year. By 2010, demand could reach 410-450 billion cu m/year.

To meet this increase, Europe must look to greater imports mainly from Algeria, Russia, and Norway. Pipeline import capacity at the time of the EIB report was 200 billion cu m/year with 40 billion cu m/year of LNG coming into the region.

Increasing capacity on the Trans-Med pipeline to Italy is one project that could begin to meet the increased demand, along with completion in late 1997 or early 1998 of the entire Maghreb pipeline from Algerian gas fields to Spain and Portugal. Gas could flow through these countries into France. European LNG terminals may also be in for expansion.

Two major projects from the Norwegian North Sea will move ahead to attempt to meet increased European demand. Den norske stats oljeselskap AS (Statoil) let contracts in late 1996 for its 528-mile, 42-in. NorFra gas pipeline from Sleipner field to Dunkirk, France.

Also, Statoil expected by 2000 to have started operating the nearly 870-mile, 36-42-in. Europipe II, making deliveries to Germany.

And construction on the long-planned, much-discussed pipeline between England and France, known as Interconnector, got into full swing in 1997. Pipelay from Bacton began, along with work from the Zeebrugge, Belgium, end.

Interconnector will be a 150-mile, 40-in., 1.9 bcfd line that will deliver as much as 815 MMcfd of gas to Britain. Start-up was slated for Oct. 1, 1998.

Offshore gas, eastern oil

Another major European pipeline prospect is a gas line from Danish discoveries in the North Sea and from Norwegian and U.K. offshore pipeline systems to Denmark.

Dansk Olie & Naturgas AS (DONG) expects Danish gas demand to rise to about 9.5 billion cu m/year by 2000. The two pipelines bringing gas from Tyra field in 1997 were running at or near capacity of 7.5 billion cu m/year.

In early 1996, DONG began talks with Norway's gas negotiating committee to secure gas for the future. Any new line would likely be rated at about 4 billion cu m/year and would probably run from the South Arne discovery area to landfall north of Esbjerg.

Another line for Norwegian gas is in the works. Norsk Hydro AS disclosed plans to build a gas pipeline from Oseberg field to the Statpipe terminal in Heimdal field. The $150 million project calls for 68 miles of 36-in. pipe; start-up would come in 2000.

Elsewhere, aggressive development by 1999 of Russia's Yubileinoye, Yamsovey, and Khavutin gas fields could lead to production of as much as 1.4 tcf/year. The gas could flow through a pipeline that would traverse Russia, Belarus, Poland, and Germany. Financing at midyear was in doubt, according to the European Investment Bank.

The puzzle of moving Caspian Sea crude oil moved a step closer to being solved in late 1996 when Mobil agreed to participate in a restructured Caspian Pipline Consortium (CPC). The new agreement allows Mobil to exercise its right to acquire a 7.5% equity interest in the planned pipeline.

Overall, the project calls for rehabilitation and upgrading of an existing line from Tengiz to Komsomolsk, construction of a new pipeline from Komsomolsk to the Black Sea, and a loading complex at or near Novorossiisk, Russia. Construction would allow Tengiz to produce more than 200,000 b/d by 2000 and nearly 800,000 b/d by 2010.

Pipeline construction is to be completed by yearend 1999 and provide export capacity of 580,000 b/d of oil.

Pipeline construction in 1997 and beyond*

	4-10 in.	12-20 in.	22-30 in.	32+ in.	Total
	Miles				
GAS PIPELINES					
U.S.	1,464	854	2,970	2,887	8,175
Canada	596	275	1,239	2,942	5,052
Latin America	693	1,510	3,071	5,535	10,809
Asia-Pacific†	487	4,063	2,225	5,529	12,304
Europe§	291	460	569	4,255	5,575
Middle East	10	127	62	2,357	2,556
Africa	—	163	27	675	865
Total gas	**3,541**	**7,452**	**10,163**	**24,180**	**45,336**
CRUDE PIPELINES					
U.S.	130	791	666	—	1,587
Canada	61	297	—	272	630
Latin America	492	538	126	1,500	2,656
Asia-Pacific†	—	2,937	4,062	—	6,999
Europe§	75	141	—	900	1,116
Middle East	62	197	129	—	388
Africa	199	1,593	42	46	1,880
Total crude	**1,019**	**6,494**	**5,025**	**2,718**	**15,256**
PRODUCT PIPELINES					
U.S.	936	850	—	—	1,786
Canada	560	120	—	—	680
Latin America	100	1,265	—	—	1,365
Asia-Pacific†	184	4,060	—	71	4,315
Europe§	—	191	—	—	191
Middle East	108	1,412	—	—	1,520
Africa	371	263	198	—	832
Total product	**2,259**	**8,161**	**198**	**71**	**10,689**
WORLD TOTAL					
Gas	3,541	7,452	10,163	24,180	45,336
Crude	1,019	6,494	5,025	2,718	15,256
Product	2,259	8,161	198	71	10,689
Total	**6,819**	**22,107**	**15,386**	**26,969**	**71,281**

*Projects planned to begin in 1997 or later. †Regions east of the Ural Mountains and south of the Caucasus Mountains, excluding the Middle East. §Regions west of the Ural Mountains and north of the Caucasus Mountains.

Canadian changes

In recent years, movement of plentiful, cheaply produced gas from western Canada to U.S. Midwest markets has been constrained by takeaway capacity from Alberta to markets east and south.

In 1996, several major pipeline projects were floated to bypass traditional export routes. The implications of some of these projects struck at the very heart of Canada's regulatory mechanisms for ensuring the economic viability of pipeline expansions.

Sidebooms maneuver concrete-coated, 24-in. pipe for Express Pipeline's crossing of the South Saskatchewan River in southern Alberta.

By far the most ambitious was Alliance Pipeline, a 1,900-mile, 36-in. dense-phase pipeline proposed to run from near Fort St. John, B.C., to near Chicago. At its initial proposal, the project was estimated to cost $2.5 billion and be designed to carry about 1 bcfd.

During an open season conducted in fall 1996, Alliance signed up 38 shippers for nearly 1.5 bcfd with eight more shippers at some point of negotiation.

The project directly challenged Alberta's principal gas pipeline, NOVA Gas Transmission, and thereby the current system of moving gas across and out of the province. Producers in southern Alberta complained that the province's system of equivalent tariffs forced them to subsidize gas from northern fields and to thereby endure diminished netbacks on gas delivered to the Midwest.

As a response to growing pressures for additional and more affordable capacity out of western Canada to midwestern U.S. markets, TransCanada PipeLines Ltd. in July 1996 revised its system expansion plans for 1997. TransCanada more than doubled what it had planned to spend to about $900 million (Canadian) from nearly $264 million.

Also, in a move aimed at projects that challenge its dominance of Alberta gas shipments, NOVA Gas Transmission requested in late 1996 regulatory approval to move up to 1997 a $99 million (Canadian) expansion originally scheduled for 1998.

Early in 1997, NOVA proposed to Alberta's Energy and Utilities Board (EUB) a new rate structure. Still another plan materialized, however.

A group of Amoco Canada, Shell Canada, and CU Gas unveiled plans to build the $450 million (Canadian) Alberta Pipeline Project with 1.1-1.4 bcfd of capacity. Tolls on the 404-

Construction advanced in 1996 on the 214-mile, 20-in. TransGas de Occidente S.A. project in Colombia. The line began operations in the second quarter 1997. Photograph courtesy of TransCanada PipeLines Ltd., Calgary.

mile, 20-36-in. pipeline would undercut NOVA's, said its backers.

Across the continent, gas movements from Nova Scotia's offshore fields to eastern Canada and the U.S. Northeast moved closer to reality.

A group of Sable Island gas developers led by Mobil Oil Canada Ltd. plans the Sable Offshore Energy Project (SOEP), formally proposed to the NEB in October 1996. SOEP calls for development of about 3 tcf of gas in Thebaud, Venture, North Triumph, South Venture, Alma, and Glenelg fields near Sable Island.

Proposed facilities include production of gas and natural gas liquids, initial treatment offshore, and transportation by two-phase gathering line to a gas plant in the Country Harbour area of Nova Scotia.

NGL will move via an onshore line to the Point Tupper area for further processing and shipping via the Maritimes & Northeast line into eastern Canada, New England, and the U.S. Northeast. SOEP's planned offshore/onshore line would be 140 miles.

To move gas from the Sable Island development, two projects have been advanced. Maritimes & Northeast Pipeline LLC is a proposed 729-mile, $975 million pipeline to bring gas from the Sable Island area to New England.

In late 1996, the project jumped the first regulatory hurdle to realization: The U.S. Department of Energy approved import-export authorization for as much as 636 bcf for 2 years.

Phase I of Maritimes & Northeast in the U.S. is to be a 64-mile, 24-in. line between Dracut, Mass., and Wells, Me.

Phase II, in the U.S., will involve about 230 miles of 24-in. and nearly 2 miles of 30-in. line from the Phase I connect near Wells to near Woodland, Me., near the international border.

Alternatively, TransCanada and utility Gaz Metropolitain Co., Montreal, want to build a line from the Sable Island development that would run through Quebec to the U.S. TransCanada also wants to ship some Sable Island gas on the proposed Portland Natural Gas System (PNGS) to Boston. TransCanada owns an interest in PNGS.

The Express crude oil pipeline made swift transition from idea to reality in 1996 and early in 1997.

Express Pipeline Ltd. is a 785-mile, 24 in., 172,000-b/d capacity line to bring Canadian crude oil from near Hardisty, Alta., to Casper, Wyo. From there, much of the crude moves via the Platte Pipeline to near Wood River, Ill., and U.S. Midwest refineries. Some will likely supply Rocky Mountain refineries.

U.S. gulf oil lines

Crude oil began moving through a major new pipeline in the Gulf of Mexico in 1996.

Phase 1, 16 and 20-in., Poseidon pipeline began moving crude oil 117 miles from Garden Banks Block 72 to a Leviathan Gas Pipeline Partners LP platform on Ship Shoal South Addition Block 332.

The 24-in. Phase 2 section came on stream later, delivering as much as 400,000 bbl of oil through a landing at Caillou Island, La. Poseidon connects near Houma, La., with Texaco Pipeline Inc. systems.

A unit of Texaco Inc. operates the system through Poseidon Oil Pipeline Co. LLC, a 50-50 venture of Texaco and Leviathan, Houston.

Also in 1996, Shell Oil Co.'s Amberjack pipeline began moving crude oil from the Bullwinkle tension leg platform (TLP) in 2,860 ft of water on Green Canyon Block 143 to Fourchon, La.

Another Shell offshore pipeline began shipping crude to Fourchon from the Mars TLP in 2,933 ft of water on Mississippi Canyon Block 807. Both pipelines deliver to Louisiana Offshore Oil Port.

Units of Amoco Pipeline Co., CNG Energy Services Corp., and PanEnergy Field Services Inc. placed in service Dec. 1, 1996, a $50 million oil gathering system in the Central Gulf of Mexico.

The 160,000 b/d pipeline serves Main Pass and Viosca Knoll, where several producers have made discoveries that will begin production by 2000. The system can also gather oil from deepwater Mississippi Canyon wells.

The project consists of 64 miles of 18 in. line from Main Pass Block 225 to a Shell crude oil terminal on Main Pass Block 69. From there, oil flows into Louisiana through the Shell Delta Pipeline System. PanEnergy Field Services managed construction for the partners. Amoco Pipeline is operating it and marketing capacity on the system.

Gulf gas plans

Among the many systems proposed to bring Gulf of Mexico gas ashore, Texaco Natural Gas plans to build a gas gathering, transmission, and processing system to support deepwater natural gas developments in the central Gulf of Mexico.

A $300 million construction program includes a 105-mile, 30-in. pipeline across five federal planning areas, gas processing at Larose in Lafourche Parish, La., and a natural gas liquids fractionator at Paradis, St. Charles Parish, La. The line will extend from about 130 miles offshore in about 2,000 ft of water to the Larose cryogenic gas processing plant.

Both line and plant will have design capacities of 600 MMcfd, expandable to 750 MMcfd.

Also in the central gulf, units of Shell, Marathon Oil Co., and DeepTech International Inc., Houston, want to spend $220 million on a gas gathering and transportation system.

The project consists of a new interstate line to shore and an expansion of an existing gathering system linking several fields. Nautilus will be a 30-in., 87-mile line from Ship Shoal Block 207 to gas processing facilities near South Bend, La. Nautilus will be able to carry as much as 600 MMcfd.

The existing Manta Ray system upstream of Ship Shoal 207 will be extended to serve both Outer Continental Shelf and deepwater developments around Ewing Bank Block 873 to the east and Green Canyon Block 65 to the west.

In addition, ANR Pipeline Co. filed with the Federal Energy Regulatory Commission to build 37 miles of 30-in. offshore and onshore pipeline loop to boost capacity by as much as 461 MMcfd.

ANR already delivers 1.1 bcfd via Eugene Island and Ship Shoal blocks. Current maximum throughput capacity is 1.35 bcfd.

Transcontinental Gas Pipe Line Corp. (Transco) plans a two-phase, $129 million project to add 660 MMcfd to its offshore Southeast Louisiana Gathering System (Selags).

Selags' total capacity after both phases will exceed 1.9 bcfd. Phase 1 of Selags consists of a 50.7-mile, 30-in. loop from Ship Shoal Block 14 to Ship Shoal 214, increasing Selags' capacity by about 380 MMcfd.

Phase 1 was to be in service by November 1997. Phase 2 calls for installation of 27 miles of 30-in. loop from Ship Shoal Block 214 to a platform to be installed on South Timbalier-South Addition Block 301, at the edge of the shelf. It will add 280 MMcfd by November 1998.

Transco's is the fifth project for the region. All five would add more than 3.5 bcfd of capacity in the central gulf by January 1999.

Off Alabama

In the Main Pass and Viosca Knoll areas off Southeast Louisiana, Destin Pipeline Co., a unit of Southern Natural Gas Co. (SNG), Birmingham, wants to lay 207 miles of 30-36-in. line to transport as much as 1 bcfd of gas.

A 36-in., 73-mile portion will move from a gathering platform in 350 ft of water at Main Pass Block 248 to landfall near Pascagoula, Miss. Included is a junction platform on Viosca Knoll Block 119.

The 134-mile, 30 and 36-in. shore segment would move gas through central Mississippi, interconnecting with interstate pipelines of Florida Gas Transmission Co. at Lucedal, Miss.; Transco at Quitman, Miss.; and SNG and Tennessee Gas Pipeline Co., at Enterprise, Miss. Destin is to be in service by January 1999.

Off Alabama, Dauphin Island Gathering Partners, Houston, plans several projects.

It wants to extend and expand the current Dauphin Island Gathering System (DIGS) to serve producers bringing on line new wells in Viosca Knoll and eastern Main Pass. Demand for takeaway capacity from these producers is expected to exceed current capacity by 376-400 MMcfd.

First-phase work included installation of 60 miles of 24-in. line.

Second-phase work includes construction of a 15-mile, 24-in. loop from a point on the current system in Alabama state waters north of Dauphin Island to the system's onshore terminus near Mobile.

The work was to boost DIGS capacity to more than 900 MMcfd from 450-500 MMcfd.

For deepwater and OCS gas off Louisiana, units of Shell and Amerada Hess Corp. want to lay a 1-bcfd gathering system in the Garden Banks area.

The Garden Banks Gas Pipeline LLC would be a 50-mile, 30-in. line to extend from Enchilada platform on Garden Banks Block 128 to a new platform on South Marsh Island Block 76. IPE

New technology, improved economics boost EOR hopes

Worldwide production from enhanced oil recovery (EOR) and heavy oil projects at the beginning of 1996 reached 2.2 million b/d, about 3.6% of the oil produced, compared with an estimated 1.9 million b/d at the beginning of 1994.

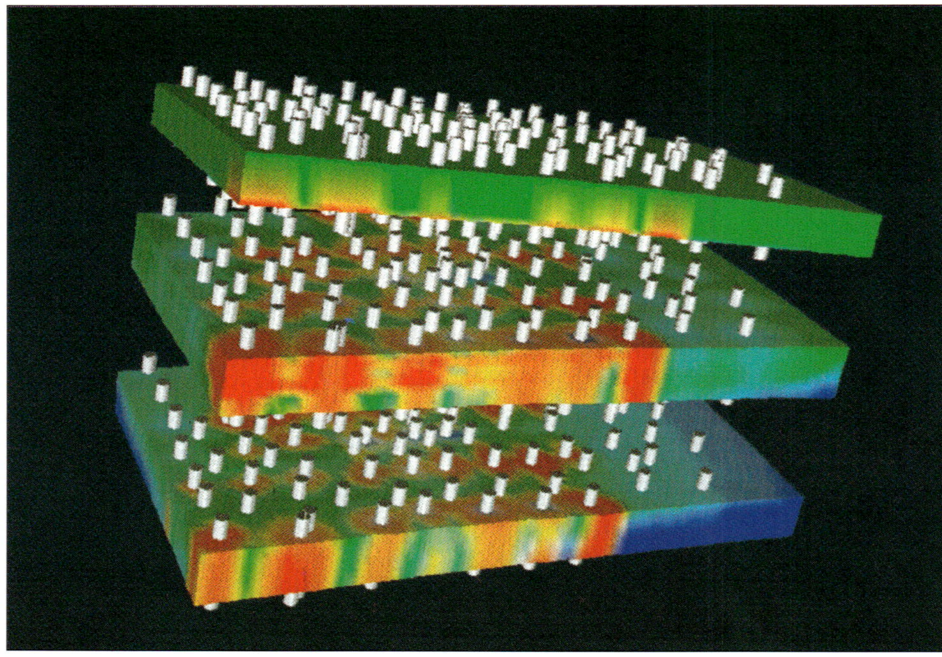

Simulations with fully compositional models reduce the risk of starting CO_2 floods. This 60,000 grid block simulation of Shell Western E&P Inc.'s Bennett Ranch Unit project (CO_2 flooding started in 1995) shows the expected fluid distribution after 15 years of CO_2-alternating-water injection. The model encompasses 2 sq miles and 120 wells. (Red=CO_2, green=oil, blue=water)

According to Oil & Gas Journal's biennial EOR survey and other published material, EOR production in the U.S. rose by 2% from the previous survey to 724,000 b/d—11% of average U.S. oil flow for 1995.

The number of U.S. EOR projects fell again in the 1996 OGJ survey, as it has in each survey since 1996, to 212 from 226 in 1994. U.S. EOR production peaked in 1992 at 761,000 b/d (Fig. 1 and Tables 1 and 2).

EOR includes thermal, gas miscible/immiscible, chemical, and other methods such as microbial (Fig. 2).

In Canada, EOR and heavy oil production identified in the 1996 survey averaged 500,000 b/d, in China and the former Soviet Union (FSU) 200,000 b/d each, and in remaining countries 600,000 b/d.

Worldwide thermal recovery (steam or in situ combustion) dominates EOR processes, accounting for about 1.8 million bo/d. In the U.S., thermal represents 60% of EOR production. Gas injection (light hydrocarbons, CO_2, and nitrogen) accounts for most of the rest.

In Canada, excluding mining and steam projects for recovering bitumen, light hydrocarbon injection dominates EOR processes and accounts for about 90,000 bo/d.

U.S. EOR production increases slightly — Fig. 1

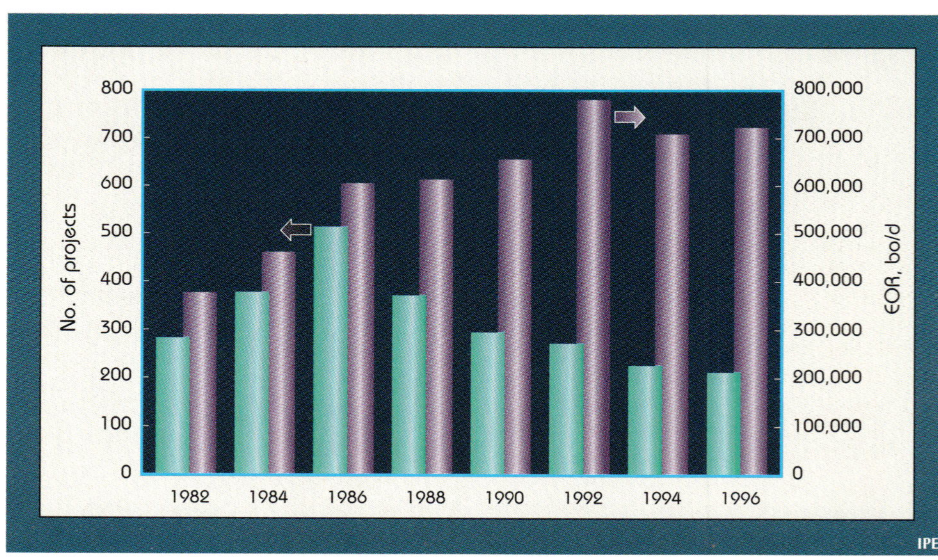

Carbon dioxide

The U.S. continues to see an increase in miscible carbon dioxide (CO_2) activity. Production in the 1996 survey was up 5.3% from the previous survey, exceeding 170,000 b/d.

During 1996 as CO_2 activity picked up, mostly from existing projects, CO_2 supplies became tight. Available supply was expected to increase by about 300 MMscfd in early 1997 once Shell Oil Co. completes a drilling and workover program to boost deliverability from the McElmo Dome CO_2 field in southwestern Colorado.

The 500 mile Cortez pipeline transports the CO_2 from the McElmo Dome to a terminal near Denver City, Tex.

Tighter CO_2 supplies raised the CO_2 price at Denver City to about 65¢/Mscf from about 50¢/Mscf in 1995. In the 1980s, the price at times exceeded $1/Mscf.

Shell estimates that CO_2 project costs decreased to $10.25/bbl of oil equivalent (boe) in 1995 from $18.20/boe in 1985. Costs, 1985 vs. 1995, break down as follows:

- Capital – $1.50/boe vs. $0.80/boe.
- Operating expense – $5.00/boe vs. $2.60/boe.
- CO_2 purchase – $6.50/boe vs. $3.25/boe.
- Royalty and production tax, property tax and insurance – $5.20/boe vs. $3.60/boe.

In 1996, the company most active starting CO_2 floods was Fina Oil & Chemical Co., which initiated three floods in West Texas (Fig. 3).

Starting three CO_2 floods in 1 year is the most for a single company since the mid-1980s, when in 1 year Amoco Production Co. kicked off four and Exxon Co. U.S.A. three.

Fina's West Brahaney Unit project represents the first time

an operator has traded CO_2 supply for a working interest in a field.

Outside of West Texas and New Mexico, CO_2 flooding prospects improved after Transpetco Transportation Co. completed a 120 mile, 12.75 in. CO_2 pipeline from Bravo Dome to Guymon, Okla.

Mobil was to purchase part of the pipeline's CO_2 capacity for its Postle flood, but Transpetco expected other operators in the Oklahoma and Texas panhandles to take advantage of the remaining CO_2 capacity.

Heavy oil

Operators planned to increase primary bitumen and tar sands recovery in Canada and Venezuela. Syncrude Canada Inc. and Suncor Inc. mining projects were to be expanded. A third mining project by Solv-ex Corp. was proposed.

Imperial Oil Ltd. at Cold Lake and Amoco Canada Petroleum Co. Ltd. at Wolf Lake and Primrose also planned sizable expansions in their steam projects.

Imperial's \$175 million investment at Cold Lake was expected boost bitumen output about 30% to 130,000 b/d by 1997.

Amoco at Wolf Lake and Primrose may be producing a combined 55,000 b/d, up from the current 10,000 b/d.

Syncrude's production averaged 202,000 b/d in 1995. Its expansion plans have been helped by prices of about \$18.40/bbl for Syncrude sweet blend and continued cost reduction, from \$10.57/bbl in 1994 to \$9.34/bbl in 1995.

Syncrude plans included a production increase of about 15,000 b/d by 2000.

Suncor Inc. planned to invest more than \$600 million (Canadian) in oil sand mining through 2000. It expected production to climb to 85,000 b/d by 1997 from 76,000 b/d in 1995. And by 2001, it forecast 105,000 b/d from reserves that may last for another 50 years.

In Burnt Lake, Suncor began injecting steam in Phase 1 of a steam-assisted gravity drainage heavy oil project. By 1999, Suncor expected 2,500 b/d from Burnt Lake and may start an expansion.

Alberta's heavy oil sands may eventually produce in excess of 1.2 million b/d. Alberta contains an estimated 300 billion bbl of recoverable bitumen.

Venezuela

In Venezuela, Maraven SA, Lagoven SA, and Corpoven SA negotiated or in 1996 were negotiating contracts with Conoco Inc., Mobil Corp., Arco Corp., and Total Petroleum to exploit areas in the Orinoco tar sands.

The synthetic crude projects were at various stages of being approved and could be producing about 600,000 b/d by 2000. Venezuela's recoverable heavy oil and EOR reserves are estimated to be about 289 billion bbl.

EOR recovery mechanisms Fig. 2

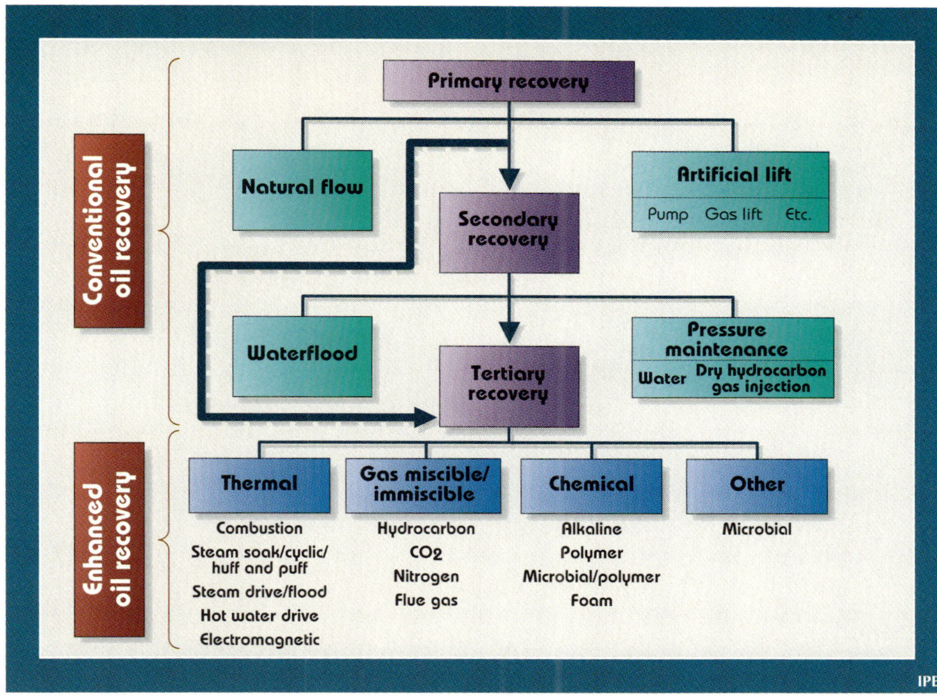

CO_2 activity Fig. 3

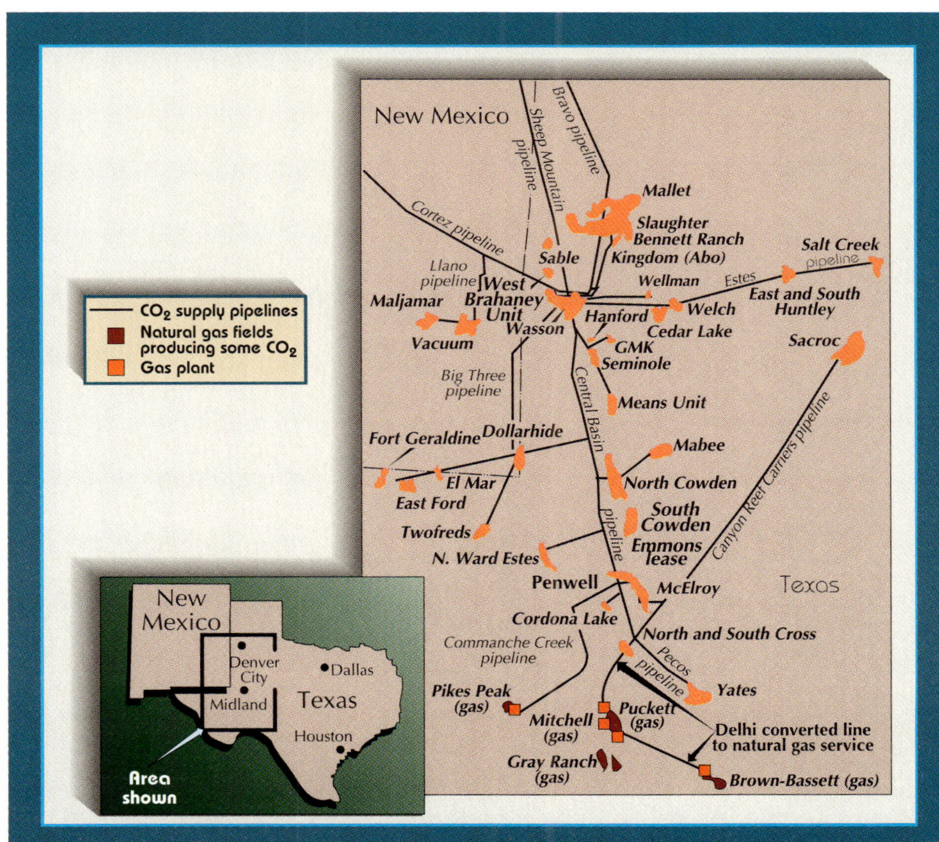

China

For 1995, China National Petroleum Corp. produced 152,000 b/d of heavy crude from 7,100 thermal recovery

Table 1

U.S. EOR production

	b/d							Change from
	1984	1986	1988	1990	1992	1994	1996	1994, %
Thermal								
Steam	358,115	468,692	455,484	444,137	454,009	415,801	419,349	0.9
Cumbustion in situ	6,445	10,272	6,525	6,090	4,702	2,520	4,485	78.0
Hot water		705	2,896	3,985	1,980	250	250	0.0
Total thermal	**364,560**	**479,669**	**464,905**	**454,212**	**460,691**	**418,571**	**424,084**	**1.3**
Chemical								
Micellar-polymer	2,832	1,403	1,509	617	254	64	0	–100.0
Polymer	10,232	15,313	20,992	11,219	1,940	1,828	139	–92.4
Caustic/alkaline	334	185						
Surfactant				20				
Total chemical	**13,398**	**16,901**	**22,501**	**11,856**	**2,194**	**1,892**	**139**	**–92.7**
Gas								
Hydrocarbon miscible/ immiscible	14,439	33,767	25,935	55,386	113,072	99,693	96,263	–3.4
CO_2 miscible	31,300	28,440	64,192	95,591	144,973	161,486	170,715	5.7
CO_2 immiscible	702	1,349	420	95	95			
Nitrogen	7,170	18,510	19,050	22,260	22,580	23,050	28,017	21.5
Flue gas (miscible and immiscible)	29,400	26,150	21,400	17,300	11,000	–	–	
Other					6,300	4,400	4,350	–1.1
Total gas	**83,011**	**108,216**	**130,997**	**190,632**	**298,020**	**288,629**	**299,345**	**3.7**
Other								
Microbial					2	2	0	–100.0
Total other	**0**	**0**	**0**	**0**	**2**	**2**	**0**	**–100.0**
Grand total	**460,969**	**604,786**	**618,403**	**656,700**	**760,907**	**709,094**	**723,568**	**2.0**

*See OGJ, June 29, 1992, p. 70.

Table 2

Active U.S. EOR projects

	Number of projects											Change from
	1976	1978	1980	1982	1984	1986	1988	1990	1992	1994	1996	1994, %
Thermal												
Steam	85	99	133	118	133	181	133	137	119	109	105	–3.7
Cumbustion in situ	21	16	17	21	18	17	9	8	8	5	8	60.0
Hot water						3	10	9	6	2	2	0.0
Total thermal	**106**	**115**	**150**	**139**	**151**	**201**	**152**	**154**	**133**	**116**	**115**	**–0.9**
Chemical												
Micellar-polymer	13	22	14	20	21	20	9	5	3	2	0	–100.0
Polymer	14	21	22	55	106	178	111	42	44	27	11	–59.3
Caustic, alkaline	1	3	6	10	11	8	4	2	2	1	1	0.0
Surfactant								1				
Total chemical	**28**	**46**	**42**	**85**	**138**	**206**	**124**	**50**	**49**	**30**	**12**	**–60.0**
Gas												
Hydrocarbon miscible/ immiscible	15	15	9	12	16	26	22	23	25	15	14	–6.7
CO_2 miscible	9	14	17	28	40	38	49	52	52	54	60	11.1
CO_2 immiscible				1	18	28	8	4	2	1	1	0.0
Nitrogen			1	4	7	9	9	9	7	8	9	12.5
Flue gas (miscible and immiscible)			3	3	3	3	2	3	2	0	0	0
Other			4	2					1	1	0	–100.0
Total gas	**24**	**29**	**34**	**50**	**84**	**104**	**90**	**91**	**89**	**79**	**84**	**6.3**
Other												
Microbial									2	1	1	0.0
Total other	**0**	**0**	**0**	**0**	**0**	**1**	**0**	**0**	**2**	**1**	**1**	**0.0**
Grand total	**158**	**190**	**226**	**274**	**373**	**512**	**366**	**295**	**273**	**226**	**212**	**–6.2**

* See OGJ, June 29, 1992, p. 70.

Guide to EOR tables

A. Planned EOR projects
B. Producing Canadian EOR projects
C. Completed, terminated Canadian projects
D. Producing EOR projects outside U.S. and Canada
E. Completed, terminated postponed projects outside U.S., Canada
F. Producing thermal EOR in U.S.
G. Producing CO_2, gas EOR in U.S.
H. Producing chemical and microbial EOR projects in U.S.
I. Completed, terminated , postponed, and delayed U.S. projects
J. Producing worldwide heavy oil EOR projects*

*Projects employing EOR for primary production

Abbreviations

Formation type
S: Sandstone
LS: Limestone
Dolo.: Dolomite
Congl.: Conglomerate
Tripol.: Tripolite
US: Unconsolidated sand

Project maturity
JS: Just started
HF: Half finished
NC: Nearing completion
C: Completed
PP: Postponed
Term: Terminated
Del: Deleted

Previous production
Prim.: Primary
WF: Waterflood
GI: Gas injection
C: Cyclic steam
HW: Hot water
SS: Steam soak
S: Steam
SD: Steam drive
SF: Steam flood
HC: Hydrocarbon

Project evaluation
TETT: Too early to tell
Prom.: Promising
Succ.: Successful
Disc.: Discouraging

Project scope
P: Pilot project
FW: Field wide
LW: Lease wide
RW: Reservoir wide
Exp. L: Expansion likely
Exp. UL: Expansion unlikely

wells. Liaohe, Xinjiang, Shengli, and Henan are its four heavy oil production basis.

Heavy oil production represented 8% of China's 1994 production.

CNPC estimates China's proven geological heavy oil reserves at about 8.4 billion bbl in 70 discovered heavy oil fields.

Romania, Tatarstan

In 1994, Petrom R.A., the Romanian national oil company, operated several in situ combustion and steam injection projects in the Videle, Moreni, and Supalcu de Barcau areas. Its first thermal projects started in 1964.

Petrom also mines three reservoirs in the Sarata Montiaru, Matita, and Slolont areas.

Text continues following tables

Planned EOR projects — Table A

Type and operator	Field	Location	Pay zone	Size, acres	Depth, ft	Gravity, °API	Start date
U.S. PROJECTS							
CO_2 miscible							
Amoco	Anton Irish	Hale & Lamb Co., Tex.	Clearfork	1,680	5,900	28	10/96
Oxy USA	West Welch	Dawson Co., Tex.	San Andres	640	4,900	34	4/97
Oxy USA	North Dollarhide	Andrews Co., Tex.	San Andres	1,280	8,000	38	1/97
Phillips	South Cowden	Extor Co., Tex.	San Andres	900	4,500	34	4/96
Transpetco Transport	Various fields	Okla.-Tex. panhandles	Morrow		5,000-6,800	40	1996
Texaco	Harris & Robertson	Gaines Co. Tex.	Glorietta	4,000	5,875	30.8	3/97
Texaco	Vacuum	Lea Co. NM	Grayburg, San Andres	2,240	4,550	39	1-3/97
Texaco	Garden Island Bay	Plaquemines Parish, La.	189 Sand	103	8,100	36	2/96
Fina	West Brahaney Unit	Yoakum Co., Tex.	San Andres	320	5,300	32	6/96
Fina	East Penwell (SA) Unit	Ector Co., Tex	San Andres	400	4,000	31	6/96
Fina	South Cowden, Emmons Lease	Ector Co., Tex.	San Andres	320	4,500	31	6/96
Hydrocarbon miscible							
Arco	Kuparuk	Alaska	A&C Sands	50,000	6,000	24	9/96
Arco	Kuparuk	Alaska	A&C Sands	2,600	6,000	24	12/96
Arco	Kuparuk	Alaska	A&C Sands	5,200	6,000	24	12/96
Steam							
Texaco	McKittrick	Kern Co., Calif.	Tulare	5	1,000	13	9/96
Texaco	Midway-Sunset	Kern Co., Calif.	Spelecy	5	1,500	12	8/96
Texaco	Midway-Sunset	Kern Co., Calif.	Potter	5	1,500	13	8/96
Tidelands	Wilmington (DOE)	Los Angeles Co., Calif	Tar	55	2,500	30	5/96
Tidelands	Wilmington (Parcel A)	Los Angeles Co., Calif	Tar	55	2,500	30	6/96
PROJECTS OUTSIDE OF U.S.							
CO_2 miscible							
Vikor	Jofffre Viking	Alta., Canada	Viking	590	5,000	42	8/96
Combustion							
ONGC	Balol	India, Gujarat	Kalol sand-I	3,377	3,450	15.6	10/96
ONGC	Santhal	India, Gujarat	Kalol sand-I & II	5,660	3,450	17	6/96
ONGC	Bechraji	India, Gujarat	Kalol sand-I	90	3,120	15.6	11/96
CNCP	Xerxing	Namangu, China	Shahej	6	1,640-2065	29	1996
Microbial							
CNPC-Jilin	Fuyu	Jilin, China			935-1,575	31.5	4/96
Steam Drive							
Qi-40	Panjin	Liaoning, China	Lianbua	1,962	2,132-3,464	12	1996
Zheo-20	Dongyin	Shandong, China	Ng	964	2,886-3,149	14-20	1996
Polymer							
CNPC, Liupukang	Lamadian	Daquing, China	K	3,803	3,215	33	7/96
CNPC, Liupukang	Sarto	Daquing, China	K	4,740	3,376	33.5	1/97
CNPC, Liupukang	Gudao	Shengli, China	N	2,989	3,911	15.5	8/96
CNPC, Liupukang	Gudong	Shengli, China	N	1,536	3,921	13.6	9/96
CNPC, Liupukang	Shuanghe	Henen, China	E	2,717	4,560	32.08	9/96

Producing Canadian EOR Projects

Type/ Operator	Field	Province	Start date	Area, acres	Wells Prod.	Wells Inj.	Pay zone	Formation type	Porosity, %	Permeability, md
CO_2 miscible										
Shell Canada	Harmattan East	Alta.	8/88	1,600	20	8	Mississippian Turner Valley	Dolo	14	10-300
Shell Canada	Midale	Sask.	1992	2,560	60	8	Mississippian Midale	LS/Dolo.	10-35	1-100
Vikor	Joffre Viking	Alta.	8/85	480	6	2	Viking	S	13	500
Vikor	Joffre Viking	Alta.	6/88	480	4	1	Viking	S	13	500
Vikor	Joffre Viking	Alta.	11/91	1,280	5	2	Viking	S	13	500
Combustion										
Mobil Oil Canada	Battrum	Sask.	10/66	4,920	94	15	Battrum/Roseray	S	26	1,265
Mobil Oil Canada	Battrum	Sask.	8/67	2,400	35	7	Battrum/Roseray	S	25	930
Mobil Oil Canada	Battrum	Sask.	11/65	680	22	3	Roseray	S	27	930
Hydrocarbon miscible										
Amoco Canada	Bigoray Nisku B	Alta.	2/80	251	5	1	Nisku D-2	LS	5	1,130
Amoco Canada	Kaybob South	Alta.	7/84	8,000	40	9	Triassic	Dolo.	11.5	92
Amoco Canada	Nipisi	Alta.	2/84	28,480	168	68	Gilwood	S	18	200
Canadian Hunter Expl.	Brassey	B.C.	8/89	6,043	13	7	Artex Triassic	S	16.6	137
Chevron Canada Resources	Acheson D-3A	Alta.	7/87	650	16	1	Leduc D3	Dolo.	12	5,000
Chevron Canada Resources	Mitsue, Stage 1 & 2	Alta.	5/85	17,280	140	55	Gilwood	S	13.4	282
Chevron Canada Resources	Pembina Nisku F	Alta.	6/86	200	3	1	Nisku F	Dolo.	12.7	660
Imperial Oil	Pembina 'G' Pool	Alta.	9/89	328	2	1	Nisku	Dolo.	8	900
Imperial Oil	Pembina 'K' Pool	Alta.	1984	126	1	1	Nisku	Dolo.	12.7	2,020
Imperial Oil	Pembina 'L' Pool	Alta.	1985	625	4	2	Nisku	Dolo.	10.5	1,060
Imperial Oil	Pembina 'M' Pool	Alta.	1983	192	2	1	Nisku	Dolo.	9	540
Imperial Oil	Pembina 'O' Pool	Alta.	11/83	346	2	1	Nisku	Dolo.	11.8	3,100
Imperial Oil	Pembina 'P' Pool	Alta.	10/83	420	3	1	Nisku	Dolo.	10.3	2,400
Imperial Oil	Pembina 'Q' Pool	Alta.	2/85	301	2	1	Nisku	Dolo.	9.8	1,970
Imperial Oil	Wizard Lake	Alta.	1969	2,725	49	14	Leduc D-3A	Dolo.	10.5	1,375
Imperial Oil	Judy Creek 'A' Pool	Alta.	5/85	29,050	96	64	Beaverhill Lake	LS	9	43
Imperial Oil	Judy Creek 'B' Pool	Alta.	1/87	8,290	30	15	Beaverhill Lake	LS	9.2	41
Imperial Oil	Rainbow "FF" Pool	Alta.	9/71	102	2	1	Keg River 344 feet	Dolo.	7.3	
Imperial Oil	Rainbow "T" Pool	Alta.	6/69	222	2	1	Keg River 394 feet	Dolo.	8.6	
Imperial Oil	Rainbow "Z" Pool	Alta.	2/71	221	6	2	Keg River 265 feet	Dolo.	4.25	
Gulf Canada	Fenn-Big Valley	Alta.	4/83	1,268	26	7	Nisku	Dolo.	8	400
Gulf Canada	Goose River	Alta.	10/86	2,847	24	7	Beaverhill Lake	LS	8	240
Home Oil	Swan Hills	Alta.	10/85	19,440	150	50	Beaverhill Lake	LS	8.5	54
Husky Oil	Rainbow B Pool	Alta.	6/84	2,500	32	10	Keg River	LS	8	300
Husky Oil	Rainbow E Pool	Alta.	6/72	173	6	1	Keg River	LS	12	300
Husky Oil	Rainbow EEE Pool	Alta.	4/70	150	2	1	Keg River	LS	16.8	500
Husky Oil	Rainbow G Pool	Alta.	10/72	163	3	1	Keg River	LS	8	300
Husky Oil	Rainbow H Pool	Alta.	6/73	165	3	1	Keg River	LS	9.4	200
Husky Oil	Rainbow KRA Pool	Alta.	12/68	633	17	2	Keg River	Dolo.	10.1	100
Husky Oil	Rainbow KRD Pool	Alta.	3/76	85	1	1	Keg River	LS	10	200
Husky Oil	Rainbow O Pool	Alta.	2/70	703	9	1	Keg River	Dolo.	6	150
Husky Oil	Rainbow South E	Alta.	3/94	320	2	2	Keg River	LS	9.1	50
Husky Oil	Rainbow South G Pool	Alta.	5/95	180			Keg River	Dolo.	8	50
Mobil Oil Canada	Rainbow	Alta.	7/83	320	5	1	Keg River	Dolo./LS	8.5	100-5,000
Mobil Oil Canada	Rainbow	Alta.	9/72	800	14	2	Keg River	Dolo./LS	8.6	100-5,000
Mobil Oil Canada	Rainbow South	Alta.	8/72	490	5	2	Keg River	Dolo.	6	40
Petro-Canada	Brazeau River D	Alta.	9/81	640	2	1	Nisku	LS	7	50
Petro-Canada	Caroline	Alta.	9/84	8,680	16	11	Cardium	S	10	12
Shell Canada	Virginia Hills	Alta.	11/89	4,575	50	14	Beaverhill Lake	LS	9	1-500
Hydrocarbon immiscible										
Husky Oil	Rainbow F Pool	Alta	6/93	1,920	12	4	Keg River	Dolo.	5	1,000
Hot water										
Alberta Energy	S. Jenner Up. Mannville J Pool	Alta.	9/89	2	3	1	Glauconitic	S	25.0	1,560
Polymer										
Encor Energy	Rapdan Unit	Sask.	1/86	440	12	5	Upper Shaunavon	S	17	85
Steam										
Norcen	Provost	Alta.	3/86	20	8	1	McLaren	S	27-30.0	4,000
Sceptre Resources	Tangleflags North	Sask.	12/87	285	8	17	Lloydminster Sand	S	32.5	3,000-5,000
Sceptre Resources	Tangleflags East	Sask.	9/94	412	4		Lloydminster Sand	S	33	3,000-5,000

Table B

Depth, ft	Gravity, °API	Oil, cp	Oil, °F.	Prev. Prod.	Satur. % start	Satur. % end	Proj. Matur.	Tot. prod., b/d	Enh. prod., b/d	Proj. Eval.	Profit	Project Scope
8,500	39	0.3	198	WF	40		HF	600	500	Prom.		Exp. L
4,500	27	3	145	WF	50		JS	750	250	Prom.		10% of field
5,140	42	1.14	133	WF	38	28	NC			Succ.		FW
5,075	42	1.14	133	WF	36	28	HF			Succ.		FW
5,000	42	1.14	133	WF	38	28	HF			Succ.		FW
2,900	18	70.3	110	Prim.	66		HF	3,700	3,700	Succ.	Yes	FW
2,900	18	70	110	Prim.	62		HF	1,200	1,200	Succ.	Yes	FW
2,900	18	70	110	Prim.	70		HF	1,350	1,350	Succ.	Yes	FW
7,500	34	1.4	169	Prim.	70	30	HF	800	660	Succ.	Yes	FW
6,981	40	0.419	190	WF	46	31	NC	1,890	400	Prom.	Yes	FW
5,500	41	0.84	131	WF	30	5	HF	12,578	6,000	Succ.	Yes	FW
9,850	57	0.097	210		98	33	HF	4,000	4,000	Succ.	Yes	FW
5,000	39	0.85	139	Prim.	90	18	NC	1,600	1,600	Succ.	Yes	LW
5,000	41	0.65	147	WF	30	19	NC	9,200	8,000	Succ.	Yes	FW
8,000	40	0.5	208	WF	75	43.3	NC	2,271	705	Succ.	Yes	FW
9,541	43.2	0.33	204	Prim.	80	5	NC	708	708	Succ.	Yes	FW
9,469	43.6	0.37	198	Prim	82	5	NC	864	864	Succ.	Yes	FW
9,415	40.9	0.42	199	WF	88	5	NC	2,258	2,258	Succ.	Yes	FW
9,333	41.1	0.14	198	Prim.	93	5	NC	1,649	1,649	Succ.	Yes	FW
9,332	43.4	0.32	190	Prim	84	5	NC	569	569	Succ.	Yes	FW
9,531	45.4	0.36	200	Prim.	87	5	NC	1,185	1,185	Succ.	Yes	FW
9,421	41.3	0.42	196	Prim.	91	5	NC	704	704	Succ.	Yes	FW
6,500	38	0.54	167	Prim.	93	5	NC	2,800	2,800	Succ.	Yes	FW
8,850	41.6	0.38	206	WF	84	10	NC	9,500	9,500	Succ.	Yes	FW
9,150	42.1	42	206	WF	83	10	NC	3,200	3,200	Succ.	Yes	FW
4,160	37	0.59	188	Prim.	90		NC	250	250	Succ.	Yes	RW
4,330	40	0.69	188	Prim.	88		NC	400	400	Succ.	Yes	RW
4,040	38	0.547	190	Prim.	73.5		NC	2,200	2,200	Succ.	Yes	RW
5,249	32.8	1.34	136	Prim.	33		HF	590	590	Succ.	Yes	FW
9,200	41	0.4	234	WF			HF	9,600	3,014	Prom.		Exp. L.
8,300	41	0.4	225	WF	30	5	JS	17,500	4,900	Succ.	Yes	FW (Exp. L)
6,000	39	0.83	180	WF	52	23	JS	4,635	4,635	Prom.	Yes	FW
5,932	39	0.439	175	Prim.	91	27	HF	1,900	1,900	Succ.	Yes	FW
6,085	37	0.542	180	Prim.	95	29	NC	70	70	Succ.	Yes	FW
6,151	39	0.485	185	Prim.	92	28	HF	1,528	1,528	Succ.	Yes	FW
6,210	39	0.596	187	Prim.	92	28	HF	572	572	Succ.	Yes	FW
6,380	43	0.29	195	Prim.	90	30	HF	2,610	2,610	Succ.	Yes	FW
6,310	40	0.426	195	Prim.	90	27	NC	141	141	Succ.	Yes	FW
6,053	42	0.28	180	Prim.	87	26	NC	650	650	Succ.	Yes	FW
6,300		0.39	195	WF	67	0.5	JS	900		TETT		FW
6,500	39	0.4	195	WF	67	0.5	JS	500	0	TETT		FW
5,500	39	0.46	190	WF	45	15	HF	600	600	Prom.	Yes	FW
5,500	39	0.47	184	GI/WF	92	15	NC	1,100	1,100	Succ.	Yes	FW
6,200	40	0.3	183	Prim.			NC	1,075	955	Succ.	Yes	FW
10,091	42	0.38	216	Prim.	90	35	NC	1,200	1,200	Succ.	Yes	FW
8,200	46	0.25	173	GI	85	45	HF	900	850	Succ.	Yes	FW
9,500	34	0.53	221	WF	56	36	HF	8,000	4,000	Succ.		Exp. L
6,000	48	0.25	180	WF	50	40	JS	2,800	400	TETT		FW
2,950	14	170	90	Prim	75		JS	95		TETT		P
4,500	23	10	132	WF	55	43	HF	880	660	Succ.	Yes	P(Exp.L)
2,430	12	2,000	80	Prim.	82	45	JS	420	420	Prom.	No	P(Exp.L)
1,476	13	13,000	66	Prim.	90	38	JS	3,773	3,773	Succ.	Yes	FW
1,924	11.5	32,000	68	Prim.	75	40	JS	509	258	TETT		P

Completed, terminated Canadian projects

Type/ Operator	Field	Province	Start date	Area, acres	Wells Prod.	Wells Inj.	Pay zone	Formation type	Porosity, %	Permeability, md
Hydrocarbon miscible										
Chevron Canada Resources	Acheson D-3A	Alta.	1990	2,700	0	0	Leduc D3	Dolo.	12	5,000
Chevron Canada Resources	Bigoray Nisku F	Alta.	3/87	150	2	1	Nisku F	Dolo.	10	250
Chevron Canada Resources	Kaybob North BHL Unit #1	Alta.	1/88	10,400	70	20	Beaverhill Lake	LS	7.5	50
Chevron Canada Resources	Pembina Nisku A	Alta.	2/84	400	3	1	Nisku A	Dolo.	8	250
Chevron Canada Resources	Pembina Nisku D	Alta.	11/85	400	5	1	Nisku	Dolo.	12	750
Chevron Canada Resources	W. Pembina Nisku A	Alta.	8/81	200	2	1	Nisku A	Dolo.	10	750
Petro-Canada	Brazeau River E	Alta.	11/80	640	2	1	Nisku	LS	10	250
Amoco Canada	South Swan Hills Unit	Alta.	1973	28,480	121	46	Beaverhill Lake	LS	8	49
Steam										
Shell Canada Ltd	Peace River	Alta.	10/79	49	24	7	Cretaceous-Bullhead	S	28	100-2,000
Carbon dioxide miscible										
Vikor	Joffre Viking	Alta.	12/82	320	2	2	Viking	S	13	500
Polymer										
Chevron Canada Resources	Taber Mannville D Unit #1	Alta.	1/87	480	7	2	Mannville D	S	22.3	1,140

Producing EOR projects outside U.S. and Canada

State/Area	Operator	Type Project	Field	Start date	Area, acres	No. wells prod	No. wells inj.	Pay zone	Formation	Porosity, %
China										
Jilin Province	CNPC-Jilin	Microbial	Fuju	1994		44	44		S	22-26
Dongyin, Shandong Province	CNPC-Shengli Bureau	Steam	Sanjasi	1984	3,162	280		Ng, Ea, El, Eo	S	30
Dongyin, Shandong Province	CNPC-Shengli Bureau	Steam	Lean	1989	10,613	658		Ea, Ng	S/Cong.	15-30
Liaoling Province	CNPC-Liaohe Bureau	Steam	Gaoshen 2-3	1982	3,583	450		3rd sand	S/Dolo.	20-25
Nanyang, Henan Province	CNPC-Henan Bureau	Steam	Jinglou	1986	1,210	177		E	S	32
Nanyang, Henan Province	CNPC-Henan Bureau	Steam	Gueheng	1987	1,655	132		E	S	27-34
Panjin, Liaoning Province	CNPC-Liaohe Bureau	Steam	Shu I 7-5	1990	237	38	11	Middle	S	25.6
Panjin, Liaoning Province	CNPC-Liaohe Bureau	Steam	Shu I	1984	5,718	1,149		Middle & Upper	S	23-28
Panjin, Liaoning Province	CNPC-Liaohe Bureau	Steam	Xiao Wa	1992	2,100	311		2nd Dongying, 3rd sand	S	27.5
Panjin, Liaoning Province	CNPC-Liaohe Bureau	Steam	Huanxiling	1985	7,067	1,848		2nd and 3rd sand	S	32
Xinjiang Province	CNPC-Xinjiang Bureau	Steam	Karamay 9-1	1984	469	128	41	Qigu	S	32
Xinjiang Province	CNPC-Xinjiang Bureau	Steam	Karamay 9-2	1986	444	79	21	Qigu	S	32
Xinjiang Province	CNPC-Xinjiang Bureau	Steam	Karamay 9-3	1986	115	62	31	Qigu	S	31
Xinjiang Province	CNPC-Xinjiang Bureau	Steam	Karamay 9-4	1988	963	358	32	Qigu	S	30
Xinjiang Province	CNPC-Xinjiang Bureau	Steam	Karamay 9-5 - 9-9	1991	2,495	1,136		Qigu	S	32
Xinjiang Province	CNPC-Xinjiang Bureau	Steam	Karamay 6	1989	963	211	45	Qigu	S	31
Heilongjiang Province	CNPC-Daqing	Polymer	Lamadian-2	1/94	516	21	9	K	S	26
Heilongjiang Province	CNPC-Daqing	Polymer	Sarto	1/93	273	36	25	K	S	25
Heilongjiang Province	CNPC-Daqing	Polymer	Lamadian-1	6/94	559	25	16	K	S	26
Henan Province	CNPC-Henan	Polymer	Shuanghe	2/96	744	12	3	E	S	20
Jilin Province	CNPC-Jilin	Polymer	Fuyu	6/93	519	86	21	K	S	25
Liaoling Province	CNPC-Liaohe Bureau	Polymer	Huanxiling-16	3/93	346	11	3	B	S	28.5
Shandong Province	CNPC-Shengli Bureau	Polymer	Guodao, Pilpt	9/92	138	10	4	N	S	32
Shandong Province	CNPC-Shengli Bureau	Polymer	Guodong	1/91	1,008	52	39	N	S	33
Shandong Province	CNPC-Shengli Bureau	Polymer	Guodao	12/94		82	40	N	S	32
Tianjin City	CNPC-Dagang	Polymer	Gangxi 3-2, West	12/91	255	19	6	N	S	31
Tianjin City	CNPC-Dagang	Polymer	Dagang-West	10/91	277	11	6	N	S	31
Colombia										
Mid. Magdalena basin	Omimex	Steam	Teca	2/84	3,448	342		Oligocene A & B	S	28
Mid. Magdalena basin	Omimex	Steam	Teca	1/91	60	20	12	Oligocene B	S	28
France										
Paris	Elf Aquitaine	Polymer	Chateaurenard (Courtenay)	1/89	250	12	4	Neocomian	S	30
Germany										
Lower Saxony	BEB	Steam	Ruhlermoor II	8/86	360	37	4	Valanginian	S	27-31
Lower Saxony	BEB	Steam	Georgsdorf I	1/75	165	15	1	Valanginian	S	25
Lower Saxony	BEB	Steam	Georgsdorf II	12/79	144	15	3	Valanginian	S	25
Lower Saxony	BEB	Steam	Georgsdorf II	10/90	60	6	1	Valanginian	S	25
Lower Saxony	BEB	Steam	Ruhlermoor I	11/80	220	30	4	Valanginian	S	28-30
Lower Saxony	BEB	Steam	Ruhlermoor III	12/87	400	40	5	Valanginian	S	25-28
Northwest	Preussag AG	Polymer	Vorhop-Knesebeck	11/89	345	3	1	Dogger-Beta	S	28
	RWE-DEA	Polymer	Ploen OST	1/89	30	3	1	Dogger-Beta	S	19
Lower Saxony	Wintershall AG	Hot water	Emlichheim 17	10/74	82	9	1	Valenginian	S	30
Lower Saxony	Wintershall AG	Hot water	Emlichheim 1	10/67	115	7	1	Valenginian	S	30

Table C

Depth, ft	Gravity, °API	Oil, cp	Oil, °F.	Prev. Prod.	Satur. % start	Satur. % end	Proj. Matur.	Tot. prod., b/d	Enh. prod., b/d	Proj. Eval.	Profit	Project Scope
5,000	39	0.8	135	WF	25-35	7	Term	0	0	Disc.	No	FW
10,500	37	0.8	175	WF	90	5	C	4,000	1,100	Succ.	Yes	FW
9,780	42	0.19	234	WF	30	5	C	8,200	4,500	Succ.	Yes	FW
10,000	41	0.3	210	WF	80	5	C	4,450	1,700	Succ.	Yes	FW
9,000	41	0.7	176	WF	90	5	C	6,400	1,700	Succ.	Yes	FW
10,000	42	0.3	228	Prim.	90	5	C	4,466	2,766	Succ.	Yes	FW
10,544	46	0.2	222	Prim.	90	20	C	1,200	1,200	Succ.	Yes	FW
8,500	38	0.4	225	Prim./WF	35	13	NC	8,176	1,022	Succ.	Yes	FW
1,800	7.5	100,000	60		80		C	1,000	1,000	Succ.		P
4,000	42	1.14	133	WF	40	28	C			Succ.	No	P(Exp.L)
3,200	18	55	121	WF	92	7	Sold	17,600	16,400	TETT	Yes	FW

Table D

Permea-bility, md	Depth, ft	Gravity, °API	Oil, cp	Oil, °F.	Prev. Prod.	Satur. % start	Satur. % end	Proj. Matur.	Tot. prod., b/d	Enh. prod., b/d	Proj. Eval.	Profit	Project Scope
180	935-1,572	31.5	19-31	86		54		NC			Succ.	Yes	Exp. L
5,000	3,673-3,938	11-19	9,200	131	Prim	65		HF	9,116	9,116	Succ.		FW
3,000-4,500	2,885-3,132	11-18	10,000-40,000	129	Prim	60		HF	21,735	21,735	Succ.		FW
2,200	5,081-5,740	16-19	1,000-2,000	150	Prim.	65		HF	10,136	7,868	Succ.		RW
1,500-3,000	459-1,936	16-25	9,600-16,000	70-90	Prim.	65		HF	1,965	1,965	Succ.		FW
1,351-7,134	513-1,627	14-22	6,000-137,000	66	Prim.	65-73		HF	1,663	1,663	Succ.		FW
1,601	3,345	13	15,000-18,900	129	C	65		HF	2,117	920	Succ.		RW
560-1500	2,755-5,051	13-20	620-25,900	118-134	Prim.	65		HF	32,124	25,760	Succ.		FW
1,683	3,772-4,592	11-13	4,000-11,000	115-122	Prim.	65		JS	15,020	15,020	Succ.		FW
450-512	2,050-3,440	14	700-14,000	104	Prim.	65		HF	59,595	42,122	Succ.		FW
3,170	820	16-24	2,000	66	Prim.	65		HF	1,329	1,329	Prom.		RW
2,290	754	16-24	2,240	66	Prim.	65		HF	951	951	Prom.		RW
1,730	525-1,180	16-24	4,000	65	Prim.	65		HF	913	913	Disc.		RW
3,000	656-1,312	16-24	7,200	66	Prim.	65		HF	2,709	2,709	Prom.		RW
1,350-2,000	721-1,146	16-24	5,400-54,000	66	Prim.	65		HF	16,632	16,632	Succ.		RW
2,500-3,100	853-1,016	16.5-23	6,400-80,000	66	Prim.	65		HF	2,948	2,948	Succ.		RW
580	3,212	33	10	108	WF	70		HF	3,313	1,492	Prom.		Exp. L
871	3,376	34	9	115	WF	72		NC	8,913	4,149	Succ.		Exp. L
622	3,215	33	10	108	WF	70		HF	7,620	4,884	Succ.		Exp. L
173	4,568	33	7	162	WF	68		NC	953	391	Succ.		Exp. L
180	1,311	31.5	32	87	WF	73		JS	812	53	Prom.		RW
908	4,626	30	17	133	WF	65		HF	1,179	596	Succ		Exp. L
875	3,911	15.5	46	154	WF	69		NC	1,072	387	Succ		Exp. L
901	3,921	14	80	149	WF	71		HF	2,084	707	Prom.		Exp. L
875	3,911	15.5	46	158	WF	69		NC	3,984	1,026	Prom.		RW
412	3,238	21	19	127	WF	60		NC	1,082	446	Succ.		Exp. L
538	3,346	21	22	123	WF	60		NC	365	211	Succ.		Exp. L
1,200	2,100	12.8	2,965	108	Prim.	57		NC	13,000	8,000	Succ.	Yes	FW
1,200	2,100	12.8	2,965	108	SS	57	10	HF	1,000	500	Disc.	No	P(Exp. UL)
2,000	1,950	27	40	86	Prim.	45		HF	635	459	Succ.	Yes	RW
600-1,000	1,700-2,100	25	120		Prim.	78		HF	1,940	1,620	Succ.	Yes	
460-1,150	2,130-2,790	27	120	95	Prim.			NC	690	610	Succ.	Yes	Exp. UL
1,000-1,300	2,130-2,790	27	120	95	Prim.			NC	500	280	Succ.	Yes	Exp. L
1,000-1,200	2,130	27	120	95	WF	65		JS	700	630	Prom.		
300-1,000	2,070-2,460	25	120	96	Prim.			HF	1,310	1,150	Succ.	Yes	
300-800	1,700-2,100	25	120	96	WF			HF	2,410	1,840	Succ.	Yes	Exp. L
1,000	3,600	33	4	133	WF	65.5	55.2	HF	250	50	Succ.	Yes	P (Exp. L)
200-1,500	9,400	35	1.3	195	WF	34		NC					P
6,000	2,300	24.5	175	95	WF	66	55	NC	295	295	Succ.	Yes	FW
6,000	2,560	24.5	175	95	WF	76	62	HF	240	200	TETT		FW

Producing EOR projects outside U.S. and Canada (continued)

State/Area	Operator	Type Project	Field	Start date	Area, acres	No. wells prod	No. wells inj.	Pay zone	Form-ation	Porosity, %
Lower Saxony	Wintershall AG	Hot water	Emlichheim 3	6/90	95	6	1	Valenginian	S	30
Lower Saxony	Wintershall AG	Steam	Ruehlertwist	12/78	237	26	2	Valenginian	S	28
Lower Saxony	Wintershall AG	Steam	Emlichheim 11	3/92	80	10	3	Valenginian	S	28
Lower Saxony	Wintershall AG	Steam	Emlichheim 10	6/94	47	7	1	Valenginian	S	30
India										
Gujarat	ONGC	Polymer	Jhalora	6/93	11	4	1	Kalol Sand IX+X	S	33
Gujarat	ONGC	Combustion	Balol	3/90	6	4	1	Kalol Sand I	US	28
Gujarat	ONGC	Combustion	Lanwa	8/92	10	4	1	Kalol Sand I	US	30
Indonesia										
Pekanbaru	PT Caltex	Steam	Duri	4/85	7,020	1,654	703	Pertama - Kedua	US	34
	Total	Micellar polymer	Handil	1982	4	1	3		S	30
Libya										
	Zueitina Oil	HC miscible	Intisar 103D	1/69	3,325	20	6	" D" Reef	LS	23.9
Trinidad										
Forest Reserve	Petrotrin	CO_2 immiscible	Area 2102	6/76	58	6	2	Forest Sands	S	32
Forest Reserve	Petrotrin	CO_2 immiscible	Area 2121	1/74	29	2	2	Forest Sands	S	30
Forest Reserve	Petrotrin	CO_2 immiscible	Area 2124	1/86	184	3	1	Forest Sands	S	31
Oropouche	Petrotrin	CO_2 immiscible	Oropouche	6/90	175	4	3	Retrench	S	30
Guapo	Petrotrin	Steam	Cruse E	8/70	531	125	29	Cruse E	S	25
Point Fortin	Petrotrin	Steam	Cruse E	2/86	66	17	7	Cruse E	S	31
Point Fortin	Petrotrin	Steam	Parrylands	7/81	86	20	10	Forest	S	30
Forest Reserve	Petrotrin	Steam	Project III	7/65	135	36	12	Forest Zone 5.1	S	33
Forest Reserve	Petrotrin	Steam	Phase I Cyclic	8/76	58	10	0	Forest Sands	S	31
Forest Reserve	Petrotrin	Steam	Phase I West	12/88	50	10	10	Forest Sands	S	30
Fyzabad	Petrotrin	Steam	Fyzabad Forest	8/79	129	37	11	Forest	S	28
Fyzabad	Petrotrin	Steam	Fyzabad Cruse	8/79	150	29	4	Cruse	S	25
Palo Seco	Petrotrin	Steam	Central Los Bajos	2/74	280	123	34	LMLE	S	28
Palo Seco	Petrotrin	Steam	Palo Seco North	11/69	438	170	62	LMLE	S	28
Palo Seco	Petrotrin	Steam	Palo Seco B.V.	11/85	150	49	10	LMLE	S	28
Quarry	Petrotrin	Steam	Apex Quarry	2/81	278	86	18	LMLE	S	28
Premier Consolidated Oilfields		Steam	Fyzabad	1989	21	19	3	Lower Forest	US	28
Turkey										
Batman	TPAO	CO_2 immiscible	Bati Raman	3/86	10,709	145	41	Garzan	LS	18
U.A.E.										
Abu Dhabi	Total	Hydrocarbon misc.	Abu Al Bu Khoosh	8/91	50	3	1	Arab D	LS	15
Venezuela										
Anzoategui	Corpoven S.A.	Steam	Bare (F.O)	3/85	16,452	55	48	U1,3(YAC.MFB-53)	US	31.9
Anzoategui	Corpoven S.A.	Steam	Bare (F.O).	3/87	8,066	66	65	U2,3(YAC.MFB-23)	US	28.6
Anzoategui	Corpoven S.A.	Steam	Arecuna (F.O.)	2/85	1,668	5	5	5	US	30.7
Anzoategui	Corpoven S.A.	Steam	Arecuna (F.O)	12/83	1,544	15	15	T(YAC.MFA-52)	US	30.6
Campo Cerro Negro	Lagoven S.A.	Steam	B.E.P.-Cerro Negro	1984	49,090	186		Morichal-Memb.	S	35
Campo Jobo	Lagoven S.A.	Steam	Jobo	12/69	25,410	88		Jobo Member	S	31
Campo Jobo	Lagoven S.A.	Steam	Jobo - P.E.T.C.	8/85	267	17		Morichal	S	30
Campo Jobo	Lagoven S.A.	Steam	Jobo	12/69	34,099	301		Morichal	S	30
Campo Pilon	Lagoven S.A.	Steam	West Pilon	12/69	1,065	8		Oficina-1	S	31
Zulia	Lagoven S.A.	Steam	Bachaquero	12/80	343	2		Bachaquero Superior	S	23
Zulia	Lagoven S.A.	Steam	Lagunillas	2/71	9,343	522	2	Bachaquero	S	34
Zulia	Lagoven S.A.	Steam	Tia Juana	2/70	1,692	25		Lagunillas Inferior	S	31
Zulia	Maraven S.A.	Steam	Lagunillas	4/65	420	59		U.L.H.	S	35
Zulia	Maraven S.A.	Steam	Lagunillas	8/64	76	7		L.L.	S	33.7
Zulia	Maraven S.A.	Steam	Lagunillas	7/67	618	54		U.L.H.	S	35
Zulia	Maraven S.A.	Steam	Lagunillas	1/70	3,025	147		L.L.	S	33.7
Zulia	Maraven S.A.	Steam	Lagunillas	4/70	2,565	220		U.L.H.	S	35
Zulia	Maraven S.A.	Steam	Lagunillas	8/70	2,114	175		U.L.H.	S	35
Zulia	Maraven S.A.	Steam	Lagunillas	11/79	3,101	261		L.L.	S	33.7
Zulia	Maraven S.A.	Steam	Lagunillas	10/80	3,565	297		U.L.H.	S	35
Zulia	Maraven S.A.	Steam	Bachaquero	11/84	7,795	640		Post-Eoceno	S	33.5
Zulia	Maraven S.A.	Steam	East Tia Juana	4/59	341	32		L.L.	S	33.5
Zulia	Maraven S.A.	Steam	East Tia Juana	2/61	35	7		L.L.	S	38.1
Zulia	Maraven S.A.	Steam	East Tia Juana	9/64	411	36		L.L.	S	38
Zulia	Maraven S.A.	Steam	East Tia Juana	5/68	2,755	201		L.L.	S	38.1
Zulia	Maraven S.A.	Steam	East Tia Juana	8/68	3,218	250		L.L.	S	38.1
Zulia	Maraven S.A.	Steam	East Tia Juana	12/68	1,961	168		L.L.	S	38
Zulia	Maraven S.A.	Steam	East Tia Juana	3/69	1,768	145		L.L.	S	38.1
Zulia	Maraven S.A.	Steam	East Tia Juana	8/69	1,642	148		L.L.	S	38.1
Zulia	Maraven S.A.	Steam	East Tia Juana	12/69	392	36		L.L.	S	38.1
Zulia	Maraven S.A.	Steam	East Tia Juana	11/74	1,848	135	21	L.L.	S	38.1
Zulia	Maraven S.A.	Steam	East Tia Juana	9/86	1,380	88		L.L.	S	36
Zulia	Maraven S.A.	Steam	Main Tia Juana	10/63	867	82		L.L.	S	38.1
Zulia	Maraven S.A.	Steam	Main Tia Juana	6/66	144	15		L.L.	S	38.1
Zulia	Maraven S.A.	Steam	Main Tia Juana	7/67	1,271	114		L.L.	S	38
Zulia	Maraven S.A.	Steam	Main Tia Juana	7/67	1,500	134		L.L.	S	38.1
Zulia	Maraven S.A.	Steam	Main Tia Juana	10/67	2,323	197		L.L.	S	38.1
Zulia	Maraven S.A.	Steam	Main Tia Juana	10/67	1,286	86		L.L.	S	38.1

Table D

Permea- bility, md	Depth, ft	Gravity, °API	Oil, cp	Oil, °F.	Prev. Prod.	Satur. % start	Satur. % end	Proj. Matur.	Tot. prod., b/d	Enh. prod., b/d	Proj. Eval.	Profit	Project Scope
6,000	2,500	24.5	175	95	WF	72	60	HF	235	225	TETT		FW
5,000	2,650	25	175	100	WF	51	42	NC	760	750	Succ.	Yes	P (Exp. L)
5,500	2,800	24.5	175	100	HW	71	45	HF	880	870	Succ.	Yes	FW
5,000	2,600	24.5	175	100	WF,HW	72	50	JS	710	710	TETT	c	FW
5,000	4,000	25.7	10	185	Prim.	82		HF			TETT		P
8,000-15,000	3,440	15.6	100-150	158	Prim.	70		NC	190	190	Succ.		P (FW)
8,000-15,000	3,440	13.5	550	158	Prim.	80		HF	165	165	Prom.		P (Exp. L)
1,550	625	22	157	101	Prim.	62	25	JS	300,000	300,000	Succ.	Yes	Exp. L
1,000	4,500	33	0.4	115	WF	35			400	400			
226	8,849	39.2	0.46	226		80	18	NC	40,000	40,000	Succ.	Yes	FW
150	2,600	17	32	120	Prim	60		HF	50	50	Prom.		RW
300	4,200	25	6	130	WF	44		HF	77	77	Prom		RW
36	2,400	29	5	120	Prim.	53	48	HF	88	88	Prom.		P
250	2,300	14	3,500	108	Prim.	65		HF	1,500	1,500	Succ.	Yes	RW
95	1,400	17	175	110	Prim.	58	18	HF	310	310	Prom.		P
500	1,100	11	5,500	104	Prim.	75	20	HF	300	300	Succ.	Yes	RW
340	1,100	15	140	110	Prim.	70	20	NC	800	800	Succ.	Yes	RW
205	1,200	19	32	105	Prim.	57	15	NC	50	50	Disc.	No	RW
430	1,500	17	160	105	Prim.	67	25	JS	50	50	Disc.	No	RW
275	1,100	14	220	98	Prim.	70		NC	230	230	Succ.	Yes	RW
19	2,000	20	150	105	Prim.	65		NC	120	120	Succ.	Yes	RW
250	1,500	16	550	102	Prim.	70		HF	1,800	1,800	Succ.	Yes	RW
250	1,700	16	550	102	Prim.	70		HF	2,500	2,500	Succ.	Yes	RW
250	1,200	21	160	98	Prim.	70		HF	400	400	Succ.	Yes	RW
250	2,100	19	185	105	Prim.	65		HF	1,100	1,100	Succ.	Yes	RW
350	350-700	14	1,100	100	Prim.	70	40	JS	120	94	Prom.		P
175	3,000	19	16	120	Prim.	56		HF	270	270	Succ.	Yes	RW
58	4,265	13	592	129		78		NC	14,000	13,500	Succ.	Yes	FW
200	8,000	32		200	Prim.	45	25	JS	500	300	TETT	Yes	P
6,600	2,650	9.3	376	131	Prim.	88	75	HF	33,401	23,385	Succ.	Yes	RW (Exp. L)
5,000	3,050	9.2	351	136	Prim.	83	75	HF	6,305	4,013	Succ.	Yes	RW (Exp. L)
5,800	2,850	10	370	135	Prim.	82	74	NC	703		Disc.	No	P (Exp. UL)
4,500	3,150	9.8	560	140	Prim.	80	72	NC	230	41	Prom.	Yes	RW
10,000	2,000	8.5	5,500	125	Prim.	80		HF	25,000	15,000	Succ.	Yes	P (Exp. L)
2,500	3,260	13.5	138	130	Prim.	80		HF	4,200	1,870	Succ.	Yes	FW
5,000	3,600	9	1,952	132	Prim.	85		NC	1,531	875	Succ.	Yes	P (Exp. L)
5,000	3,600	9	1,952	132	Prim.	85		JS	34,960	16,500	Succ.	Yes	FW
8,000	3,350	10	727	139	Prim.	82		JS	2,360	1,260	Succ.	Yes	RW
1,500	3,400	14	185	135	Prim.	85		JS			TETT	No	P (Exp. L)
4,000	2,690	12	600	128	Prim.	84		HF	24,000	11,000	Succ.	Yes	FW
1,250	2,537	15	93	119		72		HF				Yes	
	2,300	11.4	3,500	117	Prim.	75	44	NC	3,183	3,091	Succ.	Yes	FW
	2,850	15.2	2,500	125	Prim.	80	50	NC	127	118	Succ.	Yes	P
	2,300	11.4	3,500	117	Prim.	75	46	NC	4,835	4,438	Succ.	Yes	FW
	2,850	15.2	2,500	122	Prim.	87	54	HF	3,220	1,307	Prom.	Yes	FW
	2,300	11.8	7,000	115	Prim.	75	54	HF	24,017	12,045	Prom.	Yes	FW
	2,300	11.4	3,500	118	Prim.	75	63	HF	11,478	11,120	Prom.	Yes	FW
	2,850	15	580	126	Prim.	87	66	HF	6,053	4,160	Prom.	Yes	FW
	2,300	11	20,000	125	Prim.	75	63	HF	26,106	21,089	Prom.	Yes	FW
575	2,000	13	500	117	Prim.	84.5	40	JS	42,048	39,104	Prom.	Yes	FW
	1,500	12	1,000	108	Prim.	85	48	HF	673	355	Prom.	Yes	FW
1,300	1,746	13.6	13,000	100	Prim.	85	45	NC	65		Prom.	Yes	P
3,000	1,250	12	3,000	104	Prim.	85	65	HF	760	493	Prom.	Yes	FW
	1,200	12	750	104	Prim.	85	64	HF	6,878	4,150	Prom.	Yes	FW
3,000	872	12	5,000	104	Prim.	81	74	HF	6,115	4,201	Prom.	Yes	FW
	1,250	12	7,500	106	Prim.	85	67	HF	9,651	8,879	Prom.	Yes	FW
780	1,700	12.1	2,000	111	Prim.	85	67	HF	6,623	3,566	Prom.	Yes	FW
1,300	1,250	10	12,000	102	Prim.	85	77	HF	6,350	5,018	Prom.	Yes	FW
	1,000	11.1	10,000	95	Prim.	85	72	HF	1,572		Prom.	Yes	FW
780	1,597	12	1,000	111	Prim.	85	46	HF	3,799	2,097	Succ.	Yes	FW
1,000-4,000	760	9-11	5,000-30,000	110	Prim.	85	82	HF	10,595		Prom.	Yes	FW
1,400	1,750	13.1	750	113		85	57	NC	1,546	195	Prom.	Yes	FW
675	1,250	13.1	1,300	104	Prim.	85	65	NC	160	32	Prom.	Yes	FW
675	1,209	13.1	5,000	123	Prim.	85	61	HF	5,403	439	Prom.	Yes	FW
1,000	1,400	13.1	1,000	110	Prim.	85	65	HF	3,827	2,438	Prom.	Yes	FW
1,000	1,746	13.1	4,100	110	Prim.	85	62	HF	6,328	5,346	Prom.	Yes	FW
1,000	1,746	13.1	1,200	110	Prim.	85	76	HF	3,107	2,622	Succ.	Yes	FW

Completed, terminated and postponed projects outside U.S. and Canada

Country/ State/Area	Operator	Type Project	Field	Start date	Area, acres	No. wells prod	No. wells inj.	Pay zone	Form-ation	Porosity %
Colombia										
Mid. Magdalena basin	Texas Petroleum	Steam	Cocorna	3/87	15	8	3	Oligocene B	S	28
Germany										
Lower Saxony	Wintershall AG	Hot water	Emlichheim 14	10/67	64	5	1	Valenginian	S	30
Lower Saxony	Wintershall AG	Hot water	Emlichheim 07	10/67	82	5	1	Valenginian	S	30
Lower Saxony	Wintershall AG	Polymer	Bockstedt	9/84	57	4	1	Valenginian	S	23
Lower Saxony	Wintershall AG	Steam	Emlichheim 06	5/81	121	15	4	Valenginian	S	30
Hungary										
	Mol Rt KFV	CO_2	Nagylengyel	10/88	2,890	104	10	I-IV Rudistic	LS	1.06
	Mol Rt KFV	CO_2	Nagylengyel	9/80	200	5	1	Triassic	Dolo.	2.5
	Mol Rt KFV	CO_2	Budafa	1981	1,013	77	60	Zala Kerettye	S	22
Russia										
Tatarstan	Tatneft	Surfactant	Romashkino	3/88	936	28	6	Devonian	S	19.5
Tatarstan	Tatneft	Polymer	Romashkino	1983-84	1,646	55	10	Carbon	S	20-23
Tatarstan	Tatneft	Microbial	Romashkino	5/87	917	15	6	Devonian	S	20

Producing thermal EOR in U.S.

Type/ Operator	Field	State	County	Start date	Area, acres	No. wells, prod	No. wells, inj.	Pay zone	Form-ation	Porosity %
Steam										
Amoco	Winkleman Dome	Wyo.	Fremont	1964	160	19	13	Nugget	S	22.8
ARCO	Kern River	Calif.	Kern	1970	80	112	33	Kern River Series	S	31
ARCO	Kern River	Calif.	Kern	1970	95	71	29	Kern River Series	S	33
ARCO	Kern River	Calif.	Kern	9/72	38	32	16	Kern River Series	S	31
ARCO	Kern River	Calif.	Kern	1972	50	41	20	Kern River Series	S	31
ARCO	Midway-Sunset	Calif.	Kern	1/72	8	31	4	Potter	S	32
ARCO	Midway-Sunset	Calif.	Kern	1971	108	98	15	Potter	S	34
ARCO	Midway-Sunset	Calif.	Kern	1983	34	13	2	L. Monarch	S	30
ARCO	Midway-Sunset	Calif.	Kern	1981	40	70	10	Monarch	S	32
ARCO	Midway-Sunset	Calif.	Kern	8/72	9	35	4	Monarch	S	32
ARCO	Midway-Sunset	Calif.	Kern	1984	15	12	0	Sub Lakeview	S	30
ARCO	Midway-Sunset	Calif.	Kern	1969	50	60	15	Metson	S	30
ARCO	Midway-Sunset	Calif.	Kern	2/72	200	50	3	Potter	S	32
ARCO	Midway-Sunset	Calif.	Kern		40	139	1	Potter/Tulare	S	30
ARCO	Midway-Sunset	Calif.	Kern	1977	107	210	18	Potter	S	36
ARCO	Midway-Sunset	Calif.	Kern	1986	40	77	0	Potter	S	27
ARCO	Midway-Sunset	Calif.	Kern		80	95	11	Potter/Tulare	S	30
ARCO	Midway-Sunset	Calif.	Kern		70	59	4	Potter/Tulare	S	30
ARCO	Midway-Sunset	Calif.	Kern	3/90	80	188	5	Potter/Crocker/Tulare	S	30
ARCO	Midway-Sunset	Calif.	Kern	3/90	120	247	4	Potter	S	30
ARCO	Midway-Sunset	Calif.	Kern		80	36	4	Marviz	S	30
ARCO	Midway-Sunset	Calif.	Kern	1965	160	236	80	Potter	S	26
ARCO	Placerita	Calif.	Los Angeles	1986	95	70	17	L. Kraft	S	28
Berry	North Midway-Sunset	Calif.	Kern	1965	160	120		Potter	S	30
Berry	South Midway-Sunset	Calif.	Kern	1964	300	650		Monarch	S	30
Chevron	Cymric 26W	Calif.	Kern	10/89	30	31	19	Tulare/Amnicola	S	33
Chevron	Cymric 35/36W	Calif.	Kern	5/75	285	130	47	Tulare/Amnicola	S	33
Chevron	Cymric 6Z	Calif.	Kern	2/86	30	31	19	Tulare/Amnicola	S	33
Chevron	Cymric 5Z	Calif.	Kern	2/91	12	14	4	Tulare/Amnicola	S	36
Chevron	Cymric 7Z	Calif.	Kern	5/91	177	30	30	Tulare	S	36
Chevron	Kern River KCL 39	Calif.	Kern	10/75	118	67	42	Kern River	S	33
Chevron	Kern River MC1	Calif.	Kern	4/76	132	120	76	Kern River	S	34
Chevron	Kern River MCII	Calif.	Kern	4/71	80	129	30	Kern River	S	34
Chevron	Kern River Sec. 3	Calif.	Kern	9/68	424	345	155	Kern River	S	34
Chevron	Kern River Sec. 4	Calif.	Kern	6/78	156	200	64	Kern River	S	34
Chevron	Kern River Sec. 9 HHF	Calif.	Kern	1/92		8		Kern River	S	34
Chevron	Kern River-ANO	Calif.	Kern	5/74	160	177	82	Kern River	S	32
Chevron	Midway-Sunset Sec. 15A	Calif.	Kern	5/78	23	36	5	Potter	S	36
Chevron	Midway-Sunset Sec. 26C	Calif.	Kern	11/75	84	243	81	Monarch	S	32
Chevron	Midway-Sunset Sec. 2F	Calif.	Kern	10/83	84	44	10	Webster	S	32
Chevron	West Coalinga 31A/36Z	Calif.	Fresno	3/89	100	70	21	Temblor	S	33
Chevron	West Coalinga 6C	Calif.	Fresno	7/84	105	131	18	Temblor	S	33
Chevron	West Coalinga 12-D	Calif.	Fresno	2/82	120	89	31	Temblor	S	33
Chevron	West Coalinga 13-D	Calif.	Fresno	5/73	550	182	104	Temblor	S	35
Chevron	West Coalinga 25-D	Calif.	Kern	5/80	36	131	95	Temblor	S	29
Carrizo	Camp Hill	Tex.	Anderson	4/89	58	45	24	Carrizo	S	37
Exxon	Midway-Sunset	Calif.	Kern	8/90	200	136	75	Monarch Sand	S	30
Exxon	South Belridge	Calif.	Kern	12/87	90	48	24	Tulare	S	38
Fluor Daniel	Teapot Dome NPR-3	Wyo.	Natrona	10/85	90	190	30	Shannon	S	18
MacPherson Oil Co.	Mt. Poso field-West area	Calif.	Kern	5/89	240	40	2	Vedder	US	35

Table E

Permea-bility, md	Depth, ft	Gravity °API	Oil, cp	Oil, °F.	Prev. Prod.	Satur. % start	Satur. % end	Proj. Matur.	Tot. prod., b/d	Enh. prod., b/d	Proj. Eval.	Profit	Project Scope
700	2,100	12.8	2,965	108	SS	57	19	C	0	0	Succ.	Yes	P (Exp. UL)
6,000	2,550	24.5	175	95	WF	73	58	C	225	225	Succ.	Yes	FW
6,000	2,400	24.5	175	95	WF	70	56	C	295	295	Succ.	Yes	FW
4,000	4,100	34.0	11	130	WF	39	33	C	45	28	Prom.	Marg.	P
6,000	2,400	24.5	175	95	HW	62	45	C	540	540	Succ.	Yes	P (Exp. L)
1,000	6,700	18	22	237	Prim.			JS	3,700	3,700	Succ.		
1,000	7,400	16	92	248	Prim.			NC	60	60	Succ.		
110	3,000	42	1	147	Prim.			NC	400	400	Succ.		
475	5,740	44.3	5	95	WF			NC	1,624	587	Succ.	Yes	Exp. L
300-1,000	3,770	25-28	25-41	75	Prim.			NC	12,245	1,053	Succ.	Yes	FW
465	5,740	44.3	5	95	WF			NC	740	181	Succ.	Yes	Exp. L

Table F

Permea-bility, md	Depth, ft	Gravity °API	Oil, cp	Oil, °F.	Prev. Prod.	Satur. % start	Satur. % end	Proj. Matur.	Tot. prod. b/d	Enh. prod. b/d	Proj. Eval.	Profit	Project Scope
481	1,225	14	1,000	81	Prim.	71		NC	140	140	Succ.		FW
2,000	600	13	5,000	78	Prim.	63	15	NC	700	700	Succ.	Yes	LW
4,000	1,200	13	8,000	90	SS	55	20	NC	1,000	1,000	Succ.	Yes	LW
2,500	900	13	7,000	84	Prim.	70	15	HF	400	400	Succ.	Yes	LW
2,000	800	13	8,000	90	SS	60	15	NC	1,100	1,100	Succ.	Yes	LW
1,675	1,200	12	2,000	100	SS	65	15	HF	880	880	Succ.	Yes	LW
3,700	1,500	11.5	9,000	65	SS	67	15	HF	3,800	3,800	Succ.	Yes	LW
2,000	1,500	13	5,000	10	C	60	30	HF	1,300	1,300	Succ.	Yes	LW
1,500	1,200	13	30	200	SS	50	10	HF	2,475	2,475	Succ.	Yes	LW
1,500	1,000	13	1,500	100	SS	50	10	JS	485	485	Succ.	Yes	LW
4,500	1,300	13	4,000	90	Prim.	60	35	HF	105	105	Succ.	Yes	LW
3,000	1,100	11.4	9,500	130	Prim.	75	57	JS	1,125	1,125	TETT		LW
2,500	1,200	14	1,500	100	Prim.	65		NC	900	900	Succ.	Yes	LW
3,500	1,500	12	4,000	105	Prim.	70	15	NC	2,100	2,100	Succ.	Yes	LW
2,000-5,000	600	13	6,000	110	SS	70	8-12	HF	7,000	7,000	Succ.	Yes	LW
2,200	700	11.9	74,000	80	Prim.	60	15	HF	750	750	Prom.		LW
1,500-3,000	800	12	10,000	95	Prim.	70	15	NC	900	900	Succ.	Yes	LW
3,500	800	12	10,000	95	SS	70	15	NC	600	600	Succ.	Yes	LW
2,500	900	11.5	10,000	95	SS	60	15	JS	5,000	5,000	Prom.		LW
3,500	900	11.5	10,000	95	Prim.	60	15	JS	7,000	7,000	Prom.	Yes	LW
300	1,100	12.7	3,500	104	SS	65	15	HF	650	650	Succ.	Yes	LW
4,000	810	13	10,000	90	SS	70	15	NC	3,200	3,200	Prom.	Yes	LW
3,000	1,800	12	7,500	100	Prim.	62	15	JS	2,550	2,550	Prom.		FW
3,000	1,300	14	4,000	85	Prim.	70	15	HF	1,000	700	Succ.	Yes	FW
2,000	1,000	13	8,000	80	Prim.	70	15	HF	7,000	5,000	Succ.	Yes	FW
2,900	1,200	12	5,500	100	SS	51	15	HF	1,461	1,461	Succ.	Yes	P
1,800	1,200	13	4,000	100	SS	52		NC	6,518	6,518	Succ.	Yes	LW
2,900	1,200	12	5,500	100	SS	51	15	HF	900	900	Succ.	Yes	LW
2,900	1,200	12	5,500	100	Prim.	51	15	HF	591	591	Succ.	Yes	LW
2,900	600	12	5,500	100	CS	53	15	NC	70	70	Succ.	Yes	LW
3,100	1,400	14	2,000	90	Prim.	65		HF	379	379	Succ.	Yes	P
2,800	960	14	2,000	90	Prim.	59		HF	2,072	2,072	Succ.	Yes	FW
2,800	960	14	2,000	90	Prim.	59		HF	2,274	2,274	Succ.	Yes	FW
3,389	775	14	2,000	90	Prim.	55		HF	8,340	8,340	Succ.	Yes	FW
3,000	850	14	2,000	90		60		HF	3,778	3,778	Succ.	Yes	FW
3,000	800	14	2,000	90	SS	55		HF	158	158	Succ.	Yes	FW
3,000	1,000	14	2,000	90	Prim.	55		HF	3,643	3,643	Succ.	Yes	FW
3,900	1,400	14	900	120	SS	61	20	NC	1,600	1,600	Succ.	Yes	P
1,100	1,300	14	1,500	150	SS	58	20	HF	7,381	7,381	Succ.	Yes	FW
2,000	1,800	12	7,000	90	SS	60		HF	2,251	2,251	Succ.	Yes	RW
2,300	1,700	13	6,000	100	SS	44	15	JS	1,382	1,382	Succ.	Yes	LW
2,400	1,500	13	5,700	100	SS	49	15	HF	689	689	Succ.	Yes	LW
2,400	1,600	13	6,000	100	SS	50	15	HF	617	617	Succ.	Yes	LW
1,000	1,200	13	1,000	90	Prim.	46	15	NC	2,465	2,465	Succ.	Yes	FW
1,000	2,500	12	2,300	100	Prim.	50	12	HF	5,441	5,441	Succ.	Yes	FW
2,500	400	18.4	1,200	75	Prim.	62	33	NC	200	200	Succ.	No	LW
2,500	1,500	12	11,000	95				HF	1,200	1,200	Succ.	Yes	FW
2,000	1,250	13	450	95				HF	1,100	800	Succ.	Yes	FW
63	325	33	10	65	Prim.	50	15	NC	700	500	Succ.	Yes	RW
2,000	2,500	17	350	105	Prim.	50	20	JS	250	150	TETT		LW (Exp. L)

Producing thermal EOR in U.S. (continued)

Type/ Operator	Field	State	County	Start date	Area, acres	No. wells, prod	No. wells, inj.	Pay zone	Form-ation	Porosity %
Mobil	Midway-Sunset	Calif.	Kern	10/70	400	381	32	Monarch	S	34
Mobil	North Midway-Sunset	Calif.	Kern	11/67	410	376	21	Potter	S	35
Mobil	San Ardo	Calif.	Monterey	6/68	470	100	28	Aurignac	S	34.5
Mobil	Lost Hills	Calif.	Kern	6/90	125	100	36	Etchegoin	US	40
Mobil	Lost Hills	Calif.	Kern	6/90	150	125	37	Tulare	US	40
Mobil	San Ardo	Calif.	Monterey	3/80	95	42	14	Lombardi	S	32.5
Mobil	South Belridge	Calif.	Kern	1969	870	510	263	Tulare	US	36.8
Mobil	South Belridge	Calif.	Kern	1965	1,987	50		Tulare	US	36.8
Naftex	Edison 27-RT	Calif.	Kern	7/77	30	65	29	Chanac	S	30
Oxy USA	Kern Front	Calif.	Kern	11/81	3,240	491	28	Etchegoin Chanac	S	33
Saba	North Belridge	Calif.	Kern	11/65	160	14	0	Tulare	S	38
Santa Fe Energy	Coalinga	Calif.	Fresno	3/91	40	38	11	Upper Temblor	S	30
Santa Fe Energy	Coalinga	Calif.	Fresno	3/79	35	36	7	Lower Temblor	S	30
Santa Fe Energy	Coalinga	Calif.	Fresno	5/92	20	18	4	Etchegoin	S	35
Santa Fe Energy	Midway	Calif.	Kern	1/85	350	530	78	Potter S.D.	S	30
Santa Fe Energy	Midway	Calif.	Kern	1964	740	770		Potter Cyclic	S	30
Santa Fe Energy	Midway	Calif.	Kern	1970	400	500		Spellacy Cyclic	S	30
Santa Fe Energy	Midway	Calif.	Kern	6/82	800	250		Tulare Cyclic	S	33
Santa Fe Energy	Midway	Calif.	Kern	1991	30	30	8	Spellacy S.D.	S	30
Santa Fe Energy	Midway	Calif.	Kern	1991	10	9	4	Tulare S.D.	S	33
Santa Fe Energy	Belridge	Calif.	Kern	6/82	180	75	24	Tulare S.D.	S	33
Santa Fe Energy	Kern River	Calif.	Kern	10/89	235	314	0	Kern River Series	S	33
Shell	Arroyo Grande	Calif.	San Luis Obispo	1/87	20	65	18	M6	S	31
Shell	Belridge	Calif.	Kern	1961	3,489	2900	975	Tulare	S	36
Shell	Cat Canyon	Calif.	Santa Barbara	3/85	1,000			Basal Sisquoc	S	32
Shell	Coalinga	Calif.	Fresno	1980	550	190	22	Temblor Zone I	S	32
Shell	Coalinga	Calif.	Fresno	11/87	260	172	48	Etchegoin	S	34
Shell	Kern River	Calif.	Kern	1970	600	840	270	Kern River Series	S	30
Shell	Midway-Sunset	Calif.	Kern	1979	70	66	0	Upper Spellacy	S	28
Shell	Midway-Sunset	Calif.	Kern	1/89	68	78	8	Lower	S	25
Shell	Midway-Sunset	Calif.	Kern	1983	143	205	25	Sub-Hoyt	S	31
Shell	Midway-Sunset	Calif.	Kern	1971	400	650	34	Potter	US	22-32
Shell	Midway-Sunset	Calif.	Kern	1980	85	145	8	Monarch	S	25
Shell	Mount Poso	Calif.	Kern	1971	800	75	16	Vedder	S	33
Shell	Cymric	Calif.	Kern	12/86	200	100	46	Tulare	S	36
Shell	McKittrick	Calif.	Kern	3/88	226	145	115	Tulare	S	36
Shell	Yorba Linda	Calif.	Orange	1971	310	203	11	Upper Conglomerate	S	22
Stockdale	Kern Front	Calif.	Kern	2/93	160	54	6	Etchegoin	S	30
Texaco/Four Star	Lost Hills	Calif.	Kern	8/77	35	43	12	Etchegoin	S	40
Texaco/Four Star	Lost Hills	Calif.	Kern	11/75	60	65	21	Tulare	S	38
Texaco	Kern River	Calif.	Kern	8/62	5,830	4762	1319	Kern River Series	S	31
Texaco	McKittrick	Calif.	Kern	1984	18	17	2	Tulare	S	38
Texaco	North Midway	Calif.	Kern	11/81	77	27	9	Potter	US	30
Texaco	Midway-Sec 35	Calif.	Kern	1977	27	51	7	Potter	US	35
Texaco	Midway-Sec. 36	Calif.	Kern	1989	38	62	11	Potter	US	36
Texaco	Midway-Sec. 36	Calif.	Kern	1991	24	24	6	Potter	US	36
Texaco	Midway-Security	Calif.	Kern	11/77	36	72	15	Potter	US	33
Texaco	Midway-Sunset	Calif.	Kern	1/94	9.5	15	3	Potter A	S	28
Texaco	San Ardo	Calif.	Monterey	7/87	51	24	7	Lombardi	S	32
Tidelands	Wilmington	Calif.	Los Angeles	4/89	180	58	40	Tar	S	30
Torch Operating	Cymric	Calif.	Kern	1964	370	305	53	Tulare	S	35
Torch Operating	Midway-Sunset	Calif.	Kern	1974	81	52	17	Potter	S	34.5
Torch Operating	Midway-Sunset	Calif.	Kern	1983	81	50	0	Tulare	S	31
Torch Operating	Midway-Sunset	Calif.	Kern	6/77	50	79	20	Potter	S	24
Torch Operating	Midway-Sunset	Calif.	Kern	5/69	150	185	0	Potter	S	24
Hot water										
ARCO	Kern River	Calif.	Bakersfield	1986	50	45	10	Kern River Series	S	31
Texaco	San Ardo	Calif.	Monterey	9/86	240	20	16	Aurignac	S	33.0
Combustion										
Bayou State	Bellevue	La.	Bossier	1970	200	85	15	Nacatoch	S	32.0
Chevron	W. Heidelberg Cotton Valley	Miss.	Jasper	12/71	362	9	3	Cotton Valley 4 & 5	S	14
Greenwich Oil	Forest Hill	Tex.	Wood	9/76	1,900	100	21	Harris Sand	S	28
Santa Fe Energy	Midway-Sunset	Calif.	Kern	1982	24	47	10	Potter	S	35
Continental Resources	Medicine Pole Hills	N.D.	Bowman	1985	8,960	17	7	Red River B & C	Dolo.	18.9
Continental Resources	Buffalo	S.D	Harding	1979	7,680	21	12	Red River B	Dolo.	20
Continental Resources	West Buffalo	S.D	Harding	1987	4,640	15	6	Red River B	Dolo.	20
Continental Resources	South Buffalo	S.D	Harding	1983	20,800	40	19	Red River B	Dolo.	20

Producing CO_2 and other gas EOR in U.S.

Type/ Operator	Field	State	County	Start date	Area, acres	No. wells prod	No. wells inj.	Pay zone	Form-ation	Porosity, %
CO_2 miscible										
Amerada Hess	Seminole Unit	Tex.	Gaines	7/83	15,699	408	160	San Andres	Dolo.	12
Amoco	Cedar Lake	Tex.	Gaines	8/94	2,500	175	166	San Andres	Dolo.	14
Amoco	Lost Soldier	Wyo.	Sweetwater	5/89	1,345	54	60	Tensleep	S	9.9

Table F

Permea-bility, md	Depth, ft	Gravity °API	Oil, cp	Oil, °F.	Prev. Prod.	Satur. % start	Satur. % end	Proj. Matur.	Tot. prod. b/d	Enh. prod. b/d	Proj. Eval.	Profit	Project Scope
4,000	950	13	800	85	Prim.	64	53	HF	8,300	8,300	Succ.	Yes	FW
1,000	1,000	12	2,000	100	Prim.	65	30	HF	10,500	10,500	Succ.	Yes	FW
2,000	2,300	12	1,000	130	SS	55	27	HF	1,900	1,900	Succ.	Yes	FW
1,500	350	14	1,500	95	SS	55	20	JS	2,500	2,400	Prom.	Yes	FW
1,000	200	13	1,500	82	SS	60	20	JS	1,600	1,600	Prom.	Yes	FW
2,260	2,100	11	3,000	125	SS	55	27	HF	3,000	3,000	Succ.	Yes	P (Exp. L)
3,000	1,000	14	1,600	95	SS	62.9	21.1	HF	41,000	41,000	Succ.	Yes	Exp. L
3,000	1,000	14	1,600	95	Prim.	64.5	60.6	NC	460	460	Succ.	Yes	Exp. L
2,800	1,000	14	2,000	90	Prim.	50	15	NC	550	550	Succ.	Yes	FW
3,250	1,300-1,500	14	1,525	95	Prim.	50	15	JS	5,400	5,400	Succ.	Yes	FW
2,500	800	13.6	450	130	Prim.	63	49	HF	166	66	Prom.	No	FW
100-3,000	1,200	14	1,900	75	SS	45	15	HF	650	600	Succ.	Yes	LW
100-3,000	850-1800	14	1,900	75	SS	35	15	NC	550	500	Succ.	Yes	LW
4,000-6,000	530	11	3,500	70	Prim.	65	25	HF	180	150	Succ.	Yes	Exp. L
2,500	1,500	12	4,000	100	SS	60	20	HF	11,500	11,000	Succ.	Yes	FW
2,500	1,300	12	4,000	100	Prim.	60	33	HF	16,000	15,200	Succ.	Yes	FW
2,250	900	11.5	6,500	100	Prim.	60	33		3,200	2,700	Succ.	Yes	FW
1,300	1,200	11	5,000	100	Prim.	50	43		400	350	Succ.	Yes	Exp L
2,250	1,700	13	5,000	100	SS	60	25	HF	325	300	Prom.		Exp. L
1,300	1,300	11	5,000	100	SS	50	20	HF	100	100	Prom.		P
1,100	650	14	2,200	100	SS	65	25	HF	2,000	2,000	Succ.	Yes	FW
1,500-2,200	100-900	13	1,500-15,000	90	Prim., SS, SD	46	37	HF	5,000	5,000	Succ	Yes	FW
500-800	200-2,000	13-15	2,500-3,000	80-100	Prim.	56		JS	1,300	1,100	Prom.		FW
2,400	400-1,400	13	1,900	95	Prim.	65		HF	39,000	39,000	Succ.	Yes	FW
500-1,000	2,500-4,500	6-12		90-150	Prim.	55		PP			TETT	Yes	FW
200-2,500	825-1,650	12-13	2,000-1E4	84-98	Prim.	60	10	NC	2,100	2,100	Succ.	Yes	FW
800-1,000	650-1000	9-10		80-90	Prim.	55		HF	5,000	5,000	Succ.		FW
500-2,500	150-1,500	12-13	1E5-2E5	78-85	Prim.	55	10	HF	12,000	11,900	Succ.	Yes	FW
1,500-2,500	900	13	2,235	90	Prim.	70		HF	900	800	Succ.	Yes	FW
700-2,500	800	11.6	5,000	90	Prim.	70		JS	1,700	1,500	Prom.		LW
2,000-3,000	1,080	13	3,000	100	Prim.	80		HF	6,000	5,900	Succ.	Yes	FW
	500-1,400	8.5-14		95	Prim.	75		HF	7,500	7,500	Succ.	Yes	FW
900	1,300	13	2,700	95	SS	75		HF	2,200	2,200	Succ.	Yes	FW
2,000-10,000	1,500-1,800	15-18	275	90-130	Prim.	55	10	NC	3,400	2,400	Succ.	Yes	FW
1,000-2,000	1,000	11-14	1,000-2,000	95-105	Prim.	65		JS	5,500	5,500	Succ.	Yes	LW
1,000-2,000	600	10-12		90-100	None	60		JS	2,500	2,500	Prom.		LW
500-3,000	500-1,000	10-14		70-100	SS	66	20	NC	1,000	750	Succ.	Yes	FW
1,000	2,000	13		80	SS	70		JS	500	400	Succ.	Yes	Exp. L
2,000	400	13	10	250	SS	63	30	NC	1,200	1,200	Succ.	Yes	LW
2,000	200	13	20	220	SS	70	30	NC	1,000	1,000	Succ.	Yes	LW
4,000	1,000	13	4,060	90	Prim.	50	20	HF	90,000	90,000	Succ.	Yes	FW
2,800	1,000	13	35	220	SS	60	30	HF	115	115	Disc.	No	P
3,400	1,000	13	1,500	220	S	60	20	HF	2,400	1,462	Succ.	Yes	FW
2,000	1,600	12	6,500	230	SS	55	20	JS	700	590	TETT	Yes	FW
3,000	1,600	14		220	SS	61	21	HF	1,880	1,061	Succ.	Yes	FW
3,000	1,600	14		90	SS	61	21	JS	640	121	TETT	No	FW
5,000	950	12	1,500	280	S	60	20	NC	1,100	825	Succ.	Yes	FW
3,000	1,500	12	3,000	115	SS	50	20	JS	60	60	Disc.	No	P
5,500	1,900	11	1,200	135	C	58	15	JS	2,200	2,200	TETT	No	P (Exp. L)
1,500	2,500	14	300	123	WF	55	20	HF	2,800	2,800	Succ.		LW
1,500	1,100	11.8	2,921	100	Prim.	65	45	NC	6,654	6,319	Succ.	Yes	FW
3,700	1,100	11.4	10,000	110	SS	57.2	32.3	HF	727	700	Succ.	Yes	FW
1,146	700	11.4	10,000	100	Prim.	54	37.8	HF	1,082	1,050	Succ.	Yes	FW
1,500	1,000	11.3	100	220	SS	55	34	NC	1,559	1,520	Succ.	Yes	FW
1,500	1,000	11.3	500	170	Prim.	57	35	NC	2,255	1,980	Succ.	Yes	FW
3,000	900	13.5	8,000	90	S	30	20	HF	150	150	Succ.	Yes	FW
3,000	2,200	13.0	4,000	100	S	38	31.0	JS	100	100	TETT	Yes	RW
650	400	19.0	660		Prim.	94	49.0	HF	420	420	Succ.	Yes	FW
85	11,300	18.0-27.0	6	221	Prim.	80		NC	200	200	Succ.	Yes	FW
950	5,000	10	1,060	185		63	32	JS	400	400	Prom.	No	FW
500-4,000	1,700	11.5	2,770	110	SS	70	11.5	HF	1,000	900	Succ.	Yes	Exp. L
14.9	9,500	39	0.48	230	Prim.	52	30	HF	855	575	Succ.	Yes	FW
10	8,450	30	2.1	215	Prim.	55	20	NC	590	575	Succ.	Yes	FW
10	8,450	30	2.1	215	Prim.	55	20	HF	330	285	Succ.	Yes	FW
10	8,450	30	2.1	215	Prim.	55	20	HF	1,220	1,130	Succ.	Yes	FW

Table G

Permea-bility, md	Depth, ft	Gravity °API	Oil, cp	Oil, °F.	Prev. Prod.	Satur. % start	Satur. % end	Proj. Matur.	Tot. prod., b/d	Enh. prod., b/d	Proj. Eval.	Profit	Project Scope
1.3-123	5,300	35	1.07	104	WF			HF	35,035	30,000	Succ.	Yes	FW
5	4,700	32	2.40	103	WF			JS	6,365	1,744	TETT	Yes	LW
31	5,000	35	1.30	178	WF			HF	6,000	4,700	Succ.	Yes	FW

Producing CO_2 and other gas EOR in U.S. (continued)

Type/ Operator	Field	State	County	Start date	Area, acres	No. wells prod	No. wells inj.	Pay zone	Form- ation	Porosity, %
Amoco	Lost Soldier	Wyo.	Sweetwater	5/89	790	20	41	Darwin-Madison	S/LS-Dolo	10.3
Amoco	North Cowden	Tex.	Ector	2/95	200	30	18	San Andres	Dolo.	10
Amoco	Slaughter (Central Mallet)	Tex.	Hockley	1984	6,412	175	134	San Andres	Dolo./LS	10.8
Amoco	Slaughter Estate	Tex.	Hockley	12/84	5,700	185	161	San Andres	Dolo./LS	12
Amoco	Slaughter Frazier	Tex.	Hockley	12/84	1,600	59	52	San Andres	Dolo./LS	10
Amoco	Wasson ODC	Tex.	Yoakum	11/84	7,800	293	290	San Andres	Dolo./LS	9
Amoco	Wertz	Wyo.	Carbon, Sweetwater	10/86	1,400	28	41	Tensleep	S	10
ARCO	Wasson-Willard	Tex.	Yoakum	1/86	8,000	282	226	San Andres	Dolo.	10
Chevron	North Ward Estes	Tex.	Ward	3/89	3,840	190	194	Yates	S	16
Chevron	Rangely Weber Sand	Colo.	Rio Blanco	10/86	15,000	204	200	Weber SS	S	12
Conoco	Ford Geraldine Unit	Tex.	Reeves & Culberson	2/81	3,850	91	69	Delaware	S	23
Conoco	Maljamar	N.M.	Lea and Eddy	1/89	1,760	94	2	Grayburg-San Andres	Dolo/S	10.8
Conoco	East Huntley	Tex.	Garza	1/94	700	38	15	San Andres	Dolo.	16.9
Conoco	South Huntley	Tex.	Garza	1/94	560	31	7	San Andres	Dolo.	15.1
Exxon	Cordona Lake	Tex.	Crane	12/85	2,084	42	30	Devonian	Tripol.	22
Exxon	Means (San Andres)	Tex.	Andrews	11/83	8,500	480	286	San Andres	Dolo	9
Exxon	Slaughter	Tex.	Hockley	5/85	569	36	15	San Andres	Dolo.	12.5
Exxon	Wasson (Cornell Unit)	Tex.	Yoakum	7/85	1,923	62	51	San Andres	Dolo.	8.6
Fasken	Hanford	Tex.	Gains	7/86	1,120	23	26	San Andres	Dolo.	10.5
George R. Brown	Rose City North	Tex.	Orange	4/81	800	3	5	Hackberry	S	37
George R. Brown	Rose City South	Tex.	Orange	1/83	900	4	5	Hackberry	S	37
Henry Petroleum	Sho-Vel-Tum	Okla.	Stephens	9/82	1,100	60	40	Sims	S	16
Meridian Oil	El Mar	Tex.	Loving	4/94	6,000	32	17	Delaware	S	21.8
Mitchell Energy	Alvord South Field	Tex.	Wise	1980	2,291	12	3	Caddo	Congl.	12.8
Mobil	GMK South	Tex.	Gaines	1982	1,143	24	24	San Andres	Dolo.	9.8
Mobil	Greater Aneth Area	Utah	San Juan	2/85	13,440	143	120	Ismay Desert Creek	LS	14
Mobil	Postle	Okla	Texas	11/95	11,000	140	110	Morrow	SS	16
Mobil	Salt Creek	Tex.	Kent	10/93	12,000	85	48	Canyon	LS	20
Mobil	Slaughter	Tex.	Hockley	6/89	2,495	84	47	San Andres	Dolo	10.3
Mobil	Wasson	Tex.	Yoakum	10/85	640	30	26	San Andres	Dolo.	13
Orla Petco	East Ford	Tex.	Reeves	7/95	1,953	12	8	Delaware, Ranosen	S	23
Oxy USA	Northeast Purdy	Okla.	Garvin	9/82	3,400	75	44	Springer	S	13
Oxy USA	South Welch	Tex.	Dawson	10/93	2,800	80	57	San Andres	Dolo.	15.5
Pennzoil	SACROC Unit	Tex.	Scurry	1/72	49,900	400	230	Canyon Reef	LS	3.93
Phillips	Vacuum	N.M.	Lea	2/81	4,900	192	100	San Andres	Dolo.	11.7
Shell	Bennett Ranch Unit	Tex.	Yoakum	6/95	160	15	7	San Andres	Dolo.	10
Shell	N. Cross	Tex.	Crane & Upton	4/72	1,155	25	12	Devonian	Tripol	22
Shell	S. Cross	Tex.	Crockett	6/88	1,200	21	10	Devonian	Tripol	21
Shell	Little Creek Field	Miss.	Lincoln & Pike	12/85	6,200	19	19	Lower Tuscaloosa	S	23
Shell	Olive	Miss.	Pike	10/87	1,280	8	4	Lower Tuscaloosa	S	26
Shell	Wasson (Denver)	Tex.	Yoakum & Gaines	4/83	27,848	735	365	San Andres	Dolo.	12
Shell	Wasson (South)	Tex.	Gaines	1/86	4,960	105	70	Clearfork	Dolo.	6
Shell	West Mallalieu	Miss.	Lincoln	11/86	5,760	6	2	Lower Tuscaloosa	S	25
Stanberry Oil	Farnsworth, North	Tex.	Ochiltree	6/80	1,431	9	5	Marmaton B	LS	11.5
Stanberry Oil	Hansford Marmaton	Tex.	Hansford	6/80	2,010	9	10	Marmaton	S	18.1
Texaco	Mabee	Tex.	Andrews-Martin Co.	1/92	12,824	390	85	San Andres	Dolo.	9
Texaco	Slaughter Sundown	Tex	Hockley Co.	1/94	8,685	280	187	San Andres	Dolo.	11
Texaco	Paradis	La.	St. Charles	2/82	347	20	1	Lower 9,000-ft	S	26
Texaco	Paradis	La.	St. Charles	1/88	44	1	1	9,500 ft	S	24
Texaco/MVP	Paradis	La.	St. Charles	5/89	298	4	2	#16 Sand	S	24
Texaco/MVP	Paradis	La.	St. Charles	5/90	102	1	1	10,000 ft sand	S	26
Texaco	Garden Island Bay	La.	Plaquemines	12/95	91	1	1	8,500 Sand	S	29
Texaco	Port Neches	Tex.	Orange	7/93	235	5	4	Marginulina	S	30
Unocal	Dollarhide	Tex.	Andrews	5/85	6,183	83	66	Devonian	Dolo./Tripol	13.5
Unocal	Dollarhide (Clearfork)	Tex.	Andrews	11/95	160	21	4	Clearfork	Dolo.	11.5
Weiser Oil	Wellman	Tex.	Terry	7/83	1,400	14	9	Wolfcamp	LS	9.2
Whiting	Sable	Tex.	Yoakum	3/84	825	33	32	San Andres	Dolo.	8.4
CO_2, N_2 flue gas immiscible										
Marathon Oil	Yates	Tex.	Pecos & Crockett	f1/85	14,300	619	29	Grayburg/San Andres	Dolo.	17
Hydrocarbon miscible										
ARCO	Kuparuk River	Alas.		6/88	5,800	27	26	A H C Sands	S	24
ARCO	Kuparuk River	Alas.		8/93	2,900	13	13	A H C Sands	S	24
ARCO	Prudhoe Bay	Alas.		12/82	3,650	42	11	Sadlerochit	S	23
ARCO	Prudhoe Bay	Alas.		2/87	55,000	450	190	Sadlerochit	S	22
Exxon	South Pass Block 89	OCS		12/83	204	15	7	X and Y Series	S	26
Exxon	South Pass Block 89	OCS		7/89	20	3	3	X Series	S	26
Hunt	Fairway	Tex.	Anderson/Henderson	3/66	22,618	92	51	James	LS	12.6
Kerr-McGee	North Buck Draw(Dakota)	Wyo.	Campbell	12/88	5,700	11	8	Dakota	S	9.3
Kerr-McGee	Sand Dune (Muddy) Unit	Wyo.	Converse	7/91	12,438	15	9	Muddy	S	11.8
Oryx	Fordoche W-12	La.	Pt. Coupee	5/80	3,400	7		Wilcox	S	19
Oryx	Fordoche W-8	La.	Pt. Coupee	5/80	3,300	8		Wilcox	S	20
True Oil	Red Wing Creek	N. D.	McKenzie	1/82	640	8	1	Mission Canyon	LS	10
Phillips	Chatom	Ala.	Washington	8/76	3,200	7	2	Smackover lime	Dolo.	22
Hydrocarbon immiscible										
ARCO	Kuparuk River	Alas.		2/86	50,000	170	157	A & C Sands	S	24
Nitrogen & Hydrocarbon immiscible										
ARCO	Block 31	Tex.	Crane	6/49	7,840	152	77	Devonian	LS	15

Table G

Permea-bility, md	Depth, ft	Gravity °API	Oil, cp	Oil, °F.	Prev. Prod.	Satur. % start	Satur. % end	Proj. Matur.	Tot. prod., b/d	Enh. prod., b/d	Proj. Eval.	Profit	Project Scope
4	5,400	35	1.40	181	WF			JS	1,600	1,100	Prom.	Yes	FW
2-5	4,200	34	1.46	91	WF			JS	17,600	839	TETT	Yes	LW
2	4,900	31	1.40	105	WF			HF	4,400	2,600	Succ.	Yes	FW
5	4,950	31	1.40	105	WF			HF	7,400	4,200	Succ.	Yes	FW
4	4,950	31	1.40	105	WF			HF	2,500	1,600	Succ.	Yes	FW
5	5,100	32	1.30	110	WF			HF	13,313	9,300	Succ.	Yes	FW
20	6,000	35	1.16	163	WF			NC	1,800	1,300	Succ.	Yes	FW
1.5	5,100	32	2.01	105	WF	55.5	41	JS	6,000	4,900	Succ.	Yes	FW
37	2,600	35	1.40	83	WF	25	10	HF	1,491	1,491	Disc.		Exp. UL
10	6,000	35	1.70	160	WF	38	29	JS	23,881	13,881	Succ.		FW
64	2,680	40	1.4	83	Prim./WF	41	35	NC	1,300	1,300	Succ.	No	FW
5	3,650-4,200	37	1	95	Prim/GI/WF	55.6	40	NC	1,300	200	TETT	No	Exp. UL
5.6	3,100	37	2.1	100	WF	45	31	JS	430	130	TETT	TETT	FW
6	3,400	37	2.6	105	WF	45	34	JS	1,000	150	TETT	TETT	FW
4	5,500	40	0.50	101	WF			HF	1,450	1,320	Prom.	Yes	LW
20	4,300	29	6.00	97	WF			HF	11,900	8,700	Succ.	Yes	FW
6	4,900	32	1.30	110	WF			HF	1,200	530	Succ.	Yes	LW
2	4,500	33	1.00	106	WF			HF	1,800	1,100	Prom.	Prom.	LW
4	5,500	32	1.38	104	Prim.	60.7	18.7	HF	840	710	Succ.		LW
4,500	8,200	37	2.00	180	WF	50	35	NC	100	100	Prom.	Yes	FW
4,500	8,200	37	2.00	180	WF	50	35	HF	350	350	Prom.	Yes	FW
70	6,200	30	3.30	115	WF	59	42	HF	1,700	1,700	Succ.	Yes	LW
24	4,500	40.5		97	Prim./WF	40.3		JS	160	160			RW
55	5,700	44	0.39	154	WF	60	52	NC	80	80	Prom.	No	FW
3	5,400	30	2.57	101	WF	55	28	JS	1,300	400	Succ.	Yes	LW
5	5,600	41	0.50	125	Prim.	50		JS	6,000	3,000	Succ.	Yes	LW
30	6,100	36	1.30	147	WF	37	25	JS	2,200	0	TETT		Exp. L
12	6,300	39.2	0.95	125	WF	89	15	JS	25,000	10,000	Succ	Yes	Exp. L
3	5,000	32	1.60	107	WF	45	8	JS	5,000	1,500	Succ.	Yes	LW
6	5,100	33	0.97	110	WF	54.4	39.2	HF	1,700	300	Succ.	Yes	LW
64	2,680	40	0.77	83	Prim.	49	36	JS			TETT		FW
44	9,400	38	1.20	148	WF	46	40	HF	2,600	1,950	Succ.		FW
4	4,900	34	2.40	95	WF	50	38	JS	1,900	950	TETT		RW (Exp. L)
19	6,700	41	0.35	130	Prim./WF	63.3	46.8	NC	10,000	10,000	Succ.	Yes	FW
11	4,500	38	1.00	101	Prim.	70	50	HF	8,200	4,500	Succ.	Yes	FW
7	5,200	33	1.20	105	WF	55	37	JS	3,200	100	TETT		P
5	5,300	44	0.42	106	GI	49	21	HF	1,345	1,345	Succ.	Yes	FW
4	5,200	43	0.60	104	GI	43	24	JS	1,570	1,500	Prom.		Exp. L
33	10,640	39	0.40	248	WF	15	2	NC	850	850	Prom.		FW
50	10,500	39	0.34	250	WF	17	2	NC	320	320	Succ.	Yes	FW
8	5,200	33	1.24	105	WF	51	30.5	JS	36,600	30,700	Succ.	Yes	FW
2	6,700	35	1.00	105	WF	60		JS	5,000	1,000	Prom.		FW
20	10,365	38	0.50	245	Prim.	15	1	NC	225	225	Disc.		P (Exp. UL)
140	6,400	44	1.61	131	WF	57		NC	200	200	Succ.	Yes	FW
48	6,500	44	1.56	142	Prim.	43		HF	390	390	Succ.	Yes	FW
4	4,700	32	2.30	104	WF	36	10	JS	6,736	2,165	Prom	No	FW
6	4,950	33	1.40	105	WF	41	25	JS	3,000		TETT	Yes	LW
770	10,400	37	0.50	205	Prim.	62	48	HF	100	100	Prom.	No	RW
252	9,800	38	35.0	192	Prim.	45	33	HF	100	100	Prom.	No	RW
245	9,950	38	35.0	190	Prim.	44	24	HF	270	270	Prom.		P
162	11,400	38.5	0.30	192	Prim.	45	33	HF	40	40	Prom.	No	RW
500	8,000	36	0.50	190	Prim.	48	31	JS	0	0	TETT		P
750	5,800	38	2.40	165	WF	30		JS	225	225	TETT	No	RW
9	8,000	40	0.44	122	Prim./WF	35	22	JS	2,350	900	Yes		FW
4	6,500	40	0.44		Prim./WF			JS	355		TETT		P
>100.0	9,800	43.5	0.54	151	WF	35	10	HF	3,200	3,200	Succ.		FW
2	5,200	32	1.46	107	WF			NC	520	300	Succ.	Yes	FW
175	1,100-1,700	30	5.50	82	GI			HF	54,400		Succ.		FW
50-500	6,000	24	2.00	160	WF	50	25	JS	17,000	8,000	Succ.	Yes	P
50-500	6,000	24	2.00	160	Hyd. Imm.	50	25	JS	8,000		Succ.		P
300	8,800	27	0.90	200	Prim.	65	25	NC	7,000	5,000	Succ.		P (Exp. UL)
400	8,800	27	0.90	210	WF	50	25	HF	220,000	55,000	Succ.		FW
100-1,500	9,500	38.0-40.0	0.40-0.60	165	Prim.			HF	7,700	3,100	Succ.	Yes	RW
1,000	11,000	38	0.70	165	Prim.			NC	1,450	580	Succ.	Yes	RW
11	9,900	48	0.15	260	Prim.	73	36	HF	6,010	6,010	Succ.	Yes	FW
3	12,450	46	0.12	282	Prim.	85	35	JS	11,000	8,000	Succ.		RW
70	12,500	41	0.30	240	Prim.	83	40	JS	10,000	10,000	Succ.	Yes	FW
5	13,650	45	0.13	274				NC	47	47	Succ.	Yes	FW
9	13,200	44	0.13	267				NC	96	96	Succ.	Yes	FW
0.1	9,000	40	0.25	241	Prim.	60	20	JS	1,200		Succ.	Yes	FW
12	15,900	54	0.04	293	Prim.			NC	430	430	Succ.	Yes	FW
50-500	6,000	24	2.00	160	WF	55	50	JS	150,000		Prom.	Yes	FW
5	8,600	48	0.25	130	Prim.			NC	4,350	4,350	Succ.	Yes	FW

Producing CO_2 and other gas EOR in U.S. (continued)

Type/ Operator	Field	State	County	Start date	Area, acres	No. wells prod	No. wells inj.	Pay zone	Form-ation	Porosity, %
Nitrogen miscible										
Exxon	Jay-Little Escambia Creek	Fla/Ala.	Santa Rosa/Escambia	1/81	14,415	56	30	Smackover	LS	14
Unocal	Chunchula Fieldwide Unit	Ala.	Mobile	4/82	2,600	33	8	Smackover Carbonate	Dolo.	12.35
Phillips	Binger	Okla.	Caddo	1977	12,960	55	23	Marchand	S	7.5
Nitrogen immiscible										
Chevron	East Painter	Wyo.	Uinta	11/83	1,500	17	7	Nugget	S	11
Chevron	Painter	Wyo.	Uinta	6/80	1,360	33	13	Nugget	S	11.9
Exxon	Hawkins	Tex.	Woodbine-East FB	8/87	2,800	24	6	Woodbine	S	28
Exxon	Hawkins	Tex.	Woodbine-West FB	1/94	7,790	264	17	Woodbine	S	28
Unocal	Chunchula Fieldwide Unit	Ala.	Mobile	4/82	26,000	33	8	Smackover Carbonate	Dolo.	12.35

Producing chemical and microbial EOR projects in U.S.

Type/ Operator	Field	State	County	Start date	Area, acres	No. wells prod	No. wells inj.	Pay zone	Form-ation	Porosity, %
Polymer										
Bison Production	N. Kremlin	Okla.	Garfield	1/94		10	8	Misener	S	10.4
Gallagher Drilling	Stewart East	Wyo.	Campbell	7/82		4	1	Minnelusa	S	15.7
Kerr-McGee	Horse Creek	Wyo.	Campbell	2/88	24,200	69	61	Sussex	S	12
Mitchell Energy	Alba Northeast Unit	Tex.	Wood	7/80	410	7	3	Sub-Clarksville	S	21.4
Mitchell Energy	Alba SEFB Unit	Tex.	Wood	2/72	731	12	6	Sub-Clarksville	S	23.3
Mitchell Energy	Alba North Central Unit	Tex.	Wood	1/91	512	11	6	Sub-Clarksville	S	21
Mitchell Energy	Alba West Unit	Tex.	Wood	12/91	567	8	8	Sub-Clarksville	S	21
Coleman Oil & Gas	Jacksboro S.	Tex.	Jack	5/82	270	5	6	Strawn	S	19.9
Plains Petroleum	Bracken Unit	Wyo.	Campbell	7/86	120	3	2	Minnelusa	S	16.5
Presidio	Culp Draw Unit	Wyo.	Campbell	7/85		40	43	Shannon	S	
Presidio	Table Mountain	Wyo.	Campbell	8/91		18	8	Shannon	S	
Alkaline/surfactant										
True	Driscoll	Wyo.	Crook	12/95	1	1	1	Minnelusa	S	16
Microbial										
Hughes Eastern	North Blowhorn Creek	Ala.	Lamar	1/94		14	4	Carter	S	12

Completed, terminated, postponed, and delayed U.S. projects*

Type/ Operator	Field	State	County	Start date	Area, acres	No. wells prod	No. wells inj.	Pay zone	Form-ation	Porosity, %
Polymer										
Oxy USA	Harmony Hill	Kan.	Rooks	10/84	130	5	3	Lansing/Kansas City	LS	12.5
Phillips	North Burbank	Okla.	Osage	9/80	1,440	41	29	Burbank	S	15.5
Phillips	C.B. Long Unit	Tex.	Stonewall & King	2/94	90	6	1	4,800 Sand (Katz)	S	15.9
Consolidated Oil & Gas	Ottie Draw Unit	Wyo.	Campbell	3/90		1	2	Minnelusa	S	14
Ampolex	Little Missouri Creek	Wyo.	Crook	8/89	197	6	2	Minnelusa	S	15.1
Ampolex	Ash	Wyo.	Campbell	12/92	97	2	1	Minnelusa	S	16.8
Bridge Oil	Candy Draw	Wyo	Campbell	6/87	480	9	4	Minnelusa	S	15.1
Cenex	Rule	Wyo.	Campbell	12/91		1	1	Minnelusa	S	17
Enron Oil & Gas	Saddle Ridge Unit	Wyo.	Sublette	12/74	376	8	5	Mesaverde	S	22
Fancher Oil	Ash	Wyo.	Campbell	1/93	96	2	1	Minnelusa	S	16.8
Petroleum Inc.	Kiehl Unit	Wyo.	Crook	2/87	248	6	2	Minnelusa	S	22.4
Quintana	Stagg Draw	Wyo.	Campbell	1/94	10	8		Misener	S	10.4
Unocal	Dos Cuadras	Calif.	Santa Barbara	6/83	320	37	10	EP/FP	S	27.0-31.0
Unocal	Farnsworth	Tex.	Ochiltree	9/83	13,005	37	41	Morrow	S	14.5
Unocal	Healdton	Okla.	Carter	12/82	2,010	156	111	Healdton Sands	S	26.2
Unocal	Osage-Hominy	Okla.	Osage	4/83	2,880	96	37	Miss. Chat	LS	30
Alkaline/surfactant										
Cockrell Prod.	Doris	Tex.	Nolan	6/93	400	10	4	Cook	S	15
Micellar polymer										
Plains Petroleum	Lawrence Robins102B Maraflood	Ill.	Lawrence	8/82	25	12	5	Bridgeport	S	21
Plains Petroleum	Lawrence-Robins202-B Project	Ill.	Lawrence	10/85	1	4	1	Bridgeport Main	S	20.6
Steam										
Chevron	Cymric Sec. 31X	Calif.	Kern	4/79	69	38	17	Amnicola	S	35
Chevron	Cymric 1Y	Calif.	Kern	11/89	98			Tulare	S	33
Chevron	Lost Hills Sec. 30	Calif.	Kern	1/80	190	37	0	Etchegoin A	S	40
Texaco	North Antelope Hills	Calif.	Kern	11/94	14	6	3	Packwood	US	35
Berry	McKittrick	Calif.	Kern	1993	100	0	0	Tulare	S	35

Table G

Permea-bility, md	Depth, ft	Gravity °API	Oil, cp	Oil, °F.	Prev. Prod.	Satur. % start	Satur. % end	Proj. Matur.	Tot. prod., b/d	Enh. prod., b/d	Proj. Eval.	Profit	Project Scope
35	15,400	51	0.20	285	WF			NC	11,100	11,100	Succ.	Yes	FW
10	18,500	54	0.07	325	Prim.	80	45	JS	7,100	2,300	Succ.	Yes	FW
0.2	10,000	38	0.30	190	Prim.	76	59	HF	1,050	1,050	Succ.	Yes	FW
3	12,000	46	0.20	185	HC	98.5	52	HF	9,065	9,065	Succ		FW
4	11,500	46	0.20	174	HC	47		HF	1,102	1,102	TETT		FW
2,800	4,600	24	3.70	168				HF	1,100	1,100	Succ.	Yes	RW
2,800	4,600	24	3.70	168				JS	9,500		Prom.		RW
10	18,500	54	0.07	325	Prim.	80	45	JS	7,100	2,300	Succ.	Yes	FW

Table H

Permea-bility, md	Depth, ft	Gravity, °API	Oil, cp	Oil, °F.	Prev. Prod.	Satur. % start	Satur. % end	Proj. Matur.	Tot. prod., b/d	Enh. prod., b/d	Proj. Eval.	Profit	Project Scope
10	6,300	42.5		136							TETT	Yes	P
215	7,950	20	20	124							Succ.	Yes	FW
14	8,200	36	0.96	179	Prim.	59	35	JS	1,450		TETT	Yes	FW
471	4,100	15.1	75	150	WF	62.6	52.1	NC	70	70	Disc.	Yes	FW
525	4,200	15.5	75	150	Prim.	69.5	51.8	NC	100	100	Succ.	Yes	FW
471	4,010	15	75	150	Prim.	62	56	JS	150	150	Prom.	TETT	FW
471	4,050	15	75	150	Prim.	65	56	JS	110	110	Prom	TETT	FW
86	1,975	40	1.73	100	Prim.	50	22	NC	20	20	Succ.	Yes	FW
173	7,150	20.2	16.6	150	Prim.	76.1	59.4	HF	189	139	Succ.	Yes	FW
	9,300				Prim.			NC			Succ.	Yes	FW
	9,600				Prim.			HF			Succ.	Yes	Exp. L
60	5,300	22	16	155	WF	43.5		JS	50	0	TETT	TETT	FW
1-200	2,300	33	15	90	WF	55	45	JS	290	0	Prom.	TETT	P, Exp. L

Table I

Permea-bility, md	Depth, ft	Gravity, °API	Oil, cp	Oil, °F.	Prev. Prod.	Satur. % start	Satur. % end	Proj. Matur.	Tot. prod., b/d	Enh. prod., b/d	Proj. Eval.	Profit	Project Scope
	3,130	38.6	3.7	105	Prim.	49	34	Term	50	50	Succ.	Yes	FW
50	2,900	39	3	120	WF	53	47	Term	300	180	Succ.	Yes	FW
136	4,800	37	1.7	116	WF			C			Prom		P
	7,700	30	4	154	Prim.	69	45.3	JS	130		Succ.	Yes	FW
243	5,600	22	25.5	137	Prim.	79.6	51.4	HF	700	40	Succ.	Yes	FW
300	7,775	20	30	138	Prim.	84.5	59.2	HF	500	450	Succ.	Yes	FW
85	7,300	25	10	146							Succ.	Yes	FW
100	8,350	25	15	155							Succ.	Yes	FW
40	1,800	44	2.33	85	Prim.	37.5	27.3	NC	210	13	Succ.	Yes	FW
300	7,775	20	29	138							Succ.	Yes	FW
265	6,350	24.2	12	123	Prim.	55.7	39.3	NC	635	300	Succ.	Yew	FW
10	7,290	24.6	7.8	184							Succ.	Yes	FW
260.0-680.0	1,280-1,650	25.0-26.0	5-24	95-103	WF	54-59	52-57	NC	2,300		Disc.	Yes	FW
22	7,400	38	1	141	WF	43	40	HF	491	0	Disc.	Yes	FW
346	800	30.3	10	80	WF	56	47	HF	871	0	Succ.	Yes	FW
27	2,880	38.7	3	100	WF	51	48	HF	926	36	Succ.	Yes	FW
10	3,900	46	1	89							Succ.	Yes	P
398	950	29	18	70	Prim./WF	45		C	56	56	Prom.	No	P (Exp. UL)
352	900	29	18	70	WF	45		C	8	8	Prom.	No	P (Exp. UL)
2,700	1,300	12	3,000	100	Prim.	50	15	C	507	507	Succ.	Yes	FW
3,000	1,200	12	5,500	100	Prim.	56	10	Term	409	0	Disc	No	P
800	550	18	300	90	Prim.	55	15	Term	100	100	Disc	No	P
2,500	800	12	3,000	90	SS	48	19	Sold	20	120	Prom.	Yes	P
2,000	750	10	12,000	86	SS	65	30	PP	0	0		No	P

Completed, terminated, postponed, and delayed U.S. projects* (continued)

Type/ Operator	Field	State	County	Start date	Area, acres	No. wells prod	No. wells inj.	Pay zone	Form- ation	Porosity, %
Unocal	Guadalupe	Calif.	San Luis	1955	2,970	150	0	Sisquoc	S	35
Combustion										
Santa Fe Energy	Midway	Calif.	Kern	1991	3	4	1	Tulare	S	33
Hydrocarbon miscible										
Amoco	Levelland	Tex.	Hockley	5/71	1,422	81	50	San Andres	Dolo.	10.2
Microbial										
Phoenix Oil & Gas Ltd.	Chelsea-Alluwe	Okla.	Rogers	6/90	520	47	19	19-23 ft	S	20
Nitrogen immiscible										
Exxon	Hawkins	Tex.	Woodbine	4/77	10,590			Woodbine	S	28
CO_2 projects										
Pennzoil	Kane	Pa.	Elk	11/91	41	9	4	Kane	S	12

Producing Worldwide heavy oil EOR projects (Primary production)

Type/ Operator	Field	Country/ prov.	Start date	Area, acres	No. wells prod	No. wells inj.	Pay zone	Form- ation	Porosity, %
Steam									
Amoco	Wolf Lake/Primrose	Alta.	4/85	10,130			Clearwater	S	31-35
Gibson	Athabasca Oil Sands	Alta.	7/84	50,000	3	3	McMurray	US	30-35
Imperial Oil	Cold Lake	Alta.	1964		2,100	2,100	Clearwater	US	35
Husky Oil	Pikes Peak	Sask.	1/81	400	102	27	Waseca	US	33
Murphy Oil	Lindbergh	Alta.	1/74	212	68	68	Lower Grand Rapids	US	33
Shell Canada Ltd	Peace River	Alta.	10/86	450	163	53	Cretaceous-Bullhead	S	28

UTF SAGD wells

Fig. 4

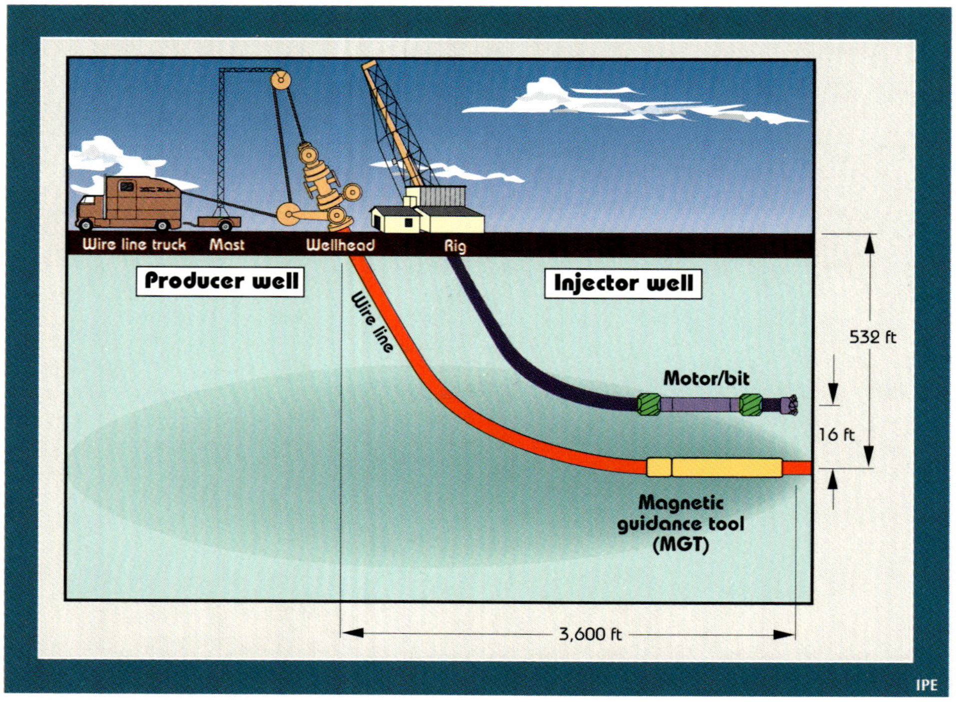

Supalcu de Barcau is the largest in situ combustion project in the world. In 1994, 507 wells produced about 8,800 b/d. Both air and steam were injected into the 33-52 ft thick reservoir encountered at depths of 115-772 ft. Tatarstan planned steam injection in seven bitumen areas. The first project was to have started in 1996 with production forecast at 17,000 b/d by 2015.

Prices, costs

The price of heavy oil was increasing in 1996. At the beginning of 1994 the Kern River 13° API heavy oil price was just above $7/bbl; in 1996 it had risen to $13-17.50/bbl.

Also, heavy oil production costs had declined. In Cold Lake the 1986 costs were more than $7/bbl (Canadian). They dropped to about $4.50/bbl in 1994. Likewise, Texaco's costs in Kern River dropped from $6.27/bbl in 1990 to $4.86/bbl in 1994.

SAGD

Steam-assisted gravity drainage (SAGD) continues to interest Canadian operators. One such innovative project, originally operated by the Alberta Oil Sands Technology and Research Authority (Aostra), extracts bitumen with dual horizontal wells drilled from a tunnel. In 1995, Gibson Petroleum Co. Ltd., became operator of the underground test facility (UTF).

Phase A of the UTF started in 1987 with three pairs of 197 ft laterals. In Phase B, producing since December 1992, production from the longer laterals averaged 2,000 b/d. The UTF site has produced over 2 million bbl of 8° API bitumen.

Table I

Permeability, md	Depth, ft	Gravity, °API	Oil, cp	Oil, °F.	Prev. Prod.	Satur. % start	Satur. % end	Proj. Matur.	Tot. prod., b/d	Enh. prod., b/d	Proj. Eval.	Profit	Project Scope
1,550	3,000	9	580	135	Prim.	80	60	HF	1,200	700	Succ.	Yes	FW
1,300	1,300	11	5,000	100	SS	70	11	PP	40	20	TETT		P
2	4,900	30	2.30	105	Prim.	90		NC	2,000	2,000	Succ.		P (Exp. UL)
16	400	34	6-7		WF			C	30	2	Prom.		P
2,800	4,530	24	3.70	168	Prim.			C			Succ.	Yes	FW
4	2,500	48	2.50	80	WF	70	40	JS	35	10	TETT		P

Table J

Permeability, md	Depth, ft	Gravity, °API	Oil, cp	Oil, °F.	Satur. % start	Satur. % end	Proj. Matur.	Tot. prod., b/d	Enh. prod., b/d	Proj. Eval.	Profit	Project Scope
1,000-3,000	1,600	10-12	30-230,000	60	54-66		HF	10,000	10,000			
0.1-10	500	8	5,000,000	45	85	15	HF	2,000	2,000	Succ.	Yes	Exp. L
1,500	1,509	10.2	100,000	55	70		HF	95,000	95,000	Succ.		FW
7,500	1,640	12	25,000	70	85		HF	7,500	7,500	Succ.	Yes	RW
2,500	1,600	11	102,500	70	82	65	PP	2,500	2,500	Prom.	Yes	Exp. L
100-2,000	1,800	7.5	100,000	60	80		HF	8,000	8,000	Succ.		Exp. L

Phase B recovered about 40% of the bitumen in place and Gibson expects ultimate recovery will be about 60% of bitumen in place. Steam/oil ratios have been about 2.5.

In the next phase, Gibson will determine if SAGD wells drilled from the surface are more economical than wells drilled from a tunnel (Fig. 4).

Gibson expects each pair of laterals to produce about 1,000 b/d.

Microbial methods

Although chemical and polymer flooding has waned, China is starting new projects. Also, microbial enhanced oil recovery (MEOR) seems to be attaining commercial success.

Although only two survey respondents described microbial EOR, one in the U.S. and one in China, there were indications of other MEOR projects. Romania had about nine experimental projects active in 1994.

Biodynamics Corp. (formerly Alpha Environmental Midcontinent Inc.), Oklahoma City, indicated having used MEOR processes in more than 2,000 wells over the past 9 years. It recently was involved in about 400 active projects. Biodynamics's targets have been single wells in primary recovery and waterfloods. It says customers have been able to qualify for U.S. enhanced oil recovery tax incentives.

Biodynamics estimates that incremental recovery with its process costs $2/bbl.

In another MEOR process, Alan Sheehy of the University of Canberra, Australia, says some North Sea operators have used a new microbial process, Biological Oil Stimulation (BOS).

Sheehy describes BOS as the use of microbes and nutrient substrates that occur naturally in virtually all petroleum reservoirs.

Growth of indigenous and resident microbes is stimulated by the addition of minor amounts of the missing organic nutrients.

Polymer flooding

Although polymer injection for augmenting waterfloods in the U.S. has declined over the years, a number of international projects were under way in 1996.

CNPC had polymer floods in the Daqing, Dagang, Shengli, Liaohe, and Jilin oil fields. CNPC expected oil recovery to increase by 8-10% of the original oil in place.

The Daqing Petroleum Administration Bureau indicated that by 2000 polymer flooding might account for 150,000-200,000 b/d of production. Full-scale polymer operations were expected in 1997.

Tiorco Inc., Englewood, Colo, installed an alkaline-surfactant-polymer waterflood chemical process and water injection facility for a pilot waterflood pattern in Xinjiang Petroleum Administration Bureau's (XPAB) Karamay reservoir in the Junggar basin of northwest China.

Tiorco described the field as shallow, depth about 2,200 ft, having viscous, light to heavy oil with very little natural energy produced under primary recovery from the 96 ft thick pay zone. The field currently has 7,000 producing wells. About 35% of the original oil in place has been recovered.

AEA Technology, of the U.K., completed a study for CNPC of polymer flooding in the Henan Petroleum Exploration Bureau's (HPEB) Shuanghe oil field. AEA's simulation indicates that polymer-augmented waterflooding would increase recovery by 4-9% of the oil in place.

AEA's economics indicate that with western oil prices and polymer costs, the project's return on investment is 14-18%/year.

Tiorco also commissioned two polymer systems at Oil & Natural Gas Corp.'s polymer-augmented waterflood project in Ahmedabad, India.

Six experimental and one commercial chemical flood were active in Romania in 1996. IPE

World 1996: Oil production, refining capacity, oil movements, reserves

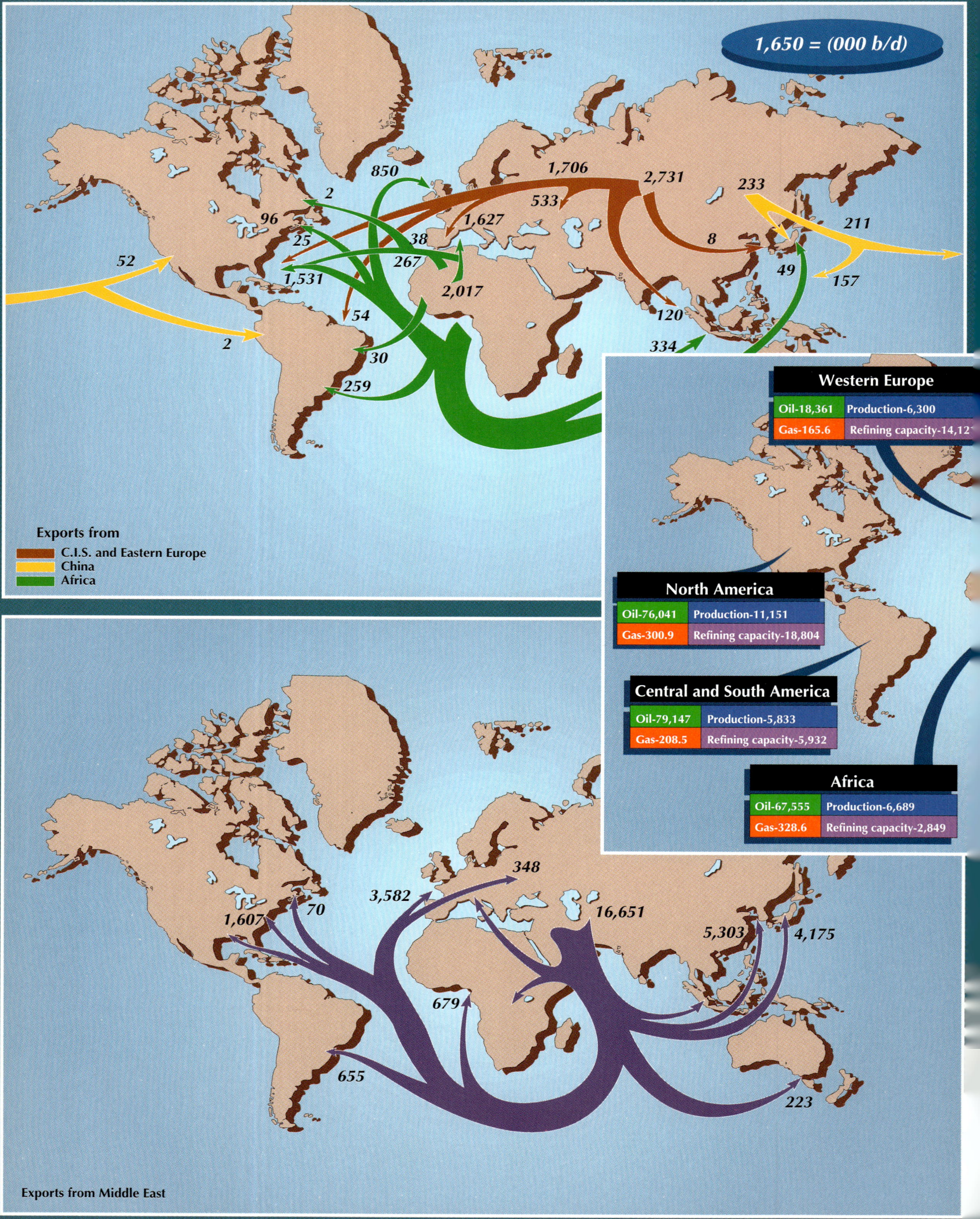

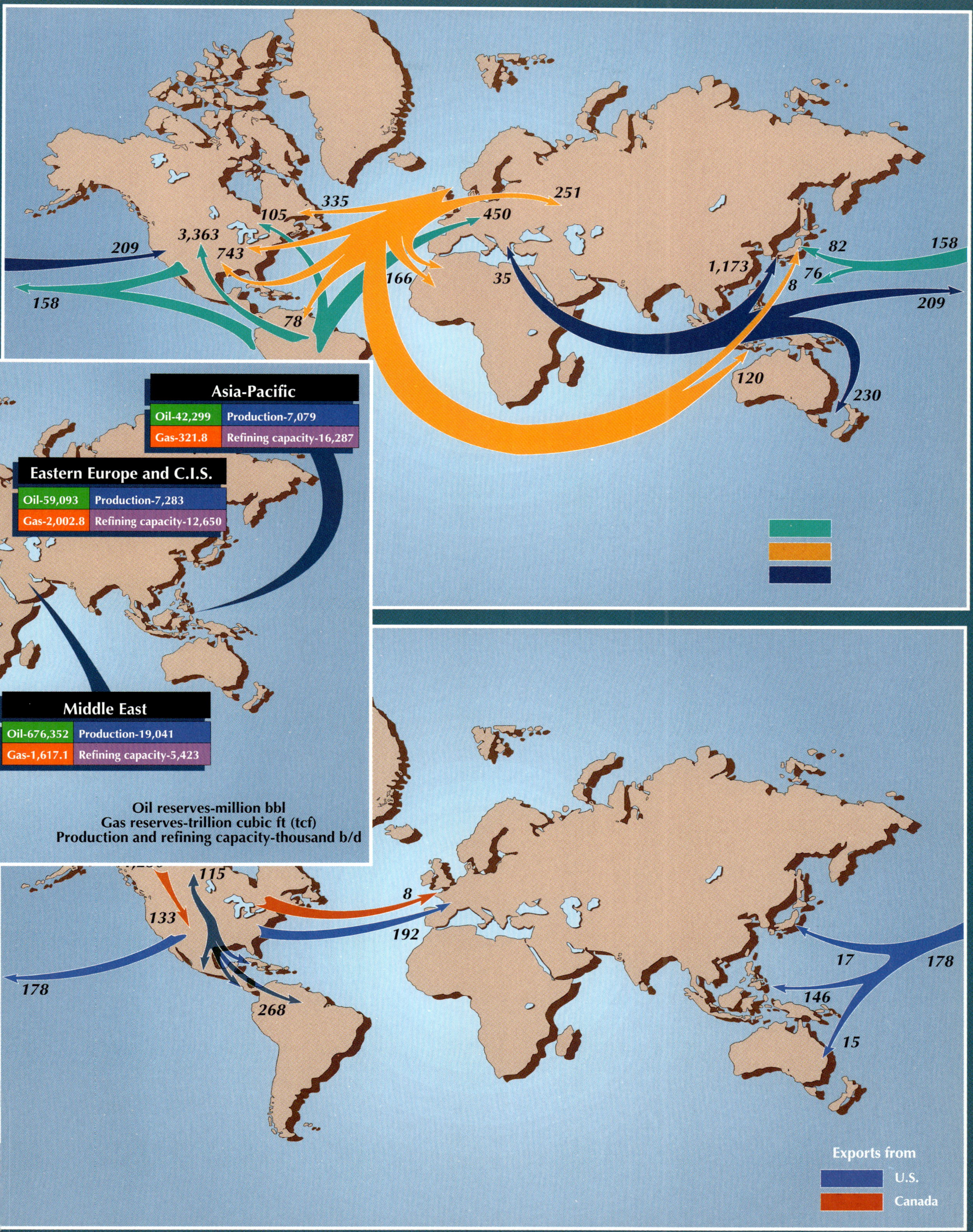

209
3,363
105
335
251
450
743
158
166
35
1,173
82
158
76
8
209
78
120
230
Asia-Pacific
Oil-42,299
Production-7,079
Gas-321.8
Refining capacity-16,287
Eastern Europe and C.I.S.
Oil-59,093
Production-7,283
Gas-2,002.8
Refining capacity-12,650
Middle East
Oil-676,352
Production-19,041
Gas-1,617.1
Refining capacity-5,423
Oil reserves-million bbl
Gas reserves-trillion cubic ft (tcf)
Production and refining capacity-thousand b/d
115
133
8
192
178
268
17
178
146
15
Exports from
U.S.
Canada

WORLDWIDE LOOK AT RESERVES AND PRODUCTION

COUNTRY	ESTIMATED PROVED RESERVES Jan. 1, 1997 Oil (1,000 bbl)	Jan. 1, 1997 Gas (bcf)	Jan. 1, 1996 Oil (1,000 bbl)	Jan. 1, 1996 Gas (bcf)	OIL PRODUCTION Producing oil wells* Dec. 31, 1995	Estimated 1996 (1,000 b/d)	Change from 1995 (%)	Actual 1995 (1,000 b/d)
ASIA-PACIFIC								
Afghanistan	....	3,500	....	3,500	....	....	....	....
Australia	1,800,180	19,429	1,560,090	20,082	1,231	535.0	5.7	506.2
Bangladesh	5,439	10,163	5,439	10,087	35	1.4	27.3	1.1
Brunei	1,350,000	14,100	1,350,000	14,000	766	150.0	−1.0	151.5
China	24,000,000	41,357	24,000,000	59,000	49,700	3,127.3	4.0	3,007.0
China, Taiwan	4,000	2,700	4,000	2,400	77	1.0	0.0	1.0
India	4,333,064	24,200	5,814,000	24,967	3,351	642.5	−4.6	673.4
Indonesia	4,979,710	72,268	5,166,867	68,916	8,504	1,515.7	1.2	1,498.2
Japan	50,407	1,052	48,873	958	229	14.3	−0.7	14.4
Malaysia	4,000,000	80,200	4,300,000	68,000	780	650.0	0.0	650.0
Myanmar (Burma)	50,000	11,000	50,000	10,000	450	15.0	−6.3	16.0
New Zealand	135,050	2,398	104,000	2,842	70	34.3	3.9	33.0
Pakistan	208,000	22,000	203,284	27,000	249	54.0	−0.4	54.2
Papua New Guinea	275,000	1,500	400,000	3,000	29	107.4	7.8	99.6
Philippines	213,000	3,850	216,100	3,880	11	1.2	−58.6	2.9
Thailand	295,260	7,120	230,749	5,901	365	59.3	16.5	50.9
Viet Nam	600,000	5,000	500,000	4,000	28	171.0	−3.4	177.0
Total Asia-Pacific	**42,299,110**	**321,837**	**43,953,402**	**328,533**	**65,875**	**7,079.4**	**2.1**	**6,936.4**
WESTERN EUROPE								
Austria	76,486	770	100,800	777	1,074	21.3	0.9	21.1
Denmark	957,100	3,853	1,031,529	4,026	151	205.8	10.6	186.0
France	117,312	683	138,312	1,074	498	43.6	−11.4	49.2
Germany	385,350	11,619	338,720	11,301	1,385	56.5	−1.7	57.5
Greece	12,000	300	14,000	300	12	8.0	−11.1	9.0
Ireland	....	377	....	418	....	....	....	....
Italy	684,615	10,506	620,500	13,200	208	101.3	2.6	98.7
Netherlands	88,057	64,096	106,927	65,156	209	60.0	−12.8	68.8
Norway	11,233,600	47,745	8,422,056	47,498	474	3,085.7	10.9	2,782.0
Spain	30,000	600	20,000	600	36	16.3	8.7	15.0
Turkey	260,046	312	487,670	400	779	68.8	2.1	67.4
United Kingdom	4,516,930	24,720	4,292,950	23,308	1,563	2,633.0	2.7	2,565.0
Total Western Europe	**18,361,496**	**165,581**	**15,573,464**	**168,058**	**6,389**	**6,300.3**	**6.4**	**5,919.7**
EASTERN EUROPE and C.I.S.								
Albania	165,000	70	165,000	70	2,510	9.4	0.0	9.4
Bulgaria	15,000	140	15,000	250	100	1.0	0.0	1.0
Croatia	55,111	786	150,000	1,250	867	34.0	8.6	31.3
Czech Rebublic	6,000	140	6,000	140	200	2.0	0.0	2.0
F.S.U.	57,000,000	1,977,000	57,000,000	1,977,000	123,970	7,043.6	−1.1	7,120.0
Hungary	119,542	3,302	128,535	3,354	987	30.5	−10.0	33.9
Poland	40,057	5,262	31,334	5,336	2,073	5.0	−16.7	6.0
Romania	1,606,000	14,000	1,606,000	13,000	6,000	136.0	−1.4	138.0
Serbia	77,500	1,580	77,500	1,580	646	20.0	0.0	20.0
Slovakia	9,000	530	9,000	530	200	1.0	0.0	1.0
Total Eastern Europe and C.I.S.	**59,093,210**	**2,002,810**	**59,188,369**	**2,002,510**	**137,553**	**7,282.5**	**-1.1**	**7,362.6**
MIDDLE EAST								
Abu Dhabi	92,200,000	189,000	92,200,000	188,400	993	1,846.0	0.8	1,832.0
Bahrain	210,000	5,200	210,000	5,295	359	103.8	−1.1	105.0
Dubai	4,000,000	4,100	4,300,000	4,400	150	320.0	−0.6	322.0
Iran	93,000,000	741,609	88,200,000	741,609	900	3,675.3	1.8	3,612.0
Iraq	112,000,000	118,000	100,000,000	109,500	58	600.0	0.0	600.0
Israel	4,090	12	4,107	13	9	0.1	0.0	0.1
Jordan	300	200	300	200	4	0.1	0.0	0.1
Kuwait	94,000,000	52,400	94,000,000	52,400	730	1,817.5	1.4	1,792.0
Neutral Zone	5,000,000	1,000	5,000,000	1,000	275	484.3	12.6	430.0
Oman	5,138,000	30,000	5,138,000	25,200	2,111	882.5	3.9	849.0
Qatar	3,700,000	250,000	3,700,000	250,000	318	479.8	5.7	454.0
Ras al Khaimah	100,000	1,100	100,000	1,100	7	0.8	0.0	0.8
Saudi Arabia	259,000,000	188,600	258,703,000	185,400	1,372	7,841.0	−0.2	7,859.0
Sharjah	1,500,000	10,700	1,500,000	10,700	52	50.0	0.0	50.0
Syria	2,500,000	8,300	2,500,000	7,000	964	601.5	−0.6	605.0
Yemen	4,000,000	16,900	4,000,000	15,000	283	338.0	0.0	338.0
Total Middle East	**676,352,390**	**1,617,121**	**659,555,407**	**1,597,217**	**8,585**	**19,040.7**	**1.0**	**18,849.0**

	ESTIMATED PROVED RESERVES				OIL PRODUCTION			
	Jan. 1, 1997		Jan. 1, 1996					
COUNTRY	Oil (1,000 bbl)	Gas (bcf)	Oil (1,000 bbl)	Gas (bcf)	Producing oil wells* Dec. 31, 1995	Estimated 1996 (1,000 b/d)	Change from 1995 (%)	Actual 1995 (1,000 b/d)
AFRICA								
Algeria	9,200,000	130,300	9,200,000	128,000	1,273	816.0	6.8	764.0
Angola	5,412,212	1,700	5,412,212	1,800	416	705.5	13.6	621.0
Benin	28,900	43	28,900	43	7	1.8	0.0	1.8
Cameroon	400,000	3,900	400,000	3,900	228	90.0	−11.9	102.1
Congo	1,505,913	3,200	1,505,913	4,311	357	202.8	15.9	175.0
Egypt	3,696,170	20,356	3,879,420	22,100	1,208	923.0	0.1	922.0
Equatorial Guinea	12,000	1,300	12,000	1,300	2	9.3	32.9	7.0
Ethiopia	428	880	428	880	....	....	....	....
Gabon	1,340,000	500	1,340,000	500	374	370.0	1.6	364.0
Ghana	16,510	219	16,000	800	3	6.0	0.0	6.0
Ivory Coast	100,000	800	100,000	800	7	20.0	81.8	11.0
Libya	29,500,000	46,300	29,500,000	45,800	1,866	1,402.5	0.9	1,390.0
Madagascar	....	70	....	70	....	....	....	....
Morocco	1,190	40	1,190	40	9	0.1	0.0	0.1
Mozambique	....	2,000	....	1,740	....	....	....	....
Namibia	....	3,000	....	2,000	....	....	....	....
Nigeria	15,520,880	104,717	20,828,000	109,710	2,005	2,013.5	6.5	1,890.0
Rwanda	....	2,000	....	2,000	....	....	....	....
Somalia	....	200	....	200	....	....	....	....
South Africa	26,700	900	26,700	959	9	10.0	0.0	10.0
Sudan	300,000	3,000	300,000	3,000	9	1.5	−25.0	2.0
Tanzania	....	726	....	2,000	....	....	....	....
Tunisia	307,560	2,401	416,000	2,600	191	86.5	−1.4	87.7
Zaire	187,000	35	187,000	50	124	30.0	7.1	28.0
Total Africa	**67,555,463**	**328,587**	**73,153,763**	**334,603**	**8,088**	**6,688.5**	**4.8**	**6,381.7**
WESTERN HEMISPHERE								
Argentina	2,386,366	21,870	2,225,895	18,583	12,564	753.3	4.5	720.7
Barbados	2,411	5	2,541	5	92	1.1	−8.3	1.2
Bolivia	131,931	4,504	138,874	4,460	299	30.0	5.6	28.4
Brazil	4,800,000	5,449	4,200,000	5,170	6,025	780.0	13.1	689.6
Canada	4,893,642	68,118	4,898,460	67,027	45,554	1,819.8	0.8	1,806.0
Chile	300,000	3,600	300,000	3,900	317	9.0	−10.0	10.0
Colombia	2,800,000	8,250	3,500,000	10,000	2,888	620.8	8.0	574.8
Cuba	100,000	100	100,000	100	228	27.0	−3.6	28.0
Ecuador	2,115,000	3,700	2,115,000	3,800	1,030	385.5	−0.3	386.7
Guatemala	200,000	10	488,000	10	20	13.8	40.8	9.8
Mexico	48,796,000	67,668	49,775,000	68,413	4,740	2,853.8	4.8	2,722.1
Peru	808,400	7,046	808,400	7,046	3,883	121.3	−2.2	124.0
Suriname	74,000	....	74,000	....	317	7.7	6.9	7.2
Trinidad & Tobago	551,000	12,360	490,000	10,570	3,337	127.8	−1.2	129.3
United States	22,351,000	165,146	22,457,000	163,837	578,080	6,477.5	−1.3	6,559.6
Venezuela	64,878,000	141,600	64,477,000	139,900	14,971	2,955.3	13.3	2,609.0
Total Western Hemisphere	**155,187,750**	**509,426**	**156,050,170**	**502,821**	**674,345**	**16,983.7**	**3.5**	**16,406.4**
TOTAL WORLD	**1,018,849,419**	**4,945,362**	**1,007,474,575**	**4,933,742**	**900,835**	**63,375.1**	**2.5**	**61,855.8**
Total OPEC	**788,578,590**	**2,051,694**	**776,874,867**	**2,036,835**	**33,474**	**25,818**	**2.8**	**25,103**

EDITOR'S NOTE: All reserves figures except those for the C.I.S. (and gas for Canada) are reported as proved reserves recoverable with present technology and prices. C.I.S. figures are "explored reserves" which are understood to be proved plus some probable. Canadian gas figure, under criteria adopted by Canadian Petroleum Association in 1980, includes proved and some probable. *Does not include shut in, injection, or service wells.

Worldwide Production

• Offshore (e) Estimated (c) Condensate

WORLDWIDE PRODUCTION

Name of field, discovery date	Depth, ft	Producing oil wells	1995 production avg., b/d	°API gravity
ABU DHABI (e)				
ANDOC, OTHERS				
• Abu Al Bukhoosh, 1969	8,900-10,900	42		32.0
• Arzanah, 1973	11,000-11,300	14		42.0
Asab, 1965	8,000-8,700	106		41.0
Bab, 1958	8,600-9,300	100		44.0
Bu-Hasa, 1962	8,300-9,200	201		39.0
• Bunduq, 1964	9,400-10,900	23		40.0
• Mubarraz, 1969	8,300-10,000	28		37.0
Sahil, 1967	9,500-9,800	22	1,832,000	39.7
• Satah, 1975	8,550-9,550	10		39.8
• Umm Addalkh, 1969	7,700-8,500	32		32.5
• Umm Shaif, 1958	9,800-12,000	142		37.0
• Zakum Lower, 1963	8,000-9,000	131		39.0
• Zakum Upper, 1963	7,000-8,000	142		35.0
Total Abu Dhabi		**993**	**1,832,000**	
ALBANIA				
ALB PETROL				
Ballsh-Hekal, 1967	4,921	130	518	13.0
Cakran-Mollaj, 1977	10,826	28	1,087	24.0
Delvina, 1989	12,800	2	6	31.0
Gorisht-Kocul, 1967	3,609	170	1,137	19.0
Kucova, 1928	1,970-4,265	1,150	736	16.0
Marinza-Patos, 1957	4,265-4,920	920	5,273	13.0
Other, 1980	6,234	30	157	22.0
Visoka, 1963	4,921	80	501	13.0
Total Albania		**2,510**	**9,416**	
ALGERIA *				
SONATRACH				
Acheb/Acheb West, 1963	7,360	7	2,571	48.1
Ait Kheir, 1971	8,860	16	22,197	51.1
Alrar (c), 1961	8,202	....	29,855	65.6
Amassak/Tin-Yaguene, 1970	6,565	22	9,817	42.4
Askarene, 1962	8,200	3	841	44.5
Assekaifaf South, 1958	2,800	2	333	43.7
Bab El Hattabet, 1982	11,880	1	1,079	44.9
Djebel Bissa (c), 1977	....	....	1,801	67.3
Djebel Onk, 1960	3,940	5	508	38.8
Djoua West, 1967	5,580-6,240	3	436	42.5
Draa Ettamra, 1971	11,600	68	56	44.5
Edeyen, 1964	5,580	3	500	43.2
Edjeleh, 1956	1,500-2,800	144	7,619	37.1
El Adeb Larache, 1958	4,100	3	238	43.8
El Borma/Zemiet Nouss, 1967	8,200	23	8,769	41.7
El Gassi-El Agreb, 1959	10,170	25	30,831	49.4
Gara, 1962	9,420	2	794	41.1
Gassi-Touil (c), 1961	6,562	8	11,190	50.5
Gassi-Touil/East, 1961	6,890	30	730	50.8
Guellala, 1969	11,320	17	9,888	44.8
Guelta, 1962	8,960	3	516	44.9
Haniet El Beida, 1978	12,045	1	278	45.0
Hassi Chergui, 1963	8,200	5	2,405	50.8
Hassi Mazoula South, 1963	4,430	3	532	40.8
Hassi Mazoula (B)/North, 1965	4,920-5,118	0	95	40.8
Hassi Messaoud North, 1956	10,500	173	153,038	47.2
Hassi Messaoud South, 1956	10,500	198	238,445	48.8
Hassi R'Mel, 1979	7,760	34	18,015	46.1
Hassi R'Mel (c), 1956	7,218	....	273,038	65.9
Hassi-Touareg (c)	....	....	1,897	....
H. Berkaoui/Ben Kahla, 1965	11,000	2	33,268	43.8
La Reculee, 1957	5,414-5,742	7	421	41.5
Makouda, 1975	6,000	1	206	51.2
Mereksen, 1974	8,200	11	10,436	50.0
Mesdar East & West, 1972	11,155	8	8,777	41.3
Mokh El Kebch, 1984	12,870	2	1,040	44.9
Nezla (c), 1965	7,382	....	1,714	....
Ngoussa, 1974	11,715	....	0	43.9
Nord In Amenas (c), 1959	....	....	206	67.2
Ohanet North & South, 1960	7,878	28	4,333	46.5
Oued Gueterini, 1946	6,600	12	32	37.6
Oued Noumer, 1969	8,860	11	6,809	51.3
Ras Toumb, 1976	9,190	4	214	37.4
Rhourde Chegga, 1959	10,170	1	3,651	49.9
Rhourde El Baguel, 1962	9,850	16	26,887	42.6
Rhourde Nouss, 1972	8,530	9	3,944	36.3
Rhourde Nouss (c), 1962	8,202-8,859	....	43,346	64.2
Sahane, 1972	12,649	2	87	44.9
Sidi Mezghiche, 1976	8,085	1	1,032	51.2
Stah, 1971	9,515	18	19,443	47.3
Tamendjelt, 1970	5,585-6,890	3	1,127	42.8
Tiguentourine, 1966	2,160-4,265	36	1,619	46.6
Timedratine/East, 1964	8,155	17	4,889	41.0-41.5
Tin Fouye Tabankort Ordo., 1966	4,600-6,560	106	68,377	42.3
Tin Fouye Tabankort (c), 1962	4,600-6,560	....	556	80.6
Tiraremine North/West	6,565	1	167	42.5
T.F.F6/T.F. North/ T.F NW/Tml., 1962	4,265	32	10,722	39.6
T.F.T. Devo East/Zone 100, 1966	4,600-6,560	14	4,055	43.6
Zarzaitine, 1957	4,700	132	32,450	42.2
Total Algeria		**1,273**	**1,118,119**	

*Table shows 1994 field production of crude oil, condensate and NGL. 1995 crude production estimated at 764,000 B/D.

WORLDWIDE PRODUCTION

ANGOLA

Name of field, discovery date	Depth, ft	Producing oil wells	1995 production avg., b/d	°API gravity
CHEVRON				
• Kali, 1969	14,416	0	0	30.0
• Kambala, 1971	10,278	4	4,943	32.8
• Kokongo, 1989	12,200	11	28,823	38.0
• Kungulo, 1976		22	19,374	32.2
• Lifuma, 1984	7,800	1	30	31.4
• Limba, 1965	2,660	13	7,464	31.6
• Livuite, 1980	8,000	2	322	31.7
• Malongo North, 1966	1,170	58	15,113	30.0
• Malongo South, 1966	1,150	26	6,310	25.0
• Malongo West, 1969	1,660	19	14,187	22.5
N'Sano, 1992	8,770	7	17,734	....
• Numbi, 1980	3,446	43	67,345	34.0
• Takula, 1971	3,070	78	156,730	31.5
• Vuko, 1983	3,572	8	8,561	35.0
• Wamba, 1982	2,507	14	30,288	29.0
ELF ANGOLA				
• Bufalo, 1982	10,500	9	15,700	39.5
• Cobo-Pambi, 1990	10,177	11	47,681	37.6
• Impala, 1983	9,022	1	1,932	37.5
• Impala SE, 1985	8,500	7	16,094	37.0
• Pacassa, 1982	11,500	16	55,604	38.0
• Palanca, 1981	8,860	9	34,845	40.0
FINA ANGOLA (e)				
Benfica, 1955	8,300	0		30.0
Bento, 1972	7,350	1		26.0
C. Cobra, 1969	4,200	0		41.0
Cacuaco, 1958	8,100	1		30.0
Galinda, 1959	7,270	0		30.0
Ganda, 1975	5,000	0		39.0
Legua, 1972	6,300	1		32.0
Luango, 1977	3,800	0		39.0
Lumueno, 1977	4,300	0		39.0
Mulenvos, 1966	5,900-6,600	5		25.0
N' Zombo, 1973	5,000-6,300	0		33.0
Pambo, 1982	4,400	0		39.0
Pangala, 1974	5,200	0		31.0
Quenguela, 1968	6,000	17		32.0
Quinfuquena, 1975	5,462-7,100	0		30.0
Quinguila, 1972	3,400	0	71,903	34.0
Sereia, 1974	6,200	0		28.0
Tobias, 1961	5,900	2		30.0
Kitona, 1973	5,200-6,102	0		27.0
TEXACO-SONANGOL TOTAL-BRASPETRO (e)				
• Cuntala, 1978	7,200	0		31.0
• Essungo, 1975	6,500	0		35.0
• Lombo Este, 1984	7,800	9		41.0
• Raia, 1988	8,700	0		36.4
• Sulele, 1982	6,900	1		40.0
• Sulele South, 1986	7,600	7		39.0
• Sulele West, 1985	7,600	6		41.0
• Tubarao, 1984	7,600	7		38.2
Total Angola		**416**	**620,983**	

ARGENTINA

Name of field, discovery date	Depth, ft	Producing oil wells	1995 production avg., b/d	°API gravity
AJAX				
K20	....	68	1,106	....
ALBERTA ENERGY				
Anticlinal Campamento	....	27	199	....
Rio Negro Norte	....	13	990	....
AMOCO				
Cerro Dragon, 1932	7,218	1,325	52,408	24.0
ASTRA				
Bloque 127, 1970	4,200	26	365	23.6
Canadon Leon, 1947	....	....	....	....
Canadon Seco-Mesta Espinosa, 1943	6,400	136	3,000	23.6
Cerro Overo, 1959	3,600	4	76	23.6
La Ventana, 1957	7,500	241	17,391	29.5
Manantiales Behr, 1929	8,500	143	4,836	21.3
Meseta Espinosa Norte, 1949	6,700	33	770	23.6
Quiamare-La Ceiba, 1942	6,500	....	....	30.0
Restinga Ali, 1933	7,200	11	224	25.3
Rio Tunuyan, 1957	7,500	17	430	29.7
Tres Picos, 1951	9,200	27	498	23.6
Vizacheras, 1962	6,000	168	13,044	28.5
BRIDAS				
Acambuco	....	8	163	....
Al Sur de la Dorsal, 1941	2,850-4,265	56	2,796	24.6
CNQ-24 Estacion Fernadez Oro	8,530	13	2,375	38.6
El Cordon, 1955	3,600-5,900	64	957	27.5
Lindero Atravesado (c), 1961	6,550-9,850	2	1,301	63.3
Los Chorrillos	....	13	316	....
Piedra Clavada, 1964	4,900-6,230	240	12788	21.0
Tierra del Fuego	....	92	4644	....
CADIPSA				
CC-4 Los Tordillos Oeste	....	....	....	....
Cerro Wenceslao, 1962	900	127	1,920	29.0
CGSJ-14 Barranca Yancovsky	....	....	....	....
CGSJ-21 Sur Piedra Clavada, 1961	1,500	1	27	29.0
CGSJ-3 Las Heras, 1962	900-1,400	83	1,033	22.1
CGSJ-7 Canadon Minerales, 1959	1,200-1,700	123	3,652	20.2
CAPSA				
CNQ-14 Agua del Cajon	....	25	892	....
Km. 27-Diadema	....	219	5,507	....
CHANARES HERRADOS				
CC-5 Puesto Pozo Cercado	....	1	28	....
Chanares Herrados	....	15	781	....
CHAUVCO RESOURCES				
Al Norte de la Dorsal	....	55	1,347	....
Dadio	....	8	234	....
Loma Negra Ni	....	5	186	....
CIA GRAL. DE COMBUSTIBLES				
CNO-4 El Chivil	....	1	135	....
CNO-5 Ipaguazu	....	1	40	....
CNO-7 Surubi	....	....	....	....
EDIVAL-CIELMEC				
CA-2 Laguna de los Capones	....	5	126	....
EPP PETROLEO				
CA-5 Del Mosquito	....	5	180	....
CNO-8 Puesto Guardian	....	9	721	....
CNO-2 El Vinalar	....	1	132	....
GIAPRO-OLMATIC				
CNQ-26 La Calera	....	....	....	....
CNO-6 Selva Maria	....	....	....	....
GLACCO				
CA-1 Campo Bremen	....	1	98	....
CA-3 La Terraza	....	....	....	....
CA-4 Moy Aike	....	2	70	....
CA-8 San Cristobal	....	....	....	....
CA-9 Oceano	....	4	109	....
La Carmen	....	....	....	....
HOME OIL				
Refugio Tupungato	....	39	1,587	....
INALRUCO				
Nuequen del Medio, 1956	5,200	14	303	30.0
MEXPETROL				
Chihuido de la Salina	....	3	841	....
El Porton	....	18	6,290	....
MISAHAR				
Mata Magallanes	....	31	492	....
NORCEN				
El Santiagueno	....	23	610	....
O.E.A.				
CA-6 Chorrillos, 1965	5,610-5,735	7	221	36.1
CA-10 Palermo Aike, 1976	6,092-7,014	2	35	36.1
CA-14 Angostura, 1961	5,935-6,942	6	322	40.1
PEREZ COMPANC				
25 de Mayo-Medanito S.E.	....	281	8,549	....
CA-11 Faro Virgenes	....	6	410	....
Cacheuta	....	21	147	....
Can. Amarillo, 1969	6,234	7	378	32.5
Catriel Oeste, 1959	2,953	127	2,484	22.5
CNQ-11 Baj. del Palo, 1978	7,874	10	131	30.0
CNQ-37 Veta Escondida	....	....	....	....
CNQ-38 Rincon de Aranda	....	....	....	....
CNQ-4 El Manzano, 1978	5,906	1	31	25.0
CNQ-9 Jaguel de los Machos	4,757	15	740	30.0
Entre Lomas, 1966	4,757	244	9,327	33.0
Koluel Kaiake-El Valle, 1957	5,413	175	6,058	24.0
Pampa del Castillo-La Guitarra	5,906	172	6,862	22.5
Puesto Hernandez, 1969	3,937	404	44,115	33.5
P. Color.-E. Interm.	....	87	3,092	....

WORLDWIDE PRODUCTION

Name of field, discovery date	Depth, ft	Producing oil wells	1995 production avg., b/d	°API gravity
Rio Neuquen	....	34	2,413	....
Santa Cruz II, 1968	6,070	21	4,093	46.8
PETROLERA ARG. SAN JORGE				
CNQ-16 El Sauce	....	....	....	....
CNQ-26 Confluencia	....	....	....	....
CNQ-8 Huantraico	....	74	50,499	....
PETROLERA SANTA FE				
Sierra Chata	....	9	314	....
PETROQ. COMOD. RIVADAVIA				
CGSJ-12 Caleta Cordova	....	....	....	....
CNQ-1 El Sosneado, 1965	3,770-4,900	28	734	19.0
CNQ-28 Vega Grande, 1985	6,900	4	182	31.0
Km. 8-Don Alberto, 1921	1,480-6,300	43	640	20.0
Medanito, 1963	3,280-3,600	12	305	28.0
Medianera, 1962	3,400	2	46	28.0
PETROLEOS SUD-AMERCANOS NECON U.T.E.				
Caimancito	....	10	582	....
CNQ-6 Centro Este	....	21	1,152	....
Loma Montosa Oeste	....	1	26	....
PLUSPETROL SA				
Aguada Baguales, 1963	3,300	31	731	38.0-39.0
Balbuena Este	....	3	1,156	....
Centenario, 1961	8,200	68	2,955	39.2
Cuchuma, 1990	1,300	6	210	31.3
El Porvenir, 1941	3,800	77	3,105	24.0
Loma Jarillosa E., 1990	10,500	1	43	....
Palmar Largo, 1983	12,600	17	5,929	....
Ramos, 1975	13,000	1	4,202	61.0
QUINTANA				
Santa Cruz I	....	41	24,339	....
ROCH				
CA-13 Las Violetas-Rio Cullen, 1949	6,560	5	615	39.0
CGSJ-13 Canadon Ramirez, 1974	7,200	....	....	....
CGSJ-2 Bella Vista Oeste, 1970	9,200	26	2,880	25.7
CNQ-3 Cajon de los Caballos, 1966	6,240	18	1,322	19.0
Mata Magallanes Este, 1985	5,900	....	....	....
SIPETROL				
• Area Magallanes	....	11	9,008	....
CNQ-17 Puesto Rojas	....	9	210	....
TECNICAGUA				
CNQ-30 Cerro Moliar Oeste, 1990	1,800	2	619	18.0
TECPETROL				
Agua Salada	5,455	3	216	53.0
Atamisqui	7,193	20	1,084	29.0
Atuel Norte	6,262	5	57	22.0
Bajo Baguales	3,320	3	23	37.0
Catriel Viejo	3,628	5	83	30.0
El Tordillo	7,640	369	15710	23.0
Jose Segundo	6,645	21	794	24.0
Los Bastos	5,731	16	140	37.0
Sierra de Aguarague	29,445	13	3,384	56.0
TECSA				
Rinconada Puestp Morales	....	9	157	....
TOTAL AUSTRAL				
Aguada San Roque & Loma Las Yeguas, 1987	4,100-6,400	14	8,223	38.0
• Ara-Alfa, 1981	5,250	39	5,803	38.0
El Huemul, 1957	5,250	422	11,991	31.0
• Hidra, 1982	5,410	9	9,327	38.0
YPF SA				
Chubut, 1907	1,908-9,168	662	20,489	21.1-26.0
Mendoza, 1932	2,178-16,778	602	38,408	23.7-32.0
Neuquen, 1918	1,312-12,498	1,168	147,034	24.0-41.0
Rio Negro, 1960	2,953-7,546	441	13,178	22.5-41.0
Santa Cruz, 1946	1,468-17,060	3,057	95,405	21.1-30.0
Total Argentina		**12,564**	**720,736**	

AUSTRALIA

Name of field, discovery date	Depth, ft	Producing oil wells	1995 production avg., b/d	°API gravity
AMPOLEX				
• Wandoo, 1991	2,000	5	13,190	19.5
APACHE				
• Alkimos, 1994	6,207	1	39	39.0
• Harriet, 1983	6,230	13	10,904	38.2
• Tanami, 1991	6,010	1	683	43.0
BHP PETROLEUM PTY. LTD.				
• Challis/Cassini, 1984	5,000	7	8,400	39.5
• Griffin area, 1989	8,630	9	53,700	55.0
• Jabiru, 1983	4,786	5	12,300	42.3
• Skua, 1986	7,545	2	3,700	42.5
BORAL ENERGY RESOURCES LTD.				
Beharra Springs (c), 1990	10,827	3	57	62.0
Katnook (c), 1989	9,394	2	41	52.0
CONSOLIDATED GAS PTY. LTD.				
Woodad (c), 1980,	7,800	6	6	53.6
DISCOVERY PETROLEUM				
Mount Horner, 1965	4,987	7	380	35.5
ESSO-BHP				
• Barracouta, 1965	4,550	8	2,100	62.8
• Bream, 1969	6,200	16	17,800	45.4
• Cobia, 1972	7,700	9	8,400	44.6
• Dolphin, 1967	4,000	1	5,800	45.0
• Flounder, 1968	8,200	13	22,600	46.7
• Fortescue, 1978	7,700	17	20,200	43.0
• Halibut, 1967	7,700	15	28,800	43.3
• Kingfish, 1967	7,500	32	36,000	46.9
• Mackerel, 1969	7,700	25	18,600	45.6
• Marlin, 1966	5,100	18	10,000	50.0
• Perch, 1968	3,700	1	3,700	41.0
• Seahorse, 1978	4,700	1	500	53.0
• Snapper, 1968	4,350	8	5,200	47.0
• Tarwhine, 1981	4,500	1	4,900	65.0
• Tuna, 1968	6,500	15	13,300	40.5
• West Kingfish, 1968	7,500	20	29,400	46.9
• Whiting, 1983	4,800	4	1,500	52.9
MOSAIC OIL N.L.				
Fairymount, 1985	6,700	4	96	50.3
WAPET GROUP				
Barrow Island, 1964	1,200-6,700	438	13,393	37.7
Dongara, 1969	5,250-5,577	1	56	35.5
Thevenard Island, 1985	4,600-5,750	21	46,339	48.2
WESTERN MINING CORP.				
• Chervil, 1983	3,450	2	520	44.0
• North Herald, 1983	4,000	1	170	42.0
• South Pepper, 1982	4,000	7	3,000	42.0
WOODSIDE OFFSHORE PETROLEUM PTY. LTD.				
• Goodwyn, 1972	9,680	5	29,400	29.4
• North Rankin, 1972	9,840	19	35,600	54.5
AGL PETROLEUM (e)				
Mereenie, 1964	4,000	24		48.9
Moonie, 1961	58,000	19		44.5
Roma		....		
OIL COMPANY OF AUSTRALIA LTD. (e)				
Bargie, 1994	5,682	1		45.6
Black Stump, 1986	3,815	1		45.2
Bodalla South, 1984	4,789-5,215	6		47.8
Cogoon River West, 1990	4,660	1		
Kenmore, 1985	4,593-4,986	14		48.2
Riverslea, 1981	4,950	2		37.0
Waratah, 1982	5,350	1		34.0
Washpool, 1985	5250	1		35.0
Wilga, 1991	4,884	1		38.0
BHP PETROLEUM (e)				
Beechwood (c), 1981	5,692	1		....
Boxleigh (c), 1970	5,300	2		....
Broadway (c), 1983	....	1		....
Glen Fosslyn (c), 1970	5,790	1		....
Lark (c), 1993	5,817	1		....
North Boxleigh (c), 1991	5,463	1		....
Roswin North (c), 1992	5,873	1		....
Roswin (c), 1984	5,756	1		....
Silver Springs/Renlim (c), 1974	5,300	6		....
Sirrah (c), 1982	5,430	2		....
Taylor (c), 1988	5,538	5		47.0
Tinker (c), 1989	5,817	1		....
SANTOS (e)				
Blina, 1981	4,300	6		37.0
Boundary, 1990	3,940	1		37.0
Dilkera, 1986	3,446	1		45.0
Koora, 1986	3,176	1		45.0
Lloyd, 1987	4,806	0		39.0
Maxwell South, 1989	2,890	1		45.0
Maxwell, 1987	2,952	3		45.0

WORLDWIDE PRODUCTION

Name of field, discovery date	Depth, ft	Producing oil wells	1995 production avg., b/d	°API gravity
Muthero, 1989	4,367	2		45.0
Nockatunga, 1983	3,318	3		45.0
Sundown, 1983	3,600	3		33.0
Thungo, 1986	3,998	5		45.0
West Terrace, 1985	3,800	0		32.8
Winna, 1985	3,334	2		45.0
SANTOS (e)				
Bogala, 1984	6,900		45,443	....
Bolan	....			....
Boweri	....			....
Challum, 1983	....			....
Chookoo, 1985	6,000			45.0
Cook, 1985	....			....
Cooroo, 1986	....			....
Corella, 1989	....			....
Echuburra	....			....
Genoa	....			....
Genoa North	....			....
Gunna, 1983	6,000			40.0
Jackson, 1981	4,750			40.0-48.0
Jackson South, 1982	4,800			40.0
Jarran	....			....
Judga	....	346		....
Mooliampah, 1985	6,000			....
Munro, 1988	....			....
Naccowlah, 1989	....			....
Naccowlah South, 1983	6000			....
Naccowlah South, 1983	6,000			....
Naccowlah West, 1983	5,700			....
Patroclus	....			....
Patroclus East	....			....
Pitchery, 1988	....			....
Sigma, 1983	5700			....
Tickalara, 1984	5,600			....
Tinpilla, 1983	6,000			....
Wandilp	....			....
Watson, 1985	....			....
Watson South, 1985	5,500			40.0
Wilson, 1983	5,000			....
Yanda, 1984	8,000			....
OTHER (e)				
• Talisman, 1984	9,600	....		42.0
Total Australia		**1,231**	**506,217**	

BAHRAIN

Name of field, discovery date	Depth, ft	Producing oil wells	1995 production avg., b/d	°API gravity
BANOCO				
Awali, 1932	1,850-4,600	359	39,593	33.0
Total Bahrain		**359**	**39,593**	

BANGLADESH

Name of field, discovery date	Depth, ft	Producing oil wells	1995 production avg., b/d	°API gravity
PETROBANGLA				
Bakhrabad, 1969	9,309	8	172	40.2
Feni, 1981	10,496	2	45	44.5
Habiganj, 1963	11,506	6	8	30.3
Kailastila, 1962	13,576	2	355	45.0
Rashidpur, 1960	9,886	4	155	45.4
Shahbazpur, 1995	10,929	....	....	....
Syl-7, 1986	6,773	1	....	29.3
Sylhet, 1955	7,803	1	20	46.0
Titas, 1962	12,326	11	351	39.1
Total Bangladesh		**35**	**1,106**	

BARBADOS

Name of field, discovery date	Depth, ft	Producing oil wells	1995 production avg., b/d	°API gravity
BARBADOS NATIONAL OIL CO.				
Woodbourne, 1966	1,924-6,563	92	1,243	26.0
Total Barbados		**92**	**1,243**	

BENIN

Name of field, discovery date	Depth, ft	Producing oil wells	1995 production avg., b/d	°API gravity
PROJET PETROLIER DE SEME				
Seme, 1968	6,500	7	1,820	23.0
Total Benin		**7**	**1,820**	

BOLIVIA

Name of field, discovery date	Depth, ft	Producing oil wells	1995 production avg., b/d	°API gravity
MAXUS ENERGY				
Surubi, 1992	14,078	10	6,347	44.0
OCCIDENTAL BOLIVIA				
Porvenir, 1978	9,600	6	422	60.5
PEREZ COMPANC				
Caranda, 1960	13,032	18	205	60.0
Colpa, 1962	9184	12	320	65.0
PLUSPETROL				
Bermejo, 1925	2,085	1	361	42.0
Toro, 1954	2982	0	169	27.0
Tigre, 1966	5,741	0	12	26.7
TESORO BOLIVIA				
Escondido (c), 1980	11,293	2	494	60.0
La Vertiente (c), 1977	15230	5	581	50.0
Taiguati (c), 1981	10,174	1	42	63.0
SOPETROL				
Palmar, 1964	10,758	1	64	65.0
YPFB				
Buena Vista, 1956	2,085	2	16	45.8
Bulo Bulo, 1964	8500	....	....	55.5
Caigua, 1973	3,280	....	....	42.4
Camatindi, 1929	4,110	4	49	42.4
Cambeiti, 1976	5,787	7	67	48.0
Camiri, 1927	3,936	42	284	55.0
Carrasco, 1991	15,650	4	2,440	56.1
Cascabel, 1985	11,319	4	514	45.6
Guairuy, 1950	3,300	4	58	50.0
H. Suarez R., 1982	7,820	1	89	35.0
Katari, 1992	16,210	2	587	57.5
La Pena, 1965	8,856	14	880	43.0
Los Cusis, 1994	8100	2	360	33.6
Monteagudo, 1967	4,592	20	767	41.0
Montecristo, 1976	11349	1	25	....
Naranjillos, 1964	4,806	12	49	65.3
Patujusal, 1993	7,200	7	2,146	66.0
Rio Grande, 1962	9,512	24	753	62.0
San Alberto, 1967	2,500	2	14	42.0
San Roque, 1981	7,170	16	1,586	71.0
Santa Cruz, 1965	9,350	2	10	65.0
Sirari, 1985	13,999	10	1,232	65.0
Tatarenda, 1964	2,296	8	99	65.3
Tita-Techi, 1976	12949	1	14	51.0
Tundy, 1992	10597	5	495	48.6
Vibora, 1988	12,949	21	4,710	67.9
Villamontes, 1987	9770	1	14	57.7
Vuelta Grande, 1978	8,220	25	1,850	57.0
Yapacani, 1968	8,400	2	246	34.1
Others	....	....	....	....
Total Bolivia		**299**	**28,371**	

BRAZIL

Name of field, discovery date	Depth, ft	Producing oil wells	1995 production avg., b/d	°API gravity
PETROBRAS				
AMAZONAS				
Leste do Urucu	....	....	4,975	....
Rio Urucu, 1983	9,000	17	7,530	42.0
BAHIA				
+ Area do BAS-60	....	....	244	....
Ilha da Cacumba	....	....	248	....
+ Candeias, 1941	3,300-7,415	56	358	30.0
+ Dom Jao, 1947	920-3,000	94	1,340	38.0
Agua Grande, 1951	820-4,265	120	4,632	40.0
Apraius	....	....	48	....
Aracas, 1965	3,280-8,856	142	5,058	41.0
Aratu	....	....	13	....
Bela Vista	....	....	13	....
Briba	....	....	37	....
Bom Lugar	....	....	9	....
Bom Sucesso	....	....	1,083	....
Brejinho	....	....	121	....
Buracica, 1959	1,476-1,840	160	6,754	35.0
Canabrava	....	....	112	....
Candeias, 1941	3,300-7,415	....	2,895	30.0
Cassarongongo, 1959	1,475-4,755	104	764	32.0
Cexis, 1983	1,670-5,230	47	2,463	30.0
Cidade de Entre Rios	....	....	1,708	....
Conceicao	....	....	34	....
Dias D'Avila	....	....	0	....
Dom Joao, 1947	920-1,350	59	452	38.0
Fazenda Alvorada, 1983	2,100-4,900	67	1,777	31.0
Fazenda Azevedo	....	....	198	...
Fazenda Balsamo, 1983	2,500-4,000	130	5,185	31.0
Fazenda Belem, 1980	1,150-2,500	312	26	13.0
Fazenda Boa Esperanca	....	....	1,466	....
Fazenda Imbe, 1964	2,130-5,575	41	451	40.0
Fazenda Onca	....	....	23	....
Fazenda Panelas	....	....	175	....
Fazenda Rio Branco	....	....	287	....

WORLDWIDE PRODUCTION

Name of field, discovery date	Depth, ft	Producing oil wells	1995 production avg., b/d	°API gravity
Fazenda Santo Estevao	....	....	203	....
Gomo	....	....	45	....
Ilha de Bimbarra	....	....	0	....
Itaparica	....	....	0	....
Jacuipe	....	....	25	....
Lagoa do Pauolo	....	....	64	....
Lagao Verde	....	....	0	....
Lamarao	....	....	44	....
Leodorio	....	....	8	....
Malombe, 1966	3,280	11	317	41.0
Mandacaru	....	....	0	....
Massape	....	....	89	....
Massui	....	....	27	....
Mata de Sao Joao, 1971	4,445-4,560	13	255	35.0
Miranga, 1965	3,280-3,936	243	4,125	40.0
Miranga Leste	....	....	4	....
Miranga Norte	....	....	92	....
Norte de Fazenda Caruacu	....	....	160	....
Paramirim do Vencimento	....	....	0	....
Pedrinhas	....	....	0	....
Pojuca	....	....	12	....
Pojuca Norte	....	....	0	....
Quiambina	....	....	17	....
Remanso	....	....	881	....
Riacho da Barra, 1982	2,910-3,998	27	1,652	39.0
Riacho de Sao Pedro	....	....	15	....
Riacho Ouricuri	....	....	742	....
Rio da Serra	....	....	18	....
Rio do Bu, 1984	2,900-3,000	63	3,195	33.0
Rio dos Ovos, 1979	2,410-3,750	8	174	35.0
Rio Itariri	....	....	384	....
Rio Joanes	....	....	0	....
Rio Pipiri	....	....	26	....
Rio Pojuca, 1982	5,600-6,200	25	1,406	35.0
Rio Sauipe	....	....	12	....
Santana	....	....	22	....
Sao Domingos	....	....	98	....
Sao Pedro	....	....	39	....
Sauipe	....	....	6	....
Sesmaria, 1963	3,100-4,600	22	626	40.0
Socorro	....	....	51	....
Sussuarana	....	....	0	....
Taquipe, 1958	3,115-3,935	87	2,248	50.0
Vale do Quirico	....	....	69	....
RIO DE JANERIO				
Albacora, 1984	8,430	13	48,368	26.0
Anequim, 1981	8,500	2	1,713	27.0
Area do 1-RJS-046	....	....	140	....
Area do 1-RJS-095	....	....	0	....
Area do 3-RJS-450	....	....	0	....
Area do 4-RJS-322	....	....	0	....
Area do 4-RJS-377	....	....	2,759	....
Area do 4-RJS-403	....	....	2,328	....
Area do 4-RJS- 410	....	....	0	....
Area do 4-RJS-448	....	....	0	....
Area do 4-RJS- 493	....	....	2,207	....
Badejo, 1981	3,500-10,500	6	2,118	28.0
Bagre, 1983	8,700-9,000	6	2,276	25.0
Bicudo, 1982	8,000-11,000	12	11,929	22.0
Bijupira, 1993	2,885-2,945	2	10,145	28.0
Bonito, 1977	7,000-8,000	12	13,428	27.0
Carapeba, 1982	10,100	32	35,353	23.0
Cherne, 1982	9,900-10,200	31	24,545	27.0
Corvina, 1983	9,000-11,000	6	15,858	25.0
Enchova, 1976	6,973-7,885	8	12,568	23.0
Enchova Oeste, 1983	8,410	1	806	26.0
Garoupa, 1974	11,382	15	7,140	30.0
Garoupinha, 1974	12,693	3	2,334	30.0
Leste de Malhado, 1989	11,100	1	2,083	27.0
Linguado, 1981	9,000-11,000	13	11,432	30.0
Malhado, 1990	10,824	1	3,727	22.0
Marimba, 1983	8,900-9,200	15	57,173	28.0
Marlim, 1991	11,808	13	84,294	15.0
Marlim Sul, 1988	9,200	1	7,651	26.0
Moreia, 1984	8,200-9,500	5	3,984	22.0
Namorado, 1975	10,083	29	32,843	28.0
Nordeste de Namorado	....	....	457	....
Pampo, 1977	6,215	26	22,173	21.0
Parati, 1982	8,900-9,200	1	592	35.0
Pargo, 1975	11,840	11	6,353	20.0
Pirauna, 1982	8,000-10,500	8	11,117	27.0
Salema, 1990	9,200	1	2,202	30.0
Trilha, 1983	8,800-11,000	3	681	28.0
Vermelho, 1985	10,600	43	19,613	25.0
Viola, 1985	12,200	8	5,056	25.0
ESPIRITO SANTO				
+ Cacao, 1978	9,184	6	1,188	32.0
Barra do Ipiranga	....	....	105	....
Cacimbas	....	....	52	....
Campo Grande	....	....	58	....
Corrego Cedro Norte	....	....	3	....
Corrego Grande	....	....	2	....
Faz, Cedro Norte	....	....	273	....
Faz, Queimadas	....	....	716	....
Faz, Sao Jorge	....	....	192	....
Faz, Queimadas Oeste	....	....	1	....
Fazenda Cedro, 1962	5,248	11	234	28.0
Fazenda Santa Luzia	....	....	1,468	....
Guriri	....	....	56	....
Lagoa Bonita	....	....	14	....
Lagoa Parda	....	....	1,897	....
Lagoa Parda Norte	....	....	74	....
Lagoa Parda Sul	....	....	0	....
Lagoa Piabanha	....	....	76	....
Lagoa Suruaca, 1962	6,400	14	524	30.0
Mariricu	....	....	46	....
Mariricu Norte	....	....	2	....
Mariricu Oeste	....	....	4	....
Nativo Oeste	....	....	1	....
Rio Barra Seca	....	....	5	....
Rio Itaunas, 1977	5,400	33	525	28.0
Rio Itaunas Leste	....	....	7	....
Rio Mariricu	....	....	85	....
Rio Preto, 1976	1,460-2,600	15	284	....
Rio Preto Oeste	....	....	232	....
Rio Sao Mateus	....	....	125	....
Sao Mateus, 1969	5,750	32	893	27.0
CEARA				
+ Atum, 1983	2,300-3,200	12	3,823	31.0
+ Curiman, 1978	6,888	8	3,379	32.0
+ Espada, 1983	5,750-6,900	3	2,278	26.0
+ Xareu, 1977	5,717-5,766	6	2,315	39.0
Fazenda Belem, 1980	1,150-2,500		2,553	13.0
RIO GRANDE DO NORTE				
+ Agulha, 1975	5,412	5	1,366	33.0
+ Aratum	....	....	406	....
+ Ubarana, 1973	7,216-8,365	66	8,462	40.0
Alto Alegre			12	
Alto do Rodrigues, 1981	990-1,220	506	7,680	18.0
Baixa do Algodao	....	....	386	....
Baixo Vermelho	....	....	2	....
Barrinha	....	....	13	....
Boa Vista	....	....	436	....
Brejinho	....	....	418	....
Cachoeirinha	....	....	322	....
Canto do Amaro, 1986	2,500-3,600	894	29,939	25.0
Estreito, 1983	650-820	709	11,440	16.0
Fazenda Canaan	....	....	20	....
Fazenda Curral	....	....	179	
Fazedna Malaquias	....	....	520	
Fazenda Pocinho	....	....	3,441	....
Guamareh, 1983	1,400-1,600	17	203	25.0
Janduih	....	....	3	....
Juazeiro	....	....	222	....
Lagoa Aroeira	....	....	27	....
Livramento, 1986	2,500-3,300	27	784	41.0
Logradouro	....	....	1	....
Lorena, 1984	1,200-1,700	27	501	28.0
Macau	....	....	136	....
Monte Alegre	....	....	317	....
Morrinho	....	....	43	....
Mossoroh, 1980	3,280	27	672	28.0
Noroeste do Morro do Rosado			16	....
Pajeu	....	....	12	....
Pereiro	....	....	1	....
Poco Verde	....	....	12	....
Poco Xavier	....	....	453	....
Ponta do Mel	....	....	259	....
Porto Carao	....	....	92	....
Porto do Mangue	....	....	1	....
Redonda	....	....	80	....
Redonda Profundo	....	....	1,352	....
Riacho Alazao	....	....	28	....
Riacho Forquilha	....	....	5,136	....
Rio Mossoro	....	....	33	....
Salina Cristal	....	....	2,126	....
Sao Manuel	....	....	4	....
Sao Miguel	....	....	329	....
Serra Vermelha	....	....	14	....
Serraria, 1982	3,200-3,900	31	713	27
Tres Marias	....	....	145	....
Upanema, 1985	1,110-1,800	12	844	28.0
Varzea Redona	....	....	352	....
ALAGOAS				
Cidade Sao Miguel dos Campos	....	....	37	....
Coqueiro Seco	....	....	30	....
Fazenda Pau Brazil	....	....	44	....
Furado, 1969	1,440-5,500	42	805	35.0
Piacabucu	....	....	61	....
Pilar, 1981	4,100-5,100	41	2,862	40.0
Rio Satuba	....	....	0	....
Sao Miguel dos Campos	....	....	66	....
Sul de Coruripe	....	....	96	....
Tabuleiro do Martins, 1957	3,900-4,950	16	284	27.0

WORLDWIDE PRODUCTION

Name of field, discovery date	Depth, ft	Producing oil wells	1995 production avg., b/d	°API gravity
SERGIPE				
+ Area SES-102	....	....	219	....
+ Area SES-107D	....	....	414	....
+ Caioba, 1969	6,232-6,890	8	704	36.0
+ Camorim, 1970	6,232	44	3,020	25.0
+ Dourado, 1970	3,620-3,635	7	1,258	36.0
+ Guaricema, 1968	3,335-4,430	8	2,901	41.0
+ Salgo	....	....	187	....
Anguilhadas	....	....	110	....
Angelim	....	....	50	....
Aruari	....	....	27	....
Atalaia Sul, 1961	1,450	1	31	24.0
Brejo Grande, 1967	1,670	7	379	26.0
Carmopolis, 1963	2,460	884	20,923	24.0
Castanhal	....	....	32	....
Cidade de Aracaju	....	....	2	....
Foz do Vaza Barris	....	....	7	....
Ilha Pequena	....	....	159	....
Mato Grosso	....	....	173	....
Riacho Agua Boa	....	....	3	....
Riachuelo, 1961	1,475	172	2,287	28.0
Siririzinho, 1967	1,640	157	2,967	30.0
Vaza Barris	....	....	1	....
PARANA				
+ Caravela, 1993	4,910-4,930	1	6,820	43.0
+ Estrela do Mar	....	....	256	....
SANTA CATARINA				
+ Caravela Sul	....	....	16	....
SAO PAULO				
+ Merluza	....	....	3,862	....
Total Brazil		**6,025**	**689,612**	

BRUNEI

Name of field, discovery date	Depth, ft	Producing oil wells	1995 production avg., b/d	°API gravity
SHELL				
• Ampa SW, 1963	7,068-8,155	151	43,731	41.0
• Champion, 1970	4,300	229	60,470	23.0
• Enggang		2	639	....
• Fairley, 1969	10,740	28	6,990	40.0
• Fairley-Baram, 1973	9,500	3	2,630	40.0
• Gannet	....	....	0	40.0
• Iron Duke, 1973	....	4	5,955	....
• Magpie, 1975	....	20	9,651	31.0
Rasau, 1929	....	17	6,313	30.0
Seria-Tali, 1929	....	312	15,115	34.0
Total Brunei		**766**	**151,494**	

CAMEROON

Name of field, discovery date	Depth, ft	Producing oil wells	1995 production avg., b/d	°API gravity
ELF				
• Asoma Centre, 1977	4,000	9	1,200	26.1
• Asoma Marine, 1973	3,600	3	2,200	19.0
• Bakassi Marine, 1976	6,500	1	1,800	37.1
• Barombi Marine, 1975	7,400	1	2,500	34.1
• Bavo, 1976	5,600	17	7,000	29.3
• Betika, 1972	5,300	5	1,200	42.5
• Betika S. Marine, 1979	6,300	2	1,500	30.0
• Biboundi, 1974	6,400	0	....	34.6
• Boa, 1976	5,900	4	2,800	35.0
• Ekoundou Horst plus Center, 1972	7,200	17	13,700	29.0
• Ekoundou N. Marine, 1977	5,250	12	1,000	36.0
• Ekoundou S., 1975	6,200	11	2,800	24.0
• Inoua Marine, 1976	6,200	9	2,700	32.8
• Itindi, 1977	5,600	14	6,100	26.1
• Kita E. Marine, 1978	6,900	9	2,300	40.8
• Kole, 1974	5,500	7	1,500	31.0
• Kole Superieur, 1978	4,100	5	1,300	23.0
• Kombo Center, 1976	5,900	14	13,400	37.0
• Kombo Nord, 1978	5,700	4	2,500	36.0
• Nyangassa, 1977	5,100	4	3,912	29.8
KELT				
Moudi, 1979	5,250-5,900	3	2,300	40.0
Moudi D., 1980	3,300	5	1,700	21.3
PECTEN INERNATIONAL				
• Makoko NE plus Abana, 1977	4,600	45	16,000	29.0
• Makoko S. Marine, 1977	3,300	27	10,700	17.0
Total Cameroon		**228**	**102,112**	

CANADA

Name of field, discovery date	Depth, ft	Producing oil wells	1995 production avg., b/d	°API gravity
ALBERTA				
Acheson, 1950	3,390	52	2,411	38.0
Bantry, 1940	2,574-3,300	221	9,219	....
Bellshill Lake, 1955	2,950	463	11,575	....
Bonnie Glen, 1952	3,959-6,779	101	3,998	34.0-44.0
Caroline	....	169	4,742	....
Carson Creek N., 1958	8,787-8,935	44	5,099	44.0
Cessford, 1950	2,800-3,028	234	3,818	....
Clive, 1951	6,074-6,208	112	4,841	....
Countess, 1951	2,858-4,272	147	10,447	....
Fenn Big Valley, 1950	3,900-5,400	89	2,570	32.0
Gilby, 1962	4,201-7,000	136	7,728	....
Golden Spike, 1949	3,570-5,961	55	1,572	36.0
Grand Forks	....	428	18,759	....
Harmattan East, 1954	6,358-8,766	72	3,368	....
Harmatton Elkton, 1955	8,796-10,757	60	2,881	....
Hayter, 1968	2,030-2,815	479	17,679	....
Innisfail, 1956	6,730-8,440	28	1,009	....
Joarcam, 1949	3,179	124	3,736	....
Joffre, 1953	4,983-6,779	86	3,577	....
Judy Creek, 1951	8,307-8,701	134	12,465	43.0
Kaybob, 1957	4,870-9,577	66	4,740	....
Kaybob S., 1958	5,600-10,042	55	9,095	....
Leduc-Woodbend, 1947	3,062-5,380	96	1,570	....
Lloydminster, 1933	1,690-1,945	324	4,398	....
Medicine River, 1954	5,435-7,600	244	8,418	....
Mitsue, 1964	5,908	273	20,071	....
Nipisi, 1965	5,648-5,726	268	19,876	41.0
Pembina, 1953	3,000-6,133	3,331	57,036	32.0-37.0
Provost, 1946	2,760-2,898	3,446	107,213	....
Rainbow, 1965	4,994-6,160	252	30,206	38.0-42.0
Rainbow South, 1965	6,102-6,400	51	5,697	....
Red Earth, 1956	4,184-4,878	185	6,730	....
Redwater, 1948	2,012-3,200	614	11,887	35.0
Simonette, 1958	10,500	35	7,860	....
Snipe Lake, 1962	8,500	35	1,572	....
Sturgeon Lake S., 1953	4,912-8,471	83	7,086	37.0
Swan Hills, 1957	8,100	510	30,951	40.0
Swan Hills S., 1959	8,400	145	7,702	....
Taber, N., 1966	3,110-3,270	235	12,999	....
Turner Valley, 1913	3,100-9,150	106	2,155	39.0
Utikuma Lake, 1963	5,624	128	9,149	....
Valhalla, 1973	1,815-7,060	484	21,423	....
Virginia Hills, 1957	9,210	110	12,637	34.0
Wainwright, 1925	1,903-2,200	597	6,902	....
Westerose, 1952	6,818	33	3,065	....
Westpem	....	17	2,913	....
Willisden Green, 1956	5,157	480	5,757	....
Wizard Lake, 1951	4,044-5,973	47	2,766	....
Zama, 1966	3,702	108	5,494	33.0-37.0
Other	....	10,464	396,145	....
BRITISH COLUMBIA				
Boundary Lake, 1957	3,418-4,575	254	7,663	40.0
Eagle West, 1976	2,170-3,940	44	2,283	....
Other	....	498	24,726	....
EAST COAST				
• Cohasset	....	8	18,845	....
• Panuke	....	2	2,553	....
MANITOBA				
Total for all fields	....	1,354	11,080	....
NEW BRUNSWICK				
Total for all fields	....	....	....	....
NORTHWEST TERRITORIES & ARCTIC ISLANDS				
Bent Horn	....	1	633	....
Norman Wells	....	163	29,272	....
ONTARIO				
Total for all fields	....	1,140	4,921	....
SASKATCHEWAN				
Steelman, 1950	....	591	6,881	....
Weyburn, 1955	4,600	931	27,157	....
Other	....	14,512	287,930	....
Total Canada		**45,554**	**1,378,951**	

CHILE

Name of field, discovery date	Depth, ft	Producing oil wells	1995 production avg., b/d	°API gravity
ENAP-CONTINENTE				
Canadon, 1962	6,090	4	34	38.4
Daniel, 1960	5,806	25	509	25.4
Daniel Este, 1961	5,523	9	95	25.0
Delgada Este, 1958	7,694	10	144	35.0
Dungeness, 1962	5,251	8	141	28.6
Faro Este, 1959	7,381	5	128	35.0
Posesion, 1960	5,622	39	298	63.6

WORLDWIDE PRODUCTION

Name of field, discovery date	Depth, ft	Producing oil wells	1995 production avg., b/d	°API gravity
ENAP-COSTA AFUERA				
Anguila AN-1, 1989	5,758	9	404	32.0
Atun AT-1, 1992	5,722	6	104	33.0
Catalina Norte, 1989	5,807	6	288	38.0
Daniel, 1990	5,840	14	188	35.0
Daniel Este-Dungeness, 1984	6,126	22	383	35.9
Ostion, 1979	7,156	12	224	33.0
Pejerrey, 1984	7,229	16	315	39.0
Posesion, 1980	6,727	15	243	34.5
Skua, 1988	5,932	24	1,179	32.0
Spiteful, 1979	6,288	13	393	34.5
Spiteful Norte, 1980	7,150	5	128	39.0
Terramar, 1991	6,211	8	946	33.0
ENAP-ISLA				
Calafate, 1956	6,045	7	150	49.3
Catalina, 1956	5,756	4	94	38.7
Catalina Sur, 1962	5,779	4	56	44.0
Cullen, 1954	5,730	14	360	41.8
Cullen Este, 1988	5,479	1	58	40.0
Flamenco, 1954	6,545	5	208	40.2
Gaviota Norte, 1990	7,000	5	123	38.0
Golondrina, 1978	5,906	1	72	37.0
Gorrion, 1986	6,025	3	75	39.0
Lago Mercedes, 1992	12,468	1	65	....
Punta Baja, 1954	7,545	4	120	39.0
Sombrero Este, 1992	6,506	2	301	36.0
Tres Lagos, 1957	5,724	16	132	40.1
Total Chile		**317**	**7,960**	

CHINA

Name of field, discovery date	Depth, ft	Producing oil wells	1995 production avg., b/d	°API gravity
CNPC				
Northeast:				
Daqing	....		1,123,207	....
Liaohe	....		311,313	....
Jilin	....		68,192	....
North:				
Huabei	....		93,455	....
Dagang	....		86,236	....
Jidong	....		10,232	
East:				
Shengli	....		601,698	....
Zhongyuan	....		82,293	....
Jiangshu	....		20,338	....
Anhui	....		1,009	
Central & South:				
Henan	....	49,700	38,431	....
Jianghan	....		17,053	....
Northwest:				
Xinjiang	....		158,501	....
Changqing	....		44,121	....
Qinghai	....		24,407	....
Yanchang	....		14,746	....
Tarim	....		50,763	....
Turpan-Hami	....		44,285	....
Yumen	....		8,102	
Southwest:				
Sichuan	....		3,455	
Y, G&G	....		2,048	
Other	....		11,315	....
• Offshore	....		168,789	....
Total China		**49,700**	**2,983,989**	

CHINA, TAIWAN

Name of field, discovery date	Depth, ft	Producing oil wells	1995 production avg., b/d	°API gravity
CHINESE PETROLEUM				
Chingtsohu & CBK, 1967	5,346-12,000	7	207	50.0
Chinshui & Yunghoshan, 1971	5,248-12,000	19	55	45.0
Chuhuangkeng, 1904	6,560-15,600	29	174	50.0
Tiechengshan, 1962	9,840	16	597	51.0
Other	6,560-8,800	6	4	....
Total China, Taiwan		**77**	**1,037**	

COLOMBIA

Name of field, discovery date	Depth, ft	Producing oil wells	1995 production avg., b/d	°API gravity
AMERICAN INTERNATIONAL PETROLEUM CORP.				
Toqui Toqui, 1985	3,000	21	847	21.4
ARGOSY ENERGY INTERNATIONAL				
Linda, 1990	9,100	2	....	28.0
Mary, 1990	8,000	3	3,171	28.3
Miraflor, 1991	7,000	1	753	27.5
Toroyaco, 1989	9,400	3	2,110	27.6
BP EXPLORATION				
Cusiana, 1988	12,000	15	128,500	35.5
CHEVRON PETROLEUM CO.				
Castilla, 1969	6,500	21	15,868	13.5
Chichimene, 1969	6,500	11	9,598	21.3
COPLEX				
Rubiales, 1989	2,600	3	702	12.6
ECOPETROL ALTO MAGDALENA				
Brisas, 1973	5,900	4	527	22.9
Cebu, 1981	6,800	8	745	20.1
Dina Cretaceos, 1961	7,000	17	2,938	22.0
Dina Terciarios, 1961	4,100	57	4,761	19.8
Hato Nuevo Loma Larga, 1969	7,500	2	104	36.4
Palogrande, 1971	6,700	25	4,175	20.3
Pijao, 1981	7,900	7	387	20.4
Santa Clara, 1987	3,000	10	1,180	18.4
Tenay, 1985	12,400	3	1,123	36.5
ECOPETROL BOGOTA				
Apiay Este, 1987	10,650	1	185	18.0
Apiiay, 1981	10,650	12	7,515	22.0
Austral, 1987	11,012	1	2,722	33.0
Boquete-Zanon, 1961	8,000	8	192	42.0
Caipal, 1957	6,000	2	58	17.0
Castilla Este, 1989	7,050	1	363	13.0
Castilla Norte, 1988	7,050	2	1,113	13.0
Cicuco, 1957	8,000	4	296	41.0
Gavan, 1995	11,200	1	279	14.2
Guatiquia, 1985	10,750	1	1,271	25.0
Guayuriba, 1984	10,600	....	70	37.8
La Reforma, 1985	11,050	1	359	33.7
Libertad, 1985	11,200	1	71	36.0
Libertad Norte, 1987	11,050	2	1,149	33.0
Ocoa, 1987	10,600	....	14	26.0
Ortega, 1951	6,000	4	248	28.4
Pacande, 1989	6,000	2	335	28.0
Palagua, 1954	5,000	99	3,686	25.0
Pompeya, 1988	10,400	1	1,089	33.0
Quenane, 1972	11,900	1	77	29.5
Quimbaya, 1988	6,000	2	360	17.0
Saurio, 1988	10,858	1	5	42.8
Suria, 1985	10,350	5	12,546	35.0
Suria Sur, 1985	10,350	4	9,596	33.0
Tanane, 1986	10,600	....	9	33.0
Toldado, 1987	6,000	5	1,473	20.0
Toy, 1987	900	2	116	19.0
ECOPETROL EL CENTRO				
Aguas Blancas, 1962	7,000	3	60	30.0
Bajo Rio, 1958	8,000	1	3	23.0
Cantagallo, 1943	7,500	9	623	20.0
Casabe, 1941	4,000	305	9,887	19.0
Colorado, 1925	4,000	8	152	30.0
Cristalina, 1959	9,500	1	147	29.0
Gala, 1985	7,500	10	968	20.0
Galan, 1943	5,000	36	736	19.0
Garzas, 1957	6,000	1	70	31.0
Infantas, 1917	2,000	186	1,828	23.0
La Cira, 1926	3,300	534	6,609	23.0
Lisama, 1965	8,000	75	1,917	30.0
Llanito, 1961	7,000	41	2,177	20.0
Nutria, 1981	8,000	18	550	30.0
Pavas, 1981	11,000	....	0	21.0
Penas Blancas, 1957	4,000	4	251	22.0
Peroles, 1977	7,000	6	57	30.0
San Luis, 1926	5,000	2	93	35.0
San Silvestre, 1958	3,500	2	54	19.0
Sogamoso, 1973	10,000	1	32	29.0
Tenerife, 1968	7,500	....	0	18.0
Tesoro, 1979	8,000	21	538	30.0
Totumal, 1950	8,000	....	0	24.0
Yarigui, 1955	8,500	53	5,360	16.0
ECOPETROL ORIENTE				
Bonanza, 1962	4,400	12	458	21.6
Campo Yuca, 1957	5,500	....	1	....
Carbonera, 1939	3,000	3	33	21.0
Conde, 1960	9,900	11	644	26.7
Petrolea, 1933	600	6	185	44.0
Provincia, 1961	....	....	....	25.7
Puerto Barco, 1958	7,000	3	95	43.0
Rio de Oro, 1920	8,000	12	194	35.0
Rio Zulia, 1962	6,200	17	1,169	41.1
Sabana, 1986	10,200	2	120	26.7
Santos, 1960	9,500	65	2,634	....
Sardina D.N., 1941	7,000	6	177	36.0

WORLDWIDE PRODUCTION

Name of field, discovery date	Depth, ft	Producing oil wells	1995 production avg., b/d	°API gravity
Sardina D.S., 1941	7,000	....	....	45.0
Suerte, 1963	9,600	26	1,189	26.7
Tibu, 1940	4,500	179	3,297	35.0
ECOPETROL D. SUR				
Acae Sur, 1965	10,800	9	3,336	30.1
Alborada, 1991	9,580	....	12	32.0
Caribe, 1959	7,900	3	269	30.7
Cencella, 1991	9,620	1	315	32.0
Churuyaco, 1968	9,200	2	165	31.9
Loro, 1968	10,600	4	560	30.5
Mansoya, 1929	9,600	1	340	32.7
Orito Norte, 1963	6,800	47	5,457	32.6
Orito Sur, 1963	6,800	2	163	30.0
Quilili, 1958	9,600	1	42	30.0
San Antonio, 1969	9,600	1	21	31.9
San Miguel, 1967	10,800	1	137	30.0
Sibundoy, 1988	9,600	1	112	27.6
Sucio, 1970	7,900	3	316	30.7
Sucombios, 1959	9,000	1	539	32.6
Yurilla, 1991	9,700	....	....	28.7
ESSO COLOMBIANA LTD.				
Arauca, 1980	5,000	4	1,420	39.0
Rio Ceibas, 1988	4,500	4	650	22.9
Yaguara, 1987	3,000	32	7,605	22.6
KELT DE COLOMBIA				
Abejas, 1990	5,600	1	472	33.0
Barquerena, 1982	9,300	2	677	32.3
Cano Garza, 1979	7,900	2	640	40.2
Cano Garza Este, 1992	8,490	1	289	36.8
Cano Garza Norte, 1983	7,900	1	348	40.2
Chaparrito, 1988	5,400	1	1,819	34.4
Chap. Nte., 1989	5,470	1	2	33.0
Cravo Este, 1987	11,376	1	7	42.0
Cravo Sur, 1982	10,600	2	940	40.2
Guanapalo, 1986	5,640	1	221	29.8
Guarilaque, 1988	5,430	3	3,442	24.4
Guasar, 1991	5,430	1	6	25.0
Jordan, 1985	5,570	1	853	29.3
Jordan Nte., 1986	5,570	1	248	27.3
La Flora, 1985	8,600	2	1,434	34.2
La Gloria, 1987	14,000	4	3,623	17.8
La Gloria Norte, 1983	12,100	3	2,814	17.2
Los Toros, 1989	5,300	3	2,502	34.2
Morichal, 1984	15,500	2	838	30.0
Palmarito, 1988	5,200	3	3,985	41.1
Paravare, 1986	6,240	1	380	28.0
Sardinas, 1982	5,420	2	1,486	26.3
Tierra Blanca, 1987	14,493	1	122	32.0
Tocaria, 1980	13,500	3	349	32.1
Trinidad, 1974	9,000	6	2,651	32.4
LASMO OIL (COLOMBIA) LTDD.				
Juncal, 1991	9,190	1	1,102	28.7
Los Trompillos, 1990	8,840	1	612	29.5
Matachin Norte, 1992	6,800	1	....	27.0
Matachin Sur, 1994	6,700	2	....	24.0
Palmar, 1990	9,930	1	914	21.7
Purificacion, 1991	4,860	2	6,747	35.0
Santiago, 1985	10,000	7	6,016	22.5
Santiago Este, 1988	8,770	1	1,289	22.1
NOMECO				
Guacamayo, 1988	6,700	1	361	40.0
Guahibos, 1989	7,000	1	135	34.0
OCCIDENTAL				
Cano Limon, 1983	7,600	15	21,279	29.0
Cano Yarunal, 1987	7,600	10	31,148	29.0
La Yuca, 1984	7,600	67	106,224	29.4
Matanegra, 1984	7,600	19	24,203	29.7
Redondo, 1984	7,600	7	7,470	30.2
OMINEX DE COLOMBIA LTD.				
Cocorna	....	25	602	12.8
Nare Asociacion, 1981	2,400	48	2,288	12.8
Teca, 1981	2,400	250	9,741	12.8
PETROBRAS				
Guarimena, 1988	7,300	2	482	33.4
PETROLEOS COLOMBIANOS				
Andalucia, 1980	2,200	16	1,570	32.9
PETROLEOS DE NORTE				
Dona Maria, 1989	8,500	2	45	....
Los Angeles, 1983	....	4	384	14.3
Rio Zulia	6,650	....	....	41.0
Santa Lucia, 1988	9,700	3	862	20.3
Tisquirama	.....	4	423	....
PETROMINEROS				
Totare, 1987	1,200	4	88	22.0

Name of field, discovery date	Depth, ft	Producing oil wells	1995 production avg., b/d	°API gravity
PETROSANTANDER COLOMBIA				
Corazon, 1963	8,000	8	45	28.0
Payoa, 1961	10,200	29	990	27.9
Salina, 1946	3,400	57	1,830	27.6
SHELL DE COLOMBIA				
Balcon/Colomb., 1988	10,200	5	4,441	34.0
Olini, 1989	6,186	1	....	18.0
Palermo, 1988	3,200	2	274	18.3
Rio Saldana, 1990	3,700	2	....	15.0
San Francisco, 1985	2,800	61	24,945	27.0
Tello, 1972	7,500	28	1,711	22.0
Total Colombia		**2,888**	**574,822**	

CONGO

Name of field, discovery date	Depth, ft	Producing oil wells	1995 production avg., b/d	°API gravity
AGIP				
• Loango, 1972	3,000	52	18,828	25.1
• Zatchi, 1980	2,000	21	29,251	24.4
ELF				
• Emeraude, 1969	820	79	9,897	22.3
• Likouala, 1979	4,270	25	7,147	33.0
Pointe Indienne, 1951	5,000	3	135	35.0
• Sendji, 1973	3,940	54	18,333	29.3
• Tchendo, 1979	1,600	23	11,248	33.0
• Tchibouela, 1983	2,110	34	59,614	26.0
• Yanga, 1979	2,950	48	11,606	29.4
WALTER INTERNATIONAL CONGO (e)				
• Yombo, 1988	3,300	18	8,941	16.2
Total Congo		**357**	**175,000**	

CROATIA

Name of field, discovery date	Depth, ft	Producing oil wells	1995 production avg., b/d	°API gravity
INA-NAFTAPLIN				
Benicanci, 1966	6,752-5,938	18	989	30.2
Bilogora, 1966	3,346-5,052	20	516	40.8
Bizovac, 1989	5,483-5,499	8	437	33.8
Boksic-Klokocevci, 1975	7,218-10,171	5	23	31.0
Bunjani, 1951	1,800-2,550	20	99	30.2
Crnac, 1977	6,814-8,061	9	558	34.6
Deletovci, 1982	3,143-3,422	....	....	28.9
Dugo Selo, 1953	3,445-4,183	13	282	31.1
Ferdinandovac, 1959	5,625-5,915	6	100	36.0
Galovac-Pavljani	1,250-1,938	5	144	34.4
Ilaca, 1982	3,445-4,183	....	....	31.1
Ivanic Grad, 1959	5,282-5,709	46	1,828	33.4
Jagnjedovac, 1961	2,864-3,570	22	310	33.0
Jamarice, 1965	3,281-5,512	96	2,136	37.6
Jezevo, 1963	6,234-7,382	9	118	36.7
Kalinovac (c), 1978	11,841-14,682	14	4,529	51.5
Klostar, 1952	2,297-4,593	60	926	36.3
Kozarice, 1972	3,281-3,609	19	277	23.6
Kriz, 1948	1,600-2,250	23	51	17.4
Kucanci-Kapelna, 1973	6,562-7,218	10	430	25.2
Lacici, 1979	7,605-8,012	7	841	35.6
Lepavina, 1969	1,780-2,200	8	60	22.8
Leticani, 1989	4,584-4,817	4	60	35.0
Lipovljani, 1960	3,937-5,709	73	1,833	36.7
Lupoglav, 1971	3,860-5,600	5	46	33.4-37.0
Mihovljani, 1973	5,150-5,760	4	67	32.5
Molve (c), 1974	10,263-11,345	17	1,789	57.2
Mramor Brdo, 1949	2,625-4,101	3	15	31.1
Obod, 1967	6,378-7,550	3	131	32.5
Okoli, 1962	7,382-8,366	4	95	35.5
Okoli (c), 1962	7,218-7,874	13	879	80.6
Privlaka, 1983	2,933-3,041	....	....	25.9
Sandrovac, 1962	2,250-3,700	88	2,437	37.8
Stari Gradac (c), 1980	11,720-13,630	4	1,050	51.4
Stevkovica, 1978	7,710-9,843	14	469	31.9
Struzec, 1956	2,362-3,773	53	3,611	38.8
Vezisce, 1965	6,135-6,562	1	5	31.6
Zutica, 1963	5,742-6,923	159	4,124	33.8
Zutica (c), 1963	....	1	38	87.9
Other (c)	5,250-11,800	3	22	....
Total Croatia		**867**	**31,325**	

CUBA (e)

Name of field, discovery date	Depth, ft	Producing oil wells	1995 production avg., b/d	°API gravity
MINISTRY				
Boca Jaruco, 1968	5,000	80		13.0
Perifericos, 1972	5,000	18		21.0
Pina, 1989	3,500	45	28,000	27.0
Varsoero, 1969	6,000	85		10.0
Total Cuba		**228**	**28,000**	

WORLDWIDE PRODUCTION

Name of field, discovery date	Depth, ft	Producing oil wells	1995 production avg., b/d	°API gravity
DENMARK				
DUC				
• Dagmar, 1983	4,600	2	601	36.9
• Dan, 1971	6,060	48	64,013	30.5
• Gorm, 1971	6,800	30	43,006	33.5
• Kraka, 1966	6,000	6	8,092	32.8
• Regnar, 1979	5,700	1	1,482	32.6
• Rolf, 1981	5,900	2	3,720	30.6
• Skjold, 1977	5,250	14	34,118	28.7
• Tyra, 1968	6,575	45	28,117	40.4
• Valdemar, 1977	8,550	3	2,852	48.1
Total Denmark		**151**	**186,001**	
DUBAI				
ARCO				
Margham, 1981	11,200	9	8,882	43.5
DUPETCO (e)				
• Falah, 1972	8,100	....		25.5
• Fateh, 1966	7,900-9,000	....		31.8
• Rashid, 1973	9,400-11,500	141	313,118	38.0
• S.W. Fateh, 1970	7,500-9,000	....		30.3
Total Dubai		**150**	**322,000**	
ECUADOR				
OCCIDENTAL				
Jivino-Laguna, 1990	10,000	11	5,664	18.3
Laguna, 1991	10,000	9	12,216	18.3
Limoncocha, 1985	9,800	9	9,125	19.0
Napo, 1994	9,900	2	4,440	18.3
ESPOL (e)				
Ancon, 1921	4,000	439		35.7
Carpet Zona Norte, 1921	4,000	99		36.4
Cautivo, 1921	4,000	79		36.4
CITY INVESTING (e)				
Fanny-18B, 1972	7,700	8		22.5
Joan	....	....		20.0
Mariann, 1971	7,700	5		20.0
Tarapoa, 1973	8,300	1		20.0
TRIPETROL (e)				
Pacoa, 1992	....	....		....
MAXUS - YPF (e)				
Amo, 1994	....	....		....
Bogi-Capiron (7%), 1994	9,300	....		....
Tivacuno, 1994	....	....		....
ORYX (e)				
Coca-Payamino (46%), 1991	8,500	....		24.0
Gacela, 1993	8,800	....		....
Lobo, 1994	....	....		....
ELF (e)				
Sunka-Wanke, 1993	9,300	....		....
Shiripuno, 1994	9,050	....		....
PETROECUADOR - ORIENTE (e)				
Anaconda, 1991	10,200	1	355,269	25.0
Atacapi, 1968	9,855	4		31.0
Auca, 1970	10,578	28		28.0
Auca Este, 1992	10,330	....		....
Auca Sur, 1980	9,100-10,300	1		25.6
Bermejo Sur•Norte, 1967	5,000	21		32.5
Bogi-Capiron (93%), 1994	9,300	....		....
Chanangue, 1990	....	1		32.0
Charapa, 1967	10,000	1		29.0
Coca - Payamino, 1991	8,500	....		24.0
Conga, 1994	10,300	....		....
Cononaco, 1972	11,233	12		33.3
Culebra, 1973	10,626	2		17.5
Cuyabeno, 1972	8,050	14		27.4
Dureno/Guanta, 1968	9,575-10,290	9		31.0
Frontera, 1991	10,175	2		29.0
Lago Agrio, 1967	10,175	20		28.5
Libertador	9,800	49		29.7
Limoncocha, 1993	9,850	....		....
Palanda, 1991	10,700	1		29.0
Parahuacu, 1968	10,173	2		30.0
Paraiso, 1991	9,700	2		28.0
Parayacu, 1991	9,500	1		24.0
Pindo, 1991	10,800	1		30.0
Pucuna, 1990	9,500	5		30.0
Puma, 1993	10,200	....		....
Sacha, 1972	10,300	101		28.0
Sansahuari, 1984	8,300	5		26.0
Shushufindi, 1972	10,900	57		30.0

Name of field, discovery date	Depth, ft	Producing oil wells	1995 production avg., b/d	°API gravity
Singue, 1991	9,500	1		28.0
Tapi, 1991	9,400	....		29.1
Tetete, 1984	9,400	8		29.1
Tiguino, 1990	11,150	4		27.0
V.H. Ruales, 1991	8,400	5		31.0
Yuca, 1980	10,300	6		28.0
Yuca Sur, 1985	10,300	1		14.5
Yulebra, 1981	10,400	3		21.4
Total Ecuador		**1,030**	**386,714**	
EGYPT				
AGIP				
Aghar, 1985	6,000	8	5,220	33.0
Aman, 1985	5,210	21	7,050	41.0
Ashrafi (c), 1987	6,000	....	200	58.0
• Ashrafi (c), 1987	6,000	7	20,450	58.0
• Emry, 1985	5,190	1	170	35.0
Falak, 1986	6,000	....	....	42.5
Karnak, 1986	5,140	....	....	32.6
Lotus, 1986	5,000	1	140	33.0
Meleiha N.E., 1986	5,210	13	2,840	42.5
Meleiha S.E., 1986	5,575	5	1,300	43.0
Meleiha West, 1980	5,120	24	8,750	39.0
Ras El-Hekma, 1990	3,000	1	220	42.0
Zahra, 1986	5,120	1	270	44.0
Zarif, 1993	6,000	6	2,090	36.0
AMOCO EGYPT				
Abu El Gharadig, 1971	10,500	11	2,390	33.0
• Badri, 1981	6,000	34	39,000	32.0
• East Razzak, 1972	6,000	3	770	37.0
• E-Tanka	....	....	....	....
• E. Badri, 1990	6,000	3	2,560	....
• GH 376, 1981	11,000	2	760	24.0
• GS 160, 1977	11,200	2	1,210	31.0
• GS 172, 1988	10,800	11	31,300	27.0
• GS 173, 1978	10,700	1	1,330	31.0
• GS 277, 1982	10,700	1	1,460	33.0
• GS 327, 1987	6,600	3	1,800	20.0
• GS 345, 1982	7,800	2	1,300	35.0
• GS 365, 1980	11,000	1	2,000	32.0
• GS 373, 1993	10,500	....	....	....
• GS 381, 1985	10,500	....	....	37.0
G.O.S. fields (c)	....	....	4,460	59.0
• Hilal, 1982	11,500	10	15,060	32.0
• July, 1973	11,000	30	23,740	32.0
• Morgan, 1965	6,300	84	59,800	31.0
NA/G, 1985	12,200	2	350	33.0
NE A/G, 1984	11,000	3	410	34.0
• Nessim, 1981	6,800	1	60	30.0
• October, 1978	12,000	47	111,913	31.0
• Ramadan, 1974	11,500	35	24,800	33.0
Razzak, 1972	6,500	5	1,780	37.0
• SB 294, 1982	11,500	3	1,300	34.0
• SB 367, 1983	7,800	....	....	39.0
• SB339, 1981	4,200	1	610	30.0
• SG 184	....	....	....	....
• SG 300, 1974	6,500	4	3,400	24.0
SG 325	....	....	....	....
• SG 374, 1987	12,500	1	600	36.0
Shoab Ali, 1977	5,500	26	8,392	33.0
Sidki, 1976	10,500	5	15,000	36.0
Waly, 1982	7,500	1	349	35.0
WD 19/1, 1972	9,500	1	1,250	45.0
WD 33/15, 1985	5,200	2	1,000	30.0
WD other	....	....	....	....
WD33/1, 1972	10,000	1	420	35.0
Younis, 1981	4,700	3	2,210	35.0
AL-ALAMEIN				
Horus, 1984	6,714	5	980	35.6
AMAPETCO				
• Al-Amal, 1983	8,109	5	2,360	42.5
BAPETCO (SHELL)				
Badr El Din-1, 1981	11,485	8	11,320	39.0
Badr El Din-2 (c), 1982	7,000	4	2,700	53.0
Badr El Din-3, 1982	12,140	6	2,700	29.0
Badr El Din-3 (c), 1982	12,140	6	2,500	50.0
Badr El Din-4, 1983	9,157	1	50	35.0
Badr El Din-11, 1986	10,151	....	....	37.0
Badr El Din-15, 1988	10,368	2	2,075	38.0
Badr El Din-16, 1989	11,795	1	35	38.0
Badr El Din-17, 1989	8,531	....	....	40.0
Badr El Din-18, 1990	10,340	....	....	30.0
Sitra-5, 1985	10,378	1	40	32.0
Sitra-8, 1993	9,198	1	755	40.0
EPEDECO				
West Bakr, 1978	4,200	33	4,760	20.0

WORLDWIDE PRODUCTION

Name of field, discovery date	Depth, ft	Producing oil wells	1995 production avg., b/d	°API gravity
ETEPCO				
West Qarun, 1993	6,600	3	1,150	40.0
EGYPTIAN GENERAL				
Abu Sennan, 1981	5,950	35	5,000	42.3
Abu Sennan (c), 1981	5,950	....	650	57.0
Amer, 1965	3,400	22	2,330	21.8
Assal, 1981	3,750	3	820	21.3
Assran, 1981	1,400	1	80	12.0
Bakr, 1958	4,000	60	4,360	18.7
Behar, 1981	4,850	8	380	30.8
Eleyon, 1968	3,450	3	130	19.5
Ghareb, 1938	2,430	104	4,880	26.0
Kareem, 1984	1,950	21	819	17.2
Kheir, 1973	3,400	1	30	21.5
Matarma, 1982	2,050	2	101	21.3
North Amer, 1965	3,450	4	5,548	34.0
Shukeir, 1987	2,500	5	514	34.5
Sudr, 1981	3,000	12	1,230	21.9
Um-Elysr, 1968	4,500	24	1,290	....
Ush-El-Malaha, 1982	4,000	3	68	41.4
GEISUM				
• N. Geisum, 1981	5,200	10	15,000	....
• S. Geisum, 1981	4,500	9	3,500	19.0
• S.E. Geisum, 1981	4,500	2	1,500	19.0
• West Tawila, 1980	5,000	1	2,100	....
GEPETCO (MARATHON)				
• Gazwarina, 1987	6,704	1	250	43.0
KHALDA				
Hayat, 1986	12,500	11	5,500	41.0
Kahrman, 1987	11,600	6	2,250	39.0
Kalabsha, 1989	14,250	1	100	45.0
Khalda, 1986	15,340	12	3,340	36.7
Nader, 1995	8,800	1	483	....
Safir, 1986	11,700	1	180	43.0
Safir North, 1986	10,420	2	610	41.0
Salam, 1986	12,200	14	5,110	44.0
Salam Area (c)	....	....	1,550	46.0
S. Umbarka, 1989	14,500	7	2,950	40.0
Tut, 1986	13,200	14	4,830	32.0
Tut West, 1986	8,953	1	410	40.0
Umbarka, 1969	11,117	5	2,730	44.0
Yasser, 1987	7,000	6	4,380	50.6
OSOCO				
Gamma, 1990	4,240	1	520	45.0
Sukeir Bay, 1980	4,350	1	480	33.8
PETROBEL				
Belayim, 1959	8,600	112	40,500	22.0
• Belayim, 1961	8,300	90	160,000	28.0
Sinai, 1987	6,500	3	10,630	27.0
Belayim fields (c)	....	....	2,100	59.0
RACEBROOK				
S. Ramadan, 1984	11,960	2	270	33.9
SUCO (SUEZ OIL CO.)				
• Ras Budran, 1979	11,400	14	31,475	26.0
• Ras Fanar, 1980	2,200	8	19,000	31.0
• Zeit Bay, 1980	4,450	26	16,210	36.0
• Zeit Bay (c), 1980	4,450	....	825	59.0
SUESSO				
• East Zeit, 1981	11,600	11	21,000	40.0
• East Zeit (c), 1981	11,600	....	250	58.0
WESTERN OPERATING PETROLEUM CO.				
Alamein, 1966	8,000	17	1,700	38.0
Yidma, 1971	8,000	3	510	44.0
ZAFCO (ZAAFARANA OIL CO.)				
• Warda, 1955	8,400	5	17,320	23.0
Total Egypt		**1,208**	**850,702**	

EQUATORIAL GUINEA (e)

Name of field, discovery date	Depth, ft	Producing oil wells	1995 production avg., b/d	°API gravity
WALTER INTERNATIONAL				
• Alba (c), 1984	8,528	2	7,000	47.0-48.0
Total Equatorial Guinea		**2**	**7,000**	

FORMER SOVIET UNION (e)

Name of field, discovery date	Depth, ft	Producing oil wells	1995 production avg., b/d	°API gravity
Azerbaijan	....	2,102	183,000	....
Belarus	....	....	39,000	....
Georgia	....	....	4,000	....
Kazakhstan	....	11,715	416,000	....
Kyrgyzstan	....	....	2,000	....
Lithuania	....	....	2,000	
Tajikistan	....	....	2,000	....
Turkmenistan	....	2,460	79,000	....
Ukraine	....	1,353	80,000	....
Uzbekistan	....	2,190	163,000	....
Russia:				
European Russia:				
North & Northwest	....		118,080	....
Vo/Ga/Ural	....		1,584,855	....
North Caucasus	....		53,505	....
Asian Russia:	....			
Western Siberia	....	104,150	3,964,905	....
Eastern Siberia	....		3,690	....
Far East	....		33,825	....
Other	....		391,140	....
Total Former Soviet Union		**123,970**	**7,120,000**	

* Includes gas condensate.

FRANCE

Name of field, discovery date	Depth, ft	Producing oil wells	1995 production avg., b/d	°API gravity
ALSACE				
GEOPETROL				
Eschau, 1956	....	2	25	32
Schelbenhard, 1956	....	7	105	31.5-40.6
Schelmenberg, 1982	....	3	47	39
AQUITAINE				
ELF AQUITAINE				
Castera-Lou, 1976	9,600	6	270	21.7
Lacq Superieur, 1949	2,170	27	254	22.3
Lagrave, 1984	6,500	3	2,472	42.5
Lameac, 1970	9,000	1	2	12.9
Pecorade, 1974	10,660	4	1,396	29.3
Vic Bilh, 1979	7,100	24	2,133	26.6
ESSOREP				
Cabell, 1955	6,810	1	26	37.0
Cazaux, 1959	7,550	27	2,745	34.2-37.3
Les Arbousiers, 1991	10,180	3	3,078	34.4
Les Pins, 1994	10,460	2	2,909	29.7
Lucats, 1956	6,890	1	27	38.4
Lugos, 1956	5250	11	252	20.8
Mothes, 1955	8200	3	90	21.1
Parentis, 1954	7710	41	3,217	33.4
BASSIN DE PARIS				
COPAREX				
Courdemanges, 1983	5,480	3	66	35.2
Fontaine-au-Bron, 1958	6,130	4	73	34.4
Grandville, 1959	6,760	4	104	36.2
Grandville Est, 1983	6,590	2	61	36.2
Hautefeuille, 1987	6,100	3	88	35.7
La Motte Noire, 1987	7,870	2	123	35.0
Linthelles, 1981	8,130	1	9	34.8
Soudron, 1976	4,600	16	294	34.4
Vert-la-Gravelle, 1985	8,030	1	107	35.0
Villleperdue, 1959	6,100	92	3,946	34.4
ELF AQUITAINE				
Dommartin-Lettree, 1985	7,020	3	579	35.0
Fontaine-au Bron, 1986	6,140	9	520	35.4
Itteville, 1990	5,020	7	4,888	32.3
La Croix Blanche, 1987	6,200	3	484	34.8
La Vignotte, 1991	8,050	2	288	35.0
Neocomien, 1958	1,800	66	195	27.5
Pezarches, 1994	8,050	1	113	35.0
Vert-le Petit, 1987	5,050	2	167	31.1
Vert-le-Grand, 1986	6,230	7	2,461	34.8
ESSOREP				
Bremonderie, 1984	8,670	1	27	31.1
Champotran, 1985	8,400	5	440	31.1
Chaunoy, 1983	7,350	46	12,891	37.1
Donnemarie, 1979	8,040	1	80	36.2
Malnoue, 1985	8,910	3	191	34.0-35.0
Vulalnes, 1977	6,102	1	154	31.3
GEOPETROL				
Bagneaux, 1988	4,070	3	45	30.2
Brie, 1968	7,230	1	25	33.5
L'Orme, 1990	5,630	1	16	32.1
St. Germain, 1984	7,200	3	195	35.4
Slvry, 1984	7,420	3	71	32.3
St. Martin-Bossenay, 1959	4,590	4	142	33.0
MIDLAND MADISON				
Champrose, 1990	7,600	1	25	34.4
Charmottes, 1984	5,910	7	72	35.0-36.6
PETROREP				
Bechevret, 1988	6,180	1	56	32.5
Coulommes, 1958	6,230	15	230	32.6

WORLDWIDE PRODUCTION

Name of field, discovery date	Depth, ft	Producing oil wells	1995 production avg., b/d	°API gravity
Ile-du-Gord, 1986	7,260	6	917	35.0
Montlevee, 1986	6,230	1	33	37.0
REPLOR				
Forcelles, 1978	800	1	5	45.4
Total France		**498**	**49,229**	

GABON

Name of field, discovery date	Depth, ft	Producing oil wells	1995 production avg., b/d	°API gravity
ELF				
• Anguille, 1962	7,380-9,350	22	10,501	30.5
• Anguille NE, 1968	6,200-7,050	8	3,177	32.5
• Anguille SE, 1962	8,200-9,200	4	330	32.2
Avocette, 1989	5,740	4	33,783	35.8
• Ayol Marine, 1978	7,320-7,580	6	1,620	19.6
• Baliste, 1975	4,900-5,050	5	873	27.5
• Barbier, 1972	5,700-6,300	10	5,398	29.2
Batanga, 1960	5,940-6,140	1	37	39.2
• Baudroie Marine, 1968	8,200-9,200	5	2,875	29.6
• Baudroie N., 1980	7,100-7,850	6	7,161	30.7
• Breme/NAT, 1976	4,460-5,310	4	3,722	36.5
Clairette, 1956	4,400	0	0	34.4
Coucal, 1987	3,800-4,000	4	11,073	32.2
• Doree, 1972	6,900-7,500	0	0	31.9
• Girelle, 1973	9,400	3	1,438	29.8
• Gonelle, 1972	5,500-6,000	15	9,493	26.2
• Grand-Anguille, 1983	8,400	5	2,032	29.8
• Grondin Marine, 1971	7,150-7,770	16	6,365	27.9
• Hylia, 1993	4,200-5,100	7	12,948	25.3
• Konzi, 1962	3,450-3,700	7	2,131	37.6
• Mandaros, 1972	4,900-6,150	8	4,385	19.8
M'Boumba, 1978	2,300-3,180	4	1,957	28.5
• M'Bya, 1969	5,700-6,800	29	1,810	35.9
• Merou Sardine, 1984	8,600-9,400	1	296	30.1
M'Polunie, 1980	1,950-2,070	0	0	27.2
M'Polunie W., 1982	1,700-1,950	0	0	18.0
N'Tchengue, 1957	2,800-5,700	2	692	28.0
N'Tchengue Ocean, 1963	5,100-5,700	0	0	29.5
Olende, 1976	6,600-6,800	0	0	34.3
• Pageau, 1972	8,950-9,100	1	287	19.0
• Pelicon Est, 1985	8,800-9,500	1	491	31.7
• Port Gentil Ocean, 1964	6,500	2	498	32.9
• Port Gentil Sud Marine, 1975	7,300-8,000	2	307	31.6
• Torpille, 1968	8,530-9,450	18	6,349	34.4
• Torpille,NE, 1982	8,150-8,700	4	1,280	29.5
• Vanneau, 1993	7,400-9,200	4	1,435	33.0
SHELL GABON (e)				
Echira, 1984	4,745-4,810	3		36.3
Gamba/Ivinga, 1963	2,800-3,100	48		32.2
• Lucina, 1972	4,290-4,930	11		38.3
• Lucina W., 1982	4,530-5,580	2		38.3
Rabi, 1985	3,500-3,640	75		34.3
KELT (e)				
Gombe Maria Beta, 1962	2,500-3,900	2	229,263	24.0
Oguendjo Band C, 1981	3,800-5,100	13		36.0
• Oguendjo Z, 1988	4,600-5,300	2		36.0
• Obando, 1984	8,200-8,680	3		32.0
• Octopus, 1984	9,850-10,365	3		33.0
• Pelican, 1985	6,700-9,580	4		31.0
Total Gabon		**374**	**364,007**	

GERMANY

Name of field, discovery date	Depth, ft	Producing oil wells	1995 production avg., b/d	°API gravity
BEB				
Barenburg, 1953	2,300-3,300		1,675	31.1
Bodenteich, 1960	4,641		29	31.3
Eich, 1983	5,995		1,955	39.4
Eldingen, 1949	5,028		587	36.2
Georgsdorf, 1944	1,800-2,600		3,797	24.5
Gross Lessen, 1969	3,300		595	31.4
Hankensbuttel-Ost, 1954	5,182		76	31.3
Hankensbuttel-Mitte, 1955	5,182		640	31.3
Hankensbuttel-Nord, 1954	5,182		305	31.3
Lingen-Dalum (incl. Wd), 1942	3,129		72	33.0
Luben, 1955	3,950		571	33.6
Meerdorf, 1954	6,077	544	3	40.0
Meppen-Schwefingen, 1959	4,257		2,282	29.5
Molme-Feldbergen, 1934	1,410		8	30.8
Nienhagen, 1909	3,079		162	30.2
Pfullendorf-Ostrach, 1962	3,558		120	37.8
Ruhlermoor-Malm, 1962	4,519		40	30.4
Ruhlermoor-Valendis, 1949	2,381		8,248	24.5
Ruhme, 1954	1,950		569	33.4
Sulingen, 1973	3,345		297	30.0
Varloh, 1984	4,129		73	32.7
Wehrbleck, 1947	3,400		416	32.1
Wietingsmoor, 1954	2,820		306	30.6
MOBIL				
Bavaria	4,660-6,190		115	20.0-25.0
Elbe-Weser (c)	....	159	537	....
Weser-Ems	2,000-2,450		2,066	24.0
PREUSSAG ENERGIE GMBH				
Adorf, 1948	4,265		387	35.0
Allermohe, 1979	6,700		26	28.0
Bramberge, 1958	2,560-3,300		5,305	29.0
Eddesse-Nord, 1950	460		65	26.0
Fronhofen, 1964	3,800		36	37.0
Hover, 1957	2,200		44	25.0
Kronsberg, 1953	2,000		118	25.0
Lahner Heide, 1982	4,570		4	34.0
Lehrte, 1952	4,000		28	31.0
Oelheim-Sud/Rhat, 1968	2,000	282	455	33.0
Ostenwalde, 1953	4,570		41	34.0
Reitbrook-Kreide, 1937	2,300		235	21.0
Reitbrook-West, 1960	6,100		181	30.0
Scheerhorn, 1949	3,550-3,750		1,759	30.0
Sinstorf, 1960	7,100		311	30.0
Sogel, 1983	4,570		17	34.0
Vorhop, 1952	5,000		536	39.0
Vorhop-Knesebeck, 1958	4,100		859	35.0
RWE-DEA A.G.				
Boostedt, 1952	5,220		327	31.0
Hankensbuettel-Sued, 1954	4,530		1,131	27.0-35.0
Hebertshausen, 1982	2,840		125	26.0
Hohne, 1951	4,170-5,955		524	33.0-34.0
Holzkirchen, 1969	12,075		113	39.0
Leiferde, 1956	2,360	137	172	33.0
• Mittelplate, 1980	7,005-8,860		8,814	18.0-30.0
Oerrel-Sued, 1954	4,135		201	25.0-26.0
Ploen-Ost, 1958	7,860		335	34.0
Preetz	....		287	24.0-35.0
• Schwedeneck-See, 1978	4,495		2,575	28.0
Wesendorf, 1943	3,300-5,905		74	25.0-40.0
WINTERSHALL A.G.				
Aitingen, 1977	6,232		669	31.1
Aldorf, 1952	4,100		175	33.0
Arlesried, 1964	4,920-8,550		98	38.5
Bockstedt, 1954	4,264		481	27.4
Dueste, 1954	3,936		218	33.0
Emlichheim, 1944	3,116		3,191	24.5
Hauerz, 1985	8,639	263	23	40.4
Kirchdorf, 1982	5,737		3	38.5
Landau, 1955	3,936		873	36.9
Moenchsrot, 1958	5,248		49	38.1
Ruehlertwist, 1949	2,350-2,900		1,100	25.0
Ruelzheim, 1984	7,544		28	37.7
Total Germany		**1,385**	**57,537**	

GHANA

Name of field, discovery date	Depth, ft	Producing oil wells	1995 production avg., b/d	°API gravity
GHANA NATIONAL PETROLEUM CORP.				
North Tano, 1980	7,500			32.0
• Saltpond, 1977	8,500	3	3,000	36.0-39.0
South Tano, 1978	6,000			29.0-32.0
Total Ghana		**3**	**3,000**	

GREECE

Name of field, discovery date	Depth, ft	Producing oil wells	1995 production avg., b/d	°API gravity
NORTH AEGEAN PETROLEUM CORP.				
• Prinos, 1974	8,000-10,000	12	9,000	28.5
Total Greece		**12**	**9,000**	

GUATEMALA

Name of field, discovery date	Depth, ft	Producing oil wells	1995 production avg., b/d	°API gravity
MINISTERIO DE ENERGIA Y MINAS				
Atzam, 1993	4,274	1	0	38.0
Caribe, 1981	6,830-7,280	2	322	22.0-24.0
Chocop, 1985	5,014	3	0	13.0
Rubelsanto, 1974	5,300-7,000	2	535	26.0-30.0
San Diego, 1981	17,150	1	0	35.0
Tierra Blanca, 1983	11,230	2	409	19.5-23.0
Tortugas, 1970	2,300	2	0	25.0
West Chinaja, 1977	3,200-3,800	0	0	31.0-35.0
Xan, 1985	8,427	6	7,820	17.0
Yalpemach, 1980	15,351	1	0	31.0-35.0
Total Guatemala		**20**	**9,086**	

WORLDWIDE PRODUCTION

HUNGARY

Name of field, discovery date	Depth, ft	Producing oil wells	1995 production avg., b/d	°API gravity
MOL HUNGARIAN OIL & GAS CO.				
Algyo, 1965	5,301-8,136	360	16,892	31.1-65.2
Asotthalom, 1967	2,493-3,199	8	449	32.1
Battonya, 1959	1,286-3,041	4	73	36.0
Battonya-East, 1970	2,765-2,913	113	677	45.4
Belezna, 1963	8,176	1	4	41.1
Budafa-Kiscsehi, 1937	2,168-4,167	59	401	41.1-45.4
Csanadapaca, 1967	5,710-6,063	4	83	37.0
Dany, 1994	5,930	1	3	17.4
Demjen, 1954	725-3,937	65	171	31.4-39.0
Devavanya, 1986	7,634-8,034	1	9	46.7
Ferencszallas, 1969	5,101-7,674	7	184	41.1-50.0
Ferencszallas East-Kiszomber, 1973	7,012-7,283	6	37	41.1
Kaba South, 1978	6,363-6,548	3	49	34.1
Kaszaper South, 1971	2,634-5,056	2	13	32.0
Kelebia NE, 1968	3,011-3,258	1	11	37.0
Kelebia South, 1970	2,171-2,428	6	304	17.4
Kiskundorozsma, 1964	4,824-9,711	16	2,074	36.0-43.4
Kiskunhalas NE, 1974	5,380-6,594	32	696	27.5-31.2
Kiskunhalas NW, 1994	5,958	1	6	41.1
Kismarja, 1979	1,963-2,536	14	51	23.1-43.2
Lovaszi, 1940	3,083-5,692	40	189	41.1-45.4
Mezocsokonya West, 1987	5,785-5,938	2	127	27.5
Mezohegyes, 1960	2,285-3,589	6	41	38.9
Mezosas, 1978	7,349-8,394	7	168	36.4-48.3
Mezosas West, 1994	8,855	1	8	41.1
Nagylengyel-Barasszeg-Szilvagy, 1951	5,545-8,235	58	5,948	11.4-35.0
Ortahaza, 1970	4,460-6,089	7	92	31.1-45.4
Ortahaza East, 1986	4,347-5,413	4	131	31.1
Ottomos East, 1992	2,936-2,573	3	197	27.5
Pitvaros North, 1994	6,234	1	92	37.0
Pusztaapati, 1973	8,300	2	30	22.3
Pusztafoldvar, 1958	2,767-5,538	56	403	30.2-31.1
Pusztaszentlaszlo East, 1990	3,346-3,608	1	1	36.5
Ruzsa, 1979	6,445-9,403	3	237	35.2-39.7
Savoly, 1980	4,856	5	1,288	25.7
Savoly SE, 1994	6,570	1	16	21.7
Savoly West, 1994	5,622	1	18	21.7
Szank, 1964	5,239-5,932	29	585	34.5-39.0
Szank NW, 1977	5,347-5,495	2	108	41.1
Szegd-Moravaros, 1971	8,038-8,629	7	676	41.7
Szeghalom, 1980	5,813-6,608	35	921	43.9-44.7
Szeghalom West, 1989	7,163-7,526	1	50	39.0
Tazlar, 1966	4,263-6,890	3	28	24.0
Tazlar North, 1986	6,669-7,415	2	85	29.0-33.4
Totkomlos South, 1992	5,272-5,429	1	5	35.6
Tura, 1991	2,611-2,628	1	22	21.6
Ulles, 1962	5,508-10,400	4	295	31.2-50.0
Total Hungary		**987**	**33,948**	

INDIA

Name of field, discovery date	Depth, ft	Producing oil wells	1995 production avg., b/d	°API gravity
BOMBAY OFFSHORE				
• B-38 (Heera) & S. Heera, 1977	4,267-6,564	68	73,500	37.0
• Bombay High, 1974	3,282-7,877	413	281,000	39.0
• Neelam, 1987	4,606-4,836	62	72,700	38.0
• Panna (North Bassein), 1976	4,923-7,549	30	9,700	38.0
EASTERN				
Champang, 1973	8,861-10,502	10	805	30.0
Demulgaon, 1976	9,646-11,840	8	2,200	33.0
Geleki, 1968	9,518-14,769	106	9,250	30.0
Lakwa-Lakhmani, 1964	6,564-14,113	212	26,000	33.0
Rudrasagar, 1960	7,877-13,128	42	3,900	26.0
SOUTHERN				
Adikamangalam, 1989	....	6	410	....
Kamalapuram, 1990	....	4	800	....
Kovilkallappal, 1990	....	4	340	....
Lingala, 1989	....	2	250	45.0
Mori, 1990	....	3	295	45.0
Nannilam, 1988	....	3	335	....
Narimanam, 1985	6,236-7,549	23	5,150	43.0-45.0
Ravva, 1987	2,687-8,599	4	3,400	45.0
Tiruvarur, 1990	....	2	875	....
WESTERN				
Ahmedabad, 1967	....	32	980	....
Ankleshwar, 1960	1,969-6,564	135	9,528	47.6-60.0
Balol, 1970	3,280-3,600	112	3,080	16.0
Bechraji, 1987	2,858	134	4,545	16.0
Gandhar, 1984	9,846-12,145	123	42,200	49.9
Jhalora, 1976	3,940-4,270	80	8,240	25.7
Jotana, 1977	3,600-4,930	55	4,840	39.0
Kadi North, 1967	3,610-7,220	189	9,825	22.3
Kadi South, 1968	6,892-9,846	17	1,345	41.1
Kalol, 1961	4,595-10,830	262	5,835	37.0
Kathana, 1965	5,250-5,906	17	445	25.0
Kosamba, 1963	1,313-8,533	4	295	45.0
Lanwa, 1972	4,595-10,830	77	1,265	15.0
LLimbodra, 1985	....	23	2,500	....
Motwan and Sisodara, 1974	4,920-5,580	7	1,100	45.4
Nada, 1988	9,180-11,490	9	1,945	47.6
Nandasan, 1975	....	19	1,800	....
Nawagam, 1963	4,595-10,174	115	3,290	35.0
Sanand, 1962	4,267-10,174	53	1,780	25.7
Santhal, 1974	3,280-3,600	105	5,580	17.0
Sobhasan & W. Sobhasan, 1968	4,595-9,846	142	10,775	33.0
Viraj, 1978	4,595-4,923	39	1,550	22.3
Wasna, 1969	....	34	700	....
OTHER FIELDS				
Digboi, 1890	300-7,500	167	450	25.0-34.0
Dikom, 1990	10,000-13,000	8	7,600	32.0
Hapjan, 1987	10,000-11,000	19	5,700	25.0-34.0
Jorajan, 1972	7,000-12,000	132	13,500	25.0-34.0
Kathaloni, 1991	10,000-13,000	9	9,100	25.0-34.0
Kharsang/Ningru/Kumehai, 1976	3,500-5,500	23	700	....
Moran, 1956	10,000-12,000	58	4,900	....
Nahorkatiya, 1953	8,500-10,000	130	11,000	32.0
Shalmari, 1986	11,000-12,000	20	6,100	25.0-34.0
Total India		**3,351**	**673,403**	

INDONESIA

Name of field, discovery date	Depth, ft	Producing oil wells	1995 production avg., b/d	°API gravity
AMOSEAS				
• Anoa, 1984	3,415-6,610	11	7,030	44.5-45.0
ARBNI				
Pagerungan (c), 1994	6,550-8,455	9	3,563	....
ARCO				
• Ardjuna, 1969	2,380-7250	365	87,846	37.0
• Arimbi, 1972	2,943	24	3,387	33.0
• Bima, 1983	3,000-3,888	34	4,288	34.0
• Northwest Corner, 1974	5,411-5,800	15	3,173	31.5
ASAMERA				
Alur Cimon, 1972	3,098			50.8
APP, 1950	701			....
Bago, 1977	2,250			....
Bentayan, 1932	4,446			22.0
Bertak, 1988	4,364			27.4
Bijak, 1987	1,705			21.3
Geodondong, 1965	3,192			52.0
Grisik, 1986	1,160			....
Julo Rayeu, 1968	2,832			53.6
Keban, 1941	1,358			49.0
Kebon Jaro	....			....
Keri, 1985	3,957			41.5
Kluang, 1913	2,591			42.6
Le Tabue	.....			....
Mangunjaya, 1934	2,700	300	21,568	32.0
Merbau, 1979	600			....
Meuranti, 1978	750			....
Panarukan, 1976	4,915			39.4
Peudawa, 1980	3,083			48.1
Peureulaw	....			....
Ramba, 1982	3,150			37.0
Rantau Panjang	....			....
Rawa, 1985	4,086			37.0
South Rawa, 1985	4,086			37.0
Supat, 1984	4,626			33.6
Tanjung Laban, 1982	3,590			38.1
Tempino, 1931	1,647			40.9
Tengah, 1984	3,245			34.7
Tualang, 1973	2,631			49.9
BONHAM/ENIM/ENERGY EQUITY				
Harimau	....	5	423	....
BOW VALLEY/TALISMAN				
Air Serdang, 1988	5,248	79	12,397	30.1-32.0
Guruh, 1991	5,861			30.0
CALTEX PACIFIC INDONESIA				
Aman, 1974	4,700			39.0
Ampuh, 1981	6,000			38.0
Antara, 1978	1,425			36.0
Arak	....			....
Ayu	....			....
Balam SE, 1972	4,500			29.0
Balam S., 1969	1,600			33.0
Bangko, 1970	1,950			34.0
Batang, 1975	690			19.0

WORLDWIDE PRODUCTION

Name of field, discovery date	Depth, ft	Producing oil wells	1995 production avg., b/d	°API gravity
Bekasap, 1955	2,950			34.0
Bekasap S, 1968	3,900			34.0
Bekasap SE, 1968	....			34.0
Benar, 1973	2,450			33.0
Benua, 1978	2,400			37.0
Beruk, 1974	1,850			38.0
Beruk NE, 1976	1,800			40.0
Beruk NO, 1985	1,900			38.0
Buaya, 1978	2,035			28.0
Bungsu, 1976	2,050			38.0
Butun, 1982	4,000			44.0
Cebakan, 1974	4,700			30.0
Cucut, 1981	5,800			33.0
Damar, 1974	4,650			34.0
Doral	....			....
Duri, 1941	770			22.0
Dusan, 1979	2,550			42.0
Garuk, 1980	4,600			31.0
Gatam, 1977	2,385			34.0
Genting	....			....
Giti	....			....
Hitam, 1975	6,690			39.0
Hiu, 1983	5,900			40.0
Idris, 1983	2,450			39.0
Intan, 1977	3,350			33.0
Jambon	....			....
Jingga, 1984	6,500			45.0
Jorang, 1972	5,500			38.0
Kasikan, 1972	660			28.0
Kerang, 1977	3,900			39.0
Kopar, 1974	5,300			37.0
Kotabatak, 1952	5,500			29.0
Kulin, 1970	2,050			20.9
Langgak, 1976	1,380			32.0
Libo, 1968	6,000	4,414	697,135	35.0
Libo SE, 1973	3,300			42.0
Lincak, 1981	2,570			35.0
Lindai, 1971	1,100			32.0
Mangga, 1988	7,800			....
Menggala North, 1968	3,850			33.0
Menggala South, 1968	3,375			34.0
Mengkapan, 1981	4,000			44.0
Minas, 1944	2,600			35.0
Mindal, 1971	3,400			37.0
Mutiara, 1976	3,500			34.0
Nella, 1977	5,000			35.0
Obor, 1978	7,370			40.0
Osam, 1978	900			32.0
Pager, 1974	4,300			38.0
Paitan, 1978	2,315			32.0
Pak, 1988	3667			35.0
Pedada, 1973	950			33.0
Pelita, 1977	6,600			39.0
Pematang, 1959	3,750			32.0
Pematang Bow, 1969	5,300			33.0
Pemburu, 1981	2,300			35.0
Perkebunan, 1977	2,300			29.0
Petani, 1964	4,750			33.0
Petapahan, 1971	4,500			28.0
Pinang, 1971	3,950			30.0
Pinggar South, 1973	3,300			39.0
Pinggir, 1972	3,300			35.0
Pudu, 1972	5,950			35.0
Pukat	....			....
Puncak, 1979	2,400			36.0
Pungut, 1951	3,400			38.0
Pusaka, 1977	2,250			36.0
Rangau, 1968	6,100			42.0
Rantau Bais, 1972	1,070			18.0
Rintis, 1984	6,450			39.7
Rokiri	....			....
Sabak, 1974	2,350			36.0
Sakti	....			....
Sebanga	....			....
Seruni, 1972	3,000			35.0
Sidingin	....			....
Sikladi, 1975	4,340			40.0
Singa, 1977	3,200			31.0
Sintong, 1971	3,900			32.0
Sintong SE, 1973	....			36.0
Suram, 1971	1,750			28.0
Tandun, 1969	3,000			33.0
Tanggul	....			....
Tanjung Medan, 1976	2,770			34.0
Tegar	....			....
Telinga, 1975	4,205			33.0
Terantam, 1973	900			32.0
Titian	....			....
Topas, 1977	5,200			33.0
Topi, 1979	3,630			37.0
Tunas, 1983	4,819			35.0
Ubi, 1976	4,350			35.0
Ujung Tanjung, 1975	3,600			34.0
Waduk, 1982	6,100			38.0
Zambrud, 1975	3,600			40.0

Name of field, discovery date	Depth, ft	Producing oil wells	1995 production avg., b/d	°API gravity
CITRA PATENINDO N.P.				
Abab, 1951	600			36.0
Dewa, 1936	8,337	....	1,393	....
Raja, 1950	600			38.0
CONOCO GROUP				
• Belida, 1989	5,000	28	113,233	47.0
Ikan Pari, 1983	4,100-4,500	....	1,618	47.4
Sembilang, 1994	....	4	8,690	....
• Udang, 1974	5,595	....	....	39.0
EKSITA PATRANAGARI				
Mamburungan, 1989	5,020-5,131	2	125	....
ENTERPRISE/GFB RESOURCES				
Camar, 1970	4,350	2	1,736	....
EXSPAN/ETAKSATRIA PETRASANGA				
Tarakan, 1906				
Juata, 1926	1,278-3,600			19.0-20.5
Mengatal, 1938	1,050-5,250			19.0-32.0
Pamusian, 1906	213-2,772			18.0-19.0
Sesanip, 1938	750-1,050			19.0-20.0
Sanga-sanga				
Anggana, 1903	230-2,772			25.0-29.0
Kutai Lama N., 1938	426-5,637			27.0-33.0
Kutai Lama S., 1902	1,640-2,953			25.0-30.0
Louise C., 1898	102-1,898	275	5,019	25.0-30.0
Louise N., 1902	62-2,264			25.0-29.0
Louise S., 1897	82-2,379			25.0-30.0
Maura, 1902	869-2,297			25.0-29.0
Nonny, 1975	295-3,248			27.0-31.0
T. Una, 1936	163-2,297			27.0-29.0
Samboja				
Jambatan B., 1934	951-213			26.0
Samboja, 1909	65-4,387			18.0-27.0
GENINDO				
Sembakung, 1976	7,956	....	2,709	35.0
GOLDEN SPIIKE				
Tanjung Kurung	....	3	1,116	....
HUSKY				
Belimbing, 1965	5,371			35.5
Karangan, 1975	5,250			23.0
Limau Barat, 1928	3,898-4,626	....	5,622	....
Limau Niru, 1954	5,118			....
Limau Timur, 1928	3,898-4,626			....
JAPEX				
Arbey Selo	....	9	2,332	....
KODECO				
KE-3/Camar, 1970	4,178-4,260			36.6-37.0
Madura KE-2, 1978	3,370-4,080	8	987	45.5-47.2
Madura KE-23, 1987	6,700-8,350			35.1-45.0
Madura KE-5	....			....
MALAKA STRAIT/LASMO/KONDUR PETROLEUM				
• Kurau, 1986	4,500-9,000			47.4
• Lalang, 1980	3,100-3,600			39.6
• Melibur JS, 1984	900-1,300			35.6
• Mengkapan, 1981	3,850-4,450	89	20,889	42.0
MSBV, 1993	4,500-9,000			....
• Selatan, 1987	3,900-4,500			....
MARATHON				
• Kakap KH, 1980	6,350	7	1,397	43.0
• Kapap KF, 1984	2,875	14	8,122	50.5
• Kakap KG, 1978	4,500	3	16,194	45.0
• Kakap KRA, 1991	5,200	4	3,618	43.0
MAXUS ENERGY				
• Cinta, 1970	3,500			34.0
• Duma, 1983	2,300			16.0
• Farida, 1982	7,000			32.0
• Gita, 1972	5,000			33.0
• Indri, 1989	3,500			34.2
• Intan, 1987	3,200			32.0
• Intan NE, 1987	3,300			32.6
• Karmila, 1983	4,650			36.0
• Kitty, 1971	2,700			18.0
• Krisna, 1976	4,500	316	126,863	37.0
• Nora, 1973	2,800			29.0
• Rama, 1974	3,200			31.0
• Selatan, 1978	2,800			20.0
• Sundari, 1981	4,400			25.0
• Titi, 1981	6,100			33.0
• Wanda, 1982	4,800			36.0
• Widuri, 1988	3,500			24.0
• Yvonne, 1980	5,000			36.0
• Zelda, 1971	6,300			32.0

WORLDWIDE PRODUCTION

Name of field, discovery date	Depth, ft	Producing oil wells	1995 production avg., b/d	°API gravity
MOBIL				
Arun (c), 1971	9,367	64	87,839	55.0
P. LIRIK PETROLEUM				
Andan, 1950	1,969			29.0
Blimbing, 1952	4,922			....
Lirik, 1939	1,600			34.0
N. Pulai, 1941	1,800	....	1,470	34.0
Sago, 1940	1,800			34.0
S. Pulai, 1941	1,800			34.0
PT. SURYA RAYA TELADAN				
Benakat, 1932	4,167	....	1,573	35.0
PT. EXSPAN SUMATERA CENTRAL SUMATERA				
Binio, 1952	1,600	14	132	34.0
Gemuruh, 1983	2,800	17	496	34.0
Kayuara East, 1983	3,500	46	1,610	35.0
Kayuara, 1982	3,700	5	128	35.0
Kerumutan, 1980	3,000	10	317	35.0
Merbau North, 1980	2,600	4	31	36.0
Merbau, 1979	2,700	21	699	36.0
Mutiara, 1985	2,700	1	5	34.0
Panduk, 1981	2,500	6	109	46.0
Parum, 1987	4,200	17	693	35.0
Pekan, 1976	3,700	12	135	35.0
PT. EXSPAN SUMATERA SOUTH SUMATERA				
Gunung Kembang, 1987	3,600	4	986	36.0
Ibul, 1970	5,700	3	89	36.0
Jene, 1985	6,500	28	5,372	35.0
Kerang, 1984	2,900	2	76	35.0
Lagan, 1986	2,400	5	134	56.8
Langkap, 1987	2,900	11	581	34.0
Pian, 1986	6,000	1	74	36.0
Rambutan, 1972	4,500	6	2	42.0
Rimbabat, 1984	3,200	....	....	34.0
South Tabuan, 1981	2,200	....	....	34.0
Tabuan, 1986	4,000	6	390	34.0
Teras, 1976	4,500	3	24	42.0
PERTIMINA UEP I				
Besitang, 1977	3,973			51.5
Gebang, 1977	2,917			54.0
Kuala Dalam, 1983	3,872			50.8
K. Simpang Barat, 1971	3,740-5,019			45.0
K. Simpang Timur, 1967	3,576			45.0
P. Tabuhan Barat, 1937	3,350-5,893			50.8
P. Tabuhan Timur, 1968	2,460	188	5,319	50.8
Pulau Panjang, 1928	3,300			....
Rantau, 1929	2,764			45.3
Serang Jaya, 1926	3,701			47.5
Securai, 1980	4,100-6,890			....
Sungal Buluh, 1984	3,701			51.0
PERTAMINA UEP II				
Air Serdang, 1988	4,860			....
Bajubang, 1930	3,822-3,225			25.7
Benakat East, 1973	4,167			35.0
Betung, 1966	4,003			....
Betang Jambi, 1951	328			....
Candi, 1937	8,012			....
Deras, 1937	6,618			....
Jirak, 1930	2,093			....
Kenali Asam, 1931	2,077			29.0
Ketaling Timur, 1985	1,837	379	7,997	....
Kruh N., 1935	4,652			....
Molek, 1956	2,600			34.0
Musi, 1985	2,717			....
Setiti, 1960	1,837			....
Sukaraja, 1934	7,379			....
Sungai Gelam, 1958	5,479-6,201			....
Sungai Lilin, 1964	2,690			....
Talang Akar, 1922	6,562-8,681			35.0
Talang Jimar, 1937	4,123			31.0
Tempino, 1931	1,647			23.0
Ukui/Pondok, 1950	1,378-1,641			....
PERTAMINA UEP III				
Banyubang, 1980	1,312			....
Cemara, 1976	3,964-7,104			....
Kandang Haui Timur, 1979	7,546			....
Kawengan, 1926	1,600-2,625			....
Ledok, 1893	1,380			....
MB STR, 1985	10,400	188	7,724	....
Nglobo & Semanggi, 1986	1,182			....
Pegaden, 1986	6,890			....
Randegan, 1973	5,578			....
Tugu Barat, 1979	3,014			....
PERTAMINA UEP IV				
Bangkadulia, 1960	3,250			39.5
Dahor Selatan, 1966	3,610			....
Kambilin, 1981	3,491			....
Sangkinah	4,265-4,539			....
Sangatta, 1939	2,600			33.0
Tanjung, 1938	....			39.9
Tanta, 1975	6,660	77	2,934	....
Tapa-Teritip, 1975	4,396			....
Tapian Timur, 1967	2,067			38.8
Warukin, 1966	3,250			26.9
PERTAMINA UEP V				
Klamono, 1936	574			19.0
Linda, 1977	3,281			19.0
Sele, 1951	2,156	98	1,629	35.0
Wiriagar, 1984	3,500			39.7
PETROMER TREND/SANTA FE ENERGY RESOURCES				
Arar Gas (c), 1977	8,748			50.0
Cenderawasih, 1976	3,226			26.7
Jaya, 1973	2,843			39.6
Kasim, 1972	3,031			36.5
Kasim Barat, 1975	4,129			34.5
Kasim Utara, 1973	4,832			25.7
Kasuari	....			....
Klagagi	....			....
Klalin, 1990	8,460			43.5
Klalin (c), 1986	8,025	281	11,191	55.0
Klaserai, 1981	....			....
Lao-lao	....			....
Maniwar	....			....
Moi, 1979	4,372			16.2
Walio Kais, 1973	2,337			34.3
Walio Text II, 1973	2,268			34.3
Walio "U", 1975	2,284			34.3
West Klagagi	....			....
PETRONUSA BUMI BHAKTI				
Selat Panjang, 1994	....	1	203	....
SANTA FE				
Salawati, 1992	....	18	7,377	34.0
SANTOS/AGL				
• Bula, 1897	280-1,300	88	900	23.0
SIDHAKARYA PILONA				
Sabaku, 1977	....			....
Salawati, 1977	5,500	....	191	....
TRITON				
Batu Keras, 1903	100-800			46.0-52.0
Kampung Minyak, 1896	100-500			46.0-52.0
Suban Jeriji, 1905	300-800	74	858	46.0-52.0
Sungai Taham, 1904	300-1,000			46.0-52.0
TOTAL INDONESIE				
• Bekapai, 1972	4,600-15,600			40.0
• Handil, 1974	2,900-19,200			33.0
Semanlu, 1990	8,850-10,158	244	62,348	30.8-32.7
• Tambora, 1984	8,000-13,000			33.0
Tunu (c), 1985	8,001-13,000			55.0
UNOCAL				
• Attaka, 1970	1,200-11,000	117	45,908	32.0-42.0
• Kerindingan, 1972	3,100-7,100	6	433	20.0-36.0
• Melahin, 1972	2,900-4,900	5	1,847	16.0-29.0
• Sepinggan, 1973	3,400-11,600	32	11,031	25.0-38.0
• Serang, 1973	6,000-10,000	17	27,517	40.0-42.0
• Yakin C., 1976	670-2,235	6	790	13.0-22.5
• Yakin N., 1977	2,180-6,600	9	1,979	16.2-28.9
• Yakin W., 1982	2,050-2,530	5	600	18.4-21.1
USTRAINDO				
Benuang, 1942	6,103			35.1
Beringin, 1975	6,365-6,925			38.8
Bunya Nibung, 1926	5,315			33.2
Gunung Kemala, 1938	5,548			38.0
Jatibarang/Karang Ampel, 1969	7,136			29.0
Kuang, 1940	5,249	....	7,352	25.1
Ogan Timur, 1943	3,898-4,626			....
Prabumulih Barat, 1953	5,315			....
Tanjung Miring, 1935	3,511			....
Tanjung Tiga, 1938	3,750			28.0
VIRGINIA INDONESIA				
Badak, 1972	4,350-12,600			34.4
Lampake, 1981	7,000-9,000			....
Mutiara, 1984	1,500-8,500			38.5
Nilam, 1974	7,300-14,700	365	49,903	33.4
Pamaguan, 1974	500-6,000			26.8
Semberah, 1974	2,000-8,500			30.0
Wailawi (c), 1974	2,600-4,800			32.0
Total Indonesia		**8,504**	**1,521,469**	

WORLDWIDE PRODUCTION

IRAN (e)

NIOC

Name of field, discovery date	Depth, ft	Producing oil wells	1995 production avg., b/d	°API gravity
• Abouzar, 1969	2,800			26.0
Ab-Teymur, 1967	10,500			32.6
Agha Jari, 1936	7,440			34.0
Ahwaz Asmari, 1958	8,150			32.0
Ahwaz Bangestan, 1958	12,000			25.5
• Bahregansar, 1960	9,000			30.0
Bibi Hakimeh, 1961	4,570			29.9
Binak, 1959	10,440			29.9
Chesmeh Khush, 1967	10,700			29.0
Chillingar, 1974	33,500			36.6
Dehluran, 1972	11,900			35.5
• Dorood, 1961	11,000			34.0
• Forozan, 1966	7,000			28.5
Gachsaran, 1937	3,400			32.0
Haft Kel, 1927	1,980			31.1
• Hendijan, 1968	11,000			....
Karanj, 1963	5,360			34.4
Kupal, 1965	10,500			32.0
Lab-e Safid, 1968	4,350			35.3
Lali, 1948	5,500			24.0
Mansuri, 1963	7,100	900	3,612,000	27.5
Marun, 1963	9,400			34.0
Masjid-e Suleiman, 1908	1,600			40.0
Naft Safid, 1938	5,000			44.5
Naft-Shahre, 1923	2,000-3,000			43.0
Nosrat, 1986	8,250			32.6
• Nowruz, 1966	8,200			21.0
Par-e Siah, 1964	4,250			31.7
Parsi, 1964	4,670			33.9
Pazanan, 1961	7,250			35.0
Rag-e Safid, 1964	7,230			28.8
Ramin, 1966	12,200			32.9
Ramshir, 1962	8,750			27.8
• Resalat, 1969	7,650			34.0
• Reshadat, 1966	7,000			34.4
• Salman, 1965	7,500-8,100			34.0
Shadegan, 1989	7,850			35.6
Sirri-C, 1979	7,050			31.0
Sirri-D, 1978	8,000			31.0
• Soroosh, 1962	7,000			19.0
Sulabedar, 1971	3,400			39.5
Total Iran		**900**	**3,612,000**	

IRAQ (e)

INOC

Name of field, discovery date	Depth, ft	Producing oil wells	1995 production avg., b/d	°API gravity
Abu Ghurab, 1971	9,800			24.0
Ain Zalah, 1939	5,200-6,500			31.0
Bai Hassan, 1953	4,800-5,400			34.0
Balad, 1983	6,000-7,000			25.0
Butmah, 1953	3,900			31.0
Buzurgan, 1970	12,000			24.0
East Baghad, 1975	6,000-7,000			23.0
Hamrin, 1973	2,000			30.0
Jabal Fauqui, 1974	10,000	58	600,000	25.5
Jambur, 1954	5,500-12,500			38.0
Kirkuk, 1927	2,800-4,200			36.0
Luhais, 1961	8,200			33.0
Naft Khaneh, 1909	3,500			42.5
Nahr Umar, 1949	8,200			42.0
Qaiyanah, 1929	650			16.0
Rumaila North, 1958	10,300			33.0
Rumaila South, 1953	10,200			34.0
Suffayah, 1978	3,900			25.0
West Tikrit, 1985	8,200			23.0
Zubair, 1949	10,200			35.0
Total Iraq		**58**	**600,000**	

*820 wells prior to conflict in the Persian Gulf.

ISRAEL

Name of field, discovery date	Depth, ft	Producing oil wells	1995 production avg., b/d	°API gravity
EMOG				
Gurim, 1984	3,280	....	....	17.0
LAPIDOTH				
Heletz-Brur, 1955	5,200	2	43	29.4
Kochav, 1962	5,500	4	40	29.0
OEIL				
Zuk Tamrur, 1995	6,890	1	92	23.6
Ashdod, 1976	8,400	2	5	32.8
Total Israel		**9**	**180**	

ITALY

Name of field, discovery date	Depth, ft	Producing oil wells	1995 production avg., b/d	°API gravity
AGIP				
Cavone, 1973	9,350	8	1,632	21.5
Gaggiano, 1982	14,764	1	86	37.2
Gela, 1956	10,827	61	6,805	10.0
Giaurone, 1982	10,170	5	1,584	10.0
Monte Alpi, 1988	9,870	4	2,863	37.2
• Perla, 1976	7,874	4	507	13.3
Pisticci-S. Cataldo, 1960	6,980	4	704	12.0
Ponte-Drillo, 1958	9,514	7	1,164	15.6
• Prezioso, 1982	15,748	6	2,287	19.7
Ragusa, 1954	4,593	36	4,607	19.3
Torrente Tona, 1963	4,101	8	922	31.9
Villafortuna, 1984	18,044	16	62,736	46.3
ELF				
• Rospo Mare, 1975	4,600	28	9,756	12.2
• Santa Maria a Mare, 1974	7,900	....	....	23.0
• Sarago Mare, 1979	5,200	....	....	8.0
MONTEDISON (e)				
• Vega, 1980	8,500	20	2,997	16.0
Total Italy		**208**	**98,650**	

IVORY COAST (e)

Name of field, discovery date	Depth, ft	Producing oil wells	1995 production avg., b/d	°API gravity
PETROCI				
• Lion, 1994	11,280	5	11,000	36.5
• Panthere (c), 1994	10,575	2		52.5
Total Ivory Coast		**7**	**11,000**	

JAPAN

Name of field, discovery date	Depth, ft	Producing oil wells	1995 production avg., b/d	°API gravity
JAPEX				
• Aga-Oki, 1972	7,590	2	612	24.8
Higashi-Niigata, 1965	4,500-9,200	3	1,577	53.9
• Iwafune-Oki, 1984	5,050-8,660	6	6,734	....
Katakai, 1960	3,310-16,300	0	496	50.0
Sarukawa, 1958	2,000-3,200	43	695	32.3
Yoshii, 1968	8,000	0	687	61.8
Yurihara, 1976	1,310-7,610	5	331	43.5
Other	....	39	767	....
TEIKOKU OIL CO. LTD.				
Higashi-Kashiwazaki, 1970	6,000-8,900	6	421	62.0
Kubiki, 1959	1,100-6,400	60	417	29.7
Minami-Aga, 1964	7,300-9,600	8	491	38.5
Minami-Nagaoka, 1984	13,200-15,100	9	888	55.7
Yabase, 1933	1,100-5,800	48	316	33.0
Total Japan		**229**	**14,432**	

JORDAN

Name of field, discovery date	Depth, ft	Producing oil wells	1995 production avg., b/d	°API gravity
NRA				
Hamzah, 1984	9,500	4	38	29.0
Total Jordan		**4**	**38**	

KUWAIT

Name of field, discovery date	Depth, ft	Producing oil wells	1995 production avg., b/d	°API gravity
KOC				
Ahmadi, 1952	4,800			31.7
Bahra, 1956	8,500			....
Burgan, 1938	4,800			30.8
Magwa, 1951	4,800	730	1,792,000	33.0
Minagish, 1959	10,000			34.4
Raudhatain, 1955	8,600			34.4
Sabriya, 1957	8,300			36.3
Umm Gudair, 1962	9,000			26.9
Total Kuwait		**730**	**1,792,000**	

LIBYA

Name of field, discovery date	Depth, ft	Producing oil wells	1995 production avg., b/d	°API gravity
AGIP				
• Bouri, 1979	8,300	46	57,192	26.1
Bu Attifel, 1968	14,000	43	159,649	40.6
OO-82, 1985	11,500	4	7,864	36.1
R-82, 1965	11,000-14,000	2	2,608	33.9
Y-82, 1969	12,300	0	0	33.2
UU-82, 1990	15,100	2	4,422	40.5
XX-82, 1992	....	1	1,942	40.5
NC 125, 1982	....	2	290	40.8

WORLDWIDE PRODUCTION

Name of field, discovery date	Depth, ft	Producing oil wells	1995 production avg., b/d	°API gravity
LNOC				
Ali, 1975	3,000	1		51.0
Almas, 1974	3,100	5		52.0
Amal, 1959	3,180-11,130	83		34.0-39.0
Ar Rachmat, 1976	4,770	1		36.0
Aswad, 1965	9,540	1		49.0
As-Sarah, 1989	12,150	13		37.0
Aswad, 1977	5,200	7		44.0
Bahi, 1968	2,590-4,900	40		40.6-43.4
Balat, 1964	4,440-4,880	12		32.0-35.1
Beda, 1959	3,000-3,500	27		32.0-36.5
Belhedan, 1962	6,500	10		35.1
Bualawn, 1971	6,000	1		40.0
Bu Mras, 1966	2,280	3		42.0
Choboc, 1971	2,960	1		50.7
Daba, 1975	4,550	2		37.0
Dahra, 1958	2,090-2,480	50		39.8-42.5
Defa, 1959	4,980-5,300	151		35.6-36.5
Dor Mansour, 1967	5,800	3		32.5
Ed Dib, 1964	3,350	6		35.0
El-Meheiriga, 1970	10,300	1		45.0
Eteila, 1977	6,420-8,400	3		35.0-37.0
Facha, 1963	2,450-4,200	7		33.0-35.0
Farigh, 1969	11,500	5		42.6
Farrud, 1964	2,250	8		42.0
Fidaa, 1978	5,100	16		42.0
Ghani, 1978	2,940-5,070	39		35.0-41.0
Ghazzun, 1974	5,090-7,250	2		34.0-36.0
Gialo, 1961	1,940-10,290	207		25.8-39.4
Gsur, 1978	4,670	3		37.0
Hakim, 1978	5,700	11		48.0
Hamada NC5, 1961	6,880-7,440	3		37.4-41.7
Hamada NC8, 1959	1,250-3,200	64		37.0-42.0
Hamid, 1967	9,630	6		43.0
Harash, 1961	6,930	6		35.9
Intisar, 1967	4,800-9,810	73		25.8-51.4
Jakhira, 1969	12,150	6		33.0
Jebel, 1962	1,510-7,100	26		36.7-37.5
Jofra, 1974	2,660-2,700	6		29.2-47.0
Khalifa, 1961	4,530-6,550	9	1,156,033	32.5-38.3
Kotla, 1963	5,100	28		34.0
Lehib Dor Marada, 1965	8,540	11		52.0
Mabruk, 1959	2,800	13		36.2
Magid, 1968	9,200-9,960	9		35.5-40.0
Masrab, 1961	2,440-9,960	10		26.4-40.6
Meghil, 1961	5,470	1		32.5
Mellugh, 1974	3,420	1		35.0
Messla, 1971	8,550	66		38.0
Nafoora Augila, 1965	8,700	42		35.5
Nafoora Non-unit, 1965	2,150-10,000	59		31.0-39.6
Nakhla, 1970	12,150	4		43.0
Nasser, 1959	5,050-7,120	131		36.8-38.5
Raguba, 1961	5,250	33		42.5
Rakb, 1967	2,400-9,330	10		36.0-41.8
Ralah, 1964	7,220	5		37.0
RR-82, 1994	13,700	2		38.0
Sabah, 1964	4,600	43		43.0
Safsaf, 1985	6,200	5		50.0
Sahabi-D, 1968	10,050	3		39.0
Samah, 1961	5,610	11		33.4
Sarir, 1961	8,200-8,400	242		37.0-38.7
Shatirah, 1992	9,130	2		37.5
Tibisti, 1962	4,880-7,250	22		33.0-35.0
Tmed, 1974	5,090	1		39.0
Tuama, 1979	14,150	2		36.0-40.5
Wadi, 1970	11,600	10		48.0
Waha, 1960	6,050-6,140	40		35.4-38.4
Zaggut, 1961	5,880	8		34.2
Zella, 1960	5,500	25		41.0
Zenad, 1980	5,260	9		38.0
Total Libya		**1,866**	**1,390,000**	

MALAYSIA (e)

Name of field, discovery date	Depth, ft	Producing oil wells	1995 production avg., b/d	°API gravity
ESSO MALAYSIA				
• Bekok, 1976	5,500			47.0
• Guntong, 1978	5,200			44.0
• Irong Barat, 1979	3,300			35.0
• Kepong, 1979	6,000			47.0
• Palas, 1979	6,300			49.0
• Pulai, 1973	4,300			42.3
• Seligi, 1971	4,300			50.0
• Semangkok, 1980	3,700			42.5
• Tabu, 1978	5,600			44.0
• Tapis, 1975	6,700			45.0
• Tinggi, 1980	4,400			48.0
• Tiong, 1978	5,800			47.0
PETRONAS CARIGALI				
• Tembungo, 1971	6,000			40.0
SABAH SHELL PETROLEUM (SSPC)				
• Erb West, 1971	6,785	780	650,000	30.0
• Samarang, 1972	5,700			37.0
• St. Joseph, 1975	2,200			32.0
SARAWAK SHELL BERHAD (SSB)				
• Bayan, 1976	4,200			37.3
• D-18, 1981	4,000			39.9
• Temana, 1972	3,100			35.0
SARAWAK SHELL/ PETRONAS CARIGALI				
• Bakau	....			
• Baram	....			
• Baronia, 1967	7,900			42.0
• Betty, 1967	7,900			38.0
• Bokor, 1972	2,000			35.0
• Fairley Baram, 1973	8,655			39.5
• Siwa, 1973	4,100			25.0
• Tukau, 1966	5,000			29.2
• West Lutong	....			39.5
Total Malaysia		**780**	**650,000**	

MEXICO

Name of field, discovery date	Depth, ft	Producing oil wells	1995 production avg., b/d	°API gravity
MARINE REGION				
Abkatun, 1978	11,800		246,560	28.7
Bacab , 1991	....		6,980	17.7
Batab , 1986	....		5,565	33.6
Caan , 1985	....		166,471	38.5
Cantarell, 1976	8,528		905,568	19.9
Chac, 1994			55,510	18.0
Chuc, 1982	13,100		112,452	12.6
Ek , 1991	....		1,598	28.0
Ixtoc, 1974	....		9,038	29.3
Ku, 1979	10,000		192,931	20.9
Pol, 1979	12,600		120,497	32.4
Taratunich , 1990	....		64,012	24.5
Other	....		50,261	26.2
Other (c)	....		87,825	....
NORTHERN REGION				
Acuatempa, 1955	4,085		332	20.3
Agua Fria, 1978	....		4,187	44.8
Angostura, 1954	....		1,000	14.2
Arenque, 1970	11,362		6,516	34.5
Atun, 1966	9,040		587	37.6
Bagre, 1973	10,919		1,407	33.3
Cerro Azul, 1938	....		1,662	20.9
Constotuciones, 1956	6,350		7,463	17.3
Copite, 1975	....		303	34.3
Escolin, 1942	7,216		3,482	26.6
Haliazgo, 1955	10,170		2,011	29.0
Isla de Lobos, 1963	6,875		215	39.8
Jillapa, 1958	7,390		1,305	35.8
Marsopa, 1974	10,198		516	20.0
Matapionche, 1974	11,129		534	35.9
Mecatepec, 1941	7,544		1,557	30.2
Miquetia, 1959	6,480		881	30.1
Muro, 1965	3,966		377	16.6
Ocotepec, 1953	3,737		333	21.2
E. Ordonez, 1952	5,220		1,291	16.2
Panuco, 1901	....		6,048	11.7
Poza Rica, 1930	17,090		8,600	30.7
Pres. Aleman, 1949	8,036		1,479	24.0
Remolino, 1962	10,745		624	29.8
San Andrez, 1956	10,410		6,709	28.6
Santa Agueda, 1953	4,780		4,316	16.1
Tamaulipas, 1956	4,200		7,795	16.7
Tres Hermanos, 1959	6,960		4,229	26.9
Other	....		19,551	27.4
Other	....		620	....
SOUTHERN REGION				
Agata, 1966	3,830		755	32.6
Agave, 1977	13,450		6,334	41.3
Arroyo Zanapa, 1978	14,599		1,524	41.0
Ayapa, 1972	8,200		137	29.1
Bacal, 1976	3,500		2,176	33.0
Bellota, 1982	17,056		21,627	37.1
Blasillo, 1967	7,216		4,245	41.9
Cactus, 1972	14,100		8,581	44.3
Caparroso, 1982	....		6,730	38.5
Cardenas, 1979	17,548		33,633	37.7
Carmito, 1980	10,050		2,789	46.3
Carrizo, 1962	3,500		1,099	18.1
Chiapas, 1979	12,136		566	45.4
Cinco Presidentes, 1960	6,862		6,205	36.1
Comoapa, 1979	14,432		2,002	37.4
Concepcion, 1974	1,600		623	33.8
Copano, 1977	11,890		8,476	47.3
Cuichapa, 1935	2,200		3,829	30.8
Cunduacan, 1974	13,775	4,740	18,954	35.1
Eden, 1983	17,590		8,382	38.7
El Burro, 1931	2,200		392	35.0

WORLDWIDE PRODUCTION

Name of field, discovery date	Depth, ft	Producing oil wells	1995 production avg., b/d	°API gravity
El Golpe, 1963	3,500		2,519	33.9
El Plan, 1931	1,700		292	29.7
Fenix, 1979	17,876		2,648	36.9
Fortuna Nacional, 1927	....		176	52.9
Giraldas, 1977	15,225		4,900	40.0
Iride, 1974	13,775		28,129	28.8
Iris, 1970	14,432		136	44.6
Ixhuatian Oriente, 1965	....		552	16.1
Jacinto, 1987	....		17,962	43.1
Jolote, 1983	18,119		25,071	37.7
Jose Colomo, 1951	....		12	35.9
Jujo, 1980	17,548		75,924	35.4
La Venta, 1954	4,730		280	35.6
Lacamango, 1973	1,700		1,781	30.5
Los Soldados, 1953	4,492		1,331	32.1
Luna, 1987	....		15,387	39.2
Moloacan, 1962	....		1,557	17.6
Mora, 1981	....		11,358	38.2
Mundo Nuevo, 1977	11,800		1,323	54.2
Muspac, 1982	9,676		12,559	53.7
Nispero, 1974	14,100		3,928	38.0
Oaxiacaque, 1977	11,150		4,205	28.2
Ogarrio, 1957	5,790		6,184	33.3
Otates, 1965	7,469		713	37.5
Paredon, 1978	15,690		8,028	39.7
Platanal, 1978	15,900		3,432	38.0
Rio Nuevo, 1975	14,950		2,848	37.0
Rodador, 1971	....		1,100	35.7
Samaria (Cret.), 1973	....		61,146	29.3
Samaria (Terc.), 1965	4,920		733	28.5
San Ramon, 1967	9,515		2,393	31.8
Santa Rosa, 1952	....		118	23.0
Santuario, 1966	9,617		2,249	42.1
Sen, 1986	....		35,105	41.3
Sitio Grande, 1972	13,766		7,616	33.5
Sunuapa, 1976	12,887		252	30.3
S. Magallanes, 1957	4,240		4,008	33.3
Tecominoacan, 1982	19,519		45,332	40.6
Tintal, 1968	5,904		326	26.9
Tonala, 1928	1,770		747	33.4
Topen, 1978	11,172		344	27.9
Tupilco, 1959	9,685		929	38.5
Vernet, 1954	....		279	43.8
Other	....		49,475	42.9
Other	....		16,485	....
Total Mexico		**4,740**	**2,722,129**	

MOROCCO

Name of field, discovery date	Depth, ft	Producing oil wells	1995 production avg., b/d	°API gravity
ONAREP				
Meskala (c), 1976	10,500	4	17	65.0
Sidi Fili, 1951	4,590	1	0	39.0
Sidi Rhalem 2, 1962	6,722	1	55	39.0
Sidi Rhalem 8, 1962	6,722	1	2	39.0
Toukimt (c), 1976	10,500	2	33	65.0
Total Morocco		**9**	**107**	

MYANMAR (e)

Name of field, discovery date	Depth, ft	Producing oil wells	1995 production avg., b/d	°API gravity
MYANMA				
Chauk-Lanywa, 1902	1,500-4,000			36.0
Mann, 1970	1,600-1,700			37.5
Myanaung, 1964	2,000-4,000	450	16,000	40.5
Prome, 1965	850-5,000			36.0
Yenangyaung, 1902	100-6,700			36.0
Total Myanmar		**450**	**16,000**	

NETHERLANDS

Name of field, discovery date	Depth, ft	Producing oil wells	1995 production avg., b/d	°API gravity
CONOCO				
• Kotter K/18, 1980	5,618	9	5,340	33.0
• Logger L/16, 1982	6,022	3	2,677	33.5
UNOCAL				
• Haven, 1980	5,300	2	1,133	25.5
• Helder, 1980	4,800	14	3,696	21.6
• Helm, 1979	4,400	8	1,057	17.9
• Hoorn, 1981	5,000	8	1,231	25.8
• Horizon, 1982	6,350	8	6,775	33.5
AMOCO (e)				
• Rijn, 1982	6,500	10	1,275	35.0
ELF PETROLAND (e)				
F6	....	....	738	....
NAM (e)				
Rijswijk	....	....	11,613	....
Schoonebeek, 1944	2,500	134	4,181	....
F3	....	....	7,970	....
RWE-DEA (e)				
F2	....	....	1,765	....
OTHER (e)				
P/6 (c), 1968	8,800	8		66.0
P/12 (c), 1986	9,200	5	19,333	54.0
Other fields (c)	....	....		....
Total Netherlands		**209**	**68,784**	

NEUTRAL ZONE (e)

Name of field, discovery date	Depth, ft	Producing oil wells	1995 production avg., b/d	°API gravity
AOC				
• Hout, 1969	4,900-8,800			33.0
• Khafji, 1961	4,400-7,300			28.2
TEXACO & KOC		275	415,000	
S. Fuwaris, 1963	6,300			25.0
S. Umm Gudair, 1966	8,900			24.3
Wafra, 1953	1,100-7,000			18.9-23.5
Total Neutral Zone		**275**	**415,000**	

NEW ZEALAND

Name of field, discovery date	Depth, ft	Producing oil wells	1995 production avg., b/d	°API gravity
FLETCHER CHALLENGE				
Ahuroa (c), 1987	8,688	0	0	46.1
Kaimiro, 1982	11,900	10	815	42.0
McKee, 1980	7,848-8,251	25	6,150	38.5
Tariki (c), 1986	9,065	0	0	52.7
Waihapa, 1988	10,125-10,643	6	3,165	36.6
NEW ZEALAND OIL & GAS				
Ngatoro, 1992	....	2	627	35.0
SHELL/BP/TODD				
Kapuni (c), 1959	11,700	12	3,390	54.0
• Maui, 1969	11,000	15	18,866	51.0
WESTERN MINING				
• Kupe S., 1987	9,514-12,467	0	0	....
Total New Zealand		**70**	**33,013**	

NIGERIA

Name of field, discovery date	Depth, ft	Producing oil wells	1995 production avg., b/d	°API gravity
AGIP				
• Agbara, 1981	7,500-12,000	14	10,556	36.5
Agwe, 1975	10,800	2	1,603	52.6
Akri, 1967	9,600-10,600	6	11,910	42.2
Akri West, 1972	9,900-10,200	0	0	43.0
Ashaka, 1968	9,700-12,000	1	1,173	37.5
Azuzuama, 1975	9,700-14,900	2	3,458	36.6
• Beniboye, 1978	9,000-10,000	6	2,410	25.1
Beniku, 1974	12,000	0	0	28.0
Clough Creek, 1976	10,000-12,400	9	6,978	34.2
Ebegoro, 1975	11,500-12,000	9	8,003	34.2
Ebegoro South, 1975	14,100	0	0	36.0
Ebocha, 1965	8,000-10,900	7	4,033	30.2
Idu, 1973	7,750-10,700	0	0	30.0
Kwale, 1967	10,000-11,500	8	5,126	35.8
M'Bede, 1966	7,300-9,400	14	11,866	41.5
Obama, 1973	11,600-14,300	10	13,307	29.1
Obiafu, 1967	9,300-12,200	22	21,227	41.5
Obrikom, 1967	8,000-10,000	9	5,463	38.6
Odugri, 1972	12,500	1	655	23.3
Ogbainbiri, 1989	7,700-16,400	6	15,570	26.5
Ogbogene, 1972	10,000	2	600	30.6
Ogbogene West, 1982	13,000	0	0	45.0
Okpai, 1968	10,000-12,000	6	3,066	43.3
Omoku West, 1975	11,500	1	438	35.3
Oshi, 1972	9,600-11,300	12	11,492	33.4
Pirigbene, 1987	13,700	1	2,759	25.3
Taylor Creek, 1985	9,300-10,400	1	1,271	25.4
Tebidaba, 1975	10,300-11,300	11	13,668	27.0
Umuoru, 1975	14,100	2	2,195	27.6
ASHLAND				
• Adanga, 1980	8,500	8	3,387	31.9
• Akam, 1980	6,700	10	2,862	34.0
• Bogi, 1989	7,500	3	715	28.7
• Ebughu, 1983	7,250	4	614	23.8
Izombe, 1974	8,000	9	7,816	34.3

WORLDWIDE PRODUCTION

Name of field, discovery date	Depth, ft	Producing oil wells	1995 production avg., b/d	°API gravity
• Mimbo, 1984	7,500	3	785	31.1
• Ossu, 1974	8,000	3	697	31.6
• Ukpam, 1989	5,500	2	1,630	40.6
CHEVRON				
Abigborodo, 1974	9,850-10,850	2	673	38.7
Abiteye, 1970	5,750-9,400	21	5,817	39.7
• Belema North, 1989	6,573-12,130	....	1,447	34.0
Benin River, 1990	6,470-7,614	2	7,630	41.8
• Delta, 1965	5,600-9,500	27	20,429	37.3
• Delta South, 1965	7,100-10,179	33	20,813	38.4
• Idama, 1974	8,100-11,250	4	10,741	33.4
• Inda, 1982	7,250-11,030	4	18,219	44.8
• Isan, 1970	5,900-9,000	11	2,511	40.4
Jisike, 1975	6,300-7,600	7	8,816	41.1
Jokka, 1993	9,280-9,880	1	4,820	22.7
Kito, 1988	4,842-8,347	1	1,919	31.1
Makaraba, 1973	7,100-12,005	28	14,727	27.7
• Malu, 1969	4800-6,300	20	11,387	40.4
• Mefa, 1965	8,570-12,030	13	13,449	38.1
• Meji, 1965	5,200-10,900	24	21,552	31.9
• Meren, 1965	5,000-7,500	69	85,687	31.9
• Mina, 1985	6,700-9,300	4	4,163	40.3
• Okan, 1964	5,500-9,245	72	47,583	38.1
• Opuekeba, 1975	6,000-10,200	9	17,436	36.7
• Parabe/Eko, 1968	4,500-8,200	31	16,988	40.4
Robertkiri, 1964	11484-13,190	15	30,828	40.2
• Tapa, 1978	8,150-10,842	11	9,082	39.5
Utonana, 1971	7,400-9,165	5	880	20.4
• West Isan, 1971	7,825-10,229	10	3,834	40.4
Yorla South, 1974	11,389-12,635	0	0	41.0
ELF				
• Afia, 1982	3,780	11	20,904	25.6
Aghigo, 1972	7,303	27	4,737	22.5
• Edikan, 1989	4,980	9	15,564	28.6
Erema, 1972	11,211	7	1,578	33.6
Obagi, 1964	8,377	109	37,463	23.4
Obodo-Jatumi, 1966	7,656	13	6,285	34.6
• Odudu, 1977	4,930	8	15,384	35.8
Okpoko, 1967	6,745	19	5,655	21.7
Olo, 1988	8,130	3	4,885	37.0
Upomami, 1965	6,256	16	3,425	19.0
Ime, 1989	4,350	7	11,173	23.0
MOBIL				
• Adua, 1967	6,970	6	10,300	34.8
• Asabo, 1966	5,600	13	31,200	34.6
• Asabo D, 1979	7,621	2	1,800	34.6
• Ata, 1964	8,823	....	....	....
• Edop, 1988	9,215	25	77,300	37.4
• Ekpe, 1966	8,200	13	15,100	34.9
• Ekpe-WW, 1977	6,810	6	3,200	31.9
• Eku, 1966	5,420	7	6,800	30.4
• Enang, 1968	6,600	28	17,200	37.4
• Etim, 1968	6,200	8	15,400	37.1
• Idoho, 1966	9,020	3	900	30.5
• Inim, 1966	5,850	10	8,000	37.5
• Isobo, 1968	7,345	4	3,300	30.4
• Iyak	....	11	13,300	....
• Iyak SE, 1979	7,441	6	4,600	38.6
• Mfem, 1968	5,200	2	7,000	36.1
• Ubit, 1968	5,400	50	39,100	36.1
• Unam, 1967	5,180	10	21,100	33.3
• Usari, 1965	8,431	....	....	....
• Utue, 1966	5,700	6	10,400	36.8
Inanga, 1994	7,600	1	200	38.0
Oso, 1967	10,266	18	106,400	48.0
SHELL (e)				
Adibawa, 1966	11,950	14		26.4
Opukushi, 1962	7,823	11		28.3
Obigbo North, 1963	8,250	30		23.2
Odeama Creek, 1981	12,897	5		35.5
Odidi, 1967	10,980	30		36.2
Oguta, 1965	10,300	13		43.2
Olomoro, 1963	8,500	24		21.5
Otumara, 1969	8,176	23		24.9
Nembe Creek, 1973	12,213	39		31.0
Sapele, 1969	12,788	8		42.9
Soku, 1958	11,500	15		27.7
Ughelli East, 1959	....	....		....
Agbada, 1960	10,000	32		23.9
Etelebou, 1971	12,000	8		31.3
Oben, 1972	12,036	18		37.6
Kolo Creek, 1971	12,000	18		39.1
Afisere, 1966	8,500	24		19.6
Egwa, 1967	9,350	17		34.1
Afremo, 1972	9,263	8		36.8
Akaso, 1979	13,122	6		37.1
Awoba, 1981	....	....		....
Benisede, 1973	8,941	13		21.9
Cawthorne Chan, 1963	11,000	21		36.9
Ekulama, 1958	10,483	23		31.6
Kalaekule, 1972	9,236	7	811,584	40.5

Name of field, discovery date	Depth, ft	Producing oil wells	1995 production avg., b/d	°API gravity
Eleilenwa, 1960	11,000	6		35.8
Escravos Beach, 1969	8,176	7		31.2
Forcados Yorki, 1968	10,859	55		24.4
Imo River, 1959	7,900	37		30.3
Jones Creek, 1967	80,000	29		29.7
Nun-River, 1960	14,200	5		32.7
TEXACO-CHEVRON-NNPC (e)				
• Funiwa, 1978	8,000	19		35.5
• Middleton, 1972	9,000	6		33.3
• North Apoi, 1973	8,500	26		35.5
• Pennington, 1965	11,000	2		38.5
• Sengana, 1987	12,000	....		....
PAN OCEAN (e)				
Ogharefe, 1973	9,900	5		46.6
DUBRIL (e)				
Gilli-Gilli, 1967	9,357	2		47.1
TENNECO (e)				
Abura, 1979	13,471	3		44.7
OTHER OPERATIONS (e)				
All Fields	....	310		
Total Nigeria		**2,005**	**1,890,000**	

NORWAY

Name of field, discovery date	Depth, ft	Producing oil wells	1995 production avg., b/d	°API gravity
AMOCO				
• Hod, 1974	8,860	5	9,026	34.0
• Valhall, 1978	8,200	23	60,169	35.0
BP				
• Gyda, 1981	13,123	18	59,435	48.0
• Ula, 1976	11,800	11	65,495	44.6
ORYX UK ENERGY				
• Murchison *, 1975	9,900	21	4,210	38.0
ELF NORGE				
• Lille-Frigg, 1975	12,060	1	7,538	40.9
• Froy, 1987	10,330	12	15,014	40.9
• Heimdal, 1972	6,950	8	8,071	68.6
NORSK HYDRO				
• 30/6 Oseberg Vest,	....	1	2,313	....
• Brage, 1980	8,200	12	109,036	37.0
• Oseberg B & C, 1979	8,200	44	498,923	34.0
• Troll	....	10	49,504	28.6
NORSK SHELL				
• Draugen, 1984	....	2	120,125	....
PHILLIPS				
• Albuskjell (c), 1979	10,400	7	1,274	45.0
• Cod (c), 1977	9,500	5	809	55.0
• Edda, 1979	10,480-10,600	7	2,514	41.5
• Ekofisk, 1971	10,000	62	221,164	41.1
• Eldfisk, 1979	9,350-10,000	41	46,418	41.1
• Embla, 1988	13,800	4	21,942	42.0
• Tor, 1978	10,000	12	5,839	38.0
• West Ekofisk (c), 1971	10,300	8	1,223	43.9
SAGA				
• Snorre, 1979	....	10	196,007	....
• Tordis, 1987	....	....	71,440	....
STATOIL				
• Gulfaks, 1978	9,500-9,700	59	473,033	29.3
• Gullfaks Vest, 1978	....	....	11,040	
• Heidrun, 1985	....	....	15,587	
• Statfjord *, 1974	9,500	71	456,073	38.2
• Statfjord Nord	....	....	43,902	
• Statfjord Ost, 1979	....	....	55,650	
• Tommeliten Gamma (c), 1976	10,400	6	3,866	53.0
• Veslefrikk, 1981	10,100	14	76,819	37.0
Total Norway		**474**	**2,713,459**	

*Norway share (22.2%) of total production.

OMAN

Name of field, discovery date	Depth, ft	Producing oil wells	1995 production avg., b/d	°API gravity
ELF				
Ramlat, 1977	12,000	1	18	46.0
Sahmah, 1978	12,400	20	4,230	46.0
INTERNATIONAL PETROLEUM CORP.				
• Bukha, 1979	11,000	2	4,985	60.0

WORLDWIDE PRODUCTION

Name of field, discovery date	Depth, ft	Producing oil wells	1995 production avg., b/d	°API gravity
OCCIDENTAL OMAN INC.				
Al Barakah, 1992	5,000	9	1,594	37.8
Madiq, 1995	7,200	2	410	38.0
Safah, 1983	6,500	110	33,907	42.0
Salmah, 1995	6,500	1	662	38.0
Wadi Latham, 1993	5,000	1	148	40.0
JAPEX (OMAN) LTD. (e)				
Daleel, 1989	4,950	28		39.0
PETROLEUM DEVELOPMENT OMAN (e)				
Al Burj, 1984	4,065	19		28.0
Al Dhabi, 1985	2,790	3		19.0
Al Ghubar, 1978	1,916	7		29.0
Al Huwaisah, 1969	5,320	64		39.0
Al Noor, 1992	13,038	1		48.0
Alam, 1987	4,200	4		33.0
Amal South, 1982	3,940	8		30.0
Amal, 1972	2,950	45		19.0
Amin, 1975	2,300	11		20.0
Anzauz, 1984	7,098	8		46.5
Bahja, 1984	5,697	13		47.2
Barik, 1978	8,856	3		47.4
Basma, 1991	3,365	2		20.0
Birba, 1978	8,500	3		32.0
Burhaan, 1984	2,650	2		34.0
Dhiab, 1985	3,280	5		26.5
Dhulaima, 1975	3,700	3		39.0
Fahud NW, 1964	2,499	124		32.0
Fahud SE, 1963	2,499	50		32.0
Fahud West, 1965	2,499	6		34.0
Fayyadh, 1983	3,600	1		27.0
Ghaba North, 1972	4,800	11		33.5
Ghanuq, 1990	3,600	1		27.0
Habur, 1972	1,400	1		15.0
Haima, 1984	4,230	1		23.3
Hasirah, 1981	8,708	6		48.8
Hazar, 1991	8,364	1		44.0
Ihsan, 1984	3,674	7		23.5
Jadeer, 1991	5,100	1		20.0
Jalmud North, 1980	350	3		19.0
Jalmud, 1979	2,900	3		24.0
Jawdah, 1984	3,570	8		28.5
Karim W., 1982	2,755	44	803,046	23.0
Kaukab, 1983	8,282	1		31.0
Lekhwair, 1974	4,352	202		37.5
Mabrouk, 1979	9,725	1		....
Maqtaa, 1991	7,150	1		44.0
Marmul NW, 1992	1,900	1		20.0
Marmul, 1977	2,000	181		21.5
Mawhoob, 1985	3,674	1		25.0
Musallim, 1971	4,690	2		27.0
Natih, 1963	4,788	76		33.4
Nimr, 1980	2,400	231		21.0
Qaharir East, 1978	4,936	1		25.5
Qaharir, 1977	3,116	30		30.4
Qam Alam, 1972	1,100	4		17.0
Qarat Al Milh, 1987	6,900	1		29.0
Qata, 1979	4,430	14		28.0
Rahab, 1977	2,000	21		25.5
Rajaa, 1988	3,430	5		25.0
Ramlat Rawl, 1987	6,560	4		50.0
Rasha, 1982	2,920	4		37.0
Reihan, 1986	3,540	2		21.3
Rima, 1979	2,755	82		33.0
Runib South, 1984	3,600	4		20.0
Runib, 1979	2,500	23		21.1
Sadad, 1986	2,263	4		25.0
Saih Nihaydah SE, 1972	3,350	....		39.0
Saih Nihayda, 1972	8,700	25		39.6
Saih Rawl, 1971	9,826	35		39.0
Salwa, 1986	4,972	1		29.0
Sayyala, 1982	3,690	17		50.1
Shahin, 1981	4,750	1		21.0
Simsim, 1985	4,100	16		30.6
Suwaihat, 1982	4,953	....		37.5
Thamoud, 1987	3,773	5		23.0
Thayfut, 1981	2,200	4		19.0
Thuleilat, 1986	1,804	26		25.5
Wadi Haka, 1990	4,300	2		32.0
Wafra, 1983	5,510	7		38.8
Warad, 1985	3,608	7		....
Yibal, 1963	8,465	398		38.5
Zahra, 1986	5,773	4		32.0
Zareef, 1985	3,264	10		47.0
Zauliyah, 1981	7,300	9		44.3
Zumurrud, 1988	1,837	5		29.0
Total Oman		**2,111**	**849,000**	

PAKISTAN

Name of field, discovery date	Depth, ft	Producing oil wells	1995 production avg., b/d	°API gravity
OCCIDENTAL OF PAKISTAN, INC.				
Bhangali-1, 1989	12,650	2	447	32.9
Dhurnal, 1984	13,100	7	2,247	41.8
Ratana, 1988	16,400	2	566	47.0
OGDC				
Bobi, 1988	9,514	3	680	51.0
Chak-Naurang, 1986	9,186	3	952	46.9
Dakhni, 1983	15,092	4	630	57.4
Dhodak, 1977	7,109	7	2,765	....
Fimkassar, 1989	9,842	2	2,362	31.0
Kal, 1995	9,299	2	653	29.5
Kunnar, 1988	6,562	3	1,103	45.7
Lashari Centre, 1988	7,382	2	2,114	40.4
Messa-Keswal, 1991	7,382	3	3,969	40.6
Pasahki, 1989	8,406	2	2,121	401.0
Pasahki North, 1989	7,323	1	1,431	42.5
Rajian, 1994	12,355	2	1,388	23.0
Sadkal, 1992	14,764	4	2,025	45.3
Sono, 1988	7,546	5	2,283	40.5
Tando Alam, 1984	8,202	10	974	40.3
Thora & Thora East, 1987	7,218	4	2,283	40.8
Toot, 1968	14,764	15	440	39.4
PAKISTAN OILFIELDS LTD.				
Bulkassar, 1946	9,398	15	321	26.0
Dhulian, 1936	8,899	34	19	48.0
Joya Mair, 1944	6,900	3	278	15.0
Khaur, 1915	9,306	32	6	33.0
Meyal, 1968	12,513	14	1,354	41.0
Pariwali, 1994	15,976	1	1,007	....
Pindori, 1991	14,141	2	62	....
PAKISTAN PETROLEUM LTD.				
Adhi (c), 1978	8,360-9,115	5	2,343	51.1
UNION TEXAS				
Bachal, 1993	5,000	1	11	47.0
Bari, 1992	2,600	2	1,745	42.0
Bhatti, 1989	5,800	3	....	44.0
Dabhi, 1984	5,975	2	413	42.0
Ghunghro, 1988	4,620	2	667	42.0
Halipota, 1986	6,000	2	310	44.4
Jalal, 1993	1,768	2	65	....
Khaskeli, 1981	3,600	4	853	39.0
Laghari, 1983	2,500	3	1,523	42.0
Liari, 1988	6,600	1	814	42.5
Mazari, 1984	3,800	6	5,096	43.0
M. Ismail, 1991	7,760	1	828	44.5
N. Akri, 1988	5,540	2	1,314	46.7
South Buzdar, 1993	5,007	1	9	41.8
South Mazari, 1985	3,920	3	2,600	43.0
S.M. Deep, 1993	7,500	1	110	42.0
Tajedi, 1984	5,460	2	549	44.4
Tangri, 1995	2,408	2	465	....
Zaur, 1993	6,750	1	....	40.7
Bukhari (c), 1985	5,800	4	....	53.0
Golarchi (c), 1984	6,200	1	....	51.1
Khorewah (c), 1988	6,300	4	....	51.0
Makhdumpur (c), 1986	7,000	1	....	54.7
Matli (c), 1986	5,400	1	....	43.7
Nari (c), 1985	5,900	3	....	51.0
Turk (c), 1985	6,150	3	....	37.8
Sonro (c), 1985	3,960	2	....	43.7
Total Pakistan		**249**	**54,195**	

PAPUA NEW GUINEA

Name of field, discovery date	Depth, ft	Producing oil wells	1995 production avg., b/d	°API gravity
CHEVRON				
Agogo, 1989	4,200-5,400	8	11,430	44.0
Iagifu/Hedinia, 1986	7,400-8,500	21	88,142	45.0
Total Papua New Guinea		**29**	**99,572**	

PERU

Name of field, discovery date	Depth, ft	Producing oil wells	1995 production avg., b/d	°API gravity
GMP SA				
Lote I (Block), 1869	2,000-9,000	69	756	33.0
Lote V (Block), 1869	2,000-9,000	33	225	35.0
MAPLE GAS				
Agua Caliente, 1939	1,000-15,000	17	161	40.0
Maquia, 1957	2,100-2,400	28	515	37.0
OCCIDENTAL				
Bartra, 1979	8,000-8,930	11	3,438	11.6
Capahuari Norte, 1988	12,000-13,500	6	5,443	31.0
Capahuari Sur, 1973	11,800-12,900	16	4,677	33.7
Carmen, 1986	10,680	1	374	18.4
Dorissa, 1989	9,800-10,600	10	6,249	32.0

WORLDWIDE PRODUCTION

Name of field, discovery date	Depth, ft	Producing oil wells	1995 production avg., b/d	°API gravity
Forestal, 1973	9,000-9,900	8	3650	18.5
Huayuri Sur, 1977	10,000-10,800	11	2,529	28.5
Jibarito, 1981	9,000-9,650	7	8,765	10.5
Jibaro, 1974	10,110-10,155	6	2,596	10.6
San Jacinto, 1978	7,200-9,760	19	7,326	14.9
Shiviyacu, 1973	9,100-10,100	21	9,314	20.3
OCCIDENTAL/BRIDAS				
Carrizo, 1978	1,343-6,080	111	517	35.0
Central, 1978	1,343-6,080	286	1,247	35.0
Cruz I, 1978	1,343-6,080	6	26	35.0
Cruz II, 1978	1,343-6,080	13	68	35.0
Folche, 1978	1,343-6,080	14	54	35.0
Folche Norte, 1978	1,343-6,080	6	27	35.0
Organos Norte, 1978	1,343-6,080	64	208	35.0
Organos Sur, 1978	1,343-6,080	82	428	35.0
Patria, 1978	1,343-6,080	48	93	35.0
Somatito, 1978	1,343-6,080	95	526	35.0
Zapotal, 1978	1,343-6,080	235	1,099	35.0
PETROPERU - LOTE X				
Ballena, 1924	3,500-5,000		1,214	30.0
Carrizo, 1953	4,000-5,500		963	31.0
Central	....		273	....
Coyonitas	....		79	....
La Tuna	....		326	....
Laguna	....		1,306	....
Laguna Zapotal, 1953	7,000-8,000	1,242	992	29.0
Merina	....		823	....
Organos, 1947	6,000-7,000		227	30.0
Patria	....		73	....
Pena Negra, 1914	4,000-5,000		1,010	35.5
Reventones	....		2,050	....
Somatito	....		380	....
Taiman, 1922	3,000-6,500		2,739	30.0
Tunal	....		61	....
Verde	....		550	....
PETROPERU - LOTE 8				
Capirona, 1978	9,800-12,000	3	225	25.0
Chambira, 1994	12,600-14,600	3	715	26.5
Corrientes, 1974	10,000-12,600	31	10,024	24.9
Pavayacu, 1978	9,600-11,300	22	14,926	36.0
Yanayacu, 1977	11,400-13,600	5	986	18.8
PETRO-TECH				
• Litoral, 1955	1,500-6,000	79	1,277	36.0-40.0
• Lobitos, 1960	3,500-7,500	193	10,099	38.0
• Organos	....	....	....	38.0
• Pena Negra, 1960	3,000-8,500	214	6,767	38.0
• Providencia, 1967	3,000-7,000	53	1,275	38.0-40.0
PROVISA/MERCANTILE				
Lote III (Block), 1869	2,000-9,000	60	266	35.0
RIO BRAVO				
Lote IV (Block), 1869	2,000-9,000	72	468	33.0
SAPET DEVELOPMENT				
Lote VI (Block)	....	265	1,562	33.0
Lote VIII (Block)	3,000	260	982	36.0
UNIPETRO ABC				
Lote IX (Block), 1869	2,000-9,000	51	418	32.0
VEGSA				
Lote II (Block), 1869	2,000-9,000	107	634	28.0
Total Peru		**3,883**	**124,001**	

PHILIPPINES (e)

Name of field, discovery date	Depth, ft	Producing oil wells	1995 production avg., b/d	°API gravity
ALCORN PALAWAN				
• Cadlao, 1977	5,734-5,881	0		45.6
South Tara, 1977	4,335-4,436	0		40.4
ALCORN PHILIPPINES				
• Galoc, 1981	7,260-7,280	0		37.2
• Matinloc, 1978	6,656-6,750	4		43.8
• Nido, 1977	6,576-6,885	4	2,900	27.2
• North Matinloc, 1987	6,830-7,021	0		43.2
• West Linapacan, 1990	7,025-8,140	3		32.3
SHELL/OXY				
• Camago, 1989	11,167	0		48.7
• Malampaya, 1992	11,648-12,343	0		29.0
Total Philippines		**11**	**2,900**	

POLAND

Name of field, discovery date	Depth, ft	Producing oil wells	1995 production avg., b/d	°API gravity
PETROBALTIC				
B-3, 1981	4,900	5	2,382	42.0
POLISH OIL AND GAS CO.				
Buk, 1974	8,540	2	392	40.6
Dominkowice-Kryg, 1860	200-2,250	132	37	30.2
Grabownica, 1896	980-3,840	114	85	45.4
Grobla, 1962	2,460	31	155	44.3
Jeniniec, 1986	9,580	1	104	36.2
Kamien Pomorski, 1972	7,360	4	178	34.0
Kije, 1976	6,540	2	70	39.2
Kosarzyn, 1991	5,650	1	216	37.0
Kosarzyn South, 1992	5,480	1	254	37.0
Nosowka, 1988	10,870	4	342	29.3
Osobnica, 1953	1,310-2,230	78	78	36.2
Plawowice, 1962	1,970	24	85	35.9
Wankowa, 1848	490-2,030	277	95	36.9
Weglowka, 1890	980-3,770	64	83	34.6
Wysoka Kamienska, 1979	9,960	3	153	30.7
Other	....	1,330	1,297	....
Total Poland		**2,073**	**6,006**	

QATAR

Name of field, discovery date	Depth, ft	Producing oil wells	1995 production avg., b/d	°API gravity
MAERSK				
• Al-Shaheen, 1994	3,000-4,000	8	19,000	31.0
OCCIDENTAL				
• Idd El Shardi, 1960	4,400-13,300	48	38,997	33.0
QATAR GENERAL PETROLEUM CORP.				
• Bul Hanine, 1970	6,000	208	273,000	35.0
Dukhan, 1940	6,500	28	80,000	41.1
• Idd El Shargi, 1960	4,500-8,250	26	43,000	35.0
Total Qatar		**318**	**453,997**	

RAS al KHAIMAH (e)

Name of field, discovery date	Depth, ft	Producing oil wells	1995 production avg., b/d	°API gravity
RAS al KHAIMAH GAS COMMISSION				
• Saleh, 1983	14,500	7	750	50.0
Total Ras al Khaimah		**7**	**750**	

SAUDI ARABIA (e)

Name of field, discovery date	Depth, ft	Producing oil wells	1995 production avg., b/d	°API gravity
ARAMCO				
Abqaiq, 1940	6,690			37.0
Abu Hadriya, 1940	9,340			35.0
Abu Jifan	....			....
• Abu-Safah, 1963	6,600			30.0
Bakr	....			....
• Berri, 1964	8,300			32.0-34.0
Dammam, 1938	4,800			35.0
Dawl, 1980	....			....
Dhib	....			....
Dibdibah	....			....
El Haba	....			....
Fadhili, 1949	8,050			39.0
Farhah	....			....
Faridah	....			....
Ghawar, 1948	6,920			34.0
Habari	....			....
• Hamur	....			....
Harmaliyah, 1971	8,430			35.0
• Harqus	....			....
• Hasbah	....			....
Jaham	....			....
Jaladi	....			....
• Jana	....			....
Jauf	....			....
Jawb	....	1,372	7,859,000	....
Juraybi'at	....			....
• Jurayd	....			....
• Karan	....			....
Khurais, 1957	5,200			33.0
Khursaniyah, 1956	6,560			31.0
• Kurayn	....			....
• Lawhah	....			....
Lughfah	....			....
• Maharah	....			....
• Manifa, 1957	7,950			29.0
• Marjan, 1967	6,800			33.0
Mazalij	....			....
• Qatif, 1945	7,100			33.0-34.0
Qirdi	....			....

WORLDWIDE PRODUCTION

Name of field, discovery date	Depth, ft	Producing oil wells	1995 production avg., b/d	°API gravity
• Ribyan	....			....
Rimthan	....			....
• Safaniyah, 1951	5,100			27.0
Sahba	....			....
Samin	....			....
Sharar	....			....
Suban	....			....
Tinat	....			....
Wari`ah	....			....
Watban	....			....
• Zuluf, 1965	5,800			32.0
Total Saudi Arabia		**1,372**	**7,859,000**	

SERBIA (e)

Name of field, discovery date	Depth, ft	Producing oil wells	1995 production avg., b/d	°API gravity
NIS/NAFTAGAS				
Boka, 1956	3,969-4,100	25		32.7
Coka, 1975	4,888-5,046	9		44.3
Elemir, 1959	5,002-5,376	29		32.7
Itebej, 1978	6,973-7,327	5		26.4
Janosik, 1958	2,148-3,293	1		24.2
Jermenovci, 1952	2,919-3,148	56		24.2
Karadjordjevo, 1973	8,308-8,846	6		26.4
Kelebija, 1970	2,0691-2,788	12		21.2
Kikinda, 1960	3,543-5,735	166	20,000	34.9
Kikinda-varos, 1963	3,740-6,490	50		27.9
Lokve, 1953	2,909-3,099	9		25.1
Morkrin, 1961	6,232-7,216	105		35.1
Mokrin-jug, 1982	6,658-6,740	16		41.1
Majdan, 1972	7,708-7,790	14		37.4
Palic, 1968	3,345-3,427	6		45.9
V. Greda-jug, 1981	3,237-3,427	10		23.8
Velebit, 1965	2,434-2,575	122		22.8
Zrenjanin, 1974	6,829-6,986	5		25.0
Total Serbia		**646**	**20,000**	

SHARJAH

Name of field, discovery date	Depth, ft	Producing oil wells	1995 production avg., b/d	°API gravity
AMOCO				
Kahaif (c), 1992	10,200-12,300	6	7,000	50.0
Saaja and Moveyid (c), 1980	10,200-12,300	34	20,800	50.0
CRESCENT				
• Mubarek, 1972	12,650-14,100	12	3,650	47.0
Total Sharjah		**52**	**31,450**	

SOUTH AFRICA

Name of field, discovery date	Depth, ft	Producing oil wells	1995 production avg., b/d	°API gravity
SOEKOR				
• Mossel Bay, F-A, 1980	8,900	9	9,400	91.0
Total South Africa		**9**	**9,400**	

SPAIN

Name of field, discovery date	Depth, ft	Producing oil wells	1995 production avg., b/d	°API gravity
REPSOL				
Albatros	....		34	....
• Casablanca, 1975	8,900	36	12,678	33.0
• Gaviota, 1980	8,300		24	52.7
Lora	....		279	....
Total Spain		**36**	**13,015**	

SUDAN (e)

Name of field, discovery date	Depth, ft	Producing oil wells	1995 production avg., b/d	°API gravity
ARAKIS ENERGY				
Al-Toor, 1996	....	....		....
Greater Heglig	5,390-6,125	9		29.6-35.0
Talih	7,532-8,220	....	2,000	42.3-43.4
Toma South, 1996	....	....		....
Unity	6,240-7,225	....		33.0-35.1
Total Sudan		**9**	**2,000**	

SURINAME (e)

Name of field, discovery date	Depth, ft	Producing oil wells	1995 production avg., b/d	°API gravity
STAATSOLIE				
Tambaredjo, 1981	1,050	317	7,240	15.9
Total Suriname		**317**	**7,240**	

SYRIA (e)

Name of field, discovery date	Depth, ft	Producing oil wells	1995 production avg., b/d	°API gravity
AL FURAT OIL CO. (SHELL)				
Azraq, 1991	....	....		35.5
El Isba, 1988	....	....		37.0
El Ward N, 1986	....	....		38.1
Galban, 1991	....	....		32.4
Maleh, 1990	....	....		34.0
Omar, 1987	....	....		41.5
Sijan, 1989	....	....		35.0
Tanak, 1987	....	....		36.5
Thayyem, 1983	....	....		36.5
S.P.C. (e)				
Alian, 1974	5,900	25	605,000	19.0
Gbebeh, 1976	2,300	54		18.0
Jebisseh, 1968	2,000-3,000	132		18.0
Karachok, 1956	6,500	103		20.0
Rumailan, 1962	6,500	59		24.0
Soudie, 1959	6,500	532		24.0
Tichrine, 1976	2,600	58		18.0
OTHER (e)				
Wadi Aabbeid, 1989	9,000	1		24.4
Total Syria		**964**	**605,000**	

THAILAND

Name of field, discovery date	Depth, ft	Producing oil wells	1995 production avg., b/d	°API gravity
CAIRN ENERGY FAR EAST LTD.				
Wichian Buri, 1988	3,526	1	244	26.6
PTTEP INTERNATIONAL				
Kamphaeng Saen, 1986	3,780	1	80	25.2
U Thong, 1987	3,550	5	1,200	33.2
SINO-U.S. PETROLEUM				
Bung Ya, 1984	7,800	1	59	34.5
Bung Nuang, 1987	8,900	6	203	35.8
THAI SHELL				
Nang Nuan, 1987	9,000	1	3,086	40.0
Sirikit, 1981	5,500	97	17,643	41.0
TOTAL				
• Bongkot, 1973	7,000	29	3,760	56.0
UNOCAL				
• Baanpot, 1974	7,000	5	160	54.6
• Erawan, 1972	7,000	93	8,298	54.6
• Funan, 1981	6,100	60	4,425	45.0
• Gomin, 1988	7,300	7	1,405	47.0
• Jakrawan, 1976	6,500	9	547	45.1
• Kaphong, 1973	8,000	4	320	55.0
• Platong, 1976	8,500	11	2,144	59.1
• Satun, 1980	8,500	32	6,913	55.1
• Surat, 1971	6,800	3	411	50.0
Total Thailand		**365**	**50,898**	

TRINIDAD AND TOBAGO

Name of field, discovery date	Depth, ft	Producing oil wells	1995 production avg., b/d	°API gravity
AMOCO TRINIDAD OIL CO. LTD.				
• Banyan (c), 1995	15,000	1	1,644	45.0
• Cassia (c), 1973	12,700	8	668	45.0
• Flambouyant (c), 1993	13,700	2	2,027	43.0
• Immortelle, 1993	13,000	5	5,804	47.0
• Poui, 1974	11,650	36	14,336	34.0
• Samaan, 1971	11,780	42	13,734	36.8
• Teak, 1971	15,191	63	20,839	29.3
ENRON GAS & OIL TRINIDAD LTD.				
• Ibis, 1995	15,000	3	1,657	43.0
• Kiskadee (c), 1993	15,000	5	4,813	43.0
MORAVEN				
• Mora, 1986	8,500	4	505	....
PCOL				
Barrackpore, 1970	1,900	8	69	18.0
Fysabad, 1918	2,100	63	216	22.0
Icacos, 1955	3,500	2	9	26.0
Palo Seco, 1915	2,000	9	22	20.0
San Francique, 1929	2,200	29	335	23.0
Siparia, 1957	9,500	1	8	39.0
PETROTRIN				
Antilles Trinity, 1959	9,700	15	251	....
Antilles Vessigny	....	27	136	....
Apex Quarry, 1920	11,000	19	146	....
Balata East	....	18	123	....

WORLDWIDE PRODUCTION

Name of field, discovery date	Depth, ft	Producing oil wells	1995 production avg., b/d	°API gravity
Barrackpore, 1911	11,100	78	1,330	....
Beach	....	25	135	....
Brighton Land, 1908	7,500	6	30	....
• Brighton Marine	....	32	331	....
Catshill, 1950	9,693	27	751	....
Central Los Bajos, 1973	....	151	1,656	....
Coora, 1936	14,000	33	273	....
Cruse, 1913	....	35	194	....
Erin, 1926	12,718	2	2	....
Erin, 1926	12,718	21	426	....
Forest Reserve, 1913	11,000	308	3,315	....
Fyzabad, 1920	11,000	241	1,819	....
• Galeota, 1963	6,304	35	1,570	....
Guapo	....	189	2,086	....
Guayaguayare, 1902	10,750	24	56	....
Inniss, 1950	9,693	5	37	....
Los Bajos, 1973	....	32	72	....
Mackenzie, 1926	12,718	26	346	....
Marcelle Valley	....	22	133	....
Morne Diablo	....	1	3	....
Morne Diablo	....	3	10	....
Moruga East	....	16	80	....
Moruga West	....	28	189	....
Navette	....	63	783	....
New Dome	....	4	20	....
Oropouche, 1944	9,100	36	213	....
Palo Seco, 1926	12,700	524	6,026	....
Parrylands, 1913	10,626	113	1,001	....
Pebal, 1936	11,067	66	646	....
Point Fortin Central, 1907	10,626	196	2,436	....
Point Fortin East	....	59	433	....
Point Fortin West, 1907	10,626	35	288	....
Point Ligoure, 1937	....	1	235	....
Quarry	11,000-14,000	160	1,044	....
Quinam	....	13	11	....
Siparia	....	3	16	....
Tabaquite	6,519	11	971	....
Wilson	....	18	108	....
TNA				
• Fortin Offshore (FOS), 1954	....	13	147	14.3
• Soldado, 1955	11,000	319	31,579	17.3
Pt. Ligoure	....	1	4	33.0
TRINTOMAR				
• Pelican (c), 1990	13,000-14,000	2	1,168	37.3
Total Trinidad and Tobago		**3,337**	**129,315**	

TUNISIA

Name of field, discovery date	Depth, ft	Producing oil wells	1995 production avg., b/d	°API gravity
AGIP-SITEP				
El Borma, 1964	8,250-8,900	91	32,373	41.2
AGIP-SAMEDAN-EAT				
Zinnia, 1989	9,850	2	16	50.5
AGIP				
Choueches Saida, 1971	12,600	1	227	49.2
Ech Chouech, 1971	11,800	1	11	51.1
Sanrhar, 1989	7,200	1	40	35.0
BRITISH GAS				
• Cercina, 1992	4,920	4	3,500	29.0
El Ain/Gremda, 1980	8,700	3	1,100	42.0
El Hajeb/Guebiba, 1982	7,050	1	170	29.0
Rhemoura, 1991	8,850	1	1,900	33.0
ETAP-AGIP-FINA (SODEPS)				
Debech, 1980	7,550	1	0	42.8
Larich, 1979	7,550	2	122	41.0
Makrouga, 1980	6,230	4	4,541	45.6
ELF-ETAP				
ELF-SEREPT				
• Ashtart (ELF-ETAP), 1971	10,500	21	18,100	29.6
Douleb/Semmama, 1966	3,937	13	450	39.0
Tamesmida, 1967	3,937	2	360	36.0
MARATHON				
• Belli, 1991	4,800	2	276	38.0
Ezzaouia, 1986	6,800	6	4,305	40.0
Robbana, 1988	6,600-7,000	1	133	43.0
CFPT/EGEP (e)				
Mahares, 1982	8,460-8,560	1		33.0
Sidi Elltayem, 1971	7,500-7,800	24		44.0
OTHER (e)			20,047	
Sidi El Kilani, 1989	9,200	3		39.6
• Tazerka, 1979	4,200	6		31.1
Total Tunisia		**191**	**87,671**	

TURKEY

Name of field, discovery date	Depth, ft	Producing oil wells	1995 production avg., b/d	°API gravity
ALADDIN MIDDLE EAST LTD.				
Bulgurdag, 1960	5,050	4	82	37.7
Kahta, 1958	3,412	11	107	11.0
Molla, 1974	6,400	1	2	30.0
Nemrut, 1991	5,085	1	1	18.0
Zeynel, 1990	4,823	5	37	23.1
MOBIL				
Selmo, 1964	6,562	21	2,244	34.4
ROYAL DUTCH/SHELL				
Barbes, 1972	7,454	3	557	29.7
Baysu, 1985	6,398	7	517	33.3
Bektas, 1985	6,070	2	87	33.7
Beykan, 1964	6,198	32	2,797	33.2
Karaali, 1989	9,941	2	4	24.6
Kastel, 1990	7,874	6	2,126	34.7
Katin, 1971	8,566	1	26	29.5
Kayakoy, 1961	6,834	15	945	38.2
Kayakoy (Foreland), 1964	6,188	12	2,093	34.7
Kayakoy-West, 1970	7,510	2	197	33.5
Kopru, 1990	6,237	....	....	35.2
Kurkan, 1963	5,318	22	1,450	31.4
Kurkan South, 1967	6,417	6	678	34.7
Malatepe, 1970	5,528	7	748	33.9
Piyanko, 1968	8,304	1	61	35.3
Sahaban, 1966	5,869	8	563	34.5
Sahaban SE, 1983	5,995	....	....	35.1
Sincan, 1980	5,200	6	209	31.1
Yatir East, 1974	5,128	7	437	30.9
Yenikoy East, 1974	6,516	3	636	31.3
Yesildere, 1986	6,890	5	427	34.5
TPAO				
Adiyaman, 1971	5,741	11	823	27.6
Bati Raman, 1961	4,265	199	11,078	13.0
Besikli, 1990	6,234	9	984	25.6
B. Firat, 1985	8,432	9	189	35.2
B. Kozluca, 1984	4,970	22	560	12.4
B. Selmo, 1981	5,971	3	21	34.3
Camurlu, 1976	4,757	17	292	12.2
Caylarbasi, 1993	5,250	2	139	11.8
Celikli, 1963	10,500	11	253	35.2
Cemberlitas, 1983	10,499	13	762	31.0
Cendere (J.V.), 1989	8,858	11	2,991	29.0
Devecatak, 1973	4,757	1	8	37.0
Dodan-Usak, 1965	3,445	1	33	40.0
D. Besikli, 1991	6,100	6	1,462	19.4
D. Silivanka, 1995	8,136	1	13	21.4
Garzan, 1951	4,732	39	1,392	24.0
G. Dincer, 1981	5,335	9	329	15.5
G. Karakus, 1989	7,776	9	3,525	26.5
G. Kayakoy, 1976	8,596	3	252	30.4
G. Sahaban, 1978	5,446	8	336	33.2
G. Saricak, 1973	5,250	9	259	31
Ikizce, 1991	7,500	3	109	26.4
Ikiztepe, 1976	4,888	7	21	11.3
Karaali (J.V.), 1989	9,941	....	....	24.6
Karadut, 1992	9,514	1	20	38.4
Karakus, 1988	8,858	25	8,756	30.1
Karteltepe, 1982	6,562	3	145	32.0
Kastel (J.V.), 1990	7,874	....	....	34.7
Kavakdere, 1995	6,725	1	3	37.0
K. Karakus, 1990	8,497	13	7,295	29.0
K. Osmancik, 1971	3,773	2	121	37.6
Magrip, 1961	5,700	13	294	18.5
Mehmetdere, 1982	6,562	1	24	32.0
O. Sungurlu, 1991	9,186	3	552	37.2
Raman, 1945	4,462	82	4,299	18.0
Saricak, 1973	5,250	2	80	31.5
Sarisogut, 1994	8,825	1	18	29.2
Silivanka, 1962	7,791	10	773	23.0
S. Sinan, 1987	4,265	3	47	15.7
Tokaris, 1991	7,900	5	337	24.1
Yanankoy, 1994	5,741	1	595	18.4
Yenikoy, 1973	6,627	20	1,216	32.5
Total Turkey		**779**	**67,437**	

UNITED KINGDOM

Name of field, discovery date	Depth, ft	Producing oil wells	1995 production avg., b/d	°API gravity
AGIP				
• Tiffany, 1977	....	7	40,484	33.6
• Toni, 1979	....	4	30,321	34.7

WORLDWIDE PRODUCTION

Name of field, discovery date	Depth, ft	Producing oil wells	1995 production avg., b/d	°API gravity
AMERADA HESS LTD.				
• Fife, 1991	....	3	15,227	36.0
• Hudson, 1987	6,500	5	36,310	33.0
• Ivanhol/Rob Roy/Hamish, 1975	8,000	11	42,211	30.0-41.0
• Scott, 1984	11,000	16	179,940	36.0
AMOCO				
• Arbroath, 1969	8,100	14	35,337	38.0
• Everest, 1982	....	11	6,203	....
• Lomond, 1972	....	7	3,644	....
• Montrose, 1971	8,150	22	2,644	38.5
• NW Hutton, 1975	11,500	50	6,995	35.0
ARCO				
• Blenheim, 1990	....	3	22,521	39.0
BP				
• Beatrice (A & B), 1976	6,750	36	9,803	39.0
• Bruce, 1974	....	18	39,214	38.0
• Buchan, 1974	8,700	9	10,008	33.5
• Clyde, 1978	12,400	20	16,271	37.5
• Deveron, 1972	9,000	3	1,121	38.0
• Don, 1976	11,200	5	4,833	40.0
• Donan, 1987	6,480	2	7,414	39.0
• Forties and Echo, 1970	7,000	95	112,011	37.0
• Leven, 1981	12,400	2	1,707	39.0
• Machar, 1975	....	3	17,200	40.0
• Magnus, 1974	9,500	32	112,822	39.0
• Medwin, 1989	....	1	1,090	38.5
• Miller, 1983	13,400	13	134,058	39.0
• Thistle, 1973	9,000	40	13,770	38.4
Wareham, 1964	....	7	1,159	34.0
Wytch Farm, 1973	3,031-5,198	61	95,441	37.0-38.0
CAIRN				
Herriard	....	2	82	....
Horndean, 1982	....	5	373	35.4
Humbly Grove/Herriad, 1980	....	24	1,058	35.8
Palmers Wood, 1983	....	7	745	36.5
Singleton, 1989	....	12	726	37.7
CANDECCA				
Nettleham, 1983	3,870	1	0	35.6
Scampton North, 1985	4,850	6	145	35.2
Stainton, 1984	4,364	1	22	27.6
Welton, 1981	4,450	42	2,573	36.0
CHEVRON				
• Alba, 1984	6,100-6,600	11	77,405	19.0
• Ninian, 1974	10,000	99	56,258	37.0
EAST MIDLAND				
Farley's Wood, 1983	....	2	22	39.7
Whisby, 1985	....	2	82	32.7
EDINBURGH OIL & GAS				
Crosby Warren, 1986	5,500	1	41	40.8
ELF ENTERPRISE				
• Chanter, 1985	12,000	1	1,890	37.8
• Claymore, 1974	8,100	28	44,852	30.0
• Piper, 1973	8,100	12	82,665	37.0
• Saltire, 1988	10,900	6	36,186	42.5
• Scapa, 1975	8,500	6	16,942	32.5
ENTERPRISE				
• Nelson, 1988	....	17	136,419	40.0
KERR-MCGEE				
• Gryphon, 1987	....	11	45,227	21.4
LASMO				
• Staffa, 1985	....	0	0	39.6
• Birch, 1985	....	2	6,090	38.0
MARATHON				
• Beinn, 1987	13,700	4	9,082	45.0
• Central Brae, 1976	14,100-15,000	6	9,907	33.0
• East Brae, 1980	12,800-13,700	15	74,178	39.0-49.0
• North Brae, 1975	11,900-12,475	18	11,510	41.0-45.0
• South Brae, 1972	12,700-13,437	31	10,844	33.0-35.0
MIDLAND AND SCOTTISH ENERGY				
• Emerald, 1981	....	9	7,907	23.0
MOBIL				
• Beryl, 1972	9,900-11,500	49	90,658	37.0
• Linnhe, 1988	11,500-12,065	0	0	37.8
• Ness, 1986	9,900-10,112	3	1,885	37.0
ORYX				
• Hutton, 1973	10,000	15	23,764	34.5
• Lyell, 1975	....	....	9,205	36.2
• Murchison*, 1975	9,900	22	12,181	36.0
PENTEX				
Beckingham West, 1985	....	1	0	35.6
East Glentworth, 1987	....	1	0	37.0
Kirklington, 1985	....	1	0	29.6
Long Clawson, 1986	....	5	145	35.8
Rempstone, 1985	....	2	104	34.2
Stockbridge, 1984	....	9	1,884	36.8
PHILLIPS				
• Joanne, 1981	....	11	866	39.0
• Judy, 1985	....	6	570	39.0
• Maureen, 1973	8,000-8,700	13	10,553	36.0
• Moira, 1988	8,800	1	781	42.0
RANGER				
• Columba D	....	3	6,863	....
SHELL				
• Auk, 1971	....	14	12,403	38.0
• Brent, 1971	....	151	187,337	38.0
• Cormorant North, 1974	....	32	42,310	36.0
• Cormorant South, 1972	....	16	16,666	35.0
• Dunlin, 1973	....	41	19,364	35.0
• Eider, 1976	....	10	18,521	34.0
• Fulmar, 1975	....	22	26,159	40.0
• Gannet A, 1973	....	12	20,540	38.0
• Gannet B, 1979	....	2	4,038	....
• Gannet C, 1982	....	6	33,274	38.0
• Gannett D, 1987	....	4	7,458	43.0
• Kittiwake, 1981	....	5	28,195	38.0
• Osprey, 1974	....	6	28,340	31.0
• Tern, 1975	....	12	68,170	34.0
STATOIL				
• Statfjord*, 1975	9,500	99	72,058	38.0
SUN				
• Balmoral, 1975	7,000	14	13,337	39.3
• Glamis, 1982	10,000	4	3,181	42.0
• Stirling, 1983	8,000	1	1,288	37.0
TEXACO NORTH SEA				
• Highlander, 1976	8,759-9,372	6	6,288	35.0
• Petronella, 1975	8,110	1	6,115	39.0
• Strathspey, 1975	10,000-10,500	9	34,644	39.0-45.0
• Tartan, 1975	10,217-12,614	13	9,337	38.0
TOTAL OIL MARINE				
• Alwyn N., 1975	10,170-11,155	27	28,636	39.0
• Dunbar, 1973	10,990-12,370	6	36,041	40.3-44.8
• Ellon, 1972	10,330-10,770	1	2,074	....
TULLOW				
W. Firsby, 1988	5,500	3	290	38.0
UNOCAL				
• Heather, 1973	10,800	23	5,863	32.0-37.0
Total United Kingdom ...		**1,563**	**2,524,376**	

*U.K. share (77.8%) of total production.

UNITED STATES *

Alabama, 1944	....	900	51,318	....
Alaska, 1905	....	1,872	1,483,984	....
Arizona, 1958	....	22	195	....
Arkansas, 1921	....	8,179	24,411	....
California, 1861	....	40,194	960,784	....
Colorado, 1887	....	8,445	76,647	....
Florida, 1943	....	85	15,597	....
Illinois, 1889	....	31,254	44,356	....
Indiana, 1889	....	7,187	7,611	....
Kansas, 1889	....	43,267	119,910	....
Kentucky, 1860	....	23,558	9,567	....
Louisiana, 1902	....	29,234	1,169,392	....
Michigan, 1900	....	4,057	31,186	....
Mississippi, 1889	....	1,520	54,551	....
Missouri, 1889	....	444	329	....

WORLDWIDE PRODUCTION

Name of field, discovery date	Depth, ft	Producing oil wells	1995 production avg., b/d	°API gravity
Montana, 1916	....	3,660	45,285	....
Nebraska, 1939	....	1,770	10,395	....
Nevada, 1954	....	67	3,677	....
New Mexico, 1911	....	18,059	176,734	....
New York, 1865	....	3,714	833	....
North Dakota, 1951	....	3,333	80,370	....
Ohio, 1860	....	29,707	22,625	....
Oklahoma, 1891	....	91,833	239,701	....
Pennsylvania, 1859	....	18,617	5,312	....
South Dakota, 1954	....	147	3,682	....
Tennessee, 1860	....	776	1,047	....
Texas, 1889	....	177,562	1,643,863	....
Utah, 1907	....	1,827	54,762	....
Virginia, 1943	....	23	33	....
West Virginia, 1860	....	16,593	5,337	....
Wyoming, 1894	....	10,174	216,121	....
Total United States		**578,080**	**6,559,615**	

*Discovery date indicates first year of production in state. There are 33,179 oil fields in the U.S.

VENEZUELA

Name of field, discovery date	Depth, ft	Producing oil wells	1995 production avg., b/d	°API gravity
PDVSA/ANZOATEGUI				
Adas, 1957	5,000	19	288	13.9
Araibel, 1955	11,300	1	8	35.0
Araibel-R, 1954	11,400	....	....	34.2
Arecuna, 1979	4,070	90	6,659	11.2
Bare, 1980	3,800	338	58,169	10.2
Boca, 1951	9,500	7	767	32.2
Boca-R, 1951	8,400	4	468	28.2
Bote, 1959	8,800	1	167	26.0
Bucaral, 1958	10,400	5	74	46.0
Cachama-R, 1952	8,700	10	3,500	28.6
Cachicamo, 1949	4,600	....	....	21.0
Caico Este, 1951	8,600	4	1,252	30.3
Caico Seco, 1946	7,700	....	....	38.1
Cantaura, 1959	12,300	....	....	41.5
Capacho, 1945	6,100	....	....	23.3
Caracoles, 1952	7,400	15	1,500	28.7
Caricari, 1977	5,500	....	....	21.0
Carina, 1982	4,000	5	260	10.9
Caz-501x, 1952	....	....	....	36.3
Chimire, 1948	7,000-7,200	16	2,260	34.1
Chimire-Chv, 1949	7,500	....	.....	30.0
Chimire Norte, 1953	8,900	6	1,088	35.0
Chimire-R, 1946	7,400	16	1,441	33.9
Dacion, 1957	6,700	111	10,220	21.0
El Robie, 1939	3,500-11,000	20	948	49.3
El Toco, 1948	8,000	23	1,077	44.3
Elotes, 1954	5,000-6,470	37	2,570	34.1
Elotes Norte, 1973	....	3	414	36.1
Esquina-R, 1951	6,800	1	140	36.1
Esquina Sur, 1952	6,800	4	816	34.2
Finca, 1953	....	6	770	37.3
Freites, 1949	10,400	3	230	37.1
Ganso, 1948	6,300	5	732	18.7
GG-401, 1951	8,100	13	2,058	28.7
GM-2, 1941	6,800	5	619	19.2
GM-4, 1946	7,000	21	2,715	29.7
Guara Central, 1946	5,000-10,000	2	244	18.2
Guara Este, 1942	7,300	59	4,108	23.6
Guara Oeste, 1942	7,000	29	2,964	28.9
Guario, 1940	8,000	22	1,945	49.9
Guere, 1950	8,000	4	512	38.6
Guico, 1944	4,500-7,000	9	649	29.7
Guico Oeste, 1946	7,300	1	70	35.5
Guico Sur, 1946	6,900	3	280	29.2
Inca Isia, 1948	7250	22	2,304	35.8
Ira, 1957	6,300	9	353	37.5
Junta, 1953	8,000	2	280	17.6
Kaki, 1955	10,200	5	395	41.1
La Ceiba, 1946	9,450	11	863	41.9
La Ceibita, 1963	9,878	17	1,405	38.3
La Viejo, 1950	5,200	....	....	19.3
Lejos, 1952	5,500	45	1,644	12.1
Leona, 1938	2,200-12,800	29	3,170	24.8
Lestes, 1956	7,400	....	....	15.7
Levas, 1952	6,500	11	1,115	20.1
Libro, 1956	6,700	1	66	12.7
Lido, 1940	9,000	25	2,466	25.4
Limon, 1947	9,500	42	2,436	25.9
Lobo, 1952	7,100	5	304	23.9
Mapiri, 1949	10,500	10	468	39.5
Mapiri C., 1950	10,200	6	274	32.2
Mapiri E., 1952	10,500	....	....	35.8
Mapuey, 1953	8,000	....	....	39.2
Mata, 1954	9,900-12,500	41	3,760	28.4
Mata-R, 1953	12,300	22	764	40.1
Melones, 1952	4,900	161	5,220	11.4
Melones C., 1974	4,622	114	11,086	11.4
Merey, 1937	5,400-5,700	26	1,027	12.5
Miga, 1953	4,600	102	5,261	12.3
Nardo, 1952	10,100	29	2,907	25.5
Nieblas, 1954	9400	1	159	30.6
Nigua, 1953	11,600	9	1,419	26.0
Nipa, 1945	6,000-8,500	17	1,219	27.4
Nipa 100, 1957	9,600	9	989	26.8
Nipa C, 1946	8,100	....	....	32.5
Nipa Oeste, 1954	9,200	7	712	29.2
Oca, 1953	5,600	4	131	16.7
Oficina Central, 1937	5,900	25	2,046	30.6
Oficina Norte, 1946	6,900	5	1,266	29.6
Oleos, 1934	5,000	34	1,095	13.0
Oscurote, 1952	10,300	1	38	18.9
Oscurote-Norte, 1952	9,513	8	293	24.2
Ostra, 1943	5,700	43	3,351	16.9
Oueja, 1942	4,800	74	4,611	16.5
Pato Este, 1988	13,700	2	30	41.9
Pradera-R, 1949	7,300	1	114	30.6
Quiamare, 1942	8,500	17	2,531	39.6
Rincon Largo, 1941	8,900	....	....	40.5
Rosa R.V., 1958	11,600	....	....	38.8
San Joaquin, 1938	8,600	109	5,346	42.9
San Roque, 1936	8,500	....	....	48.3
Santa Ana, 1936	9,200	21	981	40.1
Santa Fe, 1953	11,900	1	23	36.9
Santa Rosa, 1941	9,800	117	6,461	45.7
Sanvi, 1959	6,100	....	....	31.7
Socororo, 1940	5,000	6	589	20.2
Soto Este, 1950	11,100	6	474	33.0
Soto Norte, 1953	11,700	6	282	35.8
Tascabana, 1951	7,500	5	726	29.0
Torta-Maulpa	....	1	57	41.0
Trico, 1941	6,100	18	1,564	31.1
Yopales Central, 1937	4,600	33	2,875	22.6
Yopales Norte, 1943	5,400	6	1,180	29.0
Yopales Sur, 1953	4,700	40	2,657	13.3
Zacarias, 1959	15,100	3	383	40.6
Zanjas, 1958	13,270	8	2,074	38.1
Zapatos, 1955	11,500	19	3,454	32.4
Zarza, 1957	13,200	2	271	43.2
Zorro, 1953	11,100	5	666	29.3
Zuata Principal, 1975	900-4,900	10	2,340	8.6
Zulus, 1957	12,710	6	783	35.8
Zumo, 1954	9,200	7	1,551	25.3
Zumo Norte, 1955	11,100	1	1,123	22.0
PDVSA/BARINAS				
Caipe, 1967	10,900	3	192	24.7
Estero, 1958	10,700	....	....	27.3
Guafita, 1982	8,500	61	47,462	29.1
Hato Viejo, 1956	9,550	10	2,052	28.4
La Victoria, 1987	10,900	31	48,085	29.8
Maporal, 1957	10,950	14	2,098	25.7
Paez (Mingo), 1963	8,900	41	3,716	19.9
Palmita, 1957	10,600	1	126	27.8
Sinco, 1953	8,500-9,100	46	8,746	23.7
Silvan, 1949	10,860	16	2,454	26.8
Silvestre, 1948	8,860	22	1,967	25.5
Torunos, 1994	11,800-12,400	4	1,137	24.8
PDVSA/GUARICO				
Anibal, 1955	5,500	....	....	31
Barso, 1959	5,800	3	293	29.3
Belen, 1953	4,500	....	....	28
Bella Vista, 1952	4,300	7	252	24.6
Budare, 1958	4,523	38	3,508	31.1
Copa, 1951	7,800	3	282	32.6
Coporo, 1954	6,500	8	2,751	30.0
Dakoa, 1954	5,400	....	....	30.0
Grico, 1946	4,200	....	....	30.5
Guavinta, 1948	3,900	1	16	27.0
Ipire, 1958	5,400	1	219	26.6
Jobal, 1960	7,600	8	156	28.0
Las Mercedes, 1942	4,500	....	....	41.3
Macoya, 1972	7,700	3	41	25.4
Palacio, 1946	3,800	....	....	48.3
Piragua, 1949	4,500	....	....	23
Punzon, 1947	4,900	....	....	26.9
Retumbo, 1955	5,200	....	....	32
Ruiz, 1949	4,500	1	131	38.6
Saban, 1947	4,000	10	356	38.8
Taman, 1949	4,100	3	36	47.3
Tucupido, 1946	5,000	1	3	38.7

WORLDWIDE PRODUCTION

Name of field, discovery date	Depth, ft	Producing oil wells	1995 production avg., b/d	°API gravity
Valle 13, 1947	5,700	....	....	42
Valle 3, 1957	5,000	....	....	42.0
Yucal-Placer	....	....	....	....
PDVSA/MONAGAS				
Acema A, 1960	13,100	21	2,592	26.4
Acema B, 1971	12,600	2	192	24.6
Acema Casma Anaco, 1972	12,000	5	1,320	22.8
Acema Casma S.T., 1972	12,000	45	9,364	20.6
Aguasay 3, 1957	13,800	1	118	29.2
Aguasay C, 1955	8,100-13,400	7	1,597	35.8
Aguasay E, 1959	13,950	1	120	29.0
Aguasay N, 1972	1,590	1	430	42.4
Amarillis, 1989	....	1	183	41.9
Boqueron, 1990	....	5	7,178	30.2
Carisito, 1984	15,100	4	1,393	41.7
Carito, 1988	16,000	15	13,002	31.4
Cerro Negro	1,200	160	38,157	7.5
El Corozo, 1987	....	1	1,644	26.8
El Furrial, 1986	15,000	54	295,903	26.3
Florida, 1987	14,100	....	....	39.2
Las Piedritas, 1993		2	2,732	25.8
Jobo II, 1956	3,600-4,000	230	36,612	10.8
Jusepin, 1938	4,253	4	12,549	28.2
Manresa, 1954	....	....	....	27.0
Mata Acema, 1954	9,500-12,500	31	7,038	33.5
Mata Grande, 1946	5,700	....	....	26.1
Morichal, 1958	3,312	29	4,890	10.2
Mulata, 1941	16,500	37	137,255	28.8
Onado, 1961	4,800-15,300	....	....	23.2
Oritupano Norte, 1954	....	30	6,082	23.4
Oritupano Sur, 1954	....	43	5,116	17.7
Oritupano, 1950	7,657	55	10,005	18.4
Orocual, 1953	....	31	19,912	38.0
Pilon, 1937	....	69	11,663	10.7
Pirital, 1958	450-12,000	9	18,386	29.9
Quiriquire, 1928	7,000-7,200	2	1,008	33.1
Santa Barbara, 1941	5,020-18,000	35	83,113	29.3
Tacat, 1953	1,820-3,670	....	....	15.0
Temblador, 1936	3,500-4,500	....	....	14.3
Travieso, 1946	53,000	....	....	....
Uracoa	....	33	12,139	16.0
PDVSA/AMACURO				
Pedernales	3,490-7,000	2	3,920	20.0
Tucupita, 1945	5,754	....	....	16.0
PDVSA/ZULIA				
Ambrosio	2,337	1	150	46.8
Alpuf, 1926	2,200-17,100	2	509	28.2
Alturitas, 1948	11,400-18,500	20	14,076	29.7
+ Bachaquero, 1930	1,800-14,185	2,619	254,835	22.4
Barua, 1928	9,200-15,500	22	12,562	20.8
Boscan, 1946	9,708	265	64,617	10.2
Cabimas, 1917	2,200	160	2,738	22.4
+ Centro, 1959	9,800-11,000	348	94,764	33.6
+ Ceuta, 1956	16,380	137	50,528	30.2
Garcia, 1928	5,400-17,500	2	441	22.5
La Concepcion, 1953	3,148-8,000	28	2,655	36.3
La Ensenada, 1984	15,400	....	....	36.5
+ Lago, 1959	11,450	28	5,774	34.3
+ Lagunillas, 1925	3,490	2,577	201,951	22.0
+ Lama, 1957	8,320	298	97,983	32.2
+ Lamar, 1958	13,000	152	61,256	33.5
La Paz, 1925	4,268-8,000	29	6,451	31.2
Machiques, 1981	13,500	1	161	35.9
Mara, 1928	5,240	40	8,275	20.4
Mene Grande, 1914	4,130	156	5,129	21.7
Motatan, 1952	8,400-15,900	26	29,367	22.0
Punta Icotea La Rosa, 1917	2,337	....	....	....
San Jose, 1947	10,900-17,200	1	556	28.9
San Julian, 1980	18,500	2	373	32.7
Sibucara, 1948	3,000-15,000	1	216	37.0
+ Sur del Lago, 1967	13,900-19,000	9	10,244	33.6
+ Tia Juana, 1926	2,100	4,105	289,708	25.0
Totumos, 1980	11,900-14,000	1	326	30.0
+ Urdaneta, 1955	11,477	289	73,020	13.5
West Tarra, 1942	4,250-5,500	11	2,419	36.9
Total Venezuela		**14,971**	**2,378,190**	

VIET NAM (e)

Name of field, discovery date	Depth, ft	Producing oil wells	1995 production avg., b/d	°API gravity
PETROVIETNAM P.I.C.				
• White Tiger (Bach Ho), 1981	120-160	20		34.0
• Rong (Dragon), 1983	120-160	4	177,000	34.0
• Dai Hung, 1985	200-330	4		34.0
Total Viet Nam		**28**	**177,000**	

YEMEN

Name of field, discovery date	Depth, ft	Producing oil wells	1995 production avg., b/d	°API gravity
CANADIAN OXY				
Camaal, 1991	2,150	16	61,517	30.0-33.0
Haru, 1992	2,523	1	350	28.0
Heijah, 1991	2,313	10	31,527	25.0-30.0
Nazaih, 1993	2,474	1	96	30.0
Sunah, 1991	2,564	5	16,729	30.0-34.0
Tawila, 1992	2,656	7	45,313	34.0
N. Camaal, 1992	2,350	2	10,229	31.0-36.0
Hemiar, 1991	1,914	4	3,425	18.0-22.0
S. Heimar, 1993	1,942	2	213	19.0
W. Heimar, 1994	1,950	1	190	19.0
N.E. Sunah, 1994	2,536	1	5,019	30.0
YEMEN HUNT OIL CO.				
Alif, 1984	5,750	118	80,010	45.0
Al-Raja, 1989	8,000	11	14,555	53.0
Al-Sa'idah, 1989	7,000	1	842	52.0
Al-Shura, 1989	7,600	6	3,903	45.0
Al-Wihdah, 1990	7,500	1	280	40.3
Asa'ad Al-Kamil, 1987	6,100	42	44,498	48.0
Azal, 1987	6,850	29	16,334	43.0
Jabal Nuqum, 1988	3,780	1	387	44.0
Jabal Ras, 1995	6,220	1	149	43.0
Raydan, 1986	2,875	5	350	26.0
Saif Ben The-Yazen, 1988	7,600	1	1,144	40.0
Shaharah, 1991	8,900	1	158	40.5
Suquatrah, 1995	8,345	1	31	43.2
Wadi Bana, 1992	6,670	15	6,430	41.0
Total Yemen		**283**	**343,679**	

ZAIRE

Name of field, discovery date	Depth, ft	Producing oil wells	1995 production avg., b/d	°API gravity
CHEVRON				
• GCO, 1970	7,000-9,000	4	181	38.7
• Libwa, 1981	5,500	3	1,560	33.0
• Lukami, 1983	12,400	5	440	33.2
• Mibale, 1973	5,000-6,000	12	7,603	30.0
• Moko, 1972	12,310	1	66	32.0
• Motoba, 1976	11,098	10	4,281	31.5
• Mwambe, 1979	6,150	0	0	29.7
• Tshiala East, 1994	8,000	2	5,477	31.0
ZAIREP (FINA)				
East Mibale, 1978	6,000	1		34.0
Kifuku, 1986	3,400	1		31.0
Kinkasi, 1972	3,700	34		31.0
Liawenda, 1972	3,900	31		31.0
Makelekese, 1983	3,600	8	8,392	31.0
Muanda, 1972	3,600	6		31.0
Nsiamfumu, 1977	8,300	0		34.0
Tshiende, 1978	6,000	6		34.0
Total Zaire		**124**	**28,000**	

U.S. fields with ultimate oil recovery exceeding 100 million bbl

State Field Disc. year	Est. 1996 prod. (1,000 bbl)	Cum prod. 1-1-97 (1,000 bbl)	Est. rem. reserves (1,000 bbl)	Est. No. prod. wells
ALABAMA				
Citronelle, 1955	1,214	158,209	4,500	168
ALASKA				
• Endicott, 1978	26,520	346,500	191,300	52
• Granite Point, 1965	2,544	130,221	18,400	38
Kuparuk River, 1969	100,752	1,392,200	1,206,600	421
Lisburne, 1967	5,100	126,500	34,900	31
• McArthur River, 1965	5,976	586,997	48,900	85
• Middle Ground Shoal,1962	2,364	178,998	14,600	51
• Milne Point, 1969	13,500	65,800	241,500	93
• Point McIntyre, 1988	59,556	154,700	299,800	31
Prudhoe Bay, 1968	*312,200	†9,474,200	3,292,800	860
Swanson River, 1957	1,524	224,958	12,500	39
*Includes 68.5 million bbl of condensate. †Includes 552 million bbl of condensate.				
ARKANSAS				
Magnolia, 1938	392	165,479	2,919	53
Smackover, 1922	1,560	572,845	5,300	1,471
CALIFORNIA				
San Joaquin Valley				
Belridge North, 1912	1,680	104,665	11,862	466
Belridge South, 1911	42,232	1,067,104	313,780	4,462
Buena Vista, 1909	936	658,326	19,417	597
Coalinga, 1890	9,456	839,355	67,040	2,033
Coalinga Nose, 1938	333	503,730	4,677	75
Coles Levee North, 1938	228	162,901	1,821	61
Cuyama South, 1949	372	221,214	3,779	101
Cymric, 1909	11,364	280,057	82,742	1,202
Edison, 1928	720	140,951	5,428	732
Elk Hills, 1911	20,604	1,097,752	310,155	1,030
Fruitvale, 1928	444	119,647	6,378	252
Greeley, 1936	140	114,201	980	21
Kern Front, 1912	2,172	191,276	25,667	905
Kern River, 1899	49,380	1,569,773	377,944	7,542
Kettleman North Dome, 1928	47	457,837	2,451	43
Lost Hills, 1910	11,892	254,571	63,577	1,740
McKittrick, 1896	2,388	279,088	5,811	579
Midway-Sunset, 1894	59,844	2,298,368	394,363	10,387
Mount Poso, 1926	1,440	290,512	31,409	495
Rio Bravo, 1937	47	116,540	361	13
Round Mountain, 1927	242	98,359	2,384	187
Yowlumne, 1974	1,385	15,030	12,142	52
Coastal Area				
• Carpinteria, 1966	816	974,928	10,437	47
Cat Canyon E. & W., 1908	864	297,098	22,901	288
• Dos Cuadras, 1969	552	236,904	19,918	130
• Hondo, 1969	17,148	141,790	137,494	32
Orcutt, 1901	600	171,642	6,371	128
• Pescado, 1969	19,540	43,727	65,284	15
• Point Arguello, 1981	16,620	114,617	169,289	34
• Point Pedernales, 1982	3,792	52,328	22,155	14
• Rincon, 1927	804	155,402	4,587	109
San Ardo, 1947	4,476	442,510	87,536	359
Santa Maria Valley, 1934	289	203,751	14,890	93
South Mountain, 1916	684	151,662	5,343	367
Ventura, 1919	4,896	940,069	71,976	416
Los Angeles basin				
• Beta, 1976	3,264	73,129	43,371	66
Beverly Hills, 1900	1,320	134,104	13,497	85
Brea-Olinda, 1880	1,380	396,932	41,759	608
Coyote East, 1909	372	112,317	9,512	81
Coyote West, 1909	0	252,960	2,552	0
Dominguez, 1923	432	273,383	3,463	86
• Huntington Beach, 1920	3,372	1,095,785	42,370	424
Inglewood, 1924	2,280	363,086	270,162	280
• Long Beach, 1921	1,704	924,319	20,239	271
Montebello, 1917	336	195,375	6,628	99
Richfield, 1919	448	196,999	5,942	175
San Miguelito, 1931	1,041	108,557	29,410	54
Santa Fe Springs, 1919	1,032	619,395	13,327	135
• Seal Beach, 1924	516	208,328	8,158	141
• Torrance, 1922	813	220,063	18,845	206
Yorba Linda, 1930	483	90,602	10,694	235
• Wilmington, 1932	19,500	2,477,073	311,085	1,381
*Revised to reflect only developed portion of field. Original estimate of total field reserves is 350 million bbl.				
COLORADO				
Rangely, 1933	8,659	826,379	77,621	491
FLORIDA				
Jay, 1970	3,799	391,522	20,000	54
ILLINOIS				
Clay City, 1938	1,117	408,769	5,300	474
Dale Consolidated, 1940	87	105,468	725	42
Lawrence, 1906	1,774	413,084	5,000	230
Louden, 1938	873	395,656	2,500	228
Main, 1906	1,096	245,795	4,771	401
New Harmony, 1938	627	159,724	2,201	128

State Field Disc. year	Est. 1996 prod. (1,000 bbl)	Cum prod. 1-1-97 (1,000 bbl)	Est. rem. reserves (1,000 bbl)	Est. No. prod. wells
Salem, 1938	904	233,899	2,850	21
KANSAS				
Bemis-Shutts, 1928	1,011	253,115	5,250	716
Chase-Silica, 1931	714	308,732	3,100	652
El Dorado, 1917	743	305,253	3,850	594
Hall-Gurney, 1931	761	153,332	2,950	807
Kraft-Prusa, 1937	325	131,232	2,300	343
Trapp, 1937	685	233,548	4,243	579
LOUISIANA				
Offshore				
• Bay Marchand Block 2, 1949	9,296	689,848	46,212	181
• Breton Sound Block 20, 1953	2,896	112,603	9,410	64
• Eugene Island Block 126, 1950	996	122,084	4,559	19
• Eugene Island Block 175, 1956	2,886	91,813	15,500	24
• Eugene Island Block 276, 1964	1,905	87,327	17,403	36
• Eugene Island Block 330, 1971	10,444	333,267	55,500	97
• Eugene Island Block 361, 1973	4,155	40,568	61,000	23
• Garden Banks Block 426, 1987	22,811	49,087	105,413	8
• Grand Isle Block 16, 1948	2,298	282,800	11,500	42
• Grand Isle Block 43, 1956	3,355	300,365	57,579	72
• Grand Isle Block 47, 1955	1,699	93,411	23,030	44
• Green Canyon Block 65, 1984	11,625	89,630	50,370	16
• Main Pass Block 35, 1951	482	99,015	4,258	40
• Main Pass Block 41, 1957	1,845	254,232	7,006	51
• Main Pass Block 69, 1948	3,003	260,430	14,500	86
• Main Pass Block 144, 1967	2,216	112,303	13,770	47
• Main Pass Block 299, 1962	7,540	102,705	51,667	68
• Main Pass Block 306, 1969	1,175	211,510	5,255	66
• Main Pass Block 311, 1977	3,071	73,823	30,000	49
• Mississippi Canyon Block 194, 1980	4,029	158,031	71,969	30
• Ship Shoal Block 113, 1955	2,679	98,881	25,552	40
• Ship Shoal Block 207, 1967	822	94,206	6,610	26
• Ship Shoal Block 208, 1962	2,259	181,835	10,000	33
• South Marsh Island Block 128, 1974	1,802	112,975	10,275	39
• South Marsh Island Block 130, 1975	2,895	165,917	13,500	71
• South Pass Block 24, 1950	2,773	277,965	16,671	224
• South Pass Block 27, 1954	2,297	148,911	12,500	233
• South Pass Block 61, 1968	5,996	193,290	32,000	183
• South Pass Block 62, 1965	2,901	125,913	14,500	50
• South Pass Block 65, 1965	1,637	119,648	10,533	49
• South Pass Block 89, 1969	8,000	147,232	48,500	55
• South Timbalier Block 21, 1939	2,010	232,932	10,000	43
• South Timbalier Block 135, 1956	874	148,208	4,967	23
• West Delta Block 30, 1949	5,218	491,954	29,500	103
• West Delta Block 73, 1962	3,611	226,670	53,321	59
• West Delta Block 79, 1966	1,258	147,065	13,870	42
Onshore South				
Avery Island, 1942	667	99,450	2,693	14
Bay de Chene, 1941	359	98,791	2,563	16
Bay St. Elaine, 1928	215	167,216	1,253	10
Bayou Sale, 1941	332	165,005	1,371	15
Black Bay West, 1953	1,441	158,422	3,250	61
Caillou Island, 1930	2,508	622,204	14,500	116
Cote Blanche Bay West, 1940	470	187,887	3,133	58
Cote Blanche Island, 1948	1,156	187,115	5,500	15
Delta Farms, 1944	296	119,980	2,504	27
Garden Island Bay, 1934	850	229,640	4,500	50
Golden Meadow, 1938	129	138,487	1,492	53
Grand Bay, 1938	703	176,890	1,331	49
Hackberry, East, 1927	302	112,309	4,381	34
Hackberry, West, 1928	317	148,179	2,430	95
Iberia, 1917	296	99,413	1,298	36
Jennings, 1901	159	118,101	1,327	142
Lafitte, 1935	906	264,112	3,522	45
Lake Barre, 1929	1,014	212,206	5,449	32
Lake Washington, 1931	1,555	258,270	5,900	68
Leeville, 1931	268	145,467	3,400	23
Quarantine Bay, 1937	659	178,686	7,494	21
Romere Pass, 1950	434	100,643	1,359	19
Timbalier Bay, 1938 onshore	898	305,703	13,433	65
Venice, 1937	271	185,909	3,559	18
Vinton, 1910	214	163,216	2,000	71
Weeks Island, 1945	3,395	242,786	12,500	27
West Bay, 1940	954	236,308	8,293	36
White Castle, 1929	219	93,257	6,869	28
North				
Caddo-Pine Island, 1905	2,188	381,822	6,649	9,423
Delhi, 1944	14	213,416	2,942	2
Haynesville, 1921	818	177,041	4,287	75
Homer, 1919	288	101,156	1,117	147
Nebo-Hemphill, 1940	1,880	101,215	10,262	259
Rodessa, 1935	259	108,849	1,271	73
MISSISSIPPI				
Baxterville, 1944	961	251,266	6,163	123
Heidelberg, 1944	2,217	194,037	5,174	180

U.S. fields with ultimate oil recovery exceeding 100 million bbl (continued)

Disc. State Field year	Est. 1996 prod. (1,000 bbl)	Cum prod. 1-1-97 (1,000 bbl)	Est. rem. reserves (1,000 bbl)	Est. No. prod. wells
Tinsley, 1939	445	224,509	1,608	58
MONTANA				
Cabin Creek, 1953	1,444	101,002	7,061	108
Cut Bank, 1926	443	167,667	1,990	419
Elk Basin, 1915	496	99,640	1,800	46
Pennel, 1955	2,169	93,571	13,281	170
Pine, 1951	846	112,965	4,087	84
NEW MEXICO				
Blinebry-Drinkard, 1945	956	141,224	4,564	626
Denton, 1949	650	144,628	1,715	76
Empire-Abo, 1957	609	227,773	2,808	255
Eunice-Monument, 1929	2,412	144,947	4,621	432
Grayburg-Jackson, 1929	3,595	114,273	14,500	1,046
Hobbs, 1928	3,230	336,571	15,500	269
Langlie-Mattix, 1935	1,020	134,174	5,500	608
Maljamar, 1926	1,394	156,886	7,000	516
Vacuum, 1929	7,950	500,671	26,000	678
NORTH DAKOTA				
Beaver Lodge, 1951	1,088	122,463	6,106	55
OKLAHOMA				
Bowlegs, 1927	89	163,587	1,220	84
Burbank, 1920	597	542,903	3,591	833
Cement, 1917	889	141,798	5,217	713
Cushing, 1912	1,074	507,459	5,722	1,234
Earlsboro, 1926	106	203,434	890	50
Eola-Robberson, 1921	655	139,602	1,869	402
Fitts, 1933	1,732	217,607	8,210	478
Glenn Pool, 1905	489	333,429	5,082	417
Golden Trend, 1945	2,727	500,061	23,276	1,248
Healdton, 1913	1,411	347,421	5,500	931
Hewitt, 1919	1,796	284,073	6,520	687
Little River, 1927	52	142,254	1,974	34
Oklahoma City, 1928	541	822,976	6,159	212
Postle, 1960	760	114,347	6,967	239
Seminole, 1926	130	194,827	1,196	91
Sho-Vel-Tum, 1919	12,613	1,286,820	46,000	6,161
Sooner Trend, 1965	3,063	324,685	19,751	2,741
St. Louis, 1925	439	180,518	1,960	325
TEXAS				
Dist. 1-Southwest				
Darst Creek, 1929	604	158,654	2,100	519
Luling-Branyon, 1922	967	154,711	2,314	1,326
Pearsall, 1936	2,011	151,012	36,000	584
Dist. 2-Central Gulf Coast				
Greta, 1933	227	150,563	919	56
Lake Pasture, 1953	1,045	99,126	3,500	159
Tom O'Connor, 1934	3,185	784,845	17,885	582
West Ranch, 1938	846	391,037	6,078	161
Dist. 3-Upper Gulf Coast				
Anahuac, 1935	170	288,056	1,399	29
Barbers Hill, 1916	243	113,265	1,022	88
Conroe, 1931	1,303	741,205	5,500	186
Giddings, 1971	18,880	440,093	62,745	2,308
Goose Creek, 1906	435	122,384	1,700	184
Hastings East, 1934	1,278	706,033	2,758	126
High Island, 1922	186	137,428	1,000	78
Hull, 1918	444	171,262	2,616	230
Humble, 1905	143	99,465	954	137
Magnet Withers, 1936	909	120,323	6,416	123
Manvel, 1931	308	103,139	1,541	52
Oyster Bayou, 1941	401	164,250	1,528	28
Raccoon Bend, 1927	313	104,314	1,351	88
Sour Lake, 1902	585	102,193	7,540	355
Thompson, 1921	1,169	486,805	6,242	131
Tomball, 1933	143	122,877	700	33
Webster, 1937	1,777	594,281	11,114	153
West Columbia, 1917	179	102,343	2,132	64
Dist. 4-South				
Agua Dulce-Stratton, 1928	198	148,070	1,430	56
Borregos, 1945	62	114,874	605	18
Kelsey, 1938	64	116,015	841	28
Plymouth, 1925	102	124,162	1,961	31
Seeligson, 1925	127	272,693	750	34
TCB, 1944	61	113,568	615	8
White Point, E., 1938	32	104,631	589	10
Dist. 5-East				
Van, 1928	1,592	540,125	7,052	461
Dist. 6-East				
East Texas, 1930	23,311	5,252,730	116,879	6,611
Fairway, 1960	2,080	208,380	12,500	109
Hawkins, 1940	3,535	862,072	23,500	327
Neches, 1953	449	109,707	2,000	107
Quitman, 1948	664	128,951	2,579	89
Talco, 1931	791	284,021	7,427	239
Dist. 7B-West				
Stephens County Reg., 1916	3,454	169,459	16,000	969
Dist. 7C-West Central				
Big Lake, 1923	302	133,208	1,500	73
McCamey, 1925	151	126,122	750	270
Pegasus, 1949	894	142,572	4,500	178
Dist. 8-West				
Andector, 1946	517	185,841	2,800	35
Block 31, 1945	1,265	237,446	8,973	178
Cowden, N., 1930	10,311	588,754	50,000	1,360
Cowden, S., Foster Johnson, 1930	5,119	555,833	27,500	1,375
Dollarhide, 1945	2,815	215,991	19,794	289
Dune, 1938	1,237	198,173	7,000	566
Fuhrman-Mascho, 1930	1,008	115,868	4,500	683
Fullerton, 1942	6,749	405,283	34,000	1,015
Goldsmith, 1934	4,119	794,947	25,294	1,241
Hendrick, 1926	402	256,021	2,200	170
Howard-Glasscock, 1925	4,232	443,633	19,000	1,753
Iatan, E., 1926	2,190	163,138	14,865	1,183
Jordan, 1937	775	135,060	3,172	204
Kermit, 1928	309	116,240	1,917	389
Keystone, 1930	1,287	324,127	6,043	567
Mabee, 1943	2,390	105,547	13,301	377
McElroy, 1926	7,773	532,438	36,052	1,232
Means, 1934	4,545	271,367	27,528	715
Midland Farms, 1944	1,588	259,535	8,435	197
Penwell, 1926	1,585	120,701	8,210	330
Sand Hills, 1931	2,244	265,760	12,279	1,092
Shafter Lake, 1947	1,030	104,427	5,418	428
Spraberry Trend, 1951	21,250	791,596	95,253	8,420
TXL, 1944	1,187	274,320	9,764	509
Waddell, 1927	889	105,503	2,595	157
Ward, S., 1938	350	108,740	1,720	538
Ward Estes, N., 1929	2,070	388,629	25,984	699
Westbrook, 1920	1,294	101,640	6,769	504
Yates, 1926	20,340	1,336,028	618,477	672
Dist. 8A-West				
Adair, 1947	881	114,854	3,221	131
Anton-Irish, 1944	1,544	194,813	11,702	189
Cedar Lake, 1939	2,511	93,490	15,240	211
Cogdell, 1949	551	299,226	4,167	160
Diamond M, 1948	1,227	250,729	6,997	236
Garza, 1926	2,190	125,106	11,251	523
Jo-Mill, 1953	2,335	145,181	10,909	304
Kelly-Snyder, 1948	3,330	1,292,337	57,663	427
Levelland, 1938	13,296	604,740	49,615	3,017
Prentice, 1951	3,075	195,463	27,662	366
Robertson, N., 1956	5,229	108,274	32,015	608
Salt Creek, 1950	9,569	322,037	49,824	184
Seminole, 1936	12,611	644,329	62,500	434
Sharon Ridge, 1923	1,431	99,013	12,240	1,923
Slaughter, 1936	15,501	1,162,318	81,436	2,399
Wasson, 1936	27,689	1,936,490	150,134	1,951
Welch, 1942	2,388	165,262	22,522	724
Dist. 9-North				
Archer County Reg., 1911	1,020	188,807	6,461	3,683
Cooke County Reg., 1926	690	106,848	3,935	1,416
K-M-A, 1931	832	146,717	3,127	607
Walnut Bend, 1938	377	126,671	2,325	139
Wichita County Reg., 1910	2,006	351,998	10,051	6,804
Wilbarger County Reg., 1915	475	149,939	2,375	834
Young County Reg., 1917	945	106,523	3,230	2,435
Dist. 10-Panhandle				
Panhandle, 1921	5,197	1,470,454	36,445	10,243
UTAH				
Altamont, 1955	2,070	110,620	17,510	205
Bluebell, 1949	2,880	138,122	18,602	216
Greater Aneth, 1956	5,684	398,900	27,127	474
WYOMING				
Byron, 1918	677	126,760	2,757	61
Elk Basin, 1915	1,833	450,273	12,784	162
Frannie, 1928	308	120,044	1,597	40
Garland, 1906	1,911	180,851	7,807	254
Grass Creek, 1914	1,411	199,898	6,624	227
Hamilton Dome, 1918	1,870	247,769	6,310	230
Hartzog Draw, 1976	2,202	94,392	13,232	146
Lance Creek, 1918	111	108,948	1,040	19
Little Buffalo Basin, 1914	855	130,547	3,386	103
Lost Soldier, 1916	2,650	234,874	26,443	87
Oregon Basin, 1912	4,515	437,367	21,060	424
Salt Creek, 1889	2,413	656,448	19,699	908
Steamboat Butte, 1943	262	93,363	2,108	27
Wertz, 1921	625	112,948	12,200	38

Sources: OGJ estimates from operator, Petroleum Information Corp., state geological survey, and oil and gas agency data

• Field partly or wholly offshore.

Anonima petroli italiana Spa (API) group's refinery at Falconara Maritima, Italy. Photo courtesy of API.

Refining survey

YOUR USE OF THE INTERNATIONAL REFINING survey may be aided by the following information:

All country-by-country volumes are presented in calendar-day figures. When an asterisk (*) appears beside a location, this indicates that the figure was reported as a stream-day figure and has been converted to a calendar-day figure using the conversion factor of 0.95 for crude oil, and 0.90 for cat cracking and cat reforming units.

Barrels per calendar day (b/cd) is the maximum number of barrels of input that can be expressed during a 24-hr period, after making allowances for the following:

- Types and grades of inputs to be processed
- Types and grades of products to be manufactured
- Environmental constraints associated with refining operations
- Scheduled downtime such as technical problems, repairs, and slowdowns.

Barrels per stream day (b/sd) is the amount a unit can process when running at full capacity under optimal feedstock and product slate conditions. IPE

LEGEND

Catalytic cracking
1. Fluid
2. Other

Catalytic reforming
1. Semiregenerative
2. Cyclic
3. Continuous regeneration
4. Other

Cat reforming definitions are:

- **Semiregenerative** reforming is characterized by shutdown of the reforming unit at specified intervals, or at the operator's convenience, for in situ catalyst regeneration.
- **Cyclic regeneration** reforming is characterized by continuous or continual regeneration of catalyst in situ in any one of several reactors that can be isolated from and returned to the reforming operation. This is accomplished without changing feed rate or octane.
- **Continuous regeneration** reforming is characterized by the continuous regeneration of part of the catalyst in a special regenerator, followed by continuous addition of this regenerated catalyst to the reactor.
- **Other** includes nonregenerative reforming (catalyst is replaced by fresh catalyst) and moving-bed catalyst systems.

Footnotes:
A. Merger of Ampol and Caltex. **B.** TCC. **C.** Houdry. **D.** Joint venture of Trans Hydrocarbon Ltd. and Kyrgyzneft. **E.** Previously listed as Kremenchugne. **F.** Previously listed as Suez Oil Processing Co. **G.** Merger of Oberrheinische Mineralolwerke GmbH and Esso AG. **H.** Estimate. **I.** Previously listed as Kyung In Energy Co. Ltd. **J.** Previously listed as Kukdong Oil Co. Ltd. **K.** Previously listed as Rafinerija Skopje. **L.** Previously listed as Petromed. **M.** Previously listed as Ertoil SA. **N.** Previously listed as OK Raffinaderi AB. **O.** Joint venture of LG-Caltex and Government of Thailand. **P.** Gulf Oil's share of Pembroke CC Complex. **Q.** Previously listed as Louisiana Land & Exploration Co. **R.** Previously listed as Shell Oil Products Co. **S.** Leased by Gold Line Refining Ltd. **T.** Previously listed as Phibro Refining Co. **U.** Nonregenerative. **V.** Joint venture of Citgo and Conoco. **W.** Previously listed as Bayway Refining Co. **X.** Previously listed as Wynnwood Refining Co. **Y.** Includes assets of Southwestern Refining Co. Inc. **Z.** HOC.

Survey of operating refineries worldwide

(capacities as of January 1, 1997)

Country	No. plants	b/cd Crude capacity	b/cd Catalytic cracking	b/cd Catalytic reforming
Abu Dhabi	2	212,800	....	29,880
Albania	3	40,000	....	....
Algeria	5	465,000	....	59,000
Angola	1	32,100	....	1,900
Argentina	12	664,980	181,876	58,678
Australia	10	771,250	219,900	192,400
Austria	1	210,000	25,800	33,700
Bahrain	1	248,900	41,400	15,300
Bangladesh	1	31,200	....	1,650
Barbados	1	4,000	....	....
Belgium	4	629,750	110,900	98,440
Bolivia	3	47,888	....	13,104
Brazil	13	1,256,060	333,604	3,000
Brunei	1	8,600	....	5,700
Bulgaria	3	300,000	....	....
Cameroon	1	42,000	....	7,000
Canada	22	1,851,810	386,900	348,900
Chile	3	192,290	45,757	16,497
China	34	2,867,000	855,000	142,000
Colombia	5	248,850	90,000	....
C.I.S.	57	9,848,876	564,338	1,168,155
Congo	1	21,000	....	2,000
Costa Rica	1	15,000	....	1,200
Croatia	3	294,275	32,000	37,400
Cuba	4	301,400	14,700	20,000
Cyprus	1	26,000	....	5,100
Czech Republic	4	187,139	....	24,798
Denmark	3	189,100	....	32,300
Dominican Republic	2	50,000	....	9,700
Ecuador	4	148,000	....	2,800
Egypt	8	546,060	....	33,540
El Salvador	1	20,500	....	....
Eritrea	1	18,000	....	2,400
Finland	2	200,000	45,200	42,800
France	14	1,785,580	356,060	245,280
Gabon	1	17,300	....	1,400
Germany	18	2,108,300	275,750	398,503
Ghana	1	26,600	....	5,850
Greece	4	395,500	66,400	51,600
Guatemala	2	20,000	....	3,000
Honduras	1	14,000	....	1,800
Hungary	3	232,000	24,000	29,600
India	12	1,086,371	138,205	28,874
Indonesia	7	804,745	18,450	92,970
Iran	8	1,242,000	30,000	124,570
Iraq	8	347,500	....	43,500
Ireland	1	65,000	....	12,000
Israel	2	220,000	49,500	26,500
Italy	17	2,261,818	298,400	286,795
Ivory Coast	2	64,000	....	9,000
Jamaica	1	35,500	....	3,540
Japan	40	4,989,020	758,450	704,972
Jordan	1	100,000	4,350	8,640
Kenya	1	85,500	....	9,000
Korea, North	2	71,000	....	7,300
Korea, South	6	2,211,250	108,000	166,370
Kuwait	3	824,000	28,000	48,000
Lebanon	2	37,500	7,250	7,442
Liberia	1	15,000	....	2,000
Libya	3	348,400	....	14,440
Lithuania	1	240,000	41,063	24,335
Macedonia	1	51,180	....	10,780
Madagascar	1	15,000	....	2,000
Malaysia	4	330,000	....	52,600
Martinique	1	16,000	....	3,000
Mexico	6	1,520,000	343,000	227,800
Morocco	2	155,600	5,040	26,800
Myanmar	2	32,000	....	....
Netherlands	6	1,186,500	137,400	168,780
Netherlands Antilles	2	525,000	49,000	20,000
New Zealand	1	91,200	....	22,500
Nicaragua	1	16,500	3,500	....
Nigeria	4	433,250	82,700	70,070
Norway	3	307,000	48,000	48,700
Oman	1	85,000	....	16,000
Pakistan	3	137,325	....	6,500
Panama	1	60,000	11,000	....
Paraguay	1	7,500	....	....
Peru	5	182,250	23,300	....
Philippines	4	323,050	26,000	43,200
Poland	7	352,000	46,000	39,000
Portugal	2	304,172	31,500	50,182
Puerto Rico	2	134,000	14,200	26,000
Qatar	1	57,500	....	11,500
Romania	10	558,770	108,192	75,629
Saudi Arabia	8	1,650,700	103,600	193,360
Senegal	1	17,000	....	2,000
Serbia	2	167,264	21,000	21,610
Sierra Leone	1	10,000	....	....
Singapore	4	1,157,000	59,600	127,900
Slovakia	1	115,000	....	22,270
Slovenia	1	12,000	....	....
Somalia	1	10,000	....	....
South Africa	4	414,150	87,000	72,700
Spain	10	1,295,650	178,100	194,450
Sri Lanka	1	47,500	....	3,375
Sudan	1	21,700	....	1,900
Sweden	5	427,000	29,700	69,900
Switzerland	2	132,000	....	26,000
Syria	2	245,890	....	28,581
Taiwan	2	770,000	50,000	140,000
Tanzania	1	15,865	....	8,721
Thailand	4	558,250	71,500	67,850
Trinidad	2	245,000	25,000	31,000
Tunisia	1	34,000	....	3,300
Turkey	5	683,095	37,740	64,757
United Kingdom	15	1,940,990	484,550	333,700
United States	163	15,459,240	5,178,061	3,646,073
Uruguay	1	40,000	9,000	3,000
Venezuela	6	1,177,000	234,900	47,200
Virgin Islands	1	545,000	110,000	125,000
Yemen	2	120,000	....	8,500
Zaire	1	17,000	....	3,500
Zambia	1	24,500	....	5,600
Total	**700**	**75,871,303**	**12,759,836**	**10,939,911**

WORLDWIDE REFINING	b/cd Crude capacity	Catalytic cracking	Catalytic reforming
ABU DHABI			
Abu Dhabi National Oil Co.—Ruwais*	132,050	....	[1]17,280
Umm Al-Nar 2*	80,750	....	[3]12,600
Total	**212,800**	**....**	**29,880**
ALBANIA			
Government-owned refineries at Ballsh, Cerrik, Stalin	40,000	....	....
Total	**40,000**	**....**	**....**
ALGERIA			
Sonatrach—Ain Amenas	7,000	....	....
Arzew	60,000	....	11,600
Hassi Messaoud	30,000	....	2,400
Maison Carree	58,000	....	15,000
Skikda	310,000	....	30,000
Total	**465,000**	**....**	**59,000**
ANGOLA			
Fina Petroleos De Angola—Luanda	32,100	....	[1]1,900
Total	**32,100**	**....**	**1,900**
ARGENTINA			
Destileria Argentina de Petroleo SA—Dock Sud	4,000	....	....
Lomas de Zamora	8,000	....	....
Eg[3] SA—Bahia Blanca*	28,980	[1]7,076	[1]5,378
Esso SAPA—Campana	88,100	[1]27,300	[1]11,200
Galvan	19,000	....	....
Refinor SA—Campo Duran	32,000	....	....
Refisan SA—San Lorenzo	37,600	....	....
Shell Cia. Argentina de Petroleo SA—Buenos Aires	121,700	[1]29,200	[1]17,900
Sol Petroleo SA—San Francisco Solama, Quilmes	6,000	....	....
YPF SA—La Plata	176,000	[1]73,600	[1]11,700
Lujan de Cuyo	120,000	[1]44,700	[1]9,500
Plaza Huincul	23,600	....	[1]3,000
Total	**664,980**	**181,876**	**58,678**
AUSTRALIA			
Ampol Refineries (NSW) Pty. Ltd.[A]—Kurnell	115,000	[1]46,000	[1]28,500
Ampol Refineries (Q'land) Ltd.[A]—Lytton	100,000	[1]32,000	[3]25,000
Australian Lubricating Oil Refinery Ltd.—Kurnell	....	....	....
BP Australia—Bulwer Island*	69,350	[1]18,000	[1]12,600
Kwinana*	125,400	[1]27,900	[3]19,800
Inland Oil Refiners (Qld) Pty. Ltd.—Eromanga	1,500	....	....
Mobil Oil Australia, Ltd.—Adelaide	67,000	....	[1]24,000
Altona	103,000	[B2]23,000	[1]31,500
Shell Refining (Australia) Pty. Ltd.—Clyde	80,000	[1]35,000	[3]20,000
Geelong	110,000	[1]38,000	[1]11,000 [3]20,000
Total	**771,250**	**219,900**	**192,400**
AUSTRIA			
OeMV AG—Schwechat	210,000	[1]25,800	[1]15,600 [3]18,100
Total	**210,000**	**25,800**	**33,700**
BAHRAIN			
Bahrain Petroleum Co.—Sitra*	248,900	[1]41,400	[1]15,300
Total	**248,900**	**41,400**	**15,300**
BANGLADESH			
Eastern Refinery Ltd.—Chittagong	31,200	....	[1]1,650
Total	**31,200**	**....**	**1,650**
BARBADOS			
Mobil Oil Barbados Ltd.—Bridgetown	4,000	....	....
Total	**4,000**	**....**	**....**
BELGIUM			
Belgian Refining Corp. NV—Antwerp*	80,750	....	[1]9,900
Esso Belgium—Antwerp	246,000	[1]33,300	[3]38,540
Fina Raffinaderij Antwerpen—Antwerp	288,000	[1]77,600	[3]50,000
Nynas Petroleum NV—Antwerp	15,000	....	....
Total	**629,750**	**110,900**	**98,440**
BOLIVIA			
Yacimientos Petroliferos Fiscales Bolivianos—Cochabamba*	25,888	....	[1]7,344
Santa Cruz*	19,000	....	[1]5,760
Sucre	3,000	....	....
Total	**47,888**	**....**	**13,104**
BRAZIL			
Petroleo Brasileiro SA—Araucaria, Parana	159,210	[1]45,700	....
Betim, Minas Gerais	136,470	[1]33,080	....
Canoas, Rio Grande do Sul	68,230	[1]14,040	....
Capuava, Sao Paulo	38,100	[2]11,580	....
Cubatao, Sao Paulo	....	[1]49,620	....
Duque de Caxias, Rio de Janeiro	225,730	[1]41,360	....
Fortaleza, Ceara	....	....	....
Manaus, Amazonas	10,230	[1]2,200	....
Mataripe, Bahia	117,960	[1]24,810	....
Paulinia, Sao Paulo	272,930	[1]50,314	....
Sao Jose dos Campos, Sao Paulo	204,700	[1]57,900	....
Refinaria de Petroleo Ipiranga SA—Rio Grande do Sul	12,500	[1]3,000	....
Refinaria de Petroleos de Manguinhos SA—Rio de Janeiro	10,000	....	[1]3,000
Total	**1,256,060**	**333,604**	**3,000**
BRUNEI			
Brunei Shell Petroleum Co. Sdn. Bhd.—Seria	8,600	....	[1]5,700
Total	**8,600**	**....**	**5,700**
BULGARIA			
Total Bulgaria—Government-owned refineries at Burgas, Pleven, Ruse	300,000	....	....
Total	**300,000**	**....**	**....**
CAMEROON			
Ste. Nationale de Raffinage—Cape Limboh Limbe	42,000	....	[1]7,000
Total	**42,000**	**....**	**7,000**
CANADA			
Alberta			
Husky Oil Operations Ltd.—Lloydminster	23,500	....	....
Imperial Oil Ltd.—Edmonton	176,000	[1]50,000	[2]20,900
Parkland Refining Ltd.—Bowden	6,000	....	[1]2,800
Petro-Canada Products Inc.—Edmonton	119,000	[1]34,300	[1]15,300
Shell Canada Ltd.—Scotford	75,700	....	[3]21,500
Total	**400,200**	**84,300**	**60,500**

WORLDWIDE REFINING	b/cd Crude capacity	Catalytic cracking	Catalytic reforming
British Columbia			
Chevron Canada Ltd.—North Burnaby	50,000	[1]18,000	[1]10,000
Husky Oil Operations Ltd.—Prince George	9,500	[1]3,300	[1]1,400
Total	**59,500**	**21,300**	**11,400**
New Brunswick			
Irving Oil Ltd.—St. John	237,500	[1]24,000	[1]34,650
Total	**237,500**	**24,000**	**34,650**
Newfoundland			
North Atlantic Refining Ltd.—Come By Chance*	99,750	....	[1]23,400
Total	**99,750**	**....**	**23,400**
Nova Scotia			
Imperial Oil Ltd.—Dartmouth	84,360	[1]28,500	[2]10,300
Total	**84,360**	**28,500**	**10,300**
Ontario			
Imperial Oil Ltd.—Nanticoke	112,000	[1]40,850	[3]27,400
Sarnia	118,000	[1]25,650	[1]16,150
			[2]16,600
Novacor Chemicals (Canada) Ltd.—-Corunna	80,000	....	....
Petro-Canada Products Inc.—Mississauga	....	....	[3]9,800
Oakville	80,500	[1]25,400	[1]13,400
Shell Canada Ltd.—Sarnia	71,400	[1]14,400	[1]21,000
Sunoco Inc.—Sarnia	83,400	[C2]15,500	[1]24,700
Total	**545,300**	**121,800**	**129,050**
Quebec			
Petro-Canada Products Inc.—Montreal	92,500	[1]18,400	[1]30,400
Shell Canada Ltd.—Montreal	125,500	[1]24,000	[1]20,700
Ultramar Canada Inc.—St. Romuald	150,000	[1]47,000	[1]19,500
Total	**368,000**	**89,400**	**70,600**
Saskatchewan			
Consumers' Cooperative Refineries Ltd.—Regina	45,200	[1]17,600	[1]9,000
Moose Jaw Asphalt Inc.—Moose Jaw	12,000	....	....
Total	**57,200**	**17,600**	**9,000**

CHILE

ENAP—Gregorio-Magallanes	9,650	....	....
Petrox SA—Talcahuano	100,640	[1]20,757	[2]4,497
Refineria de Petroleo Concon SA—Concon	82,000	[1]25,000	[1]12,000
Total	**192,290**	**45,757**	**16,497**

CHINA

Sinopec—Anqing	60,000	24,000	....
Anshan	50,000	2,000	....
Baling	100,000	50,000	3,000
Cangzhou	24,000	9,000	....
Dalian	142,000	70,000	3,000
Daqing	110,000	14,000	4,000
Dushanzi	66,000	12,000	6,000
Fujian	50,000	16,000	....
Fushun	174,000	66,000	23,000
Gaoqiao	146,000	38,000	4,000
Guangzhou	104,000	44,000	8,000
Harbin	30,000	6,000	....
Jinan	60,000	22,000	....
Jingmen	100,000	20,000	3,000
Jinling	134,000	44,000	3,000
Jinshan	106,000	....	8,000
Jinxi	100,000	24,000	3,000
Jinzhou	110,000	16,000	6,000
Jiujiang	50,000	24,000	3,000
Lanzhou	100,000	24,000	2,000
Lanzhou Pet.	17,000	....	....
Liaoyang	30,000	....	3,000
Linyuan	30,000	17,000	....
Luoyang	60,000	40,000	14,000
Maoming	170,000	32,000	3,000
Qianguo	30,000	24,000	....
Qilu	160,000	46,000	3,000
Shjiazhuang	70,000	24,000	....
Tianjin	74,000	35,000	4,000
Urumqi	50,000	16,000	3,000
Wuhan	50,000	20,000	....

WORLDWIDE REFINING	b/cd Crude capacity	Catalytic cracking	Catalytic reforming
Yangzi	60,000	....	21,000
Yanshan	140,000	48,000	3,000
Zhenhai	110,000	28,000	9,000
Total	**2,867,000**	**855,000**	**142,000**

COLOMBIA

Empresa Colombiana de Petroleos—Apiay	2,250	....	....
Barrancabermeja-Santander	173,000	[1]64,000	....
Cartagena, Bolivar	70,000	[1]26,000	....
Orito, Putumayo	1,800	....	....
Tibu, N. de Santander	1,800	....	....
Total	**248,850**	**90,000**	**....**

COMMONWEALTH OF INDEPENDENT STATES (and former Soviet Union)

Azerbaijan			
Baku	238,978	....	....
Novo-Baku	202,830	[1]71,342	[3]24,466
Total	**441,808**	**71,342**	**24,466**
Belarus			
Mozyr	323,323	....	[1]49,176
P.O. Naftan Refinery —Novopolotsk	150,000	....	[1]20,000
Total	**473,323**	**....**	**69,176**
Georgia			
Batumi	106,436	....	[1]10,276
Total	**106,436**	**....**	**10,276**
Kazakhstan			
Atyrau	104,427	....	[1]8,808
Vitol Beheer BV—Chimkent	160,000	....	[1]24,466
Pavlodar	162,666	[1]38,356	[1]26,178
Total	**427,093**	**38,356**	**59,452**
Kyrgyz			
Kyrgoil[D]—Dzhalalabad	10,000	....	....
Total	**10,000**	**....**	**....**
Russia			
Joint Stock Co. Achinsk Refinery—Achinsk	146,584	....	[1]25,519
Lukoil—Perm	279,142	[2]15,726	[1]42,326
Volgograd	188,733	....	[1]18,839
Government —Angarsk	463,899	[1]33,753	[1]33,029
			[4]12,233
Aripsky	28,115	....	[1]16,147
Astrakhan	66,000	....	[1]24,466
Cracking-Saratov	176,723	....	[1]27,891
Groznyi-former Lenin	389,595	[1]38,356	....
Groznyi-Sheripov	40,164	....	[1]8,074
Khabarovsk	114,468	....	[1]9,786
Kirishi	387,586	....	[1]67,281
Komsomolsk	116,477	....	....
Kondpetroleum	6,000	....	....
Krasnodar	34,140	....	....
Kutshui	8,000	....	[1]1,750
Makhachkala	4,000	....	....
Moscow	242,995	[1]38,356	[1]33,029
Nizhnekamsk	120,493	....	....
Norsi-Nizhniy Novgorod	437,792	....	[1]45,506
Novo-Grozny	....	....	[1]16,881
Novo-Kuibishev	309,266	[2]13,616	[1]33,518
Novo-Ufa	379,553	[2]22,247	[1]50,399
Omsk	566,318	[1]65,589	[1]48,687
			[3]24,710
Orsk	158,649	....	[1]17,860
Ryazan	361,479	[1]18,219	[1]53,335
Salavatnefteorgsintez	247,011	[2]21,096	[1]48,687
Samara-Kuibishev	120,493	[2]18,795	[1]43,794
Surgut	88,000	....	5,000
Syzran	210,863	[2]17,068	[1]43,060
Tuapse	46,189	....	[1]7,829
Ufa-former Lenin	234,962	[1]38,356	[1]14,679
Ufaneftekhim	251,027	[1]17,260	[1]17,371
			[3]21,775
Ukhta	126,518	....	[1]9,297
Urayneftegaz	2,000	....	....
Urengol	9,000	....	....

WORLDWIDE REFINING	Crude capacity (b/cd)	Catalytic cracking (b/cd)	Catalytic reforming (b/cd)
Yakutsk	2,500	....	....
Yaroslavnefteorgsintez	359,471	[1]21,096	[1]25,689
Yaraslav-Mendeleev	8,700	....	....
Total	**6,732,905**	**379,533**	**848,447**
Turkmenistan			
Chardzou	120,493	....	[1]24,466
Turkmenbashi	116,477	[1]15,151	[1]8,074
Total	**236,970**	**15,151**	**32,540**
Ukraine			
Drogobich	78,321	....	[1]8,074
Lisitchansk	481,973	[1]30,356	[1]56,761
Kherson	172,707	....	[1]16,637
Uktatnafta[E]—Kremenchug*	360,000	[1]29,600	....
Nadvornaja	74,304	....	[1]8,563
Odessa	78,321	....	[1]10,276
Total	**1,245,626**	**59,956**	**100,311**
Uzbekistan			
Alty-Arik	66,271	....	....
Fergana	108,444	....	[1]23,487
Total	**174,715**	**....**	**23,487**

CONGO

Coraf—Pointe-Noire	21,000	....	[1]2,000
Total	**21,000**	**....**	**2,000**

COSTA RICA

Refinadora Costarricense de Petroleo SA—Limon	15,000	....	[1]1,200
Total	**15,000**	**....**	**1,200**

CROATIA

Ina d.d. Zagreb Rafinerija Rijeka—Rijeka	150,000	[1]22,000	[1]18,400
Ina-Industrija Nafte d.d. Zagreb—Sisak	143,472	[1]10,000	[1]19,000
Ina d.d. Rafinerija Zagreb—Zagreb	803	....	....
Total	**294,275**	**32,000**	**37,400**

CUBA

Cienfuegos	76,000	....	[1]7,500
Ermonos Dias, Santjago	101,500	....	[1]7,500
Niko Lopes, Habana	121,800	[1]14,700	[1]5,000
Serhio Soto, Cabaiguan	2,100	....	....
Total	**301,400**	**14,700**	**20,000**

CYPRUS

Cyprus Petroleum Refinery Ltd.—Larnaca	26,000	....	[1]5,100
Total	**26,000**	**....**	**5,100**

CZECH REPUBLIC

Chemopetrol a.s.—Litvinov	100,000	....	16,600
Kaucuk s.p.—Kralupy*	66,850	....	[1]8,198
Koramo Kolin—Kolin	....	....	....
Paramo A.S.—Pardubice	20,289	....	....
Total	**187,139**	**....**	**24,798**

DENMARK

AS Dansk Shell—Fredericia	66,700	....	[1]12,900
Dansk Statoil AS—Kalundborg	65,000	....	[1]8,600
Kuwait Petroleum Refining (Danmark) A/S—Gulfhavn	57,400	....	[1]10,800
Total	**189,100**	**....**	**32,300**

DOMINICAN REPUBLIC

Falconbridge Dominicana C por A—Bonao	16,000	....	....
Refineria Dominicana de Petroleo SA—Haina	34,000	....	[1]9,700
Total	**50,000**	**....**	**9,700**

ECUADOR

WORLDWIDE REFINING	Crude capacity (b/cd)	Catalytic cracking (b/cd)	Catalytic reforming (b/cd)
Petroecuador—Esmeraldas	90,000	....	[1]2,800
La Libertad	47,000	....	....
Refineria Amazonas	10,000	....	....
Lago-Agrio	1,000	....	....
Total	**148,000**	**....**	**2,800**

EGYPT

Alexandria Petroleum Co.—Alexandria (El-Mex)	94,860	....	....
Ameria Petroleum Refining Co.—Alexandria	68,620	....	[1]12,000
Assyout Petroleum Refining Co.[F]—Assyout	43,540	....	....
Cairo Petroleum Refining Co.—Mostorod	141,160	....	[1]9,000
Tanta	29,000	....	....
El-Nasr Petroleum Co.—El-Suez	99,300	....	....
Wadi-Feran	7,060	....	....
Suez Petroleum Processing Co.—El-Suez	62,520	....	[1]12,540
Total	**546,060**	**....**	**33,540**

EL SALVADOR

Refineria Petrolera Acajutla SA—Acajutla	20,500	....	....
Total	**20,500**	**....**	**....**

ERITREA

Petroleum Corp. of Eritrea—Assab	18,000	....	[2]2,400
Total	**18,000**	**....**	**2,400**

FINLAND

Neste Oy—Naantali	40,000	[2]14,200	[4]6,800
Porvoo	160,000	[1]31,000	[4]36,000
Total	**200,000**	**45,200**	**42,800**

FRANCE

Cie. de Raffinage et de Distribution Total France—Gonfreville L'Orcher	211,000	[1]40,000	[1]45,000
La Mede	127,000	[1]30,000	[2]24,000
Mardyck	127,000	[1]32,000	[2]22,000
Cie. Rhenane de Raffinage—Reichstett-Vendenheim*	76,000	[1]12,600	[1]14,400
Elf France—Donges	214,300	[1]49,400	[1]29,280
Feyzin	128,130	[1]24,940	[1]9,200
Grandpuits	98,000	[1]30,720	[1]14,800
Esso SAF—Fos sur Mer	117,000	[1]25,000	....
Port Jerome	156,000	[1]29,500	[1]18,000
Mobil Oil Francaise—Notre Dame de Gravenchon*	63,650	....	[1]10,800
Ste. des Petroles Shell—Berre l'Etang	127,000	[1]34,000	[1]19,000
Petit Couronne	141,000	[1]20,000	[1]28,000
Ste. Francaise des Petroles BP—Dunkirk	....	....	....
Lavera*	199,500	[1]27,900	[1]10,800
Total	**1,785,580**	**356,060**	**245,280**

GABON

Ste. Gabonaise de Raffinage—Port Gentil	17,300	....	[1]1,400
Total	**17,300**	**....**	**1,400**

GERMANY

Addinol Mineralol GmbH—Krumpa	....	....	....
Beta Raffineriegesellschaft Wilhelmshaven mbH—Wilhelmshaven	180,000	....	[1]40,200
BP Oil Deutschland GmbH—Hamburg	....	....	....
DEA Mineraloel AG—Heide/Grasbrook	80,000	[B2]9,000	[2]20,000
Wesseling	120,000	....	[2]21,000
Deutsche Shell AG—Godorf	170,000	....	[1]17,000 [3]21,000
Harburg	98,000	[1]16,000	[3]17,000
Erdoel Raffinerie Neustadt GmbH—Neustadt-Donau	125,400	[1]23,400	[1]18,000
Esso AG—Ingolstadt	105,000	[1]27,500	[1]18,200
Holborn Europa Raffinerie GmbH—Harburg	78,000	[1]18,750	[1]14,700
Leuna Raffineriegesellschaft mbH—Leuna	100,000	....	[1]15,000
Mineraloelraffinerie Oberrhein GmbH[G]—Karlsruhe	325,800	[1]74,000	[1]45,800 [3]21,300
OMV AG—Burghausen	72,000	....	....
PCK Schwedt AG—Schwedt	230,000	[1]51,000	[1]16,000 [3]18,000
Raffineriegesellschaft—Vohburg/Ingolstadt*	114,000	[1]35,100	[1]16,200 [3]17,100

WORLDWIDE REFINING	Crude capacity (b/cd)	Catalytic cracking (b/cd)	Catalytic reforming (b/cd)
Veba Oel/Ruhr Oel GmbH—Gelsenkirchen	227,000	[1]21,000	[3]27,000
Wintershall AG—Lingen	80,000	....	[1]13,843 [3]21,160
Schmierstoff Raffinerie—Salzbergen	3,100	....	....
Total	**2,108,300**	**275,750**	**398,503**

GHANA

WORLDWIDE REFINING	Crude capacity	Catalytic cracking	Catalytic reforming
Tema Oil Refinery Co. Ltd.—Tema*	26,600	....	[1]5,850
Total	**26,600**	**....**	**5,850**

GREECE

WORLDWIDE REFINING	Crude capacity	Catalytic cracking	Catalytic reforming
EKO-Hellenic Refineries & Chemicals of Macedonia Industrial & Commerical Co. SA—Thessaloniki	66,500	....	[2]8,100
Hellenic Aspropyrgos Refinery SA—Aspropyrgos	121,000	[1]36,000	[1]9,800 [3]21,000
Motor Oil (Hellas) Corinth Refineries SA—Aghii Theodori	100,000	[1]30,400	[2]12,700
Petrola Hellas SA—Elefsis	108,000	....	....
Total	**395,500**	**66,400**	**51,600**

GUATEMALA

WORLDWIDE REFINING	Crude capacity	Catalytic cracking	Catalytic reforming
Basic Resources International—Peten	4,000	....	....
Texas Petroleum Co.—Escuintla	16,000	....	[1]3,000
Total	**20,000**	**....**	**3,000**

HONDURAS

WORLDWIDE REFINING	Crude capacity	Catalytic cracking	Catalytic reforming
Refineria Texas de Honduras SA—Puerto Cortes	14,000	....	[1]1,800
Total	**14,000**	**....**	**1,800**

HUNGARY

WORLDWIDE REFINING	Crude capacity	Catalytic cracking	Catalytic reforming
Mol Rt. - Danube Refinery—Szazhalombatta	161,000	[1]24,000	[1]16,000 [3]13,600
Mol Rt. - Tiszai Refinery—Tiszaujvaros	61,000	....	....
Mol Rt. - Zalai Refinery—Zalaegerszeg	10,000	....	....
Total	**232,000**	**24,000**	**29,600**

INDIA

WORLDWIDE REFINING	Crude capacity	Catalytic cracking	Catalytic reforming
Bharat Petroleum Co. Ltd.—Mahul Bombay	134,860	[1]28,755	[1]5,503
Bongaigaon Refinery & Petrochemicals Ltd.—Bongaigaon Assam	27,110	....	[1]1,833
Cochin Refineries Ltd.—Ambalamugal	93,400	[1]27,000	[1]5,800
Hindustan Petroleum Co. Ltd.—Mahul Bombay	110,452	[1]12,000	....
Visakhapatnam	90,369	[1]19,200	....
Indian Oil Co. Ltd.—Barauni, Bihar	65,800	....	....
Digboi, Assam	11,700	....	....
Gawahati, Assam	19,920	....	....
Koyali, Gujarat	185,100	[1]20,000	[1]8,300
Haldia, West Bengal	61,000	....	[1]5,300
Mathura, Uttar Pradesh	156,000	[1]20,000	....
Madras Refineries Ltd.—Madras	130,660	[1]11,250	[1]2,138
Total	**1,086,371**	**138,205**	**28,874**

INDONESIA

WORLDWIDE REFINING	Crude capacity	Catalytic cracking	Catalytic reforming
Pertamina—Balikpapan, Kalimantan	240,920	....	[3]18,720
Cepu	3,420	....	....
Cilacap, Central Java	285,000	....	[3]30,690
Dumai, Central Sumatra	114,000	....	[3]12,870
Musi, South Sumatra	109,155	[1]18,450	[3]30,690
Pangakalan Brandan, North Sumatra	4,750	....	....
Sungai Pakning, Central Sumatra	47,500	....	....
Total	**804,745**	**18,450**	**92,970**

IRAN

WORLDWIDE REFINING	Crude capacity	Catalytic cracking	Catalytic reforming
National Iranian Oil Co.—Abadan	400,000	[1]30,000	[1]26,000
Arak	150,000	....	[3]21,600
Isfahan	265,000	....	[1]29,600
Kermanshah	30,000	....	[1]2,775
Lavan Island	20,000	....	....
Shiraz	40,000	....	[1]6,215
Tabriz	112,000	....	[1]11,120
Tehran	225,000	....	[1]27,260
Total	**1,242,000**	**30,000**	**124,570**

IRAQ

WORLDWIDE REFINING	Crude capacity	Catalytic cracking	Catalytic reforming
Oil Refineries Administration—Baiji	150,000	....	38,500
Basra	70,000	....	....
Daura	100,000	....	5,000
K3-Haditha	7,000	....	....
Khanaqin	12,000	....	....
Mufthia	4,500	....	....
Qaiyarah Mosul	2,000	....	....
Iraqi Company for Oil Operations—Kirkuk	2,000	....	....
Total	**347,500**	**....**	**43,500**

IRELAND

WORLDWIDE REFINING	Crude capacity	Catalytic cracking	Catalytic reforming
Irish National Petroleum Corp.—Whitegate	65,000	....	[1]12,000
Total	**65,000**	**....**	**12,000**

ISRAEL

WORLDWIDE REFINING	Crude capacity	Catalytic cracking	Catalytic reforming
Oil Refineries Ltd.—Ashdod	90,000	[1]27,500	[1]11,500
Haifa	130,000	[1]22,000	[1]15,000
Total	**220,000**	**49,500**	**26,500**

ITALY

WORLDWIDE REFINING	Crude capacity	Catalytic cracking	Catalytic reforming
Agip Plas SpA—Livorno	84,000	....	[3]12,000
Agip Raffinazione—Porto Marghera	80,000	....	[3]15,000
Sannazzaro, Pavia	200,000	[1]34,000	[2]12,000 [3]16,700
Taranto	84,000	....	[2]17,000
Anonima Petroli Italiana—Falconara, Marittima	77,000	....	[1]19,700
Arcola Petrolifera SpA—La Spezia	33,000	....	....
Esso Italiana SpA—Augusta, Siracusa	182,500	[1]43,200	[1]21,900
Iplom SpA—Busalla	46,500	....	....
Isab SpA—Priolo Gargallo	235,000	....	[2]38,000
Italiana Energia E Servizi SpA —Frassino, Mantova	50,318	....	[1]7,445
Praoil—Gela, Ragusa	105,000	[1]35,000	[2]13,850
Priolo, Siracusa	220,000	[1]32,000	[2]9,000
Raffineria di Roma SpA—Rome	81,500	....	[1]14,300
Raffineria Mediterranea SpA—Milazzo, Messina	160,000	[1]49,000	[2]13,500
Saras SpA—Sarroch	285,000	[1]80,000	[3]27,000
Sarpom—S. Martino Di Trecate	248,000	[1]25,200	[1]18,000 [2]7,800
Tamoil Raffinazione SpA—Cremona	90,000		[1]8,600 [3]15,000
Total	**2,261,818**	**298,400**	**286,795**

IVORY COAST

WORLDWIDE REFINING	Crude capacity	Catalytic cracking	Catalytic reforming
Ste. Ivoirienne de Raffinage —Abidjan	54,000	....	[1]9,000
Ste. Multinationale de Bitumes—Abidjan	10,000	....	....
Total	**64,000**	**....**	**9,000**

JAMAICA

WORLDWIDE REFINING	Crude capacity	Catalytic cracking	Catalytic reforming
Petrojam Ltd.—Kingston	35,500	....	[1]3,540
Total	**35,500**	**....**	**3,540**

JAPAN

WORLDWIDE REFINING	Crude capacity	Catalytic cracking	Catalytic reforming
Cosmo Oil Co. Ltd.—Chiba*	228,000	[1]31,500	[1]32,850
Sakaide*	133,000	[1]17,100	[1]12,600
Sakai*	104,500	[1]19,800	[1]7,200
Yokkaichi*	147,250	[1]22,500	[1]5,400 [3]12,150
Fuji Oil Co. Ltd.—Sodegaura*	153,900	[1]13,950	[3]27,000
General Sekiyu Seisei KK—Sakai	140,400	[1]36,000	[1]30,600
Idemitsu Kosan Co. Ltd.—Chita, Aichi*	152,000	[1]36,000	[3]16,200
Himeji, Hyogo*	133,000	....	[1]15,300
Ichihara, Chiba*	237,500	[1]37,800	[1]15,300
Tokuyama, Yamaguchi*	114,000	[1]22,500	[3]18,000
Tomakomai, Hokkaido*	123,500	[1]23,400	[1]16,200
Japan Energy Co.—Chita, Aichi	86,000	[1]15,300	[1]21,200
Funakawa	6,000	....	....
Okayama, Mizushima	171,000	[1]34,400	[3]21,600
Kashima Oil Co. Ltd.—Kashima, Ibaragi*	171,000	[1]24,300	[3]19,800
Koa Oil Co. Ltd.—Yamaguchi	127,000	[1]22,000	[2]22,000
Takaishi, Osaka	104,000	[1]25,000	[1]14,000
Kygnus Sekiyu Seisei KK—Kawasaki	66,500	....	....
Kyokuto Petroleum Ltd.—Chiba	143,000	[1]28,000	[1]22,000
Kyushu Oil Co. Ltd.—Oita	130,000	[1]16,500	[1]8,000
Mitsubishi Oil Co. Ltd.—Kawasaki	75,000	....	[1]10,000

WORLDWIDE REFINING	b/cd Crude capacity	Catalytic cracking	Catalytic reforming
Mizushima	250,000	[1]40,000	[1]25,000 [3]20,000
Nansei Sekiyu KK—Okinawa	100,000	....	[1]12,000
Nihonkai Oil Co. Ltd.—Toyama	60,000	....	[1]6,000
Nippon Oil Co. Ltd.—Niigata*	24,700	....	[1]4,500
Nippon Petroleum Refining Co. Ltd.—Muroran*	161,500	[1]20,700	[1]19,800
Negishi*	365,750	[1]63,900	[1]18,000 [3]27,000
Yokohama*	....	....	[1]3,600
Okinawa Sekiyu Seisei—Yonashiro, Okinawa	110,000	....	[3]17,000
Seibu Oil Co. Ltd.—Yamaguchi	114,000	[1]19,800	[1]15,300
Showa Shell Sekiyu KK—Kawasaki	110,100	....	[1]19,100
Niigata	36,700	....	[1]5,300
Showa Yokkaichi Sekiyu Co. Ltd.—Yokkaichi	220,300	[1]22,600	[1]40,600
Taiyo Oil Co. Ltd.—Kikuma, Ehime*	84,550	....	[3]27,000
Toa Oil Co. Ltd.—Kawasaki	61,750	[1]27,000	[1]7,200
Toho Oil Co. Ltd.—Owase	35,000	....	....
Tohoku Oil Co. Ltd.—Sendai	83,900	[1]25,000	[1]12,000
Tonen Corp.—Kawasaki	217,350	[1]79,380	[1]17,660 [3]26,600
Wakayama	156,870	[1]34,020	[1]33,912
Wakayama Petroleum Refining Co. Ltd.—Kainan City, Wakayama	50,000	....	....
Total	**4,989,020**	**758,450**	**704,972**

JORDAN

	Crude capacity	Catalytic cracking	Catalytic reforming
Jordan Petroleum Refinery—Zerka	100,000	[1]4,350	[1]8,640
Total	**100,000**	**4,350**	**8,640**

KENYA

	Crude capacity	Catalytic cracking	Catalytic reforming
Kenya Petroleum Refineries Ltd.—Mombasa*	85,500	....	[1]9,000
Total	**85,500**	**....**	**9,000**

KOREA, NORTH

	Crude capacity	Catalytic cracking	Catalytic reforming
Government[H]	29,000	....	....
Government—Ungi	42,000	....	[1]7,300
Total	**71,000**	**....**	**7,300**

KOREA, SOUTH

	Crude capacity	Catalytic cracking	Catalytic reforming
Hanwha Energy Co. Ltd.[I]—Inchon*	261,250	....	[1]5,400 [3]22,500
Honam Oil Refinery Co. Ltd.—Yocheon*	361,000	[1]63,000	[1]17,100
Hyundai Lube Oil[J]—Busan*	9,500	....	....
Hyundai Oil Refinery Co.[J]—Daesan	310,000	....	[3]20,000
Ssangyong Oil Refining Co. Ltd.—Onsan	500,000	....	[1]4,800 [4]27,000
Yukong Ltd.—Ulsan*	769,500	[1]45,000	[1]20,070 [3]49,500
Total	**2,211,250**	**108,000**	**166,370**

KUWAIT

	Crude capacity	Catalytic cracking	Catalytic reforming
Kuwait National Petroleum Co.—Mina Abdulla	255,000	....	....
Mina Al-Ahmadi	415,000	[1]28,000	[1]34,000
Shuaiba	154,000	....	[1]14,000
Total	**824,000**	**28,000**	**48,000**

LEBANON

	Crude capacity	Catalytic cracking	Catalytic reforming
Tripoli Oil Installations—Tripoli	20,000	[1]7,250	[1]4,392
Zahrani Oil Installations—Sidon	17,500	....	[1]3,050
Total	**37,500**	**7,250**	**7,442**

LIBERIA

	Crude capacity	Catalytic cracking	Catalytic reforming
Liberia Petroleum Refining—Monrovia	15,000	....	[1]2,000
Total	**15,000**	**....**	**2,000**

LIBYA

	Crude capacity	Catalytic cracking	Catalytic reforming
Azzawiya Oil Refining Co.—Azzawiya and Benghazi	120,000	....	[1]13,440
Ras Lanuf Oil & Gas Processing Co.—Ras Lanuf	220,000	....	....
Sirte Oil Co.—Brega	8,400	....	[1]1,000
Total	**348,400**	**....**	**14,440**

LITHUANIA

WORLDWIDE REFINING	b/cd Crude capacity	Catalytic cracking	Catalytic reforming
Mazheikiai State Oil Refinery Nafta—Mazeikia*	240,000	[1]41,063	[1]24,335
Total	**240,000**	**41,063**	**24,335**

MACEDONIA

	Crude capacity	Catalytic cracking	Catalytic reforming
OKTA Crude Oil Refinery[K]—Skopje	51,180	....	[1]10,780
Total	**51,180**	**....**	**10,780**

MADAGASCAR

	Crude capacity	Catalytic cracking	Catalytic reforming
Solima Raffinerie—Toamasina	15,000	....	[1]2,000
Total	**15,000**	**....**	**2,000**

MALAYSIA

	Crude capacity	Catalytic cracking	Catalytic reforming
Esso Malaysia Berhad—Port Dickson	80,000	....	[1]15,600
Petronas Penapisan (Melaka) Sdn. Berhad—Melaka	100,000	....	[3]20,000
Sarawak Shell Berhad—Lutong	45,000	....	....
Shell Refining Co. Berhad—Port Dickson	105,000	....	[1]4,000 [3]13,000
Total	**330,000**	**....**	**52,600**

MARTINIQUE

	Crude capacity	Catalytic cracking	Catalytic reforming
Ste. Anonyme de la Raffinerie des Antilles—Fort-de-France	16,000	....	[1]3,000
Total	**16,000**	**....**	**3,000**

MEXICO

	Crude capacity	Catalytic cracking	Catalytic reforming
Petroleos Mexicanos—Cadereyta	235,000	[1]40,000	[1]20,000
Ciudad Madero	195,000	[1]43,000	[1]20,000
Minatitlan	200,000	[1]40,000	[1]48,000
Salamanca	240,000	[1]60,000	[1]24,800
Salina Cruz	330,000	[1]80,000	[3]50,000
Tula Hidalgo	320,000	[1]80,000	[1]65,000
Total	**1,520,000**	**343,000**	**227,800**

MOROCCO

	Crude capacity	Catalytic cracking	Catalytic reforming
Samir—Mohammedia	129,000	....	[1]24,000
Ste. Cherifienne des Petroles—Sidi Kacem	26,600	[1]5,040	[1]2,800
Total	**155,600**	**5,040**	**26,800**

MYANMAR

	Crude capacity	Catalytic cracking	Catalytic reforming
Myanma Petrochemical Enterprise—Chauk	6,000	....	....
Thanlyin	26,000	....	....
Total	**32,000**	**....**	**....**

NETHERLANDS

	Crude capacity	Catalytic cracking	Catalytic reforming
Esso Nederland BV—Rotterdam	180,000	....	[3]28,080
Kuwait Petroleum Europoort BV—Rotterdam	75,500	....	[3]22,600
Netherlands Refining Co.—Europoort & Pernis*	399,000	[1]50,400	[1]53,100
Shell Nederland Raffinaderij BV—Pernis	374,000	[1]87,000	[3]42,000
Smid & Hollander Raffinaderij BV—Amsterdam	10,000	....	....
Total Raffinaderij Nederland NV—Vlissingen	148,000	....	[3]23,000
Total	**1,186,500**	**137,400**	**168,780**

NETHERLANDS ANTILLES

	Crude capacity	Catalytic cracking	Catalytic reforming
Coastal Aruba Refining Co. NV—San Nicolas	205,000	....	....
Refineria Isla Curazao SA—Emmastad	320,000	[1]49,000	[1]20,000
Total	**525,000**	**49,000**	**20,000**

NEW ZEALAND

	Crude capacity	Catalytic cracking	Catalytic reforming
New Zealand Refining Co. Ltd.—Whangarei	91,200	....	[1]22,500
Total	**91,200**	**....**	**22,500**

NICARAGUA

	Crude capacity	Catalytic cracking	Catalytic reforming
Esso Standard Oil SA Ltd.—Managua	16,500	[1]3,500	....
Total	**16,500**	**3,500**	**....**

WORLDWIDE REFINING	Crude capacity (b/cd)	Catalytic cracking (b/cd)	Catalytic reforming (b/cd)

NIGERIA

	Crude capacity	Catalytic cracking	Catalytic reforming
Kaduna Refinery & Petrochemical Co. (NNPC)—Kaduna	104,500	[1]18,000	[1]15,300
Port Harcourt Refining Co. (NNPC)—Port Harcourt, Alesa Eleme	60,000	....	[1]6,000
Port Harcourt, Rivers State	150,000	[1]40,000	[4]33,000
Warri Refinery & Petrochemical Co. (NNPC)—Warri	118,750	[1]24,700	[1]15,770
Total	**433,250**	**82,700**	**70,070**

NORWAY

	Crude capacity	Catalytic cracking	Catalytic reforming
Esso Norge AS—Slagen	100,000	....	[1]12,100
Norske Shell AS—Sola	53,000	....	[1]11,000
Statoil Division Mongstad—Mongstad	154,000	[1]48,000	[1]9,800
			[3]15,800
Total	**307,000**	**48,000**	**48,700**

OMAN

	Crude capacity	Catalytic cracking	Catalytic reforming
Oman Refinery Co.—Mina Al Fahal	85,000	....	[3]16,000
Total	**85,000**	**....**	**16,000**

PAKISTAN

	Crude capacity	Catalytic cracking	Catalytic reforming
Attock Refinery Ltd.—Rawalpindi*	28,975	....	....
National Refinery Ltd.—Korangi, Karachi	62,050	....	[3]3,800
Pakistan Refinery Ltd.—Karachi	46,300	....	[2]2,700
Total	**137,325**	**....**	**6,500**

PANAMA

	Crude capacity	Catalytic cracking	Catalytic reforming
Refineria Panama SA—Las Minas	60,000	[1]11,000	....
Total	**60,000**	**11,000**	**....**

PARAGUAY

	Crude capacity	Catalytic cracking	Catalytic reforming
Petroleos Paraguayos—Villa Elisa	7,500		
Total	**7,500**	**....**	**....**

PERU

	Crude capacity	Catalytic cracking	Catalytic reforming
Maple Gas Corp.—Pucallpa	3,250	....	....
Petroperu S.A.—Conchan	6,500	....	....
Iquitos Loreto	10,500	....	....
La Pampilla Lima	100,000	[1]6,700	....
Talara	62,000	[1]16,600	....
Total	**182,250**	**23,300**	**....**

PHILIPPINES

	Crude capacity	Catalytic cracking	Catalytic reforming
Caltex (Philippines) Inc.—Batangas	72,000	[1]12,500	[1]9,000
Petron Corp.—Limay, Bataan*	147,250	[2]13,500	[1]15,300
Philippine Petroleum Corp.—Pililla	....	....	....
Pilipinas Shell Petroleum Corp.—Tabangao	103,800	....	[3]18,900
Total	**323,050**	**26,000**	**43,200**

POLAND

	Crude capacity	Catalytic cracking	Catalytic reforming
Government-owned refineries at Czechowice, Gorlice, Jaslo, Jedlicze, Trzebinia	32,000	....	....
Petrochemia—Plock	260,000	[1]46,000	[1]25,000
Rafineria Gdanska S.A.—Gdansk	60,000	....	[3]14,000
Total	**352,000**	**46,000**	**39,000**

PORTUGAL

	Crude capacity	Catalytic cracking	Catalytic reforming
Petrogal—Leca da Palmeira Porto*	91,277	....	[1]14,831
			[3]10,601
Sines*	212,895	[1]31,500	[3]24,750
Total	**304,172**	**31,500**	**50,182**

PUERTO RICO

	Crude capacity	Catalytic cracking	Catalytic reforming
Caribbean Petroleum Corp.—Bayamon	49,000	[1]14,200	[1]6,000
Puerto Rico Sun Oil Co.—Yabucoa	85,000	....	[1]20,000
Total	**134,000**	**14,200**	**26,000**

QATAR

	Crude capacity	Catalytic cracking	Catalytic reforming
National Oil Distribution Co.—Umm Said	57,500	....	[1]2,100
			[3]9,400
Total	**57,500**	**....**	**11,500**

ROMANIA

	Crude capacity	Catalytic cracking	Catalytic reforming
Arpechim SA—Pitesti	70,288	[1]19,178	[1]12,233
Astra SA—Ploiesti	56,000	....	....
Rafinaria Darmanesti SA—Darmanesti	33,000	....	[2]2,500
Petrobrazi SA—Ploiesti	69,280	[1]21,400	[1]13,440
Petrolsub SA—Barcau	8,000	....	....
Petromidia SA—Midia	110,000	[1]23,700	[1]11,500
Petrotel SA—Ploiesti	104,000	[1]20,900	[1]11,490
Rafo SA—Onesti	87,358	[1]23,014	[1]24,466
Steaua Romania SA—Campina	9,272	....	....
Vega SA—Ploiesti	11,572	....	....
Total	**558,770**	**108,192**	**75,629**

SAUDI ARABIA

	Crude capacity	Catalytic cracking	Catalytic reforming
Arabian Oil Co. Ltd.—Ras Al Khafji	30,000	....	....
Petromin-Shell—Al-Jubail	292,000	....	[3]19,000
Saudi Arabian Oil Co. (Saudi Aramco)—Rabigh	325,000	....	....
Ras Tanura	300,000	....	[1]54,000
Jeddah	42,000	[1]13,000	[1]3,000
Riyadh	140,000	....	[1]35,660
Yanbu	190,000	....	[1]35,000
Saudi Aramco-Mobil—Yanbu	331,700	[1]90,600	[2]46,700
Total	**1,650,700**	**103,600**	**193,360**

SENEGAL

	Crude capacity	Catalytic cracking	Catalytic reforming
Ste. Africaine de Raffinage—M'Bao (Dakar)	17,000	....	[1]2,000
Total	**17,000**	**....**	**2,000**

SERBIA

	Crude capacity	Catalytic cracking	Catalytic reforming
Novi Sad	60,246	....	[1]12,233
Rafinerija Nafte Pancevo—Pancevo	107,018	[1]21,000	[1]9,377
Total	**167,264**	**21,000**	**21,610**

SIERRA LEONE

	Crude capacity	Catalytic cracking	Catalytic reforming
Sierra Leone Petroleum Refining Co. Ltd.—Freetown	10,000	....	....
Total	**10,000**	**....**	**....**

SINGAPORE

	Crude capacity	Catalytic cracking	Catalytic reforming
Esso Singapore Pty. Ltd.—Pulau Ayer Chawan	227,000	....	[1]11,400
Mobil Oil Singapore Pty. Ltd.—Jurong	255,000	....	[1]18,000
			[3]48,000
Shell Eastern Petroleum (Pte.) Ltd.—Pulau Bukom	405,000	[1]28,600	[1]6,900
			[3]30,100
Singapore Petroleum Co. Ltd.—Pulau Merlimau	270,000	[1]31,000	[2]13,500
Total	**1,157,000**	**59,600**	**127,900**

SLOVAKIA

	Crude capacity	Catalytic cracking	Catalytic reforming
Slovnaft, Joint Stock Co.—Bratislava	115,000	....	[1]22,270
Total	**115,000**	**....**	**22,270**

SLOVENIA

	Crude capacity	Catalytic cracking	Catalytic reforming
Nafte Lendava d.o.o.—Lendava	12,000	....	....
Total	**12,000**	**....**	**....**

SOMALIA

	Crude capacity	Catalytic cracking	Catalytic reforming
Iraqsoma Ref. Co.—Mogadishu	10,000	....	....
Total	**10,000**	**....**	**....**

SOUTH AFRICA

	Crude capacity	Catalytic cracking	Catalytic reforming
Caltex Oil SA Pty. Ltd.—Cape Town*	106,400	[1]22,500	[1]13,500
Engen Refinery—Durban	65,000	[1]15,000	[1]15,000
National Petroleum Refiners of South Africa Pty. Ltd.—Sasolburg	86,000	[1]18,000	[1]14,500

WORLDWIDE REFINING	Crude capacity (b/cd)	Catalytic cracking (b/cd)	Catalytic reforming (b/cd)
Shell and BP South Africa Petroleum Refineries Pty. Ltd.— Durban*	156,750	[1]31,500	[1]29,700
Total	**414,150**	**87,000**	**72,700**

SPAIN

WORLDWIDE REFINING	Crude capacity	Catalytic cracking	Catalytic reforming
Asfaltos Espanoles SA—Tarragona	21,000	....	....
BP Oil Espana[L]—Castellon de la Plana*	101,650	[1]22,500	[1]15,300
Compania Espanola de Petroles[M]—Huelva	100,000	[1]18,000	[1]17,000
San Roque (Cadiz)	205,000	[1]40,000	[1]35,000
Tenerife	89,000	....	[1]16,000
Petronor SA—Somorrostro Vizcaya*	209,000	[1]39,600	[1]30,150
Repsol Petroleo SA—Cartagena Murcia	120,000	....	[1]25,000
La Coruna	135,000	[1]28,000	[1]22,000
Puertollano, Ciudad Real	135,000	[1]30,000	[1]18,000
Tarragona	180,000	....	[1]16,000
Total	**1,295,650**	**178,100**	**194,450**

SRI LANKA

WORLDWIDE REFINING	Crude capacity	Catalytic cracking	Catalytic reforming
Ceylon Petroleum Corp.—Sapugaskanda*	47,500		[1]3,375
Total	**47,500**	**....**	**3,375**

SUDAN

WORLDWIDE REFINING	Crude capacity	Catalytic cracking	Catalytic reforming
Port Sudan Refinery Ltd.—Port Sudan	21,700		[1]1,900
Total	**21,700**	**....**	**1,900**

SWEDEN

WORLDWIDE REFINING	Crude capacity	Catalytic cracking	Catalytic reforming
AB Nynas Petroleum—Gothenburg	12,500	....	....
Nynashamn	28,000	....	....
Preem Raffinaderi AB[N]—Gothenburg	106,000	....	[1]20,500
Shell Raffinaderi AB—Gothenburg	81,000	....	[1]17,000
Skandinaviska Raffinaderi AB—Brofjorden-Lysekil*	199,500	[1]29,700	[3]32,400
Total	**427,000**	**29,700**	**69,900**

SWITZERLAND

WORLDWIDE REFINING	Crude capacity	Catalytic cracking	Catalytic reforming
Raffinerie de Cressier SA—Cressier	60,000	....	[1]16,000
Raffinerie du Sud-Ouest SA—Collombey	72,000	....	[1]10,000
Total	**132,000**	**....**	**26,000**

SYRIA

WORLDWIDE REFINING	Crude capacity	Catalytic cracking	Catalytic reforming
Banias Refining Co.—Banias	135,000	....	[3]16,000
Homs Refinery Co.—Homs	110,890	....	[3]12,581
Total	**245,890**	**....**	**28,581**

TAIWAN

WORLDWIDE REFINING	Crude capacity	Catalytic cracking	Catalytic reforming
Chinese Petroleum Corp.—Kaohsiung	570,000	[1]50,000	[1]15,000
			[3]80,000
Tao-Yuan	200,000	....	[1]20,000
			[3]25,000
Total	**770,000**	**50,000**	**140,000**

TANZANIA

WORLDWIDE REFINING	Crude capacity	Catalytic cracking	Catalytic reforming
Tanzanian & Italian Petroleum Refining Co. Ltd.—Kigambori Dar es Salaam*	15,865	....	[1]8,721
Total	**15,865**	**....**	**8,721**

THAILAND

WORLDWIDE REFINING	Crude capacity	Catalytic cracking	Catalytic reforming
Esso Standard Thailand Ltd.—Sriracha	166,000	[1]27,000	[1]9,500
Petroleum Authority of Thailand—Bangchak Bangkok	61,750	....	[1]9,450
Star Petroleum Refining Co., Ltd.[O]—Map Ta Phut, Rayong*	123,500	[1]33,300	[3]13,500
Thai Oil Co. Ltd.—Sriracha	207,000	[1]11,200	[3]35,400
Total	**558,250**	**71,500**	**67,850**

TRINIDAD

WORLDWIDE REFINING	Crude capacity	Catalytic cracking	Catalytic reforming
Petroleum Co. of Trinidad & Tobago Ltd.—Pointe-a-Pierre	165,000	[1]25,000	[1]25,000
Point Fortin	80,000	....	[1]6,000
Total	**245,000**	**25,000**	**31,000**

TUNISIA

WORLDWIDE REFINING	Crude capacity	Catalytic cracking	Catalytic reforming
Ste. Tunisienne Industries des Raffinage—Bizerte	34,000		3,300
Total	**34,000**	**....**	**3,300**

TURKEY

WORLDWIDE REFINING	Crude capacity	Catalytic cracking	Catalytic reforming
Anadolu Tasfiyehanesi AS—Mersin*	95,000	....	[1]12,600
Turkish Petroleum Refineries Corp.—Aliaga-Izmir	226,440	[1]15,095	[1]9,810
Batman, Siirt	22,015	....	[1]1,302
Izmit	226,440	[1]22,645	[1]6,920
			[3]14,000
Kirikkale	113,200	....	[1]20,125
Total	**683,095**	**37,740**	**64,757**

UNITED KINGDOM

WORLDWIDE REFINING	Crude capacity	Catalytic cracking	Catalytic reforming
England			
Conoco Ltd.—South Killingholme	180,000	[1]50,000	[1]50,000
Eastham Refinery Ltd.—Ellesmere Port	22,000	....	....
Esso Petroleum Co. Ltd.—Fawley	317,000	[1]85,000	....
Lindsey Oil Refinery Ltd.—Killingholme South Humberside	192,000	[1]48,400	[1]32,600
Mobil Oil Co. Ltd.—Coryton Essex*	171,000	[1]56,250	[3]34,200
Phillips Imperial Petroleum Ltd.—Port Clarence	100,000	....	....
Shell U.K. Ltd.—Shell Haven	92,000	....	[3]39,000
Stanlow	262,000	[1]73,000	[1]29,000
			[3]30,000
Total	**1,336,000**	**312,650**	**214,800**
Scotland			
BP Refinery Grangemouth Ltd.—Grangemouth*	194,750	[1]18,900	[1]39,600
Nynas UK AB—Dundee	10,240	....	....
Total	**204,990**	**18,900**	**39,600**
Wales			
BP Refinery Llandarcy Ltd.—Llandarcy Neath	....	....	....
Elf Oil UK Ltd.—Milford Haven	108,000	[1]32,500	[1]17,800
Gulf Oil—Milford Haven	112,000	[P1]30,500	[1]22,500
Pembroke Cracking Co. (65% Texaco, 35% Gulf Oil GB)—Milford Haven	....	[1]90,000	....
Texaco Ltd.—Pembroke, Dyfed	180,000	....	[4]39,000
Total	**400,000**	**153,000**	**79,300**

UNITED STATES

WORLDWIDE REFINING	Crude capacity	Catalytic cracking	Catalytic reforming
ALABAMA			
Coastal Mobile Refining Co.—Mobile Bay	18,700	....	....
Hunt Refining Co.—Tuscaloosa	43,225	....	[1]6,480
Shell Chemical Co.[Q]—Saraland	76,000	....	[1]20,000
Total	**137,925**	**....**	**26,480**
ALASKA			
ARCO Alaska Inc.—Prudhoe Bay	15,000	....	....
Kuparuk	12,000	....	....
Mapco Alaska Petroleum—North Pole	130,000	....	....
Petro Star Inc.—North Pole	14,000	....	....
Valdez	40,000	....	....
Tesoro Alaska Petroleum Corp.—Kenai	72,000	....	[1]12,000
Total	**283,000**	**....**	**12,000**
ARKANSAS			
Berry Petroleum Co.—Stephens	6,700	....	....
Cross Oil & Refining Co. Inc.—Smackover	6,000	....	....
Lion Oil Co.—El Dorado	52,500	[1]19,100	[3]12,400
Total	**65,200**	**19,100**	**12,400**
CALIFORNIA			
Anchor Refining Co.—McKittrick	10,000	....	....
Atlantic Richfield Co.—Carson	255,000	[1]92,000	[1]52,000
Chevron USA Products Co.—El Segundo	258,000	[1]61,000	[3]40,000
Richmond	225,000	[1]65,000	[1]45,000
Exxon Co. USA—Benicia	128,000	[1]66,000	[2]33,000
Huntway Refining Co.—Benicia	8,400	....	....
Wilmington	5,500	....	....
Kern Oil & Refining Co.—Bakersfield	21,400	....	[1]3,000
Lunday-Thagard Co.—South Gate	7,000	....	....
Mobil Oil Corp.—Torrance	130,000	[1]85,000	[1]42,000
Paramount Petroleum Corp.—Paramount	42,200	....	[1]7,500

WORLDWIDE REFINING	Crude capacity (b/cd)	Catalytic cracking (b/cd)	Catalytic reforming (b/cd)
San Joaquin Refining Co. Inc.—Bakersfield	18,000	....	....
Santa Maria Refining Co.—Santa Maria	10,000	....	....
Shell Martinez Refining Co.[R]—Martinez	155,200	[1]67,100	[2]29,000
Sunland Refining Corp.—Bakersfield	15,000	....	[1]1,350
Ten By, Inc.—Oxnard	4,500	....	....
Texaco Refining & Marketing Inc.—Los Angeles/ Wilmington*	90,725	[1]26,100	[1]22,500
Bakersfield*	57,380	....	[1]13,050
Tosco Refining Co.—Martinez	156,000	[1]66,000	[1]18,500
			[3]21,500
Ultramar Inc.—Wilmington	68,000	[1]35,000	[3]14,000
Unocal Corp.—Los Angeles/Wilmington*	118,750	[1]42,300	[1]48,600
San Francisco/Santa Maria*	103,645	....	[1]30,600
Witco Corp.—Oildale*	9,785	....	....
Total	**1,897,485**	**605,500**	**421,600**
COLORADO			
Conoco Inc.—Commerce City	57,500	[1]19,000	[1]10,000
Total Petroleum Inc.—Denver	28,000	[1]8,000	[1]9,000
Total	**85,500**	**27,000**	**19,000**
DELAWARE			
Star Enterprise—Delaware City	140,000	[1]63,000	[1]9,000
			[3]36,900
Total	**140,000**	**63,000**	**45,900**
GEORGIA			
Citgo Petroleum Corp.—Savannah	28,000	....	....
Young Refining Corp.—Douglasville	6,000	....	....
Total	**34,000**	**....**	**....**
HAWAII			
BHP Hawaii Inc.—Kapolei	95,000	....	[1]13,000
Chevron USA Products Co.—Barber's Point	54,000	[1]21,000	....
Total	**149,000**	**21,000**	**13,000**
ILLINOIS			
Clark Oil & Refining Corp.—Blue Island	66,500	[1]23,800	[1]29,000
Hartford	57,000	[1]24,700	....
Marathon Oil Co.—Robinson	166,000	[1]43,000	[2]35,000
			[3]38,500
Joliet	203,700	[1]93,500	[3]39,600
Shell Wood River Refining Co.[R]—Wood River	271,000	[1]85,000	[1]15,000
			[2]69,000
			[4]84,000
The UNO-VEN Co.—Lemont*	145,350	[1]52,200	[1]26,820
Total	**909,550**	**322,200**	**336,920**
INDIANA			
Amoco Oil Co.—Whiting	410,000	[1]149,200	[2]85,500
Countrymark Cooperative, Inc.—Mt. Vernon	22,000	[1]7,850	[3]6,500
Laketon Refining Corp.—Laketon*	3,990	....	....
Total	**435,990**	**157,050**	**92,000**
KANSAS			
Farmland Industries Inc.—Coffeyville	110,000	[1]28,000	[1]17,000
National Cooperative Refinery Association— McPherson	73,600	[1]19,800	[3]19,800
Texaco Refining & Marketing Inc.—El Dorado*	99,750	[1]31,320	[1]23,670
Total	**283,350**	**79,120**	**60,470**
KENTUCKY			
Ashland Petroleum Co.—Catlettsburg	219,300	[1]58,200	[3]42,195
		[2]38,800	
Somerset Refinery Inc.—Somerset	5,500	....	[1]1,000
Total	**224,800**	**97,000**	**43,195**
LOUISIANA			
American International Refining, Inc.[S]—Lake Charles	27,600	....	....
Atlas Processing Co. Div. of Pennzoil—Shreveport	46,200	....	[1]4,500
Basis Petroleum, Inc.[T]—Krotz Springs	67,100	[1]30,700	[1]11,800
BP Oil Co.—Belle Chasse*	242,250	[1]92,700	[1]37,800
Calcasieu Refining Co.—Lake Charles	14,000	....	....
Calumet Lubricants Co.—Cotton Valley	8,740	....	....
Princeton	8,000	....	....
Canal Refining Co.—Church Point	9,000	....	[U2]1,300
Cit-Con Oil Corp.[V]—Lake Charles	....	....	....
Citgo Petroleum Corp.—Lake Charles	304,000	[1]117,000	[1]46,800
			[3]45,000
Conoco Inc.—Westlake	226,000	[1]50,000	[3]43,600
Exxon Co.—Baton Rouge	432,000	[1]204,000	[2]68,000
Marathon Oil Co.—Garyville	225,000	[1]90,000	[3]42,500
Mobil Oil Corp.—Chalmette	176,400	[1]62,000	[1]28,000
			[3]17,500
Murphy Oil USA Inc.—Meraux	95,000	[1]36,000	[3]17,000
Placid Refining Co.—Port Allen	48,000	[1]19,000	[1]9,700
Shell Chemical Co.—Saint Rose	40,000	....	....
Shell Norco Refining Co.[R]—Norco	218,000	[1]108,000	[1]14,700
			[2]39,000
Star Enterprise—Convent	230,000	[1]76,500	[1]36,000
Total	**2,417,290**	**885,900**	**463,200**
MICHIGAN			
Lakeside Refining Co.—Kalamazoo	5,600	....	[1]900
Marathon Oil Co.—Detroit	70,000	[1]27,000	[1]15,000
Total Petroleum Inc.—Alma	45,600	[1]18,500	[1]12,000
Total	**121,200**	**45,500**	**27,900**
MINNESOTA			
Ashland Petroleum Co.—St. Paul	69,000	[1]22,310	[1]22,795
Koch Refining Co. L.P.—Rosemount	286,000	[1]86,500	[2]15,000
			[3]38,000
Total	**355,000**	**108,810**	**75,795**
MISSISSIPPI			
Chevron USA Products Co.—Pascagoula	295,000	[1]63,000	[1]71,000
Ergon Refining Inc.—Vicksburg	25,000	....	....
Southland Oil Co.—Lumberton	5,800	....	....
Sandersville	11,000	....	....
Total	**336,800**	**63,000**	**71,000**
MONTANA			
Cenex—Laurel	41,450	[1]13,500	[1]12,000
Conoco Inc.—Billings	49,400	[1]17,100	[1]9,000
Exxon Co.—Billings	46,000	[1]20,000	[1]9,500
Montana Refining Co.—Great Falls	7,000	[1]2,400	[1]1,000
Total	**143,850**	**53,000**	**31,500**
NEVADA			
Petro Source Refining Partners—Eagle Springs	7,000	....	....
Total	**7,000**	**....**	**....**
JERSEY NEW			
Amerada-Hess Corp.—Port Reading	....	[1]54,000	....
Chevron USA Products Co.—Perth Amboy	80,000	....	....
Citgo Asphalt Refining Co.—Paulsboro	80,000	....	....
Coastal Eagle Point Oil Co.—Westville	140,000	[1]50,000	[1]30,000
Mobil Oil Corp.—Paulsboro	149,000	[1]43,700	[1]23,000
			[4]40,400
Tosco Refining Co.[W]—Linden	240,000	[1]135,000	[2]28,000
Total	**689,000**	**282,700**	**121,400**
NEW MEXICO			
Giant Refining Co.—Bloomfield	16,800	[1]5,331	[1]4,000
Gallup	20,800	[1]8,500	[1]6,800
Navajo Refining Co.—Artesia	60,000	[1]18,500	[1]6,000
			[3]15,000
Total	**97,600**	**32,331**	**31,800**
NORTH DAKOTA			
Amoco Oil Co.—Mandan	58,000	[1]24,700	[2]11,500
Total	**58,000**	**24,700**	**11,500**
OHIO			
Ashland Petroleum Co.—Canton	65,900	[1]24,250	[3]19,400
BP Oil Co.—Lima*	161,500	[1]33,300	[2]50,400
Toledo*	147,250	[1]54,000	[2]37,800
Sun Refining & Marketing Co.—Toledo	125,000	[1]62,000	[1]45,600
Total	**499,650**	**173,550**	**153,200**
OKLAHOMA			
Conoco Inc.—Ponca City	155,000	[1]53,000	[1]36,000
Gary-Williams Energy Corp.[X]—Wynnewood*	45,000	[1]17,500	[3]11,250
Sinclair Oil Corp.—Tulsa	50,000	[1]16,200	[1]10,800
Sun Refining & Marketing Co.—Tulsa	85,000	....	[1]15,000

WORLDWIDE REFINING	b/cd Crude capacity	Catalytic cracking	Catalytic reforming
Total Petroleum Inc.—Ardmore	68,000	[1]23,000	[3]15,000
Total	**403,000**	**109,700**	**88,050**
OREGON			
Chevron USA Products Co.—Portland	....	....	....
Total	**....**	**....**	**....**
PENNSYLVANIA			
Pennzoil Products Co.—Rouseville	15,700	....	[1]5,238
Sun Refining & Marketing Co.—Marcus Hook	175,000	....	[1]24,000
Philadelphia-Girard Point	177,000	[1]59,500	[1]31,600
Philadelphia-Point Breeze	130,000	[1]40,000	[1]50,000
United Refining Co.—Warren	66,700	[1]23,000	[2]16,000
Witco Corp.—Bradford	10,000	....	[1]1,650
Total	**574,400**	**122,500**	**128,488**
TENNESSEE			
Mapco Petroleum Inc.—Memphis	105,000	[1]50,000	[1]16,000
Total	**105,000**	**50,000**	**16,000**
TEXAS			
AGE Refining & Manufacturing—San Antonio	5,000	....	....
Amoco Oil Co.—Texas City	433,000	[1]196,700	[2]133,000
Basis Petroleum, Inc.[T]—Houston	67,600	[1]58,500	[1]11,300
Texas City	125,400	[1]48,000	[1]10,000
			[3]12,000
Chevron USA Products Co.—El Paso	90,000	[1]28,000	[1]23,000
Citgo Petroleum Corp.—Corpus Christi	130,000	[1]77,000	[3]52,000
Clark Oil & Refining Corp.—Port Arthur	185,000	[1]63,000	[2]45,000
Coastal Refining & Marketing Inc.—Corpus Christi	100,000	[1]20,000	[1]10,000
			[3]19,000
Crown Central Petroleum Corp.—Pasadena	100,000	[1]56,000	[1]14,000
			[3]22,000
Deer Park Refining Limited Partnership[R]—Deer Park	255,700	[1]64,900	[1]22,800
			[2]43,500
Diamond Shamrock Corp.—Three Rivers	80,000	[1]20,000	[1]10,000
			[3]20,000
McKee	135,000	[1]45,000	[1]15,000
			[3]25,000
Exxon Co. USA—Baytown	411,000	[1]190,000	[2]119,000
Fina Oil & Chemical Co.—Big Spring	58,000	[1]22,500	[1]21,000
Port Arthur	178,500	[1]61,000	[3]36,000
Howell Hydrocarbons & Chemicals Inc.—Channelview	2,400	....	....
Koch Refining Co. L.P.—Corpus Christi[Y]	280,000	[1]92,000	[1]19,000
			[2]16,000
			[3]50,000
LaGloria Oil & Gas Co.—Tyler	52,000	[1]16,500	[1]4,000
			[3]12,000
Lyondell-Citgo Refining Co.—Houston	258,000	[1]92,000	[1]72,000
Marathon Oil Co.—Texas City	70,000	[1]32,000	[1]10,000
Mobil Oil Corp.—Beaumont	320,000	[1]100,000	[3]130,000
Neste Trifinery Petroleum Services—Corpus Christi	30,000	....	....
Phillips Petroleum Co.—Borger	120,000	[Z2]57,000	[1]27,700
Sweeny	200,000	[1]80,500	[1]34,000
		[2]11,100	
Pride Refining Inc.—Abilene	44,800		[1]5,800
Shell Odessa Refining Co.[R]—Odessa	28,300	[1]9,600	[1]9,500
Star Enterprise—Port Arthur	235,000	[1]83,000	[3]45,000
Valero Refining Co.—Corpus Christi	29,900	[2]64,000	[3]33,000
Total	**4,024,600**	**1,588,300**	**1,131,600**
UTAH			
Amoco Oil Co.—Salt Lake City	52,000	[1]17,700	[2]10,000
Big West Oil Co.—Salt Lake City	25,000	[B2]5,000	[1]5,500
Chevron USA Products Co.—Salt Lake City	45,000	[1]13,000	[1]7,000
Crysen Refining Inc.—Woods Cross	12,500	....	[1]2,100
Phillips Petroleum Co.—Woods Cross	25,000	[1]7,700	[1]6,800
Total	**159,500**	**43,400**	**31,400**
VIRGINIA			
Amoco Oil Co.—Yorktown	56,700	[1]25,700	[2]10,800
Total	**56,700**	**25,700**	**10,800**
WASHINGTON			
Atlantic Richfield Co.—Ferndale	202,000	....	[1]57,000
Chevron USA Products Co.—Seattle	....	....	....
Shell Anacortes Refining Co.[R]—Anacortes	108,200	[1]42,000	[2]24,300
		[2]2,800	
Sound Refining Inc.—Tacoma	11,900	....	....
Texaco Refining & Marketing Inc.—Anacortes*	140,125	[1]48,600	[1]27,900
Tosco Refining Co.—Ferndale	88,500	[B2]25,000	[2]14,500
US Oil & Refining Co.—Tacoma	40,800	....	[1]5,750
Total	**591,525**	**118,400**	**129,450**
WEST VIRGINIA			
Quaker State Oil Refining Corp.—Newell	10,500	....	[1]3,300
Total	**10,500**	**....**	**3,300**
WISCONSIN			
Murphy Oil USA Inc.—Superior	36,000	[1]10,400	[1]7,600
Total	**36,000**	**10,400**	**7,600**
WYOMING			
Frontier Oil & Refining Inc.—Cheyenne*	38,950	[1]10,350	[1]6,750
Little America Refining Co.—Casper	22,000	[1]13,300	[2]5,700
Sinclair Oil Corp.—Sinclair	54,000	[1]20,600	[1]14,200
Wyoming Refining Co.—Newcastle*	11,875	[B2]4,950	[1]2,475
Total	**126,825**	**49,200**	**29,125**
URUGUAY			
ANCAP—La Teja Montevideo	40,000	[1]9,000	[2]3,000
Total	**40,000**	**9,000**	**3,000**
VENEZUELA			
Corpoven SA—El Palito, Puerto Cabello	115,000	[1]52,000	[1]9,200
El Toreno Barinas	4,800	....	....
Puerto La Cruz, Anzoategui	195,000	[1]13,000	....
San Roque, Anzoategui	5,200	....	....
Lagoven—Judibana Falcon	571,000	[1]97,200	....
Maraven—Punta Cardon Falcon	286,000	[1]72,700	38,000
Total	**1,177,000**	**234,900**	**47,200**
VIRGIN ISLANDS			
Hess Oil Virgin Islands Corp.—St. Croix	545,000	[1]110,000	[1]125,000
Total	**545,000**	**110,000**	**125,000**
YEMEN			
Aden Refinery Co.—Little Aden	110,000	....	[1]6,000
Yemen Hunt Oil Co.—Marib	10,000	....	[1]2,500
Total	**120,000**	**....**	**8,500**
ZAIRE			
Sozir—Muanda	17,000	....	[1]3,500
Total	**17,000**	**....**	**3,500**
ZAMBIA			
Indeni Petroleum Refinery Co. Ltd.—Bwana Nkubwa Area, Ndola	24,500	....	[1]5,600
Total	**24,500**	**....**	**5,600**

Texaco Refining & Marketing Inc.'s 100,000 b/d refinery in El Dorado, Kan.

UNITED STATES

Survey of operating refineries in the U.S. (state capacities as of January 1, 1997)

Country	No. plants	b/cd Crude capacity	b/cd Catalytic cracking	b/cd Catalytic reforming
Alabama	3	137,925	....	26,480
Alaska	6	283,000	....	12,000
Arkansas	3	65,200	19,100	12,400
California	23	1,897,485	605,500	421,600
Colorado	2	85,500	27,000	19,000
Delaware	1	140,000	63,000	45,900
Georgia	2	34,000	....	....
Hawaii	2	149,000	21,000	13,000
Illinois	6	909,550	322,200	336,920
Indiana	3	435,990	157,050	92,000
Kansas	3	283,350	79,120	60,470
Kentucky	2	224,800	97,000	43,195
Louisiana	19	2,417,290	885,900	463,200
Michigan	3	121,200	45,500	27,900
Minnesota	2	355,000	108,810	75,795
Mississippi	4	336,800	63,000	71,000
Montana	4	143,850	53,000	31,500
Nevada	1	7,000	....	....
New Jersey	6	689,000	282,700	121,400
New Mexico	3	97,600	32,331	31,800
North Dakota	1	58,000	24,700	11,500
Ohio	4	499,650	173,550	153,200
Oklahoma	5	403,000	109,700	88,050
Oregon	1	....	....	....
Pennsylvania	6	574,400	122,500	128,488
Tennessee	1	105,000	50,000	16,000
Texas	28	4,024,600	1,588,300	1,131,600
Utah	5	159,500	43,400	31,400
Virginia	1	56,700	25,700	10,800
Washington	7	591,525	118,400	129,450
West Virginia	1	10,500	....	3,300
Wisconsin	1	36,000	10,400	7,600
Wyoming	4	126,825	49,200	29,125
TOTAL	**163**	**15,459,240**	**5,178,061**	**3,646,073**

Worldwide crude oil production statistics

NORTH AMERICA

Upper figures = 1,000 b/d
Lower figures = million t/y

	1940	1950	1960	1970	1980	1988	1989	1990	1991	1992	1993	1994	1995	1996
Canada	23.5	79.6	525.6	1,263.6	1,412.0	1,604.6	1,588.0	1,508.0	1,548.4	1,603.7	1,676.6	1,742.0	1,806.0	1,819.8
	1.2	4.0	26.2	62.9	70.3	79.9	79.1	75.1	77.1	79.9	83.5	86.8	89.9	90.6
U.S.	3,707.4	5,407.1	7,054.6	9,630.0	8,569.0	8,165.9	7,675.6	7,220.0	7,416.5	7,171.1	6,846.6	6,661.6	6,559.6	6,477.5
	184.6	269.3	351.3	479.6	426.7	406.7	382.2	359.6	369.3	357.1	341.0	331.7	326.7	322.6
Total	**3,730.9**	**5,486.7**	**7,580.2**	**10,893.6**	**9,981.0**	**9,770.5**	**9,263.6**	**8,728.0**	**8,964.9**	**8,774.8**	**8,523.2**	**8,403.6**	**8,365.6**	**8,297.3**
	185.8	**273.3**	**377.5**	**542.5**	**497.0**	**486.6**	**461.3**	**434.7**	**446.4**	**437.0**	**424.5**	**418.5**	**416.6**	**413.2**

MIDDLE EAST

Upper figures = 1,000 b/d
Lower figures = million t/y

	1940	1950	1960	1970	1980	1988	1989	1990	1991	1992	1993	1994	1995	1996
Abu Dhabi	...	...	...	693.8	1,350.0	1,012.6	1,359.0	1,587.0	1,947.0	1,842.0	1,800.0	1,835.0-	1,832.0	1,846.0
	...	...	...	34.6	67.2	50.4	67.7	79.0	97.0	91.7	89.6	91.4	91.2	91.9
Bahrain	19.3	30.2	45.1	76.6	48.0	42.3	42.2	42.0	38.1	36.7	106.0	105.0	105.0	103.8
	1.0	1.5	2.2	3.8	2.4	2.1	2.1	2.1	1.9	1.8	5.3	5.2	5.2	5.2
Dubai	...	...	...	...	349.0	355.3	410.6	469.0	434.0	402.0	350.0	337.0	322.0	320.0
	...	...	...	...	17.4	17.7	20.4	23.4	21.6	20.0	17.4	16.8	16.0	15.9
Iran	181.2	664.3	1,067.6	3,328.8	1,467.0	2,207.5	2,934.3	3,120.0	3,358.0	3,455.0	3,670.8	3,585.0	3,612.0	3,675.3
	9.0	33.1	53.2	165.8	73.1	109.9	146.1	155.4	167.2	172.1	182.8	178.5	179.9	183.0
Iraq	60.7	136.2	1,004.2	1,548.6	2,638.0	2,679.2	2,830.0	2,083.0	283.0	425.0	447.5	550.0	600.0	600.0
	3.0	6.8	50.0	77.1	131.4	133.4	140.9	103.7	14.1	21.2	22.3	27.4	29.9	29.9
Israel	...	...	2.5	70.2	1.0	0.3	0.3	0.3	0.2	0.2	0.1	0.1	0.1	0.1
	...	...	0.1	3.5	...	...	...	...	...	...	...	...	...	...
Jordan	...	...	...	...	...	0.5	0.3	0.4	0.1	0.1	0.1	0.1	0.1	0.1
	...	...	...	...	...	...	...	...	...	...	...	...	...	...
Kuwait	...	344.4	1,628.2	2,734.5	1,382.0	1,254.2	1,542.6	1,080.0	136.0	880.0	1,690.0	1,811.0	1,792.0	1,817.5
	...	17.2	81.1	136.2	68.8	62.5	76.8	53.8	6.8	43.8	84.2	90.2	89.2	90.5
Neutral Zone	...	...	136.2	500.6	540.0	316.3	396.6	315.0	129.0	341.0	360.0	378.0	430.0	484.3
	...	...	6.8	24.9	26.9	15.8	19.8	15.7	6.4	17.0	17.9	18.8	21.4	24.1
Oman	...	...	...	332.4	283.0	596.7	622.7	658.0	700.7	742.0	779.1	806.4	849.0	882.5
	...	...	...	16.6	14.1	29.7	31.0	32.8	34.9	37.0	38.8	40.2	42.3	43.9
Qatar	...	33.6	175.1	362.4	472.0	349.2	394.6	387.0	386.0	425.0	429.2	407.0	454.0	479.8
	...	1.7	8.7	18.0	23.5	17.4	19.7	19.3	19.2	21.2	21.4	20.3	22.6	23.9
Ras Al Khaimah	...	...	...	...	...	10.0	10.0	10.0	0.8	1.0	1.0	1.0	0.8	0.8
	...	...	...	...	...	0.5	0.5	0.5	...	...	...	...	...	...
Saudi Arabia	13.9	546.7	1,247.1	3,548.9	9,630.0	4,708.3	4,935.6	6,215.0	8,158.0	8,137.0	7,907.1	7,811.0	7,859.0	7,841.0
	0.7	27.2	62.1	176.7	479.6	234.5	245.8	309.5	406.3	405.2	393.8	389.0	391.4	390.5
Sharjah	...	...	...	...	10.0	65.0	65.0	35.0	34.6	40.0	44.0	50.0	50.0	50.0
	...	...	...	...	0.5	3.2	3.2	1.7	1.7	2.0	2.2	2.5	2.5	2.5
Syria	...	...	...	83.1	165.0	273.3	300.6	385.0	478.0	518.0	554.5	574.0	605.0	601.5
	...	...	...	4.1	8.2	13.6	15.0	19.2	23.8	25.8	27.6	28.6	30.1	30.0
Yemen	...	...	...	...	...	172.4	186.6	179.0	197.8	182.0	222.3	338.0	338.0	338.0
	...	...	...	...	...	8.6	9.3	8.9	9.9	9.1	11.1	16.8	16.8	16.8
Total	**275.1**	**1,755.4**	**5,306.0**	**13,279.9**	**18,335.0**	**14,043.1**	**16,031.0**	**16,565.7**	**16,281.3**	**17,427.0**	**18,361.7**	**18,588.6**	**18,849.0**	**19,040.7**
	13.7	**87.5**	**264.2**	**661.3**	**913.1**	**699.3**	**798.3**	**825.0**	**810.8**	**867.9**	**914.4**	**925.7**	**938.5**	**948.1**

WESTERN EUROPE

Upper figures = 1,000 b/d
Lower figures = million t/y

	1940	1950	1960	1970	1980	1988	1989	1990	1991	1992	1993	1994	1995	1996
Austria	7.7	27.9	45.4	53.3	29.0	23.2	23.3	24.0	24.3	23.1	23.6	23.7	21.1	21.3
	0.4	1.4	2.3	2.7	1.4	1.2	1.2	1.2	1.2	1.2	1.2	1.2	1.1	1.1
Denmark	...	...	...	...	6.0	95.5	111.0	118.0	142.3	156.9	167.6	184.9	186.0	205.8
	...	...	...	...	0.3	4.8	5.5	5.9	7.1	7.8	8.3	9.2	9.3	10.2
France	1.4	2.5	38.6	45.8	26.0	68.7	65.3	62.0	59.7	58.0	55.3	57.9	49.2	43.6
	0.1	0.1	1.9	2.3	1.3	3.4	3.3	3.1	3.0	2.9	2.8	2.9	2.5	2.2
Germany	20.1	23.2	108.3	148.4	100.0	85.9	81.7	78.0	68.8	65.0	60.2	56.7	57.5	56.5
	1.0	1.2	5.4	7.4	5.0	4.3	4.1	3.9	3.4	3.2	3.0	2.8	2.9	2.8
Greece	...	...	...	...	...	21.8	17.0	15.0	14.0	13.7	11.3	10.7	9.0	8.0
	...	...	...	...	...	1.1	0.8	0.7	0.7	0.7	0.6	0.5	0.4	0.4
Italy	0.2	0.2	37.5	26.3	39.0	92.9	94.7	97.0	87.6	83.0	87.4	88.0	98.7	101.3
	...	...	1.9	1.3	1.9	4.6	4.7	4.8	4.4	4.1	4.4	4.4	4.9	5.0
Netherlands	...	13.4	36.0	35.8	25.0	83.7	87.0	71.0	65.0	57.6	51.9	81.8	68.8	60.0
	...	0.7	1.8	1.8	1.2	4.2	4.3	3.5	3.2	2.9	2.6	4.1	3.4	3.0
Norway	...	...	...	...	528.0	1,069.1	1,469.8	1,574.0	1,876.1	2,144.3	2,263.6	2,579.5	2,782.0	3,085.7
	...	...	...	...	26.3	53.2	73.2	78.4	93.4	106.8	112.7	128.5	138.5	153.7
Spain	...	...	...	3.1	32.0	30.4	18.0	14.3	20.3	20.7	17.3	16.1	15.0	16.3
	...	...	...	0.2	1.6	1.5	0.9	0.7	1.0	1.0	0.9	0.8	0.7	0.8
Turkey	...	0.3	7.0	67.9	44.0	50.0	55.5	70.0	85.2	82.0	75.1	71.0	67.4	68.8
	...	...	0.3	3.4	2.2	2.5	2.8	3.5	4.2	4.1	3.7	3.5	3.4	3.4
United Kingdom	0.3	0.9	1.7	1.7	1,619.0	2,376.3	1,743.0	1,860.0	1,823.2	1,863.8	1,921.7	2,469.0	2,565.0	2,633.0
	...	...	0.1	0.1	80.6	118.3	86.8	92.6	90.8	92.8	95.7	123.0	127.7	131.1
Total	**29.7**	**68.4**	**274.5**	**382.3**	**2,448.0**	**3,997.5**	**3,766.3**	**3,983.3**	**4,266.5**	**4,568.1**	**4,735.0**	**5,639.3**	**5,919.7**	**6,300.3**
	1.5	**3.4**	**13.7**	**19.2**	**121.8**	**199.1**	**187.6**	**198.3**	**212.4**	**227.5**	**235.9**	**280.9**	**294.8**	**313.7**

AFRICA

Upper figures = 1,000 b/d
Lower figures = million t/y

	1940	1950	1960	1970	1980	1988	1989	1990	1991	1992	1993	1994	1995	1996
Algeria	...	...	182.7	1,029.1	1,016.0	666.8	698.0	797.0	803.0	772.0	747.3	750.0	764.0	816.0
	...	...	9.1	51.2	50.6	33.2	34.8	39.7	40.0	38.4	37.2	37.4	38.0	40.6
Angola (inc. Cabinda)	...	...	1.3	13.7	150.0	449.3	454.7	480.0	497.0	531.0	513.0	549.0	621.0	705.5
	...	...	0.1	0.7	7.5	22.4	22.6	23.9	24.8	26.4	25.5	27.3	30.9	35.1
Cameroon	...	...	...	...	58.0	170.0	172.7	164.0	152.0	137.0	117.5	110.0	102.1	90.0
	...	...	...	...	2.9	8.5	8.6	8.2	7.6	6.8	5.9	5.5	5.1	4.5
Congo	...	...	...	...	56.0	134.8	150.0	161.0	159.2	172.0	185.5	185.0	175.0	202.8
	...	...	...	...	2.8	6.7	7.5	8.0	7.9	8.6	9.2	9.2	8.7	10.1
Egypt	18.1	44.9	61.6	327.3	596.0	851.3	854.3	873.0	878.0	873.0	884.3	894.0	922.0	923.0
	0.9	2.2	3.1	16.3	29.7	42.4	42.5	43.5	43.7	43.5	44.0	44.5	45.9	46.0
Gabon	...	...	16.1	108.8	180.0	175.0	197.3	269.0	294.0	300.0	312.3	329.0	364.0	370.0
	...	...	0.8	5.4	9.0	8.7	9.8	13.4	14.6	14.9	15.6	16.4	18.1	18.4
Ivory Coast	...	...	...	...	...	12.9	2.0	2.1	1.3	1.0	0.5	0.0	11.0	20.0
	...	...	...	...	...	0.6	0.1	0.1	0.1	...	...	...	0.5	1.0
Libya	...	...	...	3,318.0	1,785.0	1,012.5	1,100.6	1,369.0	1,509.0	1,493.0	1,361.0	1,380.0	1,390.0	1,402.5
	...	...	...	165.2	88.9	50.4	54.8	68.2	75.1	74.4	67.8	68.7	69.2	69.8
Nigeria	...	...	17.3	1,083.3	2,057.0	1,358.3	1,605.3	1,808.0	1,867.0	1,902.0	1,905.2	1,883.0	1,890.0	2,013.5
	...	...	0.9	53.9	102.4	67.6	79.9	90.0	93.0	94.7	94.9	93.8	94.1	100.3
Tunisia	...	...	3.0	87.7	110.0	102.8	102.0	93.0	107.6	106.2	96.6	91.0	87.7	86.5
	...	...	0.1	4.4	5.5	5.1	5.1	4.6	5.4	5.3	4.8	4.5	4.4	4.3
Zaire	...	...	...	...	20.0	29.5	27.5	28.0	29.1	23.8	22.7	25.0	28.0	30.0
	...	...	...	...	1.0	1.5	1.4	1.4	1.4	1.2	1.1	1.2	1.4	1.5
Others	...	0.8	3.0	1.5	4.0	5.0	4.8	4.3	4.2	10.4	25.2	26.0	26.9	28.7
	...	...	0.1	0.1	0.2	0.2	0.2	0.2	0.2	0.5	1.3	1.3	1.3	1.4
Total	**18.1**	**45.7**	**285.0**	**5,969.4**	**6,032.0**	**4,968.2**	**5,369.2**	**6,048.4**	**6,301.4**	**6,321.4**	**6,171.1**	**6,222.0**	**6,381.7**	**6,688.5**
	0.9	**2.2**	**14.2**	**297.2**	**300.5**	**247.3**	**267.3**	**301.2**	**313.8**	**314.7**	**307.3**	**309.8**	**317.6**	**333.0**

Falcon drilling tests 1 Suriya, one of two gas discoveries and a confirmation well drilled by Carigali-Triton Operating Co. off Thailand in 1995. Carigali-Triton is owned by a unit of Triton Energy Corp., Dallas, in partnership with Malaysia's Petronas-Carigali (JDA) Sdn. Bhd. Photo courtesy of Triton Energy.

ASIA-PACIFIC

Upper figures = 1,000 b/d
Lower figures = million t/y

	1940	1950	1960	1970	1980	1988	1989	1990	1991	1992	1993	1994	1995	1996
Australia	...	...	...	175.6	379.0	552.3	488.8	582.0	544.0	533.0	495.7	535.0	506.2	535.0
	...	...	...	8.7	18.9	27.5	24.3	29.0	27.1	26.5	24.7	26.6	25.2	26.6
Bangladesh	...	...	...	...	...	0.9	0.9	0.9	0.5	1.1	1.0	1.1	1.1	1.4
	...	...	...	...	...	...	...	...	...	0.1	...	0.1	0.1	0.1
Brunei	19.3	84.8	92.9	148.0	230.0	138.3	143.3	143.0	144.7	165.3	157.8	162.0	151.5	150.0
	1.0	4.2	4.6	7.4	11.5	6.9	7.1	7.1	7.2	8.2	7.9	8.1	7.5	7.5
China	...	4.0	100.0	500.0	2,119.0	2,733.0	2,770.0	2,755.0	2,800.0	2,835.0	2,907.9	2,961.0	3,007.0	3,127.3
	...	0.2	5.0	24.9	105.5	136.1	137.9	137.2	139.4	141.2	144.8	147.5	149.7	155.7
China, Taiwan	...	...	0.4	1.8	5.0	2.6	2.6	2.5	1.9	1.2	1.1	1.1	1.0	1.0
	...	...	...	0.1	0.2	0.1	0.1	0.1	0.1	0.1	0.1	0.1	...	...
India	3.9	5.1	9.0	138.6	182.0	631.8	673.3	679.0	625.0	547.0	533.8	622.0	673.4	642.5
	0.2	0.3	0.4	6.9	9.1	31.5	33.5	33.8	31.1	27.2	26.6	31.0	33.5	32.0
Indonesia	169.4	132.6	411.2	853.6	1,576.0	1,137.5	1,208.6	1,274.0	1,410.7	1,346.0	1,327.3	1,319.0	1,498.2	1,515.7
	8.4	6.6	2.05	42.5	78.5	56.6	60.2	63.4	70.3	67.0	66.1	65.7	74.6	75.5
Japan	7.2	5.6	10.2	16.3	10.0	12.3	11.3	10.5	15.1	17.2	15.7	15.0	14.4	14.3
	0.4	0.3	0.5	0.8	0.5	0.6	0.6	0.5	0.8	0.9	0.8	0.7	0.7	0.7
Malaysia	...	...	...	...	288.0	540.0	557.3	605.0	652.0	661.0	645.0	640.0	650.0	650.0
	...	...	...	...	14.3	26.9	27.8	30.1	32.5	32.9	32.1	31.9	32.4	32.4
Myanmar (Burma)	21.1	1.5	11.1	16.4	30.0	15.0	12.0	13.0	12.0	13.0	14.0	16.0	16.0	15.0
	1.1	0.1	0.6	0.8	1.5	0.7	0.6	0.6	0.6	0.6	0.7	0.8	0.8	0.7
New Zealand	...	...	...	...	7.0	28.0	28.0	39.0	40.0	36.8	40.4	42.0	33.0	34.3
	...	...	...	...	0.3	1.4	1.4	1.9	2.0	1.8	2.0	2.1	1.6	1.7
Pakistan	2.4	3.5	7.2	9.9	10.0	47.0	45.0	60.0	72.0	75.0	61.6	57.0	54.2	54.0
	0.1	0.2	0.4	0.5	0.5	2.3	2.2	3.0	3.6	3.7	3.1	2.8	2.7	2.7
Papua New Guinea	...	4.8	4.2	...	...	...	...	...	0.2	52.4	127.2	120.6	99.6	107.4
	...	0.2	0.2	...	...	...	...	...	...	2.6	6.3	6.0	5.0	5.3
Philippines	...	...	...	...	15.0	9.2	4.0	5.0	3.0	8.9	9.1	5.0	2.9	1.2
	...	...	...	...	0.7	0.5	0.2	0.2	0.1	0.4	0.5	0.2	0.1	0.1
Thailand	...	...	...	0.4	...	38.4	39.0	41.0	43.4	51.4	52.2	54.4	50.9	59.3
	...	...	...	...	...	1.9	1.9	2.0	2.2	2.6	2.6	2.7	2.5	3.0
Viet Nam*	...	...	...	...	...	...	...	40.0	80.0	105.0	122.5	140.0	177.0	171.0
	...	...	...	...	...	...	...	2.0	4.0	5.2	6.1	7.0	8.8	8.5
Total	**223.3**	**241.9**	**646.2**	**1,860.6**	**4,851.0**	**5,886.3**	**5,984.1**	**6,249.9**	**6,444.5**	**6,449.3**	**6,512.3**	**6,691.2**	**6,936.4**	**7,079.4**
	11.2	**12.1**	**32.2**	**92.6**	**241.5**	**293.0**	**297.8**	**310.9**	**321.0**	**321.0**	**324.4**	**333.3**	**345.2**	**352.5**

*Prior to 1990, included in other Eastern Europe - C.I.S.

LATIN AMERICA

Upper figures = 1,000 b/d
Lower figures = million t/y

	1940	1950	1960	1970	1980	1988	1989	1990	1991	1992	1993	1994	1995	1996
Argentina	56.3	64.0	171.9	382.9	487.0	449.6	459.0	473.0	489.2	554.0	588.0	666.0	720.7	753.3
	2.8	3.2	8.6	19.1	24.3	22.4	22.9	23.6	24.4	27.6	29.3	33.2	35.9	37.5
Bolivia	0.8	1.7	9.8	16.3	30.0	18.8	20.3	19.2	22.2	21.2	21.9	25.7	28.4	30.0
	...	0.1	0.5	0.8	1.5	0.9	1.0	1.0	1.1	1.1	1.1	1.3	1.4	1.5
Brazil	...	0.9	80.9	160.5	182.0	555.6	597.1	633.0	623.6	625.7	638.0	665.1	689.6	780.0
	...	...	4.0	8.0	9.1	27.7	29.7	31.5	31.1	31.2	31.8	33.1	34.3	38.8
Chile	...	1.7	19.8	34.6	29.0	24.8	23.7	20.3	17.8	15.8	14.2	12.3	10.0	9.0
	...	0.1	1.0	1.7	1.4	1.2	1.2	1.0	0.9	0.8	0.7	0.6	0.5	0.4
Colombia	69.9	93.3	152.7	214.0	125.0	346.7	405.0	445.0	429.0	458.3	455.0	456.0	574.8	620.8
	3.5	4.6	7.6	10.7	6.2	17.3	20.2	22.2	21.4	22.8	22.7	22.7	28.6	30.9
Cuba*	...	...	...	...	...	...	...	15.0	15.0	20.0	19.0	23.0	28.0	27.0
	...	...	...	...	...	...	...	0.7	0.7	1.0	0.9	1.1	1.4	1.3
Ecuador	6.4	7.2	7.7	4.1	222.0	310.1	286.6	287.0	300.2	321.0	340.1	379.1	386.7	385.5
	0.3	0.4	0.4	0.2	11.1	15.4	14.3	14.3	14.9	16.0	16.9	18.9	19.3	19.2
Guatemala	...	...	...	...	5.0	3.7	3.7	4.0	4.1	5.6	6.9	7.7	9.8	13.8
	...	...	...	...	0.2	0.2	0.2	0.2	0.2	0.3	0.3	0.4	0.5	0.7
Mexico	120.3	198.5	270.6	430.2	1,936.0	2,527.3	2,618.0	2,633.0	2,774.0	2,667.7	2,673.0	2,685.0	2,722.1	2,853.8
	6.0	9.9	13.5	21.4	96.4	125.9	130.4	131.1	138.1	132.9	133.1	133.7	135.6	142.1
Peru	33.2	41.1	52.6	72.2	191.0	141.7	129.0	132.0	114.9	117.0	126.3	128.0	124.0	121.3
	1.7	2.0	2.6	3.6	9.5	7.1	6.4	6.6	5.7	5.8	6.3	6.4	6.2	6.0
Trinidad & Tobogo	60.9	56.5	115.7	139.8	211.0	149.3	153.7	151.0	144.0	135.4	122.3	129.4	129.3	127.8
	3.0	2.8	5.8	7.0	10.5	7.4	7.7	7.5	7.2	6.7	6.1	6.4	6.4	6.4
Venezuela	507.0	1,498.0	2,846.1	3,708.0	2,167.0	1,658.0	1,731.6	2,118.0	2,349.6	2,314.0	2,335.0	2,463.0	2,609.0	2,955.3
	25.2	74.6	141.7	184.7	107.9	82.6	86.2	105.5	117.0	115.2	116.3	122.7	129.9	147.2
Others	...	...	...	...	...	3.7	4.9	5.2	5.4	5.8	6.7	7.6	8.4	8.8
	...	...	...	...	...	0.2	0.2	0.3	0.3	0.3	0.3	0.4	0.4	0.4
Total	**854.8**	**1,962.9**	**3,727.8**	**5,162.6**	**5,585.0**	**6,189.3**	**6,432.6**	**6,935.7**	**7,289.0**	**7,261.5**	**7,346.4**	**7,647.9**	**8,040.8**	**8,686.4**
	42.5	**97.7**	**185.7**	**257.2**	**278.1**	**308.3**	**320.4**	**345.5**	**363.0**	**361.7**	**365.8**	**380.9**	**400.4**	**432.4**
World Total, excl. E. Europe-C.I.S.	**5,131.9**	**9,561.0**	**17,819.7**	**37,048.4**	**47,232.0**	**44,854.9**	**46,846.8**	**48,511.0**	**49,547.6**	**50,802.1**	**51,649.7**	**53,192.6**	**54,439.2**	**56,092.6**
	255.6	**476.2**	**887.5**	**1,870.0**	**2,352.0**	**2,233.6**	**2,332.7**	**2,415.6**	**2,467.4**	**2,529.8**	**2,572.3**	**2,649.1**	**2,713.1**	**2,792.9**

*Prior to 1990, included in other Eastern Europe - C.I.S.

EASTERN EUROPE — C.I.S.

Upper figures = 1,000 b/d
Lower figures = million t/y

	1940	1950	1960	1970	1980	1988	1989	1990	1991	1992	1993	1994	1995	1996
Bulgaria	...	...	4.0	6.7	6.0	5.0	5.0	5.0	4.0	1.0	0.9	1.0	1.0	1.0
	...	...	0.2	0.3	0.3	0.2	0.2	0.2	0.2	...	...	...	...	...
C.I.S.*	624.9	760.6	2,969.1	7,089.2	12,031.0	12,452.0	12,140.0	11,500.0	10,296.0	8,949.0	7,854.0	7,030.0	7,120.0	7,043.6
	31.1	37.9	147.9	353.0	599.1	620.1	604.6	572.7	512.7	445.7	391.1	350.1	354.6	350.8
Croatia	...	...	...	...	...	...	...	...	44.5	43.0	39.5	37.0	31.3	34.0
	...	...	...	...	...	...	...	...	2.2	2.1	2.0	1.8	1.6	1.7
Czech Republic & Slovakia	...	0.8	2.7	4.1	1.9	3.0	3.0	3.0	3.0	2.0	3.4	8.0	3.0	3.0
	...	...	0.1	0.2	0.1	0.1	0.1	0.1	0.1	0.1	0.2	0.4	0.1	0.1
Hungary	...	10.1	24.3	38.7	40.6	40.0	39.0	40.0	38.6	33.4	58.0	70.0	33.9	30.5
	...	0.5	1.2	1.9	2.0	2.0	1.9	2.0	1.9	1.7	2.9	3.5	1.7	1.5
Poland	...	3.3	3.9	8.5	6.6	4.0	3.0	3.0	3.3	3.6	4.6	13.0	6.0	5.0
	...	0.2	0.2	0.4	0.3	0.2	0.1	0.1	0.2	0.2	0.2	0.6	0.3	0.2
Romania	...	87.7	231.0	268.6	230.9	188.0	180.0	160.0	140.0	136.0	138.0	138.0	138.0	136.0
	...	4.4	11.5	13.4	11.5	9.4	9.0	8.0	7.0	6.8	6.9	6.9	6.9	6.8
Serbia†	0.3	2.1	18.8	57.8	84.5	73.0	70.0	65.0	22.2	22.0	22.8	20.0	20.0	20.0
	...	0.1	0.9	2.9	4.2	3.6	3.5	3.2	1.1	1.1	1.1	1.0	1.0	1.0
Others	...	2.7	14.9	37.1	50.0	85.0	86.0	30.0	30.0	11.0	9.9	11.5	9.4	9.4
	...	0.1	0.7	1.8	2.5	4.2	4.3	1.5	1.5	0.5	0.5	0.6	0.5	0.5
Total	**625.2**	**867.3**	**3,268.7**	**7,510.7**	**12,451.5**	**12,850.0**	**12,526.0**	**11,806.0**	**10,581.6**	**9,201.0**	**8,131.1**	**7,328.5**	**7,362.6**	**7,282.5**
	31.1	**43.2**	**162.7**	**373.9**	**620.0**	**639.8**	**623.7**	**587.8**	**526.9**	**458.2**	**404.9**	**364.9**	**366.7**	**362.6**
World Total	**5,757.1**	**10,428.3**	**21,088.4**	**45,059.1**	**59,683.5**	**57,704.9**	**59,372.8**	**60,317.0**	**60,129.2**	**60,003.1**	**59,780.8**	**60,521.1**	**61,855.8**	**63,375.1**
	286.7	**519.4**	**1,050.2**	**2,243.9**	**2,972.0**	**2,873.4**	**2,956.4**	**3,003.4**	**2,994.3**	**2,988.0**	**2,977.2**	**3,014.0**	**3,079.8**	**3,155.5**

*Includes gas liquids. †Prior to 1993 listed as Yugoslavia.

Worldwide oil consumption

Upper figures = 1,000 b/d
Lower figures = million t/y

	1993	1994	1995
U.S.	16,470 789.3	16,950 809.8	16,935 806.8
Canada	1,680 77.0	1,720 78.7	1,750 80.0
Mexico	1,555 71.4	1,680 77.6	1,560 71.6
Total North America	**19,705** **937.7**	**20,350** **966.1**	**20,245** **958.4**
Argentina	420 19.7	435 20.4	440 20.6
Brazil	1,355 62.9	1,420 65.7	1,510 69.9
Chile	175 8.0	190 8.8	210 9.7
Colombia	245 11.0	255 11.4	265 12.1
Venezuela	430 19.4	440 19.6	430 19.1
Others	1,200 58.3	1,245 60.5	1,285 62.4
Total S. & Cent. America	**3,825** **179.3**	**3,985** **186.4**	**4,140** **193.8**
Austria	235 11.4	235 11.3	230 11.1
Belgium & Luxembourg	545 26.5	555 27.0	535 25.9
Czech Republic & Slovakia	220 10.6	230 10.9	245 11.8
Denmark	195 9.5	210 10.1	220 10.6
Finland	205 9.9	215 10.4	210 10.0
France	1,940 91.1	1,880 88.2	1,895 89.0
Germany	2,905 136.3	2,880 135.1	2,880 135.1
Greece	340 16.7	345 16.9	350 17.0
Hungary	160 7.7	175 8.5	170 8.1
Italy	1,910 92.1	1,915 92.3	1,975 94.9
Netherlands	790 36.4	790 36.4	830 38.0
Norway	210 9.5	210 9.6	210 9.6
Poland	295 14.0	315 14.8	330 15.4
Portugal	250 12.0	255 12.0	270 12.9
Romania	240 12.1	225 11.2	260 13.0
Spain	1,080 51.3	1,120 53.5	1,170 56.1
Sweden	335 16.1	355 17.0	355 17.1
Switzerland	265 12.3	270 12.7	255 11.8
Turkey	575 27.0	555 25.8	610 28.4
United Kingdom	1,790 84.1	1,785 83.4	1,750 81.7
Others	515 25.0	525 25.6	575 28.1
Total Europe	**15,000** **711.6**	**15,045** **712.7**	**15,325** **725.6**
Azerbaijan	165 8.2	165 8.1	170 8.5

	1993	1994	1995
Belarus	280 14.0	255 12.8	245 12.3
Kazakhstan	315 15.7	245 12.3	240 12.0
Russian Federation	3,790 188.6	3,265 162.7	2,935 146.1
Ukraine	500 24.8	400 19.8	380 18.9
Uzbekistan	165 8.1	145 7.2	135 6.7
Others	255 12.7	195 9.7	205 10.2
Total Former Soviet Union	**5,470** **272.1**	**4,670** **232.6**	**4,310** **214.7**
Iran	1,075 52.7	1,135 55.3	1,190 58.0
Saudi Arabia	1,115 52.1	1,160 53.5	1,120 51.6
United Arab Emirates	315 16.3	320 16.4	320 16.5
Others	1,130 54.8	1,180 57.4	1,245 60.4
Total Middle East	**3,635** **175.9**	**3,795** **182.6**	**3,875** **186.5**
Egypt	440 21.6	435 21.5	445 21.7
South Africa	385 18.0	400 18.8	425 20.0
Others	1,250 58.6	1,275 59.9	1,300 61.0
Total Africa	**2,075** **98.2**	**2,110** **100.2**	**2,170** **102.7**
Australia	720 32.7	755 34.0	780 35.2
China	2,915 140.5	3,145 149.6	3,310 157.5
India	1,300 62.7	1,400 67.4	1,510 72.5
Indonesia	785 37.7	775 37.0	810 38.6
Japan	5,455 252.7	5,765 268.4	5,780 267.3
Malaysia	330 15.6	370 17.4	430 20.1
New Zealand	110 5.2	115 5.4	120 5.6
Pakistan	270 13.5	295 14.8	305 15.3
Philippines	290 14.1	305 14.9	345 16.8
Singapore	425 22.3	495 26.0	510 26.9
South Korea	1,675 79.3	1,840 87.0	2,010 94.8
Taiwan	625 30.5	665 32.4	725 35.4
Thailand	555 26.8	615 29.8	690 33.3
Others	475 23.1	510 24.4	540 25.9
Total Asia & Australasia	**15,930** **756.7**	**17,050** **808.5**	**17,865** **845.2**
Total World	**65,640** **3,131.5**	**67,005** **3,189.1**	**67,930** **3,226.9**
Of which OECD*	39,680 1,876.3	40,690 1,921.9	40,805 1,922.3

*Organisation for Economic Cooperation and Development
Source: British Petroleum

Worldwide refining capacity

NORTH AMERICA

Upper figures = 1,000 b/d
Lower figures = million t/y

	1940	1950	1960	1970	1980	1989	1990	1991	1992	1993	1994	1995	1996	1997
Canada	203	329	920	1,400	2,222	1,856	1,852	1,882	1,905	1,872	1,880	1,908	1,849	1,852
	10.1	16.4	45.8	69.7	110.7	92.4	92.2	93.7	94.9	93.2	93.6	95.0	92.1	92.2
U.S.	4,460	6,696	10,250	12,600	17,720	15,557	16,244	15,559	15,327	15,210	15,142	15,319	15,354	15,432
	222.1	333.5	510.5	627.5	882.5	774.7	809.0	774.8	763.3	757.5	754.1	762.9	764.6	768.5
Total	**4,663**	**7,025**	**11,170**	**14,000**	**19,942**	**17,413**	**18,096**	**17,441**	**17,232**	**17,082**	**17,022**	**17,227**	**17,203**	**17,284**
	232.2	**349.9**	**556.3**	**697.2**	**993.2**	**867.1**	**901.2**	**868.5**	**858.2**	**850.7**	**847.7**	**857.9**	**856.7**	**860.7**

WESTERN EUROPE

Upper figures = 1,000 b/d
Lower figures = million t/y

	1940	1950	1960	1970	1980	1989	1990	1991	1992	1993	1994	1995	1996	1997
Austria	...	26	47	94	280	204	204	204	210	210	210	210	210	210
	...	1.3	2.3	4.7	13.9	10.2	10.2	10.2	10.5	10.5	10.5	10.5	10.5	10.5
Belgium	12	16	171	669	1,064	631	614	602	602	607	607	614	610	630
	0.6	0.8	8.5	33.3	53.0	31.4	30.6	30.0	30.0	30.2	30.2	30.6	30.4	31.4
Cyprus	...	...	...	...	16	17	18	19	19	19	22	22	22	26
	...	...	...	...	0.8	0.8	0.9	0.9	0.9	0.9	1.1	1.1	1.1	1.3
Denmark	1	1	1	186	214	177	187	186	186	184	184	188	189	189
	...	...	...	9.3	10.7	8.8	9.3	9.3	9.3	9.2	9.2	9.4	9.4	9.4
Finland	...	...	25	174	336	241	241	241	241	200	200	200	200	200
	...	...	1.2	8.7	16.7	12.0	12.0	12.0	12.0	10.0	10.0	10.0	10.0	10.0
France	152	306	769	2,317	3,385	1,876	1,820	1,816	1,816	1,851	1,861	1,768	1,782	1,786
	7.6	15.2	38.3	115.4	168.6	93.4	90.6	90.4	90.4	92.2	92.7	88.0	88.7	88.9
Germany	48	81	573	2,359	2,986	1,518	1,507	2,065	2,062	2,233	2,265	2,317	2,126	2,108
	2.4	4.0	28.5	117.5	148.7	75.6	75.0	102.8	102.7	111.2	112.8	115.4	105.9	105.0
Greece	...	...	30	102	431	385	385	395	396	396	396	401	401	395
	...	...	1.5	5.1	21.5	19.2	19.2	19.7	19.7	19.7	19.7	20.0	20.0	19.7
Ireland	11	...	40	55	56	56	56	56	56	56	53	53	55	65
	0.5	...	2.0	2.7	2.8	2.8	2.8	2.8	2.8	2.8	2.6	2.6	2.7	3.2
Italy	41	107	773	2,963	4,131	2,450	2,804	2,385	2,386	2,420	2,262	2,260	2,285	2,262
	2.0	5.3	38.5	147.6	205.7	122.0	139.6	118.8	118.8	120.5	112.6	112.5	113.8	112.6
Netherlands	15	77	359	1,362	1,828	1,381	1,381	1,197	1,219	1,231	1,184	1,187	1,187	1,187
	0.7	3.8	17.9	67.8	91.0	68.8	68.8	59.6	60.7	61.3	59.0	59.1	59.1	59.1
Norway	1	1	2	123	264	239	295	288	288	285	287	285	307	307
	...	...	0.1	6.1	13.1	11.9	14.7	14.3	14.3	14.2	14.3	14.2	15.3	15.3
Portugal	4	8	23	37	378	313	313	294	294	294	294	304	304	304
	0.2	0.4	1.1	1.8	18.8	15.6	15.6	14.6	14.6	14.6	14.6	15.1	15.1	15.1
Spain	11	17	146	685	1,455	1,285	1,293	1,321	1,321	1,301	1,283	1,283	1,327	1,296
	0.5	0.8	7.3	34.1	72.5	64.0	64.4	65.8	65.8	64.8	63.9	63.9	66.1	64.5
Sweden	4	26	48	230	458	427	428	428	435	428	428	428	436	427
	0.2	1.3	2.4	11.5	22.8	21.3	21.3	21.3	21.7	21.3	21.3	21.3	21.7	21.3
Switzerland	...	...	...	106	137	132	132	132	132	132	132	132	132	132
	...	...	...	5.3	6.8	6.6	6.6	6.6	6.6	6.6	6.6	6.6	6.6	6.6
Turkey	...	1	7	149	356	725	725	729	704	714	713	713	713	683
	...	...	0.3	7.4	17.7	36.1	36.1	36.3	35.1	35.6	35.5	35.5	35.5	34.0
United Kingdom	133	197	963	2,301	2,527	1,803	1,831	1,867	1,856	1,843	1,867	1,869	1,888	1,941
	6.6	9.8	48.0	114.6	125.8	89.8	91.2	93.0	92.4	91.8	93.0	93.1	94.0	96.7
Total	**433**	**864**	**3,977**	**13,912**	**20,302**	**13,860**	**14,234**	**14,225**	**14,223**	**14,404**	**14,248**	**14,234**	**14,174**	**14,148**
	21.3	**42.7**	**197.9**	**692.9**	**1,010.9**	**690.3**	**708.9**	**708.4**	**708.3**	**717.4**	**709.6**	**708.9**	**705.9**	**704.6**

LATIN AMERICA

Upper figures = 1,000 b/d
Lower figures = million t/y

	1940	1950	1960	1970	1980	1989	1990	1991	1992	1993	1994	1995	1996	1997
Argentina	103	152	238	457	676	690	689	696	696	709	709	665	661	665
	5.1	7.6	11.9	22.8	33.7	34.4	34.3	34.7	34.7	35.3	35.3	33.1	32.9	33.1
Bahamas	...	...	...	...	500	...	...	...	...	...	...	...	...	...
	...	...	...	...	24.9	...	...	...	...	...	...	...	...	...
Barbados	...	...	...	3	3	3	3	3	3	3	3	3	4	4
	...	...	...	0.1	0.1	0.1	0.1	0.1	0.1	0.1	0.1	0.1	0.2	0.2
Bolivia	1	7	12	12	74	58	58	45	45	45	45	45	45	48
	...	0.3	0.6	0.6	3.7	2.9	2.9	2.2	2.2	2.2	2.2	2.2	2.2	2.4
Brazil	4	12	156	502	1,205	1,407	1,397	1,412	1,406	1,403	1,253	1,253	1,256	1,256
	0.2	0.6	7.8	25.0	60.0	70.1	69.6	70.3	70.0	69.9	62.4	62.4	62.5	62.5
Chile	1	4	24	91	139	147	147	146	143	144	165	165	178	192
	...	0.2	1.2	4.5	6.9	7.3	7.3	7.3	7.1	7.2	8.2	8.2	8.9	9.6
Colombia	15	24	51	137	193	227	227	247	274	264	249	249	249	249
	0.7	1.2	2.5	6.8	9.6	11.3	11.3	12.3	13.6	13.1	12.4	12.4	12.4	12.4
Costa Rica	...	...	...	8	11	16	16	15	15	15	15	15	15	15
	...	...	...	0.4	0.5	0.8	0.8	0.7	0.7	0.7	0.7	0.7	0.7	0.7
Cuba	4	7	87	93	160	160	160	280	280	280	280	280	301	301
	0.2	0.3	4.3	4.6	8.0	8.0	8.0	13.9	13.9	13.9	13.9	13.9	15.0	15.0
Ecuador	2	5	7	33	86	123	145	142	142	147	148	148	148	148
	0.1	0.2	0.3	1.6	4.3	6.1	7.2	7.1	7.1	7.3	7.4	7.4	7.4	7.4
El Salvador	...	...	...	14	16	17	17	16	16	15	18	19	19	20
	...	...	...	0.7	0.8	0.8	0.8	0.8	0.8	0.7	0.9	0.9	0.9	1.0
Guatemala	...	...	...	21	16	16	16	16	16	16	20	20	20	20
	...	...	...	1.0	0.8	0.8	0.8	0.8	0.8	0.8	1.0	1.0	1.0	1.0
Honduras	...	...	...	10	14	14	14	14	14	14	14	14	14	14
	...	...	...	0.5	0.7	0.7	0.7	0.7	0.7	0.7	0.7	0.7	0.7	0.7
Jamaica	...	...	...	32	34	34	34	34	34	32	36	36	36	36
	...	...	...	1.6	1.7	1.7	1.7	1.7	1.7	1.6	1.8	1.8	1.8	1.8
Mexico	98	160	357	495	1,394	1,354	1,514	1,679	1,574	1,524	1,524	1,524	1,520	1,520
	4.9	8.0	17.8	24.7	69.4	67.4	75.4	83.6	78.4	75.9	75.9	75.9	75.7	75.7
Netherlands Antilles	495	617	680	840	792	320	320	320	470	470	477	490	490	490
	24.7	30.7	33.9	41.8	39.4	15.9	15.9	15.9	23.4	23.4	23.8	24.4	24.4	24.4
Nicaragua	...	...	...	22	14	15	15	16	16	16	16	17	17	17
	...	...	...	1.1	0.7	0.7	0.7	0.8	0.8	0.8	0.8	0.8	0.8	0.8
Panama	...	...	...	78	100	100	100	100	40	100	100	40	60	60
	...	...	...	3.9	5.0	5.0	5.0	5.0	2.0	5.0	5.0	2.0	3.0	3.0
Paraguay	...	...	...	5	7	8	8	8	8	8	8	8	8	8
	...	...	...	0.2	0.3	0.4	0.4	0.4	0.4	0.4	0.4	0.4	0.4	0.4
Peru	22	35	49	92	170	172	172	189	189	189	184	184	182	182
	1.1	1.7	2.4	4.6	8.5	8.6	8.6	9.4	9.4	9.4	9.2	9.2	9.1	9.1
Puerto Rico	...	...	84	155	284	123	123	125	123	127	127	127	127	134
	...	...	4.2	7.7	14.1	6.1	6.1	6.2	6.1	6.3	6.3	6.3	6.3	6.7
Trinidad & Tobago	49	104	182	430	456	300	300	246	246	246	305	245	245	245
	2.4	5.2	9.1	21.4	22.7	14.9	14.9	12.3	12.3	12.3	15.2	12.2	12.2	12.2
Uruguay	5	16	28	40	40	33	33	33	29	29	35	35	37	40
	0.2	0.8	1.4	2.0	2.0	1.6	1.6	1.6	1.4	1.4	1.7	1.7	1.8	2.0
Venezuela	55	254	886	1,313	1,446	1,201	1,201	1,167	1,171	1,167	1,167	1,167	1,177	1,177
	2.7	12.6	44.1	65.4	72.0	59.8	59.8	58.1	58.3	58.1	58.1	58.1	58.6	58.6
Virgin Islands	...	...	...	220	728	545	545	545	545	545	545	545	545	545
	...	...	...	11.0	36.3	27.1	27.1	27.1	27.1	27.1	27.1	27.1	27.1	27.1
Others	...	...	...	11	62	60	61	60	60	64	64	64	66	66
	...	...	...	0.5	3.1	3.0	3.0	3.0	3.0	3.2	3.2	3.2	3.3	3.3
Total	**854**	**1,397**	**2,841**	**5,114**	**8,620**	**7,143**	**7,315**	**7,554**	**7,555**	**7,572**	**7,507**	**7,358**	**7,420**	**7,452**
	42.3	**69.4**	**141.5**	**254.5**	**429.2**	**355.5**	**364.0**	**376.0**	**376.0**	**376.8**	**373.7**	**366.1**	**369.3**	**371.1**

ASIA-PACIFIC

Upper figures = 1,000 b/d
Lower figures = million t/y

	1940	1950	1960	1970	1980	1989	1990	1991	1992	1993	1994	1995	1996	1997
Australia	4 0.2	14 0.7	237 11.8	594 29.6	725 36.1	644 32.1	675 33.6	706 35.2	703 35.0	698 34.8	705 35.1	705 35.1	733 36.5	771 38.4
Bangladesh	... ...	... ...	... ...	... ...	31 1.5	31 1.5	31 1.5	31 1.5	31 1.5	31 1.5	31 1.5	31 1.5	31 1.5	31 1.5
Brunei-Malaysia-Singapore	10 0.5	10 0.5	46 2.3	320 15.9	1,093 54.4	1,071 53.3	1,049 52.2	1,098 54.7	1,113 55.4	1,301 64.8	1,333 66.4	1,386 69.0	1,498 74.6	1,496 74.5
China	... ...	8 0.4	98 4.9	300 14.9	1,600 79.7	2,200 109.6	2,200 109.6	2,200 109.6	2,200 109.6	2,200 109.6	2,200 109.6	2,867 142.8	2,867 142.8	2,867 142.8
China, Taiwan	... ...	... ...	28 1.4	119 5.9	425 21.2	570 28.4	570 28.4	543 27.0	543 27.0	543 27.0	543 27.0	543 27.0	543 27.0	770 38.3
Guam*	... ...	... ...	... ...	... ...	44 2.2	... ...	... ...	... ...	... ...	... ...	... ...	... ...	... ...	... ...
India	10 0.5	6 0.3	112 5.6	446 22.2	557 27.7	1,051 52.3	1,080 53.8	1,122 55.9	1,122 55.9	1,047 52.1	1,086 54.1	1,086 54.1	1,086 54.1	1,086 54.1
Indonesia	170 8.5	203 10.1	274 13.6	268 13.3	528 26.3	714 35.6	714 35.6	814 40.5	860 42.8	860 42.8	860 42.8	805 40.1	805 40.1	805 40.1
Japan	53 2.6	34 1.7	640 31.9	3,140 156.4	5,509 274.3	4,363 217.3	4,198 209.1	4,383 218.3	4,612 229.7	4,741 236.1	4,810 239.5	4,847 241.4	4,867 242.4	4,989 248.5
Korea, North†	... ...	... ...	... ...	... ...	... ...	... ...	... ...	42 2.1	42 2.1	42 2.1	42 2.1	42 2.1	71 3.5	71 3.5
Korea, South	... ...	... ...	... ...	180 9.0	601 29.9	880 43.8	867 43.2	867 43.2	1,163 57.9	1,147 57.1	1,147 57.1	1,170 58.3	1,244 62.0	2,210 110.1
Myanmar	... ...	... ...	9 0.4	26 1.3	26 1.3	26 1.3	32 1.6	32 1.6	32 1.6	32 1.6	32 1.6	32 1.6	32 1.6	32 1.6
New Zealand	... ...	... ...	... ...	66 3.3	74 3.7	88 4.4	95 4.7	95 4.7	95 4.7	84 4.2	93 4.6	89 4.4	91 4.5	91 4.5
Okinawa*	... ...	... ...	... ...	... ...	198 9.9	... ...	... ...	... ...	... ...	... ...	... ...	... ...	... ...	... ...
Pakistan	... ...	5 0.2	6 0.3	107 5.3	98 4.9	130 6.5	121 6.0	121 6.0	121 6.0	121 6.0	133 6.6	139 6.9	137 6.8	137 6.8
Philippines	... ...	... ...	22 1.1	182 9.1	253 12.6	254 12.6	284 14.1	279 13.9	287 14.3	278 13.8	279 13.9	280 13.9	323 16.1	323 16.1
Sri Lanka	... ...	... ...	... ...	44 2.2	38 1.9	50 2.5	50 2.5	50 2.5	50 2.5	50 2.5	50 2.5	50 2.5	48 2.4	48 2.4
Thailand	... ...	... ...	1 ...	62 3.1	186 9.3	191 9.5	215 10.7	221 11.0	221 11.0	221 11.0	314 15.6	347 17.3	426 21.2	558 27.8
Others	27 1.3	4 0.2	... ...	12 0.6	... ...	... ...	... ...	... ...	... ...	... ...	... ...	... ...	... ...	... ...
Total	**274** **13.6**	**284** **14.1**	**1,472** **73.3**	**5,866** **292.1**	**11,986** **596.9**	**12,263** **610.7**	**12,181** **606.6**	**12,604** **627.7**	**13,195** **657.0**	**13,396** **667.0**	**13,658** **680.0**	**14,419** **718.0**	**14,802** **737.1**	**16,285** **811.0**

***Prior to 1980, included in others**

†Prior to 1991, included in other C.I.S.—Eastern Europe

AFRICA

Upper figures = 1,000 b/d
Lower figures = million t/y

	1940	1950	1960	1970	1980	1989	1990	1991	1992	1993	1994	1995	1996	1997
Algeria	...	...	...	48	122	465	465	465	465	530	530	465	465	465
	...	...	...	2.4	6.1	23.2	23.2	23.2	23.2	26.4	26.4	23.2	23.2	23.2
Angola	...	...	2	14	36	32	32	38	32	32	32	32	32	32
	...	...	0.1	0.7	1.8	1.6	1.6	1.9	1.6	1.6	1.6	1.6	1.6	1.6
Cameroon	...	...	...	...	...	42	43	42	42	42	42	42	42	42
	...	...	...	...	...	2.1	2.1	2.1	2.1	2.1	2.1	2.1	2.1	2.1
Congo	...	...	...	14	...	21	21	21	21	21	21	21	21	21
	...	...	...	0.7	...	1.0	1.0	1.0	1.0	1.0	1.0	1.0	1.0	1.0
Egypt	17	39	87	175	234	489	489	523	523	532	532	532	532	546
	0.8	1.9	4.3	8.7	11.7	24.4	24.4	26.0	26.0	26.5	26.5	26.5	26.5	27.2
Eritrea*	...	...	...	11	14	18	18	18	18	18	18	18	18	18
	...	...	...	0.5	0.7	0.9	0.9	0.9	0.9	0.9	0.9	0.9	0.9	0.9
Gabon	...	...	...	13	20	24	24	24	24	24	17	17	17	17
	...	...	...	0.6	1.0	1.2	1.2	1.2	1.2	1.2	0.8	0.8	0.8	0.8
Ghana	...	...	...	29	26	27	27	27	27	27	27	25	25	27
	...	...	...	1.4	1.3	1.3	1.3	1.3	1.3	1.3	1.3	1.2	1.2	1.3
Ivory Coast	...	...	...	19	50	60	69	69	69	69	63	64	64	64
	..	...	...	0.9	2.5	3.0	3.4	3.4	3.4	3.4	3.1	3.2	3.2	3.2
Kenya	...	...	...	44	95	90	95	90	90	90	90	90	90	85
	...	...	...	2.2	4.7	4.5	4.7	4.5	4.5	4.5	4.5	4.5	4.5	4.2
Liberia	...	...	...	10	15	15	15	15	15	15	15	15	15	15
	...	...	...	0.5	0.7	0.7	0.7	0.7	0.7	0.7	0.7	0.7	0.7	0.7
Libya	...	...	...	10	138	329	329	348	348	348	348	348	348	348
	...	...	...	0.5	6.9	16.4	16.4	17.3	17.3	17.3	17.3	17.3	17.3	17.3
Madagascar	...	...	...	13	11	16	16	16	16	16	16	16	15	15
	...	...	...	0.6	0.5	0.8	0.8	0.8	0.8	0.8	0.8	0.8	0.7	0.7
Morocco	...	...	2	35	72	155	155	155	155	155	155	155	155	156
	...	...	0.1	1.7	3.6	7.7	7.7	7.7	7.7	7.7	7.7	7.7	7.7	7.8
Mozambique	...	...	...	20	16	...	...	...	...	...	...	...	...	...
	...	...	...	1.0	0.8	...	...	...	...	...	...	...	...	...
Nigeria	...	...	...	46	160	415	433	433	433	433	433	433	433	433
	...	...	...	2.3	8.0	20.7	21.6	21.6	21.6	21.6	21.6	21.6	21.6	21.6
Senegal	...	...	...	13	20	30	24	24	24	23	23	17	17	17
	...	...	...	0.6	1.0	1.5	1.2	1.2	1.2	1.1	1.1	0.8	0.8	0.8
Sierra Leone	...	...	...	10	10	10	10	10	10	10	10	10	10	10
	...	...	...	0.5	0.5	0.5	0.5	0.5	0.5	0.5	0.5	0.5	0.5	0.5
South Africa	1	...	25	184	478	434	434	431	431	431	364	401	401	414
	...	...	1.2	9.2	23.8	21.6	21.6	21.5	21.5	21.5	18.1	20.0	20.0	20.6
Sudan	...	...	...	21	26	21	25	22	22	22	22	22	22	22
	...	...	...	1.0	1.3	1.0	1.2	1.1	1.1	1.1	1.1	1.1	1.1	1.1
Tanzania	...	...	...	14	17	14	14	17	17	17	17	17	16	16
	...	...	...	0.7	0.8	0.7	0.7	0.8	0.8	0.8	0.8	0.8	0.8	0.8
Togo	...	...	...	...	20	...	...	...	...	...	...	...	...	...
	...	...	...	...	1.0	...	...	...	...	...	...	...	...	...
Tunisia	...	...	...	23	34	34	34	34	34	34	34	34	34	34
	...	...	...	1.1	1.7	1.7	1.7	1.7	1.7	1.7	1.7	1.7	1.7	1.7
Zaire	...	...	...	21	16	17	17	17	17	17	17	17	17	17
	...	...	...	1.0	0.8	0.8	0.8	0.8	0.8	0.8	0.8	0.8	0.8	0.8
Others	...	...	...	...	35	31	35	35	34	34	34	34	35	35
	...	...	...	...	1.7	1.5	1.7	1.7	1.7	1.7	1.7	1.7	1.7	1.7
Total	**18**	**39**	**116**	**787**	**1,665**	**2,789**	**2,824**	**2,874**	**2,867**	**2,940**	**2,860**	**2,825**	**2,824**	**2,849**
	0.8	**1.9**	**5.7**	**38.8**	**82.9**	**138.8**	**140.4**	**142.9**	**142.6**	**146.2**	**142.1**	**140.5**	**140.4**	**141.6**

*Prior to 1995 listed as Ethiopia.

MIDDLE EAST

Upper figures = 1,000 b/d   Lower figures = million t/y

	1940	1950	1960	1970	1980	1989	1990	1991	1992	1993	1994	1995	1996	1997
Abu Dhabi	...	...	...	...	14	180	180	193	193	193	193	193	213	213
	...	...	...	...	0.7	9.0	9.0	9.6	9.6	9.6	9.6	9.6	10.6	10.6
Bahrain	33	150	187	205	250	243	243	243	243	243	250	250	250	249
	1.6	7.5	9.3	10.2	12.4	12.1	12.1	12.1	12.1	12.1	12.4	12.4	12.4	12.4
Iran	333	502	495	645	921	530	530	720	720	1,089	1,162	1,184	1,168	1,242
	16.6	25.0	24.7	32.1	45.9	26.4	26.4	35.9	35.9	54.2	57.9	59.0	58.2	61.9
Iraq	4	9	56	104	168	319	319	319	319	319	348	348	348	348
	0.2	0.4	2.8	5.2	8.4	15.9	15.9	15.9	15.9	15.9	17.3	17.3	17.3	17.3
Israel	...	83	87	107	195	180	180	180	208	221	208	220	220	220
	...	4.1	4.3	5.3	9.7	9.0	9.0	9.0	10.4	11.0	10.4	11.0	11.0	11.0
Jordan	...	...	...	7	21	100	100	100	100	100	100	100	100	100
	...	...	...	0.3	1.0	5.0	5.0	5.0	5.0	5.0	5.0	5.0	5.0	5.0
Kuwait*	...	25	270	569	645	817	819	819	819	368	624	759	801	824
	...	1.2	13.5	28.4	32.1	40.7	40.8	40.8	40.8	18.3	31.1	37.8	39.9	41.0
Lebanon	...	6	24	38	53	37	37	38	38	38	38	38	38	38
	...	0.3	1.2	1.9	2.6	1.8	1.8	1.9	1.9	1.9	1.9	1.9	1.9	1.9
Qatar	...	...	1	1	11	62	62	62	60	60	58	58	58	58
	...	...	...	...	0.5	3.1	3.1	3.1	3.0	3.0	2.9	2.9	2.9	2.9
Saudi Arabia*	...	140	189	377	487	1,375	1,484	1,863	1,863	1,863	1,614	1,661	1,656	1,656
	...	7.0	9.4	18.8	24.3	68.5	73.9	92.8	92.8	92.8	80.4	82.7	82.5	82.5
Syria	...	...	...	59	223	244	244	237	237	237	242	242	242	246
	...	...	...	2.9	11.1	12.2	12.2	11.8	11.8	11.8	12.1	12.1	12.1	12.3
Yemen	...	...	120	178	175	162	162	172	115	115	120	120	120	120
	...	...	6.0	8.9	8.7	8.1	8.1	8.6	5.7	5.7	6.0	6.0	6.0	6.0
Others	...	...	...	...	...	87	87	76	80	80	76	85	85	85
	...	...	...	...	...	4.3	4.3	3.8	4.0	4.0	3.8	4.2	4.2	4.2
Total	**370**	**916**	**1,429**	**2,290**	**3,163**	**4,336**	**4,447**	**5,022**	**4,995**	**4,926**	**5,033**	**5,258**	**5,299**	**5,399**
	18.4	**45.5**	**71.2**	**114.0**	**151.4**	**216.1**	**221.6**	**250.3**	**248.9**	**245.3**	**250.8**	**261.9**	**264.0**	**269.0**
Total, exclu. C.I.S.-E. Europe	**6,612**	**10,524**	**21,005**	**41,969**	**65,678**	**57,804**	**59,097**	**59,720**	**60,067**	**60,320**	**60,328**	**61,321**	**61,722**	**63,417**
	328.6	**523.5**	**1,045.9**	**2,089.5**	**3,270.5**	**2,878.5**	**2,942.7**	**2,973.8**	**2,991.0**	**3,003.4**	**3,003.9**	**3,053.3**	**3,073.4**	**3,158.0**

*Includes Neutral Zone.

C.I.S.-EASTERN EUROPE

Upper figures = 1,000 b/d   Lower figures = million t/y

	1940	1950	1960	1970	1980	1989	1990	1991	1992	1993	1994	1995	1996	1997
Albania*	...	...	...	...	...	...	...	40	40	40	40	40	40	40
	...	...	...	...	...	...	...	2.0	2.0	2.0	2.0	2.0	2.0	2.0
Bulgaria*	...	...	...	...	...	...	...	300	300	300	300	300	300	300
	...	...	...	...	...	...	...	14.9	14.9	14.9	14.9	14.9	14.9	14.9
C.I.S.	...	900	2,800	5,640	10,950	12,300	12,300	12,300	12,300	9,851	9,846	9,975	10,061	10,100
	...	44.8	139.4	280.9	545.3	612.5	612.5	612.5	612.5	490.6	490.3	496.8	501.0	503.0
Croatia	...	...	...	...	...	...	...	...	...	143	293	294	294	294
	...	...	...	...	...	...	...	...	...	7.1	14.6	14.6	14.6	14.6
Czech Republic†	...	16	46	220	455	455	455	455	455	457	307	307	187	187
	...	0.8	2.3	11.0	22.7	22.7	22.7	22.7	22.7	22.8	15.3	15.3	9.3	9.3
Hungary	...	20	58	130	290	220	220	220	220	235	242	242	232	232
	...	1.0	2.9	6.5	14.4	11.0	11.0	11.0	11.0	11.7	12.1	12.1	11.6	11.6
Lithuania	...	...	...	...	...	...	...	...	...	267	263	267	263	240
	...	...	...	...	...	...	...	...	...	13.3	13.1	13.3	13.1	12.0
Macedonia	...	...	...	...	...	...	...	...	...	51	51	51	51	51
	...	...	...	...	...	...	...	...	...	2.5	2.5	2.5	2.5	2.5
Poland	...	4	20	156	385	385	385	385	333	333	333	352	352	352
	...	0.2	1.0	7.8	19.2	19.2	19.2	19.2	16.6	16.6	16.6	17.5	17.5	17.5
Romania	...	182	260	356	608	617	617	617	657	737	681	651	655	559
	...	9.1	12.9	17.7	30.3	30.7	30.7	30.7	32.7	36.7	33.9	32.4	32.6	27.8
Serbia	5	8	10	179	296	609	609	609	609	444	282	168	168	167
	0.2	0.4	0.5	8.9	14.7	30.3	30.3	30.3	30.3	22.1	14.0	8.4	8.4	8.3
Slovakia	...	...	...	...	...	...	...	...	...	...	193	193	115	115
	...	...	...	...	...	...	...	...	...	...	9.6	9.6	5.7	5.7
Slovenia	...	...	...	...	...	...	...	...	...	15	15	11	12	12
	...	...	...	...	...	...	...	...	...	0.7	0.7	0.5	0.6	0.6
Others	...	4	40	332	852	910	852	...	...	...	...	...	...	...
	...	0.2	2.0	16.5	42.4	45.3	42.4	...	...	...	...	...	...	...
Total	**5**	**1,134**	**3,234**	**7,013**	**13,836**	**15,496**	**15,438**	**14,926**	**14,914**	**12,873**	**12,846**	**12,851**	**12,730**	**12,649**
	0.2	**56.5**	**161.0**	**349.3**	**689.0**	**771.7**	**768.8**	**743.3**	**742.7**	**641.0**	**639.6**	**639.9**	**633.8**	**629.8**
World Total	**6,617**	**11,658**	**24,239**	**48,982**	**79,514**	**73,300**	**74,535**	**74,646**	**74,981**	**73,193**	**73,174**	**74,172**	**74,452**	**76,066**
	328.8	**580.0**	**1,206.9**	**2,438.8**	**3,959.5**	**3,650.2**	**3,711.5**	**3,717.1**	**3,733.7**	**3,644.4**	**3,643.5**	**3,693.2**	**3,707.2**	**3,787.8**

***Prior to 1991, included in others. †Prior to 1994 listed as Czechoslovakia.**

World natural gas production

Country	1990	1991	1992	1993	1994	1995	1996*
				Bcf			
Argentina	805.0	747.3	542.8	760.0	781.2	886.0	931.8
Barbados	0.6	0.6	0.6	0.6	0.6	0.6	0.6
Bolivia	108.2	105.9	107.9	106.7	115.8	116.3	90.7
Brazil	113.3	100.4	109.5	117.3	107.8	113.3	113.3
Canada	4,258.6	4,579.8	5,069.4	5,441.3	5,855.1	6,196.2	6,462.3
Chile	39.2	32.2	37.9	40.2	40.5	41.2	40.4
Colombia	141.5	143.6	150.8	156.8	162.4	180.1	192.1
Ecuador	3.6	3.6	3.6	3.6	3.6	3.6	3.6
Guatemala	0.3	0.3	0.3	0.3	0.3	0.3	0.3
Mexico	1,322.7	1,343.8	1,311.6	1,310.6	1,323.0	1,372.1	1,536.5
Peru	46.0	45.3	32.1	33.9	34.6	32.8	34.2
Trinidad	177.7	164.6	194.2	217.9	249.7	268.0	245.4
United States	18,594.0	18,532.0	18,712.0	18,982.0	19,710.0	19,506.0	20,105.0
Venezuela	862.0	870.0	763.5	815.1	876.2	928.4	1,052.6
Western Hemisphere	**26,472.7**	**26,669.4**	**27,036.2**	**27,986.3**	**29,260.8**	**29,644.9**	**30,808.8**
Austria	38.3	44.7	50.2	51.4	47.4	52.3	51.6
Denmark	101.4	133.0	135.1	148.7	161.1	174.8	203.6
France	116.1	122.0	117.5	125.8	125.2	118.9	105.7
Germany	666.4	655.1	662.9	659.7	654.4	675.3	718.6
Greece	3.1	3.6	3.6	2.8	4.7	4.0	3.4
Ireland	81.9	88.6	88.7	88.4	88.3	88.3	98.0
Italy	610.9	614.5	641.0	687.5	728.9	719.8	720.1
Netherlands	2,618.1	2,918.7	3,001.2	3,053.0	2,771.8	2,766.9	3,297.5
Norway	901.6	868.7	899.9	871.0	947.1	981.9	1,341.2
Spain	47.3	46.6	42.7	22.2	6.4	6.7	7.1
Turkey	7.5	7.0	6.9	7.0	7.0	7.1	7.2
United Kingdom	1,750.2	1,953.2	1,975.9	2,313.1	2,470.6	2,649.6	3,105.7
Western Europe	**6,942.8**	**7,455.7**	**7,625.6**	**8,030.6**	**8,012.9**	**8,245.6**	**9,659.7**
Albania	4.9	4.9	3.5	1.1	0.7	0.7	0.7
Bulgaria	0.4	0.4	1.4	2.5	2.1	1.8	1.8
C.I.S.	28,861.0	28,682.3	27,828.1	26,871.0	25,673.8	24,893.3	25,684.4
Croatia	68.0	68.0	68.0	68.0	68.5	69.6	69.6
Czech Rep. and Slovakia	24.0	24.0	13.1	12.0	14.1	16.2	16.2
Hungary	175.0	175.5	169.2	189.3	172.0	172.3	158.4
Poland	145.8	145.8	142.0	174.8	163.5	170.2	168.4
Romania	876.2	876.2	781.8	745.8	691.8	678.0	680.0
Serbia	27.0	27.0	27.0	27.0	27.0	27.0	27.0
East Europe and C.I.S.	**30,182.3**	**30,004.1**	**29,034.1**	**28,091.5**	**26,813.5**	**26,029.1**	**26,806.5**
Algeria	1,900.0	1,903.8	1,970.5	1,902.0	1,776.3	2,051.8	2,192.2
Angola	20.5	20.5	20.1	19.8	19.8	19.8	19.9
Egypt	320.7	320.7	346.8	398.7	423.4	439.0	467.4
Gabon	3.6	3.6	3.6	3.6	3.6	3.6	3.6
Libya	202.9	231.1	238.2	224.6	226.1	223.9	226.5
Morocco	1.4	1.4	0.7	1.1	0.9	0.6	0.6
Nigeria	155.3	155.3	166.7	178.3	161.3	157.5	168.5
South Africa	—	—	1.4	63.6	68.9	69.2	68.1
Tunisia	8.5	8.5	14.1	13.1	12.4	11.9	11.9
Africa	**2,612.9**	**2,644.9**	**2,762.1**	**2,804.8**	**2,692.7**	**2,977.3**	**3,158.7**
Bahrain	209.8	157.0	165.8	180.2	182.8	185.3	201.0
Iran	854.7	909.4	882.9	956.0	1,123.0	1,239.5	1,254.9
Iraq	60.0	61.4	80.2	90.0	111.9	111.3	122.9
Israel	0.9	0.9	0.7	0.7	0.7	0.8	0.5
Jordan	4.2	4.2	6.0	7.1	10.0	10.4	10.1
Kuwait	147.8	17.7	92.5	191.4	210.8	210.8	216.0
Oman	107.0	107.7	122.5	139.8	153.3	170.9	176.9
Qatar	269.5	445.7	476.7	476.7	476.7	480.3	484.0
Saudi Arabia	1,130.0	1,130.0	1,200.1	1,267.8	1,331.4	1,424.6	1,428.1
Syria	123.0	123.6	127.1	130.7	141.6	169.2	168.1
United Arab Emirates	900.0	911.5	782.9	811.9	897.3	1,064.0	1,067.4
Middle East	**3,806.9**	**3,869.1**	**3,937.4**	**4,252.3**	**4,639.5**	**5,067.1**	**5,129.9**

World natural gas production (continued)

Country	1990	1991	1992	1993	1994	1995	1996*
	Bcf						
Afghanistan	10.4	10.4	10.4	10.4	10.4	10.4	10.4
Australia	731.6	745.6	839.2	841.3	997.0	1,050.0	1,051.6
Bangladesh	170.0	174.8	202.7	215.8	223.0	261.1	268.3
Brunei	285.5	291.2	308.9	310.0	317.4	364.9	355.8
China	517.7	526.8	549.9	584.9	599.3	607.7	669.3
India	480.0	488.8	541.0	565.0	600.7	693.3	761.6
Indonesia	1,247.9	1,360.3	1,538.1	1,799.7	1,852.6	2,179.3	2,228.7
Japan	75.0	75.2	76.6	76.6	77.0	76.7	76.7
Malaysia	746.0	746.9	796.3	880.4	922.7	1,052.0	1,053.5
Myanmar (Burma)	30.0	30.4	30.7	38.8	50.5	61.8	57.9
New Zealand	171.0	171.6	180.8	175.2	170.5	168.2	168.7
Pakistan	530.0	534.3	548.8	610.9	626.5	643.4	620.4
Papua New Guinea	0.0	0.0	2.1	2.8	3.4	3.5	4.8
Taiwan-China	32.0	32.2	27.6	27.0	29.6	29.8	29.5
Thailand	210.2	262.0	282.8	314.5	350.5	370.4	427.1
Viet Nam	0.0	20.0	24.0	24.3	24.6	47.3	45.4
Asia-Pacific	5,237.3	5,470.5	5,959.9	6,477.6	6,855.7	7,619.8	7,829.7
TOTAL WORLD	**75,254.9**	**76,113.7**	**76,355.3**	**77,643.1**	**78,275.1**	**79,583.8**	**83,393.3**

*Estimated.

Source: Oil & Gas Journal

World natural gas consumption

Country	1990	1991	1992	1993	1994	1995
	Bcf					
Argentina	649.79	721.48	619.77	833.07	856.38	955.97
Barbados	21.19	21.19	21.19	21.19	21.19	21.19
Bolivia	24.72	25.78	32.84	30.02	34.96	43.44
Brazil	113.01	117.60	130.31	145.85	152.21	159.27
Canada	2,337.83	2,384.45	2,533.48	2,713.23	2,781.39	2,835.42
Chile	52.97	54.03	56.15	61.80	68.51	67.10
Colombia	151.85	155.38	150.79	156.80	162.45	180.10
Ecuador	3.53	3.53	3.53	3.53	3.53	4.24
Guatemala	10.59	10.59	10.59	10.59	10.59	10.59
Mexico	1,000.11	996.23	1,019.89	936.19	952.79	994.11
Peru	35.31	35.31	32.14	33.90	34.61	32.84
Trinidad	194.23	201.29	194.23	217.89	249.67	268.04
United States	18,716.79	19,034.62	19,543.15	20,277.70	21,187.05	21,386.23
Venezuela	776.92	773.39	763.50	815.06	876.16	928.42
Western Hemisphere	**24,088.86**	**24,534.89**	**25,111.58**	**26,256.83**	**27,391.49**	**27,886.96**
Austria	226.01	234.14	233.78	244.73	246.85	292.76
Belgium	353.15	383.16	415.30	418.83	408.24	449.56
Denmark	88.29	99.59	88.99	102.77	110.18	125.72
Finland	98.88	100.29	104.18	109.48	120.07	127.13
France	1,172.45	1,222.95	1,274.51	1,198.23	1,253.32	1,309.12
Germany	2,577.97	2,705.81	2,707.22	2,881.68	2,956.55	3,127.47
Greece	3.88	3.88	3.53	2.47	1.77	1.41
Ireland	82.99	84.05	82.99	95.00	97.82	99.94
Italy	1,698.64	1,802.11	1,860.38	1,853.67	1,773.86	1,956.08
Luxembourg	21.19	22.25	22.95	24.01	24.01	24.01
Netherlands	1,398.46	1,543.96	1,517.83	1,524.54	1,446.14	1,447.20
Norway	79.46	80.87	85.81	90.05	92.88	92.88
Spain	211.89	211.89	246.85	237.67	264.51	308.30
Sweden	17.66	18.72	25.43	30.02	29.66	28.96
Switzerland	70.63	74.51	83.34	80.52	89.70	95.00
Turkey	141.26	149.38	163.86	183.99	193.17	250.73
United Kingdom	2,030.60	2,189.16	2,160.91	2,439.89	2,542.31	2,692.39
Western Europe	**10,273.40**	**10,926.72**	**11,077.87**	**11,517.54**	**11,651.03**	**12,428.66**

World natural gas consumption (continued)

Country	1990	1991	1992	1993	1994	1995
			Bcf			
Albania	4.94	4.94	3.53	1.06	1.06	0.71
Bulgaria	201.29	202.71	195.64	171.98	168.10	206.59
C.I.S.	24,914.52	25,014.81	23,791.51	23,278.04	21,663.80	20,726.55
Croatia	194.23	173.75	129.60	142.67	91.11	79.10
Czech Rep. and Slovakia	427.31	473.57	444.61	481.69	501.47	542.43
Hungary	395.52	391.64	347.85	376.45	355.62	394.82
Poland	427.31	379.28	364.45	383.16	382.46	424.48
Romania	1,296.05	1,062.62	953.50	908.29	850.73	893.46
Serbia, Slovenia and Bosnia	89.35	80.16	51.21	56.50	122.54	115.83
East Europe and C.I.S.	**27,950.53**	**27,783.49**	**26,281.91**	**25,799.86**	**24,136.89**	**23,383.98**
Algeria	706.29	707.00	729.95	655.09	690.40	728.19
Angola	20.48	20.48	20.13	19.78	18.36	19.78
Egypt	317.83	320.66	346.79	398.70	423.42	438.96
Gabon	3.53	3.53	3.53	3.53	3.53	3.53
Ivory Coast	0.00	0.00	0.00	0.00	0.00	1.41
Libya	173.04	175.16	174.10	168.10	173.40	171.28
Morocco	1.41	1.41	0.71	1.06	1.06	0.71
Nigeria	155.38	155.38	166.69	178.34	160.68	157.50
Senegal	0.00	0.00	0.00	0.71	1.41	1.77
South Africa	0.00	0.00	0.00	63.57	68.86	69.22
Tunisia	28.25	31.43	38.85	52.97	68.86	64.27
Africa	**1,406.23**	**1,415.06**	**1,480.75**	**1,541.84**	**1,610.00**	**1,656.61**
Bahrain	183.64	186.46	219.30	233.78	229.19	229.19
Iran	776.92	803.06	882.87	938.31	1,123.01	1,236.01
Iraq	60.03	61.45	80.16	90.05	111.95	111.24
Israel	1.41	1.41	1.06	1.06	1.06	0.71
Jordan	4.24	4.24	6.00	7.06	9.89	10.59
Kuwait	70.63	17.66	92.52	191.41	210.83	210.83
Oman	105.94	107.71	122.54	139.85	146.56	162.09
Qatar	247.20	269.45	445.67	476.75	476.75	480.28
Saudi Arabia	1,130.07	1,130.07	1,200.70	1,267.80	1,331.36	1,424.59
Syria	120.07	123.60	127.13	130.66	134.20	169.16
United Arab Emirates	776.92	789.64	662.15	693.58	765.27	833.43
Middle East	**3,477.09**	**3,494.74**	**3,840.12**	**4,170.31**	**4,540.06**	**4,868.13**
Afghanistan	10.59	10.59	10.59	10.59	10.59	10.59
Australia	552.68	512.77	557.97	539.96	595.76	628.60
Bangladesh	158.92	174.81	202.71	215.77	234.84	259.56
Brunei	28.25	30.02	34.26	28.60	24.72	32.49
China	519.13	526.19	536.43	558.33	588.70	601.41
India	395.52	448.85	541.02	531.84	593.64	657.56
Indonesia	706.29	764.92	796.70	849.67	965.15	1,059.09
Japan	1,744.55	1,863.56	1,938.07	1,949.37	2,083.92	2,119.59
Malaysia	342.55	409.65	412.83	457.68	481.69	542.08
Myanmar (Burma)	30.02	30.37	30.72	38.85	50.50	61.80
New Zealand	159.27	171.63	180.81	175.16	170.57	166.33
Pakistan	529.72	534.31	548.79	610.94	627.19	643.43
Papua New Guinea	0.00	0.00	2.12	2.83	1.77	1.77
Singapore	35.31	35.31	38.85	52.97	52.97	52.97
South Korea	109.83	128.19	161.74	204.83	278.99	336.55
Taiwan-China	66.04	104.88	109.12	111.24	140.55	150.79
Thailand	211.89	260.27	274.40	310.42	341.85	367.63
Viet Nam	0.00	6.00	7.42	8.83	8.83	47.32
Asia-Pacific	**5,600.56**	**6,012.33**	**6,384.54**	**6,657.88**	**7,252.23**	**7,739.57**
TOTAL WORLD	**72,796.66**	**74,167.23**	**74,176.76**	**75,944.26**	**76,581.69**	**77,963.91**

Source: Oil & Gas Journal and Cedigaz

PRODUCT CONSUMPTION

World petroleum product consumption

Area	1985	1986	1987	1988	1989	1990	1991	1992	1993	1994	1995
	1,000 b/d										
U.S.											
Gasolines	7,085.3	7,291.8	7,544.6	7,744.2	7,785.9	7,644.4	7,521.4	7,683.8	7,783.6	7,871.8	7,999.4
Middle distillates	4,300.8	4,481.4	4,590.6	4,823.7	4,865.7	4,840.5	4,731.3	4,806.9	4,928.7	5,172.3	5,216.4
Fuel oil	1,238.3	1,438.9	1,277.0	1,398.4	1,380.0	1,236.5	1,159.2	1,093.0	1,072.7	1,013.8	839.0
Others	2,976.8	2,995.6	3,164.7	3,281.6	3,196.0	3,227.3	3,196.0	3,396.4	3,356.7	3,530.0	3,509.1
Total USA	15,601.2	16,207.6	16,576.9	17,247.8	17,227.6	16,948.7	16,607.9	16,980.1	17,141.7	17,587.9	17,563.9
CANADA											
Gasolines	642.6	677.4	677.4	656.6	665.8	658.9	635.7	547.5	587.0	598.6	598.6
Middle distillates	466.2	474.6	478.8	508.2	527.1	504.0	470.4	499.8	514.5	546.0	564.9
Fuel oil	103.0	117.8	130.6	141.7	173.0	160.1	141.7	152.7	138.0	125.1	123.3
Others	271.4	269.3	290.2	344.4	357.0	346.5	361.1	398.7	411.2	419.6	430.0
Total Canada	1,483.3	1,539.1	1,577.0	1,650.9	1,722.9	1,669.5	1,608.9	1,598.8	1,650.7	1,689.3	1,716.8
MEXICO											
Gasolines	355.0	366.6	385.1	399.0	447.8	477.9	510.4	510.4	517.4	540.6	515.0
Middle distillates	256.2	239.4	243.6	235.2	243.6	258.3	273.0	291.9	294.0	310.8	283.5
Fuel oil	357.0	364.3	404.8	403.0	428.7	432.4	417.7	401.1	390.1	461.8	399.3
Others	227.5	215.0	215.0	217.1	223.4	238.0	265.1	283.9	292.3	302.7	296.4
Total Mexico	1,195.7	1,185.3	1,248.5	1,254.3	1,343.4	1,406.6	1,466.2	1,487.3	1,493.7	1,615.9	1,494.2
WESTERN EUROPE											
Gasolines	3,236.4	3,387.2	3,459.1	3,579.8	3,628.5	3,781.6	3,793.2	3,837.3	3,783.9	3,753.8	3,765.4
Middle distillates	4,788.0	5,014.8	5,058.9	5,121.9	5,084.1	5,205.9	5,441.1	5,483.1	5,554.5	5,571.3	5,699.4
Fuel oil	2,220.9	2,235.6	2,101.3	2,029.5	2,040.6	2,029.5	2,013.0	2,077.4	2,035.0	1,983.5	1,981.7
Others	1,872.5	1,960.2	2,016.5	2,112.6	2,131.3	2,158.5	2,210.7	2,302.5	2,292.1	2,363.1	2,390.2
Total Western Europe	12,117.8	12,597.8	12,635.8	12,843.7	12,884.5	13,175.5	13,457.9	13,700.3	13,665.5	13,671.6	13,836.6
JAPAN											
Gasolines	962.8	999.9	1,030.1	1,083.4	1,146.1	1,183.2	1,225.0	1,296.9	1,308.5	1,394.3	1,498.7
Middle distillates	1,335.6	1,398.6	1,459.5	1,612.8	1,663.2	1,745.1	1,816.5	1,856.4	1,881.6	1,934.1	2,003.4
Fuel oil	1,148.2	1,089.3	1,047.0	1,137.1	1,157.4	1,306.4	1,267.8	1,258.6	1,104.0	1,282.5	1,118.7
Others	810.0	826.7	803.7	822.5	862.1	889.3	916.4	958.2	974.9	970.7	968.6
Total Japan	4,256.5	4,314.5	4,340.2	4,655.8	4,828.8	5,124.0	5,225.6	5,370.0	5,268.9	5,581.6	5,589.4
AUSTRALASIA											
Gasolines	313.2	310.9	313.2	324.8	336.4	341.0	338.7	343.4	345.7	352.6	357.3
Middle distillates	218.4	228.9	241.5	254.1	264.6	270.9	273.0	277.2	300.3	312.9	331.8
Fuel oil	53.4	47.8	46.0	46.0	49.7	44.2	46.0	38.6	35.0	42.3	44.2
Others	81.4	108.6	114.8	119.0	121.1	133.6	121.1	121.1	144.0	148.2	150.3
Total Australasia	666.4	696.2	715.5	743.9	771.8	789.7	778.8	780.3	825.0	856.1	883.5
ASIAN EMERGING MARKET ECONOMIES (EMEs)											
Gasolines	872.3	953.5	1,076.5	1,136.8	1,252.8	1,496.4	1,607.8	1,814.2	1,976.6	2,303.8	2,487.0
Middle distillates	2,179.8	2,366.7	2,410.8	2,625.0	2,841.3	2,996.7	3,204.6	3,565.8	3,906.0	4,181.1	4,523.4
Fuel oil	1,584.2	1,635.8	1,729.6	1,898.9	2,051.6	2,057.1	2,169.4	2,323.9	2,450.9	2,531.8	2,688.2
Others	736.9	849.6	901.8	985.3	987.4	1,052.1	1,116.8	1,235.8	1,281.7	1,348.5	1,427.9
Total Asian EME'S	5,373.2	5,805.6	6,118.7	6,646.0	7,133.1	7,602.3	8,098.5	8,939.8	9,615.2	10,365.2	11,126.5
NON-ASIAN EMERGING MARKET ECONOMIES (excluding East Europe)											
Gasolines	1,767.8	1,795.7	1,842.1	1,874.6	1,941.8	2,004.5	2,039.3	2,115.8	2,187.8	2,340.9	2,440.6
Middle distillates	2,906.4	2,923.2	3,019.8	3,017.7	3,103.8	3,198.3	3,238.2	3,324.3	3,429.3	3,616.2	3,723.3
Fuel oil	2,001.9	2,082.9	2,128.9	2,176.7	2,233.8	2,259.5	2,353.4	2,323.9	2,300.0	2,314.7	2,368.1
Others	1,137.7	1,175.3	1,271.3	1,354.8	1,365.2	1,404.9	1,359.0	1,542.7	1,553.1	1,542.7	1,580.2
Total Non-Asian EME'S	7,813.8	7,977.0	8,262.0	8,423.8	8,644.6	8,867.2	8,989.8	9,306.7	9,470.2	9,814.5	10,112.3
TOTAL WORLD (excluding East Europe)											
Gasolines	15,235.4	15,783.0	16,328.2	16,799.1	17,205.1	17,587.9	17,671.4	18,149.4	18,490.4	19,156.2	19,662.0
Middle distillates	16,451.4	17,127.6	17,503.5	18,198.6	18,593.4	19,019.7	19,448.1	20,105.4	20,808.9	21,644.7	22,346.1
Fuel Oil	8,706.9	9,012.3	8,865.1	9,231.3	9,514.6	9,525.7	9,568.0	9,669.2	9,525.7	9,755.7	9,562.5
Others	8,114.1	8,400.1	8,777.9	9,237.2	9,243.5	9,450.1	9,546.1	10,239.2	10,306.0	10,625.4	10,752.7
TOTAL WORLD	**48,507.8**	**50,323.0**	**51,474.7**	**53,466.2**	**54,556.6**	**55,583.4**	**56,233.7**	**58,163.1**	**59,131.0**	**61,182.0**	**62,323.3**

Notes:
Western Europe = European members of OECD plus Cyprus, Gibralter, and Malta. Australasia = Australia, New Zealand. Asian EMEs = Non-OECD Asia. Other EMEs = South and Central America, Africa, and Middle East.

Gasolines = aviation and motor gasolines and light distillate feedstock. Middle distillates =- jet and heating kerosines, and gas and diesel oils (including marine bunkers). Fuel oil = heavy fuel oil and marine bunkers. Others = refinery gas LPG solvents, petroleum coke, lubricants, bitumen, wax, and refinery fuel and loss.

Source: Source: BP Statistical Review of World Energy   Conversion from metric tons to barrels per day by Oil & Gas Journal.

World oil supply and demand balance

	1992	1993	1994	1Q95	2Q95	3Q95	4Q95	1995	1Q96	2Q96	3Q96	4Q96	1996
	Million b/d												
DEMAND													
OECD													
North America	19.0	19.2	19.8	19.7	19.5	19.8	20.1	19.8	20.4	20.0	20.3	20.5	20.3
Europe	13.6	13.6	13.6	14.0	13.5	13.6	14.3	13.9	14.3	13.5	14.0	14.5	14.1
Pacific	6.3	6.3	6.6	7.3	6.2	6.3	6.9	6.7	7.4	6.2	6.3	7.0	6.7
TOTAL OECD	**38.8**	**39.0**	**40.0**	**41.1**	**39.2**	**39.8**	**41.3**	**40.3**	**42.1**	**39.6**	**40.6**	**42.1**	**41.1**
NON-OECD													
Former USSR	7.0	5.7	4.9	5.1	4.5	4.5	4.9	4.7	4.6	4.2	4.2	4.8	4.5
Europe	1.3	1.3	1.3	1.4	1.3	1.3	1.4	1.4	1.5	1.4	1.3	1.4	1.4
China	2.7	3.0	3.1	3.2	3.3	3.4	3.4	3.3	3.4	3.6	3.6	3.7	3.6
Asia	6.4	6.9	7.4	8.1	7.9	7.6	8.5	8.0	8.8	8.3	8.1	9.0	8.6
Latin America	5.5	5.7	6.0	6.2	6.0	6.1	6.2	6.1	6.2	6.3	6.4	6.4	6.3
Middle East	3.5	3.9	4.0	4.0	4.0	4.1	4.1	4.1	4.1	4.0	4.2	4.2	4.1
Africa	2.0	2.1	2.1	2.2	2.2	2.1	2.2	2.2	2.2	2.2	2.1	2.2	2.2
TOTAL NON-OECD	**28.4**	**28.5**	**28.9**	**30.3**	**29.1**	**29.0**	**30.6**	**29.8**	**30.8**	**30.1**	**30.0**	**31.8**	**30.7**
TOTAL DEMAND	**67.3**	**67.6**	**68.9**	**71.3**	**68.3**	**68.8**	**71.9**	**70.1**	**72.9**	**69.7**	**70.6**	**73.9**	**71.8**
SUPPLY													
OECD													
North America	11.1	11.0	10.9	11.1	11.0	10.9	11.0	11.0	11.0	11.0	11.0	11.3	11.1
Europe	4.8	5.1	6.0	6.4	6.0	6.2	6.7	6.3	6.6	6.6	6.5	7.3	6.8
Pacific	0.7	0.7	0.7	0.7	0.7	0.7	0.6	0.7	0.7	0.7	0.7	0.8	0.7
TOTAL OECD	**16.6**	**16.8**	**17.6**	**18.1**	**17.7**	**17.7**	**18.4**	**18.0**	**18.3**	**18.2**	**18.2**	**19.4**	**18.6**
NON-OECD													
Former USSR	8.9	7.9	7.3	7.1	7.1	7.1	7.1	7.1	7.0	7.0	7.1	7.1	7.0
Europe	0.3	0.3	0.3	0.3	0.3	0.3	0.3	0.3	0.3	0.3	0.3	0.3	0.3
China	2.8	2.9	2.8	3.0	2.9	3.0	3.0	3.0	3.1	3.1	3.1	3.2	3.1
Asia	1.8	1.8	1.9	2.0	2.1	2.1	2.1	2.1	2.0	2.0	2.0	2.0	2.0
Latin America	5.4	5.8	5.9	6.1	6.0	6.3	5.9	6.1	6.5	6.5	6.4	6.7	6.5
Middle East	1.5	1.6	1.8	1.9	1.9	1.9	1.9	1.9	1.9	1.9	1.9	1.9	1.9
Africa	2.0	2.3	2.4	2.5	2.6	2.6	2.6	2.6	2.6	2.7	2.7	2.8	2.7
Processing Gains	1.4	1.4	1.4	1.5	1.4	1.4	1.5	1.5	1.5	1.5	1.5	1.5	1.5
TOTAL NON-OPEC	**40.6**	**40.8**	**41.5**	**42.4**	**42.0**	**42.4**	**42.8**	**42.4**	**43.2**	**43.2**	**43.2**	**44.9**	**43.6**
OPEC													
Crude	24.4	24.4	24.7	24.8	24.9	25.2	25.3	25.1	25.7	25.6	26.0	26.0	25.8
NGLs	2.1	2.3	2.4	2.4	2.4	2.4	2.5	2.4	2.5	2.6	2.7	2.7	2.6
TOTAL OPEC	**26.5**	**26.6**	**27.0**	**27.2**	**27.3**	**27.6**	**27.8**	**27.5**	**28.2**	**28.2**	**28.6**	**28.6**	**28.4**
TOTAL SUPPLY	**67.1**	**67.5**	**68.6**	**69.6**	**69.3**	**70.1**	**70.5**	**69.9**	**71.3**	**71.4**	**71.9**	**72.6**	**72.0**
STOCK CHANGE AND MISCELLANEOUS													
REPORTED OECD													
Industry	−0.1	0.1	0.1	−1.3	0.7	0.4	−1.2	−0.3	−1.3	1.1	0.5	—	—
Government	0.1	0.1	0.1	0.1	−0.1	0.1	0.1	0.0	0.0	−0.1	−0.1	—	—
TOTAL OECD	0.0	0.2	0.2	−1.2	0.7	0.5	−1.2	−0.3	−1.3	1.0	0.4	—	—
Floating Storage/Oil in transit	0.0	0.1	−0.1	−0.3	0.1	0.2	0.3	0.1	−0.3	0.1	0.0	—	—
Other & Misc. to balance	−0.2	−0.4	−0.4	−0.2	0.2	0.5	−0.5	0.0	0.0	0.6	0.9	—	—
TOTAL STOCK CHANGE & MISC.	**−0.2**	**−0.1**	**−0.3**	**−1.7**	**0.9**	**1.2**	**−1.4**	**−0.2**	**−1.6**	**1.7**	**1.3**	**−1.3**	**0.2**

Source: International Energy Agency and Oil & Gas Journal

Refinery throughput

	1986	1987	1988	1989	1990	1991	1992	1993	1994	1995
	(Thousand barrels per calendar day)									
U.S.	12,715	12,855	13,245	13,400	13,410	13,300	13,410	13,615	13,865	13,970
Canada	1,380	1,440	1,530	1,560	1,600	1,535	1485	1,550	1,560	1,560
Mexico	1,305	1,355	1,360	1,420	1,490	1,510	1,495	1,540	1,425	1,315
South & Central America	4,310	4,410	4,640	4,745	4,800	4,665	4,735	4,835	4,915	4,835
Europe	12,475	12,460	12,745	13,630	13,570	13,795	13,980	14,215	14,335	14,395
Former Soviet Union	9,665	9,755	9,655	9,575	9,175	8,840	7,175	5,940	5,090	4,900
Middle East	3,765	3,935	4,265	4,350	4,340	3,800	4,325	4,825	4,935	5,145
Africa	1,920	2,000	2,100	2,185	2,355	2,360	2,355	2,330	2,270	2,315
China	1,865	1,950	2,035	2,110	2,155	2,280	2,450	2,570	2,545	2,710
Japan	2,990	2,910	2,990	3,175	3,435	3,655	3,880	3,980	4,165	4,170
South Asia	1,120	1,150	1,150	1,230	1,235	1,215	1,280	1,285	1,345	1,365
Other Asia	2,800	2,785	3,170	3,410	3,645	4,040	4,435	4,760	4,970	5,430
Australasia	580	645	680	700	715	745	745	755	785	805
Total world	**56,890**	**57,650**	**59,565**	**61,490**	**61,925**	**61,740**	**61,750**	**62,200**	**62,205**	**62,915**
Of which OECD*	29,480	29,590	30,530	31,855	32,540	33,265	33,905	34,485	34,890	34,915
Of which other EMEs†	15,780	16,230	17,360	18,030	18,530	18,360	19,580	20,605	20,980	21,800

*Organisation for Economic Cooperation and Development.
†Emerging Market Economics excluding Central Europe and Former Soviet Union.
Source: British Petroleum

Historical reserve data (billion bbl crude oil)

	1960	1970	1980	1985	1990	1991	1992	1993	1994	1995	1996	1997
Asia-Pacific												
Australia	—	2.0	2.4	1.4	1.7	1.6	1.5	1.8	1.6	1.6	1.6	1.8
Brunei	—	1.0	1.7	1.4	1.4	1.4	1.4	1.4	1.4	1.4	1.4	1.4
India	—	—	2.5	3.5	7.5	7.9	6.1	6.0	5.9	5.8	5.8	4.3
Indonesia	9.5	10.0	9.5	8.6	8.2	11.0	6.6	5.8	5.8	5.8	5.8	4.9
Malaysia	—	—	3.0	3.0	3.0	2.9	3.0	3.7	4.3	4.3	4.3	4.0
Europe												
Norway	—	1.0	5.5	8.3	11.5	7.6	7.6	8.8	9.3	9.4	8.4	11.2
United Kingdom	—	1.0	14.8	13.6	4.2	3.8	3.9	4.1	4.6	4.5	4.3	4.5
Middle East												
Abu Dhabi	—	11.8	29.0	30.5	92.2	92.2	92.2	92.2	92.2	92.2	92.2	92.2
Divided Zone	6.0	25.7	6.0	5.4	5.2	5.0	5.0	5.0	5.0	5.0	5.0	5.0
Dubai	—	—	1.4	1.4	4.0	4.0	4.0	4.0	4.0	4.3	4.3	4.0
Iran	35.0	70.0	57.5	48.5	92.8	92.9	92.9	92.9	92.9	89.3	88.2	93.0
Iraq	27.0	32.0	30.0	44.5	100.0	100.0	100.0	100.0	100.0	100.0	100.0	112.0
Kuwait	62.0	67.1	64.9	90.0	94.5	94.5	94.0	94.0	94.0	94.0	94.0	94.0
Oman	—	—	2.3	3.5	4.2	4.3	4.3	4.5	4.7	4.8	5.1	5.1
Qatar	2.5	3.5	3.6	3.4	4.5	4.5	3.7	3.7	3.7	3.7	3.7	3.7
Saudi Arabia	50.0	128.5	165.0	169.0	254.9	257.5	258.7	257.8	258.7	258.7	258.7	259.0
Syria	1.0	1.0	1.3	1.4	1.7	1.7	1.7	1.7	1.7	2.5	2.5	2.5
Yemen	—	—	—	—	3.0	4.0	4.0	4.0	4.0	4.0	4.0	4.0
Africa												
Algeria	5.2	7.0	8.2	9.0	9.2	9.2	9.2	9.2	9.2	9.2	9.2	9.2
Angola-Cabinda	—	—	1.2	1.8	2.0	2.1	1.8	1.5	1.5	5.4	5.4	5.4
Egypt	—	4.5	2.9	3.2	4.5	4.5	4.5	6.2	6.3	3.3	3.9	3.7
Gabon	—	—	—	—	0.7	0.7	0.7	0.7	0.7	1.3	1.3	1.3
Libya	2.0	29.2	23.0	21.1	22.8	22.8	22.8	22.8	22.8	22.8	29.5	29.5
Nigeria	—	9.3	16.7	16.7	16.0	17.1	17.9	17.9	17.9	17.9	20.8	15.5
Tunisia	—	—	1.7	1.5	1.8	1.7	1.7	1.7	1.7	0.4	0.4	0.3
Western Hemisphere												
Argentina	2.2	4.5	2.5	2.3	2.3	2.3	1.6	1.6	1.6	2.2	2.2	2.4
Brazil	—	—	1.3	1.9	2.8	2.8	2.8	3.0	3.6	3.8	4.2	4.8
Canada	—	10.7	6.4	7.1	6.1	5.8	5.6	5.3	5.1	5.0	4.9	4.9
Colombia	—	1.7	1.0	0.624	2.0	2.0	1.9	1.9	1.9	3.4	3.5	2.8
Ecuador	—	—	1.1	1.4	1.5	1.4	1.6	1.6	2.0	2.0	2.1	2.1
Mexico	2.3	3.2	44.0	48.6	56.4	51.9	51.3	51.3	50.9	50.8	49.8	48.8
Venezuela	18.5	14.0	17.9	25.8	58.5	59.0	59.1	62.7	63.3	64.5	64.5	64.9
U.S.	33.5	37.0	26.4	27.3	25.9	26.2	26.3	24.7	23.7	22.9	22.5	22.4
Subtotal*	**268.5**	**511.4**	**562.2**	**614.6**	**917.5**	**916.3**	**932.3**	**937.9**	**939.8**	**940.6**	**948.4**	**959.9**
C.I.S.†	33.5	77.0	63.0	63.0	24.0	57.0	57.0	57.0	57.0	57.0	57.0	59.1
China	—	—	—	19.1	24.0	24.0	24.0	24.0	24.0	24.0	24.0	24.0
Other	—	—	—	—	1.7	1.8	1.8	2.2	2.2	2.2	2.2	2.1
Total world*	**302.0**	**611.4**	**648.5**	**698.7**	**1,001.6**	**999.1**	**991.0**	**997.0**	**999.1**	**999.8**	**1,007.5**	**1,018.8**

*Columns do not add to totals because countries with lesser reserves are omitted. †U.S.S.R. before 1992.

Crude oil prices

	$/bbl												
	U.S. refiner acquisition cost			U.S. landed cost of imports	Selected countries						Average export prices		
Year	Domestic	Imported	Composite	Total	Canada	Mexico	United Kingdom	Nigeria	Saudi Arabia	Venezuela	Worldwide	OPEC	Non-OPEC
1979	14.27	21.67	17.72	21.45	20.22	20.77	22.97	22.97	18.95	17.65	NA	NA	NA
1980	24.29	33.89	28.07	33.67	30.11	31.77	35.68	37.15	29.80	25.92	NA	NA	NA
1981	34.93	37.05	35.24	36.47	32.32	33.70	37.29	39.66	34.20	29.91	34.81	34.42	36.16
1982	31.22	33.55	31.87	33.18	27.15	28.63	34.25	36.16	34.99	24.93	33.33	33.71	32.30
1983	28.87	29.30	28.99	28.93	25.63	25.78	30.87	30.85	29.27	22.94	29.66	29.89	29.13
1984	28.53	28.88	28.63	28.54	26.56	26.85	29.45	30.36	29.20	25.19	28.60	28.61	28.60
1985	26.66	26.99	25.75	26.67	25.71	25.63	28.36	28.96	24.72	24.43	27.60	28.00	26.98
1986	14.82	14.00	14.55	13.49	13.43	12.17	14.63	15.29	12.84	11.52	14.98	15.45	14.21
1987	17.76	18.13	17.90	17.65	17.04	16.69	18.78	19.32	16.81	15.76	17.41	17.31	17.57
1988	14.74	14.56	14.67	14.08	13.50	12.58	15.82	15.88	13.37	13.66	13.79	13.67	14.04
1989	17.87	18.08	17.97	17.68	16.81	16.35	18.74	19.19	17.34	16.78	16.65	16.40	17.11
1990	22.59	21.76	22.22	21.13	20.48	19.64	22.65	23.33	21.82	20.31	21.35	20.98	22.07
1991	19.33	18.70	19.06	18.02	17.16	15.89	21.37	21.39	17.22	15.92	17.82	17.36	18.52
1992	18.63	18.20	18.43	17.75	17.04	15.60	20.63	20.78	17.48	15.13	17.95	17.65	18.51
1993	16.67	16.14	16.41	15.72	15.27	14.11	17.92	18.73	15.40	13.39	15.81	15.45	16.44
1994	15.67	15.51	15.59	15.18	14.83	14.09	16.64	17.21	15.11	13.12	15.28	15.02	15.56
1995	17.33	17.14	17.24	16.77	16.64	16.20	17.95	18.25	16.82	14.84	16.78	16.51	17.11

From: Oil & Gas Journal Energy Database
Source: U.S. Department of Energy

Petroleum product prices

	(¢/gallon												
	Motor gasoline-pump price					Refiner resale (wholesale) product prices							
Year	Leaded Regular	Unleaded Regular	Unleaded Premium	Average All-Types	Heating Oil Residential	Motor Gasoline	Aviation Gasoline	Kerosene Jet Fuel	Kerosene	No. 2 Fuel Oil	No. 2 Diesel Oil	Propane	Resid
1979	85.7	90.3	NA	88.2	70.4	63.7	72.1	66.0	62.4	56.9	57.4	29.1	39.9
1980	119.1	124.5	NA	122.1	97.4	94.1	112.8	86.8	86.4	80.3	80.1	41.5	52.8
1981	131.1	137.8	147.0	135.3	119.4	106.4	125.0	101.2	106.6	97.6	97.2	46.6	66.3
1982	122.2	129.6	141.5	128.1	116.0	97.3	122.8	95.3	101.8	91.4	91.4	42.7	61.2
1983	115.7	124.1	138.3	122.5	107.8	88.2	117.8	85.4	89.2	81.5	80.8	48.4	60.9
1984	112.9	121.2	136.6	119.8	109.1	83.2	116.5	83.0	91.6	82.1	80.3	45.0	65.4
1985	111.5	120.2	134.0	119.6	105.3	83.5	113.0	79.4	87.4	77.6	77.2	39.8	57.7
1986	85.7	92.7	108.5	93.1	83.6	53.1	91.2	49.5	60.6	48.6	45.2	29.0	30.5
1987	89.7	94.8	109.3	95.7	80.3	58.9	85.9	53.8	59.2	52.7	53.4	25.2	38.5
1988	89.9	94.6	110.7	96.3	81.3	57.7	85.0	49.5	54.9	47.3	47.3	24.0	30.0
1989	99.8	102.1	119.7	106.0	90.0	65.4	95.0	58.3	66.9	56.5	56.7	24.7	36.0
1990	114.9	116.4	134.9	121.7	106.3	78.6	106.3	77.3	83.9	69.7	69.4	38.6	41.3
1991	112.5	114.0	132.1	119.6	101.9	69.9	100.1	65.0	72.2	62.2	61.5	34.9	31.4
1992	111.2	112.7	131.6	119.0	93.4	67.7	99.1	60.4	63.2	57.9	59.0	32.8	30.8
1993	N.A.	110.8	130.2	117.3	91.1	62.6	96.5	57.7	60.4	54.4	57.0	35.1	29.3
1994	N.A.	111.2	130.5	117.4	88.4	59.9	93.3	53.4	61.8	50.6	52.9	32.4	31.7
1995	N.A.	114.7	133.6	120.5	87.1	62.6	97.5	53.9	58.0	51.1	53.8	34.4	36.2

From: Oil & Gas Journal Energy Database
Source: U.S. Department of Energy

Comparative energy prices

	Natural gas delivered to consumers ($/MCF)					Cost of fossil fuels delivered to utilities (¢/Million BTU)				Electricity retail prices ¢/Kilowatt Hour)			
Year	Residential	Commercial	Industrial	Electric Utilities	Consumer Average	Coal	Heavy oil	Natural gas	All fuels	Residential	Commercial	Industrial	Total
1979	2.98	2.73	1.99	1.81	2.21	122.4	298.8	174.9	163.9	4.64	4.68	3.05	3.99
1980	3.68	3.39	2.56	2.27	2.80	135.1	426.7	219.9	192.8	5.36	5.48	3.69	4.73
1981	4.29	4.00	3.14	2.89	3.39	153.2	533.4	280.5	225.6	6.20	6.29	4.29	5.46
1982	5.17	4.82	3.87	3.48	4.15	164.7	483.0	337.6	224.9	6.86	6.86	4.95	6.13
1983	6.06	5.59	4.18	3.58	4.82	165.6	457.0	347.4	220.6	7.18	7.01	4.97	6.29
1984	6.12	5.55	4.22	3.70	4.85	166.4	481.0	360.3	219.1	7.54	7.33	5.04	6.52
1985	6.12	5.50	3.95	3.55	4.72	164.8	424.4	344.4	209.4	7.79	7.47	5.16	6.71
1986	5.83	5.08	3.23	2.43	4.13	157.9	240.1	235.1	175.0	7.41	7.13	4.90	6.42
1987	5.54	4.77	2.94	2.32	4.05	150.6	297.6	224.0	170.6	7.41	7.01	4.72	6.32
1988	5.47	4.63	2.95	2.33	4.09	146.6	240.5	226.3	164.3	7.49	7.07	4.62	6.31
1989	5.64	4.74	2.96	2.43	4.22	144.5	284.6	235.5	167.5	7.64	7.23	4.69	6.43
1990	5.80	4.83	2.93	2.39	4.19	145.5	331.9	232.1	168.9	7.85	7.34	4.75	6.57
1991	5.82	4.81	2.69	2.18	4.07	144.7	246.5	215.3	160.3	8.05	7.51	4.85	6.75
1992	5.89	4.88	2.84	2.36	4.17	141.2	247.5	232.8	159.0	8.23	7.63	4.84	6.83
1993	6.16	5.22	3.07	2.61	4.43	138.5	236.2	256.0	159.5	8.34	7.72	4.86	6.92
1994	6.41	5.44	3.05	2.28	4.51	135.5	240.9	223.0	152.6	8.41	7.75	4.72	6.92
1995	6.06	5.01	2.66	2.02	4.10	131.8	258.6	198.4	145.3	8.42	7.70	4.69	6.90

From Oil & Gas Journal Energy Database
Source: U.S. Department of Energy

Price history, crude oil, natural gas and motor gasoline

	Actual current prices						Inflation adjusted real prices				
	Crude oil			Natural gas			Crude oil			Natural gas	
Year	U.S. average wellhead $/bbl	West Texas Inter-mediate posted $/bbl	Motor* Gasoline pump price $/gal	U.S. average wellhead $/Mcf	Consumer average $/Mcf	Producer Price index 1982-100	U.S. average wellhead $/bbl	West Texas Inter-mediate posted $/bbl	Motor Gasoline pump price $/gal	U.S. average wellhead $/Mcf	Consumer average $/Mcf
1925	1.68	1.79	0.222	0.094	0.223	17.8	9.438	10.056	1.247	0.528	1.253
1927	1.30	1.28	0.211	0.088	0.220	16.5	7.879	7.758	1.278	0.533	1.333
1929	1.27	1.45	0.214	0.082	0.216	16.4	7.744	8.841	1.306	0.500	1.317
1931	0.65	0.77	0.170	0.070	0.233	12.6	5.159	6.111	1.348	0.556	1.849
1932	0.87	0.69	0.179	0.064	0.247	11.2	7.768	6.161	1.601	0.571	2.205
1933	0.67	1.00	0.178	0.062	0.237	11.4	5.877	8.772	1.563	0.544	2.079
1934	1.00	1.00	0.189	0.060	0.223	12.9	7.752	7.752	1.461	0.465	1.729
1935	0.97	1.00	0.188	0.058	0.224	13.8	7.029	7.246	1.365	0.420	1.623
1936	1.09	1.10	0.195	0.055	0.220	13.9	7.842	7.914	1.399	0.396	1.583
1937	1.18	1.22	0.200	0.051	0.220	14.9	7.919	8.188	1.342	0.342	1.477
1938	1.13	1.02	0.195	0.049	0.218	13.5	8.370	7.556	1.445	0.363	1.615
1939	1.02	1.02	0.188	0.049	0.216	13.3	7.669	7.699	1.410	0.368	1.624
1940	1.02	1.02	0.184	0.045	0.217	13.5	7.556	7.556	1.364	0.333	1.607
1941	1.14	1.17	0.192	0.049	0.221	15.1	7.550	7.748	1.274	0.325	1.464
1942	1.19	1.17	0.204	0.051	0.227	17.0	7.000	6.882	1.202	0.300	1.335
1943	1.20	1.17	0.205	0.052	0.223	17.8	6.742	6.573	1.153	0.292	1.253
1944	1.21	1.17	0.206	0.051	0.215	17.9	6.760	6.536	1.150	0.285	1.201
1945	1.22	1.17	0.205	0.049	0.214	18.2	6.703	6.429	1.126	0.269	1.176
1946	1.41	1.36	0.208	0.053	0.220	20.8	6.779	6.524	0.999	0.255	1.058
1947	1.93	1.84	0.231	0.060	0.232	25.6	7.539	7.188	0.903	0.234	0.906
1948	2.60	2.57	0.259	0.065	0.241	27.7	9.386	9.278	0.934	0.235	0.870
1949	2.54	2.57	0.268	0.063	0.254	26.3	9.658	9.772	1.019	0.240	0.966
1950	2.51	2.57	0.268	0.065	0.266	27.3	9.194	9.414	0.980	0.238	0.974
1951	2.53	2.57	0.272	0.073	0.298	30.4	8.322	8.454	0.893	0.240	0.980
1952	2.53	2.57	0.276	0.078	0.332	29.6	8.547	8.682	0.931	0.264	1.122
1953	2.68	2.72	0.287	0.092	0.355	29.2	9.178	9.298	0.983	0.315	1.216
1954	2.78	2.82	0.290	0.101	0.381	29.3	9.488	9.625	0.991	0.345	1.300
1955	2.77	2.82	0.291	0.104	0.400	29.3	9.454	9.625	0.992	0.355	1.365
1956	2.79	2.82	0.299	0.108	0.415	30.3	9.208	9.307	0.988	0.356	1.370
1957	3.09	3.04	0.310	0.113	0.431	31.2	9.904	9.753	0.992	0.362	1.381
1958	3.01	3.06	0.304	0.119	0.462	31.6	9.525	9.677	0.961	0.377	1.462
1959	2.90	2.98	0.305	0.129	0.477	31.7	9.148	9.385	0.962	0.407	1.505
1960	2.88	2.97	0.311	0.140	0.500	31.7	9.085	9.369	0.982	0.442	1.577
1961	2.89	2.97	0.308	0.151	0.510	31.6	9.146	9.399	0.973	0.478	1.614
1962	2.90	2.97	0.306	0.155	0.514	31.7	9.148	9.369	0.967	0.489	1.621
1963	2.89	2.97	0.304	0.158	0.512	31.6	9.146	9.399	0.963	0.500	1.620
1964	2.88	2.95	0.304	0.154	0.519	31.6	9.114	9.320	0.962	0.487	1.642
1965	2.86	2.92	0.312	0.156	0.522	32.3	8.854	9.040	0.966	0.483	1.616
1966	2.88	2.94	0.321	0.157	0.523	33.3	8.649	8.817	0.964	0.471	1.571
1967	2.92	3.03	0.332	0.160	0.520	33.4	8.743	9.060	0.994	0.479	1.557
1968	2.94	3.07	0.337	0.164	0.504	34.2	8.596	8.977	0.985	0.480	1.474
1969	3.09	3.30	0.348	0.167	0.515	35.6	8.680	9.256	0.978	0.469	1.447
1970	3.18	3.35	0.357	0.171	0.550	36.9	8.618	9.079	0.967	0.463	1.491
1971	3.39	3.56	0.364	0.182	0.590	38.0	8.921	9.368	0.958	0.479	1.553
1972	3.39	3.56	0.361	0.186	0.630	39.8	8.518	8.945	0.907	0.467	1.583
1973	3.89	3.87	0.388	0.216	0.680	45.0	8.644	8.604	0.862	0.480	1.511
1974	6.74	10.37	0.532	0.304	0.840	53.5	12.598	19.383	0.994	0.568	1.570
1975	7.56	11.16	0.567	0.445	1.120	58.4	12.945	19.110	0.971	0.762	1.918
1976	8.14	12.65	0.590	0.580	1.370	61.1	13.322	20.704	0.966	0.949	2.242
1977	8.57	14.30	0.622	0.790	1.660	64.9	13.205	22.034	0.958	1.217	2.558
1978	8.96	14.85	0.626	0.905	1.850	69.9	12.818	21.245	0.896	1.295	2.647
1979	12.51	22.40	0.857	1.178	2.210	78.7	15.896	28.463	1.089	1.497	2.808
1980	21.59	37.37	1.191	1.590	2.800	89.7	24.069	41.661	1.328	1.773	3.122
1981	31.77	36.67	1.311	1.980	3.390	98.0	32.418	37.418	1.338	2.020	3.459
1982	28.52	32.75	1.296	2.460	4.150	100.0	28.520	32.750	1.296	2.460	4.150
1983	26.19	30.25	1.241	2.590	4.820	101.2	25.879	29.891	1.226	2.559	4.763
1984	25.88	29.83	1.212	2.660	4.850	103.6	24.981	28.793	1.170	2.568	4.681
1985	24.09	28.08	1.202	2.510	4.720	103.1	23.366	27.236	1.166	2.435	4.578
1986	12.51	16.44	0.927	1.940	4.130	100.1	12.498	16.421	0.926	1.938	4.046
1987	15.40	18.21	0.948	1.670	4.050	102.8	14.981	17.714	0.922	1.625	3.940
1988	12.58	15.52	0.946	1.690	4.090	106.9	11.768	14.518	0.885	1.581	3.826
1989	15.86	18.29	1.021	1.690	4.220	112.2	14.135	16.301	0.910	1.506	3.761
1990	20.03	23.17	1.164	1.710	4.190	116.3	17.223	19.923	1.001	1.470	3.603
1991	16.54	20.42	1.140	1.640	4.071	116.5	14.197	17.528	0.979	1.408	3.494
1992	15.99	19.67	1.127	1.740	4.173	117.2	13.643	16.783	0.962	1.485	3.561
1993	14.25	18.17	1.108	2.040	4.429	118.9	11.985	15.282	0.932	1.716	3.725
1994	13.19	16.46	1.112	1.880	4.509	120.4	10.955	13.671	0.924	1.561	3.745
1995	14.62	17.50	1.147	1.590	4.095	124.7	11.724	14.034	0.920	1.275	3.284

*Leaded gasoline price prior to 1982, unleaded gasoline price beginning in 1982.
From: Oil & Gas Journal Energy Database
Source: U.S. Department of Energy

International active rig count

Region	1989	1990	1991	1992	1993	1994			1995			1996		
						Land	Off.	Total	Land	Off.	Total	Land	Off.	Total
NORTH AMERICA														
Canada	130	138	121	96	184	261	0	261	229	1	230	269	1	270
United States*	869	1,010	860	721	754	673	102	775	621	101	722	671	108	779
Subtotal	**999**	**1,148**	**981**	**817**	**938**	**934**	**102**	**1,036**	**850**	**102**	**952**	**940**	**109**	**1,049**
LATIN AMERICA														
Argentina	55	64	60	49	42	70	1	71	91	1	92	67	1	68
Bolivia	6	6	10	16	11	10	0	10	8	0	8	7	0	7
Brazil	28	23	21	26	25	14	9	23	11	9	20	11	11	22
Chile	5	6	6	4	4	2	1	3	2	1	3	1	1	2
Colombia	15	11	9	12	13	15	0	15	16	0	16	14	0	14
Costa Rica	0	0	0	0	0	0	0	0	0	0	0	0	0	0
Ecuador	5	2	7	4	6	6	0	6	3	0	3	3	0	3
Mexico	103	90	109	80	36	12	16	28	20	14	34	33	13	46
Peru	10	6	3	6	6	3	1	4	4	2	6	6	1	7
Trinidad	6	8	6	23	2	1	4	5	1	4	5	0	4	4
Venezuela	28	32	45	50	58	41	28	69	59	26	85	78	30	108
Other	0	0	0	0	0	0	0	0	0	0	0	0	0	0
Subtotal	**261**	**248**	**276**	**250**	**203**	**174**	**60**	**234**	**215**	**57**	**272**	**220**	**61**	**281**
FAR EAST														
Australia	14	14	12	10	11	6	6	12	6	6	12	9	5	14
Bangladesh	5	4	0	0	0	0	0	0	0	0	0	0	0	0
Brunei	4	5	4	2	1	0	2	2	0	1	1	1	1	2
China-offshore	4	3	2	3	21	6	6	12	5	7	12	0	9	9
India	135	137	136	124	105	69	13	82	58	12	70	51	10	61
Indonesia	46	52	53	50	40	26	12	38	25	10	35	31	12	43
Japan	6	7	6	7	8	6	1	7	7	1	8	7	0	7
Malaysia	12	13	13	10	10	1	9	10	0	8	8	0	6	6
Myanmar (Burma)	23	19	22	18	15	10	0	10	10	0	10	10	1	11
New Zealand	2	1	1	1	2	1	1	2	1	1	2	1	0	1
Papua New Guinea	3	3	2	2	1	2	0	2	2	0	2	2	0	2
Philippines	7	6	5	7	9	9	1	10	7	0	7	5	1	6
Taiwan	5	3	3	4	3	2	1	3	1	1	2	1	1	2
Thailand	6	5	4	5	5	1	4	5	0	4	4	1	6	7
Viet Nam	N/A	N/A	N/A	N/A	N/A	0	8	8	0	6	6	0	6	6
Other	1	1	0	0	0	0	1	1	0	0	0	0	1	1
Subtotal	**273**	**273**	**263**	**243**	**231**	**139**	**65**	**204**	**122**	**57**	**179**	**119**	**59**	**178**
AFRICA														
Algeria	24	35	31	30	29	28	0	28	28	0	28	28	0	28
Angola	8	8	6	4	4	0	5	5	0	7	7	0	10	10
Congo	1	2	3	4	2	0	2	2	0	2	2	0	3	3
Gabon	6	5	5	3	3	2	0	2	1	2	3	2	1	3
Kenya	3	1	0	1	0	0	0	0	0	0	0	0	0	0
Libya	17	15	15	15	15	13	0	13	11	0	11	13	0	13
Nigeria	14	18	21	16	10	1	6	7	1	8	9	0	14	14
South Africa	3	3	2	1	2	0	1	1	0	1	1	0	0	0
Tunisia	3	3	6	3	3	1	2	3	2	1	3	1	1	2
Other	4	2	0	1	2	1	2	3	0	3	3	0	4	4
Subtotal	**83**	**92**	**89**	**78**	**70**	**46**	**18**	**64**	**43**	**24**	**67**	**44**	**33**	**77**
EUROPE														
Austria	2	1	2	2	1	0	0	0	1	0	1	0	0	0
Croatia†	32	31	15	1	0	0	0	0	0	0	0	3	0	3
Denmark	2	2	2	3	3	0	2	2	0	2	2	0	2	2
France	7	6	4	3	3	2	0	2	1	0	1	1	0	1
Germany	8	9	7	6	7	8	0	8	9	0	9	9	0	9
Greece	1	0	0	0	0	0	0	0	0	0	0	0	0	0
Hungary	N/A	N/A	4	2	2	2	0	2	2	0	2	2	0	2
Italy	22	21	25	23	14	10	1	11	10	1	11	11	2	13
Netherlands	12	14	11	10	7	2	3	5	3	5	8	5	6	11

International active rig count — continued

Region	1989	1990	1991	1992	1993	1994 Land	1994 Off.	1994 Total	1995 Land	1995 Off.	1995 Total	1996 Land	1996 Off.	1996 Total
Norway	12	12	16	15	13	0	14	14	0	13	13	0	15	15
Poland	N/A	N/A	22	18	18	18	0	18	18	0	18	18	0	18
Romania	N/A	N/A	N/A	1	4	4	0	4	4	0	4	3	0	3
Spain	3	1	1	0	0	0	0	0	0	0	0	0	0	0
Turkey	20	17	19	15	16	16	0	16	15	0	15	10	0	10
United Kingdom	46	48	39	33	24	1	22	23	1	26	27	1	30	31
Other	0	0	1	1	1	1	1	2	2	0	2	2	1	3
Subtotal	**167**	**162**	**168**	**133**	**113**	**64**	**43**	**107**	**66**	**47**	**113**	**65**	**56**	**121**
MIDDLE EAST														
Abu Dhabi	6	9	13	15	15	7	8	15	7	7	14	7	7	14
Dubai	3	3	3	3	3	1	1	2	1	2	3	0	3	3
Egypt	18	15	17	16	13	7	7	14	7	10	17	10	9	19
Iran	20	19	21	39	45	19	2	21	20	1	21	20	2	22
Iraq§	26	23	N/A	0	0	0	0	0	0	0	0	0	0	0
Jordan	3	2	2	2	0	0	0	0	0	0	0	0	0	0
Kuwait§	4	2	1	4	9	9	0	9	7	0	7	5	0	5
Oman	13	17	14	12	16	16	0	16	17	0	17	19	0	19
Pakistan	13	11	10	11	9	10	0	10	11	0	11	11	0	11
Qatar	3	2	3	4	4	1	3	4	1	3	4	2	6	8
Saudi Arabia	5	10	16	22	21	13	4	17	14	3	17	14	3	17
Syria	24	17	14	17	15	12	0	12	13	0	13	15	0	15
Yemen	2	3	5	8	6	4	0	4	3	0	3	3	0	3
Other	1	1	0	2	1	2	0	2	1	0	1	1	0	1
Subtotal	**141**	**134**	**119**	**155**	**157**	**101**	**25**	**126**	**102**	**26**	**128**	**107**	**30**	**137**
Total	**1,924**	**2,057**	**1,896**	**1,676**	**1,712**	**1,458**	**313**	**1,771**	**1,398**	**313**	**1,711**	**1,495**	**348**	**1,843**

*U.S. land includes inland water rigs: 17 in 1994, 16 in 1995, 19 in 1996. †Prior to 1996 listed as Yugoslavia. §1990 data for Iraq and Kuwait is average rigs January through August.

Source: Baker Hughes Inc.

International refining margins*

		1987	1988	1989	1990	1991	1992	1993	1994	1995	1996
		$/bbl									
U.S. Gulf Coast											
West Texas sour	Cracking	1.40	3.15	3.05	4.03	3.69	2.47	2.33	2.20	2.19	3.37
West Texas sour	Coking	1.92	4.28	4.15	5.97	5.71	3.94	3.71	3.05	2.78	4.20
Arab light	Coking	2.29	4.63	5.31	5.80	5.91	4.25	4.15	4.40	3.56	3.63
Bonny light	Coking	1.59	3.05	3.66	4.11	4.61	3.11	2.73	2.64	2.37	2.41
U.S. PADD II											
Chicago (WTI)	Coking	1.15	3.10	5.26	6.06	4.50	3.35	3.22	3.70	3.00	3.74
U.S. East Coast											
NY Harbor (Arab med)	Cracking	2.29	3.92	4.59	2.98	3.48	1.71	2.53	3.94	3.40	2.89
U.S. West Coast											
Los Angeles (ANS)	Coking	3.78	5.84	6.68	7.56	6.63	6.11	6.98	5.00	4.33	5.13
NW Europe											
Rotterdam (Brent)	Cracking	1.48	2.98	3.25	4.68	5.16	3.16	3.33	2.59	2.48	2.78
Mediterranean											
Italy (Urals)	Cracking	0.92	1.63	1.86	2.36	3.58	2.52	2.80	1.33	1.67	1.82
Far East											
Singapore (Dubai)	Cracking	1.79	2.32	3.14	4.85	5.92	3.43	3.69	2.52	2.52	2.57

*Gross margins before costs.

Source: The Pace Consultants, Inc.

Assays of world crude oils

This year's assays are of crude oil from two important new oil fields: Cusiana in central Colombia and Mars in federal waters of the Gulf of Mexico off Louisiana.

Cusiana is owned by Empresa Colombiana de Petroleos (50%), BP (19%), Total Exploratie en Produktie (19%), and Triton Colombia Inc. (12%). Operator is BP Exploration Co. (Colombia) Ltd.

Cusiana crude is shipped from the field in Colombia's Central Pipeline System to Coveñas, on Colombia's northern coast. From there, the crude can reach the U.S. Gulf Coast in 5 days or the Philadelphia harbor in 6 days.

The light, sweet crude has low concentrations of nitrogen and metals, low acidity, and low residual yields. It has excellent characteristics for producing feeds for reforming, fluid catalytic cracking, and coking.

Table 1 shows Cusiana's distillation data and Table 2, detailed analyses of its heavy distillate and residue fractions.

Mars field is owned by Shell Oil Co. (71.5%) and BP (28.5%). Final crude quality may differ slightly from the values shown here, which were determined on a preproduction well sample.

The light, medium-sulfur crude is piped ashore to Fourchon, La. From there it can enter a number of pipelines. Table 3 summarizes the distillation data for Mars crude oil.

Cusiana
Colombia

Whole crude
Gravity, °API: 36.35
Sulfur, wt %: 0.25
Visc. @ 68° F., cSt: 7.26
Visc. @ 86° F., cSt: 4.73
Visc. @ 104° F., cSt: 3.31
Pour pt., °F.: 32
Acidity, mg KOH/g: <0.05
Conradson carbon, wt %: 1.2
Asphaltenes, wt %: 0.09
V/Ni, ppm(wt): <2/<2
Salt, lb/1,000 bbl: <1
Water, vol %: <0.05

Range: Light hydrocarbons
Yield C_1-C_4, wt %: 1.85
Isopentane, wt %: 1.05
n-Pentane, wt %: 1.09

Range, °F.: C_5-203
Yield, wt %: 7.45
Yield, vol %: 9.2
Gravity, °API: 75.92
Sulfur, wt %: <0.001
Mercaptan S, wt %: <0.0002
Paraffins, wt %: 74.9
Naphthenes, wt %: 21.4
Aromatics, wt %: 3.7
n-Paraffins, wt %: 31.8

Range, °F.: 203-347
Yield, wt %: 15.3
Yield, vol %: 16.8
Gravity, °API: 52.79
Sulfur, wt %: <0.001
Mercaptan S, wt %: <0.0002
Paraffins, wt %: 44.9
Naphthenes, wt %: 33.1
Aromatics, wt %: 22.0
n-Paraffins, wt %: 15.7

Range, °F.: C_5-300
Yield, wt %: 17.9
Yield, vol %: 20.8
Gravity, °API: 63.54
Sulfur, wt %: <0.001
Mercaptan S, wt %: <0.0002
Paraffins, wt %: 57.1
Naphthenes, wt %: 29.1
Aromatics, wt %: 13.8
n-Paraffins, wt %: 22.6

Range, °F.: 300-450
Yield, wt %: 15.15
Yield, vol %: 15.9
Gravity, °API: 44.39
Sulfur, wt %: 0.002
Mercaptan S, wt %: <0.0002
Visc. @ 104° F., cSt: 1.12
Visc. @ 140° F., cSt: 0.89
Acidity, mg KOH/g: 0.018
Aromatics, vol %: 18.9
Smoke pt., mm: 22
Freeze, pt., °F.: –83
Aniline pt., °F.: 130.3
Cetane index (ASTM D976/1P380): 36.8/40.4
Hydrogen, wt %: 13.8
Color stability: Stable
Naphthalenes, vol %: 1.52

Range, °F.: 450-648
Yield, wt %: 24.9
Yield, vol %: 24.3
Gravity, °API: 32.16
Sulfur, wt %: 0.12
Visc. @ 122° F., cSt: 3.01
Visc. @ 212° F., cSt: 1.38
Cloud pt., °F.: 0
Pour pt., °F.: 0
Wax, wt %: 4.9
Total nitrogen, ppm(wt): 40
Acidity, mg KOH/g: <0.01
Aromatics, vol %: 20.4*
Smoke pt., mm: 15
Freeze, pt., °F.: –8†
Aniline pt., °F.: 153.9
Cetane index (ASTM D976/IP380): 44.9/47.4
Aromatics, wt %: 23.0*
Color stability: Stable
Naphthalenes, vol %: 8.87

Range, °F.: 648-696
Yield, wt %: 5.8
Yield, vol %: 5.5
Gravity, °API: 27.26
Sulfur, wt %: 0.39
Visc. @ 122° F., cSt: 8.69
Visc. @ 212° F., cSt: 2.77
Cloud pt., °F.: 53
Pour pt., °F.: 53
Wax, wt %: 15.9
Total nitrogen, ppm(wt): 290
Aniline pt., °F.: 173.3
Cetane index: 45.8
Refractive index @ 158° F.: 1.4747

Range, °F.: 696-948
Yield, wt %: 23.25
Yield, vol %: 21.65
Gravity, °API: 24.68
Sulfur, wt %: 0.44
Visc. @ 140° F., cSt: 21.05
Visc. @ 212° F., cSt: 6.65
Pour pt., °F.: 102
Wax, wt %: 23.0
Total nitrogen, ppm(wt): 750
Basic nitrogen, ppm(wt): 185
Organic oxygen, wt %: 0.2
Acidity, mg KOH/g: <0.01
Conradson carbon wt %: 0.02
Aniline pt., °F.: 200.8
Refractive index @ 158° F.: 1.4825

Dewaxed oil
Gravity, °API: 20.59
Visc. @ 104° F., cSt: 113.0
Visc. @ 140° F., cSt: 37.90
Visc. @ 212° F., cSt: 9.02
Viscosity index: 21
Pour pt., °F.: –11

Range, °F.: 948-1,022
Yield, wt %: 3.15
Yield, vol %: 2.8
Gravity, °API: 18.70
Sulfur, wt %: 0.66
Visc. @ 140° F., cSt: 188
Visc. @ 212° F., cSt: 29.55
Wax, wt %: 16.2
Total nitrogen, ppm(wt): 1,700
Basic nitrogen, ppm(wt): 375
Acidity, mg KOH/g: <0.01
Conradson carbon, wt %: 1.4
Aniline pt., °F.: 211.1
Refractive index @ 158° F.: 1.5058

Range, °F.: 648+§
Yield, wt %: 40.2
Yield, vol %: 36.8
Gravity, °API: 22.05
Sulfur, wt %: 0.54
Visc. @ 122° F., cSt: 62.4
Pour pt., °F.: 102
Wax, wt %: 19.5
Total nitrogen, ppm(wt): 1,210
Carbon residue, wt %: 2.9
Asphaltenes, wt %: 0.2
V/Ni, ppm(wt): <2/<2

Range, °F.: 696+
Yield, wt %: 34.4
Yield, vol %: 31.3
Gravity, °API: 21.14

Table 1

Cusiana distillation

TBP cut point, °C.	50	55	60	65	70	75	80	85	90	95
Total distillate, wt %	4.37	4.76	5.17	5.62	6.10	6.63	7.22	7.85	8.55	9.30
Total distillate, vol %	5.56	6.05	6.56	7.10	7.69	8.32	9.00	9.74	10.54	11.40
TBP cut point, °C.	100	105	110	115	120	125	130	135	140	145
Total distillate, wt %	10.11	10.98	11.89	12.84	13.82	14.82	15.85	16.88	17.91	18.94
Total distillate, vol %	12.32	13.30	14.32	15.39	16.48	17.60	18.73	19.86	20.99	22.12
TBP cut point, °C.	150	155	160	165	170	175	180	185	190	195
Total distillate, wt %	19.95	20.95	21.91	22.85	23.75	24.60	25.41	26.18	26.95	27.73
Total distillate, vol %	23.22	24.29	25.34	26.34	27.29	28.20	29.05	29.87	30.68	31.50
TBP cut point, °C.	200	205	210	215	220	225	230	235	240	245
Total distillate, wt %	28.55	29.42	30.35	31.32	32.33	33.38	34.46	35.57	36.69	37.83
Total distillate, vol %	32.35	33.26	34.22	35.23	36.27	37.35	38.45	39.58	40.71	41.85
TBP cut point, °C.	250	255	260	265	270	275	280	285	290	295
Total distillate, wt %	38.97	40.12	41.25	42.37	43.48	44.59	45.70	46.82	47.95	49.10
Total distillate, vol %	43.00	44.13	45.26	46.37	47.46	48.55	49.64	50.73	51.82	52.93
TBP cut point, °C.	300	305	310	315	320	325	330	335	340	345
Total distillate, wt %	50.26	51.42	52.59	53.76	54.91	56.05	57.17	58.27	59.37	60.45
Total distillate, vol %	54.05	55.17	56.30	57.41	58.52	59.61	60.69	61.74	62.79	63.82
TBP cut point, °C.	350	355	360	365	370	375	380	385	390	395
Total distillate, wt %	61.53	62.61	63.68	64.75	65.81	66.88	67.93	68.98	70.00	71.00
Total distillate, vol %	64.85	65.87	66.88	67.89	68.90	68.91	70.90	71.89	72.85	73.80
TBP cut point, °C.	400	410	420	430	440	450	460	470	480	490
Total distillate, wt %	71.99	73.92	75.84	77.77	79.69	81.50	83.11	84.54	85.82	86.97
Total distillate, vol %	74.73	76.54	78.34	80.15	81.94	83.61	85.10	86.41	87.58	88.63
TBP cut point, °C.	500	510	520	525	530	540	550	600	650	700
Total distillate, wt %	88.00	88.94	89.81	90.21	90.60	91.33	92.00	94.65	96.55	97.85
Total distillate, vol %	89.58	90.43	91.21	91.57	91.92	92.57	93.15	95.48	97.13	98.25

Sulfur, wt %: 0.57
Visc. @ 122° F., cSt: 98.3¶
Visc. @ 140° F., cSt: 59.9
Visc. @ 176° F., cSt: 26.6
Visc. @ 212° F., cSt: 14.10
Pour pt., °F.: 108
Wax, wt %: 20
Melting pt. of wax, °F.: 126
Total nitrogen, ppm(wt): 1,370
Acidity, mg KOH/g: <0.05
Carbon residue, wt %: 3.4
Asphaltenes, wt %: 0.25
V/Ni, ppm(wt): <2/<2
Xylene equivalent: 5
Saturates, wt %: 60
Aromatics, wt %: 38
Resins A, wt %: 2
Resins B, wt %: 0

Range, °F.: 948+
Yield, wt %: 11.15
Yield, vol %: 9.65
Gravity, °API: 13.78
Sulfur, wt %: 0.85
Visc. @ 212° F., cSt: 155.0
Visc. @ 248° F., cSt: 66.8
Visc. @ 302° F., cSt: 24.7
Pour pt., °F.: 118
Wax, wt %: 14
Melting pt. of wax, °F.: 151
Total nitrogen, ppm(wt): 2,660
Carbon residue, wt %: 10.5§
Asphaltenes, wt %: 0.75§
V/Ni, ppm(wt): 3/3

Range, °F.: 1,022+
Yield, wt %: 8.0
Yield, vol %: 6.85
Gravity, °API: 11.86
Sulfur, wt %: 0.92
Visc. @ 212° F., cSt: 375
Visc. @ 248° F., cSt: 139.0
Visc. @ 302° F., cSt: 44.8
Total nitrogen, ppm(wt): 3,040
Carbon residue, wt %: 14.0§
Asphaltenes, wt %: 1.1§
V/Ni, ppm(wt): 4/4
Xylene equivalent: 7.5
Saturates, wt %: 21
Aromatics, wt %: 69
Resins A, wt %: 8
Resins B, wt %: 2

* 450-650° F. aromatics: 1-ring = 12.1 wt % (11.6 vol %); 2-ring = 8.7 wt % (7.2 vol %); 3-ring = 2.2 wt % (1.6 vol %).

† Temperature difference between cloud/clear is >5° F.
§ Calculated. ¶ Extrapolated.

Mars blend, Offshore Louisiana

Whole crude
Gravity, °API: 31.0
Sulfur, wt %: 2.0
Rvp @ 100° F, psia: 8.0
H_2S, g/100 ml: 0.0011
Pour pt. °F.: –33
Total acid no., mg KOH/g: 0.45
Visc. @ 80° F., SSU: 82.8
Visc. @ 100° F., SSU: 64.2
Visc. @ 140° F., SSU: 45.9

Light ends
Range, °F.: IBP-68
Yield, vol %: 2.8
Iso-to-normal ratio: 0.30
Parrafins, vol %: 100.0
Naphthenes, vol %: 0.0
Aromatics, vol %: 0.0

Gasoline
Range, °F.: 68-155
Yield, vol %: 6.9
Gravity, °API: 85.1
Rvp @ 100° F., psia: 12.8
RON (calculated): 68.0
MON (calculated): 66.9
Sulfur, wt %: <0.02
Iso-to-normal ratio: 0.89
Paraffins, vol %: 92.0
Naphthenes, vol %: 7.3
Aromatics, vol %: 0.7

Light naphtha
Range, °F.: 155-265
Yield, vol %: 9.0
Gravity, °API: 62.9
Sulfur, wt %: <0.02
Nitrogen, ppm(wt): <1
Iso-to-normal ratio: 1.14
Paraffins, vol %: 62.6
Naphthenes, vol %: 32.3
Aromatics, vol %: 5.1

Heavy naphtha
Range, °F.: 265-350
Yield, vol %: 8.0
Gravity, °API: 52.4
Hydrogen, wt %: 14.25
Sulfur, wt %: 0.13
Nitrogen, ppm(wt): <1
Iso-to-normal ratio: 1.68
Total acid no., mg KOH/g: 0.00

Table 2

Cusiana heavy distillate and residue data

Cut points, °C.	369+	369-509	509-550	550-600	600-625	625-705	369-700	700+
Position in crude, wt %	65.6-100	65.60-88.85	88.85-92	92-94.65	94.65-95.7	95.7-97.95	65.6-97.95	97.95-100
Yield, wt %	34.40	23.25	3.15	2.65	1.05	2.25	32.35	2.05
Density @ 15° C., kg/l.	0.9270	0.9062	0.9430	0.9569	0.9699	0.9999	0.9212	1.0086
Sulfur, wt%	0.57	0.44	0.68	0.76	0.82	1.00	0.54	0.92
V, ppm	<2	<0.1*	<0.1*	<0.1*	0.2*	4†	0.2*	14†
Ni, ppm	<2	<0.1*	0.1*	0.2*	1.2*	3†	0.2*	5†
Refr. index @ 70° C.	1.4982	1.4827	1.5063	1.5163	1.5266	§	1.4930	§
Carbon residue, wt %	3.4	0.02	1.35	4.8	9.2	18.3	1.5	24
Kin. visc. @ 80° C., cSt	26.6	10.94	68.4	164	¶	¶	—	—
Kin. visc. @ 100° C., cSt	14.10	6.62	30.5	63.3	¶	¶	11.47	1,850
Kin. visc. @ 120° C., cSt	—	—	—	—	¶	¶	7.12	535

* Ashing ICP-OES. † Direct ICP-OES. § Sample out of range. ¶ Insufficient sample.

Paraffins, vol %: 59.0
Naphthenes, vol %: 25.5
Aromatics, vol %: 15.5

Kerosine
Range, °F.: 350-500
Yield, vol %: 12.9
Gravity, °API: 42.8
Cetane index: 47.0
Hydrogen, wt %: 13.74
Sulfur, wt %: 0.49
Mercaptan S, wt %: 0.0010
Nitrogen, ppm(wt): <1
Basic N, ppm (wt): 2
Smoke pt, mm: 21
Freeze pt., °F.: –49.6
Pour pt., °F.: –66
FIA aromatics, vol %: 21.3
UV diaromatics, vol %: 2.1
UV monoaromatics, wt %: 8.26
UV diaromatics, wt %: 2.92
UV triaromatics, wt %: 0.20
UV tetra-aromatics, wt %: 0.00
UV total aromatics, wt %: 11.23
Refractive index @ 20° C.: 1.4516
Total acid no., mg KOH/g: 0.04

Heavy gas oil
Range, °F.: 350-500
Yield, vol %: 12.7
Gravity, °API: 32.6
Cetane index: 48.1
Hydrogen, wt %: 12.94
Sulfur, wt %: 1.28
Mercaptan S, wt %: 0.0010
Nitrogen, ppm(wt): 44
Basic N, ppm (wt): 30
Pour pt., °F.: 0
UV monoaromatics, wt %: 5.49
UV diaromatics, wt %: 5.60
UV triaromatics, wt %: 1.28
UV tetra-aromatics, wt %: 0.56
UV total aromatics, wt %: 12.93
Refractive index @ 20° C.: 1.4793
Total acid no., mg KOH/g: 0.24

FCC feed
Range, °F.: 650-1,000
Yield, vol %: 24.6
Gravity, °API: 21.8
Hydrogen, wt %: 12.15
Sulfur, wt %: 2.13
Nitrogen, ppm(wt): 953
Basic N, ppm (wt): 280
UV monoaromatics, wt %: 4.82
UV diaromatics, wt %: 3.30
UV triaromatics, wt %: 3.79
UV tetra-aromatics, wt %: 2.42
UV total aromatics, wt %: 14.31
Total acid no., mg KOH/g: 0.32
Conradson C, wt %: 0.20
Ramsbottom C, wt %: 0.29
Visc. @ 140° F., SSU: 117.1
Visc. @ 210° F., SSU: 50.3

Long residue
Range, °F.: 650+
Yield, vol %: 47.7
Gravity, °API: 14.3
Hydrogen, wt %: 11.24
Sulfur, wt %: 3.24
Nitrogen, ppm(wt): 2,986
Basic N, ppm (wt): 826
UV monoaromatics, wt %: 5.50
UV diaromatics, wt %: 3.65
UV triaromatics, wt %: 4.81
UV tetra-aromatics, wt %: 6.34
UV total aromatics, wt %: 20.30
Fe/Cu/Na ppm(wt): 0/0/7
V/Ni ppm(wt): 84/34
Total acid no., mg KOH/g: 0.34
Conradson C, wt %: 9.30
Ramsbottom C, wt %: 7.10
Visc. @ 210° F., SSU: 316.1

Pitch
Range, °F.: 1,000+
Yield, vol %: 23.1
Gravity, °API: 4.7
Sulfur, wt %: 4.38
Basic N, ppm (wt): 1,476
UV monoaromatics, wt %: 6.00
UV diaromatics, wt %: 3.79
UV triaromatics, wt %: 5.67
UV tetra-aromatics, wt %: 10.25
UV total aromatics, wt %: 25.72
Fe/Cu/Na, ppm(wt): 0/1/13
V/Ni, ppm(wt): 168/66
Total acid no., mg KOH/g: 0.23
Conradson C, wt %: 18.70
Abs. visc. @ 140° F., poise: 1,430.0
Kin. visc. @ 275° F., cSt: 348.8
Penetration @ 77° F., dmm: 76

Table 3

Mars distillation data

Fraction, °F.	Yield, vol %	Gravity, °API	Sulfur, wt %
IBP-68	2.8	—	—
68-155	6.9	85.1	<0.02
155-265	9.0	62.9	<0.02
265-350	8.0	52.4	0.13
350-400	4.4	46.2	0.34
400-500	8.5	41.1	0.59
500-600	8.6	33.8	1.17
600-650	4.1	30.1	1.51
650-750	2.2	26.4	1.83
750-900	14.3	23.2	2.05
900-1,000	8.1	18.3	2.51
1,000+	23.1	4.7	4.38
Total	**100.0**		

Directory of national oil companies, energy ministries

A

Abu Dhabi

Abu Dhabi National Oil Co. (ADNOC)
Box 898
Abu Dhabi, UNITED ARAB EMIRATES
Ph: 971 2 66-60-00
Fax: 971 2 602-3389
Telex: 949 22215, 23688
Cable: ADNOC

Ministry of Petroleum & Mineral Resources
Box 59
Abu Dhabi, UNITED ARAB EMIRATES
Ph: 971 2 62810
Telex: 2544 MPMR AH

Afghanistan

Afghan National Petroleum Co. (ANPC)
Shari Nau
Kabul, AFGHANISTAN

Albania

Albpetrol (formerly DPNG)
c/o Geological Institute for Oil & Gas
Fieri, ALBANIA
Ph: 355 423-4542
Fax: 355 423-4204
Telex: 4204 MIN EN

National Petroleum Agency
Agjensia Kombetare e Hidrokarbureve
Rruga "Diressit," No. 83
Tirana, ALBANIA
Ph. & Fax: 355 42 34031

Algeria

Sonatrach Inc.
Immeuble Mauretania Pl. Perou
80 Ave. Ahmed Ghermoul
Algiers, ALGERIA
Ph: 213 2 77-12-77
Fax: 213 2 59-57-58
Telex: 62115 DZ
Cable: SONATRACH ALGIERS

Ministry of Energy & Petrochemical Industries
80 Rue Ahmed Ghermoul
Algiers, ALGERIA
Ph: 213 2 66-33-00
Telex: 52790, 52916

Angola

Sociedad Nacional de Combustiveis de Angola (SONANGOL)
Box 1316
Luanda, ANGOLA
Ph: 244 2 33-41-43
Telex: 3148

Argentina

Gas del Estado SE
Alsina 1169
C. Postal 1311
Buenos Aires, ARGENTINA
Ph: 54 1 383-2091
Fax: 54 1 381-4462
Telex: 33 19021 GASES AR

Yacimientos Petroliferos Fiscales SA (YPF)
C.P. 1364
Buenos Aires, ARGENTINA
Ph: 54 1 326-7271, 326-2545
Fax: 54 1 326-0641
Telex: 21999 21792

Yacimientos Petroliferos Fiscales SA (YPF)
5 Greenway Plaza Suite 210
Houston, Texas 77046
Ph: 713 621-4850
Telex: 0762441

Armenia

Republic of Armenia
Ministry of Energy
Petroleum Project Implementation Unit
2 Government House
Republic Square
Yerevan 375010, ARMENIA
Ph: 3742 52-85-34
Fax: 3742 15-16-87

Australia

Petroleum and Fisheries Division
Department of Primary Industries & Energy
GPO Box 858
Canberra, ACT 2600, AUSTRALIA
Ph: 61 6 272-4585
Fax: 61 6 272-4137

Austria

Federal Ministry of Economic Affairs
Department VII/3
Landstrasser Hauptstrasse 55-57
A-1030 Vienna, AUSTRIA
Ph: 43 222 711-0270, 711-0271
Fax: 43 222 711-0252
Telex: 131300

OMV Aktiengesellschaft
Otto Wagner-Platz 5
A-1090 Vienna, AUSTRIA
Ph: 43 222 404-4090
Fax: 43 222 404-4091
Telex: 114801
Cable: ERDOEL-WIEN

Azerbaijan

State Oil Co. of Azerbaijan (SOCAR)
Neftchilar Ave. 73
Baku 370004, AZERBAIJAN
Ph: 78922 92-35-11
Fax: 788922 92-32-97
Telex: 142 187 CWET SU

B

Bahrain

Bahrain National Oil Co.
P.O. Box 25504
Awali, BAHRAIN
Ph: 973 75-46-66
Fax: 973 75-32-03
Telex: 8670 BANOCO BN

Bangladesh

Bangladesh Oil, Gas & Mineral Corp. (PETROBANGLA)
Chamber Bldg.
122-124, Motijheel Comm'l Area
Dhaka 1000, BANGLADESH
Ph: 880 2 81-49-72
Fax: 880 2 81-16-13
Telex: 642765
Cable: BOGMC, DHAKA

Minister of Energy & Mineral Resources
Dhaka, BANGLADESH

Belize

Ministry of Natural Resources
Geology & Petroleum Office
34-36 Unity Blvd.
Belmopan, BELIZE
Ph: 501 8 22-651, 22-178
Fax: 501 8 23-538

Benin

Ministry of Mines, Energy & Hydrocarbons
P.O. Box 955
Cotonou, BENIN
Ph: 229 30-03-75
Fax: 229 30-11-38
Telex: 5237 MINERH

Ste. Nat. de Commercialisation des Produits Petrolieres (SONACCP)
B.P. 245
Cotonou, BENIN
Ph: 229 30-03-75
Fax: 229 30-11-38
Telex: 5173

Bolivia

Yacimientos Petrolifero Fiscales Bolivianos (YPFB)
Box 401
La Paz, BOLIVIA
Ph: 591 2 56-541, 56-540, 25-289
Telex: YACIBOL BX2567, 3560006
Cable: YACIBOL

Botswana

Director of Geological Survey
Private Bag 14
Lobatse, BOTSWANA

Ph: 267 31 330-428
Fax: 267 31 332-013
Telex: 2293

Brazil

Petroleo Brasileiro SA (PETROBRAS)
Caixa Postal 809
Avenida Republica do Chile 65
20031.170 Rio de Janeiro, RJ, BRAZIL
Ph: 55 21 534-1731, 534-1745, 534-4477
Fax: 55 21 262-2627, 262-0145, 262-0271
Telex: 038 212-3335 PETRA BR
Cable: PETROBRASRIO

Brunei

Director of Petroleum Unit
Petroleum Unit
Jabatan Perdana Menteri
Bandar Seri Begawan 2007
Negara BRUNEI Darussalam
Ph: 673 2 28-932
Fax: 673 2 40-270
Telex: BRUPET BU 2209

Bulgaria

Committee of Geology & Mineral Resources
22 Princess Marie-Louisa Blvd.
Sofia 1000, BULGARIA
Ph: 359 2 83-53-52
Fax: 359 2 83-21-69
Telex: 22 502

Burkina Faso

Burkina & Shell
(formerly Petrovolta)
Box 601
Ouagadougou, BURKINA FASO
Ph: 226 31-00-71
Fax: 226 33-39-36
Telex: 5929

C

Cameroon

Societe Nationale des Hydrocarbures (SNH)
Box 955
Yaounde, CAMEROON
Ph: 237 20-19-10, 21-04-30
Fax: 237 20-46-51
Telex: 8514 HYDROCAM KN
Cable: HYDROCAM 8514 KN

Central African Republic

Ministry of Energy, Mines, and Hydrology
Bangui
CENTRAL AFRICAN REPUBLIC
Ph. & Fax: 236 61-46-72

Chile

Empresa Nacional del Petroleo (ENAP)
Ahumada 341, 8 Piso
Box 3556
Santiago, CHILE
Ph: 56 2 638-1845
Fax: 56 2 638-0164
Telex: 034 240427, 240447 ENAPCL
Cable: ENAP 40447, 40427

China

Ministry of Petroleum Industry
P.O. Box 1411
Beijing
PEOPLE'S REPUBLIC OF CHINA

China National Offshore Oil Corp. (CNOOC)
Jia 1 Sidaokou Rd., Haidan
Box 9623
Beijing
PEOPLE'S REPUBLIC OF CHINA
Ph: 86 1 201-4906
Telex: 22611, 222301 CNOOC CN
Cable: 3113

China National Petroleum Corp.
P.O. Box 766
Beijing
PEOPLE'S REPUBLIC OF CHINA
Ph: 86 1 201-5544
Telex: 22312 PCPRC CN

China National Petroleum Corp.
One Westchase Center Suite 840
10777 Westheimer Rd.
Houston, Tex. 77042
Ph: 713 784-8598
Fax: 713 784-9197
Telex: 378-7801

Colombia

Empresa Colombiana del Petroles (ECOPETROL)
Carrera 13, No. 3624
Apartado Aereo 5938
Bogota, COLOMBIA
Ph: 57 1 287-9308
Fax: 57 1 288-0071
Telex: 035 44464, 42237, 44707 ECP CO
Cable: ECOPETROL

Ministerio de Minas y Energia de Colombia
Centro Administrative Nacional
Avenida El Dorado
Bogota, COLOMBIA
Ph: 57 1 44-520, 44-525
Telex: MINENERGIA

Congo

General Direction of Hydrocarbons
Ministry of Mines & Energy - S.P. 2120
Brazzaville, CONGO
Ph: 242 83-12-81, 83-58-73, 83-59-74
Fax: 242 83-62-43
Telex: 55 47 KG

Hydro Congo
B.P. 2008
Pointe Noire, Brazzaville, CONGO
Ph: 242 81-35-60, 81-40-23
Fax: 242 83-12-38
Telex: 5215, 5220

Costa Rica

Direccion General de Hidrocarburos
Ministerio de Ambiente y Energia
Barrio Los Yoses, Avenida 8, Calle 35
San Jose, COSTA RICA
Ph: 506 2 34-79-79
Fax: 506 2 34-84-02

Cote d'Ivoire

Director of the Office of the Minister, Ministere des Mines
Box V 50
Abidjan, COTE D'IVOIRE
Ph: 225 21-50-03
Fax: 225 21-53-20

Societe Nationale d'Operations Petrolieres de la Cote d'Ivoire (PETROCI)
Box V 194
Abidjan, COTE D'IVOIRE
Ph: 225 20-25-00, 20-25-10
Fax: 225 21-68-24
Telex: 969 22135

Croatia

INA-NAFTAPLIN
Subiceva ulica 29
Zagreb, CROATIA
Ph: 385 41 41-80-11, 44-00-11, 44-00-22
Telex: 22428

Cuba

Ministerio de la Industria Basica
Empedarado 113
Havana, CUBA

Comercial Cupet SA (CUPET)
km 37.5 Via Blanca
Caribe, Sta. Cruz del Norte
Havana 32900, CUBA
Ph: 53 7 62-40-11
Fax: 53 7 33-34-60, 33-80-27, 33-30-72
Telex: 511452 MMG CU

Czech Republic

Ministry of Economic Policy & Development
tr. SNG 65 - 101 60 Prague 10
CZECH REPUBLIC
Ph: 42 2 712-1111
Fax: 42 2 73-13-57
Telex: 122298

D

Denmark

Danish Energy Agency
Energiministeriet
DK-1216 Copenhagen, DENMARK
Ph: 45 33 92-67-00
Fax: 45 33 11-47-43
Telex: 22450

Ministry of Energy
Slotsholmsgade 1
DK-1216 Copenhagen K, DENMARK
Ph: 45 3 392-3350
Fax: 45 3 392-7508

Dominican Republic

Estado de Industria y Comercio
Av. Mexico, Esq. Leopoldo Navarro
Edif. Gubernamental, P. 10
Santo Domingo, DOMINICAN REPUBLIC
Ph: 809 685-8191
Fax: 809 686-8327

Dubai

Dubai Petroleum Co. (DUPETCO)
Box 2222
Dubai, UNITED ARAB EMIRATES
Ph: 971 4 44-29-90
Telex: 45423
Cable: DUPETCO DUBAI

E

Ecuador

Petroleos del Ecuador (Petroecuador)

Av. Amazonas y La Nina
Edifico Torrealba 10« Piso
Box 5007 y 5008
Quito, ECUADOR
Ph: 593 2 55-06-11, 52-14-36
Fax: 593 2 56-97-38
Telex: 0308 22213, 22297 PETROEC ED
Cable: CEPE QUITO

Ministerio de Recursos Naturales y Energeticos
Direccion General de Geologia y Miras
Carrion 1016 y Paez
Casilla 23-A
Quito, ECUADOR
Ph: 593 2 23-12-04
Telex: 2271

Organizacion Latinoamericana
de Energia (Olade)
Casilla 6412 C.C.I.
Quito, ECUADOR
Ph: 593 2 53-82-80
Fax: 593 2 53-96-84

Egypt

Egyptian General Petroleum Corp. (EGPC)
Box 2130
Cairo, EGYPT
Ph: 20 2 353-1335
Fax: 20 2 353-1591
Telex: 92049
Cable: PETMISR CAIRO

Ministry of Petroleum
2 Latin America St.
Garden City
Cairo, EGYPT
Ph: 20 2 25-022, 25-023
Telex: 92049 PETMISR UM

Equatorial Guinea

Ministry of Mines & Energy
Malabo, C/12 de Octubre S/N
Equatorial Guinea
Ph: 240 9 3567
Fax: 240 9 3353
Telex: GBNOM 5405 EG

Eritrea

Ministry of Energy, Mines and
Water Resources
P.O. Box 5285
Asmara, ERITREA
Ph: 291 1 11-68-72
Fax: 291 1 12-76-52

Estonia

Geological Centre of Estonia
67 Pik.K. str.
Tallinn, ESTONIA 0001
Ph: 372 2 44-87-19
Fax: 372 2 44-65-01

Ministry of Economy
Energy Department
6 Kiriku St.
Tallinn, ESTONIA
Ph: 372 2 44-39-41
Fax: 372 2 44-80-91

Ethiopia

Ethiopian Institute for General Surveys
(EIGS)
P.O. Box 2302
Addis Ababa, ETHIOPIA
Ph: 251 1 15-64-15
Fax: 251 1 51-38-77

Ethiopian Petroleum Corp.
Box 3375
Addis Ababa, ETHIOPIA
Ph: 251 1 51-32-88
Fax: 251 1 51-29-38
Telex: 21054
Cable: REFINERY ADDIS

Ministry of Mines and Energy
Box 486
Addis Ababa, ETHIOPIA
Ph: 251 1 614-523
Fax: 251 1 614-574, 515-788

F

Falkland Islands

British Geological Survey
Murchison House
West Mains Road
Edinburgh EH9 3LA
UNITED KINGDOM
Ph: 44 131 667-1000
Fax: 44 131 668-4930
E-mail: N.Fannin@bgs.ac.uk
Telex: 727343 SEISED G

Faroe Islands

Faroese Petroleum Administration
Debesartro
100 Torshaun
FAROE ISLANDS
Ph: 298 12-306
Fax: 298 18-438

Fiji

Mineral Resources Department Ministry of Lands, Energy &
Mineral Resources
Private Mail Bag
Suva, FIJI
Ph: 679 38-16-11
Fax: 679 38-66-84
Telex: 2330
Cable: GEOLOGY

Finland

Ministry of Trade & Industry
00170 Helsinki 17, FINLAND
Ph: 358 0 1601
Fax: 358 0 160-3666
Telex: 124645

France

Service de Conservation des Gisements d'Hydrocarbures
Ministry of Industry
366 Avenue Napoleon Bonaparte
Rueil-Malmaison, FRANCE

G

Gabon

Petrogab
Box 564
Libreville, GABON

Direction Generale des Hydrocarbures
Immeuble du Petrole
Box 2199
Libreville, GABON
Ph: 241 76-39-18
Fax: 241 76-39-17
Telex: 5499/5578 90

Ghana

Ghana National Petroleum Corp.
Petroleum House, Harbour Road
Private Mail Bag
Tema, GHANA
Ph: 233 21 6596, 71-29-30
Fax: 233 21 77-41-43, 71-29-16
Telex: 2188 GNPC GH, 2704 GNPC GH
E-mail: gnpc@ncs.com.gh

Greece

Ministry for Industry, Energy & Technology
80 Michalakopoulos St.
Athens 611, GREECE
Ph: 30 1 770-5111
Telex: 21 5089, 21 6620

Public Petroleum Corp. of Greece
199 Kifissias Ave. GR, 151 24
15124 Athens, GREECE
Ph: 30 1 806-9801
Fax: 30 1 806-4212
Telex: DEP 226205 EKY

Greenland

Geological Survey of Greenland
Oster Voldgade 10
DK-1350 Copenhagen K
DENMARK
Ph: 45 33 47-85-64
Fax: 45 33 93-53-52
Telex: 19066 GGUTEL DK

Mineral Resources Administration
for Greenland
Kompagnistraede 15
DK-1208 Copenhagen K
DENMARK
Ph: 45 33 92-75-00
Fax: 45 33 13-30-17

Guatemala

Ministerio de Energia y Minas
Directorate of Hydrocarbons
Apartado Postal 1421
01901 Guatemala City, GUATEMALA
Ph: 502 2 77-09-01, 77-09-03
Fax: 502 2 76-20-44, 76-31-75

Guinea

Office National des Hydrocarbures
Societe Guineane des Petroles (SOGUIP)
Conakry, GUINEA
Ph: 224 4 46-12-56
Telex: 776

Guinea-Bissau

Empresa Nacional de Pesquisa e Exploracao Petroliferas e Mineras E P (PETROMINAS)
Caixa Postal 387
Bissau, GUINEA-BISSAU
Ph: 245 21-23-89

H

Honduras

Direccion General de Minas e Hidrocarburos
Apartado Postal 981

Ministerio de Recursos Naturales
Boulevard a la Colonia Kennedy
Tegucigalpa, DC, HONDURAS
Ph: 504 32-78-48, 32-67-21, 32-84-55

Hungary

Hungarian National Oil & Gas Corp.
H-1502, P.O. Box 22
Xi, Schonherz Z. U. 18
1117 Budapest
HUNGARY
Ph: 36 1 166-2646
Fax: 36 1 186-8281
Telex: 22 4762 OKGT H

I

India

Oil & Natural Gas Corp. Ltd. (ONGC)
7th Floor, Bank of Baroda Bldg.
Parliament Street
New Delhi 110 001, INDIA
Ph: 91 11 331-7205, 371-5291
Fax: 91 11 331-6413
Telex: 031-65184, 031-66262

Director General of Hydrocarbons
Ministry of Petroleum & Natural Gas
2nd Floor, Shastri Bhavan
New Delhi 110 001, INDIA

Indonesia

Perusahaan Pertambangan Minyak Dan Gas Bumi Negara (PERTAMINA)
Jalan Merdeka Timur No. 1
Box 12
Jakarta 10110, INDONESIA
Ph: 62 21 381-5111, 381-6111
Fax: 62 21 384-3882, 384-6865
Telex: 796 44152, 44302, 46554, 46549

Iran

National Iranian Oil Co. (NIOC)
Ave. Takhte Jamshid
Box 1863
Tehran, IRAN
Ph: 98 21 6151
Telex: 2114
Cable: NAFTMELLI-TEHRAN

Petroleum Ministry of Islamic Republic of Iran
Box 1863
Tehran, IRAN
Ph: 98 21 66-11-20
Fax: 98 21 66-62-93
Telex: 215582 DVNI
Cable: NAFTMELLI

Iraq

Iraq National Oil Co. (INOC)
Al-Khullani Square
Box 476
Baghdad, IRAQ
Ph: 964 1 80-066, 80-069
Telex: 943 212204
Cable: PETROLNA

Ministry of Oil
Box 6178
Al-Mansour, Baghdad, IRAQ
Ph: 964 1 541-0031
Telex: 943 212216
Cable: NAFTIYAH BAGHDAD

Ireland

Department of Transport, Energy and Communications
Beggars Bush, Haddington Road
Dublin, IRELAND
Ph: 353 1 671-5233
Fax: 353 1 660-4462
Telex: 90335

Minerals and Petroleum Unit
Department of Economic Development
Netherleigh
Massey Ave.
Belfast BT4 2JP
NORTHERN IRELAND
Ph: 232 52-99-00
Fax: 232 52-95-50

Isle of Man

Department of Industry
Illiam Dhone House
2 Circular Road
Douglas, ISLE OF MAN 1M1 1PJ
Ph: 44 624 68-56-76
Fax: 44 624 68-56-83

Israel

Israel National Oil Co. Ltd.
Beit Gibor, 6 Kaufman St.
Tel-Aviv 68012, ISRAEL
P.O. Box 50199
Tel-Aviv 61500, ISRAEL
Ph: 972 3 514-2020
Fax: 972 3 514-2061
Telex: 341751
Cable: ISNEFT TEL AVIV

Ministry of Energy & Infrastructure
234 Yaffo St.
Box 1442/91013
Jerusalem, ISRAEL
Ph: 972 2 31-61-11
Fax: 972 2 38-14-44

Italy

Ufficio Nazionale Idrocarburi
Ministero dell Industria del Commercio e dell Artigianato
Via Veneto
33 Roma, ITALY

Ente Nazionale Idrocarburi (ENI)
1, Piazzale Enrico Mattei
00144 Rome, ITALY
Ph: 39 6 59002
Fax: 39 6 5900-2141
Telex: 610082, 610086
Cable: ENIDRO-ROMA

J

Jamaica

Petroleum Corp. of Jamaica (PCJ)
PCJ Resource Center 5th Floor
36 Trafalgas Rd.
P.O. Box 579
Kingston 10, JAMAICA W.I.
Ph: 809 929-5380
Fax: 809 929-2400
Telex: 291 2356 PETCORP J

Japan

Japan National Oil Corp. (JNOC)
Fukoku-Seimei Bldg.
2-2 Uchisaiwaicho, 2-chome
Chiyoda-ku, Tokyo 100, JAPAN
Ph: 81 3 3580-5411
Fax: 81 3 3591-0172
Telex: 22166 J
Cable: SEKIYUKODAN TOKYO

Jordan

Ministry of Energy & Mineral Resources
Natural Resources Authority
Bayadir Wadi Esseer 8th Circle
P.O. Box 7
Amman, JORDAN
Ph: 962 6 81-42-42
Fax: 962 6 81-18-66
Telex: 925 21415 Jo
Cable: NRA JO

K

Kazakhstan

Ministry of Fuel & Energy
Bakenbay-Batyj St. 142
480091 Almaty
KAZAKHSTAN
Ph: 327 2 62-64-10, 62-60-80
Fax: 327 2 62-66-30

Kenya

Ministry of Energy & Regional Development
Nyayo House
Box 30582
Nairobi, Kenya
Ph: 254 2 33-88-18
Fax: 254 2 22-83-14
Telex: 23094
Cable: MINIPOWER NAIROBI

National Oil Corp. of Kenya
National Bank Bldg., Harambee Ave.
Box 58567
Nairobi, KENYA
Ph: 254 2 340-030
Fax: 254 2 340-039
Telex: 23094
Cable: MINIPOWER NAIROBI

Kuwait

Kuwait Petroleum Corp. (KPC)
Box 26565
13126 Safat, KUWAIT
Ph: 965 245-5455
Fax: 965 246-7159
Telex: 44874/5/6/7/8
Cable: PETCORP KUWAIT

Ministry of Oil
P.O. Box 5077
Safat, KUWAIT
Telex: PETROL 959 22363KT

L

Latvia

Geological Survey of Latvia
LV 1484
11 November krastmala 31
Riga, LATVIA
Ph: 3712 22-23-90
Fax: 3712 22-81-59

Liberia

Ministry of Lands, Mines & Energy
Box 10-9024
1000 Monrovia-10, LIBERIA
Ph: 231 22-14-88, 22-15-80
Fax: 231 22-52-17
Telex: 4532

Libya

General Department of Technical Affairs
Ministry of Petroleum
P.O. Box 256
Tripoli, LIBYA

National Oil Corp. (NOC)
Box 2655
Tripoli, LIBYA
Ph: 218 21 46-181
Telex: 20270 LINAFT LY
Cable: LINAFT

Lithuania

Geological Survey of Lithuania
2600, Vilnius, LITHUANIA
35 Konarskio str.
Ph: 632889
Fax: 370 67 06-376

M

Madagascar

Office des Mines Nationales et des Industries Strategiques (OMNIS)
21 Lalana Razanakombana
B.P. 1 Bis
Antananarivo, MADAGASCAR
Ph: 261 2 24-439
Fax: 261 2 22-985
Telex: 22370

Malaysia

Petroliam Nasional Berhad (PETRONAS)
Menara Dayabumi, Komplex Dayabumi
Jalan Sultan Hishamuddin
Box 12444
50778 Kuala Lumpur, MALAYSIA
Ph: 60 3 274-3833, 274-8011, 274-8022
Fax: 60 3 274-0217
Telex: 31123 PETRON MA
Cable: PETRONAS

Mali

Direction Nationale de la Geologie et des Mines (DNGM)
P.O. Box 223
Bamako, MALI
Ph: 223 222-466, 225-821
Fax: 223 229-111, 227-174

Malta

Government of Malta
Oil Exploration Division
Office of the Prime Minister
Auberge de Castille
Valletta, MALTA
Ph: 356 23-79-21, 24-08-42
Fax: 356 24-80-15
Telex: 1458 OED OPM

Mauritania

Direction des Mines et de la Geologie
Box 199
Nouakchott, MAURITANIA
Ph: 222 2 53-225
Fax: 222 2 53-225
Telex: 531 BMTN

Mauritius

Permanent Secretary
Ministry of Energy & Water Resources
Government Centre
Port Louis, MAURITIUS
Ph: 230 454-3694
Fax: 230 208-6497

Mexico

Petroleos Mexicanos (PEMEX)
Avenida Marina Nacional 329
Mexico 17, D.F., MEXICO
Ph: 52 5 250-2611, 254-2044
Fax: 52 5 625-4385, 533-0418
Telex: PMX GRP MEX 017-7-912
Cable: PEMEX

Mongolia

Mongol Petroleum Co. (MGT)
Uildverchnii Street 37
Ulaanbaatar, MONGOLIA
Ph: 976 1 38-34-83
Fax: 976 1 33-11-76

Petroleum Authority of Mongolia
Ulaanbaatar-37
Uildverchnii gudamj
MGT, MONGOLIA
Ph: 976 1 38-34-83
Fax: 976 1 33-11-76
Telex: 79235 MGT MH

Morocco

Bureau de Recherches et de Participations Minieres Morocco (BRPM)
5-7 Carli Moulay Hassan
Box 99
Rabat, MOROCCO
Ph: 212 7 63-035
Fax: 212 7 76-24-10
Telex: 310-66

Office National de Reserches & Exploitations Petrolieres (ONAREP)
Avenue Al Fadila
Quartier Industriel, C.Y.M.
Rabat, MOROCCO
Ph: 212 7 79-40-80, 79-50-05 (Ext. 282)
Fax: 212 7 79-44-75
Telex: OFREP 317-15M

Mozambique

Empresa Nacional de Hidrocarbonetos de Mocambique
Avenida Fernao de Magalhaes 31
P.O. Box 4787
Maputo, MOZAMBIQUE
Ph: 258 1 42-94-56, 42-94-67
Fax: 258 1 42-48-08
Telex: 6-478 ENH-MO
Cable: PETRO MO

Republic Popular de Mocambique
Ph: 258 1 42-94-56, 42-94-67
Fax: 258 1 30931
Telex: 6-478 ENH MO

Myanmar

Burma Ministry of Mines
Minister's Office
Yangon, MYANMAR
Cable: BURMIN

Myanma Oil & Gas Enterprise
Box 1049
74-80 Min Ye Kyawzwa Rd.
Yangon, MYANMAR
Ph: 95 1 21-394, 21-027
Fax: 95 1 22-964, 22-965
Telex: MYCORP BM 21307

N

Namibia

Ministry of Mines & Energy
Trust Bank Centre, Kaiser St.
Private Bag 13297
Windhoek, NAMIBIA
Ph: 264 61 226-571
Fax: 264 61 38-643, 220-386
Telex: 50 908 487 WK

National Petroleum Corp. of Namibia Pty. Ltd. (NAMCOR)
Private Bag 13196
Windhoek, NAMIBIA
Ph: 264 61 22-16-99, 22-57-23
Fax: 264 61 22-17-85

Nepal

Ministry of State for Industry & Labor
Petroleum Exploration Promotion Project
Department of Mines & Geology
Lainchour
Kathmandu, NEPAL
Ph: 977 1 41-35-41, 41-47-40
Fax: 977 41-17-83
Telex: 2320 MINES NP

Nepal Oil Corp. Ltd.
Babar Mahal
Box 1140
Kathmandu, NEPAL
Ph: 977 21-46-00
Fax: 977 22-67-99
Telex: 2246 NEANI NP
Cable: NEANI

Netherlands

Ministry of Economic Affairs
General Energy Policy Division
Postbus 20101
2500 The Hague
NETHERLANDS
Ph: 31 70 79-89-11
Fax: 31 70 79-63-58

Newfoundland & Labrador

Government of Newfoundland & Labrador
Department of Mines and Energy
P.O. Box 8700
St. John's, Newfoundland
CANADA A1B 4J6
Ph: 709 729-6877
Fax: 709 729-2508

New South Wales

Director General
Department of Mineral Resources
P.O. Box 536

St. Leonards, NSW 2065, AUSTRALIA
Ph: 61 2 9901 8888
Fax: 61 2 9901 8520

New Zealand

Ministry of Commerce
P.O. Box 1473
Wellington, NEW ZEALAND
Ph: 64 4 472-0030
Fax: 64 4 499-0968
Telex: ENMIN NZ 31488

Nicaragua

Instituto Nicaragua de Energia
Direccion General de Hydrocarburos
Iglesia Santo Domingo 2c. abajo
P.O. Box 3104
Managua, NICARAGUA
Ph: 505 2 22-78-17
Fax: 505 2 22-73-23, 22-70-52, 62-30-68
E-mail: dgh-ine@ibw.com.ni

Empresa Nicaraguense del Petroleo (PETRONIC)
Iglesia Santo Domingo 2 Cuadras Abajo
Escombros de Managua
P.O. Box 3104
Managua, NICARAGUA
Ph: 505 2 27-140, 27-156, 27-168, 27-513
Fax: 505 2 62-10-84, 62-10-49, 27-244
Telex: 0375 1278 CABLE PETRONIC

Niger

Ministere des Mines et de l'Energie
Direction de l'Energie
Naimey, NIGER
Ph: 227 73-55-21
Telex: 5418 Minimi

Ste. Nigerienne de Produits Petroliers (SONIDEP)
Box 1735 & 11702
Naimey, NIGER
Ph: 227 73-33-34
Telex: 5343

Nigeria

Ministry of Petroleum Resources
44, Eric Moore, Surulere
P.M.B. 12701
Lagos, NIGERIA
Ph: 234 1 60-31-00
Telex: 961 21-126

Nigerian National Petroleum Corp. (NNPC)
Falomo Office Complex
Private Mail Bag 12701 (Ikoyi)
Lagos, NIGERIA
Ph: 234 1 261-4650, 4228, 4871, 4959
Telex: 21610 NG
Cable: NAPECOR

Northern Territory

Secretary, Dept. of Mines & Energy
P.O. Box 2901
Darwin, N.T. 0800 AUSTRALIA
Ph: 61 089 99 5511
Fax: 089 99 5530

Norway

Den Norske Stats Oljeselskap AS (STATOIL)
Box 300
N-4001 Stavanger, NORWAY
Ph: 47 4 80-80-80
Fax: 47 4 80-70-42
Telex: 73600 STAST N
Cable: STATOIL

Royal Ministry of Petroleum & Energy
Ploensgt 8
Box 8148 Dep. 0033
Oslo 1, NORWAY
Ph: 47 2 34-90-90
Fax: 47 2 34-95-65
Telex: 21486 OEDEP N

O

Oman

Director General of Petroleum and Gas Affairs
Ministry of Petroleum & Minerals
Sultanate of Oman
Box 551
Muscat, OMAN
Ph: 968 60-33-33
Telex: 5280 ON

Petroleum Development Oman (PDO)
Box 81
Mina Al-Fahal, OMAN
Ph: 968 67-81-11
Fax: 968 67-71-06
Telex: 5212
Cable: PETRO MUSCAT

P

Pakistan

Directorate General of Petroleum Concessions
Ministry of Petroleum & Natural Resources
1019-A, Pak Plaza
Fazal-e-Haq Rd., Blue Area
Islamabad, PAKISTAN
Ph: 92 51 82-49-93, 81-83-52
Fax: 92 51 21-32-45
Telex: 54089 TWPET

Oil & Gas Development Corp.
Markaz F-8
Islamabad, PAKISTAN
Ph: 92 51 85-39-74
Fax: 92 51 85-89-39
Telex: 5692 OGDC PK
Cable: OILGASCORP

Papua New Guinea

Papua New Guinea Department of Mining & Petroleum (Petroleum Division)
Private Mail Bag
Port Moresby Post Office
PAPUA NEW GUINEA
Ph: 675 22 4200
Fax: 675 22 4222
Telex: 22211

Paraguay

Petroleos Paraguayos (PETROPAR)
Oliva 299 Casi Chile
Edificio Finamericana 3RO y 4TO Piso
Casilla Correo 571
Asuncion, PARAGUAY
Ph: 595 21 44-85-03
Fax: 595 21 49-62-32
Telex: 0305 25025 PY

Peru

Ministerio de Energia & Minas y Direccion General de Hidrocarburos
Esq. Avenida Javier Prado Este y Avenida Aviacion
Edifico Sol Gas, 5 Piso
Lima 34, PERU
Ph: 51 14 35-29-96, 36-62-36
Telex: 25731 PU MEM

Perupetro SA
Av. Luis Aldana No. 320
Lima 41, PERU
Ph: 51 1 475-9590
Fax: 51 1 475-9644, 475-7722

Philippines

Department of Energy
PNPC Complex, Merritt Rd.
Fort Bonifacio
Makati, Metro Manila, PHILIPPINES
Ph: 63 2 844-1021
Fax: 63 2 812-4016
E-mail: oil&gas@doe.gov.ph

Ministry of Energy
7901 Makati Ave.
Box 1031 MCC
Makati, Metro Manila, PHILIPPINES
Ph: 63 2 85-88-56/9
Telex: 22259, 63667, 5270
Cable: PHILNOCO MANILA

Philippine National Oil Co.
PNOC Bldg.
7901 Makati Ave.
Makati, Metro Manila 1200, PHILIPPINES
Ph: 63 2 85-90-61, 85-88-56, 88-75-51
Fax: 63 2 815-3094, 810-6728
Telex: 22259 PNO PH
Cable: PHILNOCO MANILA

Poland

Bureau of Geological Concessions
Ministry of Environmental Protection, Natural Resources, and Forestry
Wawelska 52/54
00-922 Warsaw, POLAND
Ph: 48 22 25-43-93
Fax: 48 22 25-39-72
Telex: 817857 PL

Polish Oil & Gas Co. (PGNiG)
6/14 Krucza St.
00-537 Warsaw, POLAND
Ph: 48 22 628-2769
Fax: 48 22 623-5862
Telex: 813466 PGNG PL

Portugal

Petroleos de Portugal EP (PETROGAL)
Edificio Europeia
Av. Fontes Pereira de Meio, No. 6-10
1100 Lisboa, PORTUGAL
Ph: 351 1 353-8821
Fax: 351 1 310-2950
Telex: 12521
Cable: PETROGAL, LISBON

Gabinete Para a Pesquisa e Exploracao de Petroleo (GPEP)
Rua Vale do Pereiro, 4
1200 Lisbon, PORTUGAL
Ph: 351 1 388-3541
Fax: 351 1 388-2775

Q

Qatar

Ministry of Finance & Petroleum
Department of Petroleum Affairs
Box 2233
Doha, QATAR
Ph: 974 41-41-23, 41-35-71
Telex: 957-4891
Cable: PETROFAIRS DOHA

Qatar General Petroleum Corp. (QGPC)
Box 3212
Doha, QATAR
Ph: 974 49-14-91
Fax: 974 83-19-95
Telex: 4343
Cable: PETROL DOHA

Queensland

Director General
Department of Mines and Energy
GPO Box 194
Brisbane, QLD 4001, AUSTRALIA
Ph: 61 7 3224 2180
Fax: 61 7 3224-8380

R

Romania

National Agency for Mineral Resources
36-38 Mendeleev St.
70169 Bucharest, ROMANIA
Ph: 40 1 613-2204
Fax: 40 1 210-7440

Petrom RA
109 Calea Victoriei
70176 Bucharest, ROMANIA
Ph: 40 1 650-3485
Fax: 40 1 312-9635
Telex: 11720

Russia

Ministry of Fuel & Energy of the
Russian Federation (Roskomnedra)
4/6 Bol'shaya Gruzinskaya St.
Moscow 123812, RUSSIA
Ph: 7 95 254-8277
Fax: 7 95 943-0013

S

Saudi Arabia

Saudi Arabian Oil Co. (SAUDI ARAMCO)
Administration Bldg. Room 2220
Box 5000
Dhahran 31311, SAUDI ARABIA
Ph: 966 3875-6110
Fax: 966 3873-8190
Telex: 801220 A SAO SJ
Cable: ARAMCO DAMMAM

Senegal

Ministry of Industries, Commerce, and Crafts
Societe des Petroles du Senegal (PETROSEN)
19, Rue Parchappe Immeuble Faycal
P.O. Box 2076
Dakar, SENEGAL
Ph: 221 22-04-44, 22-05-95
Fax: 221 22-83-40
Telex: (0906) 61 249 PETRO SG

Seychelles

Seychelles National Oil Co. Ltd. (SNOC)
P.O. Box 230
Victoria, Mahe, SEYCHELLES
Ph: 248 22-51-82, 22-52-93
Fax: 248 22-51-77
Telex: 2342 SNOCN SZ

Sharjah

The Director
Petroleum & Mineral Department
P.O. Box 188
Sharjah, UNITED ARAB EMIRATES

Somalia

Ministry of Mineral Resources &
Water (SOMALIA)
Government of Somalia
Box 774
Mogadishu, Southern Region, SOMALIA
Telex: 639

National Petroleum Agency
Box 573
Mogadishu, Southern Region, SOMALIA
Ph: 252 20747, 20561
Telex: 605

South Africa

Department of Mineral and Energy Affairs
Pretoria, SOUTH AFRICA
Ph: 27 12 317-9121
Fax: 27 12 322-0810

Soekor (Pty.) Ltd.
P.O. Box 307
Parow 7500
Cape Province
SOUTH AFRICA
Ph: 27 21 938-3911
Fax: 27 21 938-3405
Telex: 555307
Cable: SOEKOR

South Australia

Director General
Department of Mines and Energy
P.O. Box 151
Eastwood, S.A. 5063, AUSTRALIA
Ph: 61 8 274-7500
Fax: 61 8 373-3269

South Korea

Korea Petroleum Development Corp.
Songam Bldg.
84 Nonhyun-Dong
Gangnam-Gu
Seoul, KOREA
Ph: 82 2 547-5321/9
Fax: 82 2 540-0880, 546-4776
Telex: PEDCO K24593

Spain

Jefe del Servicio de Hidrocarburos dela Direccion General de la Energia del Ministerio de Industria y Energia
Madrid 16, SPAIN

Hispanica de Petroleos SA
(HISPANOIL)
Box 14355
Madrid 30, SPAIN
Ph: 34 1 274-7200, 274-9700
Telex: 22114

Sri Lanka

Ceylon Petroleum Corp.
113 Galle Rd.
Colombo 3, SRI LANKA
Ph: 94 1 25-231
Fax: 94 1 44-81-43
Telex: 21167, 21235
Cable: CEYPETCO

Sudan

General Petroleum Corp. of Sudan
Khartoum, SUDAN

Suriname

Staatsolie Maatschappij Suriname NV
Industrieterrein 21, Flora
P.O. Box 4069
Paramaribo, SURINAME
Ph: 597 49-96-49
Fax: 597 49-11-05, 48-08-11
Telex: 217 SUROIL SN
Cable: 597 91105

Syria

Ministry of Petroleum & Mineral Resources
Government of Syria
Jadet Al Katib
Damascus, SYRIAN ARAB REPUBLIC

Syrian Petroleum Co.
Box 2849
Damascus, SYRIAN ARAB REPUBLIC
Ph: 963 11 22-82-98, 22-82-71
Telex: 924 411031 SY, 411726
Cable: PETSYRIA

T

Taiwan

Chinese Petroleum Corp.
83 Chung Hwa Road
Taipei 10031, TAIWAN
Ph: 886 2 361-0221, 371-7121
Fax: 886 2 331-9645
Telex: TP 11215
Cable: CHINOL TAIPEI

Tanzania

Tanzania Petroleum Development Corp.
P.O. Box 5233
Dar-Es-Salaam, TANZANIA
Ph: 255 51 29-663, 32-963
Fax: 255 51 20-775
Telex: 41219 PETROL, 41293 OILSEARCH
Cable: MAFUTA

Tasmania

Director of Mines & State Chief Geologist
Tasmania Development & Resources
P.O. Box 56
Rosny Park, Tas. 7018, AUSTRALIA
Ph: 61 02 33 8333
Fax: 61 02 33 8338

Thailand

Department of Mineral Resources
Ministry of Industry
Rama VI Rd.
Bangkok 10400, THAILAND
Ph: 66 2 511-0215, 511-0749
Fax: 66 2 245-9855
Telex: 84763
Cable: MINDEPT BANGKOK THAILAND

Petroleum Authority of Thailand (PTT)
14 Vighavadi Rangsit Rd.
Bangkok 10900, THAILAND
Ph: 66 2 537-2000
Fax: 66 2 537-3499
Telex: 87940
Cable: PTT BANGKOK

Trinidad & Tobago

Ministry of Energy & State Enterprises
4th Floor, Salvatori Bldg.
Box 96
Port of Spain, TRINIDAD
Ph: 809 6238-8416

Petroleum Co. of Trinidad & Tobago Ltd.
(PETROTRIN)
Administration Bldg.
Pointe-a-Pierre, TRINIDAD
Ph: 809 658-4200, 648-4354
Fax: 809 658-1213, 658-1315
Telex: 0294 39366, 39367 TTOCPAP WG

Tunisia

Entreprise Tunisienne d'Activites
Petrolieres (ETAP)
27 Bis, Ave. Kherreddine Pacha
B.P. 367, 1002 Tunis de Belvedere
TUNISIA
Ph: 216 1 78-22-88, 78-32-33
Fax: 216 1 78-40-92, 78-57-56
Telex: 15128, 13877
Cable: ETAPETROLE

Turkey

General Directorate of Mineral
Research & Exploration (MTA)
Ankara, TURKEY
Ph: 90 41 287-3430
Fax: 90 41 222-2878
Telex: 42-721
Cable: METEA ANKARA

Turkiye Petrolleri Anonim Ortakligi (TPAO)
Mustafa Kemal Mahallesi
2. Cadde No. 86
06520 Ankara, TURKEY
Ph: 90 41 286-9100
Fax: 90 41 286-9000, 9001
Telex: 42426 TPAO TR

Turkmenistan

Ministry of Oil and Gas of Turkmenistan
Institute "Balkannipineft"
Maglymguly Street, 44
Nebit-Dag, TURKMENISTAN 745100
Ph: 7-363-233-770
Fax: 7-363-251-1581

U

Uganda

Ministry of Natural Resources
Petroleum Exploration & Production Dept.
P.O. Box 9
Entebbe, UGANDA
Ph: 256 422-0714
Fax: 256 422-0437
Telex: 61531 PETROL UG

Uganda Petroleum Co. Ltd.
Box 2133
Kampala, UGANDA
Ph: 256 41 25-85-16, 25-70-66, 24-18-49, 24-18-07
Telex: 61299

Ukraine

Counsel of Ministries
Vladimirskaya St. 34
252003 Kiev, UKRAINE
Ph: 7 044 226-2007
Telex: 131419 TOPAZ

State Committee on Geology &
Utilization of Mineral Resources
34 Volodymyrska St.
252601 Kiev, UKRAINE
Ph: 7 044 228-5671
Fax: 7 044 228-6221
Telex: 131419 TOPAZ

United Kingdom

U.K. Department of Energy
1 Palace St.
London SW1E 5HE
UNITED KINGDOM
Ph: 44 1 238-3000
Fax: 44 1 834-03771
Telex: 918777

Uruguay

Administracion Nacional de Combustibles,Alcohol y Portland (ANCAP)
Casilla 1090
Montevideo, URUGUAY
Ph: 598 2 92-06-08, 98-95-04, 98-93-55
Fax: 598 2 92-11-36
Telex: ANCAP UY 23168

Asistencia Reciproca Petrolera
Empresa Latinoamericana (ARPEL)
Javier de Viana 2345
Casilla de Correo 1006
11200 Montevideo, URUGUAY
Ph: 598 2 40-69-93, 40-74-54
Fax: 598 2 23-70-23
Telex: ARPEL UY 22560

Uzbekistan

Ministry of Foreign Economic Relations
Buyuk Ipak Iuli 75
700077 Tashkent, UZBEKISTAN
Ph: 7 371 2 68-76-31
Fax: 7 371 2 68-72-31, 68-74-77

State Committee for Geology &
Mineral Resources
T. Shevchenko St., 11
70060 Tashkent, UZBEKISTAN
Ph: 7 371 2 56-19-98
Fax: 7 371 2 56-32-83

Uzneftegazdobycha
Amir Temir Ulitsa 66
700084 Tashkent, UZBEKISTAN
Ph: 371 2 35-83-23
Fax: 371 2 35-83-37

V

Venezuela

Ministerio de Energia y Minas
Edificio Parque Central
Caracas, VENEZUELA
Ph: 58 2 483-2033, 483-4033, 483-2317

Petroleos de Venezuela SA (PDVSA)
Avenida Libertador, Torre Este,
La Campina
Apartado 169
Caracas 1010-A, VENEZUELA
Ph: 58 2 708-4111
Fax: 58 2 708-4461, 708-4420
Telex: 031 23489, 21890 PDVSA VE

Victoria

Secretary
Dept. of Natural Resources and Environment
P.O. Box 2145MDC
Fitzroy, Victoria 3065, AUSTRALIA
Ph: 61 3 9412 7000
Fax: 61 3 9412 7888

Viet Nam

Ministry of Petroleum & Gas
193/6A Nam Ky Khoi Nghia
Ho Chi Minh City 3, VIET NAM

Vietnam Oil & Gas Co. (PETROVIETNAM)
Oil & Gas General Dept.
80 Nguyen Du Ha Noi
Hanoi, VIET NAM
Ph: 84 4 25-25-26, 25-23-57, 25-29-10
Fax: 84 4 26-59-42
Telex: 412280 PVN-VT

W

Western Australia

Director General
Department of Minerals and Energy
Mineral House
100 Plain St.
East Perth, W.A. 6004, AUSTRALIA
Ph: 61 9 222-3333
Fax: 61 9 325-3515

Y

Republic of Yemen

Ministry of Oil & Mineral Resources
Yemen Republic
Sanaa, YEMEN
Ph: 967 2 52-268
Fax: 967 2 52-253

Yemen Petroleum Co.
YPC Bldg.
Box 3360
Al Hudaydah
YEMEN

Z

Zaire

Petrozaire
B.P. 7617
Kinshasa/Gombe, ZAIRE
Ph: 243 12 20-344, 20-492
Telex: 21066 EPZ DGZR

INDEX

ADVERTISERS' INDEX INTERNATIONAL PETROLEUM ENCYCLOPEDIA 1997

38
39
20-21
36-37
26-27
18-19
22
29
30-31
22
24
28
34
34-35
32-33
16-17